Culinary Arts Institute®

Cover Photo:
Roast Beef Filet with Burgundy Sauce,
Book II, page 182

Kitchen TREASURY

Culinary Arts Institute
A DIVISION OF DELAIR PUBLISHING COMPANY INC.

ISBN: 0-8326-0636-7

BOOK I

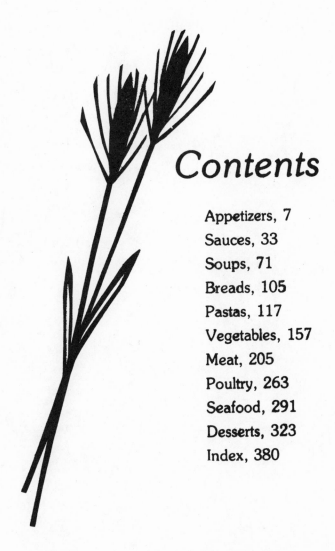

Contents

Note. In some recipes you will find a dot • before an ingredient or in the instructions. This indicates that an additional recipe is needed to complete the dish you are making. You will find the added recipe title, exactly as cited, in heavy type in the index.

Appetizers

1 *Fried Cheese (Saganaki)*

Kefalotyri or kasseri cheese,
  sliced lengthwise in
  ¼-inch-thick wedges (about
  1 pound for 4 people)
2 egg yolks mixed with 2
  tablespoons water
Flour
Olive oil
2 lemons, cut in quarters

1. Dip cheese slices into egg-yolk mixture, then into flour, coating each side evenly. Shake off excess flour.
2. In a 10-inch skillet, heat a ¼-inch layer of olive oil. When the oil begins to smoke, add the cheese. Fry first on one side, then on the other.
3. Remove from skillet and squeeze some lemon juice on each slice. Serve immediately. Allow 2 slices of Saganaki for each person.

2 *Crisp Cheese Crackers* *(Tyrobiskota)*

¼ cup sesame seed
 2 cups all-purpose flour
   Salt (optional)
½ teaspoon ground red pepper
1½ cups grated kefalotyri cheese
¾ cup butter, softened
¼ cup olive oil
 2 egg yolks, beaten, for brushing
   Sesame seed

1. Combine ¼ cup sesame seed, flour, salt, red pepper, and cheese. Work in butter and oil, using hands. Mix until dough holds together.
2. Roll dough out on lightly floured board. Cut into small diamond shapes. Transfer to cookie sheets. Brush with egg yolks and sprinkle with sesame seed.
3. Bake at 350°F about 12 minutes, or until golden.

About 3 dozen

3 *Marrow Canapés*

8 large marrow bones, cut in
   2-inch pieces
  Salted water
½ cup butter
1 loaf cocktail-size black bread,
   cut in thick slices
¼ cup minced parsley
  Ground red pepper

1. Using a thin sharp knife, loosen marrow from bones and remove. Soak marrow in salted water for 24 hours. Drain.
2. Cut marrow into ½-inch-thick rounds and poach in simmering water until tender (2 to 3 minutes). Remove with a slotted spoon. Drain on paper towels.
3. Melt butter in a skillet. Fry slices of bread on both sides.
4. Spread slices with marrow. Sprinkle with parsley and red pepper.
5. Place under broiler for a moment. Serve hot.

12 to 15 pieces

4 *Peppery Peanut Butter and Coconut Sandwiches*

8 slices white bread
6 tablespoons peanut butter
2 tablespoons butter, softened
1 teaspoon Tabasco
½ cup freshly grated or chopped
   flaked coconut

1. Remove crusts from bread. Flatten each slice with a rolling pin and cut into 3 strips.
2. Combine peanut butter, butter, and Tabasco.
3. Spread peanut butter mixture on bread; dip in coconut. Roll each bread strip to form a pinwheel.
4. Chill thoroughly before serving.

2 dozen appetizers

5 *Cocktail Meatballs (Keftethes)*

1 large onion, minced
2 tablespoons olive oil
1½ pounds freshly ground round steak (half each of lamb and veal)
3 tablespoons cracker meal
2 cups firm-type bread, crusts removed
2 eggs
6 tablespoons chopped parsley
2 teaspoons oregano, crushed
1½ teaspoons mint
2 tablespoons vinegar
Salt and pepper to taste
Flour
Olive or corn oil for deep frying heated to 365°F

1. Brown half of onion in 2 tablespoons oil in a small frying pan. Mix with the uncooked onion and add to meat in a large bowl. Add the remaining ingredients except flour and oil. Toss lightly with two forks to mix thoroughly.
2. Dust hands with flour. Roll a small amount of meat at a time between palms, shaping into a ball.
3. To heated fat in deep fryer, add the meatballs a layer at a time. Fry until browned on all sides (about 12 minutes). Serve hot.

30 to 40 meatballs

6 *Eggplant Appetizer (Salata Melitzana)*

1 large eggplant
1 medium onion, minced
1 garlic clove, crushed in a garlic press
1 teaspoon chopped parsley
½ teaspoon freshly dried mint
½ cup olive oil
1 tablespoon wine vinegar (or more to taste)
Juice of 1 large lemon
Salt and pepper to taste

1. To prepare eggplant, place in a baking pan and prick top in four or five places with a fork.
2. Bake at 350°F about 45 minutes, or until skin is wrinkled and the surface is soft.
3. Cool eggplant slightly and cut in half. Scoop out the flesh and place in a blender. Add onion, garlic, parsley, and mint. Blend until well mixed.
4. Combine olive oil, vinegar, and lemon juice. Add to the eggplant mixture and blend well. Season with salt and pepper.
5. Chill. Serve with **toasted French** or **pita bread.** May also be used as a dip for fresh vegetables, or served separately as a first course.

About 4 cups

7 *Olive Canapés*

1 pound Greek olives, pitted
2 tablespoons olive oil
4 hard-cooked eggs, mashed
Pinch dry mustard
1 clove garlic, crushed in a garlic press
Pepper to taste
Egg yolks, hard-cooked and chopped for garnish
Scallions (green part), minced for garnish

1. Put olives and olive oil into a blender; purée. Blend in remaining ingredients except yolks and scallions.
2. Serve on **crackers,** or mound in a dish and serve crackers separately. Garnish with egg yolks and scallions.

1 cup

8 *Yogurt Dip*

2 cups plain yogurt
1 garlic clove, crushed in a garlic press
1 teaspoon dill
1 teaspoon mint
1 teaspoon wine vinegar

1. Combine all ingredients. Chill.
2. Serve with **toasted pita bread** or as a dip for **fresh vegetables.** May also be served as an accompaniment to roast meats or with pilaf.

2 cups

9 *Red Caviar Dip* *(Taramosalata)*

1 jar (4 ounces) tarama (fish roe)
10 slices firm-type whole wheat bread, crusts removed
Water
1 medium onion, minced
2 cups olive oil
Juice of 2 or 3 lemons

1. Beat tarama in a mixer for 5 minutes at medium speed.
2. Sprinkle bread lightly with water and squeeze very dry. Add bread, slice by slice, to tarama, beating after each addition. Add onion and beat. Slowly pour in olive oil, alternating with lemon juice to taste. Beat until fluffy. Refrigerate.
3. Serve with **crackers** or small pieces of crusty **Greek bread.**

5 cups

Note: Store in the refrigerator no longer than a week.

10 *Salami Cornucopias*

1 package (8 ounces) cream cheese
¼ cup grated kefalotyri cheese
¼ teaspoon pepper
Pinch dry mustard
½ pound salami, sliced very thin

1. Combine cheeses, pepper, and mustard. Beat well.
2. With a small knife or spoon, put a teaspoon of the mixture at the bottom of a salami slice.
3. Roll over to form a cornucopia. Secure with a wooden pick.

18 to 20 cornucopias

11 *Kalamata Olives*

2 pounds kalamata olives preserved in brine
¾ cup wine vinegar
¼ cup olive oil

1. Rinse olives in ½ cup wine vinegar. Drain.
2. Pour olive oil and remaining vinegar in a glass jar. Add the olives. Shake well. Store in refrigerator until ready to serve.

12 *Baked Clams Oregano*

12 clams
3 tablespoons minced onion
Salt and pepper to taste
1 teaspoon oregano
1 teaspoon minced parsley
5 tablespoons olive oil
Juice of 1 lemon

1. Open clams. Arrange side by side in a small baking dish.
2. Combine onion, salt, pepper, oregano, parsley, olive oil, and lemon juice. Spoon on clam meat.
3. Bake at 325°F about 7 minutes, or until clams curl slightly at the edges.

3 servings

13 *Yialandji Dolmathes*

1 jar (32 ounces) grapevine leaves
1 quart water
½ cup olive oil
3 medium onions, finely chopped
1½ cups long-grain rice
Juice of 2 lemons
2 tablespoons pine nuts
1 tablespoon dried black currants
2 teaspoons dill
2 teaspoons mint
¼ cup minced parsley
Salt and pepper to taste
Water (about 1 cup)
Olive oil (about 1 cup)

1. To prepare grapevine leaves, rinse leaves thoroughly in cold running water to remove brine.
2. Bring 1 quart water to a boil. Add leaves and parboil 3 minutes. Drain.
3. Select 4 or 5 heavy leaves and line bottom of a medium-size Dutch oven. Set aside.
4. To prepare filling, heat ½ cup olive oil in a medium skillet. Add onion and cook until translucent. Remove with a slotted spoon.
5. In a saucepan, parboil rice in 1 cup water until liquid is absorbed.
6. Combine rice, onion, lemon juice, pine nuts, currants, dill, mint, and parsley. Season with salt and pepper. Cool.
7. To fill grapevine leaves, place a leaf on a working surface, rough side up with stem pointing toward you. Place about a teaspoon of the rice mixture at the base of the leaf. Lift the bottom sides of the leaf up onto the filling. Fold both the right and left sides of the leaf over the filling. Roll up, tucking the edges in.
8. Place the stuffed grape leaves (dolmathes) side by side in the Dutch oven to cover the bottom. Put a second layer on top of the first one. Continue to do this until all the stuffed leaves have been put in.
9. Add water and olive oil to cover. Place an inverted plate on the dolmathes. Bring to boiling. Cover Dutch oven, lower heat, and simmer 1 hour. Taste a dolma to see if rice is tender. If necessary, continue cooking.
10. Cool dolmathes in liquid. Remove carefully with a spoon. Chill in refrigerator 24 hours before serving. Serve cold.

About 50 dolmathes

Note: Dolmathes will keep 10 days in the refrigerator.

14 *Sesame Seed Dip* (Tahi)

½ cup tahini (sesame seed paste)
2 tablespoons olive oil (or more to taste)
¾ cup water
Juice of 1 lemon
2 garlic cloves, crushed in a garlic press
½ cup walnuts
Salt and pepper to taste
¼ cup sesame seed, toasted

1. In a blender, combine all the ingredients except sesame seed until smooth and milky white in color. Refrigerate.
2. Garnish with sesame seed. Serve with **crackers** or as a vegetable dip.

About 1¾ cups

15 *Anchovy Fillets*

½ pound anchovy fillets
    preserved in salt
Wine vinegar (2 or more cups)
2 tablespoons olive oil

1. Separate fillets. Scrape scales and as much of the salt as possible from each fillet.
2. Soak in wine vinegar 5 to 10 minutes, changing as often as necessary until the vinegar remains clear.
3. Drain fillets on paper towels.
4. Arrange fillets on a serving platter. Drizzle with 1 tablespoon fresh vinegar and the olive oil.
5. Serve as an hors d'oeuvre or in anchovy salad.

16 *Fried Calf, Lamb, or Chicken Livers* (Sikotakia Tyganita)

1 pound livers, cut in small
    pieces (do not cut chicken
    livers)
1½ cups flour, seasoned with
    pepper for dredging
Olive oil for frying
2 lemons, quartered
Salt to taste

1. Rinse livers in cool water. Drain on absorbent paper.
2. Dip livers in flour. Shake off excess.
3. In a deep skillet, heat olive oil to smoking. Brown livers on both sides over medium heat.
4. Squeeze lemon juice on each piece. Season with salt. Serve at once.

4 servings

17 *Barbecued Lamb Innards* (Splinandero Karsaniko)

1 large intestine
Innards (heart, liver, kidneys,
    lungs, and sweetbreads) from
    a milk-fed calf
Salt to taste
1 tablespoon vinegar
¾ cup olive oil
Juice of 2 to 3 lemons
2 garlic cloves, crushed in a
    garlic press
2 teaspoons pepper
2 teaspoons oregano
1 teaspoon thyme
2 lamb casings, washed and
    drained
Pepper to taste

1. Rinse intestine in lukewarm water. Using a long spit, turn inside out. Rub salt over surface. Wash thoroughly in lots of lukewarm water.
2. Put innards in a large bowl. Cover with lukewarm water. Add salt and vinegar. Let stand ½ hour. Drain. Discard membranes and connective tissues. Cut into pieces.
3. Combine olive oil, lemon juice, garlic, 2 teaspoons pepper, oregano, and thyme. Add innards. Marinate in refrigerator 4 to 6 hours, turning occasionally.
4. Drain innards, reserving marinade. Knot one end of casing, then stuff with innards and knot other end.
5. Put a skewer beside the filled casing (splinandero). Tie the splinandero to the skewer with the empty casing by turning the casing around the length of the skewer.
6. Charcoal-broil over embers heated until they are white, turning about every 10 minutes and brushing frequently with the marinade. Cook until tender (about 2½ hours). Remove from spit. Cut into 2-inch pieces. Sprinkle with pepper. Serve hot.

10 to 20 pieces

18 *Pickled Mushrooms (Grzybki Marynowane)*

4 pounds small mushrooms
4 cups boiling water
1½ tablespoons salt
Marinade:
1¾ cups water
15 peppercorns
2 bay leaves
2½ tablespoons salt
¾ cup sugar
¾ cup vinegar

1. Cut the mushroom stems off even with the caps.
2. Cook over medium heat in boiling water with salt until they sink to the bottom, about 10 to 15 minutes.
3. Remove mushroom caps; place in small sterilized jars.
4. Make marinade. Boil water with peppercorns and bay leaves for 30 minutes. Add salt and sugar. Stir until dissolved. Add the vinegar, bring to boiling.
5. Pour hot marinade over mushroom caps. Close the jars. Keep refrigerated 2 or 3 days before serving.

4 pints

19 *Beet Relish (Ćwikła)*

1 can (16 ounces) whole beets, drained
¼ cup prepared horseradish
¼ cup sugar
¼ cup vinegar
¼ cup water
1 tablespoon grated onion
1 teaspoon salt
⅛ teaspoon pepper

1. Grate or mince beets.
2. In casserole or other container with a cover, mix beets with remaining ingredients. Cover.
3. Store in refrigerator for at least 1 day before serving.

About 2 cups

20 *Feet in Aspic (Galareta z Nóżek Wieprzowych)*

1½ pounds pigs' feet or calves' feet
½ pound lean pork or veal shanks
3 carrots, pared
1 onion, cut in quarters
2 stalks celery or 1 small celery root
2 bay leaves
5 peppercorns
3 whole allspice
2 cloves garlic, crushed (optional)
Water
1 tablespoon salt
½ cup chopped fresh parsley
⅓ cup vinegar
Lemon wedges
Parsley sprigs

1. Have the butcher skin and split pigs' feet.
2. Cook pigs' feet, pork, vegetables, bay leaves, peppercorns, allspice, garlic, and water to cover in a covered saucepot 2 hours on low heat. Skim off foam and add salt, parsley, and vinegar; cook 2 hours.
3. Strain off the stock; set aside. Take out pigs' feet and carrots. Discard onion and spices. Dice meat and slice carrots.
4. Arrange sliced carrots on bottom of an oiled 2-quart mold. Put meat on top of carrots in mold. Add parsley. Pour stock into mold.
5. Chill until set, at least 4 hours. Skim off fat.
6. Unmold onto platter. Garnish with lemon wedges and parsley sprigs.

8 servings

21 *Pickled Watermelon Rind*

3 pounds watermelon rind
Salted water (use 3 tablespoons salt for each quart of water)
2 pounds sugar
3 cups distilled white vinegar
6 pieces stick cinnamon (3 inches each)
2 tablespoons whole allspice
2 tablespoons whole cloves
2 tablespoons whole mustard seed

1. Cut rind into 1-inch cubes; trim off outer green skin and bright pink flesh.
2. Soak overnight in enough salted water to cover. Drain.
3. Heat sugar and vinegar to boiling.
4. Tie spices in cheesecloth bag.
5. Add spice bag and melon rind to vinegar mixture. Cook, uncovered, until melon is transparent, about 45 minutes.
6. Discard spice bag.
7. If desired, add a few drops red or green food coloring to the rind.
8. Pack watermelon rind tightly into hot, sterilized jars. Pour boiling syrup over watermelon to within ⅛ inch from top, making sure vinegar solution covers rind. Seal each jar at once.

3 pints

22 *Dill Pickles (Kiszenie Ogórków)*

3 pounds 4-inch cucumbers
2 cloves garlic, crushed
1 cup distilled white vinegar
5 cups water
½ cup salt
3 tablespoons dried dill weed

1. Scrub cucumbers.
2. Place a layer of dill on bottom of a large ceramic bowl or crock. Cover with half the cucumbers. Add another layer of dill, then the remaining cucumbers. Add garlic. Top with a final layer of dill.
3. Mix vinegar, water, and salt. Pour over dill and cucumbers. Add more water, if needed, to cover completely.
4. Cover bowl with a china plate to hold pickles under the brine. Let stand in a cool place 4 days.
5. Seal in sterilized jars.

4 pints pickles

23 *Fresh Mushrooms in Sour Cream* (*Grzyby ze Smietaną*)

1 pound fresh mushrooms, sliced
⅔ cup sliced green onions with tops
2 tablespoons butter or margarine
1 tablespoon fresh lemon juice
1 tablespoon flour
1 cup dairy sour cream
2 tablespoons chopped fresh dill or
    1 tablespoon dill weed
¼ teaspoon salt
⅛ teaspoon pepper
    Small rounds of rye or Melba
    toast

1. Sauté mushrooms and onions in butter and lemon juice for 4 minutes. Stir in flour. Cook slowly, stirring 1 minute. Add sour cream, dill, salt, and pepper. Cook and stir 1 minute.
2. Serve warm on toast.

About 2 cups

24 *Pork Pâté* (*Pasztet Wieprzowy*)

1½ pounds ground fresh pork
½ pound salt pork, diced
5 medium onions, quartered
2 pounds sliced pork liver
3 eggs, beaten
1½ teaspoons salt
½ teaspoon black pepper
1 teaspoon marjoram
½ teaspoon nutmeg
¼ teaspoon allspice
1 tablespoon beef flavor base
½ pound sliced bacon

1. Combine fresh pork and salt pork in a roasting pan. Roast at 325°F 1 hour, stirring occasionally.
2. Remove pork from pan and set aside. Put onions and liver into the pan. Roast 20 minutes, or until liver is tender. Discard liquid in pan or use for soup.
3. Combine pork, liver, and onion. Grind twice.
4. Add eggs, dry seasonings, and beef flavor base to ground mixture; mix well.
5. Line a 9×5×3-inch loaf pan (crosswise) with bacon slices. Pack ground mixture into pan. Place remaining bacon (lengthwise) over top of ground mixture.
6. Bake at 325°F 1 hour. Cool in pan.
7. Remove paté from pan. Chill.
8. To serve, slice paté and serve cold with **dill pickles** and **horseradish.**

About 4 pounds

25 *Flybanes* (*Muchomorki*)

8 hard-cooked eggs
4 small tomatoes
    Salt and pepper
    Mayonnaise
    Lettuce

1. Peel the eggs. Cut off both ends so eggs will stand evenly. Stand the eggs on a small tray; they will serve for mushroom stems.
2. Cut the tomatoes in halves lengthwise. Remove cores. Sprinkle with salt and pepper. Put each tomato half over an egg as a mushroom cap. Dot the caps with mayonnaise. Garnish the tray with lettuce.

8 flybanes

26 *Ham Pudding (Budyń z Szynki)*

3 cups (about 1 pound) ground ham
2 cups warm unseasoned mashed potatoes
2 tablespoons melted butter
4 eggs, separated
1 teaspoon salt
½ teaspoon pepper
Ham fat or drippings
Fine bread crumbs
Mustard Sauce (page 63) or Horseradish Sauce (page 88)

1. Mix ham and potatoes well.
2. Put butter and egg yolks into a small bowl of electric mixer; beat until thick and creamy.
3. Fold egg yolks into ham mixture; add salt and pepper.
4. With clean beaters, beat egg whites until stiff, but not dry.
5. Fold half of egg whites into the ham mixture; stir gently. Fold in the rest of the egg whites.
6. Grease a 1½-quart casserole with ham fat. Coat with bread crumbs. Spoon ham mixture into prepared casserole; cover.
7. Bake at 350°F 45 minutes.
8. Serve with sauce.

About 6 servings

27 *Ham and Egg Rolls (Jajka Zawijane w Szynce)*

6 hard-cooked eggs
12 thin slices cooked ham
Lettuce leaves
Mayonnaise
Pickles

1. Peel the eggs; cut in halves.
2. Roll each half of egg in a slice of ham. Secure with wooden pick.
3. Arrange lettuce leaves around ham and egg rolls on serving plate. Decorate with mayonnaise and garnish with pickles.

12 rolls

28 *Mustard Butter (Masło Musztardowe)*

½ cup butter (at room temperature)
½ cup prepared mustard

1. Beat the butter with the mustard until creamy.
2. Spread on toast rounds to serve with **sardines** or **herring**.

1 cup

29 *Onion-Chive Butter*
(Masło Szczypiorkowe lub Koperkowe)

1 tablespoon sliced green onion
1 tablespoon snipped chives
½ cup butter (at room temperature)

1. Blend onion, chives, and butter.
2. Form into a roll about 1 inch in diameter. Chill.
3. Cut into small disks.

About ⅔ cup

30 *Spring Cottage Cheese Spread*
(Twarożek Wiosenny)

1 carton (12 to 14 ounces) cottage cheese
½ cup dairy sour cream
8 radishes, shredded
3 tablespoons sliced green onion
½ teaspoon salt
Lettuce leaves
Radish roses
Rye or French bread

1. Mix cottage cheese with sour cream. Add radishes, onion, and salt; toss to mix well.
2. Mound on lettuce leaves. Garnish with radish roses. Surround with bread.

About 2⅓ cups

31 *Chicken Liver Spread* *(Pasta z Kurzej Wątróbki)*

½ pound chicken livers
1 cup milk
¼ cup rendered chicken fat or margarine
1 medium onion, cut in quarters
3 hard-cooked eggs, peeled and cut in half
½ pound cooked ham or cooked fresh pork, cut up
¼ teaspoon salt
¼ teaspoon pepper
⅛ teaspoon garlic powder (optional)

1. Soak livers in milk 2 hours. Drain livers and discard milk.
2. Melt fat in skillet. Add livers and onion and cook over medium heat until tender.
3. Combine livers, pan drippings, and all remaining ingredients. Grind or mince.
4. Add extra melted chicken fat or margarine, if desired, to make spread of desired spreading consistency.

About 4 cups

32 *Purée of Anchovies* *(Purée Sardelowe)*

1 can (2 ounces) flat anchovy fillets, drained
3 slices stale white bread
Water
½ cup dairy sour cream or mayonnaise
1½ teaspoons vinegar

1. Mince or pound anchovy fillets.
2. Moisten bread with enough water to cover; then squeeze dry. Break into bits or mince with a fork. Blend in sour cream and vinegar to make a smooth purée. Serve as a spread with **dark bread rounds.**

About 1 cup

33 *Tangerine Yakatori*

This colorful Japanese-style appetizer is as pleasing to the eye as it is to the taste.

½ cup tangerine or orange juice
¼ cup dry white wine
3 tablespoons light soy sauce
½ bunch green onions, cut in
   1-inch pieces
2 large tangerines or oranges,
   peeled, sectioned, and seeded
2 large whole chicken breasts,
   skinned, boned, and cut in
   1x¼-inch strips

1. Combine all ingredients in a mixing bowl. Refrigerate covered 2 hours, stirring occasionally. Drain; reserve marinade.
2. Thread ingredients alternately on wooden skewers. Broil 4 inches from heat until chicken is done (about 3 minutes on each side).
3. Heat marinade until bubbly. Serve in individual cups as a dipping sauce.

4 servings

34 *Individual Chicken Terrines*

Crisp carrots and the delicate flavor of brandy enliven this appetizing dish.

½ cup thinly sliced small carrots
¼ cup brandy
2 pounds boned chicken, coarsely
   chopped
1 small onion
1 small carrot
1 teaspoon salt
¼ teaspoon nutmeg
1 egg, lightly beaten
2 teaspoons vegetable oil
2 tablespoons ice water
1½ tablespoons matzo meal or
   white cornmeal
   Vegetable oil
   Watercress
● Cucumber Sauce, if
   desired

1. Simmer carrot slices in brandy in a covered saucepan just until tender (about 3 minutes). Remove carrots with a slotted spoon; reserve. Mix a quarter of the chicken with brandy; remove from heat and let stand 45 minutes. Drain.
2. Mince remaining chicken, the onion, and carrot in a food processor or blender; remove to a mixing bowl. Stir in marinated chicken, salt, nutmeg, egg, oil, and ice water; mix well. Sprinkle matzo meal over mixture; mix well.
3. Layer the carrot slices in bottom of 8 lightly oiled 6-ounce custard cups. Spoon chicken mixture over carrots, smoothing top of mixture. Cover cups tightly with aluminum foil; place in a baking pan. Pour boiling water into baking pan, halfway up sides of custard cups.
4. Bake at 325°F 40 to 45 minutes, or until mixture is set. Remove cups from water. Remove foil. Let stand 5 minutes.
5. Terrines can be served hot, or refrigerated until chilled and served cold. To unmold, run knife around edge of cups and invert on individual plates. Garnish with watercress. Serve with Cucumber Sauce, if desired.

8 servings

Note: For a luncheon entrée, follow directions above, using six 10-ounce glass dishes. Bake until mixture is set.

35 *Crab Meat and Bean Sprouts with Omelet Strips*

2 eggs
3 tablespoons water
1 tablespoon dry sherry
1 tablespoon light soy sauce
1 tablespoon walnut or vegetable oil
4 green onions, chopped
¾ cup chopped green pepper
1 cup sliced fresh mushrooms
2 cups drained fresh or canned bean sprouts
1 tablespoon light soy sauce
8 ounces fresh or 1 can (7 ¾ ounces) crab meat, drained and flaked
1 teaspoon toasted sesame seed

1. Beat eggs with water, sherry, and 1 tablespoon soy sauce. Heat half the walnut oil in a small skillet. Cook egg mixture in skillet until set but still moist on top; remove to plate and cut egg into strips.
2. Heat remaining walnut oil in a wok or medium skillet. Cook and stir vegetables and 1 tablespoon soy sauce until vegetables are just tender (about 3 minutes). Add crab meat and omelet strips; cook and stir until thoroughly heated (about 1 minute). Sprinkle with toasted sesame seed. Serve immediately.

4 servings

36 *Broiled Fish Quenelles*

The traditional method of poaching is given along with our new, easy broiling method. The quenelles puff to a light texture when cooked.

2 pounds skinned fish fillets (all trout or a combination of trout, whitefish, or pike)
½ cup chopped onion
⅓ cup chopped carrot
1 egg, beaten
2 teaspoons vegetable oil
1½ teaspoons salt
1½ teaspoons matzo meal or white cornmeal
3 tablespoons ice water
Watercress

1. Place all ingredients except 1 tablespoon of the ice water and watercress in a blender or food processor; purée until the consistency of a paste. Add remaining ice water if necessary (mixture should hold together and be easy to handle).
2. Form fish mixture into oval patties, using ½ cup for each. Place on a lightly oiled cookie sheet.
3. Broil 4 inches from heat until patties are well browned and slightly puffed (8 to 10 minutes on each side). Serve immediately. Garnish with watercress.

8 servings

Note: Fish quenelles can be poached, if desired. Simmer covered in a large skillet in 1½ quarts Fish Stock (page 26) until puffed and cooked through the center (about 10 minutes). Remove from stock with slotted spoon. Serve hot or refrigerate until chilled. Garnish as above.

37 *Oysters in Mushroom Purée*

1 pound mushrooms, coarsely chopped
1 quart oysters, liquor reserved
¼ cup dry sherry
½ cup soft bread crumbs
2 garlic cloves, minced
1 teaspoon salt
¼ teaspoon freshly ground pepper
● Beef Stock
Watercress

1. Simmer mushrooms and 1 cup of the oysters in the sherry in a covered saucepan 8 to 10 minutes. Drain; press all moisture out of mushrooms.
2. Purée mushrooms and cooked oysters in a food processor or blender; pour into a shallow 1½-quart casserole. Stir in the bread crumbs, garlic, salt, and pepper. Stir in reserved oyster liquor. Stir in stock, if necessary, to make purée of a thick sauce consistency. Arrange remaining oysters in purée.
3. Bake covered at 350°F 20 minutes.
4. Serve in shallow bowls or ramekins. Garnish with watercress.

6 to 8 servings

38 Seviche

In this specialty of Mexico, the lemon juice actually "cooks" the fish.

1¼ pounds whitefish fillets,
   skinned and cut in 2x¼-inch
   strips
1 cup fresh lemon juice
2 green chilies, seeded and
   minced
1 teaspoon snipped fresh or ½
   teaspoon dried oregano
   leaves
1 tablespoon snipped fresh or
   1½ teaspoons dried coriander
   leaves
1 tablespoon olive oil
1 teaspoon salt
¼ teaspoon freshly ground
   pepper
2 large tomatoes, peeled, seeded,
   and chopped
1 medium green pepper, finely
   chopped
1 small yellow onion, finely
   chopped
¼ cup fresh lime juice
   Radish slices
   Ripe olives

1. Place fish in a shallow glass bowl; pour lemon juice over it. Refrigerate covered 6 hours, stirring occasionally. Drain; discard lemon juice.
2. Mix remaining ingredients except radish slices and olives with fish in a medium bowl. Refrigerate 30 minutes.
3. Serve on chilled plates; garnish with radish slices and olives. Or spoon into **fluted lemon shells.**

8 servings (½ cup each)

39 Chilled Artichoke Plate

Elegant in flavor and appearance. Serve with Individual Chicken Terrines (●) or Broiled Fish Quenelles (●) for an exquisite luncheon.

   4 medium artichokes
●   Chicken Stock
¼ cup lemon juice
1 teaspoon salt
½ pint cherry tomatoes
● ¾ cup Mock Béarnaise Sauce
*1 pound fresh asparagus, cut in
   2-inch pieces

1. Snip tips from artichoke leaves with scissors. Simmer artichokes in 1 inch of the stock with lemon juice and salt in a large covered saucepan until tender (about 45 minutes). Lift from pan with tongs; let cool. Refrigerate until chilled.
2. Carefully scoop seeds from tomatoes, using small end of a melon-ball cutter. Fill tomatoes with ¼ cup of the sauce; refrigerate.
3. Scrape choke from artichoke bottoms. Place artichokes in center of individual plates and dollop each with 2 tablespoons sauce. Arrange raw asparagus pieces and tomatoes attractively on plates. Serve immediately.

4 servings

*The flavor and texture of raw young asparagus is delightful. If asparagus is tough, simmer in 1 inch of stock until just tender (about 8 minutes); drain and refrigerate until chilled.

Frozen asparagus (10 ounces) can be used; cook according to package directions and refrigerate until chilled.

40 *Celery Appetizer*

This lovely first course can be expanded to a luncheon entrée with the addition of shrimp or chicken.

8 stalks celery, cut in julienne
   strips (about 3 cups)
● ½ cup Mock Mayonnaise
½ teaspoon celery seed, crushed
¼ teaspoon salt
2 teaspoons minced shallots
½ teaspoon wine vinegar
   Lettuce cups
   Pimento strips

Mix all ingredients, except lettuce and pimento, just until combined. Refrigerate covered until cold. Serve in lettuce cups; garnish with pimento.

6 servings

Note: If desired, mix in 1 cup cooked diced shrimp or chicken breast, increasing Mock Mayonnaise by 2 tablespoons. Season to taste with salt.

41 *Lombardy Green Tart*

1 package (10 ounces) frozen
   chopped spinach, thawed
2 cups low-fat cottage cheese
1 medium zucchini, minced
2 stalks celery, minced
1 bunch green onions, green part
   only, minced
2 tablespoons snipped parsley
2 teaspoons snipped fresh or 1
   teaspoon dried marjoram
   leaves
2 teaspoons snipped fresh or 1
   teaspoon dried thyme leaves
4 eggs, lightly beaten
½ teaspoon salt
⅛ teaspoon freshly ground
   pepper
   Lettuce leaves

1. Press all liquid from spinach.
2. Combine all ingredients, except lettuce leaves, in a bowl. Mix thoroughly. Spoon mixture into a lightly oiled 9-inch pie plate.
3. Bake at 375°F 45 minutes. Cut into wedges to serve. Serve hot, or refrigerate until chilled and serve on lettuce.

6 servings

Lombardy Green Salad: Follow recipe for Lombardy Green Tart. Omit eggs, baking, and lettuce. Serve chilled on a bed of **fresh spinach leaves.**

42 *Vegetable Mélange with Mustard Sauce*

1 large yellow squash or
   zucchini, pared and minced
3 medium carrots, minced
¼ cup minced onion
¼ cup minced dill pickle
4 ounces Swiss cheese, minced
⅓ cup prepared mustard
⅓ cup dill pickle juice
1 teaspoon sugar
½ teaspoon curry powder
1 garlic clove, minced
   Lettuce cups

Combine squash, carrot, onion, pickle, and cheese in a medium bowl. Mix remaining ingredients, except lettuce cups; pour over vegetables and stir to coat well. Refrigerate until well chilled. Serve in lettuce cups.

6 servings

43 *Tomato Toast (Crostini di Pomodori)*

¼ cup finely chopped onion
2 tablespoons butter or margarine
Italian-style tomatoes (canned), drained
1 teaspoon sugar
⅛ teaspoon salt
1 egg yolk, fork beaten
¼ to ½ teaspoon Worcestershire sauce
¼ cup shredded Parmesan cheese
4 slices white bread, toasted, crusts removed, and toast cut in quarters
Snipped fresh parsley or crushed dried basil or oregano

1. Add onion to heated butter in a heavy saucepan and cook until tender, stirring occasionally.
2. Force enough of the drained tomatoes through a sieve to yield 1½ cups. Add to onion with sugar and salt; cook, stirring occasionally, until liquid evaporates and mixture is thick (about 25 minutes).
3. Stir a small amount of tomato mixture into egg yolk; blend thoroughly and return to saucepan. Cook and stir 5 minutes.
4. Mix in Worcestershire sauce and half of cheese; spread generously on toast quarters. Sprinkle half of appetizers with the remaining cheese and half with the parsley.
5. Broil appetizers 3 to 4 inches from heat until bubbly. Serve hot.

16 appetizers

44 *Avocado Cocktail Dip*

1 large ripe avocado
2 teaspoons lemon juice
1 small slice onion
¼ cup mayonnaise
6 drops of Tabasco
Salt to taste
Potato chips

1. Halve and peel avocado, reserving 1 shell. Cube avocado and put into container of an electric blender. Add lemon juice, onion, mayonnaise, Tabasco, and salt. Process until puréed.
2. To serve, pile avocado mixture into reserved shell; place on a serving dish and surround with potato chips for dipping.

About 1 cup

45 *Savory Cheese Custards*

1 large yellow onion
¼ teaspoon salt
1½ teaspoons poppy seed
1 cup instant nonfat dry-milk solids
2 cups water
2 teaspoons Worcestershire sauce
2 teaspoons Dijon mustard
¼ teaspoon salt
2 eggs
2 ounces Jarlsberg or Parmesan cheese, finely shredded

1. Bake onion at 400°F until tender when pierced with a fork (about 1½ hours). Let cool. Peel onion and chop finely (about 1½ cups). Mix onion with ¼ teaspoon salt and the poppy seed; spoon mixture into the bottom of 4 ramekins or custard cups.
2. Process dry-milk solids, water, Worcestershire sauce, mustard, ¼ teaspoon salt, and eggs in a food processor or blender until very smooth.
3. Pour mixture into ramekins; sprinkle cheese over mixture. Place ramekins in a shallow baking pan; pour 1 inch boiling water into pan.
4. Bake at 325°F 30 to 40 minutes, or until custard is set and a knife inserted between center and edge comes out clean. Serve warm, or refrigerate and serve cold.

4 servings

46 *Eggs with Anchovies (Jajka ze Sardelkami)*

4 hard-cooked eggs
Lettuce leaves
16 anchovy fillets
2 tablespoons mayonnaise
1 dill pickle, sliced
1 tomato, sliced

1. Peel the eggs; cut in halves.
2. Arrange eggs, yolks up, on a dish covered with lettuce leaves.
3. Place 2 anchovy fillets over each egg to form an "X."
4. Garnish with mayonnaise, pickle, and tomato slices.

8 egg halves

47 *Veal Pâté (Pasztet z Cielęciny)*

1 pound pork liver, cut up
2 cups milk
6 dried mushrooms or 8 ounces fresh mushrooms
1 large onion, quartered
1 bay leaf
5 peppercorns
1 pound veal, cut up
1 pound sliced bacon
2 cups chicken bouillon
3 slices white bread
3 eggs
½ teaspoon nutmeg
Pinch allspice
Salt and pepper

1. Soak liver in milk 1 hour. Drain; discard milk.
2. Scrub mushrooms gently with a brush. Put dried mushrooms into a large saucepan. Add onion, bay leaf, peppercorns, veal, bacon, and bouillon; simmer 1 hour. Add the liver and fresh mushrooms (if used). Simmer 30 minutes longer.
3. Strain off the bouillon and soak bread in it.
4. Combine mushrooms, onion, veal, ¾ of the bacon, liver, and bread. Grind twice.
5. Combine eggs with ground mixture, season with nutmeg, allspice, and salt and pepper to taste. Mix very well.
6. Line a 9×5×3-inch pan with the remaining bacon. Pack with the meat mixture. Cover with foil.
7. Bake at 350°F 1 hour. Cool.
8. Serve with Horseradish Sauce (page 88), or Red Beets with Horseradish (page 79).

About 12 servings

Turkey Pâté: Follow recipe for Veal Pâté, using **turkey** or **chicken livers** instead of pork liver and **turkey meat** instead of veal. Omit allspice.

48 *Liver Pâté*

This is not baked, but made with gelatin and chilled. Calories can be cut by serving with vegetables rather than the usual crackers.

1½ cups chopped onion
1 cup chopped celery
• 1½ cups Chicken Stock
1 cup dry white wine
1 teaspoon paprika
⅛ teaspoon ground allspice or cloves
¼ teaspoon garlic powder
4 drops Tabasco
1¼ teaspoons salt
1½ pounds chicken livers, membranes removed
2 envelopes unflavored gelatin
½ cup cold water
Assorted vegetable relishes

1. Simmer onion and celery in stock and wine in an uncovered saucepan until liquid is reduced to 2 cups (about 15 minutes). Stir in paprika, allspice, garlic powder, Tabasco, and salt; simmer 2 minutes. Stir in livers; simmer covered until livers are tender (about 15 minutes). Drain; discard liquid.
2. Sprinkle gelatin over cold water; let stand 3 minutes. Set over low heat, stirring occasionally, until gelatin is dissolved (about 5 minutes).
3. Purée half the livers and vegetables along with half the gelatin mixture in a food processor or blender. Repeat with remaining ingredients; combine the two mixtures.
4. Pour mixture into a lightly oiled 1½-quart mold or bowl or ten 6-ounce custard cups. Chill until set (about 4 hours).
5. Serve from mold, or unmold onto platter and accompany with assorted vegetables.

10 to 12 servings

49 *Pickled Zucchini (Zucchini con Olio e Aceto)*

3 to 4 zucchini
5 tablespoons olive oil
2 cloves garlic, quartered
½ teaspoon oregano
¼ teaspoon salt
1 bay leaf
Wine vinegar

1. Wash zucchini and trim off ends. Cut crosswise into ¼-inch slices.
2. Heat 3 tablespoons olive oil in a skillet. Add zucchini and cook slowly until browned. Drain on absorbent paper. Cool and put into a pint screw-top jar.
3. Combine 2 tablespoons oil, garlic, oregano, salt, and bay leaf. Pour into jar. Add enough wine vinegar to cover zucchini.
4. Store, covered, in refrigerator at least 24 hours. Serve cold.

1 pint pickle

50 *Pickled Mushrooms (Funghi con Olio e Aceto)*

1 pound fresh mushrooms (½-inch caps)
White vinegar
Hot water
¼ cup olive oil
2 teaspoons salt
2 teaspoons peppercorns
2 cloves garlic, quartered
1 teaspoon ground mace

1. Clean mushrooms and put into a saucepan. Pour in equal amounts of white vinegar and hot water to cover mushrooms. Bring to boiling; cook 6 minutes. Drain and cool.
2. Pack mushrooms into a pint screw-top jar and add a mixture of oil, salt, peppercorns, garlic, and mace. Add enough white vinegar to cover mushrooms.
3. Store, covered, in refrigerator 2 days. Drain and serve cold.

1 pint pickle

51 *Italian Shrimp (Scampi Italiano)*

½ cup olive or other cooking oil
¾ teaspoon salt
¼ teaspoon black pepper
½ teaspoon garlic powder
¼ cup minced parsley
1 whole pimento, mashed
2 pounds large fresh shrimp, shelled and deveined
3 tablespoons butter or margarine
3 tablespoons lemon juice

1. Mix oil, salt, pepper, garlic powder, parsley, and pimento. Dip shrimp in mixture and cook in a hot skillet over low heat about 2 minutes on each side. Spoon 2 or 3 tablespoons of the oil mixture over shrimp; cover and cook until tender (5 to 8 minutes), turning once.
2. Transfer shrimp to a serving dish. Add butter and lemon juice to the skillet; stir and heat until mixture begins to sizzle. Pour over shrimp and serve hot.

About 6 dozen shrimp

52 *Pickled Carrots (Carote con Olio e Aceto)*

6 to 8 medium carrots, pared and cut in strips
Boiling salted water
2 tablespoons olive oil
1 clove garlic, cut in halves
1 hot green pepper
½ teaspoon salt
Wine vinegar

1. Cook carrots in a small amount of boiling salted water in a covered saucepan until just tender. Drain and cool.
2. Pack carrots in a pint screw-top jar and add oil, garlic, hot pepper, and salt. Cover carrots with wine vinegar.
3. Store, covered, in refrigerator at least 24 hours. Drain and serve cold.

1 pint pickle

53 *Marinated Pimentos*

2 to 3 tablespoons red wine vinegar
2 cloves garlic, minced
1 bay leaf
½ teaspoon salt
½ teaspoon pepper
2 tablespoons olive or other
    cooking oil
2 tablespoons chili sauce
2 jars or cans (7 ounces each)
    whole pimentos, drained and
    torn in half or in large pieces
1 can anchovy fillets
¼ cup slivered ripe olives
1 tablespoon lemon juice

1. Put the vinegar, garlic, bay leaf, salt, and pepper into a saucepan; simmer 5 minutes.
2. Blend in oil and chili sauce; pour over pimentos. Let stand about 3 hours.
3. To serve, drain pimentos and garnish with anchovy fillets and ripe olives. Drizzle lemon juice over all.

About 6 servings

54 *Eggplant Appetizer-Relish (Caponata)*

¾ cup olive oil
2 cloves garlic, crushed or minced
1 large eggplant, sliced, pared, and
    cut in small cubes (about 3
    cups)
½ cup chopped green pepper
½ cup chopped onion
¼ cup finely chopped parsley
1 tablespoon sugar
½ teaspoon crushed oregano
¼ teaspoon crushed basil
1 teaspoon seasoned salt
    Few grains black pepper
1 cup canned tomato paste
¼ cup water
3 tablespoons red wine vinegar
1 can (4 ounces) mushroom stems
    and pieces (do not drain)
½ cup very small pimento-stuffed
    olives

1. Heat the oil and garlic in a large, heavy skillet. Add the eggplant, green pepper, onion, and parsley; toss to mix. Cover tightly and cook over low heat about 10 minutes.
2. Meanwhile, blend sugar, oregano, basil, salt, and pepper. Add tomato paste, water, and wine vinegar; mix well. Add to mixture in skillet and stir in remaining ingredients. Cover and cook gently until eggplant is just tender (not mushy).
3. Turn into a bowl and store, covered, in refrigerator overnight to allow flavors to blend.
4. Serve with **crackers.**

About 4 cups relish

55 *Pears with Roquefort*

This recipe can be served appropriately as a dessert as well as a first course.

4 small pears
2 tablespoons Roquefort or blue
    cheese, crumbled
½ cup low-fat cottage cheese
¼ cup Neufchatel cheese
2 teaspoons brandy
2 tablespoons water
    Watercress

1. Cut entire top off pears; reserve. Using melon-ball cutter, carefully scoop out pears, leaving a ¼-inch shell. Discard core and seeds. Finely chop pulp.
2. Purée pulp with cheeses, brandy, and water in a food processor or blender. Fill cavity of pears with cheese mixture. Replace tops on pears. Garnish with watercress. Serve with a knife and fork.

4 servings

56 George's Greek-Style Artichokes
(Carciofi alla Greca George's)

6 artichokes
4 ounces fresh mushrooms, sliced
⅔ cup coarsely chopped onion
½ cup olive oil
½ cup dry white wine
Juice of 1 lemon
30 fennel seeds
¼ teaspoon coriander
Salt and pepper to taste

1. Rinse artichokes and discard the hard outer leaves. Quarter artichokes, remove and discard "choke" or fuzzy part, and arrange the pieces in a large baking pan or shallow heat-resistant casserole having a cover. Allow plenty of space for the artichokes.
2. Cover artichoke pieces with the mushrooms and onion. Then pour over them a mixture of oil, wine, lemon juice, and dry seasonings.
3. Cover and place over medium heat. Bring to a rapid boil and cook about 1 minute.
4. Set in a 350°F oven about 30 minutes, or until artichokes are tender.
5. Remove from oven; cool at room temperature, then refrigerate to chill thoroughly. Serve cold.

About 8 servings

57 Deep-Fried Plantain

Green plantain
Ice water
Peanut oil for deep frying, heated
    to 365°F
Salt

1. Peel plantain; reserve the skin. Slice the plantain on the slant in 2½-inch pieces. Soak in water.
2. Without draining, drop a few pieces of plantain into the oil. Fry for 2 minutes. Remove, using a spoon with a long handle. Repeat until all pieces are fried.
3. Place a fried plantain piece inside the reserved skin. Press between the palms of the hands to flatten the fried plantain; the edges will be jagged. Remove from skin and deep-fry again until golden brown. Flatten and refry all pieces. Drain on absorbent paper. Sprinkle with salt and serve hot.

58 Pasties (Pâtes Chauds)

1 cup ice-cold water
1 teaspoon salt
3 cups all-purpose flour
1¼ cups vegetable shortening
    Cold milk (about ¼ cup)
    Beef Filling (½ recipe)
1 egg yolk, beaten

1. Combine water and salt. Place flour in a large mixing bowl and make a well in the center. Pour salted water into well and mix lightly with a spoon without kneading. Place dough in refrigerator 30 minutes.
2. Roll the dough into a rectangle ¼ inch thick. Spread half the shortening on the dough. Fold one side over the middle and spread this section with the remaining shortening. Fold over the remaining section and again roll out to ¼-inch thickness. Fold again into thirds and roll out. Repeat this rolling process a third time. Refrigerate dough overnight.
3. Roll the dough to about ½-inch thickness. Cut the dough into 2½-inch rounds. Roll out trimmings to cut more rounds.
4. Place a tablespoonful of filling in the center of half the dough rounds. Brush the edges with milk. Cover with remaining rounds, lightly pressing the edges down. Brush the tops with egg yolk. Place pasties on a baking sheet with sides. Place a pan of hot water on the bottom rack of the oven.
5. Bake at 400°F 30 minutes, then turn the oven control to 300°F and bake 20 minutes, or until golden brown.

1 dozen

59 Beef Filling

2 parsley sprigs
¼ small green hot pepper or
    6 dried Italian pepper pods
2 shallots, chopped
1 garlic clove
½ pound ground beef, cooked
● 1 cup Béchamel Sauce
    (use beef broth)

1. In a mortar, pound to paste the parsley, pepper, shallot, and garlic.
2. Add seasoning paste and cooked beef to Béchamel Sauce; mix well.

Note: Half of the filling is needed for Pasties; use remainder for hot sandwiches or as desired.

    Filling may also be made with leftover cooked chicken, fish, tongue, ham, or mushrooms. Follow above procedure, using chicken or fish broth in Béchamel Sauce.

60 Pork Tidbits (Grio)

2 pounds pork loin
½ orange
½ lime
    Salt, pepper, and garlic to taste
2 cups water
½ cup bacon drippings
● Ti-Malice Sauce
● Deep-Fried Plantain

1. Remove bones from pork loin and cut meat into small cubes, keeping all the fat on the meat. Rub meat first with the cut side of orange, then with cut side of lime. Season with salt, pepper, and garlic.
2. Put the meat and water into a Dutch oven and cook covered over high heat until all water has evaporated, leaving the fat only.
3. Add bacon drippings to meat in Dutch oven and fry meat over medium heat, stirring occasionally, until meat is brown and crisp.
4. Heap meat on a round platter, sprinkle generously with sauce, and surround with plantain pieces.

61 *Meatballs with Breadfruit*

1 breadfruit (about 1 pound)
1 garlic clove
1 teaspoon lime juice
1 tablespoon chopped chives
2 parsley sprigs
3 eggs
1 cup cooked ground meat
½ cup finely ground peanuts
Oil for frying, heated to 365°F
● Tomato Sauce Creole

1. Peel breadfruit. Boil about 20 minutes in salted water, or until soft; drain. Mash as for potatoes.
2. In a mortar, pound to a paste the garlic, lime juice, chives, and parsley. Combine paste with mashed breadfruit, 2 eggs, and cooked ground meat; beat until fluffy. Roll into walnut-size balls; coat with beaten egg and then peanuts.
3. Fry in heated fat until golden. Drain on absorbent paper. Serve hot with the sauce as a dip.

Note: Breadfruit may also be combined with ham, poultry, game, salt cod, or salt herring.

62 *Meatballs à l'Haitienne*

4 white bread slices
1 cup milk
1 pound freshly ground lean beef
2 slices smoked ham or bacon, minced
Salt and pepper to taste
1 garlic clove, crushed in garlic press
1 tablespoon tomato paste
½ cup flour
½ cup grated Parmesan cheese
Fat for frying, heated to 365°F
● Tomato Sauce Creole

1. Soak bread in milk 5 minutes, then mash and mix with ground beef, minced ham, salt, pepper, garlic, and tomato paste. Roll into walnut-size balls; coat with flour and then with cheese.
2. Fry in heated fat until golden brown. Drain on absorbent paper. Serve hot with the sauce as a dip.

Note: These meatballs may be made larger for a main course and are usually served with Cornmeal (●) and a salad.

63 *Cocktail Puffs* (Marinades)

1 tablespoon coarse salt
2 peppercorns
1 scallion or green onion, cut in pieces
2 parsley sprigs
⅛ teaspoon ground mace
1 teaspoon lime juice
4 drops Tabasco
1 cup all-purpose flour
1 tablespoon baking powder
2½ cups water
1 egg yolk
1 cup chopped cooked calf's brains, chicken, turkey, smoked herring, shrimp, lobster, or fish
2 egg whites, stiffly beaten
Peanut oil for frying, heated to 365°F

1. In a mortar, pound to a paste the salt, peppercorns, scallion, parsley, mace, lime juice, and Tabasco.
2. Sift flour with baking powder into a bowl. Mix in water, seasoning paste, egg yolk, and desired cooked ingredient. Fold in beaten egg white.
3. Pour the batter by tablespoonfuls into the heated fat; it will spread. Gather the batter with a circular motion as it floats on top of the fat and looks like a wafer. Fry until crisp, golden, and lacelike. Drain on absorbent paper. Serve hot.

64 *Codfish Fritters*

½ pound salt cod
3 dried Italian pepper pods or
   1 very small piece hot pepper
2 garlic cloves
2 green onions, cut in pieces
2 parsley sprigs
2½ cups all-purpose flour
1 teaspoon baking powder
1 cup light beer
   Peanut oil, heated to 365°F
● Dilled Avocado Sauce for Fish

1. Soak cod in cold water overnight. The next day, drain the cod, add fresh water, and bring to a boil. Drain, cool, and shred finely.
2. In a mortar, pound together to a paste the pepper pods, garlic, onion, and parsley.
3. Sift flour with baking powder into a bowl; stir in beer. Add the seasoning paste and shredded cod; mix well.
4. Drop batter by teaspoonfuls into heated oil. Fry until golden. Drain on absorbent paper. Serve hot with the sauce.

65 *Haitian Rarebit*

8 kaiser rolls
16 slices American or Cheddar cheese
½ cup sweet pickle relish
1 cup chopped cooked ham, chicken, beef, or tongue
8 tablespoons butter or margarine, melted

1. Split rolls. On bottom half of each roll, place in the following order: 1 slice cheese, 1 tablespoon sweet pickle relish, 2 tablespoons chopped meat, and another slice cheese. Replace top of roll.
2. Generously brush top and bottom of sandwiches with melted butter.
3. Place rolls in a large skillet over medium heat. Cover with a lid slightly smaller than the skillet and weight it down over the rolls. Brown both sides until cheese melts. Serve immediately.

8 servings

66 *Shrimp Paste à la Creole*

Fresh shrimp
● Court Bouillon for Fish and Shellfish
¼ cup butter, melted
1 garlic clove, crushed in a garlic press
⅛ teaspoon ground mace
⅛ teaspoon pepper
   Tabasco to taste

1. Cook enough shrimp in bouillon to make 4 cups shelled shrimp.
2. Put shrimp, hot melted butter, garlic, mace, pepper, and Tabasco into container of an electric blender; process 10 seconds.
3. Serve on **toasted cassava** or **Melba toast**.

67 Chicken Fritters Guadeloupe

2 cups minced cooked chicken
3 tablespoons finely chopped parsley
2 tablespoons finely chopped chives
3 tablespoons fresh bread crumbs
1 tablespoon grated onion
1 tablespoon curry powder
  Salt to taste
¼ teaspoon cayenne or red pepper
¼ cup Dijon mustard
½ cup dry bread crumbs
1 egg, beaten with 1 teaspoon
    peanut oil
  Oil for frying, heated to 365°F

1. Mix chicken with parsley, chives, fresh bread crumbs, onion, and seasonings. Shape mixture into walnut-size balls, roll in dry bread crumbs, then in beaten egg, and again in bread crumbs. Chill in refrigerator.
2. Just before serving, fry in hot oil until golden brown. Drain on absorbent paper and serve hot.

68 Eggplant Fritters

3 long thin eggplants
1 tablespoon lime juice
  Salt, pepper, and cayenne or
    red pepper to taste
1½ cups all-purpose flour (about)
¾ cup beer (about)
  Oil for deep frying
    heated to 365°F
  Salt

1. Slice eggplants into eighteen ½-inch rounds. Season with lime juice, salt, and ground peppers. Marinate 15 minutes.
2. Make a batter the consistency of whipping cream by mixing flour with beer.
3. Dip and coat eggplant slices in batter. Fry in heated oil until golden brown. Drain on absorbent paper. Sprinkle lightly with salt. Serve hot.

Artichoke Fritters: Follow recipe for Eggplant Fritters. Substitute **artichoke hearts** or **bottoms** for eggplant rounds.

69 Corn Fritters

1 cup fresh corn kernels
½ cup butter
1 cup all-purpose flour
4 eggs
  Corn oil for frying,
    heated to 365°F

1. Cook corn until soft in boiling salted water in a saucepan; drain thoroughly, reserving 1 cup liquid. Melt butter with corn liquid in saucepan, add flour, and cook, stirring rapidly, until mixture is smooth and rolls away from the sides of pan.
2. Remove from heat and add the eggs, one at a time, beating well after each addition. Stir in cooked corn.
3. Drop batter by spoonfuls into heated oil and fry until golden and well puffed. Drain on absorbent paper. Serve hot.

70 Acra

5 dried Italian pepper pods or
    1 small piece hot pepper
1 tablespoon coarse salt
6 peppercorns
½ medium onion, chopped
2 garlic cloves
1 egg
1 cup finely grated malanga root*
  Peanut oil for frying,
    heated to 365°F

1. In a mortar, pound together to a paste the pepper pods, salt, peppercorns, onion, and garlic.
2. Add seasoning paste and egg to grated malanga root; beat until light.
3. Drop mixture by spoonfuls into heated oil and fry until golden. Drain on absorbent paper.

20 fritters

*Malanga root can be found in Puerto Rican markets.

71 *Oysters Barquettes Gourmet Club Port-au-Prince*

- Pastry (see Turnovers Aquin,
- 1 jar pickled oysters, drained
- ¾ cup Béchamel Sauce
  (use fish broth)
- 1 cup coarsely chopped artichoke
  hearts
  Finely shredded Swiss cheese

1. Prepare pastry, roll out, and cut to fit barquette or other small molds. Press dough firmly into molds against bottom and sides. Prick with a fork. Fill with beans or lentils, if desired.
2. Bake at 375°F 12 minutes. Pour out beans, if used. Unmold and set aside.
3. Measure 1 cup oysters; reserve remainder for garnish.
4. Combine sauce, artichoke hearts, and 1 cup oysters. Spoon mixture into barquettes and sprinkle with cheese. Glaze under a broiler; top each with an oyster. Serve hot.

72 *Turnovers Aquin*

Aquin is a small town in the south of Haiti renowned for its mangrove oysters.

- 1½ cups all-purpose flour
- ¼ teaspoon salt
- ⅓ cup peanut oil
- 2 tablespoons ice-cold water
- 1 jar pickled oysters
  Milk for brushing
  Peanut oil for deep frying,
  heated to 365°F

1. For pastry, combine flour and salt in a bowl. Mix in oil and ice-cold water. Gather dough into a ball and roll out very thin between 2 sheets of waxed paper. Cut out 3-inch rounds with cookie cutter or inverted glass.
2. Slightly off center on round, place 3 oysters. Fold in half, coming to within ¼ inch of the opposite edge. Moisten rim with a pastry brush dipped in milk. Fold rim back over itself to seal.
3. Fry in heated fat until golden. Drain on absorbent paper.

73 *Salt Cod Salad (Mor Marinée)*

- 1 pound dried cod fillet
- 3 peppercorns, cracked
- 1 whole clove, cracked
- ⅛ teaspoon nutmeg
- 5 dried Italian pepper pods or
  1 small hot pepper
- 1 sweet pepper, cored, seeded, and
  julienned
- 4 shallots, chopped
- 2 garlic cloves, crushed in a
  garlic press
- 1 cup olive oil
- ¼ cup wine vinegar
- ¼ cup chopped mixed chives and
  parsley
- Biscuits Port-au-Prince

1. Put cod into a sieve and slowly pour 2 quarts very hot water over it. Shred fish and remove all bones and skin. Add peppercorns, clove, nutmeg, pepper pods, julienne of pepper, shallots, and garlic; mix well. Add olive oil and vinegar; mix again. Marinate 3 days in refrigerator.
2. Mound marinated mixture on a serving platter. Sprinkle with mixture of chives and parsley. Serve on halved hot buttered biscuits.

74 Pickled Herring in Sour Cream
(Śledzie Marynowane w Śmietanie)

6 pickled herring, drained
1 large onion, peeled and chopped
6 hard-cooked eggs, peeled and
   chopped
1 apple, cored and chopped
1 teaspoon lemon juice
1 cup dairy sour cream
1 clove garlic, crushed (optional)
¼ teaspoon salt
⅛ teaspoon pepper
2 tablespoons chopped fresh dill or
   parsley

1. Cut herring into small cubes. Mix herring with onion, eggs, apple, and lemon juice.
2. Combine sour cream, garlic (if desired), salt, and pepper; add to herring mixture and mix well. Sprinkle with dill.
3. Serve with **dark bread.**

4 to 6 servings

75 Egg Crowns

 6 hard-cooked eggs, peeled and
    sliced
30 small rounds of buttered bread
 1 package (3 ounces) cream cheese
    (at room temperature)
 2 tablespoons mayonnaise
 1 teaspoon prepared mustard
 ½ teaspoon salt
 ½ teaspoon vinegar
 1 jar (2 ounces) pimento strips,
    drained
   Watercress

1. Remove yolks from eggs; put into a sieve over a bowl. Place rings of white on buttered bread.
2. Sieve egg yolks and ends of whites.
3. Mix sieved eggs, cream cheese, mayonnaise, mustard, salt, and vinegar. Beat until smooth.
4. With 2 spoons or pastry tube and star tip, fill each egg white ring with yolk mixture. Garnish with pimento strips and watercress.

30 canapés

Chilled Artichoke Plate, page 20
Cucumber Sauce, page 39
Individual Chicken Terrines, page 18

Sauces

76 Mayonnaise (Mayoneza)

2 egg yolks
½ teaspoon salt
¼ teaspoon white pepper
½ teaspoon dry mustard
  Wine or tarragon vinegar
    (about 3 tablespoons)
1½ cups olive oil

Beat egg yolks until thick and lemon colored. Beat in salt, pepper, dry mustard, and half of the vinegar. Beating constantly, trickle in 1/3 cup olive oil, add ½ teaspoon vinegar, and trickle in remaining olive oil. Check for consistency. If the Mayonnaise is too thick, add vinegar drop by drop and mix by hand until the appropriate consistency is achieved. Adjust seasoning.

About 1½ cups

Note: If Mayonnaise curdles, wash beater. Beat an egg yolk until thick in a small bowl. Slowly add curdled mixture, beating constantly, to form a new emulsion. Another egg yolk may be necessary. If so, beat again until thick, add mixture slowly.

77 Garlic Mayonnaise (Mayoneza me Skortho)

4 garlic cloves, crushed in a
    garlic press
¼ teaspoon salt
2 egg yolks
  Olive oil (about 1 cup)
  Juice of ½ lemon, or more to
    taste
  Salt and white pepper

Combine garlic, salt, and egg yolks. Slowly add oil, a drop at a time, beating vigorously until 2 to 3 tablespoons have been added. Add remaining oil in a steady stream, beating constantly. Add lemon juice, beating well. Season with salt and pepper.

About 1½ cups

78 Tomato Sauce (Saltsa me Domates)

3 tablespoons butter
1 large onion, chopped
2 pounds fresh ripe tomatoes,
    peeled and chopped
2 teaspoons sugar
2 whole cloves
1 bay leaf
1 garlic clove, crushed in a garlic
    press
1 teaspoon vinegar
  Salt and pepper to taste

Melt butter in a saucepan; add onion and cook until translucent. Add tomatoes and remaining ingredients. Simmer uncovered 20 minutes.

3 cups

Note: A variation served during Lent is Anchovy Tomato Sauce. To prepare, use **olive oil** instead of butter, decrease sugar to 1 teaspoon, increase vinegar to 2 teaspoons; and add ½ **tube anchovy paste** or **1 can (2 ounces) anchovies**, drained and cut into small pieces.

79 Mustard Sauce (Sos Musztardowy)

¾ cup dairy sour cream
⅓ cup mayonnaise
2 tablespoons prepared mustard
¼ teaspoon salt
¼ teaspoon sugar

1. Mix all ingredients well.
2. Serve with cold pork, ham, or hard-cooked eggs.

About 1¼ cups

80 Sour Cream Sauce (Sos Śmietanowy)

2 hard-cooked eggs
1 cup dairy sour cream
1 teaspoon prepared mustard or dill
¼ teaspoon sugar
¼ teaspoon salt
⅛ teaspoon pepper

1. Press eggs through a sieve. Add sour cream and beat with a mixer at medium speed 3 minutes. Add mustard, sugar, salt, and pepper. Beat 1 minute at high speed.
2. Serve with ham or veal.

1½ cups

81 Mushroom Sauce (Sos Grzybowy)

1 pound mushrooms, sliced
1 large onion, chopped
1 cup chicken or meat broth or bouillon
3 tablespoons flour
2 tablespoons melted butter
½ cup dairy sour cream
1 teaspoon lemon juice
Salt and pepper

1. Simmer mushrooms with onion in bouillon 15 minutes.
2. Blend flour into butter. Stir into mushrooms. Bring to boiling, stirring.
3. Remove from heat. Stir in sour cream, lemon juice, and salt and pepper to taste.

3 cups

82 Green Onion Sauce (Sos Szczypiorkowy)

1 cup dairy sour cream
3 tablespoons sliced green onion
1 egg yolk, beaten
2 tablespoons prepared mustard
1 teaspoon lemon juice
½ teaspoon sugar
¼ teaspoon salt

1. Combine sour cream, green onion, egg yolk, prepared mustard, lemon juice, sugar, and salt.
2. Serve hot or cold.

About 1⅓ cups

83 Cold Horseradish Sauce (Sos Chrzanowy Zimny)

6 ounces prepared cream-style horseradish
1 large apple, pared and shredded
1½ cups dairy sour cream
½ teaspoon sugar
¼ teaspoon salt

1. Mix horseradish with apple. Add sour cream; stir in sugar and salt.
2. Serve with cold meat, hard-cooked eggs, and fish.

About 2½ cups

84 Tartar Sauce (Sos Tatarski)

2 hard-cooked eggs
2 tablespoons finely chopped mushrooms
2 tablespoons salad oil
2 teaspoons prepared mustard
2 teaspoons pickle liquid
¼ teaspoon salt
¼ teaspoon sugar
½ cup mayonnaise
½ cup dairy sour cream
¼ cup finely chopped dill pickles

1. Mash cooked egg yolks. Chop whites separately.
2. Sauté mushrooms in oil. Blend in mashed egg yolks, mustard, pickle liquid, salt, and sugar.
3. Blend mayonnaise into sour cream. Add chopped egg whites, egg yolk mixture, and pickles; mix well.

About 2 cups

85 Mock Crème Fraîche

Crème fraîche is a heavy cream which is fermented naturally. It is very thick and nutlike in flavor and is used in French cooking to give body to sauces. Unlike sour cream, it will not curdle when cooked. Crème fraîche has recently become available in this country; it is very high in calories and very expensive. Our version has half the calories and is simple and inexpensive to make.

1½ cups Neufchatel cheese
● 6 tablespoons Low-Fat Yogurt

1. Mix cheese and yogurt in a blender or food processor until smooth and fluffy. Place in small jars; cover tightly.
2. Set jars in a warm place (100° to 125°F) for 2 hours; see Note. Cool and refrigerate. Stir before using.

About 2 cups

Note: Use an oven thermometer in making Mock Crème Fraîche, as temperature is very important. A gas oven with a pilot light will be about 125°F. Turn electric oven to as warm a setting as necessary to maintain temperature. Mock Crème Fraîche can be refrigerated up to 3 weeks.

86 Madeira Sauce

¼ cup chopped celery
¼ cup chopped carrot
2 tablespoons chopped green onion
1 tablespoon cooking oil
1 quart water
2 beef bouillon cubes
1 chicken bouillon cube
½ bay leaf
Pinch ground thyme
Few grains freshly ground black pepper
1 tablespoon tomato sauce
¼ cup water
2 tablespoons flour
⅓ cup Madeira

1. Cook celery, carrot, and onion in hot oil in a large saucepot until dark brown, but not burned.
2. Stir in 1 quart water, bouillon cubes, bay leaf, thyme, and pepper. Bring to boiling, and simmer until liquid is reduced by half.
3. Strain the liquid. Stir in tomato sauce and bring to boiling.
4. Vigorously shake ¼ cup water and flour in a screw-top jar. While stirring the boiling mixture, slowly add the flour mixture. Cook 1 to 2 minutes, then simmer about 30 minutes, stirring occasionally.
5. Just before serving, stir Madeira into sauce and bring sauce to boiling.

About 2⅓ cups sauce

87 Green Garlic Sauce (Pesto Genovese)

3 cloves garlic, peeled
3 tablespoons minced sweet basil leaves or 2½ teaspoons dried basil leaves
3 tablespoons grated Parmesan or Romano cheese
1 tablespoon chopped pinenuts or walnuts
¼ teaspoon salt
4 to 6 tablespoons olive oil
1 tablespoon chopped fresh parsley

1. In a mortar, mix garlic, basil, cheese, nuts, and salt. Grind mixture with a pestle to a smooth paste.
2. Still grinding, add very gradually enough olive oil to make a smooth sauce. Stir in parsley.
3. To serve, add desired amount of sauce and a tablespoon of butter to hot pasta and mix well at the table. Accompany with grated cheese, if desired.

About ½ cup sauce

Note: Sauce may be stored in refrigerator with a little olive oil on top.

88 *Low-Fat Yogurt*

1 quart 2% milk
¼ cup instant nonfat dry-milk
    solids
2 tablespoons low-fat natural
    yogurt

1. Mix milk and dry-milk solids in a medium saucepan. Heat to scalding (150°F); cool to 110°F. Stir in yogurt.
2. Transfer mixture to a glass or crockery bowl. Cover with plastic wrap; wrap bowl securely in a heavy bath towel. Set in a warm place (100° to 125°F)* for 4 to 6 hours, until yogurt has formed.
3. Place several layers of paper toweling directly on yogurt; refrigerate covered until cold.

About 1 quart

*A gas oven with a pilot light will be about 125°F; however, use an oven thermometer, as temperature is very important. Turn an electric oven to as warm a setting as necessary to maintain temperature.

Excess liquid and a coarse texture will result if temperature is too high. Liquid can be drained with a nylon baster. Blend yogurt in a food processor or blender to restore texture.

Note: This recipe can be made using skim or reconstituted dry milk, although the product will not be as rich.

Purchased low-fat natural yogurt can be substituted in any recipe.

89 *Avocado Sauce*

Mexican guacamole was the idea behind this flavorful sauce.

2 medium avocados, peeled and
    chopped
1 small pared zucchini, chopped
1 tablespoon minced onion
2 teaspoons lemon juice
¼ teaspoon chili powder
1 small tomato, seeded and
    chopped
¼ teaspoon salt

1. Purée avocados, zucchini, onion, lemon juice, and chili powder in a food processor or blender; stir in tomato and salt. Refrigerate covered until chilled (about 1 hour).
2. Serve over pork, veal, poultry, fish, or vegetable salads.

About 3 cups

90 *Cauliflower Sauce*

This sauce has a rich, creamy texture and lends itself well to any recipe calling for a white sauce.

¾ pound cauliflower
● Chicken Stock
½ teaspoon salt
¼ teaspoon freshly ground white
    pepper
2 tablespoons dry white wine
1 teaspoon snipped fresh or ½
    teaspoon dried thyme leaves
2 ounces Swiss cheese, shredded
    Snipped parsley (optional)

1. Remove leaves and tough stalks from cauliflower; separate into flowerets. Simmer cauliflower, covered, in 1 inch of stock until tender (about 8 minutes); drain.
2. Purée cauliflower with remaining ingredients, except cheese and parsley, in a food processor or blender. Heat thoroughly over low heat. Stir in cheese; heat, stirring constantly, until cheese is melted (about 2 minutes).
3. Stir parsley into sauce, if desired, and serve immediately as a sauce or soup.

About 1⅓ cups

91 *Garlic-Parsley Sauce*

Garlic cloves lose their pungency and develop a delicate flavor when poached. Flavors of garlic, mushrooms, green onion, and parsley merge in this hearty sauce.

30 large garlic cloves, peeled
    Water
● ¾ cup Chicken Stock
1½ cups sliced fresh mushrooms
1 teaspoon minced green onion
1 tablespoon snipped parsley
¼ teaspoon salt
½ teaspoon bottled brown
    bouquet sauce

1. Cover garlic cloves with water in a saucepan; heat to boiling and drain. Repeat 2 more times. Add remaining ingredients, except brown bouquet sauce, to garlic in saucepan; simmer, covered, 15 minutes.
2. Purée all ingredients and brown bouquet sauce in a food processor or blender. Heat in a saucepan to serve hot, or refrigerate and serve cold.
3. Serve on roast beef, steak, or veal. Or fill **mushroom caps** with sauce; bake at 300°F 15 minutes.

About 2 cups

Note: Substitute ¼ cup stock for red wine, if desired.

92 *Seasoned Dark Green Sauce*

*1 pound spinach, washed and
    stems removed
1 teaspoon anchovy paste
1 large garlic clove, minced
1 drop Tabasco
1 tablespoon instant nonfat
    dry-milk solids
● ¾ to 1 cup Chicken Stock

1. Simmer spinach with water clinging to leaves in a covered saucepan until spinach is tender (about 7 minutes); drain.
2. Purée in a food processor or blender with remaining ingredients, adding amount of stock necessary for a medium sauce consistency. Heat in a saucepan to serve hot or refrigerate to serve cold.
3. Serve over poultry, fish, or cooked vegetables. Or serve as a vegetable in small bowls and top with yogurt.

About 2 cups

*1 package (10 ounces) frozen leaf spinach can be used. Cook according to package instructions; drain well.

93 *Green Peppercorn Sauce*

Green peppercorns are the whole unripe berries from the pepper vine. They are generally processed and packed in brine. Their pungent flavor makes this a distinctive sauce.

● 1 cup Chicken Stock
2 tablespoons brandy
1 tablespoon arrowroot
    Cold water
¼ pound fresh mushrooms,
    chopped
● ¼ cup Mock Crème Fraîche
½ teaspoon salt
¼ teaspoon freshly ground
    pepper
2 tablespoons drained green
    peppercorns

1. Heat stock and brandy.
2. Mix arrowroot with a little cold water; stir into stock. Simmer, stirring constantly, until stock has thickened (about 4 minutes). Stir in remaining ingredients. Heat thoroughly. Serve immediately.

About 2½ cups

94 *Light Green Sauce*

1 cup finely chopped lettuce
    Peel of 1 large zucchini
¼ cup parsley sprigs, stems
    removed
1 tablespoon chopped green
    onion
⅔ cup low-fat ricotta cheese
¾ teaspoon salt
⅛ teaspoon freshly ground white
    pepper
2 teaspoons fresh lemon juice
● ⅓ to ½ cup Chicken Stock

1. Purée all ingredients in a food processor or blender, adding amount of stock necessary for a medium sauce consistency.
2. Serve over hot or cold vegetables, poached fish, or chicken.

About 1¼ cups

95 *Artichoke Sauce*

This sauce is so elegant in flavor that you would never guess it is so easy to make.

1 can (8 ounces) artichoke hearts,
    cut in quarters
¼ cup low-fat ricotta cheese
● ⅓ to ½ cup Chicken Stock
¼ teaspoon salt
⅛ teaspoon freshly ground white
    pepper

1. Purée all ingredients in a food processor or blender, adding more stock if necessary for a fairly thick consistency. Heat in a saucepan to serve hot, or refrigerate and serve cold.
2. Serve with veal, pork, fish, vegetables, or eggs.

About 1½ cups

Note: To serve as a soup, add more stock to sauce for desired consistency.

96 *Cucumber Sauce*

1 medium cucumber, pared,
    seeded, and finely chopped
●   Chicken Stock
● 1½ cups Low-Fat Yogurt
1 tablespoon snipped fresh or
    1½ teaspoons dried dill
    weed
¼ teaspoon salt
    Dash freshly ground white
    pepper

1. Simmer cucumber in 1 inch of stock in a covered saucepan until tender (about 5 minutes); drain off and discard stock.
2. Mix cucumbers with remaining ingredients. Serve cold, or heat and serve warm.

About 2 cups

Note: Snipped coriander or mint can be used in place of dill in this recipe.

97 *Cumberland Sauce*

½ cup fresh cranberries
2 teaspoons grated orange peel
1 large navel orange, peeled and finely chopped
2 tablespoons brandy
½ cup port wine
¼ cup orange juice
● ¼ cup Beef Stock
1 teaspoon prepared mustard

1. Process cranberries, orange peel and chopped orange, and brandy in a food processor or blender until finely ground.
2. Transfer mixture to a saucepan; stir in remaining ingredients. Simmer uncovered until sauce is of medium thick consistency (about 15 minutes). Serve hot, or refrigerate and serve cold.
3. Serve over duck, pork, ham, or over cottage cheese or fruit salads.

About 1½ cups

98 *Mock Hollandaise Sauce*

Our recipe boasts one-third the calories of the traditional hollandaise sauce. It has an enjoyable, smooth texture and tart flavor with no butter or egg yolks added.

½ cup Neufchatel cheese
● 3 tablespoons Low-Fat Yogurt
Dash salt
Juice of ½ lemon

1. Mix all ingredients in a blender or food processor until smooth and fluffy.
2. Cook over simmering water until hot and thickened. Serve immediately or refrigerate and serve cold. Stir before using.

¾ cup

Mock Béarnaise Sauce: Stir **1½ teaspoons snipped fresh** or **½ teaspoon dried tarragon leaves** and **½ teaspoon minced shallots** into sauce before heating.

Mock Mayonnaise: Stir **1½ teaspoons Dijon mustard** and **½ teaspoon sugar** into sauce before heating. Refrigerate until cold.

Note: The above sauces can be refrigerated up to 3 weeks.

99 *Herbed Mock Mayonnaise*

Mock Mayonnaise given a new flavor twist can be used as a sauce, a salad dressing, or a dip for raw vegetables.

● 1 cup Mock Mayonnaise
2 teaspoons snipped fresh or 1 teaspoon dried crumbled tarragon leaves
2 teaspoons snipped fresh chervil or parsley
½ garlic clove, minced
½ teaspoon minced onion

Mix all ingredients. Refrigerate 3 hours or overnight. Stir before serving.

1 cup

100 *Citrus Mayonnaise*

- 1 cup Mock Mayonnaise
- 1 tablespoon fresh orange juice
- 1 tablespoon fresh lemon juice
- 1 teaspoon grated orange peel
  Dash ground white pepper

Mix all ingredients in a small bowl. Refrigerate covered ½ hour. Stir before serving.

About 1 cup

101 *Madeira Sauce*

- 1 cup Chicken Stock
  Juice of 1 lemon
- 1 teaspoon Worcestershire sauce
- ¼ teaspoon salt
- ⅓ cup Madeira wine
- 1 tablespoon arrowroot
  Cold water
- 1 tablespoon snipped parsley

1. Heat stock, lemon juice, Worcestershire sauce, salt, and Madeira in a small saucepan.
2. Mix arrowroot with a little cold water; stir into stock mixture. Simmer, stirring constantly, until thickened (about 3 minutes). Stir in parsley. Serve immediately.

About 1½ cups

102 *Savory Tomato Sauce*

- 5 large tomatoes, peeled, cored, and coarsely chopped
- ⅔ cup chopped green onions
- ⅔ cup chopped celery
- 1 large green pepper, cored and chopped
- 2 tablespoons snipped parsley
- ¾ cup tomato juice
- ½ teaspoon cumin
- ¼ teaspoon chili powder
- ¼ teaspoon garlic powder
- ⅛ teaspoon ground cloves
- 1½ teaspoons salt

Mix all ingredients in a 3-quart saucepan. Simmer uncovered until sauce is of medium, not thick, consistency (about 1 hour).

About 1 quart

103 *Green Onion Sauce*

- 2 bunches green onions, sliced
- 1 medium zucchini, cut in 1-inch pieces
- 1½ to 1⅔ cups Chicken Stock
- ½ teaspoon salt

1. Simmer onions and zucchini in 1½ cups stock in a covered saucepan until tender (about 10 minutes).
2. Purée vegetables, stock, and salt in a food processor or blender, adding more stock if necessary for a medium sauce consistency. Heat in a saucepan to serve hot, or refrigerate and serve cold.
3. Serve over cooked vegetables, roast beef, pork, or lamb, or . as a dip for raw vegetables.

About 2 cups

Note: To serve as a cold soup, thin with ½ cup stock and top with a **dollop of yogurt.**

104 *Middle Eastern Sauce*

1 cup raw soybeans
3 cups water
1 teaspoon salt
● ½ cup Low-Fat Yogurt
1 teaspoon cumin
½ teaspoon sesame or vegetable oil
¼ teaspoon curry powder
1 teaspoon minced garlic
¼ to ½ teaspoon salt

1. Simmer soybeans in water with 1 teaspoon salt in a covered saucepan 3 hours; drain, reserving ½ cup liquid.
2. Purée soybeans with remaining ingredients in a food processor or blender; add reserved liquid as necessary for a medium sauce consistency.
3. Serve warm over steamed vegetables, chicken, or lamb. Or refrigerate until chilled and serve as a dip for assorted vegetables.

About 2½ cups

105 *Vinaigrette Dressing*

Chicken stock replaces most of the oil in this recipe. Great as a sauce, salad dressing, or marinade.

1 tablespoon fresh lemon juice
1 tablespoon olive or vegetable oil
● ¼ cup Chicken Stock
2 teaspoons snipped parsley
1 teaspoon snipped fresh or
½ teaspoon dried basil leaves
2 teaspoons distilled white vinegar
1 teaspoon Dijon mustard
1 small garlic clove, minced
⅛ teaspoon salt
Freshly ground white pepper

Measure all ingredients into a jar with a tight cover; shake vigorously. Refrigerate dressing until chilled. Shake before serving.

About ½ cup

106 *White Vegetable Purée*

You will enjoy the rich texture of this hearty sauce—puréed turnips and potatoes form the base.

¾ pound white potatoes, pared and cut in 1-inch pieces
¾ pound turnips, pared and cut in 1-inch pieces
Water
¼ cup instant nonfat dry-milk solids
½ cup 2% milk
1 teaspoon salt
¼ teaspoon freshly ground white pepper
1 tablespoon clarified butter
● ¼ to ⅓ cup Mock Crème Fraîche if desired

1. Simmer potatoes and turnips in 1½ inches water in a large covered saucepan until tender (about 20 minutes). Drain vegetables; reserve cooking liquid.
2. Purée vegetables with milk solids, milk, salt, pepper, and butter in a food processor or blender. Add reserved cooking liquid and Mock Crème Fraîche, if used, for desired consistency. Return mixture to saucepan and heat thoroughly.

About 2 cups

Note: This recipe can be served as a soup if thinned with skim milk.

107 *Custard Sauce*

- 1 cup Low-Fat Yogurt
  1 egg yolk
  2 teaspoons honey or apple
     concentrate

Beat all ingredients until fluffy. Serve immediately or refrigerate until chilled.

About 1¼ cups

108 *Beef Stock*

1 pound lean beef stew cubes
1 pound lean veal stew cubes
½ pound beef soup bones
3 carrots, cut in 2-inch pieces
1 tomato, quartered and seeded
2 medium yellow onions,
   quartered
1 stalk celery,
   cut in 2-inch pieces
1 garlic clove, minced
1 teaspoon salt
Bouquet garni:
   ½ teaspoon dried thyme
      leaves
   1 bay leaf
   2 sprigs parsley
Water

1. Place meats, vegetables, garlic, salt, and bouquet garni in an 8-quart Dutch oven. Pour in water to cover (about 3 quarts). Simmer covered 2 to 2½ hours. Cool slightly.
2. Strain stock through a double thickness of cheesecloth into a storage container. Taste for seasoning. If a more concentrated flavor is desired, return stock to saucepan and simmer 20 to 30 minutes, or dissolve **1 to 2 teaspoons instant beef bouillon** in the stock.
3. Store covered in refrigerator or freezer. Remove solidified fat from top of stock before using.

2 to 2½ quarts

Note: Refrigerated stock is perishable. If not used within several days, heat to boiling, cool, and refrigerate or freeze to prevent spoilage. Stock can be kept frozen up to 4 months.

109 *Chicken Stock*

5 pounds chicken backs and
   wings, or stewing chicken,
   cut up
3 carrots, cut in 2-inch pieces
2 medium yellow onions,
   quartered
1 stalk celery, cut in 2-inch
   pieces
2 teaspoons salt
Bouquet garni:
   ¾ teaspoon dried thyme
      leaves
   ¾ teaspoon dried rosemary
      leaves
   1 bay leaf
   4 sprigs parsley
   2 whole cloves
Water

1. Place chicken, vegetables, salt, and bouquet garni in an 8-quart Dutch oven. Pour in water to cover (about 4 quarts). Simmer covered 2 to 2½ hours.
2. Strain stock through a double thickness of cheesecloth into a storage container. Taste for seasoning. If more concentrated flavor is desired, return stock to saucepan and simmer 20 to 30 minutes, or dissolve 1 to 2 teaspoons instant chicken bouillon in the stock.
3. Store covered in refrigerator or freezer. Remove solidified fat from top of stock before using.

3 to 3½ quarts

Note: Refrigerated stock is perishable. If not used within several days, heat to boiling, cool, and refrigerate or freeze to prevent spoilage. Stock can be kept frozen up to 4 months.

110 *Fish Stock*

2 pounds fresh lean fish with heads and bones, cut up
1 medium yellow onion, quartered
½ teaspoon salt
1 cup dry white wine
Bouquet garni:
   4 sprigs parsley
   1 bay leaf
   ½ teaspoon dried thyme leaves
   1 sprig celery leaves
   2 peppercorns
Water

1. Rinse fish under cold water. Place fish, onion, salt, wine, and bouquet garni in a 3-quart saucepan. Pour in water to cover (about 1½ quarts). Simmer covered 2 hours. Cool slightly.
2. Strain stock through a double thickness of cheesecloth into a storage container. Taste for seasoning. Add a small amount of salt and lemon juice, if desired. If a more concentrated flavor is desired, return stock to saucepan and simmer 30 to 45 minutes.
3. Store covered in refrigerator or freezer.

About 1 quart

Note: Use white firm-fleshed fish such as halibut, cod, flounder, or lemon sole. Frozen fish can be used if necessary.

Refrigerated stock is highly perishable. If not used within 2 days, heat to boiling, cool, and refrigerate or freeze to prevent spoilage. Stock can be kept frozen up to 2 months.

111 *Canned Stock*

6 cups canned chicken or beef bouillon or clam juice
2 medium carrots, cut in 2-inch pieces
2 medium onions, peeled and quartered
¾ cup dry white wine, if desired
Bouquet garni:
   4 sprigs parsley
   2 bay leaves
   1 teaspoon dried thyme leaves

1. Combine all ingredients in a 2-quart saucepan. Simmer covered 45 minutes.
2. Strain stock through a double thickness of cheesecloth into a storage container. Refrigerate.

About 1½ quarts

112 *White Clam Sauce (Salsa alla Vongole)*

¼ cup olive oil
1 clove garlic, thinly sliced
¼ cup water
½ teaspoon chopped parsley
½ teaspoon salt
¼ teaspoon oregano
¼ teaspoon pepper
1 cup (8-ounce can) whole littleneck clams with juice

1. Heat oil and garlic in a skillet until garlic is lightly browned.
2. Remove from heat. Add water, parsley, and dry seasonings; mix well. Stir in clams with juice. Heat thoroughly.
3. Serve hot on **cooked spaghetti** or **macaroni**.

About 1½ cups sauce

Red Clam Sauce: Follow recipe for White Clam Sauce. Sieve **3½ cups canned tomatoes**, stir in with water and seasonings, and simmer about 10 minutes. Add clams and heat.

About 5 cups sauce

113 *Tomato Sauce*

1 clove garlic
2 tablespoons olive oil
3 pounds fully ripe plum tomatoes, peeled, seeded, and diced; or use 9 cups canned peeled plum tomatoes, sieved
1 teaspoon salt
¼ teaspoon freshly ground black pepper
1 tablespoon dried basil

1. Peel garlic and cut in thirds. Put into a deep skillet with olive oil. Heat until garlic is browned. Flatten garlic and move it around in the oil. Discard garlic.
2. Add tomatoes all at one time to skillet. Mix in salt, pepper, and basil. Cook over low heat, stirring occasionally, about 10 minutes. Continue cooking, stirring occasionally, until sauce thickens (about 20 minutes).

About 6 cups sauce

114 *Rosy Sauce (Salsa Rosata)*

From Antico Martini, a famous restaurant on St. Mark's Square in Venice, comes this delightfully smooth and piquant dressing for seafood.

¾ cup ketchup
½ cup mayonnaise
½ cup whipping cream
2 tablespoons cognac
1½ teaspoons Worcestershire sauce
1 teaspoon prepared horseradish
4 drops Tabasco

1. Mix all ingredients; chill thoroughly.
2. Arrange chilled **cooked seafood** on **lettuce**, drizzle with **lemon juice** and spoon on sauce.

About 1½ cups sauce

115 *Italian Dressing*

6 tablespoons olive oil
3 tablespoons wine vinegar
1 clove garlic, crushed in a garlic press
¼ teaspoon salt
⅛ teaspoon pepper

1. Place all ingredients in a screw-top jar, shake well, and chill.
2. Just before serving, beat or shake thoroughly.

About ½ cup dressing

Anchovy Dressing: Follow recipe for Italian Dressing. Add **1 teaspoon prepared mustard** and **2 finely chopped anchovy fillets** to jar before shaking.

116 *Butter and Garlic Sauce (Salsa al Burro e Aglio)*

¾ cup butter
2 cloves garlic, peeled and thinly sliced
¼ cup water
½ teaspoon finely chopped parsley

1. Melt butter in skillet. Stir in garlic and cook slowly until slightly browned. Remove from heat and cool slightly.
2. Slowly add water and parsley. Cook about 10 minutes and serve over **cooked spaghetti.**

About 1 cup sauce

Butter and Cheese Sauce: Follow recipe for Butter and Garlic Sauce. Omit garlic. Mix butter sauce with spaghetti and sprinkle with **¼ cup grated Parmesan cheese.**

117 Clam Sauce (Salsa di Vongole)

¼ cup finely chopped onion
3 tablespoons butter
2 tablespoons flour
¼ teaspoon salt
⅛ teaspoon white pepper
1 can (12 ounces) clam juice
3 tablespoons finely chopped
   parsley
¼ to ½ teaspoon thyme
1 jar (7½ ounces) whole clams,
   drained and cut in pieces
1 can (2½ ounces) minced clams,
   drained

1. Add onion to hot butter in a saucepan and cook until soft. Blend in a mixture of flour, salt, and pepper. Heat until bubbly.
2. Remove from heat and add the clam juice gradually, stirring constantly. Mix in parsley and thyme. Bring to boiling; stir and cook 1 to 2 minutes. Stir in the clams; heat thoroughly.

About 2¼ cups sauce

118 Tomato Sauce with Meat

1 cup chopped onion
1 clove garlic, minced
3 tablespoons olive oil
½ pound ground beef
½ pound ground pork
1 can (28 ounces) Italian-style
   tomatoes, drained
3 cans (6 ounces each) tomato
   paste
2 cups water
2½ teaspoons salt
½ teaspoon pepper
1 teaspoon oregano

1. Add the onion and garlic to hot oil in a large, deep skillet and cook until onion is soft.
2. Add the ground meat, separate it into small pieces, and cook until lightly browned. Stir in tomatoes, tomato paste, water, and a mixture of salt, pepper, and oregano. Cook, uncovered, over low heat about 1 hour, stirring occasionally.

About 7½ cups sauce

119 Marinara Sauce

2 medium cloves garlic, sliced
½ cup olive oil
1 can (28 ounces) tomatoes,
   sieved
1¼ teaspoons salt
⅛ teaspoon pepper
1 teaspoon oregano
¼ teaspoon chopped parsley

1. Brown garlic in hot olive oil in a large, deep skillet. Add gradually, stirring constantly, a mixture of the tomatoes, salt, pepper, oregano, and parsley. Cook rapidly uncovered about 15 minutes, or until sauce is thickened; stir occasionally. If sauce becomes too thick, stir in ¼ to ½ **cup water**.
2. Serve sauce hot on **cooked spaghetti**.

4 cups sauce

120 *Medium White Sauce*

2 tablespoons butter
2 tablespoons flour
½ teaspoon salt
⅛ teaspoon pepper
1 cup milk (use light cream for a
  richer sauce)

1. Heat butter in a saucepan. Blend in flour, salt, and pepper; heat and stir until bubbly.
2. Gradually add the milk, stirring until smooth. Bring to boiling; cook and stir 1 to 2 minutes longer.

About 1 cup

Thick White Sauce: Follow recipe for Medium White Sauce. Use 3 to 4 tablespoons flour and 3 to 4 tablespoons butter.

Thin White Sauce: Follow recipe for Medium White Sauce. Use 1 tablespoon flour and 1 tablespoon butter.

Béchamel Sauce: Follow recipe for Medium White Sauce. Substitute ½ **cup chicken broth** for ½ cup milk; use ½ cup cream for remaining liquid needed. Stir in **1 tablespoon minced onion.**

121 *Quick Italian Tomato Sauce (Salsa di Pomodoro)*

1 cup chopped onion
¼ cup olive oil or cooking oil
1 clove garlic, minced
¼ cup grated carrot
1 tablespoon finely snipped parsley
¼ teaspoon basil, crushed
⅛ teaspoon thyme, crushed
2 cans (8 ounces each) tomato
  sauce
½ cup beef broth (dissolve ½ beef
  bouillon cube in ½ cup boiling
  water)

1. Add onion to hot oil in a saucepan and cook until tender. Stir in the garlic, carrot, and parsley; cook about 3 minutes, stirring frequently.
2. Blend in remaining ingredients. Simmer gently until flavors are blended (about 10 minutes).

About 3 cups sauce

122 *Green Sauce (Salsa Verde)*

1 tablespoon chopped parsley
1 tablespoon chopped watercress
1 tablespoon chopped capers
1 small clove garlic, peeled and
  chopped
¼ teaspoon salt
⅛ teaspoon pepper
6 tablespoons olive oil
3 tablespoons lemon juice

1. Place parsley, watercress, capers, garlic, salt, and pepper in a mortar. Crush with a pestle to make a smooth paste.
2. Add olive oil, 1 tablespoon at a time, beating vigorously with a fork or spoon after each addition. Slowly add lemon juice, beating constantly.
3. Serve with **artichokes, cooked spaghetti, shrimp,** or **any fried fish.**

About ½ cup sauce

123 *Tomato Meat Sauce (Ragù di Pomodoro)*

¼ cup olive oil
½ cup chopped onion
½ pound beef chuck
½ pound pork shoulder
7 cups canned tomatoes with liquid, sieved
1 tablespoon salt
1 bay leaf
1 can (6 ounces) tomato paste

1. Heat olive oil in a large saucepot. Add onion and cook until lightly browned. Add the meat and brown on all sides. Stir in tomatoes and salt. Add bay leaf. Cover and simmer about 2½ hours.
2. Stir tomato paste into sauce. Simmer, uncovered, stirring occasionally, about 2 hours, or until thickened. If sauce becomes too thick, add ½ **cup water.**
3. Remove meat and bay leaf from sauce (use meat as desired). Serve sauce over **cooked spaghetti.**

About 4 cups sauce

Tomato Sauce with Ground Meat: Follow recipe for Tomato Meat Sauce. Brown ½ **pound ground beef** in **3 tablespoons olive oil,** breaking beef into small pieces. After removing meat from sauce, add ground beef and simmer 10 minutes longer.

Tomato Sauce with Mushrooms: Follow recipe for Tomato Meat Sauce. Clean and slice ½ **pound mushrooms.** Cook slowly in 3 tablespoons melted butter until lightly browned. After removing meat from sauce, add mushrooms and simmer 10 minutes longer.

Tomato Sauce with Chicken Livers: Follow recipe for Tomato Meat Sauce. Rinse and pat dry ½ **pound chicken livers.** Slice livers and brown in **3 tablespoons olive oil.** After removing meat from sauce, add livers and simmer 10 minutes longer.

Tomato Sauce with Sausage: Follow recipe for Tomato Meat Sauce. Brown about ½ **pound Italian sausage,** cut in 2-inch pieces, in **1 tablespoon olive oil.** After removing meat from sauce, add sausage and simmer 10 minutes longer.

124 *Oil and Garlic Sauce (Salsa all' Olio e Aglio)*

½ cup olive oil
4 cloves garlic, thinly sliced
½ cup water
1 tablespoon chopped parsley
⅛ teaspoon pepper

1. Heat olive oil in a skillet. Stir in garlic and cook until browned. Remove skillet from heat and cool slightly.
2. Slowly stir in water. Add parsley and pepper. Simmer about 10 minutes. Serve over **cooked spaghetti.**

About 1 cup sauce

Garlic Sauce with Anchovies: Follow recipe for Oil and Garlic Sauce. Stir in **5 chopped anchovy fillets** with the parsley.

Garlic Sauce with Walnuts: Follow recipe for Oil and Garlic Sauce. Add **2 tablespoons chopped walnuts** with the parsley.

Garlic Sauce with Capers: Follow recipe for Oil and Garlic Sauce. Add **2 tablespoons capers** with the parsley.

Oil and Onion Sauce: Follow recipe for Oil and Garlic Sauce, substituting **1 medium onion**, thinly sliced, for the garlic.

125 *Bolognese Meat Sauce (Ragù Bolognese)*

2 tablespoons butter
1 medium onion, finely chopped
1 small carrot, finely chopped
1 small stalk celery, finely chopped
¾ pound ground beef
¼ pound ground lean pork
¼ cup tomato sauce or tomato paste
½ cup white wine
1 cup beef broth or stock
½ teaspoon salt
¼ teaspoon pepper

1. Melt butter in a skillet. Stir in onion, carrot, and celery. Cook until tender. Add meat and cook over low heat 10 to 15 minutes.
2. Add tomato sauce, wine, ¼ cup broth, salt, and pepper; mix well. Simmer about 1¼ hours. Stir in remaining broth, a small amount at a time, while the sauce is simmering. Sauce should be thick.

About 2½ cups sauce

126 *Fresh Tomato Sauce*

Following is a recipe for a simple uncooked table sauce which is ideal for topping tacos and tostadas. If preferred, one of the many bottled hot sauces of chilies and/or tomatoes may be used as well.

2 large ripe tomatoes, peeled and cored
¼ cup chopped onion
2 canned jalapeño chilies, finely chopped (more or less may be used, to taste)
1 tablespoon chopped cilantro (optional)
¼ teaspoon salt
Pepper (optional)

1. Chop tomatoes into small pieces. Add remaining ingredients and allow flavors to blend at least 30 minutes before using.
2. Store in refrigerator.

About 2 cups sauce

127 *Chicken Stock*

1 large stewing chicken, cut in serving pieces
4 quarts water
1 large onion, chopped
1 stalk celery, sliced
1 carrot, pared and sliced
1 clove garlic, minced
2 teaspoons salt
¼ teaspoon pepper

1. Rinse chicken and place in large kettle. Cover with the water. Bring to boiling. Add all remaining ingredients. Cover kettle, reduce heat, and simmer until chicken is tender (about 2 hours).
2. Cool; remove chicken and use in other recipes calling for cooked chicken. Strain broth, skim fat, and refrigerate broth until ready to use. (Or the broth, with or without vegetables, may be used as a simple soup.)

About 3 quarts stock

128 *Béchamel Sauce*

2 tablespoons butter
3 tablespoons flour
1½ cups hot milk, beef broth, or
    chicken broth
Salt and pepper to taste
½ cup whipping cream

Melt butter over medium heat; stir in flour. Using a whisk, stir rapidly until smooth. Gradually add milk or other liquid, stirring constantly. Bring sauce to a rapid boil and boil 4 minutes, or until sauce is thick and reduced to half its original volume. Season with salt and pepper. Reduce heat and stir in cream. Heat thoroughly, but do not boil.

About 1⅔ cups

129 *Ti-Malice Sauce*

8 large shallots, sliced
    Juice of 3 limes
1 cup water
¼ cup bacon drippings
3 garlic cloves
1 fresh green hot pepper or
    2 preserved cherry peppers,
    centers removed and peppers
    thinly slivered
⅛ teaspoon ground thyme
5 parsley sprigs

1. Marinate shallots in lime juice 30 minutes, or until they turn pink.
2. Put shallots into a saucepan, add water and bacon drippings, and bring to the boiling point. Set aside.
3. In a mortar, pound together to a paste the garlic, pepper, thyme, and parsley.
4. Add seasoning paste to shallots in saucepan and bring to a boil, stirring to blend.
5. Serve in a sauceboat to accompany fried foods.

130 *Four Thieves Sauce (Sauce des Quatre Voleurs)*

2 tablespoons butter
2 tablespoons flour
1½ cups chicken broth
Salt and freshly ground pepper
    to taste
1 egg yolk
● 3 tablespoons Four Thieves
    Vinegar
1 egg white, beaten stiff but not dry

1. Melt butter in a saucepan over medium heat. Add flour and, stirring constantly with a whisk, make a lightly browned roux. Continue to stir rapidly with a whisk while gradually adding broth. When all the broth is added, boil 4 minutes to reduce the liquid. Season with salt and pepper.
2. Remove from heat and beat a small amount of hot sauce into egg yolk; return mixture to saucepan. Cool thoroughly.
3. Blend sauce into vinegar. Just before serving, fold in beaten egg white.
4. Serve sauce with cold fish or poultry.

131 *Dilled Avocado Sauce for Fish*

1 large firm avocado, peeled and
    cubed
¼ cup olive oil
3 tablespoons lime juice, strained
    Salt, pepper, and cayenne or red
    pepper to taste
½ teaspoon dried dill or
    4 fresh dill sprigs

Put all ingredients into container of an electric blender; process until puréed.

132 *Creole Barbecue Sauce*

1 can (28 ounces) Italian plum
    tomatoes, drained
1 medium onion, finely chopped
⅔ cup olive oil
2 garlic cloves, crushed in a
    garlic press
¼ cup lime juice
1 teaspoon salt
⅛ teaspoon dried basil
    Dash pepper
    Bouquet garni
5 drops Tabasco

1. Chop tomatoes; put tomato and onion into a saucepan and cook uncovered over medium heat for 15 minutes.
2. Force tomato mixture through a fine sieve into another saucepan. Discard remaining solids.
3. Add remaining ingredients to saucepan. Stir until blended. Simmer uncovered about 1 hour, stirring occasionally.
4. Brush sauce over meat for barbecuing.

About 3½ cups

133 *Beef Stock*

2 pounds beef pot roast or brisket
    or beef for stew
2 pounds beef short ribs
1 marrow bone
4 quarts water
1 large onion, chopped
1 stalk celery, sliced
2 carrots, pared and sliced
1 cup canned tomatoes
1 clove garlic, minced
2 teaspoons salt
¼ teaspoon pepper
1 bay leaf (optional)

1. Put meats and bone into a large kettle. Cover with the water. Bring to boiling. Add all remaining ingredients. Cover kettle, reduce heat, and simmer until meat is tender (3 to 4 hours).
2. Skim fat from broth. Cool, remove meat, and use in recipes such as Picadillo (●). Strain broth and refrigerate until ready to use. (Or the broth, with or without vegetables, may be used as a simple soup.)

About 3 quarts stock

134 *French Dressing Antillaise for Salads*

½ cup olive oil
1 teaspoon salt
½ teaspoon freshly ground pepper
2 garlic cloves
    Tarragon, dill, or oregano to taste
5 parsley sprigs
2 scallions or green onions,
    finely chopped
1 tablespoon wine vinegar

1. Pour oil into a salad bowl; add remaining ingredients. With a pestle or wooden spoon, rub herbs against the side of the bowl and mix with oil.
2. For salad, marinate your choice of **celery pieces, chickpeas, onion slices, cherry tomatoes, sliced mushrooms, sliced cooked beets,** or **beans** (never more than two) in dressing for at least 1 hour before serving.
3. To serve, toss chilled **salad greens** with marinated vegetables.

135 *Tomato Sauce Creole*

⅓ cup peanut oil
2 medium onions, thinly sliced
6 Italian plum tomatoes, peeled, seeded, and finely chopped
½ cup beef stock
  Salt and freshly ground pepper to taste
3 drops Tabasco
1 garlic clove, crushed in a garlic press

1. Heat oil in a saucepan, add onion, and cook over low heat until translucent but not browned. Add tomato, stock, and seasonings; stir with a wooden spoon until tomato pulp is cooked to a fine purée.
2. Serve with rice or grilled meats.

136 *Mayonnaise*

2 egg yolks
½ teaspoon salt
¼ teaspoon white pepper
1 teaspoon prepared mustard
1 cup olive oil
1½ teaspoons vinegar*

Rinse a soup plate with hot water and dry well. Put egg yolks and seasoning into plate. Pour a few drops of oil over these ingredients and, with a fork or wooden spoon, stir in a slow circular motion until all the ingredients have been blended together. Continue the dripping of oil and the slow, even motion until ¼ cup oil has been blended in, then add ½ teaspoon vinegar, still stirring, then begin to pour the oil in a thin stream, never changing the pace of the beating. If the emulsion gets too thick and forms a ball, add a little more vinegar. To do it right takes about 20 minutes. The result is much richer than with the electric beater used at medium speed. When all the oil is blended in, finish with 1 teaspoon vinegar.

*The quality of the vinegar is important. Herb-flavored vinegar should be used to enhance certain dishes and salads.

137 *Watercress Mayonnaise*

  Handful watercress, finely chopped
● ¾ cup Mayonnaise
  4 drops Tabasco

Blend all ingredients and serve with cold fish or shellfish.

Note: Dill, capers, chervil, or horseradish may be substituted for the watercress.

138 *Herbal Mayonnaise Odette Mennesson*

3 parsley sprigs
3 basil sprigs
2 fennel or dill sprigs
6 watercress sprigs
3 leaves Boston or Bibb lettuce
2 scallions or green onions
2 hard-cooked eggs
● 1 cup Mayonnaise

Stem herbs, watercress, and lettuce. Chop very finely along with scallions and eggs. Blend in Mayonnaise.

2 cups

139 *Bean Sauce*

3 scallions or green onions, chopped
2 parsley sprigs
2 shallots
1 green hot pepper or
    6 dried Italian pepper pods
2 tablespoons peanut oil
2 cups dried red beans, rinsed
    Bouquet garni
2 quarts water (see Note)
1 small ham hock
1 cup cubed ham
    Salt and pepper to taste

1. In a mortar, pound to a paste the scallions, parsley, shallots, and hot pepper.
2. Heat oil in a Dutch oven over medium heat, add seasoning paste, beans, and bouquet garni. Stir until beans are lightly coated with oil.
3. Add water, ham hock, and cubed ham and bring to boiling. Cover and simmer 2 hours, or until beans are tender.
4. Remove ham hock. Process beans and juice in an electric blender or force through a food mill.
5. Return sauce to Dutch oven and bring to boiling. Season with salt and pepper. Serve warm over Caribbean Rice ● or meats.

1½ quarts

Note: If using fresh beans, add only 1 quart water.

140 *Four Thieves Vinegar*

The "four thieves" are, like the bouquet garni, a standard combination of narrow-leaved basil, rosemary, sage, and marjoram commonly used in eighteenth-century French cuisine.

Several sprigs each of
    narrow-leaved basil, rosemary,
    sage, and majoram
10 cloves
 1 cinnamon stick
10 peppercorns, cracked
 2 garlic cloves
 1 bay leaf
    Thyme sprig
 2 tablespoons salt
 8 dried Italian pepper pods
3½ cups wine vinegar
 2 garlic cloves

1. Stem the basil, rosemary, sage, and majoram and put into a 1-quart jar along with the spices, 2 garlic cloves, bay leaf, thyme, salt, and pepper pods. Pour vinegar into jar; cover. Allow to stand 1 month in a sunny window, then strain through wet cheesecloth.
2. Put a garlic clove into each of 2 decorative 1-pint bottles; cover tightly.
3. Use for sauces and to make Condiments ●

141 *Condiments*

Some people like their food very spicy, so on every table in the islands sits a bottle of pickled mixture of hot peppers and vegetables. A great deal of pride is taken in the coloring and general aspect of the condiment, as well as in the container which, in certain families, is of the most precious antique crystal.

1 medium head cabbage, very
    finely shredded
2 small heads cauliflower
    (tips of flowerets only)
1 cup frenched green beans
1 cup green onions (white part only)
1 cup thinly sliced small carrots
1 cucumber, diced
1 cup julienned red and green
    sweet pepper
  Snow peas (fresh or frozen),
    halved
  Small shallots
  Lime juice
6 peppercorns, cracked
2 cloves
2 bay leaves
2 cherry peppers (fresh or pickled)
4 small green hot peppers
    (fresh or pickled)
2 fresh cayenne pepper pods
    (if available)

1. Combine the vegetables.
2. Marinate desired number of shallots in lime juice 30 minutes, or until a deep purple color.
3. Drain vegetables and shallots well on paper towels. Arrange mixture decoratively in jars, then add spices and pepper to each so they can be seen from the outside.

142 *Orange Rum Sauce*

1½ cups orange juice
½ cup amber rum
  Sugar to taste
1 tablespoon butter
1 tablespoon cornstarch
½ teaspoon grated orange peel

1. Combine orange juice, rum, and sugar in a small saucepan. Bring to a boil.
2. Mix butter and cornstarch and add to sauce. Cook until thickened. Remove from heat. Mix in orange peel.
3. Cool before serving.

About 2 cups

Salads

143 *Cucumber Salad* (*Tsatziki*)

2 cups plain yogurt
1 scallion, chopped
1 teaspoon mint
½ teaspoon salt
   Freshly ground pepper
   Pinch dill
1 garlic clove, crushed in a garlic
   press
4 cucumbers, pared and thinly
   sliced

Mix yogurt with scallion, mint, salt, pepper, dill, and garlic. Add cucumber and toss to coat with dressing. Refrigerate 1 hour.

6 servings

144 *Potato Salad* (*Patatosalata*)

½ cup olive oil
3 tablespoons wine vinegar
1 teaspoon oregano, crushed
2 tablespoons chopped parsley
1 medium onion, finely sliced
5 large red potatoes
   Salt and pepper to taste

1. Combine olive oil, vinegar, oregano, parsley, and onion. Mix well. Set aside to marinate.
2. Scrub potatoes. Boil them in salted water in their jackets. When just tender (about 40 minutes), remove and plunge into cold water so they can be handled at once. Peel while hot and cut into even slices.
3. Pour the dressing over the potatoes; toss lightly. Add salt and pepper.

6 servings

145 *Anchovy Potato Salad*

Dressing:
1 cup olive oil
½ cup wine vinegar
¼ teaspoon sugar
1 teaspoon dill
1 teaspoon marjoram
   Pepper to taste

Salad:
- 8 Anchovy Fillets or 1
   can (2 ounces) anchovies
   preserved in olive oil,
   drained
1 bunch escarole, torn in
   bite-size pieces
2 potatoes, boiled and diced
1 small jar pickled beets, drained
   and diced
2 green peppers, cleaned and
   thinly sliced
4 scallions, minced
3 hard-cooked eggs, sliced, for
   garnish
1 teaspoon capers for garnish
   Salt and pepper to taste

1. For dressing, combine all ingredients in a jar. Shake well. Refrigerate 1 or 2 hours before serving.
2. For salad, combine anchovies with remaining ingredients, except eggs, capers, salt, and pepper. Add the salad dressing and toss to coat. Garnish with eggs and capers. Season with salt and pepper.

4 to 6 servings

146 *Cucumber and Tomato Salad* *(Angourodomatosalata)*

3 firm-ripe homegrown tomatoes,
    cut in wedges
3 pickle cucumbers (as straight
    as possible), pared and sliced
    ¼ inch thick
4 scallions, finely chopped
¼ pound feta cheese, crumbled
    Kalamata olives (about 8)
    Oregano and freshly dried dill,
    a generous pinch of each
    Salt and pepper to taste
3 tablespoons wine vinegar
⅓ cup olive oil

1. In a salad bowl, combine tomatoes, cucumbers, scallions, cheese, and olives. Season with oregano, dill, salt, and pepper.
2. Combine vinegar and olive oil in a small jar; shake well. Add to salad and toss.

6 to 8 servings

147 *Lobster Salad* *(Astakos Mayoneza)*

6 cups diced fresh lobster meat,
    chilled
3 hard-cooked eggs, mashed
    through a sieve
1 large scallion, minced
1 small leek, finely chopped
2 teaspoons tarragon
½ teaspoon thyme
2 garlic cloves, crushed in a
    garlic press
2 cups Mayonnaise
1 tablespoon capers
    Juice of 1 lemon
    Cucumber, sliced paper thin
    Tomato wedges for garnish

1. Combine all ingredients except cucumber and tomato. Adjust seasoning.
2. Spoon into heated **pastry shells,** a **lobster** cavity, or on a bed of **lettuce.** Garnish with cucumber slices and tomato wedges.

About 12 servings

148 *Russian Salad* *(Salata Roseiki)*

⅓ cup olive oil
3 tablespoons vinegar
1 cup diced cooked carrots
1 cup diced cooked beets
2 potatoes, cooked and diced
1 cup french-cut green beans,
    cooked and diced
1 cup cooked peas
¼ cup minced parsley
● Mayonnaise
    Salt and pepper to taste
2 teaspoons capers

1. Mix olive oil and vinegar and pour over vegetables; allow to marinate 1 to 2 hours. Drain. Discard dressing.
2. Mix vegetables and parsley with enough Mayonnaise to bind together (about 1 cup). Season with salt and pepper. Garnish with capers to serve.

6 servings

Note: Russian Salad makes an excellent appetizer. Serve in small dishes with heated **Sourdough Greek Bread** ●

149 *Warsaw Salad (Sałatka Warszawska)*

1 cup mayonnaise
⅓ cup dairy sour cream
1 tablespoon prepared mustard
2 cups julienne beets, cooked or canned
1½ cups kidney beans, cooked or canned
1½ cups cooked or canned peas
1 cup diced dill pickles
6 ounces (about 1¼ cups) cooked crab meat
3 scallions, chopped
1 hard-cooked egg, sliced
Carrot curls and radish roses to garnish

1. Combine mayonnaise, sour cream, and mustard in a large bowl.
2. Add remaining ingredients, except egg, carrots, and radishes; toss gently to mix.
3. Garnish with egg slices, carrot curls, and radish roses.

8 to 12 servings

150 *Sauerkraut Salad with Carrots and Apples (Surówka z Kiszonej Kapusty)*

¼ cup salad or olive oil
1½ teaspoons sugar
1 teaspoon caraway seed
½ teaspoon salt
1 teaspoon vinegar
1 pound sauerkraut, drained
2 medium tart apples, peeled, cored, and diced
¾ cup grated carrot

1. Combine oil, sugar, caraway seed, salt, and vinegar.
2. Rinse and drain sauerkraut well; chop. Stir into oil mixture.
3. Add apples and carrot; toss to mix.

About 6 servings

151 *Potato Salad with Wine (Sałatka Kartoflana z Winem)*

2 pounds potatoes
2 teaspoons salt
Boiling water
1 cup white wine
1 stalk celery
⅓ cup olive oil
¼ cup chopped fresh dill
¼ cup chopped parsley
3 tablespoons lemon juice
2 tablespoons chopped chives
¼ teaspoon pepper

1. Cook potatoes with salt in enough boiling water to cover until tender, about 30 minutes. Peel and slice; put into a bowl.
2. Pour wine over potatoes; let stand 30 minutes.
3. Cook celery in a small amount of boiling water until soft. Press celery through a sieve. Combine 2 tablespoons cooking liquid with puréed celery, oil, dill, parsley, lemon juice, chives, and pepper.
4. Add celery mixture to potatoes; mix.

6 servings

152 *Rose Salad*

10 small potatoes (about 2½ pounds), cooked
¼ cup olive oil
3 tablespoons lemon juice or vinegar
1 tablespoon water
1 tablespoon sugar
1 teaspoon salt
¼ teaspoon pepper
2 cups shell beans, cooked or canned
¼ pound sauerkraut, drained
4 stalks celery, sliced lengthwise
6 cups shredded red cabbage
Boiling water
3 tablespoons tarragon vinegar
4 cooked or canned beets, sliced

1. Slice potatoes. Mix olive oil, lemon juice, 1 tablespoon water, sugar, salt, and pepper. Pour over potatoes. Add beans, sauerkraut, and celery.
2. Add red cabbage to boiling water. Let stand 2 minutes. Drain well. Stir in tarragon vinegar; mix until cabbage is pink.
3. Mound red cabbage in center of a large platter. Arrange beet slices in cabbage to form a rose.
4. Place potatoes and other vegetables around edges. Use **celery** for rose stem. Garnish with **lettuce leaves.**

8 to 12 servings

153 *Green Bean and Onion Salad*

1 pound small boiling onions
1½ pounds fresh green beans
● Chicken Stock
● ½ cup Mock Crème Fraîche
¼ cup low-fat cottage cheese
2 tablespoons snipped fresh chives
1 teaspoon snipped fresh or ½ teaspoon dried thyme leaves
1 teaspoon snipped fresh or ½ teaspoon dried marjoram leaves
Salt
Freshly ground pepper
Juice of ½ lemon

1. Simmer onions and beans in 1 inch of stock in a covered saucepan until tender (15 to 18 minutes). Drain; refrigerate covered until chilled (about 2 hours).
2. Mix remaining ingredients except salt, pepper, and lemon juice; refrigerate covered until chilled.
3. Arrange vegetables on a platter; sprinkle lightly with salt and pepper. Squeeze lemon juice over. Spoon sauce over or pass sauce separately.

6 servings

154 *Beet Mousse*

Both elegant and unusual, this salad is worth the effort to make. Try as a first course, too.

8 medium beets
1 tablespoon vinegar
1½ teaspoons unflavored gelatin
¼ cup orange juice
½ cup instant nonfat dry-milk
    solids
2 to 3 ice cubes
1½ teaspoons prepared horseradish
Salad greens

1. Cut greens from beets; discard. Simmer beets in 2 inches water and vinegar until tender (about 30 minutes). Slip off skins. Cut thin slice from bottoms of beets; hollow out centers with melon-baller, leaving ½-inch shells; reserve centers. Refrigerate beets until chilled.
2. Sprinkle gelatin over orange juice in a small saucepan; let stand 5 minutes. Set over low heat, stirring occasionally, until gelatin is dissolved (about 3 minutes). Pour gelatin mixture into a food processor or blender; add beet centers and dry-milk solids. Process, adding ice cubes one at a time, until mixture is the consistency of thick whipped cream. Stir in horseradish. Fill beets with mixture; refrigerate until serving time. Serve on salad greens.

4 servings

155 *Red Cabbage-Apple Salad*

In this cross between coleslaw and Waldorf salad, you will enjoy crisp textures and tart flavors.

3 cups shredded red cabbage
1 red apple, cut in 1½x¼-inch
    strips
1 sweet red pepper, cut in
    1½x¼-inch strips
2 tablespoons cider vinegar
¼ cup apple juice
¼ teaspoon caraway seed
⅛ teaspoon salt
⅛ teaspoon freshly ground
    pepper
Salad greens

Mix all ingredients except salad greens in a medium bowl. Refrigerate covered 2 hours. Serve on salad greens on individual plates.

4 servings

156 *Raw Broccoli Salad*

If you have never eaten broccoli raw, you have a treat in store.

3 cups raw bite-size pieces
    broccoli spears
● ½ cup Low-Fat Yogurt
½ teaspoon salt
¼ teaspoon freshly ground
    pepper
2 ounces Cheddar cheese,
    shredded
1 large carrot, cut in thin slices

Mix broccoli with yogurt, salt, and pepper. Spoon mixture on 4 salad plates. Sprinkle tops of salads with cheese; arrange carrot slices around salads.

4 servings

Note: See recipe for Garden Vegetables in Sweet Seasoned Vinegar (●) to use broccoli stalks.

157 *Fresh Spinach Salad*

This is an example of a composed salad, where ingredients have been carefully arranged for eye and appetite appeal.

4 cups bite-size pieces spinach
1 cup ½-inch pieces yellow
    squash
1 can (7¾ ounces) water
    chestnuts, drained and sliced
2 hard-cooked eggs, chopped
½ cup sliced green onions
    Salt
    Freshly ground pepper
● ½ cup Mustard Sauce
● ½ cup Low-Fat Yogurt

Arrange spinach, squash, water chestnuts, eggs, and onion attractively in rows on a medium platter; sprinkle lightly with salt and pepper. Mix Mustard Sauce and yogurt; drizzle over salad.

6 servings

Note: This recipe will make 4 luncheon servings with the addition of **2 cups flaked tuna.**

158 *Greek Salad in Peppers*

The natural juice from the tomato and the lemon juice are the "salad dressing" for this salad. Add a dollop of yogurt, if desired.

1 large tomato, chopped
1 green onion, sliced
⅛ teaspoon salt
1 teaspoon snipped fresh or ½
    teaspoon dried basil leaves
1 tablespoon fresh lemon juice
4 small green peppers, cored
½ cup crumbled feta cheese
8 anchovies, drained and rinsed
8 lemon wedges

1. Mix tomato, onion, salt, basil, and lemon juice; refrigerate covered 1 hour.
2. Spoon half the tomato mixture into green peppers; layer cheese over tomatoes. Spoon remaining tomato mixture over cheese. Arrange 2 anchovies over top of each pepper. Serve with lemon wedges.

4 servings

159 *Cucumbers with Buttermilk Dressing*

1 medium cucumber, pared,
    seeded, and finely chopped
1 teaspoon salt
1 tablespoon fresh lemon juice
● 1 tablespoon Mock Crème
    Fraîche
¾ cup buttermilk
1 tablespoon snipped fresh or 1
    teaspoon dried dill weed
½ teaspoon salt
⅛ teaspoon freshly ground
    pepper
1 cucumber, sliced
2 large tomatoes, sliced

1. Sprinkle chopped cucumber with 1 teaspoon salt; let stand 10 minutes. Rinse cucumber; pat dry and place in a mixing bowl. Mix lemon juice, crème fraîche, buttermilk, dill, ½ teaspoon salt, and the pepper; pour over cucumber and refrigerate covered 1 hour.
2. Arrange sliced cucumber and tomatoes on individual plates; spoon buttermilk mixture over.

4 servings

Note: This recipe can be increased and served as a first-course soup; stir in skim milk if thinner consistency is desired.

160 *Fruited Carrot Salad*

Tart apple pieces would be an interesting addition to this salad.

4 carrots
1 cup unsweetened pineapple
   juice
2½ cups orange juice
   Lettuce cups
   Snipped mint

1. Pare carrots into strips with a vegetable peeler. Place in a shallow glass dish; pour fruit juices over. Refrigerate covered 6 hours or overnight, stirring occasionally.
2. Drain carrots, spoon into lettuce cups, and garnish with mint.

4 servings

161 *Oriental Cucumber Salad*

10 baby cucumbers (about 3
   inches long), sliced in very
   thin rounds
1 bunch green onions, tops only,
   finely chopped
2 teaspoons honey or sugar
2 teaspoons toasted sesame seed
½ cup distilled white vinegar
½ teaspoon sesame oil
5 tablespoons light soy sauce
   Salad greens

1. Arrange cucumber and onion in a shallow glass dish. Shake remaining ingredients except salad greens in a covered jar; pour over the vegetables. Refrigerate for 2 hours, stirring occasionally.
2. Drain cucumber and onion; marinade can be strained and refrigerated for use again. Serve salad on lettuce or other salad greens.

4 servings

162 *Garden Vegetables in Sweet Seasoned Vinegar*

1½ cups very thinly sliced baby
   cucumbers
2 cups very thinly sliced broccoli
   stalks
½ cup cider vinegar
½ teaspoon salt
¼ teaspoon freshly ground
   pepper
1½ teaspoons sugar
   Salad greens

1. Arrange vegetable slices in a shallow glass dish. Shake remaining ingredients except salad greens in a covered jar; pour over vegetables. Refrigerate covered 30 minutes; stir occasionally. Drain; marinade can be strained and refrigerated for use again.
2. Serve vegetables on salad greens.

4 servings

163 *Vegetable Salad with Yogurt Dressing*

Vivid colors dominate this unusual salad combination.

- ● ¾ cup Low-Fat Yogurt
  2 tablespoons snipped parsley
  ½ cup finely chopped dill pickle
  ½ cup chopped tomato
  1 teaspoon salt
  1 cup sliced radishes
  1 medium zucchini, shredded
  2 medium carrots, shredded
  1 large beet, shredded

1. Mix yogurt, parsley, pickle, chopped tomato, and salt; refrigerate covered 1 hour.
2. Arrange radish slices around edge of a serving plate. Arrange zucchini, carrots, and beet decoratively in center of plate. Serve yogurt mixture with salad.

4 servings

164 *Vegetable Platter Vinaigrette*

Use any fresh vegetables that you want in this recipe—let your imagination be your guide.

- 1 pound fresh green beans
  1 small head cauliflower
- ● Chicken Stock
- ● 1 cup Vinaigrette Dressing
  1 pint cherry tomatoes, halved
  Salt
  Freshly ground pepper
  1 medium red onion, thinly sliced

1. Steam green beans and whole cauliflower in separate covered saucepans in 1 inch of stock until tender (about 15 minutes). Drain. Mix beans with ½ cup dressing and refrigerate covered 3 hours, stirring occasionally. Refrigerate cauliflower. Mix cherry tomatoes with ½ cup dressing; refrigerate covered 3 hours, stirring occasionally.
2. Drain beans and tomatoes; reserve dressing. Place cauliflower in center of a platter; arrange beans and tomatoes around cauliflower. Sprinkle vegetables lightly with salt and pepper. Arrange onion slices over beans and tomatoes. Cut cauliflower into wedges to serve. Pass reserved dressing.

8 to 10 servings

165 *Red Vegetable Salad*

- 1 pint cherry tomatoes, stems removed, cut in half
  20 radishes, sliced
  1 small red onion, sliced
  3 tablespoons wine vinegar
  2 teaspoons salad oil
  1 teaspoon salt
  2 teaspoons snipped fresh mint
  ⅛ teaspoon freshly ground white pepper
  Lettuce leaves

1. Combine all ingredients except lettuce leaves in a medium bowl; refrigerate covered 2 hours, stirring occasionally.
2. Serve vegetables on lettuce.

4 to 6 servings

166 *Pineapple-Mint Salad*

1 can (20 ounces) unsweetened
   pineapple chunks, drained
2 cups low-fat cottage cheese
½ bunch mint, snipped
   Bibb lettuce
1 cup sliced celery
   Mint sprigs
8 orange slices

1. Dice 1 cup of the pineapple; mix with cottage cheese and snipped mint.
2. Arrange lettuce leaves on a platter or individual plates; mound pineapple mixture on lettuce. Arrange remaining pineapple and the celery around mounds of pineapple mixture. Garnish with mint sprigs and orange slices.

4 to 6 servings

167 *California Fruit Plate*

Fresh fruits are a must for this recipe. If figs and raspberries are not available, substitute other ingredients such as strawberries and melon.

2 cups low-fat cottage cheese
8 fresh figs, cut in quarters
2 cups fresh raspberries
2 tablespoons honey
4 lemon wedges

Place ½ cup cottage cheese on each of 4 salad plates. Surround cottage cheese with 8 quarters of fig; sprinkle raspberries over figs. Drizzle honey over fruit and cottage cheese. Squeeze lemon over all.

4 servings

168 *Broccoli Salad (Insalata di Broccoli)*

1 pound broccoli
3 tablespoons olive oil
3 tablespoons lemon juice
1 medium clove garlic
¼ teaspoon salt
⅛ teaspoon pepper

1. Trim off leaves and bottoms of broccoli stalks, and split thick stems lengthwise. Cook, covered, in a small amount of salted water until just tender. Drain and chill.
2. Combine olive oil, lemon juice, garlic, salt, and pepper. Drizzle over thoroughly chilled broccoli and serve.

About 3 servings

Cauliflower Salad: Follow recipe for Broccoli Salad. Substitute **1 medium head cauliflower** for broccoli. Separate into flowerets and cook as for broccoli. Peel and dice **1 boiled potato**; combine with cauliflower and chill. Substitute **wine vinegar** for the lemon juice and add **¼ teaspoon oregano.**

Green Bean Salad: Follow recipe for Broccoli Salad. Clean and cook **½ pound green beans** and substitute for broccoli. Use wine vinegar instead of lemon juice.

Asparagus Salad: Follow recipe for Broccoli Salad. Clean and cook **1 pound asparagus** and substitute for the broccoli.

169 *Pickled Pepper Salad (Insalata di Peperoni)*

2 cups sliced pickled red peppers
¾ cup chopped celery
½ cup sliced ripe olives
8 anchovy fillets, chopped
2 tablespoons olive oil
2 tablespoons wine vinegar
¼ teaspoon oregano
⅛ teaspoon salt
¼ teaspoon pepper

1. Gently combine the red peppers, celery, olives, and anchovy fillets. Mix oil, vinegar, oregano, salt, and pepper; pour over the red pepper mixture. Toss gently.
2. Serve very cold.

6 to 8 servings

170 *Red Kidney Bean Salad (Insalata di Fagioli)*

1 can (16 ounces) kidney beans
¼ cup wine vinegar
3 tablespoons olive oil
¼ teaspoon oregano
¼ teaspoon salt
⅛ teaspoon pepper
¼ cup sliced celery
2 tablespoons chopped onion
Lettuce cups

1. Thoroughly rinse and drain kidney beans.
2. Combine vinegar, oil, oregano, salt, and pepper; mix with beans. Blend in celery and onion; chill.
3. Serve in crisp lettuce cups.

About 4 servings

171 *Italian Potato Salad (Insalata di Patate)*

2 medium potatoes, boiled, peeled, and diced
⅓ cup chopped celery
½ cup diced pared cucumber
½ cup chopped ripe olives
2 tablespoons minced onion
● ¾ cup Italian Dressing
¼ teaspoon oregano

1. Lightly toss together the potatoes, celery, cucumber, olives, and onion. With a fork, thoroughly but carefully blend in the dressing mixed with oregano.
2. Cover the salad. Chill about 1 hour before serving.

About 4 servings

172 *Green Salad (Insalata Verde)*

1 large head lettuce, or an equal
   amount of another salad green
   (curly endive, romaine,
   escarole, chicory, or dandelion
   greens)
1 clove garlic
  Italian Dressing

1. Wash lettuce in cold water, removing core, separating leaves, and removing any bruised leaves. Drain; dry thoroughly and carefully. Tear lettuce into bite-size pieces, put into a plastic bag, and chill 1 hour.
2. Just before serving, cut garlic in half and rub a wooden bowl. Put greens in bowl and pour on desired amount of dressing. Turn and toss the greens until well coated with dressing and no dressing remains in the bottom of the bowl.

About 6 servings

Green Salad with Anchovy Dressing: Follow recipe for Green Salad. Add **2 tomatoes**, cut in wedges, **¼ cup diced celery**, and **½ cup chopped ripe olives** to lettuce in bowl. Toss with **Anchovy Dressing.**

Mixed Salad: Follow recipe for Green Salad. Add **¼ cup chopped cucumber, ¼ cup chopped celery, ¼ cup sliced radishes,** and **¼ cup chopped ripe olives** to lettuce before tossing with dressing.

173 *Fresh Bean Sprout Salad*

A crisp, colorful, light salad.

1 pound fresh bean sprouts,
   rinsed (see Note)
2 medium carrots, shredded
1 tablespoon toasted sesame seed
2 teaspoons vegetable oil
⅓ cup distilled white vinegar
2 teaspoons sugar

1. Mix bean sprouts and carrots in a shallow glass dish.
2. Shake remaining ingredients in a covered jar; pour over vegetables.
3. Refrigerate covered 1½ hours; stir occasionally. Serve in shallow bowls.

4 to 6 servings

Note: If fresh bean sprouts are not available, you can substitute **1 large pared, seeded, shredded cucumber.**

174 *Guacamole I*

2 very ripe avocados
1 medium fresh tomato
1 small onion, chopped (about ⅓ cup)
2 tablespoons lemon juice
1 teaspoon salt
1 to 2 teaspoons chili powder

1. Peel avocados and mash pulp, leaving a few small lumps throughout.
2. Peel and chop tomato and add to mashed avocado. Add onion, lemon juice, salt, and chili powder to taste. If not serving immediately, refrigerate in covered bowl, with avocado pits immersed in guacamole; this is said to help keep avocado from darkening on standing.
3. Serve on lettuce as a salad, as a "dip" with tostada chips, or as a condiment to top taco fillings.

About 2 cups guacamole

Note: If you prefer a smoother guacamole, ingredients may be blended to desired consistency.

175 *Guacamole II*

2 large ripe avocados
3 tablespoons lemon juice
1 medium tomato
1 slice onion
1 small green chili
1 small clove garlic, minced
⅛ teaspoon coriander
Salt

1. Halve avocados, peel, remove pits, and cut avocado into pieces. Put into an electric blender with lemon juice.
2. Peel, halve, and seed tomato. Add to blender along with onion, chili, garlic, coriander, and salt to taste. Blend.
3. Serve as a dip with **corn chips, cauliflowerets,** and **carrot** and **celery sticks.**

About 3 cups dip

176 *Christmas Eve Salad* (Ensalada de Noche Buena)

This salad is customarily served at the traditional Mexican midnight supper on Christmas Eve. It usually precedes a turkey entrée. You might enjoy it in a similar menu. Or, it could provide an interestingly different light luncheon main dish.

1 cup diced cooked beets
1 cup diced tart apple, not peeled
1 cup orange sections
1 cup sliced bananas
1 cup diced pineapple (fresh or canned)
Juice of 1 lime
Oil and Vinegar Dressing (see below)
Shredded lettuce
½ cup chopped peanuts
Seeds from 1 pomegranate

1. Drain beets well. Combine beets, apple, oranges, bananas, and pineapple. Refrigerate until ready to serve.
2. Add lime juice to beet-fruit mixture. Add desired amount of dressing and toss until evenly mixed and coated with dressing.
3. To serve, make a bed of shredded lettuce in salad bowl. Mound salad on top. Sprinkle with peanuts and pomegranate seeds.

8 to 10 servings

Oil and Vinegar Dressing: Mix **2 tablespoons white wine vinegar, 1½ teaspoons sugar,** and **¼ teaspoon salt.** Add **⅓ cup salad oil;** mix well.

177 *Rooster's Bill* (Pico de Gallo)

1 medium jícama*
1 large orange
¼ cup chopped onion
   Juice of 1 lemon
1 teaspoon salt
1 teaspoon chili powder
½ teaspoon oregano, crumbled

*3 large tart crisp apples may be
substituted for jícama.

1. Wash, pare, and chop jícama into ½-inch chunks.
2. Pare and section orange, reserving juice, and add to jícama; pour orange juice over fruit chunks. Add onion, lemon juice, and salt and stir until evenly mixed. Let stand at least 1 hour in refrigerator before serving.
3. When ready to serve, sprinkle with chili powder and oregano.

4 to 6 servings

178 *Coliflor Acapulco*

1 large head cauliflower
   Marinade (see below)
1 can (15 ounces) garbanzos,
   drained
1 cup pimento-stuffed olives
   Pimentos, drained and cut
      lengthwise in strips
   Lettuce
1 jar (16 ounces) sliced pickled
   beets, drained and chilled
1 large cucumber, thinly sliced and
   chilled
   Parsley sprigs
   Radish roses
● Guacamole I

1. Bring 1 inch of salted water to boiling in a large saucepan. Add cauliflower, cover, and cook about 20 minutes, or until just tender; drain.
2. Place cauliflower, head down, in a deep bowl and pour marinade over it. Chill several hours or overnight; occasionally spoon marinade over all.
3. Shortly before serving, thread garbanzos, olives, and pimento strips onto wooden picks for decorative kabobs. Set aside while arranging salad.
4. Drain cauliflower. Line a chilled serving plate with lettuce and place cauliflower, head up, in the center. Arrange pickled beet and cucumber slices around the base, tucking in parsley sprigs and radish roses.
5. Spoon and spread guacamole over cauliflower. Decorate with kabobs. Serve cold.

6 to 8 servings

Marinade: Combine 1½ cups vegetable oil, ½ cup lemon juice, 1½ teaspoons salt, and 1 teaspoon chili powder. Shake marinade well before using.

179 *Avocados Stuffed with Cauliflower Salad*

2 cups very small, crisp raw
    cauliflowerets
1 cup cooked green peas
½ cup sliced ripe olives
¼ cup chopped pimento
¼ cup chopped onion
● Oil and Vinegar Dressing
    Salt to taste
6 small lettuce leaves
3 large ripe avocados
    Lemon wedges

1. Combine all ingredients, except lettuce, avocados, and lemon wedges; stir gently until evenly mixed and coated with dressing.
2. Refrigerate at least 1 hour before serving.
3. When ready to serve, peel, halve, and remove pits from avocados. Place a lettuce leaf on each serving plate; top with avocado half filled with a mound of cauliflower salad. Serve with lemon wedges.

6 servings

180 *Garbanzo Salad*

1 can (15 ounces) garbanzos,
    drained
¼ cup chopped parsley
1 can or jar (4 ounces) pimentos,
    drained and chopped
3 green onions, chopped
¼ cup wine vinegar
2 tablespoons olive or salad oil
1 teaspoon salt
½ teaspoon sugar
¼ teaspoon pepper

Combine all ingredients in a bowl; cover and refrigerate until chilled.

About 6 servings

181 *Shrimp Salad*

1½ cups cooked shrimp, sliced in
    half lengthwise
½ cup diced cooked potatoes
2 hard-cooked eggs, sliced
½ cup chopped celery
¼ cup chopped green onions
½ cup mayonnaise or salad
    dressing
½ cup dairy sour cream
½ teaspoon chili powder
    Salt to taste
    Lettuce leaves
    Lemon wedges

1. Combine all ingredients, except lettuce and lemon wedges, and stir gently until evenly mixed and coated with dressing.
2. Refrigerate at least 1 hour before serving.
3. When ready to serve, place on lettuce leaves. Serve with lemon wedges.

6 servings

Note: Shrimp salad also makes a delicious avocado filling.

182 *Cucumber Mousse*

1 package (3 ounces) lime-flavored
   gelatin
¾ cup boiling water
1 cup cottage cheese
1 cup mayonnaise or salad dressing
2 tablespoons grated onion
¾ cup grated cucumber
1 cup slivered almonds

1. Dissolve gelatin in boiling water. Stir in cottage cheese, mayonnaise, and onion until well blended. Fold in cucumber and almonds.
2. Pour mixture into a 1-quart mold. Refrigerate until set.

4 to 6 servings

Soups

183 *Beef Stock*

6 to 8 pounds beef soup bones
Salt to taste
2 large onions, peeled and left whole
10 peppercorns
2 whole allspice
2 carrots, scraped
4 parsley sprigs
2 bay leaves
2 celery stalks
Water to cover bones

1. Combine all ingredients in a 12-quart saucepot. Bring to boiling, lower heat, and simmer 10 to 12 hours, skimming off foam from top.
2. Strain. Discard solids. Cool. Skim off fat. Taste for salt.

7 to 8 quarts

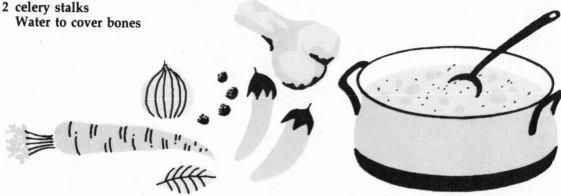

184 *Creamed Avgolemono Soup* (*Soupa Xerokosta Avgolemono*)

1 cup butter, softened
6 tablespoons flour
2 cups milk, scalded
2 cups cream, scalded
1½ quarts homemade chicken stock, strained
2 cups cooked rice
4 egg yolks
Juice of 3 lemons
1 lemon, thinly sliced for garnish

1. Beat butter in a small bowl. Beating constantly, slowly add flour.
2. Combine butter mixture with scalded milk and cream in a soup pot. Cook over medium heat, stirring frequently, until boiling. Reduce heat at once.
3. Pour in stock and add rice. Simmer 30 minutes, skimming off fat.
4. Beat egg yolks in a large bowl until fluffy. Pour in lemon juice a little at a time, while beating. Add 2 cups hot stock, a tablespoon at a time, while beating.
5. Pour stock mixture into soup. Heat, but do not boil. Garnish with sliced lemon.

6 servings

185 *Egg and Lemon Soup* *(Avgolemono Soupa)*

1½ quarts chicken stock
    (homemade or canned)
1½ cups uncooked parboiled rice
1 whole egg
3 egg yolks
    Juice of 2 lemons
    Salt and pepper to taste

1. Heat stock in a saucepan. Add rice and simmer, covered, until tender (about 20 minutes).
2. Beat egg and yolks until light. Beating constantly, slowly add lemon juice.
3. Measure 2 cups hot chicken stock and add, tablespoon by tablespoon, to egg mixture, beating constantly to prevent curdling. Add this mixture to the remaining hot chicken stock with rice. Season with salt and pepper.
4. Serve at once.

6 servings

186 *Egg and Lemon Soup with Sour-Dough Noodles*

(Trahana Avgolemono)

1½ quarts chicken broth
1 cup trahana (see Note)
    Salt and pepper to taste
2 eggs, separated
    Juice of 2 lemons

1. Bring broth to boiling; boil 6 minutes. Add trahana, salt, and pepper. Simmer covered 10 minutes.
2. In a small bowl, using a wire whisk, beat egg whites until frothy. In another bowl, beat egg yolks. Combine. Slowly beat in lemon juice, then 1 cup hot broth. Add to soup. Serve immediately.

About 2½ cups

Note: There are three varieties of trahana dough—sour, sweet, sweet-sour. It may be made at home (see recipe for Sweet-Sour Trahana and variations) or purchased at a Greek grocery store.

187 *Sweet-Sour Trahana*

2 eggs, slightly beaten
½ cup plain yogurt
½ cup milk
1 teaspoon salt
1½ cups all-purpose flour
    Semolina (about 1½ cups)

1. Blend eggs, yogurt, milk, and salt. Add flour and semolina, a little at a time, to form a stiff dough.
2. Knead for about 5 minutes (dough will be very sticky). Divide into small portions. Roll with hands into balls. Place on a clean cloth.
3. Flatten each piece as thin as possible. Let dry undisturbed on trivets at least 12 hours.
4. Cut into small pieces. Turn pieces over and continue drying for another 12 hours or more.
5. When completely dry, mash into crumbs with rolling pin. Spread on a baking sheet.
6. Bake at 200°F for 2 hours.

Note: The weather affects the drying of the trahana. When it is humid, allow more time for drying. Homemade trahana is far superior to the commercially made product. Store in an airtight jar indefinitely.

Sweet Trahana: Follow recipe for Sweet-Sour Trahana; omit yogurt and increase milk to 1 cup.

Sour Trahana: Follow recipe for Sweet-Sour Trahana; omit milk and increase yogurt to 1 cup.

188 *Bean Soup* (Fassoulatha)

1 cup large dried white beans
2 quarts water
1 cup sliced celery (½-inch pieces)
2 cups chopped onion
4 medium carrots, cut in ½-inch slices
½ cup chopped parsley
1 tablespoon tomato paste
1 cup olive oil
1 tablespoon oregano, crushed
3 tablespoons wine vinegar

Bring beans to a boil in the water. Reduce heat and simmer 1 hour. Add remaining ingredients. Simmer 2 hours more. Add **salt** and **pepper** to taste. Serve with **toasted bread.**

6 to 8 servings

189 *Lentil Soup* (Faki)

1 package (16 ounces) dried lentils
2 quarts water
½ cup olive oil
1 cup chopped celery
½ cup grated carrot
1 onion, quartered
1 tablespoon tomato paste
3 garlic cloves, peeled
2 bay leaves
Salt and pepper to taste
Vinegar

1. Rinse lentils several times. Drain.
2. In a kettle, put lentils, water, olive oil, celery, carrot, onion, tomato paste, garlic, bay leaves, salt, and pepper. Bring to a boil. Reduce heat and simmer covered 2 hours. Adjust salt and pepper.
3. Serve with a cruet of vinegar.

6 to 8 servings

190 *Soupa Aravanaiko*

This soup is a delicious main course with homemade bread on a cold night.

3 quarts beef stock
3 pounds lean beef, cut in 2½-inch squares
2 cans (15 ounces each) tomato sauce or 4 cups Tomato Sauce
4 medium ripe tomatoes, peeled, seeded, and diced (optional)
1 pound macaroni, cooked according to directions on package
1 cup freshly grated kefalotyri cheese, or more to taste

1. Heat stock to boiling. Add meat and tomato sauce. Simmer until meat is tender (about 2 hours).
2. Add tomato pieces. Simmer 20 minutes. Add cooked macaroni. Heat thoroughly.
3. Top with grated cheese before serving.

8 servings

191 *Fish Soup* (Psarosoupa)

2 small cleaned fish or 2 heads
  and bones from large fish
  such as red snapper or
  mackerel (tied together in
  cheesecloth)
1 bay leaf
2 quarts water or enough to
  cover
8 or 10 small onions, peeled and
  left whole
8 or 10 small new potatoes,
  pared and left whole
3 or 4 carrots, pared and sliced in
  1-inch pieces
1 stalk celery, sliced in 1-inch
  pieces
3 tomatoes, peeled, seeded, and
  chopped
2 garlic cloves, crushed in a
  garlic press
2 pounds mackerel fillets
1 pound red snapper fillets
1 pound codfish fillets
  Parsley sprigs
  Juice of 1 large lemon
½ cup olive oil

1. Put fish heads and bones into a stock pot with bay leaf and water. Bring to a boil and cook 20 minutes, removing scum as it forms. Strain broth; return to pot. Discard heads and bones. Add onions, potatoes, carrots, celery, tomatoes, and garlic. Place mackerel and snapper on top of vegetables. Add water if necessary to cover. Bring to a boil quickly. Boil 10 minutes. Add codfish. Boil another 10 minutes. Remove fish and place in a heated serving dish. Garnish with parsley.
2. Blend lemon juice and olive oil. Drizzle half over fish and add the rest to the stock. Pour soup and vegetables into a tureen. Serve the fish and soup in separate dishes.

8 servings

192 *Tripe Soup*

4 pounds prepared tripe
1½ quarts water
  Salt and pepper to taste
5 tablespoons butter
2½ tablespoons flour
3 eggs
  Juice of 2 lemons
1 teaspoon paprika
  Pinch red pepper seeds
  Croutons

1. Rinse tripe thoroughly. Place in a large saucepan. Add water, cover, and simmer for 3 hours, adding more water as the water in the pan boils away.
2. Remove tripe from the stock. Put through a meat grinder. Return to the stock. Season with salt and pepper. Cook over medium heat for 2 hours.
3. Meanwhile, melt 3 tablespoons butter in a saucepan, add flour and cook over low heat, stirring constantly, for 3 minutes. Add 1 cup stock in a thick stream to the butter and flour, stirring constantly with a whisk to prevent lumps. Pour this mixture into the soup. Simmer 15 minutes.
4. Beat eggs until frothy. Slowly add lemon juice while beating. Add 2 cups of stock in a thin stream, stirring constantly. Season with paprika and red pepper.
5. Add remaining butter just before serving. Serve with croutons and a cruet of **garlic-flavored vinegar.**

6 to 8 servings

193 *Traditional Greek Easter Soup* (*Mayeritsa Avgolemono*)

1 small bunch green onions,
  trimmed
2 cups diced celery root
4 parsley sprigs
1 dill sprig
2½ quarts water
  Salt and freshly ground pepper
  to taste
½ cup lamb's intestines
½ pound lamb's liver
½ pound lamb's heart
  Cold water
½ cup finely chopped parsley
2 tablespoons finely chopped dill
6 egg yolks
  Juice of 1 lemon

1. Tie green onions, celery root, parsley, and dill in cheesecloth and place in a kettle. Add the 2½ quarts water, salt, and pepper; bring to a boil.
2. Meanwhile, clean lamb's intestines. Rinse them well, then turn them inside out. To do this, use a small stick about the size of a pencil. Tie one end of one length of intestine. Fit this onto the tip of the stick, then reverse the intestine down the stick much as you would a stocking, pushing the inside out with the fingers. Rinse well and add the intestines to the kettle. Bring to a boil and cook about 1 hour.
3. Place liver and heart in a saucepan and add cold water to cover. Add salt and pepper and simmer until tender (20 minutes or longer).
4. Remove the intestines from the stock. Discard the cheesecloth bag. Chop the intestines. Dice the heart and liver. Add all this to the stock, then add parsley and dill. Heat thoroughly. Strain, reserving stock.
5. Heat small bowl of an electric mixer. Add egg yolks to the bowl and beat well. Add lemon juice, a little at a time, beating rapidly. Beat in 2 cups strained hot stock, tablespoon by tablespoon, beating rapidly. Beat in the remaining stock, strained, and serve immediately.

8 to 10 servings

194 *Bread Kvas*

1 quart hot water
1 pound beets, pared and sliced
1 rye bread crust

1. Pour hot water over beets in a casserole. Add bread. Cover with a cloth. Let stand 3 to 4 days.
2. Drain off clear juice and use as a base for soup.

About 3 cups

195 *Beet Kvas*

5 to 6 cups boiling water
3 cooked beets, sliced
½ cup vinegar

1. Pour boiling water over beets; add vinegar. Let stand at room temperature 2 to 4 days.
2. Drain off juice and use as a base for soup.

About 4 cups

196 *Rye Flour Kvas*

4 cups rye flour
6 to 8 cups lukewarm water

1. Put flour into a crock and gradually mix water into flour until smooth and the consistency of pancake batter. Cover with a cloth.
2. Keep in warm place 48 hours. Mixture will bubble. When brown liquid comes to top and bubbling stops, it is done. Skim off foam.
3. Fill crock with cold water; stir. Flour settles to bottom in a few hours. Pour off clear liquid and refrigerate in jars.

About 6 cups

197 "Nothing" Soup (Zupa Nic)

4 eggs, separated
⅓ cup sugar
1 quart milk
½ teaspoon vanilla extract
¼ teaspoon salt
  Dash of cinnamon or nutmeg
    (optional)

1. Beat egg yolks with 3 tablespoons of the sugar until very fluffy.
2. With clean beaters, beat the egg whites until frothy. Gradually beat in the remaining sugar. Continue beating until stiff, not dry, peaks form.
3. Heat milk over medium heat in a deep 10-inch skillet or 5- or 6-quart Dutch oven just until a "skin" forms on top, about 3 minutes.
4. Drop beaten egg whites by rounded spoonfuls into hot milk. Cook until the egg white "kisses" are set and firm to the touch, about 5 minutes. Remove kisses with a slotted spoon to waxed or absorbent paper.
5. Stirring constantly, gradually add hot milk to egg yolks. Strain into a heavy saucepan. Add vanilla extract and salt. Cook and stir over medium low heat about 3 minutes, until thickened, and soup coats a spoon.
6. Serve soup with 2 or 3 meringues in each portion. Sprinkle with cinnamon, if desired. Serve hot or cold.

4 servings

198 Pumpkin Soup (Zupa z Dynią)

1 quart milk
1 can (16 ounces) pumpkin
½ teaspoon allspice
¼ teaspoon nutmeg
¼ teaspoon pepper
½ teaspoon salt
1 cup cooked rice
2 tablespoons butter or margarine

1. Beat milk into pumpkin in saucepan. Stir in spices and salt. Bring just to boiling.
2. Stir in rice and butter. Cook and stir 5 to 10 minutes, or until rice is heated through; do not boil.

8 to 10 servings

199 Mushroom Soup (Zupa Grzybowa)

1 carrot
2 sprigs parsley
1 stalk celery
2 small onions, sliced
1 teaspoon salt
2 cups water
½ pound fresh mushrooms, sliced,
    or 2 cans (4 ounces each)
    mushrooms
1 cup water or mushroom liquid
1 teaspoon dill weed
1 teaspoon chopped parsley
1 tablespoon flour
¼ cup cold water
½ cup dairy sour cream or whipping
    cream

1. Cook carrot, parsley, celery, 1 onion, and salt in 2 cups water 20 minutes. Strain; discard vegetables.
2. Cook mushrooms and remaining onion in ½ cup water 8 minutes. Add to the vegetable broth along with ½ cup water, dill, and parsley.
3. Mix flour with ¼ cup cold water. Stir into soup. Bring to boiling. Cook and stir 3 minutes. Remove from heat.
4. Beat in sour cream. Serve hot.

About 4 servings

200 *Duck Soup (Czarnina)*

    1 duck (5½ to 6½ pounds), cut up
    1 quart duck, goose, or pork blood
 1½ pounds pork loin back ribs
    2 quarts water
    2 teaspoons salt
    1 stalk celery
    1 sprig parsley
    5 whole allspice
    2 whole cloves
    1 pound dried prunes, pitted
 ½ cup raisins
    1 small tart apple, chopped
       (optional)
    2 tablespoons flour
    1 tablespoon sugar
    1 cup whipping cream or dairy
       sour cream
       Salt, pepper, lemon juice, or
       vinegar

1. Purchase duck and blood from butcher. The blood will contain vinegar. (If preparing your own poultry, put ½ cup vinegar into glass bowl with blood to prevent coagulation. Set aside.)
2. Cover duck and back ribs with water in a large kettle. Add salt. Bring to boiling. Skim off foam.
3. Put celery, parsley, allspice, and cloves into cheesecloth bag and add to soup. Cover and cook over low heat until meat is tender, about 1½ hours.
4. Remove spice bag from kettle. Discard bones, cut up meat. Return meat to soup. Add prunes, raisins, and apple (if desired); mix. Cook 30 minutes.
5. With beater, blend flour and sugar into cream until smooth. Then add blood mixture, a little at a time, continuing to beat.
6. Add about ½ cup hot soup stock to blood mixture, blending thoroughly. Pour mixture slowly into the soup, stirring constantly until soup comes just to boiling.
7. Season to taste with salt, pepper, and lemon juice or vinegar. Serve with homemade noodles, if desired.

About 2½ quarts

Note: If a thicker soup is desired, increase flour to 3 to 4 tablespoons or add 1 cup puréed prunes.

201 *Dill Pickle Soup (Zupa Ogórkowa)*

    4 large dill pickles, diced or
       thinly sliced
    2 tablespoons flour
    2 tablespoons butter or margarine
    3 cups meat broth, bouillon, or
       meat stock
 ⅔ cup liquid from pickles or water
 2½ cups cubed boiled potatoes
       (optional)
    1 cup dairy sour cream

1. Coat pickles with flour.
2. Melt butter in a large skillet. Add pickles and stir-fry over medium heat 3 minutes.
3. Stir in beef broth, pickle liquid, and potatoes, if desired. Cook over medium heat 15 minutes, stirring occasionally.
4. To serve, mix in sour cream or spoon dollops of sour cream into each bowl before ladling in soup.

About 6 servings

202 *Kohlrabi Soup (Zupa z Kalarepy)*

    5 cups meat broth or bouillon or
       meat stock
    1 pound kohlrabi, peeled and diced
    2 tablespoons water
    1 tablespoon cornstarch or potato
       flour
    1 teaspoon salt
 ¼ teaspoon pepper
    1 tablespoon butter, melted
    2 egg yolks

1. Boil broth and kohlrabi in large saucepan. Cover; reduce heat and simmer 20 to 30 minutes, until kohlrabi is tender.
2. Mash or purée the kohlrabi.
3. Make a smooth paste by stirring water into cornstarch. Add to soup. Season with salt and pepper. Cook soup over medium heat until it boils.
4. Beat melted butter into egg yolks. Then beat in a little of the hot soup.
5. Remove soup from heat. Beat in egg yolk mixture. Serve hot with **croutons.**

About 8 servings

203 *Barley Soup* (*Krupnik*)

1 cup pearl barley
2 quarts meat stock
¼ cup butter or margarine, cut in pieces
2 carrots, diced
2 potatoes, diced
4 ounces (canned or frozen) mushrooms, sliced
1 stalk celery, chopped
Giblets from 1 chicken or turkey, diced (optional)
1 teaspoon dried parsley flakes
1½ teaspoons salt
½ teaspoon pepper
1 cup dairy sour cream (optional)
Sprigs of fresh dill

1. Combine barley with 1 cup of the meat stock in large saucepan. Bring to boiling; reduce heat and simmer until all stock is absorbed. Add butter piece by piece, stirring.
2. Boil vegetables and, if desired, giblets in the remaining stock until crisp-tender. Then add barley, parsley, salt, and pepper. Cook until barley is tender.
3. Garnish each serving with sour cream, if desired, and dill.

About 2½ quarts

204 *Black Bread Soup* (*Zupa Chlebowa*)

2 cups stale dark bread pieces (rye or whole wheat)
2 medium onions, quartered
1 carrot, quartered
1 leek, sliced
3 sprigs parsley
½ cup cut fresh or frozen green beans, lima beans, or peas
1 stalk celery, sliced
1 celery root or parsnip, sliced
1½ quarts water or meat broth or bouillon
1½ teaspoons salt
½ teaspoon pepper
Dash nutmeg
1 cup milk or water
3 egg yolks (optional)
Croutons or sliced hard-cooked eggs (optional)

1. Combine bread, all vegetables, and water in a 3-quart saucepan. Simmer 30 or 40 minutes, or until vegetables are tender.
2. Purée vegetables by pressing through a sieve or using an electric blender. Add vegetable purée to broth in pan. Stir in salt, pepper, nutmeg, and milk. Cook until soup simmers; do not boil.
3. If using egg yolks, beat them and then stir in a small amount of hot soup. Immediately beat mixture into soup. Remove from heat.
4. Serve hot with croutons or sliced hard-cooked eggs, if desired.

About 6 servings

205 *Caraway Soup* (*Zupa Kminkowa*)

5 cups meat broth or bouillon or meat stock
2 tablespoons caraway seed
● 2 tablespoons browned flour
2 tablespoons melted butter
½ pound diced cooked or smoked kiełbasa (Polish sausage) or salami (optional)
Buttered croutons
Dairy sour cream (optional)

1. Rapidly simmer broth with caraway seed 15 minutes. Strain and discard seed.
2. Blend flour into butter until smooth.
3. Return broth to saucepan. Stir in flour mixture and sausage. Bring just to boiling, stirring.
4. Serve garnished with croutons and, if desired, sour cream.

About 6 servings

206 *Sauerkraut Soup (Kapuśniak)*

2 pounds pork shanks, ham hocks, or pigs' feet
1 quart water
1 medium onion, sliced
1 bay leaf
5 peppercorns
1 sprig parsley or ¼ teaspoon dried parsley flakes
1 pound sauerkraut
2 cups meat broth, bouillon, or meat stock
8 to 12 ounces bacon or smoked link sausage, diced (optional)
¼ cup raisins or 2 tablespoons sugar (optional)
3 tablespoons lard or margarine (at room temperature)
3 tablespoons flour
½ teaspoon salt
¼ teaspoon pepper

1. Cook pork shanks in water in a 5-quart kettle 20 minutes. Skim off foam. Add onion, bay leaf, peppercorns, and parsley. Cook about 45 minutes, or until meat is tender.
2. Remove meat from broth. Strain broth; return to kettle.
3. Remove meat from bones; discard skin and bones. Dice meat.
4. Rinse sauerkraut with cold water; drain.
5. Add diced meat, drained sauerkraut, beef broth, and if desired, bacon and raisins to kettle. Simmer 1 hour.
6. Mix lard and flour to a smooth paste; stir into simmering soup. Cook and stir over medium heat until thickened. Mix in salt and pepper.
7. Serve with plain boiled potatoes or potato dumplings, if desired.

About 10 servings

207 *Fish Broth (Rosół z Ryby)*

1 large onion, quartered
2 tablespoons butter or margarine
½ small head savoy cabbage
2 carrots, cut up
2 celery stalks, cut up
1 parsley root, cut up
3 quarts water
6 peppercorns
1 bay leaf
Salt
2 pounds fish fillets
1 teaspoon lemon juice
1 teaspoon salt
½ teaspoon nutmeg

1. Brown onion in butter in a small skillet.
2. Meanwhile, simmer the vegetables in water with peppercorns, bay leaf, and salt to taste 15 minutes.
3. Add onion and fish to vegetables; simmer about 10 minutes, or until fish flakes easily.
4. Remove fish and vegetables. Use for another dish, if desired, or discard.
5. Strain broth. Add lemon juice, salt, and nutmeg.
6. Boil broth rapidly 10 minutes. Strain again, if desired. Serve as a clear soup.

About 2 quarts

208 *Chicken Broth (Rosół z Kury)*

1 chicken (3½ pounds)
2 teaspoons salt
7 cups boiling water
2 carrots
¼ small head savoy cabbage
2 stalks celery
1 parsley root (optional)
1 large onion, quartered
5 whole peppercorns
1 tablespoon chopped parsley

1. Simmer chicken with salt in boiling water 30 minutes.
2. Add carrots, cabbage, celery, parsley root (if desired), onion, peppercorns, and parsley.
3. Remove chicken. Strain broth. Quickly chill broth, then skim off fat. Store broth in refrigerator or serve hot with dumplings.
4. Use chicken meat for other dishes. Fat can be used in cooking instead of butter.

About 1½ quarts

209 *Meat Broth (Rosół z Mięsa)*

2 pounds beef shank or short ribs,
   or pork neckbones
1 pound marrow bones
3 quarts water
1 large onion, quartered
2 leaves cabbage
2 sprigs fresh parsley or 1
   tablespoon dried parsley flakes
1 carrot, cut up
1 parsnip, cut up
1 stalk celery, cut up
5 peppercorns
1 tablespoon salt

1. Combine beef, bones, and water in a 6-quart kettle. Bring to boiling. Boil 15 minutes, skimming frequently.
2. Add remaining ingredients. Simmer rapidly about 1½ hours, or until meat is tender.
3. Strain off broth. Chill quickly. Skim off fat.
4. Remove meat from bones. Set meat aside for use in other dishes. Discard bones, vegetables, and peppercorns.
5. Return skimmed broth to kettle. Boil rapidly about 15 minutes, or until reduced to about 6 cups. Store in refrigerator until needed.

About 1½ quarts

Meat Stock: Prepare Meat Broth as directed. Chill. Lift off fat. Boil until reduced to 3 cups, about 45 minutes.

210 *Borscht with Meat (Barszcz z Mięsa)*

¼ pound salt pork, diced
1 large leek, thinly sliced
1 medium onion, sliced
1 celery or parsley root (about 6
   ounces), peeled and cut in
   thin strips
3 beets (about ½ pound), peeled
   and shredded
½ head cabbage (about ½ pound),
   thinly sliced
2 quarts water
1½ pounds cooked meat such as
   kiełbasa (Polish sausage),
   ham, beef, or pork, diced
1 can (8 ounces) whole tomatoes
● 1 cup Rye Flour Kvas
2 tablespoons butter (at room
   temperature)
2 tablespoons flour
1 teaspoon salt
½ teaspoon pepper
1½ tablespoons lemon juice or
   vinegar
1 cup whipping cream or dairy
   sour cream
Prepared horseradish (optional)

1. Fry salt pork until golden in a 5-quart kettle. Add leek and onion. Fry until onion is transparent.
2. Add celery root, beets, cabbage, water, and meat. Cook until celery root is crisp tender; about 25 minutes.
3. Add tomatoes and kvas; mix. Cook over medium heat 30 minutes.
4. Make a smooth paste of butter and flour; stir into the simmering soup. Cook and stir until soup thickens. Add salt, pepper, and lemon juice; mix.
5. To serve, spoon a small amount of cream and horseradish into each bowl. Ladle hot soup into bowl and stir to blend with the cream and horseradish.

About 2½ quarts

211 *Volhynian Beet Soup (Barszcz Wołński)*

¼ cup dried navy or pea beans
2 cups water
● 2 cups Bread Kvas
2 cups meat broth, bouillon, or
    meat stock
6 medium beets, cooked and peeled
1 can (16 ounces) tomatoes
    (undrained)
1 small head cabbage (about 1½
    pounds)
1 small sour apple
    Salt and pepper
1 tablespoon butter (optional)
    Dairy sour cream

1. Bring beans and water just to boiling in a large kettle. Remove from heat. Let stand 1 hour. Then boil for 20 minutes, or until beans are tender. Add kvas and meat broth.
2. Slice beets. Mash tomatoes or make a purée by pressing through a sieve or using an electric blender. Add beets and tomatoes to beans.
3. Cut cabbage into sixths; remove core. Pare apple, if desired; core and dice. Add cabbage and apple to beans.
4. Season to taste with salt and pepper. Stir in butter, if desired. Cook soup over medium heat 30 minutes.
5. To serve, spoon a small amount of sour cream into each bowl. Ladle in hot soup and stir.

About 2½ quarts

212 *Fresh Cabbage Soup*
(Kapuśniak ze Świeżej Kapusty)

5 slices bacon, diced
1 pound cabbage, chopped
2 carrots, sliced
2 potatoes, sliced
1 stalk celery, sliced
1½ quarts water
2 tablespoons flour
2 tablespoons butter or margarine
    (at room temperature)
    Salt and pepper

1. Fry bacon until golden but not crisp in a 3-quart saucepan.
2. Add vegetables and water. Simmer 30 minutes, or until vegetables are tender.
3. Blend flour into butter; stir into soup. Bring soup to boiling, stirring. Season to taste with salt and pepper. If desired, serve with dumplings or pierogi.

6 to 8 servings

213 *Cold Cucumber-Beet Soup (Chłodnik)*

1 small bunch beets with beet
    greens (about 1 pound)
1½ quarts water or chicken broth
1 teaspoon salt
2 medium cucumbers, pared and
    diced
6 radishes, sliced
6 green onions with tops, sliced
2 tablespoons fresh lemon juice
2 cups dairy sour cream or
    buttermilk
1 dill pickle, minced (optional)
3 tablespoons chopped fresh dill
    or 4 teaspoons dill weed
    Salt and pepper
1 lemon, sliced
2 hard-cooked eggs, chopped or
    sliced
12 large shrimp, cooked, peeled,
    and deveined (optional)

1. Scrub beets and carefully wash greens. Leave beets whole; do not peel. Put beets and greens into a kettle with water and salt. Bring to boiling. Cover. Reduce heat, and cook slowly until tender, about 30 minutes, depending on size of beets. Drain, reserving liquid in a large bowl.
2. Peel and chop beets, mince the greens.
3. Add beets and greens to reserved liquid along with cucumber, radish, green onion, lemon juice, sour cream, pickle (if desired), and dill. Season with salt and pepper to taste; mix. Chill.
4. Serve garnished with lemon slices and hard-cooked egg and, if desired, whole shrimp.

About 2 quarts soup

214 *Clear Borscht (Barszca Klarowny)*

● 1 cup Beet Kvas
5 cups meat or vegetable broth (or use 3 beef and 3 vegetable bouillon cubes dissolved in 5 cups boiling water)
2 tablespoons brown sugar
Dairy sour cream (optional)

1. Heat kvas and broth to boiling in a saucepan. Skim surface if necessary.
2. Serve hot or chilled with **rye bread** and a large dollop of sour cream, if desired.

About 1½ quarts

215 *Wine Soup (Polewka z Wina)*

1 quart white wine
2 cups water
1 piece cinnamon stick (3 inches)
3 whole cloves
3 whole allspice
5 egg yolks
2 tablespoons sugar

1. Bring wine, water, and spices to boiling. Strain; discard spices.
2. Beat egg yolks with sugar until thick. Slowly add the hot wine mixture, beating constantly until a thick foam forms at the top. Be careful not to curdle the yolks by pouring hot wine too fast. Serve in cups with **wafers.**

8 to 10 servings

216 *Beer Soup (Polewka z Piwa)*

2 cans (12 ounces each) beer
3 egg yolks
4 teaspoons sugar
Croutons or grated cheese

1. Bring beer to boiling.
2. Meanwhile, beat egg yolks with sugar until thick.
3. Stirring constantly, gradually add a small amount of beer to egg yolks. Then carefully stir egg yolk mixture into boiling beer, reduce heat, and stir 1 minute; do not boil.
4. At once remove from heat. Serve with hot croutons.

About 4 servings

217 *Apple Soup (Zupa Jabłkowa)*

6 large apples (see Note)
1 quart water
¾ cup sugar
½ teaspoon cinnamon (optional)
½ cup lemon juice
1 cup whipping cream
⅔ cup white wine (optional)

1. Pare and core 5 apples. Cook in water until soft. Rub through a sieve, or purée in an electric blender to make an applesauce.
2. Combine applesauce, sugar, and cinnamon (if desired) in a large bowl.
3. Shred or mince remaining apple; mix with lemon juice. Stir into applesauce mixture. Chill.
4. To serve, blend cream into applesauce mixture. Stir in wine, if desired.

8 to 10 servings

Note: If desired, substitute 1 can or jar (16 ounces) applesauce and 1 cup water for apples and water.

218 *Prune Soup* (Zupa z Suszonych Śliwek)

1 package (12 ounces) pitted dried
    prunes
3 cups hot water
½ pound rhubarb, cut in pieces
2 cups boiling water
½ teaspoon cinnamon
¼ teaspoon cloves
⅔ cup sugar
1 tablespoon cornstarch or potato
    flour (optional)
¼ cup cold water (optional)
¾ cup dairy sour cream
    Cooked macaroni or croutons

1. Soak prunes in 3 cups hot water 1 hour. Cook in the same water 3 to 5 minutes.
2. Cook rhubarb in 2 cups boiling water 10 minutes.
3. Combine cooked fruits; press through a sieve, or purée in an electric blender.
4. Combine purée in a saucepan with cinnamon, cloves, sugar, and, if desired, a blend of cornstarch and cold water. Bring to boiling, stirring constantly. Remove from heat.
5. Cool slightly; beat in sour cream. Mix in macaroni. Or top with croutons and serve after the meat course.

8 to 10 servings

219 *Plum or Apricot Soup* (Zupa ze Śliwek lub Moreli)

1 pound fresh apricots or plums
1 quart water
1 tablespoon potato flour
⅓ cup sugar or ½ cup apricot or
    plum jam
    Peel and juice of ½ lemon
    (optional)
¼ teaspoon salt
1 pint dairy sour cream
    Buttered croutons

1. Cook fruit in water until tender, 20 to 30 minutes.
2. Discard pits. Purée fruits by pressing through a sieve or using an electric blender. (Fruit may be pitted raw for easier handling, but the taste will be less subtle.)
3. Stir potato flour into liquid in which fruit was cooked. Bring to boiling, stirring until thickened.
4. Pour thickened liquid into fruit purée. Stir in sugar, lemon peel and juice, if desired, and salt. Cook, stirring, 3 minutes.
5. Serve hot or cold. Spoon sour cream on top of each serving of soup. Garnish with croutons.

8 to 10 servings

220 *Berry Soup* (Zupa Jagodowa)

1 quart fresh blueberries,
    blackberries, raspberries, or
    strawberries; or 2 packages (10
    ounces each) frozen berries
1 cup fresh currants (optional)
2 cups water
1 tablespoon cornstarch or potato
    flour
2 tablespoons water
    Peel and juice of ½ lemon
⅔ cup sugar
½ teaspoon cinnamon or ¼
    teaspoon cloves
1 pint whipping cream or dairy
    sour cream

1. Using a potato masher, crush 3 cups of the berries in a large kettle. Reserve 1 cup berries for garnish. Purée fruits by pressing through a sieve, or use an electric blender.
2. Add the 2 cups water; simmer 15 minutes.
3. Mix cornstarch with 2 tablespoons water. Stir in soup. Bring to boiling, stirring until soup thickens.
4. Stir in lemon peel and juice, sugar, and cinnamon. Chill.
5. To serve, beat in cream. Or spoon soup over dollops of sour cream. Garnish with reserved whole berries.

6 to 8 servings

221 *Cherry Soup (Zupa Wiśniowa)*

3 pints pitted fresh red tart cherries
  or 3 cans (16 ounces each)
  pitted red tart cherries, drained
½ teaspoon cinnamon
¼ teaspoon cloves
1 quart water
½ cup sugar
¾ cup dairy sour cream
  Cooked noodles or croutons

1. Combine cherries, cinnamon, and cloves with the water in large saucepan. Bring to boiling. Reduce heat and simmer 15 minutes.
2. If desired, purée fruits by pressing through a sieve, or use an electric blender.
3. Add sugar and stir until it dissolves. Cool thoroughly.
4. Beat in sour cream. Serve with noodles or croutons after the meat course.

8 to 10 servings

222 *Easter Soup (Żurek Wielkanocny)*

2 cups rolled oats
2 cups warm water
  Crust of sour rye bread
1½ pounds Polish sausage
  (kiełbasa)
1½ quarts water
1 tablespoon prepared horseradish
1 teaspoon brown sugar
1 teaspoon salt
¼ teaspoon pepper

1. Mix oats and warm water. Add bread crust. Let stand until mixture sours, at least 24 hours. Strain; reserve liquid.
2. Cook sausage in 1½ quarts water 1 hour. Remove sausage. Skim off fat. Combine skimmed broth and oatmeal liquid.
3. Add horseradish, brown sugar, salt, and pepper. Slice sausage; add to broth. Bring just to boiling.
4. Serve hot with **boiled potatoes** and **hard-cooked eggs.**

About 4 servings

223 *Borscht without Meat (Barszcz Postny)*

7 medium beets (about 1½
  pounds)
2 medium potatoes (about ½
  pound) (optional)
½ cup chopped parsley root or 2
  tablespoons dried parsley
  flakes
⅓ cup chopped celery leaves
4 dried mushrooms or 4 fresh
  mushrooms
1 clove garlic, crushed (optional)
2 quarts water
● 1½ cups Beet Kvas
3 beef bouillon cubes or 1 tablespoon concentrated meat
  extract
2 teaspoons salt
1 tablespoon sugar
  Dairy sour cream (optional)

1. Pare beets and potatoes, then dice them.
2. Combine all ingredients in a 6-quart kettle. Bring to boiling. Reduce heat. Cover and cook over medium heat until vegetables are tender, 30 to 40 minutes.
3. Remove vegetables and force through a sieve or purée in an electric blender. Return purée to kettle. (This is optional and may be omitted.)
4. Various ingredients may be added to soup: prepared horseradish, lemon juice or vinegar, dill, more salt and sugar, pepper, chunks of rye bread, or filled pastries such as pierogi. Sometimes sliced or chopped hard-cooked eggs, beet tops, and baked beans are added. Simmer just long enough to heat thoroughly.
5. Serve in large bowls with dollops of sour cream, if desired.

About 5 quarts

224 *Almond Soup (Zupa Migdałowa)*

5 cups milk
½ pound blanched almonds, ground twice
5 bitter almonds (optional)
1 teaspoon almond extract
2 cups cooked rice
⅓ cup sugar
¼ cup raisins or currants

1. Heat milk just to simmering in a large saucepan.
2. Add all the ingredients; stir until well mixed. Cook over low heat 3 to 5 minutes.
3. Serve hot as is traditional for Christmas, or chill before serving.

About 2 quarts

225 *Jellied Consommé*

2 envelopes unflavored gelatin
½ cup cold water
● 5 cups Beef Stock
1 teaspoon Worcestershire sauce
1 tablespoon dry sherry
2 teaspoons lemon juice
Lemon twists
2 tablespoons chopped ripe olives

1. Pour gelatin over cold water in a medium saucepan; let stand 5 minutes. Set over low heat until gelatin is dissolved (about 3 minutes), stirring occasionally. Stir in remaining ingredients, except lemon twists and olives. Heat thoroughly, then cool slightly.
2. Pour consommé into a mixing bowl; refrigerate covered until set (3 to 4 hours).
3. Beat slightly before serving. Spoon into consommé cups or wine glasses. Garnish with lemon twists and chopped olives.

6 servings (about ¾ cup each)

226 *Fragrant Mushroom Soup*

The flavor of the dried mushrooms is "woodsy" and full-bodied. The combination of fresh and dried mushrooms is unusual.

● 1½ quarts Chicken Stock
1 cup dried mushrooms
1 small onion, chopped
Salt
Freshly ground pepper
10 fresh mushrooms, cleaned and sliced
● Low-Fat Yogurt, if desired

1. Pour 2 cups of the stock over the dried mushrooms in a bowl. Cover with a plate to keep mushrooms submerged. Let stand until mushrooms are soft (about 45 minutes). Drain; reserve liquid. Remove tough center stems with a sharp knife and discard; chop mushrooms.
2. Combine reserved mushroom liquid, remaining chicken stock, dried mushrooms, and onion in a medium saucepan. Simmer covered 30 minutes. Season to taste with salt and pepper. Stir fresh mushrooms into stock; cook 1 minute.
3. Serve immediately in soup cups. Top with dollops of yogurt, if desired.

8 servings (¾ cup each)

227 *Egg-Drop Soup*

The addition of rice and chicken livers adds heartiness to this Oriental favorite.

- 6 cups Chicken Stock
  2 teaspoons clarified butter
  ¼ cup uncooked long-grain rice
  6 chicken livers, cooked and
    chopped
  1 egg yolk, beaten
  2 tablespoons snipped parsley
    Salt
    Freshly ground white pepper
  1 tablespoon snipped chives

1. Heat stock to boiling in a medium saucepan.
2. Heat butter in a small skillet until bubbly; stir in rice. Cook and stir rice until lightly browned; stir into boiling stock. Simmer covered until rice is tender (about 25 minutes).
3. Stir liver, egg yolk, and parsley into stock; cook and stir until egg is cooked and liver hot (about 2 minutes). Season to taste with salt and pepper.
4. Spoon into bowls; garnish with chives.

6 servings (1⅓ cups each)

228 *Spinach Soup with Onion Petals*

  8 small onions, peeled
- 6 cups Chicken Stock
  2 pounds fresh spinach, washed
    and stems removed
  3 cups water
    Salt
  1 tablespoon finely chopped
    green onion tops

1. Cut each onion into ¼-inch slices, cutting almost to, but not through, base. Give onion a quarter turn; cut into ¼-inch slices, intersecting previous slices.
2. Simmer onions in stock in a large covered skillet or saucepan until onions are tender (about 20 minutes).
3. Simmer spinach in water in a covered saucepan 10 minutes; drain, adding cooking liquid to stock with onions. Reserve spinach for other use.
4. Taste stock; add salt if necessary. Lift onions from stock and into individual soup bowls with slotted spoon. Ladle stock around onions in each bowl. Sprinkle with green onion tops. Serve with knives, forks, and spoons.

8 servings (1 cup each)

229 *Jellied Gazpacho*

Colorful Mexican fare that is a traditional crowd pleaser.

  4 cups chilled tomato juice
  2 envelopes unflavored gelatin
- 1 cup Low-Fat Yogurt
  1 garlic clove, minced
  1 pound tomatoes, peeled,
    seeded, and chopped
  1 small cucumber, pared, seeded,
    and chopped
  1 medium green pepper, chopped
  ⅓ cup shredded carrot
  2 tablespoons minced red onion
  ½ cup finely chopped celery
  3 tablespoons fresh lemon juice
  1 to 1½ teaspoons salt
  ¼ teaspoon freshly ground
    pepper
  ⅛ teaspoon chili powder
  2 garlic cloves, minced
    Salad greens

1. Pour ½ cup of the tomato juice into a small saucepan. Sprinkle the gelatin over the juice; let stand 5 minutes. Set over low heat, stirring constantly, until gelatin is dissolved (about 3 minutes).
2. Pour mixture and remaining tomato juice into a large mixing bowl. Refrigerate until slightly thickened, but not set.
3. Mix yogurt and garlic; refrigerate covered.
4. Stir vegetables, lemon juice, salt, pepper, chili powder, and 2 garlic cloves into tomato mixture. Mix well.
5. Spoon tomato mixture into 6 individual soup bowls or a 2-quart bowl. Refrigerate covered until mixture has set (about 4 hours).
6. Unmold on salad greens and serve with the garlic yogurt.

6 servings (about 1 cup each)

Note: Jellied Gazpacho is excellent for lunch served with steamed shrimp.

230 *Yogurt Soup*

Middle Eastern influence has been translated for this rich, filling, but low-calorie soup.

- ● 1½ quarts Chicken Stock
  - 2 tablespoons cornstarch
- ● 1 cup Low-Fat Yogurt
  - Juice of ½ lemon, if desired
  - 2 teaspoons clarified butter
  - ¼ teaspoon paprika
  - Snipped parsley

1. Heat stock to boiling. Mix cornstarch thoroughly with yogurt; stir into stock. Simmer, stirring rapidly, until stock mixture thickens slightly (about 4 minutes). Taste; add lemon juice if needed for tartness.
2. Melt butter; stir in paprika. Spoon butter mixture onto top of soup. Pour soup into bowls. Sprinkle with parsley.

8 servings (¾ cup each)

231 *Chicken-Mushroom Pudding*

Though soufflélike in texture, this recipe has only half the eggs, flour, and butter of a soufflé.

- 1 tablespoon butter
- 1 tablespoon flour
- ½ cup nonfat dry-milk solids
- ½ cup cold water
- ● ½ cup Chicken Stock
- 1¼ cups finely chopped cooked chicken
- 1 cup finely chopped mushrooms
- 2 teaspoons snipped parsley
- 1 tablespoon finely snipped chives or green onion tops
- 2 teaspoons Dijon mustard
- ½ teaspoon salt
- ¼ teaspoon freshly ground pepper
- 2 egg yolks
- 3 egg whites
- Shredded carrot or radish roses

1. Melt butter in a medium skillet; mix in flour, stirring constantly until mixture is smooth and bubbly. Remove from heat. Mix milk solids, water, and stock; stir into flour mixture gradually. Return sauce to heat; boil and stir until thickened (about 2 minutes). Stir in remaining ingredients, except eggs and carrot. Cook and stir 3 minutes; let cool to room temperature.
2. Beat egg yolks; stir into chicken mixture. Beat egg whites until stiff but not dry peaks form; fold gently into chicken mixture until blended. Spoon mixture into lightly buttered 1-quart soufflé dish.
3. Bake at 350°F 35 to 40 minutes, or until puffy and light brown. Garnish with carrot. Serve immediately.

6 to 8 servings

Note: Chicken-Mushroom Pudding is also delicious served cold. Let cool 30 minutes after baking, then refrigerate covered until completely chilled (about 4 hours).

232 *Spiced Pumpkin Soup*

The crunchy green pepper garnish adds an interesting texture and flavor contrast to this soup.

- 1 small pumpkin (about 3 pounds), pared and cut in 2-inch pieces; or 2½ cups canned pumpkin
- 1 cup chopped onion
- 1 teaspoon minced ginger root
- ● 3 cups Chicken Stock
- ½ teaspoon salt
- ½ teaspoon freshly ground pepper
- ½ teaspoon ground cloves
- ½ cup white wine
- 1¼ cups chopped green pepper

1. Simmer pumpkin, onion, and ginger root in stock in a covered saucepan until pumpkin is tender (about 20 minutes).
2. Purée mixture in two batches in a food processor or blender. Pour purée back into saucepan; stir in remaining ingredients except green pepper. Simmer uncovered 10 minutes.
3. Serve soup in bowls; garnish with green pepper.

6 servings (about ¾ cup each)

Note: This soup is also excellent served cold. If desired, Low-Fat Yogurt (●) can be used in place of the wine, or as a garnish.

233 *Minestrone*

Derived from the Latin "to hand out," this soup was a staple in the days when the monks kept it always on the fire to be ready for sojourners or travelers. Even today, it is a favorite.

6 cups water
1¼ cups (about ½ pound) dried navy beans, rinsed
¼ pound salt pork
3 tablespoons olive oil
1 small onion, chopped
1 clove garlic, chopped
¼ head cabbage
2 stalks celery, cut in ½-inch slices
2 small carrots, pared and cut in ½-inch slices
1 medium potato, pared and diced
1 tablespoon chopped parsley
½ teaspoon salt
¼ teaspoon pepper
1 quart hot water
¼ cup packaged precooked rice
½ cup frozen green peas
¼ cup tomato paste
Grated Parmesan cheese

1. Bring the 6 cups water to boiling in a large saucepot. Gradually add the beans to the boiling water so the boiling does not stop. Simmer the beans 2 minutes, and remove from heat. Set aside to soak 1 hour.
2. Add salt pork to beans and return to heat. Bring to boiling, reduce heat, and simmer 1 hour, stirring once or twice.
3. While beans are simmering with salt pork, heat the olive oil in a skillet, and brown the onion and garlic lightly. Set aside.
4. Wash the cabbage, discarding coarse outer leaves, and shred finely.
5. After the beans have simmered an hour, add the onion, garlic, celery, carrots, potato, cabbage, parsley, salt, and pepper. Slowly pour in 1 quart hot water and simmer about 1 hour, or until the beans are tender.
6. Meanwhile, cook the rice according to package directions. About 10 minutes before the beans should be done, stir in the rice and peas. When the peas are tender, stir in the tomato paste. Simmer about 5 minutes. Serve sprinkled with cheese.

About 6 servings

234 *"Little Hats" in Broth (Cappelletti in Brodo)*

½ cup (4 ounces) ricotta or cottage cheese
2 tablespoons grated Parmesan cheese
½ cup finely chopped cooked chicken
1 egg, slightly beaten
⅛ teaspoon salt
Few grains nutmeg
Few grains pepper
2 cups sifted all-purpose flour
¼ teaspoon salt
2 eggs
3 tablespoons cold water
2 quarts chicken broth or bouillon

1. Combine cheeses, chicken, 1 egg, ⅛ teaspoon salt, nutmeg, and pepper; set aside.
2. Combine flour and ¼ teaspoon salt in a large bowl. Make a well in the center of the flour. Place 2 eggs, one at a time, in the well, mixing slightly after each one is added. Gradually add the water; mix well to make a stiff dough. Turn dough onto a lightly floured surface and knead until smooth and elastic (5 to 8 minutes).
3. Roll dough out to about 1/16 inch thick. Cut into 2½-inch circles. Place ½ teaspoon of the chicken-cheese mixture in the center of each round. Dampen the edges with water, fold in half, and press together to seal. Bring the two ends together, dampen, and pinch together.
4. Bring the chicken broth to boiling. Add pasta and cook 20 to 25 minutes, or until pasta is tender. Pour broth and pasta into soup bowls, and serve immediately.

8 servings

235 *Zuppa di Pesce: Royal Danieli*

This fish soup recipe is from the Danieli Royal Excelsior, a hotel in Venice.

3 pounds skinned and boned fish (haddock, trout, cod, salmon, and red snapper)
1 lobster (about 1 pound)
1 pound shrimp with shells
1 quart water
½ cup coarsely cut onion
1 stalk celery with leaves, coarsely cut
2 tablespoons cider vinegar
2 teaspoons salt
¼ cup olive oil
2 cloves garlic, minced
1 bay leaf, crumbled
1 teaspoon basil
½ teaspoon thyme
2 tablespoons minced parsley
½ to 1 cup dry white wine
½ cup chopped peeled tomatoes
8 shreds saffron
1 teaspoon salt
½ teaspoon freshly ground black pepper
6 slices French bread
¼ cup olive oil

1. Reserve heads and tails of fish. Cut fish into bite-size pieces.
2. In a saucepot or kettle, boil lobster and shrimp 5 minutes in water with onion, celery, vinegar, and 2 teaspoons salt.
3. Remove and shell lobster and shrimp; devein shrimp. Cut lobster into bite-size pieces. Set lobster and shrimp aside.
4. Return shells to the broth and add heads and tails of fish. Simmer 20 minutes.
5. Strain broth, pour into saucepot, and set aside.
6. Sauté all of the fish in ¼ cup oil with garlic, bay leaf, basil, thyme, and parsley 5 minutes, stirring constantly.
7. Add to reserved broth along with wine, tomatoes, saffron, 1 teaspoon salt, and the pepper. Bring to boiling; cover and simmer 10 minutes, stirring occasionally.
8. Serve with slices of bread sautéed in the remaining ¼ cup olive oil.

About 2½ quarts soup

236 *Roman Egg Soup with Noodles*
(Stracciatella con Pasta)

4 cups chicken broth
1½ tablespoons semolina or flour
1½ tablespoons grated Parmesan cheese
⅛ teaspoon salt
⅛ teaspoon pepper
4 eggs, well beaten
1 cup cooked noodles
Snipped parsley

1. Bring chicken broth to boiling.
2. Meanwhile, mix semolina, cheese, salt, and pepper together. Add to beaten eggs and beat until combined.
3. Add noodles to boiling broth, then gradually add egg mixture, stirring constantly. Continue stirring and simmer 5 minutes.
4. Serve topped with parsley.

4 servings

Roman Egg Soup with Spinach: Follow recipe for Roman Egg Soup with Noodles; omit noodles. Add ½ **pound chopped cooked fresh spinach** to broth before adding egg mixture.

237 *Escarole Soup*

3 pounds beef shank cross cuts
1 can (6 ounces) tomato paste
1 tablespoon salt
1 teaspoon basil, crushed
½ teaspoon oregano, crushed
8 cups water
1 pound escarole, chopped
1 medium onion, peeled and diced
1 medium potato, pared and diced
2 stalks celery, diced
   Fresh parsley, snipped
   Freshly ground black pepper

1. Put beef shank into a saucepot or Dutch oven. Add tomato paste, salt, basil, oregano, and water; stir. Cover; bring to boiling, reduce heat, and simmer until meat is tender (about 3 hours).
2. Add escarole, onion, potato, and celery; stir. Bring to boiling; simmer, uncovered, 45 minutes, or until vegetables are tender.
3. Remove meat and bone; cut meat into pieces and transfer to soup plates. Ladle hot soup over meat and garnish each serving with parsley and pepper.

About 3 quarts soup

238 *Vegetable Soup Italienne (Minestrone)*

1 cup thinly sliced carrots
1 cup thinly sliced zucchini
1 cup thinly sliced celery
1 cup finely shredded cabbage
2 tablespoons butter
2 tablespoons cooking oil
2 beef bouillon cubes
8 cups boiling water
2 teaspoons salt
2 medium tomatoes, cut in pieces
½ cup uncooked broken spaghetti
½ teaspoon thyme

1. Add carrots, zucchini, celery, and cabbage to hot butter and oil in a saucepot. Cook, uncovered, about 10 minutes, stirring occasionally.
2. Add bouillon cubes, water, and salt to the vegetables. Bring to boiling; reduce heat and simmer, uncovered, 30 minutes.
3. Stir in tomatoes, spaghetti, and thyme; cook 20 minutes longer.
4. Serve hot from soup tureen with shredded Parmesan cheese sprinkled over the top of each serving.

About 6 servings

239 *Chicken Broth (Brodo di Pollo)*

1 stewing chicken (4 to 5 pounds)
5 cups water
2 teaspoons salt
5 pieces (3 inches each) celery with leaves
3 small carrots, washed and scraped
2 medium onions
1 large tomato, rinsed and quartered

1. Clean chicken, disjoint, cut into pieces, and rinse. Put into a saucepot. Rinse giblets, refrigerate liver, and put remaining giblets into pot. Add water, salt, celery, carrots, onions, and tomato. Cover and bring to boiling. Uncover and skim off foam.
2. Cover tightly. Simmer 2 to 3 hours. When chicken is almost tender, add liver. Cook about 15 minutes.
3. Remove chicken and giblets from broth, cool slightly, and remove skin. Remove meat from bones, and use as needed in recipes.
4. Strain broth and cool slightly. Remove fat that rises to surface. Refrigerate fat; use as needed. Cool broth and refrigerate until needed.

About 1 quart broth

240 *Zuppa Pavese*

● 1 quart Chicken Broth
  4 slices bread (½ inch thick),
      toasted and generously
      buttered
  4 eggs
  ¼ cup freshly grated Parmesan
      cheese

1. Heat Chicken Broth.
2. Place slices of buttered toast in individual heat-resistant soup bowls. Break an egg over each toast slice. Carefully pour broth into bowls, taking care not to break the egg yolks.
3. Set bowls in a 350°F oven and cook until egg whites are firm.
4. Before serving, sprinkle generously with grated cheese.

4 servings

Note: Instead of toasting and buttering the bread, the slices may be browned on both sides in butter in a skillet or on a griddle. If desired, use poached eggs and omit oven cooking.

To poach eggs, grease the bottom of a deep skillet. Add enough water to come about 1 inch above eggs. Lightly salt the water; bring to boiling, then reduce heat to simmering. Break the eggs, one at a time, into a small dish and slip each into the water. Cook 3 to 5 minutes, depending on firmness desired. Remove with slotted spoon.

241 *Miniatures Florentine*

Float these vivid green cutouts on individual servings of hot bouillon or consommé.

  1 egg, well beaten
  ¼ cup finely chopped fresh
      spinach
  1 tablespoon finely chopped
      unblanched almonds
  ¼ clove garlic, minced
  ⅛ teaspoon salt
    Few grains black pepper

1. Mix all ingredients thoroughly in a bowl.
2. Meanwhile, heat a griddle or heavy skillet until moderately hot.
3. Lightly butter the griddle. Spoon the batter onto it, spreading to make a round about 7 inches in diameter. Bake until lightly browned, about 3 minutes; turn and brown second side.
4. Using hors d'oeuvre cutters (½ inch in diameter), cut out shapes from the griddlecake. Serve a spoonful in each serving of **soup.**

242 *Specialty Soup (Zuppa Specialita)*

6 cups canned chicken broth
2 tablespoons minced parsley
2 tablespoons flour
3 eggs, well beaten
3 tablespoons shredded Parmesan
   cheese

1. Heat broth to boiling in a large saucepan.
2. Meanwhile, add parsley and flour to beaten eggs; stir in cheese and blend thoroughly.
3. Gradually add the egg mixture to boiling broth; while stirring with a fork. Cook over low heat several minutes, or until egg mixture is set.

About 6 servings

243 *Tortilla Soup*

This is a light soup, good for a first course at dinner, and is one use for stale tortillas.

2 quarts chicken or beef stock,
   canned consommé, or water
   plus bouillon cubes
½ cup chopped onion
1 cup canned tomato sauce or
   purée
1 teaspoon salt
¼ teaspoon pepper
6 to 8 stale tortillas
   Oil for frying
1½ cups shredded Monterey Jack or
   mild Cheddar cheese
   (optional)

1. Heat stock with onion to boiling. Reduce heat and simmer about 5 minutes. Stir in tomato sauce, salt, and pepper; simmer about 5 minutes.
2. Meanwhile, cut tortillas into ½-inch strips and fry in hot oil until crisp; drain on absorbent paper.
3. To serve soup, place a handful of crisp tortilla strips in soup bowl and ladle soup on top. Sprinkle with cheese, if desired.

About 2 quarts soup

244 *Pozole*

This hearty soup comes from Guadalajara, capital of the Mexican state of Jalisco. The everyday variety calls for pork head as the only meat. This richer version uses pork hocks and loin as well as chicken, and obviously is a meal in itself. Pozole is always served with a variety of crisp vegetable garnishes which are sprinkled on top of the hot soup at the diner's discretion.

2 pork hocks, split in two or three
   pieces each
1 large onion, sliced
2 cloves garlic, minced
   Water
1 stewing chicken, cut in serving
   pieces
1 pound pork loin, boneless, cut in
   1-inch chunks
2 cups canned hominy or canned
   garbanzos
1 tablespoon salt
½ teaspoon pepper
1 cup sliced crisp radishes
1 cup shredded cabbage
1 cup shredded lettuce
½ cup chopped green onions
   Lime or lemon wedges

1. Put split pork hocks, onion, and garlic into a kettle, cover with water, and cook until almost tender (about 3 hours).
2. Add chicken and pork loin and cook 45 minutes, or until chicken is almost tender.
3. Add hominy, salt, and pepper. Cook about 15 minutes, or until all meat is tender.
4. Remove pork hocks and chicken from soup. Remove meat from bones and return meat to soup.
5. Serve in large soup bowls. Accompany with a relish tray offering the radishes, cabbage, lettuce, green onions, and lime or lemon wedges as garnishes.

8 to 10 servings

245 *Fish Soup*

1 head and bones from large fish,
   such as red snapper
1 bay leaf
1 onion, coarsely chopped
2 stalks celery
1½ quarts water
2 cups (16-ounce can) tomatoes
   with juice
1 cup sliced carrots
1 cup diced pared potatoes
1 or 2 diced jalapeño chilies
1 cup dry sherry
1 pound diced, boneless fillets of
   white fish, or deveined
   shrimp
½ teaspoon garlic salt
½ teaspoon marjoram
   Salt and pepper

1. Put fish head and bones into a kettle with bay leaf, onion, celery, and water. Boil 15 minutes. Remove from heat and strain liquid, returning it to kettle. Discard solids.
2. Add tomatoes, carrots, potatoes, and chilies to liquid in kettle. Simmer until carrots and potatoes are almost tender (about 15 minutes).
3. Add sherry, diced fish, garlic salt, marjoram, and salt and pepper to taste to kettle. Cook about 5 minutes, or until fish flakes easily with fork.

2½ to 3 quarts soup

246 *Soup Mexicana*

1 chicken breast
1½ quarts chicken broth
2 onions, chopped
1 tablespoon butter or margarine
1½ teaspoons grated onion
2 cups chopped zucchini
1 cup drained canned whole
   kernel corn
⅓ cup tomato purée
2 ounces cream cheese, cut in
   small cubes
2 avocados, sliced

1. Combine chicken breast, broth, and onion in a large saucepan. Cover, bring to boiling, reduce heat, and cook 30 minutes, or until chicken is tender.
2. Remove chicken; dice and set aside. Reserve broth.
3. Heat butter and grated onion in a large saucepan; stir in zucchini and corn. Cook about 5 minutes, stirring occasionally. Mix in broth and tomato purée. Cover and simmer about 20 minutes.
4. Just before serving, mix in diced chicken, cream cheese, and avocado slices.

6 to 8 servings

Note: Any remaining soup may be stored, covered, in refrigerator.

247 *Avocado Soup*

4 fully ripe avocados, peeled and
   pitted
3 cups cold chicken broth
2 teaspoons lime juice
½ teaspoon salt
⅛ teaspoon garlic powder
2 cups chilled cream

1. Put all ingredients except cream into an electric blender container. Cover and blend until smooth. Mix with the cream and chill thoroughly.
2. Serve with **lemon slices** or garnish as desired.

6 servings

248 *Corn Soup I*

½ cup finely chopped onion
2 tablespoons butter
1 quart beef stock or canned beef broth
2½ cups cooked whole kernel golden corn
3 tomatoes, peeled, halved, and seeded
Salt and pepper
1 cup whipping cream
Dairy sour cream

1. Cook onion in butter in a saucepan until onion is soft.
2. Put onion and a small amount of stock into an electric blender. Add 2 cups corn and tomato halves; blend until smooth.
3. Turn purée into saucepan and mix in remaining stock. Season to taste with salt and pepper. Bring to boiling, reduce heat, and cook 5 minutes. Add cream gradually, stirring constantly. Heat thoroughly, but do not boil.
4. Garnish soup with dollops of sour cream and remaining corn.

6 to 8 servings

249 *Corn Soup II*

2 tablespoons butter or margarine
½ cup chopped onion
2 cups (17-ounce can) cream-style corn
1 cup canned tomato sauce
3 cups chicken stock, canned chicken broth, or 3 cups water plus 3 chicken bouillon cubes
1 cup cream
Salt and pepper

1. Melt butter in a large saucepan. Add onion and cook until soft. Add corn, tomato sauce, and stock. Bring to boiling, reduce heat, and simmer about 10 minutes to blend flavors, stirring frequently.
2. Remove from heat and stir in cream. Season to taste with salt and pepper. Serve hot.

6 to 8 servings

250 *Bean Soup*

● 2 cups cooked Basic Mexican Beans or canned kidney beans with liquid
1 cup beef stock, canned beef broth, or 1 cup water plus 1 beef bouillon cube
1 cup cooked tomatoes with liquid
1 clove garlic, minced
½ teaspoon oregano
½ teaspoon chili powder
Salt and pepper

1. Put beans into a large saucepan. Mash with a potato masher, leaving some large pieces. Add meat stock, tomatoes, garlic, oregano, and chili powder. Bring to boiling, reduce heat, and simmer about 10 minutes, stirring frequently.
2. Add salt and pepper to taste. Serve hot.

About 1 quart soup

251 Black Bean Soup

1 pound dried black beans, washed
2 quarts boiling water
2 tablespoons salt
5 cloves garlic
1½ teaspoons cumin (comino)
1½ teaspoons oregano
2 tablespoons white vinegar
10 tablespoons olive oil
½ pound onions, peeled and chopped
½ pound green peppers, trimmed and chopped

1. Put beans into a large, heavy saucepot or Dutch oven and add boiling water; boil rapidly 2 minutes. Cover tightly, remove from heat, and set aside 1 hour. Add salt to beans and liquid; bring to boiling and simmer, covered, until beans are soft, about 2 hours.
2. Put the garlic, cumin, oregano, and vinegar into a mortar and crush to a paste.
3. Heat olive oil in a large skillet. Mix in onion and green pepper and fry until onion is browned, stirring occasionally. Thoroughly blend in the paste, then stir the skillet mixture into the beans. Cook over low heat until ready to serve.
4. Meanwhile, mix a small portion of **cooked rice, minced onion, olive oil**, and **vinegar** in a bowl; set aside to marinate. Add a soup spoon of rice mixture to each serving of soup.

About 2 quarts soup

252 Gazpacho

Gazpacho is a refreshing cold soup made with fresh, raw vegetables. It is so filled with vegetable chunks that it seems almost like a salad. Serve it very well chilled, and keep bowls over ice, or place an ice cube in each bowl just as it is served.

1 clove garlic
2 cups chopped peeled fresh tomatoes
1 large cucumber, pared and chopped
½ cup diced green pepper
½ cup chopped onion
1 cup tomato juice
3 tablespoons olive oil
2 tablespoons vinegar
Salt and pepper
Dash Tabasco
½ cup crisp croutons

1. Cut garlic in half and rub onto bottom and sides of a large bowl. Add tomatoes, cucumber, green pepper, onion, tomato juice, olive oil, and vinegar to bowl and stir until evenly mixed. Season to taste with salt, pepper, and Tabasco.
2. Chill in refrigerator at least 1 hour before serving.
3. Serve soup in chilled bowls. Top each serving with a few croutons.

8 to 10 servings

253 Avocado Yogurt Soup

Here is another cold soup, very different from Gazpacho, and perfect as a warm-weather meal appetizer.

1 cup avocado pulp (2 to 3 avocados, depending on size)
⅔ cup unsweetened yogurt
⅔ cup beef stock, or bouillon made with ⅔ cup water and 1 bouillon cube, then chilled
1 tablespoon lemon juice
1 teaspoon onion juice or grated onion
½ teaspoon salt
Dash Tabasco

1. Put avocado pulp and yogurt into an electric blender and blend until evenly mixed. Adding gradually, blend in beef stock, lemon juice, onion juice, salt, and Tabasco. Chill well.
2. Serve soup in chilled bowls.

4 to 6 servings

Fruit Bread, Milan Style, page 112

254 Cream-Style Gazpacho with Avocado

4 hard-cooked eggs
¼ cup oil
1 tablespoon prepared mustard
1 tablespoon Worcestershire sauce
¼ cup lemon juice
1 teaspoon garlic salt
¼ teaspoon pepper
5 fresh medium tomatoes
1 large cucumber
1 medium onion
1 ripe avocado
1 cup dairy sour cream

1. Peel eggs; slice in half and remove yolks; set whites aside. Put egg yolks into a small bowl and mash with fork; blend in oil until of paste consistency. Blend in mustard, Worcestershire sauce, lemon juice, garlic salt, and pepper. Set aside.

2. Peel tomatoes; set aside one for garnish; coarsely chop remaining 4 and put into an electric blender. Pare and seed cucumber. Set aside ¼ as garnish; chop remaining ¾ and place in blender with tomatoes. Peel, coarsely chop, and add onion to blender. Peel avocado and place half in blender with vegetables. Reserve remaining half for garnish. Blend contents of blender until smooth. Add egg yolk mixture and blend until thoroughly mixed. Add sour cream gradually, blending well.

3. Pour soup into container with cover.

4. Chop remaining tomato, cucumber, and hard-cooked egg whites and add to soup. Slice remaining avocado half thinly and add to soup. Stir in lightly. Cover and refrigerate until well chilled.

About 6 servings

255 Breadfruit Soup Guadeloupe

1 breadfruit (about 1½ pounds)*
2 bacon slices, fried and crumbled
● 4 cups Coconut Milk
2 tablespoons soft butter (optional)

1. Bake breadfruit at 350°F 45 minutes. Open it and remove the center; peel and dice the meat. Put breadfruit, bacon, and Coconut Milk in a bowl. Purée a little at a time in an electric blender or in a food mill, adding butter if necessary. Heat.

2. Serve in bouillon cups and garnish with **toasted grated coconut**.

*Breadfruit can now be found in many supermarkets and most Puerto Rican markets.

256 Chili con Carne

Chili con Carne is not, strictly speaking, an authentic Mexican soup. However, it is so associated with Mexican food in the minds of most North Americans, and besides, is so delicious, that a recipe is included here.

1½ pounds ground beef
1 large onion, chopped
1 clove garlic, minced
4 cups (two 16-ounce cans) cooked tomatoes
2 cups (one 15-ounce can) red kidney beans
1 tablespoon chili powder
2 teaspoons salt
¼ teaspoon pepper

1. Cook ground beef in a large skillet, stirring until crumbled into small pieces and well browned.

2. Add onion and garlic to meat; cook about 5 minutes, stirring frequently.

3. Add tomatoes to skillet and chop into bite-size chunks. Stir in kidney beans, chili powder, salt, and pepper. Reduce heat to simmering and cook, stirring occasionally, about 30 minutes.

6 to 8 servings

Island Bread, page 107
Yogurt, page 36
Drop Doughnuts, page 106

257 *Quick Tomato-Fish Stew*

3 tablespoons oil
½ cup chopped onion
1 clove garlic, minced
2 cups canned tomatoes with juice
    (16-ounce can)
2 cups cooked garbanzos, drained
    (16-ounce can)
½ pound boned white fish, flaked
    Salt and pepper

1. Heat oil in a kettle. Add onion and garlic and cook until soft (about 5 minutes). Add tomatoes and garbanzos and bring to boiling. Add flaked fish, reduce heat, and cook about 15 minutes longer. Season to taste with salt and pepper.
2. Serve with **pickled hot chilies**.

6 to 8 servings

258 *Spinach-Ball Soup*

Here is another example of the Mexican way with unusual soups. The little deep-fried spinach-wrapped balls give the soup its name. They're so delicious by themselves that you might like to serve them as a hot appetizer.

Spinach Balls:
2 pounds fresh spinach
½ cup cooked cubed ham
½ cup cubed Cheddar cheese
3 eggs, separated
1 tablespoon flour
    Dash salt
    Oil for deep frying
Soup:
2 tablespoons oil
½ cup chopped onion
1 clove garlic, minced
1 can (6 ounces) tomato paste
3 cups chicken or meat stock or
    canned bouillon
    Salt and pepper

1. For spinach balls, wash spinach well and remove hard stalks. Steam until tender, in a small amount of boiling salted water in a large saucepot. Drain. Cool slightly and form into balls about 1¼ inches in diameter. Push a piece of ham or cheese into center of each ball.
2. Beat egg whites until stiff; gradually beat in yolks, flour, and salt. Coat spinach balls with egg batter and fry one layer of balls at a time in hot oil until lightly browned.
3. Meanwhile, prepare soup. Heat 2 tablespoons oil in a large kettle. Add onion and garlic and cook until soft (about 5 minutes). Stir in tomato paste and stock. Heat to boiling, reduce heat, and simmer gently about 15 minutes. Season to taste with salt and pepper.
4. Serve the spinach balls in the soup.

4 to 6 servings

259 *Green Rice*

1 cup (1 small can) salsa verde
    mexicana (Mexican green
    tomato sauce)
1 cup (lightly packed) fresh parsley
1 clove garlic
2 tablespoons vegetable oil
2 cups beef or chicken stock, or 2
    cups water plus 2 bouillon
    cubes
    Salt and pepper
1 cup uncooked rice

1. Put salsa verde, parsley, and garlic in an electric blender and blend until liquefied.
2. Heat oil in a large saucepan. Add blended sauce and mix well; cook about 5 minutes.
3. Add stock to saucepan and bring to boiling, stirring to blend ingredients. Season to taste with salt and pepper. Add rice, stir, cover tightly, and cook until all liquid is absorbed (about 25 minutes).

6 servings

260 *Tortilla-Ball Soup*

8 large stale tortillas
1 cup milk
1 small onion, coarsely chopped
1 clove garlic, minced
¼ cup grated Parmesan cheese
1 whole egg plus 1 egg yolk,
    beaten
½ teaspoon salt
⅛ teaspoon pepper
    Lard or oil for frying
● 2 quarts meat stock , or
    2 quarts canned
      beef broth (3 cans condensed
      beef broth plus equal amount
      water)
1 cup canned tomato sauce

1. Tear tortillas into pieces and soak in milk until soft. Place in an electric blender with onion and garlic and blend until puréed. Turn purée into a bowl. Beat in cheese, whole egg and egg yolk, salt, and pepper. Shape into small balls.
2. Fry in hot lard until lightly browned.
3. Meanwhile, heat meat stock and tomato sauce together in a large kettle. When bubbling, add tortilla balls. Serve at once.

6 to 8 servings

261 *Baked Noodles with Chorizo*

¼ pound chorizo sausage (see
  ● Chorizo Filling, or
    use bulk pork sausage
2 to 4 tablespoons lard or oil
1 package (7 ounces) fine noodles
¼ cup chopped onion
2 cups beef or chicken stock, or
    water plus bouillon cubes
1 cup cottage cheese
1 cup dairy sour cream
    Dash Tabasco (if bulk pork
      sausage used)
    Salt and pepper
    Grated Parmesan cheese

1. Fry chorizo in a large skillet with heat-resistant handle until cooked through, crumbling and stirring as it cooks.
2. Remove meat from skillet and set aside. Add lard or oil to skillet to make about 1¼-inch layer in bottom. Stir in uncooked noodles and onion and fry until noodles are lightly browned and onion is soft, stirring often to prevent burning.
3. Return cooked chorizo to skillet. Stir in stock.
4. Bake at 350°F about 15 minutes, or until all liquid is absorbed by noodles.
5. Remove skillet from oven. Stir in cottage cheese and sour cream. Season to taste with Tabasco, if using, and salt and pepper to taste. Sprinkle with Parmesan cheese. Return to oven and bake about 10 minutes, or until bubbling hot.

6 servings

262 Dry Soup of Tortillas with Tomatoes and Cheese

½ cup oil
1 cup chopped onion
1 clove garlic, minced
2 cups (16-ounce can) cooked
    tomatoes with juice, slightly
    chopped
1 teaspoon salt
¼ teaspoon pepper
½ teaspoon oregano
10 to 12 stale tortillas, cut in
    ½-inch strips
1 cup whipping cream
1 cup (about ¼ pound) grated
    Parmesan cheese
    Paprika

1. Heat 2 tablespoons oil in a heavy saucepan. Cook onion and garlic in hot oil until onion is soft (about 5 minutes). Add tomatoes, salt, pepper, and oregano and stir until blended. Heat to simmering and cook about 10 minutes to blend flavors.
2. Meanwhile, heat remaining oil in a heavy skillet. Fry tortilla strips in hot oil until limp, not crisp; drain on paper towels.
3. In an ovenproof casserole arrange layers as follows: a little tomato sauce, a handful of tortilla strips, some cream, then cheese. Repeat until all ingredients are used, ending with cheese. Sprinkle with paprika.
4. Bake at 350°F about 20 minutes, or until bubbling hot.

6 servings

263 Bouillon Cocq

This soup is traditionally served on Christmas Eve when the family and guests return from midnight mass.

1 meaty smoked ham hock
1 capon (7 to 8 pounds)
½ lime
½ orange
2 tablespoons bacon drippings
1 tablespoon butter
1 tablespoon peanut oil
3 quarts water
    Bouquet garni
1 pound cabbage, cut in chunks
4 small potatoes, pared and
    cut in chunks
2 carrots, pared and cut in chunks
2 white turnips, pared and
    cut in chunks
2 onions studded with
    8 whole cloves
2 celery stalks, cut in pieces
2 leeks, washed and cut in chunks
    Salt, pepper, and cayenne or red
    pepper to taste
● Caribbean Rice

1. Soak ham hock in cold water to remove excess salt. Drain.
2. Truss capon as for roasting. Rub skin with cut side of lime half, then cut side of orange half. Let stand to drain.
3. Heat bacon drippings, butter, and peanut oil in a deep soup kettle. Brown capon. Add ham hock, water, and bouquet garni; bring to a boil, reduce heat, and simmer 30 minutes, skimming twice.
4. Add vegetables and seasonings, bring to a boil, skim, then cook over low heat 30 minutes, or until vegetables and meats are tender.
5. Put the capon on a large platter and surround with drained vegetables and rice. Drink the broth from cups.

264 *Consommé with Oxtails*

3 tablespoons olive oil
1 medium oxtail (about 4 pounds)
8 large tomatoes, peeled and seeded
2 medium onions
2 quarts beef broth
  Freshly ground pepper
  Coarse salt
1 large garlic clove, crushed in a
    garlic press
  Sprig fresh basil or ⅛ teaspoon
    dried basil
1 cup sliced carrot
1 cup fresh peas
4 plantains, boiled

1. Heat oil in a soup kettle. Add oxtail and cook until well browned.
2. Mince tomatoes and onions together. Add to meat in kettle, reduce heat, and simmer 3 minutes. Add broth and seasonings. Cook uncovered 1½ hours, then add carrot and peas; continue to cook until meat easily comes from the bones.
3. Serve consommé with a piece of meat and a plantain half in each soup plate.

8 servings

265 *Congo Soup* *(Gros Bouillon Habitant)*

3 tablespoons lard
3 pounds beef shin bones
1 pound lean beef for soup
  Marrow bone
3 quarts water
2 tablespoons coarse salt
1 teaspoon ground pepper
8 dried Italian pepper pods or
    1 green hot pepper, pricked
3 carrots, pared and cubed
3 leeks, washed and cubed
3 parsnips, pared and cubed
3 plantains, peeled and cubed
12 shallots, halved
4 cups cubed pumpkin
1 pound cabbage, cut in chunks
1 pound malanga root or rutabaga,
    peeled and cubed
  Handful spinach or sorrel leaves
2 tablespoons tomato purée
¾ cup cooked rice

1. Heat lard in a large soup kettle. Add shin bones, soup beef, and marrow bone and brown to a rich golden color. Add water and bring to a boil. Add salt, ground pepper, and pepper pods. Simmer covered 45 minutes, skimming soup twice.
2. Add remaining ingredients except spinach, tomato purée, and rice; simmer covered 40 minutes, or until vegetables are tender.
3. Remove bones and meat. Slice marrow and cube the meat; reserve.
4. Press vegetables against side of kettle with the back of a large wooden spoon. Add spinach and cook 5 minutes, then stir in tomato purée.
5. Spoon 1 tablespoon cooked rice in center of each soup plate and pour in soup.

12 servings

266 *Pumpkin Bread Soup* *(Panade of Pumpkin)*

4 garlic cloves
1 green hot pepper or
    6 dried Italian pepper pods
4 cups beef broth
4 slices white bread
2 tablespoons peanut oil
1¼ cups minced onion
1 can (16 ounces) pumpkin or
    1 pound pared and cubed
    fresh pumpkin (see Note)
¼ pound spinach leaves

1. Put garlic and hot pepper into a mortar and pound to a paste. Set aside.
2. Pour beef broth over bread; set aside.
3. Heat peanut oil in a large saucepan; sauté onion. Add bread with beef broth, pumpkin, and seasoning paste; mix well. Simmer 10 minutes.
4. Add spinach; bring to boiling, reduce heat, and cook 5 minutes.

About 1½ quarts

Note: If fresh pumpkin is used, process the soup in an electric blender before adding the spinach.

267 Purée of Malanga Soup

3 tablespoons peanut oil
1 bunch scallions or green onions, minced
3 pounds malanga root, peeled and diced
2 quarts rich stock
   Salt, black pepper, and cayenne or red pepper to taste
⅛ teaspoon nutmeg
1 garlic clove, crushed in a garlic press
   Bouquet garni
   Few celery leaves
   Fresh basil sprig

1. Heat peanut oil in a soup kettle. Add minced scallions and cook until translucent but not brown. Add malanga root, stock, and seasonings and cook until malanga root is tender.
2. Purée through a food mill or in an electric blender.
3. Serve with **toasted white bread**.

About 12 servings

268 Creamy Fresh Tomato Soup

2 shallots
1 tablespoon coarse salt
1 large garlic clove
8 peppercorns
8 large tomatoes, peeled, seeded, and quartered
2 quarts beef broth or rich stock
1 small beet, pared
1 cup uncooked rice
1 cup whipping cream
½ cup chopped mixed parsley and chives

1. In a mortar, pound shallots, salt, garlic, and peppercorns to a paste.
2. Put tomato quarters into a soup kettle and add broth, seasoning paste, and beet. Cook 12 minutes, then add rice, bring to a boil, reduce heat, and cook 30 minutes.
3. Purée tomato-rice mixture in an electric blender or force through a food mill. Return to kettle, bring to a boil, and stir in cream.
4. Serve in soup cups and sprinkle with parsley and chive mixture.

269 Cream of Turnip Soup

¼ cup peanut oil
½ cup minced onion
6 medium white turnips, pared and quartered
1½ quarts chicken broth
   Marrow bone
   Bouquet garni
   Salt and pepper to taste
3 dried Italian pepper pods or 1 whole pink hot pepper
1 cup whipping cream

1. Heat oil in a soup kettle. Add onion and cook over low heat until translucent but not brown, stirring constantly. Add turnips, broth, marrow bone, and seasonings; bring to a boil, reduce heat, and cook 30 minutes. Remove marrow bone and pepper pods. Slice bone marrow thinly and set aside.
2. Purée turnip mixture in an electric blender or force through a food mill. Return to kettle, add cream, and stir to blend. Bring to boiling point.
3. Serve garnished with **avocado cubes**, **red sweet pepper strips**, and reserved bone-marrow slices.

Note: This soup can also be served iced, but then omit the bone marrow which will congeal and be unappetizing.

270 *Head Soup*

1 veal, pork, or lamb head
2 limes, halved
¼ pound salt pork
6 dried Italian pepper pods or
   1 green hot pepper
2 garlic cloves
5 parsley sprigs
1½ to 2 quarts chicken broth or stock
4 tomatoes, peeled, seeded, and
   quartered
3 carrots, pared and cut in chunks
2 onions, cut in chunks
2 leeks, washed and cut in chunks
2 plantains or green bananas, peeled
   and cut in chunks
2 purple yams, pared and cut
   in chunks
1 parsnip, pared and cut in chunks
2 cups cubed pared pumpkin
½ cup corn kernels
½ pound lima beans
¼ pound cabbage, cut in chunks
   Bouquet garni
   Pepper to taste
● Caribbean Rice

1. Have your meat man trim the head and prepare it with the tongue separated. Rub the head with cut sides of lime halves, squeezing gently and going into all cavities.
2. Render the salt pork in a small skillet over low heat.
3. Meanwhile, in a mortar pound the pepper pods, garlic, and parsley to a paste.
4. Pour the fat from the salt pork into a large soup kettle, add the head, tongue, and seasoning paste (no salt is needed). Pour in enough broth to cover, bring to a boil, skim twice, reduce heat, and simmer 1 hour.
5. Add vegetables and seasonings; bring to a boil and simmer until vegetables are tender and meat comes from the bones. Remove the bones and meat. Cut meat into pieces.
6. Crush the vegetables against side of kettle with a spatula, potato masher, or large wooden spoon.
7. Serve in soup plates with a generous portion of meat and a small mound of rice in each.

271 *Velouté Martinique*

1 cup crab meat from boiled crab
1 cup fish broth from a fish head or
   boiled crab
2 chicken breasts
2 tablespoons olive oil
1 cup water
   Bouquet garni
3 dried Italian pepper pods
● 1 cup Coconut Milk

1. Have crab meat and broth ready.
2. Sauté chicken breasts in oil until golden. Add water, bouquet garni, and pepper pods; cover and simmer until chicken is tender. Remove chicken and reserve liquid.
3. Cut the chicken into small pieces; add crab meat, reserved liquid, fish broth, and Coconut Milk. Purée, a little at a time, in an electric blender.
4. Serve hot in soup cups and garnish with **grated coconut**.

272 *Pickled Oyster Stew*

1 cup milk
1 jar pickled oysters, drained
¼ cup peanut oil
½ pound onions, minced
   Salt and freshly ground pepper
   to taste
1½ quarts stock
2 egg yolks
1 cup whipping cream

1. Pour milk over oysters and let stand 2 hours.
2. Meanwhile, heat oil in a soup kettle. Add onion and cook slowly until translucent but not brown. Season with salt and pepper and add stock; cook 30 minutes.
3. Beat egg yolks with cream and set aside.
4. Drain oysters, rinse with water, and pat dry on absorbent paper. Add to the stock and bring to a boil. Immediately stir in cream-egg mixture and remove from heat.
5. Serve from a tureen and sprinkle each serving with **freshly ground pepper** and **cayenne** or **ground red pepper**.

273 *Fisherman's Soup* *(Bouillon Pecheur)*

1 pound each halibut, whiting, sea trout, and red snapper
Juice of 1 lime (reserve halves)
Juice of 1 orange
Salt and pepper to taste
1 pound shrimp
8 small crabs
1 small lobster
1 pound conches removed from shells
Meat tenderizer
4 garlic cloves
5 parsley sprigs
5 scallions or green onions, cut in pieces
8 dried Italian pepper pods or 1 pink hot pepper
1 tablespoon coarse salt
¼ cup peanut oil
12 shallots
8 small potatoes, pared and cut in chunks
4 onions, sliced
3 carrots, pared and cut in chunks
3 plantains, peeled and cut in chunks
1 chayote, cut in chunks
1 leek, washed and cut in chunks
1 parsnip, pared and cut in chunks
1 yam, pared and cut in chunks
1 pound pumpkin meat, cut in chunks
½ pound malanga root, peeled and cut in chunks (optional)
3 quarts water
1 cup amber rum
12 slices white bread with crusts removed, fried

1. Cut fish into serving pieces and put into a shallow dish. Season with lime juice, orange juice, salt, and pepper; let stand 30 minutes.
2. Shell and devein shrimp; rub crabs and lobster with pieces of lime. Set aside.
3. Rinse shelled conches in many waters. Sprinkle them with meat tenderizer and beat them with a meat hammer to make them soft. Cut into strips. Set aside.
4. In a mortar, pound to a paste the garlic, parsley, scallions, pepper pods, and salt.
5. Heat oil in a large soup kettle. Sauté onion, adding the seasoning paste, until mixture is golden but not brown. Add conch strips, vegetables, water, and rum; bring to a boil, then reduce heat and simmer 30 minutes. Add lobster and crabs; cook 10 minutes. Add fish and cook 10 minutes, then add shrimp and cook 5 minutes.
6. With a wooden spoon or potato masher, press some of the vegetables against side of kettle. Remove lobster and cut into serving pieces.
7. Put fried bread into deep soup plates and add the soup.

12 servings

274 *Snapper Chowder à l'Ancienne*

4 pounds red snapper fillets
Juice of 1 lime
Salt, freshly ground pepper, and cayenne or red pepper to taste
8 tomatoes, peeled and seeded
5 scallions or green onions
2 tablespoons soybean or peanut oil
● Court Bouillon for Fish and Shellfish
2 cups potato balls
1 cup diced carrot
1 cup diced turnip
8 bread slices, fried

1. Drizzle fish with lime juice and season with salt and peppers. Set aside.
2. Chop tomatoes and scallions together finely.
3. Heat oil in a large saucepan, add tomato-scallion mixture, and cook slowly until mixture is like a liquid paste. Add bouillon and bring to a boil. Add vegetables and cook 20 minutes.
4. Cut fish into small portions, add to saucepan mixture, and simmer 7 minutes, or until fish flakes.
5. To serve, spoon chowder over fried bread in soup plates.

8 servings

Breads

275 *Greek Easter Bread* (Lambropsomo)

2 packages active dry yeast
½ cup warm water
½ cup milk, scalded and cooled
1 cup unsalted butter, melted and cooled to lukewarm
4 eggs, slightly beaten
1 egg yolk
¾ cup sugar
1 tablespoon anise seed, crushed
1 teaspoon salt
7 cups all-purpose flour
1 egg white, slightly beaten
¼ cup sesame seed

1. Blend yeast with warm water in a large bowl and stir until dissolved. Add milk, butter, eggs, egg yolk, sugar, anise seed, and salt; blend thoroughly. Add flour gradually, beating until smooth.
2. Turn dough onto a lightly floured board and knead for 10 minutes, or until dough is smooth and elastic.
3. Place dough in a lightly oiled large bowl, turning dough to coat surface. Cover and let rise in a warm place for about 2 hours, or until double in bulk. Test by inserting a finger about ½ inch into dough. If indentation remains, the dough is ready to shape.
4. Punch dough down. Knead on unfloured board to make a smooth ball. Cut off four pieces, each the size of a large egg. Place remaining dough in a greased round pan, 10 inches in diameter and 2 inches high. Shape small pieces into twists about 4½ inches long. Arrange the twists from the center of the dough so they radiate out to the edge. Brush the loaf lightly with beaten egg white. Sprinkle with sesame seed. Cover loaf lightly and set in a warm place until double in bulk (about 1½ hours).
5. Bake at 375°F for 30 minutes, or until a wooden pick inserted in center of loaf comes out clean. Transfer to wire rack to cool.

1 large loaf

Note: For Easter, place a red egg in center of the dough in pan. Shape small pieces of dough into loops and place a red egg in the center of each.

New Year's Day Bread (Vasilopita):
Follow recipe for Greek Easter Bread; substitute **grated peel of 1 large orange** for the anise seed. Wrap a coin in foil and knead into the dough. Proceed as directed.

276 *Drop Doughnuts* (Svingi)

4 eggs
1 cup buttermilk
2 teaspoons vanilla extract
1 teaspoon grated lemon or orange peel (optional)
3 cups all-purpose flour
1½ teaspoons baking powder
Cooking oil for deep frying
Honey
Cinnamon

1. Beat eggs; stir in buttermilk, vanilla extract, and grated peel. Combine flour and baking powder. Stir into the egg mixture. Cover with a cloth. Let stand at room temperature for 1 hour.
2. In a deep fryer, heat oil to 375°F. Drop batter by the tablespoon. Cook 4 minutes, or until doughnuts are golden brown. Drain on paper towels. Drizzle with honey and sprinkle with cinnamon. Serve hot.

About 30 doughnuts

Note: Batter keeps well in the refrigerator. Bring to room temperature before cooking.

277 *Christmas Bread* (Christopsomo)

2 envelopes active dry yeast
2 cups scalded milk, cooled to 105° to 115°F
1 cup sugar
1 teaspoon salt
4 eggs (or 8 yolks), well beaten
½ cup unsalted butter, melted
7½ to 8 cups all-purpose flour
1½ teaspoons cardamom, pounded, or 1 teaspoon mastic
½ cup dried golden currants
¾ cup chopped walnuts
2 egg whites, beaten
3 to 4 tablespoons sugar

1. Sprinkle yeast over 1 cup warm milk in a small bowl; stir until dissolved. Set aside.
2. Reserve 2 teaspoons sugar for pounding with mastic, if using. Put sugar into a bowl and add salt, eggs, remaining 1 cup milk, and butter; mix well.
3. Put 7 cups flour into a large bowl. Stir in cardamom, or pound mastic with 2 teaspoons sugar (so it will not become gummy) and add. Make a well and add dissolved yeast, egg mixture, currants, and nuts; mix well.
4. Knead dough on a floured board, adding the remaining 1 cup flour as required. Knead dough until smooth (5 to 6 minutes).
5. Place dough in a greased bowl. Turn until surface is completely greased. Cover. Set in a warm place until double in bulk.
6. Punch dough down. Form into two round loaves and place in buttered 10-inch pans.
7. Cover and let rise again in a warm place until double in bulk.
8. Bake at 375°F 15 minutes. Remove from oven and brush with beaten egg whites, then sprinkle with sugar. Return to oven. Turn oven control to 325°F and bake about 35 to 40 minutes, or until bread is done.

2 loaves

278 *Island Bread*

2 packages active dry yeast
1½ cups warm water (105° to 115°F)
¼ cup packed dark brown sugar
2 tablespoons honey
3 cups whole wheat flour
¼ cup olive oil
2 tablespoons grated orange peel
1 tablespoon grated lemon peel
2½ teaspoons salt
1 teaspoon anise seed, crushed
2 cups all-purpose flour

1. Dissolve yeast in warm water; stir in brown sugar, honey, and whole wheat flour. Beat with a wooden spoon until smooth. Cover and let rise in a warm place until almost double in bulk (about 2 hours).
2. Stir in oil, orange and lemon peels, salt, and anise seed. Gradually add 1¾ cups all-purpose flour, beating vigorously. Cover for 10 minutes.
3. Sprinkle remaining ¼ cup flour on a board and work it in. Put dough on board, cover, and let rise until double in bulk. Shape into a round loaf; put onto a well-greased cookie sheet.
4. Let rise until dough is double in bulk.
5. Bake at 375°F 45 minutes. Turn out of pan immediately and cool on a rack.

1 loaf

279 *Sourdough Greek Bread*

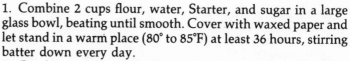

5 to 5½ cups all-purpose flour
2 cups warm water (105° to 115°F)
½ cup Starter
3 tablespoons sugar
1 package active dry yeast
2 teaspoons salt
1½ teaspoons baking soda

1. Combine 2 cups flour, water, Starter, and sugar in a large glass bowl, beating until smooth. Cover with waxed paper and let stand in a warm place (80° to 85°F) at least 36 hours, stirring batter down every day.
2. Combine yeast, salt, baking soda, and 1 cup flour. Add to starter mixture and stir until well blended. Stir in the remaining flour, using enough to make a moderately stiff dough. Turn onto lightly floured surface and knead until smooth and satiny (10 to 15 minutes).
3. Put into a large deep bowl and cover with plastic wrap or aluminum foil. Let rise in a warm place until double in bulk (about 2 hours).
4. Divide dough in half, shape into balls, and place in 2 greased 2-quart round baking dishes. Make a crisscross with a sharp knife on the top of each ball of dough. Cover and let rise in a warm place until double in bulk.
5. Brush loaves with water and place a shallow pan of boiling water on bottom rack of the oven.
6. Bake at 400°F 45 minutes, or until loaves test done. Brush loaves with water twice during baking. Remove from baking dishes immediately; cool.

2 round loaves

280 *Starter*

1 package active dry yeast
2 cups warm water
2 cups all-purpose flour

1. Combine yeast, water, and flour in a large glass bowl, mixing until well blended. Let stand uncovered in a warm place for 48 hours, stirring occasionally. Stir well before use.
2. Measure out required amount and replenish remaining starter by mixing in equal parts of flour and water. If ½ cup starter is removed, mix in ¼ cup water and ¼ cup flour to replace. Let starter stand until it bubbles again before covering loosely and refrigerating. Use and replenish every two weeks.

281 *Corn Bread* (Bobota)

2 eggs
2 cups buttermilk
3 tablespoons shortening, melted
1½ teaspoons salt
2½ cups cornmeal
1 teaspoon baking powder
½ teaspoon baking soda

1. Beat eggs until light. Add buttermilk and melted shortening; mix well.
2. Mix dry ingredients together. Add to egg mixture; beat until smooth. Pour into a greased 9-inch square baking pan.
3. Bake at 425°F about 25 minutes. Serve hot.

About 16 pieces

282 *Whole Wheat Bread*

¼ cup warm water (105°F for dry
    yeast, 95°F for compressed
    yeast)
1 package yeast, active dry or
    compressed
1½ cups scalded milk, cooled to
    105° or 95°F
½ cup honey
2 tablespoons olive oil
2 tablespoons salt
6 to 6½ cups whole wheat flour

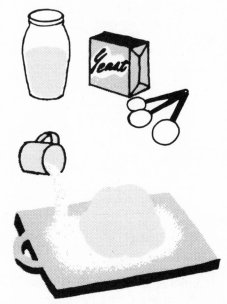

1. Pour water into a bowl; add yeast and stir until dissolved. Add milk, honey, olive oil, and salt. Stir with a wooden spoon until well blended.
2. Stir in 4 cups of flour, 1 cup at a time. Beat until dough is smooth and elastic. Mix in another cup of flour. The dough will be very stiff.
3. Measure another cup of flour; sprinkle half of it on a board. Turn dough onto the board. Knead dough, adding flour to board until the dough no longer sticks. Continue kneading until dough is not sticky (about 8 minutes).
4. Put dough into a greased bowl about three times the size of the dough. Turn dough to grease surface lightly. Cover bowl with a towel and let rise in a warm place for about 2 hours, or until double in bulk. Test by inserting a finger about ½ inch into dough. If indentation remains, the dough is ready to shape.
5. Punch dough down; squeeze out air bubbles and shape into a smooth ball. Let rise again in warm place for about 30 minutes.
6. Divide into equal portions for 2 loaves. Form each into a smooth oval loaf. Let stand covered for 15 minutes.
7. Place the loaves seam side down in 2 greased 9x5x3-inch loaf pans. Cover with a towel and let rise in warm place until almost double in bulk (about 1 hour).
8. Bake at 375°F about 30 minutes, or until crust is medium brown.
9. Turn out of pans at once. Cool on wire racks.

2 loaves

283 *Oregano and Kefalotyri Cheese Bread*
(Psomi me Rigani ke Kefalotyri)

3 to 3½ cups all-purpose flour
2 tablespoons sugar
1½ teaspoons salt
2 packages active dry yeast
¾ cup milk
¼ cup water
¼ cup shortening
1 egg
3 tablespoons oregano
¼ teaspoon garlic powder
½ cup grated kefalotyri cheese
1 teaspoon mint
2 tablespoons basil
¼ cup instant minced onion
1 tablespoon sesame seed

1. Combine 1 cup flour, sugar, salt, and dry yeast in a large bowl.
2. Heat milk, water, and shortening in a saucepan until warm. (Shortening will not melt completely.) Add milk mixture and egg to flour mixture. Beat until smooth.
3. Mix oregano, garlic powder, cheese, mint, basil, onion, and sesame seed. Stir into dough. Gradually add more flour to form a stiff dough.
4. Turn into a greased loaf pan. Cover with a towel. Let rise in a warm place until double in bulk (about 1 hour).
5. Bake at 350°F about 40 minutes, or until golden brown.

1 loaf

284 *Church Bread* *(Prosphoron)*

1 package active dry yeast
2½ cups warm water (105° to 115°F)
6 cups all-purpose flour
1 teaspoon salt
Prosphoron seal

1. Sprinkle yeast over ¼ cup warm water; stir until dissolved.
2. Combine 5½ cups of flour and salt in a large bowl and make a well in the center. Pour in yeast and remaining warm water. Mix with a wooden spoon.
3. Sprinkle remaining flour over a board. Knead 10 minutes, adding as little flour as possible to the board. Dough will be sticky.
4. Put dough into a large bowl, cover with a cloth, and let rise in a warm place until double in bulk.
5. Sprinkle board with a little flour, punch dough down, and knead 15 minutes. (Dough should be firm and smooth.)
6. Form into a large round loaf and place in a heavily floured 12-inch round pan. Lightly flour the top of the loaf. Flour the prosphoron seal. Press seal down firmly in the center to make a sharp impression and leave on the dough.
7. Cover and allow to rise in a warm place until double in bulk. Remove seal.
8. Bake at 350°F for 1 hour. Remove from pan to cool.

285 *Dark Rye Bread*

2 cups milk, scalded
2 tablespoons butter
2 tablespoons sugar
1 teaspoon salt
1 package active dry yeast
½ cup lukewarm water
4 cups rye flour
2½ cups whole-wheat flour
2 tablespoons caraway seed

1. Pour scalded milk over butter, sugar, and salt in a large bowl; stir. Cool.
2. Dissolve yeast in lukewarm water.
3. Add softened yeast and 3 cups rye flour to milk mixture. Beat thoroughly, then beat in remaining rye flour.
4. Cover and let rise in warm place until doubled in bulk. Turn onto well-floured surface. Knead in whole-wheat flour and caraway seed. Knead until dough is smooth.
5. Divide dough in half and shape into 2 round or oblong loaves. Place round loaves in greased round pans; oblong loaves in greased loaf pans. Cover and let rise in warm place until doubled in bulk.
6. Bake at 450°F 15 minutes; reduce heat to 350°F and bake 35 to 40 minutes longer. Brush with melted butter 5 minutes before done if a more tender crust is desired.

2 large loaves

286 *Croutons for Fruit Soups*

4 stale dinner rolls or slices baba or bread
½ cup whipping cream
2 tablespoons butter or margarine
¼ cup confectioners' sugar

1. Cut rolls into 1-inch cubes.
2. Dip cubes in cream; quickly sauté in butter.
3. Dust with confectioners' sugar.

About 14 to 18

287 *Croutons (Grzanki)*

2 slices stale bread
2 tablespoons butter or margarine

1. Trim crusts from bread. Cut bread into ½-inch cubes. Spread cubes on bottom of a shallow pan or baking sheet.
2. Bake at 350°F until golden but not browned.
3. Melt butter in a large skillet. Add toasted bread cubes. Stir-fry until all cubes are coated with butter. Cool and drain croutons on paper towels.

About ¾ cup

Cheese Croutons: Prepare croutons as directed. Mix **4 teaspoons grated Parmesan or Romano cheese** and **½ teaspoon paprika.** Toss hot croutons with cheese mixture.

288 *Poppy Seed Rolls (Strucle z Makiem)*

Dough:
2 packages active dry yeast
½ cup warm water
4½ cups all-purpose flour
¾ cup sugar
½ teaspoon salt
½ cup butter or margarine
2 eggs
2 egg yolks
½ cup dairy sour cream
1 teaspoon vanilla extract

Filling:
2 tablespoons butter
10 ounces poppy seed, ground twice (may be purchased already ground in gourmet shops)
2 tablespoons honey
2 teaspoons lemon juice or vanilla extract
¼ cup raisins, steamed
2 egg whites
½ cup sugar
¼ cup finely chopped candied orange peel
2 teaspoons grated lemon peel

Icing:
1 cup confectioners' sugar
2 tablespoons lemon juice

1. For dough, soften yeast in warm water in a bowl.
2. Mix flour with sugar and salt. Cut in butter with a pastry blender or two knives until mixture has a fine, even crumb.
3. Beat eggs and egg yolks; mix with yeast, then stir into flour mixture. Add sour cream and vanilla extract; mix well.
4. Knead dough on floured surface for 5 minutes. Divide in half. Roll each half of dough into a 12-inch square. Cover.
5. For filling, melt butter in a large saucepan. Add poppy seed. Stir-fry 3 minutes.
6. Add honey, lemon juice, and raisins to poppy seed. Cover and remove from heat; let stand 10 minutes.
7. Beat egg whites with sugar until stiff, not dry, peaks form. Fold in orange and lemon peels. Gently fold in poppy seed mixture.
8. Spread half of filling over each square of dough. Roll up, jelly-roll fashion. Seal edges. Place on greased baking sheets. Cover. Let rise until doubled in bulk, about 1½ hours.
9. Bake at 350°F about 45 minutes. Cool.
10. For icing, blend sugar and lemon juice until smooth. Spread over rolls.

2 poppy seed rolls

289 *Christmas Bread* (*Placek Świąteczny*)

5 eggs
2 cups confectioners' sugar
2¼ cups all-purpose flour
¾ cup finely chopped walnuts
⅔ cup raisins
4 ounces candied orange peel, finely chopped
2 teaspoons baking powder
½ teaspoon salt
1 cup butter or margarine (at room temperature)
1 tablespoon grated lemon peel
1 teaspoon vanilla extract
3 tablespoons vodka or brandy

1. Beat eggs with sugar 5 minutes at high speed of electric mixer.
2. Mix nuts, raisins, and orange peel with 2 tablespoons flour. Mix remaining flour with baking powder and salt.
3. Cream butter, lemon peel, and vanilla extract until fluffy. Beat in vodka. Add egg mixture gradually, beating constantly. Add flour mixture and beat 5 minutes. Fold fruit-nut mixture into the batter. Turn into a generously greased and floured 9×5×3-inch loaf pan or 1½-quart ring mold.
4. Bake at 350°F 1 hour.
5. Cool cake in pan on wire rack 10 minutes. Turn cake out onto rack; cool completely.
6. Wrap in plastic wrap. Store 1 or 2 days to mellow. Sprinkle with confectioners' sugar, if desired, or ice with Lemon Icing (page 70).

1 loaf

290 *Fruit Bread, Milan Style* (*Panettone*)

The traditional Christmas bread of Italy.

2 packages active dry yeast
¼ cup warm water
1 cup butter, melted
1 cup sugar
1 teaspoon salt
2 cups sifted all-purpose flour
½ cup milk, scalded and cooled to lukewarm
2 eggs
4 egg yolks
3½ cups all-purpose flour
1 cup dark seedless raisins
¾ cup chopped citron
½ cup all-purpose flour
1 egg, slightly beaten
1 tablespoon water

1. Dissolve yeast in the warm water.
2. Pour melted butter into large bowl of electric mixer. Add the sugar and salt gradually, beating constantly.
3. Beating thoroughly after each addition, alternately add the 2 cups flour in thirds and lukewarm milk in halves to the butter mixture. Add yeast and beat well.
4. Combine eggs and egg yolks and beat until thick and piled softly. Add the beaten eggs all at one time to yeast mixture and beat well. Beating thoroughly after each addition, gradually add the 3½ cups flour. Stir in raisins and citron.
5. Sift half of the remaining ½ cup flour over a pastry canvas or board. Turn dough onto floured surface; cover and let rest 10 minutes.
6. Sift remaining flour over dough. Pull dough from edges toward center until flour is worked in. (It will be sticky.) Put dough into a greased deep bowl and grease top of dough. Cover; let rise in a warm place (about 80°F) about 2½ hours.
7. Punch down dough and pull edges of dough in to center. Let rise again about 1 hour.
8. Divide dough into halves and shape each into a round loaf. Put each loaf into a well-greased 8-inch layer cake pan. Brush surfaces generously with a mixture of slightly beaten egg and water. Cover; let rise again about 1 hour.
9. Bake at 350°F 40 to 45 minutes, or until golden brown. Remove to wire racks to cool.

2 panettoni

291 *Italian Bread (Pane)*

1 package active dry yeast
2 cups warm water
1 tablespoon salt
5 to 5½ cups sifted all-purpose flour

1. Soften yeast in ¼ cup warm water. Set aside.
2. Combine remaining 1¾ cups warm water and salt in a large bowl. Blend in 3 cups flour. Stir softened yeast and add to flour mixture, mixing well.
3. Add about half the remaining flour to the yeast mixture and beat until very smooth. Mix in enough remaining flour to make a soft dough. Turn dough onto lightly floured surface. Allow to rest 5 to 10 minutes. Knead 5 to 8 minutes, until dough is smooth and elastic.
4. Shape dough into a smooth ball and place in a greased bowl, just large enough to allow dough to double. Turn dough to bring greased surface to the top. Cover bowl with waxed paper and a towel. Let stand in warm place (about 80°F) until dough is doubled (1½ to 2 hours).
5. When dough has doubled in bulk, punch down with fist. Knead on a lightly floured surface about 2 minutes. Divide into 2 equal balls. Cover with towel and let stand 10 minutes.
6. Roll each ball into a 14×8-inch rectangle. Roll up lightly from wide side into a long, slender loaf. Pinch ends to seal. Place loaves on a lightly greased 15×10-inch baking sheet. Cover loaves loosely with a towel and set aside in a warm place until doubled.
7. Bake at 425°F 10 minutes. Turn oven control to 350°F and bake 1 hour, or until golden brown.

2 loaves

Note: To increase crustiness, place shallow pan on the bottom of the oven and fill with boiling water at the beginning of the baking time.

292 *Corn Bread*

1   cup all-purpose flour
1   cup yellow cornmeal
2   teaspoons baking powder
½   teaspoon baking soda
1   teaspoon salt
1   cup milk
2½ teaspoons lime juice
1   egg, beaten
2   tablespoons lard, melted

1. Combine flour, cornmeal, baking powder, baking soda, and salt in a bowl.
2. Mix milk and lime juice; add to dry ingredients along with egg and lard. Mix well, but do not beat. Pour into a greased 11x7x1½-inch baking pan.
3. Bake at 450°F 15 to 20 minutes, or until it is brown and tests done. Cool slightly and cut into squares.

About 8 servings

293 Tomato-Cheese Pizza
(Pizza al Formaggio e Pomodoro)

½ package active dry yeast
1 cup plus 2 tablespoons warm water
4 cups sifted all-purpose flour
1 teaspoon salt
3 cups drained canned tomatoes
8 ounces mozzarella cheese, thinly sliced
½ cup olive oil
¼ cup grated Parmesan cheese
1 teaspoon salt
½ teaspoon pepper
2 teaspoons oregano

1. Soften yeast in 2 tablespoons warm water. Set aside.
2. Pour remaining cup of warm water into a large bowl. Blend in 2 cups flour and 1 teaspoon salt. Stir softened yeast and add to flour-water mixture, mixing well.
3. Add about 1 cup flour to yeast mixture and beat until very smooth. Mix in enough remaining flour to make a soft dough. Turn dough onto a lightly floured surface and allow to rest 5 to 10 minutes. Knead 5 to 8 minutes, until dough is smooth and elastic.
4. Shape dough into a smooth ball and place in a greased bowl just large enough to allow dough to double. Turn dough to bring greased surface to top. Cover with waxed paper and let stand in warm place (about 80°F) until dough is doubled (about 1½ to 2 hours).
5. Punch down with fist. Fold edge towards center and turn dough over. Divide dough into two equal balls. Grease another bowl and place one of the balls in it. Turn dough in both bowls so greased side is on top. Cover and let rise again until almost doubled (about 45 minutes).
6. Roll each ball of dough into a 14×10-inch rectangle, ⅛ inch thick. Place on two lightly greased 15½×12-inch baking sheets. Shape edges by pressing dough between thumb and forefinger to make a ridge. If desired, dough may be rolled into rounds, ⅛ inch thick.
7. Force tomatoes through a sieve or food mill and spread 1½ cups on each pizza. Arrange 4 ounces of mozzarella cheese on each pizza. Sprinkle over each pizza, in the order given, ¼ cup olive oil, 2 tablespoons grated Parmesan cheese, ½ teaspoon salt, ¼ teaspoon pepper, and 1 teaspoon oregano.
8. Bake at 400°F 25 to 30 minutes, or until crust is browned. Cut into wedges to serve.

6 to 8 servings

Mushroom Pizza: Follow Tomato-Cheese Pizza recipe. Before baking, place on each pizza 1 cup (8-ounce can) drained **button mushrooms.**

Sausage Pizza: Follow Tomato-Cheese Pizza recipe. Before baking, place on each pizza 1 pound **hot Italian sausage** (with casing removed), cut in ¼-inch pieces.

Anchovy Pizza: Follow Tomato-Cheese Pizza recipe. Omit mozzarella and Parmesan cheeses, decrease amount of oregano to ¼ teaspoon, and top each pizza with 8 **anchovy fillets,** cut in ¼-inch pieces.

Miniature Pizza: Follow Tomato-Cheese Pizza recipe. After rolling dough, cut dough into 3½-inch rounds. Shape edge of rounds as in Tomato-Cheese Pizza recipe. Using half the amount of ingredients in that recipe, spread each pizza with 2 tablespoons sieved canned tomatoes. Top with a slice of mozzarella cheese. Sprinkle cheese with ½ teaspoon olive oil, ½ teaspoon grated Parmesan cheese, and a few grains salt and pepper. Bake at 400°F 15 to 20 minutes, or until crust is browned.

About 24 miniature pizzas

English Muffin Pizza: Split 12 **English muffins** and spread cut sides with **butter or margarine.** Toast under the broiler until lightly browned. Top each half as for Miniature Pizza. Bake at 400°F 5 to 8 minutes, or until tomato mixture is bubbling hot.

294 *Easter Egg Bread (Pane di Pasqua all' Uovo)*

2 packages active dry yeast
½ cup warm water
1 cup all-purpose flour
⅓ cup water
¾ cup butter or margarine ,
1 tablespoon grated lemon peel
1½ tablespoons lemon juice
¾ cup sugar
1 teaspoon salt
2 eggs, well beaten
3¾ to 4¼ cups all-purpose flour
6 colored eggs (uncooked)

1. Soften yeast in the warm water in a bowl. Mix in the 1 cup flour, then the ⅓ cup water. Beat until smooth. Cover; let rise in a warm place until doubled (about 1 hour).
2. Cream butter with lemon peel and juice. Add beaten eggs in halves, beating thoroughly after each addition.
3. Add yeast mixture and beat until blended. Add about half of the remaining flour and beat thoroughly. Beat in enough flour to make a soft dough.
4. Knead on floured surface until smooth. Put into a greased deep bowl; turn dough to bring greased surface to top, Cover; let rise in a warm place until doubled.
5. Punch down dough; divide into thirds. Cover; let rest about 10 minutes.
6. With hands, roll and stretch each piece into a roll about 26 inches long and ¾ inch thick. Loosely braid rolls together. On a lightly greased baking sheet or jelly-roll pan shape into a ring, pressing ends together. At even intervals, gently spread dough apart and tuck in a colored egg. Cover; let rise again until doubled.
7. Bake at 375°F about 30 minutes. During baking check bread for browning, and when sufficiently browned, cover loosely with aluminum foil.
8. Transfer coffee cake to a wire rack. If desired, spread a confectioners' sugar icing over top of warm bread.

1 large wreath

295 *Biscuits Port-au-Prince*

2 cups sifted all-purpose flour
2 teaspoons baking powder
1 teaspoon salt
5 tablespoons vegetable shortening
¾ cup milk

1. Combine flour, baking powder, and salt in a bowl. Cut in shortening with pastry blender or two knives until mixture resembles small peas.
2. Make a well in center of mixture and add milk. Stir with fork until dough holds together.
3. Knead on a lightly floured board 30 seconds. Roll dough to ½-inch thickness. Cut with a floured 1½-inch cutter.
4. Place on greased baking sheets about 1 inch apart.
5. Bake at 425°F 15 to 20 minutes, or until golden brown.

About 2 dozen biscuits

296 *Kings' Bread Ring* (*Rosca de Reyes*)

2 packages active dry yeast or 2
    cakes compressed yeast
½ cup water water (hot for dry
    yeast, lukewarm for
    compressed)
½ cup milk, scalded
⅓ cup sugar
⅓ cup shortening
2 teaspoons salt
4 cups all-purpose flour (about)
3 eggs, well beaten
2 cups chopped candied fruits
    (citron, cherries, and orange
    peel)
    Melted butter or margarine
    Confectioners' Sugar Icing

1. Soften yeast in water.
2. Pour hot milk over sugar, shortening, and salt in large bowl, stirring until sugar is dissolved and shortening melted. Cool to lukewarm. Beat in 1 cup of the flour, then eggs and softened yeast. Add enough more flour to make a stiff dough. Stir in 1½ cups candied fruits, reserving remainder to decorate baked ring.
3. Turn dough onto a floured surface and knead until smooth and satiny. Roll dough under hands into a long rope; shape into a ring, sealing ends together. Transfer to a greased cookie sheet. Push a tiny china doll into dough so it is completely covered. Brush with melted butter.
4. Cover with a towel and let rise in a warm place until double in bulk (about 1½ hours).
5. Bake at 375°F 25 to 30 minutes, or until golden brown.
6. Cool on wire rack. Frost with Confectioners' Sugar Icing and decorate with reserved candied fruit.

1 large bread ring

Confectioners' Sugar Icing: Blend 1⅓ cups confectioners' sugar, 4 teaspoons water, and ½ teaspoon vanilla extract.

297 *Sweet Rolls* (*Molletes*)

2 packages active dry yeast
½ cup warm water
½ cup sugar
½ teaspoon salt
1 tablespoon anise seed
½ cup butter or margarine, melted
3 eggs, at room temperature
3¾ to 4¾ cups all-purpose flour
1 egg yolk
2 tablespoons light corn syrup

1. Sprinkle yeast over water in a large warm bowl. Stir until yeast is dissolved. Add sugar, salt, anise seed, melted butter, eggs, and 2 cups of flour; beat until smooth. Stir in enough additional flour to make a soft dough.
2. Turn dough onto a lightly floured surface; knead until smooth and elastic (8 to 10 minutes).
3. Put dough into a greased bowl; turn to grease top. Cover; let rise in a warm place until double in bulk (about 1 hour).
4. Punch dough down and turn onto lightly floured surface; roll into a 12-inch square. Cut into fourths and cut each square into 4 triangles.
5. Allowing space for rising, place triangles on greased cookie sheets. Cover; let rise in warm place until double in bulk (about 1 hour).
6. Beat egg yolk and corn syrup together until blended. Generously brush over triangles.
7. Bake at 350°F 10 to 15 minutes. Serve warm.

16 large rolls

Pastas

298 *Pasta with Fresh Tomatoes and Artichoke Hearts*

For each serving:
- 1 **medium ripe tomato, peeled, seeded, and diced**
- 2 **cooked artichoke hearts, cut in half**
- 1 **teaspoon oregano**
- ½ **teaspoon basil**
- 1 **garlic clove, crushed in a garlic press**
- **Salt and pepper to taste**
- 1 **tablespoon wine vinegar**
- 3 **tablespoons olive oil**
- ½ **cup macaroni, cooked according to package directions**
- **Mizithra cheese, cut in slices, for garnish**
- **Kalamata olives for garnish**

1. Combine all ingredients except macaroni and garnishes in a bowl. Cover and marinate several hours.
2. Turn macaroni onto a plate. Cover with marinated mixture. Garnish with cheese and olives. Serve cool.

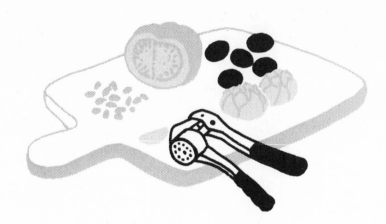

299 *Spaghetti Timbale*

- 2 **tablespoons oil**
- 1 **medium onion, minced**
- 2 **tomatoes, peeled and coarsely chopped, or ½ cup drained canned Italian-style tomatoes**
- **Salt and pepper to taste**
- 2 **tablespoons chopped fresh parsley**
- 1 **package (16 ounces) spaghetti**
- 2 **tablespoons oil**
- 4 **eggs, lightly beaten with a fork**
- ¾ **cup freshly grated mizithra cheese**
- 3 **tablespoons butter**
- 1 **cup cubed salami or Pork**
- ● **Sausage with Orange Peel**

1. Heat 2 tablespoons oil in a heavy saucepan. Cook onion over low heat until translucent. Add tomatoes, salt, and pepper, stirring often, until mixture thickens. Stir in parsley.
2. Cook spaghetti according to package directions; add 2 tablespoons oil to water.
3. Toss cooked spaghetti with eggs, cheese, salt, and pepper until thoroughly mixed.
4. Butter a baking dish with some of the butter. Add a layer of half the spaghetti and a layer of salami; spoon the tomato sauce over. Cover with spaghetti and dot with remaining butter.
5. Bake at 300°F 20 minutes.

6 servings

300 *Cracked Wheat Pilafi* *(Pligouri)*

- 3 **tablespoons butter**
- 1¼ **cups cracked wheat**
- 3 **cups stock, heated**
- **Salt and pepper to taste**

Melt butter in a large saucepan, add wheat, and cook over low heat, tossing lightly with a fork until lightly browned. Add stock, cover, and simmer about 30 minutes until wheat is done. Season with salt and pepper.

4 servings

301 *Macaroni with Sausage* (Makaronatha me Loukanika)

- 2 pounds Pork Sausage with Orange Peel
- 1 garlic clove, sliced
- 1 large onion, minced
- 1 can (24 ounces) tomato sauce or 3 cups Tomato Sauce, heated
- Salt and pepper to taste
- 1 teaspoon oregano
- 1 tablespoon chopped parsley
- ½ cup water
- 1 package (16 ounces) macaroni
- ½ to ¾ cup grated kefalotyri cheese

1. Pull off sausage casings.
2. Brown meat in a large skillet. Add garlic and onion, cook until lightly browned. Discard fat. Add tomato sauce, salt, pepper, oregano, parsley, and water; cover. Simmer over low heat 30 minutes.
3. Boil macaroni according to directions on the package; drain. Put macaroni into a serving dish and cover with sauce. Sprinkle with cheese. Serve hot.

6 to 8 servings

302 *Macaroni in Browned Butter with Grated Cheese* (Makaronatha me Voutero ke Kefalotyri)

- 1 pound macaroni
- 1 cup butter
- ½ cup freshly grated kefalotyri or Parmesan cheese (or more to taste)

1. Cook macaroni according to directions on the package, adding ¼ **cup cooking oil** and **1 tablespoon salt.** Drain. Rinse under hot water.
2. Brown butter in a saucepan, stirring constantly.
3. Return the macaroni to the pot in which it was cooked, or place it in a warm serving dish. Drizzle the browned butter over it. With two spoons lift the macaroni to coat all the strands evenly. Cover with freshly grated kefalotyri. Serve at once.

4 to 6 servings

303 *Homemade Noodles* (Hilopites)

- 3 cups semolina
- 3 eggs
- 3 tablespoons olive oil (do not substitute)
- 1½ teaspoons salt
- 1½ teaspoons warm water

1. Combine all ingredients in a mixing bowl and work with fingers until dough holds together and can be shaped into a ball. A few drops of water may be added, if necessary, but do not let dough get sticky.
2. Knead dough on a board until smooth and shiny. Cover and let rest 15 minutes. Divide dough into 4 portions. Roll out each portion into a paper-thin sheet.
3. Lay sheets on a linen cloth and allow to dry for 1 to 2 hours.
4. Loosely fold sheets over jelly-roll fashion. Cut strips no more than ¼ inch wide. Holding in place, cut again at right angles, the same width, to make square noodles. Hilopites may be cooked right away or dried.
5. To dry, transfer to a large tray, and spread on a linen surface for about 3 days, turning occasionally.
6. To cook, bring a large quantity of water, with **salt** and **2 tablespoons oil** added, to a rolling boil. Add noodles and boil until they have doubled in size (about 5 minutes).
7. Serve hot with **browned butter** or **tomato sauce.** Sprinkle with **grated kefalotyri cheese.**

About 2 pounds noodles

304 *Spanakopeta*

10 pounds fresh spinach or 8
    packages (10 ounces each)
    frozen leaf spinach
1½ cups olive oil
 2 large onions, chopped
 1 bunch scallions, chopped
 1 bunch parsley, chopped
 ½ cup freshly dried dill leaves
 ¼ cup freshly dried mint leaves
 ¼ cup oregano, crushed
    Salt and pepper to taste
1½ pounds feta cheese, crumbled
 2 cups milk
 4 eggs, lightly beaten
    Olive oil (about 1 cup) or ½
      olive oil and ½ vegetable oil
 2 packages filo

1. Prepare the fresh spinach by removing the coarse stems and washing it well in cool water. Set aside for 10 minutes. Pat all the leaves dry with paper towels. If frozen spinach is used, thaw it completely and squeeze out all the moisture with the hands or with a heavy weight.
2. In a large skillet, heat 1½ cups olive oil. Add onion, scallion, parsley, dill, mint, oregano, salt, and pepper. Cook 5 minutes over low heat, stirring constantly.
3. In a bowl, crumble cheese. Mix in milk and eggs. Pour over the spinach. Add the cooked herbs and mix well. Adjust the seasoning.
4. Oil an 18x12-inch baking pan. Line the bottom of the pan with 10 layers of filo, brushing each layer with oil before adding the next. After the last layer of filo has been oiled, spread the spinach mixture evenly over the surface.
5. Cover with the remaining filo, oiling each layer. With a sharp knife or a single-edge razor blade, using a ruler as a guide, cut into the topmost layers, tracing square shapes.
6. Bake at 350°F 30 minutes. Turn oven control to 275°F and bake an additional 30 minutes. Cool. Cut through to separate each piece.
7. Serve as a main course, an appetizer, or vegetable dish. Freeze, if desired.

20 to 50 pieces depending on size

305 *Feta Cheese Triangles* (Tyropites)

 1 pound feta cheese, crumbled
 2 egg yolks
 1 whole egg
 3 tablespoons chopped parsley
    Dash finely ground pepper
 ¾ pound butter, melted and kept
      warm
 1 pound filo

1. Mash feta cheese with a fork. Add egg yolks, egg, parsley, and pepper.
2. Melt butter in a saucepan. Keep warm, but do not allow to brown.
3. Lay a sheet of filo on a large cutting board. Brush with melted butter. Cut into strips about 1½ to 2 inches wide. See pages 80-81 for how to handle filo. Place ½ teaspoon of the cheese mixture on each strip about 1 inch from base. Fold to form a triangle. Continue until all cheese mixture and filo have been used.
4. Place triangles, side by side, in a shallow roasting pan or baking sheet.*
5. Bake at 350°F about 20 minutes, or until golden brown. Serve at once.

About 100 pieces

Note: Tyropites freeze well. Before serving, remove from freezer and let stand 15 to 20 minutes. Bake at 325°F until golden brown.

*Pan must have four joined sides; otherwise butter will fall to bottom of the oven and burn.

306 *Meat Pasties (Trigonopitakia me Kima)*

3 tablespoons butter, melted
1 pound lean ground beef
1 medium onion, finely chopped
2 tablespoons tomato sauce
½ cup dry white wine
  Salt and pepper to taste
1 tablespoon minced parsley
1 tablespoon mint
1 cup crumbled feta cheese
1 egg, beaten
2 teaspoons cracker meal
1 package filo
  Butter for filo

1. Melt butter in a skillet. Add beef, onion, tomato sauce, wine, salt, pepper, parsley, and mint. Cook over low heat, stirring frequently until all liquid evaporates. Cool.
2. Add cheese, egg, and cracker meal to meat mixture; stir to mix.
3. See pages 80-81 for how to handle filo.
4. Arrange the pasties in a shallow baking pan.
5. Bake at 350°F about 15 minutes, or until golden brown. Serve hot.

50 to 100 pieces depending on size

307 *Meat Pie Ioannina (Kreatopita Yianniotiki)*

½ cup butter, melted
2 pounds ground lean lamb
1 large onion, chopped
2 scallions, chopped
2 tablespoons tomato paste
  mixed with 1 cup wine
  Salt and pepper to taste
½ teaspoon cinnamon or more to
  taste
¼ cup chopped parsley
2 cups fresh bread crumbs
½ cups milk
1½ cups stock
7 eggs, separated
¾ cup grated kefalotyri cheese
1 package filo or 2 double recipes
  of pie crust
  Butter, melted and kept warm,
  or equal parts olive oil and
  vegetable oil

1. Melt butter in a large skillet. Add meat, onion, and scallions, and cook until browned, stirring occasionally. Add tomato paste with wine, salt, pepper, cinnamon, and parsley; mix well. Cover. Simmer 20 minutes.
2. Toss bread crumbs with milk and stock. Stir into meat mixture.
3. Beat egg whites in a bowl to form soft peaks. Beat yolks in another bowl until thick. Fold yolks into whites. Mix in cheese. Set aside.
4. Line bottom and sides of a 12x9-inch baking pan with 4 filo leaves. (See pages 80-81 for how to handle filo.) Spread with the meat filling. Cover with egg and cheese mixture. Top with remaining filo sheets. Score the top 2 or 3 filo sheets in squares, using a sharp knife. If using pie crust, prick with a fork.
5. Bake at 350°F 40 minutes. Let stand 15 minutes before cutting.

10 to 12 servings

308 *Kefalonian Meat Pie (Kreatopita Kefalonias)*

¼ **cup butter**
2 **pounds lean lamb, cut in**
    1-inch cubes
2 **cups lamb stock or water**
½ **pound feta cheese, crumbled**
1 **large onion, chopped**
4 **medium potatoes, parboiled,**
    peeled, and diced
1 **tablespoon olive oil**
¼ **cup chopped parsley**
1 **teaspoon grated orange peel**
1 **garlic clove, crushed in a garlic**
    press
2 **teaspoons dill**
½ **teaspoon cinnamon**
    Salt and pepper
4 **hard-cooked eggs, sliced**
1 **package filo**
    Butter, melted and kept warm
    without browning

1. Melt butter in a skillet, add meat, and brown lightly on all sides. Pour in lamb stock and simmer covered about 20 minutes, or until meat is just tender. Remove from heat. Cool. Add cheese, onion, potatoes, oil, parsley, orange peel, garlic, dill, cinnamon, salt, and pepper; mix well. Set aside.
2. Place 1 sheet of filo in a 12x9-inch baking dish, allowing the filo to hang over the dish a little on all sides. Lightly butter filo. (See pages 80-81 for how to handle filo.) Repeat 4 times. Pour filling evenly in the pan. Arrange sliced eggs over the filling. Adjust salt and pepper. Flip the edges of filo onto the filling. Cover with remaining filo. Score the top 2 or 3 filo sheets in squares with a sharp knife.
3. Bake at 325°F about 1 hour, or until filo is golden brown.

10 to 12 servings

Note: Pie crust can be substituted for filo. Use a double recipe. Prick top crust with a fork.

309 *Chiffon Noodles (Kluski z Piany)*

2 **eggs, separated**
2 **tablespoons flour**
¼ **teaspoon salt**

1. Beat egg whites and salt until stiff, not dry, peaks form.
2. Beat yolks separately just until frothy. Fold into whites. Fold in flour.
3. Gently spoon onto **boiling soup or broth.** Cover; cook 2 minutes. Turn; cook a few seconds longer.
4. To serve, break into separate portions with a spoon.

About 4 servings

310 *Beaten Noodles (Kluski Rozcierane)*

1 **tablespoon butter or margarine**
    (at room temperature)
2 **whole eggs**
2 **egg yolks**
3 **tablespoons flour**
¼ **teaspoon salt**

1. Beat butter until fluffy. Beat in whole eggs and egg yolks, one at a time. Mix in flour and salt.
2. Spoon into **boiling soup or bouillon.** Cover; cook 2 minutes. Turn. Cover and cook a few seconds longer.
3. To serve, break noodles into separate portions with a spoon.

About 6 servings

311 *Rice Noodles (Kluski z Ryżu)*

1½ cups cooked rice
2 eggs
1 tablespoon butter or margarine
¼ teaspoon salt

1. Combine all ingredients. Beat until well mixed.
2. Drop by small spoonfuls into **boiling soup or broth.** Cook until noodles float, about 3 minutes.

About 2 cups

312 *Egg Barley (Zacierki)*

1 egg
3 tablespoons grated Parmesan cheese (optional)
Dash salt
1 cup all-purpose flour (about)

1. Beat egg with cheese (if desired) and salt, then add flour until a thick dough forms.
2. On a floured surface, knead in more flour until a stiff, dry dough forms.
3. Grate dough onto waxed paper. Let dry 1 to 2 hours.
4. Cook in **boiling soup** about 5 minutes, or until egg barley floats.

About 1 cup dry; about 1¾ cups cooked

313 *Egg Noodles (Makaron)*

1 cup all-purpose flour
1 large egg
¼ teaspoon salt
½ eggshell of water (about 1 tablespoon)

1. Mound flour on a board. Make a well in center; drop in egg and salt. Beat in water with a fork.
2. Knead from center to outer edges until dough is smooth.
3. Roll out very thin on a floured surface. Place sheet of dough on a cloth; let dry until not sticky but not too brittle to handle.
4. Sprinkle the sheet of noodle dough with flour. Roll up tightly and slice into thin threads. Toss the threads lightly to separate. Let dry 2 hours.
5. To cook, boil in **salted water** until the noodles rise to the top. Drain. Rinse in cold water. Drain again. Toss in **hot melted butter.**

About 2 cups uncooked

314 *Egg Drops (Kluski Lane)*

2 eggs, beaten
¼ teaspoon salt
1 tablespoon water
⅓ cup all-purpose flour

1. Combine all ingredients and stir until smooth.
2. Hold spoonfuls of batter about 12 inches from **boiling soup;** pour slowly from end of spoon. Let boil 2 to 3 minutes, until egg drops float.

About 4 servings

String Dumplings: Prepare Egg Drops batter. Pour almost continuously from a cup or spoon into boiling soup to form long "strings." Break apart after cooking.

315 *Potato Dumplings (Kartoflane Kluski)*

2 cups hot mashed potatoes
⅓ cup fine dry bread crumbs
2 egg yolks
¾ teaspoon salt
¼ teaspoon pepper
⅓ cup all-purpose flour
2 egg whites, beaten until stiff, but not dry

1. Mix ingredients in a large bowl in the order given.
2. Place on floured board and roll to pencil thickness. Cut into 2- or 3-inch strips.
3. Drop into **boiling salted water.** Cook until dumplings float to top.

Croquettes: Sauté ½ cup chopped onion in 2 table-spoons butter. Proceed as in recipe for Potato Dumplings; add onion to potatoes. Roll strips in **fine dry bread crumbs.** Pan-fry in **butter** until golden brown.

316 *Suet or Marrow Balls (Pulpety z Łoju lub Szpiku)*

½ pound white beef suet from kidneys, or marrow
2 eggs, slightly beaten
½ teaspoon salt
¼ teaspoon pepper
½ cup fine dry bread crumbs or cracker meal
2 teaspoons chopped fresh dill or parsley
Flour
Broth or desired soup

1. Remove membrane from suet or marrow. Chop fine and put into a bowl.
2. Add eggs, salt, pepper, bread crumbs, and dill to suet; mix thoroughly but lightly. Form into small round balls.
3. Roll in flour and drop into gently boiling broth or soup. Cook 10 minutes, or until balls float.

About 2½ dozen balls

317 *Egg Balls (Kluski z Żółtek)*

4 hard-cooked egg yolks
4 raw egg yolks
¼ teaspoon salt
⅛ teaspoon nutmeg
⅛ teaspoon pepper

1. Mash the cooked egg yolks or press through a sieve. Add raw yolks and seasonings. Mix until a smooth thick paste forms.
2. Drop by spoonfuls into **boiling soup or broth.** Cook a few seconds until egg balls float. Serve immediately.

4 to 6 servings

318 *Fish Dumplings (Pulpety z Ryby)*

1 onion, minced
1 tablespoon butter or margarine
1 pound cooked fish or 2 cups flaked cooked fish
1 slice white bread, soaked in water and squeezed
2 eggs
¾ teaspoon salt
2 tablespoons fine dry bread crumbs
1 teaspoon dill weed
1 teaspoon chopped parsley
2 tablespoons flour

1. Fry onion in butter until golden.
2. Flake or chop fish very fine. Or, grind fish with the onion.
3. Mix fish with bread and eggs. Season with salt and pepper. Stir in bread crumbs, dill, and parsley.
4. Form balls about 1½ inches in diameter. Roll in flour.
5. Cook in **boiling water** until dumplings float, about 4 minutes.

4 to 6 servings

319 *Liver Mounds (Babki z Wątróbek)*

¾ pound chicken, turkey, or capon livers
1 cup milk
1 tablespoon butter or margarine
⅓ cup minced onion
⅓ cup fine dry bread crumbs
3 eggs, separated
½ teaspoon salt

1. Soak livers in milk in a glass or pottery bowl 3 hours in refrigerator. Drain livers, discarding milk. Mince livers.
2. Melt butter in a skillet. Add onion and stir-fry until golden. Remove from heat.
3. Combine minced liver, onion with butter, bread crumbs, and egg yolks. Mix until thoroughly combined.
4. Beat egg whites with salt until stiff, not dry, peaks are formed. Fold into liver mixture.
5. Spoon liver mixture into well-greased muffin-pan wells. Grease a piece of brown paper or waxed paper on one side. Place paper, greased side down, on top of muffin pan.
6. Bake at 350°F 25 to 35 minutes. Remove at once from pan. Serve hot with **a piquant sauce** or in **chicken broth**.

About 6 servings

320 *Raw Potato Dumplings (Kartoflane Kluski)*

2 cups grated raw potatoes
2 eggs
1 teaspoon salt
½ cup fine dry bread crumbs
1½ cups all-purpose flour (about)
Boiling salted water

1. Rinse potatoes in cold water; drain well.
2. Combine potatoes in a large bowl with eggs, salt, crumbs, and enough flour to make a stiff dough.
3. Using a wet spoon, drop tablespoonfuls of dough into boiling salted water.
4. Cook until dumplings float to the top. Dumplings should be about 1½ × ½ inches when done.

About 6 servings

321 *Yeast Pierogi (Pierożki)*

4 eggs
1 tablespoon melted butter
1 teaspoon salt
1 package active dry yeast
¼ cup warm water
1 cup dairy sour cream
1 tablespoon sugar
1½ teaspoons grated lemon peel (optional)
4 cups all-purpose flour (about)
● Filling

1. Beat eggs with melted butter and salt until thick and fluffy.
2. Dissolve yeast in warm water in a large bowl. Let stand 10 minutes.
3. Add egg mixture to yeast. Beat in sour cream, sugar, and, if desired, lemon peel. Stir in flour, 1 cup at a time, until dough is firm but not stiff.
4. Turn dough on floured surface; knead 3 minutes. Place dough in a greased bowl. Cover with plastic wrap. Let rise in a warm place until doubled, about 1 hour.
5. Roll out dough to ⅜-inch thickness on floured surface. Cut into 3-inch rounds.
6. Place a spoonful of filling a little to one side of each round. Moisten edges. Fold over and seal. Place on greased baking sheet.
7. Bake at 350°F about 20 to 35 minutes, or until golden brown.

About 3 dozen

322 *Pierogi*

2 cups all-purpose flour
2 eggs
½ teaspoon salt
⅓ cup water
● Filling

1. Mound flour on a bread board and make a well in the center.
2. Drop eggs and salt into well. Add water; working from the center to outside of flour mound, mix flour into liquid in center with one hand and keep flour mounded with other hand. Knead until dough is firm and well mixed.
3. Cover dough with a warm bowl; let rest 10 minutes.
4. Divide dough into halves. On floured surface, using half of dough at a time, roll dough as thin as possible.
5. Cut out 3-inch rounds with large biscuit cutter.
6. Place a small spoonful of filling a little to one side on each round of dough. Moisten edge with water, fold over and press edges together firmly. Be sure they are well sealed to prevent the filling from leaking out.
7. Drop pierogi into **boiling salted water.** Cook gently 3 to 5 minutes, or until pierogi float. Lift out of water with perforated spoon.

1½ to 2 dozen

Note: The dough will have a tendency to dry. A dry dough will not seal completely. Work with half the dough at a time, rolling out a large circle of dough and placing small mounds of filling far enough apart to allow for cutting. Then cut with biscuit cutter and seal firmly.

Never put too many pierogi in cooking water. The uncooked will stick together and the cooked get lumpy and tough.

323 *Little Ears* (*Uszka*)

2 cups all-purpose flour
½ cup water
1 egg
⅛ teaspoon salt
● Filling

1. Mound flour on a bread board and make a well in the center. Place remaining ingredients in the well. Mix flour into liquid in center until a dough is formed. Knead thoroughly.
2. Roll dough very thinly on a floured surface. Cut into 2-inch squares.
3. Put a spoonful of filling in center of each square. Fold so that the corners meet in the middle. Press together with fingers to seal. Fold in half diagonally, so the square becomes a triangle. Seal edges. Then bring the 2 long ends of triangle together; press firmly to seal.
4. Drop into **boiling soup.** Cook until the uszka float.

About 3 dozen

324 *Thin Pancakes* (*Naleśniki*)

½ cup all-purpose flour
1 egg
1 egg yolk
½ cup milk
1 teaspoon sugar
⅛ teaspoon salt

1. Combine flour, egg, and egg yolk in a small bowl of electric mixer. Beat just to mix. Add milk, sugar, and salt; beat at low speed 2 minutes.
2. Heat a small, heavy skillet. Brush bottom with oil.
3. Pour about 2 tablespoons batter into skillet; at once tilt skillet to spread batter evenly over bottom of skillet. When

Salad oil
● Filling

edges are dry, turn pancake and cook other side.

4. Repeat until all batter is used, reserve some batter for coating stuffed pancakes, if desired.

5. For stuffed pancakes, place 1 heaping tablespoonful of filling in center of pancake. Fold sides toward center, over filling, and roll up pancakes.

6. Dip in **egg** beaten with **water** or in reserved batter. Coat with **fine dry bread crumbs.**

7. Quickly fry coated pancakes in a small amount of hot oil. Turn and cook until golden on all sides.

12 pancakes

325 *Thick Pancakes (Naleśniki)*

1 cup milk
1 egg
1 cup all-purpose flour
⅓ cup water
¼ teaspoon salt
Salad oil or melted butter
● Filling

1. Beat milk and egg until frothy. Add flour and beat rapidly 1 minute. Add water and salt. Beat rapidly 1 minute longer.

2. Heat a small, heavy skillet. Brush bottom with oil or wipe with cloth dipped in oil. (Do not use too much oil.)

3. Pour about 2 tablespoons batter onto bottom of skillet; at once tilt skillet so batter spreads evenly. When edge of pancake begins to dry, turn and cook other side.

4. Repeat until all the batter is used.

12 pancakes

326 *Yeast Fingers (Drożdżowe Paluszki)*

2 cups all-purpose flour
1 package active dry yeast
1 teaspoon sugar
½ teaspoon salt
½ cup butter or margarine
1 egg
2 egg yolks
2 tablespoons dairy sour cream
1 egg white
2 tablespoons caraway seed or
poppy seed

1. Combine flour, yeast, sugar, and salt in a bowl. Cut in butter with a pastry blender or two knives until well mixed. Stir in egg, egg yolks, and sour cream.

2. Knead the dough in the bowl a few minutes until it forms a smooth ball.

3. Break off small bits of dough, about 1 tablespoonful each; roll between palms of hands to form long, thin rolls.

4. Place on a greased baking sheet. Let rise in a warm place until doubled in bulk.

5. Brush with egg white, then sprinkle with caraway seed.

6. Bake at 375°F 15 minutes, or until golden. Remove immediately from the baking sheet.

About 40 fingers

Stuffed Yeast Fingers: Two ways are typical, either a long roll which is sliced after baking, or individual fingers.

For long roll, roll out the dough on a floured surface to form a rectangle about 18×6 inches. Spoon filling lengthwise down center of dough. Fold over both long sides and seal the top seam and ends. Carefully place, seam-side down, on a greased baking sheet. Cover with plastic wrap. Let rise in a warm place 30 minutes. Brush top with slightly beaten **egg white.** Cut ½-inch deep slashes across top, about 1 inch apart. Bake at 375°F 1 hour. Cool 15 minutes before slicing.

For individual fingers, roll out dough as directed. Cut into 48 pieces and roll each piece into a rectangle. Place 1 tablespoon filling on each rectangle. Fold dough lengthwise over filling and pinch to seal all seams. Place on greased baking sheet. Cover; let rise, and brush with egg white as directed. Do not slash. Bake at 375°F about 20 to 35 minutes, or until golden brown.

327 *Beef Filling*

1 large onion, halved and sliced
2 tablespoons margarine or
    shortening
1¾ cups ground cooked beef
¾ cup cooked rice
2 teaspoons instant bouillon or
    meat extract
3 tablespoons hot water
1 tablespoon chopped fresh
    parsley
    Salt and pepper

1. Stir-fry onion in margarine in a large skillet until golden. Stir in meat and rice.
2. Dissolve bouillon in hot water. Add to meat mixture with parsley and salt and pepper to taste.

About 2½ cups

328 *Cooked Meat Filling*

2 onions, minced
2 tablespoons butter or margarine
1 cup ground cooked meat
2 slices stale white bread
    Milk or water
½ teaspoon salt
¼ teaspoon pepper

1. Stir-fry onion in butter in a heavy skillet 5 minutes. Add ground meat. Remove from heat.
2. Soak bread in just enough milk to cover. When thoroughly soaked, about 10 minutes, squeeze out excess milk.
3. Stir bread, salt, and pepper into onion mixture until well combined.

2 to 3 cups

329 *Meat Filling*

¼ pound suet, chopped
2 cups grated onion
½ pound ground lean beef
½ pound ground lean lamb
½ pound ground lean veal
1 teaspoon salt
¾ teaspoon marjoram
¾ teaspoon sweet basil
¼ teaspoon pepper
⅓ cup fine dry bread crumbs
    Meat stock

1. Fry suet and onion just until onion is tender. Add meat; fry until meat changes color.
2. Stir in all seasonings and bread crumbs. Add just enough meat stock to make a paste.

About 3½ cups

330 *Sausage Filling*

10 ounces Polish sausage (kiełbasa),
    skinned and chopped
½ cup grated cheese or chopped
    mushrooms
¼ cup fine dry bread crumbs
1 egg

Combine all ingredients thoroughly.

About 2 cups

Red Vegetable Salad, page 63
Brussels Sprouts and Grapes, page 175
Herbed Stuffed Mushrooms, page 172

331 *Brains Filling*

1 pair fresh veal or pork brains
   (about 12 ounces)
Water
1 teaspoon salt
5 peppercorns
1 bay leaf
1 tablespoon vinegar
⅓ cup finely chopped onion
3 tablespoons butter
1 egg yolk
Salt and pepper

1. Rinse brains under running cold water.
2. Put brains into a saucepan with water to cover, 1 teaspoon salt, peppercorns, bay leaf, and vinegar. Bring to boiling and cook 3 minutes.
3. Drain brains; remove and discard white tough membrane. Chop brains coarsely.
4. Sauté onion in butter until golden. Add the brains and stir to mix well. Cook 2 minutes. Add egg yolk to mixture and blend well. Season to taste with salt and pepper.

About 1 cup

332 *Mushroom Filling*

1½ cups chopped mushrooms
½ cup chopped onion
2 tablespoons butter or margarine
¼ teaspoon salt
⅛ teaspoon pepper
2 egg yolks or 1 egg, beaten

1. Stir-fry mushrooms and onion in butter until onion is soft. Remove from heat.
2. Stir in remaining ingredients.

About 1 cup

333 *Cabbage and Mushroom Filling with Egg*

1 small head cabbage (about 1 pound) shredded
⅓ cup water
1 large onion, halved and sliced
1 can (4 ounces) mushroom stems and pieces
2 tablespoons butter or margarine
1 teaspoon salt
¼ teaspoon pepper
2 hard-cooked eggs, chopped

1. Combine the cabbage, water, onion, mushrooms, and butter in a large saucepan. Cook, covered, over low heat until tender, about 30 minutes.
2. Add salt, pepper, and chopped eggs; mix well.

About 3½ cups

334 *Sauerkraut Filling*

⅓ cup chopped onion
1 tablespoon butter or margarine
1½ cups finely chopped sauerkraut
2 tablespoons dairy sour cream

1. Stir-fry onion in butter in a saucepan 3 minutes.
2. Rinse and drain sauerkraut. Add to onion and cook 2 minutes.
3. Remove from heat. Stir in sour cream.

About 1½ cups

335 *Potato Filling*

½ cup chopped onion
2 tablespoons butter
½ teaspoon salt
¼ teaspoon white pepper
2 cups mashed potatoes

1. Sauté onion in butter 5 minutes. Stir in salt and pepper.
2. Combine potatoes and onion mixture. Blend well.

About 2 cups

Fish Stew, page 305
Sole with Shrimp Pate in Champagne, page 302

336 Sauerkraut and Mushroom Filling

2½ cups sauerkraut
    Boiling water
2 tablespoons fat
½ cup chopped onion
4 ounces mushrooms, sliced
¼ teaspoon salt
¼ teaspoon pepper
1 hard-cooked egg, chopped
2 tablespoons dairy sour cream

1. Rinse sauerkraut and drain. Put into a saucepan. Cover with a small amount of boiling water. Cook 20 minutes; drain.
2. Heat fat in a skillet. Add onion and fry until golden. Add mushrooms and fry 3 minutes. Stir in sauerkraut, salt, and pepper. Fry until the sauerkraut becomes golden, about 20 minutes.
3. Remove from heat. Add chopped egg and sour cream; mix well.

About 2 cups

337 Savory Cheese Filling

1½ cups pot cheese or farmer cheese
1 teaspoon lemon juice
1 teaspoon sugar
1 egg
1 egg yolk
¼ teaspoon salt

Press cheese through a sieve into a bowl. Add remaining ingredients; mix well.

About 1½ cups

338 Sweet Cheese Filling

1½ cups pot cheese, farmer cheese, or ricotta
1 egg, beaten
3 tablespoons sugar
¼ cup raisins or currants
½ teaspoon vanilla extract
¼ teaspoon cinnamon

Press cheese through a sieve into a bowl. Add remaining ingredients; mix well.

About 1¾ cups

339 Cooked Fruit Filling

2 cups pitted cherries, apples, or blueberries
¾ cup water
⅓ cup sugar (optional)
½ teaspoon cinnamon or cardamom (optional)
1 teaspoon lemon juice (optional)
2 to 4 tablespoons fine dry bread crumbs

1. Combine fruit, water, and sugar in a saucepan. Bring to boiling; cook and stir until fruit is tender and water is almost gone. Remove from heat.
2. Mash fruit slightly with potato masher. Add cinnamon and lemon juice. Cook and stir over low heat just until fruit mixture is thick.
3. Stir in enough bread crumbs to make filling very thick.

About 1½ cups

340 Prune Filling

2 cups dried prunes
1 tablespoon lemon juice
1 tablespoon brown sugar

1. Cover prunes with **water.** Bring just to boiling. Cover. Remove from heat and let stand 20 minutes. Remove and discard pits.
2. Add lemon juice and sugar. Cook until almost all liquid is gone.

About 1½ cups

341 Egg Noodles with Poppy Seed
(Kluski z Makiem)

1½ quarts boiling water
1 teaspoon salt
3 cups egg noodles
½ cup milk
½ cup poppy seed, ground
3 tablespoons sugar or 2 tablespoons honey

1. Combine boiling water and salt in a large saucepan. Add noodles and cook until tender. Drain.
2. Meanwhile, scald milk; mix in poppy seed and sugar. Cook 5 minutes.
3. Combine poppy seed mixture with the noodles. Serve hot.

4 to 6 servings

342 Noodles with Poppy Seed and Raisins
(Kluski z Makiem i Rodzynkami)

2 cups cooked egg noodles
2 tablespoons butter, melted
1 can (12 ounces) poppy seed cake and pastry filling
1 teaspoon vanilla extract
1 teaspoon lemon juice
1½ teaspoons grated lemon peel
⅓ cup raisins

1. Toss noodles with butter in a saucepan.
2. Combine poppy seed filling with vanilla extract, lemon juice and peel, and raisins. Add to noodles and mix well. Cook just until heated through.

About 6 servings.

343 Lasagne with Green Garlic Sauce
(Lasagne al Pesto)

1 pound lasagne noodles
● Green Garlic Sauce
1 cup grated Parmesan cheese

1. Cook lasagne noodles according to package directions. Drain. Alternate layers of lasagne, sauce, and cheese in a 2-quart baking dish.
2. Bake at 425°F 15 to 20 minutes, or until hot.

8 to 10 servings

344 Spaghetti Genoese (Spaghetti alla Genovese)

1 pound long spaghetti
¼ cup olive oil
½ cup butter
2 cloves garlic, finely minced
6 tablespoons chopped parsley
1 pint half-and-half
½ cup grated Parmesan cheese

1. Cook spaghetti according to package directions. Drain.
2. In a large skillet, heat oil and butter over low heat. Add garlic, but do not brown. Stir in parsley and half-and-half; heat slightly, but do not boil.
3. Add spaghetti to cream sauce in skillet; mix well. Blend in cheese, a little at a time, coating all the spaghetti well. Serve on hot plates.

6 to 8 servings

345 *Soup Dumplings (Canederli)*

1 slice bacon, diced
1 teaspoon butter
½ cup minced onion
½ cup peeled fresh Italian sausage, cut in small pieces
2½ cups coarsely crumbled dry bread
1 cup milk
3 eggs
1 tablespoon minced parsley
2 tablespoons grated Parmesan cheese
Dash nutmeg
½ teaspoon salt
Dash pepper
2 cups all-purpose flour
2 quarts chicken consommé or broth, boiling

1. Place bacon, butter, onion, and sausage in saucepan. Cook until onion is soft. Mix in bread and cook 1 or 2 minutes.
2. Remove mixture from heat and stir in milk. Set aside for at least 1 hour.
3. Add eggs, one at a time, mixing well after each is added. Stir in parsley, cheese, nutmeg, salt, and pepper. Add the flour, stirring until mixture holds together.
4. Form mixture into balls no larger than a walnut, and drop, one at a time, into the boiling consommé in a large pot. Reduce heat and allow dumplings to cook 20 to 25 minutes.
5. Serve broth and dumplings, sprinkled with grated Parmesan cheese.

6 to 8 servings

Note: If desired, dumplings may be cooked in boiling salted water, drained, and served with melted butter or a meat sauce.

346 *Polenta*

3 cups water
2 chicken bouillon cubes
1 cup yellow cornmeal
2 tablespoons butter or margarine

1. Bring water to boiling. Stir in bouillon cubes to dissolve. Slowly stir in cornmeal. Reduce heat and cook, stirring, until very thick (about 7 minutes).
2. Remove from heat and stir in butter until melted.
3. Spoon onto plates and top each serving with 1 tablespoon butter or 2 tablespoons shredded mozzarella, Monterey Jack, or Cheddar cheese. Serve as a meat accompaniment.

4 servings

347 *Polenta with Sausage (Polenta con Salsiccia)*

1 pound Italian sausage
2 tablespoons olive oil
1 pound mushrooms, cleaned and sliced
2½ cups canned tomatoes
1 teaspoon salt
¼ teaspoon pepper
3 cups water
1½ teaspoons salt
1 cup yellow cornmeal
1 cup cold water
Grated Parmesan or Romano cheese

1. Cut sausage casing, remove sausage, and crumble into small pieces with a fork.
2. Heat olive oil in large skillet. Add sausage and mushrooms to skillet. Cook slowly, stirring occasionally, until the mushrooms and sausage are lightly browned.
3. Slowly stir in the tomatoes, 1 teaspoon salt, and pepper. Simmer 20 to 30 minutes.
4. While the tomato and sausage mixture is simmering, bring 3 cups water with 1½ teaspoons salt to boiling. Gradually stir in the cornmeal and 1 cup cold water. Continue boiling, stirring constantly, until the mixture is thickened.
5. Cover, lower the heat, and cook slowly 10 minutes or longer, if necessary. Transfer the cooked cornmeal to warm platter, and top with the tomato mixture.
6. Sprinkle with cheese and serve immediately.

6 to 8 servings

348 *Baked Green Lasagne Bolognese*
(Lasagne Verdi al Forno Bolognese)

- 6 quarts water
- 1 teaspoon salt
- ● ¾ pound Green Lasagne
- ● 2½ cups Bolognese Meat Sauce
- 2 cups Cream Sauce
- ¾ cup grated Parmesan cheese

1. Bring water to boiling in a large saucepot. Add salt and cook lasagne strips a few at a time for 3 minutes. Remove from boiling water with a strainer, and drop into cold water. Drain again and spread on damp towels.

2. Cover the bottom of a buttered 2-quart baking dish with meat sauce, a small amount of Cream Sauce, and a sprinkling of cheese. Next form a layer of noodles with the ends turning part way up at the sides of the dish. Repeat layering with meat sauce, Cream Sauce, cheese, and lasagne, forming about 6 layers. Finish top with meat sauce, Cream Sauce, and a generous amount of cheese.

3. Bake at 375°F 20 to 25 minutes, or until hot and bubbly.

6 servings

Cream Sauce: Melt **2 tablespoons butter** in a saucepan and blend with **2 tablespoons flour**. Gradually stir in **1 cup milk** and **1 cup half-and-half**. Season with **½ teaspoon salt** and a **dash nutmeg**. Cook, stirring constantly, until sauce boils and thickens. Cover with a sheet of waxed paper on surface and keep warm until ready to use.

2 cups sauce

349 *Green Lasagne (Lasagne Verdi)*

- ½ pound spinach
- 4 cups all-purpose flour
- 1 teaspoon salt
- 2 large eggs, beaten

1. Wash spinach and place in heavy saucepan. Do not add water; cook only in moisture remaining on leaves from washing. Partially cover and cook 5 minutes, stirring occasionally with a fork.

2. Drain spinach, press out the water, chop it, and force it through a sieve; or drain, press out water, and purée in an electric blender. It should retain its fresh green color and become a smooth purée. If the purée is very wet, heat it in the saucepan, about a minute, over very high heat to evaporate some of the moisture. Allow it to cool.

3. Sift the flour and salt into a large mixing bowl. Make a well in the center of the flour and put the beaten eggs and puréed spinach in it. Mix gradually with one hand, or with a fork, until the paste is well blended. If the mixture is too dry, add some water until it forms a ball. If the dough is too sticky, add more flour.

4. Knead the dough at least 12 minutes, until it is smooth and elastic. Divide dough in 4 pieces and roll out to 1⁄16-inch thick. Cut the sheets of dough into 4×2-inch rectangles, or longer, if desired. The dough may also be cut in squares. Let cut pieces of dough dry on towels for an hour. If not using immediately, store at room temperature.

About 1¼ pounds pasta

Green Noodles: Follow recipe for Green Lasagne. Roll the sheets of dough up and cut in ¼-inch-wide strips. Unroll and place on towels for half an hour to dry. Place in **boiling salted water** and cook 5 minutes; drain. Serve tossed with **butter** and **grated cheese**, or any sauce desired.

350 *Stuffed Pasta Rings in Cream* (*Tortellini alla Bolognese*)

½ turkey breast (about 2½ pounds), boned
4 slices prosciutto
1 medium-size veal sweetbread, blanched and cleaned
¼ pound lean pork
¼ pound lean beef
7 tablespoons butter
¼ pound Parmesan cheese, grated
2 egg yolks, beaten
Pinch grated nutmeg
Pinch ground cinnamon
Salt and pepper
Pasta Dough for Tortellini
4 quarts chicken broth
1 cup whipping cream

1. Cut turkey breast, prosciutto, sweetbread, pork, and beef into pieces.
2. Melt 4 tablespoons of the butter in a large skillet. Sauté meats until sweetbread pieces are cooked. Remove from heat and cool.
3. Put meat mixture through a meat grinder twice, so it is very finely ground. Place the ground meat in a large bowl and stir in half the cheese, the egg yolks, nutmeg, cinnamon, and salt and pepper to taste. Blend well.
4. Prepare Pasta Dough for Tortellini, using turkey mixture for filling. Set aside on a cloth, cover with another cloth, and allow to dry 30 minutes.
5. Bring the chicken broth to a gentle simmer, not a violent boil or the pasta will break apart. Melt the remaining 3 tablespoons butter in a large saucepot over low heat.
6. Carefully drop filled tortellini, a few at a time, into the gently simmering broth. Simmer until cooked through, but still a little firm (about 10 minutes). Remove, using a slotted spoon, and place in melted butter in saucepot. When all the tortellini are cooked and in the saucepot, pour in the whipping cream and sprinkle remaining cheese over tortellini. Stir gently with a wooden spoon until sauce is smooth.
7. Serve immediately in heated soup bowls. Accompany with additional grated Parmesan cheese.

About 8 servings

Note: A 2-pound frozen boneless turkey roast (thawed) may be substituted for the turkey breast.

351 *Pasta Dough for Tortellini*

3½ cups all-purpose flour
1 teaspoon salt
2 eggs, beaten
1 tablespoon olive oil
Warm water (about ½ cup)

1. Put flour on a board and sprinkle with salt. Make a well and add eggs and oil. Mix well until a soft smooth dough is formed. Add warm water gradually, if necessary, to soften dough. Knead 5 to 10 minutes until dough is smooth and elastic. Cover with a bowl for 30 minutes.
2. Divide dough in quarters. Roll each quarter into a round as thin as possible. Cut into 2-inch rounds.
3. For each tortellini, place ¼ to ½ teaspoon filling in center of round. Moisten edges with water. Fold in half; seal edges. Shape into rings by stretching the tips of half circle slightly and wrapping the ring around your index finger. Gently press tips together.
4. Cook as directed.

About 12 dozen tortellini

352 *Manicotti Tuscan Style (Manicotti alla Toscana)*

● **Egg Pasta Dough for Manicotti**
● **Tomato Sauce**
3 tablespoons butter
1 tablespoon olive oil
1 clove garlic, minced
6 mushrooms, minced
1 pound ground beef round
1 teaspoon salt
¼ teaspoon pepper
½ pound ricotta
¼ pound Parmesan cheese, grated

1. Prepare pasta dough and Tomato Sauce.
2. Heat butter and oil in a skillet. Add garlic; sauté until soft. Stir in mushrooms, beef, salt, and pepper. Cook until meat is brown, stirring often. Add ricotta and half the Parmesan cheese, blending well.
3. When dough squares are dry, spread ½ tablespoon of the beef mixture on each square and roll up tightly. Press edges together to seal, moistening edges with water if necessary. Filling must be sealed in completely, or it will fall out during the cooking in boiling water.
4. Cook manicotti in gently boiling salted water until just tender. Remove with a slotted spoon and drain. Arrange a layer of manicotti (about 30) in a buttered 3-quart casserole. Cover with Tomato Sauce and sprinkle with half of remaining Parmesan cheese. Arrange remaining manicotti crosswise in another layer, cover with Tomato Sauce, and sprinkle with remaining Parmesan cheese.
5. Bake at 350°F 25 minutes, or until cheese browns and sauce bubbles.

About 60 manicotti

353 *Egg Pasta Dough for Manicotti*

4 cups all-purpose flour
4 eggs, beaten
1½ teaspoons salt
2 teaspoons olive oil
Warm water (about ½ cup)

1. Put flour onto a board, make a well in center, and add eggs, salt, and olive oil. Mix until a soft dough is formed, adding warm water as needed.
2. Knead about 10 minutes until dough is smooth and elastic. Add more flour if dough is too soft.
3. Divide dough in quarters. Roll each quarter into as thin a sheet as possible. Cut the sheets into 3-inch squares. Dry on cloth or cloth-covered board for 1 hour before using.

About 1¾ pounds dough

354 *Fettuccine Alfredo*

1 pound green noodles
Boiling salted water
2 tablespoons olive oil
1 teaspoon chopped fresh basil
1 clove garlic, minced
Grated Parmesan cheese
Butter

1. Cook noodles in boiling salted water until just tender; drain.
2. In a chafing dish, heat olive oil, basil, and garlic. Toss the noodles in hot oil with a fork until they are very hot.
3. Sprinkle generously with Parmesan cheese, adding a generous piece of butter, and toss again a moment before serving.

About 8 servings

Fettuccine al Burro Alfredo: Cook egg noodles in boiling salted water until barely tender, *al dente*; drain thoroughly. Bring quickly to the table in a heated serving bowl and rapidly toss and twirl with a generous amount of unsalted butter and finely grated Parmesan or Romano cheese so that the butter and cheese melt so quickly that the fettuccine can be served piping hot.

355 *Meat-Stuffed Manicotti*

2 tablespoons olive oil
½ pound fresh spinach, washed, dried, and finely chopped
2 tablespoons chopped onion
½ teaspoon salt
½ teaspoon oregano
½ pound ground beef
2 tablespoons fine dry bread crumbs
1 egg, slightly beaten
1 can (6 ounces) tomato paste
8 manicotti shells (two thirds of a 5½-ounce package), cooked and drained
1½ tablespoons butter, softened (optional)
1 to 2 tablespoons grated Parmesan or Romano cheese (optional)
Mozzarella cheese, shredded

1. Heat olive oil in a skillet. Add spinach, onion, salt, oregano, and meat. Mix well, separating meat into small pieces. Cook, stirring frequently, until meat is no longer pink.
2. Set aside to cool slightly. Add bread crumbs, egg, and 2 tablespoons tomato paste; mix well. Stuff manicotti with mixture. Put side by side in a greased 2-quart baking dish. If desired, spread butter over stuffed manicotti and sprinkle with the grated cheese.
3. Spoon remaining tomato paste on top of the manicotti down the center of the dish. Sprinkle mozzarella cheese on top of tomato paste. Cover baking dish.
4. Bake at 425°F 12 to 15 minutes, or until mozzarella melts.

4 servings

356 *Gnocchi*

● **Tomato Meat Sauce**
3 medium (about 1 pound) potatoes, pared and quartered
1¾ cups sifted all-purpose flour
Grated Parmesan cheese

1. Prepare sauce, allowing 4½ hours for cooking.
2. While sauce is cooking, place the potatoes in enough boiling salted water to cover. Cook, covered, about 20 minutes, or until tender when pierced with a fork. Drain. Dry potatoes by shaking in pan over low heat.
3. Mash or rice the potatoes with a potato masher, food mill, or ricer that has been scalded with boiling water. Keep the potatoes hot.
4. Place the flour in a bowl, make a well in the center, and add the mashed potatoes. Mix well to make a soft dough. Turn dough onto lightly floured surface and knead 5 to 8 minutes until it is smooth and elastic.
5. Break off small pieces of dough and, using palms of hands, roll to pencil thickness. Cut into ¾-inch pieces. Curl each piece by pressing lightly with the index finger and pulling the finger along the dough toward you. Gnocchi may also be shaped by pressing each piece with a lightly floured fork.
6. Gradually add the gnocchi to 3 quarts boiling water, cooking about half at a time. Boil rapidly, uncovered, 8 to 10 minutes, or until gnocchi are tender and float to the surface.
7. Drain gnocchi in a colander or large sieve, and mix with 2 cups Tomato Meat Sauce, top with remaining sauce, and sprinkle generously with cheese. Serve immediately.

About 6 servings

357 *Lasagne I*

- ● Tomato Sauce with Meat
- 3 tablespoons olive oil
- 1 pound ground beef
- 1 pound lasagne noodles, cooked and drained
- ¾ pound mozzarella cheese, thinly sliced
- 2 hard-cooked eggs, sliced
- ¼ cup grated Parmesan cheese
- ½ teaspoon pepper
- 1 cup ricotta

1. Prepare sauce, allowing 4½ hours for cooking.
2. Heat olive oil in a skillet. Add ground beef and cook until browned, separating into small pieces.
3. Spread ½ cup sauce in a 2-quart baking dish. Top with a layer of noodles and half the mozzarella cheese. Spread half the ground beef and half the egg slices on top. Sprinkle on half the Parmesan cheese and ¼ teaspoon pepper. Top with ½ cup ricotta.
4. Beginning with sauce, repeat layering, ending with ricotta. Top ricotta with ½ cup sauce. Arrange over this the remaining lasagne noodles. Top with more sauce.
5. Bake at 350°F about 30 minutes, or until mixture is bubbling. Let stand 5 to 10 minutes to set the layers. Cut in squares and serve topped with remaining sauce.

6 to 8 servings

358 *Egg Noodles Abruzzi (Maccheroni alla Chitarra)*

- 1 tablespoon butter
- ¼ cup olive oil
- 1 pound ground lamb
- 2 green peppers, chopped
- 1 teaspoon salt
- ¼ teaspoon pepper
- ½ cup dry white wine
- 2 large tomatoes, peeled and coarsely chopped
- 1 pound egg noodles

1. Heat butter and oil in a large skillet. Stir in lamb and green peppers; season with salt and pepper. Brown the meat slightly, stirring occasionally.
2. Add wine and simmer until liquid is almost evaporated. Stir in tomatoes and simmer mixture 30 minutes, or until sauce is thick.
3. Cook noodles according to package directions; drain. Place noodles on a hot platter, pour sauce over noodles, and serve.

4 to 6 servings

359 *Stuffed Pancakes (Scrippelle Imbusse)*

- 4 eggs
- 1 cup all-purpose flour
- ½ teaspoon salt
- ¾ cup water
  Cooking oil
- ½ cup freshly grated Parmesan or Romano cheese
- 1 cup minced prosciutto
- 1 cup chicken broth

1. Beat eggs well in a medium-size mixing bowl. Gradually add flour and salt; mix well. When the mixture is smooth and creamy, add water, more if needed to make a thin batter.
2. Heat a 5-inch skillet and brush with oil. Pour in 2 tablespoons batter, spreading over bottom of skillet to form a thin pancake. As soon as bubbles appear on the top, turn and brown other side.
3. Continue making pancakes, greasing the skillet between each one. Combine cheese with prosciutto; sprinkle each pancake with about 1½ tablespoons of the mixture. Roll up pancakes tightly and place side by side in a shallow baking dish.
4. Bring chicken broth to boiling and pour over rolled pancakes. Cover the dish and set in a hot place (a heated oven with the heat turned off) for a few minutes, so the broth will be partially absorbed. Serve immediately.

16 filled pancakes

360 *Pasta with Potatoes (Lumachine con Patate)*

2 white onions, chopped
2 tablespoons olive oil
2 tablespoons butter
1 pound potatoes, pared and diced
2 pounds very ripe tomatoes, peeled and coarsely chopped
1½ teaspoons salt
½ teaspoon freshly ground pepper
1 tablespoon minced Italian parsley
1 pound lumachine
6 tablespoons grated Romano cheese

1. Sauté onions in oil and butter until soft. Stir in potatoes and simmer, covered, 15 minutes.
2. Stir in tomatoes, salt, pepper, and parsley. Simmer, covered, 25 minutes, then uncovered 10 minutes, stirring often.
3. Cook lumachine according to package directions; drain. Add to tomatoes and potatoes; mix well. Blend in 4 tablespoons cheese.
4. Serve immediately in hot soup bowls with remaining cheese sprinkled on top.

6 to 8 servings

361 *Basic Noodle Dough (Pasta)*

4 cups sifted all-purpose flour
½ teaspoon salt
4 eggs
6 tablespoons cold water

1. Mix flour and salt in a bowl; make a well in center. Add eggs, one at a time, mixing slightly after each addition. Add water gradually, mixing to make a stiff dough.
2. Turn dough onto a lightly floured surface and knead until smooth.
3. Proceed as directed in recipes.

362 *Pasta with Beans Sorrento Style (Conchigliette con Fagioli alla Sorrento)*

2 cups dried Great Northern beans
5 cups water
1 teaspoon salt
1 cup chopped celery
1 cup chopped onion
3 tablespoons olive oil
1 teaspoon salt
6 ripe tomatoes, peeled and diced
1 tablespoon chopped Italian parsley
4 fresh basil leaves, chopped, or 1 teaspoon dried basil
½ pound conchigliette

1. Rinse beans and put into a heavy saucepot or kettle. Add water and bring rapidly to boiling; boil 2 minutes and remove from heat. Cover; set aside 1 hour.
2. Stir 1 teaspoon salt into beans, cover, and bring to boiling. Cook until beans are nearly done, but still firm (about 2 hours). Drain and set aside.
3. Sauté the celery and onion in olive oil until soft. Sprinkle in 1 teaspoon salt, then stir in tomatoes, parsley, and basil.
4. Simmer 15 minutes, uncovered. Add the beans to tomato mixture; stir well. Cook the conchigliette according to package directions, drain, and stir into bean mixture. Serve in hot soup bowls.

4 to 6 servings

363 *Spaghetti Sicilian Style (Spaghetti alla Siciliana)*

½ cup olive oil
2 cloves garlic, peeled and quartered
½ medium-size eggplant, pared and diced
6 large ripe tomatoes, peeled and coarsely chopped
2 green peppers
1 tablespoon chopped fresh basil or ½ teaspoon dried sweet basil
1 tablespoon capers
4 anchovy fillets, cut in small pieces
12 ripe olives, pitted and halved
1 teaspoon salt
¼ teaspoon pepper
1 pound spaghetti

1. Heat olive oil in a skillet; stir in garlic. Remove garlic from oil when brown. Stir eggplant and tomatoes into skillet; simmer 30 minutes.
2. Cut peppers vertically in half; remove membrane and seeds. Place peppers under broiler, skin side up, to loosen skins. Peel off skin, slice peppers, and add to tomato mixture.
3. Stir basil, capers, anchovies, olives, salt, and pepper into tomato mixture. Cover the skillet and simmer 10 minutes, or until sauce is well blended and is thickened.
4. Cook spaghetti according to package directions and drain. Immediately pour sauce over spaghetti and serve.

About 6 servings

364 *Lasagnette*

● Tomato Meat Sauce (half recipe)
  Basic Noodle Dough
8 quarts water
¼ cup salt
1 tablespoon olive oil
1 cup (8 ounces) ricotta
2 tablespoons grated Parmesan cheese
¼ teaspoon salt
⅛ teaspoon pepper

1. Prepare Tomato Meat Sauce.
2. Prepare noodle dough. Roll lightly ⅛ inch thick to form a rectangle about 12 inches long. Cut dough lengthwise with pastry cutter into strips ½ to ¾ inch wide.
3. Bring water to boiling in a large saucepot. Add ¼ cup salt, then noodles. Boil rapidly, uncovered, about 15 minutes, or until tender. Drain by pouring into a colander or large sieve; keep warm.
4. Put ½ cup meat sauce into a saucepan. Mix in ricotta, Parmesan cheese, ¼ teaspoon salt, and pepper. Cook over low heat until thoroughly heated.
5. Put noodles on a warm serving platter and pour cheese sauce over them. Cover with meat sauce. Serve immediately.

About 8 servings

365 *Lasagne II*

● Tomato Sauce with Meat
1 pound lasagne noodles, cooked, drained, and rinsed
2 pounds ricotta
1 pound mozzarella or scamorze cheese, shredded
1 cup shredded Parmesan cheese

1. Prepare Tomato Sauce with Meat.
2. Spread about 1 cup tomato sauce in a buttered 13×9×2-inch baking dish. Using a fourth of each, add a layer of noodles and then one of tomato sauce. Using a third of each, top evenly with 3 cheeses. Repeat layering and end with sauce.
3. Heat in a 375°F oven about 30 minutes, or until bubbly. Allow to stand 10 to 15 minutes to set layers before serving. Cut into squares.

12 to 15 servings

366 *Shells with Clam Sauce* (*Conchiglie con Salsa alle Vongole*)

4 quarts water
1 tablespoon salt
2 cups (8-ounce package) macaroni
   shells
● White Clam Sauce
1 tablespoon minced parsley

1. Bring water to boiling in a large saucepan or saucepot. Add salt, then macaroni. Boil rapidly, uncovered, 10 to 12 minutes, or until tender.
2. Meanwhile, prepare clam sauce.
3. Drain macaroni and put into a warm serving bowl. Pour clam sauce over macaroni and sprinkle with parsley.

4 to 6 servings

367 *Macaroni Muffs* (*Manicotti*)

● Tomato Meat Sauce
2 tablespoons olive oil
½ pound ground beef
2 cups (about 1 pound) ricotta
¼ pound mozzarella cheese, diced
2 teaspoons grated Parmesan
   cheese
2 eggs, well beaten
¾ teaspoon salt
¼ teaspoon pepper
● Basic Noodle Dough (one-half
   recipe)
5 quarts water
1 tablespoon salt

1. Prepare Tomato Meat Sauce.
2. While sauce is cooking, heat oil in a skillet. Add ground beef and cook until no pink color remains.
3. Combine cheeses, eggs, ¾ teaspoon salt, and pepper. Mix in meat. Set aside.
4. Prepare noodle dough. Divide dough into halves. Lightly roll each half ⅛ inch thick to form a rectangle. Cut dough lengthwise with pastry cutter into strips 5 inches wide. Cut strips every 6 inches to form noodles 5×6 inches.
5. Bring water to boiling in a large saucepot. Add 1 tablespoon salt, then noodles. Boil rapidly, uncovered, 10 to 12 minutes, or until noodles are tender. Drain.
6. Lay noodles out flat on a working surface. About ½ inch from the lengthwise edge of the noodle, put 4 tablespoons filling. Spread filling from narrow edge to narrow edge so filling is in a ½-inch-wide mound. Roll the ½-inch edge of the dough over filling and continue to roll. Press edges to seal. Put 4 to 6 manicotti into each of two 11×7×1½-inch baking dishes in a single layer. Cover with sauce.
7. Bake at 400°F 15 to 20 minutes, or until tomato sauce is bubbly hot. Serve with remaining sauce.

8 to 12 manicotti

368 *Mostaccioli and Cheese* (*Mostaccioli al Formaggio*)

● Tomato Meat Sauce
4 quarts water
1 tablespoon salt
2 cups (8-ounce package)
   mostaccioli
1 cup chopped mozzarella cheese
2 tablespoons grated Parmesan
   cheese
¼ teaspoon pepper
   Grated Parmesan or Romano
   cheese

1. Prepare Tomato Meat Sauce.
2. Heat water to boiling in a large saucepan. Add salt, then mostaccioli. Boil rapidly, uncovered, 12 to 15 minutes, or until tender. Drain.
3. Returned drained mostaccioli to saucepan and mix in 2 tablespoons meat sauce. Turn half of mostaccioli into an 8-inch square baking dish. Add cheeses and pepper in layers, then the remaining mostaccioli. Cover with additional meat sauce.
4. Bake at 350°F 15 to 20 minutes, or until sauce is bubbling.
5. Serve with remaining meat sauce. Sprinkle with grated cheese.

4 to 6 servings

369 *Green Noodles in Pastry* *(Tagliatelle Verdi Pasticciate)*

1 unbaked deep 9-inch pie shell
6 large mushrooms, cleaned
    and sliced
2 tablespoons butter
12 ounces green noodles
1 tablespoon butter
¼ cup grated Parmesan cheese
● 1 cup Bolognese Meat Sauce
● 1½ cups Cream Sauce
1 mushroom cap
6 to 8 mushroom halves
1 tablespoon butter, melted
    Grated Parmesan cheese

1. Thoroughly prick bottom and sides of pie shell. Bake at 450°F about 7 minutes, or until lightly browned; set aside.
2. Sauté mushrooms in 2 tablespoons butter 3 minutes. Cook noodles according to package directions and drain.
3. Combine noodles, mushrooms, 1 tablespoon butter, ¼ cup cheese, meat sauce, and 1 cup Cream Sauce. Turn mixture into pie shell. Spread remaining ½ cup Cream Sauce over top. Put mushroom cap in center and surround with mushroom halves. Drizzle melted butter over all and sprinkle with additional cheese.
4. Bake at 400°F about 8 minutes, or until heated through and top is slightly browned.

About 6 servings

370 *Green Noodles (Pasta Verde)*

¼ pound spinach
3 cups sifted all-purpose flour
½ teaspoon salt
3 eggs
6 quarts water
1 tablespoon salt
¾ cup grated Parmesan cheese
½ teaspoon salt
¼ cup butter

1. Wash spinach and put into a heavy saucepan. Do not add water; cook only in moisture remaining on leaves from washing. Partially cover and cook 5 minutes, stirring occasionally with a fork.
2. Drain spinach, pressing out water, and chop finely.
3. Mix flour and ½ teaspoon salt in a bowl; make a well in center. Add eggs, one at a time, mixing slightly after each addition. Add the chopped spinach and mix well.
4. Turn dough onto a lightly floured surface and knead until smooth, adding flour if needed for a stiff dough.
5. Divide dough in half. Lightly roll each half into a rectangle, about ⅛ inch thick. Cover; let stand 1 hour. Beginning with a narrow end, gently fold over about 2 inches of dough and continue folding over so final width is about 3 inches. (Dough must be dry enough so layers do not stick together.) Beginning at a narrow edge, cut dough into strips ¼ inch wide. Unroll strips and arrange on waxed paper on a flat surface. Let stand until noodles are dry (2 to 3 hours).
6. Bring water to boiling in a large saucepot. Add 1 tablespoon salt. Add noodles gradually. Boil rapidly, uncovered, 8 to 10 minutes, or until tender.
7. Drain noodles and put a third of them into a greased 2-quart casserole. Top with a third each of the cheese and remaining salt. Dot with a third of butter. Repeat layering twice.
8. Bake at 350°F 15 to 20 minutes, or until cheese is melted.

About 8 servings

371 *Ravioli*

- ● Tomato Meat Sauce
-   3 cups (about 1½ pounds) ricotta
- 1½ tablespoons chopped parsley
-   2 eggs, well beaten
-   1 tablespoon grated Parmesan cheese
-   ¾ teaspoon salt
-   ¼ teaspoon pepper
- ● Basic Noodle Dough
-   7 quarts water
-   2 tablespoons salt
    Grated Parmesan or Romano cheese

1. Prepare Tomato Meat Sauce.
2. Mix ricotta, parsley, eggs, 1 tablespoon grated Parmesan, ¾ teaspoon salt, and pepper.
3. Prepare noodle dough. Divide dough in fourths. Lightly roll each fourth ⅛ inch thick to form a rectangle. Cut dough lengthwise with pastry cutter into strips 5 inches wide. Put 2 teaspoons filling 1½ inches from narrow end in center of each strip. Continuing along strip, put 2 teaspoons filling at 3½-inch intervals.
4. Fold each strip in half lengthwise, covering mounds of filling. To seal, press the edges together with the tines of a fork. Press gently between mounds to form rectangles about 3½ inches long. Cut apart with a pastry cutter and press cut edges of rectangles with tines of fork to seal.
5. Bring water to boiling in a large saucepot. Add 2 tablespoons salt. Add ravioli gradually; cook about half of ravioli at one time. Boil, uncovered, about 20 minutes, or until tender. Remove with slotted spoon and drain. Put on a warm platter and top with Tomato Meat Sauce. Sprinkle with grated cheese.

About 3 dozen ravioli

Ravioli with Meat Filling: Follow recipe for Ravioli. Prepare sauce. Omit ricotta and parsley. Heat **2 tablespoons olive oil** in a skillet. Add **¾ pound ground beef** and cook until no pink color remains. Cook **½ pound spinach** until tender (see step 1 of Green Noodles, page 61); drain. Mix spinach and ground beef with egg mixture. Proceed as directed.

372 *Seafood-Sauced Green Noodles*

- 1½ pounds medium-size fresh shrimp
-   3 tablespoons olive oil
-   2 tablespoons lemon juice
-   1 clove garlic, minced
-   2 tablespoons butter
- ● Clam Sauce
-   8 ounces green noodles (packaged or homemade), cooked and drained

1. Shell and devein shrimp; rinse under running cold water and drain.
2. Mix olive oil, lemon juice, and garlic in a bowl. Add shrimp; cover and marinate about 2 hours, tossing occasionally. Remove shrimp; set marinade aside.
3. Add shrimp to hot butter in a skillet; cook, turning frequently, until pink and tender, about 10 minutes.
4. Remove shrimp with a slotted spoon. Cut about two thirds of shrimp into pieces; reserve remainder. Blend pieces into Clam Sauce; keep warm.
5. Add reserved marinade to skillet; heat. Toss cooked noodles with hot marinade; turn into a heated serving dish. Pour sauce over noodles, sprinkle with **grated Romano cheese,** and garnish with whole shrimp.

About 6 servings

373 *Macaroni alla Savonarola*

½ pound ground veal
¾ cup fine dry bread crumbs
1 egg, beaten
2 tablespoons shredded Parmesan cheese
¼ teaspoon ground nutmeg
¼ teaspoon salt
1 cup uncooked green peas, fresh or frozen
2 tablespoons butter
⅓ cup finely chopped onion
1 cup finely chopped cooked ham
3 tablespoons butter
3 hard-cooked eggs, cut in ¼-inch cubes
2 cups whipping cream
1 pound maccaroncini (big spaghetti with a hole), cooked and drained
½ cup shredded Parmesan cheese

1. Mix half of the ground veal with bread crumbs, egg, 2 tablespoons cheese, nutmeg, and salt to make a smooth mixture. Form into small balls.
2. In a large ovenware skillet, cook peas in 2 tablespoons hot butter until lightly browned. Add the meatballs to the skillet. Set in a 375°F oven for 20 minutes.
3. Lightly brown onion, ham, and remaining veal in 3 tablespoons butter in a saucepan.
4. Add the ham-veal mixture, hard-cooked eggs, and cream to the skillet; mix well. Bring to boiling; simmer about 15 minutes.
5. Turn maccaroncini onto a platter, pour sauce over it, and sprinkle remaining Parmesan cheese over all.

6 to 8 servings

374 *Spaghetti with Meatballs (Spaghetti con Polpette)*

● Tomato Meat Sauce
½ pound ground beef
½ pound ground pork
1 cup soft bread crumbs
1 tablespoon grated Parmesan cheese
1 tablespoon minced parsley
1 egg, well beaten
1 teaspoon salt
¼ teaspoon pepper
2 tablespoons olive oil
1 clove garlic, minced
4 quarts water
1 tablespoon salt
8 ounces long spaghetti
Grated Parmesan or Romano cheese

1. Prepare Tomato Meat Sauce.
2. While sauce is cooking, lightly mix ground meat with bread crumbs, 1 tablespoon Parmesan cheese, parsley, egg, 1 teaspoon salt, and pepper. Shape mixture into balls about 1 inch in diameter.
3. Heat oil and garlic in a skillet. Add meatballs and brown on all sides. Add meatballs to sauce about 20 minutes before sauce is cooked.
4. Heat water to boiling in a saucepot. Add 1 tablespoon salt. Add spaghetti and stir with a fork. Boil rapidly, uncovered, 10 to 12 minutes, or until tender. Drain.
5. Put spaghetti on a warm platter and top with sauce. Sprinkle with grated cheese.

4 to 6 servings

Spaghetti with Wine Tomato Sauce: Follow recipe for Spaghetti with Meatballs. About 30 minutes before sauce is done, add ½ cup dry red wine.

Spaghetti with Tomato Sauce: Follow recipe for Spaghetti with Meatballs. Omit meatballs. Top spaghetti with Tomato Meat Sauce or a variation.

375 *Pasta with Broccoli* (Pasta e Broccoli)

4 quarts water
2 teaspoons salt
4 cups (1-pound package) ditalini
1 pound broccoli, washed and
    trimmed
¼ cup olive oil
2 cloves garlic, sliced
⅛ teaspoon pepper
    Grated Parmesan or Romano
    cheese

1. Heat water to boiling in a large saucepan. Add salt, then ditalini. Boil rapidly, uncovered, about 12 minutes, or until tender. Drain, reserving 3 cups liquid. Set aside.
2. Put broccoli into a small amount of boiling salted water. Cook uncovered 5 minutes, then cover and cook 10 to 15 minutes, or until just tender. Drain if necessary and keep warm.
3. Heat oil and garlic in a large saucepan until garlic is lightly browned.
4. Add broccoli and ditalini with the reserved cooking liquid. Season with pepper. Simmer about 10 minutes.
5. Top with grated cheese and serve immediately.

About 6 servings

376 *Pasta with Peas* (Pasta e Piselli)

2 quarts water
1 teaspoon salt
2 cups (8-ounce package) ditalini
¼ cup olive oil
¼ cup chopped onion
½ cup canned tomatoes, sieved
¾ teaspoon salt
⅛ teaspoon pepper
⅛ teaspoon oregano
2 cans (16 ounces each) green peas,
    drained
    Grated Parmesan or Romano
    cheese

1. Heat water to boiling in a large saucepan. Add 1 teaspoon salt, then ditalini. Boil rapidly, uncovered, about 12 minutes, or until tender. Drain, reserving 2 cups liquid.
2. Heat oil in a large saucepan. Add onion and cook until lightly browned. Add tomatoes, ¾ teaspoon salt, pepper, and oregano; mix well. Simmer about 10 minutes.
3. Add cooked ditalini, reserved cooking liquid, and drained peas. Simmer about 10 minutes.
4. Top with grated cheese and serve immediately.

4 to 6 servings

377 *Pasta with Beans* (Pasta e Fagioli)

3 cups water
1¼ cups (about ½ pound) dried
    navy beans, rinsed
½ teaspoon salt
2 quarts water
1 teaspoon salt

1. Heat 3 cups water to boiling in a large saucepan. Add beans gradually to water. Boil 2 minutes. Remove from heat and cover, and set aside 1 hour.
2. Add ½ teaspoon salt to soaked beans. Bring to boiling, reduce heat, and simmer, covered, 2 hours, or until beans are tender; stir once or twice.

2 cups (8-ounce package) ditalini
¼ cup canned tomatoes, sieved
1 tablespoon olive oil
¼ teaspoon pepper
¼ teaspoon oregano
   Grated Parmesan cheese

3. Meanwhile, heat 2 quarts water to boiling in a large saucepan. Add 1 teaspoon salt, then ditalini. Boil rapidly, uncovered, about 12 minutes, or until ditalini is tender. Drain, reserving 1 cup liquid.

4. When beans are tender, add the drained ditalini, the 1 cup reserved liquid, tomatoes, oil, pepper, and oregano. Simmer 10 to 15 minutes.

5. Sprinkle with grated cheese and serve immediately.

About 6 servings

378 *Gnocchi alla Semolino*

1 quart milk
1 teaspoon salt
⅛ teaspoon freshly ground nutmeg
1 cup uncooked farina or semolina
¼ cup butter
3 eggs, well beaten
½ cup freshly shredded Parmesan
   cheese
   Butter
   Freshly shredded Parmesan
   cheese

1. Put milk, salt, and nutmeg into a heavy saucepan and bring to boiling. Add farina gradually, stirring constantly to prevent lumping. Cook and stir over low heat 10 minutes, or until very thick.

2. Remove from heat and beat in ¼ cup butter, eggs, and ½ cup cheese. Spread mixture about ½ inch thick on a greased baking sheet with sides. Chill thoroughly.

3. When ready to bake, top with bits of butter and a generous sprinkling of Parmesan cheese.

4. Heat in a 425°F oven until top is browned.

5. To serve, cut into squares.

About 8 servings

379 *Corn Tortillas*

1 teaspoon salt
2 cups dehydrated masa flour
(masa harina)
1⅓ cups hot water

1. Stir salt into masa flour. Add water and stir until all flour is moistened and dough sticks together. Add a little more water if necessary; dough should be soft, but not sticky.
2. Break off pieces of dough about the size of a large egg, form into balls, and flatten slightly. Press with a tortilla press (or roll with rolling pin) between two sheets of waxed paper to 6-inch rounds.
3. Bake on a preheated ungreased griddle, about 2 minutes per side; tortillas are ready to be turned when edges begin to curl. Stack hot baked tortillas in a towel-lined bowl. Serve hot.

12 tortillas

Note: Unused tortillas may be wrapped in moisture-proof wrap and stored in the refrigerator. To reheat, simply dampen slightly and warm on a medium-hot griddle, turning several times. Immediately wrap in towel to retain heat until served. Do not let them dry out.

380 *Wheat Flour Tortillas*

2 cups all-purpose flour
1 teaspoon salt
1 teaspoon baking powder
¼ cup lard or shortening
½ to ¾ cup cold water

1. Stir flour with salt and baking powder in bowl. Cut in lard until pieces are the size of small peas. Sprinkle water on top and mix lightly until all dry ingredients are moistened, adding only enough water to make a soft dough.
2. Turn out on a lightly floured surface or pastry canvas and knead gently, about 30 seconds. Divide into 12 equal balls; cover with a towel or waxed paper and let stand about 15 minutes. Roll each ball to a 7-inch round.
3. Bake on an ungreased griddle until lightly browned, turning once; use 2 to 3 minutes total baking time.

12 tortillas

381 *Ground Beef Filling*

This filling may be used alone, but is particularly good sprinkled with shredded mild Cheddar cheese.

1½ pounds ground beef
¼ cup chopped onion
1 clove garlic, minced
1 teaspoon salt
¼ teaspoon pepper
1 teaspoon chili powder
½ teaspoon cumin (optional)
1 cup canned tomato sauce

1. Crumble beef into skillet and brown well; if beef is very fat, pour off excess fat.
2. Add onion and garlic and cook about 5 minutes until onion is soft, stirring frequently.
3. Stir in dry seasonings, then tomato sauce. Continue cooking about 15 minutes longer.

About 3 cups filling

382 *Beef-Onion Filling*

3 tablespoons lard
1 cup finely chopped onion
1 clove garlic, minced
1 pound ground beef
1 teaspoon salt
2 teaspoons chili powder
Pinch ground cumin (comino)

Heat lard in a large, heavy skillet. Add onion and garlic and cook until tender. Add beef and seasonings; mix well. Cook until meat is lightly browned.

About 2½ cups filling

383 *Chicken Filling*

2 cups diced cooked chicken
● 1 cup Guacamole I , or 1
  fresh avocado
1 large fresh tomato, peeled, cored,
  and chopped

1. Combine chicken with guacamole; or, if using fresh avocado, peel and slice avocado into thin strips.
2. To assemble tacos, spoon chicken onto soft tortillas (top with avocado slices, if using fresh avocado). Spoon on a little chopped tomato and close tacos.

384 *Picadillo I*

1½ pounds beef (chuck or pot roast
    may be used)
    Water
¾ cup chopped onion
1 clove garlic, minced
¼ cup cooking oil
1 cup chili sauce
1 cup cooked peas and diced
    carrots
½ cup beef broth (from cooked
    meat)
1 teaspoon salt
¼ teaspoon pepper
¼ teaspoon ginger
1 bay leaf, crumbled
1 or more chopped canned
    jalapeño chilies

1. Cook meat in water to cover until tender (1 to 3 hours, depending upon cut of meat chosen); add more water during cooking if necessary to prevent drying out. Pour off and reserve beef broth.
2. Shred the meat by pulling it apart into small strips.
3. Sauté the onion and garlic in hot oil until onion is soft; add to the meat. Add remaining ingredients and stir until evenly mixed.

About 3 cups filling

385 *Picadillo II*

1 pound coarsely chopped beef
1 pound coarsely chopped pork
1 cup chopped onion
1 clove garlic, minced
1 cup chopped raw apple
1½ cups chopped tomatoes (fresh
    peeled tomatoes or canned
    tomatoes, drained, may be
    used)
½ cup raisins
1 or more chopped canned
    jalapeño chilies
1½ teaspoons salt
¼ teaspoon pepper
⅛ teaspoon cinnamon
⅛ teaspoon cloves
½ cup chopped almonds

1. Cook beef and pork together in large skillet until well browned. Add onion and garlic and cook until onion is soft. Add remaining ingredients, except almonds, and simmer 15 to 20 minutes longer until flavors are well blended and filling is slightly thickened.
2. Stir in almonds.

About 4½ cups filling

386 *Grilled Meat Filling*

1½ pounds thinly sliced beef steak
    (cubed steaks may be used if
    no more than ¼ inch thick)
    Salt and pepper
    Oil for frying

1. Sprinkle meat with salt and pepper and rub in slightly.
2. Pour oil into heavy skillet to just cover bottom; heat until sizzling. Quickly fry steaks, turning once; allow about 5 minutes total cooking time.
3. Remove steaks to a heated platter or cutting board and immediately slice into ½-inch squares. Serve at once with **hot soft tortillas** and Fresh Tomato Sauce (●).

387 *Chorizo Filling*

Chorizo is spicy Mexican sausage which is frequently used as filling for tacos, topping for tostadas, in combination with eggs, or in various soups and casserole dishes. It is popular as a taco filling combined with cubed cooked potatoes. You may be able to purchase chorizo in a Mexican specialty store. If not, here is a simple recipe for making your own.

1 pound ground lean pork
½ cup chopped onion
1 clove garlic, minced
2 tablespoons chili powder
1 teaspoon salt
1 teaspoon oregano
½ teaspoon cumin (comino)
¼ cup vinegar

1. Combine all ingredients and let stand several hours, or overnight, in refrigerator.
2. To use as a filling, fry in skillet until well browned, stirring until crumbled.
3. Serve in tacos, combined with cubed cooked potatoes, refried beans, and/or guacamole.

About 2½ cups filling

Note: Chorizo is also delicious formed into patties and fried. The cooked patties make a good breakfast dish.

388 *Flautas*

Flautas are another form of taco, formed with two overlapping tortillas, filled, rolled, and fried until crisp.

Soft tortillas
● Meat filling
Oil for frying

1. To prepare each flauta, arrange 2 soft tortillas on a flat surface, overlapping one about halfway over the other. Spoon desired amount of meat filling down center length. Roll up, starting with one long side and rolling toward other. Pin closed with wooden picks or small skewers, or hold closed with tongs.
2. Fry in oil in a skillet until crisp. Drain. Eat while hot.

389 *Enrollados*

Still another type of taco—batter dipped and then deep fried—is named Enrollados. Use one of the fillings on page 17, or try this version, which is a kind of pork picadillo containing potatoes.

Filling:
- ½ pound boneless pork loin (lomo)
- ½ pound potatoes, pared
- 2 tablespoons oil or lard
- 1 cup chopped onion
- 1 cup tomato purée
  Salt and pepper
- 12 soft tortillas
- ¼ cup flour
- 3 eggs, beaten
- ¾ cup oil for frying

Garnish:
- ¼ cup shredded Monterey Jack
- 1½ cups canned enchilada sauce
  Avocado slices

1. Prepare filling by cooking pork in a small amount of salted water until tender; shred.
2. Chop potatoes.
3. Heat oil; cook onion in oil until soft (about 5 minutes). Add shredded pork and potatoes. Stir in tomato purée. Season to taste with salt and pepper. Simmer until thick, stirring frequently.
4. Spoon a scoop of this mixture on center of each tortilla. Roll up tortilla; dip in flour and then in beaten eggs.
5. Fry in hot fat until crisp on all sides.
6. Serve hot, sprinkled with shredded cheese, topped with sauce, and garnished with avocado slices.

12 enrollados

390 *Swiss Enchiladas*

- 2 cans (6 ounces each) tomato paste
- ¼ cup coarsely chopped onion
- 1 clove garlic
- 1 teaspoon salt
- ⅛ teaspoon pepper
- 2 cups water
- 1 chicken bouillon cube
  Oil for frying
- 12 soft corn tortillas
- 1½ cups finely diced cooked chicken
- 1½ cups shredded cheese (Monterey Jack, Chihuahua, or process Swiss)
- ½ cup whipping cream

1. Combine tomato paste, onion, garlic, salt, pepper, and 1 cup of the water in an electric blender. Blend until liquefied.
2. Pour into a medium-size skillet; stir in remaining water and bouillon cube. Bring to boiling and simmer until bouillon cube is dissolved, stirring frequently. Continue to simmer over low heat until smooth and slightly thickened. Remove from heat.
3. Pour about ¼ inch oil into a small skillet and heat to sizzling.
4. To prepare enchiladas, first dip each tortilla into hot sauce, turning to coat both sides; then fry coated tortilla in hot oil, about 30 seconds per side. Remove from oil; drain slightly.
5. Put about 2 tablespoons chicken at one side of tortilla and roll up. Place in a shallow casserole with open flap on bottom. Repeat until all tortillas are filled. Sprinkle with shredded cheese and drizzle with cream. Pour remaining sauce over all.
6. Bake at 350°F about 30 minutes, or until bubbling hot.

About 6 servings

391 *Quesadillas*

1½ cups shredded Monterey Jack or
mild Cheddar cheese
2 ancho chilies, peeled, seeded,
stemmed, and chopped; or 2
or 3 chopped canned jalapeño
chilies
12 soft corn tortillas
Oil for frying

1. Combine cheese and chopped chilies.
2. Use as a filling for folded crisp-fried tacos, spooning about 1 heaping tablespoon of filling onto center of each soft tortilla before folding and frying. As taco is fried, cheese will melt and help hold tortilla in folded position.

12 quesadillas

392 *Burritos*

Burritos are a type of taco made with wheat flour tortillas. The filling may be refried beans alone, or combined with meat as in the following recipe.

12 wheat flour tortillas
1½ cups hot refried beans (use
canned beans or ●
● 1½ cups hot Ground Beef Filling
Oil for frying (optional)

1. Spread each tortilla with about 1 tablespoon refried beans, spreading only to about ½ inch of edge. Spoon a heaping tablespoon of ground beef filling along one side. Fold in ends about 1 inch to cover filling, then roll up tortilla starting with side on which meat has been placed. Serve at once.
2. Or, fry in hot oil until crisp, placing each burrito in skillet with open flap on bottom to start, then turning to fry top and sides. Drain on absorbent paper. Serve hot.

12 burritos

393 *Totopos*

1 small onion, finely chopped
1 tablespoon butter
1 can (15 ounces) kidney beans
(undrained)
Salt and pepper
6 tortillas
Oil for frying
Shredded lettuce
2 ripe avocados, peeled, pitted, and
sliced
2 cups slivered cooked chicken
3 jalapeño chilies, seeded and
thinly sliced, or 3 pickles,
thinly sliced
● Oil and Vinegar Dressing
1 fresh tomato, sliced
¾ cup shredded Monterey Jack or
mild Cheddar cheese

1. Sauté onion in butter in a skillet. Add kidney beans with liquid and cook until liquid is reduced by half.
2. Remove beans from skillet to a bowl. Mash beans and season to taste with salt and pepper.
3. Fry tortillas, one at a time, in oil in a skillet. Drain and cool. Spread tortillas with mashed beans and put on individual plates.
4. Toss lettuce, avocado slices, chicken, and chilies with a small amount of dressing.
5. Pile salad mixture on mashed beans, top with tomato slices, and sprinkle with cheese.

6 servings

394 *Chicken Enchiladas*

3 cups shredded cooked chicken
  white meat
● Green Chili Sauce (double
  recipe)
12 tortillas
  Dairy sour cream

1. Lightly toss chicken with ¾ cup sauce.
2. Dip each tortilla in hot sauce, spoon ¼ cup of chicken down center, and roll up. Place enchiladas, open edge down, in a baking dish, then spoon hot sauce over them; cover dish.
3. Set in a 400°F oven about 10 minutes, or until thoroughly heated.
4. Serve with sour cream.

6 servings

395 *Cheese Enchiladas with Chili Sauce*

6 dried ancho chilies
¼ cup water
¼ teaspoon garlic salt
  Oil for frying
24 soft corn tortillas
1½ pounds shredded Monterey Jack
½ cup chopped onion
1 teaspoon oregano
1 cup whipping cream

1. Put chilies into a saucepan with small amount of water; cook until softened. Drain; remove seeds and pith.
2. Put into an electric blender with ¼ cup water. Blend until puréed. Pour into saucepan, add garlic salt, and heat to bubbling.
3. In another saucepan, pour in oil to about ½-inch depth; heat to boiling.
4. Pass tortillas through oil, one at a time, then through warm sauce. Spoon cheese on tortilla and sprinkle with onion and oregano. Roll up and arrange filled tortillas in a single layer in the bottom of a baking dish. Pour a third of the cream over all and sprinkle with a little cheese. Repeat for two more layers.
5. Bake at 350°F about 15 minutes, or until heated through and cheese is melted.

8 to 10 servings

396 *Ranch-Style Enchiladas*

Sauce:
- 5 ancho chilies
- 1 clove garlic
- ⅛ teaspoon salt
- 1 cup chicken stock or bouillon or 1¼ cups canned enchilada sauce

Enchiladas:
- Oil for frying
- 12 corn tortillas (6- or 7-inch size)
- 2 cups diced cooked chicken or pork
- ½ cup chopped onion
- Shredded lettuce

1. To make sauce, toast and peel chilies; remove stems and seeds.   Put into an electric blender with garlic, salt, and chicken broth. Blend until liquefied. Pour into a medium-size skillet and cook about 5 minutes.
2. Pour about ¼ inch oil into a small skillet and heat to sizzling.
3. To prepare enchiladas, first dip each tortilla in hot sauce, turning to coat both sides; they fry coated tortilla in hot oil, about 30 seconds per side. Remove from oil; drain slightly.
4. Put about 2 tablespoons chicken or pork along one side; sprinkle with onion. Roll up and place in a shallow casserole with open flap on bottom. Repeat until all tortillas are filled.
5. When ready to serve, heat in a 350°F oven about 20 minutes.
6. Serve topped with shredded lettuce.

About 6 servings

397 *Pastel de Tortilla*

- 2 large ancho chilies
- 2 cups canned salsa verde mexicana (Mexican green tomato sauce)
- 1 cup chicken stock or bouillon
- 20 tortillas
- Oil for frying
- 1 pound diced cooked pork
- 1 cup cream
- 1 cup shredded Monterey Jack or mild Cheddar cheese

1. Toast and peel chilies; remove stems and seeds and cut into thin strips.
2. Combine chilies with salsa verde and chicken stock.
3. Meanwhile, slice tortillas into strips and fry in hot oil until crisp; drain on absorbent paper.
4. Layer ingredients in a 2-quart casserole as follows: first ⅓ of fried tortilla strips, next ⅓ of diced pork, then ⅓ of salsa verde mixture. Repeat twice more. Pour cream over all. Sprinkle cheese over top.
5. Heat in a 350°F oven about 30 minutes, or until heated through.

8 servings

398 *Chicken Chalupa*

12 corn tortillas
1¼ cups chicken stock or bouillon
1 cup dairy sour cream
¼ cup chopped onion
1 clove garlic, minced
1 to 3 canned jalapeño chilies,
    finely chopped
1 teaspoon salt
2 cups diced cooked chicken
2 cups shredded Monterey Jack or
    mild Cheddar cheese
    Paprika

1. Soak tortillas in 1 cup of the chicken stock.
2. Combine remaining ¼ cup chicken stock, sour cream, onion, garlic, chilies, and salt and stir until well mixed.
3. Layer ingredients in a casserole as follows: single layer of soaked tortillas, chicken, sauce, and then cheese; repeat until all ingredients are used, ending with cheese on top. Sprinkle with paprika.
4. Let stand overnight (or about 8 hours) in refrigerator before baking.
5. Bake at 350°F 1 hour.

6 to 8 servings

399 *Meat or Poultry Tamales*

3½ dozen large dry corn husks
1 cup lard
4 cups dehydrated masa flour
    (masa harina)
2½ to 3 cups warm meat or poultry
    stock (or water)
2 teaspoons salt
3½ cups meat or poultry filling of
    ● your choice (Picadillo,
        ● Ground Beef Filling,
        ● or Chicken or Turkey
            Mole Poblano)

1. Wash corn husks in warm water, put into a saucepan, and cover with boiling water. Let soak at least 30 minutes before using.
2. Beat lard until light and fluffy, using spoon or electric mixer. Gradually beat in masa flour and stock until dough sticks together and has a pastelike consistency. Taste dough before adding salt; if stock is salty you will not need all 2 teaspoons of salt.
3. Shake excess water from each softened corn husk and pat dry on paper towels. Spread about 2 tablespoons tamale dough on center portion of husk, leaving at least a 2-inch margin at both ends and about ½-inch margin at right side. Spoon about 1½ tablespoons filling onto dough. Wrap tamale, overlapping left side first, then right side slightly over left. Fold bottom up and top down.
4. Lay tamales in top section of steamer with open flaps on bottom. (If husks are too short to stay closed, they may be tied with string or thin strips of corn husk.) Tamales may completely fill top section of steamer but should be placed so there are spaces between them for circulation of steam.
5. Steam over simmering water about 1 hour, or until corn husk can be peeled from dough easily.

3½ dozen tamales

400 *Chicken Tamale Pie*

Filling:
- ¼ cup lard or cooking oil
- 1 cup chopped onion
- 1 clove garlic, minced
- 2 cups (16-ounce can) cooked tomatoes
- 1½ teaspoons salt
- 1 tablespoon chili powder
- ½ teaspoon cumin (comino)
- 3 cups diced cooked chicken

Tamale Dough:
- ½ cup lard
- 3 cups dehydrated masa flour (masa harina)
- 1 teaspoon baking powder
- ½ teaspoon salt
- 1 cup chicken stock (or 1 cup water plus 1 chicken bouillon cube)

1. For filling, heat lard in a large skillet. Add onion and garlic and cook until onion is soft, about 5 minutes. Add tomatoes and seasonings and bring to boiling, stirring until evenly mixed. Reduce heat and simmer about 10 minutes. Stir in chicken and simmer about 5 minutes.

2. For the tamale dough, beat lard until light and fluffy, using spoon or electric mixer. Combine masa flour, baking powder, and salt. Gradually beat flour mixture and chicken stock into lard until dough sticks together and has a pastelike consistency.

3. Grease a 2-quart casserole. Press tamale dough onto bottom and sides of casserole in a layer about ½ inch thick, reserving enough dough to cover top. Pour in prepared filling. Cover filling with remaining dough patted into a layer of same thickness as lining.

4. Bake at 350°F about 1 hour.

6 to 8 servings

401 *Pork Tamale Pie*

Filling:
- 1½ pounds ground lean pork
- ½ cup chopped onion
- 2 cups cooked tomatoes (19-ounce can)
- 1 clove garlic
- 1 tablespoon chili powder
- 1½ teaspoons salt
- ½ teaspoon oregano
- ¼ teaspoon pepper

Cornmeal Topping:
- 1 cup yellow or white cornmeal
- 2 tablespoons flour
- 1 tablespoon sugar
- 2 teaspoons baking powder
- ½ teaspoon salt
- 1 egg
- ½ cup milk
- 1 tablespoon melted shortening, bacon drippings, or oil

1. For the filling, brown pork in a large skillet, crumbling and stirring until all meat is browned.

2. Put onion, some of the tomatoes, garlic, and chili powder into an electric blender; blend to a thick purée. Gradually add remaining tomatoes and continue blending until puréed.

3. Pour tomato purée into skillet with meat. Bring to boiling; reduce heat to simmering. Stir in salt, oregano, and pepper. Cover and simmer 30 minutes.

4. Meanwhile, for cornmeal topping, mix cornmeal with flour, sugar, baking powder, and salt in a bowl.

5. Beat egg slightly; beat in milk and shortening. Add liquid ingredients to dry ingredients all at once and stir lightly, just until all dry ingredients are moistened. Do not beat.

6. Spoon batter over simmering filling.

7. Bake at 425°F 20 to 25 minutes, or until topping is golden brown.

About 6 servings

402 *Dessert Tamales*

3½ dozen large dry corn husks
1 cup lard (or ½ cup lard and ½ cup butter or margarine)
4 cups dehydrated masa flour (masa harina)
1 cup sugar
1 teaspoon salt
2½ to 3 cups warm water or fruit
Date-Pecan Filling (or other fruit or nut filling of your choice)

1. Wash corn husks in warm water, put into a saucepan, and cover with boiling water. Let soak at least 30 minutes before using.
2. Beat lard until light and fluffy, using spoon or electric mixer.
3. Combine masa flour, sugar, and salt. Gradually beat in this mixture and water until dough sticks together and has a pastelike consistency.
4. Shake excess water from each softened corn husk and pat dry on paper towels. Spread about 2 tablespoons tamale dough on center portion of husk, leaving at least a 2-inch margin at both ends and about ½-inch margin at right side. Spoon about 1½ tablespoons filling onto dough. Wrap tamale, overlapping left side first, then right side slightly over left. Fold bottom up and top down.
5. Lay tamales in top section of steamer with open flaps on bottom. (If husks are too short to stay closed, they may be tied with string or thin strips of corn husk.) Tamales may completely fill top section of steamer but should be placed so there are spaces between them for circulation of steam.
6. Steam over simmering water about 1 hour, or until corn husks can be peeled from dough easily.

3½ dozen tamales

Date-Pecan Filling: Blend **1 cup brown sugar, ¼ cup butter or margarine,** and **½ teaspoon cinnamon** until smooth. Add **1 cup chopped pitted dates** and **1 cup chopped pecans;** toss until evenly mixed.

Vegetables

403 *Artichokes in White Wine* *(Angynares Krasata)*

12 whole small onions, peeled
1 cup wine
1 cup water
¾ cup olive oil
Salt and pepper to taste
1 teaspoon sugar
1 teaspoon marjoram
1 bay leaf
4 parsley sprigs, minced
Juice of 1 lemon
8 artichokes, cleaned and cut in
quarters

1. Combine all ingredients in a deep saucepan. Simmer covered until artichokes are tender.
2. Serve either hot or cold.

4 servings

404 *Beans Plaki*

3 cups dried white beans
½ cup olive oil
2 medium onions, chopped
2 garlic cloves, crushed in a
garlic press
1 can (8 ounces) tomato sauce or
● 1 cup Tomato Sauce
2 celery stalks, diced
1 carrot, diced
1 bay leaf
1 teaspoon oregano
1 teaspoon sugar
Salt and pepper to taste
Wine vinegar

1. Place beans in a pot and cover with water. Bring to a boil. Simmer covered 2 to 3 hours, until just tender. Drain.
2. Heat oil in a saucepan, add onion, and cook until translucent. Add garlic, tomato sauce, celery, carrot, bay leaf, oregano, sugar, salt, and pepper. Simmer 5 minutes. (If sauce is too thick, add a little water.)
3. Add beans to sauce and simmer covered about 20 minutes, or until tender.
4. Serve hot or cold with a cruet of wine vinegar.

About 12 servings

405 *Green Beans with Tomatoes* (Fasolakia me Domates)

2 pounds green beans or 3
    packages (9 ounces each)
    frozen green beans
1 teaspoon salt
½ cup olive oil
1 can (20 ounces) tomatoes
    (undrained)
1 medium onion, chopped
    Juice of 1 lemon
1 teaspoon oregano, crushed
    Salt and pepper

1. Wash green beans, cut off ends, and cut in half lengthwise. Bring a small amount of water to a boil. Add ½ teaspoon salt and the beans. Cover and cook about 20 minutes. Drain. If frozen beans are used, cook according to directions on the package.
2. Heat olive oil in a skillet. Add tomatoes, onion, lemon juice, oregano, and salt and pepper to taste. Simmer covered 10 minutes. Pour over beans. Simmer together an additional 10 minutes.

8 servings

406 *Green Beans with Onion Rings*

1 cup water
1 onion, thinly sliced
2 pounds green beans, ends
    snipped off and beans sliced
½ cup butter
    Salt and pepper to taste
    Lemon juice to taste

Bring water to boiling. Separate onion slices into rings and add. Add green beans, butter, salt, pepper, and lemon juice. Boil until beans are tender (about 20 minutes).

6 servings

407 *Stewed Cabbage in Tomato Sauce* (Lahana Brasto me Domata)

1 head cabbage
    Boiling salted water
½ cup olive oil
1 medium onion, chopped
1 can (16 ounces) tomatoes
    (undrained)
1 celery stalk, diced
1 carrot, diced
1 bay leaf
1 teaspoon sugar
    Salt and pepper to taste

1. Remove outer leaves from cabbage and trim off part of the core. Drop into boiling salted water to cover. Cook until just tender (about 8 minutes). Drain.
2. Meanwhile, heat olive oil in a saucepan and add onion; cook until translucent. Add tomatoes, celery, carrot, bay leaf, and sugar. Simmer 15 minutes.
3. Pour sauce over cabbage. Season with salt and pepper.

4 servings

408 *Baked Carrot Ring*

¾ cup butter
2 eggs, separated
½ cup packed brown sugar
1 teaspoon cinnamon
½ teaspoon nutmeg
½ teaspoon mint
   Juice of ½ lemon
2 teaspoons water
1½ cups grated carrots
1 cup dried black currants
1 cup pine nuts
1 cup all-purpose flour
1 teaspoon baking powder
½ teaspoon baking soda
½ teaspoon salt
½ cup cracker meal

1. Using an electric mixer, cream butter, egg yolks, brown sugar, cinnamon, nutmeg, and mint until fluffy. Add lemon juice, water, carrots, currants, and pine nuts; blend thoroughly.
2. Mix flour, baking powder, baking soda, and salt. Add to carrot mixture.
3. Beat egg whites until fluffy. Fold into batter.
4. Grease a 9-inch ring mold or a square cake pan. Sprinkle with cracker meal. Pour in the batter.
5. Bake at 350°F 50 to 55 minutes.
6. Cool on wire rack. Place a serving dish over the top of carrot ring. Invert to unmold.

8 servings

409 *Dilled Carrots* (Karota me Anitho)

1 cup water
¼ cup white wine vinegar
1 medium onion, quartered
½ teaspoon salt
1 tablespoon dill
6 large carrots, pared and cut in thick slices

1. Bring water and vinegar to boiling. Put in onion, salt, dill, and carrots. Reduce heat and simmer 10 minutes. Cool.
2. Refrigerate in liquid until chilled.
3. Drain and serve cold.

4 to 6 servings

410 *Cauliflower in Béchamel Sauce* (Kounoupidi me Béchamel Saltsa)

1 head cauliflower
   Boiling water
   Juice of 1 small lemon
● 2 cups Béchamel Sauce
½ cup grated mizithra cheese
¼ cup fresh bread crumbs
¼ teaspoon ground allspice
   Salt and pepper to taste

1. Remove leaves from the cauliflower and cut off tough end. Soak in cold salted water for 15 minutes. Rinse and drain. Keep whole or break into flowerets.
2. Boil enough water to cover cauliflower. Add lemon juice and the cauliflower. Cook until stalks are just tender (10 to 20 minutes). Drain.
3. Place cauliflower in a baking dish. Cover with Béchamel Sauce, sprinkle with cheese, bread crumbs, allspice, salt, and pepper.
4. Bake at 375°F 20 minutes.

4 to 6 servings

Vegetable (Cauliflower) Polonaise, page 167

411 *Stewed Cauliflower* *(Kounoupidi Sigovrasmeno)*

1 head cauliflower
½ cup olive oil
1 medium onion, chopped
1 garlic clove
1 bay leaf
1 tablespoon wine vinegar
¼ cup chopped parsley

1. Remove leaves from cauliflower and cut off tough end. Soak in cold salted water for 15 minutes. Rinse and drain. Keep whole or break into flowerets.
2. Heat olive oil in a saucepan. Add onion and cook until translucent. Add garlic, bay leaf, wine vinegar, parsley, cauliflower, and enough water to cover. Cover. Simmer, turning several times until tender (10 to 20 minutes).
3. Serve hot or cooled.

4 servings

412 *Fried Eggplant* *(Melitzanes Tyganites)*

2 medium eggplants
Salt
¾ cup olive oil
¾ cup vegetable oil
2 cups all-purpose flour
Salt and pepper to taste

1. Slice eggplants horizontally 1/3 inch thick. Sprinkle both sides generously with salt. Arrange in a single layer in baking dish. Allow to stand 1 hour.
2. Squeeze each eggplant slice firmly between palms of hands or use a heavy weight wrapped in aluminum foil to press out excess liquid.
3. Heat oils together to smoking.
4. Meanwhile, season flour with salt and pepper. Dip each slice in the flour. Fry the eggplant slices until golden brown, turning once. Remove. Serve immediately.

About 6 servings

413 *Stuffed Eggplant* *(Melitzanes Yemistes)*

¼ cup olive oil
2 large onions, minced
1 cup minced celery
1 carrot, thinly sliced
1 tablespoon long-grain rice
1 garlic clove, crushed in a garlic press
⅓ cup chopped parsley
1 teaspoon mint
½ teaspoon oregano
½ teaspoon thyme
1 can (8 ounces) whole tomatoes, drained
Salt and pepper to taste
1 firm ripe eggplant

1. Heat oil in a large skillet, add onion, and sauté. Remove from heat. Add celery, carrot, rice, garlic, parsley, mint, oregano, thyme, tomatoes, salt, and pepper. Cover. Simmer 10 to 15 minutes.
2. Cut off the stem end of the eggplant. Scoop out the center pulp. Sprinkle inside with salt. Set shell aside. Mash pulp and add to vegetables. Simmer, stirring occasionally, for 10 minutes.
3. Rinse inside of eggplant with a little water. Spoon in vegetable mixture. Replace top and secure with wooden picks.
4. Pour ½ cup water into a baking pan. Place eggplant on a trivet in pan.
5. Bake at 350°F 1 hour.
6. To serve, slice eggplant in half from top to bottom. Lay portions flat. Slice each lengthwise again.

4 servings

Chicken Vesuvio, page 279

414 *Boiled Endive with Lemon Juice and Olive Oil*
(Vrasta Antithia)

2 bunches young curly endive
3 cups water
1 teaspoon salt
1 lemon, cut in wedges, or use
　　wine vinegar
　Olive oil

1. Slice endive in half lengthwise. Rinse several times to remove all traces of dirt. Cut stem 1 inch from bottom and discard.
2. Boil the endive in water with salt added in a covered pot until tender (about 20 to 25 minutes).
3. Serve with lemon juice and olive oil.

4 servings

415 *Braised Leeks* *(Prassa Vrasta)*

¼ cup lemon juice
6 tablespoons olive oil
1½ cups chicken stock
1 teaspoon fennel seed, crushed
1 teaspoon coriander seed,
　　crushed
½ teaspoon thyme
1 bay leaf
1 garlic clove, sliced
　Salt and pepper to taste
9 medium leeks, white part only,
　　split and cleaned, attached at
　　the root

1. Combine lemon juice, olive oil, chicken stock, fennel seed, coriander seed, thyme, bay leaf, garlic, salt, and pepper in a skillet and bring to boiling. Simmer covered 15 minutes.
2. Arrange the prepared leeks in skillet in one layer. Simmer covered 20 to 30 minutes, or until tender.
3. Remove leeks carefully, arrange on serving platter, and pour liquid over.

3 servings

416 *Okra with Tomatoes* *(Bamies Giahni me Lathi)*

2 pounds fresh okra
½ cup olive oil
1 large onion, minced
5 tomatoes, peeled, seeded, and
　　coarsely chopped
3 garlic cloves, halved
1 teaspoon sugar
　Salt and pepper to taste
　Juice of 1 lemon

1. Wash okra and cut off any hard stems. Blanch in salted water for 3 minutes.
2. Heat olive oil. Add onion and cook until translucent. Add okra and cook until it begins to soften. Add tomatoes, garlic, sugar, salt, and pepper. Cook 2 to 3 minutes. Pour in enough water to cover. Cover and simmer about 1 hour, or until okra is tender. Stir in lemon juice. Serve hot.

8 servings

417 *Simmered Zucchini*

6 zucchini (5 inches long), cut in
　　thick slices
1 cup water
½ cup olive oil
¼ cup wine vinegar
1 parsley sprig
1 garlic clove
　Salt and pepper to taste

Combine all ingredients in a saucepan. Bring to a boil and reduce heat. Simmer covered about 8 minutes, or until just tender. Let cool in the liquid. Serve hot or chilled.

6 servings

418 *Potato Cakes* (Patates Keftethes)

2 pounds potatoes
3 tablespoons grated kefalotyri cheese
2 tablespoons chopped parsley
Salt and pepper to taste
6 eggs, beaten
1 garlic clove, crushed in a garlic press
Flour for coating
Oil for frying

1. Boil potatoes in skins until tender. Peel and mash thoroughly. Mix in cheese, parsley, salt, pepper, eggs, and garlic. Shape into flat cakes. Coat with flour.
2. Heat oil in a skillet and add cakes, a few at a time. Fry until golden brown, turning once.

6 servings

419 *Spinach Casserole*

4 packages (10 ounces each) frozen spinach, defrosted
7 slices day-old whole wheat bread with crusts removed
Water
¼ cup olive oil
3 garlic cloves, crushed in a garlic press
2 bunches scallions, minced
1 leek, minced
½ pound mushrooms
Salt and pepper to taste
2 tablespoons dill weed
1 tablespoon oregano
½ teaspoon cinnamon
1 tablespoon mint
6 eggs, beaten
¾ cup grated kefalotyri cheese
1½ cups water or chicken broth
1 cup freshly toasted coarse bread crumbs
Olive oil

1. Squeeze excess liquid from spinach. Sprinkle bread slices with water. Squeeze water out.
2. Heat olive oil in a large skillet. Sauté garlic, scallions, leek, and mushrooms for 3 minutes. Remove from heat. Add salt, pepper, dill, oregano, cinnamon, mint, and spinach. Sauté the mixture for 3 minutes. Add bread, eggs, cheese, and water; mix well.
3. Oil a 3½-quart baking dish and sprinkle bottom with bread crumbs. Pour in the spinach mixture.
4. Bake at 350°F 40 to 50 minutes, or until mixture is firm.

8 to 12 servings

420 *Spinach with Rice* (Spanakorizo)

1 medium onion, finely chopped
3 tablespoons olive oil
1 pound fresh spinach, washed well and drained, or 2 packages (10 ounces each) frozen leaf spinach, partially thawed
1 tablespoon tomato paste
¼ cup water
2 tablespoons long-grain rice
Salt and pepper to taste

In a saucepan, cook onion in olive oil until translucent. Add the spinach. Mix tomato paste with the water and add along with rice; cover. Simmer until rice is tender (about 20 minutes). Season with salt and pepper.

4 servings

421 *Stuffed Tomatoes with Rice and Pine Nuts*
(Domates Yemistes Neptisima)

8 large firm tomatoes with tops
   sliced off and reserved
Salt, pepper, and sugar to taste
¾ cup olive oil
4 onions, minced
1 cup long-grain rice
½ cup water
½ cup chopped parsley
½ cup dried currants
½ cup pine nuts
1 teaspoon mint
Juice of 1 lemon
2 cups water

1. Scoop out pulp from tomatoes and reserve. Sprinkle insides of tomatoes with salt, pepper, and sugar. Arrange in a baking dish.
2. Heat ¼ cup oil in a large skillet. Add onion, pulp, rice, water, parsley, currants, pine nuts, mint, and lemon juice. Simmer, covered, stirring occasionally, until liquid is absorbed. Cool slightly. Adjust seasonings.
3. Fill tomatoes with rice mixture. Replace tops and put into baking dish. Drizzle remaining olive oil between tomatoes. Add water.
4. Bake at 350°F about 40 minutes, or until rice is cooked; baste occasionally. If necessary, add a little water. Serve hot or chilled.

6 servings

422 *Grilled Tomatoes with Rosemary and Dill*

6 large ripe red tomatoes, cored
   and sliced in half
   horizontally
¼ cup olive oil
3 teaspoons rosemary
2 teaspoons dill
12 teaspoons grated kefalotyri
   cheese
Salt and pepper to taste

1. Arrange tomatoes, cut side up, in a baking dish. Pour olive oil onto tomatoes, letting some fall into the dish.
2. Sprinkle with rosemary, dill, and cheese. Season with salt and pepper.
3. Broil until topping begins to brown (about 5 minutes).

6 servings

423 *Steamed Yellow Squash* *(Kolokithia Vrasta)*

1 can (10 ounces) plum tomatoes
1 large onion, minced
1 tablespoon minced parsley
1 teaspoon mint
1 teaspoon oregano
Salt and pepper to taste
1 cup chicken stock
3 tablespoons butter
2 pounds small yellow squash,
   sliced in half lengthwise

Combine all ingredients except squash. Bring to a boil. Add squash. Reduce heat and simmer about 15 minutes, or until squash is tender.

6 servings

424 *Mixed Baked Vegetables* *(Tourlou Tava)*

1 pound fresh green beans, ends snipped off and beans sliced vertically

2 large potatoes, pared and quartered

2 medium zucchini, pared and cut in ½-inch slices

4 celery stalks, cut in ½-inch slices

1 can (20 ounces) whole tomatoes, quartered, or 4 fresh tomatoes, peeled and cut in wedges

2 large onions, peeled and sliced

3 tablespoons olive oil

2 garlic cloves, crushed in a garlic press

½ cup chopped parsley

½ cup chopped dill
Salt and pepper to taste
Warm water

1. Oil a 2½-quart casserole. Arrange green beans, potatoes, zucchini, celery, tomatoes, and onions in layers, drizzling with oil and seasoning layers with garlic, parsley, dill, salt, and pepper. Add enough water to reach three fourths the depth of vegetables. Cover casserole.

2. Bake at 400°F about 15 minutes, or until liquid begins to simmer. Turn oven control to 325°F and bake 20 minutes longer. Remove cover and bake another 10 minutes. Adjust seasoning.

6 servings

425 *Cooked Vegetables with Garlic Mayonnaise*

1 cup french-cut green beans, cooked

1 cup green peas, cooked

4 artichoke hearts, cooked

1 cup broccoli pieces, cooked

1 cup cauliflowerets, cooked
Paprika
Garlic Mayonnaise
Parsley sprigs for garnish

Arrange vegetables in separate mounds in a serving dish, leaving a space in the center. Sprinkle with paprika. Mound Garlic Mayonnaise in the center. Garnish with parsley.

6 to 8 servings

426 *Rice with Pine Nuts* *(Pilafi me Koukounaria)*

¼ cup butter

1 small onion, minced

4 cups rice, cooked in chicken broth

¼ cup pine nuts
Juice of 1 lemon

1 teaspoon dill

½ teaspoon mint
Salt and pepper to taste

Melt butter in a saucepan. Add onion and sauté until translucent. Add cooked rice, pine nuts, lemon juice, dill, mint, salt, and pepper. Heat thoroughly.

6 servings

427 *Rice in Tomato Sauce* (*Pilafi me Domata*)

½ cup canned tomato sauce
1½ cups water
¼ cup butter
1 small onion, minced
Juice of 1 lemon
1 cup long-grain rice
Salt and pepper to taste

In a saucepan, combine tomato sauce, water, butter, onion, and lemon juice. Simmer covered until butter is melted. Add rice. Continue simmering until the liquid is absorbed (about 20 minutes). Season with salt and pepper.

4 to 6 servings

428 *Mushroom Cutlets* (*Kotlety z Grzybów*)

1 pound fresh mushrooms or 2 cups drained canned mushrooms
1 cup chopped onion
2 tablespoons butter
2 cups stale bread cubes
½ cup milk or water
3 eggs, beaten
1 tablespoon chopped parsley
½ teaspoon salt
¼ teaspoon pepper
Fine dry bread crumbs

1. Chop mushrooms. Sauté with onion in butter.
2. Soak bread cubes in milk 10 minutes. Add to mushrooms. Stir in eggs, parsley, salt, and pepper.
3. Shape into patties, using about 3 tablespoons for each. Coat with bread crumbs.
4. Fry in **butter** in a skillet until golden brown on both sides.

About 12 to 14 cutlets

Baked Mushroom Mounds: Prepare Mushroom Cutlets as directed; add ¼ **teaspoon mace** along with salt. Spoon mushroom mixture into well-greased muffin pans. Dot tops with small pieces of **butter.** Bake at 350°F 15 to 20 minutes, or until set.

429 *Beets* (*Buraki*)

6 cooked beets, peeled
2 tablespoons butter
1 tablespoon flour
1 tablespoon vinegar
½ teaspoon salt
1 tablespoon sugar
¼ teaspoon caraway seed
½ cup dairy sour cream

1. Grate the beets.
2. Melt butter in a saucepan; add flour and blend. Stir in vinegar, salt, sugar, and caraway seed.
3. Add beets. Cook over high heat 2 or 3 minutes. Stir in sour cream. Serve at once.

4 servings

430 *Cucumbers in Sour Cream (Mizeria ze Śmietaną)*

3 cups sliced cucumbers
Salt
¼ cup chopped fresh dill or 2 tablespoons dill weed
1 cup dairy sour cream or yogurt

1. Sprinkle cucumbers with salt. Let stand 30 minutes. Pat dry with paper towels.
2. Stir dill into sour cream. Add cucumbers; mix well.

4 to 6 servings

Radishes with Sour Cream: Follow directions for Cucumbers in Sour Cream; substitute **radishes** for cucumbers and omit step 1.

431 *Vegetables Polonaise (Jarzyny po Polsku)*

1½ pounds vegetables (Brussels sprouts or savoy cabbage or carrots or cauliflower or green beans or leeks)
1 cup boiling water
1 teaspoon salt
½ teaspoon sugar (optional)
2 tablespoons butter
¼ teaspoon salt
⅛ teaspoon pepper
1 tablespoon lemon juice (optional)
2 tablespoons fine dry bread crumbs

1. Choose one vegetable to prepare at a time. Trim and pare as necessary. (Leave Brussels sprouts and green beans whole. Cut cabbage into six wedges. Leave cauliflower whole or break into flowerets. Slice leeks.)
2. Cook vegetable, covered, in boiling water with 1 teaspoon salt and the sugar, if desired, until tender. Drain off water.
3. Melt butter. Stir in ¼ teaspoon salt, pepper, and lemon juice. Add bread crumbs. Sauté until golden. Spoon over top of vegetable.

About 4 servings

432 *Sauerkraut (Kapusta Kiszona)*

1 pound sauerkraut, drained
5 slices bacon, diced
1½ cups water
1 tablespoon flour
½ cup dairy sour cream (optional)

1. Rinse sauerkraut if mild favor is desired. Drain well.
2. Fry bacon in a skillet until golden. Drain off 1 tablespoon fat; set aside.
3. Add sauerkraut to skillet. Fry 3 minutes, stirring often.
4. Add water. Cover and cook 45 minutes over medium heat.
5. Blend flour into reserved bacon fat. Stir into sauerkraut. Cook and stir over high heat 2 minutes. Stir in sour cream, if desired. Remove from heat.

About 4 servings

433 *Stuffed Tomatoes (Pomidory Faszerowane)*

4 medium tomatoes
⅓ cup chopped onion
2 tablespoons butter or margarine
½ pound ground beef or pork (optional)
1 cup cooked rice
1 tablespoon chopped fresh dill or 1 teaspoon dill weed
½ teaspoon salt
¼ teaspoon pepper
⅓ cup dairy sour cream
Fine dry bread crumbs

1. Remove cores and seeds from tomatoes.
2. Sauté onion in butter. Add meat; cook until browned. Add rice, dill, salt, pepper, and sour cream; mix well.
3. Stuff tomatoes with rice mixture. Sprinkle bread crumbs on top. Place in a shallow casserole or baking dish. Cover.
4. Bake at 375°F 20 minutes. Remove cover. Continue baking until tender.

4 servings

Note: Green peppers may be substituted for tomatoes, if desired.

434 *Smothered Green Peas or Salad Greens*
(Groszek Zielony lub Sałata Duszona)

2 packages (10 ounces each) frozen
    peas or 1¼ pounds escarole or
    endive, trimmed
1 teaspoon salt
2 cups boiling water
½ cup dairy sour cream
1 teaspoon dill weed
2 tablespoons melted butter or
    bacon drippings
2 tablespoons flour
¼ teaspoon pepper
1 tablespoon chopped parsley

1. Add peas and salt to boiling water. Cover; remove from heat. Let stand 10 minutes. Drain.
2. Combine sour cream, dill weed, butter, flour, pepper, and parsley; mix well. Add to vegetables. Cover. Cook over medium-low heat 10 to 15 minutes, or until tender; stirring occasionally. Garnish with croutons, if desired.

4 to 6 servings

435 *Stuffed Vegetables (Jarzyny Faszerowane)*

6 turnips, kohlrabi, cucumbers, or
    celery roots (about 1½
    pounds)
2 cups boiling water or chicken
    broth
1½ teaspoons salt
½ teaspoon sugar (optional)
¼ pound ground beef or pork
¼ cup sliced mushrooms
¼ cup chopped onion
1 tablespoon grated Parmesan
    cheese (optional)
¼ teaspoon salt
⅛ teaspoon pepper
1 egg, beaten
2 tablespoons fine dry bread
    crumbs

1. Trim and pare vegetables. Cook in boiling water with 1½ teaspoons salt and sugar, if desired, until tender.
2. Scoop out centers of vegetables until a thick, hollow shell is left.
3. Fry ground beef with mushrooms and onion in a skillet until onion is golden. Add cheese, salt, and pepper; mix well. Remove from heat. Blend in egg.
4. Mash scooped-out portion of vegetables. Combine with meat mixture.
5. Fill vegetable shells with stuffing. Sprinkle bread crumbs on top.
6. Place stuffed vegetables in a shallow casserole or baking dish.
7. Bake at 400°F 10 to 15 minutes, or until lightly browned on top.

6 servings

436 *Smothered Vegetables (Jarzyny Duszone)*

1½ pounds potatoes, carrots,
    turnips, or celery roots
1 cup boiling water
1 teaspoon salt
4 teaspoons butter
4 teaspoons flour
¼ teaspoon pepper
1 tablespoon lemon juice
    (optional)
1 cup bouillon

1. Choose one vegetable to prepare at a time. Pare and slice or dice. Cook in boiling water with 1 teaspoon salt about 10 minutes, until crisp-tender. Drain.
2. Melt butter in a saucepan. Stir in flour, pepper, and, if desired, lemon juice. Gradually stir in bouillon. Add vegetable; stir to coat with sauce.
3. Cook, covered, 15 minutes, or until vegetable is tender. Garnish with Croutons if desired.

About 4 servings

Note: For extra flavor, dice **2 slices bacon.** Stir-fry until golden but not crisp. Substitute for butter.

437 *Stuffed Artichokes or Tomatoes* (Karczochy lub Pomidory Faszerowane)

4 cooked artichokes or 4 small
  tomatoes
¾ cup chopped onion
1 clove garlic, crushed
2 tablespoons butter
⅓ cup fine dry bread crumbs
1 tablespoon chopped fresh parsley
½ teaspoon dried basil leaves
½ teaspoon salt
¼ teaspoon pepper
1 tablespoon grated Parmesan
  cheese (optional)
4 teaspoons butter or margarine

1. Remove center leaves of artichokes; remove chokes. (Remove core from tomatoes and scoop out seeds; sprinkle inside with sugar and salt.)
2. Sauté onion and garlic in 2 tablespoons butter. Stir in bread crumbs, parsley, basil, salt, and pepper.
3. Fill vegetables with onion mixture. Sprinkle cheese on top. Set in a shallow casserole or baking dish. Place 1 teaspoon butter on top of each stuffed vegetable.
4. Bake at 375°F about 20 minutes, or until tender and browned on top.

4 servings

438 *Red Beets with Horseradish* (Ćwikła)

3 cups cooked or canned red beets,
  drained and coarsely chopped
6 ounces prepared cream-style
  horseradish
1 tablespoon brown sugar
1 teaspoon vinegar
¼ teaspoon salt

1. Combine all ingredients. Cover; refrigerate 3 days.
2. Serve with cold meats.

About 3 cups

439 *Sauerkraut with Dried Peas (for Christmas Eve)* (Kapustą z Grochem)

1 cup dried split green or yellow
  peas, rinsed
2⅔ cups boiling water
1 quart sauerkraut, rinsed and
  drained
½ cup chopped mushrooms
3 cups water
  Salt and pepper
1 can (2 ounces) anchovies,
  drained

1. Combine peas and 2⅔ cups boiling water in a saucepan. Bring to boiling and boil 2 minutes. Remove from heat. Cover and let soak 30 minutes. Bring to boiling; simmer 20 minutes.
2. Cover sauerkraut and mushrooms with 3 cups water in a saucepan; cover and cook 1 hour.
3. Add cooked peas to sauerkraut mixture. Season to taste with salt and pepper; mix well. Turn into a buttered baking dish. Top with anchovies. Cover.
4. Bake at 325°F 30 minutes.

4 to 6 servings

Sauerkraut with Dried Peas (for nonfast days): Prepare Sauerkraut with Dried Peas; omit anchovies and baking. Fry **1 onion, chopped,** with ½ **pound salt pork or bacon,** chopped, until lightly browned. Blend in **2 tablespoons flour** and add **1 cup sauerkraut cooking liquid.** Cook and stir until smooth. Mix with sauerkraut and peas; heat thoroughly.

440 *Mushrooms with Sour Cream*
(Grzybki z Kwaśną Śmietaną)

1 large onion, minced
2 tablespoons butter
1 pound fresh mushrooms, diced
1 tablespoon flour
½ teaspoon salt
¼ teaspoon pepper
½ cup whipping cream
½ cup dairy sour cream
¼ cup grated cheese (Parmesan, Swiss, or Cheddar)
2 tablespoons butter, melted

1. Sauté onion in 2 tablespoons butter in a skillet 5 minutes. Add mushrooms; sauté 5 minutes longer.
2. Blend flour, salt, and pepper with skillet mixture. Add whipping cream and sour cream gradually; mixing thoroughly. Turn into 1-quart casserole. Top with cheese. Drizzle melted butter over top.
3. Bake at 350°F about 20 minutes, or until thoroughly heated.

4 to 6 servings

441 *Stewed Sauerkraut with Mushrooms*
(Kapusta Kiszona z Grzybami)

1 ounce dried mushrooms or ¼ pound fresh mushrooms
½ cup warm water
1 large onion, diced
2½ tablespoons butter or shortening
1½ pounds sauerkraut, rinsed and drained
⅓ cup water
2 tablespoons flour
Salt and pepper

1. Soak the dried mushrooms in ½ cup warm water 1 hour.
2. Sauté mushrooms and onion in butter in a skillet 3 minutes.
3. Add sauerkraut to mushrooms; cook and stir 10 minutes.
4. Blend ⅓ cup water into flour. Mix with sauerkraut and simmer 15 minutes. Season to taste with salt and pepper. Serve with fish.

About 6 servings

442 *Pickled Beets (Ćwikła)*

3 cups sliced cooked or canned beets
1 tablespoon grated fresh horseradish or 4 teaspoons prepared horseradish
8 whole cloves or ½ teaspoon caraway seed
2 cups vinegar
1 tablespoon brown sugar
2 teaspoons salt

1. Layer beets in a glass or earthenware bowl, sprinkling layers with horseradish and cloves.
2. Boil vinegar with sugar and salt 2 minutes. Pour over the beets. Cover; refrigerate 24 hours.

About 3 cups

443 *Asparagus Extraordinaire*

1½ pounds fresh asparagus
1 medium sweet red pepper, cut
  in ¼-inch strips
● Chicken Stock
  Salt
  Freshly ground pepper
¼ pound prosciutto or boiled
  ham, cut in 1x⅛-inch strips
● ½ cup Mock Hollandaise Sauce

1. Break off and discard tough parts of asparagus stalks. Pare stalks. Simmer asparagus and pepper strips in 1 inch of stock in a covered skillet until tender (about 7 minutes); drain.
2. Arrange asparagus spears on a serving platter; arrange pepper strips over center of asparagus. Sprinkle lightly with salt and pepper. Arrange ham along sides of asparagus. Spoon hollandaise over all.

4 servings

Note: For a special luncheon entrée, increase amount of asparagus to 2 pounds and the ham to ½ pound. Arrange on individual plates; top each with a **poached egg.**

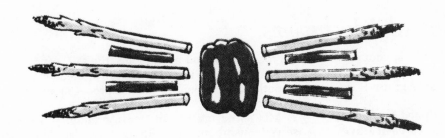

444 *Herbed Cabbage*

3 cups shredded cabbage
1 large onion, sliced
½ teaspoon snipped fresh or ¼
  teaspoon dried tarragon
  leaves
½ teaspoon snipped fresh or ¼
  teaspoon dried basil leaves
2 teaspoons snipped fresh or 1
  teaspoon dried marjoram
  leaves
¼ teaspoon freshly ground
  pepper
● Chicken Stock
2 teaspoons clarified butter
½ pound mushrooms, sliced
1 teaspoon salt
  Snipped parsley

1. Place cabbage and onion in a medium saucepan: sprinkle with tarragon, basil, marjoram, and pepper. Pour in 1 inch of stock; simmer covered until cabbage is tender (about 10 minutes). Drain.
2. Heat butter in a medium skillet until bubbly; add mushrooms and cook 4 minutes, stirring occasionally. Stir mushrooms and salt into cabbage mixture. Sprinkle with snipped parsley. Serve with Mock Crème Fraîche (●) or yogurt, if desired.

4 to 6 servings

445 *Vegetable Kabobs*

Colorful vegetables, threaded on a skewer and covered with Cauliflower Sauce, make an elegant presentation.

24 Brussels sprouts
2 small zucchini, each cut in 6 pieces
● Chicken Stock
12 cherry tomatoes
12 mushrooms
Salt
● 1⅓ cups Cauliflower Sauce

1. Simmer Brussels sprouts and zucchini in 1 inch of stock in a covered saucepan 5 minutes. Drain vegetables; cool.
2. Thread vegetables alternately on skewers. Sprinkle lightly with salt. Arrange kabobs in a shallow baking dish.
3. Bake at 400°F about 10 to 15 minutes, or until vegetables are tender; baste occasionally with stock. Serve hot sauce over kabobs.

6 servings

446 *Herbed Stuffed Mushrooms*

*¾ pound mushrooms, chopped
¼ teaspoon salt
⅛ teaspoon freshly ground pepper
1½ teaspoons snipped fresh or ½ teaspoon dried basil leaves
1 tablespoon snipped parsley
½ cup chopped onion
8 large mushrooms, stems removed and sliced into rounds; reserve caps
2 tablespoons brandy
1 tablespoon clarified butter
Parsley for garnish (optional)

1. Process ¾ pound mushrooms, the salt, pepper, basil, parsley, and onion in a food processor or blender until thick and smooth. Layer ½ cup of the mushroom mixture in bottom of a baking dish.
2. Mix sliced mushroom stems, brandy, and butter. Fill reserved mushroom caps with mixture; place filled caps in baking dish. Spoon remaining mushroom mixture around mushrooms.
3. Bake at 400°F 20 minutes. Garnish with parsley.

4 servings

Note: This recipe is also excellent for a first course.

*If desired, chop mushrooms in food processor or blender, following manufacturer's directions.

447 *French-Style Peas*

2 cups shelled peas (see Note)
8 small boiling onions, cut in half
1 cup shredded lettuce
1 teaspoon sugar
2 teaspoons snipped parsley
2 teaspoons clarified butter
½ teaspoon salt
¼ teaspoon freshly ground pepper
¾ cup water

Combine all ingredients except water; let stand 1 hour, stirring occasionally. Transfer mixture to a saucepan; add water. Simmer covered until peas and onions are tender (about 15 minutes). Serve hot.

4 servings

Note: Two packages (10 ounces each) frozen peas can be substituted in this recipe; do not mix with other ingredients. Add to saucepan during last 5 minutes of cooking.

448 *Whipped Carrots with Dill*

1 pound carrots, sliced
● Chicken Stock
● ½ cup Mock Crème Fraîche
2 tablespoons snipped fresh or 1
tablespoon dried dill weed
1 teaspoon salt

1. Simmer carrots in 1 inch of stock in a covered saucepan until tender (about 15 minutes); drain.
2. Purée in a food processor or blender with remaining ingredients. Return to saucepan; heat thoroughly.

4 servings

449 *Whipped Carrots and Pears*

Vegetables no longer need to be dull or monotonous; this unexpected combination proves how exciting they can be.

1 pound carrots, sliced
Chicken Stock (page 25)
2 medium pears, pared, cored, and chopped
½ cup Citrus Mayonnaise
¼ teaspoon salt
1 teaspoon toasted sesame seed

1. Simmer carrots in 1 inch of stock in a covered saucepan until tender (about 10 minutes); drain.
2. Purée in a food processor or blender with pears, mayonnaise, and salt. Return to saucepan; heat thoroughly. Sprinkle with sesame seed.

6 servings

450 *Stewed Okra and Tomatoes*

1 pound okra, cut in 1-inch pieces
4 medium onions, chopped
4 large tomatoes, cored and chopped (see Note)
● ½ cup Beef Stock
2 tablespoons fresh lemon juice
½ teaspoon coriander seed, crushed
1 teaspoon salt
¼ teaspoon freshly ground pepper
Lemon wedges

Combine all ingredients except lemon wedges in a medium saucepan. Simmer covered over low heat 45 minutes. Serve hot, or refrigerate and serve cold. Accompany with lemon wedges.

6 to 8 servings

Note: If fully ripe fresh tomatoes are not available, use drained tomatoes from a 29-ounce can.

451 *Squash and Tomatoes Parmesan*

2 large yellow squash, pared and cut in thirds lengthwise
● Chicken Stock
¾ teaspoon salt
¼ teaspoon freshly ground pepper
1½ teaspoons snipped fresh or ¾ teaspoon dried basil leaves
1½ teaspoons snipped fresh or ¾ teaspoon dried oregano leaves
¼ teaspoon garlic powder
3 medium tomatoes, cut in thin slices
3 tablespoons freshly grated Parmesan cheese

1. Simmer squash in a large covered skillet in 1 inch stock until tender (about 8 minutes).
2. Remove squash to broiler pan. Sprinkle with half the salt, pepper, basil, oregano, and garlic. Top squash with tomato slices; sprinkle with remaining spices and cheese.
3. Broil 3 inches from heat until cheese browns (3 to 5 minutes).

6 servings

452 *Broiled Tomatoes with Piquant Sauce*

Serve this versatile recipe as a first course, too.

6 medium tomatoes, cut in half
   Salt
   Freshly ground pepper
1 hard-cooked egg, minced
1 egg, slightly beaten
1 tablespoon wine vinegar
1 tablespoon Worcestershire sauce
1 teaspoon curry powder
½ teaspoon sugar
½ teaspoon dry mustard
3 tablespoons low-fat ricotta cheese
½ teaspoon salt
¼ cup water

1. Arrange tomatoes cut side up on a broiler pan. Season with salt and pepper. Broil 5 inches from heat 8 minutes.
2. Mix remaining ingredients except water in top of a double boiler. Cook and stir over simmering water 2 minutes; add ¼ cup water. Stir until sauce has thickened (about 3 minutes). Spoon sauce over tomatoes.

6 servings

Note: The sauce in this recipe can be served over any cooked vegetables. It is also delicious over steaks or roast beef.

453 *Cauliflower with Seasoned Dark Green Sauce*

1 medium head cauliflower
● Chicken Stock
   Juice of ½ lemon
   Fresh spinach leaves
● 1 cup Seasoned Dark Green Sauce

1. Remove leaves and tough parts of stalks from cauliflower. Place whole cauliflower in a deep saucepan. Pour in 2 inches of stock and the lemon juice. Simmer covered until cauliflower is tender (20 to 25 minutes). Drain and remove cauliflower to a platter.
2. Arrange spinach leaves on platter. Pour sauce over cauliflower. Cut into wedges to serve.

6 servings

454 *Brussels Sprouts and Grapes*

1½ pounds fresh Brussels sprouts,
    cut in half
1½ cups beer
 2 teaspoons clarified butter
 ¼ teaspoon salt
 ⅛ teaspoon freshly ground white
    pepper
 1 cup seedless white grapes
    Snipped parsley

1. Simmer Brussels sprouts in beer in covered saucepan until tender (about 8 minutes); drain.
2. Drizzle butter over sprouts; sprinkle with salt and pepper. Add grapes; heat thoroughly. Sprinkle with parsley.

4 to 6 servings

455 *Green Onions with Mock Hollandaise*

 4 bunches green onions, cleaned
    and trimmed
● 1¼ cups Chicken Stock
    Salt
● ⅔ cup Mock Hollandaise Sauce
 ¼ teaspoon freshly grated nutmeg
    Orange wedges

1. Arrange green onions in a large skillet; pour stock over. Simmer until onions are tender (about 10 minutes). Drain; arrange onions on a platter; sprinkle lightly with salt.
2. Blend hollandaise and nutmeg. Serve over onions. Garnish platter with orange wedges.

4 to 6 servings

456 *Baked Cheddar Onions*

 6 medium onions
 3 cups chopped carrots
1½ cups (6 ounces) shredded
    Cheddar cheese
 1 teaspoon thyme
 ½ teaspoon salt
● Chicken Stock

1. Cut a thin slice off both ends of each onion; peel. Carefully scoop out inside of onions with a sharp knife or melon-baller, leaving a shell 2 or 3 rings thick. Chop onion centers; mix with carrots, cheese, thyme, and salt. Fill onions with mixture; place in a shallow baking pan. Pour ½ inch stock around onions.
2. Bake at 400°F 1 to 1¼ hours, or until onions are tender.

6 servings

Note: This recipe is also excellent served as a first course.

457 *Zucchini Squares*

Mint and zucchini are an interesting and refreshing combination. Cut into smaller squares, the mixture can be served as a first course.

1 pound zucchini, shredded
2 teaspoons salt
4 ounces feta cheese, crumbled
2 eggs, beaten
2 teaspoons flour
2 teaspoons snipped fresh or 1 teaspoon crumbled dried mint leaves
¼ cup finely chopped green onion tops
¼ teaspoon freshly ground pepper
● 1 cup Low-Fat Yogurt
1 teaspoon snipped fresh or ½ teaspoon crumbled dried mint leaves

1. Mix zucchini with 2 teaspoons salt. Let stand 10 minutes; rinse and drain well between paper toweling. Mix zucchini with remaining ingredients except yogurt and 1 teaspoon mint. Beat mixture well with a fork. Pour mixture into a lightly oiled 8-inch square baking pan.
2. Bake at 375°F 45 minutes. If further browning is desired, place under broiler 1 minute. Cut into squares to serve.
3. Mix yogurt and 1 teaspoon snipped mint. Serve over zucchini squares.

6 to 8 servings

Note: **Dill weed** can be substituted for the mint in this recipe, using the same amounts.

458 *Gingered Turnips*

Oriental seasonings give this often neglected vegetable new flavor appeal.

2 pounds yellow turnips, pared and cubed
1 tablespoon minced onion
● 1¼ cups Beef Stock
½ teaspoon ground ginger
½ teaspoon sugar
2 teaspoons soy sauce

Combine all ingredients in a saucepan; simmer covered until turnips are tender (about 15 minutes). Drain; mash turnips with potato masher or electric mixer until fluffy, adding cooking liquid as needed for desired consistency.

6 servings

459 *Composed Vegetable Platter*

Eye appeal promotes appetite appeal—add other fresh vegetables if desired.

1 large sweet red pepper, cut in 1-inch pieces
3 large green peppers, sliced
3 medium kohlrabi, pared, cut in half lengthwise, and sliced
6 carrots, sliced
● Chicken Stock
● Herbed Mock Mayonnaise

1. Simmer vegetables in a covered saucepan in 1 inch of stock just until tender (about 10 minutes). Drain.
2. Arrange red pepper pieces in center of a large round platter. Arrange remaining vegetables in circles around the red pepper. Pass the mayonnaise or spoon over vegetables.
3. The vegetable platter can be refrigerated and served cold as a salad.

8 servings

Note: You may desire to serve 2 or 3 sauces with the vegetable platter; Cucumber Sauce, Seasoned Dark Green Sauce, and Green Onion Sauce (●   ) would be excellent.

460 *Vegetable-Stuffed Grapevine Leaves*

For a Greek accent, serve this tasty vegetable combination with a lamb entrée.

1 small eggplant, pared and cut
   in ¼-inch cubes
   Water
⅔ cup chopped onion
⅔ cup chopped celery
⅔ cup chopped carrot
1¼ teaspoons salt
¼ teaspoon freshly ground
   pepper
½ teaspoon poultry seasoning
½ teaspoon cinnamon
2 tablespoons snipped parsley
2 teaspoons snipped fresh or 1
   teaspoon dried mint leaves
*1 jar (8 ounces) grapevine leaves
   preserved in brine
   Cold water
1 cup water
2 tablespoons fresh lemon juice
● ¾ cup Mock Hollandaise Sauce

1. Simmer eggplant in 1 inch of salted water in a covered saucepan until tender (about 10 minutes); drain.
2. Process onion, celery, and carrot in a food processor or blender until finely ground; transfer mixture to mixing bowl. Mix in eggplant, salt, pepper, poultry seasoning, cinnamon, parsley, and mint. Spoon vegetable mixture into a 1-quart casserole.
3. Bake at 325°F 40 minutes; cool slightly.
4. Soak grapevine leaves in cold water 20 minutes; pat dry. Cover bottom of large skillet with four leaves. Place a rounded tablespoon of vegetable mixture on stem end of each leaf; roll up leaf, tucking in sides. Place filled leaf seam side down in skillet. Repeat with remaining leaves and vegetable mixture.
5. Pour 1 cup water and the lemon juice over rolls. Simmer covered 30 to 35 minutes. Serve hot, or refrigerate and serve cold. Pass hollandaise. This recipe can also be served as a first course.

8 servings (4 rolls each)

*Grapevine leaves can be purchased in a gourmet shop or in the specialty department of a supermarket.

461 *Soy Pilaf with Fresh Vegetables*

A Middle Eastern influence is found in the ingredients of this unusual recipe.

1½ cups chopped onion
½ cup soy grits or granules (see
   Note)
1 small eggplant, pared and cut
   in ½-inch cubes
● 1½ cups Chicken Stock
½ teaspoon curry powder
¼ teaspoon salt
½ teaspoon paprika
½ teaspoon cumin
¼ teaspoon chili powder
⅛ teaspoon garlic powder
¼ teaspoon salt
2 medium tomatoes, chopped
1 green onion, chopped
1½ tablespoons lemon juice
¼ teaspoon salt
⅛ teaspoon freshly ground
   pepper
1 tablespoon snipped parsley

1. Spread onion in a 9x5x2-inch baking dish; sprinkle with soy. Layer eggplant over top. Mix stock with curry, salt, paprika, cumin, chili powder, and garlic; pour over eggplant.
2. Bake covered at 350°F 1 hour. Mound mixture on a serving platter; sprinkle with ¼ teaspoon salt.
3. While eggplant mixture is baking, mix tomatoes and remaining ingredients in a small bowl. Refrigerate covered. Spoon around pilaf on platter.

4 to 6 servings

Note: Soy grits can be purchased in specialty or health food stores. They have a flavor similar to cracked wheat.

Cracked wheat can be used in this recipe. You will need **2 cups cooked cracked wheat;** cook according to package directions.

462 *Vegetable Mélange*

In our version of scalloped tomatoes, eggplant replaces the bread cubes.

- 1 medium eggplant, pared and cut in ¾-inch pieces
- 1 can (16 ounces) tomatoes, cut in thirds; use juice
- 4 stalks celery, cut in ¾-inch pieces
- ½ cup snipped parsley
- ½ cup dry vermouth
- 1½ teaspoons salt
- ¼ teaspoon freshly ground pepper
- 2 tablespoons snipped fresh or 1½ teaspoons dried fennel leaves
- 1 cup coarsely chopped onion
- 1½ cups coarsely chopped green pepper

Combine all ingredients except onion and green pepper in a Dutch oven; simmer covered 30 minutes. Add onion and green pepper; simmer uncovered 20 minutes, stirring occasionally. Serve in small bowls.

6 to 8 servings

Note: Try different herb combinations in place of the fennel: **2 teaspoons snipped fresh basil** and **1 teaspoon snipped fresh oregano**, or **2 teaspoons curry powder** and **1 teaspoon cumin.**

463 *Vegetable Casserole Niçoise*

- ½ head iceberg lettuce, cut in 2-inch pieces
- 3 tomatoes, cut in quarters
- 4 heads Belgian endive, cut in ½-inch slices
- ½ cup ripe olives, sliced
- 4 slices prosciutto or 2 slices boiled ham, cut in 2x⅛x⅛-inch strips
- 4 anchovies, minced
- ½ teaspoon salt
- ¼ teaspoon freshly ground pepper
- ● ¾ cup Beef Stock
- ¼ cup dry white wine or Beef Stock
- ¼ cup grated Gruyère cheese

1. Arrange lettuce, tomatoes, and endive in a 9x5x2-inch casserole. Sprinkle with olives, prosciutto, anchovies, salt, and pepper. Pour stock and wine over all.
2. Bake at 350°F 25 minutes. Sprinkle with cheese and bake until cheese is melted (about 5 minutes).

6 to 8 servings

464 *Cheese-Spinach Gnocchi (Gnocchi Verdi)*

1½ cups milk
 1 tablespoon butter
 ¼ teaspoon salt
   Few grains ground nutmeg
 ¼ cup uncooked farina
 ½ cup well-drained cooked
     chopped spinach
 1 egg, well beaten
 1 tablespoon chopped onion,
     lightly browned in 1 teaspoon
     butter
1½ cups shredded Swiss cheese
 2 eggs, well beaten
 ¾ cup milk
 1 tablespoon flour
 1 teaspoon salt
   Few grains ground nutmeg

1. Bring milk, butter, salt, and nutmeg to boiling in a saucepan. Add farina gradually, stirring constantly over low heat until mixture thickens.
2. Stir in spinach, egg, onion, and 1 cup shredded cheese; mix well. Remove from heat and set aside to cool slightly.
3. Drop mixture by tablespoonfuls close together in a well-greased 9-inch shallow baking pan or casserole. Sprinkle mounds with remaining cheese.
4. Combine remaining ingredients and pour over spinach mounds.
5. Bake at 350°F 35 to 40 minutes, or until topping is golden brown.

About 6 servings

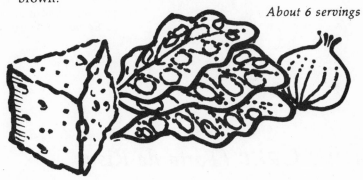

465 *Venetian Rice and Peas (Risi e Bisi)*

3 tablespoons olive oil
3 tablespoons unsalted butter
2 slices prosciutto, cut in pieces
1 small onion, minced
3 tablespoons chopped parsley
1 package (10 ounces) frozen green
    peas (or 1 pound fresh)
  Water
1 cup uncooked rice, long or short
    grain
1 quart chicken broth
  Grated Parmesan cheese

1. Put oil and butter into a large saucepan over medium heat. Add prosciutto, onion, and parsley. Sauté until onion is translucent. Add peas and enough water to cover (about ½ inch), and cook 5 minutes.
2. Stir in rice and chicken broth; bring to a boil. Reduce heat and simmer about 15 minutes, stirring frequently, or until the rice is tender.
3. Serve with Parmesan cheese.

6 to 8 servings

466 *Braised Rice with Saffron (Risotto alla Milanese)*

¼ cup butter
¼ cup finely chopped onion
1 cup uncooked rice
3 cups chicken broth
½ cup Marsala
1 teaspoon salt
¼ teaspoon saffron
2 tablespoons hot water
¼ cup grated Parmesan cheese

1. Melt butter in a heavy 1½-quart saucepan with a tight-fitting cover. Add onion and cook until lightly browned. Stir in uncooked rice. Cook slowly until rice is lightly browned, stirring occasionally with a fork.
2. Slowly stir in broth, wine, and salt. Place over high heat and stir with a fork until mixture boils. Cover pan, reduce heat, and allow rice to simmer without stirring 18 minutes.
3. Turn off heat, leave pan in place, and keep on cover to allow rice to steam. While rice is steaming, dissolve saffron in hot water.
4. After 30 minutes, the rice should absorb all the liquid and be tender, fluffy, and dry. Add saffron mixture to rice and mix well, using a fork to lift and turn the rice.
5. Serve rice warm, topped with cheese.

4 or 5 servings

467 *Rice Cake (Torta de Riso)*

3 cups milk
¼ cup uncooked long grain white rice
½ cup sugar
¼ teaspoon salt
2 tablespoons butter
1 cup all-purpose flour
2 tablespoons sugar
6 tablespoons firm butter
1 egg yolk, beaten
½ cup chopped blanched almonds
3 eggs, beaten
¼ teaspoon almond extract

1. Combine milk, rice, ½ cup sugar, salt, and 2 tablespoons butter in the top of a double boiler. Set over simmering water, cover, and cook 2¼ to 2½ hours, or until rice is soft; stir occasionally.
2. While the rice is cooking, prepare the pastry. Combine flour, 2 tablespoons sugar, and 6 tablespoons butter. Rub mixture between fingers until butter is the size of rolled oats. Stir in egg yolk and work dough until it forms a ball. Press dough onto bottom and sides of a 9-inch layer cake pan with removable bottom.
3. Bake pastry at 325°F 30 minutes, or until lightly browned. Cool on a wire rack. Place almonds in a shallow pan. Bake at 325°F 15 minutes, or until golden; stir occasionally.
4. Stir some of the hot cooked rice mixture into the beaten eggs. Immediately stir back into mixture in double boiler. Stir in almonds and almond extract, and pour filling into baked pastry crust.
5. Bake at 400°F 20 minutes, or until center is set. Remove pan sides, leaving cake on pan bottom. Serve warm or cool, cut in wedges.

About 8 servings

468 Cauliflower à la Romagna
(Cavolfiore alla Romagna)

1 head cauliflower, washed and trimmed
⅔ cup fine dry bread crumbs
1 teaspoon grated Parmesan cheese
½ teaspoon salt
¼ teaspoon pepper
2 eggs, slightly beaten
¼ cup milk
Fat for deep frying heated to 365°F

1. Put whole cauliflower into a saucepan containing a 1-inch depth of boiling salted water. Cook, uncovered, 5 minutes. Cover and cook 15 to 20 minutes, or until cauliflower is tender. Drain, separate into flowerets, and set aside to cool.
2. Combine crumbs, cheese, salt, and pepper. Mix eggs and milk in a small bowl. Coat flowerets with egg mixture, then with crumbs.
3. Put only as many flowerets into fat at one time as will float uncrowded. Fry 2 to 4 minutes, or until golden brown; turn occasionally during frying.
4. Drain and serve hot.

About 4 servings

469 Artichoke Pie (Tortino di Carciofi alla Fiorentina)

1 package (9 ounces) frozen artichoke hearts
Lemon juice
2 tablespoons olive oil
1½ tablespoons butter
Flour
4 eggs
½ teaspoon salt
Pinch pepper
2 tablespoons milk or water

1. Thinly slice the artichoke hearts vertically and spread out on paper towels. Pat dry when thawed, and drizzle with lemon juice.
2. Heat olive oil and butter in a 10-inch skillet with an ovenproof handle. Coat artichoke heart slices with flour and brown on both sides in hot fat.
3. Beat eggs slightly. Mix in salt, pepper, and milk. Pour over artichoke slices in skillet.
4. Bake at 350°F 5 to 10 minutes, or until egg mixture is set.

4 servings

470 Broccoli Florentine (Broccoli alla Fiorentina)

1 pound broccoli, washed and trimmed
2 tablespoons olive oil
2 cloves garlic, sliced thin
¼ teaspoon salt
¼ teaspoon pepper

1. Split the heavy broccoli stalks (over ½ inch thick) lengthwise through stalks up to flowerets. Put into a small amount of boiling salted water. Cook, uncovered, 5 minutes, then cover and cook 10 to 15 minutes, or until broccoli is just tender.
2. Meanwhile, heat oil and garlic in a large skillet until garlic is lightly browned.
3. Drain broccoli and add to skillet; turn to coat with oil. Cook about 10 minutes, stirring occasionally. Season with salt and pepper. Serve hot.

4 servings

Broccoli Roman Style: Follow recipe for Broccoli Florentine. Omit cooking broccoli in boiling water. Cook broccoli in oil only 5 minutes. Add **1½ cups dry red wine** to skillet. Cook, covered, over low heat about 20 minutes, or until broccoli is tender; stir occasionally.

Spinach Sautéed in Oil: Follow recipe for Broccoli Florentine; substitute **2 cups chopped cooked spinach** for broccoli. Add spinach, **1 tablespoon chopped pinenuts or almonds,** and **1 tablespoon raisins** to oil mixture.

471 *Florentine Spinach (Spinaci alla Fiorentina)*

2 pounds spinach
● 2 cups Medium White Sauce
3 eggs, slightly beaten
3 tablespoons minced onion
½ teaspoon salt
½ teaspoon pepper

1. Wash spinach. Put into a large saucepan with only the water clinging to the leaves; cover. Cook rapidly about 5 minutes, or until tender. Drain well.
2. Prepare white sauce. Pour hot sauce into beaten eggs, stirring vigorously to blend. Set aside to cool to lukewarm.
3. Finely chop spinach. Combine spinach, sauce mixture, onion, salt, and pepper. Turn into a thoroughly greased 9-inch ring mold.
4. Set filled mold in a pan and pour hot water into pan to a depth of 1 inch.
5. Bake at 350°F 45 to 55 minutes, or until set.
6. Remove from oven; remove mold from water and let stand 5 minutes. Loosen spinach from mold and unmold onto a warm serving plate.

6 servings

472 *Eggplant Pugliese Style (Melanzane alla Pugliese)*

3 medium-size eggplants (about ½ pound each)
2 tablespoons olive oil
1 tablespoon chopped parsley
1 medium onion, chopped
1 clove garlic, peeled and chopped
1½ cups chopped cooked meat (see Note)
½ cup fine dry bread crumbs
1 tablespoon chopped pinenuts or almonds
Salt and pepper
3 or 4 tablespoons olive oil
1 can (8 ounces) tomato sauce

1. Wash and dry eggplants; remove stems. Cut eggplants in half crosswise, and scoop out most of the pulp; reserve pulp.
2. Heat 2 tablespoons olive oil in a skillet. Sauté pulp, parsley, onion, and garlic. Add meat, bread crumbs, and pinenuts. Season with salt and pepper; set aside.
3. Heat 3 or 4 tablespoons olive oil in another skillet. Cook eggplant shells in hot oil until the skins start to brown. Fill each half with the meat mixture. Pour tomato sauce over each half and cover skillet.
4. Cook eggplant slowly 20 to 30 minutes, or until tender.
5. If desired, place eggplant in a serving dish, add more tomato sauce, and keep in warm oven until ready to serve.

4 to 6 servings

Note: If desired, ¾ pound uncooked chopped beef, lamb, or pork may be used. Sauté with pulp, parsley, onion, and garlic until browned before combining with other ingredients.

473 *Artichokes in Lemon (Carciofi con Limone)*

1 can (14 ounces) artichoke hearts
3 tablespoons lemon juice
2 tablespoons olive oil
1 clove garlic, peeled and finely
    chopped
¼ teaspoon salt
⅛ teaspoon pepper

1. Drain artichoke hearts and place in refrigerator to chill. Combine remaining ingredients and chill.
2. When ready to serve, stir lemon-olive oil mixture and pour over artichoke hearts.

6 appetizer servings

474 *Stuffed Eggplant (Melanzane Ripiene)*

3 medium eggplants (about 3
    pounds)
1½ teaspoons salt
1 cup boiling water
¼ cup butter
1 cup chopped onion
2 cups coarsely chopped peeled
    tomatoes
1 to 2 teaspoons salt
¼ teaspoon pepper
1 teaspoon dried basil
½ teaspoon oregano
2 cups chopped cooked ham
1 cup fine dry bread crumbs
¼ teaspoon oregano
¼ cup butter, melted
6 slices mozzarella cheese, halved
12 anchovy fillets
2 tablespoons chopped parsley

1. Cut the eggplants in half lengthwise. Make several cuts into the pulp, being careful not to pierce skin. Sprinkle cut sides with 1½ teaspoons salt. Let stand 30 minutes.
2. Pat eggplant halves dry with paper towels. Place flat-side down in a baking pan. Add boiling water.
3. Bake at 375°F, uncovered, 15 minutes, or until just tender. Cool on wire rack. Scoop out pulp, leaving ¼-inch-thick shell walls. Chop pulp coarsely and drain. Set pulp and shells aside.
4. Melt ¼ cup butter in a large skillet. Add the onion and sauté about 5 minutes, or until golden. Stir in tomatoes, 1 to 2 teaspoons salt, pepper, basil, ½ teaspoon oregano, ham, ½ cup of the bread crumbs, and the eggplant pulp. Simmer, covered, 5 minutes.
5. Fill eggplant shells with mixture, mounding slightly. Place in a shallow baking pan. Combine remaining ½ cup bread crumbs, ¼ teaspoon oregano, and melted butter; sprinkle over each eggplant.
6. Place 2 pieces cheese on top of each eggplant half. Lay 2 anchovy fillets on each half.
7. Bake at 375°F about 15 minutes, or until cheese melts and filling is heated through. Sprinkle each half with 1 teaspoon chopped parsley.

6 servings

475 *Vegetable Omelet (Frittata)*

3 tablespoons olive oil
½ cup chopped onion
½ cup sliced mushrooms
½ cup sliced zucchini
10 frozen artichoke heart halves,
    thawed
1 teaspoon salt
¼ teaspoon freshly ground black
    pepper
6 eggs
¼ cup canned tomato sauce

1. Heat oil in a 9-inch skillet with an oven-proof handle. Sauté onion 5 minutes. Add mushrooms, zucchini, and artichoke heart halves; cook 10 minutes over low heat. Sprinkle ½ teaspoon salt and ⅛ teaspoon pepper over vegetables.
2. Beat eggs with remaining ½ teaspoon salt and ⅛ teaspoon pepper; pour over vegetables. Spoon tomato sauce over the top.
3. Bake at 350°F 15 minutes, or until eggs are set. Cut in wedges and serve immediately.

4 to 6 servings

476 Artichokes Basilicata Style (Carciofi alla Basilicata)

1 package (9 ounces) frozen
    artichoke hearts
1 tablespoon lemon juice
½ cup fine dry bread crumbs
1 tablespoon grated Parmesan or
    Romano cheese
1 teaspoon chopped fresh basil
    leaves or ½ teaspoon dried
    basil
1 egg
½ teaspoon salt
⅛ teaspoon pepper
½ cup olive oil

1. Slice artichoke hearts vertically into thin slices. Spread out on paper towels to thaw. Sprinkle with lemon juice and let stand 30 minutes.
2. Combine bread crumbs, cheese, and basil. Beat egg with salt and pepper. Dip artichoke heart slices in egg, then roll in bread-crumb mixture.
3. Heat olive oil in skillet. Add artichoke heart slices and cook over low heat until browned. Serve while crisp.

3 or 4 servings

477 Green Beans Basilicata Style (Fagiolini alla Basilicata)

1½ pounds fresh green beans
1 teaspoon salt
2 quarts boiling water
¼ cup chopped onion
2 tablespoons olive oil
½ teaspoon salt
⅛ teaspoon pepper
2 tablespoons chopped fresh mint
    or basil leaves
3 tablespoons wine vinegar

1. Wash beans and break off ends. Leave whole or cut as desired.
2. Add 1 teaspoon salt to boiling water, stir in beans, cover, and bring to boiling. Cook 10 minutes, or until crisp-tender.
3. While beans are cooking, sauté onion in olive oil until transparent (about 8 minutes). When beans are done cooking, drain and add to onion. Season with ½ teaspoon salt and the pepper. Add mint leaves and vinegar; toss gently. Serve while hot.

4 to 6 servings

478 Buttered Carrots (Carote al Burro)

1½ pounds carrots
1 teaspoon sugar
½ teaspoon salt
⅛ teaspoon pepper
3 tablespoons butter
¾ cup water
1 tablespoon chopped parsley

1. Pare carrots and cut into julienne strips. Place in a large, heavy saucepan with sugar, salt, pepper, butter, and water. Cover.
2. Bring to boiling, then simmer 10 to 15 minutes, or until carrots are tender and moisture is evaporated. Remove cover to evaporate moisture, if necessary.
3. Turn carrots into a serving bowl and sprinkle with parsley.

6 servings

479 *Baked Rice Balls (Arancine)*

1½ pounds ground beef
1 small onion, chopped
1 can (6 ounces) tomato paste
¾ cup water
1 teaspoon salt
⅛ teaspoon pepper
1 tablespoon chopped parsley
6 cups cooked rice, hot
½ cup grated Romano cheese
¼ cup butter
1 cup all-purpose flour
2 eggs, slightly beaten
   All-purpose flour (1 to 1½ cups)
3 eggs, slightly beaten
2 cups fine dry bread crumbs
1 can (8 ounces) tomato sauce

1. Brown ground beef with onion in a skillet. Add tomato paste, stir, and cook 5 minutes. Add water, salt, pepper, and parsley. Mix well and cool about 15 minutes.
2. Combine rice, cheese, butter, 1 cup flour, and 2 eggs. Mix until butter is melted and ingredients are well blended.
3. With well-floured hands, shape some rice into a small ball. Flatten slightly and top with 1 tablespoon of the meat mixture. Top with more rice to cover meat, and make into a ball the size of a small orange.
4. Hold the ball over a shallow pan filled with about 1 cup flour; add more flour when needed. Sprinkle rice ball with flour while gently packing and turning in palm of hand.
5. Carefully dip ball in beaten eggs, then roll gently in bread crumbs to coat. Repeat with remaining rice. Place finished rice balls in a jelly-roll pan or baking sheet lined with aluminum foil.
6. Bake at 350°F 30 minutes. While rice balls are baking, stir tomato sauce into meat sauce and heat. Serve sauce over baked rice balls.

7 or 8 servings

480 *Stuffed Artichokes Sicilian*
(Carciofi Imbottiti alla Siciliana)

4 medium artichokes
1 teaspoon salt
⅔ cup fine dry bread crumbs
1 clove garlic, peeled and thinly
   sliced
1 teaspoon grated Parmesan cheese
1 teaspoon chopped parsley
1 teaspoon salt
¾ teaspoon pepper
2 cloves garlic, peeled and thinly
   sliced
1 tablespoon chopped parsley
2 cups boiling water
2 tablespoons olive oil

1. Cut off 1 inch from the top and base of each artichoke. Remove lower outer leaves. If desired, snip off tips of remaining leaves. Cover with cold water and add 1 teaspoon salt. Let stand 5 to 10 minutes. Drain upside down.
2. Mix together bread crumbs, 1 clove garlic, thinly sliced, cheese, 1 teaspoon chopped parsley, 1 teaspoon salt, and pepper. Set aside.
3. Spread leaves of drained artichokes open slightly. Place 3 slices garlic in each artichoke. Sprinkle bread crumb mixture between leaves and over top of artichokes. Sprinkle with chopped parsley.
4. Place artichokes close together in a 10-inch skillet so they will remain upright during cooking. Pour the boiling water in the skillet and sprinkle the artichokes with olive oil.
5. Cook, covered, about 30 minutes, or until artichoke leaves are tender.

4 servings

481 *Lemon Rice with Egg (Riso all' Uovo e Limone)*

1¾ cups chicken broth
¾ cup uncooked long grain rice
1 egg
1 tablespoon lemon juice
¼ cup grated Parmesan cheese

1. Bring broth to boiling in a saucepan. Stir in rice; cover tightly. Cook 15 to 20 minutes, or until rice is tender and liquid is absorbed.
2. Place egg, lemon juice, and cheese in a bowl; beat until foamy. Stir into rice over low heat. Serve immediately.

About 4 servings

482 *Asparagus Parmesan (Asparagi alla Parmigiana)*

1½ pounds asparagus
½ cup butter, melted
½ cup grated Parmesan or Romano cheese
1 teaspoon salt
½ teaspoon pepper

1. Wash asparagus. Put into a small amount of boiling salted water in a skillet. Bring to boiling, reduce heat, and cook 5 minutes, uncovered; cover and cook 10 minutes, or until just tender.
2. Pour melted butter into a greased 1½-quart casserole. Put cooked asparagus into casserole and sprinkle with mixture of grated cheese, salt, and pepper.
3. Bake at 450°F 5 to 10 minutes, or until cheese is melted.

About 6 servings

483 *Green Beans with Onions (Fagiolini con Cipolla)*

8 to 12 small whole onions, peeled
1 pound green beans
¼ teaspoon salt
2 tablespoons olive oil
1 clove garlic, chopped
½ teaspoon salt
⅛ teaspoon pepper

1. Put onions into a small amount of boiling salted water in a saucepan. Cover and cook 15 to 20 minutes, or until onions are tender.
2. Meanwhile, wash beans, break off ends, and cut beans lengthwise into fine strips. Bring a small amount of water to boiling in a saucepan, add ¼ teaspoon salt and beans. Cover and cook 10 to 15 minutes, or until beans are tender. Drain.
3. Heat oil and garlic in a skillet until garlic is lightly browned. Add green beans and onions, season with salt and pepper, and cook 5 to 10 minutes, or until thoroughly heated, stirring occasionally.

About 4 servings

484 *Green Beans in Sauce (Fagiolini al Sugo)*

2 tablespoons olive oil
1 clove garlic, chopped
2½ cups canned tomatoes, sieved
1 cup boiling water
½ teaspoon salt
⅛ teaspoon pepper
⅛ teaspoon oregano
2 teaspoons chopped parsley
1 pound green beans
¼ teaspoon salt

1. Heat olive oil and garlic in a skillet until garlic is lightly browned. Add tomatoes and water slowly. Stir in ½ teaspoon salt, pepper, oregano, and parsley. Bring to boiling, cover, and simmer 20 minutes, stirring occasionally.
2. Meanwhile, wash beans, break off ends, and cut crosswise into pieces. Bring a small amount of water to boiling in a saucepan. Add ¼ teaspoon salt and beans. Cover and cook about 15 minutes, or until beans are tender. Drain.
3. Turn beans into a warm serving bowl and pour sauce over them. Serve immediately.

About 4 servings

485 *Broccoli, Southern Style*

1 medium onion, thinly sliced
1 clove garlic, thinly sliced
2 tablespoons olive oil
1½ tablespoons flour
½ teaspoon salt
⅛ teaspoon pepper
1 cup chicken broth
4 anchovy fillets, chopped
½ cup sliced ripe olives
2 cups shredded process Cheddar
   cheese
2 pounds broccoli, cooked and
   drained

1. Cook onion and garlic in hot olive oil in a saucepan until onion is soft. Blend in a mixture of flour, salt, and pepper. Heat until bubbly.
2. Add chicken broth, stirring constantly. Bring to boiling and cook 1 or 2 minutes, or until sauce thickens.
3. Blend in anchovies, olives, and cheese. Pour sauce over hot broccoli.

About 6 servings

486 *Italian Cauliflower (Cavolfiore Italiana)*

1 large head cauliflower, washed
   and trimmed
2 tablespoons butter
½ clove garlic, minced
2 teaspoons flour
1 teaspoon salt
2 cups canned tomatoes
1 small green pepper, coarsely
   chopped
¼ teaspoon oregano

1. Separate cauliflower into flowerets. Put into a saucepan containing a small amount of boiling salted water. Cook, uncovered, 5 minutes. Cover and cook 8 to 10 minutes, or until cauliflower is tender. Drain if necessary and keep hot.
2. Heat butter with garlic; stir in flour and salt and cook until bubbly.
3. Add tomatoes and bring to boiling, stirring constantly; cook 1 to 2 minutes. Mix in green pepper and oregano.
4. Pour sauce over hot cauliflower.

About 6 servings

487 *Baked Eggplant (Melanzane alla Sardegna)*

4 eggplants (about ¾ pound each)
½ cup olive oil
2 teaspoons salt
1 teaspoon pepper

1. Wash and dry eggplants; remove stems. Leave eggplant whole and unpeeled. Make a slit the length of each eggplant only to the center, not completely through to the other side.
2. In each slit, drizzle 1 tablespoon olive oil and season with ½ teaspoon salt and ¼ teaspoon pepper. Gently press eggplant together and rub completely with olive oil. Rub an 11×7-inch baking dish with olive oil. Place eggplants in dish.
3. Bake at 375°F about 30 minutes, or until eggplants are tender.

6 to 8 servings

488 *Eggplant Parmesan (Melanzane alla Parmigiana)*

- ● **Tomato Meat Sauce**
- **4 quarts water**
- **1 tablespoon salt**
- **3 cups (about 8 ounces) noodles**
- **1 eggplant (about 1 pound)**
- **2 eggs, slightly beaten**
- **¼ cup cream**
- **3 tablespoons olive oil**
- **⅔ cup fine dry bread crumbs**
- **1 cup grated Parmesan cheese**
- **6 slices (3 ounces) mozzarella cheese**

1. Prepare Tomato Meat Sauce.
2. Heat water in a large saucepan. Add salt, then noodles; stir with a fork. Boil rapidly. uncovered, 10 to 15 minutes, or until noodles are tender. Drain. Set aside.
3. Wash eggplant, pare, and cut into ½-inch-thick slices.
4. Combine eggs and cream.
5. Heat oil in a skillet. Dip eggplant into egg mixture, then into bread crumbs. Put eggplant slices into skillet and brown slowly on both sides.
6. Put a third of the drained noodles into a greased 2-quart casserole. Layer with a third of eggplant slices. Add 1 cup meat sauce. Sprinkle with a third of grated cheese. Repeat layers, ending with eggplant slices. Top with cheese slices. Cover casserole.
7. Bake at 350°F about 20 minutes. Remove cover and bake 10 to 15 minutes, or until cheese is lightly browned. Serve with remaining meat sauce.

About 6 servings

489 *Mushrooms Parmesan (Funghi alla Parmigiana)*

- **1 pound mushrooms with 1- to 2-inch caps**
- **2 tablespoons olive oil**
- **¼ cup chopped onion**
- **½ clove garlic, finely chopped**
- **⅓ cup fine dry bread crumbs**
- **3 tablespoons grated Parmesan cheese**
- **1 tablespoon chopped parsley**
- **½ teaspoon salt**
- **⅛ teaspoon oregano**
- **2 tablespoons olive oil**

1. Clean mushrooms and remove stems. Place caps open-end up in a shallow greased 1½-quart baking dish; set aside. Finely chop mushroom stems.
2. Heat 2 tablespoons olive oil in a skillet. Add mushroom stems, onion, and garlic. Cook slowly until onion and garlic are slightly browned.
3. Combine bread crumbs, cheese, parsley, salt, and oregano. Mix in the onion, garlic, and mushroom stems. Lightly fill mushroom caps with mixture. Pour 2 tablespoons olive oil into the baking dish.
4. Bake at 400°F 15 to 20 minutes, or until mushrooms are tender and tops are browned.

6 to 8 servings

Anchovy-Stuffed Mushrooms: Follow recipe for Mushrooms Parmesan. Omit cheese. Mix in **4 anchovy fillets,** finely chopped.

490 *Stuffed Onions (Cipolle Imbottite)*

6 large onions
2 tablespoons butter
1 cup soft bread crumbs
2 tablespoons olive oil
¼ pound ground beef
2 cups soft bread crumbs
1 egg yolk
2 teaspoons chopped parsley
1 teaspoon salt
¼ teaspoon pepper
¼ teaspoon marjoram
2 tablespoons olive oil
1 tablespoon chopped parsley

1. Cut off root ends of onions; peel, rinse, and cut off a ½-inch slice from top of each.
2. Put onions in boiling salted water to cover in a large saucepan. Cook 10 to 15 minutes, or until onions are slightly tender. Drain well and cool.
3. Meanwhile, heat butter in a skillet. Stir in 1 cup bread crumbs. Turn into a small bowl and set aside.
4. With a sharp knife, cut down around onions, about ¼ inch from edge, leaving about 3 outside layers. With a spoon, scoop out centers and chop them.
5. Heat 2 tablespoons oil in skillet. Add chopped onion and ground beef to heated oil; cook until beef is browned.
6. Combine beef mixture with 2 cups bread crumbs, egg yolk, 2 teaspoons parsley, salt, pepper, and marjoram. Lightly fill onions with mixture.
7. Put filled onions into a greased 2½-quart casserole. Spoon buttered crumbs on top and sprinkle with remaining oil and parsley.
8. Bake at 350°F about 1 hour.

6 servings

491 *Stuffed Peppers (Peperoni Imbottiti)*

4 green peppers
¼ cup olive oil
1 pound ground beef
1⅓ cups cooked rice
2 tablespoons minced onion
1 tablespoon minced parsley
½ teaspoon salt
¼ teaspoon pepper
1½ cups canned tomatoes, sieved
¼ cup water
¼ cup minced celery
1 tablespoon olive oil
½ teaspoon salt
¼ teaspoon pepper
Mozzarella cheese, cut in strips

1. Rinse peppers and cut a thin slice from stem end of each. Remove white fiber and seeds; rinse. Drop peppers into boiling salted water to cover and simmer 5 minutes. Remove peppers from water; invert and set aside to drain.
2. Heat ¼ cup oil in a skillet. Add ground beef and cook until browned. Stir in cooked rice, onion, parsley, ½ teaspoon salt, and ¼ teaspoon pepper. Lightly fill peppers with rice-meat mixture, heaping slightly. Set in a 2-quart baking dish.
3. Mix tomatoes, water, celery, and remaining oil, salt, and pepper; pour around peppers. Put strips of cheese on each pepper.
4. Bake at 350°F about 15 minutes.

4 servings

492 *Baked Tomatoes, Genoa Style*
(Pomodori alla Genovese)

4 firm ripe tomatoes, cut in halves
  and seeded
Sugar
¼ cup olive oil
2 cloves garlic, minced
1½ teaspoons salt
½ teaspoon pepper
1½ teaspoons marjoram, crushed
¼ cup finely snipped parsley
½ cup shredded Parmesan cheese

1. Put tomato halves, cut side up, in a shallow baking dish. Sprinkle lightly with sugar.
2. Mix olive oil, garlic, salt, pepper, and marjoram. Spoon an equal amount onto each tomato half. Sprinkle with parsley and cheese.
3. Bake at 350°F about 20 minutes, or until lightly browned.

4 servings

493 *Deep-Fried Potatoes*

Fat for deep frying heated to
  360°F
2 pounds potatoes (about 6
  medium)
Salt

1. Start heating fat for deep frying.
2. Wash and pare potatoes. Trim off sides and ends to form large blocks. Cut lengthwise into sticks about ⅜ inch wide. Pat dry with absorbent paper.
3. Fry about 1 cup of potatoes at a time in hot fat until potatoes are tender and golden brown. Drain over fat, then put on paper toweling. Sprinkle with salt.
4. Serve hot.

About 4 servings

494 *Zucchini Parmesan (Zucchini alla Parmigiana)*

8 to 10 small zucchini squash
  (about 2½ pounds)
3 tablespoons olive oil
⅔ cup coarsely chopped onion
¼ pound mushrooms, cleaned and
  sliced
⅔ cup grated Parmesan cheese
2 cans (6 ounces each) tomato
  paste
1 clove garlic, minced
1 teaspoon salt
⅛ teaspoon pepper

1. Wash and trim off ends of zucchini; cut crosswise into ⅛-inch-thick slices.
2. Heat olive oil in a large saucepan; add zucchini, onion, and mushrooms. Cover saucepan and cook vegetables over low heat 10 to 15 minutes, or until tender, stirring occasionally.
3. Remove vegetable mixture from heat; stir in about half the cheese. Combine tomato paste, garlic, salt, and pepper; pour into vegetable mixture, blending lightly but thoroughly. Turn mixture into a 2-quart casserole. Sprinkle with remaining cheese.
4. Bake at 350°F 20 to 30 minutes.

About 8 servings

495 *Zucchini in Salsa Verde*

Fat for deep frying
¼ cup olive oil
2 tablespoons wine vinegar
2 tablespoons minced parsley
1 clove garlic, crushed in a garlic press or minced
2 anchovy fillets, finely chopped
Few grains black pepper
4 zucchini squash, washed and thinly sliced
Flour
Salt

1. Start heating the fat to 365°F.
2. Meanwhile, blend oil, vinegar, parsley, garlic, anchovies, and pepper in a small bowl and set mixture aside.
3. Coat zucchini slices slightly with flour. Fry in hot fat, turning frequently, until lightly browned (2 to 3 minutes). Remove from fat and drain. Sprinkle lightly with salt.
4. Put zucchini into a bowl; pour the sauce over it and toss lightly to coat well. Cover and set aside at least an hour before serving.

4 servings

496 *Zucchini Romano*

8 small zucchini (about 1½ pounds)
1 egg, fork beaten
½ cup shredded mozzarella cheese
3 tablespoons bottled Italian salad dressing
1/16 teaspoon black pepper
2 tablespoons melted butter or margarine
½ pound ground ham or veal
● ½ cup Quick Italian Tomato Sauce

1. Wash zucchini and trim ends. Slice off a narrow lengthwise strip. Using an apple corer, remove seeds to make a hollow about ¾ inch deep in each zucchini. Cover with boiling water, simmer about 5 minutes, and drain well.
2. Meanwhile, combine egg, cheese, dressing, pepper, and butter in a bowl. (If using veal, add ¼ teaspoon salt.) Lightly mix in meat. Fill zucchini with meat mixture, using about 3 tablespoons in each hollow.
3. Arrange zucchini, stuffed side up, in a single layer in an oiled shallow 1½-quart baking dish; spread tops with sauce. (Or omit sauce and brush tops with olive oil.)
4. Bake at 375°F about 15 minutes, or until meat is cooked. Serve hot.

8 servings

497 *Basic Mexican Beans*

1 pound dried pinto, pink, black, or red kidney beans
1 cup chopped onion
Water
Salt to taste

1. Wash beans well and put into a large saucepan. Add onion, then add enough water to cover beans completely. Cover, bring water to boiling, reduce heat, and simmer until beans are tender, about 3 hours. Add more water if needed, but add it gradually so water continues to boil.
2. When beans are tender, add salt to taste.
3. Use in recipes calling for cooked beans.

About 5 to 6 cups cooked beans

Soupy Beans: Beans prepared as above are sometimes served in soup bowls without further preparation, or with a sprinkling of grated cheese and chopped green onion.

498 *Refried Beans* (*Frijoles Refritos*)

- 2 to 3 cups cooked beans (see Basic Mexican Beans ; or use canned kidney beans)
- ½ cup lard or bacon drippings
- 1 cup chopped onion
- 1 clove garlic, minced
- ½ cup cooked tomatoes or tomato sauce
- 1 teaspoon chili powder
  Salt and pepper

1. Mash beans with a potato masher with half of the lard or bacon drippings (drippings make the best-flavored beans).
2. Heat remaining lard or drippings in skillet. Add onion and garlic and cook until onion is soft, about 5 minutes. Add mashed beans and continue cooking until all fat is absorbed by beans, stirring constantly to prevent sticking. Stir in tomatoes, chili powder, and salt and pepper to taste.

3 to 4 cups beans

499 *Hot Bean Dip*

- ¼ cup lard or bacon drippings
- 1 to 3 canned jalapeño chilies, chopped
- 1 cup refried beans (see above; or use canned)
- ½ cup tomato sauce

1. Heat lard in a small skillet or saucepan. Add chopped chilies and fry in hot fat about 5 minutes. Add beans and tomato sauce and stir until well blended.
2. Transfer dip to a small chafing-dish-type server and keep hot during serving. Serve with **tostada chip "dippers."**

About 1½ cups dip

500 *Chili con Queso*

- 2 tablespoons butter or margarine
- ½ cup finely chopped onion
- 1 cup chopped peeled fresh tomatoes
- 1 cup chopped peeled fresh green California chilies or canned peeled green chilies
- 1 package (8 ounces) cream cheese
- ¾ cup whipping cream
  Salt and pepper
  Crisp tortilla chips

1. Melt butter in a large skillet. Add onion and cook about 5 minutes, or until soft. Add tomatoes and chilies and cook about 10 minutes, stirring occasionally.
2. Cut cheese into chunks and stir into skillet mixture. When cheese melts, stir in cream. Add salt and pepper to taste.
3. Serve hot over toasted tortilla chips, or keep warm in chafing dish and serve as a dip with tortilla chips.

About 2½ cups dip

Variation: Substitute 1 or 2 chopped jalapeño chilies for the California green chilies and 8 ounces shredded sharp Cheddar cheese for the cream cheese.

501 *Red Chili Sauce*

- 4 fresh or dried ancho chilies
- 1 cup canned tomatoes with juice
- 1 cup chopped onion
- 1 clove garlic
- 1 teaspoon oregano
- ¼ teaspoon cumin (comino)
- ¼ cup olive oil
  Salt and pepper
- 1 tablespoon vinegar
  Few drops Tabasco

1. Prepare the chilies (see this page). Put prepared chilies, tomatoes, onion, garlic, oregano, and cumin into an electric blender and blend to a purée.
2. Heat oil in a skillet. Add puréed sauce and cook about 10 minutes. Stir in salt and pepper to taste, then vinegar and Tabasco to taste. Cool before serving.

About 2 cups sauce

502 *Green Chili Sauce*

1 cup chopped canned peeled green
    chilies
1 cup canned Mexican green
    tomatoes (tomatillos)
¼ cup chopped fresh parsley
¼ cup chopped onion
1 clove garlic
1 canned jalapeño chili, chopped
    Salt and pepper
¼ cup olive oil

1. Put green chilies, green tomatoes, parsley, onion, garlic, and jalapeño chili into an electric blender. Blend to a purée. Add salt and pepper to taste.
2. Heat oil in skillet. Add puréed sauce and cook about 5 minutes, stirring constantly. Cool before serving.

About 2 cups sauce

503 *Chilies Rellenos*

6 fresh or canned California green
    chilies (see Note) or 6 green
    bell peppers
● 2 cups Picadillo or ½
    pound Monterey Jack or mild
    Cheddar cheese
2 eggs, separated
    Flour
    Oil for frying
Sauce:
1 cup chopped onion
1 clove garlic, minced
2 cups canned tomato sauce
1 tablespoon oil
1 cup chicken stock, or water plus
    1 chicken bouillon cube
    Salt and pepper

1. Make a slit in the side of each chili and with a spoon carefully remove seeds and pith, leaving stems intact. (If using peppers, cut around stem with a sharp knife, leaving attached at one side, if possible; slit side. Remove seeds and pith.)
2. Fill chilies with desired filling.
3. Beat egg whites until stiff, not dry, peaks form; beat egg yolks until thick and lemon colored. Fold whites into yolks. Dust chilies with flour, then dip into beaten egg to coat on all sides.
4. Heat oil (about 1-inch depth) in a heavy skillet or large heavy saucepan to about 350°F. Fry stuffed chilies in hot oil, turning to brown on all sides. Stems may be used as "handles" to help turn the chilies.
5. Drain on absorbent paper and set aside while preparing sauce.
6. For sauce, put onion, garlic, and tomato sauce into an electric blender. Blend until liquefied.
7. Heat 1 tablespoon oil in skillet. Cook sauce in oil about 5 minutes. Stir in chicken stock. Season to taste with salt and pepper.
8. Place fried stuffed chilies in sauce and cook a few minutes until they reach serving temperature.

6 servings

Note: If chilies are very hot, they may be soaked in a solution of 1 quart water, 1 tablespoon salt, and 1 tablespoon vinegar for an hour before using.

504 *Stuffed Peppers with Nogada Sauce*
(Chilies Rellenos en Nogada)

6 medium green peppers
3 tablespoons lard
2 cloves garlic, minced
¼ cup chopped onion
1 pound lean ground pork
½ pound ham with fat, ground
2 cups chopped ripe tomatoes
2 tablespoons snipped parsley
3 tablespoons cider vinegar
½ teaspoon vanilla extract
2 tablespoons sugar
4 whole cloves, crushed
5 peppercorns, crushed
¼ teaspoon nutmeg
⅛ teaspoon powdered saffron
¼ cup finely chopped almonds
¼ cup dark seedless raisins
1 teaspoon chopped capers
2 tablespoons chopped candied
    lemon peel
¼ cup pitted chopped green olives
Nogada Sauce (see below)
Flour
2 eggs, beaten
Lard for deep frying, heated to
    365°F (see Note)
Pomegranate seeds

1. Cut out stems of peppers; remove seeds and membrane. Place peppers in a large saucepan; cover with boiling water, bring to boiling, and cook about 2 minutes. Drain and invert peppers on absorbent paper.
2. Heat 3 tablespoons lard in a heavy skillet; add garlic, onion, and meat. Cook until meat is browned, stirring occasionally.
3. Meanwhile, mix tomatoes, parsley, vinegar, vanilla extract, sugar, and spices.
4. Add tomato mixture to meat along with almonds, raisins, capers, lemon peel, and olives; stir. Cook over low heat, stirring frequently, until mixture is almost dry (30 to 40 minutes).
5. Meanwhile, prepare Nogada Sauce.
6. Spoon filling into peppers, packing lightly so mixture will remain in cavities during frying.
7. Roll peppers in flour, coating entire surface. Dip in beaten eggs.
8. Fry peppers in hot deep fat until coating is golden. Remove peppers with a slotted spoon and drain on absorbent paper.
9. Arrange stuffed peppers on a serving plate and top with Nogada Sauce. Sprinkle with pomegranate seeds.

6 servings

Note: If desired, use 2 inches of fat in a deep skillet, heat to 365°F, and fry peppers, turning to brown evenly.

505 *Nogada Sauce*

1 cup walnuts, ground
½ clove garlic, ground
5 peppercorns, crushed
¼ cup fine dry bread crumbs
2 tablespoons sugar
½ teaspoon salt
2 tablespoons cider vinegar
6 to 8 tablespoons water

Mix walnuts, garlic, peppercorns, crumbs, sugar, and salt. Add to vinegar, then stir in enough water to make a very thick sauce. Let stand 30 minutes.

506 *Garbanzos with Condiments*

¼ pound bulk pork sausage
½ cup chopped onion
1 clove garlic, minced
1 teaspoon chili powder
2 cups (16-ounce can) cooked
    garbanzos, drained and rinsed
1 can (4 ounces) pimentos, drained
    and cut in strips
    Salt
¼ teaspoon oregano
⅛ teaspoon pepper

1. Brown sausage in skillet, crumbling and stirring as it cooks. Add onion, garlic, and chili powder and cook until onion is soft. Add garbanzos and pimentos and stir to mix well. Bring to simmering. Season to taste with salt; add oregano and pepper.
2. Serve as an accompaniment to meat.

4 to 6 servings

507 *Cauliflower Tortas*

1 head cauliflower
2 eggs, separated
2 tablespoons flour
1 teaspoon salt
    Dash pepper
    Oil or shortening for deep frying
    heated to 375°F

1. Rinse cauliflower, remove outer leaves, and separate into cauliflowerets. Cook in boiling salted water until almost tender (about 8 to 10 minutes). Drain.
2. Beat egg whites until they form rounded peaks. Beat egg yolks until smooth. Pour yolks into whites gradually, beating lightly with fork to combine.
3. In separate small bowl combine flour, salt, and pepper. Roll cooked cauliflowerets, a few at a time, in flour, then dip in eggs, coating well.
4. Fry in heated fat until golden brown, turning to brown on all sides. Serve very hot.

8 to 10 servings

508 *Lima Beans Mexicana*

2 packages (10 ounces each) frozen
    green lima beans
2 tablespoons butter or margarine
½ cup chopped onion
1 clove garlic, minced
1 cup canned tomatoes
1 jalapeño chili, chopped
    Salt and pepper
1 hard-cooked egg, chopped

1. Cook beans until tender, following package directions.
2. Meanwhile, heat butter in a small skillet. Add onion and garlic and cook about 5 minutes, until onion is soft. Stir in tomatoes and chili. Season to taste with salt and pepper.
3. Drain beans. Pour tomato sauce over beans and stir gently until evenly mixed. Turn into a serving dish and garnish with chopped hard-cooked egg.

6 servings

509 *Corn-Chili Casserole*

1 can (17 ounces) cream style corn
1 can (4 ounces) chopped green
    chilies (undrained)
2 eggs, beaten
2 tablespoons flour
1 teaspoon sugar
½ teaspoon salt
⅛ teaspoon oregano
1 tablespoon butter

1. Mix corn, chilies, and eggs. Blend flour, sugar, salt, and oregano; stir into corn mixture. Turn into a greased 1-quart casserole. Dot with butter.
2. Bake at 350°F 55 to 60 minutes, or until set.

About 6 servings

510 *Chili-Hominy Casserole*

2 cans (15 ounces each) whole hominy, drained and rinsed
1 can (4 ounces) green chilies, drained (discard seeds) and finely chopped
1 tablespoon butter
1½ cups dairy sour cream
Salt and pepper
1 cup shredded Monterey Jack or mild Cheddar cheese

1. Layer half of hominy and the chopped chilies in a well-buttered 1½-quart baking dish. Dot with butter and spread with half of sour cream. Add a layer of remaining hominy, cover with remaining sour cream, and sprinkle with salt and pepper to taste. Top with cheese.
2. Bake at 350°F about 25 minutes, or just until thoroughly heated.

About 6 servings

511 *Hominy and Bacon*

½ pound sliced bacon
1 green pepper, chopped
1 small onion, chopped
1 can (16 ounces) tomatoes (undrained)
1 tablespoon sugar
1 teaspoon salt
2 cans (15 ounces each) whole hominy, drained

1. Fry bacon in a skillet until lightly browned; drain. Reserve 2 tablespoons drippings in skillet. Mix in green pepper and onion; cook until tender. Add tomatoes with liquid, sugar, and salt; simmer 10 minutes.
2. Turn hominy into a greased shallow baking dish; crumble bacon over top and mix with hominy. Pour tomato mixture over all.
3. Bake at 325°F about 45 minutes.

6 to 8 servings

512 *Hominy in Tomato Sauce*

1 can (15 ounces) whole hominy, drained
1 can (16 ounces) tomatoes
1 tablespoon chili powder
½ teaspoon salt
1 medium onion, chopped
8 ounces sharp Cheddar cheese, shredded

1. Combine hominy and tomatoes in a saucepan. Cook, stirring occasionally, until thickened (about 15 minutes). Stir in chili powder, salt, and onion.
2. Layer hominy and cheese in a shallow 1½-quart baking dish, ending with cheese.
3. Bake at 350°F about 20 minutes.

About 6 servings

513 *Green Chili Cornbread I*

1 cup yellow cornmeal
2 teaspoons baking powder
½ teaspoon salt
2 eggs
¼ cup vegetable oil
1 can (4 ounces) green chilies, drained, seeded, and finely chopped
1 can (8 ounces) cream style corn
½ cup dairy sour cream
2 cups shredded mild Cheddar cheese

1. Mix cornmeal, baking powder, and salt; set aside.
2. Beat eggs with oil until blended. Add chilies, corn, sour cream, cornmeal mixture, and 1½ cups cheese; mix well.
3. Turn into a greased 9-inch round pan. Sprinkle with remaining cheese.
4. Bake at 350°F 45 minutes, or until lightly browned.
5. Serve warm with butter, if desired.

6 to 8 servings

514 *Green Chili Cornbread II*

1½ cups cornmeal
1½ tablespoons flour
1 tablespoon salt
½ teaspoon baking soda
1 cup buttermilk
⅔ cup vegetable oil
2 eggs, beaten
1 can (8 ounces) cream style corn
1 can (about 4 ounces) chopped green chilies, drained
4 green onions, chopped
1½ cups shredded Monterey Jack

1. Mix cornmeal, flour, salt, and baking soda in a bowl. Add buttermilk, oil, eggs, and corn; mix well. Stir in chilies and onions.
2. Grease a 13×9-inch baking dish with **bacon fat;** heat in oven.
3. Pour half of batter into heated pan and sprinkle with half of cheese; repeat, using remaining batter and cheese.
4. Bake at 375°F about 35 minutes.
5. Cut into squares and serve warm.

8 to 12 servings

515 *Cornbread Pie*

1 cup soft butter or margarine
1 cup sugar
4 eggs
2 cups (17-ounce can) cream style corn
1 cup shredded Monterey Jack
1 can (4 ounces) green chilies, drained, seeded, and chopped
1 cup yellow or white cornmeal
1 cup sifted all-purpose flour
4 teaspoons baking powder
½ teaspoon salt

1. Cream butter and sugar until light and fluffy. Beat in eggs, one at a time. Stir in corn, cheese, chilies, and cornmeal.
2. Sift flour, baking powder, and salt together and stir into batter.
3. Pour into greased 13×9-inch baking pan or two 9-inch pie pans.
4. Bake at 300°F 60 to 70 minutes, or until a wooden pick inserted in center comes out clean.
5. To serve, cut while still hot into squares or wedges. Serve with butter, if desired.

6 to 8 servings

516 *Mexican Eggplant*

1 eggplant (¾ to 1 pound)
2 cloves garlic
1 large green pepper
1 can (4 ounces) hot green chilies, drained and seeded
2 tablespoons olive oil
1 can (6 ounces) tomato paste
⅔ cup water
1 teaspoon salt
⅛ teaspoon pepper
2 eggs
¼ cup olive oil
1 cup shredded Monterey Jack or mild Cheddar cheese

1. Pare eggplant and cut into ¼-inch slices; set aside.
2. Finely chop garlic, pepper, and chilies. Sauté in olive oil until soft. Add tomato paste, water, and salt and pepper to taste. Simmer, stirring occasionally, until sauce is thickened.
3. Beat eggs and coat eggplant slices with egg.
4. Heat olive oil in a large skillet, add eggplant, and quickly brown on both sides.
5. Put browned eggplant into a shallow baking dish, cover with sauce, and sprinkle with cheese.
6. Bake at 350°F about 30 minutes, or until eggplant is tender and cheese is lightly browned.

About 6 servings

517 *Greens with Chilies*

3 fresh or dried ancho chilies
1½ pounds fresh greens (spinach, kale, collard greens, mustard greens, Swiss chard, etc.)
2 tablespoons butter or margarine
½ cup chopped onion
1 clove garlic, minced
Salt and pepper

1. Prepare chilies and chop them.
2. Wash greens well. Cook in small amount of boiling salted water until tender. Drain and chop. Return to saucepan.
3. Melt butter in a small skillet. Add chilies, onion, and garlic and cook until onion is soft, about 5 minutes. Stir chili mixture into chopped greens. Season to taste with salt and pepper. Heat thoroughly.

6 servings

518 *Peas with Condiments*

2 packages (10 ounces each) frozen green peas
2 tablespoons butter or margarine
½ cup chopped onion
3 canned pimentos, cut in 1-inch strips
Salt and pepper

1. Cook peas until tender, following package directions.
2. Meanwhile, heat butter in a small skillet. Add onion and cook about 5 minutes, or until onion is soft. Stir in pimento.
3. Drain peas. Stir onion and pimento into peas. Season to taste with salt and pepper.

6 servings

519 *Aztec Patties*

This unique use for leftover mashed potatoes is a well-known Mexican side dish. If you live in an area where fresh masa is available, use that in place of the dehydrated masa flour and water.

1 cup dehydrated masa flour (masa harina)
¾ cup warm water
1½ cups mashed potatoes
Salt (about 1 teaspoon)
½ cup shredded Monterey Jack
1 egg, beaten
Lard or oil

1. Mix masa flour with warm water until dough can be formed into a soft ball. Combine with mashed potatoes and mix well. Stir in salt to taste, then add cheese and beaten egg. Form into patties about ¾ inch thick.
2. Fry patties in hot lard in a skillet.
3. Serve as an accompaniment to meat.

6 to 8 servings

520 *Squash and Corn Dish*

2 tablespoons oil
⅓ cup chopped onion
1 small clove garlic, minced
2 pounds summer squash, pared and cubed
1 cup whole kernel corn, drained
1 large fresh tomato, peeled and cubed
1 jalapeño chili, finely chopped
1 teaspoon salt
¼ teaspoon pepper
½ cup milk
Grated Parmesan cheese

1. Heat oil in a skillet that can be transferred to oven. Add onion and garlic and cook until soft (about 5 minutes). Add squash, corn, tomato, chili, salt, and pepper and cook over low heat about 10 minutes, stirring occasionally. If skillet cannot be put into oven, transfer mixture to an ovenproof dish; pour milk over top.
2. Bake at 350°F about 30 minutes.
3. Remove from oven and sprinkle with Parmesan cheese.

About 8 servings

521 *Spinach with Tomato*

2 packages (10 ounces each) fresh
    spinach
3 slices bacon
2 tablespoons bacon fat
½ cup chopped onion
1 cup chopped fresh tomato
¾ teaspoon salt
⅛ teaspoon pepper

1. Wash spinach thoroughly. Put spinach with water that clings to leaves into a large saucepan. Cook rapidly about 5 minutes, or until tender. Drain.
2. Meanwhile, fry bacon until crisp in a large skillet. Drain bacon, crumble, and set aside. Add onion to 2 tablespoons bacon fat in skillet and cook until soft. Add tomato, spinach, salt, and pepper. Heat thoroughly.
3. Garnish with sliced hard-cooked egg, if desired.

About 6 servings

522 *Green Tomatoes and Zucchini*

2 tablespoons butter
1 large onion, chopped
¾ cup chopped canned Mexican
    green tomatoes (tomatillos)
3 medium zucchini, thinly sliced
½ teaspoon oregano
½ teaspoon salt
1 tablespoon water
¼ cup grated Parmesan cheese

1. Heat butter in a large skillet. Add onion and cook until soft. Add green tomatoes, zucchini, oregano, salt, and water; stir. Cover; bring to boiling, reduce heat, and cook until zucchini is crisp-tender (5 to 7 minutes).
2. Stir in cheese just before serving.

6 to 8 servings

523 *Baked Zucchini*

2 pounds zucchini
1 cup shredded mild Cheddar
    cheese
½ cup cottage cheese
4 eggs, beaten
¾ cup dry bread crumbs
3 tablespoons chopped parsley
1½ teaspoons salt
½ teaspoon pepper
3 tablespoons butter

1. Wash zucchini and slice crosswise into ¼-inch slices. (It is not necessary to peel zucchini, unless skin seems very tough.)
2. Combine cheeses, eggs, bread crumbs, parsley, salt, and pepper until evenly mixed. Layer into baking dish, alternating zucchini with sauce. Dot top with butter.
3. Bake at 375°F about 45 minutes, or until slightly set.

6 to 8 servings

524 Artichokes à la Four Thieves

8 artichokes
Boiling salted water
● Four Thieves Sauce

1. Wash artichokes under running water. Let them stand 10 minutes in cold salted water; drain.
2. With a sharp kitchen knife, remove stem and bottom leaves from each artichoke, and with kitchen shears snip ¼ inch off the top of each leaf.
3. Cook the artichokes uncovered in a pot of boiling salted water 30 minutes; drain and cool.
4. To serve, gently spread artichoke leaves to the sides and, with a grapefruit knife, remove the very small purplish leaves and the choke that covers the bottom, scraping it clean. Accompany with hot Four Thieves Sauce.

8 servings

525 Braised Lettuce

8 small heads Boston lettuce or
  16 heads Bibb lettuce
1 cup chicken broth
Juice of 1 lime
6 tablespoons butter
Salt and freshly ground pepper
  to taste

1. Rinse lettuce under running cold water; tie each head firmly with string.
2. Put lettuce into a skillet with broth, lime juice, butter, salt, and pepper. Bring to a boil, then cover, reduce heat, and simmer 15 minutes.
3. Remove cover, increase heat, and boil rapidly until no liquid remains and edges of lettuce are golden. Remove the string. Serve with roasts.

526 Barbecued Sweet Peppers

4 red sweet peppers
4 green sweet peppers
Peanut oil
French dressing

1. Core the peppers and cut each into three strips.
2. Coat both sides of pepper strips with oil; let them stand 40 minutes.
3. Brush pepper strips lightly with oil and place in a hinged grill. Barbecue 2 inches from ash-covered coals, allowing peppers to blister.
4. Chill and serve with French dressing as an antipasto or with other marinated vegetables.

527 Cooked Hearts of Palm

To obtain this vegetable a full-grown palm tree has to be felled. It is, therefore, understandable that heart of palm is expensive. It looks like a chunk of ivory and is rarely found in the market stalls.

½ cup cubed salt pork
2 cups cubed heart of palm
1 cup chicken broth

1. Render salt pork in a Dutch oven. Add heart of palm and broth; simmer covered over medium heat until no liquid remains and heart of palm is tender.
2. Serve hot with Béchamel Sauce (●) or cold with **French dressing**.

528 *Raw Heart of Palm Salad*

1 pound heart of palm
Mayonnaise or French dressing

1. Slice the heart of palm paper thin. Soak it 1 hour in cold water. Drain well on absorbent paper.
2. Serve heart of palm with mayonnaise or in a tossed green salad with French dressing.

529 *Smothered Cabbage (Chou Touffe)*

2 small heads cabbage
2 tablespoons peanut oil
1 onion, minced
1 garlic clove, crushed in a
    garlic press
8 bacon slices
½ cup stock
    Freshly ground pepper to taste
3 drops Tabasco
1 tablespoon butter
1 tablespoon cornstarch
1 teaspoon tomato paste
1 teaspoon lime juice
    Lime wedges

1. Remove wilted leaves from cabbage. Quarter and core cabbage.
2. Heat oil in a top-of-range casserole, add onion and garlic and sauté until golden. Add cabbage pieces and lay a bacon slice on each. Add stock, pepper, and Tabasco. Bring to a boil, reduce heat, and simmer covered 15 minutes; cabbage will still be a little crisp.
3. Meanwhile, mix butter and cornstarch.
4. Transfer cabbage to a heated platter. Mix tomato paste and lime juice into cooking liquid and bring rapidly to a boil, then add butter-cornstarch mixture and stir until liquid is slightly thicker.
5. To serve, pour sauce over cabbage. Accompany with lime wedges.

8 servings

530 *Fried Okra Pods*

2 pounds large okra pods, washed
    and stems trimmed
    Salt, pepper, and cayenne or
    red pepper to taste
1 egg yolk
1 tablespoon olive oil
1 cup dried bread crumbs
    Oil for deep frying,
    heated to 365°F
    Watercress and wedges of avocado
    and tomato for garnish

1. Cook okra in lightly salted boiling water 7 minutes. Drain and season.
2. Roll them in egg yolk beaten with oil, then in bread crumbs.
3. Fry the pods in heated oil until golden and drain on absorbent paper.
4. Serve surrounded with watercress, avocado, and tomato.

531 *Sweet Potato Soufflé*

2 cups hot mashed sweet potatoes
⅓ cup hot milk
⅓ cup amber rum
¼ cup butter
⅛ teaspoon nutmeg
    Dash Tabasco
1 teaspoon grated lime peel
4 egg yolks, beaten
5 egg whites, stiffly beaten

1. Beat sweet potatoes, milk, rum, and butter together until smooth. Add nutmeg, Tabasco, lime peel, and beaten egg yolk; beat well. Fold in beaten egg white.
2. Pour into a well-greased 1½-quart soufflé dish. Set in pan of hot water.
3. Bake at 425°F 25 to 30 minutes. Serve at once.

532 *Ratatouille of Pumpkin*

1 cup diced salt pork
4 slices ham or Canadian bacon
3 scallions or green onions including green tops, cut in pieces
3 garlic cloves
5 parsley sprigs
6 dried Italian pepper pods or ½ green hot pepper
2½ pounds pumpkin meat, pared and cubed
2 cups stock or chicken broth
3 tablespoons butter
¼ cup chopped parsley

1. Sauté salt pork and ham in a Dutch oven until brown.
2. In a mortar, pound together to a paste the scallions, garlic, parsley, and pepper pods.
3. Add pumpkin, seasoning paste, and stock to Dutch oven. Cover and simmer until pumpkin is tender enough to mash with a fork.
4. Remove cover and, stirring constantly, cook off most of the liquid, being careful that pumpkin does not stick. Add butter and stir until melted.
5. Serve sprinkled with parsley.

533 *Smothered Mixed Vegetables (Touffé)*

8 small carrots, sliced
8 small potatoes
4 medium white turnips, pared and sliced
4 medium tomatoes, peeled, seeded, and quartered
2 small chayote or zucchini, sliced
1 green and 1 red sweet pepper, cut in strips
1 small eggplant (unpeeled), diced
Cauliflower chunks
½ cup green peas
½ cup lima beans
2 tablespoons peanut oil
1 large Spanish onion, sliced
1 cup stock or beef broth
¼ cup peanut oil
1 tablespoon salt
Freshly ground pepper
1 garlic clove, crushed in a garlic press
4 dried Italian pepper pods or 1 pink hot pepper
1 tablespoon tomato paste

1. Arrange in a top-of-range casserole with lid the sliced carrot, potatoes, turnip slices, tomato quarters, sliced chayote, pepper strips, diced eggplant, cauliflower chunks, peas, and beans.
2. Heat 2 tablespoons oil in a skillet over medium heat. Add onion and sauté until golden. Add stock, ¼ cup oil, salt, pepper, and garlic; pour over vegetables in casserole. Lay pepper pods over vegetables; cover and cook covered over low heat 45 minutes.
3. Remove cover, increase heat, and cook off most of the liquid. Remove peppers and stir tomato paste into vegetable mixture. Serve with **pepper steak** or well-browned **spareribs** or **pork chops**.

534 *Yams and Sweet Potatoes*

Yams or sweet potatoes
Salt
Butter (optional)

Boil yams and serve plain sprinkled with salt and, if desired, topped with butter. Or barbecue yams on a grill 4 inches from ash-covered coals, turning frequently, until soft. Or bake yams until tender.

535 *Stuffed Sweet Peppers*

4 red or green sweet peppers,
    halved lengthwise
Stock
1 cup cooked rice
2 cups cooked ground beef, ham,
    or poultry
Shredded cheese
● Tomato Sauce Creole

1. Parboil pepper halves in stock to cover. Drain peppers and reserve stock.
2. Mix rice and meat; stuff peppers. Sprinkle tops with cheese. Arrange peppers in a baking dish; add reserved stock to dish.
3. Bake at 350°F 30 minutes, or until well browned. Serve in the baking dish and accompany with the sauce.

4 servings

536 *Cornmeal*

1 cup ground cornmeal
3 cups water
4 dried Italian pepper pods or
    1 piece hot pepper
3 garlic cloves
1 parsley sprig
1 tablespoon coarse salt
¼ cup peanut oil
1 medium onion, chopped
¼ cup unsalted butter
● Bean Sauce

1. Stir cornmeal into water and let stand 5 minutes.
2. Meanwhile, in a mortar, pound together to a paste the pepper pods, garlic, parsley, and salt.
3. Heat oil in a Dutch oven over medium heat, add onion, and sauté until translucent but not brown. Add the seasoning paste and the cornmeal with water; mix well. Bring to a boil, reduce heat, and simmer covered 30 minutes. Remove cover, add butter, and fluff the cornmeal. Serve with Bean Sauce.

Cornmeal with Beans: Drain **1 large can Puerto Rican red or black beans**, reserving liquid. Add enough **stock** to liquid to make 3 cups. Follow recipe for Cornmeal, substituting bean liquid for water. Add the beans when you fluff the cornmeal.

Cornmeal with Kippers: Follow recipe for Cornmeal. Add desired amount of **flaked canned fillet of kippered herring** when you fluff the cornmeal.

Fried Cornmeal: Follow recipe for Cornmeal or Cornmeal with Beans. Spread 4 cups cornmeal mixture in a rectangular dish; refrigerate overnight. Cut chilled mixture into finger-size strips. Heat **3 tablespoons butter** and **3 tablespoons peanut oil** in a skillet and fry cornmeal over medium heat until golden and crisp.

537 *French-Fried Breadfruit*

1 large heavy breadfruit
Oil for deep frying,
    heated to 365°F
Salt to taste

1. Cut the breadfruit into wedges about 1½ inches thick; discard the center. Soak the wedges in lightly salted water 30 minutes. Dry with absorbent paper.
2. Fry breadfruit wedges, a few at a time, in heated oil until golden (about 8 minutes). Drain on absorbent paper. Salt lightly and serve very hot where you would serve French-fried potatoes.

Rice and Beans

2 quarts water
2 cups dried red beans, rinsed
1 can (13¾ ounces) beef broth
   Water
1 tablespoon salt
8 parsley sprigs
3 scallions or green onions, chopped
3 garlic cloves
¼ teaspoon dried rosemary
3 tablespoons peanut oil
2 cups rice

1. Bring water to boiling. Add red beans and cook covered for 1½ hours.
2. Drain beans, reserving liquid, and set aside. Add beef broth and enough water to bean liquid to equal 4¾ cups liquid. Set aside.
3. In a mortar, pound together to form a paste the salt, parsley, scallions, garlic, and rosemary.
4. Heat oil and seasoning paste in a Dutch oven over medium heat. Put rice in Dutch oven and stir until well coated with oil. Add reserved liquid and bring to a boil, stirring. Add beans and again bring to a boil. Reduce heat, cover, and cook undisturbed for 20 minutes.
5. Remove cover, stir, and cook about 5 minutes longer, or until no liquid remains.

8 to 10 servings

Caribbean Rice

4 parsley sprigs
3 peppercorns
2 garlic cloves
2 scallions or green onions,
   cut in pieces
1½ teaspoons salt
½ teaspoon thyme
2 tablespoons peanut oil
2 cups rice
4½ cups chicken broth
1 bay leaf
1 green hot pepper or
   ½ teaspoon cayenne or
   red pepper

1. In a mortar, pound parsley, peppercorns, garlic, scallions, salt, and thyme to a paste. Set aside.
2. Heat oil in a large, heavy saucepan; add rice. Stir until all the rice is coated with oil and turns chalky.
3. Add seasoning paste and chicken broth; bring to a boil. Reduce heat and add bay leaf and pepper. Cover saucepan and cook undisturbed for 20 minutes.
4. Remove the cover; continue to cook over low heat for 5 minutes, or until no liquid remains.
5. Discard bay leaf and whole pepper. Fluff rice and serve.

8 servings

Rice and Avocado: Follow recipe for Caribbean Rice. Place **cubed avocado** on top of the rice for the last 5 minutes of cooking. Mix in avocado when rice is fluffed. Serve with Bean Sauce (page 65).

Coconut and Rice: Follow recipe for Caribbean Rice, using **brown rice** and an additional ½ **cup chicken broth**. Add **1 cup freshly grated coconut** along with bay leaf and pepper. Proceed as directed.

Saffron Rice: Steep ½ **teaspoon Spanish saffron** in 2¼ **cups boiling water** until it turns bright orange. Strain. Follow recipe for Caribbean Rice, using saffron water in place of some of the chicken broth to cook the rice.

Meat

538 *Roast Beef with Wine* (Roz Bif)

1 beef rolled rump roast (5 pounds or more)
Salt and pepper
2 garlic cloves, crushed in a garlic press
1 tablespoon oregano
2 tablespoons grated kefalotyri cheese
Chicken stock (about ¾ cup)
1 medium onion, quartered
½ cup red wine
1 package macaroni, cooked according to directions on package
1 cup grated kefalotyri cheese

1. Sprinkle beef roast with salt and generously cover with pepper. Slit the meat with a small sharp knife in several places on a diagonal slant about 1 inch deep.
2. Mix garlic, oregano, and 2 tablespoons cheese. Fill each incision with some of this mixture. Pinch to close incision.
3. Place beef on a trivet in a roasting pan. Pour enough stock into the pan to barely reach top of trivet. Add the quartered onion.
4. Roast at 325°F until done to taste. (A meat thermometer will register 140°F for rare, 160°F for medium, and 170°F for well-done meat.)
5. During the last 15 minutes of roasting, pour in wine.
6. Remove meat to a platter. Keep warm. Remove fat from pan juices. Toss in cooked pasta. Sprinkle with remaining cheese. Serve hot.

About 8 servings

539 *Meatballs with Lemon Sauce* (Youverlakia Avgolemono)

2 pounds lean beef, ground
1 large onion, minced
3 tablespoons minced parsley
2 tablespoons mint leaves
½ cup long-grain rice
Salt and pepper to taste
1 garlic clove, crushed in a garlic press
½ cup flour
2 cups water
Salt to taste
2 tablespoons butter
Juice of 1 or 2 lemons
2 eggs, separated

1. Mix thoroughly meat, onion, parsley, mint, rice, salt, pepper, and garlic. Dip hands in flour. Shape meat into round balls about 1 inch in diameter.
2. Bring water and salt to boiling in a large Dutch oven. Add butter and meatballs in a single layer. Simmer covered 40 minutes.
3. Pour stock into a small bowl and add lemon juice. Beat egg yolks until frothy. In another bowl, beat whites until peaks form. Fold in yolks. In a thin stream, pour stock into eggs. Pour over meatballs. Serve hot.

6 servings

540 *Tournedos*

6 slices beef loin tenderloin steak
(1½ inches thick)
Salt and pepper to taste
½ cup butter
¼ cup flour
¾ cup dry white wine
½ cup chopped parsley
Juice of 1 lemon

1. Season meat with salt and pepper on both sides.
2. Melt butter in a heavy skillet. Add meat and brown quickly on each side. Remove to a dish.
3. Using a whisk, stir flour into pan juices. Cook, stirring constantly, over low heat for 2 minutes.
4. Stir in wine and cover. Simmer 5 minutes.
5. Add meat, parsley, and lemon juice. Simmer 5 minutes.

6 servings

541 *Braised Beef Corfu Style (Soffrito)*

3 cups all-purpose flour
Salt and pepper to taste
1 teaspoon paprika
Olive oil for frying
4 pounds beef round top round,
cut in slices ¼ inch thick or
less
4 garlic cloves, crushed in a
garlic press
1 cup red wine vinegar
1½ cups water
1 teaspoon sugar
1 bay leaf
¼ cup chopped parsley

1. Season flour with salt, pepper, and paprika.
2. Heat olive oil in a skillet. Lightly dip meat slices in flour. Shake off excess. Brown meat on each side in the olive oil. Arrange in a casserole.
3. Combine garlic, vinegar, water, sugar, bay leaf, and parsley in a small saucepan; heat to boiling. Pour over the meat.
4. Bake at 325°F 1 hour, or until the meat is tender and almost all the liquid is absorbed.
5. Serve with **mashed potatoes.**

About 8 servings

542 *Beef Stew with Lentils or Lima Beans*

5 pounds beef chuck roast
¼ cup olive oil
2 large onions, thinly sliced
4 celery stalks, chopped
2 large carrots, chopped
1½ pounds fresh tomatoes, peeled
and diced
2 parsley sprigs, minced
1 pound dried lentils (or lima
beans)
Salt and pepper to taste
3 garlic cloves, crushed in a
garlic press
1 cup dry red wine
3 cups beef stock (or more if
necessary)

1. Trim excess fat from beef roast. Cut meat into large cubes.
2. Heat oil in a large Dutch oven. Brown meat on all sides and remove to platter.
3. Put onions into the Dutch oven and cook until translucent. Pour off excess fat.
4. Return meat to the Dutch oven. Arrange vegetables, parsley, and lentils around the meat. Season with salt and pepper.
5. Combine garlic, wine, and stock in a saucepan. Bring to boiling. Pour over meat and vegetables. Cover. Simmer until meat is tender. (Meat should be covered with liquid throughout cooking.)

8 to 10 servings

Note: This dish is tastier when made early and allowed to rest several hours or overnight, then reheated.

543 *Beef with Baby Onions* *(Stifatho)*

¼ cup olive oil
4 pounds beef shoulder, cut in large pieces
Salt and pepper to taste
1 can (16 ounces) tomatoes (undrained)
1 tablespoon tomato paste mixed with ½ cup water
5 garlic cloves, crushed in a garlic press
1 cup red wine
1 teaspoon sugar
1 tablespoon lemon juice
1 bay leaf
Pinch cinnamon
1 teaspoon oregano
¼ cup chopped parsley
3 tablespoons pickling spice (put in a tea infuser or wrapped and securely tied in cheesecloth)
3 pounds whole fresh baby onions, peeled

1. Heat oil in a large Dutch oven. Brown meat well on all sides. Season with salt and pepper.
2. Add tomatoes and diluted tomato paste. Cover and simmer 10 minutes.
3. Add remaining ingredients, except onions. Cover. Bring to a boil. Reduce heat. Simmer 2 to 3 hours until meat is tender.
4. Meanwhile, cut a small cross at the base of each onion. During the last ½ hour of cooking, add onions. Adjust salt and pepper.
5. Serve with **rice** or **pasta.**

8 servings

544 *Moussaka*

Fried Eggplant:
3 medium eggplants
Salt
2 cups flour (about)
Olive oil combined with vegetable oil for frying

Meat Filling:
¼ cup butter
2 pounds lean beef or lamb, ground
1 large onion, minced
¼ cup minced parsley
1½ teaspoons tomato paste mixed with ½ cup water
½ cup dry white wine
Salt and pepper to taste
3 egg whites, beaten until stiff
6 tablespoons fine bread crumbs

Béchamel Sauce with Egg Yolks:
7 tablespoons butter
7 tablespoons flour
1½ quarts milk, scalded
3 egg yolks, beaten
1 cup grated kefalotyri cheese

1. Slice eggplants ¼ inch thick, and place on a large platter in a single layer. Sprinkle with salt on both sides. Let stand at least 30 minutes, or until liquid beads form on surfaces. Take each slice, squeeze well between both hands or press down with a heavy weight, being sure all liquid is squeezed out.
2. Dip each slice lightly in flour. Shake off excess. Heat oil in a large skillet. Fry eggplant, turning once, until golden brown. Drain on paper towels. Set aside.
3. For Meat Filling, melt butter in a large skillet; add meat and onion, and cook until browned. Add parsley, tomato paste and water, wine, salt, and pepper. Cook until all liquid has evaporated (about 30 minutes). Cool.
4. Beat egg whites until they form soft mounds. Fold in half the bread crumbs. Fold egg-white mixture into meat mixture.
5. For Béchamel Sauce, heat butter until melted. Stir in flour. Cook 4 minutes over low heat, stirring constantly; do not brown. Pour in warm milk slowly. Cook over low heat until sauce thickens. Cool. Stir in yolks with a whisk.
6. To assemble, oil an 18x12-inch baking pan. Dust with remaining bread crumbs. Line bottom of pan with 1 layer of eggplant. Cover with meat. Layer remaining eggplant on top. Sprinkle with cheese. Pour Béchamel Sauce over.
7. Bake at 350°F about 40 minutes, or until golden brown. Cool. Cut into squares and serve.

About 10 servings

545 *Pastichio*

3 tablespoons olive oil
2 pounds ground beef or lamb
1 large onion, grated
Few parsley sprigs, chopped
1 tablespoon tomato paste mixed
with ½ cup water
1 pound elbow macaroni, cooked
according to directions on
package and drained
1 pound fresh kefalotyri cheese,
grated

Béchamel Sauce:
½ cup butter, melted
7 tablespoons flour
1½ quarts milk, heated to
lukewarm
10 eggs, separated

1. Heat oil in a large skillet. Add meat and onion and cook until meat is brown. Add chopped parsley and diluted tomato paste. Cover and simmer for 30 minutes. If any liquid remains, cook meat uncovered until liquid has evaporated.
2. Spread half the cooked macaroni in an 18x12-inch baking dish and cover with all the meat mixture. Sprinkle top with three fourths of the cheese. Form a layer with remaining macaroni.
3. Meanwhile, to make sauce, melt butter in a large saucepan. Add flour and mix with a whisk for several minutes. Gradually add milk while stirring; simmer until sauce thickens, stirring frequently.
4. Separate eggs. Beat whites in a bowl until they pile softly. Beat yolks in another bowl. Fold yolks and whites together, then fold in sauce. Spoon over meat and macaroni. Sprinkle with remaining cheese.
5. Bake at 325°F about 45 minutes, or until golden brown. Cool slightly before serving.

8 servings

Note: Pastichio may be prepared and baked in advance. To reheat, cover tightly with foil and heat in a 200°F oven.

546 *Meatballs with Tomato Sauce (Giouverlakia me Domata)*

1 pound beef, freshly ground
1 large onion, minced
3 tablespoons long-grain rice
1 garlic clove
½ cup minced parsley
1 tablespoon basil
Salt and pepper to taste
1 cup flour for rolling
Olive oil for frying
2 tablespoons tomato paste
mixed with 1 cup water or
beef stock

1. In a large bowl, combine meat, onion, rice, garlic, parsley, basil, salt, and pepper. Dip hands in flour. Shape meat mixture into round balls about 1½ inches in diameter.
2. Heat oil in a skillet. Sauté the meatballs, turning to brown on all sides. Remove to a baking dish.
3. Pour tomato paste liquid into the skillet. Simmer 3 minutes, stirring and scraping constantly. Strain the juices over the meatballs and add as much water or beef stock as needed to half cover them. Loosely cover with foil.
4. Bake at 350°F about 40 minutes. Once or twice during the cooking, turn meatballs with a wooden spoon. Serve hot with **pilafi** or **mashed potatoes.**

About 6 servings

547 *Sautéed Sweetbreads (Glykathia Tyganita)*

4 pairs sweetbreads from
milk-fed calves
Ice water
2 teaspoons salt
1 tablespoon lemon juice
5 tablespoons butter or olive oil
for frying
Flour seasoned with salt and
pepper

1. Soak sweetbreads in ice water mixed with salt for 1 hour. Drain.
2. Place sweetbreads in boiling water to cover. Add lemon juice and simmer 10 minutes. Drain. Plunge at once into ice water. Remove membranes and connective tissue, and split into 2 pieces.
3. Melt butter or heat olive oil in a skillet. Dip sweetbreads into flour. Fry until golden brown on all sides.

2 servings

548 *Stuffed Grapevine Leaves with Egg and Lemon Sauce*

(Dolmathes Avgolemono)

1 jar (32 ounces) grapevine leaves
1 quart water
¼ cup butter
2 medium onions, minced
1 pound ground lean beef or
    lamb or a combination of the
    two
    Salt and pepper to taste
2 tablespoons mint
2 tablespoons minced parsley
½ cup long-grain rice
2½ cups lukewarm water or more
    to barely cover dolmathes
4 egg yolks
½ cup lemon juice

1. Rinse grapevine leaves thoroughly in cold running water to remove brine. Bring 1 quart water to boiling. Add the leaves and parboil 3 minutes. Strain. Select 4 to 6 coarse, large leaves and line the bottom of a Dutch oven with them.
2. For filling, melt butter in a skillet. Add onion and cook until translucent. Remove from heat. Add meat, salt, pepper, mint, parsley, and rice. Toss lightly with 2 forks.
3. To fill, place a leaf, glossy side down, with the stem pointing toward you. (If a leaf is too small, use 2, overlapping 1 over the other by ¾ inch.) Place 2 teaspoons filling just above where the stem begins. Tuck base up and over. To seal, loosely fold one side, then the other, over toward the middle. Roll up to form oblong rolls, leaving room for the rice to expand while cooking.
4. To cook, arrange the dolmathes side by side in Dutch oven, layer upon layer. Place a ceramic plate on the last layer to keep dolmathes from floating to the surface during cooking. Pour water into pan to cover dolmathes. Cover pot and simmer 50 to 60 minutes. Check occasionally to see if too much water has evaporated. Add a little at a time, if necessary.
5. To make sauce, beat egg yolks until frothy. While continuing to beat, add lemon juice, a tablespoon at a time. Drain 1 cup broth from the cooked dolmathes and add slowly to the egg mixture, beating constantly.
6. Remove plate from dolmathes. Pour egg and lemon sauce over. Set over low heat until hot; do not boil. Serve immediately.

20 to 30 dolmathes

549 *Tomatoes Stuffed with Meat and Rice*

(Domates Yemistes me Kimake Rizi)

12 large firm tomatoes
1 teaspoon sugar
½ teaspoon salt
¾ cup olive oil
2 onions, minced
1 garlic clove, crushed in a garlic
    press
1 pound lean ground beef or
    lamb
¼ cup long-grain rice
¼ cup chopped parsley
1 teaspoon mint
½ teaspoon cinnamon
    Salt and pepper to taste
½ cup water

1. Slice tops from tomatoes and save. Remove pulp and save. Sprinkle insides of tomatoes with sugar and salt.
2. Heat ¼ cup oil in a large skillet. Add onion and garlic and sauté until onion is translucent. Add meat and cook until no longer red. Add rice, seasonings, and tomato pulp. Simmer 10 minutes. Cool slightly.
3. Fill tomatoes two thirds full, leaving room for rice to expand. (If too much filling is added, tomatoes may break open.) Place in a baking dish. Put tops on tomatoes. Drizzle remaining olive oil between tomatoes. Add ½ cup water.
4. Bake at 350°F about 40 minutes, or until rice is tender, basting occasionally. (Add more liquid to dish, if necessary.)

12 servings

Stuffed Peppers: Follow recipe for Tomatoes Stuffed with Meat and Rice, substituting **green peppers** for tomatoes. Remove seeds from peppers and discard. Proceed as directed.

550 *Roast Leg of Lamb with Orzo (Ghiouvetsi)*

1 lamb leg (6½ to 7 pounds)
4 large garlic cloves, peeled and
    cut in half lengthwise
¼ cup oregano, crushed
1 tablespoon salt
2 tablespoons freshly ground
    pepper
    Juice of 2 lemons
1 pound orzo (a pasta)
¼ cup cooking oil
1 tablespoon salt
1 cup boiling water
2 medium onions, quartered
¾ cup shredded or grated
    kefalotyri cheese

1. First prepare the lamb by placing it on a large sheet of aluminum foil. With a small, sharp knife, make eight 1-inch-deep diagonal incisions on the top and bottom the lamb. Into each incision, insert half a garlic clove. Press meat back to cover incisions.
2. Combine oregano, 1 tablespoon salt, and the pepper. Rub this all over the lamb. Fold the four sides of foil up to form a cuff. Pour on lemon juice. Seal the foil and refrigerate at least 6 hours, or preferably overnight.
3. Place leg of lamb on a rack in a roasting pan.
4. Roast in a 450°F oven 20 minutes. Turn oven control to 350°F. Roast until meat is cooked as desired; a meat thermometer inserted in the leg will register 160°F for medium and 170°F to 180°F for well-done meat.
5. Remove from roasting pan to a carving board. Keep warm. When ready to serve, slice meat on the diagonal. Save the pan drippings to use for making gravy.
6. Prepare orzo by boiling it according to directions on the package, adding cooking oil and 1 tablespoon salt. Drain. Rinse under hot water.
7. To make gravy for the orzo, remove the fat from the pan drippings. Add boiling water while stirring with a spoon to loosen drippings on bottom of the pan. Add onions.
8. Bake at 350°F 15 minutes.
9. Pour the gravy with onions into a blender and purée. Return to the roasting pan. Combine the orzo with the gravy. Toss quickly. Serve with shredded kefalotyri as an accompaniment to the lamb.

6 to 8 servings

551 *Saddle of Lamb with Artichoke Purée*

1 (5 pounds) saddle of lamb
    (lamb loin roast)
2 tablespoons olive oil
    Salt and pepper
2 teaspoons oregano
4 garlic cloves, crushed in a
    garlic press
8 to 10 thick grapevine leaves
8 artichoke bottoms, cooked
1 pound mushrooms, cooked
2 tablespoons butter
½ cup red wine
½ cup water

1. Rub lamb with olive oil. Combine salt, pepper, oregano, and garlic. Rub over lamb. Cover with grapevine leaves. Seal with foil. Refrigerate overnight.
2. Purée artichoke bottoms and mushrooms. Combine with butter and heat.
3. Set roast in a roasting pan. Remove grapevine leaves and season with salt and pepper.
4. Roast in a 325°F oven 50 minutes. Remove from oven. Reserve juices in the pan. Separate each loin from the saddle in one piece. Cut the meat into slices. Spread each slice with some of the purée. Reassemble the loins and tie securely in place. Return the meat to the roasting pan and add wine and water. Continue roasting, basting frequently, for 15 minutes.
5. Remove to a serving platter and discard strings. Skim fat from the pan juices and strain juices over the meat.

About 10 servings

552 *Lamb Shank in Parchment Paper*

1 lamb shank per serving
For each serving:
   1 garlic clove, peeled and slivered
   1 slice hard mizithra cheese
   1 small onion, sliced
   1 small tomato, peeled and diced
   1 teaspoon minced parsley
   ¼ teaspoon dill
   ¼ teaspoon mint flakes
   ½ teaspoon oregano
   Juice of ½ lemon
   Salt and pepper to taste
   1 teaspoon olive oil
   Parchment paper
   Cotton string

1. Make several incisions in the meat, top and bottom. Insert sliver of garlic in each incision.
2. Place meat on a piece of parchment paper ample enough to seal meat and vegetables securely. Put cheese on meat, then arrange onion and tomato on top. Sprinkle with herbs, lemon juice, salt, and pepper. Drizzle with olive oil.
3. Wrap securely in parchment paper. Tie with string. Set in a roasting pan.
4. Bake at 350°F about 1½ hours, or until meat is done. Serve package unopened.

Note: Oiled brown paper may be substituted for the parchment paper.

553 *Braised Lamb Shanks*

   3 tablespoons olive oil
   6 lamb shanks
   Salt and pepper to taste
   1 can (16 ounces) tomatoes (undrained)
   2 cups red wine
   ¼ cup dried oregano
   2 bay leaves
   ¼ cup minced parsley
   2 garlic cloves, minced
   2 onions, quartered

1. Heat olive oil until it begins to smoke. Brown lamb shanks on all sides. Season with salt and pepper. Add tomatoes, wine, oregano, bay leaves, parsley, garlic, and onion. Cover. Simmer 2 to 2½ hours, or until meat is fork tender.
2. Remove from heat. Cool. Skim off fat. Reheat and serve hot.

6 servings

554 *Lamb with Endive Avgolemono (Arni me Antithia Avgolemono)*

   3 large bunches curly endive
   1 quart water
   3 tablespoons olive oil
   5 pounds lamb shoulder with bone, cut in large pieces
   1 medium onion, minced
   2 tablespoons flour
   2 cups water
   Salt and pepper to taste
   3 eggs
   Juice of 2 lemons

1. Wash endive thoroughly under running cold water to remove grit. Cut off coarse stems. Bring 1 quart water to boiling in a large saucepot. Remove from heat and add endive. Let stand 3 minutes. Drain.
2. Heat olive oil in a large Dutch oven. Add meat and brown on all sides. Add onion. Cover and simmer, stirring occasionally.
3. Combine flour with 2 cups water in a bowl; stir well. Pour into meat. Season with salt and pepper. Add endive, cover, and continue cooking 1½ to 2 hours, or until meat is tender. (There should be enough stock for avgolemono sauce.)
4. To prepare sauce, beat eggs in a bowl and, beating constantly with a whisk, add lemon juice in a steady stream. Take 1 cup stock from meat and add, a tablespoon at a time, beating constantly.
5. Pour sauce over meat and endive. Heat; do not boil.

6 servings

555 *Lamb Shish Kebob* (*Arni Souvlakia*)

¾ cup dry red wine
¼ cup lemon juice
3 tablespoons olive oil
1 teaspoon salt
Freshly ground pepper to taste
2 garlic cloves, crushed in a
garlic press
1 onion, minced
Bay leaf
2 tablespoons oregano, crushed
3 pounds leg of lamb, boneless,
cut in 1½-inch cubes
Green peppers, cored and cut
in squares
Baby onions, peeled and left
whole
Large mushroom caps
Tomato wedges

1. Make a marinade of wine, lemon juice, olive oil, salt, pepper, garlic, onion, bay leaf, and oregano in a large bowl and add lamb cubes. Cover securely and refrigerate at least 6 hours. Turn lamb several times while marinating.
2. Remove meat from marinade and place on skewers with green pepper squares, onions, mushroom caps, and tomato wedges.
3. Barbecue over hot coals or broil about 20 minutes, or until done; baste with marinade during cooking.

8 to 10 servings

556 *Lamb Stew with Eggplant* (*Arni me Melitzana*)

2 pounds lean lamb shoulder, cut
in large pieces
1 cup flour seasoned with salt
and pepper
2 tablespoons olive oil
1 large onion, minced
3 large tomatoes, peeled and
diced
¾ cup water
1 bay leaf
Salt and pepper to taste
3 cups water
2 medium eggplants, cut in large
cubes
2 garlic cloves, crushed in a
garlic press
1 tablespoon tomato paste

1. Dip lamb lightly in flour.
2. Heat oil in a large skillet. Add meat and brown on all sides. Remove meat with a slotted spoon.
3. Put onion in the oil and sauté until translucent.
4. Return meat to skillet. Add tomatoes, water, and bay leaf. Season with salt and pepper. Bring to boiling. Reduce heat and simmer, covered, for 1½ hours.
5. Meanwhile, bring water to a boil in a saucepan. Add eggplant and simmer 5 minutes (to remove bitter taste). Pour off water.
6. Add eggplant, garlic, and tomato paste to meat. Stir to blend. Cover. Simmer about 40 minutes, or until meat is tender.

4 to 6 servings

557 *Lamb Chops with Oregano* (*Kotolettes Arniou me Rigani*)

2 lamb chops (rib or loin) per
serving

For each serving:
1 tablespoon oregano
Salt to taste
1 lemon, cut in half
1 tablespoon olive oil (optional)
Pepper to taste

1. An hour before cooking, sprinkle lamb chops with oregano. Season with salt. Set aside.
2. Place lamb chops on a broiler rack and broil 7 minutes on each side.
3. Remove from broiler and squeeze lemon juice over the chops. Drizzle with oil. Season with pepper.

558 *Lamb-Stuffed Zucchini with Avgolemono Sauce*

8 medium straight zucchini
1 pound ground beef round or lamb
½ cup long-grain rice
1 small onion, minced
2 tablespoons chopped parsley
1 teaspoon chopped mint
Salt and pepper
Water (about 2 cups)

Sauce:
2 egg yolks
Juice of 2 lemons
½ cup broth

1. Remove the ends and scrape the skins of the zucchini. With a corer, scoop out the zucchini centers and discard. Soak the zucchini in cold water.
2. Meanwhile, mix meat with rice, onion, parsley, mint, salt, and pepper. Drain zucchini and stuff with meat mixture.
3. Arrange stuffed zucchini in a single layer in a Dutch oven. Add enough water to half cover the zucchini. Bring the water to a boil, reduce heat, and simmer, covered, about 35 minutes.
4. Before serving, beat egg yolks until frothy. Slowly add lemon juice, beating constantly. Add broth, tablespoon by tablespoon, beating constantly. Heat thoroughly, but do not boil. Pour over zucchini. Serve immediately.

4 servings

559 *Roast Baby Lamb's Head* (*Arni Kefalaki Psito*)

1 head per serving, split in half and tied with a string to keep brains intact
Juice of 1 lemon
2 tablespoons olive oil
1 tablespoon oregano or more to taste
Salt and pepper to taste

1. Soak head in cold salted water for 1 hour. Drain. Pat dry. Cut string and place halves in a shallow pan, brains up.
2. Combine lemon juice, olive oil, oregano, salt, and pepper. Drizzle over head.
3. Roast in a 350°F oven for about 20 minutes, basting frequently until brains are tender. Remove brains with a spoon and keep warm. Continue roasting about 45 minutes more, or until other parts are tender.

560 *Lamb Kidneys in Wine Sauce* (*Nefra Krasata*)

4 lamb kidneys
Water
1 tablespoon wine vinegar
3 tablespoons flour
¼ cup butter
1½ cups white wine
1 bay leaf
1 garlic clove
2 tablespoons minced parsley
2 teaspoons oregano
½ teaspoon cumin
Salt and pepper to taste

1. Soak kidneys in cold water and vinegar for 15 minutes. Drain. Remove opaque skin and cut out the core. Slice kidneys thinly.
2. Dip slices in flour.
3. Melt butter in a skillet. Sauté the kidneys until browned on both sides. Add wine, bay leaf, garlic, parsley, oregano, cumin, salt, and pepper. Cover and simmer 20 minutes.

4 servings

561 *Shepherdess' Pie (Pita tys Voskopoulas)*

1½ cups Béchamel Sauce
1 medium onion, minced
1 egg, beaten
¼ cup fresh cracker crumbs
¼ cup chopped parsley
1 teaspoon salt
1 teaspoon thyme
¼ teaspoon ground red pepper
1 teaspoon vinegar
1 pound coarsely ground lamb or
    lean beef
4 cups mashed potatoes
½ cup grated kefalotyri cheese
1 teaspoon paprika

1. Combine ¾ cup of Béchamel Sauce, onion, egg, cracker crumbs, parsley, salt, thyme, red pepper, and vinegar.
2. Combine sauce with meat, tossing with 2 forks to mix lightly. Spoon mixture into a baking dish. Level top lightly with the back of the spoon. Make an indentation in the center.
3. Bake at 350°F 30 minutes, removing fat as it collects in the indentation.
4. Combine potatoes with remaining sauce.
5. Remove meat from oven when done. Sprinkle with cheese. Cover with potatoes. Sprinkle with paprika. Bake 20 minutes.

4 servings

Béchamel Sauce: Melt ¼ **cup butter.** Whisk in **3 tablespoons flour.** Cook, stirring constantly, for 1 minute. Slowly pour in **1½ cups milk,** scalded. Cook, stirring constantly, until mixture coats a wooden spoon.

562 *Charcoal-Roasted Pig (Gourounipoulo tys Skaras)*

3 garlic cloves, crushed in a
    garlic press
2 cups dry white wine
    Juice of 2 lemons
1 tablespoon salt
¼ cup oregano
2 tablespoons crushed
    peppercorns
1 piglet (12 to 15 pounds), with
    eyes, tongue, and feet
    removed
½ cup olive oil
1 tablespoon paprika

1. Make a marinade by combining garlic, wine, lemon juice, salt, oregano, and peppercorns. Refrigerate 1 hour.
2. Score pig several places with a knife. Rub interior cavity and exterior surface with marinade. Allow to marinate 12 hours in refrigerator.
3. Crush aluminum foil into a firm, thick ball and put in mouth to keep open. Cover ears with foil so they will not burn. Pull front feet forward and tie together. Pull hind feet backwards and tie together. Cover feet loosely with foil.
4. Attach pig to revolving spit and roast, basting frequently with a mixture of oil and paprika, until skin is brown and crisp and meat is tender (about 5 hours). In the last hour, remove foil so ears and feet can brown.
5. Remove pig from spit. Set on a platter. Put an apple or other piece of fruit in its mouth. Pour off fat from pan juices and serve.

8 to 10 servings

563 *Pork Chops with Vegetables*

3 tablespoons vegetable oil
8 lean pork chops
1 can (15 ounces) stewed
    tomatoes
1¾ cups water
1 cup minced celery
1 large green pepper, minced
1 medium onion, minced
1 bay leaf
1 thyme sprig
¼ teaspoon paprika
    Salt and pepper to taste

1. Heat oil in a large deep skillet. Add chops and brown on both sides.
2. Turn stewed tomatoes into a bowl. Add water, celery, green pepper, onion, bay leaf, thyme, paprika, salt, and pepper; mix well.
3. Remove excess fat from skillet; add tomato mixture. Cover.
4. Bake at 325°F about 2 hours, or until tender. Serve pork chops with **pilafi** or **potatoes.** Pass gravy separately.

8 servings

564 Pork Braised with Celery in Egg and Lemon Sauce
(Hoirino Selin Avgolemono)

¼ cup butter
4 pounds lean pork, cut in 2-inch cubes
1 large onion, minced
2 cups water
2 bunches celery (stalks only), cut in 1-inch pieces

Avgolemono Sauce:
¼ cup butter
3 tablespoons flour
2 cups pork stock
Juice of 2 lemons
3 eggs, separated
Salt and pepper to taste

1. Melt butter in a Dutch oven and sauté pork until golden brown. Add onion and cook until translucent. Add water. Cover and simmer 1 to 1½ hours, or until meat is just tender. Add celery and simmer about 15 minutes, or until tender. Drain off 2 cups stock and strain. Keep meat warm.
2. To make sauce, melt butter in a saucepan; add flour and cook about 1 minute, stirring constantly; do not brown. Add pork stock and lemon juice. Simmer, stirring constantly, until sauce thickens.
3. Separate eggs. Beat whites until soft peaks form. Beat yolks until thick. Fold yolks into whites. Using a wire whisk, slowly add sauce to eggs. Pour over pork mixture. Heat and serve at once.

8 servings

565 Pork Sausage with Orange Peel (Loukanika)

2 pounds pork shoulder, ground
½ pound pork fat back, ground
Grated peel of 1 navel orange
2 garlic cloves, crushed in a garlic press
1 tablespoon minced parsley
1 tablespoon oregano
2 teaspoons salt
2 teaspoons anise seed
2 teaspoons coriander, ground
1½ teaspoons allspice, ground
1 teaspoon pepper
1 long casing, cut in 7- to 8-inch pieces

1. Combine pork shoulder, fat back, and remaining ingredients, except casings, in a bowl and mix thoroughly. Cover and refrigerate several hours.
2. Rinse casings thoroughly in lukewarm water. Tie one end of a casing and stuff by pushing meat through a funnel inserted in the untied end; tie other end. Continue until all the meat and casings have been used.
3. Poach sausages in boiling water for 1 hour. Cool. Cut into slices and fry in a skillet until browned.

Note: If desired, omit casing, form sausage into patties, and fry until cooked.

566 Roast Veal

3 pounds veal rump roast, boned, rolled, and tied
1 garlic clove
1 tablespoon dill
1 teaspoon oregano
Salt and pepper to taste
3 tablespoons butter
¼ cup water
¼ cup white wine
1 teaspoon rosemary

1. Rub roast with garlic, dill, and oregano. Season with salt and pepper.
2. Melt butter in a roasting pan. Brown veal well on all sides.
3. Place a rack under veal. Pour water and wine into bottom of pan. Add rosemary. Cover pan.
4. Roast in a 350°F oven 2 hours.
5. Serve with pan juices.

6 to 8 servings

567 *Sautéed Veal Brains in Browned Butter* (*Myala Tyganita*)

4 veal brains
Juice of 2 lemons
1 teaspoon salt
½ cup flour seasoned with salt
    and pepper
½ cup butter
2 tablespoons chopped fresh dill
1 lemon, cut in wedges

1. Rinse brains thoroughly. Soak in water with ice cubes for 15 minutes. Drain; remove membranes.
2. Pour enough water into a saucepot to cover brains. Add lemon juice and salt; bring to boiling. Reduce heat and drop in brains. Simmer 15 minutes. Drain. Plunge into ice water to cool quickly.
3. Dip brains into seasoned flour.
4. Put butter into a skillet and heat until deep brown. Add brains and sauté briefly. Remove to a warm platter. Sprinkle with dill. Serve with lemon wedges.

4 servings

568 *Braised Veal with Lemon and Anchovies*

6 thick slices veal shin, sawed
    through so marrow shows
½ cup flour
½ cup butter
1 cup dry white wine
¼ cup chicken or veal stock
1 can (16 ounces) tomatoes
    (undrained)
2 teaspoons salt
1 teaspoon ground pepper
1 teaspoon thyme
2 garlic cloves, crushed in a garlic
    press
1 teaspoon grated lemon peel
½ cup minced parsley
2 anchovies, minced

1. Roll veal shin slices lightly in flour.
2. Melt butter in a Dutch oven and add veal, browning on all sides. Add wine, stock, tomatoes, salt, pepper, thyme, and garlic. Cover. Simmer about 2 hours, or until meat is tender, adding a little liquid when necessary.
3. Sprinkle with lemon peel, parsley, and anchovies before serving.

3 servings

569 *Cypriote Sausages*

1 pound coarsely ground beef
1 pound coarsely ground pork
1 cup fresh bread crumbs
3 garlic cloves, crushed in a
    garlic press
2 teaspoons salt
2 teaspoons coriander
1 teaspoon cumin
1 teaspoon thyme
½ teaspoon paprika
¼ teaspoon ground red pepper
1 bay leaf, ground
1 egg
½ cup minced parsley
1 large onion, minced
2 tablespoons tomato paste
    mixed with ½ cup water
Flour for rolling
Oil for frying

1. Combine meats in a large bowl, tossing with 2 forks.
2. Combine remaining ingredients except flour and oil in a separate bowl. Toss with meat mixture.
3. Break off enough meat to form a 2-inch-long sausage. Lightly flour palms of hands. Roll meat into sausage shapes.
4. Heat oil to smoking in a skillet. Fry sausages until deep brown on all sides. Serve hot or cold.

20 to 30 sausages

570 *Veal Stew with Onions (Moskari Stifatho)*

Flour seasoned with salt,
   pepper, and paprika
6 veal shanks, cut in pieces
3 tablespoons olive oil
3 tomatoes, peeled, seeded, and
   cubed
2 tablespoons chopped parsley
1 cup water
1 tablespoon wine vinegar
2 garlic cloves, minced
1 teaspoon sugar
1 bay leaf
2 whole cloves
2 whole allspice
   Pinch red pepper seed
2 pounds whole baby onions
   Water

1. Put seasoned flour into a bag. Add shank pieces and shake to coat evenly.
2. Heat oil in a Dutch oven and brown meat on all sides. Add tomatoes, parsley, 1 cup water, wine vinegar, garlic, and sugar. Tie bay leaf, cloves, allspice, and red pepper seed in cheesecloth. Add to meat mixture. Cover and simmer 1 hour.
3. Meanwhile, peel onions. Cut a small cross on the bottom of each. Add to stew and pour in enough water to cover. Simmer until onions are tender (about 25 minutes). Discard spices. Serve hot with **rice** or **cracked wheat pilafi**.

3 or 4 servings

571 *Rabbit Stew (Kounelli Stifatho)*

2 rabbits, skinned, cleaned, and
   cut in four pieces each
1½ cups mild vinegar
1 cup water
1 large onion, quartered
2 teaspoons salt
1 teaspoon pepper
2 bay leaves
2 pounds whole baby onions
3 tablespoons olive oil
2 tablespoons tomato paste
   mixed with 1 cup water
1 cup red wine
1 garlic clove, crushed in a garlic
   press
1 bay leaf
⅛ teaspoon cinnamon
   Salt and pepper to taste
   Water to cover

1. Put rabbit pieces into a large bowl. Add vinegar, water, onion, salt, pepper, and bay leaves. Cover. Refrigerate 24 hours, turning occasionally. Pat dry.
2. Peel onions. Cut a small cross at the base of each (to keep onions whole during cooking).
3. Heat olive oil in a large Dutch oven and sear rabbit on all sides until reddened. Add all ingredients including onions and water to barely cover. Bring to a boil. Cover.
4. Bake at 250°F about 2 hours, or until rabbit is tender.

8 servings

Note: If a thick sauce is desired, pour the sauce into a saucepan and simmer uncovered for ½ hour. Pour over rabbit.

572 *Beef Pot Roast (Pieczeń Wołowa Duszona)*

1 beef round rump or chuck roast,
    boneless (3½ pounds)
3 tablespoons salad oil or ¼
    pound salt pork, diced
    Bouillon or meat broth (about 1½
    cups)
1 bay leaf
2 onions, quartered
2 carrots, cut in pieces
½ teaspoon salt
½ teaspoon coarse pepper
    Flour
    Salt and pepper

1. Brown the beef in oil. Add ¼ cup bouillon, bay leaf, onions, carrots, salt, and pepper; cover and simmer 2½ hours, basting with additional bouillon to prevent burning.
2. Sprinkle flour over meat and turn it over. Sprinkle with more flour. If necessary, add more bouillon for the sauce. Cook uncovered 30 minutes. Serve the pot roast with **noodles** or **potatoes** and any kind of vegetables.

8 to 10 servings

Pot Roast with Sour Cream: Prepare Beef Pot Roast as directed. Add **1½ cups dairy sour cream** instead of bouillon after flouring the meat. Finish cooking as directed.

Pot Roast with Sour Cream and Pickles or Mushrooms: Prepare Beef Pot Roast as directed. Add **1½ cups dairy sour cream** instead of bouillon after flouring the meat. Then stir in **⅔ cup chopped dill pickles** or **1 cup sliced mushrooms.** Finish cooking as directed.

573 *Beef Slices with Sour Cream and Mushrooms (Zrazy z Grzybami i ze Śmietaną)*

½ cup all-purpose flour
1 teaspoon salt
½ teaspoon pepper
2 pounds beef eye round, top
    round, or sirloin (cut in thin
    steaks)
3 tablespoons butter or fat
1 can (4 ounces) mushrooms with
    liquid
1 cup water
6 medium potatoes, cooked; or 3
    cups sauerkraut, drained
1 tablespoon flour
1 cup dairy sour cream

1. Mix flour with salt and pepper. Coat meat with seasoned flour.
2. Melt butter in a large skillet or Dutch oven. Brown meat quickly on both sides.
3. Add mushrooms with liquid and water. Cover. Simmer 1 hour, basting occasionally with sauce.
4. Add potatoes to meat; cook 10 minutes, or until meat and potatoes are tender.
5. Blend flour into sour cream. Blend into sauce. Bring to boiling, then simmer 5 minutes.

6 servings

574 *Steamed Beef (Sztuka Mięsa w Parze)*

3 to 4 pounds beef round rump or
    eye round steak
    Salt and pepper
2 onions, sliced
1 cup each diced carrot, parsley
    root, and parsnips
1 cup green peas
½ cup sliced celery
½ cup asparagus stems (optional)
1 cauliflower or cabbage core, diced
    (optional)
2 tablespoons butter

1. Pound the meat. Sprinkle with salt and pepper. Let stand 30 minutes. Pound again.
2. In a steamer top, combine meat and vegetables. Add butter. Cook over gently boiling water about 3 hours, or until meat is tender.
3. Slice meat. Serve with the steamed vegetables.

6 to 8 servings

575 *Roast Leg of Lamb* (Pieczeń Baraniha z Pieca)

Vinegar
1 lamb leg, whole
Garlic cloves, slivered
Salt and pepper

1. Soak a towel with vinegar; wrap around the leg of lamb. Let stand overnight.
2. Remove towel. Trim off fell, if necessary, and excess fat. Make small slits in fat cover on meat. Push a sliver of garlic into each slit.
3. Place lamb, fat side up, on rack in a roasting pan. Sprinkle with salt and pepper.
4. Roast in a 325°F oven until done as desired. Allow 30 minutes per pound for medium; 35 minutes per pound for well-done.

About 8 to 12 servings

576 *Roast Loin of Pork* (Schab Pieczony)

2 tablespoons flour
1½ teaspoons salt
1 teaspoon dry mustard or caraway seed
½ teaspoon sugar
¼ teaspoon black pepper
¼ teaspoon ground sage
1 pork loin roast (4 to 5 pounds)
Topping:
1½ cups applesauce
½ cup brown sugar
¼ teaspoon cinnamon or allspice
¼ teaspoon mace
¼ teaspoon salt

1. Mix flour, salt, mustard, sugar, pepper and sage. Rub over surface of meat. Set meat fat side up in a roasting pan.
2. Roast at 325°F 1½ hours.
3. For topping, mix applesauce with brown sugar, cinnamon, mace, and salt. Spread on top of meat.
4. Roast about 45 minutes longer, or until done.

8 to 10 servings

577 *Sauerkraut with Pork* (Kapusta z Wieprzowiną)

2 pounds pig's feet or ham hocks
2 pounds neck bones or spareribs
3 tablespoons lard or margarine
1 large onion
1 clove garlic, crushed
1½ quarts boiling water
1 green pepper, diced
4 whole allspice
1 bay leaf
½ teaspoon celery seed
1 quart (about 2 pounds) sauerkraut
¼ cup barley
1 small apple, chopped
½ teaspoon caraway seed
2 teaspoons salt
½ teaspoon pepper

1. Brown all meat in lard in a large kettle.
2. Add onion and garlic. Fry 1 minute.
3. Add boiling water, green pepper, allspice, bay leaf, and celery seed. Cover; cook 1 hour or until meat is tender.
4. Remove meat; cool. Boil until broth is reduced to 3 cups.
5. Discard bones and gristle from meat. Drain and rinse sauerkraut.
6. Cook barley in the broth 15 minutes. Add meat, sauerkraut, apple, caraway seed, salt, and pepper. Cook 45 minutes longer.
7. Serve with potato dumplings, if desired.

About 6 servings

578 *Pork Pot Roast (Pieczeń Wieprzowa Duszona)*

1 pork shoulder arm picnic or pork
    loin roast, boneless (3 pounds)
2 tablespoons butter or lard
2 tomatoes, peeled and cored
1 celery root
1 parsley root
1 onion, sliced
2 sprigs parsley
2 tablespoons spices to taste:
    allspice, caraway seed, whole
    cloves, juniper berries, dried
    marjoram leaves, peppercorns
    (tie in cheesecloth)
¼ cup water
½ cup bouillon or meat broth
½ cup Madeira, Marsala, or sherry

1. Rub meat with salt and pepper. Let stand 1 hour.
2. Brown meat in butter in a large, heavy skillet. Add vegetables, parsley, spice bag, and water. Cover tightly. Cook over medium heat 1½ hours; stirring as necessary and turning meat occasionally.
3. Sprinkle a small amount of flour over top of meat. Pour bouillon and wine over meat. Simmer 15 minutes.
4. Slice and arrange meat on a warm platter. Strain sauce and pour over meat.

6 to 8 servings

579 *Boiled Tongue (Ozór Szpikowany w Potrawie)*

1 beef tongue (about 3 pounds);
    fresh, smoked, or corned
    tongue may be used
    Boiling water
¼ pound salt pork, diced
2 onions, quartered
2 bay leaves
1 celery root or 3 stalks celery
2 carrots
2 parsnips or turnips
1 fresh horseradish root (optional)
1 parsley root
2 sprigs fresh parsley
1 tablespoon salt
6 whole peppercorns
Sauce:
1 cup white wine
1 bouillon cube
1 tablespoon flour
2 tablespoons butter (at room
    temperature)
2 tablespoons prepared cream-style
    horseradish

1. Rinse tongue under cold, running water. Cook in enough boiling water to cover 1 hour.
2. Add salt pork, 1 onion, and 1 bay leaf. Cover; cook 1 to 2 hours, or until tongue is tender. Remove skin, fat, and gristle. Strain liquid.
3. Combine tongue, strained liquid, remaining onion, and bay leaf with vegetables, parsley, salt, and peppercorns. Cover; simmer until vegetables are tender, 30 to 45 minutes.
4. For sauce, purée vegetables in an electric blender or press through a sieve.
5. Combine 1½ cups cooking liquid, wine, and bouillon cube. Bring to boiling. Blend flour into butter; stir into boiling broth. Add vegetable purée and prepared horseradish. Cook and stir until sauce is smooth.
6. Slice tongue. Simmer in sauce 10 minutes.

About 8 servings

580 *Liver à la Nelson*

1½ pounds sliced calf's liver
  Milk
  6 medium potatoes, pared
  1 onion, sliced
  ½ cup sliced mushrooms
  ¼ cup butter
  ½ cup all-purpose flour
  ½ teaspoon salt
  ¼ teaspoon pepper
  1 cup bouillon or meat broth
  ½ cup sweet red wine or Madeira

1. Soak liver 45 minutes in enough milk to cover.
2. Cook potatoes in boiling water until tender; cut in thick slices.
3. Sauté onion and mushrooms in butter in a large skillet until tender, about 5 minutes.
4. Mix flour with salt and pepper. Drain liver; pat dry with paper towels. Coat liver with seasoned flour.
5. Quickly brown liver in skillet with onion and mushrooms. Add sliced potatoes, bouillon, and wine. Cover. Simmer just until liver is tender, about 10 to 15 minutes.

6 servings

581 *Tripe and Vegetables Warsaw Style*
(Flaki z Jarzynami po Warszawsku)

2 pounds fresh tripe
1 pound beef or veal soup bones
  Water
  Salt
4 carrots, sliced
1 celery root, chopped, or 3 stalks celery, sliced
1 bunch green onions, sliced
1 tablespoon chopped fresh parsley
3 cups bouillon or meat broth
2 tablespoons butter or margarine
2 tablespoons flour
½ teaspoon salt
¼ teaspoon ginger
¼ teaspoon mace
¼ teaspoon marjoram
¼ teaspoon pepper
1 cup light cream or vegetable broth

1. Clean tripe well and rinse thoroughly under running cold water.
2. Combine tripe and soup bones with enough water to cover in a large kettle. Season with ½ teaspoon salt for each cup of water added. Cover. Bring to boiling; reduce heat and simmer 3 to 5 hours, or until tripe is tender.
3. Drain tripe; discard bones and cooking liquid. Cut tripe into very thin strips.
4. Cook tripe with vegetables and parsley in bouillon until vegetables are tender.
5. Melt butter in a saucepan. Stir in flour to make a smooth paste. Cook and stir until golden. Blend in a small amount of cooking liquid. Add ½ teaspoon salt and spices. Add cream gradually, stirring until smooth.
6. Drain vegetables and tripe. Stir into sauce. Simmer 5 minutes.

4 to 6 servings

582 Polish Sausage with Red Cabbage
(Kiełbasa z Czerwoną Kapustą)

1 head red cabbage, sliced (about 2 pounds)
Boiling water
2 tablespoons butter
⅓ cup lemon juice
½ cup red wine or beef broth
½ teaspoon salt
¼ teaspoon pepper
¾ pound Polish sausage, diced
2 teaspoons brown sugar
1 tablespoon cornstarch or potato flour

1. Place cabbage in a colander. Pour boiling water over cabbage. Drain well.
2. Melt butter in a Dutch oven or large heavy skillet. Add cabbage. Stir in lemon juice. Cook and stir about 5 minutes, or until cabbage is pink. Add wine, salt, and pepper. Cover. Simmer over medium-low heat 45 minutes.
3. Mix sugar and cornstarch. Stir into simmering liquid. Bring to boiling, stirring constantly. Reduce heat; add sausage. Cover; cook 30 minutes.

About 4 servings

583 Sausage in Polish Sauce
(Kiełbasa w Polskim Sosie)

2 onions, sliced
3 tablespoons butter or margarine
Ring Polish sausage (about 1½ pounds)
1½ cups bouillon or meat broth
12 ounces beer
2 tablespoons flour
1 tablespoon vinegar
2 teaspoons brown sugar
¾ teaspoon salt
¼ teaspoon pepper
4 to 6 boiled potatoes

1. Sauté onion in 2 tablespoons butter until golden. Add sausage, bouillon, and beer. Simmer 20 minutes.
2. Blend flour into remaining 1 tablespoon butter. Stir into broth. Add vinegar, brown sugar, salt, and pepper.
3. Add potatoes. Cook over medium heat 10 to 15 minutes.
4. Slice sausage into 2-inch chunks to serve.

4 to 6 servings

584 Bacon Fry (Grzybek ze Słoninką)

1 pound sliced bacon, diced
4 eggs
1 cup milk
2 cups all-purpose flour
1 tablespoon sugar
2½ teaspoons baking powder
1½ teaspoons salt

1. Fry bacon just until golden in a 10-inch skillet. Remove ⅔ cup bacon and drippings.
2. Beat eggs with milk. Add 1 cup flour, sugar, baking powder, and salt. Beat until smooth. Beat in remaining flour.
3. Pour half of batter just in center of skillet over bacon and drippings. Tilt skillet slightly to spread batter. Cook until browned on bottom and set on top. Turn.
4. Sprinkle half the reserved bacon and 1 tablespoon drippings over top. Pour on half the remaining batter. Turn when bottom is browned.
5. Sprinkle remaining bacon and 2 tablespoons drippings on top. Pour on remaining batter. Turn when bottom is browned. Cook just until browned.
6. Cut into wedges for serving.

About 4 servings

585 *Cabbage Rolls (Gołąbki)*

1 whole head cabbage (about 3
    pounds)
  Boiling water
1 pound ground beef
½ pound ground veal
¾ cup chopped onion
½ cup packaged precooked rice
1 egg, beaten
1 teaspoon salt
¼ teaspoon pepper
5 slices bacon
1 can (16 ounces) tomatoes or
    sauerkraut
⅓ cup bouillon or meat broth
½ teaspoon sugar
¼ teaspoon salt
¼ teaspoon pepper

1. Remove core from cabbage. Place whole head in a large kettle filled with boiling water. Cover; cook 3 minutes. Remove softened outer leaves. Repeat until all large leaves have been removed (about 20 leaves). Cut thick center stem from each slice.
2. Sauté meat with onion 5 minutes. Remove from heat. Stir in rice, egg, 1 teaspoon salt, and ¼ teaspoon pepper.
3. Place 3 tablespoons meat mixture on each cabbage leaf. Roll each leaf, tucking ends in toward center. Fasten securely with wooden picks. Place each roll seam side down in a large skillet or Dutch oven.
4. Lay bacon slices over top of cabbage rolls.
5: Mix tomatoes, bouillon, sugar, ¼ teaspoon salt, and ¼ teaspoon pepper. Pour over cabbage rolls.
6. Cover; simmer about 1 hour, turning occasionally.

About 10 servings

586 *Cabbage Rolls with Mushroom Sauce (Gołąbki w Grzybowym Sosie)*

1 onion, chopped
1 clove garlic, crushed (optional)
2 tablespoons butter
¾ cup uncooked raw rice
½ pound ground beef or veal
½ pound ground pork
1 teaspoon salt
¼ teaspoon pepper
1 whole head cabbage (about 3
    pounds)
  Boiling water
2 cups beef broth or stock
1 can (about 10 ounces) condensed
    cream of mushroom soup

1. Sauté onion and garlic in butter in a large skillet, about 5 minutes. Add rice, meat, salt, and pepper. Stir-fry just to mix well. Remove from heat.
2. Remove core from cabbage. Place whole head in a large kettle filled with boiling water. Cover; cook 3 minutes. Remove softened outer leaves. Repeat until all leaves are softened and have been removed. Cut thick stem from each leaf.
3. Taking one large cabbage leaf at a time, spoon about 1 rounded tablespoonful of meat mixture in center of leaf. Cover with a small leaf. Tuck ends up and just over edge of filling; place one end of leaf over filling and roll up loosely. If desired, secure with a wooden pick. Repeat until all filling and leaves are used. Place cabbage rolls in a large casserole; do not make more than 2 layers.
4. Combine beef broth and mushroom soup; pour over cabbage rolls.
5. Bake at 350°F about 1½ hours.

8 to 12 servings

Easy Hunter's Stew, page 223

587 *Stuffed Cabbage Rolls (Gołąbki)*

1 whole head cabbage (about 4
   pounds)
   Boiling salted water
1 onion, chopped
2 tablespoons oil
1½ pounds ground beef
½ pound ground fresh pork
1½ cups cooked rice
1 teaspoon salt
¼ teaspoon pepper
2 cans (about 10 ounces each)
   condensed tomato soup
2½ cups water

1. Remove core from cabbage. Place whole head in a large kettle filled with boiling salted water. Cover; cook 3 minutes, or until softened enough to pull off individual leaves. Repeat to remove all large leaves (about 30). Cut thick center stem from each leaf. Chop remaining cabbage.
2. Sauté onion in oil. Add meat, rice, salt, and pepper. Mix thoroughly. Place a heaping tablespoonful of meat mixture on each cabbage leaf. Tuck sides over filling while rolling leaf around filling. Secure with wooden picks.
3. Place half the chopped cabbage on bottom of a large Dutch oven. Fill with layers of the cabbage rolls. Cover with remaining chopped cabbage.
4. Combine tomato soup with water; mix until smooth. Pour over cabbage rolls. Cover and bring to boiling. Reduce heat and simmer 1½ hours.
5. Serve cabbage rolls with the sauce.

About 15 servings

588 *Ham in Rye Crust*

Dough:
1 package active dry yeast
½ cup warm water
⅓ cup caraway seed
¾ cup water
2 tablespoons molasses
3 cups rye flour (about)
Topping for ham:
½ cup firmly packed brown sugar
1 teaspoon dry mustard
¼ teaspoon cloves

1 canned fully cooked ham
   (5 pounds)

1. For dough, dissolve yeast in ½ cup warm water and add caraway seed; let stand 10 minutes.
2. Stir in ¾ cup water, molasses, and half of the flour.
3. Turn out dough onto floured surface. Knead in remaining flour to make a stiff dough. Cover with plastic wrap. Let rest 20 minutes.
4. Mix brown sugar with mustard and cloves.
5. Remove gelatin and wipe ham with paper towels.
6. Roll out dough on a floured surface to form a 28×10-inch rectangle.
7. Sprinkle about 1 tablespoon brown sugar mixture in center of dough. Place ham on sugar mixture. Sprinkle remaining sugar mixture over top of ham.
8. Fold dough over top of ham, cutting out corners to fit with only one layer of dough. Pinch edges to seal.
9. Set dough-wrapped ham on rack in pan lined with foil.
10. Roast at 350°F 1½ to 1¾ hours, or until meat thermometer reaches 140°F. Remove from oven; let rest 10 minutes.
11. To serve, remove crust and discard. Slice ham.

12 to 15 servings

589 *Polish Sausage (Kiełbasa)*

1½ pounds lean boneless pork
½ pound boneless veal
1 teaspoon salt
¼ teaspoon pepper
1 clove garlic, crushed
1 tablespoon mustard seed
¼ cup crushed ice
   Casing

1. Cut meat into small chunks. Grind meat with seasonings and ice; mix well.
2. Stuff meat mixture into casing.
3. Smoke in a smoker, following manufacturer's directions. Or, place sausage in a casserole; cover with water. Bake at 350°F until water is absorbed, about 1½ hours. Roast 10 minutes.

About 2 pounds

Pastichio, page 209
Braised Beef, Corfu Style, page 207
Lamb Shish Kebob, page 213

590 *Roasted Veal (Pieczeń Cielęca)*

1 veal leg round roast or shoulder
    arm roast (4 to 5 pounds)
Boiling water
3 tablespoons lemon juice
1 tablespoon salt
1 teaspoon pepper
½ cup butter, melted
Flour for dusting

1. Dip meat quickly in boiling water; drain well.
2. Mix lemon juice, salt, and pepper. Spread over surface of meat.
3. Place meat on a spit or rack in a roasting pan.
4. Roast at 400°F 20 minutes. Reduce heat to 325°F. Roast 55 minutes.
5. Baste with melted butter. Sprinkle flour over top. Roast 10 minutes longer, or until done as desired.

6 to 8 servings

591 *Roast Suckling Pig (Prosię Pieczone)*

1 suckling pig, about 25 to 30
    pounds
Salt and pepper
1½ pounds stale bread, diced
1½ cups milk
2 eggs
2 apples, sliced
2 onions, diced
⅓ cup chopped parsley
1 potato
Melted lard or salad oil
1 small whole apple
Parsley sprigs or small fruits
    and leaves

1. Wipe pig, inside and out, with a clean damp cloth. Sprinkle entire cavity with salt and pepper. If necessary to make pig fit into pan (and oven) cut crosswise in half just behind shoulders.
2. Put bread into a large mixing bowl. Add milk and let soak 20 minutes. Add eggs, sliced apples, onion, and parsley; mix well.
3. Spoon stuffing into cavity of pig. (There will not be enough stuffing to entirely fill cavity.)
4. Use metal skewers to hold cavity closed and lace with string.
5. Set pig belly side down in roasting pan. Tuck feet under body. Cover tail, snout, and ears with foil. Place whole potato in mouth.
6. Roast at 375°F 8 to 10 hours. Baste frequently with melted lard. When pig is done, juices run golden and skin is a crackling, translucent, golden-chocolate brown.
7. Set pig on platter. Remove potato from mouth; replace with apple. Make a wreath of parsley sprigs for neck or to cover joint behind shoulders.

About 25 servings

592 *Rabbit (Zając Pieczony)*

1 rabbit (2 to 3 pounds), cut in
    pieces
Salt and pepper
Flour
¼ cup butter
1 cup chopped mushrooms
1 onion, sliced
1 clove garlic, sliced
1 cup meat stock

1. Sprinkle rabbit pieces with salt and pepper. Coat with flour.
2. Melt butter in a Dutch oven or flame-proof casserole. Add mushrooms, onion, and garlic. Add rabbit pieces and brown quickly. Remove garlic.
3. Mix stock with wine, thyme, and bay leaves. Add to rabbit.
4. Bake at 350°F or simmer about 1½ hours, or until rabbit is very tender.

⅔ cup dry white wine*
½ teaspoon ground thyme
2 bay leaves
Sauce:
1 cup dairy sour cream
1 teaspoon dried parsley flakes
¼ teaspoon nutmeg

* Or substitute ½ cup water and 1 tablespoon lemon juice

5. Remove rabbit and place on heated platter. Stir sauce ingredients into broth in pan. Cook and stir just until sauce begins to simmer. Spoon over rabbit.

4 to 6 servings

593 *Leg of Venison (Sarna Duszona)*

Marinade:
1 bottle (4/5 quart) dry white wine
3 cups vinegar
2 cups olive oil or salad oil
1 cup sliced carrots
1 cup sliced onions
2 stalks celery, cut in pieces
2 cloves garlic, crushed
3 sprigs parsley
1 bay leaf
6 whole cloves
6 peppercorns
Venison and Sauce:
1 leg of venison (5 to 6 pounds)
¼ cup oil
2 tablespoons butter
1 onion, diced
1 cup red wine
3 tablespoons sugar
6 whole cloves
1 cup dairy sour cream
½ cup all-purpose flour
Salt and pepper

1. Combine all ingredients for marinade in a large crock. Soak the venison 2 or 3 days in the marinade. Remove and wipe dry with a cloth.
2. Heat oil and butter in a heavy skillet. Add venison; brown evenly on all sides. Fry onion in the same butter.
3. Strain 1 cup marinade. Add to skillet.
4. Place venison in a Dutch oven or roaster. Add liquid and onion from skillet. Add wine, sugar, and cloves.
5. Cover; simmer or bake at 350°F about 2½ hours, or until meat is tender.
6. Remove venison to carving board.
7. Make sauce by combining sour cream and flour. Gradually stir in 1 cup strained cooking broth. Return to Dutch oven; cook, stirring, until smooth and thick. Season to taste with salt and pepper.
8. To serve, carve venison; place slices on a warmed platter. Pour sauce over top.

8 to 12 servings

594 *Veal à la Nelson (Zrazy po Nelsońsku)*

3 ounces dried mushrooms (optional)
2 cups warm milk
3 slices bacon
1 pound fresh mushrooms, sliced
4 large onions, chopped
8 veal cutlets (about 3 pounds)
3 bouillon cubes
3 tablespoons flour
¼ cup butter or margarine, melted
1 cup dairy sour cream
Salt and pepper
8 medium potatoes, cooked

1. Soak dried mushrooms in warm milk 2 hours.
2. Fry bacon in a large skillet. Add mushrooms and onion. Sauté until onion is soft. Add fried bacon, mushrooms, and onion to milk.
3. Sauté veal in drippings. Add oil, if needed.
4. Add milk mixture and bouillon cubes. Cover; simmer 1 hour.
5. Stir flour into melted butter. Blend in a small amount of cooking liquid. Stir into remainder of liquid in skillet. Cook and stir until sauce is smooth and thick. Then blend in sour cream. Season to taste with salt and pepper.
6. Add potatoes. Cook 10 to 15 minutes, or until potatoes are hot.

8 servings

595 *Braised Lamb with Savoy Cabbage*
(Baranina Duszona z Włoską Kapustą)

3 pounds lamb breast
1 teaspoon salt
2 cloves garlic, crushed
2 carrots
2 stalks celery with leaves
1 large onion
1 large celery root, pared
1 leek
½ parsley root
3 tablespoons butter or margarine
  Water
1 head (about 2 pounds) savoy
  cabbage, cut in quarters
1 bay leaf
½ teaspoon salt
¼ teaspoon pepper
1 tablespoon flour

1. Rub meat with 1 teaspoon salt and garlic. Let stand 1 hour.
2. Cut meat into 2-rib pieces. Dice vegetables, except for cabbage.
3. Melt 2 tablespoons butter in a large kettle. Add meat and brown. Drain off fat. Add vegetables with just enough water to cover. Simmer covered about 1 hour, or until meat is tender. Remove vegetables; discard or reserve for other use. Reduce broth to 2 cups.
4. Add cabbage and bay leaf to meat. Season with ½ teaspoon salt and pepper. Continue simmering, tightly covered, until meat and cabbage are done.
5. Blend flour into remaining 1 tablespoon butter. Stir into simmering broth. Simmer until sauce thickens, about 15 minutes.

6 servings

Braised Lamb with Caraway Seed: Prepare Braised Lamb with Savoy Cabbage, substituting **2 tablespoons caraway seed** for carrots, celery, celery root, leek, and bay leaf.

596 *Hunter's Stew (Bigos)*

6 pounds diced cooked meat (use at least ½ pound of each of the following: beef, ham, lamb, sausage, veal, pork, venison or rabbit, wild duck, wild goose, or pheasant)*
5 ounces salt pork, diced
1 onion, minced
2 leeks, minced
2 tablespoons flour
1 pound fresh mushrooms, sliced, or 3 cans (4 ounces each) sliced mushrooms (undrained)
1 to 2 cups water or bouillon
6 pounds sauerkraut
2 teaspoons salt
1 teaspoon pepper
2 teaspoons sugar
1 cup Madeira

1. Fry salt pork until golden but not crisp in an 8-quart kettle. Add onion and leeks. Stir-fry 3 minutes. Stir in flour.
2. Add mushrooms with liquid and water to kettle; simmer 5 minutes.
3. Drain and rinse sauerkraut. Add to kettle along with cooked meat, salt, pepper, and sugar. Cover; cook over medium-low heat 1½ hours.
4. Stir in wine. Add more salt, pepper, and sugar to taste. Simmer 15 minutes; do not boil.

12 to 16 servings

*If meat must be prepared especially for this stew, each piece should be braised separately. Put meat, poultry, or game into a Dutch oven with 1 carrot, 1 stalk celery, 1 onion, 1 parsnip, 1 clove garlic or 1 sprig parsley, 5 peppercorns, 1 cup water, and 1 cup wine. Simmer, covered, until meat is tender.

Note: When wine is added, chopped apples, heavy cream, and/or cooked small potatoes may also be added.

597 *Cold Roast Beef Vinaigrette*

Use freshly cooked or leftover beef for this superb entrée. Stock replaces oil in the marinade. Your own selection of vegetables can be used for color and texture contrast.

1½ **pounds cooked medium-rare roast beef, sliced ¼ inch thick and cut in 2-inch-wide strips**

3 **stalks celery, cut in ¼-inch pieces**

1 **medium tomato, chopped**

2 **sweet red or green peppers, chopped in ¼-inch pieces**

1 **tablespoon finely chopped red onion**

1 **tablespoon olive oil**

2 **tablespoons wine vinegar**

● ¼ **cup Beef Stock**

2 **teaspoons snipped fresh or 1 teaspoon dried basil leaves**

1 **teaspoon snipped fresh or ½ teaspoon dried coriander leaves (cilantro)**

1 **tablespoon snipped parsley**

1 **teaspoon salt**

* ¼ **teaspoon freshly ground Szechuan or black pepper**

1 **teaspoon snipped fresh or ½ teaspoon dried oregano leaves**

2 **garlic cloves, finely minced**

2 **teaspoons Dijon mustard**

1. Arrange beef in a shallow glass dish. Mix remaining ingredients and pour over meat. Refrigerate covered 8 hours or overnight.
2. Taste meat and marinade; adjust seasoning, if desired. Let stand at room temperature 45 minutes before serving. Serve beef slices topped with marinade.

4 to 6 servings

*Lightly roast Szechuan pepper over medium heat in a skillet before grinding.

598 *Beef-on-Tomato Medallions*

Oriental stir-frying is a perfect technique for use in New French Cooking as little oil is used and the foods are cooked quickly to retain natural color, flavor, and texture.

3 **large ripe tomatoes**
    Salt
    Freshly ground pepper

1 **tablespoon vegetable oil**

½ **teaspoon sesame or walnut oil**

2½ **pounds lean beef sirloin steak, boneless, cut in paper-thin slices**

2 **bunches green onions, cut in ¾-inch pieces**

1 **tablespoon light soy sauce**

2 **tablespoons dry white wine**

¼ **teaspoon sugar**

½ **teaspoon salt**

1. Slice each tomato into 4 slices horizontally. Sprinkle with salt and pepper. Bake on a cookie sheet at 325°F until hot (about 15 minutes).
2. Heat vegetable and sesame oils in a wok or skillet until hot but not smoking. Add meat, stirring to coat pieces. Cook 1 minute. Add green onions. Cook and stir 1 minute. Mix soy sauce, wine, sugar, and ½ teaspoon salt; pour over meat. Cook and stir until meat is done (about 3 minutes).
3. Overlap 2 tomato slices at the side of each serving plate. Arrange meat mixture on plates, partially covering tomatoes.

6 servings

Note: Sesame and walnut oils can be purchased in specialty or gourmet shops. These oils have a delicate but distinct flavor which provides an interesting accent in this recipe. The oil can be omitted, or vegetable oil substituted.

599 *Meat-Stuffed Cabbage*

A whole cabbage encases a flavorful and moist meat-and-vegetable combination.

1 large head cabbage (about 4 pounds)
Water
1 tablespoon salt
Cheesecloth
2 pounds lean ground beef
2 bunches green onions, cut in ¼-inch pieces
1 garlic clove, minced
1 medium zucchini, finely chopped (reserve 8 thin slices for garnish)
1 large green pepper, chopped
1 egg, slightly beaten
1 cup fine soft bread crumbs made from whole-grain bread
1½ teaspoons snipped fresh or ¾ teaspoon dried basil leaves
2 teaspoons snipped fresh or 1 teaspoon dried thyme leaves
2 teaspoons snipped fresh or 1 teaspoon dried rosemary leaves
2 teaspoons salt
½ teaspoon freshly ground pepper
1 can (16 ounces) plum tomatoes (reserve liquid)
4 fresh mushrooms, cut in half, for garnish
Water

1. Place cabbage in a Dutch oven. Cover with boiling water; add 1 tablespoon salt. Simmer covered until outer leaves are softened but still firm (about 10 minutes). Drain cabbage; rinse with cold water. Have cheesecloth ready for wrapping stuffed cabbage.
2. Mix remaining ingredients, except the reserved zucchini slices and the mushrooms, until well blended.
3. Core cabbage and pull outside leaves back. Remove inside of cabbage carefully, leaving outside layer 5 or 6 leaves thick. Lay outer leaves on a double thickness of cheesecloth; fill leaves with meat mixture. Wrap stuffed cabbage tightly in cheesecloth; invert on another piece of cheesecloth so that the opening of the cabbage is on the bottom. Wrap cabbage securely, tying the cheesecloth into a handle at the top. Lift wrapped cabbage into Dutch oven. Pour reserved tomato liquid around cabbage. Cover.
4. Bake at 350°F to an internal temperature of 165°F (about 1½ hours). Check temperature by inserting a meat thermometer through leaves and into center of meat. Lift cabbage out of Dutch oven; let stand 10 minutes.
5. While cabbage is standing, place zucchini slices and mushrooms in a medium saucepan. Simmer in a small amount of water until barely tender (about 3 minutes); drain.
6. Remove outside layer of cheesecloth from cabbage; place a pie plate on cabbage and invert. Remove remaining cheesecloth; place serving platter on cabbage and invert. Gently shape cabbage with hands if necessary. Garnish top of cabbage with zucchini slices and mushrooms. Cut into wedges and serve.

8 to 10 servings

600 *Hearty Beef-Cabbage Soup*

2 cups tomato juice
● 4 cups Beef Stock
2 cups shredded red cabbage
1 medium onion, thinly sliced
1 carrot, thinly sliced
3 cups cooked beef cubes
2 tablespoons dark raisins
1 teaspoon caraway seed
1 teaspoon paprika
1 teaspoon salt
1 tablespoon cider vinegar
● Low-Fat Yogurt, if desired, for garnish

Simmer all ingredients in a Dutch oven 20 minutes, stirring occasionally. Serve in bowls. Garnish with dollops of yogurt.

6 servings (2 cups each)

Note: This recipe can be made without the meat and served as a first course.

601 *Steak Tartare with Vegetables*

2 pounds beef sirloin steak, boneless
⅓ cup finely chopped leek or green onion
1½ teaspoons Worcestershire sauce
¼ teaspoon Tabasco
1 teaspoon Dijon mustard
½ teaspoon salt
  Freshly ground Szechuan or black pepper
1 egg yolk, if desired
1 teaspoon drained capers
2 bunches parsley, stems removed
1 green pepper, cut in 1-inch pieces
1 sweet red pepper, cut in 1-inch pieces
1 large zucchini, cut in ¼-inch slices
1 medium cucumber, cut in ¼-inch slices
12 medium mushrooms, cut in half lengthwise
1 large carrot, cut in ¼-inch slices
12 large red or white radishes, cut in half

1. Chop meat coarsely in a food processor (or have butcher grind meat coarsely 2 times). Place beef, leek, Worcestershire sauce, Tabasco, mustard, salt, and pepper in a mixing bowl; mix quickly and lightly with 2 forks. Taste; adjust seasonings.
2. Mound beef on a medium serving platter. Make an indentation in top of mound; slip egg yolk into indentation. Sprinkle beef with capers. Surround beef with a thick rim of parsley. Arrange vegetables on parsley. Serve immediately with knives for spreading beef mixture on vegetables.

8 servings

Note: For a party, this recipe would make about 48 appetizer servings.

602 *Elegant Leg of Lamb*

A coating of Dijon mustard, spices, coffee, and wine lends pleasing flavor to the lamb.

1 lamb leg, whole (about 6 pounds)
2 garlic cloves, each sliced in 3 pieces
1 tablespoon Dijon mustard
1 tablespoon strong coffee
2 teaspoons ground ginger
1 cup strong black coffee
¼ cup white port wine
● 1 cup Chicken Stock
4 teaspoons arrowroot
  Cold water
2 teaspoons butter, if desired

1. Trim excess fat from roast. Cut 6 small slits in the roast and insert garlic slices. Rub mixture of mustard, 1 tablespoon coffee, and ginger over entire surface of roast.
2. Place in a shallow roasting pan. Insert meat thermometer so that tip is in center of meat, away from bone and fat.
3. Roast in a 325°F oven to an internal temperature of 175°F (about 3 hours). Mix 1 cup coffee and wine; baste roast with mixture several times during last hour of roasting time.
4. Remove roast to meat platter. Cover loosely with a tent of aluminum foil.
5. Carefully spoon fat from roasting pan. Add remaining basting mixture and stock to roasting pan. Heat to boiling, stirring to incorporate meat particles from pan. Mix arrowroot with a little cold water. Stir into stock mixture. Simmer, stirring constantly, until mixture thickens. Stir butter into gravy just before serving.

6 to 8 servings

603 *Fruited Lamb Roast*

A boned leg of lamb is filled with marinated dried fruits and roasted. The fruit is then puréed for an elegant sauce.

½ pound dried pears or apples
½ pound dried apricots
½ cup golden raisins
1 teaspoon finely minced ginger root or ½ teaspoon ground ginger
1 tablespoon grated orange peel
Juice of 1 orange
½ cup bourbon
Apple cider (about 3 cups)
1 lamb leg, boneless (about 4 pounds)
½ cup bourbon
Apple cider
Salt
2 tablespoons bourbon
Apple cider

1. Place pears, apricots, raisins, ginger root, orange peel, orange juice, and ½ cup bourbon in a medium saucepan. Pour in enough apple cider to cover fruits. Simmer uncovered 20 minutes; cool.

2. Trim roast of excess fat. Lay roast flat in a shallow glass casserole. Drain fruit. Add ½ cup bourbon to drained juice; add enough apple cider to measure 2 cups. Pour juice mixture over roast. Refrigerate roast covered 8 hours or overnight. Refrigerate fruits covered.

3. Remove roast from marinade; salt lightly on both sides. Arrange one third of the fruit on surface of meat; roll up and tie with string at intervals.

4. Place roast on rack in a roasting pan. Insert meat thermometer so tip is in center of roast.

5. Roast uncovered in a 325°F oven to an internal temperature of 175°F (about 2 hours). Add remaining fruit to roasting pan during last half hour of cooking.

6. Place roast and half the fruit on a serving platter. Cover lightly with aluminum foil. Let stand 20 minutes before carving.

7. Purée remaining fruit in a blender or food processor with 2 tablespoons bourbon and enough apple cider to make a sauce consistency. Heat thoroughly; serve with the roast.

8 to 10 servings

604 *Lamb and Pork in Cognac*

The flavors of these two meats blend uniquely while cooking. Choose your favorite fresh vegetable to add to this recipe.

⅓ cup cognac
1⅔ cups dry white wine
½ teaspoon ground mace
¼ teaspoon ground cinnamon
½ teaspoon salt
1½ pounds lean lamb stew cubes
1½ pounds lean pork stew cubes
3 stalks celery, finely chopped
3 carrots, finely chopped
1 medium yellow onion, finely chopped
2 teaspoons salt
½ pound baby carrots
½ pound fresh broccoli
½ pound baby white onions
● Chicken Stock
Salt
Freshly ground pepper

1. Mix cognac, wine, mace, cinnamon, and ½ teaspoon salt; pour over meat cubes in a shallow glass bowl. Refrigerate covered 6 hours or overnight; stir occasionally. Drain meat, reserving ¾ cup marinade.

2. Mix chopped vegetables and layer them in bottom of a Dutch oven; pour reserved marinade over and simmer on top of range 5 minutes. Layer meat cubes over vegetables and sprinkle with 2 teaspoons salt. Cover Dutch oven.

3. Bake at 350°F 1½ to 2 hours, or until meat is tender.

4. Simmer vegetables in 1 inch of stock until just tender (about 15 minutes). Season with salt and pepper.

5. Remove meat from Dutch oven with a slotted spoon to a shallow serving dish; arrange attractively with vegetables.

6 servings

605 *Lamb Ratatouille*

In this main-dish version of ratatouille, the vegetables remain crisp and flavorful.

- 1 quart Savory Tomato Sauce
- 1 tablespoon snipped fresh or 1½ teaspoons dried coriander leaves
- 2 pounds lean lamb stew cubes
- 2 teaspoons salt
  Freshly ground pepper
- 2 tablespoons fresh lemon juice
- ¼ cup dry vermouth or dry white wine
- 1 small eggplant, pared and cut in 1-inch cubes
  Salted water
- 2 green peppers, cut in 1-inch squares
- 2 medium zucchini, cut in ½-inch slices
- 2 medium yellow onions, cut in ¼-inch slices
- Chicken Stock
  Salt
  Freshly ground pepper
- 1 tablespoon olive oil
  Snipped coriander

1. Spoon tomato sauce into bottom of a Dutch oven; sprinkle with 1 tablespoon coriander. Place lamb cubes in sauce; sprinkle with 2 teaspoons salt, pepper, and lemon juice. Pour vermouth over meat. Simmer covered until lamb is tender (about 2 hours).
2. Soak eggplant in salted water to cover for 1 hour; drain and pat dry.
3. Cook vegetables during last half hour lamb is cooking. Simmer eggplant, green peppers, zucchini, and onions in ½ inch of stock in a large skillet until barely tender, so vegetables retain their shape and texture.
4. Arrange cooked vegetables attractively on a heatproof platter; keep warm in oven. Season vegetables with salt and pepper; drizzle with olive oil. Arrange lamb and tomato mixture over vegetables; sprinkle with coriander.

6 servings

606 *Pork Chops Piquant*

Green pepper and onion stay crisp in this braised pork chop dish. Capers add a hint of pungency.

- 4 pork loin chops, 1 inch thick
- ¼ cup water
- ¼ teaspoon bottled brown bouquet sauce
- ½ teaspoon salt
  Freshly ground pepper
- ½ cup Chicken Stock
- ¼ cup dry white wine
- 1 green pepper, chopped
- 1 medium yellow onion, chopped
- 2 tablespoons capers, drained
  Watercress or parsley sprigs

1. Trim excess fat from chops. Brush chops lightly with a mixture of water and brown bouquet sauce. Brown chops lightly on both sides in a nonstick skillet over medium heat. Sprinkle with salt and pepper.
2. Add stock and wine. Simmer covered 30 minutes. Skim fat from liquid. Stir in green pepper, onion, and capers. Simmer uncovered 10 to 15 minutes until vegetables are just tender. Taste vegetables and sauce; adjust seasoning.
3. Serve vegetables and sauce over chops; garnish with watercress.

4 servings

607 *Savory Veal Stew*

The meat in this stew is unbelievably tender. Caraway and fennel provide a flavorful accent to garden vegetables.

3 pounds veal stew cubes
1½ teaspoons salt
½ teaspoon freshly ground
　　pepper
2 garlic cloves
1 teaspoon caraway seed, lightly
　　crushed
1 teaspoon fennel seed, lightly
　　crushed
2 bay leaves
½ cup dry white wine
● 1 cup Beef Stock
1 small head cabbage, cut in 8
　　wedges
3 leeks, cut in 3-inch pieces
¾ teaspoon salt
½ teaspoon freshly ground
　　pepper
1 tablespoon arrowroot
　　Cold water
½ pound mushrooms, sliced
● ½ cup Mock Crème Fraîche
　　if desired

1. Place veal in a 6-quart Dutch oven; sprinkle with 1½ teaspoons salt and ½ teaspoon pepper. Mix garlic, caraway, fennel, bay leaves, wine, and stock. Pour over veal. Simmer covered over low heat 2 hours.
2. Add cabbage and leeks to Dutch oven; sprinkle with ¾ teaspoon salt and ½ teaspoon pepper. Simmer covered until vegetables and veal are just tender (about 15 minutes). Remove veal and vegetables to a shallow serving dish; keep warm.
3. Skim fat from cooking liquid in Dutch oven. Discard bay leaves. Mix arrowroot with a little cold water. Stir into cooking liquid; simmer until thickened (about 3 minutes). Stir in mushrooms and Mock Crème Fraîche; simmer 1 minute. Pour thickened mixture over veal and vegetables. Sprinkle with **parsley**.

8 servings

608 *Veal Scallops in Lemon Sauce*

This adaptation of Veal Piccata uses stock rather than butter in the sauce. Szechuan pepper adds a flavor accent to the tart sauce; fresh snipped parsley adds color.

12 veal scallops (about 2 pounds)
¼ cup water
¼ teaspoon bottled brown
　　bouquet sauce
2 teaspoons clarified butter
　　Salt
¾ cup dry white wine
● ¾ cup Chicken Stock
⅓ cup finely chopped onion
1 garlic clove, minced
½ cup fresh lemon juice
¼ teaspoon freshly ground white
　　pepper
½ teaspoon salt
1 tablespoon arrowroot
　　Cold water
1 tablespoon snipped parsley

1. Pound veal scallops with a mallet until thin and even in thickness. Brush both sides lightly with a mixture of water and brown bouquet sauce. Cook a few pieces of veal in hot butter in a skillet just until done (about 1 minute on each side). Sprinkle lightly with salt. Keep warm in oven while cooking remaining veal.
2. While veal is cooking, mix wine, stock, onion, and garlic in a small saucepan. Simmer until onion is tender (about 3 minutes). Stir in lemon juice, pepper, and salt.
3. Mix arrowroot with a little cold water. Stir into simmering stock mixture. Simmer, stirring constantly, until mixture thickens.
4. Arrange veal on warm plates. Pour sauce over. Sprinkle with parsley.

6 servings

609 *Ham Steak with Parsley Sauce*

2 bunches parsley, washed and
  stems removed
¼ cup dry white wine
1 center-cut smoked ham steak,
  ¾ inch thick (about 1½
  pounds)
● ⅔ cup Mock Hollandaise Sauce
  Salt
  Freshly ground white pepper

1. Line bottom of a shallow baking dish with half the parsley; drizzle with half the wine. Lay ham steak on parsley. Cover ham with remaining parsley; drizzle with remaining wine. Lightly cover baking dish.
2. Bake at 325°F about 30 minutes, or until ham is thoroughly heated.
3. Make Mock Hollandaise Sauce while ham is baking; keep warm.
4. Place ham on platter; cover lightly with aluminum foil. Purée cooked parsley in a blender or food processor; stir mixture into Mock Hollandaise Sauce. Season sauce with salt and pepper. Heat sauce thoroughly; serve with ham.

3 or 4 servings

610 *Ham Mousse on Medallions*

6 slices boiled ham, cut ⅓ inch
  thick (about 1½ pounds)
2 teaspoons unflavored gelatin
1 cup cold water
2 cups low-fat ricotta cheese
3 tablespoons snipped parsley
1½ tablespoons snipped fresh or 2
  teaspoons crumbled dried
  tarragon leaves
2 teaspoons Dijon mustard
⅛ teaspoon salt
  Dash freshly ground pepper
  Parsley sprigs
  Radish roses

1. Cut two 2½-inch circles from each slice ham; refrigerate covered. Mince remaining ham pieces; refrigerate covered.
2. Sprinkle gelatin over cold water in a saucepan; let stand 5 minutes. Set over low heat until dissolved (about 3 minutes), stirring occasionally.
3. Pour gelatin into a food processor or blender; add ricotta cheese, snipped parsley, tarragon, mustard, salt, and pepper. Process until mixture is smooth; transfer mixture to a medium mixing bowl. Stir in minced ham; refrigerate covered until mixture has set (about 1 hour).
4. Place 2 ham circles on each of 6 individual plates. Mound mousse by heaping tablespoonfuls on circles. Garnish with parsley and radish roses.

6 servings

Note: This recipe will make 12 first-course servings.

611 *Rack of Veal with Peppercorn Sauce*

Very easy to prepare, very elegant to serve. Green peppercorns add zest to a low-calorie version of Béarnaise Sauce.

1 veal rib roast (about 5 pounds)
1 teaspoon salt
  Freshly ground white pepper
  White wine
● 1⅓ cups Mock Béarnaise Sauce
  (double recipe)
2 tablespoons drained green
  peppercorns

1. Rub roast with salt and pepper; place in a roasting pan. Insert meat thermometer so tip is in center of meat, away from bone.
2. Roast uncovered in a 325°F oven to an internal temperature of 165°F (about 3 hours). Baste several times with white wine during last hour of roasting. Remove to a platter and cover loosely with aluminum foil; let stand 20 minutes before carving.
3. While roast is standing, make the sauce, adding peppercorns before heating. Pass sauce.

10 servings

Note: A boneless veal roast can also be used in this recipe. Roast as directed above, allowing about 35 minutes per pound.

612 *Stuffed Veal Breast*

Spinach and ricotta cheese are in the filling for this tempting dish with an Italian influence.

2½ pounds boneless breast of veal
Salt
Freshly ground pepper
1 large onion, chopped
● 2 tablespoons Chicken Stock
*½ pound fresh spinach, washed and stems removed
¾ cup low-fat ricotta cheese
¼ cup grated Jarlsberg or Parmesan cheese
2 garlic cloves, minced
1 teaspoon snipped fresh or ½ teaspoon dried thyme leaves
1½ teaspoons snipped fresh or ¾ teaspoon dried basil leaves
½ teaspoon snipped fresh or ¼ teaspoon dried oregano leaves
2 tablespoons snipped parsley
1 teaspoon salt
¼ teaspoon pepper
½ cup dry white wine or Chicken Stock

1. Trim excess fat from meat. Sprinkle meat lightly on both sides with salt and pepper.
2. Simmer onion in stock just until tender (about 5 minutes).
3. Place spinach with water clinging to leaves in a large saucepan; cook covered over medium heat just until wilted (about 3 minutes).
4. Drain onion and spinach well in a strainer, pressing moisture out with a wooden spoon. Mix onion, spinach, cheeses, garlic, thyme, basil, oregano, parsley, 1 teaspoon salt, and ¼ teaspoon pepper. Spoon mixture on surface of meat; roll up and tie with string at intervals. Place meat in a roasting pan. Pour wine over roast. Cover.
5. Roast in a 325°F oven about 1½ hours, or until tender.
6. Remove roast to a serving platter. Cover lightly with aluminum foil. Let stand 15 minutes before carving.

6 servings

*1 package (10 ounces) frozen spinach can be substituted for the fresh. Thaw and drain thoroughly in strainer.

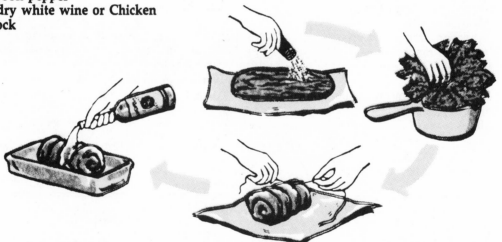

613 *Calf's Liver with Curried Onions*

The addition of curry and raisins gives this recipe an interesting Indian accent.

1 large yellow onion, sliced
¼ cup sherry
½ teaspoon curry powder
½ teaspoon salt
Freshly ground pepper
¼ cup golden raisins
2 teaspoons clarified butter
1 pound calf's liver
Clarified butter

1. Simmer onion slices in wine in a medium skillet until onion is tender and wine is absorbed (about 10 minutes). Stir in curry powder, salt, pepper, raisins, and 2 teaspoons butter.
2. While onion is cooking, brush liver slices very lightly with clarified butter.
3. Broil 4 inches from heat until lightly browned (about 3 minutes on each side). Serve with onion.

4 servings

614 *Pot Roast Jardinière*

A country-style stew with garden vegetables is hearty fare.

   1 beef chuck pot roast (4 pounds)
¼ cup prepared horseradish
   1 tablespoon salt
   1 medium tomato, chopped
● 1 cup Beef Stock
   3 medium kohlrabi or turnips, pared and cut in ½-inch cubes
   3 medium carrots, cut in ½-inch slices
*1 pound fresh Brussels sprouts, cleaned
   1 teaspoon snipped fresh or ½ teaspoon dried thyme leaves
   1 teaspoon snipped fresh or ½ teaspoon dried marjoram leaves
   1 teaspoon salt
½ teaspoon pepper
   2 leeks, cut in 1-inch pieces
   2 teaspoons arrowroot
   Cold water

1. Rub meat on both sides with a mixture of horseradish and 1 tablespoon salt; place meat in a Dutch oven. Add tomato and stock to Dutch oven. Cover.
2. Cook in a 325°F oven about 3 hours, or until meat is tender.
3. Add vegetables, thyme, marjoram, 1 teaspoon salt, and ½ teaspoon pepper to Dutch oven during last 15 minutes of cooking time; cook just until vegetables are tender.
4. Remove meat and vegetables to platter. Skim fat from cooking liquid. If thicker sauce is desired, mix arrowroot with a little cold water and stir into liquid. Simmer, stirring constantly, until sauce is thickened. Pass sauce.

6 servings

*1 package (10 ounces) frozen Brussels sprouts can be substituted for the fresh. Add to Dutch oven for length of cooking time indicated on package.

615 *Oriental One-Pot Meal*

This recipe has been borrowed from Japanese sukiyaki. The technique is perfect for New French Cooking, as foods are cooked quickly in stock to retain natural color, flavor, and texture.

● 6 cups Beef Stock
¼ cup light soy sauce
⅓ cup beer
   2 teaspoons sugar
*¼ teaspoon freshly ground Szechuan or black pepper
½ teaspoon salt
   2 cups sliced fresh mushrooms
   2 bunches green onions, cut in ½-inch pieces
   1 cup sliced bamboo shoots
**1 cup sliced Chinese cabbage or bok choy
1½ pounds lean beef sirloin or rib eye steak, cut in paper-thin slices

1. Mix stock, soy sauce, beer, sugar, pepper, and salt in a 3-quart saucepan. Boil 3 minutes. Simmer vegetables in stock mixture until vegetables are just tender (about 5 minutes). Divide vegetables among 6 shallow bowls; keep warm in oven.
2. Cook half the beef slices in the simmering stock mixture until rare to medium done (2 to 4 minutes). Divide meat among bowls. Cook remaining meat; divide among bowls. Serve hot stock mixture over meat and vegetables or in individual bowls for dipping.

6 servings

*Lightly roast Szechuan pepper over medium heat in a skillet before grinding.
**Chinese cabbage can be purchased in Oriental or specialty shops.

616 *Herbed Skirt Steak*

Mock Crème Fraîche and fresh dill enhance this creative combination.

1½ pounds lean beef skirt steak
2 teaspoons clarified butter
1 large yellow onion, finely sliced
● ½ cup Beef Stock
1 garlic clove, minced
¼ teaspoon freshly ground pepper
1½ teaspoons salt
● ½ cup Mock Crème Fraîche
¼ cup snipped fresh dill or 2 tablespoons dried dill weed

1. Slice steak in half lengthwise; cut pieces across the grain into paper-thin slices. Heat butter over high heat in a 12-inch skillet. Add meat slices, stirring quickly to coat meat with butter. Add onion; cook and stir 2 minutes. Add Beef Stock, garlic, pepper, and salt; simmer covered until onion is tender (about 3 minutes).
2. Stir ¼ cup pan juices into Mock Crème Fraîche. Stir mixture back into pan; stir in dill. Serve immediately.

4 to 6 servings

617 *Steak with Mushroom Stuffing*

The texture of fresh mushrooms and the flavor of nutmeg are memorable additions to a perfectly cooked steak.

1 small onion, finely chopped
2 shallots, finely chopped
● 2 tablespoons Beef Stock
½ pound mushrooms, cleaned and chopped
1 tablespoon brandy
3 grinds fresh or ¼ teaspoon ground nutmeg
¾ teaspoon salt
¼ teaspoon freshly ground pepper
2½ pounds lean beef sirloin steak, boneless
Snipped parsley

1. Simmer onion and shallots in stock until tender (about 5 minutes). Mix onion, shallots, mushrooms, brandy, nutmeg, salt, and pepper.
2. Trim excess fat from steak. Cut pocket in steak, cutting to, but not through opposite side and leaving 1 inch intact on each end. Fill pocket loosely with onion mixture; skewer opening with wooden picks.
3. Broil steak 3 inches from heat, 8 minutes on each side for medium rare, 10 minutes on each side for medium. Remove wooden picks. Sprinkle steak with parsley. Slice and serve.

8 servings

618 *Veal Cutlets Valle d'Aosta (Costolette alla Valdostana)*

6 veal chops, boneless, 1 inch thick
6 thin slices fully cooked ham
6 slices fontina or mozzarella cheese
1 cup all-purpose flour
1 teaspoon salt
¼ teaspoon pepper
1 egg, beaten with 1 tablespoon water
Fine bread crumbs
¼ cup butter, more if needed

1. Butterfly chops by slicing through the chop almost all the way, and laying chop open so it is ½ inch thick; pound flat.
2. Place a slice of ham, then a slice of cheese, in the center of each chop. Moisten edges of chop and press together.
3. Dip each folded chop first in flour mixed with salt and pepper, then in beaten egg, and finally in the bread crumbs.
4. Heat the butter in a large skillet. Brown the chops slowly, about 5 minutes on each side or until done.

6 servings

619 *Meatballs (Polpette)*

Peel of 1 lemon, grated
1 sprig parsley
2 cloves garlic, peeled
1 pound ground beef
1 teaspoon salt
¼ teaspoon pepper
Pinch grated nutmeg
1 slice bread, crumbled
Milk
1 egg, beaten
2 to 3 tablespoons olive oil or
  other cooking oil

1. Mince together grated lemon peel, parsley, and garlic.
2. Mix ground beef with salt, pepper, nutmeg, and lemon-peel mixture.
3. Soak bread in a small amount of milk, squeeze dry, and add with egg to meat mixture. Blend well.
4. On a lightly floured surface, form mixture into patties about ½ inch thick and 1½ inches wide.
5. Place the patties in hot oil in a skillet. Brown about 2 minutes on each side. Drain and serve hot.

4 to 6 servings

620 *Bollito Misto*

1 fresh beef tongue (3 to 4 pounds)
1 calf's head, prepared for cooking, or 2 pounds veal neck
2 pounds beef (neck, rump, or chuck roast)
2 pig's feet or 1 pound cotechino or other uncooked pork sausage
1 stewing chicken (3 to 4 pounds)
4 medium carrots, pared and cut in 3-inch pieces
2 large stalks celery, cut in pieces
3 onions, peeled and quartered
4 turnips or parsnips, pared and quartered
2 tablespoons chopped parsley
1 teaspoon tarragon
1 teaspoon thyme
Water
Salt
Salsa Verde

1. Combine meats, chicken, vegetables, parsley, tarragon, and thyme in a large sauce pot. Pour in enough water to cover meat, and salt to taste.
2. Cover pot, bring to boiling, and simmer 3 to 4 hours, or until tongue is tender.
3. Remove skin from tongue. Slice meat, cut chicken in serving pieces, and arrange with vegetables on a large platter.
4. Serve with **boiled potatoes, cooked cabbage, beets, pickles,** and Salsa Verde.

10 to 12 servings

Note: A pressure cooker may be used. Follow manufacturer's directions for use of cooker and length of cooking time.

Salsa Verde: Finely chop **3 hard-cooked eggs;** set aside. Combine **½ cup salad oil** and **3 tablespoons wine vinegar.** Add **sugar, salt,** and **pepper** to taste. Mix well and combine with the chopped eggs. Blend in **6 tablespoons chopped herbs** such as **dill, tarragon, chervil, parsley, sorrel,** and **chives.** Refrigerate several hours to allow flavors to blend.

621 *Ossobuco*

4 to 5 pounds veal shank crosscuts
Flour
⅓ cup olive oil
Salt and pepper
½ cup beef broth or bouillon
1 onion, chopped
1 clove garlic, crushed in a garlic
    press
1 medium carrot, sliced
1 leek, sliced
1 slice celery root
2 whole cloves
1 bay leaf
    Pinch each of sage, thyme, and
    rosemary
½ cup white wine
1 can (28 ounces) whole tomatoes
1 tablespoon grated lemon peel

1. Dredge crosscuts with flour. Heat several tablespoons olive oil in a skillet. Brown the veal well, season with salt and pepper, and transfer to a heatproof casserole or Dutch oven. Handle gently so the marrow remains in the bones. Pour the broth into the casserole.
2. Add more oil to skillet, if needed. In hot oil, sauté onion, garlic, carrot, leek, and celery root over medium heat about 5 minutes.
3. Stir in the cloves, bay leaf, sage, thyme, and rosemary. Pour in the wine and continue cooking until wine is almost evaporated. Stir in tomatoes and grated lemon peel. Cook over medium heat several minutes.
4. Pour tomato mixture over meat in casserole. Cover tightly and simmer about 1½ hours, or until meat is tender. Remove veal to serving dish and keep hot.
5. Force vegetables and juice in casserole through a sieve or food mill. If the resulting sauce is thin, cook over high heat to reduce liquid. Season sauce, if necessary. Pour sauce over meat or serve separately.
6. Serve with **rice** or **spaghetti** tossed with **melted butter** and topped with **grated Parmesan** or **Romano cheese**.

4 or 5 servings

622 *Mixed Fry (Fritto Misto)*

½ pound calf's brains
2 cups water
1½ teaspoons vinegar or lemon
    juice
½ teaspoon salt
¼ cup flour
½ teaspoon salt
    Pinch pepper
½ pound liver (beef, lamb, veal, or
    calf), sliced ¼ to ½ inch thick
2 cups all-purpose flour
1 teaspoon salt
¼ teaspoon pepper
1½ cups milk
3 eggs, well beaten
2 tablespoons melted shortening
    Oil for frying
6 artichoke hearts (canned in
    water), drained
2 zucchini, washed and cut
    crosswise in 1-inch slices
3 stalks celery, cut in 3-inch
    pieces

1. Wash brains in cold water. Combine with 2 cups water, vinegar, and ½ teaspoon salt in a saucepan. Bring to boiling, reduce heat, and simmer gently 20 minutes.
2. Drain the brains and drop into cold water. Drain again and remove membranes. Separate into small pieces and set aside.
3. Combine ¼ cup flour, ½ teaspoon salt, and pinch pepper. Coat the liver with the flour mixture, cut into serving-size pieces, and set aside.
4. Combine 2 cups flour with 1 teaspoon salt and ¼ teaspoon pepper; set aside. Combine milk, eggs, and shortening. Gradually add the flour mixture to the liquid, beating until smooth.
5. Fill a deep saucepan one-half to two-thirds full with oil. Heat slowly to 360°F. Dip pieces of meat and the vegetables in the batter and fry in hot oil, being careful not to crowd the pieces. Fry about 5 minutes, or until golden brown, turning occasionally.
6. Hold cooked pieces over the hot oil to drain before placing on paper towels. Place on a warm platter and serve immediately.

6 servings

Roast Stuffed with Liver (Porchetta)

on fennel seed
garlic, peeled
n salt
n sugar
n coarsely ground pepper
rubbed sage
pork loin or loin end
about 3 pounds)
rk, lamb, or beef liver,
lices ⅓ inch thick
n cornstarch
1 cup cool beef broth

1. Using a mortar and pestle, crush the fennel seed. Add the garlic, salt, sugar, pepper, and sage. Crush until mixture becomes a rough paste.
2. Open pork roast and lay flat side down; cut the meat if necessary to make it lie flat. Rub surface of the roast with about half the garlic paste. Lay liver strips lengthwise over meat.
3. Roll the roast tightly lengthwise with seasoned surface inside. Tie with heavy string at 2-inch intervals. Rub remaining garlic paste on outside of roast. Place roast on a rack in a shallow baking pan.
4. Cook, uncovered, at 375°F until meat thermometer inserted in thickest part of the roast registers 170°F (about 1½ hours). Transfer roast to a serving platter and keep warm.
5. Remove rack from roasting pan and place pan over direct heat. Stir together the cornstarch and broth until blended. Stir into drippings in roasting pan. Cook over medium heat, stirring constantly, until sauce boils and thickens. Pour sauce into a serving bowl.
6. To serve, cut and remove strings from roast, and cut meat into thin slices.

About 8 servings

624 Veal Peasant Style (Vitello alla Paesano)

2 tablespoons butter
1 tablespoon olive oil
1 cup finely chopped onion
⅓ cup finely chopped celery
1½ to 2 pounds veal, cubed
1 teaspoon salt
¼ teaspoon pepper
4 tomatoes, peeled and coarsely
    chopped
    Several basil leaves or ¼
    teaspoon dried basil leaves
¾ cup beef broth
2 tablespoons butter
1 pound fresh green peas, shelled,
    or 1 package (10 ounces)
    frozen green peas
3 carrots, diced
½ teaspoon salt
¾ cup hot water
1 tablespoon minced parsley

1. Heat 2 tablespoons butter and the olive oil in a Dutch oven or large saucepot. Add onion and celery; sauté 3 or 4 minutes.
2. Add meat and brown on all sides. Season with 1 teaspoon salt and the pepper. Stir in tomatoes and basil. Cover Dutch oven.
3. Cook at 275°F about 1¼ hours, or until meat is almost tender. Add broth, a little at a time, during cooking.
4. Heat 2 tablespoons butter in a saucepan. Stir in peas, carrots, ½ teaspoon salt, and water. Cook, covered, until vegetables are tender (about 15 minutes).
5. Skim off fat from meat. Stir in the cooked vegetables and parsley. Continue cooking in oven until meat is tender.
6. Serve meat surrounded with the vegetables and **small sautéed potatoes** on a heated platter. Pour sauce over all.

6 to 8 servings

625 *Perugia Ham and Cheese Pie (Pizzetta alla Perugina)*

2 cups all-purpose flour
½ teaspoon salt
¼ cup butter or margarine
2 eggs
3 tablespoons milk
1½ cups minced cooked ham
½ cup shredded Swiss cheese
½ cup diced Bel Paese cheese
1 egg yolk, slightly beaten

1. Combine flour and salt in a bowl. Cut in butter with pastry blender or two knives until pieces are small. Add eggs and stir in milk to form a soft dough. Knead dough lightly; divide in two equal portions.
2. Roll cut one portion on a lightly floured surface into a rectangle large enough to line the bottom and sides of an 11×7-inch baking pan. Place dough in pan and cover with ham and cheese.
3. Bring dough on sides of pan down over the meat and cheese. Roll out the remaining dough to form an 11×7-inch rectangle and place on top of filling. Press edges of top crust with a fork to seal to bottom crust. Prick top with fork in several places, and brush with egg yolk.
4. Bake at 425°F 10 minutes. Turn oven control to 350°F and bake 10 minutes. Cut into rectangles and serve warm.

6 to 8 servings

626 *Saltimbocca (Sliced Ham and Veal with Wine)*

4 large, thinly sliced veal cutlets
Salt and pepper
4 large, very thin slices ham or prosciutto
Dried sage leaves
Olive oil
¼ cup (2 ounces) Marsala

1. Place veal slices on a cutting board and pound with a mallet until very thin. Divide each slice into 2 or 3 pieces.
2. Season veal with salt and pepper.
3. Cut ham into pieces the same size as veal.
4. Place a sage leaf on each piece of veal and top with a slice of ham. Secure with a wooden pick.
5. Heat several tablespoons olive oil in a skillet; add the meat and cook slowly until golden brown on both sides. Remove meat to heated platter and keep warm.
6. Scrape residue from bottom of pan; add the Marsala and simmer over low heat several minutes. Pour over meat and serve.

4 servings

627 *Veal and Peppers Basilicata Style (Vitello e Pepe alla Basilicata)*

2 tablespoons butter
1 tablespoon lard
1½ pounds boneless veal leg, rump, or shoulder roast, cut in 1-inch pieces
1 teaspoon salt
⅛ teaspoon pepper
1 medium-size onion, sliced
4 large ripe tomatoes
1 tablespoon chopped basil leaves or 1 teaspoon dried sweet basil
4 large firm green or red peppers
3 tablespoons olive oil

1. Heat butter and lard in skillet over medium heat. Add meat and brown on all sides. Stir in salt, pepper, and onion; cook 5 minutes.
2. Cut tomatoes in half, squeeze out seeds, chop pulp, and add with basil to meat. Cover and simmer 20 minutes.
3. Cut out stems, remove seeds, and clean peppers. Cut in quarters, lengthwise. Fry peppers in hot olive oil about 10 minutes, or until softened. Add to meat, cover, and simmer 30 minutes, or until meat is tender. Serve hot.

4 servings

633 *Veal Chops Pizzaiola (Scaloppine alla Pizzaiola)*

¼ cup olive oil
6 veal rib or loin chops, cut about
    ½ inch thick
1 can (28 ounces) tomatoes, sieved
2 cloves garlic, sliced
1 teaspoon oregano
1 teaspoon salt
½ teaspoon pepper
½ teaspoon chopped parsley

1. Heat oil in a large, heavy skillet. Add chops and brown on both sides.
2. Meanwhile, combine tomatoes, garlic, oregano, salt, pepper, and parsley. Slowly add tomato mixture to browned veal. Cover and cook over low heat 45 minutes, or until meat is tender.

6 servings

Beefsteak Pizzaiola: Follow recipe for Veal Chops Pizzaiola. Substitute **2 pounds beef round steak,** cut about ¾ inch thick, for veal chops. Cook about 1½ hours.

634 *Veal Scaloppine with Mushrooms and Capers* *(Scaloppine di Vitella con Funghi e Capperi)*

1 pound veal round steak, cut
    about ½ inch thick
½ cup flour
½ teaspoon salt
⅛ teaspoon pepper
¼ cup olive oil
½ clove garlic, minced
¼ cup butter
½ pound mushrooms, cleaned and
    sliced lengthwise
1 medium onion, thinly sliced
1¾ cups sieved canned tomatoes
¼ cup capers
1 teaspoon salt
⅛ teaspoon pepper
¼ teaspoon minced parsley
¼ teaspoon oregano

1. Put meat on a flat working surface and pound on both sides with a meat hammer. Cut into 1-inch pieces. Coat evenly with a mixture of flour, ½ teaspoon salt, and ⅛ teaspoon pepper.
2. Heat oil with garlic in a large skillet. Add veal and slowly brown on both sides.
3. Meanwhile, heat butter in a skillet. Add mushrooms and onion; cook until mushrooms are lightly browned.
4. Add mushrooms to veal along with tomatoes, capers, 1 teaspoon salt, ⅛ teaspoon pepper, parsley, and oregano; mix well.
5. Cover skillet and simmer about 25 minutes, or until veal is tender; stir occasionally.

About 4 servings

635 *Veal Marsala (Scaloppine di Vitella al Marsala)*

1½ to 2 pounds veal round steak,
   cut about ½ inch thick
¼ cup flour
1 teaspoon salt
⅛ teaspoon pepper
1 clove garlic, thinly sliced
¼ cup olive oil
¼ cup Marsala
¼ cup water
¼ teaspoon chopped parsley
⅛ teaspoon salt
⅛ teaspoon pepper

1. Place meat on a flat working surface and pound with a meat hammer on both sides. Cut into 6 pieces.
2. Coat veal with a mixture of flour, 1 teaspoon salt, and ⅛ teaspoon pepper.
3. Heat garlic and oil in a large, heavy skillet until garlic is slightly browned. Add meat to oil and garlic in skillet; brown slowly on both sides.
4. Meanwhile, combine Marsala, water, parsley, ⅛ teaspoon salt, and ⅛ teaspoon pepper. Slowly add Marsala mixture to browned veal. Cover and cook over low heat 20 minutes, or until veal is tender.

6 servings

636 *Veal Cannelloni*

¼ cup finely chopped onion
¼ cup finely chopped celery
2 tablespoons finely chopped carrot
1 tablespoon minced parsley
2 tablespoons olive oil
2 cups ground cooked veal
¼ teaspoon salt
⅛ teaspoon white pepper
¼ teaspoon oregano, crushed
¼ teaspoon basil, crushed
½ cup strong chicken broth (1
   chicken bouillon cube
   dissolved in ½ cup boiling
   water)
⅛ teaspoon nutmeg
● 2 cups Medium White Sauce
   Pasta for Cannelloni
¼ cup tomato sauce
¼ cup cream
1 cup grated Parmesan cheese

1. Cook onion, celery, carrot, and parsley in hot oil in a skillet about 3 minutes. Stir in veal, salt, pepper, oregano, basil, and chicken broth. Cook about 15 minutes.
2. Stir ½ cup white sauce into veal mixture.
3. Prepare pasta.
4. Spoon veal filling equally on the pasta squares and roll up. Arrange on an oven-proof platter.
5. Blend tomato sauce and cream into remaining white sauce; pour over cannelloni. Sprinkle top with cheese.
6. Set in a 425°F oven 10 minutes, or until top is browned.

4 servings

637 *Pasta for Cannelloni*

2 cups all-purpose flour
¼ teaspoon salt
1 egg, beaten
2 egg yolks, beaten
7 tablespoons water
4 quarts water
1 tablespoon salt

1. Blend flour and ¼ teaspoon salt in a bowl. Using a fork, stir in egg and egg yolks. Gradually add 7 tablespoons water, stirring constantly to make a stiff dough.
2. Turn dough onto a lightly floured surface and knead until smooth. Divide dough into halves and roll each into a rectangle ¹/₁₆ inch thick. Cut into eight 6×4-inch rectangles. Dry 1 hour. (Any leftover dough may be cut into strips, dried, and used as noodles.)
3. Bring 4 quarts water to boiling in a large saucepan. Add 1 tablespoon salt, then cannelloni squares. Boil, uncovered, about 8 minutes, or until just tender. Drain, rinse with cold water, and drain again.

8 cannelloni squares

638 *Meat-and-Spinach-Filled Pancake Rolls*
(Cannelloni alla Piemontese "Maison")

6 thin 10-inch pancakes*
⅓ cup finely chopped onion
3 tablespoons olive oil
½ pound ground veal, cooked (or other cooked meat)
1 package (10 ounces) frozen chopped spinach, cooked and drained
1 egg
⅓ cup grated Parmesan cheese
¼ teaspoon salt
Pinch pepper
Pinch nutmeg
● 1½ cups Béchamel Sauce

1. Prepare pancakes and cut into 2½-inch squares; keep warm.
2. Cook onion in heated olive oil in a skillet about 3 minutes. Add ground meat and cook until lightly browned. Mix spinach with meat mixture; force mixture through medium blade of food chopper.
3. Mix egg, cheese, salt, pepper, and nutmeg with meat mixture until thoroughly blended. Place about 1 tablespoon meat mixture on each pancake square and roll each into a sausage shape.
4. Arrange the filled cannelloni in a shallow buttered baking dish; cover with Béchamel Sauce.
5. Heat in a 375°F oven until golden brown. Serve very hot.

4 to 6 servings

*Prepare pancakes using batter in recipe for Stuffed Pancakes ●

639 *Scamorze-Crowned Veal with Mushrooms*

2 pounds veal cutlets, cut about ½ inch thick
¼ cup lemon juice
½ teaspoon salt
1/16 teaspoon black pepper
¼ cup butter
½ cup flour
1 egg, beaten
½ cup fine dry bread crumbs
¼ pound mushrooms, cleaned and sliced
6 thin slices cooked ham
6 ounces scamorze cheese, cut in 6 slices
6 mushroom caps, browned in butter

1. Cut meat into 6 serving-size pieces; place on a flat working surface and pound both sides with a meat hammer. Put into a large, shallow dish.
2. Mix lemon juice, salt, and pepper together and spoon over veal. Cover and refrigerate 2 hours.
3. Heat butter in a large, heavy skillet. Coat veal pieces with flour, dip in egg, then in bread crumbs. Add to hot butter in skillet and fry about 5 minutes on one side, or until lightly browned.
4. Turn meat and arrange on each piece a layer of mushroom slices, a slice of ham, a slice of cheese, and a mushroom cap. Continue cooking about 5 minutes, or until second side is browned and cheese is melted.
5. Remove to a warm serving platter and serve immediately.

6 servings

640 *Veal Parmesan (Scaloppine di Vitella alla Parmigiana)*

● 2 cups Tomato Meat Sauce
1½ to 2 pounds veal round steak, cut about ½ inch thick
1⅓ cups fine dry bread crumbs
⅓ cup grated Parmesan cheese
3 eggs, beaten
1 teaspoon salt
¼ teaspoon pepper
⅓ cup olive oil
6 slices (3 ounces) mozzarella cheese

1. Prepare Tomato Meat Sauce.
2. Put meat on a flat working surface and repeatedly pound on one side with meat hammer. Turn meat over and repeat process. Cut into 6 pieces.
3. Mix bread crumbs and grated cheese; set aside.
4. Mix eggs, salt, and pepper; set aside.
5. Heat oil in a large skillet. Coat meat pieces first with egg, then with crumb mixture. Add to oil in skillet and brown on both sides.
6. Put browned meat into an 11×7×1½-inch baking dish. Pour sauce over meat. Top with slices of mozzarella cheese.
7. Bake at 350°F 15 to 20 minutes, or until cheese is melted and lightly browned.

6 servings

641 *Ham-and-Asparagus-Stuffed Veal Rolls (Manicaretti alla Lucrezia Borgia)*

6 slices (1½ pounds) veal cutlet, boneless
1 teaspoon salt
¼ teaspoon black pepper
6 slices prosciutto
6 slices Emmenthaler cheese
6 white asparagus spears, 4 inches long
¼ cup butter
½ cup port wine
2 tablespoons butter
⅓ cup finely chopped parsley
2 cloves garlic, crushed
3½ ounces dried mushrooms, hydrated (soaked in water)
¼ cup beef gravy
3 cups cream
1 teaspoon salt

1. Pound veal cutlets until thin. Season with salt and pepper.
2. Place a slice of prosciutto, then a slice of cheese and an asparagus spear, over each veal slice. Roll into fingers; skewer or secure with twine.
3. Melt the ¼ cup butter in a large, heavy skillet. Add veal rolls; brown on all sides. Add port wine; cover and simmer about 10 minutes.
4. Meanwhile, melt the 2 tablespoons butter in a saucepan. Add and lightly brown the parsley and garlic. Mix in the mushrooms, beef gravy, and cream; simmer 5 minutes. Pour sauce over veal rolls; correct seasoning, using the remaining 1 teaspoon salt. Cover and simmer until meat is tender.

6 servings

642 *Beef Stew* (Caldillo)

3 tablespoons lard or vegetable oil
3 pounds lean beef, cut in ½-inch cubes
1 large onion, finely chopped
1 clove garlic, minced
3 fresh ripe tomatoes, peeled, seeded, and chopped
2 cans (4 ounces each) mild red chilies, drained and puréed
2 cups beef broth
2 teaspoons salt
⅛ teaspoon pepper
½ teaspoon oregano

1. Heat lard in a large skillet. Brown meat quickly on all sides. Remove beef from fat and set aside.
2. Add onion and garlic to fat in skillet; cook until onion is soft. Remove from fat and add to beef.
3. Cook tomato in fat in skillet, adding more fat if necessary. Return meat and onion to skillet. Add chili purée, beef broth, and seasonings; stir. Cover; bring to boiling, reduce heat, and cook over low heat about 2 hours, or until meat is tender.

6 to 8 servings

643 *Mexican Beef Stew*

2 pounds beef for stew, cut in 2-inch chunks
1 large onion, chopped
1 clove garlic, minced
1 green pepper, cut in strips
1 cup canned tomato sauce
1 canned chipotle chili, finely chopped
1 tablespoon vinegar
1½ teaspoons salt
1 teaspoon oregano
3 cups cubed pared potatoes
4 or 5 carrots, pared and cut in strips
   Beef stock, or water plus beef bouillon cube
2 tablespoons flour

1. Put meat into a Dutch oven or large kettle. Add onion, garlic, green pepper, tomato sauce, chili, vinegar, salt, and oregano. Cover and bring to boiling; reduce heat and simmer 2½ hours, stirring occasionally.
2. Add potatoes and carrots to meat mixture. If more liquid seems needed, add up to 1 cup beef stock. Cover and cook about 30 minutes, or until meat and vegetables are tender.
3. Sprinkle flour over stew and stir in; continue to cook until sauce is thickened.

About 8 servings

644 *Beefsteak à la Mexicana*

2 pounds very thinly sliced tender beef (cubed steaks may be used)
   Salt, pepper, and garlic salt
   Fat
1 pound fresh tomatoes, peeled, cored, and chopped
1 cup chopped onion
4 jalapeño chilies, seeded and chopped

1. Sprinkle beef with salt, pepper, and garlic salt on both sides.
2. Pan-fry meat quickly in a small amount of hot fat in a skillet (about 2 minutes per side). Smother with chopped tomatoes, onion, and chilies. Cover skillet and cook over low heat about 15 minutes. Serve at once.

4 to 6 servings

645 *Mexican Meatballs* (Albóndigas)

Mexican meatballs often are centered with a chunk of hard-cooked egg as suggested in this recipe. Serve as a meat entrée, or prepare small-size meatballs as a party hors d'oeuvre.

Sauce:
- ½ cup chopped onion
- 1 clove garlic, minced
- ¼ cup oil or lard
- 1 cup tomato sauce
- 2 cups beef broth, or 2 cups water plus 2 beef bouillon cubes
- 1 teaspoon salt
- ½ teaspoon oregano
- ½ teaspoon cumin (comino)
- 2 chipotle chilies, chopped

Meatballs:
- 1 pound ground beef
- ½ pound ground pork
- ¼ pound ground cooked ham
- ½ cup chopped onion
- 2 slices dry bread
- ¼ cup milk
- 1 egg
- 1½ teaspoons salt
- ¼ teaspoon pepper
- 2 canned chipotle chilies, chopped
- 2 hard-cooked eggs, coarsely diced (optional)

1. For sauce, cook onion and garlic in hot oil in a large skillet until onion is soft. Add remaining sauce ingredients and heat to boiling, stirring constantly. Reduce heat and let simmer while preparing meatballs.
2. For meatballs, combine beef, pork, ham, and onion.
3. Tear bread into chunks and soak in milk.
4. Beat egg slightly and add salt, pepper, and chopped chilies. Add egg mixture and bread-milk mixture to meat; mix well.
5. Form into balls about 1½ inches in diameter. If desired, press a chunk of hard-cooked egg into center of each meatball.
6. Put meatballs into simmering sauce; cover and simmer 1 hour.

25 to 30 large meatballs (or about 75 small appetizer-size meatballs)

646 *Mexican Meat Loaf*

- 1 pound ground beef
- ½ pound ground pork
- ½ cup chopped onion
- ⅔ cup uncooked oats
- 1 egg, beaten
- 1 teaspoon salt
- ¼ teaspoon pepper
- ● 1 cup Red Chili Sauce or canned enchilada or taco sauce
- 2 hard-cooked eggs, cut in half lengthwise
- ¼ cup sliced pimento-stuffed green olives

1. Combine ground beef, ground pork, onion, oats, beaten egg, salt, pepper, and ½ cup of the sauce, mixing until evenly blended.
2. Pack half of the meat mixture into an 8×4×2-inch loaf pan. Arrange hard-cooked eggs in a row down center of loaf. Arrange olive slices on either side of eggs; press eggs and olives slightly into meat mixture. Cover with remaining half of meat mixture. Pour remaining ½ cup sauce over top.
3. Bake at 350°F 1 hour.

6 servings

647 *Green Chili Meat Loaf*

1½ pounds ground beef
1 cup soft bread crumbs
1 cup canned undrained tomatoes
1 can (4 ounces) green chilies,
  drained, seeded, and chopped
3 tablespoons dried onion flakes
1¼ teaspoons salt
¼ teaspoon garlic salt

1. Combine all ingredients thoroughly. Turn into a 9×5×3-inch loaf dish and press lightly.
2. Bake at 375°F 1 hour.

About 6 servings

648 *Chili con Carne with Beans*

1 pound boneless beef, cut in
  1-inch cubes
1 pound boneless pork, cut in
  1-inch cubes
3 tablespoons lard
1 cup beef broth
1 teaspoon salt
1 to 2 tablespoons chili powder
2 cloves garlic, minced
2 tablespoons lard
1 large onion, coarsely chopped
3 fresh tomatoes, peeled, seeded,
  and cut in pieces
1 can (16 ounces) white beans,
  drained
1 can (15 ounces) red kidney beans,
  drained

1. Brown meat in 3 tablespoons lard in a large skillet. Add broth; cover and cook 30 minutes.
2. Add salt, chili powder, and garlic; mix. Cook covered until meat is tender (about 1 hour).
3. Meanwhile, heat 2 tablespoons lard in a skillet. Add onion and tomato; mix well. Cover and cook until vegetables are soft. Purée vegetables.
4. Add purée and beans to meat; mix well. Heat thoroughly.

6 to 8 servings

649 *Taco Skillet Casserole*

1½ pounds ground beef
½ cup chopped onion
1 clove garlic, minced
1 teaspoon salt
¼ teaspoon pepper
1 teaspoon chili powder (see
  Note)
2 cups canned tomato sauce (see
  Note)
8 tortillas, cut into ½-inch strips
  Oil for frying
½ cup shredded Monterey Jack or
  mild Cheddar cheese
  Shredded lettuce

1. Crumble ground beef into a large skillet and brown well. If beef is very fat, pour off excess fat. Add onion and garlic and cook about 5 minutes, until onion is soft, stirring frequently. Stir in salt, pepper, chili powder, and tomato sauce and continue cooking over low heat about 15 minutes longer.
2. Meanwhile, in a separate skillet, fry tortilla strips in hot oil a few minutes until slightly crisped. Drain on absorbent paper. Stir tortilla strips into meat mixture and cook about 5 minutes longer, stirring frequently to prevent sticking. Sprinkle with cheese. As soon as cheese melts, remove from heat and serve. Top each serving with shredded lettuce.

6 servings

Note: **2 cups canned taco** or **enchilada sauce** may be substituted for chili powder and tomato sauce, if preferred.

650 *Cheese Ball Casserole*

1 pound ground lean pork
½ pound smoked ham, ground
1 green pepper, finely chopped
1 small onion, finely chopped
3 cloves garlic, minced
2 tablespoons snipped parsley
1 can (16 ounces) tomatoes, well drained
2 tablespoons tomato juice
2 teaspoons sugar
½ teaspoon salt
¼ teaspoon pepper
½ cup dark seedless raisins
¼ cup chopped green olives
1 tablespoon capers
2 cups shredded tortillas
½ pound sharp Cheddar cheese, thinly sliced
1 egg, beaten
Tortillas

1. Cook pork in a skillet until no longer pink. Mix in remaining ingredients, except cheese, egg, and whole tortillas. Heat for about 20 minutes, stirring occasionally.
2. Meanwhile, cover bottom and sides of a 1½-quart casserole with overlapping cheese slices.
3. When meat mixture is heated, quickly stir in egg and spoon into lined casserole. Around edge of dish overlap small pieces (quarters) of tortillas and remaining cheese slices.
4. Set in a 325°F oven 15 minutes, or until cheese is bubbly.
5. If desired, garnish center with green pepper strips and parsley arranged to form a flower. Serve with warm tortillas.

8 servings

651 *Empanadas*

Picadillo:
½ pound coarsely chopped beef
½ pound coarsely chopped pork
½ cup chopped onion
1 small clove garlic, minced
½ cup chopped raw apple
¾ cup chopped canned tomatoes
¼ cup raisins
¾ teaspoon salt
⅛ teaspoon pepper
Dash ground cinnamon
Dash ground cloves
¼ cup chopped almonds
Pastry:
4 cups all-purpose flour
1¼ teaspoons salt
1⅓ cups lard or shortening
⅔ cup icy cold water (about)

1. For picadillo, cook beef and pork together in large skillet until well browned. Add onion and garlic and cook until onion is soft. Add remaining ingredients, except almonds, and simmer 15 to 20 minutes longer until flavors are well blended.
2. Stir in almonds. Cool.
3. For pastry, mix flour and salt in a bowl. Cut in lard until mixture resembles coarse crumbs. Sprinkle water over flour mixture, stirring lightly with a fork until all dry ingredients hold together. Divide dough in four portions.
4. On a lightly floured surface, roll one portion of dough at a time to ⅛-inch thickness.
5. Using a 5-inch cardboard circle as a pattern, cut rounds of pastry with a knife. Place a rounded spoonful of filling in center of each round. Fold one side over filling to meet opposite side. Seal by dampening inside edges of pastry and pressing together with tines of fork.
6. Place empanadas on a baking sheet. Bake at 400°F 15 to 20 minutes, or until lightly browned. Or fry in **fat for deep frying** heated to 365°F until browned (about 3 minutes); turn once.

24 to 30 empanadas

652 *Lamb Mayan Style*

The sauce for this dish contains two ingredients typical of Mayan dishes from Yucatan: pepitas (pumpkin seeds), generally available in the United States in the roasted, salted form prepared as a cocktail snack, and annatto seeds (also called achiote). The latter would be available in Mexican specialty sections of large supermarkets and in Mexican grocery stores.

2 pounds boneless lamb for stew, cut in 2-inch chunks
½ cup chopped onion
1 clove garlic, minced
1 cup canned tomatoes, chopped
1 teaspoon salt
¼ teaspoon pepper
Water
1 cup pepitas
1 tablespoon annatto seeds
2 tablespoons oil
1 tablespoon lemon juice

1. Put lamb, onion, garlic, tomatoes, salt, and pepper into a Dutch oven or heavy saucepot; mix well. Add water to cover. Bring to boiling, reduce heat, cover, and simmer until meat is tender (about 2 hours).
2. Meanwhile, combine pepitas and annatto seeds in an electric blender and blend until pulverized.
3. Fry mixture in a small amount of hot oil in a small skillet 2 or 3 minutes, stirring constantly. Stir into the sauce with meat. Stir in lemon juice. Serve with **cooked rice.**

6 servings

653 *Lomo of Pork with Pineapple*

1 tablespoon lard or oil
3 pounds pork loin, boneless, cut in 2-inch chunks
1 cup chopped onion
2 cups pineapple chunks (a 15¼-ounce can) with juice
1 cup beef stock, or 1 cup water plus 1 beef bouillon cube
¼ cup dry sherry
⅓ cup sliced pimento
1 fresh tomato, peeled and chopped
½ teaspoon chili powder
Salt and pepper
2 tablespoons flour

1. Heat lard in a large, heavy skillet. Add meat and brown well on all sides. Add onion and cook about 5 minutes, or until soft.
2. Add pineapple with juice, beef stock, sherry, pimento, tomato, and chili powder to the skillet; stir until well mixed. Bring to boiling, reduce heat to simmering, and add salt and pepper to taste. Cover and simmer until meat is tender, about 1½ hours; stir occasionally to prevent sticking.
3. Just before serving, sprinkle flour over simmering sauce and stir in; cook and stir until sauce is thickened. Serve over **hot rice.**

6 to 8 servings

654 *Whole Lomo of Pork in Tomato Sauce*

1 pork loin roast, boneless (3 to 4 pounds)
1 can (6 ounces) tomato paste
¼ cup chopped onion
1 canned chipotle chili, very finely chopped; or 2 teaspoons chili powder
1 clove garlic, minced
1 teaspoon salt
¼ teaspoon pepper
1½ cups chicken stock, or 1½ cups hot water plus 2 chicken bouillon cubes
1 cup dairy sour cream

1. Put pork loin into a shallow baking pan; if necessary, cut in half so meat will fit into pan.
2. Combine tomato paste, onion, chili, garlic, salt, and pepper in a saucepan. Stir in chicken stock. Cook about 5 minutes.
3. Pour liquid over meat in pan.
4. Bake at 325°F about 1¼ hours. Occasionally spoon sauce over meat during baking, and check to see if additional water is needed to prevent drying.
5. When meat is tender, remove to serving platter.
6. Stir sour cream into sauce remaining in pan; warm slightly but do not boil. Pour over meat on platter.
7. To serve, slice meat about ¾ inch thick.

10 to 12 servings

655 *Lomo of Pork in Red Adobo*

3 pounds pork loin, boneless
1 onion, stuck with 1 clove
1 bay leaf
1 teaspoon salt
Water
Adobo Sauce:
6 fresh or dried ancho chilies
1 cup coarsely chopped onion
1 clove garlic
1 cup canned tomatoes
½ teaspoon oregano
½ teaspoon cumin (comino)
2 tablespoons lard or oil
1½ cups pork stock
Salt and pepper
1 avocado (optional)

1. Put pork, onion stuck with clove, bay leaf, and salt into large kettle or Dutch oven; cover with water. Cover kettle and cook until pork is tender, about 1½ hours.
2. Remove pork from stock; strain stock and save, discarding onion and bay leaf. Slice pork into 1-inch slices and return to kettle.
3. For adobo sauce, first prepare chilies (●). Put prepared chilies, onion, garlic, tomatoes, oregano, and cumin into an electric blender. Blend to a thick purée.
4. Heat lard in skillet. Add purée and cook about 5 minutes, stirring constantly. Stir in pork stock. Season to taste with salt and pepper.
5. Pour sauce over sliced pork in kettle. Cook, uncovered, over low heat for about 30 minutes, or until sauce thickens and coats the meat.
6. Peel and slice avocado. Arrange sliced meat on platter. Garnish with avocado slices, if desired.

6 to 8 servings

656 *Chili with Pork*

2 pounds lean pork, cut in 1-inch cubes
2 tablespoons flour
1 tablespoon chili powder
1½ teaspoons salt
½ teaspoon pepper
1 teaspoon sugar
½ teaspoon cumin (comino) seed
1 clove garlic, minced
2 cans (10 ounces each) mild enchilada sauce
2 cups water

1. Brown pork in a heavy skillet. Stir in flour and chili powder. Add remaining seasonings, sauce, and water. Bring to boiling; cover and simmer about 2 hours.
2. Serve with cooked rice and Mexican Beans (page 27), if desired.

About 8 servings

657 *Pork Slices in Mole Verde*

½ cup finely chopped onion
¼ cup finely chopped blanched almonds
2 tablespoons vegetable oil
2 cans (10 ounces each) Mexican green tomatoes (tomatillos)
1 tablespoon minced fresh coriander (cilantro) or 1 teaspoon dried coriander
1 to 3 tablespoons minced canned green chilies

1. Combine onion, almonds, and oil in a saucepan. Cook over medium heat until onion is soft.
2. Turn contents of cans of green tomatoes into an electric blender and blend until smooth (or force green tomatoes through a sieve).
3. Add purée to onion mixture and stir in coriander, chilies (to taste), and stock. Bring to boiling, reduce heat, and simmer, uncovered, until reduced to 2½ cups; stir occasionally.
4. Arrange meat in a large skillet, sprinkle with salt to taste, and pour sauce over meat. Cover, bring slowly to boiling,

2 cups chicken stock, or 2 cups
    water plus 2 chicken bouillon
    cubes
6 to 8 slices cooked pork loin roast
Salt
Small lettuce leaves
Whole pickled mild chilies
Dairy sour cream

reduce heat, and simmer about 10 minutes, or until thoroughly heated.

5. Arrange sauced meat on a platter. Garnish with lettuce and chilies. Accompany with sour cream.

6 to 8 servings

658 *Dried Lima Casserole*

More Mexican-style beans—limas, this time. This dish makes a delectable luncheon or supper main dish, quite out of the ordinary.

1 pound dried lima beans
1 large onion, sliced
¼ cup lard or oil
¼ pound chorizo or Italian-style
    sausage meat
¼ pound diced ham
1 cup canned enchilada sauce
½ cup shredded Monterey Jack

1. Soak lima beans in water to cover for 1 hour. Bring to boiling, reduce heat, and cook until tender; add more water if necessary.

2. Meanwhile, cook onion in lard until soft (about 5 minutes). If using sausage in casing, remove from casing and add to onion, crumbling slightly. Cook and stir until well browned. Add ham and enchilada sauce; cover and cook about 30 minutes.

3. Skim off excess fat. Add cooked beans and continue cooking about 15 minutes longer to blend flavors. Sprinkle with cheese just before serving.

6 to 8 servings

Note: This skillet-type casserole dish can be transferred to a baking dish before the cheese is sprinkled on top. It may then be refrigerated for later serving. Heat in a 350°F oven 20 to 30 minutes, or until bubbling.

659 *Pork and Beans Mexican Style*

This Mexican-style pork-and-beans dish offers more pork than the North American variety. Therefore it's definitely an entrée.

¼ pound sliced bacon
¼ pound boneless pork loin
    (lomo) or pork tenderloin,
    cubed
¼ pound ham, cubed
1 large onion, sliced
1½ cups fresh or canned, peeled,
    diced tomatoes
1 teaspoon chili powder
½ teaspoon cumin (comino)
½ teaspoon oregano
● 2 cups cooked pinto or kidney
    beans (canned or prepared as
    directed)
12 ounces beer

1. Cook bacon until crisp; drain and crumble. In bacon fat brown pork and ham. Add onion; cover and cook until soft (about 5 minutes).

2. Add tomatoes, chili powder, cumin, oregano, and the crumbled bacon. Add cooked beans; bring to boiling. Gradually stir in beer. Continue to simmer over low heat about 1 hour, or until pork is well done and mixture is consistency of rich stew, stirring occasionally.

3. Serve in bowls as a stew, or with hot, soft tortillas to make tacos.

4 to 6 servings

660 *Pork and Green Tomato Stew*

2½ pounds lean pork, cut in 1-inch cubes
1 tablespoon vegetable oil
1 onion, chopped
2 cloves garlic, minced
1 can (12 ounces) Mexican green tomatoes (tomatillos), drained and chopped
2 cans (4 ounces each) green chilies, drained, seeded, and chopped
1 tablespoon dried cilantro leaves
1 teaspoon marjoram
1 teaspoon salt
½ cup water
Cooked rice
Dairy sour cream

1. Brown meat in oil in a large skillet. Push meat to sides of skillet; add onion and garlic and cook until onion is soft. Add green tomatoes, chilies, cilantro, marjoram, salt, and water; mix well. Cover; bring to boiling, reduce heat, and cook until meat is tender (about 2 hours).
2. Serve with rice and top with dollops of sour cream.

6 to 8 servings

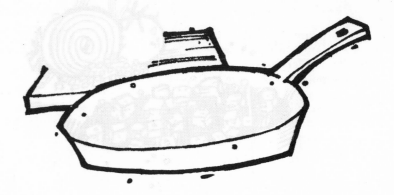

661 *Tongue in Almond Sauce*

2 veal tongues (about 2½ pounds each)
1 medium onion, stuck with 2 or 3 cloves
1 stalk celery with leaves
1 bay leaf
6 peppercorns
2 teaspoons salt
Water
Almond Sauce:
2 fresh or dried ancho chilies
½ cup canned tomatoes with juice
½ cup whole blanched almonds
½ cup raisins
1 slice bread, torn in pieces
2 tablespoons lard or oil
2 cups tongue stock
Salt and pepper
¼ cup blanched slivered almonds

1. Put tongues, onion stuck with cloves, celery, bay leaf, peppercorns, and salt into a Dutch oven or kettle. Cover with water. Cover Dutch oven, bring to boiling, and cook until meat is tender, about 2 hours. Allow to cool in liquid.
2. Remove skin from cooled tongues, trim off roots, and slice meat into ½-inch slices. Strain stock in which meat was cooked and save, discarding onion, celery, and bay leaf. Return sliced meat to kettle.
3. For almond sauce, first prepare chilies (see page 30). Put chilies, tomatoes, the whole almonds, ¼ cup of the raisins, and the bread into an electric blender. Blend to a thick purée.
4. Heat lard in a skillet. Add the puréed mixture and cook about 5 minutes. Stir in tongue stock and remaining ¼ cup raisins. Cook about 5 minutes, stirring constantly. Season to taste with salt and pepper.
5. Pour sauce over sliced meat in Dutch oven and simmer until meat is heated through.
6. Transfer meat and sauce to platter and garnish with slivered almonds.

8 to 10 servings

Baked Rice Balls, page 184

662 *Pan-Fried Steak*

⅓ cup prepared mustard
1 beef boneless sirloin steak
  (4 pounds)
¼ cup lard
1 onion, minced
2 cups beef stock
½ teaspoon beef extract or
  1 beef bouillon cube
1 teaspoon tomato paste
2 tablespoons butter
2 tablespoons cornstarch
  Salt and pepper to taste

1. Spread mustard on all sides of meat.
2. Melt lard in a large, heavy skillet and sauté onion. Add meat and brown well on all sides. Reduce heat and continue to cook until the meat is done. Transfer to a warm platter and keep hot.
3. Remove fat from skillet. Pour in stock to deglaze; add beef extract and tomato paste.
4. Mix butter and cornstarch and put into skillet juices. Stir constantly over medium heat until sauce is slightly thicker. Add salt and pepper.
5. Pour a little sauce over the meat. Serve remaining sauce in a ● sauceboat. Garnish meat with Smothered Mixed Vegetables

663 *Pepper Steak Port-au-Prince*
(Steak au Poivre Port-au-Prince)

2 tablespoons peppercorns
8 beef sirloin steaks (4 pounds),
  about 2 inches thick
2 tablespoons peanut oil
2 tablespoons butter
1 onion, minced
  Salt to taste
½ cup dry white wine
¼ cup beef stock
3 tablespoons butter
2 tablespoons chopped parsley
¼ cup amber rum

1. In a mortar, pound the peppercorns until coarsely crushed. With the heel of the hand, press peppercorns into the meat.
2. Heat oil, 2 tablespoons butter, and onion over high heat in a large skillet. Sauté steaks in the fat until meat is as done as desired. Season with salt. Transfer meat to a warm platter and keep hot.
3. Pour wine and stock into the skillet over high heat to deglaze. Add the remaining butter and parsley. Pour mixture over the meat.
4. Warm rum, ignite it, and pour it, still flaming, over the steak.
● 5. Serve immediately with Smothered Mixed Vegetables

8 servings

664 *Broiled Beef with Barbecue Sauce*

1 beef boneless sirloin steak,
  1 inch thick (about 4 pounds)
½ cup prepared mustard
  Pepper to taste
● Creole Barbecue Sauce
5 tablespoons butter
2 tablespoons chopped parsley
2 tablespoons chopped chives
  Salt to taste

1. Lay beef on a broiler rack and spread mustard over surface. Score meat deeply in a diamond pattern. Season with pepper. Brush Creole Barbecue Sauce over meat.
2. Broil 4 inches from heat 6 to 8 minutes on each side, or until as done as desired. When meat is turned, brush with the barbecue sauce.
3. While meat cooks, combine butter, parsley, and chives. Set aside.
4. Place meat on a hot platter and season with salt. Spread butter mixture over meat. This will melt and mix with meat juice. Serve with French-Fried Breadfruit (●) and Caribbean Rice with Bean Sauce (●).

8 to 10 servings

Red Snapper Veracruz Style, page 311

665 *Tournedos Caribbean*

8 beef tenderloin steaks
    (about 4 pounds)
½ cup prepared mustard
    Freshly ground pepper to taste
2 tablespoons butter
8 goose liver slices (¼ inch thick)
    Flour
½ cup beef stock
1½ teaspoons beef extract or
    3 beef bouillon cubes
⅓ cup amber rum
2 tablespoons butter
2 tablespoons cornstarch

1. Pound steaks until about 1 inch thick. Spread mustard on one side of each steak. Roll up steaks with mustard side in and secure with string. Season with pepper.
2. Melt butter over medium heat in a heavy skillet. Coat liver with flour and sauté until golden brown on both sides. Transfer liver to a warm dish and keep hot.
3. Place steak rolls in skillet and cook until as done as desired. Add more butter if necessary.
4. Arrange the steak rolls on a warm platter and place a sautéed liver slice on each one.
5. Pour the stock and beef extract into skillet to deglaze. Warm the rum, ignite it, and pour it, still flaming, into the skillet.
6. Mix butter and cornstarch and add to liquid in skillet. Bring to a boil, stirring constantly; remove from heat and pour over steak rolls.
7. Serve immediately with French-Fried Breadfruit (●).

8 servings

666 *Beef Stew*

¼ cup peanut oil
1 large onion, thinly sliced
3 to 4 pounds beef boneless chuck
    or rump, cubed
2 cups beef stock
1 can (10½ ounces) tomato purée
    Bouquet garni
1 green hot pepper or
    6 drops Tabasco
    Salt and pepper to taste
3 cups diced potato
3 cups cubed white turnip
3 cups sliced carrot
    Water
2 tablespoons butter
2 tablespoons flour
1 tablespoon chopped parsley

1. Heat oil in a Dutch oven; sauté onion until golden brown, stirring constantly. Add meat and brown on all sides.
2. Add beef stock, tomato purée, bouquet garni, hot pepper, salt, and pepper; stir to blend. Cover and simmer over low heat 2 hours, or until meat is tender.
3. Add potato, turnip, and carrot. If more liquid is needed, add water. Bring to a boil and simmer 20 minutes, or until vegetables are tender.
4. Discard the bouquet garni and hot pepper. Transfer meat and vegetables to a warm platter.
5. Combine butter and flour to make a paste; add to pan juices and boil until thickened. Add parsley, and, if desired, salt and pepper.
6. Pour gravy over meat and vegetables. Serve with Coconut and Rice and Smothered Cabbage (●).

8 to 10 servings

Note: Lamb or kid may be substituted for the beef.

667 *Scallop of Kid or Veal*
(Escalopes de Cabrit ou de Veau)

16 small kid or veal scallops,
    (about 3 pounds)
2 eggs, beaten
2 tablespoons vegetable oil
1 teaspoon lime juice
    Salt and pepper to taste
    Dry bread crumbs
2 tablespoons butter
2 tablespoons vegetable oil

1. Cut meat into pieces the size of a silver dollar, then pound between 2 sheets of waxed paper until very thin.
2. Mix eggs, 2 tablespoons oil, lime juice, salt, and pepper. Dip each piece of meat into the egg mixture, then in the bread crumbs.
3. Heat remaining butter and oil in a skillet over medium heat. Sauté the meat until golden brown on each side. Add more butter and oil to skillet if necessary.
4. Serve with Rice and Avocado (●).

8 servings

668 Braised Shanks

8 lamb shanks
1 cup cubed salt pork
½ cup each peas, coarsely chopped onion, sliced green beans, cubed white turnip, and sliced carrot
1 cup boiling water
½ cup dry white wine
7 peppercorns
3 parsley sprigs
1 thyme sprig
1 garlic clove
1 teaspoon salt
½ cup red wine
¾ cup beef broth
1 tablespoon butter
1 tablespoon cornstarch
1 tablespoon chopped parsley

1. Thoroughly wash shanks in cold water; drain. (If necessary, pull off the parchmentlike covering.)
2. In a Dutch oven render the salt pork, and in this fat sauté the shanks over high heat until brown on all sides.
3. Remove Dutch oven from heat; add vegetables, water, and white wine.
4. In a mortar, pound to a paste the peppercorns, parsley, thyme, garlic, and salt. Add to the shanks. Bring to a boil over high heat.
5. Remove Dutch oven from heat and add red wine and ½ cup beef broth.
6. Cook covered in a 375°F oven 2 hours.
7. Mix butter and cornstarch. Set aside.
8. Transfer shanks to a large serving platter; arrange vegetables around shanks.
9. Pour ¼ cup beef broth into Dutch oven to deglaze and place over high heat. Add butter mixture and stir constantly until thickened. Pour into a serving dish and sprinkle with parsley.
10. Serve with Caribbean Rice and Bean Sauce (●).

About 4 servings

Note: Beef, veal, or kid shanks may be substituted for lamb shanks.

669 Veal Roulades

6 veal cutlets (1½ pounds)
½ cup peanut oil
2 large onions, chopped
½ cup fresh bread crumbs
¼ cup chopped parsley
½ teaspoon salt
½ teaspoon freshly ground pepper
1 egg yolk, beaten
¼ cup butter
1 cup stock
12 small onions
12 small carrots
1 green hot pepper or 5 dried Italian pepper pods
1 tablespoon butter
1 tablespoon cornstarch

1. Pound the meat until flattened. Set aside.
2. Heat oil in a small skillet and sauté the chopped onion. Add bread crumbs, parsley, salt, and pepper; stir to blend. Remove from heat and stir in egg yolk. Cool.
3. Spread some of the mixture on each piece of meat. Roll up the slices of meat and secure with string.
4. Melt ¼ cup butter in a large skillet and brown the roulades. Add stock.
5. Simmer covered over low heat or cook in a 375°F oven about 2 hours, or until tender; add onions, carrots, and pepper halfway through cooking.
6. Transfer meat and vegetables to a warm platter and keep hot. Discard pepper.
7. Mix butter and cornstarch and put into skillet juices. Stir constantly over medium heat until sauce is slightly thicker. Pour sauce over roulades.
8. Serve with Caribbean Rice (●).

6 servings

670 Ham Rolls Guadeloupe

¼ cup amber rum
● 2 cups Béchamel Sauce
   use beef broth)
 8 ham slices
   (about ¼ inch thick)
1½ cups Creamed Spinach

1. Add rum to Béchamel Sauce. Pour sauce into a skillet and add ham slices; heat thoroughly.
2. Transfer ham, a slice at a time, to a baking dish, place 3 tablespoons Creamed Spinach on each slice and roll up. Secure with picks, if necessary. Pour sauce in skillet over ham slices.
3. Broil 4 inches from heat about 5 minutes, or until warmed and glazed.
4. Serve with Bananas à l'Antillaise (●).

8 servings

Creamed Spinach: Chop 1½ **cups cooked spinach** very fine. Season with **salt** and **pepper** to taste. Melt **1 tablespoon butter** and stir in **1 teaspoon flour.** Add ½ **cup milk** and cook 3 minutes, stirring constantly. Add chopped spinach and heat thoroughly.

671 Calf's Liver with Basil

1½ pounds calf's liver, cut in strips
 ½ cup flour
    Salt and pepper to taste
 ½ cup butter
 2 garlic cloves
 1 tablespoon minced onion
 ½ cup beef stock
 1 teaspoon dried basil
 2 tablespoons butter
 1 tablespoon cornstarch

1. Coat liver strips in a mixture of flour, salt, and pepper.
2. Melt butter in a skillet over medium heat. Add garlic, onion, and liver strips. Sauté meat 3 minutes on each side. Transfer the meat to a warm platter and keep hot.
3. Deglaze the skillet with the stock; add basil. Mix butter and cornstarch and add to the stock. Cook and stir mixture until slightly thickened. Pour over liver.
4. Serve liver with Sweet Potato Soufflé (●).

4 to 6 servings

672 Ragout of Brains

 2 pounds calf's brains
 6 peppercorns
 5 shallots, halved
 4 parsley sprigs
 1 small carrot, cut in pieces
 1 teaspoon salt
 ¼ teaspoon thyme
 ¼ cup butter
 2 tablespoons soybean oil
 ¼ cup beef stock
 1 tablespoon tomato paste
 2 tablespoons butter
 1 tablespoon lime juice

1. Remove membrane and blood from brains, then soak brains in cold water for 30 minutes. Simmer for 15 minutes in water. Drain and drop into cold water.
2. In a mortar, pound to a paste the peppercorns, shallots, parsley, carrot, salt, and thyme.
3. Melt ¼ cup butter with oil in a medium skillet. Add the brains and seasoning paste. Sauté, gently stirring, until the meat is golden.
4. Add stock and tomato paste; cook 5 minutes longer, then add the remaining butter and lime juice.
5. Serve immediately with Deep-Fried Plantain (●).

About 8 servings

673 *Beef Liver à la Beauharnais*

½ cup flour
1 tablespoon paprika
½ teaspoon salt
⅛ teaspoon freshly ground pepper
⅛ teaspoon cayenne or red pepper
1½ pounds beef liver, thinly sliced
1 cup minced onion
3 tablespoons peanut oil
2 tablespoons butter
1 tablespoon chopped parsley
1 tablespoon lime juice

1. Combine flour, paprika, salt, and peppers. Coat liver slices with flour mixture. Set aside.
2. Sauté onion in oil over medium heat. When onion is translucent, add butter and liver slices. Cook liver about 5 minutes; do not overcook.
3. Arrange liver on a heated platter and sprinkle with parsley and lime juice. Garnish with **watercress**.

6 servings

674 *Beef Tongue King Christophe*

1 fresh beef tongue (about 4 pounds)
Water
1 carrot
1 onion stuck with 4 cloves
½ cup lime juice
Bouquet garni

1. Wash tongue and put into a large saucepan. Add water to cover and remaining ingredients. Cover and simmer about 2 hours, or until tongue is tender.
2. Cool tongue, then remove skin; cut away roots and gristle.
3. Slice the tongue diagonally and against the grain. Arrange slices on a platter. Garnish with sliced **hard-cooked eggs**, **pickles**, **avocado wedges**, and **sliced tomatoes**.

About 12 servings

675 *Tripe à la Creole*

2 pounds tripe
1 lime, halved
Water
1 tablespoon coarse sea salt
1 tablespoon wine vinegar
4 garlic cloves
1 green hot pepper or
    3 dried Italian pepper pods
½ cup olive oil
2 large Spanish onions, sliced
1 cup cubed cooked ham
5 large tomatoes, peeled, seeded, and chopped
¼ cup amber rum
2 thyme sprigs
2 bay leaves

1. Wash tripe thoroughly in cold water; drain. Rub the cut surface of lime over entire tripe. Put into a large kettle, cover with water, and add salt and vinegar. Bring to a boil; simmer 5 hours, adding more water if necessary. (This step is generally done the day before tripe is served; tripe is left to cool in its water.)
2. Cut the tripe into 2-inch slices; set aside.
3. In a mortar, pound to a paste the garlic and green hot pepper; set aside.
4. Heat oil in a top-of-range casserole. Sauté onion, then add tripe, ham, tomato, rum, seasoning paste, thyme, and bay leaves. Simmer 20 minutes. Serve immediately.

6 to 8 servings

676 *Vegetable-Smothered Steak (Filet Touffé)*

8 beef loin tenderloin or boneless
    sirloin steaks (about 4 pounds),
    cut thin
3 garlic cloves
2 parsley sprigs
1 thyme sprig
1 teaspoon coarse salt
2 tablespoons prepared mustard
1 tablespoon orange juice
1 cup sliced carrot
1 cup shredded cabbage
4 medium onions, sliced and
    separated in rings
3 large truffles, sliced
¼ pound ham, cubed
¼ pound salt pork, cubed
    Madeira or port wine
    (about 1 cup)
¾ cup amber rum
    Beef stock
2 tablespoons butter
2 tablespoons cornstarch
    Salt and pepper to taste

1. Pound steaks until flattened.
2. In a mortar, pound to a paste the garlic, parsley, thyme, and salt. Add mustard and orange juice to the seasoning paste.
3. Combine carrot, cabbage, onion, truffles, ham, and the mustard mixture. Set aside.
4. Render salt pork in a skillet. Remove the cracklings and add to the vegetable mixture. Brown the steaks in the fat over medium heat.
5. Alternate layers of the steak and vegetable mixture in a large casserole with a tight-fitting cover. Pour wine into the casserole dish to fill it one third full.
6. Warm the rum, ignite it, and pour it, still flaming, over the meat. Cover casserole tightly.
7. Bake at 450°F 20 minutes, then turn oven control to 325°F and continue to cook 4 hours.
8. Transfer steaks and vegetables to a warm platter and keep hot.
9. Measure liquid in casserole and add enough beef stock to equal 2 cups. Pour liquid into a saucepan and set over medium heat.
10. Mix butter and cornstarch and add to liquid in saucepan. Stir constantly until thickened. Add salt and pepper.
11. Pour sauce over meat or serve in a sauceboat. Accompany with Purée of Breadfruit (●).

Poultry

677 *Chicken with Tomatoes and Onions* (Kotopoulo Riganati)

2 broiler-fryer chickens
3 tablespoons olive oil
Juice of 1 lemon
2 teaspoons salt
½ cup butter
1 can (20 ounces) tomatoes
    (undrained)
1 teaspoon pepper
1 tablespoon oregano
Salt

1. Rinse chickens well and pat dry with paper towels. Rub inside and out with a mixture of olive oil, lemon juice, and 2 teaspoons salt. Place in a large roasting pan.
2. Bake at 375°F 1 hour.
3. Melt butter in a saucepan. Add tomatoes, pepper, and oregano. Simmer 5 minutes.
4. Pour sauce over the chickens. Turn oven heat to 325°F and bake chickens an additional 45 minutes; baste frequently. Salt to taste.

4 servings

Note: Kotopoulo Riganati freezes very well.

678 *Chicken and Grapes*

6 tablespoons butter
2 broiler-fryer chickens, cut in
    pieces
Salt and pepper to taste
3 scallions, chopped
1 cup dry white wine
Clusters of seedless white
    grapes
½ teaspoon paprika

1. Melt butter in a skillet. Add chicken and brown. Season with salt and pepper. Transfer chicken to a casserole.
2. Add scallions to the skillet and cook until browned. Add wine and heat. Pour over the chicken. Cover.
3. Bake at 350°F 30 minutes. Remove cover. Add grapes and bake an additional 5 minutes. Sprinkle with paprika.

4 to 6 servings

679 *Braised Chicken with Tomatoes and Cheese*
(Kotopoulo Vorthonia)

1 chicken (3 pounds), cut in
    small pieces
¼ cup olive oil
Salt and pepper to taste
1 can (16 ounces) tomatoes
    (undrained)
1 medium onion, minced
1 garlic clove, crushed in a garlic
    press
2 tablespoons oregano
¼ teaspoon cinnamon
2 tablespoons whiskey
1 pound orzo (a pasta)
¼ cup vegetable oil
1 cup grated hard mizithra
    cheese

1. Rinse chicken and pat dry with paper towels.
2. Heat olive oil in a large skillet. Add chicken pieces. Season with salt and pepper. Brown on all sides.
3. Mash tomatoes and add to skillet. Add onion, garlic, oregano, cinnamon, and whiskey. Cover and simmer about 30 minutes, or until done. Remove chicken pieces and keep hot.
4. Cook orzo according to directions on the package, adding vegetable oil to the water. Drain thoroughly and put into a deep serving dish. Add the sauce and toss lightly until orzo is coated completely. Adjust seasoning. Add the chicken. Toss again to combine.
5. Serve with grated cheese.

6 to 8 servings

680 *Broiled Chicken in Lemon Juice and Oregano*
(Kotopoulo me Lemoni ke Rigani)

2 broiler-fryer chickens, cut up
½ cup olive oil
Juice of 2 lemons
¼ cup oregano, crushed
Salt and pepper to taste

1. Rinse chicken pieces and pat dry.
2. In a bowl, make a marinade by combining olive oil with lemon juice and oregano. Dip each piece of chicken into the marinade. Season with salt and pepper. Marinate for several hours, or overnight if possible.
3. In a preheated broiler, place the chicken fleshy side down. Broil about 6 inches from heat about 15 minutes, or until brown, basting frequently. Turn once. Broil until done.

4 servings

Note: The marinade may be served as a gravy with cooked rice or noodles.

681 *Roast Chicken with Potatoes*
(Kotopoulo tou Fournou me Patates)

1 chicken (about 4 pounds)
Salt and pepper to taste
Juice of 1 lemon
¼ cup butter
¼ teaspoon paprika
1 cup water
5 medium potatoes, pared

1. Season chicken, inside and out, with salt, pepper, lemon juice, butter, and paprika. Place chicken on a rack in a baking dish.
2. Bake at 350°F about 1¼ hours, or until chicken is tender, basting occasionally. After the first 30 minutes of cooking, pour in water; add potatoes and baste with drippings.
3. Turn oven control to 400°F. Remove chicken to a platter and keep warm. Turn potatoes over in dish. Bake an additional 5 to 10 minutes.

5 servings

682 *Rock Cornish Hens with Oranges and Almonds*

1 Rock Cornish hen per serving

For each serving:
2 tablespoons butter, melted
2 tablespoons orange juice
Salt and pepper to taste
¼ teaspoon marjoram
¼ teaspoon thyme
½ garlic clove, crushed in a garlic press
½ navel orange with peel, cut in thin slices
2 tablespoons honey (about)
5 almonds, blanched, slivered, and toasted

1. Rinse hen well. Drain and pat dry. Place in a shallow baking dish. Drizzle inside and out with butter.
2. Combine orange juice, salt, pepper, marjoram, thyme, and garlic in a small bowl. Pour over and into the bird. Marinate 2 hours; turn occasionally.
3. Set bird on a broiler rack and put under broiler about 6 inches from heat. Broil 12 minutes on each side, or until tender, basting frequently with the marinade. During the last few minutes of broiling, arrange orange slices around the bird and drizzle with honey.
4. Garnish with almonds and serve at once.

683 *Chicken Breasts with Yogurt Sauce*
(Kotopoulo me Saltsa Yaourti)

½ cup butter
6 chicken breasts, boned
Salt and pepper to taste
½ teaspoon paprika
6 fresh scallions, chopped
¼ cup minced parsley
2 cups chicken stock
Juice of 1 lemon
1 pound mushrooms, sliced
2 cups plain yogurt
1 cup coarsely ground walnuts

1. Melt butter in a large skillet. Add chicken and season with salt, pepper, and paprika. Brown on both sides.
2. Add scallions, parsley, chicken stock, and lemon juice; bring to a boil. Reduce heat and simmer covered about 20 minutes, or until chicken is tender.
3. Remove chicken and arrange on a serving platter.
4. Add mushrooms to the stock. Simmer uncovered 3 minutes. Blend in yogurt and walnuts. (If sauce is too thick, dilute with a little stock or water.) Heat just to warm yogurt; do not boil.
5. Pour sauce over chicken.

6 servings

684 *Chicken in Filo* (Kotopita)

1 stewing chicken, cut in pieces
½ cup unsalted butter
1 medium onion, minced
½ cup finely chopped leek
1 celery stalk, minced
1 garlic clove, crushed in a garlic
 press
2 tablespoons finely chopped
 parsley
2 tablespoons pine nuts
3 tablespoons flour
2½ cups chicken stock
½ cup cream
4 eggs, beaten until frothy
¼ teaspoon nutmeg
½ teaspoon dill
2 tablespoons white wine
Salt and pepper
1 package filo
Additional butter for filo

1. Rinse chicken pieces. In a large heavy Dutch oven, add ¼ cup butter. When hot, add the chicken. Cover. Cook, turning, without browning, for about 15 minutes.
2. Remove the chicken pieces and cool slightly. Remove bones and skin from chicken and discard. Chop chicken meat. Set aside.
3. Melt 2 tablespoons butter in a skillet. Add onion, leek, celery, garlic, parsley, and pine nuts. Sauté until vegetables are limp.
4. Melt remaining butter in a saucepan and blend in flour. Cook 2 minutes. Stir in stock. Simmer until sauce boils. Cool. Stir in cream, eggs, nutmeg, dill, chicken, vegetables, and wine, if sauce seems too thick. Season with salt and pepper.
5. Butter a 12x9x3-inch baking pan. Line it with 6 sheets of filo, brushing each with butter
6. Spread chicken filling evenly over filo. Top with filo according to directions.
7. Bake at 350°F about 50 minutes, or until golden in color. Let stand 15 minutes before cutting into squares. Serve warm.

8 to 10 servings

685 *Chicken with Cheese* (Kotopoulo me Tyri)

¼ cup butter
1 chicken (3 pounds), cut in
 pieces
1 medium onion, minced
Salt and pepper to taste
½ teaspoon rosemary
¼ teaspoon paprika
1 garlic clove, crushed in a garlic
 press
1½ cups chicken broth
⅓ pound kasseri cheese, cut in
 thin slices

1. Melt butter in a large skillet. Brown chicken on all sides. Add onion. Season with salt and pepper. Add rosemary, paprika, garlic, and chicken broth. Simmer, covered, about 40 minutes, or until chicken is tender.
2. Lay cheese slices on top of chicken. Simmer, covered, 5 minutes more. Serve at once.

2 to 4 servings

686 *Stuffing for a Small Turkey* (Yemisi yra Galopoulo)

½ cup butter
1 onion, minced
1 medium cooking apple, pared, cored, and diced
1 pound mushrooms, sliced
2 medium potatoes, boiled, peeled, and diced
½ cup pine nuts
½ cup dried black currants
1 cup blanched almonds, sliced
2 pounds chestnuts, boiled and cleaned
4 cups prepared bread stuffing
2 cups or more chicken stock to make a moist stuffing
1 can (4½ ounces) pâté de foie gras
Salt and pepper to taste

1. Melt butter in a large deep skillet. Add onion, apple, and mushrooms; cook until tender.
2. Add potatoes, pine nuts, currants, almonds, chestnuts, stuffing, and stock. Heat thoroughly over low heat, adding more liquid if necessary.
3. Stir in pâté. Season with salt and pepper.
4. Cool completely. Stuff bird.

Stuffing for a small turkey or 2 capons

687 *Royal Chicken*

⅓ cup butter
2 medium onions, chopped
1 cup sliced mushrooms
1 chicken or capon, cut in pieces
1 cup hot water
1 teaspoon salt
¼ teaspoon pepper
1 tablespoon flour
1 teaspoon paprika (optional)
1 cup dairy sour cream or white wine

1. Melt butter in a large skillet. Add onion, mushrooms, and chicken pieces. Stir-fry until golden.
2. Add water, salt, and pepper.
3. Cover; cook over medium heat about 35 minutes, or until chicken is tender.
4. Blend flour, paprika (if desired), and sour cream. Stir into liquid in skillet. Bring just to boiling. Simmer 3 minutes.

About 6 servings

688 *Chicken Livers in Madeira Sauce* (Wątróbki z Kur w Sosie Maderowym)

1 pound chicken livers
Milk
1 medium onion, minced
2 tablespoons chicken fat or butter
⅔ cup all-purpose flour
¾ teaspoon salt
⅔ cup chicken broth
½ cup Madeira

1. Cover chicken livers with milk; soak 2 hours. Drain; discard milk.
2. Sauté onion in fat.
3. Mix flour with salt. Coat livers with seasoned flour.
4. Add livers to onions. Stir-fry just until golden, about 5 minutes.
5. Stir in broth and wine. Cover. Simmer 5 to 10 minutes, or just until livers are tender.

4 servings

689 *Smothered Stuffed Chicken*
(Nadziewane Kurczątko Duszone)

1 chicken (about 3 pounds)
½ teaspoon salt
⅛ teaspoon pepper
2 tablespoons butter
1¼ cups dry bread cubes or pieces
¼ cup chopped onion
½ teaspoon dill weed
¼ cup hot milk
⅓ cup butter, melted

1. Sprinkle inside of chicken with salt and pepper. Tuck wing tips underneath wings. Chop liver.
2. Sauté liver in 2 tablespoons butter 2 minutes. Add bread cubes, onion, dill, and milk; mix.
3. Stuff chicken. Close and secure with poultry pins. Place in a ceramic or earthenware casserole.
4. Pour melted butter over chicken. Cover.
5. Bake at 350°F about 1 hour, or until chicken is tender.
6. If desired, remove cover. Baste. Increase temperature to 450°F. Bake 10 minutes to brown.

4 to 6 servings

690 *Chicken with Anchovies*
(Pularda Pieczona z Sardelami)

1 chicken (3 pounds), split in half
1 can (2 ounces) flat anchovy
  fillets, cut in half
1 cup chicken broth
1 tablespoon lemon juice
1 slice bacon, chopped
  Hot cooked rice
¼ cup dairy sour cream
¼ teaspoon ginger

1. Slit the skin of the chickens, and insert anchovies in slits as in larding meat.
2. Put chicken, broth, lemon juice, and bacon into a flame-proof casserole or Dutch oven. Cover; simmer about 1 hour, or until chicken is tender.
3. Spoon hot rice onto platter. Set chicken on rice.
4. Blend sour cream and ginger into liquid in casserole. Heat just until mixture bubbles; do not boil. Serve sauce over chicken.

4 to 6 servings

691 *Chicken Polish Style* *(Kurczęta po Polsku)*

1 chicken (2 to 3 pounds)
  Salt
  Chicken livers
¾ cup dry bread crumbs
1 egg
1 teaspoon dill weed
¼ teaspoon pepper
½ cup milk (about)
⅓ cup melted butter

1. Sprinkle the chicken with salt. Let stand 1 hour.
2. Chop the livers finely. Combine with bread crumbs, egg, salt to taste, dill, pepper, and as much milk as needed for a loose, sour-cream-like consistency.
3. Fill cavity of chicken with crumb mixture; truss. Place chicken in roasting pan.
4. Bake at 400°F about 45 minutes, or until chicken is tender. Baste often with melted butter.

About 4 servings

Chicken with Ham: Prepare Chicken Polish Style as directed. Substitute **6 ounces (1 cup) ground ham, ½ cup sliced mushrooms,** and **2 crushed juniper berries** for the chicken livers. Add **½ cup sherry** to pan drippings for a sauce.

692 *Roast Turkey with Anchovies*
(Pieczony Indyk z Sardelami)

1 turkey (12 to 15 pounds)
5 slices bacon
1 large onion, minced
¾ pound veal (2 cups ground)
3 slices stale bread, cubed
⅓ cup milk or chicken broth
1 can (2 ounces) flat anchovies
2 tablespoons butter
2 eggs, beaten
Grated peel and juice of 1 lemon
½ teaspoon pepper
⅔ cup melted butter

1. Rinse turkey with running water. Dry with paper towels.
2. Dice bacon. Fry until transparent. Add onion; stir-fry until golden. Stir in veal, bread cubes, and milk. Remove from heat.
3. Finely chop or mash anchovies. Mix in butter, lemon peel and juice, and pepper; beat until well combined. Add to meat mixture and stir until well blended. Stuffing should be of a paste consistency.
4. Spread stuffing in cavity of turkey. Truss.
5. Place turkey in roasting pan. If desired, insert meat thermometer in thickest part of breast.
6. Roast at 425°F about 3½ hours, basting frequently with melted butter and pan drippings. When done, leg of turkey moves easily and meat thermometer registers 180° to 185°F.

12 to 18 servings

693 *Smothered Duck in Caper Sauce*
(Kaczka Duszona w Sosie Kaparowym)

1 duck (5 to 6 pounds), cut up
1 clove garlic, crushed (optional)
Salt and pepper
3 tablespoons butter or bacon drippings
1 cup chicken or beef bouillon
2 tablespoons water
2 teaspoons cornstarch
⅓ cup capers
2 teaspoons brown or caramelized sugar
1 tablespoon lemon juice

1. Rub duck with garlic. Sprinkle cavity with salt and pepper to taste. Let stand 1 to 2 hours.
2. Melt butter in a heavy skillet or Dutch oven. Add duck and brown quickly on all sides. Drain off fat, if desired.
3. Add bouillon. Cover. Simmer over medium heat about 1 hour, or until duck is tender.
4. Remove duck to a heated platter.
5. Blend water into cornstarch. Stir into hot liquid in Dutch oven. Add capers, cook and stir over high heat until sauce boils. Reduce heat. Add sugar and lemon juice. Stir just until sauce is thickened.

About 4 servings

694 *Duck with Red Cabbage*
(Kaczka Duszona z Kapustą)

1 head red cabbage, shredded
1 onion, chopped
Salt
6 ounces salt pork, diced
½ cup red wine or chicken broth
1 duck (5 to 6 pounds)

1. Put cabbage and onion into a bowl, sprinkle with salt, and let stand 10 minutes. Squeeze out liquid.
2. Fry salt pork in a skillet until golden. Add cabbage-onion mixture and wine. Cover and simmer 20 minutes.
3. Place duck in a roasting pan.
4. Bake at 425°F 30 minutes. Drain off fat. Spoon cabbage mixture over duck. Reduce oven temperature to 350°F. Bake about 45 minutes, or until duck is tender. Baste frequently.

About 4 servings

695 *Capon in Cream (Kapłon z Kremem z Pieca)*

1 capon or chicken (5 to 6 pounds)
Salt
2 cups chicken stock or broth
4 egg yolks
1 tablespoon melted butter
4 teaspoons flour
2 cups dairy sour cream
1 teaspoon salt
¼ teaspoon pepper

1. Sprinkle cavity of bird with salt. Place in a large kettle.
2. Add stock to kettle. Cover. Simmer until just tender (about 1 hour). Allow to cool.
3. Meanwhile, cream egg yolks and butter; add flour and blend thoroughly. Stir in sour cream. Season with 1 teaspoon salt and pepper. Beat at high speed until stiff. Cook until thickened in top of a double boiler, stirring constantly to keep from curdling or sticking (handle like hollandaise sauce). Cool.
4. Make cuts in capon as for carving, but without cutting through. Place in a shallow baking pan. Fill cuts with sauce, then spread remainder over the whole surface of the bird.
5. Bake at 425°F about 20 minutes, or until sauce is browned.
6. Meanwhile, boil liquid in which chicken was cooked until it is reduced to 1 cup of stock.
7. To serve, pour stock over capon. Carve at the table.

About 6 servings

696 *Potted Pheasant (Bażant Pieczony)*

¾ cup all-purpose flour
½ teaspoon salt
¼ teaspoon pepper
1 pheasant, cut in pieces
½ cup butter
1 onion, quartered
1 stalk celery, cut up
2 cups meat stock or beef broth
3 whole allspice
½ cup whipping cream
2 tablespoons sherry

1. Mix flour with salt and pepper.
2. Coat each piece of pheasant with seasoned flour. Melt butter in a Dutch oven or flameproof casserole. Brown pheasant in butter. Add onion, celery, and 1 cup meat stock. Cover.
3. Bake at 350°F 40 minutes. Add remaining meat stock. Do not cover. Bake about 40 minutes longer, or until pheasant is tender.
4. Remove pheasant to heated platter. Strain broth; combine 1 cup broth with cream and sherry. Serve over the pheasant.

2 to 4 servings

697 *Smothered Pigeons (Potrawka z Gołębi)*

3 tablespoons butter
2 pigeons (about 2 pounds)
3 onions, sliced
1 cup meat stock or broth
2 tart apples, cored and sliced
¼ cup sliced mushrooms
Juice of ½ lemon
⅓ cup Madeira
1 tablespoon butter or margarine (at room temperature)
1 tablespoon Browned Flour
1 cup dairy sour cream

1. Melt butter in a large skillet. Sauté pigeons in butter 15 minutes. Remove pigeons.
2. Fry onions in the butter left in skillet until tender. Add stock, sliced apples, mushrooms, and lemon juice. Mix well and bring to boiling. Add wine.
3. Mix butter with flour until smooth. Stir into liquid in skillet. Cook and stir until mixture is thickened.
4. Dip pigeons in sour cream; return to skillet. Cook, covered, until tender.

2 servings

Browned Flour: Spread 1½ cups all-purpose flour in a shallow baking pan. Place on lowest position for broiler. Broil and stir about 20 minutes, or until flour is golden brown. Stirring must be almost constant to prevent burning. If flour burns, skim off burned portion and continue browning remainder. Cool. Store in tightly covered container.

About 1⅓ cups

698 *Baked Pigeon (Gołąb Pieczony)*

1 pigeon
Salt and pepper
1 strip bacon, diced
Melted butter

1. Soak the pigeon about 2 hours in cold water. Dry with paper towels.
2. Sprinkle cavity with salt and pepper.
3. Make small slits in skin; insert pieces of bacon. Place in a roasting pan.
4. Bake at 350°F 30 to 40 minutes, or until tender; baste often with butter.

1 serving

699 *Wild Duck, Goose, or Partridge*
(Dzika Kaczka, Gęś, lub Kuropatwy)

2 partridges, 1 duck, or 1 goose
12 peppercorns
1 onion, quartered
Salt
14 to 20 juniper seeds, ground or mashed
2 tablespoons bacon drippings or butter
½ cup water
2 cups sliced red cabbage
1 large onion, sliced
½ cup water
1 tablespoon cornstarch or potato starch
2 tablespoons water
½ teaspoon sugar
1 teaspoon vinegar
¾ cup red wine

1. Place partridges in a plastic bag with peppercorns and quartered onion. Refrigerate 3 days to age.
2. Discard peppercorns and quartered onion. Cut up bird. Sprinkle with salt and juniper. Let stand 1 hour.
3. Heat bacon drippings in a large skillet. Brown bird in the drippings; add ½ cup water. Cover and simmer 1 hour.
4. Add cabbage, sliced onion, and ½ cup water. Cover and simmer 30 minutes. Remove the meat to a warmed platter.
5. Mix the cornstarch with 2 tablespoons water to make a smooth paste. Stir into drippings in pan.
6. Stir in sugar and vinegar; bring to boiling. Cook and stir 2 minutes. Remove from heat. Stir in wine.

4 servings

700 *Cornish Hens with Raisin Stuffing*

Plumped raisins and rice are the base of the stuffing. Grapevine leaves cover the breasts of the Cornish hens to retain moistness.

4 Cornish hens (1 to 1½ pounds each)
Salt
*16 grapevine leaves preserved in brine
⅔ cup dark raisins
⅓ cup brandy
¾ cup cooked long-grain rice
1¼ cups finely chopped carrot
1¼ cups finely chopped celery
½ teaspoon cinnamon
1 tablespoon clarified butter
¼ teaspoon salt
⅛ teaspoon pepper
½ cup brandy

1. Rinse hens and pat dry; sprinkle lightly with salt.
2. Soak grapevine leaves in cold water 20 minutes. Pat dry. Set aside.
3. Simmer raisins in brandy 15 minutes; remove from heat and let stand 15 minutes. Stir in rice, carrot, celery, cinnamon, clarified butter, ¼ teaspoon salt, and the pepper. Spoon stuffing lightly into cavities of hens. Place hens on rack in a roasting pan. Cover breasts with grapevine leaves.
4. Roast in a 325°F oven 1¼ to 1½ hours, or until hens are tender. Baste with brandy during last ½ hour of roasting. Let hens stand 15 minutes before serving. Remove grapevine leaves.

4 servings

*Grapevine leaves can be purchased in a gourmet shop or in the specialty department of a supermarket.

701 *Roast Chicken Tarragon*

Based on the classic French recipe, the sauce is made without whipping cream, flour, and eggs. It is delicately flavored with tarragon and spooned over roasted chicken.

1 broiler-fryer chicken (2½ to 3
   pounds)
2 teaspoons clarified butter
2 teaspoons snipped fresh or 1
   teaspoon dried tarragon
   leaves
   Salt
2 carrots, cut in 1-inch pieces
1 small onion, cut in quarters
1 stalk celery, cut in 1-inch
   pieces
2 sprigs parsley
●1¼ cups Chicken Stock
1 tablespoon arrowroot
   Cold water
½ teaspoon salt
¼ teaspoon freshly ground white
   pepper
2 teaspoons snipped fresh or 1
   teaspoon dried tarragon
   leaves
2 tablespoons dry sherry

1. Rinse chicken; pat dry. Place in a roasting pan. Brush chicken with clarified butter, sprinkle with 2 teaspoons tarragon. Sprinkle cavity with salt; fill cavity with carrot, onion, celery, and parsley.
2. Roast in a 325°F oven about 2½ hours, or until chicken is done; meat on drumstick will be very tender. Remove chicken to a platter. Remove vegetables; reserve. Cover loosely with aluminum foil and let stand 20 minutes before carving.
3. Spoon fat from roasting pan. Heat stock to simmering in roasting pan, stirring to incorporate particles from pan. Mix arrowroot with a little cold water; stir into stock with salt, pepper, 2 teaspoons tarragon, and the sherry. Simmer, stirring constantly, until stock is thickened (about 5 minutes).
4. Slice chicken and arrange on platter. Garnish with reserved vegetables. Serve with sauce.

4 servings

702 *Chicken with Poached Garlic*

The garlic, poached without peeling, imparts a delicate flavor to the chicken.

1 broiler-fryer chicken (2½ to 3
   pounds)
1 garlic clove, peeled and cut in
   half
   Juice of 1 lime
   Salt
   Freshly ground white pepper
16 garlic cloves (unpeeled)
● ½ cup Chicken Stock
¼ cup dry vermouth
   Chicken Stock
2 teaspoons arrowroot
   Cold water
● ¼ cup Mock Crème Fraîche
1 tablespoon snipped parsley
   Salt
   Freshly ground white pepper

1. Rinse chicken; pat dry. Place in a roasting pan. Rub entire surface of chicken with cut garlic clove. Squeeze lime juice over chicken. Sprinkle cavity and outside of chicken lightly with salt and pepper. Place remaining garlic cloves around chicken; pour in ½ cup stock and ¼ cup dry vermouth.
2. Roast in a 325°F oven about 2½ hours, or until done; meat on drumstick will be very tender. Add stock if necessary to keep garlic covered. Remove chicken to platter. Cover loosely with aluminum foil. Let stand 20 minutes before carving.
3. Spoon fat from roasting pan. Add enough stock to pan to make 1 cup of liquid. Mix arrowroot with a little cold water; stir into stock. Simmer, stirring constantly, until thickened (about 3 minutes). Stir in Mock Crème Fraîche and parsley. Season to taste with salt and pepper. Pass sauce with chicken.

4 servings

Note: To eat garlic cloves, gently press with fingers; the soft cooked interior will slip out. The flavor of the poached garlic is very delicate.

703 *Chicken en Cocotte*

1½ cups sliced leeks, white part only
1 medium zucchini, cut in ¼-inch slices
2 large sweet red or green peppers, cut in ¼-inch strips
1 large green pepper, cut in ¼-inch strips
2 teaspoons snipped fresh or 1 teaspoon finely crushed dried rosemary leaves
2 teaspoons snipped fresh or 1 teaspoon finely crushed dried thyme leaves
1½ teaspoons salt
⅓ cup dry sauterne or other white wine
1 roasting chicken (about 3 pounds)
1 teaspoon clarified butter
Salt
1 small bunch parsley
1 cup 3-inch pieces leek, green part only
1 tablespoon dry sauterne or other white wine

1. Arrange 1½ cups leeks, the zucchini, and peppers in bottom of a Dutch oven. Mix rosemary, thyme, and 1½ teaspoons salt; sprinkle one third of herb mixture over vegetables. Pour ⅓ cup sauterne over vegetables.
2. Rinse chicken and pat dry. Rub chicken with butter and sprinkle with remaining herb mixture. Lightly salt cavity of chicken. Stuff cavity with parsley and green part of leeks; sprinkle with 1 tablespoon sauterne. Place chicken in Dutch oven; cover with lid.
3. Bake at 325°F 2 hours, or until tender. Remove chicken to platter; discard parsley and leek from cavity. Surround chicken with vegetables.

4 servings

704 *Roast Turkey with Pineapple-Stuffed Breast*

A stuffing of pineapple, cooked poultry, and curry is carefully spread beneath the skin of the turkey breast so that the flavors are absorbed while roasting.

1 turkey (10 to 12 pounds)
1½ tablespoons curry powder
2 teaspoons salt
⅓ cup minced onion
4 garlic cloves, minced
1 teaspoon minced ginger root
2 tablespoons vegetable oil
⅔ cup unsweetened pineapple juice
1 can (20 ounces) unsweetened crushed pineapple, drained
1½ cups minced cooked turkey or chicken
Unsweetened pineapple juice

1. Rinse turkey; pat dry. Carefully loosen skin over turkey breast by running fingers under the skin.
2. Mix curry powder, salt, onion, garlic, ginger root, vegetable oil, and ⅔ cup pineapple juice. Mix one quarter of the spice mixture with the drained pineapple and minced turkey. Spread pineapple mixture gently and evenly under skin of turkey breast with fingers. Place turkey in a roasting pan. Insert meat thermometer in thickest part of thigh. Brush remaining spice mixture over turkey breast.
3. Roast in a 325°F oven until thermometer registers 175°F (3½ to 4 hours); baste occasionally with pineapple juice. Remove turkey to serving platter; cover loosely with aluminum foil. Let stand 20 minutes before carving.

About 16 servings

Note: This recipe can be used for a roasting chicken of about 5 pounds. Use half the spice and pineapple mixtures; proceed as directed. Roast at 325°F about 2½ hours, or until chicken is tender; drumstick meat will feel very soft.

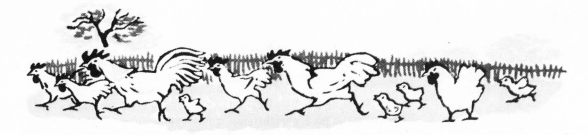

705 *Capon Roasted in Salt*

The salt casing leaves the chicken lean, moist, and tender with just a tinge of salt flavor.

1 capon (about 5 pounds)
Salt
1 carrot, cut in 1-inch pieces
1 medium onion, cut in quarters
2 sprigs parsley
6 to 7 pounds coarse kosher salt
Watercress

1. Rinse capon; pat dry. Salt inside of cavity lightly; fill cavity with vegetables.
2. Line a deep Dutch oven (that will fit size of capon, allowing 1½ to 2 inches space on bottom, sides, and top) with heavy-duty aluminum foil, allowing 2 inches of foil to fold down over top edge of pan. Fill bottom of Dutch oven with a 1½-inch layer of salt. Place capon in Dutch oven. Carefully fill Dutch oven with salt, being careful not to get salt inside cavity of capon. Layer salt over top of capon.
3. Roast uncovered in a 400°F oven 2 hours. Remove from oven. Let stand 15 minutes.
4. Lay Dutch oven on its side. Using foil lining, gently pull salt-encased capon from Dutch oven. Break salt from capon, using an ice pick or screwdriver and hammer. Place capon on serving platter; remove vegetables from cavity. Garnish with watercress. Serve immediately.

4 servings

706 *Capon with Vegetable Dressing*

The intriguing combination of vegetables gives the impression of an old-time stuffing.

1 capon (about 5 pounds)
½ can (10½-ounce size)
    condensed onion soup
1 medium eggplant, pared and
    cut in ½-inch cubes
1 cup chopped onion
1 cup chopped celery
1 cup chopped carrot
1½ to 2 teaspoons salt
¼ teaspoon freshly ground
    pepper
2 teaspoons poultry seasoning
¼ cup snipped parsley
2 eggs, beaten

1. Rinse capon; pat dry with paper toweling. Place capon on rack in a roasting pan. Pour onion soup over.
2. Roast in a 325°F oven about 2½ hours, or until capon is done; meat on drumstick will be very tender.
3. Remove capon to a serving platter; let stand 15 minutes before carving.
4. While capon is roasting, simmer eggplant in 1 inch of **salted water** until tender (about 10 minutes); drain.
5. Process onion, celery, and carrot in a food processor or blender until finely ground; transfer mixture to a mixing bowl. Mix in eggplant and remaining ingredients. Spoon vegetable mixture into a lightly oiled 2-quart casserole; do not cover.
6. Bake at 325°F 45 minutes. Remove to serving bowl.

4 servings

Note: Do not bake vegetable dressing in cavity of capon because the correct texture will not be obtained.
   This dressing is excellent served with pork.

707 *Chicken Meringue*

Meringue replaces the need for a pastry crust in this colorful chicken pot pie.

- 10 tiny boiling onions
- 2 stalks celery, cut in 1-inch pieces
- 1 large sweet red pepper, cut in ½-inch pieces
- 2 carrots, cut in ½-inch slices
- ● 2 cups Chicken Stock
- 4 cups cubed cooked chicken
- ½ pound medium mushrooms, cut in half
- ½ pound fresh pea pods, or 1 package (10 ounces) frozen pea pods, thawed
- 2 tablespoons cornstarch
  Cold water
  Salt
  Freshly ground pepper
- 4 egg whites
- ½ teaspoon salt
- ¼ teaspoon cream of tartar
- 1 tablespoon snipped fresh or 1½ teaspoons dried chervil leaves
- 2 tablespoons instant nonfat dry-milk solids

1. Simmer onions, celery, red pepper, and carrot in stock until just tender (about 8 minutes). Remove vegetables with slotted spoon and mix with chicken, mushrooms, and pea pods in a 2-quart casserole.

2. Mix cornstarch with a little cold water. Stir into stock: simmer, stirring constantly, until mixture thickens (about 4 minutes). Season to taste with salt and pepper. Pour over chicken in casserole.

3. Bake covered at 350°F 15 minutes.

4. Beat egg whites and ½ teaspoon salt until foamy. Add cream of tartar and chervil; continue beating, adding dry-milk solids gradually, until egg whites form stiff but not dry peaks. Spread meringue over casserole mixture, sealing to edges of casserole.

5. Bake at 350°F 12 to 14 minutes, or until meringue is lightly browned. Serve immediately.

4 to 6 servings

708 *Chicken Livers Marsala*

Green pepper, onion, and water chestnuts provide crisp contrast to the smooth texture of the chicken livers.

- 1 cup diced green pepper
- ½ cup finely chopped onion
- ⅔ cup water chestnuts, sliced in half
- ● 1½ cups Chicken Stock
- ¼ cup Marsala wine
- 1½ pounds chicken livers, cut in half (discard membrane)
- 2 teaspoons arrowroot
  Cold water
- ½ teaspoon bottled brown bouquet sauce
  Salt
  Freshly ground pepper
  Parsley sprigs

1. Simmer green pepper, onion, and water chestnuts in stock and wine until tender (about 5 minutes). Remove from stock with slotted spoon; keep warm. Add chicken livers to stock; simmer until livers are tender (about 8 minutes). Remove livers from stock with slotted spoon; add to vegetables and keep warm.

2. Mix arrowroot with a little cold water. Stir into stock. Simmer, stirring constantly, until it thickens (about 3 minutes). Stir brown bouquet sauce, vegetables. and livers into sauce. Season with salt and pepper to taste. Heat until hot. Spoon into ramekins. Garnish with parsley. Serve at once.

4 servings

709 *Vegetable-Stuffed Chicken Breasts*

Chicken breasts are rolled around a flavorful vegetable mixture and baked with creamy Cauliflower Sauce and Swiss cheese—elegant for entertaining.

3 whole large chicken breasts
  (about 3 pounds), boned,
  halved, and skinned
¾ pound cauliflower
¼ pound broccoli
● Chicken Stock
½ cup finely chopped celery
2 shallots, minced
½ teaspoon salt
● Cauliflower Sauce (do
  not add cheese or parsley)
3 ounces Swiss cheese, shredded
  Snipped parsley

1. Rinse chicken breasts; pat dry. Pound with mallet until even in thickness; set aside.
2. Remove leaves and tough stalks from cauliflower and broccoli; separate into flowerets. Simmer covered in 1 inch of stock until tender (about 8 minutes). Coarsely chop the cauliflower and broccoli; mix with the celery, shallots, and salt.
3. Spoon mixture onto chicken breasts; roll up carefully and place seam side down in a lightly oiled shallow baking pan. Spoon Cauliflower Sauce over breasts.
4. Bake covered at 350°F 40 minutes. Uncover and bake 15 minutes. Sprinkle cheese over breasts; bake until cheese is melted (about 5 minutes). Arrange chicken on platter; sprinkle with parsley.

6 servings

710 *Curried Breast of Chicken Salad*

6 cups bite-size pieces cooked
  chicken
1½ cups sliced celery
1 can (8½ ounces) water
  chestnuts, drained and cut in
  thirds
½ teaspoon salt
¼ teaspoon finely ground pepper
● 1 cup Mock Mayonnaise
1 teaspoon curry powder
2 tablespoons dry sherry
  Lettuce leaves
  Orange slices

1. Combine chicken, celery, water chestnuts, salt, and pepper.
2. Mix Mock Mayonnaise, curry, and sherry; stir gently into chicken mixture. Serve on lettuce-lined plates; garnish with orange slices.

6 servings

711 *Ducklings with Green Peppercorn Sauce*

2 ducklings (about 4½ pounds
  each)
1½ teaspoons salt
¼ teaspoon freshly ground
  pepper
1 teaspoon snipped fresh or
  ½ teaspoon dried crumbled
  rosemary leaves
● Chicken Stock
● Green Peppercorn Sauce

1. Rinse ducklings; pat dry. Place ducklings breast side up on rack in a roasting pan. Sprinkle with salt, pepper, and rosemary. Pierce breasts of ducklings with a fork several times.
2. Roast in a 350°F oven about 2½ hours, or until ducklings are done; drumstick meat will feel very tender. Baste ducklings occasionally with stock. Remove ducklings to a serving platter; let stand 15 minutes before carving.
3. Serve with the sauce.

6 to 8 servings

712 *Duckling with Fruit Salad*

2 ducklings (about 4½ pounds
    each)
2 teaspoons salt
½ teaspoon freshly ground
    pepper
¾ teaspoon allspice
½ cup fruit juice
6 slices fresh or canned
    pineapple
6 preserved kumquats, thinly
    sliced
3 oranges, peeled and segments
    removed
2 apples, sliced
2 papayas, peeled and sliced, if
    desired
2 bananas, sliced
1 pound white grapes
1 lime, cut in 6 wedges
1 lemon, cut in 6 wedges
● 1½ cups Low-Fat Yogurt
2 tablespoons snipped mint
    Mint sprigs

1. Rinse ducklings; pat dry. Place ducklings breast side up on rack in a roasting pan. Sprinkle with salt, pepper, and allspice. Pierce breasts of ducklings with a fork several times.
2. Roast in a 350°F oven about 2½ hours, or until ducklings are done; drumstick meat will feel very soft. Baste ducklings occasionally with fruit juice. Remove ducklings to platter; let cool.
3. While ducklings are roasting, prepare fruits; refrigerate. Mix yogurt and snipped mint; refrigerate.
4. Carefully cut skin and fat from ducklings. Remove meat from carcass carefully, keeping meat in as large pieces as possible. Arrange duckling meat and fruits attractively on individual plates. Garnish with mint. Pass chilled yogurt sauce.

6 servings

713 *Crumb-Crusted Duckling Halves*

The ducklings are covered with grapevine leaves to insure moistness. A delicious crumb coating adds crispness. Serve with a variety of sauces.

*16 grapevine leaves preserved in
    brine
2 ducklings (about 4½ pounds
    each), cut in half
2 teaspoons salt
● ½ cup Chicken Stock
    Juice of 1 lemon
    Clarified butter
⅓ cup seasoned stuffing crumbs,
    slightly crushed
●Cumberland Sauce or
● Madeira Sauce

1. Soak grapevine leaves in cold water 20 minutes. Pat dry. Set aside.
2. Using fingers and a sharp knife, remove skin and excess fat from ducklings (do not skin wings). Place ducklings breast side up on rack in a roasting pan; sprinkle with salt. Cover surface of ducks with grapevine leaves.
3. Roast in a 325°F oven about 2½ hours, or until ducklings are done; drumstick meat will feel soft. Baste ducklings every half hour with a mixture of stock and lemon juice.
4. Remove grapevine leaves. Brush ducklings very lightly with butter and sprinkle with crumbs. Broil 4 inches from heat until crumbs are browned (about 5 minutes). Remove ducklings to platter; let stand 10 minutes before serving. Serve with desired sauce.

4 servings

*Grapevine leaves can be purchased in a gourmet shop or in the specialty section of a supermarket.

714 *Fried Chicken (Pollo Fritto)*

1 frying chicken (about 3
    pounds), cut in serving pieces
½ cup flour
1½ teaspoons salt
¼ teaspoon pepper
    Olive oil
2 eggs, well beaten
¼ cup milk
1 tablespoon chopped parsley
½ cup grated Parmesan cheese
1 to 2 tablespoons water

1. Rinse chicken and pat dry with paper towels. To coat chicken evenly, shake 2 or 3 pieces at a time in a plastic bag containing the flour, salt, and pepper.
2. Fill a large, heavy skillet ½-inch deep with olive oil; place over medium heat.
3. Combine eggs, milk, and parsley. Dip each chicken piece in the egg mixture and roll in cheese. Starting with meaty pieces, place the chicken, skin-side down, in the hot oil. Turn pieces as necessary to brown evenly on all sides.
4. When chicken is browned, reduce heat, pour in water, and cover pan tightly. Cook chicken slowly 25 to 40 minutes, or until all pieces are tender. For crisp skin, uncover chicken the last 10 minutes of cooking.

3 or 4 servings

715 *Chicken Breasts Regina (Petti di Pollo Regina)*

2 whole chicken breasts, skinned,
    boned, and cut in half
4 thin slices ham
4 thin slices liver sausage or liver
    pâté
    Water
    Flour
1 egg, beaten
    Fine dry bread crumbs
3 tablespoons butter
● Madeira Sauce

1. Split chicken breast halves lengthwise, but not completely through. Open breast halves and pound until very thin.
2. Place a slice of ham, then a slice of liver sausage in center of each breast. Fold in half, enclosing the ham and liver sausage, moisten the edges with water, and press together.
3. Coat chicken breasts with flour, dip in beaten egg, and coat with bread crumbs.
4. Fry in butter in a skillet until golden brown on both sides. Serve with hot Madeira Sauce.

4 servings

716 *Wild Pigeons Perugian (Palombacci alla Perugina)*

3 pigeons or Rock Cornish hens
4 to 6 tablespoons olive oil
1 cup dry red wine
10 green olives
4 fresh sage leaves or ¼ teaspoon
    ground sage
½ teaspoon juniper berries
½ teaspoon salt
    Dash pepper

1. Brown pigeons in 2 tablespoons hot olive oil in a Dutch oven, adding more oil if necessary. Stir in wine, 2 tablespoons olive oil, olives, sage, juniper berries, salt, and pepper.
2. Cook in a 300°F oven 50 to 60 minutes, or until pigeons are tender.

4 servings

717 *Chicken Vesuvio (Pollo alla Vesuviana)*

1 broiler-fryer chicken (2 to 3
    pounds), cut in pieces
½ cup flour
1½ teaspoons salt
¼ teaspoon pepper
½ cup olive oil
2 tablespoons olive oil
1 clove garlic, sliced
2 tablespoons Marsala
½ teaspoon chopped parsley
● Deep-Fried Potatoes

1. Coat chicken pieces with a mixture of flour, salt, and pepper.
2. Heat ½ cup oil in a large skillet. Add chicken pieces and brown on all sides. Put into a large, shallow baking dish.
3. Heat 2 tablespoons oil and garlic until garlic is lightly browned. Add Marsala and parsley; mix well. Pour over chicken in baking dish.
4. Bake at 325°F about 45 minutes, or until chicken is tender; turn once.
5. Prepare potatoes and place around edges of baking dish.

4 servings

718 *Country Style Chicken (Pollo alla Paesana)*

1 frying chicken (about 3
    pounds), cut in serving pieces
2 tablespoons butter
2 tablespoons olive oil
1 medium-size onion, sliced
1 teaspoon salt
⅛ teaspoon pepper
1 pound zucchini
2 large green peppers
1½ tablespoons olive oil
1 teaspoon chopped basil leaves,
    or ¼ teaspoon dried sweet
    basil
½ cup dry white wine

1. In a large skillet, brown the chicken in butter and 2 tablespoons olive oil. Place onion around chicken; sprinkle with salt and pepper. Cover and cook slowly about 15 minutes.
2. While chicken is cooking, wash and cut zucchini in ½-inch-thick slices. Wash peppers; remove stems and seeds. Rinse in cold water and slice lengthwise into 1-inch-wide strips.
3. In another skillet, heat 1½ tablespoons olive oil and sauté zucchini and peppers until soft (about 10 minutes). Sprinkle with basil. Transfer vegetables to skillet with chicken and pour in wine.
4. Simmer, covered, about 15 minutes, or until chicken is very tender and vegetables are cooked.

About 4 servings

719 *Chicken Cacciatore*

Cacciatore, meaning "hunter" in Italian, indicates that the food (usually chicken), is prepared in the "hunter's style," that is, simmering the fowl in a well-seasoned tomato and wine sauce.

¼ cup cooking oil
1 broiler-fryer (2½ pounds), cut up
2 onions, sliced
2 cloves garlic, minced
3 tomatoes, cored and quartered
2 green peppers, sliced
1 small bay leaf
1 teaspoon salt
¼ teaspoon pepper
½ teaspoon celery seed
1 teaspoon crushed oregano or
    basil
1 can (8 ounces) tomato sauce
¼ cup sauterne
8 ounces spaghetti, cooked
    according to package directions

1. Heat oil in a large, heavy skillet; add chicken and brown on all sides. Remove from skillet.
2. Add onion and garlic to oil remaining in skillet and cook until onion is tender, but not brown; stir occasionally.
3. Return chicken to skillet and add the tomatoes, green pepper, and bay leaf.
4. Mix salt, pepper, celery seed, and oregano and blend with tomato sauce; pour over all.
5. Cover and cook over low heat 45 minutes. Blend in wine and cook, uncovered, 20 minutes longer. Discard bay leaf.
6. Put the cooked spaghetti onto a hot serving platter and top with the chicken and sauce.

About 6 servings

720 *Chicken and Mushrooms in Sour Cream Sauce*

2 frying chickens, cut in serving
  pieces
¼ cup oil
1 pound fresh mushrooms,
  cleaned and sliced
2 cups canned tomatoes with juice
  (16-ounce can)
2 canned green chilies, seeded
½ cup chopped onion
1 clove garlic, minced
1 cup chicken stock (or water plus
  chicken bouillon cube)
1½ teaspoons salt
1 cup dairy sour cream

1. Brown chicken pieces in hot oil in a large skillet. Place chicken in Dutch oven or heavy saucepot.
2. Sauté mushrooms in oil remaining in skillet; spoon mushrooms over chicken.
3. Combine tomatoes, chilies, onion, and garlic in an electric blender and blend to a purée (if amount is too large for blender container, blend in two portions).
4. Pour purée into fat remaining in skillet in which chicken and mushrooms were cooked; bring to boiling and cook about 5 minutes. Stir in chicken stock and salt.
5. Pour sauce over chicken and mushrooms in Dutch oven. Cover and cook over low heat until chicken is tender (about 1 hour).
6. Just before serving, stir in sour cream and heat through, but do not boil.

6 to 8 servings

721 *Chicken Tablecloth Stainer*

Mexicans love to give humorous names to foods, and this particular dish is undoubtedly well-named. The reason becomes obvious when you see the deep red color of the sauce, caused by the dark pasilla chilies called for in the recipe. This same sauce is often used with pork, and occasionally both pork and chicken are combined in the same recipe.

2 frying chickens (about 2½
  pounds each), cut in serving
  pieces
½ pound link sausages
½ cup canned pineapple chunks,
  drained
1 apple, pared, cored, and sliced
1 large, firm banana, sliced
Sauce:
2 fresh or dried ancho chilies and 2
  fresh or dried pasilla chilies,
  or 1 tablespoon chili powder
1 cup coarsely chopped onion
1 clove garlic
2 cups (16-ounce can) tomatoes
  with juice
½ cup whole blanched almonds
¼ teaspoon cinnamon
⅛ teaspoon cloves
2 cups chicken stock, or 2 cups
  water plus 2 chicken bouillon
  cubes
Salt and pepper

1. Put chicken pieces into a Dutch oven or heavy kettle.
2. Fry sausages in a skillet until browned. Put into Dutch oven with chicken. Arrange pineapple, apple, and banana over chicken.
3. For sauce, first prepare chilies . (If chilies are not available, substitute chili powder.) Combine chilies, onion, garlic, tomatoes, almonds, cinnamon, and cloves in an electric blender. Blend to a smooth purée.
4. Heat the fat remaining in the skillet in which the sausages were cooked. Add the blended sauce and cook about 5 minutes, stirring constantly. Stir in chicken stock. Season to taste with salt and pepper.
5. Pour sauce over chicken in Dutch oven. Cover and simmer over low heat 1 hour, or until chicken is tender.

6 to 8 servings

722 *Chicken with Rice* (*Arroz con Pollo*)

1 broiler-fryer chicken, (2 to 3 pounds), cut in pieces
¼ cup fat
½ cup chopped onion
1 clove garlic, minced
1 large tomato, chopped
3 cups hot water
1 cup uncooked rice
1 tablespoon minced parsley
2 teaspoons salt
½ teaspoon paprika
¼ teaspoon pepper
¼ teaspoon saffron
1 bay leaf

1. Rinse chicken and pat dry with absorbent paper.
2. Heat fat in a skillet over medium heat. Add onion and garlic; cook until onion is tender. Remove with a slotted spoon; set aside.
3. Put chicken pieces, skin side down, in skillet. Turn to brown pieces on all sides.
4. When chicken is browned, add tomato, onion, water, rice, parsley, and dry seasonings. Cover and cook over low heat about 45 minutes, or until thickest pieces of chicken are tender when pierced with a fork.

6 to 8 servings

723 *Marinated Chicken* (*Pollo Escabeche*)

2 broiler-fryer chickens, cut in serving pieces
1½ cups oil
1 cup cooked sliced carrots
2 large onions, sliced
2 stalks celery, cut in 2-inch pieces
1 clove garlic, minced
⅛ teaspoon thyme
⅛ teaspoon marjoram
1 small bay leaf
12 peppercorns
1 teaspoon salt
3 cups vinegar
Olives, radishes, pickled chilies

1. Brown chicken pieces in hot oil in a skillet. Place browned chicken in a Dutch oven or heavy kettle. Top with carrots, onions, celery, garlic, thyme, marjoram, bay leaf, peppercorns, and salt. Pour vinegar over all.
2. Simmer over low heat until chicken is tender (about 30 to 45 minutes).
3. Remove from heat and let cool to room temperature. Place in refrigerator and chill for at least 1 hour.
4. Garnish with olives, radishes, and chilies.

8 to 10 servings

724 *Green Chicken* (*Pollo Verde*)

1 medium onion, coarsely chopped
1 clove garlic, peeled
1 cup (small can) salsa verde mexicana (Mexican green tomato sauce)
¼ cup (lightly filled) fresh parsley
1 teaspoon salt
¼ teaspoon pepper
2 frying chickens, cut in serving pieces

1. Put onion, garlic, salsa verde, and parsley into an electric blender. Blend until liquefied. Stir in salt and pepper.
2. Rinse chicken pieces and pat dry; arrange pieces in a heavy skillet. Pour green sauce over chicken. Cover; bring to boiling. Cook over low heat until chicken is tender, about 1 hour.

6 servings

725 *Chicken or Turkey Mole Poblano I (with canned mole sauce)*

1 jar (8 ounces) mole poblano paste
1 cup canned tomato sauce
1 cup chicken stock or water
Sugar and salt
3 cups diced cooked chicken or turkey

1. Blend mole paste, tomato sauce, and stock in a large saucepan. Heat to boiling; add sugar and salt to taste. Reduce heat. Stir in chicken. Simmer about 10 to 15 minutes, stirring occasionally, to blend flavors.
2. To use as a tamale filling, the sauce must be fairly thick, so may be simmered until of desired consistency. Then spoon poultry pieces and sauce onto tamale dough spread on corn husk; use leftover sauce to serve over cooked tamales.
3. Or, Chicken or Turkey Mole Poblano may be served over hot rice.

About 4 cups filling (enough for 3½ dozen tamales)

726 *Chicken or Turkey Mole Poblano II (from basic ingredients)*

6 ancho chilies, fresh or dried
2 cups (16-ounce can) cooked tomatoes
1 large onion, coarsely chopped
1 clove garlic, peeled
½ cup salted peanuts or ½ cup peanut butter
1 tortilla or 1 piece of toast, torn in pieces
⅓ cup raisins
2 tablespoons sesame seed
¼ cup oil
1 tablespoon sugar
¼ teaspoon anise
¼ teaspoon cinnamon
¼ teaspoon cloves
¼ teaspoon coriander
¼ teaspoon cumin (comino)
1 cup chicken or turkey stock
1 ounce (1 square) unsweetened chocolate
Salt and pepper
3 cups diced cooked chicken or turkey

1. Prepare chilies. Combine with tomatoes, onion, garlic, peanuts, tortilla, raisins, and sesame seed. Put a small amount at a time into an electric blender and blend to make a thick purée.
2. Heat oil in a large skillet. Add the purée and cook, stirring constantly, about 5 minutes. Stir in sugar, anise, cinnamon, cloves, coriander, cumin, and stock. Bring to boiling, reduce heat, and simmer. Add chocolate and continue simmering, stirring constantly, until chocolate is melted and blended into sauce. Add salt and pepper to taste. Stir in chicken pieces and simmer about 10 minutes.
3. To use as a tamale filling, the sauce must be fairly thick, so it may be simmered until desired consistency is reached. Then spoon poultry pieces and a little sauce onto tamale dough spread on a corn husk. Use leftover sauce to serve over cooked tamales.
4. Or, Chicken or Turkey Mole Poblano may be served over hot rice.

About 4 cups filling (enough for 3½ dozen tamales)

727 *Piquant Chicken*

1 frying chicken, cut in serving pieces
Butter or margarine
6 limes or 4 lemons, sliced as thinly as possible
Salt and pepper

1. Brown chicken pieces in butter in a skillet.
2. Place chicken in an ovenproof casserole. Cover completely with lime or lemon slices. Sprinkle with salt and pepper. Cover tightly with foil.
3. Bake at 325°F about 1¼ hours, or until chicken is tender.
4. Serve plain or with Red Chili Sauce (●   ).

4 servings

728 *Spiced Fruited Chicken*

1½ teaspoons salt
¼ teaspoon pepper
¼ teaspoon cinnamon
¼ teaspoon cloves
2 cloves garlic, minced
2 frying chickens, cut in serving pieces
¼ cup oil
½ cup chopped onion
½ cup raisins
½ cup crushed pineapple
2 cups orange juice
½ cup dry sherry

1. Combine salt, pepper, cinnamon, cloves, and garlic. Rub into chicken pieces.
2. Heat oil in a heavy skillet. Brown chicken in hot oil. Place browned chicken in a Dutch oven or heavy saucepot.
3. Cook onion in remaining oil in skillet until soft (about 5 minutes).
4. Add onion to chicken along with raisins, pineapple, and orange juice. Add water, if needed, to just cover chicken. Bring to boiling, reduce heat, cover, and cook until chicken is tender (about 1 hour). Add sherry and cook about 5 minutes longer to blend flavors.

6 to 8 servings

729 *Stuffed Turkey*

1 turkey (12 to 16 pounds)
Salt and pepper
Juice of 1 lemon
Stuffing (see below)
Melted butter
Gravy:
　Flour
　Chicken broth
　White wine
　Salt and pepper

1. Clean turkey. Sprinkle inside and out with salt and pepper, then drizzle with lemon juice.
2. Spoon desired amount of stuffing into cavities of turkey. Secure openings with skewers and twine.
3. Put turkey, breast side up, on a rack in a shallow roasting pan. Cover bird with a double thickness of cheesecloth soaked in butter.
4. Roast in a 325°F oven 4½ to 5½ hours, or until done (180°F to 185°F on a meat thermometer inserted in inside thigh muscle or thickest part of breast); baste with drippings several times during roasting.
5. For gravy, stir a small amount of flour with pan drippings. Cook until bubbly. Stir in equal parts of broth and wine. Season to taste with salt and pepper.
6. Put turkey on a platter and garnish with **watercress.** Accompany with gravy.

12 to 16 servings

730 *Stuffing*

5 slices bacon, diced
1 onion, chopped
1 clove garlic, minced
3 pounds ground pork loin
½ cup tomato purée
¾ cup blanched almonds, chopped
½ cup ripe olives, coarsely chopped
6 jalapeño chilies, seeded and chopped
3 carrots, pared and sliced
3 bananas, peeled and sliced
3 apples, pared, cored, and diced
¾ cup raisins
2 teaspoons sugar
Salt and pepper
Cinnamon

1. Fry bacon until brown in a large skillet. Remove bacon from fat; reserve. Brown onion and garlic in fat in skillet, then brown meat. Discard excess fat.
2. Add tomato purée, almonds, olives, chilies, carrots, fruit, sugar, and salt, pepper, and cinnamon to taste; mix well. Cook several minutes. Mix in bacon. Cool before stuffing turkey.

731 *Martinique Stuffed Chicken in Rum*

1 roaster chicken (about 4 pounds)
1 lime, halved
  Salt and pepper
2 white bread slices with crusts
    trimmed
1 cup milk
1 package (3 ounces) cream cheese
2 tablespoons amber rum
½ cup chopped chicken livers
2 pork sausage links, casing removed
    and meat chopped finely
1 scallion or green onion, chopped
1 tablespoon chopped parsley
⅛ teaspoon cayenne or red pepper
  Salt and pepper (optional)

1. Rub chicken skin with the cut side of lime. Season with salt and pepper. Remove the fat deposits from the opening of the cavity. Set chicken and fat aside.
2. Soak bread in milk. Set aside.
3. Combine cream cheese, rum, chicken liver, sausage, scallion, parsley, and cayenne.
4. Squeeze bread and add to mixture; discard milk. Add salt and pepper, if desired. Mix well.
5. Stuff cavity of chicken with the mixture, then tie chicken legs and wings to hold close to body.
6. Place chicken, breast side up, on rack in a shallow roasting pan. Lay reserved fat across breast.
7. Roast in a 375°F oven about 2 hours.
8. Garnish with **watercress** and serve with Smothered Mixed Vegetables (●).

4 to 6 servings

732 *Braised Chicken and Onions*
(Maman Poule à la Chaudière)

1 stewing chicken (about 4 pounds)
  Papaya leaves
1 lime, halved
1 orange, halved
  Salt and freshly ground pepper
    to taste
3 tablespoons soybean, olive, or
    peanut oil
3 tablespoons bacon drippings
2 tablespoons water
24 small onions
2 cups chicken stock
2 tablespoons butter
2 tablespoons cornstarch
  Chopped parsley
  Chopped scallions or green onions

1. Truss chicken. Wrap in papaya leaves and refrigerate for 12 hours.
2. Rub the chicken with the cut sides of the lime and orange. Season with salt and pepper.
3. Heat oil and bacon drippings in a Dutch oven. Brown chicken. Add water and cover.
4. Cook in a 375°F oven about 2 hours, or until almost tender; turn occasionally and stir the juices. Add stock if more liquid is needed.
5. Add onions and continue cooking until onions are tender and well browned (about 30 minutes).
6. Place chicken and onions on a large serving platter. Carve bird.
7. Pour stock into Dutch oven and set over medium heat to deglaze. Mix butter and cornstarch and add to stock. Stir until sauce is slightly thicker.
8. Pour sauce over meat and sprinkle with chopped parsley and scallions. Serve with Coconut and Rice (●).

6 to 8 servings

733 *Barbecued Chicken, Quail, or Guinea Fowl*

  Chicken, quail, or guinea fowl
● Creole Barbecue Sauce

1. Split the birds in half and remove the backbone and neck.
2. Marinate birds overnight in Creole Barbecue Sauce.
3. Place bird halves on a grill 5 inches from glowing coals. Barbecue 25 minutes, turning several times and basting with the barbecue sauce.
4. Serve with **barbecued yams**

Allow ½ bird per serving

734 *Chicken with Cashews*

In the Caribbean, this dish is traditionally served with preserves made from the cashew fruit, but in the United States, guava jelly is an acceptable substitute.

2 broiler-fryer chickens (about
    2 pounds each), cut in pieces
1 lime, halved
    Salt, freshly ground pepper, and
      cayenne or red pepper
½ cup peanut oil
4 shallots, minced
¾ cup dry white wine
½ cup chicken broth
1 cup split cashews
½ cup amber rum
2 tablespoons butter
2 tablespoons cornstarch

1. Rub chicken with the cut side of lime. Season with salt, pepper, and cayenne.
2. Heat oil in a Dutch oven and sauté the chicken until golden brown. Add shallots and brown. Add wine and chicken broth. Cover. Simmer over low heat 25 minutes. Add cashews and simmer about 10 minutes.
3. Remove chicken and cashews with a slotted spoon and keep warm. Remove excess fat from Dutch oven, leaving drippings. Deglaze with rum.
4. Mix butter and cornstarch and add to drippings. Cook over high heat, stirring constantly, until sauce is slightly thicker.
5. Pour sauce over chicken and nuts. Serve with Bananas à l'Antillaise and Guava Jelly (●).

6 servings

735 *Chicken with Peas (Poulet Pois France)*

3 broiler-fryer chickens
    (3 pounds each), cut in pieces
1 tablespoon lime juice
    Salt and freshly ground pepper
¼ cup soybean oil
1 shallot
1 garlic clove
1 teaspoon dried thyme
1 green hot pepper or
    3 dried Italian pepper pods
2 cups chicken stock
3 pounds fresh green peas, shelled
2 tablespoons butter
2 tablespoons cornstarch

1. Season chicken with lime juice, salt, and pepper.
2. Heat oil in a Dutch oven and sauté the chicken pieces until golden brown on all sides.
3. In a mortar, pound to a paste the shallot and garlic. Add seasoning paste, thyme, green hot pepper, 1 cup stock, and peas to the chicken. Reduce heat and simmer 25 minutes, or until chicken and peas are tender.
4. Remove chicken, peas, and hot pepper to a heated platter and keep hot. Add remaining stock to Dutch oven; bring to a boil. Mix butter and cornstarch and add to stock. Stir until sauce is slightly thicker. Add salt and pepper, if desired.
5. Garnish chicken with **chopped parsley** and serve sauce in a sauceboat.

About 10 servings

Squab with Peas: Follow recipe for Chicken with Peas, allowing ½ **squab per serving.** Carve birds and place meat on slices of **bread fried in butter.** Pour sauce over meat and croutons.

Quail with Peas: Follow recipe for Chicken with Peas, substituting **1 cup red wine** for the cooking stock. Allow **1 quail per serving.** Carve birds and place meat on slices of **bread fried in butter.** Pour sauce over meat and croutons.

736 *Wild Duck Pâté*

2 wild ducks (about 4 pounds each);
   reserve livers
¼ cup olive oil
   Juice of 2 limes
1 garlic clove, halved
   Water
1 carrot
1 leek
1 teaspoon salt
⅛ teaspoon pepper
1 cup port wine
2 bay leaves
1 small onion, minced
1 green hot pepper
⅛ teaspoon thyme
3 tablespoons olive oil
3 tablespoons butter
½ pound beef liver, cubed
¼ cup amber rum
1 egg
   Lard
   Truffles (optional)
   Bay leaves and green hot peppers
      for garnish

1. Marinate the ducks for ½ hour in a mixture of ¼ cup oil and lime juice. Rub ducks with the cut surface of garlic clove.
2. Place birds in a Dutch oven and cover with water; add carrot, leek, salt, and pepper and bring to a boil. Simmer covered over low heat until birds are tender.
3. Remove birds from broth and cool. Reserve ¼ cup broth; store remaining broth for future use. Remove the meat from the carcasses, cutting the breast meat into long, even strips.
4. Mix port wine, bay leaves, onion, pepper, and thyme; marinate the breast meat for ½ hour. Set aside remaining duck meat.
5. Heat 3 tablespoons oil and butter in a medium skillet. Sauté duck livers and beef liver over high heat until golden. Warm the rum, ignite it, and pour it, still flaming, over the livers. Stir in ¼ cup of the reserved broth to deglaze the skillet.
6. Purée in an electric blender the liver mixture, reserved duck meat, and egg.
7. Coat heavily with lard 1 large terrine or loaf dish, or 2 small terrines or loaf dishes. Put in half the puréed mixture, then arrange the marinated strips of duck breast on top with slices of truffles, if desired. Cover with the remaining duck mixture, then with a thick coat of lard.
8. Garnish with bay leaves and green hot peppers. Cover terrine and place in a pan of hot water.
9. Bake at 375°F about 1½ hours.
10. Wipe clean the sides of the terrine. Cool and store covered in refrigerator up to a week.
11. To serve, remove bay leaves and peppers; slice pâté and accompany with salad.

737 *Curried Duck Martinique* *(Colombo de Canard Martiniquaise)*

3 cups coarsely chopped
   cooked duck
3 cups sliced mushrooms
6 tablespoons butter, melted
1 cup diced apple
⅓ cup grated onion
1 garlic clove, crushed in a
   garlic press
3 tablespoons flour
1 tablespoon curry powder
½ teaspoon salt
¼ teaspoon freshly ground pepper
1 cup whipping cream
½ cup duck stock
   (made from cooking the carcass)
3 tablespoons Madeira or
   sweet sherry

1. Cook duck and mushrooms in half the melted butter in a skillet over low heat, until the duck is slightly browned and the mushrooms are tender. Remove from heat and cover.
2. Sauté apple, onion, and garlic in remaining butter in a large skillet until soft. Remove skillet from the heat and stir in flour, curry, salt, and pepper.
3. Place skillet over low heat and blend in cream, stock, and Madeira. Stir constantly until the mixture thickens. Stir in the duck and mushroom mixture.
4. Serve with cooked white rice tossed with 1 cup diced banana.

6 servings

738 *Pot-Roasted Wild Duck*

4 wild ducks (about 2 pounds each)
  Amber rum
8 limes, peeled
8 peppercorns, cracked
  Papaya leaves
  Bacon drippings
3 tablespoons soybean oil
12 shallots
⅓ cup amber rum
½ cup stock
1 carrot
1 garlic clove, crushed in a
    garlic press
1 thyme sprig
1 parsley sprig
1 green hot pepper
2 cups hot stock
2 tablespoons butter
2 tablespoons cornstarch
  Salt and pepper to taste
8 slices bread, toasted
¼ cup butter

1. Wipe the duck with rum. Place 2 limes and 2 peppercorns in the cavity of each duck. Wrap the birds in papaya leaves to tenderize and refrigerate 12 hours.
2. Brush bacon drippings on each bird. Heat the oil in a Dutch oven and sauté ducks and shallots until the birds are brown on all sides.
3. Heat rum, ignite it, and pour it, while still flaming, over the birds. Add the ½ cup stock, carrot, garlic, thyme, parsley, and hot pepper. Cover Dutch oven.
4. Cook in a 475°F oven 30 minutes.
5. Cut the breasts in one piece and slice off remaining meat; reserve. Discard limes and peppercorns.
6. In a mortar, pound the carcasses until broken up. Pour the hot stock into the Dutch oven; add the broken carcasses and boil 10 minutes. Remove the hot pepper. Strain the stock and return to the Dutch oven.
7. Mix butter and cornstarch. Add to the stock; stir over medium heat until slightly thickened. Add salt and pepper to taste.
8. Fry toasted bread in butter until golden and crisp. Arrange meat on croutons. Pour sauce over all.
9. Garnish with Stuffed Sweet Peppers (●). Serve remaining sauce from a sauceboat.

8 servings

739 *Guinea Stew*

½ teaspoon monosodium glutamate
  Salt and freshly ground pepper
1 guinea fowl (2½ to 3 pounds)
1 lime, halved
¼ pound salt pork, cubed
4 parsley sprigs
2 scallions or green onions, chopped
2 garlic cloves
2 cloves
½ teaspoon salt
¼ cup soybean oil
½ cup amber rum
2 cups red wine
1 cup chicken stock
12 shallots
2 carrots, sliced
2 turnips, sliced
1 tablespoon butter
1 tablespoon cornstarch

1. Sprinkle monosodium glutamate, salt, and pepper over bird and refrigerate overnight. The next day, rub the skin with the cut side of the lime. Cut bird into pieces.
2. Render salt pork over medium heat in a Dutch oven. When crisp, remove the cracklings.
3. In a mortar, pound to a paste the parsley, scallions, garlic, cloves, and salt. Add the seasoning paste and oil to the Dutch oven.
4. Sauté the meat until golden brown on all sides.
5. Heat rum, ignite it, and pour it, still flaming, over the meat. Add wine and stock; reduce heat, cover, and simmer 30 mintues.
6. Add shallots, carrots, and turnips. Simmer until meat and vegetables are tender.
7. Place meat and vegetables on a serving platter.
8. Mix butter and cornstarch; add to liquid in Dutch oven and stir over high heat until sauce is slightly thickened. Season with salt and pepper, if necessary. Pour sauce over meat and vegetables.
9. Serve with Caribbean Rice (●).

2 servings

Chicken Stew: Follow recipe for Guinea Stew, substituting **1 broiler-fryer chicken (about 2 pounds)** for guinea fowl.

740 *Barbecued Wild Game Birds*

4	ready-to-cook wild game birds such as duckling, snipe, teal, or woodcock
	Amber rum
6	peppercorns
4	parsley sprigs
3	garlic cloves
1	green hot pepper
1	tablespoon salt
1	tablespoon olive or peanut oil
1	cup red wine
	Bacon drippings
	Dry bread crumbs
●	Creole Barbecue Sauce

1. Brush surface of birds with rum. Split birds in half and pound with a meat hammer.
2. In a mortar, pound to a paste the peppercorns, parsley, garlic, pepper, and salt. Mix seasoning paste with olive oil and wine. Pour marinade over birds and refrigerate 12 hours.
3. Thoroughly drain bird halves. Brush with bacon drippings and coat with bread crumbs.
4. Barbecue bird halves in a hinged grill 4 inches from glowing coals about 10 minutes on each side, basting twice with Creole Barbecue Sauce; time depends on their size. Turn birds once and baste again.
5. Birds should be eaten on the rare side; when birds are pricked with a fork, a droplet of blood should surface slowly.
6. Serve with Purée of Breadfruit (●).

741 *Teal on the Spit*

Teal, a small wild duck, is in season October to February.

4	teals; reserve livers
1	orange, halved
8	chicken livers
1	tablespoon flour
¼	teaspoon garlic powder
	Salt and pepper
2	tablespoons olive oil
4	bacon slices
2	tablespoons flour
2	tablespoons butter
1	can (13 ounces) clear consommé madrilène
1½	teaspoons lime juice
1½	teaspoons orange juice

1. Rub teals with cut sides of orange halves. Set aside.
2. Coat the teal livers and chicken livers with a mixture of 1 tablespoon flour, garlic powder, salt, and pepper. Heat oil and sauté the livers until golden brown.
3. Put the livers into the bird cavities. Wrap each bird in a slice of bacon, securing with skewers.
4. Spear birds on a spit and broil on the electric broiler about 25 minutes or, if charcoal is used, place the spitted bird 4 inches from the hot coals and turn often.
5. Brown 2 tablespoons flour in butter in a small saucepan over high heat. Add enough consommé madrilène to just moisten the mixture, stirring rapidly with a whisk. While it thickens, slowly pour in the remaining consommé in a thin stream. Boil rapidly, uncovered, stirring constantly for about 4 minutes, or until the sauce is reduced to ½ cup. Remove from heat and add lime juice and orange juice.
6. Serve teal with Tomatoes Stuffed with Rice and Peanuts (●) and the sauce separately.

4 servings

742 *Ortolans on Croutons*

8	ortolans
½	lime
	Salt and freshly ground pepper
½	cup cubed salt pork
¼	cup amber rum
½	cup red wine
1	tablespoon butter
1	tablespoon cornstarch
8	white bread slices with crusts trimmed
¼	cup butter

1. Truss ortolans. Rub the skin with the cut side of the lime half. Season with salt and pepper.
2. Render the salt pork over high heat in a Dutch oven. Sauté ortolans for 6 minutes, or until well browned.
3. Heat rum, ignite it, and pour it, still flaming, over the birds. Place birds on a serving platter.
4. Pour wine into Dutch oven to deglaze. Mix 1 tablespoon butter and cornstarch and add to wine. Stir until sauce is slightly thicker.
5. Make croutons by frying bread slices in butter until brown on both sides.
6. Serve each ortolan on a crouton, top with a slice of sautéed liver pâté, if desired, and pour sauce over all.

8 servings

Twelve-Fruit Compote, page 344

743 *Roast Turkey*

1 ready-to-cook turkey
   (reserve giblets)
1 lime, halved
1 orange, halved
1 teaspoon monosodium glutamate
   Salt and freshly ground pepper
¼ cup olive oil
1 tablespoon tomato paste
1 garlic clove, crushed in a
   garlic press
1 quart water
1 large onion, sliced
4 parsley sprigs
1 bay leaf
2 teaspoons salt
   Lettuce
   Cherry tomato
   Avocado half
   Green pepper ring
2 tablespoons butter
2 tablespoons cornstarch

1. Rub the skin of the bird with the cut side of the lime and orange. Sprinkle monosodium glutamate, salt, and pepper over surface. Refrigerate 2 hours.
2. Combine oil, tomato paste, and garlic. Brush mixture over bird. Set on a rack in a shallow roasting pan.
3. Roast, uncovered, in a 375°F oven until turkey tests done (the thickest part of the drumstick feels soft when pressed with fingers, or meat thermometer inserted in the thickest part of inner thigh muscle registers 180° to 185°F).
4. Meanwhile, prepare giblet broth. Put turkey neck and giblets (except liver), water, onion, parsley, bay leaf, and salt in a saucepan. Cover and simmer about 2 hours, or until giblets are tender. Add the liver the last 15 minutes of cooking. Strain.
5. Carve turkey and arrange meat on a bed of lettuce. Garnish with tomato, avocado, and green pepper.
6. Remove excess fat from roasting pan. Pour in 2 cups giblet broth to deglaze over medium heat.
7. Mix butter and cornstarch and add to broth. Stir until sauce is slightly thicker.
8. Serve sauce with turkey.

744 *Turkey Croquettes*

2 tablespoons butter
2 tablespoons minced shallot
1½ tablespoons flour
½ cup chicken broth
2 egg yolks, beaten
2 cups ground turkey
1 tablespoon chopped parsley
1 teaspoon salt
¼ teaspoon freshly ground pepper
2 egg yolks
2 teaspoons cooking oil
   Dry bread crumbs
   Fat for deep frying,
      heated to 375°F

1. Melt butter in a skillet. Cook shallot over low heat until translucent. Stir in flour. Gradually add chicken broth, blending until smooth.
2. Remove from heat and beat in 2 egg yolks. Add turkey, parsley, salt, and pepper; mix well.
3. Spread mixture on a platter and cool in refrigerator.
4. Shape mixture into small balls. Coat balls with a mixture of 2 egg yolks and oil and then roll in bread crumbs.
5. Fry in heated fat until golden. Drain on absorbent paper.
6. Serve with Tomato Sauce Creole (●).

Grandmother's Cheese Cake, page 340
Baba, page 336

745 *Duck Bigarade*

A bigarade is a small, bitter orange which grows in profusion in the islands. The sour orange taste can be duplicated by mixing lime and orange juices.

2 limes, halved
1 ready-to-cook duck
  (about 5 pounds)
  Salt, freshly ground pepper, and
    cayenne or red pepper
2 cups firmly packed brown sugar
1 cup water
2 teaspoons vanilla extract
½ cup orange peel strips
4 small oranges, halved and seeded
2 cups chicken broth
¼ cup orange juice
½ cup amber rum
¼ cup butter
¼ cup cornstarch

1. Squeeze lime juice over the entire duck. Season with salt, pepper, and cayenne. Place on a rack in a roasting pan.
2. Roast uncovered in a 425°F oven 25 minutes. Turn oven control to 350°F and continue to roast 30 minutes.
3. Combine brown sugar, water, and vanilla extract in a large, heavy saucepan. Bring to a boil over high heat and boil about 6 minutes. Add orange peel and orange halves and continue boiling 1 minute. Remove from heat and cool. Set ¼ cup syrup aside in a small saucepan.
4. Transfer duck to a warm platter. Remove fat from roasting pan. Stir in chicken broth and orange juice to deglaze. Heat the rum, ignite it, and when flames die down, pour it into the chicken broth.
5. Heat the reserved syrup until it caramelizes. Add to chicken broth mixture and blend well.
6. Mix butter and cornstarch and add to roasting pan. Cook over medium heat, stirring constantly, until the gravy is slightly thicker.
7. Carve the duck. Sprinkle the glazed orange peel strips over the meat. Pour a little gravy over the meat. Serve remaining gravy separately. Arrange glazed orange halves around the duck, alternating with bouquets of **watercress**. Serve with Caribbean Rice (●).

4 servings

Seafood

746 *Baked Halibut in Parchment Paper*

1 tablespoon olive oil
Juice of ½ lemon
Pinch basil
Pinch oregano
1 halibut steak (or any other
    preferred steak)
Salt and pepper
2 thin lemon slices
4 capers

1. Combine oil, lemon juice, basil, and oregano; spoon over both sides of the fish. Season with salt and pepper.
2. Place the fish on a piece of parchment paper. Lay lemon slices and capers on top of fish. Seal paper and tie. Put into a baking dish.
3. Bake at 325°F 30 minutes.
4. Serve hot sealed in parchment.

1 serving

747 *Fried Codfish in Garlic Sauce*
(Bakaliaros Tiganitos me Skorthalia)

4 frozen codfish fillets, thawed
Flour, seasoned with salt and
    pepper
Flour and water to make a
    thick paste (about 1¼ cups
    water to 1 cup flour)
Oil for frying
Garlic and Potato Sauce
Lemon wedges

1. Pat fillets dry. Coat with seasoned flour. Dip in flour and water mixture.
2. Pour oil into a deep skillet and heat to smoking.
3. Put fillets in oil. Fry until golden brown, turning once.
4. Serve with Garlic and Potato Sauce and lemon wedges.

2 to 4 servings

748 *Garlic and Potato Sauce* *(Skorthalia)*

1 pound potatoes, pared and cut
    in small pieces
4 garlic cloves, crushed in a
    garlic press
1 cup olive oil
¼ cup vinegar
Salt and freshly ground pepper

1. Boil potatoes until they can be pierced easily with a fork. Drain in a colander or on paper towels.
2. Mash potatoes in a potato ricer. Add garlic and then olive oil, a tablespoon at a time, beating well after each spoonful. Beat in vinegar. Season with salt and pepper to taste. If sauce is too thick, beat in a little warm water or more olive oil.
3. Serve with **fried** or **broiled seafood,** on **crackers** or **toasted bread,** or as a dip for **fresh vegetables.**

1 quart sauce

749 *Baked Fish à la Spetses*

4 pounds fish fillets (turbot,
    whitefish, bass, mullet)
4 fresh tomatoes, peeled and
    sliced
¾ cup olive oil
1 cup white wine
2 tablespoons chopped parsley
1 large garlic clove, crushed in a
    garlic press
  Salt and pepper to taste
1 teaspoon basil (optional)
1 cup fresh bread crumbs
1 slice feta cheese for each
    portion

1. Put fillets into a baking dish.
2. In a bowl, combine tomatoes, olive oil, wine, parsley, garlic, salt, pepper, and basil. Pour over fillets. Sprinkle with bread crumbs.
3. Bake at 375°F 40 minutes.
4. Top fillets with feta cheese slices. Broil 1 or 2 minutes.

6 to 8 servings

750 *Charcoal-Grilled Fish* (Psari tys Skaras)

Fish for grilling
¼ cup olive oil
  Juice of 1 lemon
2 tablespoons oregano, crushed
  Salt and pepper to taste

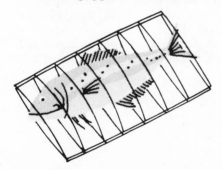

1. Fish suitable for grilling are trout, whitefish, bluefish, snapper, or mackerel. (In Greece, the fish are usually served with their heads and tails intact. You may prefer to remove the heads at least, because some people are revolted by a whole fish on their plate. However you decide to serve the fish, allow 1 pound for each person.)
2. Heat charcoal until white. Arrange grill so that it is about 4 inches from coals. Use a hinged basket grill for easier turning; oil it well to prevent fish from sticking.
3. Combine olive oil, lemon juice, oregano, salt, and pepper. Brush fish generously with mixture. Place in basket grill.
4. Cook on one side about 7 minutes. Turn over and cook an additional 7 minutes.
5. Serve fish with remaining sauce.

751 *Baked Fish with Tomatoes, Onions, and Parsley*
(Psari Plaki)

½ cup olive oil
2 large onions, coarsely chopped
1 can (20 ounces) tomatoes
    (undrained)
½ cup white wine
½ cup chopped parsley
1 garlic clove, crushed in a garlic
    press
  Salt and pepper to taste
3 pounds fish fillets (any firm
    fish such as turbot, bass,
    grouper, or red snapper may
    be used)

1. Heat olive oil in a saucepan. Add onion and cook until translucent. Add tomatoes, wine, parsley, garlic, salt, and pepper. Simmer covered 10 minutes.
2. Place fish in a large baking dish. Cover with sauce.
3. Bake at 350°F about 25 minutes, or until fish flakes easily when tested with a fork.

4 servings

752 *Fish Kebob*

2 pounds swordfish or halibut
with bones removed, cut in
large cubes
1 cup olive oil
Juice of 2 lemons
1 teaspoon oregano
1 teaspoon dill
1 bay leaf
Salt and pepper to taste
Small whole onions, peeled
Whole cherry tomatoes

1. Marinate fish in a mixture of the oil, lemon juice, oregano, dill, bay leaf, salt, and pepper for 2 hours, basting occasionally. Reserve marinade.
2. Alternate fish, onions, and tomatoes on skewers.
3. Broil, turning frequently, until done (about 5 minutes).
4. Heat marinade. Serve with Fish Kebob.

4 servings

753 *Poached Striped Bass*

1 quart water
1 quart dry white wine
Juice of 3 lemons
2 cups olive oil
2 medium onions, quartered
1 large carrot, pared and left
whole
2 celery stalks with leaves
2 leeks
Salt to taste
10 coriander seeds
8 whole peppercorns
1 bay leaf
4 parsley sprigs
1 thyme sprig
3 garlic cloves, peeled and left
whole
5 pounds bass, cleaned, with
gills removed and head and
tail left on

1. Pour water, wine, lemon juice, and olive oil into a saucepot.
2. Wrap remaining ingredients, except fish, in cheesecloth and add. Bring to boiling and simmer covered 15 minutes.
3. Wrap fish in cheesecloth. Place in a fish poacher or a deep greased baking dish.
4. Pour in stock, discarding vegetables; cover and simmer 15 minutes. Remove from heat.
5. Let fish remain in the liquid for another 15 minutes. Lift out of pan and drain; reserve fish stock for other use. Remove cheesecloth and peel off skin.
6. Serve fish at room temperature with Vinegar and Oil Dressing with Tomato, Mayonnaise, or Garlic and Potato Sauce

6 to 8 servings

754 *Poached Tuna Rolls with Garlic Mayonnaise*

1 can (9¼ ounces) solid-pack
tuna, drained and flaked
3 anchovies, minced
Salt and pepper to taste
2 eggs, lightly beaten
Bread crumbs
1 tomato, thinly sliced
1 onion, thinly sliced
1 cucumber, thinly sliced
● Garlic Mayonnaise

1. Combine tuna with anchovies. Add pepper and taste before adding salt. Mix in eggs and enough bread crumbs to make a paste firm enough to shape into four 1½-inch-thick rolls.
2. Wrap rolls tightly in cheesecloth. Tie at both ends.
3. Put into boiling salted water to cover. Reduce heat and simmer 20 minutes. Remove from water.
4. Slice rolls and garnish with tomato, onion, and cucumber. Serve with Garlic Mayonnaise.

4 servings

755 *Fish Casserole Haramogli* (Psari Haramogli)

3 pounds whitefish, sole, or any
   other lean fish (head and tail
   removed), cut in 4 portions
5 cups fish stock
● 3 cups Béchamel Sauce
2 tablespoons minced parsley
1 teaspoon basil
1 garlic clove, crushed in a garlic
   press
4 cups cooked rice
½ cup freshly grated kefalotyri
   cheese

1. Wrap fish loosely in cheesecloth. Knot the ends. Heat fish stock until boiling. Add fish and simmer until done (about 10 minutes).
2. Remove fish from liquid and discard cheesecloth.
3. Mix Béchamel Sauce with parsley, basil, and garlic.
4. Turn rice into a casserole. Put fish on top. Top with Béchamel Sauce and cheese. Cover tightly with aluminum foil.
5. Set in a 300°F oven 12 to 15 minutes, or until thoroughly heated.

8 servings

756 *Marinated Fish* (Psari Marinata)

2 pounds halibut, sole, or
   grouper fillets or fish with
   heads and tails intact
Salt
Juice of 2 lemons
2 cups flour, seasoned with salt
   and pepper
Olive oil for frying
½ cup olive oil
¼ cup flour
½ cup white wine
½ cup white wine vinegar
● 1 can (8 ounces) tomato sauce or
   1 cup Tomato Sauce
1 teaspoon sugar
1 teaspoon fennel
2 garlic cloves, minced (optional)

1. Season fish with salt and lemon juice. Dip in flour. Heat olive oil in a large skillet; add fish and fry on both sides until medium brown, being careful not to burn the oil.
2. Arrange fish in a baking dish. Discard cooking oil.
3. Combine ½ cup oil and flour in a skillet and, stirring constantly with a wooden spoon, cook until flour browns.
4. Add remaining ingredients and simmer, covered, 15 minutes. Strain over fish. Allow to marinate out of the refrigerator several hours before serving. Adjust salt and pepper. Serve at room temperature or chilled.

6 servings

757 *Vinegar and Oil Dressing with Tomato* (Ladoxido me Domata)

1 tablespoon imported mustard
   (Dijon, preferably)
2 tablespoons red wine vinegar,
   or more to taste
½ cup olive oil
1 large tomato, peeled and diced
2 whole scallions, minced
2 tablespoons minced parsley
1 tablespoon chopped capers
1 teaspoon dill

Put mustard and vinegar into a small bowl. Add olive oil while stirring with a whisk. Add remaining ingredients; mix well. Refrigerate several hours before serving.

1 ¾ cups

758 *Trout in Grapevine Leaves*

1 jar (32 ounces) grapevine
    leaves, drained
4 medium trout, cleaned, with
    heads and tails left on
2 tablespoons olive oil
2 tablespoons butter, melted
2 teaspoons oregano
1 teaspoon dill
    Additional oil to brush outside
      of trout
    Salt and pepper to taste
2 lemons, cut in wedges

1. Rinse grapevine leaves thoroughly under cold running water to remove brine.
2. Rinse trout; pat dry.
3. Drizzle 2 tablespoons olive oil and butter in trout cavities. Sprinkle with oregano and dill. Brush oil on outside of fish. Season inside and out with salt and pepper.
4. Wrap each trout in 5 or 6 grapevine leaves. Refrigerate 1 to 2 hours.
5. To charcoal-broil, adjust grill 4 inches from heated coals. Grease a rectangular, long-handled grill on all sides. Place fish in the grill, side by side. Grill one side about 8 minutes, turn, grill until fish flakes easily with a fork (about 8 minutes more).
6. Discard browned outer leaves. Serve trout in remaining leaves. Garnish with lemon wedges.

4 servings

Note: Trout may also be broiled under the broiler. For easy turning, use a long-handled grill.

759 *Sea Chowder*

¼ cup olive oil
3 garlic cloves
1 medium onion, quartered
2 bay leaves
    Water to cover fish
1 cup dry white wine
    Juice of 1 lemon
6 squid, cleaned and cut in
      pieces
    Salt and pepper to taste
2 tomatoes, peeled, seeded, and
      diced
3 pounds fish (several kinds),
      skinned and boned
1 pound shrimp, shelled and
      deveined

1. Heat oil in a deep saucepan. Add garlic, onion, and bay leaves. Cook until onion is translucent.
2. Pour in water, wine, and lemon juice. Add squid. Season with salt and pepper. Cover and simmer 40 minutes.
3. Add tomatoes and fish; simmer 8 minutes. Add shrimp; simmer just until shrimp are cooked. Adjust seasonings. Serve at once.

6 servings

760 *Pickled Octopus* (Oktapodi Tursi)

1 small octopus (about 2 pounds)
½ cup olive oil
¼ cup white wine vinegar
    Juice of ½ lemon
1 tablespoon minced parsley
½ teaspoon marjoram
    Salt and pepper to taste

1. Beat octopus with the flat side of a metal meat hammer 15 to 20 minutes; it will feel soft and excrete a grayish liquid.
2. Wash octopus thoroughly, drain, and cook in skillet without water until it becomes bright pink. Cut into bite-size pieces.
3. Make a salad dressing of the olive oil, vinegar, lemon juice, parsley, marjoram, salt, and pepper. Mix well.
4. Pour over octopus and store in the refrigerator in a covered container for 5 days before serving.
5. Serve cold as an appetizer.

4 to 6 servings

761 *Steamed Mussels in Wine Sauce (Mithia Krassata)*

2 pounds mussels
1 large onion, minced
1 large celery stalk, minced
4 peppercorns
3 cups dry white wine
¼ cup butter (at room
   temperature)
1 tablespoon flour
1 teaspoon vinegar
1 tablespoon chopped parsley
1 garlic clove
   Salt and pepper to taste

1. Scrub mussels well with a vegetable brush and rinse. Put into a kettle with onion, celery, peppercorns, and white wine. Cover and steam until they open, discarding any that are unopened.
2. Put mussels onto a deep platter. Cover and keep warm.
3. Strain liquid and simmer. Mix butter and flour together in a small bowl; stir into hot liquid. Add vinegar, parsley, garlic, salt, and pepper; continue to simmer until liquid is reduced by half.
4. To serve, pour sauce over mussels.

6 servings

762 *Shrimp Giahni with Feta Cheese*

1 medium onion, minced
½ cup olive oil
1 can (28 ounces) tomatoes
   (undrained)
4 ounces white wine
1 small bunch parsley, finely
   chopped
1 celery stalk, finely chopped
   Salt and pepper
1 pound large shrimp, cleaned
   and deveined
¼ pound feta cheese, crumbled

1. Brown onion in oil. Add tomatoes, stirring until mixture reaches boiling. Lower heat and simmer, covered, 5 minutes. Add wine, parsley, celery, and salt and pepper to taste. Simmer 30 minutes.
2. While tomato sauce is simmering, parboil shrimp 2 minutes in **3 quarts boiling water** with **2 teaspoons salt.** Drain immediately.
3. Add shrimp to sauce. Simmer 1 minute. Garnish with feta.

6 servings

763 *Spiced Shrimp with Onions*

4 quarts water
1 tablespoon salt
3 pounds raw shrimp, shelled
   and deveined
¾ cup white wine vinegar
1 cup olive oil
2 cups white wine
1 tablespoon salt
1 teaspoon pepper
2 jars whole baby onions,
   drained
3 garlic cloves
1 bay leaf
1 celery stalk, cut in half
   Juice of 1 lemon

1. Bring water and 1 tablespoon salt to a rolling boil in a saucepot. Add shrimp. Boil 1 minute. Drain.
2. Combine remaining ingredients in a saucepot and bring to boiling. Simmer uncovered 5 minutes. Cool.
3. Pour onion mixture over shrimp. Refrigerate 6 to 8 hours.
4. Drain shrimp and onions and serve chilled.

6 to 8 servings

764 *Stuffed Squid* (Kalamarakia Yemista)

32 squid, cleaned and tentacles
 removed
¾ cup olive oil
1 large onion, chopped
1½ cups water
1 cup long-grain rice
½ cup chopped parsley
1 teaspoon mint
1 teaspoon basil
2 cloves garlic, crushed in a
 garlic press
½ cup pine nuts
¼ cup dried black currants
1 cup dry white wine
 Salt and pepper to taste
 Water
 Juice of 2 lemons

1. Reserve squid. Rinse tentacles in cold water. Drain and mince finely.
2. In a large saucepan, heat 2 tablespoons of the oil, add onion and minced tentacles and cook over low heat until tentacles turn pink. Add water. Heat to boiling. Reduce heat, add rice, parsley, mint, basil, garlic, pine nuts, currants, and ½ cup of the wine.
3. Simmer until liquid is absorbed. Season with salt and pepper. Cool.
4. Using a teaspoon, stuff each squid cavity loosely with the rice mixture. Arrange squid in rows in a large baking dish. Combine the remaining wine and olive oil with enough water to reach half the depth of the squid. Season with additional salt and pepper. Cover.
5. Bake at 325°F about 40 minutes, or until squid is tender. Drizzle with lemon juice just before serving.

8 servings

Note: Stuffing may also be used as a side dish. Stuff 16 squid. Put remaining stuffing in a baking dish. Add a little water, salt, and pepper and cover. Bake at 325°F 30 minutes.

765 *Fish au Gratin* (Ryba Zapiekana)

1 cup chicken or vegetable broth
 or stock
1 tablespoon flour
1 tablespoon butter or margarine
 (at room temperature)
½ teaspoon salt
¼ teaspoon parsley flakes
¼ teaspoon pepper
 Pinch ground thyme
¼ cup whipping cream
1½ pounds sole, trout, pike, or
 other white fish
3 tablespoons grated Parmesan,
 Swiss, or Gruyère cheese
2 tablespoons dry bread crumbs
1 tablespoon melted butter or
 margarine
1 teaspoon lemon juice (optional)

1. Bring broth to boiling in a small saucepan. Blend flour into butter and stir into boiling broth. Cook and stir until thickened. Reduce heat. Stir in salt, parsley flakes, pepper, thyme, and cream.
2. Place fish in a well-buttered pan. Pour sauce over fish.
3. Bake at 375°F 15 minutes.
4. Mix cheese, bread crumbs, melted butter, and lemon juice (if desired). Sprinkle over fish in pan. Bake about 15 minutes longer, or until fish flakes easily.

4 to 6 servings

Fish au Gratin with Tomatoes: Prepare Fish au Gratin as directed, except sprinkle ½ cup chopped tomato over top of fish before covering with sauce.

Fish au Gratin with Mushrooms: Prepare Fish au Gratin as directed, adding ½ cup sliced mushrooms to partially baked fish before topping with crumb mixture.

Fish au Gratin with Horseradish: Prepare Fish au Gratin as directed, adding 4 teaspoons prepared horseradish to sauce along with cream.

766 *Sole with Vegetables* (Sola z Jarzynami)

2 tablespoons butter or margarine
1 large onion, diced
1 cup savoy cabbage, shredded
 (optional)
1 leek, thinly sliced
1 large carrot, thinly sliced
1 stalk celery, thinly sliced

1. Melt butter in a Dutch oven or large skillet. Add vegetables and stir-fry 5 minutes.
2. Sprinkle fish fillets with salt. Place on the vegetables. Add water. Cover; simmer 15 minutes.
3. For sauce, melt butter in a saucepan. Stir in flour. Cook and stir until golden. Then gradually stir in broth. Cook, stirring constantly, until sauce boils.

1 parsley root, thinly sliced
2 pounds sole or any white fish
    fillets
½ teaspoon salt
2 tablespoons water
Sauce:
    2 tablespoons butter or margarine
    2 tablespoons flour
    1 cup chicken broth or fish stock
    ½ teaspoon salt
    ¼ teaspoon pepper
    ¼ cup dairy sour cream

4. Transfer the fish to a warm platter. Stir the sauce into the vegetables. Remove from heat. Season with salt and pepper; stir in sour cream. Pour over the fish.

About 6 servings

767 Deep-Fried Squid *(Kalamarakia Tyganita)*

12 squid, cleaned, with their
    tentacles left on
Flour seasoned generously with
    salt and pepper
Vegetable oil for deep frying
3 lemons, cut in wedges

1. Rinse the cleaned squid in cold water and pat dry with paper towels. Dip the squid into the seasoned flour and coat all surfaces evenly.
2. Heat the oil in a deep fryer to 375°F. Drop in the squid, a few at a time. Fry until golden brown (about 5 minutes). Transfer the squid with a slotted spoon to a baking dish lined with paper towels. Keep in a 200°F oven until all the squid are fried.
3. Remove paper; serve squid with lemon.

3 servings

768 Baked Leftover Fish *(Potrawa Zapiekana)*

3 boiled potatoes, sliced
1½ cups diced cooked fish
¾ cup sliced cooked cauliflower or
    mushrooms (optional)
2 hard-cooked eggs, sliced
    Salt and pepper
1 tablespoon flour
1 cup dairy sour cream
¼ cup water
3 tablespoons bread crumbs
2 tablespoons grated Parmesan
    cheese
2 tablespoons butter

1. Arrange layers of half the potatoes, fish, cauliflower, eggs, and remaining potatoes in a greased 1½-quart casserole. Lightly sprinkle salt and pepper over each layer.
2. Blend flour into sour cream; stir in water. Spoon over casserole mixture.
3. Mix bread crumbs, cheese, and butter together. Sprinkle over top of casserole.
4. Bake at 350°F 30 minutes.

About 4 servings

769 Roulade of Eel *(Rolada z Węgorza)*

1 eel (2 pounds)
3 hard-cooked eggs, chopped
2 dill pickles, chopped
4 mushrooms, sliced
1 egg
1 teaspoon salt
¼ teaspoon pepper
1 quart vegetable stock or
    consommé
⅓ cup vinegar

1. Skin eel. Split in half; remove bones. Lay half the eel on a double thickness of cheesecloth.
2. Mix hard-cooked eggs, pickles, mushrooms, raw egg, salt, and pepper. Spread over the eel on cloth. Top with other half of eel. Wrap eel in the cloth. Place in a large kettle.
3. Add stock and vinegar to kettle. Boil gently 30 minutes. Let cool 1½ hours.
4. To serve, remove eel from cloth. Set on platter. Garnish, if desired. Serve with a sauce such as Mustard Sauce (●) or Horseradish Sauce (●).

About 6 servings

770 *Northern Pike Polish Style*
(Szczupak po Polsku)

1 dressed northern pike, perch, or
    other white fish (2 pounds)
1 carrot
1 onion
1 stalk celery
10 peppercorns
1½ teaspoons salt
    Water

Topping:
¼ cup butter
6 hard-cooked eggs, finely
    chopped
¼ cup lemon juice
1 tablespoon chopped fresh dill or
    parsley
¾ teaspoon salt
¼ teaspoon pepper

1. Put fish into a large kettle. Add carrot, onion, celery, peppercorns, and salt. Add enough water to cover. Cover; boil gently about 15 to 20 minutes, or until fish flakes easily.
2. Meanwhile, heat butter in a skillet. Add chopped eggs, lemon juice, dill, salt, and pepper. Cook 5 minutes, stirring frequently.
3. When fish is cooked, set it on a warm platter. Spoon topping over fish. Serve with boiled potatoes, if desired.

4 to 6 servings

771 *Pike or Carp Stuffed with Anchovies*
(Szczupak lub Karp Nadziewany Sardelami)

1 can (2 ounces) flat anchovy fillets
1 pike (3 pounds) with milt and
    liver, or other white fish
¼ cup butter or margarine (at room
    temperature)
2 eggs, separated
½ cup grated fresh bread
¼ cup melted butter for basting
1 cup dairy sour cream

1. Cut half the anchovies in thin strips. Lard the fish with strips of anchovy.
2. Chop or mash remaining anchovies; cream with 2 tablespoons of butter. Divide in half.
3. For stuffing, beat egg yolks. Chop liver. Combine grated bread, egg yolks, milt, and liver. Add half of anchovy butter; mix well. Beat egg whites until stiff peaks are formed; fold into bread mixture.
4. Fill cavity of fish with stuffing. Close cavity with skewers or wooden picks. Place fish in roasting pan. Drizzle with half the melted butter.
5. Bake at 350°F 30 minutes. Baste with remaining melted butter. Bake 10 minutes longer. Spread remaining anchovy butter over fish. Top with sour cream. Continue baking until fish is tender and flakes easily.

6 to 8 servings

772 *Stuffed Baked Fish (Nadziewana Pieczona Ryba)*

1 dressed pike, trout, or carp (4 to
    5 pounds)
    Salt and pepper
⅓ cup butter or margarine
2 onions, chopped
3 stalks celery, chopped
3 apples, cored and chopped

1. Sprinkle cavity of fish with salt and pepper.
2. For stuffing, melt ⅓ cup butter in skillet. Add onion and celery. Stir-fry until onion is transparent. Add apples, parsley, and mushrooms. Stir-fry 2 minutes longer.
3. Mix cooked vegetables with bread cubes, sugar, thyme, lemon juice, eggs, and water. Blend well.
4. Fill fish cavity with the stuffing. Close cavity with skewers

1 tablespoon chopped parsley
1 cup sliced mushrooms
4 cups dry bread cubes
2 teaspoons sugar
½ teaspoon thyme
2 teaspoons lemon juice
3 eggs
1 cup water or wine

or wooden picks. Place fish in a roasting pan and drizzle with **melted butter.**

5. Bake at 350°F about 40 minutes, or until fish flakes easily. Baste occasionally with additional melted butter.

About 8 servings

773 *Fish in Greek Sauce (Ryba po Grecku)*

1 pound carp, white fish, or
   flounder fillets
3 tablespoons olive oil
Salt
Fresh parsley sprigs
Greek Sauce:
   2 tablespoons olive oil
   ½ cup sliced celery
   ½ cup coarsely shredded carrots
   ½ cup coarsely shredded parsley root
   ¾ cup diced onion
   ½ cup water
   ½ teaspoon salt
   1 can (6 ounces) tomato paste
   ¼ teaspoon pepper
   ½ teaspoon sugar
   1 tablespoon lemon juice
   ½ teaspoon paprika

1. Cut fish fillets into 2-inch pieces.
2. Fry fish in hot oil in a skillet, then sprinkle with salt. Drain on paper towels. Arrange on a serving platter and keep warm. Garnish with parsley.
3. For sauce, heat oil in a skillet. Stir-fry celery, carrots, and parsley root for 3 minutes. Add onion, water, and salt. Cover; cook over low heat 15 minutes.
4. Add remaining sauce ingredients; stir to mix.
5. Chill sauce or serve hot over fish.

About 4 servings

774 *Fish in Horseradish Sauce*
(Ryba w Sosie Chrzanowym)

2 carrots
2 stalks celery (optional)
1 parsley root
1 onion, quartered
1 bay leaf
5 peppercorns
2 teaspoons salt
1½ quarts water
2 pounds carp, sole, or pike fillets
Horseradish Sauce:
   3 tablespoons butter or margarine
   3 tablespoons flour
   ¾ cup prepared cream-style
      horseradish
   ½ teaspoon sugar
   ¼ teaspoon salt
   ⅔ cup dairy sour cream
   2 hard-cooked eggs, peeled and
      sieved
Garnish:
   Shredded lettuce

1. Combine vegetables, dry seasonings, and water in a saucepot. Bring to boiling; simmer 20 minutes. Strain.
2. Cook fish in the strained vegetable stock 6 to 10 minutes, or until fish flakes easily.
3. Remove fish from stock. Arrange on serving platter and cover with plastic wrap. Chill.
4. Strain fish stock and reserve ¾ cup for horseradish sauce; cool.
5. For horseradish sauce, melt butter in a saucepan; blend in flour until smooth.
6. Add the cooked fish stock gradually, stirring constantly. Cook and stir until the sauce boils and becomes thick and smooth.
7. Remove from heat. Stir in horseradish, sugar, salt, sour cream, and eggs. Cool 15 minutes.
8. Pour the horseradish sauce over chilled fish. Garnish with shredded lettuce.

About 6 servings

775 *Citrus Steamed Salmon and Shrimp*

1½ pounds salmon fillets, cut in
    2x1-inch pieces
¾ pound uncooked shelled
    shrimp
½ cup lemon juice
¼ cup lime juice
¾ teaspoon salt
1 teaspoon paprika
1 teaspoon coriander seed,
    crushed
1 teaspoon cardamom seed,
    crushed (discard shells)
Parsley sprigs

1. Place salmon and shrimp in a shallow glass dish. Mix remaining ingredients except parsley and pour over fish. Refrigerate covered 30 minutes; stir twice.
2. Transfer fish and marinade to a large skillet. Simmer covered 4 minutes; stir and simmer uncovered 2 minutes. Add shrimp to skillet; simmer covered just until shrimp are done (about 3 minutes). Arrange fish and shrimp on a serving platter. Spoon pan juices over. Garnish with parsley.

6 to 8 servings

776 *Sole with Shrimp Pâté in Champagne*

Fillets are rolled with asparagus and a filling of shrimp, creamy cheese, and anchovy. Poached in champagne and served with our version of hollandaise sauce, this entrée is just right for special occasions.

*1 pound fresh asparagus, spears
    only (2-inch pieces)
● Fish Stock
8 sole fillets (about 3 pounds)
2 cups cooked, shelled shrimp
2 ounces Neufchatel cheese
2 teaspoons anchovy paste
1 cup champagne or Fish Stock
●1 cup Mock Hollandaise Sauce
    Lemon wedges

1. Simmer asparagus spears in 1 inch of stock 4 minutes; drain. Set aside.
2. Lay fillets on a flat surface. Purée shrimp with cheese and anchovy paste in a food processor or blender. Spoon shrimp mixture in center of fillets.
3. Arrange asparagus on shrimp mixture in center of fillets so spears are visible on sides; roll fillets and place seam side down in a large skillet. Pour champagne into skillet; simmer covered until fish is tender and flakes with a fork (about 5 minutes). Remove fish carefully with a slotted spoon to serving platter. Spoon hollandaise sauce over fillets; garnish with lemon wedges.

8 servings

*Frozen asparagus spears can be substituted for the fresh. Thaw and drain; do not cook.

777 *Mock Crab Meat Salad*

You will hardly be able to tell that the crab meat is mock, but use fresh fish and cook it carefully.

1¾ pounds halibut steaks
● 1 cup Fish Stock
½ cup dry white wine
1 teaspoon salt
¼ teaspoon freshly ground
    white pepper
2 tablespoons snipped fresh or 2
    teaspoons dried dill weed
● ¾ cup Mock Mayonnaise

1. Simmer halibut in stock and wine in a large skillet until fish is tender and flakes with a fork (about 10 minutes). Remove fish from skillet; let cool to room temperature. Discard skin and bones.
2. Flake two thirds of the fish; cut remaining fish into ½-inch pieces. Stir salt, pepper, and dill into mayonnaise. Mix flaked fish into ½ cup of the mayonnaise; mix fish pieces into remaining mayonnaise.
3. Arrange lettuce leaves on 4 individual salad plates; place melon rings on lettuce. Mound flaked fish mixture inside mel-

Lettuce leaves
4 rings cut from honeydew or
  cantaloupe
½ pound white grapes
1 lime, cut in 4 wedges

on rings; top with mixture of fish pieces. Garnish salads with clusters of grapes and lime wedges.

4 servings

Note: This recipe makes 8 first-course servings. Prepare recipe as directed except substitute melon pieces for the melon rings, increase grapes to ¾ pound, and use 2 limes for wedges.

778 *Steamed Red Snapper Oriental*

Soy sauce and sesame oil lend a distinctive Oriental flavor to this lively dish.

3 red snapper (about 1½ pounds
  each), drawn and scaled
5 garlic cloves, finely sliced
● Fish Stock
1 cup light soy sauce
½ cup dry white wine
3 tablespoons peanut or
  vegetable oil
1 tablespoon sesame oil
1 bunch green onions, tops only,
  cut in 2-inch matchstick-size
  pieces
*½ teaspoon freshly ground
  Szechuan or black pepper
3 zucchini slices
3 thin carrot slices
3 cloves
  Lemon or lime slices
  Watercress

1. Place fish on a piece of cheesecloth which is 18 inches longer than the fish. Using cheesecloth, lower fish onto rack in a fish steamer or large, deep roasting pan with 1½ inches of stock in bottom. Arrange garlic slices on fish. Simmer covered until fish is tender and flakes with a fork (about 40 minutes).
2. Using cheesecloth, lift fish from steamer to a heated platter. Remove cheesecloth from fish, carefully lifting fish with spatula and cutting cheesecloth with scissors if necessary.
3. Mix soy sauce, wine, and peanut and sesame oils in a small saucepan; heat to boiling. Drizzle 3 tablespoons soy mixture over fish; arrange green onion tops decoratively on fish. Sprinkle ground pepper over fish. Place zucchini and carrot slices over eyes of fish and secure with cloves. Arrange lemon slices and watercress around fish. Pass remaining soy mixture to spoon over individual servings.
4. If desired, let fish stand 45 minutes after poaching, then refrigerate until chilled (about 4 hours). Spoon hot soy mixture over fish and garnish as directed. Pass remaining soy mixture.

8 to 10 servings

Note: Whole white fish, lake trout, or other lean fish can be substituted for the red snapper.

*Lightly roast Szechuan pepper over medium heat in skillet before grinding.

779 *Baked Fish with Red Sauce*

The sauce, made with puréed red peppers, is piquant and distinctive.

*2 pounds haddock fillets, cut in
  serving-size pieces
1 teaspoon salt
¼ teaspoon freshly ground white
  pepper
1 lemon, thinly sliced
1 medium red onion, sliced
4 large sweet red peppers, cut in
  quarters
¼ cup dry vermouth
½ teaspoon salt
  Dry vermouth
  Watercress

1. Sprinkle haddock with 1 teaspoon salt and the pepper; place in a lightly oiled baking pan. Arrange lemon, onion, and peppers over fish. Pour ¼ cup vermouth over top.
2. Bake at 350°F about 20 minutes, or until fish is tender and flakes with a fork.
3. Place peppers and onion slices in a food processor or blender container; discard lemon. Arrange fish on serving platter; keep warm.
4. Purée peppers, onion, and salt, adding additional vermouth, if needed, to make a thick sauce. Heat mixture thoroughly; spoon over fish. Garnish with watercress.

6 servings

*Flounder, halibut, or whitefish fillets, or poultry can be used in this recipe.

780 *Chilled Decorated Whitefish*

1 whole whitefish (about 5 pounds), dressed
● Fish Stock
2 cups minced celery
2 cups minced carrot
2 hard-cooked eggs, minced
¾ teaspoon salt
⅛ teaspoon freshly ground white pepper
● 1⅓ cups Mock Mayonnaise
1 cup sliced carrot
1 cup ¼- to ⅛-inch strips red or green pepper
1 green olive slice
2 lemons, thinly sliced
Selection of sauces: Light
● Green Sauce, Seasoned Dark
● Green Sauce, Citrus
● Mayonnaise, Mock
● Hollandaise Sauce

1. Place fish on a piece of cheesecloth which is 18 inches longer than the fish. Using cheesecloth, lower fish onto rack in a fish steamer or a large, deep roasting pan with 1½ inches stock in bottom. Simmer covered until fish is tender and flakes with a fork (about 40 minutes). Using cheesecloth, lift fish from steamer. Let cool to room temperature. Carefully remove skin and transfer fish to a serving platter.
2. Stir celery, minced carrot, eggs, salt, and pepper into mayonnaise. Form the head and tail and fins of the fish, using the vegetable-mayonnaise mixture. Decorate the head and fins with the carrot slices. Decorate the tail and gills with strips of pepper. Place an olive slice in position for the eye. Garnish fish with lemon slices. Refrigerate until chilled (about 2 hours). Serve with 2 or 3 of the sauces.

8 to 10 servings

781 *Crab-Stuffed Trout with Tarragon*

The flavor of onions, mushrooms, crab meat, and tarragon permeates the trout while baking. Use fresh tarragon if it is available.

2 large onions, finely chopped
¼ cup dry white wine
1 cup sliced fresh mushrooms
8 ounces fresh or 1 can (7¾ ounces) chunk crab meat, drained and flaked
1 tablespoon snipped fresh or 1½ teaspoons dried tarragon leaves
¼ cup snipped parsley
½ teaspoon salt
¼ teaspoon freshly ground white pepper
6 dressed trout (1 to 1½ pounds each)
1 tablespoon snipped fresh or 1½ teaspoons dried tarragon leaves
Lemon twists

1. Simmer onion in wine until tender (about 5 minutes). Mix 1½ cups cooked onion with the mushrooms, crab meat, 1 tablespoon tarragon, the parsley, salt, and pepper. Stuff trout with onion mixture.
2. Spread remaining onion in a shallow baking pan; arrange trout over onion.
3. Bake at 400°F about 20 minutes, or until fish is tender and flakes with a fork. Remove fish to serving platter. Sprinkle with 1 tablespoon tarragon and garnish with lemon twists.

6 servings

782 *Sole Véronique in Parchment*

Baked in parchment paper, the fish retains its natural moisture and flavor.

2 pounds sole fillets
¾ teaspoon salt
3 tablespoons snipped parsley
2 teaspoons minced lemon peel
1½ cups seedless white grapes
⅔ cup dry white wine
   Lemon wedges

1. Lay each fillet on a piece of parchment paper or aluminum foil, 12x12 inches. Sprinkle fillets with salt, parsley, and lemon peel. Divide grapes over fish; sprinkle with wine. Bring edges of parchment up, crimp edges and seal; place on a jelly-roll pan.
2. Bake at 350°F 20 minutes.
3. Place parchment packets on individual plates; let each person open packet. Serve with lemon wedges.

4 servings

783 *Fish Stew*

French fish stew (bouillabaisse) is traditionally made with a selection of fresh shellfish. Our version uses fish which is more available and less expensive. Add shellfish if you like.

*3 pounds fish fillets, skinned
5 medium tomatoes, peeled and chopped
3 carrots, chopped
1 large onion, thinly sliced
2 teaspoons salt
¼ teaspoon freshly ground pepper
2 garlic cloves, minced
1 teaspoon fennel seed, crushed
1 tablespoon minced orange peel
1 cup dry white wine
● 1 quart Fish Stock

1. Cut fish into 1½-inch pieces. Set aside.
2. Simmer tomatoes, carrots, onion, salt, pepper, garlic, fennel, and orange peel in a mixture of wine and stock 15 minutes. Add fish to stock mixture; simmer covered until fish is tender and flakes with a fork (about 20 minutes).
3. Serve immediately in large shallow soup bowls.

8 servings (2 cups each)

*Flounder, haddock, cod, whitefish, halibut, bass, or other fish can be used in this recipe. For maximum flavor and variety, select at least 3 kinds of fish.

784 *Crab Meat Soup with Sherry*

1 cup 1-inch celery pieces
● 1⅓ cups Fish Stock
2 cans (7¾ ounces each) crab meat, drained (reserve 1 cup flaked crab meat)
½ cup instant nonfat dry-milk solids
½ cup water
½ cup whole milk
¼ teaspoon salt
⅛ teaspoon ground mace
4 teaspoons arrowroot
   Cold water
2 tablespoons dry sherry
3 tablespoons finely sliced celery for garnish

1. Simmer celery in stock in a covered saucepan 15 minutes. Place celery and stock in a food processor or blender; add 1 cup of flaked crab meat, the milk solids, water, milk, salt, and mace. Purée mixture; pour back into saucepan.
2. Heat crab mixture to simmering. Mix arrowroot with a little cold water; stir into crab mixture. Simmer, stirring constantly, until mixture has thickened. Stir in sherry and remaining crab meat. Heat thoroughly. Garnish with celery slices. Serve immediately.

4 servings (1½ cups each)

785 *Oysters Rockefeller*

No cream, eggs, or bread crumbs in this version of a popular classic.

  1 pint oysters
*2 pounds fresh spinach, washed and stems removed
  1 cup instant nonfat dry-milk solids
  2 tablespoons chopped onion
  2 garlic cloves, minced
  1 teaspoon salt
  ¼ teaspoon freshly ground pepper
  ⅛ teaspoon freshly ground nutmeg
  2 egg whites
  ⅓ cup grated Jarlsberg or Parmesan cheese

1. Drain oysters; reserve liquor. Cook spinach in a covered saucepan with water clinging to leaves until tender (about 7 minutes); drain. Purée spinach with reserved liquor, the milk solids, onion, garlic, salt, pepper, nutmeg, and egg whites in a food processor or blender. Pour mixture into a saucepan; heat thoroughly.
2. Layer half the spinach mixture into large shell dishes or ramekins. Top with oysters; spoon remaining spinach mixture over oysters. Sprinkle with cheese. Set on a cookie sheet.
3. Bake at 400°F about 10 minutes, or until bubbly. Broil 1 to 2 minutes to brown tops. Serve immediately.

4 servings

Note: This recipe will make 8 first-course servings. Prepare recipe as directed; serve in shell-shaped ramekins or custard cups.

*If desired, substitute 2 packages (10 ounces each) frozen chopped spinach for fresh; cook following package directions.

786 *Bay Scallops with Cucumber Rings*

Serve this entrée in a clear bowl so that the layering is visible.

  2 pounds bay scallops or sea scallops, cut in thirds
  1 tablespoon minced onion
  ½ cup minced celery
  1 cup minced carrot
● 1½ cups Chicken Stock
  ½ teaspoon salt
  2 large cucumbers, pared, sliced lengthwise, seeded, and cut in 1-inch slices
  ¼ cup dry white wine
  1 tablespoon arrowroot
  Cold water
  Salt

1. Simmer scallops, onion, celery, and carrot in the stock until scallops are tender (about 4 minutes). Strain stock into a medium saucepan. Sprinkle ½ teaspoon salt over scallop mixture; keep warm.
2. Simmer cucumbers in stock until just tender (about 4 minutes). Remove cucumbers with slotted spoon; keep warm.
3. Heat remaining stock and wine to boiling. Mix arrowroot with a little cold water; stir into stock. Simmer, stirring constantly, until thickened (about 3 minutes). Season to taste with salt. Spoon half the cucumbers into a clear glass serving bowl. Arrange scallops on top. Spoon remaining cucumbers over scallops; pour sauce over. Serve immediately.

6 servings

787 *Gingered Scallops*

- 3 cups Fish Stock
- 1 tablespoon minced fresh ginger root
- 2 tablespoons dry sherry
- ½ teaspoon ground ginger
- 1½ pounds bay scallops or sea scallops, cut in ½-inch pieces
- ¾ cup chopped celery
- 2 teaspoons arrowroot
  Cold water
  Salt
  Snipped parsley

1. Combine stock and ginger root in a medium skillet. Simmer until stock is reduced to 1 cup (about 15 minutes). Strain stock and discard ginger root. Return stock to skillet; stir in sherry and ground ginger.
2. Simmer scallops and celery in stock until tender (about 4 minutes). Remove scallops with a slotted spoon to small shell dishes. Mix arrowroot with a little cold water; stir into stock. Simmer, stirring constantly, until sauce is thickened (about 2 minutes). Taste and season with salt. Spoon sauce over scallops; sprinkle with parsley.

4 servings

Note: This recipe will make 6 first-course servings.

788 *Herbed Shrimp in Beer*

Simmer the shrimp in the marinade instead of broiling them, if you desire. Also excellent served as an appetizer with Mock Hollandaise Sauce (●) or Cucumber Sauce (●) for dipping.

- 2 pounds peeled raw shrimp
- 1½ cups beer
- 2 teaspoons lemon juice
- 2 garlic cloves, minced
- 2 tablespoons snipped chives
- 2 tablespoons snipped parsley
- 1½ teaspoons salt
- ½ teaspoon freshly ground pepper
  Shredded lettuce
- 2 green onions, finely chopped

1. Combine all ingredients except lettuce and green onions in a bowl. Refrigerate covered 8 hours or overnight; stir occasionally. Drain; reserve marinade.
2. Broil shrimp 4 inches from heat until cooked and tender (about 2 minutes on each side; less time for small shrimp). Do not overcook or shrimp will become tough. Brush occasionally with marinade. Marinade can be heated and served for dipping, if desired.
3. Serve shrimp on shredded lettuce; sprinkle with chopped green onion.

6 servings

789 *Citrus Seafood Salad*

Seafood and citrus flavors team for a refreshing salad entrée.

- 3 cups shredded iceberg lettuce
- ● ½ cup Citrus Mayonnaise
- 1 teaspoon celery seed
- 1½ pounds cooked crab meat, lobster, flounder, or whitefish, cut in ½-inch pieces
  Salt
  Freshly ground white pepper
- 1 navel orange, sliced

Arrange lettuce on a serving platter or individual plates. Mix Citrus Mayonnaise and celery seed; gently fold fish into mixture. Mound fish mixture on lettuce; sprinkle very lightly with salt and pepper. Arrange orange slices around fish mixture.

4 servings

790 *Baked Shrimp (Scampi al Forno)*

2 pounds large fresh uncooked
    shrimp
⅓ cup butter
1 teaspoon salt
4 cloves garlic, crushed in a garlic
    press
¼ cup chopped parsley
2 teaspoons grated lemon peel
2 tablespoons lemon juice

1. Remove shells from shrimp, leaving shell on tail section. Remove vein down the back, wash under cold running water, and drain on paper towels.
2. Place butter in a 13×9-inch baking dish; heat in oven at 400°F until melted. Stir in salt, garlic, and 1 tablespoon parsley. Place shrimp in a single layer in the baking dish.
3. Bake at 400°F 5 minutes. Turn the shrimp and sprinkle with lemon peel, lemon juice, and remaining parsley. Continue baking about 15 minutes, or until tender.
4. Serve shrimp with sauce over **hot fluffy rice.**

About 6 servings

791 *Shrimp San Giusto (Scampi Imperiali San Giusto)*

1 pound large uncooked shrimp
½ teaspoon salt
⅛ teaspoon pepper
1 bay leaf
3 tablespoons lemon juice
2½ cups water
1 bay leaf
1 thick slice onion
    Pinch each salt, pepper, thyme,
    and oregano
2 tablespoons olive oil
1 tablespoon butter
½ cup finely chopped onion
1 clove garlic, finely chopped
1 teaspoon finely chopped parsley
    Flour
⅓ cup dry white wine
1 large tomato, peeled, seeded,
    and chopped

1. Using scissors, cut the shells of the shrimp down middle of back; remove shells and set aside. Clean and devein shrimp.
2. Place cleaned shrimp in a bowl with salt, pepper, and a bay leaf; drizzle with lemon juice. Set shrimp aside to marinate 1 hour.
3. To make fish stock, place shrimp shells in a saucepan with water, a bay leaf, onion slice, salt, pepper, thyme, and oregano. Cover and simmer 30 minutes; strain.
4. Heat olive oil and butter in a skillet. Add chopped onion, garlic, and parsley; cook until soft. Coat marinated shrimp with flour, add to skillet with vegetables, and cook until lightly browned on both sides.
5. Add wine and simmer until it is almost evaporated. Stir in tomato and ½ cup or more of the strained fish stock. Simmer 15 to 20 minutes, or until the sauce is desired consistency.

3 or 4 servings

792 *Rice with Lobster Sardinian Style* *(Riso con Aragosta alla Sardegna)*

2 large frozen lobster tails
⅔ cup minced onion
1 large clove garlic, minced
¼ cup olive oil
2 cans (16 ounces each) tomato
    purée
1 tablespoon chopped fresh basil
    leaves, or 1 teaspoon dried
    basil
1 tablespoon mild honey
1 teaspoon salt
⅛ teaspoon pepper
4 cups hot cooked rice

1. Boil lobster tails according to package directions. Cool. Remove meat from shells and cut into chunks; set aside.
2. Sauté onion and garlic in olive oil 5 minutes. Stir in tomato purée, basil, honey, salt, and pepper.
3. Simmer sauce, covered, 45 minutes. If sauce becomes too thick while it is cooking, stir in **½ cup water.**
4. Combine lobster with rice, pour hot sauce over rice, and serve.

793 *Baked Fettuccine with Perch Florentine*
(Fettuccine con Persici alla Fiorentina)

White Sauce
12 small perch fillets
1 teaspoon salt
¼ teaspoon pepper
2 cups white wine
3 pounds spinach
1 pound fettuccine noodles, cooked according to package directions and drained
¼ cup grated Parmesan cheese

1. Prepare sauce, place a piece of waxed paper directly on surface, and keep warm.
2. Wash and dry the fillets; place in a saucepan. Sprinkle with salt and pepper and pour in the wine. Simmer 15 minutes, or less, being sure fish remains intact.
3. Wash spinach. Place in a saucepan only with water that clings to leaves from washing. Cover saucepan and cook rapidly about 5 minutes, or until tender. Drain well and chop.
4. Arrange half the spinach in a 3-quart baking dish. Place half the fettuccine over spinach, and top with 6 fillets. Repeat layering with remaining spinach, fettuccine, and fish. Pour the warm sauce over all and sprinkle cheese on top.
5. Bake at 400°F 20 minutes, or until top is browned. Serve 2 fillets per person on a mound of fettuccine and spinach.

6 servings

White Sauce: Melt **5 tablespoons butter** in a saucepan. Blend in **5 tablespoons flour, 1 teaspoon salt,** and **⅛ teaspoon pepper;** heat until bubbly. Gradually add **2½ cups milk,** stirring until smooth. Bring to boiling and cook, stirring constantly, 1 to 2 minutes. Stir in **pinch nutmeg.**

About 2½ cups sauce

794 *Fried Scampi (Scampi Fritti)*

3 pounds fresh prawns or shrimp with shells
Fat for deep frying heated to 360°F
½ cup olive oil
4 cloves garlic, minced
1 teaspoon salt
½ teaspoon oregano
¼ teaspoon pepper
1 teaspoon chopped parsley

1. Wash prawns in cold water. Remove tiny legs, peel off shells, and devein prawns. Rinse in cold water, then pat dry with absorbent paper.
2. Put only as many prawns in fat as will float uncrowded one layer deep. Fry 3 to 5 minutes, or until golden brown. Drain over fat before removing to absorbent paper. Turn fried prawns onto a warm platter.
3. Heat oil in a skillet. Add garlic, salt, oregano, and pepper and cook until garlic is lightly browned. Pour sauce over prawns and sprinkle with parsley.

About 6 servings

795 *Lobster Fra Diavolo (Aragosta alla Diavola)*

● Marinara Sauce
2 live lobsters (about 1½ pounds each)
½ cup red wine
Few grains cayenne pepper

1. Prepare Marinara Sauce.
2. While sauce is cooking, fill a large, deep kettle about two thirds full with water. Bring to boiling and plunge lobsters, one at a time, head first into boiling water. Cover and boil about 8 minutes (Lobsters will turn pink.) Remove lobsters with tongs. With a sharp knife, slit underside lengthwise and remove stomach, lungs, and vein. Keep warm.
3. When sauce is cooked, stir in wine and cayenne, bring to boiling, and pour over lobsters. Serve immediately.

2 servings

796 *Scampi Flamingo*

A recipe from the Danieli Royal Excelsior in Venice.

½ cup butter
1 cup chopped celery
¼ cup chopped carrot
¼ cup chopped onion
¼ teaspoon thyme
2 pounds fresh shrimp with shells
3 tablespoons cognac
2 cups light cream
⅓ cup sherry
½ cup butter
½ teaspoon lemon juice
⅛ teaspoon ground nutmeg
● ¼ cup Béchamel Sauce

1. Heat ½ cup butter in a large skillet. Sauté vegetables with thyme until lightly browned. Add the shrimp and brown carefully.
2. Add cognac and flame it. Add cream, sherry, and sauce; cook 15 minutes.
3. Remove shrimp; shell and devein them; keep warm.
4. Add ½ cup butter, lemon juice, and nutmeg to sauce; cook about 5 minutes. Strain through a fine sieve and pour over the shrimp.
5. Serve sauce and shrimp with hot cooked rice.

About 4 servings

797 *Ancona Fish Stew (Brodetto Anconetana)*

2 pounds assorted fish (mullet, sole, and halibut fillets)
1 large onion, thinly sliced
½ cup olive oil
2 teaspoons salt
½ teaspoon pepper
Pinch saffron
Water (about 2 cups)
Dry white wine (about 2 cups)

1. Cut fish fillets in 2½-inch pieces; set aside.
2. Sauté onion in olive oil until golden. Sprinkle in salt, pepper, and saffron. Add the fish and enough water and wine to cover the fish. Bring to boiling and cook over high heat 10 to 15 minutes.
3. Serve very hot in warmed soup bowls with crusts of fried bread, if desired.

6 servings

798 *Fillet of Sole in White Wine*
(Filetti di Sogliole al Vino)

2 pounds sole fillets
½ cup dry white wine
½ cup chopped onion
3 tablespoons butter, melted
2 bay leaves, crushed
1 teaspoon chopped parsley
½ teaspoon salt
¼ teaspoon pepper

1. Put fillets into a greased shallow 2-quart casserole.
2. Mix wine, onion, butter, and dry seasonings. Pour over fish. Cover casserole.
3. Bake at 375°F 25 minutes, or until fish flakes easily when tested with a fork.

6 servings

799 *Cod Sailor Style (Baccalà alla Marinara)*

2 pounds cod steaks, about 1 inch
    thick
2 cups canned tomatoes, sieved
¼ cup chopped green olives
2 tablespoons capers
1 tablespoon parsley
1 teaspoon salt
½ teaspoon pepper
½ teaspoon oregano

1. Put cod steaks into a greased 1½-quart casserole.
2. Combine tomatoes, olives, capers, parsley, salt, pepper, and oregano in a saucepan. Bring to boiling and pour over cod.
3. Bake at 350°F 25 to 30 minutes, or until fish flakes easily when tested with a fork.

4 servings

800 *Red Snapper Veracruz Style*

Red Snapper Veracruz Style is one of Mexico's famous fish entrées. The sauce of tomatoes, onion, olives, and capers is also frequently used with haddock, and is equally delicious with other similar fish.

¼ cup olive oil
1 cup chopped onion
1 clove garlic, minced
2 cups (16-ounce can) tomatoes
    with liquid
1 teaspoon salt
¼ teaspoon pepper
2 pounds red snapper fillets
¼ cup sliced pimento-stuffed olives
2 tablespoons capers
Lemon wedges

1. Heat oil in a large skillet. Cook onion and garlic in hot oil until onion is soft, about 5 minutes. Add tomatoes, salt, and pepper and cook about 5 minutes to blend flavors; slightly chop tomatoes as they cook.
2. Arrange red snapper fillets in a 3-quart baking dish. Pour sauce over fish. Sprinkle with olives and capers.
3. Bake at 350°F 25 to 30 minutes, or until fish can be flaked easily with a fork. Serve with lemon wedges.

About 6 servings

801 *Drunken Fish*

A number of traditional Mexican recipes call for "drunken" sauce—another example of the penchant for humorous food names. They may use dry white or red wine, tequila, or pulque (another alcoholic beverage made from the maguey cactus, like tequila). This recipe for Drunken Fish calls for dry red wine in a chili-tomato sauce.

1 whole red snapper or similar
    fish, or 5 pounds fish fillets
Flour, seasoned with salt and
    pepper
¼ cup oil
1 cup chopped onion
1 clove garlic, minced
6 fresh or dried ancho chilies
1½ cups canned tomatoes
2 tablespoons dried parsley
⅓ teaspoon oregano
½ teaspoon cumin (comino)
Salt and pepper
2 cups dry red wine
2 tablespoons capers

1. Dredge the fish with seasoned flour. Heat oil in a large skillet and brown fish on both sides. Remove fish from skillet and place in a shallow baking dish.
2. Add onion and garlic to oil remaining in skillet and cook until onion is soft, about 5 minutes.
3. Prepare chilies (see page 30); place in an electric blender and blend to a thick purée. Add to onion and garlic in skillet and cook about 5 minutes. Add tomatoes, parsley, oregano, and cumin. Bring to boiling, stirring constantly. Season to taste with salt and pepper. Stir in red wine and mix well.
4. Pour sauce over fish in baking dish.
5. Bake at 400°F about 30 minutes, or until fish flakes easily. Garnish with capers and serve.

6 to 8 servings

802 *Codfish for Christmas*

1 pound salted codfish (1 piece)
2 small onions, peeled
Salt and pepper
3 medium (1 pound) tomatoes, peeled, seeded, and cut in pieces
2 cloves garlic, peeled
3 tablespoons oil
5 pickled chilies, seeded and cut in strips
3 canned pimentos, cut in strips
½ cup pimento-stuffed olives
1 tablespoon chopped parsley

1. Soak codfish several hours in cold water; change water several times.
2. Drain codfish and put into a saucepan; add 1 onion and water to cover. Bring to simmering, cover, and cook gently about 15 minutes, or until fish flakes easily when tested with a fork. Drain. Season with salt and pepper.
3. Meanwhile, purée tomatoes, remaining onion (cut in quarters), and garlic in an electric blender.
4. Heat oil in a skillet and add the red sauce. Cook until thicker, stirring occasionally. Mix in chili and pimento strips.
5. To serve, put the codfish on a platter, pour the sauce over it, and garnish with whole olives and parsley. Accompany with **cooked rice.**

About 4 servings

803 *Pickled Tuna (Atún en Escabeche)*

This is an adaptation of a Mexican favorite, Escabeche. The word escabeche means pickled, and usually refers to one of the popular recipes for chilled pickled fish. Normally a mild-flavored white fish is called for, but in this recipe canned tuna is prepared "en escabeche." Serve as an appetizer, as Escabeche is usually served in Mexico, or as a luncheon salad.

2 cans (6½ to 7 ounces each) tuna, drained
Juice of 2 limes or 1 lemon
¼ cup oil
1 medium onion, thinly sliced (about ½ cup)
2 canned jalapeño chilies, seeded and cut in thin strips
1 clove garlic, minced
½ teaspoon oregano
½ teaspoon cumin (comino)
¾ cup wine or cider vinegar
Lettuce leaves
Sliced pimento-stuffed olives

1. Put tuna into a jar or bowl with lid; flake with fork. Pour lime juice over fish and let stand while preparing pickling mixture.
2. Heat oil in skillet. Add onion, chilies, and garlic; cook about 5 minutes, until onion is soft. Stir in oregano and cumin, then stir in vinegar. Bring to boiling.
3. Pour sauce over fish and stir until well coated.
4. Cover and refrigerate several hours. Serve on lettuce garnished with olive slices.

6 servings

804 *Fish Campeche Style*

1 pound fish fillets, fresh or frozen
½ cup orange juice
1 can (6 ounces) tomato paste
1 cup water
¼ cup chopped onion

1. Place fish fillets in a medium-sized skillet and add water to cover. Add ¼ cup of the orange juice. Bring to boiling, reduce heat, and simmer about 10 minutes, or until fish flakes when tested with a fork. Drain and skin, if necessary. Cut fish into finger-sized pieces. Return to skillet.

1 teaspoon chili powder
Salt and pepper

2. Meanwhile, in a small saucepan, combine remaining orange juice, tomato paste, 1 cup of water, onion, and chili powder. Bring to boiling; season with salt and pepper to taste. Pour over fish fingers. Simmer fish in this sauce until well coated and sauce starts to thicken.

4 to 6 servings

805 *Seviche I*

1 pound pompano (or other
    mild-flavored fish fillets)
  Juice of 6 limes (or lemons)
2 medium tomatoes, peeled and
    chopped
2 tablespoons finely chopped onion
1 or 2 canned jalapeño chilies,
    seeded and finely chopped
¼ cup olive oil
1 tablespoon vinegar
¼ teaspoon oregano
  Salt and pepper
  Sliced green olives
  Chopped parsley

1. Wash the fish very well. Cut into small chunks or strips and place in a glass jar or glass bowl with cover. Pour lime juice over fish; cover and refrigerate about 6 hours. (Lime juice will "cook" raw fish until it is white and firm.)
2. At least a half hour before serving, add tomato, onion, chili, olive oil, vinegar, oregano, and salt and pepper to taste; stir gently until evenly mixed.
3. When ready to serve, garnish with sliced olives and parsley.

6 servings

806 *Seviche II*

1 pound fresh firm-fleshed
    boneless white fish
¾ cup lemon juice
1 teaspoon salt
3 canned green chilies, seeded and
    chopped
2 ripe medium tomatoes, peeled,
    seeded, and chopped
2 small onions, thinly sliced
2 teaspoons coriander
⅓ cup olive oil
2 tablespoons vinegar

1. Remove skin from fish; cut into small pieces and put into a deep bowl. Add lemon juice and salt; toss. Cover and refrigerate 1 to 2 hours.
2. Toss gently. Add remaining ingredients; mix thoroughly. Chill.
3. Serve in shells or cocktail glasses and, if desired, garnish with avocado slices.

About 6 servings

807 *Poached Fish with Almonds*

Poached fish garnished with nuts is another seafood entrée. This sauce calls for dry white wine and Mexican green tomato sauce.

1 cup dry white wine
1 small can salsa verde mexicana (Mexican green tomato sauce)
½ cup chopped onion
1 clove garlic, minced
Salt and pepper
2 pounds fish fillets (halibut, flounder, sole, or other white fish)
½ cup toasted slivered almonds ·
Lemon wedges

1. Combine wine, salsa verde, onion, and garlic in a large skillet. Season with salt and pepper to taste. Bring to boiling, reduce heat, and simmer about 10 to 15 minutes.
2. Place fish fillets in simmering sauce and cook until fish flakes easily with a fork, about 5 to 10 minutes.
3. Transfer fish to a heated platter, spoon some of the sauce over fish, and sprinkle wtih almonds. Serve with lemon wedges.

About 6 servings

808 *Veracruz Style Crab-Filled Fish Rolls*

6 fish fillets (such as red snapper or sole), cut into long, thin slices
Juice of 1 lemon or lime
½ cup milk
2 tablespoons olive oil
½ cup chopped onion
1 clove garlic, minced
1 small tomato, peeled and chopped
1 teaspoon minced parsley
1 teaspoon salt
Dash of pepper
¼ pound crab meat, shredded
¼ pound shredded Monterey Jack
1 cup dairy sour cream
1 egg yolk
¼ pound butter or margarine

1. Rinse fish; rub with lemon or lime juice; soak in milk.
2. Meanwhile, heat olive oil in a small skillet. Sauté onion and garlic in oil; add tomato and cook until no longer juicy. Remove from heat and stir in parsley, salt, and pepper. Add crab meat and ⅓ of the cheese and mix well.
3. Remove fish from milk and pat dry with paper towels. Place a small amount of crab meat filling on one end of fillet and roll up, as for a jelly roll. Place fish rolls in one layer in a greased baking dish.
4. Beat sour cream with egg yolk and pour over fish. Dot with butter. Sprinkle remaining cheese over top.
5. Bake at 350°F until golden brown and cheese is melted (about 20 minutes).

6 servings

809 *Shrimp with Red Rice*

¼ cup oil
½ cup chopped onion
1 clove garlic, minced
1 medium green pepper, seeded and sliced in ½-inch strips
1 pound shelled green shrimp
1 can (6 ounces) tomato paste
2½ cups water
1 teaspoon salt
¼ teaspoon pepper
¼ teaspoon marjoram
1 cup uncooked rice

1. Heat oil in a large, heavy saucepan. Add onion and garlic and cook until soft (about 5 minutes). Add green pepper and uncooked shrimp and cook until shrimp turn pink.
2. Stir tomato paste, water, and seasonings into shrimp mixture and bring to boiling. Add rice; mix well. Cover and simmer over very low heat until all liquid is absorbed by rice (about 25 to 30 minutes).

4 to 6 servings

810 *Shrimp with Sesame Seed Sauce*

½ cup plain pumpkin seed
3 tablespoons sesame seed
1 small clove garlic
2 tablespoons vegetable oil
¾ teaspoon chili powder
¼ teaspoon cinnamon
⅛ teaspoon cloves
¾ cup canned chicken broth
½ teaspoon salt
1½ tablespoons lime juice
1½ pounds hot cooked shelled
    shrimp

1. Combine pumpkin seed, sesame seed, garlic, and oil in a saucepan. Stir and cook over medium heat until sesame seed is light golden brown.
2. Remove from heat and stir in chili powder, cinnamon, and cloves. Turn into an electric blender and grind. Add broth and salt; blend.
3. Turn mixture into a saucepan, mix in lime juice, and heat over low heat, stirring in one direction, until thickened.
4. Arrange hot shrimp on a platter and spoon sauce over it. If desired, garnish with sliced green onion and lime wedges.

4 servings

811 *Paella I*

1 cup sliced carrots
1 small onion, sliced
2 bay leaves
1 tablespoon dried parsley
¼ teaspoon pepper
3 cups water
½ cup oil
2 broiler-fryer chickens, cut in
    serving pieces
2 cloves garlic, minced
1 green pepper, cut in thin strips
1 teaspoon crumbled saffron
1 can (12 ounces) clams or 8 to 12
    fresh clams
1½ cups uncooked rice
1 tablespoon salt
2 large tomatoes, peeled and
    chopped
1 can (8 ounces) artichoke hearts
1 pound cooked shrimp, shelled
    and deveined

1. Place carrots, onion, bay leaves, dried parsley, pepper, and water in saucepan; simmer over low heat about 20 minutes, or until carrots are tender.
2. Meanwhile, heat oil in a large Dutch oven or heavy kettle. Brown chicken pieces in oil, a few at a time, removing as they are well browned.
3. In same oil, sauté garlic, pepper strips, and saffron. Return chicken pieces to Dutch oven. Drain liquid from clams and add enough of this liquid to vegetable liquid to make 3 cups. Pour over chicken in Dutch oven. Bring to simmering and gradually stir in rice and salt.
4. Bake at 350°F 1 hour.
5. During last part of baking, prepare clams by cutting in half; chop tomatoes; cut artichoke hearts into quarters vertically. Add clams, tomatoes, shrimp, and artichoke hearts to chicken-rice mixture, and mix in carefully. Return to oven for 10 to 15 minutes more, or until heated through. Serve hot.

8 to 10 servings

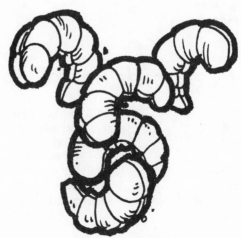

812 *Paella II*

1 cup olive oil or vegetable oil
1 broiler-fryer chicken (2 pounds), cut in pieces
½ cup diced boiled ham or smoky sausage
1 tablespoon minced onion
2 cloves garlic, minced
2 ripe tomatoes, peeled and coarsely chopped
1½ teaspoons salt
1½ pounds fresh shrimp, shelled and deveined
12 small clams in shells, scrubbed
2 cups uncooked rice
1 quart hot water
1 cup fresh or frozen green peas
¼ cup coarsely chopped parsley
Few shreds saffron
1 rock lobster tail, cooked and meat cut in pieces
1 can or jar (7 ounces) whole pimentos

1. Heat oil in paellera or large skillet; cook chicken and ham about 10 minutes, turning chicken to brown on all sides. Add onion and garlic and cook 2 minutes. Add tomatoes, salt, shrimp, and clams; cover and cook 5 to 10 minutes, or until clam shells open. Remove clams and keep warm.
2. Add rice, water, peas, parsley, and saffron; mix well. Cover and cook, stirring occasionally, 25 minutes, or until rice is just tender. Mix in lobster, half of pimento, and the reserved clams in shells; heat until very hot. Serve garnished with remaining pimento.

8 to 10 servings

813 *Court Bouillon for Fish and Shellfish*

1 onion
1 leek
1 carrot
3 celery stalks
5 parsley sprigs
1 basil sprig
2 tablespoons olive oil
2 quarts boiling water
Bouquet garni
6 peppercorns, cracked
2 whole cloves
6 dried Italian pepper pods or 1 whole pink hot pepper
½ cup amber rum

1. Finely chop fresh vegetables and herbs together.
2. Heat oil in a large saucepan, add chopped mixture, and cook until lightly browned. Add boiling water, bouquet garni, peppercorns, cloves, pepper pods, and rum. Cover; boil 30 minutes. Boil uncovered to reduce volume by half.
3. Strain and cool before using.

About 1 quart

814 *Scrambled Eggs with Salt Cod*

5 parsley sprigs
2 green onions, chopped
1 garlic clove, crushed in a garlic press
1 dried Italian pepper pod or 1 sliver green hot pepper
1½ cups shredded soaked salt cod
3 tablespoons peanut oil
1 cup hot milk
6 eggs

1. In a mortar, pound together to a paste the parsley, onion, garlic, and pepper pod. Mix this seasoning paste with the shredded cod.
2. Heat oil in a skillet, add fish mixture, and brown it, adding hot milk.
3. In another skillet, scramble eggs to a soft consistency while gradually adding the fish mixture.

4 servings

815 *Stuffed Fish Odette Mennesson*

1 large grouper or bluefish
    (4 to 5 pounds)
    Court Bouillon for Fish and
    ● **Shellfish**
6 hard-cooked eggs
2 cups Herbal Mayonnaise Odette
    ● Mennesson , chilled
1 cup crab meat
    Parsley
    Lime wedges and avocado slices
      for garnish

1. Have the fish split and boned without removing the head or tail.
2. Bring court bouillon to boiling in a large roasting pan. Wrap fish in cheesecloth and put into pan, leaving the ends of the cloth out of the pan. Poach 7 to 10 minutes, or until fish is thoroughly cooked.
3. Meanwhile, mash eggs with mayonnaise; mix in crab meat.
4. Gently remove fish from bouillon and transfer from cloth to a platter. Spoon crab mixture between the two halves of fish. Serve warm, or if desired, chill thoroughly.
5. To serve, arrange parsley around fish and garnish with slices of lime and avocado.

816 *Red Snapper Meuniere*

2 red snappers (2 pounds each)
2 limes, halved
    Salt and pepper to taste
½ cup flour
    Peanut oil (about ¼ cup)
    Butter (about 2 tablespoons)
5 drops Tabasco
¼ cup butter
1 tablespoon chopped parsley
1 tablespoon lime juice
    Lime wedges for garnish

1. Have the fins and tails trimmed from fish, without removing the heads. Rub the fish with cut side of lime halves, squeezing gently to release the juice. Season with salt and pepper. Superficially slash the skin of the fish in a diamond design.
2. Put flour into a bag large enough to hold fish; put fish into bag and coat them evenly with flour.
3. Heat enough oil and butter to cover the bottom of a skillet large enough to hold both fish. When fat is sizzling, add Tabasco. Sauté fish about 12 minutes on each side, or until done, reducing the heat if necessary so as not to scorch them.
4. Meanwhile, cream ¼ cup butter with parsley.
5. Remove fish to a heated plater and keep warm. Discard all the fat in bottom of the skillet and add butter with parsley and the lime juice; stir until blended. Spoon over fish.
6. Garnish platter with lime wedges.

6 servings

817 *Stuffed Red Snapper*

1 red snapper (about 5 pounds)
    Salt and pepper to taste
½ lime
¼ cup flour
1 cup cooked rice
1 cup chopped raw shrimp
½ cup chopped green onion
    (including top)
½ cup very thinly sliced celery
1 tablespoon grated ginger root
2 bacon slices
¼ cup dry white wine

1. Season red snapper inside and out with salt and pepper. Rub with cut side of lime. Sprinkle evenly with flour.
2. Combine rice, shrimp, onion, celery, and ginger root. Spoon into fish; skewer or sew the opening. Lay fish in a very heavily buttered baking pan. Score the top of fish in an attractive design to prevent it from buckling. Lay bacon slices over top.
3. Bake at 350°F 45 minutes, or until fish flakes. Transfer fish to a heated platter.
4. Deglaze baking pan with white wine. Pour liquid over fish.

818 *Red Snapper à l'Orange*

1 red snapper (5½ to 6 pounds)
Salt and cayenne or red pepper
   to taste
Juices of 1 lime and 1 orange
● Court Bouillon for Fish and
   Shellfish
Bouquet garni
16 potato balls
16 small carrots, cut in chunks
6 leeks (white part only), halved
8 unpeeled orange slices
3 tablespoons tomato paste
● Saffron Rice

1. Season red snapper with salt, cayenne, and juices; allow to marinate 30 minutes.
2. Pour court bouillon into a fish steamer. Place the fish in steamer along with bouquet garni, vegetables, and orange slices. Simmer uncovered on top of the range or bake at 450°F 20 minutes.
3. Transfer fish carefully to a heated platter. Arrange the vegetables around it. Garnish with orange slices.
4. Measure 2 cups fish broth and blend with tomato paste; pour over vegetables. Serve with the rice.

819 *Dr. Gagneron's Fish in Pastry*

1 cup cold water
1 teaspoon salt
2 cups all-purpose flour
½ cup butter
1 grouper (about 2½ pounds)
● Court Bouillon for Fish and
   Shellfish
●1 cup Béchamel Sauce ;
   made with strained court
   bouillon
12 raw oysters, shelled
¼ cup capers
½ cup chopped red and green sweet
   peppers
Milk

1. For pastry, chill a bowl and pastry board. Combine water and salt. Put flour into the chilled bowl, make a well, and pour in the salted water; mix without kneading. Refrigerate dough 30 minutes.
2. Roll the dough into a rectangle ¼ inch thick on chilled and floured pastry board. Lightly trace lines dividing the rectangle into 3 even sections.
3. Spread the butter on the middle section, working quickly. Fold the 2 sides over the middle. Roll again to ¼-inch thickness. Fold into thirds and roll again. Fold into thirds and refrigerate overnight.
4. For filling, poach grouper in court bouillon. When the fish flakes at the touch of a knife near the backbone, remove from broth. Cool and shred it, discarding the skin and bones.
5. Combine sauce, the shredded grouper, oysters, capers, and peppers. Set aside.
6. Roll pastry to ¼-inch thickness. Spread the filling on half the pastry; fold the other half over it. Brush the edges with milk and press to seal. Brush the top surface with milk. Put on a baking sheet with sides.
7. Bake at 400°F 30 minutes; turn oven control to 350°F and bake 15 minutes, or until pastry is browned.

820 *Macadam of Cod Martinique*

2 pounds salt cod
¼ cup olive oil
2 large onions, chopped
⅛ teaspoon cayenne or red pepper
   Bouquet garni
1 garlic clove, crushed in a
    garlic press
3 tomatoes, peeled, seeded,
    and cut in chunks
1 tablespoon olive oil
1 teaspoon lime juice
¼ cup chopped parlsey
● Caribbean Rice

1. Soak cod in cold water overnight. The next day, drain, trim edges from fish, and coarsely shred fish.
2. Heat ¼ cup oil in a large skillet. Add onion and cod; cook until lightly browned. Add pepper, bouquet garni, garlic, and tomato; mix well. Cook covered over low heat 15 minutes. Add 1 tablespoon oil and the lime juice; mix well.
3. Transfer cod mixture to a serving platter and sprinkle with parsley. Serve with the rice.

821 *Eggplant and Salt Cod (Morue e Beregenes)*

2 pounds salt cod
1 eggplant (2 pounds),
    pared and sliced
½ cup olive oil
2 garlic cloves, crushed in a
    garlic press
5 drops Tabasco
1 tablespoon tomato paste
   Bouquet garni
   Juice of ½ lime
   Salt and pepper to taste
● French-Fried Breadfruit or
● Deep-Fried Plantain

1. Soak cod in cold water overnight. The next day, place the fish in a sieve and slowly pour 1 quart boiling water over it. Bone fish, trim, and remove any skin, then shred and set aside.
2. Cook eggplant slices in salted water 3 minutes, then drain.
3. Put oil, garlic, Tabasco, and tomato paste into a Dutch oven; mix. Add reserved fish, the eggplant, and bouquet garni. Cook over medium heat until eggplant falls apart. Mix in lime juice, salt, and pepper.
4. Serve hot with breadfruit.

Crab Zoumba: Follow recipe for Eggplant and Salt Cod, substituting **2 pounds crab meat** for cod.

822 *Guadelupean Blaffe*

2 pounds salt cod
3 garlic cloves
⅛ teaspoon cayenne or red pepper
10 parsley sprigs
3 peppercorns
3 scallions or green onions,
    cut in pieces
3 celery leaves
1 fresh dill sprig or
    ⅛ teaspoon dried dill
2 quarts water
   Bouquet garni
● Caribbean Rice

1. Soak cod in cold water overnight. The next day, drain cod and reserve.
2. In a mortar, pound together to a paste the garlic, cayenne, parsley, peppercorns, scallions, celery leaves, and dill.
3. Bring water to boiling in a soup kettle. Add the seasoning paste and bouquet garni; bring to a boil. Add reserved cod and simmer until the cod flakes.
4. Serve in soup plates with the rice.

823 *Crab Meat Omelet Martinique* *(Omelette aux Ouassous)*

3 tablespoons butter or margarine
1 package (6 ounces) frozen crab meat, thawed, drained, and flaked
2 teaspoons finely chopped onion
2 teaspoons chopped parsley
¼ cup dairy sour cream
1 tablespoon dry sherry
4 eggs
2 tablespoons water
Salt and pepper to taste

1. For filling, melt 1 tablespoon butter in a skillet. Add crab meat, onion, and parsley; heat thoroughly. Stir in sour cream and sherry. Set aside.
2. For omelets, beat eggs in a bowl; add water, salt, and pepper.
3. In a small skillet, melt 1 tablespoon butter over high heat. Add half the beaten eggs. Immediately use a fork or spoon to push the edges of the thickened egg mass towards the center; the liquid will immediately fill the vacant spaces. Repeat this procedure until the eggs are cooked but still soft. Remove from heat.
4. Place half the crab filling in the middle of the omelet. Fold the omelet in thirds to enclose the filling.
5. Repeat procedure for making an omelet, using the remaining beaten eggs and crab meat filling. Serve immediately.

2 omelets

824 *Lobster Canapé*

6 rock lobster tails (at least ½ pound each)
● Court Bouillon for Fish and Shellfish
9 tablespoons olive oil
6 tablespoons butter
16 white bread slices with crusts trimmed
● 2½ cups Béchamel Sauce
2 egg yolks
⅓ cup amber rum, warmed and flamed
¾ cup chopped cashews
2 tablespoons chopped parsley
1 tablespoon chopped dill

1. Cook lobster tails in court bouillon until tender; drain, reserving bouillon. Slice lobster into chunks ½ inch thick.
2. Heat 3 tablespoons oil and 2 tablespoons butter in a large skillet. Add a few bread slices and fry until golden, turning once. Repeat frying procedure with more oil, butter, and bread slices. Set croutons aside and keep hot.
3. Prepare Béchamel Sauce with the reserved bouillon; blend in egg yolks and rum. Mix in lobster pieces. Keep warm in a chafing dish.
4. Sauté cashews in 2 tablespoons butter; stir in parsley and dill.
5. To serve, spoon lobster mixture onto croutons and sprinkle with herbed cashews.

825 *Barbecued Eel*

1 eel (about 3 pounds)
2 garlic cloves
1 scallion or green onion, cut in pieces
4 dried Italian pepper pods
1 basil sprig
3 parsley sprigs
2 peppercorns
1 tablespoon coarse salt
¼ cup lime juice
1 cup peanut or olive oil
1 cup cornmeal

1. Have eel skinned and cleaned; cut into 3-inch chunks.
2. In a mortar, pound together to a paste the garlic, scallion, pepper pods, basil, parsley, peppercorns, and salt. Blend lime juice and oil into seasoning paste. Pour over eel chunks and marinate overnight.
3. When ready to barbecue, pour cornmeal into a bag, add chunks of eel, and shake to coat. Place eel in a hinged grill and barbecue 5 inches from ash-covered coals, basting frequently with the marinade; turn pieces so they brown on both sides.
4. Serve with Creole Barbecue Sauce (●) or Ti-Malice Sauce (●) and **barbecued yams** (see Yams and Sweet Potatoes, ●

826 Cod Casserole

1 pound salt cod
12 small potatoes
12 small onions, peeled
3 tablespoons olive oil
⅛ teaspoon cayenne or red pepper
Black pepper
½ cup half-and-half

1. Soak cod in cold water overnight. The next day, drain and then rinse under running cold water.
2. Cook cod, potatoes, and onions separately in water, adding no salt. Drain when tender.
3. Remove all bones from cod, trim edges from fish, and cut into 2-inch pieces. Place fish in alternating layers with onions and potatoes in a top-of-range casserole. Drizzle with olive oil, sprinkle with cayenne and black pepper, and pour half-and-half over all. Cover and simmer over low heat 20 minutes.
4. Serve cool, but not cold, with a green salad.

827 Cod Soup (Chaudrée of Cod)

1 pound salt cod
¼ pound salt pork, cubed
1 tablespoon chopped onion
2 sprigs celery leaves
4 parsley sprigs
4 peppercorns, cracked
1 shallot, halved
¼ cup tomato paste
4 drops Tabasco
Bouquet garni
1 cup potato balls
1 quart stock
● Boiled Plantain

1. Soak cod in cold water overnight. The next day, put cod in a sieve and gently pour 1 quart boiling water over it. Flake cod and reserve.
2. Sauté salt pork and onion in a soup kettle until light brown. Set aside.
3. In a mortar, pound together to a paste the celery leaves, parsley, peppercorns, and shallot.
4. Add seasoning paste to kettle along with tomato paste, Tabasco, bouquet garni, potato balls, flaked cod, and stock; stir. Bring to a boil, reduce heat, and simmer gently until vegetables are tender.
5. To serve, put plantain into soup plates and add soup.

828 Barbecued Crabs

8 large hard-shell crabs
½ lime
● Creole Barbecue Sauce
● Caribbean Rice

1. Rinse crabs in water several times. Rub the shells with the cut side of a lime half, squeezing a little to release some of the juice. Cut off the heads just behind the eyes and discard the green sac; lift the belly apron and cut it away, too.
2. Put the crabs in a hinged grill and barbecue 5 inches away from glowing coals for about 5 minutes on each side. Immediately brush with the sauce.
3. Serve crabs with the rice.

8 servings

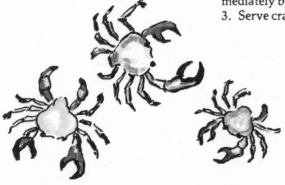

829 *Haitian Rock Lobster Salad*

8 rock lobster tails
● Court Bouillon for Fish and Shellfish
● 4 cups Caribbean Rice
16 cherry tomatoes, washed and stemmed
1 cup cubed pared cucumber
3 celery stalks, diced
1 cup cubed fresh pineapple
1 cup small Greek black olives
¼ cup capers
● 1 cup French Dressing Antillaise for Salads
4 hard-cooked eggs, peeled and quartered
¾ cup amber rum

1. Simmer lobster tails in court bouillon 20 minutes. Belly side down on a board, split the tail lengthwise with a sharp knife and keep warm in the bouillon until serving time (see Note).
2. Toss rice with vegetables, pineapple, olives, and capers. Add dressing and toss again.
3. Mound the rice mixture on a large silver platter, garnish with hard-cooked egg quarters, and edge platter with drained cooked lobster tails.
4. At the table, warm rum, ignite it, and pour it flaming over the lobster.

8 servings

Note: If you have room in the freezer, save the court bouillon to use as a base for Béchamel Sauce for fish or for a chowder.

830 *Crawfish or Jumbo Shrimp au Gratin Guadeloupe*

50 small crawfish in their shells or 50 shelled raw jumbo shrimp
● Court Bouillon for Fish and Shellfish
3 tablespoons butter
1 tablespoon peanut oil
1 pound sliced calf's liver
6 mushrooms, sliced
1 tablespoon chopped parsley
⅛ teaspoon dried marjoram
⅛ teaspoon dried rosemary
Salt, freshly ground pepper, and cayenne or red pepper to taste
3 white bread slices with crusts trimmed
1 egg, beaten
½ cup dried bread crumbs
½ cup finely shredded Swiss cheese
½ cup whipping cream
2 tablespoons amber rum, warmed and flamed

1. Cook crawfish in boiling court bouillon 10 minutes, then cool. Reserve 1 cup bouillon.
2. Heat butter and oil in a skillet; sauté liver and mushrooms until liver is firm on the outside and pink inside. Season with parsley, marjoram, rosemary, salt, and peppers.
3. Soak bread slices in reserved bouillon; stir to break up bread. Process soaked bread with bouillon and liver-mushroom mixture, a little at a time, in an electric blender or force through a food mill. Stir in egg.
4. Spread mixture on bottom of a shallow baking dish. Arrange crawfish decoratively on top. Sprinkle with a mixture of bread crumbs and cheese. Blend cream and rum; pour over all. Broil until lightly browned.

Desserts

831 *Figs with Mavrodaphne Wine* (*Syka me Mavrodaphne Krasi*)

12 ripe figs
2 cups Mavrodaphne wine
2 cups whipping cream, whipped
¼ cup walnuts

1. Peel figs. Prick each 3 or 4 times on sides and bottoms. Arrange figs in a dish and pour wine over them. Refrigerate for 2 hours, turning occasionally.
2. Remove figs to a serving platter. Reserve the wine. Arrange whipping cream around the figs. Garnish with walnuts. Serve wine separately.

4 servings

832 *Whole Wheat Porridge with Currants and Almonds* (*Kourkourti*)

5 cups whole wheat
Water
Salt, sugar, and cinnamon
1 cup coarsely ground blanched almonds
½ cup dried currants (optional)

1. Place whole wheat in a large saucepan. Cover with cold water and let stand overnight.
2. The next day, drain wheat. Cover with fresh cold water. Simmer about 4 hours, or until tender, stirring frequently to prevent scorching and adding water as needed. Stock will become very thick.
3. Drain wheat stock into a saucepan. Add salt, sugar, and cinnamon to taste. Stir in almonds, currants, and 1 cup of the boiled wheat, if desired. Serve hot.

4 servings

833 *Revani*

1 cup unsalted butter
½ cup sugar
1 teaspoon grated lemon or orange peel
5 eggs
2 cups semolina
1 cup flour
1 tablespoon baking powder
Syrup:
3 cups sugar
1 quart water
1 cinnamon stick

1. Cream butter with sugar and grated peel. Beat together 5 minutes. Add eggs, one at a time, beating until well blended after each.
2. Combine semolina, flour, and baking powder. Add to creamed mixture and mix together by hand. Spread in a buttered 9-inch square pan.
3. Bake at 350°F 40 to 45 minutes. Cool 5 minutes.
4. While Revani is baking, prepare the syrup. Combine sugar, water, and cinnamon. Bring to boiling, reduce heat at once, and simmer covered 20 minutes.
5. Pour syrup over cake. Cool, then slice into squares. Serve plain or garnished with **whipped cream** and **toasted almonds** or accompanied with **fresh fruit.**

10 to 12 servings

834 *Butter Horns* (*Rogaliki*)

1 cup sweet unsalted butter or margarine
½ cup sugar
1 egg yolk
1 teaspoon vanilla extract
¼ cup chopped blanched almonds
1⅔ cups all-purpose flour
Confectioners' sugar

1. Beat butter at high speed and add sugar gradually, creaming until light and fluffy. Beat in egg yolk and vanilla extract. Beat in almonds, then flour.
2. With hands, shape 1-inch pieces of dough into crescents. Place on ungreased baking sheets, about 1 inch apart.
3. Bake at 350°F about 20 minutes, or until just golden on edges.
4. While warm, coat crescents with confectioners' sugar.

About 3 dozen

835 *Drop Yeast Doughnuts* (Loukoumathes)

2 packages active dry yeast
2 cups warm water (105° to 115°F)
3 to 4 cups all-purpose flour
1 teaspoon salt
Vegetable oil or olive oil or a combination of the two for deep frying
Honey and cinnamon

1. Dissolve yeast in 1 cup warm water in a small bowl.
2. Add 1½ cups flour to yeast. Beat batter with a wooden spoon until smooth.
3. Cover with a towel and put into a warm place until batter is double in bulk.
4. Pour into a larger bowl, add remaining water, salt, and flour to make a thick but runny batter.
5. Cover with a towel and put into a warm place until batter is double in bulk and begins to bubble.
6. Half fill a deep fryer with oil. Heat just until smoking.
7. Drop batter by tablespoonfuls into oil; occasionally dip spoon in oil before dipping in batter. Cook until golden brown. Remove with a slotted spoon.
8. Drizzle with honey and sprinkle with cinnamon. Serve hot.

About 30

836 *Diples*

2 eggs
1 egg yolk
1 tablespoon butter, melted
Grated peel of 1 orange (optional)
¼ cup orange juice
2 tablespoons lemon juice
Semolina (about 2½ cups)
½ teaspoon baking powder
½ teaspoon salt
Oil for deep frying (4 to 5 inches deep)
Honey
Cinnamon
Chopped walnuts

1. Beat eggs and egg yolk until fluffy. Add melted butter, grated peel, orange juice, and lemon juice.
2. Mix 1 cup semolina with baking powder and salt. Stir into egg mixture. Add another cup semolina and mix well. Add remaining ½ cup semolina as necessary to make a soft dough. It will be a little sticky. Knead on a board until elastic and smooth.
3. Divide dough into 3 portions. Lightly flour a large board and roll dough as thin as for noodles. Using a sharp knife, cut dough into 4-inch-wide strips. Cover dough until ready to fry.
4. Heat oil in a deep saucepan. When oil reaches 350°F, regulate temperature and drop in a piece of dough. Using two forks, turn in one end and roll up quickly to the other. Remove with a slotted spoon as soon as light gold in color. Drain on absorbent towels.
5. To serve, pour warm honey over the Diples and sprinkle with cinnamon and walnuts.

About 4 to 5 dozen

837 *Shredded Wheat Nut Dessert* (Kataifi)

3 cups sugar
1 quart water
Grated peel of 1 lemon
2 whole cloves
4 cups walnuts, coarsely ground
½ cup sugar
2 teaspoons cinnamon
2 pounds kataifi dough
1½ cups unsalted butter, melted
1 tablespoon rosewater

1. Combine 3 cups sugar, water, peel, and cloves in a saucepan. Bring to a boil. Reduce heat, cover, and simmer 20 minutes. Set aside to cool.
2. Combine nuts, ½ cup sugar, and cinnamon in a bowl. Set aside.
3. Take enough kataifi dough to pat into a 4x3-inch flat piece. Put 1 tablespoon of the nut filling in the center, fold dough over, and shape into a roll. Continue until all the filling and dough have been used.
4. Place rolls, 1 inch apart, in a greased large baking pan. Spoon melted butter over each roll.
5. Bake at 325°F about 40 minutes, or until golden brown. Remove from oven and sprinkle with rosewater. Pour cooled syrup over. Cool several hours before serving.

About 30

838 *New Year's Day Cake* (Vasilopita)

3½ cups all-purpose flour
2 teaspoons baking powder
1 cup softened unsalted butter
1 cup sugar
2 eggs (at room temperature)
1 egg yolk
   Grated peel of 1 orange
¼ teaspoon nutmeg (optional)
¼ cup cream
1 tablespoon cognac
1 silver coin, boiled and wrapped
   in foil
   Blanched almonds (about 20)
1 egg white, beaten until frothy

1. Sift flour and baking powder; set aside.
2. Using an electric mixer, beat butter until fluffy. Add sugar gradually, beating 4 minutes. Add eggs and egg yolk, one at a time, beating after each. Add peel and nutmeg. Combine cream and cognac; add gradually while beating.
3. Add dry ingredients, using a wooden spoon to mix in well. Stir in coin.
4. Heavily grease a 10-inch round cake pan. Turn batter into pan. Press edge with fork tines to decorate. Arrange blanched almonds in a decorative pattern on top.
5. Bake at 350°F 15 to 20 minutes, or until cake is set. Pull out from oven, brush with egg white, and return to oven. Continue baking until a wooden pick inserted in the center comes out clean (about 20 minutes). Cool before serving.

8 to 10 servings

839 *Walnut Honey Cake* (Karithopeta)

Syrup:
1 cup sugar
½ cup honey
1 cup water
1 teaspoon lemon juice
1 cinnamon stick

Cake:
¾ cup unsalted butter (at room
   temperature)
½ teaspoon grated orange peel
¾ cup sugar
3 eggs
1 cup all-purpose flour
1½ teaspoons baking powder
½ teaspoon cinnamon
¼ teaspoon salt
¼ cup milk
1 cup chopped walnuts

1. For syrup, bring all ingredients to a boil in a saucepan. Simmer 20 minutes. Set aside to cool.
2. For cake, cream butter, orange peel, and sugar together until fluffy. Beat in eggs, one at a time, beating well after each addition.
3. Mix flour, baking powder, cinnamon, and salt. Fold flour mixture into butter mixture, alternating with milk. Stir in nuts.
4. Pour batter into a greased and floured 8-inch square pan.
5. Bake at 350°F 30 minutes, or until done.
6. Remove cake from oven, cool, and cut into diamonds while in the pan.
7. Pour syrup over cake. Cool. Refrigerate and let soak 24 hours before serving.

2 to 3 dozen

840 *Pasta Flora*

½ cup unsalted butter (at room
   temperature)
2 eggs
1 teaspoon vanilla extract
1 cup sugar
3 cups all-purpose flour
1 tablespoon baking powder
1 pint jam or preserves
1 egg yolk, beaten with ½
   teaspoon water

1. Beat butter 4 minutes, using an electric mixer. Add eggs, vanilla extract, and sugar. Beat until fluffy. Mix flour and baking powder. Slowly work into mixture until well blended.
2. Divide dough into 2 parts; one a ball using three fourths of the total, and one using one fourth of the total.
3. Line the bottom a 13x9-inch baking pan with the larger portion of the dough. Spread the preserves evenly over dough.
4. Roll the remaining quarter of the dough on a lightly floured board to fit the size of the pan. Cut into strips. Form a lattice over the preserves. Brush dough with the egg yolk and water.
5. Bake at 350°F about 45 minutes until pastry is golden brown or a wooden pick comes out clean when inserted. Cool. Cut into squares.

10 servings

841 *Copenhagen Pita* *(Copenhai)*

Syrup:
3 cups sugar
1½ cups honey
5 cups water
½ stick cinnamon

Cake:
1½ cups butter
1 cup confectioners' sugar
5 eggs
1½ cups flour
1 tablespoon baking powder
2 tablespoons cognac

Filling:
5 eggs
2 cups sugar
1 teaspoon cinnamon
3 pieces zwieback, ground
1½ cups almonds, blanched and ground

Topping:
1 package filo
1½ cups butter

1. For syrup, combine sugar, honey, water, and cinnamon in a large saucepan. Bring to boiling. Reduce heat and simmer 20 minutes. Set aside to cool.
2. For cake, cream butter and confectioners' sugar. Add eggs, one at a time, beating well after each. Mix flour and baking powder and add to butter mixture. Add cognac and mix well.
3. Spread mixture evenly in a greased 18x12-inch baking pan. Set aside.
4. For filling, separate eggs. Beat yolks slightly, add sugar, and beat until light and fluffy.
5. Beat egg whites in another bowl until stiff, not dry, peaks are formed. Fold whites into yolk mixture. Combine cinnamon, zwieback crumbs, and almonds and fold into egg mixture. Spread evenly over layer in pan.
6. For topping, layer 10 sheets of filo over top, buttering after each layer has been added; see pages 80-81 for how to handle filo. Drizzle a little butter over top layer. Score topmost sheets into diamond shapes.
7. Bake at 350°F about 50 minutes, or until golden in color. Remove from oven and pour cooled syrup over.
8. Let stand several hours before serving.

About 60 pieces

842 *Turkish Delight* *(Loukoumi)*

2 cups granulated sugar
½ cup light corn syrup
½ cup cornstarch plus 3 tablespoons extra for dusting
3 cups water
1 tablespoon rosewater
⅛ teaspoon ground mastic
2 tablespoons fresh lemon juice
¾ cup unsalted pistachios
Confectioners' sugar for rolling

1. Combine granulated sugar and corn syrup in a saucepan and bring to boiling, stirring constantly. Cook for 30 seconds. Cool.
2. In another saucepan, combine ½ cup cornstarch with water. Simmer mixture until thick. Mix cornstarch into syrup and bring slowly to boiling. Stir to prevent lumps from forming. Reduce heat to very low and cook uncovered, stirring occasionally, until a candy thermometer registers 220°F. Stir in rosewater, mastic, lemon juice, and pistachios.
3. Pour the hot mixture into a square pan lined on bottom and sides with a heavy cotton cloth dusted with cornstarch. Spread mixture and dust top with cornstarch. Cover with a cloth and let it stand 24 hours.
4. Cut the layer into small squares with a sharp knife, roll the pieces in confectioners' sugar, and put into candy paper cups. This confection will keep for weeks.

About 3 dozen pieces

843 *Roast Chestnuts* *(Kastana Karvoudizmena)*

4 pounds chestnuts

1. Cut a cross on the flat side of each chestnut with a small sharp knife, being careful not to damage nutmeat. Spread in a large baking pan.
2. Roast in a 425°F oven about 30 minutes, or until done; shake frequently. Serve hot.

844 *Rusks I* *(Paximathia)*

¼ cup unsalted butter
1 teaspoon vanilla extract
¾ cup sugar
3 eggs (¾ cup)
1 egg yolk
3½ cups sifted cake flour
1 tablespoon baking powder
¼ teaspoon salt
1 egg yolk for glaze

1. Beat butter and vanilla extract, then add sugar gradually, beating thoroughly. Add eggs, one at a time, beating 1 minute after each addition. Combine flour, baking powder, and salt. Add half of flour to creamed mixture and mix with a wooden spoon. Add remaining flour; mix well.
2. Divide dough into four portions. Roll each portion into a long roll about 1½ inches in diameter on a floured pastry cloth. Place rolls 3 inches apart on a well-greased and floured cookie sheet. Flatten dough slightly with hands. Brush tops with egg yolk.
3. Bake at 400°F about 20 to 25 minutes, or until golden and firm to the touch.
4. Remove from oven. Cover with a towel; let stand 2 hours.
5. Cut rolls into ½-inch slices. Place on ungreased cookie sheet, cut sides down.
6. Toast in a 400°F oven 15 to 20 minutes, turning several times until delicately brown.

About 3 dozen

845 *Rusks II* *(Paximathia)*

1 loaf Greek Easter Bread
● (Lambropsomo)
Unsalted butter
Honey

1. Cut bread into thick slices. Place on ungreased cookie sheet.
2. Bake at 225°F 20 minutes on each side.
3. Cool on wire rack. Serve with butter and honey.

846 *Rusks III* *(Paximathia)*

1 cup butter
1 teaspoon vanilla extract
2 cups sugar
2 eggs
1 cup dairy sour cream
5½ cups all-purpose flour
1 teaspoon baking soda
¼ teaspoon salt

1. Cream butter, vanilla extract, and sugar. Add eggs and beat thoroughly. Stir in sour cream.
2. Mix flour, baking soda, and salt. Add to butter mixture and mix until a dough is formed.
3. Divide dough into 3 portions. Shape each portion into a roll 1½ inches in diameter. Place each roll on a cookie sheet.
4. Bake at 350°F 15 minutes. Remove from oven and turn oven control to 425°F. Using a very sharp knife, cut into ¾-inch slices. Arrange slices cut side down on cookie sheets. Bake slices first on one side, then the other, until golden brown and firm (about 6 minutes for each side). Cool on wire racks.

About 3 dozen

847 *Sesame Seed Candy* *(Pasteli)*

½ cup honey
2 cups sugar
½ cup water
3 cups sesame seed, toasted

1. Blend honey, sugar, and water in a heavy skillet. Cook over low heat, stirring frequently. Bring to a firm ball stage, 250°F on a candy thermometer (syrup will be a light gold color). Stir in sesame seed.
2. Spread in a buttered 12x8x1½-inch pan. Break into pieces.

2 to 3 dozen pieces depending on size

848 *Koulourakia I*

1 cup unsalted butter
3 eggs
2 egg yolks
2 tablespoons cognac
2 cups confectioners' sugar
4½ cups sifted cake flour
3½ teaspoons baking powder
Egg white, beaten
Sesame seed, lightly toasted

1. Beat butter until light and fluffy. Add eggs and egg yolks, one at a time, beating well after each. Add cognac, then confectioners' sugar, beating well. Sift flour with baking powder and add to butter mixture; mix well.
2. Knead dough on a floured board until shiny.
3. Break off a small amount of dough and roll on a board to form a strip 5 to 6 inches long. Shape into a ring by joining the ends, or make a snail shape by winding up the strip. Place on a greased cookie sheet. Repeat with remaining dough.
4. Brush tops with beaten egg white. Sprinkle with sesame seed.
5. Bake at 350°F 20 to 25 minutes, or until done.

About 6 dozen

849 *Koulourakia II*

3 cups sifted all-purpose flour
2 teaspoons baking powder
½ teaspoon salt
¾ cup unsalted butter
1 teaspoon anise flavoring
½ cup sugar
1 egg
¼ cup whipping cream
1 egg yolk, beaten, for brushing

1. Sift flour, baking powder, and salt together.
2. Cream butter with anise flavoring until fluffy. Add sugar and beat thoroughly. Add egg and beat well. Pour in whipping cream; mix thoroughly. Stir in flour mixture.
3. Knead dough on a floured board until shiny. Cover and refrigerate 2 hours.
4. Remove from refrigerator 30 minutes before rolling and baking. Break off a small amount of dough and roll on a board to form a strip 5 to 6 inches long. Shape into a ring by joining the ends, or make into a snail shape by winding up the strip. Place on a greased cookie sheet. Brush with egg yolk.
5. Bake at 350°F 20 to 25 minutes, or until done.

3½ dozen

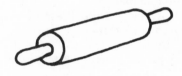

850 *Kourambiethes*

1 cup unsalted butter (at room temperature)
2 egg yolks
1 tablespoon granulated sugar
1 cup coarsely chopped blanched almonds
2 cups all-purpose flour
1 teaspoon baking powder
Whole cloves
Rosewater
2 pounds confectioners' sugar

1. Beat butter until white in an electric mixer (about 10 minutes). Add egg yolks and sugar; beat well. Add chopped almonds and mix well. Blend flour and baking powder and mix in until blended.
2. Taking a small amount of dough, roll it between palms, shaping it into a ball. Continue until all dough has been used. Or, roll dough into a round log, about 1 inch in diameter; cut diagonally into 1-inch slices. Press a clove into center of each cookie.
3. Bake at 350°F 20 minutes. Remove from oven and sprinkle lightly with rosewater. Immediately sift confectioners' sugar over them, covering the tops and sides. Cool for 1 hour.
4. Using a spatula or fork, lift the cookies, being careful not to disturb the sugar, and place them in medium-size paper cupcake cups. Store cookies at least a day before serving.

About 30 cookies

851 *Polish Pecan Cookies* (*Ciastka Kurche*)

1 cup butter
3 tablespoons vanilla extract
½ cup confectioners' sugar
1½ tablespoons water
2½ cups sifted all-purpose flour
2 cups pecan halves
Confectioners' sugar for rolling

1. Cream butter with vanilla extract; add confectioners' sugar gradually, beating until fluffy.
2. Add water and beat thoroughly.
3. Add flour in fourths, mixing until blended after each addition.
4. If necessary, chill the dough until easy to handle.
5. Shape a teaspoonful of dough around each pecan half, covering nut completely. Place on ungreased cookie sheets.
6. Bake at 400°F 10 minutes.
7. Roll in confectioners' sugar while still warm.

About 5 dozen

852 *Honey Cookies* (*Piernik*)

½ cup honey
½ cup sugar
2 eggs
½ teaspoon vanilla extract
3 cups all-purpose flour
1 teaspoon baking soda
½ teaspoon salt
½ teaspoon cinnamon
½ teaspoon ginger
½ teaspoon nutmeg
¼ teaspoon cloves
1 egg white, beaten
48 blanched almond halves (about)

1. Combine honey and sugar in a bowl; mix well. Beat in eggs and vanilla extract.
2. Blend flour, baking soda, salt, and spices. Stir into honey mixture. Knead to mix thoroughly; dough will be stiff.
3. Shape dough into a ball. Wrap in plastic wrap. Let stand 2 hours.
4. Roll dough on a floured surface to ¼-inch thickness. Cut into 2½-inch rounds or other shapes.
5. Brush top of each cookie with egg white. Press an almond onto center. Place on greased cookie sheets.
6. Bake at 375°F 8 to 10 minutes.
7. Cool on racks. Store in plastic bags for 8 to 10 days to mellow.

About 4 dozen

853 *Kolacky*

1 cup butter or margarine (at room temperature)
1 package (8 ounces) cream cheese (at room temperature)
¼ teaspoon vanilla extract
2¼ cups all-purpose flour
½ teaspoon salt
Thick jam or canned fruit filling, such as apricot or prune

1. Cream butter and cream cheese until fluffy. Beat in vanilla extract.
2. Combine flour and salt; add in fourths to butter mixture, blending well after each addition. Chill dough until easy to handle.
3. Roll dough to ⅜-inch thickness on a floured surface. Cut out 2-inch circles or other shapes. Place on ungreased baking sheets.
4. Make a "thumbprint" about ¼ inch deep in each cookie. Fill with jam.
5. Bake at 350°F 10 to 15 minutes, or until delicately browned on edges.

About 3½ dozen

854 *Polish Doughnuts (Pączki)*

1 package active dry yeast
¼ cup warm water
⅓ cup butter or margarine (at room temperature)
⅔ cup sugar
1 egg
3 egg yolks
1 teaspoon vanilla extract
1 teaspoon grated orange or lemon peel
¾ teaspoon salt
3½ cups all-purpose flour (about)
Fat for deep frying heated to 375°F
Confectioners' sugar (optional)

1. Dissolve yeast in warm water.
2. Cream butter and sugar until fluffy. Beat in egg, then egg yolks, one at a time. Add vanilla extract, orange peel, dissolved yeast, and salt. Beat until well mixed. Stir in flour gradually, adding enough to make a stiff dough.
3. Turn dough onto a floured surface. Knead until smooth and elastic, about 10 minutes. Place in a greased bowl. Cover. Let rise until doubled in bulk.
4. Turn onto lightly floured surface. Pat or roll to ½-inch thickness. Cut out with doughnut cutter. Cover. Let rise until doubled in bulk.
5. Fry in hot fat 2 to 3 minutes; turn to brown all sides.
6. Drain doughnuts on paper towels and sprinkle with confectioners' sugar, if desired.

About 2 dozen

855 *Wise Men (Mądrzyki)*

1 pound farmer or pot cheese
4 eggs, separated
3 tablespoons sugar
¼ teaspoon salt
¼ cup all-purpose flour
Fat for deep frying heated to 365°F
Dairy sour cream and sugar (optional)

1. Press cheese through a sieve.
2. Combine egg yolks and sugar; beat at high speed until mixture is thick and piles softly, about 7 minutes.
3. Add cheese and salt, then mix in flour, 1 tablespoon at a time. Add just enough flour to form a dough. (Dough will be sticky.)
4. Pat out dough on generously floured surface to ¾-inch thickness.
5. Cut into 2×1-inch rectangles with well-floured knife.
6. Fry the rectangles quickly, turning to brown both sides. (Be sure the temperature of the fat is maintained at 365°F, so the cheese will fry crisply.)
7. Serve at once with dairy sour cream and sugar, if desired.

About 2½ dozen

856 *Favors (Chrust-Faworki)*

4 egg yolks
1 whole egg
½ teaspoon salt
⅓ cup confectioners' sugar
2 tablespoons rum or brandy
1 teaspoon vanilla extract
1¼ cups all-purpose flour
Fat for deep frying heated to 350°F
Confectioners' sugar or honey for topping (optional)

1. Combine egg yolks, whole egg, and salt in small bowl of electric mixer. Beat at highest speed 7 to 10 minutes, until mixture is thick and piles softly. Beat in sugar, a small amount at a time. Then beat in rum and vanilla extract.
2. By hand, fold in flour.
3. Turn onto a generously floured surface. Knead dough until blisters form, about 10 minutes.
4. Divide dough in half. Cover half of dough to prevent drying. Use a towel or plastic wrap.
5. Roll out half of dough as thin as possible. Cut dough into 5×2-inch strips. Make a 2-inch slit from center almost to end of each strip of dough. Then pull opposite end through slit. Repeat with remaining dough.
6. Fry in hot fat until golden brown.
7. Drain on paper towels. If desired, sprinkle with confectioners' sugar or drizzle with honey.

About 2½ dozen

857 *Mazurkas (Mazurek)*

1 cup sweet unsalted butter
¾ cup eggs, beaten
2 cups ground blanched almonds
1¾ cups all-purpose flour
1 cup sugar

1. Cream butter and eggs until fluffy.
2. Mix almonds, flour, and sugar. Add flour mixture, a small amount at a time, to the butter mixture. Beat or knead after each addition.
3. Pat or roll out dough in a greased 15×10×1-inch jelly-roll pan.
4. Bake at 350°F about 20 minutes, or until golden brown.
5. Spread jam over top. Cool for 5 minutes. Cut into 2-inch squares to serve.

About 3 dozen

858 *Royal Mazurkas (Mazurek Królewski)*

1 cup butter or margarine (room temperature)
1½ cups all-purpose flour
1 cup sugar
¼ teaspoon salt
6 egg yolks
¼ cup ground or finely chopped, blanched almonds
1 teaspoon grated orange or lemon peel (optional)

1. Cream butter until fluffy in a large mixing bowl.
2. Mix flour, sugar, and salt.
3. Alternately beat in 1 egg yolk and a sixth of flour mixture. Continue until all ingredients are well combined. Stir in almonds and orange peel. Mix well.
4. Roll or pat dough to fit a greased 15×10×1-inch jelly-roll pan.
5. Bake at 325°F 35 to 40 minutes, or until golden but not browned.
6. Cool in pan on rack 10 minutes. Cut in fourths. Remove from pan. Cool on rack.

About 3 dozen

859 *Almond Mazurkas (Mazurek Migdałowy)*

1 pound blanched almonds, ground (about 4 cups)
2 cups sugar
3 eggs
2 tablespoons lemon juice.

1. Combine almonds and sugar; mix well.
2. Beat eggs with lemon juice just until foamy. Stir into almond mixture.
3. Pour batter into a well-greased 15×10×1-inch jelly-roll pan.
4. Bake at 250°F about 1 hour, or until golden.
5. Cut into 2-inch squares while still warm. Remove from pan.

About 3 dozen

860 *Mazurkas with Fruit and Nut Topping*

Mazurkas or Royal Mazurkas or
● Almond Mazurkas
Fruit Filling:
- ¾ cup raisins or currants
- ½ cup chopped dried apricots
- ¾ cup diced dried figs or dates
- ⅔ cup chopped candied lemon or orange peel
- ¾ cup chopped blanched almonds
- ½ cup chopped walnuts

Topping:
- 1 egg
- 1 egg white
- ½ cup confectioners' sugar
- ⅓ cup butter, melted
- 1 tablespoon lemon juice
- 1 teaspoon vanilla extract
- 2 ounces almonds, ground (about ¾ cup)
- 2 tablespoons bread crumbs

1. Prepare and bake mazurkas as directed. Do not cut into squares.
2. For fruit filling, combine apricots and raisins in a saucepan. Add **water**. Bring to boiling. Cover; remove from heat and let stand 10 minutes.
3. Drain raisins and apricots. Combine with other fruits and nuts. Spread evenly over mazurkas.
4. For topping, combine egg and egg white with confectioners' sugar. Beat at high speed until very thick and fluffy, about 7 minutes.
5. Gradually beat in melted butter, lemon juice, and vanilla extract. Fold in ground almonds and bread crumbs.
6. Spread egg mixture over fruit layer.
7. Bake at 350°F about 15 minutes, or until topping is golden but still moist.
8. Cool in pan on rack 5 minutes, then cut into squares.

About 3 dozen

861 *Mazurkas with Chocolate Topping*

Mazurkas or Royal Mazurkas or
● Almond Mazurkas
- 4 eggs
- 1 cup sugar
- ½ teaspoon vanilla extract
- 1 package (8 ounces) unsweetened chocolate, grated
- 1 tablespoon flour
- ½ teaspoon salt
- 1¼ cups chopped blanched almonds

1. Prepare and bake mazurkas as directed. Do not cut into squares.
2. Beat eggs with sugar and vanilla extract until fluffy. Add chocolate; beat until well mixed. Beat in flour, salt, and almonds.
3. Spread chocolate mixture over baked mazurkas.
4. Bake at 250°F 5 to 7 minutes, or until topping is set.
5. Cool. Cut into 2-inch squares.

About 3 dozen

862 *Mazurkas with Apple Topping*

Mazurkas or Royal Mazurkas or
● Almond Mazurkas
- 1 cup sugar
- ⅓ cup water
- 3 pounds apples, pared and thinly sliced
- 2 teaspoons grated lemon or orange peel
- ½ teaspoon salt (optional)
- 1½ cups finely chopped blanched almonds (optional)

1. Prepare and bake mazurkas as directed. Do not cut into squares.
2. Combine sugar and water in a large saucepan. Simmer 5 minutes. Add apples and lemon peel. Cook over medium heat until apples are soft, about 5 to 10 minutes; stir frequently to prevent sticking.
3. If desired, add salt and almonds. Cook and stir until apples are translucent on edges and mixture clings to the spoon. Remove from heat. Cool 15 to 20 minutes.
4. Spread apple filling over warm baked mazurkas. Cool completely. Cut into 2-inch squares.

About 3 dozen

863 *Mazurkas with Lemon Icing*

Mazurkas or Royal Mazurkas or
● Almond Mazurkas
Lemon Icing:
  2 cups confectioners' sugar
  2 to 3 tablespoons lemon juice

1. Prepare and bake mazurkas as directed. Cool on a wire rack.
2. Meanwhile, mix confectioners' sugar with lemon juice until smooth.
3. Spread icing over mazurkas. Cut into 2-inch squares.

About 3 dozen

864 *Black Bread Pudding (Legumina Chlebowa)*

  6 eggs, separated
  ½ cup sugar
  ¼ teaspoon salt
  1 cup fine dry bread crumbs made
    from black bread
    (pumpernickel, rye, or whole
    wheat bread)
  ¾ teaspoon cinnamon
  ¼ teaspoon cloves
  2 tablespoons melted butter
    Fine dry bread crumbs

1. Beat egg yolks at high speed in a small bowl until thick. Gradually beat in sugar. Continue beating at high speed until mixture is very thick and piles softly.
2. Using clean beaters and a large bowl, beat egg whites with salt until stiff, not dry, peaks form.
3. Fold bread crumbs, cinnamon, and cloves into beaten yolks. Then fold in 1 tablespoon melted butter. Fold in egg whites.
4. Brush a 2-quart soufflé dish or deep casserole with remaining 1 tablespoon melted butter. Coat dish with bread crumbs.
5. Gently turn soufflé mixture into prepared dish.
6. Bake at 350°F 25 to 30 minutes, or until set near center.

About 6 servings

865 *Chocolate Torte (Tort Czekoladowy)*

  8 eggs, separated
  1¼ cups sugar
  ¾ cup all-purpose flour
  ¼ cup fine dry bread crumbs
  ¼ teaspoon salt
  2 ounces (2 squares) semisweet
    chocolate, grated
  1½ teaspoons vanilla extract
    Filling (see below)
    Frosting (see below)

1. Beat egg yolks until very thick and lemon-colored, about 5 minutes. Gradually beat in sugar.
2. Combine flour, bread crumbs, and salt. Add chocolate and mix thoroughly but lightly.
3. Add flour mixture to egg yolks and sugar in 4 portions, folding until well mixed after each addition.
4. With clean beaters, beat egg whites with vanilla extract until stiff, not dry, peaks are formed. Fold into flour mixture.
5. Turn into a well-greased 10-inch springform pan or deep, round layer cake pan.
6. Bake at 325°F 50 to 60 minutes. Remove from pan and cool completely.
7. Split cake in half.
8. Spread filling on bottom half. Replace top. Spread frosting over sides and top. Refrigerate 4 hours or longer for torte to mellow.

One 10-inch torte

Filling: Whip **½ cup whipping cream** until cream piles softly. Fold in **¼ cup ground almonds or walnuts** and **3 tablespoons sugar.**

Frosting: Melt **4 ounces (4 squares) unsweetened chocolate** and **3 tablespoons butter** together in a saucepan. Remove from heat. Stir in **1 tablespoon brandy.** Add **2 to 2½ cups confectioners' sugar** and **2 to 3 tablespoons milk or cream** until frosting is of spreading consistency.

866 *Walnut Torte (Tort Orzechowy)*

12 eggs, separated
1 cup sugar
½ pound finely ground walnuts
⅓ cup all-purpose flour
½ teaspoon salt
   Fine dry bread crumbs
2 to 3 tablespoons brandy or rum
   Filling
   Frosting
   Chopped walnuts

1. Beat egg yolks until thick and lemon-colored. Add sugar gradually, beating at high speed until mixture is very thick and piles softly.
2. Fold in ground walnuts and flour; mix thoroughly.
3. Beat egg whites with salt until stiff, but not dry, peaks form. Fold beaten egg whites into egg yolk mixture.
4. Generously grease two 10-inch cake layer pans or one 10-inch springform pan. Line with waxed paper. Grease paper. Coat with bread crumbs.
5. Turn batter into prepared pans.
6. Bake at 350°F about 25 minutes.
7. Remove layers from pans. Cool on racks 15 minutes. (Cut single, high cake, from springform pan, into 2 layers. Layers shrink slightly as they cool.) Sprinkle each layer with brandy. Cool completely.
8. Meanwhile, prepare filling and frosting.
9. Spread filling over 1 layer. Set second layer on top.
10. Spread frosting over top and sides of torte. Frosting is runny and will run down sides. Let stand 30 minutes. Pat chopped walnuts around sides of torte.
11. Refrigerate until ready to serve.

One 10-inch torte

Filling: Whip **1 cup whipping cream** until it is very thick and piles softly. Gradually beat in **¾ cup sugar**, then **½ teaspoon vanilla extract** and, if desired, **2 tablespoons brandy or rum**. Fold in **1 cup finely ground walnuts**, a small amount at a time, until blended.

About 2 cups

Frosting: Beat **1 egg** until thick and foamy. Beat in **2 tablespoons melted butter or margarine, 2 tablespoons brandy or rum, pinch salt**, and about **2½ cups sifted confectioners' sugar**. Add enough confectioners' sugar to make frosting of thin spreading consistency.

867 *Plum Cake (Placek ze Śliwkami)*

2⅓ cups all-purpose flour
2½ teaspoons baking powder
¾ teaspoon salt
1 cup sugar (reserve ¼ cup)
½ cup shortening
¾ cup milk
2 eggs
2 tablespoons fine dry bread crumbs
40 fresh plums (prune, Damson, or greengage), pitted and cut in half; or use 2 cans (30 ounces) whole purple plums, drained and pitted
3 tablespoons butter, cut in pieces
¼ teaspoon cloves

1. Combine flour, baking powder, salt, and ¾ cup sugar in a large mixing bowl. Add shortening, milk, and eggs. Beat at medium speed 4 minutes.
2. Grease bottom and sides of a 13×9×2-inch pan. Coat with bread crumbs.
3. Turn batter into prepared pan. Place plums on top, pushing one edge of each half down ¼ inch into batter. Dot with butter.
4. Combine remaining ¼ cup sugar and cloves; mix well. Sprinkle over plums.
5. Bake at 350°F about 40 minutes.
6. To serve, cut into pieces.

About 32

Apple Cake: Prepare Plum Cake as directed, substituting 4 large apples, pared and thinly sliced, for the plums.

868 *Baba (Babka)*

1 package active dry yeast
½ cup milk, scalded and cooled
½ cup sugar
2 cups all-purpose flour
½ cup butter (at room temperature)
4 eggs
½ teaspoon salt
½ teaspoon cinnamon
¼ teaspoon mace
1 tablespoon grated lemon peel
½ cup raisins, chopped almonds, or chopped candied fruits (optional)
● Lemon Icing or honey

1. Dissolve yeast in milk 10 minutes. Add 1 tablespoon of the sugar and ½ cup of the flour; mix well. Cover. Let rise until doubled.
2. Cream butter, gradually adding remaining sugar. Beat until fluffy. Beat in 3 whole eggs, 1 at a time. Beat in 1 egg yolk; reserve remaining egg white.
3. Mix remaining flour with salt and spices. Beat into butter mixture. Stir in lemon peel and raisins.
4. Beat yeast mixture into butter mixture. Beat until batter is silky, about 10 to 15 minutes.
5. Turn into a well-greased and floured 10-inch baba or tube pan. Cover. Let rise until tripled in bulk, about 1½ hours.
6. Beat remaining egg white until foamy. Brush over top of baba.
7. Bake at 350°F about 40 minutes, until baba sounds hollow when tapped.
8. Cool on rack 10 minutes. Remove from pan. Drizzle with icing or brush with honey, if desired.

1 baba

Baba au Rhum: Prepare Baba as directed. Set in cake pan or shallow casserole. To prepare Rum Sauce: Boil ⅓ cup **water**, ⅓ cup **sugar**, and ⅓ cup **apricot jam** with **1 teaspoon lemon juice** 5 minutes. Add ½ cup **rum**. Bring just to simmering. Pour over baba. With wooden pick, poke holes in baba. Continue pouring syrup over baba until all syrup is absorbed.

869 *Filled Baba (Babki Śmietankowe)*

Baba:
2 cups butter or margarine (at room temperature)
1 cup sugar
2 eggs
3 egg whites
2½ cups all-purpose flour
Custard:
3 egg yolks
¾ cup whipping cream
¾ cup sugar
¼ teaspoon salt

1. For baba, beat butter at high speed. Gradually add sugar, creaming until fluffy.
2. Beat in whole eggs and 2 egg whites. Stir in flour; mix well.
3. For custard, combine egg yolks, cream, sugar, and salt in the top of a double boiler or in a heavy saucepan. Cook and stir until custard is thickened. Set aside to cool a few minutes.
4. Generously grease muffin-pan wells; coat with fine dry bread crumbs. Line each with 1 tablespoon dough. Spoon in 2 tablespoons custard. Top with more dough.
5. Beat reserved egg white just until foamy. Brush top of each baba.
6. Bake at 350°F 20 to 25 minutes.

About 1½ dozen

870 *Country Cheese Cake (Serowiec)*

Dough:
- 1¾ cups all-purpose flour
- ½ cup confectioners' sugar
- ¾ teaspoon baking powder
- ¼ teaspoon salt
- ¼ cup butter or margarine
- 3 egg yolks
- 3 tablespoons dairy sour cream

Filling:
- 4 eggs
- 1 egg white
- ¾ cup sugar
- 1½ pounds farmer or pot cheese or ricotta
- ½ cup dairy sour cream
- 2 tablespoons grated orange peel
- 1 teaspoon vanilla extract

1. For dough, combine flour, sugar, baking powder, and salt in a bowl. With pastry blender, cut butter into flour mixture until coarse and crumbly.
2. Beat egg yolks into sour cream. Stir into flour mixture. Knead in bowl until dough is well mixed and holds its shape.
3. Refrigerate dough until easy to roll out, at least 1 hour.
4. Roll out dough on a floured surface to fit a 13×9×2-inch pan, about a 15×11-inch rectangle.
5. Line bottom of pan, fitting dough so it comes about ⅔ of the way up sides of pan.
6. For filling, beat eggs and egg white at high speed of electric mixer until thick. Gradually add sugar, beating at high speed until stiff, not dry, peaks form.
7. Press cheese through a sieve. Fold into beaten egg mixture. Add remaining ingredients. Mix gently but thoroughly. Turn filling into dough-lined pan.
8. Bake at 350°F about 40 minutes, or until set.
9. Cool before cutting into squares.

About 16 servings

871 *Apples in Blankets (Jabłuszka w Cieście)*

- 1 pound apples, pared and cored
- 2 eggs
- ⅓ cup sugar
- Dash salt
- 1¼ cups all-purpose flour
- ⅓ cup dairy sour cream
- ¼ cup buttermilk
- Fat for deep frying heated to 365°F
- Confectioners' sugar
- Nutmeg or cinnamon (optional)

1. Slice apples crosswise to make rings about ⅜ inch thick.
2. Beat eggs with sugar until thick and foamy. Add salt. Beat in small amounts of flour alternately with sour cream and buttermilk. Beat until batter is well mixed.
3. Coat apple slices with batter. Fry in hot fat until golden.
4. Drain on paper towels. Sprinkle with confectioners' sugar. Add a dash of nutmeg or cinnamon, if desired.

About 14

872 *Raspberry Syrup (Sok Malinowy)*

- 2 cups sugar
- ½ cup water
- 2 cups fresh or frozen raspberries

1. Combine sugar and water in a saucepan.
2. Bring to boiling; add raspberries. Boil 3 minutes. Remove from heat.
3. Line a strainer or colander with cheesecloth. Set over a bowl. Turn cooked berries into cloth-lined strainer. Let drain 2 hours.
4. Discard seeds and pulp. Return juice to saucepan. Boil about 12 minutes, or until reduced to half the original amount. Skim off foam.
5. Pour into a clean jar. Cover. Store in refrigerator. Serve with fruit compote, fresh fruits, or as a sauce for cake.

About 2 cups

873 *Easter Baba (Babka Wielkanocna)*

1 cup milk
3⅓ cups all-purpose flour
2 packages active dry yeast
¼ cup lukewarm water
⅔ cup sugar
2 teaspoons salt
15 egg yolks
1 teaspoon vanilla extract
¼ teaspoon almond extract
½ cup melted butter
¾ cup mixed chopped candied citron and orange and lemon peel
½ cup chopped almonds
⅓ cup raisins
Blanched almond halves
Fine dry bread crumbs

1. Scald milk; pour into a large bowl. Slowly add ¾ cup flour to hot milk and beat thoroughly. Cool.
2. Dissolve yeast in lukewarm water 5 minutes; add 1 tablespoon of the sugar. Let stand 5 minutes. Add to cooled milk mixture; beat well.
3. Cover; let rise until doubled in bulk.
4. Add salt to egg yolks. Beat until thick and lemon-colored, about 5 minutes. Add remaining sugar and extracts; continue beating. Combine egg mixture with milk mixture, beating thoroughly. Add remaining flour; mix well.
5. Knead 10 minutes in bowl. Add butter and continue kneading 10 more minutes, or until dough leaves the fingers. Add candied peel, almonds, and raisins; knead to mix well.
6. Let rise until doubled in bulk. Punch down and let rise again.
7. Generously grease a 12-inch fluted tube pan or turban mold. Press almond halves around sides and bottom of pan. Coat with bread crumbs.
8. Punch down dough and put into prepared pan. Dough should fill a third of pan. Let rise 1 hour, or until dough fills pan.
9. Bake at 350°F about 50 minutes, or until hollow sounding when tapped on top.

1 large loaf

874 *Baba with Raisins (Babka z Rodzynkami)*

1 cup butter or margarine (at room temperature)
1½ cups confectioners' sugar
4 eggs, separated
¼ cup orange juice
4 teaspoons lemon juice
1 tablespoon grated orange or lemon peel
4 teaspoons baking powder
1½ cups all-purpose flour
1 cup cornstarch
⅓ cup confectioners' sugar
½ teaspoon salt
½ cup raisins
Fine dry bread crumbs
1 tablespoon whipping cream (optional)

1. Cream butter. Gradually add 1½ cups confectioners' sugar, beating at high speed of electric mixer. Beat in egg yolks, one at a time. Beat in orange juice, lemon juice, and orange peel.
2. Mix flour, cornstarch, and ⅓ cup confectioners' sugar.
3. With clean beaters, beat egg whites with salt until stiff, not dry, peaks form.
4. Fold half the flour mixture into the butter mixture. Fold in egg whites.
5. Add raisins to remaining flour mixture; mix well. Fold into batter.
6. Generously grease an 11-cup ring mold or baba pan. Coat with bread crumbs.
7. Turn batter into prepared pan. Brush top with cream.
8. Bake at 350°F about 40 minutes.

1 baba

875 Grandmother's Cheese Cake (Sernik Babci)

Dough:
- 1¼ cups all-purpose flour
- ¾ teaspoon baking powder
- ¼ teaspoon salt
- ¼ cup butter or margarine
- 1 egg
- 3 tablespoons dairy sour cream
- ⅓ cup confectioners' sugar

Filling:
- 6 eggs
- 2 cups confectioners' sugar
- 1½ teaspoons vanilla extract
- 1 pound farmer cheese or ricotta
- ⅔ cup melted butter
- 1½ cups unseasoned mashed potatoes
- 2 teaspoons baking powder
- ½ teaspoon nutmeg
- ½ teaspoon salt
- ¼ cup grated orange or lemon peel

1. For dough, combine flour, baking powder, and salt in a bowl. Cut in butter with a pastry blender.
2. Beat egg into sour cream. Stir into flour mixture. Stir in sugar. Knead dough until well mixed and smooth.
3. Roll dough on a floured surface into a rectangle. Line a 13×9×2-inch pan with dough, and bring dough part way up sides.
4. For filling, separate 1 egg and reserve the white. Beat remaining yolk and whole eggs with the sugar 5 minutes at high speed of electric mixer. Add vanilla extract. Beat at high speed until mixture piles softly.
5. Press cheese through a sieve. Blend cheese with butter; add potatoes, baking powder, nutmeg, and salt. Stir in orange peel. Fold into egg mixture. Turn into prepared crust in pan.
6. Bake at 350°F about 45 minutes, or until set. Cool.
7. Cool well before cutting.

About 32 pieces

876 Lamb Cake

- 2 cups sifted cake flour
- ¾ teaspoon baking powder
- ¼ teaspoon salt
- ¼ teaspoon mace
- 1 cup butter or margarine
- 1 cup plus 2 tablespoons sugar
- 2 teaspoons grated lemon peel
- 1½ teaspoons vanilla extract
- ½ teaspoon almond extract
- 4 eggs
- 1 tablespoon flour
- 2 tablespoons shortening
  Seven-Minute Frosting (see recipe)
  Shredded coconut

1. Sift together cake flour, baking powder, salt, and mace.
2. Cream butter. Gradually add sugar, creaming until fluffy. Add lemon peel and extracts.
3. Alternately beat in eggs and flour mixture.
4. Blend 1 tablespoon flour into shortening. Brush over both inside sections of a lamb mold.
5. Turn batter into face side of mold, filling it level. Spoon a small amount of batter into back side of mold, filling ears. Close and lock mold. Set on baking sheet.
6. Bake at 375°F 50 to 55 minutes.
7. Set mold on wire rack to cool 5 minutes. Remove back side. Cool 5 minutes longer. Turn out on rack to cool completely.
8. Frost with Seven-Minute Frosting. Coat with coconut.

1 lamb cake

877 Seven-Minute Frosting

- 1½ cups sugar
- ⅓ cup water
- 1 tablespoon light corn syrup
- ⅛ teaspoon salt
- 2 egg whites (unbeaten)
- ½ teaspoon vanilla extract

1. Combine sugar, water, corn syrup, salt, and egg whites in the top of a double boiler. Set over boiling water and beat at high speed 7 to 10 minutes, or until stiff peaks form when beater is lifted.
2. Remove from heat. Beat in vanilla extract.

About 5 cups

878 *Pear Compote (Kompot z Gruszek)*

8 pears or 4 cups pitted dark sweet cherries
1½ cups wine
⅔ cup sugar
⅓ cup red currant jelly
½ teaspoon vanilla extract or 1 tablespoon lemon juice
4 whole cloves
1 stick cinnamon

1. Pare pears, leaving whole with stems attached.
2. Combine wine, and remaining ingredients. Bring to boiling.
3. Add pears. Simmer until pears are transparent on the edges, about 45 minutes. (Boil cherries 2 minutes.)
4. Remove fruit to serving dish.
5. Boil syrup until very thick, about 20 minutes. Pour over fruit.
6. Chill. Serve with whipped cream or soft dessert cheese, if desired.

8 servings

879 *Berry Compote (Kompot z Malin lub Truskawek)*

1 pint strawberries or raspberries
1 cup water
½ cup sugar
½ cup white dessert wine

1. Wash and hull berries. Put into a glass bowl.
2. Boil water with sugar 5 minutes. Pour over berries and add wine. Let stand 2 hours before serving. Chill, if desired.

4 servings

880 *Fruit Compote in Spirits (Kompot w Spirytusie)*

2 pounds ripe peaches, pears, or apricots
1⅓ cups water
2 cups sugar
¾ cup white rum, vodka, or grain alcohol

1. Dip whole fruit, 1 piece at a time, in boiling water for a few seconds to loosen skin. Pull off skin; leave fruit whole.
2. Combine water with sugar in a saucepan. Boil 5 minutes.
3. Add fruits and simmer 3 minutes for small fruit; 5 minutes for large fruit.
4. Remove from heat. Skim off foam. Let stand overnight.
5. Remove fruit from syrup. Boil syrup 1 minute. Skim off foam. Pour syrup over fruit. Let stand overnight.
6. Remove fruits from syrup. Place in sterilized jars. Bring syrup to boiling; skim off foam. Add rum and pour over fruit. Seal.
7. Store in a cool, dry place at least 1 week before using.

6 to 8 servings

881 *Pear and Apple Compote (Kompot z Gruszek i Jabłek)*

2 cups water
⅔ cup sugar
6 pears, pared, cored, quartered
2 apples, pared, cored, quartered
8 whole cloves
½ cup currant or gooseberry jelly

1. Bring water with sugar to boiling in a large saucepan. Boil 5 minutes.
2. Add fruits and cloves. Simmer until fruits are tender, about 7 to 10 minutes.
3. Remove fruits and place in a serving bowl. Discard cloves. Boil syrup until only 1 cup remains.
4. Blend syrup into jelly. Return to saucepan. Bring just to boiling. Pour over fruits. Let stand 1 hour before serving, or chill.

6 to 8 servings

882 *Easter Cheese Cake (Sernik Wielkanocny)*

Dough for Grandmother's
●Cheese Cake or
●Country Cheese Cake

Cheese Filling:
6 eggs
2¼ cups confectioners' sugar
1½ pounds farmer cheese or ricotta
⅔ cup butter or margarine (at
    room temperature)
½ teaspoon salt
1½ teaspoons vanilla extract
2 teaspoons grated lemon peel
¼ cup finely chopped candied
    orange peel
⅓ cup raisins

Spread:
¾ cup thick raspberry jam or
    strawberry preserves

1. Prepare dough for crust; line pan.
2. Beat eggs at high speed until thickened. Slowly beat in sugar, beating until mixture piles softly.
3. Press cheese through a sieve. Beat cheese with butter, salt, vanilla extract, and lemon peel.
4. Fold eggs into cheese mixture. Stir in orange peel and raisins.
5. Spread jam over bottom of prepared crust in pan.
6. Turn cheese mixture into pan.
7. Bake at 325°F 45 minutes to 1 hour or until a knife inserted near center comes out clean.
8. Cool well before cutting.

32 pieces

883 *Cheese Pascha from Lwow (Pascha ze Lwowa)*

1 whole egg
4 egg yolks
2⅔ cups sugar
1 cup whipping cream
1 cup raisins or currants
2 pounds white farmer cheese
½ pound unsalted sweet butter
1 tablespoon vanilla extract
1 cup chopped blanched almonds
2 tablespoons grated orange peel

1. Beat whole egg and egg yolks with sugar until thick and creamy. Add half of cream. Turn into a saucepan. Heat almost to the boiling point, stirring constantly; do not boil. Remove from heat. Add raisins; cover.
2. Combine the rest of the cream, the cheese, butter, and vanilla extract in a large electric blender. Blend until smooth.
3. Turn cheese mixture into a bowl. Fold in the egg mixture. Add almonds and orange peel.
4. Refrigerate 4 hours. Place in a double thickness of cheese-cloth. Hang over a bowl in a cold place; let drain 24 hours. Chill. Garnish with **nuts** and **candied fruits** as desired. Serve cold. Cut small slices.

16 to 20 servings

884 *Cross Cake*

1 cup butter or margarine
1½ cups sugar
4 eggs
1 teaspoon vanilla extract
½ teaspoon salt
4 cups sifted cake flour
4 teaspoons baking powder
1⅓ cups milk
Basic Butter Frosting (see
    recipe)
Butter Cream Decorating
    Frosting (see recipe)

1. Beat butter until softened. Gradually add sugar, creaming until fluffy. Add eggs, 1 at a time, beating thoroughly after each. Add vanilla extract and salt; beat well.
2. Mix flour with baking powder; alternately add with milk to creamed mixture, beating thoroughly after each addition.
3. Turn into a greased and floured 13×9×2-inch baking pan and spread evenly to edges.
4. Bake at 350°F about 45 minutes, or until top springs back when lightly touched.
5. Cool in pan on rack 5 minutes. Turn out onto rack; cool completely.
6. Cut out 3-inch squares from the two top corners of cake.
7. Cut out 6×2-inch rectangles from the two corners of the lower section of cake, leaving the cake in the form of a cross. Frost and decorate as desired.

1 cross cake

885 *Basic Butter Frosting*

6 tablespoons butter or margarine
1½ teaspoons vanilla extract
3 cups confectioners' sugar
1½ tablespoons milk or cream

1. Cream butter with vanilla extract. Add confectioners' sugar gradually, beating thoroughly after each addition.
2. Stir in milk and beat until frosting is of spreading consistency.

About 2 cups

Lemon Butter Frosting: Follow recipe for Basic Butter Frosting. Substitute **lemon juice** for milk and add **1½ teaspoons grated lemon peel.** If desired, add a few drops yellow food coloring.

Orange Butter Frosting: Follow recipe for Basic Butter Frosting. Substitute **1½ teaspoons grated orange peel** for the vanilla extract and **1½ to 2½ tablespoons orange juice** for the milk. If a deeper orange color is desired, mix 4 drops red food coloring and 3 drops yellow food coloring with orange juice.

886 *Excellent Warsaw Paczki*
(Wyborne Warszawskie Pączki)

12 egg yolks
1 teaspoon salt
2 packages active dry yeast
¼ cup warm water
⅓ cup butter or margarine (at room temperature)
½ cup sugar
4½ cups all-purpose flour
3 tablespoons rum or brandy
1 cup whipping cream, scalded
1½ cups very thick jam or preserves (optional)
Fat for deep frying heated to 365°F

1. Beat egg yolks with salt in a small mixer bowl at high speed of electric mixer until mixture is thick and piles softly, about 7 minutes.
2. Soften yeast in warm water in a large bowl.
3. Cream butter; add sugar gradually, creaming until fluffy. Beat into softened yeast.
4. Stir one fourth of flour into yeast mixture. Add rum and half the cream. Beat in another one fourth of the flour. Stir in remaining cream. Beat in half the remaining flour. Then beat in egg yolks. Beat 2 minutes. Gradually beat in remaining flour until dough blisters.
5. Cover bowl with plastic wrap. Set in a warm place to rise. When doubled in bulk, punch down. Cover; let dough rise again until doubled. Punch down.
6. Roll dough on a floured surface to about ¾-inch thickness. Cut out 3-inch rounds. Use a regular doughnut cutter for plain. Use a biscuit cutter for filled doughnuts.
7. To fill doughnuts, place 1 teaspoonful of jam in center of half the rounds. Brush edges of rounds with water. Top with remaining rounds. Seal edges.
8. Cover doughnuts on floured surface. Let rise until doubled in bulk, about 20 minutes.
9. Fry doughnuts in hot fat until golden brown on both sides. Drain on absorbent paper. Sprinkle with cinnamon sugar, if desired.

About 3 dozen

887 *Butter Cream Decorating Frosting*

½ cup all-purpose shortening
¼ cup butter or margarine
1 teaspoon lemon extract
3 cups sifted confectioners' sugar

Beat shortening, margarine, and lemon extract together in an electric mixer bowl. Gradually beat in confectioners' sugar until frosting will hold the shape of a tube design.

About 2 cups

888 *Christmas Eve "Kutia" (Kutia Wigilijna)*

1 cup cracked wheat or bulgur
2 cups hot water
1 cup honey
2 cups water
1 teaspoon salt

1. Soak wheat in 2 cups hot water 30 minutes. Bring to boiling; cook covered until tender.
2. Cook honey with remaining 2 cups water 20 minutes. Add salt. Cool and serve with wheat.

About 4 servings

889 *Christmas Cake*

3 cups all-purpose flour
2 cups sugar
2 teaspoons baking soda
1 teaspoon allspice
1 teaspoon cinnamon
1 teaspoon nutmeg
1 teaspoon cloves
1 teaspoon salt
⅔ cup butter or margarine
2 cups buttermilk
1 cup chopped dates, raisins, or
   mixed candied fruits
½ cup chopped almonds or walnuts

1. Combine flour, sugar, baking soda, spices, and salt in a bowl. Cut in butter with pastry blender or two knives until particles resemble rice kernels. Add buttermilk; mix thoroughly. Mix in dates and nuts.
2. Turn batter into a generously greased and floured (bottom only) 9-inch tube pan or into two 8×4×3-inch loaf pans.
3. Bake at 350°F about 1 hour, or until a wooden pick comes out clean.
4. Cool in pan on wire rack 15 minutes. Remove from pan and cool completely on wire rack.

1 tube cake

890 *Marzipan (Marcepan)*

1 pound blanched almonds
1 pound confectioners' sugar
2 tablespoons orange water or rose
   water
Food coloring
Decorations (colored sugar,
   dragées, or chocolate shot)

1. Grind almonds very fine. Combine in a saucepan with sugar and flavoring. Cook until mixture leaves side of pan.
2. Roll almond mixture on flat surface to ½-inch thickness. Cut out small heart shapes. Or, shape into small fruits or vegetables.
3. Paint with appropriate food coloring or coat as desired, for example, with red sugar for "strawberries" and cocoa for "potatoes." Decorate with dragées or chocolate shot. Place on waxed paper to dry 2 hours.

2 pounds

891 # *Light Fruitcake from Warsaw*
(Keks Warszawski)

5 eggs or 3 whole eggs plus 3 egg whites
1¾ cups confectioners' sugar
¾ cup butter
1 teaspoon vanilla extract
¼ cup milk or brandy
½ teaspoon salt
3 cups sifted cake flour
2 teaspoons baking powder
3 ounces candied orange peel, finely chopped (about ¾ cup)
⅔ cup currants or raisins
⅔ cup finely chopped walnuts
½ cup sliced dried figs
½ cup diced pitted dried prunes
½ tablespoon cornstarch

1. Beat eggs with sugar at high speed of electric mixer 7 minutes.
2. Cream butter with vanilla extract until fluffy. Beat in milk and salt.
3. Mix half of flour with baking powder. Add to creamed mixture and mix thoroughly. Fold in beaten eggs, then remaining flour.
4. Mix fruits and nuts with cornstarch. Fold in to batter.
5. Butter an 11×7×3-inch loaf pan and sprinkle with bread crumbs. Turn batter into pan.
6. Bake at 350°F 50 minutes, or until a wooden pick comes out clean.
7. Cool before slicing.

1 fruitcake

892 # *Baked Apples with Red Wine*
(Jabłka na Winie Czerwonym)

8 apples, cored
Cherry or strawberry preserves
½ cup sugar
½ teaspoon mace or nutmeg
1 cup red wine
½ teaspoon vanilla extract

1. Place apples in a buttered casserole or baking dish. Fill each with preserves.
2. Blend sugar and mace; stir in wine and vanilla extract. Pour over apples. Cover.
3. Bake at 350°F 1 hour.
4. Chill 2 to 4 hours before serving.

8 servings

893 # *Twelve-Fruit Compote*

3 cups water
1 pound mixed dried fruits including pears, figs, apricots, and peaches
1 cup pitted prunes
½ cup raisins or currants
1 cup pitted sweet cherries
2 apples, peeled and sliced or 6 ounces dried apple slices
½ cup cranberries
1 cup sugar
1 lemon, sliced
6 whole cloves
2 cinnamon sticks (3 inches each)
1 orange
½ cup grapes, pomegranate seeds, or pitted plums
½ cup fruit-flavored brandy

1. Combine water, mixed dried fruits, prunes, and raisins in a 6-quart kettle. Bring to boiling. Cover; simmer about 20 minutes, or until fruits are plump and tender.
2. Add cherries, apples, and cranberries. Stir in sugar, lemon, and spices. Cover; simmer 5 minutes.
3. Grate peel of orange; reserve. Peel and section orange, removing all skin and white membrane. Add to fruits in kettle.
4. Stir in grapes and brandy. Bring just to boiling. Remove from heat. Stir in orange peel. Cover; let stand 15 minutes.

About 12 servings

894 *Dessert Puff with Fruit*

A fancy "show-off" dessert to impress family and friends.

4 eggs, slightly beaten
¾ cup skim milk
¾ cup flour
2 teaspoons sugar
¼ teaspoon salt
2 teaspoons clarified butter
4 cups assorted sliced fruits
● 1 cup Low-Fat Yogurt
    Freshly ground nutmeg

1. Combine eggs, milk, flour, sugar, and salt; beat with a fork until blended but still slightly lumpy. Heat butter in a 10-inch skillet until bubbly and sides of skillet are hot; pour batter into skillet.
2. Bake at 425°F 20 minutes. Turn oven control to 350°F; bake until golden (10 to 15 minutes). (Do not open oven door during baking. Sides of puff will rise very high; the center will rise only slightly.) Remove from oven and cut into 8 wedges; place on individual plates.
3. Spoon ½ cup fresh fruit on each wedge. Dollop fruit with yogurt; sprinkle with nutmeg. Serve immediately.

8 servings

895 *Squash and Apple Confection*

Apple and squash slices form a decorative pattern in this molded dessert. Try it also as a meat accompaniment.

3 large Golden Delicious apples
1 cup prune juice
1 cup water
¾ teaspoon ground ginger
3 eggs, beaten
1½ pounds acorn squash or pumpkin, pared and sliced
● Chicken Stock
3 tablespoons currants or dark raisins
● 1¼ cups Custard Sauce

1. Cut each apple into 12 slices; layer slices in a medium skillet. Pour prune juice, water, and ginger over. Simmer covered 5 minutes. Drain, pouring liquid into a small mixing bowl. Stir eggs into liquid.
2. Cook squash in 1 inch of stock in a covered saucepan until tender (about 5 minutes); drain.
3. Alternate half the apple and squash slices in rows in bottom of a lightly oiled 9x5x3-inch loaf pan. Sprinkle with currants; layer remaining apple and squash slices on top. Pour egg mixture over top. Place pan in larger baking pan; fill with 1 inch boiling water.
4. Bake at 375°F about 45 minutes, or until set. Cool to room temperature. Refrigerate covered 2 hours. Run knife around edge of plate; unmold on a platter. Slice; serve sauce over slices.

8 servings

896 *Banana-Sweet Potato Bake*

1 cup mashed cooked sweet potato or squash
2 medium bananas
1 cup water
½ cup instant nonfat dry-milk solids
2 egg yolks
2 tablespoons honey or sugar
½ teaspoon ground ginger
2 tablespoons dark rum, if desired
4 egg whites
● 1 cup Custard Sauce

1. Purée sweet potato, bananas, water, milk solids, egg yolks, honey, ginger, and rum in a food processor or blender. Pour into a mixing bowl.
2. Beat 4 egg whites until stiff but not dry peaks form. Fold into sweet potato mixture. Spoon into a lightly oiled 9x5x2-inch baking dish.
3. Bake at 325°F 45 minutes. Serve at room temperature, or refrigerate and serve cold. Cut into slices. Serve with Custard Sauce.

6 servings

897 *Molded Cheese Dessert*

A not-too-sweet dessert with the unusual flavor of bay leaf.

2 envelopes unflavored gelatin
1 cup cold water
1 cup double-strength coffee
1 pound pot cheese or low-fat cottage cheese
1 teaspoon vanilla extract
¼ cup sugar
2 bay leaves, broken in half
Mint leaves or watercress

1. Sprinkle gelatin over cold water in a small skillet; let stand 5 minutes. Heat, stirring occasionally, over low heat until dissolved (about 3 minutes). Pour gelatin mixture into a food processor or blender; add remaining ingredients except bay leaves and mint. Purée mixture.
2. Spoon mixture into a 1-quart mold. Push bay leaf pieces into mixture. Refrigerate covered 4 to 6 hours; unmold. Garnish with mint.

4 servings

898 *Carrot-Apricot Tart*

1 cup fresh or canned apricot halves, drained and cut into ¼-inch slices
1 pound baby carrots, cut in half lengthwise
½ teaspoon cinnamon
¾ cup carrot juice
2 eggs
½ cup instant nonfat dry-milk solids
¼ cup water
1 tablespoon brandy
¼ teaspoon nutmeg

1. Cover bottom of a 9-inch pie plate with apricots; arrange carrots in spoke design over apricots.
2. Mix remaining ingredients in a food processor or blender; pour over carrots.
3. Bake at 325°F about 45 minutes, or until set. Cool slightly. Cut into wedges to serve.

6 servings

899 *Cheese-Stuffed Strawberries*

A traditional French dessert, served in an elegant manner. If berries are small, slice them and serve the cheese mixture as a sauce.

½ cup low-fat ricotta cheese
1 teaspoon grated lemon peel
1 teaspoon fresh lemon juice
1 teaspoon honey or sugar
48 large strawberries
Mint sprigs (optional)

1. Mix cheese, lemon peel, lemon juice, and honey in a food processor or blender until fluffy; refrigerate until chilled (about 1 hour).
2. Gently scoop centers from strawberries with melon-baller or fruit knife. Fill with cheese mixture.
3. Arrange filled strawberries on small individual plates. Garnish with mint.

4 servings

900 *Pineapple-Berry Dessert*

Puréed strawberries are the sauce for this fruit dessert.

  1 **large pineapple**
  ½ **cup light rum or orange juice**
  1 **quart strawberries**

1. Cut stem and end off pineapple; cut into quarters lengthwise. Remove core and pare; cut into ½-inch slices and place in a shallow glass dish. Pour rum over pineapple; refrigerate covered 4 hours, turning slices several times.
2. Arrange pineapple slices in overlapping pattern on a large platter.
3. Halve some of the strawberries and arrange on pineapple. Purée remaining strawberries in a food processor or blender and pour into a bowl. Serve with knife and fork.

901 *Fresh Fruit with Brandy Cream*

● ½ **cup Mock Crème Fraîche**
  ¼ **cup low-fat ricotta cheese**
  2 **teaspoons brandy or orange juice**
  ¼ **teaspoon ground ginger**
  2 **teaspoons honey or sugar**
  3 **cups assorted fresh fruit**
  2 **teaspoons toasted sesame seed (optional)**

1. Mix crème fraîche, ricotta, brandy, ginger, and honey in a food processor or blender until fluffy. Refrigerate until chilled (about 1 hour).
2. Arrange fruit on individual plates. Spoon sauce over; sprinkle with sesame seed.

6 servings

902 *Peaches and Cream*

Rice is the secret of this fanciful dessert served in pretty parfait glasses for an elegant effect.

  3 **large ripe peaches, peeled**
  1½ **teaspoons fresh lemon juice**
  ½ **cup long-grain rice**
  1 **cup water**
  ½ **cup instant nonfat dry-milk solids**
  ½ **cup 2% milk**
  2 to 3 **tablespoons honey or sugar**
  ¼ **teaspoon almond extract**
    Mint sprigs

1. Purée 2 of the peaches in a food processor or blender; stir in lemon juice. Coarsely chop remaining peach.
2. Cook rice according to package instructions. Purée rice with remaining ingredients except almond extract and mint in a food processor or blender. Simmer rice mixture in a saucepan over medium heat 8 minutes; stir constantly. Remove from heat; stir in almond extract.
3. Spoon rice mixture and peach purée alternately into stemmed parfait glasses. Top with chopped peaches. Garnish with mint. Serve warm, or refrigerate until chilled.

6 servings

Note: Substitute pears, strawberries, or other fresh fruit if peaches are not available.

903 *Baked Banana and Orange Compote*

2 large navel oranges, peeled
½ teaspoon cinnamon
4 large bananas, peeled and cut
   in 1½-inch pieces
½ cup orange juice
   Cherries with stems

1. Cut oranges into ¼-inch slices; cut slices in half. Arrange orange slices in bottom of a shallow casserole; sprinkle with cinnamon.
2. Dip bananas in orange juice; arrange over oranges. Spoon remaining orange juice over fruit.
3. Bake at 400°F 15 minutes. Serve warm in compote dishes; garnish with cherries.

6 servings

904 *Baked Sherried Bananas*

6 medium bananas, cut in half
   lengthwise and crosswise
   Pineapple juice
¼ cup sherry or pineapple juice
1 tablespoon honey
¼ teaspoon ground ginger
1 tablespoon toasted sesame seed

1. Dip bananas in pineapple juice; arrange in a shallow casserole. Spoon sherry and honey over bananas; sprinkle with ginger.
2. Bake at 400°F 15 minutes. Serve in shallow bowls; sprinkle with sesame seed.

6 servings

905 *Broiled Oranges*

3 large navel oranges
3 tablespoons sweet vermouth
36 black cherries with stems

1. Cut oranges in half; cut around sections with fruit knife. Drizzle vermouth over oranges.
2. Broil 3 inches from heat until oranges are hot through (about 5 minutes).
3. Place one cherry in center of each orange half. Arrange remaining cherries around oranges on plates.

6 servings

906 *White Port Granite*

Serve this light, delicate dessert as a summer refresher.

1 tray ice cubes (about 14)
¼ cup white port wine
   Juice of 1 lemon
1½ to 2 tablespoons sugar
   Lemon slices

1. Drop ice cubes, one at a time, into a food processor or blender, following manufacturer's directions. When ice is finely ground, add wine, lemon juice, and sugar. Process until ice is in small crystals.
2. Immediately spoon into stemmed glasses, garnish with lemon slices, and serve.

4 servings (about ⅔ cup each)

Note: This recipe is excellent served as a first course.

907 *Meringue Cakes with Fruit and Custard Sauce*

4 egg whites (room temperature)
¼ teaspoon cream of tartar
¼ teaspoon salt
1½ tablespoons sugar
1½ tablespoons instant nonfat
   dry-milk solids
1 large pear, cut in ¼-inch cubes
¾ cup sliced strawberries
● 1 cup Custard Sauce
6 strawberries

1. Beat egg whites until foamy. Add cream of tartar and salt; beat until stiff, but not dry, peaks are formed, adding sugar and dry-milk solids gradually.
2. Drop meringue by large rounded tablespoonfuls onto cookie sheet lined with brown paper.
3. Place in a 500°F oven; turn oven control to 300°F and bake 15 to 20 minutes, or until light brown. Remove from oven and let cool. Remove from cookie sheet.
4. Slice meringues crosswise in half. Stir pear cubes and sliced strawberries into sauce; spoon mixture into hollow bottom halves of meringues; place tops on meringues. Garnish with strawberries.

6 servings (12 small meringues)

908 *Sliced Poached Pears in Wine*

● ½ cup Mock Crème Fraîche
¾ cup puréed cherries
⅛ teaspoon ground cloves
4 large firm-ripe pears
3 cups water
2 tablespoons lemon juice
2 large sticks cinnamon, broken
   in 1-inch pieces
1½ cups white or pink Chablis
   wine
¼ teaspoon ground cloves

1. Mix crème fraîche, cherries, and ⅛ teaspoon ground cloves. Refrigerate covered 1 hour.
2. Cut pears in half lengthwise; remove cores. Cut halves carefully into thin slices, keeping halves together. Dip pear halves into a mixture of water and lemon juice; place halves close together in a medium saucepan. Tuck cinnamon sticks around pears; pour wine over. Sprinkle pears with ¼ teaspoon ground cloves.
3. Simmer covered until pears are just tender (12 to 15 minutes). Cool slightly. Arrange pears in shallow dishes, fanning slices out slightly. Serve warm, or refrigerate and serve cold. Pass crème fraîche or spoon over pears.

8 servings

● *Note:* This recipe is also excellent served with Custard Sauce

909 *Hot Apple-Raisin Compote*

6 large apples, pared, cored, and
   cut in 1-inch pieces
½ cup golden raisins
1 stick cinnamon, broken in 3
   pieces
⅔ cup water
1 tablespoon lemon juice
2 tablespoons bourbon
1 tablespoon chopped walnuts

1. Put apples, raisins, cinnamon stick, water, and lemon juice into a saucepan. Cook covered until apples are tender (about 10 minutes). Drain; discard cinnamon stick.
2. Add bourbon to saucepan; simmer until liquid is reduced by half. Purée 1 cup of the apples and raisins with liquid in a food processor or blender; pour mixture over remaining fruit and sprinkle with walnuts.

8 servings

910 *Basic Mousse with Variations*

Low in calories, yet superb in flavor, this adaptable recipe can be used to create your own variations.

1 envelope unflavored gelatin
½ cup cold water
1 cup instant nonfat dry-milk solids
¼ cup sugar or honey
1 teaspoon vanilla extract
10 to 12 ice cubes
Mint sprigs or strawberries for garnish

1. Sprinkle gelatin over cold water in a saucepan; let stand 5 minutes. Set over low heat, stirring constantly until gelatin is dissolved (about 3 minutes).
2. Pour gelatin mixture into a food processor or blender container; add remaining ingredients except ice cubes. Process 10 seconds. Add ice cubes one at a time until mixture has consistency of heavy whipped cream.
3. Pour mixture into a serving bowl or individual stemmed glasses. Refrigerate until set (about ½ hour). Garnish with mint or strawberries.

6 servings

Note: Mousse can be unmolded, if desired. Run knife around side of bowl; dip briefly in hot water. Invert on serving plate.

Mocha Mousse: Follow recipe for Basic Mousse, adding **1 tablespoon instant coffee crystals** and **¼ teaspoon ground cinnamon** to ingredients.

Rum-Pineapple Mousse: Follow recipe for Basic Mousse, adding **1 tablespoon dark rum** to ingredients. When mousse is almost consistency of heavy whipped cream, add **1 cup crushed pineapple.** Continue adding ice cubes until desired consistency is achieved.

Ricotta Mousse: Prepare half the Basic Mousse recipe. When desired consistency is reached, add **1 tablespoon apple concentrate, 1 cup low-fat ricotta cheese, and ¼ teaspoon cinnamon.** Turn food processor on and off 2 times so ingredients are just blended.

Fruit Mousse: Follow recipe for Basic Mousse, adding **1 cup sliced fruit or berries** to ingredients.

Fruit Concentrate Mousse: Follow recipe for Basic Mousse; omit sugar and add **3 tablespoons natural fruit concentrate** to ingredients. Garnish with slices of fresh fruit or **1 to 2 cups of prepared fruit.**

Note: Natural fruit concentrates can be purchased in specialty sections of the supermarket or in gourmet food shops. Many flavors, such as peach, apple, blackberry, and strawberry, are available.

911 *Viennese Fried Cakes (Faschingskrapfen)*

½ envelope active dry yeast
⅓ cup warm water
¼ teaspoon salt
1½ teaspoons sugar
1 cup half-and-half (at room temperature)
3½ tablespoons melted butter
3 egg yolks, lightly beaten
3 cups all-purpose flour
Maraschino cherries or apricot jam
Milk
Clarified butter or butter and lard
Confectioners' sugar

1. Dissolve yeast in warm water. Stir in salt, sugar, half-and-half, melted butter, and egg yolks. Stir in 2 cups flour, and add enough additional flour to form a soft but manageable dough.
2. Knead the dough briefly, place in a floured bowl, and cover with a cloth. Let rise in a warm place until doubled in bulk (about 1 hour).
3. Knead dough down lightly and turn onto a floured board. Pull or roll the dough gently until it is ¼ inch thick. Cut dough into 2-inch rounds, using a biscuit cutter.
4. In the centers of half the rounds, place a maraschino cherry or 1 teaspoon apricot jam. Brush these rounds with milk and cover with remaining rounds, pressing the edges together very lightly.
5. Place the filled rounds on a floured baking sheet or towel and let stand for 30 minutes in a warm place.
6. Fry them a few at a time in hot butter 2 inches deep in a saucepan. Do not crowd. After placing in hot butter, cover the pan for a minute or two; then turn the cakes. When they are golden, remove from butter, and drain on paper towels.
7. Sprinkle generously with confectioners' sugar and serve.

20 cakes

912 *Widows' Kisses (Witwe Küsse)*

4 egg whites
½ cup plus 2 tablespoons granulated sugar
1 cup chopped nuts (almonds or walnuts)
¼ cup finely diced citron

1. In the top of a double boiler set over simmering water, beat egg whites with the sugar. Use a rotary beater and beat the mixture until it is fairly stiff.
2. Remove the top of double boiler from hot water and stir in nuts and citron. Drop by level tablespoons about 1 inch apart onto greased baking sheets.
3. Bake at 300°F 25 to 30 minutes. Cookies should be just lightly browned. Leave on baking sheet 1 to 2 minutes before removing to cooling rack.

About 3½ dozen cookies

913 *Tiny Turnovers (Cuscinetti di Teramo)*

2 cups all-purpose flour
2 teaspoons sugar
½ teaspoon salt
3 tablespoons cooking oil
½ to ¾ cup white wine
¾ cup marmalade or jam
Slivered almonds
Oil for frying heated to 370°F

1. Combine flour, sugar, salt, oil, and wine, mixing just enough to make a tender dough. Knead briefly and roll very thin (⅛ inch or less). Cut into 3¼-inch rounds.
2. Place 1 teaspoon marmalade mixed with a few slivered almonds on each round. Moisten edges of rounds, fold in half, and press together to seal. Spread on a tray or cutting board and let stand several hours to dry a little.
3. Fry in hot oil until golden. Remove, using slotted spoon, and drain on paper towels. Serve warm.

36 turnovers

914 *Cream Rolls (Cannoli)*

Filling:
    2 **cartons (15 ounces each) ricotta**
    2 **teaspoons vanilla extract**
    ½ **cup confectioners' sugar**
    ½ **cup finely chopped candied citron**
    ½ **cup semisweet chocolate pieces**

Shells:
    3 **cups all-purpose flour**
    ¼ **cup sugar**
    1 **teaspoon cinnamon**
    ¼ **teaspoon salt**
    3 **tablespoons shortening**
    2 **eggs, well beaten**
    2 **tablespoons white vinegar**
    2 **tablespoons cold water**
        Oil or shortening for deep frying
    1 **egg white, slightly beaten**
    ¼ **to ½ cup finely chopped blanched**
        pistachio nuts
        Sifted confectioners' sugar

1. To make filling, beat cheese with vanilla extract. Add ½ cup confectioners' sugar and beat until smooth. Fold in candied citron and semisweet chocolate pieces. Chill thoroughly.
2. To make the shells, combine flour, sugar, cinnamon, and salt. Using a pastry blender, cut in shortening until pieces are the size of small peas. Stir in eggs; blend in vinegar and cold water.
3. Turn dough onto a lightly floured surface and knead until smooth and elastic (5 to 10 minutes). Wrap in waxed paper and chill 30 minutes.
4. Fill a deep saucepan a little over half full with oil. Slowly heat oil to 360°F.
5. Roll out chilled dough to ⅛ inch thick. Using a 6×4½-inch oval pattern cut from cardboard, cut ovals from dough with a pastry cutter or sharp knife.
6. Wrap dough loosely around cannoli tubes (see Note), just lapping over opposite edge. Brush overlapping edges with egg white and press together to seal.
7. Fry shells in hot oil about 8 minutes, or until golden brown, turning occasionally. Fry only a few at a time, being careful not to crowd them. Using a slotted spoon or tongs, remove from oil, and drain over pan before removing to paper towels. Cool slightly and remove tubes. Cool completely.
8. When ready to serve, fill shells with ricotta filling. Sprinkle ends of filled shells with pistachio nuts and dust shells generously with confectioners' sugar.

About 16 filled rolls

Note: Aluminum cannoli tubes or clean, unpainted wooden sticks, 6 inches long and ¾ inch in diameter, may be used.

915 *Honey-Almond Cakes (Sospiri)*

    2½ **cups all-purpose flour**
    2 **tablespoons baking powder**
    ¼ **teaspoon baking soda**
    ½ **teaspoon salt**
    ½ **cup butter or lard**
    ½ **cup sugar**
    1 **egg, beaten**
    ½ **cup buckwheat honey or other**
        strong honey
    ½ **cup chopped almonds**
        Cinnamon sugar (optional)

1. Combine flour, baking powder, baking soda, and salt. Cream together butter, sugar, egg, and honey. Combine with flour mixture and mix well.
2. Add almonds, knead 1 minute, and form into two 7-inch-long rolls. Wrap each roll in waxed paper and chill 2 hours. Remove dough from waxed paper, cut into ¼-inch-thick slices, and place on greased cookie sheets.
3. Bake at 350°F 10 minutes, or until lightly browned. If desired, sprinkle with cinnamon-sugar.

About 4 dozen cookies

916 *Biscuit Tortoni*

⅓ cup confectioners' sugar
1 tablespoon sherry
½ cup plus 2 tablespoons fine dry macaroon crumbs
1 cup whipping cream, whipped
1 egg white

1. Fold sugar, sherry, and ½ cup macaroon crumbs into whipped cream until well blended.
2. Beat egg white until stiff, not dry, peaks are formed. Fold into whipped cream mixture.
3. Divide mixture equally into ten 2-inch heavy paper baking cups and sprinkle with the remaining crumbs. Freeze until firm.

10 servings

917 *Italian Fried Twists (Cenci)*

¼ cup butter
4 cups cake flour
⅓ cup sugar
4 eggs
2 tablespoons brandy
Oil or shortening for deep frying
Confectioners' sugar

1. In a large bowl, cut butter into flour with a pastry blender until the mixture resembles coarse crumbs. Stir in sugar.
2. In a small bowl, lightly beat the eggs with brandy. Add to flour mixture, stirring until all the flour is moistened. On a lightly floured surface, knead dough until smooth (about 5 minutes). Cover and let rest 10 minutes.
3. Fill a heavy saucepan with oil 4 inches deep; slowly heat to 400°F. Cut off a sixth of the dough at a time, and roll paper thin. Using a pastry cutter or sharp knife, cut into 8 × ¾-inch strips. Leave in strips or tie in knots. If desired, dough may also be cut in 2-inch-long diamonds.
4. Gently drop into hot oil, a few at a time, and cook 1 minute, or until lightly browned. Using a slotted spoon or tongs, lift out of oil and drain on paper towels. Cool slightly.
5. Sprinkle generously with confectioners' sugar and store, loosely covered, in a dry place.

About 8 dozen twists

918 *Italian Butter Cookies (Canestrelli)*

4 cups sifted all-purpose flour
1 cup sugar
2½ teaspoons grated lemon peel
1 tablespoon rum
4 egg yolks, beaten
1 cup firm unsalted butter, cut in pieces
1 egg white, slightly beaten

1. Combine flour, sugar, and lemon peel in a large bowl; mix thoroughly. Add rum and then egg yolks in fourths, mixing thoroughly after each addition.
2. Cut butter into flour mixture with pastry blender until particles are fine. Work with fingertips until a dough is formed.
3. Roll one half of dough at a time about ¼ inch thick on a lightly floured surface. Cut into desired shapes. Brush tops with egg white. Transfer to lightly greased cookie sheets.
4. Bake at 350°F about 15 minutes.

About 6 dozen cookies

Chocolate Torte, page 334
Walnut Torte, page 335

919 *Zuppa Inglese*

Zuppa Inglese, which means English soup, probably has more variations and stories about its origin than any other Italian food. That a rum-soaked cake should be called English soup has given much cause for comment on the origin of this wrongly named delicacy. Perhaps the most logical explanation has been that the name was given to tease the English about their love of rum, and the first Zuppa was so rum-soaked that it had to be eaten with a soup spoon.

Italian Sponge Cake
½ cup rum
2 tablespoons cold water
● Pineapple Cream Filling
● Chocolate Cream Filling
    chilled
● Whipped Cream
    Candied cherries

1. Trim corners of each of the sponge cake layers to form ovals. Save all pieces trimmed from cake. Place one layer on a platter; set other two aside.
2. Combine rum and water. Sprinkle a third of rum mixture over first cake layer and spread with desired amount of Pineapple Cream Filling. Top with second layer, sprinkle with half the remaining rum mixture, and spread with desired amount of Chocolate Cream Filling.
3. Place third layer on cake and sprinkle with remaining rum mixture. Cover cake with waxed paper and chill several hours.
4. Make a square, diamond, or heart shape from leftover pieces of cake. Place on top of cake and frost cake with Whipped Cream. If desired, decorate with Whipped Cream using a No. 27 star decorating tip. Garnish with candied cherries.
5. Store dessert in refrigerator until ready to serve.

16 to 20 servings

Note: If desired, **Seven-Minute Frosting (●   )** or **Butter Frosting (●   )** may be used to frost and decorate the dessert.

920 *Italian Sponge Cake (Pan di Spagna)*

5 egg yolks
½ cup sugar
2 tablespoons lemon juice
1 teaspoon grated lemon peel
1 teaspoon vanilla extract
½ teaspoon salt
5 egg whites
½ cup sugar
1 cup sifted cake flour

1. Combine egg yolks, ½ cup sugar, lemon juice, lemon peel, and vanilla extract. Beat 3 to 4 minutes with an electric mixer on medium-high speed; set aside.
2. Add salt to egg whites and beat until frothy. Gradually add ½ cup sugar, beating constantly until stiff peaks are formed.
3. Gently fold egg yolk mixture into beaten egg whites. Sift flour over the egg mixture, ¼ cup at a time, gently folding until just blended after each addition. Turn batter into a 9-inch tube pan (see Note).
4. Bake at 325°F 60 to 65 minutes, or until cake springs back when lightly touched or when a cake tester or wooden pick inserted comes out clean.
5. Invert and leave cake in pan until completely cooled.

One 9-inch tube cake

Note: For Zuppa Inglese, pour batter into three 11×7×1½-inch baking pans. Bake at 325°F 30 to 35 minutes.

921 *Pineapple Cream Filling (Crema d'Ananasso)*

½ cup sugar
2 tablespoons cornstarch
⅛ teaspoon salt
½ cup cold milk
1½ cups milk, scalded
3 eggs, slightly beaten
1 can (20 ounces) crushed
    pineapple, drained
1 teaspoon vanilla extract

1. Combine sugar, cornstarch, and salt in a saucepan. Gradually add cold milk, stirring well. Slowly stir in the scalded milk.
2. Stirring gently and constantly, rapidly bring mixture to boiling over direct heat and cook 3 minutes. Pour into top of double boiler and place over simmering water. Cover and cook about 12 minutes, stirring three or four times.
3. Vigorously stir about 3 tablespoons hot mixture into the eggs. Immediately blend into mixture in double boiler. Cook over simmering water 3 to 5 minutes. Stir slowly so mixture cooks evenly. Remove from heat and cool.
4. Stir in pineapple and vanilla extract. Chill.

About 4 cups filling

Chocolate Cream Filling: Follow recipe for Pineapple Cream Filling. Add **1½ ounces (1½ squares) unsweetened chocolate** to milk before scalding. Beat smooth with a rotary beater. Increase sugar to ⅔ cup and omit the pineapple.

About 2½ cups filling

922 *Butter Frosting (Ghiacciata di Burro)*

⅔ cup butter, softened
1½ teaspoons rum
1½ teaspoons vanilla extract
6 cups confectioners' sugar
1 egg white, slightly beaten
3 to 6 tablespoons half-and-half

1. Cream butter, rum, and vanilla extract. Gradually add confectioners' sugar, creaming until fluffy after each addition.
2. Stir in egg white and blend in half-and-half, a tablespoon at a time, until frosting is desired consistency.

Enough to frost and decorate a Zuppa Inglese

923 *Whipped Cream (Panna Montata)*

2 cups chilled whipping cream
6 tablespoons confectioners' sugar
2 teaspoons vanilla extract

1. Beat whipping cream, 1 cup at a time, in a chilled 1-quart bowl using chilled beaters. Beat until cream stands in peaks.
2. Put whipped cream into a large chilled bowl. Fold or beat confectioners' sugar and vanilla extract into whipped cream until blended.

4 cups whipped cream

924 *Stuffed Peaches (Pesche Ripiene)*

½ cup blanched almonds, finely chopped
½ cup macaroon crumbs (see Note)
¼ cup sugar
1 tablespoon chopped candied orange peel
6 large firm peaches
⅓ cup sherry or Marsala

1. Combine almonds, macaroon crumbs, 2 tablespoons sugar, and orange peel; set aside.
2. Peel peaches, cut in half, and remove pits. Lightly fill peach halves with almond mixture. Put two halves together and secure with wooden picks. Place in a 10×6-inch baking dish, pour sherry over peaches, and sprinkle with remaining sugar.
3. Bake at 350°F 15 minutes. Serve either hot or cold.

6 servings

Note: To make macaroon crumbs, grind enough Macaroons (below) in electric blender to make ½ cup crumbs.

925 *Queen's Biscuits (Biscotti di Regina)*

4 cups sifted all-purpose flour
1 cup sugar
1 tablespoon baking powder
¼ teaspoon salt
1 cup shortening
2 eggs, slightly beaten
½ cup milk
⅔ to ¾ cup sesame seed

1. Combine flour, sugar, baking powder, and salt in a mixing bowl. Cut in shortening with a pastry blender or two knives until pieces are the size of small peas.
2. Stir in eggs and milk, one tablespoon at a time. Mix together thoroughly to make a soft dough.
3. Break off small pieces of dough, and roll between palms of hands to form rolls about 1½ inches long. Flatten slightly and roll in sesame seed. Place about ¾ inch apart on lightly greased cookie sheets.
4. Bake at 375°F 12 to 15 minutes, or until cookies are lightly browned.

About 6 dozen cookies

926 *Macaroons (Amaretti)*

¾ cup whole blanched almonds
2 egg whites
¼ teaspoon salt
1 cup sugar
½ teaspoon almond extract

1. Using an electric blender or nut grinder, finely grind almonds; set aside.
2. Beat egg whites with salt until frothy. Beat in sugar, 1 tablespoon at a time, beating thoroughly after each addition. Continue beating until stiff peaks are formed.
3. Fold in ground almonds with almond extract. Drop by teaspoonfuls about 1 inch apart on unglazed paper (baking parchment or brown) on a cookie sheet.
4. Bake at 350°F about 20 minutes, or until very lightly browned.

About 3 dozen macaroons

927 *Apple Tart (Torta di Mele)*

½ cup butter
1 teaspoon grated lemon peel
1 teaspoon lemon juice
½ cup sugar
4 egg yolks, well beaten
2 cups all-purpose flour
¼ teaspoon salt
⅛ teaspoon baking soda
4 egg whites
½ teaspoon vanilla extract
⅔ cup sugar
¾ cup walnuts, finely chopped
2 large apples, coarsely shredded

1. Cream butter with lemon peel and juice. Gradually add ½ cup sugar, creaming well. Add egg yolks in halves, beating well after each addition.
2. Blend flour, salt, and baking soda. Add in thirds to creamed mixture, beating until blended after each addition. Chill thoroughly.
3. Beat egg whites with vanilla extract until frothy. Gradually add the ⅔ cup sugar, beating well; continue beating until stiff peaks are formed. Fold in nuts and apples.
4. Roll out two thirds of the dough and line bottom of a 13×9-inch baking pan. Turn nut-apple mixture into pan and spread evenly into corners.
5. Roll pieces of remaining dough into pencil-thin strips and arrange lattice-fashion over top. Press strips slightly into filling.
6. Bake at 325°F 35 to 40 minutes, or until lightly browned. Set aside on rack to cool completely. Cut into squares and, if desired, serve topped with small scoops of vanilla ice cream.

One 13×9-inch tart

928 *St. Joseph's Day Cream Puffs (Zeppole di San Giuseppe)*

1 cup hot water
½ cup butter
1 tablespoon sugar
½ teaspoon salt
1 cup sifted all-purpose flour
4 eggs
1 teaspoon grated orange peel
1 teaspoon grated lemon peel
● Ricotta filling; use one-half recipe)

1. Combine water, butter, sugar, and salt in a saucepan; bring to boiling. Add flour, all at once, and beat vigorously with a wooden spoon until mixture leaves the sides of pan and forms a smooth ball (about 3 minutes). Remove from heat.
2. Quickly beat in eggs one at a time, beating until smooth after each one is added. Continue beating until mixture is smooth and glossy. Add orange and lemon peel; mix thoroughly. Drop by tablespoonfuls 2 inches apart on a lightly greased baking sheet.
3. Bake at 450°F 15 minutes. Turn oven control to 350°F and bake 15 to 20 minutes, or until golden. Cool on wire racks.
4. To serve, cut a slit in side of each puff and fill with ricotta filling.

About 18 puffs

Note: If desired, puffs may be filled with Whipped Cream (●) or Pineapple Cream Filling (●).

929 *Spumone*

½ cup sugar
⅛ teaspoon salt
1 cup milk, scalded
3 egg yolks, beaten
1 cup whipping cream
½ ounce (½ square) unsweetened chocolate, melted
2 teaspoons rum extract
1 tablespoon sugar
⅛ teaspoon pistachio extract
2 drops green food coloring
½ cup whipping cream, whipped
1 maraschino cherry
1 tablespoon sugar
6 unblanched almonds, finely chopped
¼ teaspoon almond extract
½ cup whipping cream, whipped

1. Stir ½ cup sugar and salt into scalded milk in the top of a double boiler. Stir until sugar is dissolved.
2. Stir about 3 tablespoons of the hot milk into the egg yolks. Immediately return to double boiler top. Cook over boiling water, stirring constantly, about 5 minutes, or until mixture coats a spoon. Remove from heat and cool.
3. Stir in 1 cup whipping cream and divide mixture equally into two bowls.
4. Add melted chocolate to mixture in one bowl and mix thoroughly. Set in refrigerator.
5. Add rum extract to remaining mixture and pour into refrigerator tray. Freeze until mushy.
6. Turn into a chilled bowl and beat until mixture is smooth and creamy. Spoon into a chilled 1-quart mold and freeze until firm.
7. Fold 1 tablespoon sugar, pistachio extract, and food coloring into ½ cup whipping cream, whipped. Spoon over firm rum ice cream; freeze until firm.
8. When pistachio cream becomes firm, place the maraschino cherry in the center and return to freezer.
9. Fold 1 tablespoon sugar, chopped almonds, and almond extract into remaining ½ cup whipping cream, whipped. Spoon over firm pistachio cream. Freeze until firm.
10. When almond cream is firm, pour chocolate ice cream mixture into refrigerator tray and freeze until mushy.
11. Turn into a chilled bowl and beat until mixture is smooth and creamy. Spoon mixture over firm almond cream. Cover mold with aluminum foil or waxed paper. Return to freezer and freeze 6 to 8 hours, or until very firm.
12. To unmold, quickly dip mold into warm water and invert. Cut spumone into wedge-shaped pieces.

6 to 8 servings

930 *Rum Cream (Mascarpone in Coppe)*

2 packages (3 ounces each) cream cheese, softened
3 egg yolks
⅓ cup sugar
2 tablespoons rum
  Ladyfingers

1. Beat cream cheese until very light and fluffy; set aside.
2. Combine egg yolks and sugar, beating until very thick. Thoroughly blend in rum.
3. Pour egg-yolk mixture over cream cheese and fold in gently.
4. Fill 4 champagne or wine glasses to within ½ inch of rim. Chill 2 hours. Serve with ladyfingers.

4 servings

931 *Marsala Custard (Zabaglione)*

6 egg yolks
½ cup sugar
⅛ teaspoon salt
1 cup Marsala

1. In a bowl, beat egg yolks with sugar and salt until lemon colored. Stir in Marsala.
2. Cook in double boiler over simmering water. Beat constantly with rotary beater until mixture foams up and begins to thicken.
3. Turn into sherbet glasses and chill until serving time.

About 6 servings

932 *Cheese and Fruit (Formaggio e Frutta)*

Although used in many entrées, cheese is the most popular of Italian desserts whether served alone or accompanied by sweet, succulent fruits. An Italian family dinner usually is ended with fruit, cheese, and black coffee. Following are a few Italian dessert cheeses with a short description of each and the typical fruit they would usually accompany.

Bel Paese—a soft, mild cheese of the North and often served with ripe cherries or plums.

Gorgonzola—the most popular of the dessert cheeses, a creamy, tangy cheese veined with green mold; often served with sliced fresh pears, ripe Italian bananas, or quartered apples.

Stracchino—a tangy goat's milk cheese of Milan which may be accompanied by any number of fruits including peaches and grapes.

Provolone—whether the pear-shape Provolone, round Provolette, or sausage-shape Provolone salami, this is a favorite when accompanied by quartered apples and small slices of watermelon.

Caciocavallo—typifying a tapering beet root, this smoked cheese is delicious when served as a dessert with small crackers.

Ricotta—a soft, bland pot cheese often used in baking, this can be served as a dessert when accompanied by berries and figs.

933 *Italian Strawberry Water Ice (Granita di Fragole)*

2 cups sugar
1 cup water
4 pints fresh ripe strawberries, rinsed and hulled
⅓ cup orange juice
¼ cup lemon juice

1. Combine sugar and water in a saucepan; stir and bring to boiling. Boil 5 minutes; let cool.
2. Purée the strawberries in an electric blender or force through a sieve or food mill. Add juices to a mixture of the cooked syrup and strawberries; mix well.
3. Turn into refrigerator trays, cover tightly, and freeze.
4. About 45 minutes before serving time, remove trays from freezer to refrigerator to allow the ice to soften slightly. Spoon into sherbet glasses or other serving dishes.

About 2 quarts water ice

934 *Ricotta Pie (Torta di Ricotta)*

Pastry:
2 cups all-purpose flour
½ teaspoon salt
1 cup shortening
2 egg yolks, slightly beaten
1 to 2 tablespoons cold water

Filling:
1½ pounds ricotta
¼ cup flour
2 tablespoons grated orange peel
2 tablespoons grated lemon peel
1 tablespoon vanilla extract
⅛ teaspoon salt
4 eggs
1 cup sugar
2 tablespoons confectioners' sugar

1. To make pastry, combine flour with salt. Cut in shortening with a pastry blender until it is the size of small peas. Gradually sprinkle egg yolks over mixture; mix until thoroughly combined. Stir in just enough water to hold dough together.
2. Shape pastry into a ball and flatten on a lightly floured surface. Roll out to form a circle about 11 inches in diameter and ⅛ inch thick. Fit dough into a 9-inch round layer cake pan. (Handle dough carefully as it breaks easily.) Trim dough, leaving a ½-inch border around top of pan. Pinch dough between index finger and thumb to make it stand about ¼ inch high around edge; set aside.
3. For filling, combine cheese, flour, orange peel, lemon peel, vanilla extract, and salt; set aside. Beat eggs until foamy. Gradually add sugar, and continue beating until eggs are thick and pile softly. Stir eggs into ricotta mixture until well blended and smooth. Pour filling into pastry.
4. Bake at 350°F about 50 to 60 minutes, or until filling is firm and pastry is golden brown. Cool on wire rack. Sift confectioners' sugar over top before serving.

8 to 10 servings

935 *Bread Pudding (Capirotada)*

2 cups firmly packed dark brown sugar
1 quart water
1 stick cinnamon
1 clove
6 slices toast, cubed
3 apples, pared, cored, and sliced
1 cup raisins
1 cup chopped blanched almonds
½ pound Monterey Jack or similar cheese, cubed

1. Put brown sugar, water, cinnamon, and clove into a saucepan and bring to boiling; reduce heat and simmer until a light syrup is formed. Discard spices and set syrup aside.
2. Meanwhile, arrange a layer of toast cubes in a buttered casserole. Cover with a layer of apples, raisins, almonds, and cheese. Repeat until all ingredients are used. Pour syrup over all.
3. Bake at 350°F about 30 minutes.
4. Serve hot.

6 servings

936 *Coconut Flan*

Flan is a baked custard dessert which Mexico has adopted from Spain. A caramelized layer is prepared in the bottom of the baking dish before the custard is poured in, so when the finished dessert is turned out it has a caramel topping. This version is flavored with coconut.

Caramel Topping:
  ½ cup granulated sugar
  2 tablespoons water
Custard:
  2 cups milk
  4 eggs
  ¼ cup sugar
  ⅛ teaspoon salt
  ½ teaspoon vanilla extract
  ⅓ cup shredded or flaked coconut

1. For caramel topping, heat sugar and water in a small skillet, stirring constantly, until sugar melts and turns golden brown.
2. Pour syrup into a 1-quart baking dish or 6 custard cups, tipping to coat bottom and part way up sides. Set dish aside while preparing custard.
3. For custard, scald milk. Beat eggs; beat in sugar, salt, and vanilla extract. Gradually beat scalded milk into egg mixture. Strain into prepared baking dish or custard cups. Sprinkle top with coconut.
4. Place baking dish in pan containing hot water which comes at least 1 inch up sides of dish.
5. Bake at 325°F about 45 minutes for individual custard cups, or 1 hour for baking dish.

6 servings

937 *Quick Flan*

This is a somewhat simpler recipe for flan, made with sweetened condensed milk and "baked" in a pressure cooker. The flavor's a bit different, too.

  ¼ cup granulated sugar
  4 eggs
  1 can (14 ounces) sweetened
      condensed milk
  ½ can water
  1 teaspoon vanilla extract

1. Select a pan of at least 1-quart capacity which will fit inside pressure cooker. Spread sugar over bottom of pan. Heat over very low heat, stirring constantly, until sugar melts and turns golden brown. Remove from heat.
2. Beat eggs in a bowl; beat in milk, water, and vanilla extract.
3. Pour milk-egg mixture into sugar-coated pan.
4. Place about 1 inch of water in pressure cooker. Place filled pan inside cooker. Lay a sheet of waxed paper over top of milk-egg mixture. Place cover on cooker and heat following manufacturer's directions; cook 10 minutes.
5. Cool, then chill before serving.

6 servings

938 *Almond Snow*

  2 cups milk
  ½ cup sugar
  ¼ cup ground blanched almonds
  4 egg whites
    Pinch salt
  1 tablespoon kirsch
    Toasted slivered almonds

1. Scald milk. Stir in sugar until dissolved. Add almonds. Cook over very low heat about 15 minutes. Cool.
2. Meanwhile, beat egg whites with salt until stiff, not dry, peaks form. Fold egg whites into milk mixture. Stir in kirsch.
3. Butter top of a double boiler; pour in mixture; cover. Cook over hot (not boiling) water until mixture is firm. Chill.
4. Unmold onto serving plate and stud with slivered almonds.

6 servings

939 *Neapolitan Fondant Roll (Fondante Napoletana)*

1 egg white
3 cups confectioners' sugar
1 teaspoon vanilla extract
4 tablespoons unsalted butter, softened
3 drops red food coloring
3 drops green food coloring
½ cup finely chopped toasted almonds

1. Beat egg white until it forms soft peaks. Sift confectioners' sugar into egg white and combine thoroughly. Add vanilla extract; mix well. Cream butter until it is fluffy, add to the sugar mixture, and beat mixture until it is as fluffy as possible.
2. Divide creamed mixture into 3 equal parts. Blend red food coloring into one part, green into another, and leave remaining part white. Chill in refrigerator until firm enough to handle (about 1 hour).
3. With a spatula that has been dipped in cold water, shape the green part into a 7×3-inch rectangle on a piece of waxed paper. Spread the white part on the green, and the red on the white, forming a rectangle about ½ inch thick.
4. Using waxed paper, roll up rectangle from wide edge into a roll with the green on the outside. Chill 30 minutes, unwrap, and coat well with nuts. Rewrap in waxed paper, and chill in refrigerator 12 hours.
5. To serve, remove paper and cut in ¼-inch slices.

About 40 slices

940 *Rice with Milk (Arroz con Leche)*

This dessert is similar to rice pudding, but is not as firm. It may be served hot or cold.

1 cup uncooked rice
1 cup sugar
1 cinnamon stick
1 can (14 ounces) sweetened condensed milk
1 quart milk
1½ teaspoons vanilla extract

1. Put all ingredients into a saucepan; stir. Bring to boiling, then reduce heat to low. Cover and cook until rice is tender, about 2 minutes; stir occasionally to prevent sticking. Remove cinnamon stick.
2. The dessert will be fairly runny. Serve hot or chilled.

6 to 8 servings

941 *Sherried Almond Torte*

4 eggs, separated
½ cup sugar
1 cup sifted all-purpose flour
1 teaspoon baking powder
¼ teaspoon salt
⅓ cup melted butter or margarine, cooled
1 teaspoon vanilla extract
½ teaspoon almond extract (optional)

Sauce and Topping:
2 cups sugar
2 cups water
½ cup sherry
¾ cup toasted slivered almonds

1. Beat egg whites until foamy; gradually add 4 tablespoons of the sugar and continue beating until soft peaks form.
2. Beat egg yolks with remaining 4 tablespoons of sugar. Gradually fold beaten yolks into beaten whites.
3. Sift flour, baking powder, and salt together. Sprinkle over egg mixture about ¼ cup at a time and fold in gently. Fold in butter, vanilla extract, and almond extract (if used).
4. Pour into a greased 9-inch square baking pan.
5. Bake at 375°F about 30 minutes, or until golden brown. Remove from oven and pierce all over with a long-handled kitchen fork or ice pick, making holes through to bottom.
6. Meanwhile, prepare sauce. Combine sugar and water in a saucepan and boil over low heat, stirring occasionally, to soft ball stage (234°F). Stir in sherry. Pour hot sauce over hot cake, sprinkling entire top with almonds as last third of sauce is poured over top. Let stand in baking pan until thoroughly cooled. Serve from pan, or remove to a serving plate.

8 to 10 servings

942 Viceroy's Dessert (Mexican Trifle)

4 eggs, separated
¾ cup sugar
1 cup milk
1 cup dry sherry
1 teaspoon vanilla extract
Pinch salt
1 cup whipping cream
1 tablespoon confectioners' sugar
2 tablespoons brandy
1 pound sponge cake or ladyfingers
Apricot preserves
Grated semisweet chocolate
Toasted slivered almonds

1. Place egg yolks and sugar in top of a double boiler; beat until evenly mixed, then beat in milk. Place over boiling water and cook until thickened, stirring constantly. Stir in ½ cup of the sherry and vanilla extract. Cool; set aside.
2. Beat egg whites with salt until stiff, not dry, peaks form. Beat cream with confectioners' sugar until stiff; stir in brandy. Fold egg whites into whipped cream mixture. Set aside.
3. Slice sponge cake into ½-inch-thick slices (or split ladyfingers). Spread with apricot preserves.
4. Arrange one layer in 2-quart serving dish (preferably glass, as the finished dessert is pretty). Sprinkle with some of remaining sherry. Spread with a layer of one-third of the custard mixture. Add another layer of cake, sprinkle with sherry, and spread with a third of the cream-egg-white mixture. Repeat layers until all ingredients are used, ending with a layer of cream-egg-white mixture.
5. Sprinkle with chocolate and almonds. Chill in refrigerator several hours.

6 to 8 servings

943 Royal Eggs

This unusual dessert is typical of those created by the Spanish nuns, who were responsible for a number of the elegant dishes which combined Indian and European ingredients.

¼ cup raisins
½ cup dry sherry
12 egg yolks
2 cups sugar
1 cup water
1 cinnamon stick
¼ cup slivered almonds

1. Soak raisins in ¼ cup of the sherry.
2. Beat egg yolks until they form a ribbon when poured from the beater.
3. Pour into a buttered shallow pan. Set this pan in another larger pan with about 1 inch of water in it.
4. Bake at 325°F about 20 to 25 minutes, or until set.
5. Remove from oven and cool on a wire rack.
6. Cut cooked, cooled eggs into cubes.
7. Meanwhile, combine sugar, water, and cinnamon stick in a saucepan and bring to boiling. Reduce heat and simmer about 5 minutes, stirring until all sugar is dissolved. Remove cinnamon stick.
8. Carefully place egg cubes in saucepan of sauce. Continue simmering over very low heat until cubes are well-saturated with the syrup. Add soaked raisins and remaining sherry. Sprinkle with slivered almonds.

6 servings

944 Orange Liqueur Mousse

1 package (3 ounces)
    orange-flavored gelatin
1 cup boiling water
¼ cup cold water
¼ cup orange liqueur
1 cup whipping cream
Whipped cream (optional)
Shredded coconut (optional)

1. Dissolve gelatin in boiling water. Add cold water and cool mixture to room temperature. Stir in orange liqueur. Chill in refrigerator until mixture starts to thicken (about 30 minutes).
2. Whip cream until it piles softly. Gradually add gelatin mixture, stirring gently until evenly blended.
3. Pour into a mold. Chill until set.
4. Turn out of mold onto serving plate and top with additional whipped cream and coconut, if desired.

4 to 6 servings

945 *Almendrado*

The colors of the Mexican flag and the Mexican eagle are represented in this red, white, and green layered gelatin dessert served with creamy custard sauce.

1 tablespoon unflavored gelatin
½ cup sugar
1 cup cold water
4 egg whites
½ teaspoon almond extract
   Red and green food coloring
1 cup finely ground almonds
   Custard Sauce with Almonds

1. Mix gelatin and sugar in a saucepan. Stir in water. Set over low heat and stir until gelatin and sugar are dissolved. Chill until slightly thickened.
2. Beat egg whites until stiff, not dry, peaks are formed. Fold into gelatin mixture along with almond extract. Beat until mixture resembles whipped cream. Divide equally into 3 portions. Color one portion red, another green, and leave the last one white.
3. Pour red mixture into an 8-inch square dish or pan. Sprinkle with half of the almonds. Pour in white mixture and sprinkle with remaining almonds. Top with green layer. Chill thoroughly.
4. Cut into portions and serve with custard sauce.

12 servings

Custard Sauce with Almonds: Scald **2 cups milk**. Mix **4 egg yolks** and **¼ cup sugar** in the top of a double boiler. Add scalded milk gradually, stirring constantly. Cook over boiling water, stirring constantly until mixture coats a spoon. Remove from water and stir in **¼ teaspoon almond extract** and **½ cup toasted sliced almonds**. Cool; chill thoroughly.

About 2½ cups

946 *Coffee Liqueur Mold*

1 envelope unflavored gelatin
¼ cup coffee liqueur
1 cup strong hot coffee
¼ cup sugar
1 cup whipping cream
   Whipped cream (optional)
¼ cup chopped pecans (optional)

1. Soften gelatin in coffee liqueur. Dissolve in hot coffee. Add sugar and stir until dissolved. Cool to lukewarm. Stir in cream.
2. Pour into a mold. Chill until set.
3. To serve, turn out of mold onto serving plate. If desired, top with whipped cream and sprinkle with chopped pecans.

4 to 6 servings

947 *Buñuelos*

Buñuelos are often described as Mexican fritters, but because they are so thin and crisp they're more like a deep-fried cookies. And that's how they are usually served, as a snack or finger dessert. Sometimes they are made small, but are more fun when large.

4 cups all-purpose flour
2 tablespoons sugar
1 teaspoon baking powder
1 teaspoon salt
2 eggs, well beaten
¾ to 1 cup milk
¼ cup butter or margarine, melted
   Oil for deep frying heated to
      365°F
   Granulated sugar-cinnamon
      mixture for dusting

1. Mix flour with sugar, baking powder, and salt in a bowl.
2. Combine beaten eggs and ¾ cup of the milk. Stir into dry ingredients to make a stiff dough; add more milk if needed to moisten all dry ingredients. Stir in butter.
3. Turn dough onto a lightly floured surface and knead 1 to 2 minutes until smooth. Divide dough into 24 balls. Roll each ball into a round about 6 inches in diameter.
4. Fry each round in hot deep fat until delicately browned, turning to fry on second side. Drain on absorbent paper. Sprinkle with sugar-cinnamon mixture while still warm.

2 dozen buñuelos

948 *Churros*

Oil for deep frying
1 lime or lemon, cut in half
1 cup water
1 tablespoon sugar
1 teaspoon salt
1½ cups all-purpose flour
1 large egg
Granulated sugar

1. Start heating oil in a deep kettle or saucepan; add lime or lemon halves.
2. Put water, sugar, and salt into a saucepan and heat to boiling.
3. Remove from heat and beat in flour until smooth. Add egg and continue to beat until mixture is smooth and satiny.
4. Remove lime pieces from the oil, which should be between 365° and 375°F. Force batter through pastry tube into hot fat. Fry until golden brown.
5. Remove from fat and drain on absorbent paper. Break into 3-inch lengths. Roll in granulated sugar.

About 1 dozen 3-inch churros

949 *Sopaipillas*

Sopaipillas are little pillow-shaped deep-fried pastries. They may be served plain as a bread, or as suggested here, sprinkled with cinnamon-sugar as a dessert. Sometimes they are topped with syrup.

2 cups sifted all-purpose flour
2 teaspoons baking powder
1 teaspoon salt
2 tablespoons shortening
⅔ to ¾ cup cold water
Oil or shortening for deep frying heated to 365°F
Cinnamon sugar

1. Sift flour, baking powder, and salt together into bowl. Cut in shortening until mixture resembles coarse crumbs. Sprinkle water over top and work in gradually until dough will just hold together (as for pie pastry).
2. Turn out on a lightly floured surface and knead gently about 30 seconds. Roll out as thin as possible. Cut into 2-inch squares.
3. Fry one or two at a time in heated fat, turning until puffed and golden brown on both sides.
4. Drain on absorbent paper. Sprinkle with cinnamon sugar while still hot.

2½ to 3 dozen

950 *Gâteau du Mardi-Gras*

Meringue Circles:
3 egg whites
½ teaspoon almond extract
¼ teaspoon salt
¾ cup firmly packed brown sugar
½ cup chopped cashews
1 teaspoon multicolored nonpareilles or colored sugar
Filling:
1 package (6 ounces) semisweet chocolate pieces
1 package (8 ounces) cream cheese
1 tablespoon milk
1 teaspoon vanilla extract
⅛ teaspoon salt
¾ cup firmly packed brown sugar
½ cup whipping cream, whipped

1. For meringue circles, cut four 8-inch circles of brown or waxed paper.
2. Beat egg whites with almond extract and ¼ teaspoon salt until light and foamy. Add brown sugar gradually while beating until stiff and glossy. Fold in cashews.
3. Spread meringue on paper circles; slide onto cookie sheets. Sprinkle top of 1 circle with nonpareilles.
4. Bake at 300°F 35 minutes. Peel off paper from meringue circles.
5. For filling, melt chocolate pieces over hot, not boiling, water. Cool about 10 minutes.
6. Beat cream cheese until creamy. Blend in milk, vanilla extract, and salt. Add brown sugar gradually, beating until smooth. Add cooled melted chocolate and blend well. Fold in whipped cream.
7. Spread a fourth of the filling on each of the 3 plain meringue circles. Stack circles and top with decorated circle. Cover sides with remaining filling. Chill overnight.

12 to 15 servings

951 Sherried Raisin-Rice Pudding

⅔ cup raisins
¼ cup sherry
1 cup uncooked rice
1 teaspoon grated lemon peel
Dash salt
1½ cups water
3 cups milk
1 cup sugar
½ teaspoon cinnamon
1 egg, beaten
Whipped cream (optional)

1. Soak raisins in sherry while preparing rest of pudding.
2. Put rice, lemon peel, salt, and water in a saucepan. Bring to boiling, reduce heat, cover, and cook over very low heat until all water is absorbed (about 10 to 15 minutes).
3. Stir in milk, sugar, and cinnamon and cook over very low heat, stirring frequently, until all milk has been absorbed.
4. Stir in soaked raisins, then beaten egg. Continue to heat 1 or 2 minutes, stirring constantly, until egg has cooked.
5. Turn pudding into a serving dish. Chill in refrigerator.
6. Serve with whipped cream, if desired.

6 to 8 servings

952 Fresh Pineapple and Almond Pudding

The term "pudding" is somewhat of a misnomer for this dessert, which resembles the luscious English Trifle, but uses readily available and popular Mexican foods—fresh pineapple, almonds, and the inevitable cinnamon flavor.

2 cups pared diced fresh pineapple
½ cup sugar
½ cup ground blanched almonds
½ cup dry sherry
4 egg yolks, beaten
¼ teaspoon cinnamon
1 dozen ladyfingers, or 12 (4×1-inch) slices sponge or angel food cake
½ cup orange marmalade
½ cup dairy sour cream
1 tablespoon sugar
Toasted slivered almonds

1. Combine pineapple, ½ cup sugar, ground almonds, ¼ cup of the sherry, egg yolks, and cinnamon in a saucepan. Cook over low heat, stirring constantly, until thickened. Cool.
2. Meanwhile, split ladyfingers and spread with marmalade. (If using cake slices, they may be toasted lightly if very soft, but do not split before spreading with marmalade.)
3. Arrange half the spread ladyfingers or cake slices in bottom of a 1½-quart serving dish. Sprinkle with 2 tablespoons sherry. Spoon half the pineapple mixture on top. Repeat layers of ladyfingers, sherry, and pineapple mixture.
4. Set in refrigerator until well chilled (at least 1 hour).
5. Sweeten sour cream with 1 tablespoon sugar. Spread over top of chilled dessert. Decorate with toasted almonds.

6 to 8 servings

953 Mexican Custard (Jericalla)

This custard is light and less rich than that in flan. It is typically heavily spiced with cinnamon sticks, which are baked right with the custard.

1 quart milk
1 cup sugar
3 or 4 cinnamon sticks
⅛ teaspoon salt
4 eggs
1 teaspoon vanilla extract

1. Combine milk, sugar, and cinnamon sticks in saucepan. Bring to scalding point, stirring constantly. Remove from heat and cool to lukewarm.
2. Meanwhile, beat eggs in a 1½-quart casserole. Gradually beat in milk-sugar mixture; stir in vanilla extract. Place in a shallow pan of water.
3. Bake at 325°F about 1 hour, or until custard is set.
4. Serve warm or cooled.

About 10 servings

954 Spiked Watermelon

1 large ripe watermelon
2 cups amber rum

1. Cut a hole 2½ inches wide and 2 inches deep in the watermelon rind. Pour rum through hole and replace rind.
2. Chill 24 hours. Serve ice-cold slices.

955 *Anise Cookies*

1 package active dry yeast
½ cup warm water
2 teaspoons salt
5 cups all-purpose flour
3 tablespoons sugar
1 cup each butter and vegetable shortening (at room temperature)
4 teaspoons anise extract
1 teaspoon baking powder
Red and green decorating sugar

1. Dissolve yeast in water in a large bowl. Add salt and about 1 cup flour; mix very well. Add all other ingredients except the remaining flour and baking powder; mix thoroughly. Add remaining flour and baking powder; mix well.
2. Make 6 or 8 balls; with the palm of your hand, make long, thin rolls (about the size of the ring finger) and cut them into squares.
3. Place pieces, leaving space between them, on a cookie sheet. Make a cut on top of each.
4. Bake at 350°F about 25 minutes, or until golden brown.
5. Remove from cookie sheet and coat with red and green sugar. Cool on wire racks.

About 10 dozen

956 *Mexican Christmas Cookies* (Biscochos)

1 cup vegetable shortening
2 teaspoons grated orange peel
1¼ cups sugar
1 egg
⅓ cup fresh orange juice
3¾ cups all-purpose flour
¼ teaspoon salt
1 teaspoon cinnamon
½ teaspoon ground cloves
½ cup finely chopped pecans
Very fine sugar

1. Cream shortening, orange peel, and sugar until light. Beat in egg, then orange juice.
2. Blend flour, salt, and spices. Stir into creamed mixture. Mix in pecans.
3. Wrap dough and chill overnight.
4. Next day, roll out a small amount at a time on lightly floured surface to ⅛-inch thickness. Cut in desired shapes with fancy cookie cutter.
5. Put on lightly greased cookie sheets.
6. Bake at 375°F 8 to 10 minutes, or until golden brown.
7. Sprinkle with sugar while still warm.

About 10 dozen

957 *Polvorones*

These buttery rich pecan cookies are sometimes called Mexican Wedding Cakes, Bride's Cakes, or simply Polvorones, which Mexicans translate to mean sugar cookies—not because there is much sugar in the dough, but because the warm baked cookies are rolled in confectioners' sugar. Literally the name polvorones means "dusted ones."

1 cup butter or margarine, softened
1 teaspoon vanilla extract
½ cup confectioners' sugar
2 cups all-purpose flour
¼ teaspoon salt
1 cup finely chopped pecans
Confectioners' sugar

1. Cream butter with vanilla extract until light and fluffy. Add sugar, creaming well. Mix in flour and salt, then pecans.
2. Shape dough into 1-inch balls and flatten slightly. Place on ungreased cookie sheets.
3. Bake at 350°F 25 to 30 minutes, or until lightly browned.
4. Remove from cookie sheets and cool slightly. Roll in confectioners' sugar.

About 4 dozen cookies

958 *Baked Bananas*

6 ripe bananas
¼ cup lime juice
½ cup orange juice
¼ cup packed brown sugar
3 tablespoons amber rum
Cinnamon
Butter
1½ cups grated coconut

1. Peel bananas and coat them with lime juice to keep them from darkening. Cut bananas in half lengthwise and arrange in a well-buttered baking dish. Mix orange juice, brown sugar, and rum. Pour over bananas and sprinkle with cinnamon. Dot with butter and cover with grated coconut.
2. Bake at 400°F 12 to 15 minutes.

959 *Empanadas de Dulce*

Empanadas are Mexican-style turnovers, made with a simple pastry. Actually, they are frequently filled with meat, fish, or poultry. But this version is for Empanadas de Dulce—the sweet kind. The pastry has a bit of sugar added. The filling suggestions given are typical of those served for snacks or desserts.

Pastry:
- **2 cups all-purpose flour**
- **2 tablespoons sugar**
- **2 teaspoons baking powder**
- **1 teaspoon salt**
- **½ cup lard or shortening**
- **⅓ cup ice water (about)**

Fillings:
- **(1) 1 cup chopped pecans**
- **¼ cup brown sugar**
- **2 tablespoons butter or margarine**
- **½ teaspoon cinnamon**

- **(2) 1 cup drained crushed pineapple**
- **2 tablespoons sugar**
- **¼ cup flaked coconut**

1. Mix flour with sugar, baking powder, and salt in bowl. Cut in lard until mixture resembles coarse crumbs. Sprinkle ice water over flour mixture, stirring lightly with a fork until all dry ingredients hold together.

2. Turn dough onto a lightly floured surface and knead gently 30 seconds. Roll out to a rectangle about 16×12 inches.

3. With a floured knife, cut into twelve 4-inch squares. Place a spoonful of filling in center of each square. Fold one corner over filling to meet opposite corner. Seal by dampening inside edges of pastry and pressing together with tines of fork. Place on a baking sheet.

4. Bake at 400°F 15 to 20 minutes. While still hot, sprinkle tops with **granulated sugar.**

12 empanadas

960 *Mexican-Style French Toast* (Torrejas de Coco)

- **1 cup sugar**
- **½ cup water**
- **1 coconut, drained, shelled, pared, and shredded**
- **1 loaf egg bread (1½ pounds), sliced**
- **3 eggs**
- **1 tablespoon flour**
- **1 cup lard**
- **3 cups sugar**
- **1 cinnamon stick**
- **1 cup water**
- **3 tablespoons raisins**
- **¼ cup chopped blanched almonds or pinenuts**

1. Dissolve 1 cup sugar in ½ cup water in a saucepan over medium heat. Bring to boiling; boil 3 minutes. Add shredded coconut; let it cook until the moisture is absorbed and coconut is dry (about 15 minutes). Remove from heat and cool slightly.

2. Put the coconut paste between each two slices of egg bread.

3. Beat eggs with flour; dip both sides of sandwiches in egg and fry in lard in a skillet (about 1 minute on each side). Drain them on absorbent paper.

4. Make a syrup by heating 3 cups sugar, cinnamon, and 1 cup water to boiling in a large skillet; boil 5 minutes. Add browned sandwiches and simmer several minutes; turn once.

5. Arrange desserts on a serving dish, garnish with raisins and almonds, and strain the syrup over all.

About 12 servings

961 *Pecan Cake*

- **¾ cup cake flour**
- **1 teaspoon baking powder**
- **3 eggs, separated**
- **⅔ cup sugar**
- **1 tablespoon lemon juice**

1. Blend flour and baking powder.
2. Beat egg yolks until thick and lemon colored in large bowl of electric mixer. Gradually beat in sugar. Beat in lemon juice and grated pecans, then gradually beat in flour mixture. Slowly beat in melted butter.

½ cup finely grated pecans (use blender or fine knife of vegetable grater to get nuts very fine)
½ cup butter or margarine, melted
Pinch salt
Orange Glaze
Pecan halves for decoration

3. Beat egg whites with salt until stiff peaks form. Fold beaten egg whites into batter.
4. Pour batter into a greased and floured 9-inch round cake pan.
5. Bake at 350°F 30 to 35 minutes, or until cake tester inserted in center comes out clean.
6. Let cake cool 10 minutes before removing from pan. Cool completely on a wire rack, right side up.
7. Place cake on a serving plate and cover with hot orange glaze. Decorate with pecan halves.

6 to 8 servings

Orange Glaze: Combine ½ **cup orange marmalade** and ¼ **cup sugar** in a small saucepan and cook until sugar is dissolved (2 to 3 minutes), stirring constantly. Use while still hot.

962 *Cream-Filled Chestnut Cake*

1 pound chestnuts in the shell; or use 1¼ cups pecans, chopped
¾ cup butter
1 cup sugar
½ teaspoon vanilla extract
6 eggs, separated
1¼ cups all-purpose flour
1 teaspoon baking powder
½ cup milk
Chestnut Cream

1. Prepare chestnuts (see Note).
2. Cream butter with sugar and vanilla extract until fluffy. Mixing well after each addition, add the chestnut purée, then the egg yolks, one at a time.
3. Mix flour with baking powder, and add alternately with milk to the chestnut mixture, mixing well after each addition. Beat egg whites until stiff, but not dry. Fold into batter.
4. Turn mixture into 2 greased and floured 9-inch round layer cake pans.
5. Bake at 350°F about 25 minutes, or until done.
6. Let cool, then put layers together and decorate cake with chestnut cream.

One 9-inch layer cake

Note: To prepare chestnuts, rinse chestnuts and make a slit on two sides of each shell. Put into a saucepan; cover with boiling water and boil about 20 minutes. Remove shells and skins; return chestnuts to saucepan and cover with boiling salted water. Cover and simmer until chestnuts are tender (10 to 20 minutes). Drain and finely chop.

Chestnut Cream: Prepare ¾ **pound chestnuts** in the shell (see Note above); or use **1 cup pecans**, chopped. Whip **1 cup whipping cream** until thickened. Mix in ⅔ **cup confectioners' sugar** and ½ **teaspoon vanilla extract,** then chestnuts.

963 *Nut Cookies*

1 cup butter
¼ cup confectioners' sugar
2 cups all-purpose flour
¾ cup chopped nuts

1. Beat butter until softened. Add sugar and cream well. Add flour and nuts; mix well.
2. Shape into small balls. Place on cookie sheets.
3. Bake at 325°F 15 to 20 minutes.
4. While still warm, coat with **confectioners' sugar.**

About 5½ dozen cookies

964 *Apricot-Filled Pastries* (Pastelitos)

1 cup dried apricots
1 cup water
½ cup sugar
½ teaspoon vanilla extract
2 cups all-purpose flour
¾ teaspoon salt
½ teaspoon baking powder
⅔ cup lard
4 to 6 tablespoons icy cold water
Confectioners' Sugar Glaze

1. Put apricots and water into saucepan. Cover, bring to boiling, and cook 20 minutes.
2. Turn contents of saucepan into an electric blender; cover and blend until smooth.
3. Combine blended apricots and sugar in saucepan; cook until thick (about 5 minutes). Cool slightly; stir in vanilla extract.
4. Mix flour, salt, and baking powder in a bowl. Cut in lard until crumbly. Add cold water, 1 tablespoon at a time, tossing with a fork until dough holds together. Divide in half.
5. Roll each half of dough to a 14×10-inch rectangle on a lightly floured surface.
6. Line a 13×9×2-inch baking pan with one rectangle of dough. Spread apricot mixture evenly over dough. Place remaining dough on top; seal edges. Prick top crust.
7. Bake at 400°F 25 minutes, or until lightly browned around edges.
8. Cool slightly. Frost with confectioners' sugar glaze. Cool; cut in squares.

2 dozen filled pastries

Confectioners' Sugar Glaze: Combine **1 cup confectioners' sugar** and **½ teaspoon vanilla extract.** Blend in **milk or cream** (about 3 tablespoons) until glaze is of spreading consistency.

965 *Flaming Bananas*

2 tablespoons butter or margarine
⅔ cup sugar
6 ripe bananas, peeled
½ cup rum

1. Melt butter in a chafing dish or skillet. Stir in sugar and heat until sugar melts.
2. Slice bananas lengthwise and add to butter-sugar mixture; turn to coat on all sides. Pour in rum and keep over medium heat.
3. Flame sauce by pouring a little rum into a teaspoon and holding it over flame of chafing dish or range until it flames; then use this flaming rum to light rum on top of bananas. Spoon flaming sauce over fruit several times.
4. Serve over **vanilla or chocolate ice cream.**

6 servings

966 *Flaming Mangos*

2 fresh mangos, or 12 slices canned mango, about ½ inch thick
1 cup orange juice
2 tablespoons sugar
1 cup tequila

1. Wash and peel fresh mangos; cut each into 6 slices. Place in chafing dish or skillet. Pour orange juice over fruit and sprinkle with sugar. Heat to simmering, stirring gently to dissolve sugar and coat fruit. After 3 or 4 minutes, pour in tequila; keep over medium heat.
2. Flame sauce by pouring a little tequila into teaspoon and holding it over flame of chafing dish or range until it flames; then use this flaming tequila to light tequila on top of mangos.
3. Serve over **vanilla ice cream.**

6 servings

967 *Pinenut Balls*

1 pound pinenuts
1 cup sweetened condensed milk
3 cups confectioners' sugar
  Confectioners' sugar to coat

1. Grind pinenuts and mix with sweetened condensed milk and confectioners' sugar.
2. Shape into 1-inch balls and coat them with sugar. Put onto a waxed paper lined tray. Let stand until set.

About 6 dozen

968 *Mexican Molasses Candy*

1 cup light molasses
1 cup firmly packed brown sugar
2 tablespoons butter or margarine
1 teaspoon cider vinegar
¾ teaspoon almond extract
1½ cups toasted slivered almonds

1. Put molasses, brown sugar, butter, and vinegar into a heavy saucepan. Bring to boiling. Boil hard about 7 to 12 minutes, until mixture reaches 260°F on a candy thermometer (firm ball stage).
2. Remove from heat and add almond extract and almonds; stir.
3. Pour onto a greased baking sheet, spread as thin as possible, and cool. Break into 2-inch pieces.

About 1 pound

969 *Orange Candy*

3 cups sugar
¼ cup water
1 cup undiluted evaporated milk
  Pinch salt
2 teaspoons grated orange peel
1 cup chopped walnuts

1. Put 1 cup sugar into a heavy, light-colored skillet and stir over medium heat with a wooden spoon until sugar is melted and caramelized (cooked to a golden brown color). Add water and stir until sugar is completely dissolved.
2. Add remaining sugar, milk, and salt. Cook over low heat, stirring until mixture begins to boil. Cook, stirring frequently, to 230°F on candy thermometer (soft-ball stage).
3. Remove from heat. Cool to lukewarm; do not stir.
4. Meanwhile, lightly butter an 8-inch square pan.
5. Add grated peel and nuts to lukewarm mixture. Beat until candy loses gloss and holds its shape when dropped from a spoon.
6. Press into buttered pan and cool. Cut into small squares.

About 1½ pounds

970 *Tutti-Frutti Barbancourt*

2 quarts strawberries
1 quart honey
4 cinnamon sticks
32 whole cloves
¼ cup grated orange peel
¼ cup grated lime peel
  Mangoes, peeled and cut in pieces
  Bananas, sliced
  Pineapple, cubed
  Barbancourt rum or other
    amber rum

1. Cook strawberries in honey and enough water to cover over low heat 5 minutes. Skim thoroughly; spoon an equal amount into each of four 2-quart wide-mouthed Mason jars. Put into each jar 1 cinnamon stick, 8 cloves, and 1 tablespoon each orange and lime peel. When cool, fill jars with desired amount of remaining fruit and rum. Stir, cover tightly, and refrigerate 3 months.
2. Serve tutti-frutti over ice cream or plain, with cookies.

8 quarts tutti-frutti

971 *Caramel Candy* (Cajeta)

2 quarts milk
3 cups sugar
¼ teaspoon baking soda
1 cinnamon stick (optional)
1 teaspoon vanilla extract

1. Combine 1 quart of the milk and the sugar in a saucepan. Cook over very low heat until golden in color, stirring occasionally (this may take 2 to 3 hours).
2. Place second quart of milk in separate saucepan; add baking soda and cinnamon stick (if used). Bring to boiling; remove from heat and discard cinnamon stick. Add hot milk to caramelized milk-sugar mixture very gradually, stirring constantly. Cook over very low heat until thick, stirring occasionally (another hour of cooking may be needed).
3. Cool and stir in vanilla extract. Pour into a serving bowl or several individual cups.

About 1 quart candy

972 *Christmas Candy Balls*

2 medium potatoes, scrubbed (do not pare)
1 cup sugar
1 teaspoon vanilla extract
2 cups chopped pecans
1 cup confectioners' sugar
1 teaspoon ground cinnamon
Candied red or green cherries, cut in halves

1. Cook potatoes in their skins, peel, press through ricer or food mill. Mix in sugar, vanilla extract, and nuts. Chill.
2. Form little balls; coat them with confectioners' sugar mixed with cinnamon. Put into small fluted paper cups and garnish with cherry halves.
3. Store in refrigerator until ready to serve.

About 2 dozen balls

973 *Guava Preserves*

5 cups peeled ripe guava slices
Sugar
Limes, halved

1. Put guava slices into a deep pot and cover with water; bring to a boil, reduce heat, and simmer until fruit is tender.
2. Measure fruit and add an equal amount of sugar.
3. For 4 cups of fruit, use 2 limes. Discard center and core from lime halves and squeeze. Add the juice and shells to the fruit and sugar. Cook at a rolling boil 10 minutes. Skim.
4. Pack hot mixture into sterilized jars, seal, and store.

Guava Jelly: Follow recipe for Guava Preserves for cooking guava. Allow to drip through a jelly bag or through a strainer lined with cheesecloth. For a clear jelly, do not squeeze the bag. Measure juice and add an equal amount of sugar and 1 tablespoon lime juice per cup of liquid. Boil at a rolling boil until mixture sheets from side of spoon. Skim and cool. Pack in sterilized jars, seal, and store.

974 *Chestnuts with Coffee Cream*

1 pound chestnuts
3 tablespoons brown sugar
● Coffee Cream

1. Slit shells of chestnuts. Simmer chestnuts, in water to cover, 5 minutes. While the chestnuts are still hot, discard shells and skins. Put nuts into boiling water with brown sugar and cook 30 minutes, or until tender. Drain and chill.
2. To serve, pile chestnuts into sherbet glasses. Spoon Coffee Cream over them.

975 *Pineapple Ablaze*

1 cup packed brown sugar
1 cup water
6 fresh pineapple slices
6 raisin bread slices with
　　crusts trimmed
½ cup unsalted butter
6 tablespoons coarsely ground
　　cashews
1 teaspoon cinnamon
½ cup amber rum

1. Combine brown sugar and water in a saucepan. Bring to boiling and boil rapidly until reduced to half its volume, Add pineapple and poach for 6 minutes. Remove pineapple and keep syrup warm.
2. Fry bread slices in butter in a skillet until golden.
3. Lay these croutons in a circle in a chafing dish. Top with pineapple slices and sprinkle with cashews and cinnamon. Spoon half the syrup into chafing dish pan. Warm rum, ignite, and pour, still flaming, over all.

6 servings

976 *Pineapple Flan*

3 cups pineapple juice
2 cups sugar
½ cup water
1 cup sugar
6 eggs
2 egg yolks

1. Combine pineapple juice and 2 cups sugar in a saucepan. Bring to a boil, then reduce heat and cook until a thin syrup is formed (about 5 minutes). Remove from heat, cool, and reserve.
2. Combine water and 1 cup sugar in a saucepan. Boil rapidly until it turns the color of maple syrup (5 to 7 minutes). Immediately remove from heat and pour it into a 1-quart mold, tilting mold until it is completely coated with caramel. Set aside to cool.
3. Beat eggs and yolks with the reserved pineapple syrup. Pour into mold. Set mold in a pan of hot water.
4. Bake at 325°F 1½ hours. Cool.
5. Chill thoroughly, then unmold on a serving platter.

About 12 servings

977 *Pineapple Pyramids*

● 2½ cups crushed Coconut Macaroons
3 tablespoons amber rum
3 cups whipping cream
⅓ cup sugar
¾ cup chopped cashews
12 pineapple slices
12 whole cashews

1. Sprinkle crushed macaroons with rum.
2. Whip cream with sugar, one half at a time, until it stands in peaks. Fold crumbs and chopped cashews into the whipped cream.
3. Place 1 pineapple slice on each dessert plate, mound cream mixture in a pyramid, and put a cashew on top of each.

12 servings

978 *Rum Pineapple Snow*

1 small fresh fully ripe pineapple
4 egg whites
½ cup sugar
2 cups whipping cream
1 teaspoon vanilla extract
¾ cup amber rum
● Ladyfingers or leftover Génoise

1. Pare pineapple and grate; keep grated pineapple separate from juice.
2. Beat egg whites until frothy; gradually add sugar while beating until meringue is thick and glossy.
3. Whip cream and blend in vanilla extract; fold into meringue along with as much grated pineapple and pineapple juice as meringue will hold and still pile softly.
4. Pour rum over ladyfingers and use to line sherbet glasses. Spoon in pineapple snow.

979 *Pineapple Boat*

1 small pineapple
2 cups whipping cream
1 cup sugar
1 tablespoon lime juice
½ cup whipped cream mixed with
    chopped flaked coconut
Chopped cashews

1. Cut pineapple in half lengthwise, a little off center. Remove pulp, keeping larger shell intact, and discard core. Chop pineapple finely or process in an electric blender. Measure 2 cups of pineapple and juice. Add to whipping cream along with sugar and lime juice.
2. Cut the leafy top off the pineapple shell and reserve for decoration. Spoon pineapple mixture into the shell and freeze until firm.
3. To serve, pipe large rosettes of the whipped cream around the shell and sprinkle with cashews. Decorate with leafy top.

980 *Boiled Plantain*

Green plantain
½ lime
Boiling salted water

1. Remove the skin and scrape the threads from plantain. Rub the fruit with the cut side of a lime.
2. Cook in boiling salted water 30 minutes.

981 *Baked Pineapple*

1 large sugarloaf pineapple
1 banana, peeled and thinly sliced
¼ cup packed brown sugar
⅓ cup amber rum

1. Cut top from pineapple and remove pulp from inside the top. Reserve leafy top. With a grapefruit knife, remove the core and pulp from the pineapple, being careful to leave a ¼-inch layer of flesh inside the rind to keep juice in during baking.
2. Dice the pineapple pulp and mix with banana and brown sugar in a bowl. Warm rum, ignite it, and, when the flame subsides, pour over fruit mixture. Fill pineapple shell with fruit; replace top, moisten with water, and wrap in foil. Secure top with a few wooden picks. Set upright in oven in a deep casserole.
3. Bake at 350°F 25 minutes. Remove foil and serve hot.

982 *Pineapple Cream*

1 pineapple, pared, sliced, and cored
2 tablespoons amber rum
½ cup butter or margarine
6 tablespoons sugar
1 tablespoon flour
6 egg yolks

1. Cube pineapple pulp and put with rum into the top of a double boiler over boiling water.
2. Beat remaining ingredients together about 5 minutes.
3. Pour the cream mixture over the pineapple cubes and mix well. Cook and stir over boiling water about 6 minutes, or until thickened.
4. Pour into small bowls or **pots de crème** cups and chill before serving.

About 3 cups

983 *Coconut Milk*

1 fresh coconut
2 cups boiling water

1. Open coconut, discarding liquid. With a sharp paring knife, remove the meat in chunks and grate it (see Note). Pour boiling water over grated coconut and let stand 4 hours.
2. Place a sieve over a bowl, turn grated coconut into sieve, and press out the liquid. Reserve grated coconut, if desired, to toast in the oven and use to decorate desserts and salads.

About 2 cups

Note: If you have an electric blender, coarsely chop coconut meat and process with boiling water a small amount at a time.

984 *Coconut Chocolate Sauce*

4 ounces (4 squares) semisweet chocolate
● 1½ cups Coconut Milk
1 teaspoon vanilla extract

1. Combine chocolate and ¼ cup Coconut Milk in a saucepan. Stir over low heat until chocolate is melted. Gradually add the remaining Coconut Milk, stirring until smooth and blended.
2. Remove from heat and mix in vanilla extract.

About 2 cups

985 *Mocha Mousse*

8 ounces (8 squares) unsweetened chocolate
● ⅔ cup Coffee Extract
2 cups whipping cream
½ cup sugar
● Coconut Chocolate Sauce

1. Put chocolate and Coffee Extract into a saucepan. Stir over low heat until chocolate is blended with coffee. Cool.
2. Whip cream and gradually add sugar, continuing to beat until cream holds its shape. Fold in cooled chocolate mixture. Pour into a mold and freeze without stirring.
3. Serve mousse with the sauce.

986 *Caramel Sauce*

1½ cups sugar
1 cup water
¼ cup hot water
1 tablespoon butter

1. Put sugar and 1 cup water into a heavy saucepan and bring to a boil. Boil, stirring constantly, until syrup is golden.
2. Remove from heat and stir in hot water and butter.
3. Serve hot.

About 1½ cups

987 *Banana Compote*

½ cup sugar
½ cup apricot jam
1 cup water
6 ripe bananas
¼ cup unsalted butter

1. Combine sugar, jam, and water in a saucepan. Cook over medium heat until the syrup is heavy. Set aside.
2. Peel bananas and slice into ¼-inch pieces. Melt butter in a heavy skillet over medium heat and put in enough banana slices to cover bottom of skillet. Sauté until edges become golden. Pour reserved syrup over all bananas and boil uncovered over high heat until syrup is slightly thicker. Cool.
3. Pour into a crystal bowl, chill, and serve.

988 *Banana Fan*

4 ripe bananas
1 cup water
½ cup sugar
1 cup maraschino cherries
½ cup amber rum, warmed and flamed
1 cup whipped cream
¼ teaspoon vanilla extract

1. Peel bananas and halve them lengthwise. Arrange halves flat side down in the shape of an open fan on a round silver or glass dish.
2. Boil water and sugar together at a rolling boil 4 minutes. Add cherries, reduce heat, and simmer 2 minutes. Remove some of the cherries with a perforated spoon and arrange in a design on upper portion of fan.
3. Put the remaining fruit with syrup into an electric blender along with flamed rum; process until puréed. Or force mixture through a food mill. Spoon over upper part of fan.
4. Blend whipped cream and vanilla extract. Using a pastry bag and decorating tube, make a thick border around upper portion of fan to simulate lace. Serve well chilled.

989 *Banana Fritters*

1 cup all-purpose flour
1 teaspoon baking powder
⅛ teaspoon salt
1 egg, beaten
⅓ cup milk
1 teaspoon grated orange peel
¼ cup orange juice
4 ripe bananas
  Fat for deep frying, heated to 365°F
  Confectioners' sugar
● Orange Rum Sauce

1. Sift flour, baking powder, and salt. Combine beaten egg and milk; add to dry ingredients along with orange peel and juice; mix until smooth.
2. Peel and slice bananas; stir into batter.
3. Drop by spoonfuls into heated fat and fry until golden. Drain on absorbent paper. Sprinkle with confectioners' sugar. Serve with the sauce.

990 *Purée of Breadfruit*

1 breadfruit (1½ pounds), peeled and cubed
1 cup whipping cream
  Salt, freshly ground pepper, and cayenne or red pepper to taste

1. Cook breadfruit in lightly salted water until tender; drain.
2. Process breadfruit, a small amount at a time, with a small amount of cream, in an electric blender to make a purée. Mix in seasonings.

Note: If desired, force breadfruit through a food mill and beat in cream, slightly whipped, and the seasonings.

991 *Haitian Upside-down Cake (Gâteau Pistaches)*

Topping:
  6 **tablespoons butter, melted**
  ½ **cup firmly packed dark brown
     sugar**
  ¼ **cup light corn syrup**
  1 **cup chopped pistachios or peanuts**
Cake:
  4 **ounces (4 squares) unsweetened
     chocolate**
  6 **tablespoons butter**
1¼ **cups sugar**
  2 **egg yolks**
  1 **teaspoon vanilla extract**
  2 **cups all-purpose flour**
  1 **tablespoon baking powder**
1½ **cups milk**
  2 **egg whites, beaten stiff, but
     not dry**

1. For topping, blend butter, brown sugar, and corn syrup, then add nuts and mix well.
2. Spread nut mixture over bottom of a greased 13x9-inch baking pan.
3. For cake, melt chocolate over hot, not boiling, water.
4. Cream butter with sugar thoroughly. Beat in egg yolks, vanilla extract, and melted chocolate.
5. Sift flour with baking powder. Alternately add flour mixture with milk to the chocolate mixture, beating until blended after each addition. Fold in beaten egg white. Turn batter into pan over nut mixture.
6. Bake at 350°F about 45 minutes. Invert on a board or platter. If necessary, spread nut mixture evenly over the cake. Cool; serve cut in squares.

One 13x9-inch cake

992 *Génoise*

This light cake is something quite different from "American cake," and is well worth the effort.

  1 **cup sugar**
  6 **eggs**
  2 **teaspoons vanilla extract**
    Grated peel of 1 lime
  1 **cup all-purpose flour**
  ¼ **cup clarified butter**

1. Combine sugar, eggs, vanilla extract, and grated peel in the top of a double boiler. Beat with an electric mixer over hot water for 15 minutes, or until light and fluffy. Remove from heat. Continue beating until mixture is cooled and has reached the ribbon stage. (The mixture should flow in ribbons and softly peak.)
2. Sift the flour onto the cooled mixture a fourth at a time; fold in gently after each addition. Fold in clarified butter.
3. Pour the batter into 2 greased and floured 9-inch round layer cake pans.
4. Bake at 325°F about 25 minutes, or until cake tests done.
5. Cool on racks. Frost cooled layers with **Rich Chocolate Frosting** (●) or **Italian Meringue** (●).

One 9-inch layer cake

993 *Coconut Macaroons*

  4 **egg whites**
  ½ **teaspoon vanilla extract**
  1 **cup confectioners' sugar**
  ½ **cup all-purpose flour**
  2 **cups freshly grated or chopped
     flaked coconut**

1. Beat egg whites until rounded peaks are formed. Mix in vanilla extract. Add sugar gradually, beating until stiff, not dry, peaks form. Fold in flour and coconut.
2. Drop by tablespoonfuls 1 inch apart on a buttered and floured cookie sheet.
3. Bake at 350°F 10 to 15 minutes, or until lightly browned.

About 2½ dozen

Plantation Macaroons: Follow recipe for Coconut Macaroons. When cool, put 2 macaroons together, like a sandwich, with a filling of Rich Chocolate Frosting (●). Roll in **grated** or **flaked coconut**.

994 *Coffee Extract (Essence de Café)*

5 cups water
1½ cups ground coffee

1. Prepare very strong coffee using water and ground coffee.
2. Pour brewed coffee into a large saucepan. Bring to a boil; simmer 30 minutes. Cool.
3. Store in a tightly covered container and use to flavor custard, buttercream, and ice cream.

About ½ cup extract

995 *Coffee Cream*

4 cups milk
● 2 tablespoons Coffee Extract
3 tablespoons cornstarch
6 egg yolks, beaten
¾ cup sugar
1 tablespoon butter or margarine
¼ cup whipping cream

1. Combine ½ cup of the milk, Coffee Extract, and cornstarch. Beat in egg yolks. Set aside.
2. Put the remaining milk, sugar, and butter into the top of a metal double boiler. Bring to a boil over direct heat.
3. Half fill the bottom of the double boiler with water; bring to boiling. Place the top of the double boiler over the bottom pan.
4. Add the reserved milk-and-egg mixture to the top pan while stirring. Cook over medium heat, stirring until the custard thickens and coats the spoon.
5. Cool custard, then add cream. Pour into a large bowl or individual custard cups. Serve chilled.

Rum Cream: Follow recipe for Coffee Cream, omitting Coffee Extract and cream. Heat ¼ **cup amber rum** in a small saucepan. Ignite rum and stir it into the thickened custard. Serve chilled.

996 *Orange Cake (Gâteau à l'Orange)*

1 cup butter
1 cup sugar
3 egg yolks
2 cups sifted all-purpose flour
1 teaspoon baking powder
1 teaspoon baking soda
1 cup milk
1 teaspoon lime juice
1 tablespoon grated
    orange peel
¾ cup cashews, chopped
3 egg whites
    Pinch salt
½ cup orange juice
½ cup corn syrup
¼ cup rum

1. Cream butter with sugar until light and fluffy. Beat in egg yolks.
2. Sift flour with baking powder and baking soda. Mix milk and lime juice. Add dry ingredients alternately with milk to creamed mixture, beating until blended after each addition. Mix in orange peel and cashews.
3. Beat egg whites and salt to stiff, not dry, peaks. Fold into batter.
4. Turn batter into a buttered and lightly floured 9-inch tube pan.
5. Bake at 350°F 40 minutes.
6. Mix orange juice, corn syrup, and rum. While cake is still hot in the pan, pour orange juice mixture over it.

997 *Haitian Chocolate Rum Sauce*

● 1 cup Coffee Extract
4 ounces dark sweet Swiss chocolate
1 ounce (1 square) unsweetened
    chocolate
1 cup amber rum

1. Combine Coffee Extract and chocolates in a heavy saucepan. Cook over low heat, stirring constantly, until chocolate is melted.
2. Heat rum, ignite it, and when the flames subside, stir into the chocolate mixture.
3. Serve hot over cake.

About 2 cups

998 *Orange Coconut Filling*

1 cup sugar
½ cup orange juice
3½ tablespoons cornstarch
3 tablespoons lime juice
2 tablespoons butter
2 tablespoons water
    Grated peel of 1 orange
1 egg, slightly beaten
¾ cup freshly grated or chopped
    flaked coconut

1. Combine all the ingredients except the coconut in a saucepan. Cook over low heat, stirring constantly, about 10 minutes or until thick and clear; do not boil.
2. Remove from heat and stir in coconut. Cool before using.

About 1 cup

999 *Orange Rum Sauce*

1½ cups orange juice
½ cup amber rum
    Sugar to taste
1 tablespoon butter
1 tablespoon cornstarch
½ teaspoon grated orange peel

1. Combine orange juice, rum, and sugar in a small saucepan. Bring to a boil.
2. Mix butter and cornstarch and add to sauce. Cook until thickened. Remove from heat. Mix in orange peel.
3. Cool before serving.

About 2 cups

1,000 *Pineapple Sauce*

1½ cups cubed pineapple,
    canned or fresh
½ cup sugar
¼ cup rum, flamed
    Pineapple juice
½ cup water
1 tablespoon cornstarch

1. Process pineapple, sugar, and rum in an electric blender until completely smooth. Add pineapple juice if more liquid is needed.
2. Turn pineapple mixture into a small saucepan and bring to a boil.
3. Mix water and cornstarch, stir into mixture in saucepan, and cook until sauce is slightly thickened.

1⅔ cups

1,001 *Rich Chocolate Frosting*

1 package (6 ounces) semisweet
    chocolate pieces
⅓ cup strong black coffee
½ cup butter or margarine,
    cut in pieces

1. Put chocolate pieces and coffee in a heavy saucepan. Set over low heat and stir constantly just until chocolate is melted.
2. Pour mixture into a bowl. Add butter, piece by piece, beating until mixture is smooth.
3. Chill until frosting is of spreading consistency.

About 1½ cups frosting

Index

BOOK II

Contents

Note: A black circle: ● is used throughout this book to alert you to the fact that an additional recipe is involved in the one you are working on. The reference will be found in bold type and in its exact wording in the index.

Appetizers

1 *Appetizer Puffs*

These tiny cream puffs may be filled as you wish to make dainty and appealing hors d'oeuvres.

1 cup beer
½ cup butter or margarine
½ teaspoon salt
1 cup all-purpose flour
4 eggs

1. Heat beer, butter, and salt to boiling in a saucepan.
2. Add flour all at once. Beat vigorously with a wooden spoon until mixture leaves sides of pan and forms a smooth ball.
3. Add eggs, one at a time, beating until smooth.
4. Drop mixture by rounded teaspoonfuls onto a greased cookie sheet, 1 inch apart.
5. Bake at 450°F 10 minutes. Turn oven control to 350°F and bake 5 to 10 minutes more, or until lightly browned and puffed.
6. Cool. Split and fill with desired filling.

About 40 puffs

2 *Pickled Shrimp*

With small to medium shrimp, serve this appetizer on cocktail rye rounds. Larger shrimp may be served on fancy picks.

1 can or bottle (12 ounces) beer
¼ cup oil
1 tablespoon lemon juice
1 teaspoon sugar
1 teaspoon salt
½ teaspoon each dill seed, dry mustard, and celery salt
¼ teaspoon tarragon
⅛ teaspoon ground red pepper
2 bay leaves, halved
2 medium onions, chopped
1 package (10 ounces) small to medium frozen cooked shrimp, thawed

1. Place all ingredients except shrimp in a saucepan. Simmer 10 to 15 minutes, or until onions are just tender.
2. Add shrimp; remove from heat. Turn into a small casserole. Cover and refrigerate at least 1 day.
3. Remove bay leaves; drain off marinade. Let guests spoon shrimp and onions onto **cocktail rye rounds.**

About 25 appetizers

Note: With larger shrimp to be served on fancy picks, use only one onion and slice it. Remove onion before serving. Recipe may also be made with uncooked shrimp. Add them 4 to 5 minutes before end of cooking time; cover and simmer until shrimp turn pink. Continue as in above recipe.

3 *Shrimp Dunk*

This is the famous shrimp boiled in beer served as an appetizer. Instead of cocktail sauce or melted butter, try cold beer for dunking.

1 can or bottle (12 ounces) beer
    plus ½
    cup water
1 small onion, sliced
    Top and leaves of 1 stalk celery
1 tablespoon salt
3 or 4 peppercorns
1 bay leaf
1 garlic clove
1 pound very large shelled
    shrimp, uncooked

1. Combine ingredients except shrimp in a large saucepan. Cover; heat to boiling. Boil 10 minutes.
2. Add shrimp. Cover and boil 5 minutes, or just until shrimp turn pink. Remove from heat; chill in cooking liquid.
3. Serve cold with dunking bowls of cold beer. Serve as hors d'oeuvres or as a summertime main entrée.

25 to 30 shrimp

4 *Shrimp Spread*

Serve this spread at a cocktail party—on fancy crackers or inside tiny beer-flavored cream puffs.

½ cup butter or margarine,
    softened
2 green onions with some tops
2 parsley sprigs
¼ teaspoon salt
⅛ teaspoon garlic powder
    Dash pepper
1 package (12 ounces) frozen
    cooked shrimp, thawed
½ cup beer
1 tablespoon capers (optional)
    Fancy crackers or tiny cream
    puffs

1. Using a food processor or blender, process butter, onions, parsley, and seasonings until vegetables are minced and mixture is smooth. (With blender, prepare in 2 or 3 batches.)
2. Add shrimp, beer, and capers. Process to a smooth paste.
3. Serve at room temperature on crackers or in tiny cream puffs. Use a rounded teaspoon for each. One half recipe of Shrimp Spread fills one recipe Appetizer Puffs ●

2 ¾ cups spread for about 7 dozen crackers or tiny cream puffs

5 *Marinated Mushrooms*

Serve hot or cold as light hors d'oeuvres before a dinner party, or as part of an array of cocktail party nibbling foods.

1 pound small fresh mushrooms
⅔ cup vegetable oil
½ cup beer
¼ cup minced green onion with
    tops
2 tablespoons lemon juice
1 tablespoon chopped parsley
1 large garlic clove, minced
½ teaspoon salt
    Dash pepper

1. Wash mushrooms, remove stems, and pat dry. Reserve stems for later use.
2. Combine remaining ingredients in a shallow glass or ceramic dish. Add mushrooms. Cover and let stand at room temperature about 3 hours, stirring occasionally.
3. Place mushrooms, cup side up, on a broiler pan. Spoon some marinade over each. Broil 3 inches from heat about 2 minutes, or until lightly browned. Serve warm with picks.

40 to 50 mushrooms

Note: Marinated Mushrooms may also be served cold. Marinate in refrigerator. Do not broil. Turn into a serving bowl with marinade; serve with picks. Canned button mushrooms may also be used when serving this dish cold.

6 Tangy Cheese Dip

4 ounces Muenster cheese or
   other semisoft cheese, finely
   shredded (1 cup)
3 ounces blue cheese, crumbled
1 package (3 ounces) cream
   cheese, softened
⅛ teaspoon garlic powder
¾ cup beer (about)

1. After shredding, let Muenster cheese stand at room temperature at least 1 hour.
2. Using an electric blender or food processor, blend cheeses and garlic. Gradually add enough beer to make a mixture of dipping consistency.
3. Serve at room temperature with crackers for dipping.

About 2 cups

7 German Beer Cheese *(Bierkäse)*

Serve as a spread for hors d'oeuvres at a party or before dinner. It's especially good on rye rounds with glasses of cold beer to drink.

½ pound Cheddar cheese
½ pound Swiss cheese
2 teaspoons Worcestershire sauce
1 teaspoon dry mustard
1 small garlic clove, mashed
½ cup beer (about)

1. Shred cheeses finely. Or put through a meat grinder, using finest blade.
2. Add Worcestershire sauce, dry mustard, garlic, and enough beer to make a mixture of spreading consistency.
3. Turn into a 3-cup rounded bowl or mold; pack firmly. Chill. Unmold and serve at room temperature with **small rye rounds** or **crackers.**

3 cups

8 Cocktail Party Sausages

● 1½ cups Mustard Sauce or Savory
   Barbecue Sauce
4 dozen (about) cocktail
   frankfurters, vienna sausages,
   cocktail smoked sausage
   links, or chunks of
   frankfurters

1. Prepare desired sauce and heat with your choice of sausage.
2. Turn into a chafing dish. Serve warm with decorative picks.

About 4 dozen

9 Chili Nuts

These zippy nuts are nice to nibble on while drinking a glass of cold beer.

1 package (12 ounces) shelled
   raw peanuts
2 tablespoons peanut or
   vegetable oil
2 teaspoons chili powder
1 teaspoon salt

1. Combine ingredients in a large baking pan; spread thinly.
2. Bake at 325°F 25 minutes. Cool on waxed paper.

2 cups

10 *Hot Crab Spread*

1 package (8 ounces) cream cheese, softened
1 tablespoon milk
2 teaspoons Worcestershire sauce
1 can (7½ ounces) Alaska King crab, drained and flaked, or 1 package (6 ounces) frozen crab meat, thawed, drained, and flaked
2 tablespoons chopped green onion
2 tablespoons toasted slivered almonds

1. Combine cream cheese, milk, Worcestershire sauce, crab, and green onion. Place in small individual casseroles. Sprinkle with almonds.
2. Bake, uncovered, at 350°F 15 minutes. Serve with **assorted crackers.**

2 cups

11 *Crab Meat Newburg Appetizer*

2 tablespoons butter or margarine
2 tablespoons flour
½ teaspoon salt
2 cups milk
2 cups (8 ounces) shredded Cheddar cheese
2 cans (7½ ounces each) Alaska King crab, drained and flaked
3 hard-cooked eggs, grated
½ cup finely chopped onion
Dash ground red pepper
1 tablespoon snipped parsley

1. Melt butter in a saucepan. Add flour and salt. Gradually add milk, stirring until thickened and smooth.
2. Add cheese, stirring until blended. Blend in remaining ingredients, except parsley. Put into a 1½-quart casserole.
3. Bake, covered, at 325°F 15 minutes, or until heated through. Sprinkle with parsley. Serve with **Melba toast** or **toast-points.**

25 servings

12 *Crab Meat Quiche*

1 unbaked 9-inch pie shell
2 eggs
1 cup half-and-half
½ teaspoon salt
Dash ground red pepper
¾ cup (3 ounces) shredded Swiss cheese
¾ cup (3 ounces) shredded Gruyère cheese
1 tablespoon flour
1 can (7½ ounces) Alaska King crab, drained and flaked

1. Prick bottom and sides of pie shell. Bake at 450°F 10 minutes, or until delicately browned.
2. Beat together eggs, half-and-half, salt, and red pepper.
3. Combine cheeses, flour, and crab; sprinkle evenly in pie shell. Pour in egg mixture.
4. Bake, uncovered, at 325°F 45 minutes, or until tip of knife inserted 1 inch from center comes out clean. Let stand a few minutes. Cut into wedges to serve.

16 appetizers

13 *Barbecue Fondue*

2 cans (15¼ ounces each) barbecue
    sauce and beef for Sloppy Joes
1 teaspoon instant minced onion
1 teaspoon oregano
1½ cups (6 ounces) shredded Cheddar
    cheese

1. Combine all ingredients in a 1-quart casserole.
2. Bake, covered, at 350°F 30 minutes, or until heated through, stirring occasionally. Serve with **French bread cubes** on wooden picks.

3½ cups

14 *Mexican Chili-Bean Dip*

1 pound ground beef
½ cup finely chopped onion
½ cup ketchup
1 tablespoon chili powder
1 teaspoon salt
⅛ teaspoon garlic powder
    Dash ground red pepper
1 can (15½ ounces) red kidney beans
    (with liquid), mashed
1 cup (4 ounces) shredded Monterey
    Jack cheese

1. Brown ground beef and onion in a skillet; drain off excess fat.
2. Add remaining ingredients, except cheese. Put into a 1-quart casserole.
3. Bake, covered, at 350°F 30 minutes, or until heated through. Sprinkle with cheese. Serve with **corn chips.**

8 servings

15 *Hot Artichoke-Cheese Squares*

¼ cup finely chopped onion
1 garlic clove, minced
1 tablespoon shortening
4 eggs, well beaten
1 can (14 ounces) artichoke hearts,
    drained and chopped
¼ cup dry bread crumbs
2 cups (8 ounces) shredded Cheddar
    or Swiss cheese
2 tablespoons snipped parsley
    Few drops Tabasco

1. Sauté onion and garlic in shortening in a skillet.
2. Combine all ingredients. Pour into an 11x7-inch baking dish.
3. Bake, uncovered, at 325°F 30 minutes, or until filling is set. Let stand a few minutes. Cut into squares to serve.

24 appetizers

16 *Sausage and Applesauce Appetizers*

1 package (12 ounces) smoked link
    sausage, cut in 1-inch pieces
1 jar (15 ounces) applesauce
1 tablespoon caraway seed
1½ teaspoons instant minced onion

1. Broil sausage pieces until evenly browned.
2. Combine with applesauce, caraway seed, and onion. Put into a 1-quart casserole.
3. Bake, covered, at 250°F 2 hours. Serve with wooden picks.

About 32 appetizers

17 *Baked Carrot Spread*

1 cup grated carrot
1 cup mayonnaise
1 cup (4 ounces) grated Romano
    cheese
½ teaspoon garlic salt
½ teaspoon lemon pepper seasoning

1. Combine all ingredients in a 1-quart casserole.
2. Bake, uncovered, at 350°F 25 minutes, or until heated through. Serve with **assorted crackers.**

3 cups

18 *Baked Mushrooms*

1½ pounds fresh mushroom caps*
1 cup butter or margarine, melted
2 teaspoons finely chopped onion
1 garlic clove, minced
½ teaspoon rosemary
¾ teaspoon Worcestershire sauce

1. Place mushroom caps in a 1½-quart casserole.
2. Combine remaining ingredients. Pour over mushrooms.
3. Bake, covered, at 325°F 30 minutes, or until tender.

12 servings

* The mushroom stems can be sautéed and added to **hot, cooked green beans.**

19 *Onion Appetizers*

4 medium onions, finely chopped
3 tablespoons butter or margarine
½ cup dairy sour cream
1 tablespoon flour
½ teaspoon salt
    Dash pepper
1 teaspoon caraway seed
3 eggs, beaten
4 bacon slices, cooked and crumbled
1 unbaked 9-inch pie shell

1. Sauté onion in butter in a skillet.
2. Blend sour cream, flour, salt, pepper, and caraway seed. Beat in eggs. Stir in bacon and onion. Pour into pie shell.
3. Bake, uncovered, at 325°F 35 to 40 minutes, or until filling is set. Let stand a few minutes. Cut into wedges to serve.

16 appetizers

20 Wine-Cheese Canapés

½ cup whipped unsalted butter
4 teaspoons Roquefort cheese
4 toasted bread rounds
2 packages (3 ounces each) cream cheese
2 tablespoons sauterne
Parsley, minced
Pimento-stuffed olive slices
Paprika
Clear Glaze (see recipe)

1. Whip together butter and Roquefort cheese. Spread onto toasted bread rounds.
2. Whip cream cheese with sauterne.
3. Pipe a swirl of the mixture onto each canapé. Roll edges in minced parsley. Top with pimento-stuffed olive slice; sprinkle with paprika.
4. Glaze and chill.

Clear Glaze: Soften **1 envelope unflavored gelatin** in **⅔ cup cold water** in a bowl. Pour **1 cup boiling water** over softened gelatin and stir until gelatin is dissolved. Chill until slightly thickened. To glaze canapés: Place canapés on wire racks over a large shallow pan. Working quickly, spoon about 2 teaspoons of slightly thickened gelatin over each canapé. (Have ready a bowl of ice and water and a bowl of hot water. The gelatin may have to be set over one or the other during glazing to maintain the proper consistency.) The gelatin should cling slightly to canapés when spooned over them. Any drips may be scooped up and reused.

21

About 24 canapés

22 Liver Pâté

This is not baked, but made with gelatin and chilled. Calories can be cut by serving with vegetables rather than the usual crackers.

1½ cups chopped onion
1 cup chopped celery
1½ cups Chicken Stock
1 cup dry white wine
1 teaspoon paprika
⅛ teaspoon ground allspice or cloves
¼ teaspoon garlic powder
4 drops Tabasco
1¼ teaspoons salt
1½ pounds chicken livers, membranes removed
2 envelopes unflavored gelatin
½ cup cold water
Assorted vegetable relishes

1. Simmer onion and celery in stock and wine in an uncovered saucepan until liquid is reduced to 2 cups (about 15 minutes). Stir in paprika, allspice, garlic powder, Tabasco, and salt; simmer 2 minutes. Stir in livers; simmer covered until livers are tender (about 15 minutes). Drain; discard liquid.
2. Sprinkle gelatin over cold water; let stand 3 minutes. Set over low heat, stirring occasionally, until gelatin is dissolved (about 5 minutes).
3. Purée half the livers and vegetables along with half the gelatin mixture in a food processor or blender. Repeat with remaining ingredients; combine the two mixtures.
4. Pour mixture into a lightly oiled 1½-quart mold or bowl or ten 6-ounce custard cups. Chill until set (about 4 hours).
5. Serve from mold, or unmold onto platter and accompany with assorted vegetables.

10 to 12 servings

23 Puff Shrimp with Orange Ginger Sauce

Orange Ginger Sauce (see recipe)
Fat for deep frying heated to 375°F
2 pounds medium raw shrimp (20 to 25 per pound)
3 egg yolks
½ cup white wine
¾ cup all-purpose flour
1 teaspoon salt
¼ teaspoon pepper
3 egg whites

Orange Ginger Sauce:
1 cup orange marmalade
2 tablespoons soy sauce
¼ cup sherry
1 piece whole ginger root
1 clove garlic, minced

1. Prepare and cool Orange Ginger Sauce.
2. Fill a deep saucepan or automatic deep fryer one-half to two-thirds full with fat for deep frying; heat slowly to 375°F.
3. Shell and devein raw shrimp and set aside.
4. Beat together in a bowl egg yolks, wine, flour, salt, and pepper until smooth.
5. Beat egg whites until stiff, not dry, peaks are formed. Fold egg whites into egg yolk mixture.
6. Dry shrimp thoroughly and dip into batter, coating well.
7. Deep-fry one layer deep in heated fat 2 to 3 minutes on each side, or until golden brown. Remove from fat with a slotted spoon. Drain on absorbent paper. Be sure temperature of fat is 375°F before frying each layer. Serve shrimp hot accompanied with the Orange Ginger Sauce for dipping.
8. For Orange Ginger Sauce, combine in a saucepan marmalade, soy sauce, sherry, ginger root, and minced garlic. Stir over low heat until mixture bubbles. Remove from heat. Cool. Remove ginger before serving.

40 to 50 appetizers

24 Oysters Rockefeller

2 tablespoons butter or margarine
2 tablespoons flour
½ teaspoon salt
⅛ teaspoon pepper
1 cup milk (use light cream for richer sauce)
1 egg, well beaten
2 dozen oysters in shells
2 tablespoons sherry
2 tablespoons butter or margarine
1 tablespoon finely chopped onion
1 pound fresh spinach, cooked, drained, and finely chopped
1 tablespoon minced parsley
½ teaspoon Worcestershire sauce
6 drops Tabasco
¼ teaspoon salt
Few grains ground nutmeg
¼ cup shredded Parmesan cheese

1. For sauce, heat 2 tablespoons butter in a saucepan. Blend in flour, salt, and pepper; heat and stir until bubbly.
2. Gradually add the milk, stirring until smooth. Bring to boiling; cook and stir 1 to 2 minutes longer.
3. Stir the egg into white sauce; set aside.
4. Pour **coarse salt** into a 15×10×1-inch jelly roll pan to a ¼-inch depth. Open oysters and arrange the oysters, in the shells, on the salt; sprinkle ¼ teaspoon sherry over each.
5. Heat 2 tablespoons butter in a heavy skillet. Add the onion and cook until partially tender. Add the chopped spinach, 2 tablespoons of the white sauce, parsley, Worcestershire sauce, and Tabasco to the skillet along with salt and nutmeg; mix thoroughly. Heat 2 to 3 minutes.
6. Spoon spinach mixture over all of the oysters; spoon remaining white sauce over spinach. Sprinkle each oyster with cheese.
7. Bake at 375°F 15 to 20 minutes, or until tops are lightly browned.

4 to 6 servings

25 Avocado Sandwiches on Sour Dough

2 avocados, thinly sliced and salted
¼ cup butter (½ stick), softened
½ teaspoon oregano leaves
¼ teaspoon each chervil, parsley flakes, and grated lemon peel
Dash onion powder
8 slices sour dough or Italian bread, diagonally cut

1. Prepare avocado slices.
2. Cream butter with seasonings. Spread thinly over bread.
3. Top with avocado slices. Serve with white wine.

8 servings

26 Wine-Pickled Mushrooms

1 pound fresh mushrooms, sliced
    lengthwise
1 cup water
⅔ cup white vinegar
½ cup sugar
1 teaspoon salt
½ teaspoon monosodium gluta-
    mate
½ teaspoon celery salt
4 sprigs parsley
2 small stalks celery
1 tablespoon mixed pickling spices
1 bay leaf
6 whole cloves
12 peppercorns
½ teaspoon whole allspice
1 cup dry white wine

1. Prepare mushrooms and set aside in a bowl.
2. Mix remaining ingredients, except wine, in a saucepan; bring rapidly to boiling, reduce heat and simmer 10 minutes.
3. Strain the mixture over mushrooms and stir in the wine.
4. Cover and refrigerate several days before serving.

1 quart pickled mushrooms

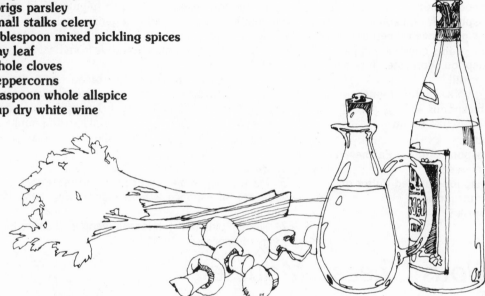

27 Cocktail Meatballs with Mushroom Curry Sauce

Meatballs:
1 pound ground beef
½ cup fine soft bread crumbs
¼ cup milk
¼ cup sherry
1 egg, slightly beaten
2 tablespoons grated onion
¼ teaspoon ground ginger
1 teaspoon salt
¼ teaspoon pepper
2 tablespoons bacon drippings
    or other fat
Mushroom Curry Sauce:
1 can (about 10 ounces) condensed
    cream of mushroom soup
¼ cup sherry
1 teaspoon curry powder

1. For meatballs, mix beef, bread crumbs, milk, wine, egg, onion, ginger, salt, and pepper; shape mixture into little balls, using about one level teaspoon for each.
2. Heat bacon drippings in a large heavy skillet; add a single layer of meatballs and cook, slowly, for about 10 minutes, or until meat is done, shaking pan gently from time to time to cook and brown evenly.
3. When all meat is cooked, spear each with a pick and arrange in hot serving dish.
4. For sauce, combine soup, wine, and curry powder. Heat through and serve piping hot with meatballs.

About 60 meatballs

28 Hot Crab Meat Canapés

2 cups (about 8 ounces) fresh lump crab meat (bony tissue removed)
1 tablespoon chopped pimento
3 tablespoons butter or margarine
1 tablespoon finely chopped green pepper
1 teaspoon finely chopped onion
3 tablespoons flour
½ teaspoon salt
¼ teaspoon dry mustard
Few grains white pepper
Few grains cayenne pepper
½ teaspoon Worcestershire sauce
¾ cup milk
1 egg yolk, slightly beaten
2 tablespoons sherry
5 slices white bread
Butter
5 teaspoons grated Parmesan cheese
2½ teaspoons melted butter or margarine
Paprika

1. Set out crab meat and pimento.
2. Heat 3 tablespoons butter in a heavy 2-quart saucepan; add green pepper and onion. Cook over low heat 2 to 3 minutes, or until partially tender. Blend in flour, salt, dry mustard, white pepper, cayenne pepper, and Worcestershire sauce. Heat until mixture bubbles. Add the milk gradually, stirring constantly. Bring mixture rapidly to boiling, stirring constantly; cook 1 to 2 minutes longer. Vigorously stir about 3 tablespoons hot mixture into egg yolk. Immediately blend into mixture in saucepan and cook, stirring constantly, about 5 minutes. Add crab meat and pimento to saucepan and mix gently until thoroughly blended. Cook over low heat, stirring gently, 2 to 3 minutes or until crab meat is thoroughly heated. Remove from heat and stir in sherry. Cool.
3. For canapés, trim crust from bread and toast until golden brown. Lightly spread toast with butter. Cover toast with crab meat mixture. Top each slice with 1 teaspoon grated cheese and ½ teaspoon of melted butter. Sprinkle with paprika.
4. Cut each toast slice diagonally into 4 triangles and place on a baking sheet.
5. Bake at 425°F 8 to 10 minutes.
6. Place canapés on broiler rack and place rack under broiler with tops of canapés 2 to 3 inches from heat. Broil 1 to 2 minutes.
7. Serve piping hot with **lemon wedges.** If desired, garnish with sprigs of parsley.

20 canapés

29 Fabulous Cheese Mousse

¼ cup cold water
1 envelope unflavored gelatin
3¾ ounces (three 1¼-ounce packages) Roquefort cheese
2⅔ ounces (two 1⅓-ounce packages) Camembert cheese
1 egg yolk, slightly beaten
1 tablespoon sherry
1 teaspoon Worcestershire sauce
½ cup chilled whipping cream
1 egg white
Pimento-stuffed olive slices

1. Lightly oil a fancy 1-pint mold with salad or cooking oil (not olive oil); set aside to drain. Chill a small bowl and rotary beater.
2. Pour the cold water into a small cup or custard cup. Sprinkle the gelatin evenly over the water. Let stand about 5 minutes to soften. Dissolve completely by placing cup over very hot water.
3. Force the Roquefort and Camembert cheeses through a fine sieve. Blend in the egg yolk, sherry, and Worcestershire sauce. Stir the dissolved gelatin and add to the cheese mixture, blending thoroughly.
4. Using the chilled bowl and beater, beat whipping cream until it is of medium consistency (piles softly).
5. Using clean beater, beat egg white until rounded peaks are formed. Fold whipped cream and egg white into the cheese mixture. Turn into the mold. Chill until firm.
6. Unmold onto chilled plate and garnish with olive slices. Serve with **crackers.**

One 1-pint mold

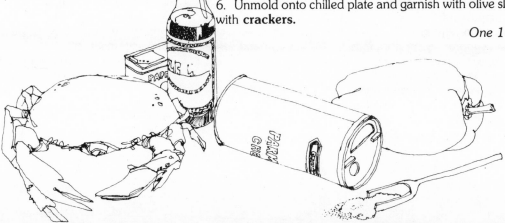

Salads

30 Sauerkraut Slaw

2 cups (16-ounce can) sauerkraut,
   drained and snipped with
   scissors
1 onion, chopped (about ½ cup)
1 green pepper, sliced (about ¾ cup)
1 unpared red apple, diced (about 1
   cup)
⅓ to ½ cup sugar
1 can (16 ounces) sliced tomatoes or
   tomato wedges, drained
   Seasoned pepper

1. Combine sauerkraut, onion, green pepper, apple, and sugar in a serving bowl; toss until well mixed. Cover and refrigerate.
2. Before serving, overlap tomato slices around edge of bowl. Sprinkle slices with seasoned pepper.

8 to 12 servings

31 Stuffed Eggplant Salad

2 large eggplants
4 medium tomatoes, peeled and
   diced
⅓ cup thinly sliced green onion
⅓ cup olive or salad oil
½ cup fresh lemon juice
¼ cup chopped parsley
1 tablespoon sugar
2½ teaspoons salt
2 teaspoons oregano
¼ teaspoon ground black pepper

1. Wash and dry eggplants; place on a cookie sheet. Bake in a 375°F oven 35 to 45 minutes, or until tender when pierced with a fork. Cool.
2. Cut a thin lengthwise slice from the side of each eggplant; carefully spoon out pulp. Chill shells.
3. Dice pulp and put into a bowl. Add tomatoes, green onion, oil, lemon juice, parsley, sugar, salt, oregano, and pepper; toss to mix. Chill.
4. Before serving, drain off excess liquid from salad mixture. Spoon salad into shells.

6 servings

32 *Bacon-Bean Salad*

⅔ cup cider vinegar
¾ cup sugar
1 teaspoon salt
1 can (16 ounces) cut green beans
1 can (16 ounces) cut wax beans
1 can (16 ounces) kidney beans,
  thoroughly rinsed and drained
1 medium onion, quartered and
  finely sliced
1 medium green pepper, chopped
½ teaspoon freshly ground black
  pepper
⅓ cup salad oil
1 pound bacon, cut in 1-inch squares
Lettuce (optional)

1. Blend vinegar, sugar, and salt in a small saucepan. Heat until the sugar is dissolved and set aside.
2. Drain all beans and toss with onion, green pepper, vinegar mixture, and ground pepper. Pour oil over all and toss to coat evenly. Store in a covered container in refrigerator.
3. When ready to serve, fry bacon until crisp; drain on absorbent paper. Toss the bacon with bean mixture. If desired, serve the salad on crisp lettuce.

About 12 servings

Note: If desired, omit bacon.

33 *Mixed Vegetable Salad*

1 cup diced cooked potatoes
1½ cups cooked sliced carrots
1½ cups cooked whole or cut green
  beans (fresh, frozen, or canned)
1½ cups cooked green peas (fresh,
  frozen, or canned)
1 cup sliced or diced cooked beets
Bottled Italian-style salad dressing
Lettuce
1 cup sliced celery
1 small onion, chopped
2 hard-cooked eggs, chopped
¾ cup small pimento-stuffed olives
¾ cup mayonnaise
¼ cup chili sauce
1 teaspoon lemon juice

1. Put potatoes, carrots, beans, peas, and beets into separate bowls. Pour salad dressing over each vegetable; chill thoroughly.
2. To serve, drain vegetables and arrange in a lettuce-lined salad bowl along with celery, onion, eggs, and olives.
3. Blend mayonnaise, chili sauce, and lemon juice. Pass with the salad.

About 8 servings

34 *Beef Salad Acapulco*

3 cups cooked beef strips
¾ cup salad oil
½ cup red wine vinegar
1½ teaspoons salt
¼ teaspoon ground pepper
⅛ teaspoon cayenne pepper
1 tablespoon chili powder
Salad greens
Avocado slices, brushed with
  marinade
Onion and green pepper rings
Tomato wedges
Ripe olives

1. Put beef strips into a shallow dish. Combine oil, vinegar, salt, pepper, cayenne pepper, and chili powder in a bottle; cover and shake vigorously. Pour over beef strips. Cover; marinate several hours or overnight.
2. Remove beef from marinade and arrange on crisp greens on chilled salad plates. Garnish with avocado slices, onion rings, green pepper rings, tomato wedges, and ripe olives. Serve the marinade as the dressing.

4 to 6 servings

35 *Greek-Style Lamb-and-Olive Salad*

Greek-Style Salad Dressing:
- ½ cup olive or salad oil
- 1 cup red wine vinegar
- 3 to 4 tablespoons honey
- 1½ teaspoons salt
- ⅛ teaspoon dry mustard
- 2 teaspoons crushed dried mint leaves
- ¼ teaspoon crushed oregano
- ¼ teaspoon crushed thyme
- ¼ teaspoon anise seed

Salad:
- 1½ pounds roast lamb, trimmed of fat and cut in strips
- Curly endive
- 1 large cucumber, pared and sliced
- 4 medium tomatoes, sliced and quartered
- 1 cup pitted ripe olives

1. For dressing, mix oil, vinegar, honey, salt, dry mustard, mint, oregano, thyme, and anise.
2. Pour the dressing over cooked lamb in a bowl, cover, and marinate in refrigerator at least 1 hour, or until thoroughly chilled.
3. To serve, arrange curly endive in a large salad bowl. Toss cucumber, tomatoes, and olives with some of the dressing and turn into salad bowl. Spoon meat over vegetables and pour more dressing over all.

6 servings

36 *Molded Spinach Cottage Cheese on Platter*

- 1 package (10 ounces) frozen chopped spinach
- 2 envelopes unflavored gelatin
- ¾ cup water
- 2 chicken bouillon cubes
- 2 tablespoons lemon juice
- 1½ cups creamed cottage cheese
- ½ cup dairy sour cream
- ½ cup sliced celery
- ⅓ cup chopped green pepper
- 2 tablespoons minced green onion

1. Cook and drain spinach, reserving liquid. Add enough water to liquid to make ½ cup. Set spinach and liquid aside.
2. Soften gelatin in ¾ cup water in a saucepan; add bouillon cubes. Set over low heat; stirring occasionally, until gelatin and bouillon cubes are dissolved. Remove from heat; stir in spinach liquid and lemon juice. Set aside.
3. Beat cottage cheese until fairly smooth with mixer or in electric blender. Blend with sour cream and then gelatin mixture. Stir in spinach, celery, green pepper, and onion. Turn into a 5-cup mold. Chill until firm.
4. Unmold onto a chilled large platter. If desired, arrange slices of summer sausage around the mold.

6 to 8 servings

37 *Chicken-Fruit Salad*

- Creamy Cooked Salad Dressing (page 82)
- 3 cups cubed cooked chicken
- Bottled French dressing
- ½ cup diced celery
- 1 cup small seedless grapes
- ½ cup drained crushed pineapple; reserve syrup for dressing
- 1 orange, sectioned and sections cut in halves
- ½ cup toasted salted almonds, coarsely chopped
- 1 tablespoon minced crystallized ginger

1. Prepare Creamy Cooked Salad Dressing; refrigerate.
2. Toss chicken in a bowl with enough French dressing to coat thoroughly; cover and set in refrigerator to marinate about 3 hours, mixing occasionally.
3. Lightly toss together chicken, celery, grapes, pineapple, orange, almonds, and ginger. Pour desired amount of the dressing over chicken mixture and toss gently. Cover and chill thoroughly.
4. To serve, line a salad bowl with chilled crisp greens. Fill bowl with chicken salad.

About 8 servings

38 Tossed Supper Salad

Dressing:
- 1 cup salad oil
- ½ cup cider vinegar
- 1 teaspoon salt
- 1 teaspoon sugar
- ½ teaspoon onion salt
- ¼ teaspoon crushed tarragon
- ¼ teaspoon paprika
- ¼ teaspoon dry mustard
- ¼ teaspoon celery salt
- ⅛ teaspoon garlic salt
- ⅛ teaspoon ground black pepper

Salad:
- 2 cans (6½ or 7 ounces each) tuna
- ½ head lettuce
- 1 cup spinach leaves, washed
- 1 cup diced celery
- ¾ cup chopped green pepper
- ½ cup cooked green peas
- 4 sweet pickles, chopped
- 4 radishes, thinly sliced
- 2 hard-cooked eggs, sliced
- 2 tablespoons chopped pimento
- 2 tomatoes, rinsed and cut in eighths
- 1 teaspoon salt
  Tomato wedges
  Ripe olives

1. For dressing, put oil and vinegar into a jar; mix salt, sugar, and seasonings; add to jar, cover, and shake well. Refrigerate until needed. Shake before using.
2. For salad, drain tuna well and separate into small chunks; put into a bowl. Toss tuna with ½ cup prepared dressing; cover and refrigerate 1 to 2 hours.
3. Tear lettuce and spinach into pieces and put into a large bowl. Add celery, green pepper, peas, pickles, radishes, eggs, and pimento; add the tuna with its dressing and tomatoes. Sprinkle with salt. Toss lightly until ingredients are mixed and lightly coated with dressing; add more dressing, if desired.
4. Garnish with tomato wedges and ripe olives.

8 to 10 servings

Note: Two cups of diced cooked chicken, turkey, veal, or pork may be substituted for tuna.

39 Hearty Bean Salad

- 1 can (15 ounces) kidney beans, drained
- 2 hard-cooked eggs, diced
- ¼ cup chopped onion
- ½ cup diced celery
- ⅓ cup drained sweet pickle relish
- ½ cup shredded sharp Cheddar cheese
- ½ cup dairy sour cream
  Lettuce

1. Mix kidney beans, eggs, onion, celery, relish, and cheese in a large bowl. Add sour cream and toss together lightly; chill.
2. Serve the salad on lettuce.

4 to 6 servings

40 Cinnamon Waldorf Molds

- ⅓ cup red cinnamon candies
- 3 cups water
- 2 packages (3 ounces each) cherry-flavored gelatin
- 1 tablespoon lemon juice

1. Heat cinnamon candies and water to boiling in a saucepan. Remove from heat and add gelatin and lemon juice; stir until gelatin and candies are dissolved.
2. Chill until slightly thickened.
3. Mix in celery, apples, marshmallows, and walnuts. Spoon

2 cups chopped celery
2 cups chopped unpared red apples
1 cup miniature marshmallows
½ cup chopped walnuts
　Lettuce

into 6 to 8 individual fancy molds or turn into a 1½-quart mold. Chill until firm.
4. Unmold onto lettuce.

6 to 8 servings

41 Chef's Fruit Salad

Cinnamon-Buttered Raisins:
1 tablespoon butter or margarine, melted
½ cup dark raisins
½ cup golden raisins
½ teaspoon ground cinnamon

Salad:
　Salad greens
1 quart shredded salad greens
6 cups mixed fruit
　Creamy Lemon Celery-Seed Dressing or Celery-Seed Salad Dressing
1½ cups Swiss cheese strips
1½ cups cooked ham or turkey strips

1. For Cinnamon-Buttered Raisins, melt butter in a skillet. Mix in raisins and cinnamon. Set over low heat 5 minutes, stirring frequently. Cool.
2. Line a salad bowl with salad greens. Add shredded greens.
3. Arrange fruit in bowl. Spoon some of the desired dressing over all. Top with cheese and ham strips alternated with Cinnamon-Buttered Raisins. Serve with remaining dressing.

About 6 servings

Creamy Lemon Celery-Seed Dressing: Blend thoroughly 1½ cups mayonnaise, ¼ cup unsweetened pineapple juice, 1 teaspoon grated lemon peel, 1 tablespoon lemon juice, ½ teaspoon celery seed, and few drops Tabasco. Cover and refrigerate at least 1 hour to blend flavors.   42

About 1½ cups dressing

Celery-Seed Salad Dressing: Combine in a small bowl ¼ cup sugar, ⅓ cup light corn syrup, ¼ cup cider vinegar, 1½ to 2 teaspoons celery seed, 1 teaspoon dry mustard, 1 teaspoon salt, few grains white pepper, and 1 teaspoon grated onion. Beat with a rotary beater until mixture is thoroughly blended. Add 1 cup salad oil very gradually, beating constantly. Continue beating until mixture thickens. Cover and chill thoroughly. Shake before serving.   43

2 cups dressing

44 Salade à la Crème (Green Salad with Cream Dressing)

1 quart mixed greens (such as iceberg, Boston, or Bibb lettuce, romaine, escarole, or chicory)
½ cup dairy sour cream
2 tablespoons chopped parsley
2 tablespoons dry white wine (such as chenin blanc)
½ teaspoon salt
⅛ teaspoon freshly ground pepper

1. Using only perfect leaves, wash, dry, tear into pieces, and chill greens before combining with dressing. Cold, dry leaves ensure a crisp salad.
2. Combine sour cream, parsley, wine, salt, and pepper.
3. At serving time, transfer greens to a large bowl, add dressing, and toss well.

About 6 servings

45 *Garden-Green Salad Mold*

1 package (3 ounces) lime-flavored
    gelatin
¼ teaspoon salt
1 cup boiling water
1 cup cold water
1 ripe medium avocado
1 tablespoon lemon juice
2 cups finely shredded cabbage
½ cup thinly sliced radishes
½ cup thinly sliced green onions with
    tops
    Crisp greens

1. Put gelatin and salt into a bowl; add boiling water and stir until completely dissolved. Blend in cold water. Chill until slightly thickened.
2. Mash avocado and stir in lemon juice; blend thoroughly with gelatin. Mix in cabbage, radishes, and green onions.
3. Turn into a 1-quart mold or individual molds and chill until firm. Unmold onto chilled serving plate and garnish with salad greens.

About 8 servings

46 *Stewed Tomato Aspic*

1 envelope unflavored gelatin
½ cup cold water
1 can (16 ounces) stewed tomatoes
1 tablespoon sugar
¼ teaspoon salt
1 tablespoon cider vinegar
1½ teaspoons prepared horseradish
1½ teaspoons grated onion
¼ teaspoon Worcestershire sauce
2 hard-cooked eggs, cut in quarters
    Salad greens

1. Sprinkle gelatin over water to soften.
2. Turn tomatoes into a saucepan and break up any large pieces with a spoon. Stir in sugar, salt, vinegar, horseradish, onion, and Worcestershire sauce and heat to boiling. Add softened gelatin and stir until dissolved.
3. Chill gelatin until slightly thickened.
4. Arrange egg quarters around bottom of a 3- or 4-cup mold. Spoon slightly thickened gelatin mixture into mold. Chill until firm.
5. Unmold and garnish with crisp greens.

4 to 6 servings

47 *Rice Salad with Assorted Sausages*

⅓ cup white wine vinegar
1 teaspoon lemon juice
¼ teaspoon French mustard
1 teaspoon salt
¼ teaspoon ground black pepper
⅓ cup salad oil
3 cups cooked enriched white rice,
    cooled
3 cups finely shredded red cabbage
½ cup raisins
½ cup walnut pieces
    Greens
    Link sausage (such as bratwurst,
      smoky links, and frankfurters),
      cooked

1. Put vinegar into a bottle. Add lemon juice, mustard, salt, and pepper. Cover and shake. Add oil and shake well.
2. Combine rice, cabbage, raisins, and walnuts in a bowl; chill.
3. When ready to serve, shake dressing well and pour over salad; toss until well mixed.
4. Arrange greens on luncheon plates, spoon salad on greens, and accompany with assorted sausages.

6 to 8 servings

48 *Shimmering Strawberry Mold*

2 packages (3 ounces each)
  strawberry-flavored gelatin
1½ cups boiling water
2 bottles (7 ounces each) lemon-lime
  carbonated beverage
1 pint fresh ripe strawberries,
  rinsed and hulled
⅓ cup sugar
  Salad greens
  Whole strawberries (optional)

1. Turn gelatin into a bowl, add boiling water, and stir until completely dissolved. Mix in carbonated beverage. Stir frequently over ice and water until slightly thicker than consistency of thick unbeaten egg white.
2. Meanwhile, cut berries lengthwise into halves, if large; sprinkle with sugar and set aside.
3. Stir the berries into the slightly thickened gelatin. Spoon into a 2-quart fancy tubed mold (or 10 individual molds). Chill until firm.
4. Unmold onto a chilled serving plate; garnish with crisp salad greens and, if desired, strawberries.

About 10 servings

Note: If desired, nut-coated cream cheese balls may be added to the salad. Soften 1 package (8 ounces) cream cheese; shape into ½-inch balls and roll in finely chopped walnuts (about ¾ cup). Arrange 5 or 6 balls in bottom of 2-quart mold; spoon enough of the slightly thickened gelatin-strawberry mixture into mold to cover cheese balls. Continue layering with remaining balls and gelatin mixture. Chill until firm.

49 *Wilted Cabbage*

4 cups shredded cabbage
6 slices bacon
½ cup cider vinegar
¼ cup water
3 tablespoons sugar
½ teaspoon salt
¼ teaspoon dry mustard

1. Turn cabbage into a bowl.
2. Cook bacon until crisp in a skillet; drain, reserving ¼ cup drippings. Crumble bacon onto cabbage; set aside.
3. Put reserved drippings into skillet. Add vinegar, water, sugar, salt, and dry mustard. Heat to boiling, stirring to blend.
4. Pour dressing over cabbage and bacon; toss lightly to mix.

6 to 8 servings

50 *Ham Mousse Piquant*

2 packages (3 ounces each)
  lemon-flavored gelatin
¼ teaspoon salt
2 cups boiling water
1 cup cold water
¼ cup cider vinegar
2 teaspoons grated onion
¼ cup water
⅔ cup chopped sweet pickle
¼ cup diced pimento
⅔ cup mayonnaise or salad dressing
1 teaspoon Worcestershire sauce
1 cup chilled whipping cream,
  whipped
4 cups firmly packed coarsely ground
  cooked ham
1 cup sliced celery
  Watercress

1. Turn gelatin and salt into a bowl. Add boiling water and stir until gelatin is dissolved. Stir in cold water, vinegar, and onion.
2. Remove 2 cups of the mixture and stir in ¼ cup water; chill until mixture thickens slightly.
3. Mix pickle and pimento into the slightly thickened gelatin. Turn into a ring mold (11 to 12 cups). Chill until just set but not firm.
4. Meanwhile, chill remaining gelatin over ice and water, stirring frequently, until slightly thickened, then whip with rotary beater until fluffy.
5. Blend mayonnaise and Worcestershire sauce; fold into whipped cream. Combine whipped cream mixture, ham, celery, and whipped gelatin. Turn into mold over pickle layer. Chill until firm.
6. Unmold onto a chilled serving plate. Fill center of mold with watercress.

About 12 servings

51 *Frosty Fruit Salad*

1 cup chopped soft dried prunes
1 cup orange pieces (1 to 2 oranges)
1 can (13¼ ounces) pineapple tidbits,
    drained; reserve ¼ cup syrup
½ cup sliced maraschino cherries,
    well drained on absorbent paper
1 envelope unflavored gelatin
⅓ cup cold water
2 cups creamed cottage cheese
1 cup dairy sour cream
1 cup whipping cream, whipped
¾ cup sugar
¾ teaspoon salt
1 large ripe banana, sliced
½ cup chopped salted almonds

1. Prepare fruits and set aside.
2. Soften gelatin in cold water in a small saucepan. Set over low heat and stir until gelatin is dissolved.
3. Sieve cottage cheese into a bowl. Blend in reserved pineapple syrup, sour cream, whipped cream, sugar, and salt; stir in the dissolved gelatin. Add the reserved fruits, banana, and almonds; mix well. Turn into refrigerator trays and freeze.
4. Allow salad to soften slightly at room temperature before serving. To serve, cut into wedges.

About 12 servings

52 *Vegetable Medley Salad Dressing Deluxe*

1 cup salad oil
3 tablespoons cider vinegar
2 tablespoons prepared horseradish
1 tablespoon sugar
1 teaspoon dry mustard
1 teaspoon paprika
½ teaspoon seasoned salt
¾ teaspoon salt
⅛ teaspoon ground black pepper
    Few grains cayenne pepper
1 medium ripe tomato, peeled and
    cut in pieces
1 small onion, peeled and cut in
    pieces
½ small cucumber, pared and cut in
    pieces
⅓ small ripe avocado, peeled and cut
    in pieces
1 large clove garlic, peeled

1. Put oil, vinegar, horseradish, sugar, seasonings, vegetables, avocado, and garlic into an electric blender container and blend thoroughly. Chill.
2. Serve on a tossed vegetable salad.

About 3½ cups dressing

53 *Jiffy French Dressing*

1 tablespoon sugar
1 teaspoon paprika
1 teaspoon dry mustard
1 teaspoon salt
⅛ teaspoon ground black pepper
1 cup salad oil
¼ cup vinegar or lemon juice

1. Blend sugar, paprika, dry mustard, salt, and pepper; put into a jar. Add oil and vinegar. Cover jar tightly and shake vigorously to blend. Store in refrigerator.
2. Before serving, shake dressing thoroughly.

1¼ cups dressing

54 Gourmet French Dressing

¾ cup olive oil
¼ cup vinegar (tarragon or cider)
¼ teaspoon Worcestershire sauce
1 clove garlic, cut in halves
1 teaspoon sugar
½ teaspoon salt
¼ teaspoon paprika
¼ teaspoon dry mustard
⅛ teaspoon ground black pepper
⅛ teaspoon ground thyme

1. Combine oil, vinegar, Worcestershire sauce, garlic, sugar, salt, paprika, dry mustard, pepper, and thyme in a jar; cover and shake well. Chill in refrigerator.
2. Before serving, remove garlic and beat or shake dressing thoroughly.

About 1 cup dressing

Roquefort French Dressing: Follow recipe for Gourmet French Dressing. Blend **3 ounces (about ¾ cup) Roquefort cheese,** crumbled, and **2 teaspoons water** until smooth. Add dressing slowly to cheese, blending well.

55

56 No-Oil Salad Dressing

½ cup water
½ cup white wine vinegar
1 tablespoon cold water
2 teaspoons cornstarch
1 tablespoon sugar
1 tablespoon chopped parsley
1 teaspoon salt
½ teaspoon basil
¼ teaspoon paprika
¼ teaspoon dry mustard
⅛ teaspoon ground white pepper

1. Heat ½ cup water and vinegar to boiling. Blend 1 tablespoon cold water and cornstarch; pour into vinegar mixture, stirring constantly.
2. Cook and stir until slightly thickened. Stir in sugar, parsley, salt, basil, paprika, dry mustard, and pepper. Chill thoroughly.
3. Serve on tossed salad greens.

About 1 cup dressing

57 Cooked Salad Dressing

¼ cup sugar
1 tablespoon flour
½ teaspoon dry mustard
½ teaspoon salt
⅛ teaspoon ground pepper
1 cup water
¼ cup cider vinegar
4 egg yolks, fork beaten
2 tablespoons butter or margarine

1. Blend sugar, flour, dry mustard, salt, and pepper in a heavy saucepan. Add water gradually, stirring constantly. Bring rapidly to boiling; cook and stir mixture 2 minutes. Stir in vinegar.
2. Stir about 3 tablespoons of the hot mixture into the beaten egg yolks. Immediately blend into mixture in saucepan. Cook and stir until slightly thickened.
3. Remove from heat and blend in butter. Cool; chill. Store in a covered jar in refrigerator.

About 1½ cups dressing

58 Creamy Cooked Salad Dressing

2 tablespoons sugar
⅛ teaspoon salt
2 tablespoons cider vinegar
2 tablespoons pineapple syrup
3 egg yolks, slightly beaten
1 tablespoon butter or margarine
1 cup chilled whipping cream, whipped

1. Mix sugar and salt in a heavy saucepan. Stir in vinegar and pineapple syrup. Bring to boiling, stirring constantly.
2. Stir about 2 tablespoons of the hot mixture into egg yolks until blended. Immediately blend into mixture in saucepan. Cook and stir until slightly thickened.
3. Remove from heat; blend in butter. Cool and chill.
4. Blend chilled mixture into whipped cream. Cover and refrigerate until ready to use.

About 2 cups dressing

59 *Refreshing Salad Mold*

A nice accompaniment to a savory meat dish, especially on warm days.

1 can or bottle (12 ounces) beer
2½ cups ginger ale
2 envelopes unflavored gelatin
2 medium grapefruit, peeled and sectioned

1. Sprinkle gelatin over beer in a saucepan; let stand to soften. Stir over low heat until gelatin is dissolved. Add ginger ale.
2. Chill until partially thickened. Fold in grapefruit sections.
3. Turn into a lightly oiled 5-cup mold. Chill until set. Unmold onto a platter before serving.

8 servings

60 Golden Glow Salad

1 package (6 ounces) lemon-flavored gelatin
2 cups boiling water
1 can (20 ounces) crushed pineapple
1 cup dry white wine, such as chablis
2 cups grated carrots
Crisp salad greens

1. Dissolve gelatin in boiling water.
2. Drain pineapple, reserving 1 cup syrup.
3. Add pineapple syrup and wine to gelatin mixture. Chill until partially set.
4. Fold in carrots and pineapple. Fill 12 individual molds or one 1½-quart mold.
5. Chill until firm and unmold on greens.

12 servings

61 *Gourmet Potato Salad*

5 cups cubed cooked potatoes
½ teaspoon salt
⅛ teaspoon ground black pepper
4 hard-cooked eggs, chopped
1 cup chopped celery
⅔ cup sliced green onions with tops
¼ cup chopped green pepper
1 cup large curd cottage cheese
¼ teaspoon dry mustard
½ teaspoon salt
Few grains black pepper
⅔ cup (6-ounce can) undiluted evaporated milk
½ cup crumbled blue cheese
2 tablespoons cider vinegar
Lettuce

1. Put potatoes into a large bowl and sprinkle with salt and pepper. Add eggs, celery, onions, and green pepper; toss lightly.
2. Put cottage cheese, dry mustard, salt, pepper, evaporated milk, blue cheese, and vinegar into an electric blender container. Blend thoroughly.
3. Pour dressing over mixture in bowl and toss lightly and thoroughly. Chill before serving to blend flavors.
4. Spoon chilled salad into a bowl lined with lettuce. Garnish as desired.

About 8 servings

62 *Piquant Perfection Salad*

1½ cups boiling water
1 package (6 ounces)
    lemon-flavored gelatin
1 can (8 ounces) crushed
    pineapple in juice
    Water
1 can or bottle (12 ounces) beer
3 medium carrots, shredded
    (about 1½ cups)
½ small head cabbage, finely
    shredded (about 3 cups)

1. Pour boiling water over gelatin; stir until dissolved.
2. Drain pineapple, thoroughly pressing out and reserving juice. Add enough water to juice to measure ¾ cup.
3. Add juice and beer to gelatin. Chill until partially thickened.
4. Stir in carrots, cabbage, and pineapple. Turn into a shallow pan or oiled 6½-cup ring mold or any 1½-quart mold. Chill until set.
5. Dip mold briefly in hot water; invert on a serving platter.
6. Serve with a dressing of **1 cup mayonnaise** blended with **2 tablespoons beer.**

12 half-cup servings

63 *Beermato Aspic*

A refreshing complement to many meat, poultry, and fish dishes.

1 can (18 ounces) tomato juice
    (2¼ cups)
1 can or bottle (12 ounces) beer
⅓ cup chopped onion
⅓ cup chopped celery leaves
    (optional)
2½ tablespoons sugar
1 tablespoon lemon juice
½ teaspoon salt
1 bay leaf
2 envelopes unflavored gelatin
¼ cup cold water

1. Combine tomato juice (reserve ¼ cup), beer, onion, celery leaves, sugar, lemon juice, salt, and bay leaf in a saucepan. Simmer, uncovered, 10 minutes.
2. Meanwhile, sprinkle gelatin over cold water and reserved tomato juice in a large bowl; let stand to soften.
3. Strain hot tomato juice mixture into bowl; stir until gelatin is completely dissolved.
4. Pour into a lightly oiled 1-quart mold. Chill until firm. Unmold onto crisp **salad greens.**

8 servings

Note: For individual aspics, turn mixture into 8 oiled ½-cup molds. Chill until firm.

64 *Beer-Curried Fruit*

An unusual accompaniment for baked ham, pork, poultry, or lamb. A nice winter brunch dish, too. It's pretty on a buffet table.

½ cup packed brown sugar
1 tablespoon cornstarch
2 to 3 teaspoons curry powder
¾ cup beer
¼ cup butter or margarine
1 tablespoon grated orange peel
1 can (30 ounces) cling peach
    slices, drained
1 can (29 ounces) pear halves or
    slices, drained
2 cans (11 ounces each) mandarin
    oranges, drained
2 bananas, thinly sliced

1. In a large saucepan, combine sugar, cornstarch, and curry powder. Stir in beer. Cook, stirring constantly, until thickened and clear.
2. Add butter and orange peel; stir until melted.
3. Add peaches, pears, and mandarin oranges. (If using pear halves, cut into slices.) Cover and simmer about 10 minutes. Stir in bananas.
4. Turn into a serving dish, chafing dish, or warming dish. Sprinkle with **flaked coconut.**

7 cups

65 *Gourmet Salad Dressing*

3 ounces Roquefort cheese, crumbled (about ¾ cup)
1 package (3 ounces) cream cheese, softened
1 cup dairy sour cream
⅓ cup sherry
1 tablespoon grated onion
½ teaspoon salt
¼ teaspoon paprika
1 or 2 drops Tabasco

1. Put Roquefort cheese into a bowl. Blend in cream cheese until smooth.
2. Add sour cream, sherry, onion, salt, paprika, and Tabasco; blend until creamy. Store dressing, covered, in refrigerator.

About 2 cups dressing

66 *Enchanting Fruit Dressing*

A fitting partner for fruit.

½ cup water
½ cup honey
8 mint leaves
⅛ teaspoon whole cardamom seed (contents of 3 cardamom pods), crushed
¼ teaspoon salt
½ cup sherry, madeira, or port
1 tablespoon lemon juice

1. Put water, honey, mint leaves (bruise the mint with the back of a spoon), and cardamom seed into a small saucepan with a tight-fitting cover. Set over low heat and stir until mixed. Cover saucepan and bring rapidly to boiling. Boil gently 5 minutes. Remove from heat and stir in salt. Set aside to cool.
2. When mixture is cool, strain it and blend in sherry and lemon juice.

About 1⅓ cups dressing

67 *Chicken Mousse Amandine*

½ cup dry white wine, such as sauterne
2 envelopes unflavored gelatin
3 egg yolks
1 cup milk
1 cup chicken broth

1. Place a small bowl and a rotary beater in refrigerator to chill.
2. Pour wine into a small cup and sprinkle gelatin evenly over wine; set aside.
3. Beat egg yolks slightly in top of a double boiler; add milk gradually, stirring constantly.
4. Stir in the chicken broth gradually. Cook over simmering

½ cup (about 3 ounces) almonds, finely chopped
3 cups ground cooked chicken
¼ cup mayonnaise
2 tablespoons minced parsley
2 tablespoons chopped green olives
1 teaspoon lemon juice
1 teaspoon onion juice
½ teaspoon salt
½ teaspoon celery salt
　Few grains paprika
　Few grains cayenne pepper
½ cup chilled heavy cream
　Sprigs of parsley

water, stirring constantly and rapidly until mixture coats a metal spoon.

5. Remove from heat. Stir softened gelatin and immediately stir it into the hot mixture until gelatin is completely dissolved. Cool; chill in refrigerator or over ice and water until gelatin mixture begins to gel (becomes slightly thicker). If mixture is placed over ice and water, stir frequently; if placed in refrigerator, stir occasionally.

6. Blend almonds and chicken into chilled custard mixture along with mayonnaise, parsley, olives, lemon juice, onion juice, and a mixture of salt, celery salt, paprika, and cayenne pepper.

7. Using the chilled bowl and beater, beat cream until of medium consistency (piles softly).

8. Fold whipped cream into chicken mixture. Turn into a 1½-quart fancy mold. Chill in refrigerator until firm.

9. Unmold onto chilled serving plate and, if desired, garnish with sprigs of parsley.

8 servings

68 *Dubonnet Chicken Salad Mold*

2 envelopes unflavored gelatin
1 cup cranberry juice cocktail
1 cup red Dubonnet
1 cup red currant syrup
1 envelope unflavored gelatin
¾ cup cold water
1 tablespoon soy sauce
1 cup mayonnaise
1½ cups finely diced cooked chicken
½ cup finely chopped celery
¼ cup toasted blanched almonds, finely chopped
½ cup whipping cream, whipped
　Leaf lettuce
　Cucumber slices, scored
　Pitted ripe olives

1. Soften 2 envelopes gelatin in cranberry juice in a saucepan; set over low heat and stir until gelatin is dissolved. Remove from heat and stir in Dubonnet and currant syrup.

2. Pour into a 2-quart fancy tube mold. Chill until set but not firm.

3. Meanwhile, soften 1 envelope gelatin in cold water in a saucepan. Set over low heat and stir until gelatin is dissolved.

4. Remove from heat and stir in soy sauce and mayonnaise until thoroughly blended. Chill until mixture becomes slightly thicker. Mix in chicken, celery, and almonds. Fold in whipped cream until blended.

5. Spoon mixture into mold over first layer. Chill 8 hours or overnight.

6. Unmold onto a chilled serving plate. Garnish with lettuce, cucumber, and olives.

About 10 servings

69 *Peach Wine Mold*

1 can (29 ounces) sliced peaches
1 package (6 ounces) lemon-flavored gelatin
1½ cups boiling water
1 cup white wine
⅓ cup sliced celery
⅓ cup slivered blanched almonds
　Curly endive

1. Drain peaches thoroughly, reserving 1¼ cups syrup. Reserve and refrigerate about 8 peach slices for garnish. Cut remaining peaches into pieces; set aside.

2. Pour gelatin into a bowl, add boiling water, and stir until gelatin is dissolved. Stir in reserved syrup and wine. Chill until partially set.

3. Mix peaches, celery, and almonds into gelatin. Turn into a 1½-quart fancy mold. Chill until firm.

4. Unmold salad onto a serving plate. Garnish with curly endive and reserved peach slices.

About 8 servings

70 *Tangy Cabbage Mold*

A cool, tart taste that is nice with a hearty main dish. If you wish, serve with mayonnaise.

1 envelope unflavored gelatin
¼ cup cold water
¼ cup sugar
2 tablespoons lemon juice
½ teaspoon salt
1 can or bottle (12 ounces) beer
1½ cups shredded cabbage (about ¼ of a 2-pound head)
½ green pepper, shredded

1. Soften gelatin in cold water in a saucepan. Stir over low heat until dissolved.
2. Add sugar, lemon juice, and salt; stir until dissolved. Add beer. Chill until partially thickened.
3. Stir in cabbage and green pepper.
4. Turn into a 3½-cup mold, a shallow 1½-quart oblong casserole (8x6 inches), or 6 individual molds.

6 servings

71 *Hot Potato Salad*

Bacon and beer flavor the slightly sweet sauce on these German-style potatoes. Serve with hot dogs, bratwurst, or Polish sausage. Beer is the perfect beverage.

6 medium boiling potatoes (2 pounds)
10 slices bacon (½ pound)
½ cup chopped onion
½ cup beer
1 to 1½ tablespoons sugar
1 to 1½ teaspoons salt
1 teaspoon celery seed

1. Place unpeeled potatoes in a large saucepan; add water to cover. Heat to boiling. Boil, uncovered, for 20 minutes, or until tender. Peel and cube; turn into a serving dish.
2. Meanwhile, cook bacon until crisp; leave drippings in skillet. Crumble bacon over potatoes.
3. Add onion to skillet. Sauté until tender. Add beer, sugar, salt, and celery seed. Heat to boiling, stirring occasionally. Pour over potatoes; toss lightly.

6 servings

72 *Shrimp Salad with Coral Dressing*

2 cups cooked, peeled, and deveined shrimp
1½ cups cooked rice
½ cup sliced celery
½ cup chopped unpeeled cucumbers
¼ cup chopped chives
⅓ cup mayonnaise
¼ cup dairy sour cream
1 tablespoon chili sauce
¼ teaspoon onion salt
⅛ teaspoon pepper
1½ teaspoons tarragon vinegar
Salad greens
Horseradish (optional)
Lemon wedges

1. Toss shrimp, rice, celery, cucumbers, and chives together.
2. Blend ingredients for dressing. Pour over shrimp mixture and toss thoroughly. Chill.
3. Serve on salad greens. Top with a little horseradish, if desired, and garnish with lemon wedges.
4. Accompany with champagne.

6 servings

73 Salde Siciliano

1 whole clove garlic
4 anchovy fillets
Juice of 1 lemon
6 tablespoons dry red wine, such as burgundy
¾ cup olive oil
Oregano leaves (¼ ounce or 2½ tablespoons)
Peppercorns, crushed (⅛ ounce or ¾ teaspoon)
2 cloves garlic, minced
1 pimento, diced
3 tomatoes, diced
1 cup cooked green beans
1 cup diced hearts of artichoke
1 cup diced hearts of palm
1 head romaine lettuce, torn in pieces
1 head iceberg lettuce, torn in chunks
2 slices bread, toasted and cut in cubes
¼ pound Gorgonzola cheese, crumbled

1. Rub a large wooden salad bowl with the whole clove of garlic. Add anchovy fillets. Rub bowl again with the garlic and anchovies; mash together forming a paste. Blend in, stirring vigorously, the lemon juice, burgundy, olive oil, oregano, and pepper. (If necessary, correct seasonings to taste.)
2. Blend in minced garlic, diced pimento, and tomatoes. Add green beans, hearts of artichoke and palm, romaine, and iceberg lettuce. Toss lightly.
3. Add croutons and cheese. Again, toss lightly. Serve immediately on chilled salad plates.

4 to 8 servings

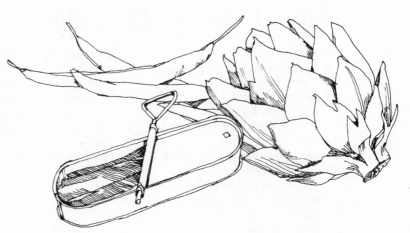

74 White Wine Aspic

1½ tablespoons unflavored gelatin
2 tablespoons sugar
¼ teaspoon salt
⅔ cup cold water
1¼ cups apple juice
1 cup dry white wine, such as chablis
1 tablespoon sweet pickle syrup
1 tablespoon lemon juice
½ cup dairy sour cream

1. Blend gelatin, sugar, and salt in a saucepan; add water. Place over low heat, stirring constantly, until gelatin and sugar are thoroughly dissolved.
2. Stir in apple juice, white wine, pickle syrup, and lemon juice. Chill until slightly thickened. Immediately blend with sour cream.
3. Pour into a fancy 1-quart ring mold and chill until firm. Unmold onto a serving plate and surround with fresh fruits, such as peach or pear halves or wedges, bunches of Tokay or green grapes, sweet red cherries, orange segments, or other colorful fruits in season.

About 6 servings

Note: If desired, fold 1½ cups shredded vegetables such as carrots, cabbage, cucumber, and green pepper into sour cream-gelatin mixture and turn into an 8×8×2-inch pan. Chill until firm, cut into squares, and serve in crisp lettuce cups.

Soups

75 *Chicken Soup Tortellini*

2 quarts water
1 broiler-fryer chicken (about 2½ pounds)
1 onion, sliced
2 teaspoons fresh minced parsley or 1 teaspoon dried parsley
1½ teaspoons salt
1 teaspoon rosemary or chervil
⅛ teaspoon pepper
1 cup sliced celery with leaves
1 cup sliced fresh mushrooms
½ cup dry white wine
32 tortellini (see recipe)

1. Place water, chicken, onion, parsley, salt, rosemary, and pepper in a large saucepan. Bring to boiling; simmer covered 1 hour, or until chicken is tender.
2. Remove chicken; cool. Discard chicken skin. Remove meat from bones and chop fine. Reserve for tortellini filling.
3. Bring stock to boiling; stir in remaining ingredients. Simmer 15 minutes, or until tortellini are done. (If using frozen tortellini, simmer about 30 minutes.)

8 to 10 servings

76 *Tortellini*

Dough:
2 eggs
2 egg whites
2 tablespoons olive or vegetable oil
2 teaspoons salt
3 cups all-purpose flour
Filling:
2½ cups finely chopped chicken
¼ cup grated Parmesan cheese
2 egg yolks

1. Prepare dough by combining eggs, egg whites, oil, and salt in a bowl. Gradually add flour, mixing well until mixture forms a soft dough. Turn onto a floured surface and knead in remaining flour to form a very stiff dough.
2. Wrap dough in waxed paper; let rest 10 minutes.
3. Combine chicken, cheese, and egg yolks in a bowl. Set aside.
4. Divide dough in quarters. Roll each quarter into a large circle as thin as possible. Cut into about 32 (2-inch) rounds.
5. For each tortellini, place about 1 teaspoon chicken mixture in center of round. Moisten edges with water. Fold in half; seal edges. Shape into rings by stretching the tips of half circle slightly and wrapping the ring around your index finger. Gently press tips together (tortellini may be frozen at this point).
6. Cook as directed in recipe for Chicken Soup Tortellini.

About 128 tortellini

77 *French Onion Soup (Soupe à l'Oignon)*

The originator of this famous French soup was King Louis XV, who returned late one night to his hunting lodge and found only onions, butter, and champagne on hand. So hungry and weary was he that he simply mixed them together. Voilà—French Onion Soup! A toasted cheese crouton is traditionally part of the recipe, so there's no need to serve additional bread.

5 medium onions, sliced (4 cups)
3 tablespoons butter or margarine
1½ quarts beef broth
½ teaspoon salt
⅛ teaspoon pepper
Cheese Croutons

1. Sauté onions in melted butter in a large saucepan. Cook slowly, stirring until golden (about 10 minutes).
2. Blend in beef broth, salt, and pepper. Bring to boiling, cover, and simmer 15 minutes.
3. Pour soup into warm soup bowls or crocks. Float a cheese crouton in each bowl of soup.

6 servings

78 *Cheese Croutons*

6 slices French bread, toasted
2 tablespoons butter or margarine
¼ cup (1 ounce) grated Gruyère or Swiss cheese

1. Spread one side of each bread slice with butter. If necessary, cut bread to fit size of bowl. Sprinkle cheese over buttered toast.
2. Place under broiler until cheese melts.

79 *Hungarian Goulash Soup*

The Hungarians use grated potato for a thickening in this soup, with wonderful results.

1½ pounds beef for stew, cut into ½-inch cubes
1 tablespoon shortening or vegetable oil
1 large onion, chopped
1 quart water
¾ cup grated potato (about 1 large)
1 tablespoon paprika
1 tablespoon tomato sauce or ketchup
1 teaspoon salt
½ teaspoon caraway seed (optional)
¼ teaspoon crushed thyme
Pinch red pepper
1 cup chopped pared raw potato (about 1 large)
1 cup uncooked egg noodles

1. Brown meat in shortening in a large saucepan. Add onion; cook until tender.
2. Add water, grated potato, and seasonings. Bring to boiling; cover. Simmer 1½ hours, or until beef is tender.
3. Stir in potatoes and noodles. Cook until tender, 10 to 20 minutes.

4 to 6 servings

Hungarian Goulash Soup with Spaetzle: Follow recipe for Hungarian Goulash Soup, omitting chopped potato and noodles. Serve with **hot buttered spaetzle.**

80

81 *Spaetzle*

2 cups all-purpose flour
1 teaspoon salt
1 egg
¼ to ½ cup water

1. Combine flour and salt; stir in egg. Gradually add water until batter is stiff, but smooth. Place on wet cutting board; flatten.
2. With a wet knife, scrape small pieces of dough off and drop into boiling salted water. Cook only one layer of spaetzle at a time, boiling gently 5 to 8 minutes, or until done. Remove with perforated spoon.

Note: Spaetzle may be served in pea, lentil, or tomato soup or as a side dish, either tossed with hot melted butter or sautéed in butter. For variety, sprinkle with toasted bread crumbs or grated Parmesan cheese.

82 *Mulligatawny Soup*

Mulligatawny soup is from India, and as you might expect, the distinctive flavor is curry. Curry recipes do not always call for curry powder. The authentic ones call for a combination of spices, such as turmeric, cumin, coriander, dill, and cardamom. This version of mulligatawny calls for both curry powder and several other seasonings.

1 cup diced uncooked chicken (see Note)
¼ cup chopped onion
¼ cup chopped celery
¼ cup diced carrot
2 tart apples, pared and sliced
¼ cup fat or margarine
¼ cup flour
1 teaspoon curry powder
1½ quarts chicken broth
1 tomato, peeled and chopped, or 1 cup drained canned tomatoes, chopped
½ green pepper, minced
1 teaspoon minced parsley
1 teaspoon salt
1 teaspoon sugar
⅛ teaspoon pepper
⅛ teaspoon mace
2 whole cloves
1 cup cooked rice (optional)

1. Cook chicken, onion, celery, carrots, and apple in melted fat in a large saucepan until lightly browned.
2. Stir in flour and curry powder. Gradually add chicken broth, stirring constantly.
3. Stir in remaining ingredients. Cook, covered, over low heat until chicken is tender.
4. Remove and reserve chicken. Strain soup, discarding cloves.
5. Purée vegetables in an electric blender or force through a sieve or food mill. Return soup and vegetable purée to saucepan. Mix in chicken and heat to serving temperature.
6. If desired, mix in hot cooked rice.

8 servings

Note: If making your own chicken broth, substitute the cooked chicken meat for the uncooked chicken and add to soup for final heating.

83 *Tomato-Cheese Soup*

1 can (about 10 ounces) condensed tomato soup
1 soup can milk
1 cup (4 ounces) shredded Cheddar, American, or Colby cheese
¼ teaspoon finely crushed basil (optional)

1. Turn soup into a large saucepan; gradually blend in milk. Stir until hot and blended.
2. Mix in cheese and, if desired, basil.

3 servings

84 *Greek Egg-Lemon Soup*

Lemons are to Greece as oranges are to Florida—they just can't seem to get enough of them. And this soup is as common to them as chicken-noodle is to Americans.

6 cups rich veal or chicken broth (page 62) or 6 bouillon cubes in 6 cups water
⅓ cup uncooked rice
3 eggs
¼ cup lemon juice

1. Bring broth to boiling in a large saucepan. Add rice; cover and simmer until rice is tender, about 20 minutes.
2. Beat eggs until frothy in a bowl; add lemon juice. Beat in 2 cups of broth very slowly; stir the mixture into the remaining soup.
3. Heat to serving temperature, being very careful not to let it boil (boiling will curdle the egg).

4 to 6 servings

Basic White Bread, page 62

85 *Alphabet Soup*

½ pound ground beef
1 onion, chopped
5 cups water
1 can (16 ounces) tomatoes
3 potatoes, cubed
2 carrots, sliced
2 stalks celery, sliced
2 teaspoons salt
1 teaspoon Worcestershire sauce
1 beef bouillon cube
¼ teaspoon garlic powder
¼ teaspoon pepper
3 sprigs fresh parsley, minced, or 2
   tablespoons dried
1 cup uncooked alphabet macaroni

1. Brown meat in a large saucepan; drain off fat.
2. Add remaining ingredients, except macaroni. Bring to boiling; cover and simmer 1 hour.
3. Stir in macaroni; cook 20 minutes.

6 to 8 servings

86 *Homemade Chicken-Noodle Soup*

2 quarts water
1 broiler-fryer chicken (about 2½
   pounds), cut up
1 finely chopped onion
1 cup finely chopped celery
2 tablespoons minced fresh parsley
   or 1 teaspoon dried
2 teaspoons salt
1 teaspoon crushed rosemary or
   chervil
⅛ teaspoon pepper
2 cups uncooked homemade (see
   page 60) or packaged noodles

1. Place all ingredients except noodles in a kettle or Dutch oven. Bring to boiling; simmer 1 hour, or until chicken is tender.
2. Remove chicken; cool. Discard skin. Remove meat from bones and chop.
3. Return chicken to stock; bring to boiling. Stir in noodles. Simmer 20 to 30 minutes, or until noodles are done.

8 servings

87 *Homemade Noodles*

2 eggs
½ teaspoon salt
1 cup all-purpose flour

1. Beat eggs and salt in a mixing bowl. Gradually add flour, mixing well until mixture forms a soft dough. Turn onto a floured surface; knead in remaining flour to form a very stiff dough.
2. Cover; let rest 10 to 15 minutes.
3. Roll dough as thin as possible, turning dough over as you roll.
4. Roll dough up tightly, jelly-roll fashion. Cut off thin slices. Toss to separate. Spread out on baking sheets; toss periodically until thoroughly dry.

2 cups noodles

88 *Hot Dog! It's Soup*

One way of improving your child's acceptance of food is to allow him or her to have a hand in its preparation. With this soup we are mixing two favorite children's foods—corn and hot dogs. You might ask your child to help you shred the cheese (under your supervision, of course) or slice the hot dogs (a table knife will do). Serve with buttered slices of homemade white bread. That's one of their favorites, too.

½ cup chopped onion
⅓ cup sliced celery
2 tablespoons margarine
1 cup water
2 cups (16-ounce can) cream-style corn
1 bay leaf
½ teaspoon basil
1½ cups milk
1 pound frankfurters, sliced
1 teaspoon salt
⅛ teaspoon pepper
½ cup shredded process American cheese
Minced parsley

1. Sauté onion and celery in margarine in a medium saucepan. Add water, corn, bay leaf, and basil. Cook 5 minutes.
2. Remove bay leaf. Add remaining ingredients except parsley. Cook over low heat until cheese melts.
3. Garnish with parsley.

6 to 8 servings

89 *Beef Stock*

Because during simmering the liquid is reduced, salt lightly initially and correct salt level before serving.

3 pounds lean beef (chuck or plate), cut in 1-inch pieces
1 soup bone, cracked
3 quarts cold water
1 tablespoon salt
2 large onions, peeled
2 whole cloves
5 carrots, cut in large pieces
3 stalks celery with leaves, sliced
4 sprigs parsley
1 bay leaf
1 teaspoon thyme
8 peppercorns

1. Put meat and soup bone into a large saucepan; add water and salt. Cover saucepan and simmer about 2 hours, removing foam as necessary.
2. Slice 1 onion; insert the cloves into second onion. Add onions, remaining vegetables, and seasonings to saucepan. Cover and bring to boiling. Reduce heat and simmer about 1½ hours.
3. Remove from heat; remove soup bone and strain stock through a fine sieve. Allow to cool. Chill. (The meat and vegetables strained from stock may be served as desired.)
4. Remove fat that rises to surface (reserve for use in other food preparation). Reheat and serve with slices of crisp toast.

About 2½ quarts stock

Brown Stock: Follow recipe for Beef Stock. Cut meat from soup bone and brown it along with beef pieces in ¼ **cup fat** in saucepan before cooking. Proceed as in Beef Stock.

90 *Baked Minestrone*

1½ pounds lean beef for stew, cut
    in 1-inch cubes
1 cup coarsely chopped onion
2 cloves garlic, crushed
1 teaspoon salt
¼ teaspoon pepper
2 tablespoons olive oil
3 cans (about 10 ounces each)
    condensed beef broth
2 soup cans water
1½ teaspoons herb seasoning
1 can (16 ounces) tomatoes
    (undrained)
1 can (15¼ ounces) kidney beans
    (undrained)
1 can (6 ounces) pitted ripe olives
    (undrained)
1½ cups thinly sliced carrots
1 cup small seashell macaroni
2 cups sliced zucchini
    Grated Parmesan cheese

1. Mix beef, onion, garlic, salt, and pepper in a large saucepan. Add olive oil and stir to coat meat evenly.
2. Bake at 400°F 30 minutes, or until meat is browned, stirring occasionally.
3. Turn oven control to 350°F. Add broth, water, and seasonings; stir. Cover; cook 1 hour, or until meat is tender.
4. Stir in tomatoes, kidney beans, olives, carrots, and macaroni. Put sliced zucchini on top. Cover; bake 30 to 40 minutes, or until carrots are tender.
5. Serve with grated cheese.

10 to 12 servings

91 *Brown Vegetable Stock*

Use assorted vegetables from your refrigerator, or purchase a package of soup vegetables from your produce counter.

2 pounds mixed vegetables
    (carrots, leeks, onions, celery,
    turnips, etc.)
¼ cup butter or margarine
2½ quarts water
½ teaspoon salt
½ teaspoon thyme
3 sprigs parsley
½ bay leaf
    Dash of pepper

1. Chop vegetables. Brown in butter.
2. Add water and seasonings. Cover.
3. Simmer 1½ hours or until vegetables are tender.
4. Strain and chill.

About 2 quarts stock

White Vegetable Stock: If a lighter, clearer stock is desired, omit butter and do not brown vegetables.

92

93 Red and White Bean Soup

There are many dried white beans on the market—great northern, navy, white, kidney, and lima are some. They may be used interchangeably and are all high in protein.

2 cups dried navy beans, soaked overnight
2 cups chopped onion
1 tablespoon salt
10 whole peppercorns
1 stalk celery with leaves, sliced
¼ cup minced parsley or 2 tablespoons dried parsley
½ teaspoon crushed thyme or basil
2 cups chopped potato
¼ cup butter or margarine
¼ cup flour
1 can (15 ounces) tomato sauce
1 can (14 ounces) brown beans in molasses sauce

1. Drain soaked beans, reserving liquid. Add enough water to bean liquid to measure 6 cups. Combine in a large saucepan soaked beans, bean liquid, onion, salt, peppercorns, celery, parsley, and thyme. Heat to boiling; simmer 45 minutes.
2. Stir in potato. Simmer 20 minutes or until tender.
3. In a separate saucepan, stir flour into melted butter; cook until bubbly. Gradually add tomato sauce; mix well.
4. Stir tomato mixture and brown beans into soup. Simmer 5 minutes.

8 servings

94 Chili Soup

½ pound ground beef
1 cup chopped onion
5 cups water
1 can (28 ounces) tomatoes
1 can (15 ounces) tomato sauce
1 clove garlic, crushed
1 tablespoon chili powder
1 teaspoon salt
1 teaspoon cumin
½ teaspoon oregano
1 cup uncooked macaroni
1 can (about 15 ounces) kidney or chili beans

1. Brown meat in a large saucepan; drain off fat. Stir in onion; cook 1 minute.
2. Add water, tomatoes, tomato sauce, garlic, chili powder, salt, cumin, and oregano. Simmer 30 minutes.
3. Add remaining ingredients; cook until macaroni is done (about 10 to 15 minutes).

8 to 10 servings

95 Farm-Style Leek Soup

2 large leeks (1 pound) with part of green tops, sliced
2 medium onions, sliced
1 large garlic clove, minced
¼ cup butter or margarine
4 cups chicken stock or bouillon
2 cups uncooked narrow or medium noodles (3 ounces)
1 can or bottle (12 ounces) beer
1½ cups shredded semisoft cheese (Muenster, brick, process, etc.)
Salt and pepper

1. Cook leek, onion, and garlic in butter for 15 minutes, using low heat and stirring often.
2. Add stock. Cover and simmer 30 minutes.
3. Add noodles. Cover and simmer 15 minutes, or until noodles are tender.
4. Add beer; heat to simmering. Gradually add cheese, cooking slowly and stirring until melted. Season to taste with salt and pepper.

6 servings, about 1½ cups each

96 *Bean and Prosciutto Soup*

2 cups (about ¾ pound) dried
    beans, soaked overnight
5 cups water
2 cups sliced celery
3 to 4 ounces sliced prosciutto, cut
    in thin strips
1 can (16 ounces) tomatoes
1 can (about 10 ounces) condensed
    beef broth
1 teaspoon salt
1 garlic clove, crushed
2 packages (9 ounces each) frozen
    Italian green beans
3 sprigs fresh parsley, minced
    (about 2 tablespoons)

1. Combine soaked dried beans, water, celery, prosciutto, tomatoes, beef broth, salt, and garlic in a 5-quart saucepot. Bring to boiling; simmer, covered, 30 minutes.
2. Mix in green beans and parsley; simmer 5 to 10 minutes.

10 to 12 servings

97 *Tomato-Lentil Soup*

2 cups chopped carrots
1 cup chopped onion
1 cup sliced celery
2 tablespoons margarine, melted
1 clove garlic, crushed
1¼ cups (½ pound) dried lentils
2 quarts water
1 tablespoon salt
1 can (6 ounces) tomato paste
¼ teaspoon crushed dill weed or
    tarragon

1. Sauté carrots, onion, and celery in margarine in a large saucepan until tender.
2. Add garlic, lentils, water, and salt. Simmer 2 hours, or until lentils are tender.
3. Add tomato paste and dill weed; stir.

6 to 8 servings

98 *Split Pea Soup with Ham Bone*

2 cups dried green split peas
1½ quarts water
1 ham bone (about 1½ pounds)
1 onion, sliced
1 cup sliced celery
1 cup grated carrot
2 teaspoons salt
1 teaspoon crushed basil
¼ cup butter or margarine
¼ cup flour
2 cups milk

1. In a large saucepan, combine peas, water, bone, onion, celery, carrot, salt, and basil. Bring to boiling; simmer 1½ to 2 hours.
2. Stir flour into melted butter in a separate saucepan; cook until bubbly. Gradually add milk, stirring constantly. Bring to boiling; cook 1 minute.
3. Stir white sauce into soup.

8 servings

99 Lentil Soup

1¼ cups (about ½ pound) lentils,
    soaked overnight
2 quarts beef broth
6 frankfurters, cut diagonally in
    ½-inch slices
2 onions, thinly sliced
2 carrots, sliced
2 stalks celery, sliced
3 sprigs chervil or parsley or 1
    tablespoon dried chervil
2 teaspoons salt
¼ teaspoon pepper

Combine all ingredients in a large saucepan. Bring to boiling; simmer 35 minutes, or until lentils are tender.

100 Chicken Succotash Soup with Parsley Dumplings

1 broiler-fryer chicken (2 to 3
    pounds), cut up
2 quarts water
2 teaspoons salt
½ teaspoon crushed rosemary
    Pinch pepper
    Parsley Dumplings
1 cup sliced carrots
¼ cup chopped onion
1 package (10 ounces) frozen corn
1 package (10 ounces) frozen lima
    beans

1. Combine chicken, water, salt, rosemary, and pepper in a large saucepan. Bring to boiling; simmer 45 minutes, covered, or until chicken is tender.
2. Remove chicken from broth; cool, skin, and cut into pieces.
3. Skim fat or chill to remove fat
4. Prepare Parsley Dumplings.
5. Add vegetables and chicken to stock. Bring to boiling. Drop dumplings by teaspoonfuls onto gently simmering soup. Cover; cook 10 minutes. Uncover; cook 5 to 10 minutes.
6. Serve each portion with one or two dumplings.

6 to 8 servings

101 Parsley Dumplings

2 cups all-purpose flour
2 teaspoons baking powder
1½ teaspoons salt
⅛ teaspoon pepper
3 tablespoons butter or margarine
1 egg
    Milk
¼ cup minced parsley

1. Combine flour, baking powder, salt, and pepper in a bowl.
2. Cut in butter until mixture resembles coarse meal.
3. Break egg into measuring cup. Add enough milk to make 1 cup liquid. Beat well. Add to dry ingredients along with parsley and stir just until flour is moistened.
4. Proceed as directed.

102 *Lebanon Lentil Soup*

2 quarts beef broth
1 ham bone
1¼ cups (about ½ pound) lentils
2 stalks celery, sliced
2 carrots, sliced
1 onion, sliced
1 teaspoon salt
¼ teaspoon pepper
½ teaspoon crushed thyme or ¼
   teaspoon dill weed

1. Combine all ingredients in a large saucepan. Bring to boiling. Cover; simmer 1 to 2 hours, or until lentils are tender.
2. Remove ham bone. Force soup mixture through a coarse sieve or food mill, or purée in an electric blender.
3. Heat, if necessary.

8 servings

Cream of Lentil Soup: Follow recipe for Lebanon Lentil Soup. After puréeing, stir in **1 cup half-and-half** or **whipping cream.**

103

104 *Italian White Bean Soup*

2 cups (about ½ pound) dried navy
   beans, soaked overnight
2 quarts water
2 cups chopped potato (about 1
   large)
1 can (16 ounces) tomatoes
   (undrained)
¼ cup chopped onion
2 teaspoons salt
1 clove garlic, crushed
1 teaspoon crushed basil
1 cup (about 2 ounces) broken
   vermicelli or shell macaroni

1. Combine in a large saucepan beans, water, potato, tomatoes, onion, salt, garlic, and basil. Bring to boiling; simmer 1 hour, or until beans are tender.
2. Stir in vermicelli; cook 20 minutes.

8 to 10 servings

105 *Lancaster County Chicken-Corn Soup*

The "rivvels" served in this soup are a Pennsylvania Dutch dumpling made by rubbing bits of the dough mixture between the palms of your hands and dropping them into the soup.

1 stewing chicken (3 to 4 pounds),
   cut up
1 large onion, chopped
3 quarts water
2 teaspoons salt
¼ teaspoon pepper
4 cups corn (three 10-ounce
   packages frozen corn or two
   16-ounce cans)
½ cup chopped celery with leaves
   Rivvels

1. Place chicken, onion, water, salt, and pepper in a large saucepot. Bring to boiling; simmer 1 hour or until chicken is tender.
2. Remove chicken from stock, strip meat from bones, cut into bite-size pieces, and return to stock. Add corn and celery; simmer 30 minutes.
3. Drop rivvels into soup by rivveling; that is, rubbing dough between palms of your hands and dropping into soup. Cook in simmering soup 15 minutes, or until done.

10 servings

Rivvels: Combine 1 cup all-purpose flour, **½ teaspoon salt, 1 egg,** and enough **milk (about ¼ cup)** to make a crumbly semimoist mixture.

106

107 Chili-Chicken Soup

1 broiler-fryer chicken (about 3 pounds), cut up
1½ quarts water
1 onion, studded with 2 or 3 whole cloves
1 tablespoon salt
3 garlic cloves, crushed
1 bay leaf
1 can (about 15 ounces) red kidney beans
1 can (6 ounces) tomato paste
1 can (4 ounces) mild green chilies or 1 hot pepper, chopped
1 tablespoon chili powder
1 teaspoon crushed basil
Cooked rice

1. Combine chicken, water, onion, salt, garlic, and bay leaf in a large saucepan. Bring to boiling; simmer 45 minutes, or until chicken is tender.
2. Remove chicken and onion from stock; cool. Discard chicken skin; remove meat from bones and chop. Skim fat from stock. Remove cloves from onion; discard. Chop onion.
3. Stir chicken, onion, and remaining ingredients, except rice, into stock. Heat. Serve with rice.

6 to 8 servings

108 Burgundy Oxtail Soup

2 oxtails (about 3 pounds), cut up
¼ cup flour (about)
3 tablespoons bacon fat or shortening
2 quarts water
1 onion, chopped
¾ cup tomato juice
2 teaspoons salt
1 bay leaf
4 peppercorns
1 garlic clove, crushed
1 cup sliced celery with leaves
1 cup sliced carrot
¾ cup burgundy or other dry red wine
½ teaspoon crushed tarragon
1 cup sliced fresh mushrooms
¼ cup chopped fresh parsley

1. Coat oxtails with flour. Brown in hot fat in a large saucepan.
2. Add water, onion, tomato juice, salt, bay leaf, peppercorns, and garlic. Bring to boiling; simmer 2 to 3 hours.
3. Strain stock. Chill; remove fat. Return stock to saucepan.
4. Bring stock to boiling; add celery, carrot, burgundy, and tarragon. Simmer 30 minutes.
5. Stir in remaining ingredients. Cook 5 minutes.

8 servings

109 Belgian Beer Soup

Soups provide great ways to cook less-tender cuts of meat. Most of these meats are flavorful and relatively inexpensive, and best of all they become tender through long, slow simmering.

2 pounds beef chuck, cut in ½-inch cubes; reserve bone
7 cups water
1 cup beer
2 teaspoons salt
1 bay leaf

1. Trim fat from meat.
2. Brown meat and bone in a large saucepan without fat. Stir in water, beer, salt, bay leaf, pepper, allspice, and bouillon cubes. Heat to boiling; simmer 2 hours.
3. Stir in onion, potatoes, celery, and carrots; simmer 30 minutes.

½ teaspoon pepper
½ teaspoon allspice
2 beef bouillon cubes
½ cup chopped onion
4 cups chopped potatoes (about 6
   medium potatoes)
2 cups sliced celery
2 cups sliced carrots
1 package (10 ounces) frozen
   Brussels sprouts

4. Stir in Brussels sprouts; simmer 15 minutes, or until sprouts are tender.

6 to 8 servings

110 *Sherried Chicken Chowder*

10 cups water
1 broiler-fryer chicken (about 2½
   pounds)
1 carrot, coarsely chopped
1 stalk celery, coarsely chopped
1 onion, halved
4 whole cloves
2 teaspoons salt
1 teaspoon crushed tarragon
1 bay leaf
½ cup uncooked barley or rice
½ teaspoon curry powder
¼ cup dry sherry
1 cup half-and-half

1. Place water, chicken, carrot, celery, onion halves studded with cloves, salt, and tarragon in Dutch oven or saucepot. Bring to boiling; simmer 1 hour, or until chicken is tender.
2. Remove chicken; cool. Discard skin; remove meat from bones; chop.
3. Strain stock. Discard cloves and bay leaf. Reserve stock and vegetables. Skim fat from stock.
4. Purée vegetables and 1 cup stock in an electric blender.
5. Return stock to Dutch oven; bring to boiling. Stir in barley and puréed vegetables. Simmer 1 hour, or until barley is tender. Stir in chicken, curry, sherry, and half-and-half.

8 servings

111 *Meatball Soup*

1 pound ground beef
1 onion, chopped
1½ quarts water
1 can (16 ounces) tomatoes
3 potatoes, cubed
2 carrots, sliced
2 stalks celery, sliced
3 sprigs fresh parsley, minced, or
   2 tablespoons dried
½ cup uncooked barley
2 teaspoons salt
½ teaspoon crushed thyme or basil
¼ teaspoon garlic powder
¼ teaspoon pepper
1 bay leaf
1 teaspoon Worcestershire sauce
1 beef bouillon cube

1. Shape beef into tiny meatballs. Brown meatballs and onion in a large saucepan, or place in a shallow pan and brown in a 400°F oven. Drain off excess fat.
2. Add remaining ingredients. Bring to boiling, simmer 1½ hours, or until vegetables are tender.

8 servings

112 *Vegetable Medley Soup*

8 slices bacon
½ cup chopped onion
½ cup sliced celery
5 cups water
1½ cups fresh corn or 1 package
   (about 10 ounces) frozen corn
½ cup sliced carrots
1 potato, pared and sliced
1 tablespoon salt
1 teaspoon sugar
¼ teaspoon pepper
¼ teaspoon crushed thyme or basil
1 cup fresh green beans, cut in
   1-inch pieces
4 cups chopped peeled tomatoes
   (4 to 5 tomatoes)

1. Cook bacon until crisp in a Dutch oven or kettle. Drain off all but 2 tablespoons fat.
2. Sauté onion and celery in bacon fat.
3. Stir in water, corn, carrots, potato, salt, sugar, pepper, and thyme. Bring to boiling; simmer covered 30 minutes.
4. Stir in green beans; simmer 10 minutes, or until beans are crisp-tender.
5. Stir in tomatoes; heat 5 minutes.

About 6 servings

113 *Vegetarian Chowder*

4 cups sliced zucchini
½ cup chopped onion
⅓ cup butter or margarine
⅓ cup flour
2 tablespoons minced parsley
1 teaspoon crushed basil
1 teaspoon salt
⅛ teaspoon pepper
3 cups water
1 chicken bouillon cube
1 package (10 ounces) frozen corn
   or 2 cups fresh corn
1 can (13½ ounces) evaporated
   milk
1 can (16 ounces) tomatoes, broken
   up, or 3 tomatoes, skinned
   and chopped
1 cup shredded Monterey Jack
   cheese (optional)

1. Sauté zucchini and onion in butter in a large saucepan. Stir in flour, parsley, basil, salt, and pepper.
2. Gradually add water, stirring constantly. Add remaining ingredients. Bring to boiling; simmer 10 to 15 minutes.
3. If desired, stir in Monterey Jack cheese.

6 to 8 servings

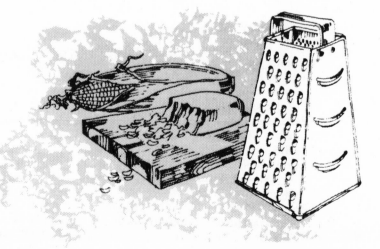

114 *Beef Barley Soup*

2 quarts water
1 soup bone with meat
½ cup chopped celery tops
1 tablespoon salt
½ teaspoon pepper
½ cup uncooked regular barley

1. Combine water, bone, celery tops, salt, and pepper in a Dutch oven. Bring to boiling; cover tightly and simmer 1 to 2 hours.
2. Remove bone from stock; cool. Remove meat from bone; chop. Return to stock.
3. Stir in barley; continue cooking 30 minutes.

3 cups coarsely chopped cabbage
1 cup sliced carrots
1 cup sliced celery
2 cups sliced parsnips
2 cups thinly sliced onion
1 can (12 ounces) tomato paste

4. Add remaining ingredients; simmer 30 minutes, or until vegetables are tender.

8 to 10 servings

115 *Cheddar-Corn Chowder*

2½ cups water
1½ cups chopped potatoes
1 cup sliced carrots
½ cup sliced celery
¼ cup chopped onion or scallions
1½ teaspoons salt
¼ teaspoon pepper
¼ cup butter or margarine
¼ cup flour
2 cups milk
2½ cups shredded sharp Cheddar cheese (10 ounces)
1 can (16 ounces) cream-style corn or 2 cups fresh corn

1. Combine water, potatoes, carrots, celery, onion, salt, and pepper in a large saucepan. Cover; bring to boiling. Simmer 10 minutes, or until vegetables are tender.
2. Melt butter in a saucepan. Stir in flour; cook until bubbly. Gradually add milk, stirring constantly. Bring to boiling; cook 1 minute. Add cheese; stir until melted.
3. Gradually add cheese sauce to soup, stirring constantly. Stir in corn.

6 servings

116 *Vegetable-Beer Chowder*

1 package (9 ounces) frozen green beans, thawed
1 package (10 ounces) frozen corn, thawed
¼ cup chopped onion
¼ cup butter or margarine
¼ cup flour
1 teaspoon salt
½ teaspoon dry mustard
2 cups milk
1 cup beer
2 cups shredded Cheddar cheese (8 ounces)

1. Sauté vegetables in melted butter in a large saucepan.
2. Stir in flour, salt, and dry mustard; cook until bubbly, stirring constantly.
3. Gradually add milk and beer, stirring constantly. Bring to boiling; cook 1 minute.
4. Stir in cheese until melted.

4 to 6 servings

117 *New England Clam Chowder*

2 tablespoons butter or margarine
½ cup finely diced celery
¼ cup thinly sliced leek (white part only)
¼ cup minced onion
¼ cup minced green pepper
3 tablespoons flour
1¾ cups milk
1 cup whipping cream or half-and-half
½ cup finely diced potato
12 large hard-shelled clams (to prepare, see Note), or 2 cans (about 7 ounces each) minced clams, drained (reserve liquid)
½ teaspoon salt
⅛ teaspoon thyme
3 drops Tabasco
Pinch white pepper
½ teaspoon Worcestershire sauce
Finely chopped parsley

1. Melt butter over low heat in a heavy 3-quart saucepan. Add celery, leek, onion, and green pepper. Stirring occasionally, cook 6 to 8 minutes, or until partially tender.
2. Blend flour into the vegetable-butter mixture; heat until bubbly. Gradually add milk and cream, stirring constantly. Bring to boiling, stirring constantly; cook 1 to 2 minutes.
3. Stir in potato, reserved clam liquid, salt, thyme, Tabasco, and pepper. Bring to boiling and simmer 25 to 35 minutes, stirring frequently. Add minced clams and Worcestershire sauce.
4. Pour into soup tureen or individual soup bowls. Garnish with parsley.

4 to 6 servings

Note: To prepare clams and broth, rinse clams thoroughly under running cold water. Place clams in saucepan and add 3 cups water. Cook over medium heat until shells open completely. Drain the clams, reserving 2 cups of broth for chowder. Remove clams from shells. Cut off the hard outsides (combs) and chop clams into small, fine pieces. Decrease milk in chowder to 1 cup.

118 *Creamy Tuna-Broccoli Soup*

¼ cup butter or margarine
3 tablespoons minced onion
3 tablespoons flour
½ teaspoon salt
½ teaspoon celery salt
½ teaspoon ground sage
¼ teaspoon white pepper
Pinch cayenne pepper
1 quart milk
1 package (10 ounces) frozen chopped broccoli
1 can (6½ or 7 ounces) tuna, drained and flaked

1. Melt butter in a large, heavy saucepan over low heat. Add onion and cook until tender. Blend in flour, salt, celery salt, sage, and peppers. Heat until bubbly.
2. Gradually add milk, stirring constantly. Bring to boiling. Stir in broccoli. Cook over low heat, stirring occasionally, 10 to 12 minutes, or until broccoli is tender when pierced with a fork.
3. Mix in tuna and heat about 3 minutes.

About 6 servings

119 *Vegetable Oyster Soup*

4 cups chopped head lettuce
2 cups chopped spinach
1 cup chopped carrots
½ cup chopped onion
1½ cups chicken broth or 1 can
    (about 10 ounces) chicken
    broth
1 can (10 ounces) frozen oysters,
    thawed
2 tablespoons butter
2 tablespoons flour
1¼ teaspoons salt
2 cups milk
1 teaspoon grated lemon peel
1 tablespoon lemon juice
Freshly ground pepper
Lemon slices

1. Put lettuce, spinach, carrots, onion, ½ cup chicken broth, and oysters into a 3-quart saucepan. Cover and cook until carrots are just tender (about 5 minutes).
2. Turn half of cooked mixture into an electric blender container and blend a few seconds; repeat. Set vegetable mixture aside.
3. Melt butter in a saucepan. Stir in flour and salt. Gradually add milk and remaining 1 cup chicken broth, stirring until smooth. Bring to boiling, stirring occasionally, and cook until thickened. Add vegetable mixture, lemon peel and juice, and pepper; heat to desired serving temperature, stirring occasionally.
4. Serve garnished with lemon slices.

About 7 cups

120 *Cream of Broccoli Soup*

2 packages (10 ounces each)
    frozen chopped broccoli
1 cup water
½ cup sliced celery
1 small onion, sliced
2 tablespoons butter or margarine
2 tablespoons flour
1½ quarts chicken stock
2 egg yolks, beaten
½ cup half-and-half or milk
½ teaspoon salt
Pinch pepper
Paprika

1. Cook broccoli in water 3 to 5 minutes; reserve liquid.
2. Sauté celery and onion in butter; stir in flour. Gradually add stock and liquid from broccoli, stirring constantly, until thickened.
3. Add broccoli; put through a food mill or purée in an electric blender, if desired.
4. Stir egg yolks into half-and-half; gradually add to soup, being careful not to boil. Season with salt and pepper.
5. Garnish each serving with a sprinkle of paprika.

6 servings

121 *Chinese Cabbage Soup*

2 cups cooked chicken, cut into
    strips (about 1 chicken breast)
7 cups chicken broth
6 cups sliced Chinese cabbage
    (celery cabbage)
1 teaspoon soy sauce
1 teaspoon salt
¼ teaspoon pepper

Combine chicken and chicken broth; bring to boiling. Stir in remaining ingredients; cook only 3 to 4 minutes, or just until cabbage is crisp-tender. (Do not overcook.)

6 servings

Note: If desired, lettuce may be substituted for the Chinese cabbage. Reduce cooking time to 1 minute.

122 *Dill Cabbage Soup*

Cook the vegetables only until crisp-tender to keep the flavor and appearance attractive.

2 quarts beef stock
1 cup thinly sliced carrots
1 cup sliced celery
½ cup chopped onion
8 cups (about ½ head) thinly sliced cabbage
Salt and pepper to taste
3 tablespoons water
2 tablespoons flour
½ cup yogurt or dairy sour half-and-half
½ teaspoon minced dill or ¼ teaspoon dried dill weed
Minced parsley

1. Pour stock into a large saucepan. Add carrots, celery, and onion. Bring to boiling, reduce heat, and cook until vegetables are tender (about 10 minutes).
2. Add cabbage; continue cooking until crisp-tender (about 5 minutes). Season to taste with salt and pepper.
3. Stir water gradually into flour, stirring until smooth. Pour slowly into soup, stirring constantly. Bring to boiling; boil 1 minute.
4. Stir in yogurt and dill.
5. Garnish with parsley.

8 to 10 servings

123 *French Cauliflower Soup*

1 head cauliflower, cut in flowerets
5 cups chicken stock or 5 chicken bouillon cubes in 5 cups water
½ cup uncooked rice
¼ cup finely chopped celery
1 cup milk or half-and-half
¼ cup flour
Salt and pepper
Sliced green onion, snipped watercress, or snipped parsley

1. Put cauliflowerets, stock, rice, and celery into a large saucepan. Bring to boiling; simmer until cauliflower is crisp-tender and rice is cooked (about 10 minutes).
2. Gradually add milk to flour, blending until smooth; stir into soup. Bring to boiling, stirring constantly until thickened. Season to taste.
3. Sprinkle each serving with green onion, watercress, or parsley.

6 servings

Creamed French Cauliflower Soup: Follow recipe for French Cauliflower Soup; strain soup after Step 1. Purée vegetables and rice in an electric blender. Return vegetables and stock to saucepot. Continue with Step 2. Stir in **¼ cup white wine** and either **½ teaspoon basil** or **¼ teaspoon dill weed.** Garnish as suggested.

124

125 *Cream of Turkey Soup*

½ cup butter
6 tablespoons flour
½ teaspoon salt
Pinch black pepper
2 cups half-and-half
3 cups turkey or chicken broth
¾ cup coarsely chopped cooked turkey

1. Heat butter in a saucepan. Blend in flour, salt, and pepper. Heat until bubbly.
2. Gradually add half-and-half and 1 cup of broth, stirring constantly. Bring to boiling; cook and stir 1 to 2 minutes.
3. Blend in remaining broth and turkey. Heat; do not boil. Garnish with grated carrot.

About 6 servings

126 *Frosty Cucumber Soup*

1 large cucumber, scored with a
    fork
¼ teaspoon salt
    Pinch white pepper
1½ cups yogurt
1¼ cups water
½ cup walnuts, ground in an
    electric blender
2 cloves garlic, minced
    Green food coloring (optional)

1. Halve cucumber lengthwise and cut crosswise into very thin slices. Rub inside of a large bowl with cut surface of ½ clove garlic. Combine cucumber, salt, and pepper in bowl. Cover; chill.
2. Pour combined yogurt and water over chilled cucumber; mix well. If desired, tint with 1 or 2 drops of food coloring. Chill.
3. Combine walnuts and garlic; set aside for topping.
4. Ladle soup into bowls. Place soup bowls over larger bowls of crushed ice. Serve with walnut topping.

4 servings

127 *Creamy Cheddar Cheese Soup*

2 tablespoons butter
2 tablespoons chopped onion
⅓ cup all-purpose flour
1¼ teaspoons dry mustard
¼ teaspoon garlic powder
¼ teaspoon paprika
2 teaspoons Worcestershire sauce
1½ quarts milk
3 tablespoons chicken seasoned
    stock base
1½ cups sliced celery
2½ cups (10 ounces) shredded
    Cheddar cheese

1. Melt butter in a 3-quart saucepan. Add onion and sauté until tender. Stir in flour, mustard, garlic powder, paprika, and Worcestershire sauce.
2. Remove from heat; gradually add milk, stirring constantly. Add chicken stock base and celery; mix well. Cook over low heat, stirring occasionally, until thickened. Add cheese and stir until cheese is melted and soup is desired serving temperature; do not boil.
3. Serve topped with **chopped green pepper, pimento strips, toasted slivered almonds, or cooked crumbled bacon.**

About 2 quarts

128 *Sweet Pea Soup*

1 small head lettuce, shredded
    (about 5 cups)
2 cups shelled fresh peas, or 1
    package (10 ounces) frozen
    green peas
1 cup water
½ cup chopped leek or green onion
2 tablespoons butter
2 teaspoons chervil
1 teaspoon sugar
½ teaspoon salt
¼ teaspoon black pepper
1 can (about 10 ounces) condensed
    beef broth
¾ cup water
2 cups half-and-half

1. Put lettuce, peas, 1 cup water, leek, butter, chervil, sugar, salt, and pepper into a large saucepan; stir and bring to boiling. Cover and cook until peas are tender.
2. Press mixture through a coarse sieve or food mill and return to saucepan. Stir in broth and ¾ cup water.
3. Just before serving, stir half-and-half into mixture and heat.

6 servings

129 Pumpkin Patch Soup

If zipped in the blender before cooking, this soup becomes light and fluffy. You'll be left with an extra cup of pumpkin, so use it in Pumpkin Spice Rolls

3 cups canned pumpkin or fresh
   cooked puréed pumpkin
2 cups milk, half-and-half, or 1
   can (13 ounces) evaporated
   milk
3 tablespoons maple syrup
1 teaspoon salt
½ teaspoon nutmeg
½ teaspoon cinnamon
¼ teaspoon cloves or allspice

Combine all ingredients in a large saucepan. Heat.

4 servings

130 Gazpacho

2 cans (6 ounces each) seasoned
   tomato juice
½ cucumber, coarsely sliced
1 tomato, quartered
¼ cup vinegar
¼ cup salad oil
1 tablespoon sugar
1 can or bottle (25.6 ounces)
   seasoned tomato juice
½ cucumber, chopped
1 tomato, chopped
1 small onion, chopped
   Minced parsley
   Chopped hard-cooked egg
   Chopped cucumber
   Croutons

1. Pour the 12 ounces tomato juice into an electric blender. Add sliced cucumber, tomato, vinegar, oil, and sugar; blend. Pour into a bowl and mix in remaining ingredients; chill.
2. Serve with bowls of parsley, hard-cooked egg, cucumber, and croutons.

4 servings

131 Tomato Cooler Gazpacho

2 cans (about 10 ounces each)
   condensed tomato soup
2 soup cans water
1 large clove garlic, crushed
1 tablespoon lemon juice
5 to 10 drops Tabasco
½ teaspoon crushed basil
½ cup chopped cucumber
½ cup chopped green pepper
2 tablespoons sliced green onion

1. Combine ingredients; chill several hours.
2. Serve in chilled sherbet glasses or bowls with garnishes suggested in Gazpacho.

6 servings

132 *Gazpacho Garden Soup*

3 large tomatoes, chopped
1 clove garlic, crushed
1 small cucumber, chopped
1 green pepper, chopped
½ cup sliced green onions
¼ cup chopped onion
¼ cup minced parsley
1 teaspoon crushed rosemary
¼ teaspoon crushed basil
½ teaspoon salt
¼ cup olive oil
¼ cup salad oil
2 tablespoons lemon juice
2 cups chicken broth or 3 chicken
    bouillon cubes dissolved in 2
    cups boiling water, then cooled

1. Combine all ingredients except chicken broth in a large bowl. Toss gently.
2. Stir in chicken broth; chill.
3. Serve in chilled bowls with garnishes suggested in Gazpacho.

6 servings

133 *Pioneer Potato Soup*

1 quart chicken stock
4 potatoes, chopped (about 4 cups)
2 cups sliced carrots
½ cup sliced celery
¼ cup chopped onion
1 teaspoon salt
½ teaspoon marjoram, dill weed, or
    cumin
⅛ teaspoon white pepper
1 cup milk or half-and-half
2 tablespoons flour
    Garnishes: paprika, sliced green
      onions, crisply cooked
      crumbled bacon, chopped
      pimento, snipped chives or
      parsley, or grated Parmesan
      cheese

1. Combine all ingredients except milk, flour, and garnishes in a large saucepan. Bring to boiling; simmer 30 minutes.
2. Gradually add milk to flour, stirring until smooth. Stir into soup.
3. Bring soup to boiling; boil 1 minute, stirring constantly.
4. Garnish as desired.

4 to 6 servings

Potato Soup with Sour Cream: Follow recipe for 134 Pioneer Potato Soup. Before serving, stir in **½ cup dairy sour cream.** Heat; do not boil.

Puréed Potato Soup: Follow recipe for either Pioneer Potato or Potato Soup with Sour Cream, omitting the 135 flour. Purée in an electric blender before serving. Reheat, if necessary.

136 *Lettuce Soup*

Lettuce need not be relegated only to the salad bowl. Chop it up, stir it into a rich broth, and eat it with some San Francisco Sourdough French Bread

2 tablespoons butter or margarine
2 tablespoons flour
1 can (about 10 ounces) condensed
    chicken broth
1 soup can water
½ small head lettuce, cored and
    coarsely chopped
¼ cup thinly sliced celery
1 tablespoon chopped watercress
    Salt and pepper

1. Melt butter in a saucepot; stir in flour and cook until bubbly.
2. Gradually stir in chicken broth and water; bring to boiling, stirring constantly. Cook 1 minute.
3. Stir in lettuce, celery, and watercress. Season with salt and pepper to taste. Cook until vegetables are crisp-tender, about 5 minutes.

About 3 servings

137 *Mixed Vegetables Soup*

3 cups beef broth or 3 beef
   bouillon cubes dissolved in 3
   cups boiling water
1 small potato, diced
2 carrots, diced
1 tomato, chopped
1 green onion, sliced
½ cup shredded cabbage or ½ cup
   sliced zucchini
½ teaspoon Beau Monde seasoning
   or seasoned salt
1 tablespoon minced parsley

1. Combine broth, potato, and carrot in a saucepan; bring to boiling. Simmer 30 minutes.
2. Add remaining ingredients; cook 5 minutes, or until cabbage is crisp-tender.

4 servings

138 *Celery-Crab Soup*

Quick, but elegant. Since it is so easy, you'll have time to make Popovers

2 cans (about 10 ounces each)
   condensed cream of celery
   soup
2 soup cans milk
1 cup flaked crab meat
1 teaspoon Worcestershire sauce
¼ teaspoon crushed tarragon
4 to 8 drops Tabasco
   Butter (optional)
   Paprika (optional)

1. Combine soup and milk in a saucepot. Stir in crab meat, Worcestershire sauce, tarragon, and Tabasco. Heat (do not boil); stir occasionally.
2. Garnish each serving with a pat of butter and a sprinkling of paprika, if desired.

6 servings

139 *Oyster Stew*

If you like oysters, you'll love this—it's hardly more than oysters and milk. Traditionally, this is served Christmas Eve with buttered toast.

¼ cup butter or margarine
1 pint fresh oysters, drained;
   reserve liquor
1½ cups milk
1 cup half-and-half
1 teaspoon salt
   Pinch black pepper or cayenne
   pepper
   Minced parsley

1. Melt butter in a saucepan. Add milk, half-and-half, and oyster liquor. Scald; do not boil.
2. Add oysters and seasonings. Heat; do not boil.
3. Garnish with parsley.

4 servings

140 *Lobster-Tomato Cream Soup*

When you use lobster, you are really going first class. Serve with a bread equally as classy—French Crescents

>   2 tablespoons minced onion
>   ¼ cup butter
>   ¼ cup flour
>   ¼ teaspoon salt
>   Pinch black pepper
>   2 cups tomato juice
>   1 cup half-and-half
>   ½ cup milk
>   1½ teaspoons Worcestershire sauce
>   4 drops Tabasco
>   1 can (about 6 ounces) lobster,
>   drained and cut in pieces
>   3 tablespoons dry sherry
>   Whipped cream

1. Sauté onion in melted butter in a large saucepan. Stir in flour, salt, and pepper. Heat until mixture bubbles.
2. Gradually stir in tomato juice, half-and-half, milk, Worcestershire sauce, and Tabasco. Cook until sauce thickens, stirring constantly.
3. Add lobster, reserving a few pieces for garnish. Heat; do not boil. Stir in sherry.
4. Pour into a tureen or individual soup bowls. Garnish with reserved lobster meat and whipped cream.

6 servings

Crab-Tomato Cream Soup: Follow recipe for Lobster-Tomato Cream Soup, except substitute **1 cup** (about 4 ounces) **flaked fresh crab meat** for the lobster. 141

142 *Creamy Shrimp and Avocado Bisque*

Seafood and fruit join to make an elegant soup. Serve with bowknot-shaped Dinner Rolls

>   2 cans (about 10 ounces each)
>   condensed cream of asparagus
>   soup
>   2 cans (about 10 ounces each)
>   condensed cream of potato soup
>   1 teaspoon curry powder
>   2 soup cans milk
>   2 soup cans half-and-half
>   2 cups cooked shrimp, cut in pieces
>   (see Note)
>   1 avocado, peeled and chopped
>   2 tablespoons minced chives

1. Combine soups and curry in a large, heavy saucepan. Stir in milk and half-and-half. Set over low heat until thoroughly heated, stirring occasionally.
2. Mix in shrimp; heat thoroughly; do not boil.
3. Pour into soup tureen; gently stir in avocado. Sprinkle with chives. Serve at once.

10 servings

Note: When using fresh or fresh-frozen shrimp, shell and devein. To remove the vein, make a shallow cut lengthwise down back of each shrimp. Remove vein with point of knife.

Cool and Creamy Shrimp and Avocado Bisque: Follow recipe for Creamy Shrimp and Avocado Bisque; chill before serving. 143

144 *Consommé*

More than just a clear stock, consommé derives its special flavor from the vegetables used. Egg whites and shells clarify this traditional and elegant appetizer soup.

>   ½ cup coarsely chopped celery
>   leaves
>   ½ cup chopped leek (green part
>   only)
>   ½ cup chopped carrots
>   ¼ cup chopped parsley leaves and
>   stems
>   2 tomatoes, chopped
>   3 egg whites
>   3 egg shells, crushed
>   2 quarts beef stock

1. Combine ingredients in a heavy 4- or 5-quart saucepot. Bring to boiling. Reduce heat; simmer 20 minutes, uncovered and undisturbed.
2. Pour soup into a sieve lined with a double thickness of dampened cheesecloth which has been placed over a large bowl. Serve hot.

6 servings

Double Consommé: Follow recipe for Consommé, adding **1 pound beef,** cut in pieces, with vegetables. Simmer 45 minutes. 145

Consommé with Vegetables: Follow recipe for Consommé. After straining, add **1 cup thinly sliced cooked vegetables.** Heat. 146

147 *Bouillabaisse*

Truly a bouillabaisse should be served after you've been fishing all day—so you can include your catch! But when you are buying, select 3 different fish plus seafood. Other possibilities besides those listed here are red snapper and whole clams.

⅔ cup chopped onion
2 leeks, chopped (white part only)
¼ cup olive oil
1 clove garlic, crushed
1 can (16 ounces) tomatoes
1 tablespoon minced parsley
½ bay leaf
½ teaspoon savory
½ teaspoon fennel
⅛ teaspoon saffron
1½ teaspoons salt
¼ teaspoon pepper
1 lobster (1½ to 2 pounds) cleaned
   and cut up, or 8 lobster tails
1½ pounds bass, boned and cut in
   1-inch pieces
1 pound perch, boned and cut in
   1-inch pieces
1 pound cod, boned and cut in
   1-inch pieces
1 pound fresh shelled deveined
   shrimp
1 pound sea scallops (fresh or
   thawed frozen)
1 pint oysters
6 slices French bread, toasted

1. Sauté onion and leeks in olive oil in a large Dutch oven. Stir in garlic, tomatoes, parsley, bay leaf, savory, fennel, saffron, salt, pepper, lobster, and bass, and just enough water to cover (1 to 1½ quarts). Bring to boiling; simmer 10 minutes.
2. Add perch and cod; continue to simmer 10 minutes, or until fish are almost tender.
3. Add shrimp and scallops; cook 5 minutes longer.
4. Meanwhile, drain oysters, reserving liquor. Remove any shell particles. Simmer oysters in liquor in a saucepan 3 minutes, or until edges begin to curl. Add to fish mixture.
5. Line a deep serving dish with toasted bread. Cover with fish and pour sauce in which fish has been cooked over all. Serve at once.

About 8 servings

Note: If desired, substitute 1 cup sherry for 1 cup of the water in step 1.

148 *Vichyssoise (Chilled Leek and Potato Soup)*

Surprisingly enough, this is an American soup with a French name. Gourmets will insist that it be made with the white part of leeks. (The rest of us will settle for green onions.) Serve very cold.

4 to 6 leeks
2 tablespoons butter or margarine
4 potatoes, pared and sliced
1 quart chicken broth or 6 chicken
   bouillon cubes dissolved in 1
   quart boiling water
1 cup half-and-half
1 cup chilled whipping cream
   Snipped chives

1. Finely slice the white part and about an inch of the green part of each leek to measure about 1 cup.
2. Sauté leeks in butter in a heavy saucepan. Stir in potatoes and broth; bring to boiling. Simmer 40 minutes, or until potatoes are tender.
3. Sieve the cooked vegetables or blend until smooth in an electric blender. Mix in half-and-half; chill thoroughly.
4. Just before serving, stir in whipping cream. Garnish with chives.

8 servings

149 *Sour Cream Garlic Soup*

Garlic lovers—this one would be a nice beginning to a pork entrée.

8 cloves garlic, crushed or minced
⅓ cup butter or margarine
⅓ cup flour
¼ teaspoon crushed basil
⅛ teaspoon salt
⅛ teaspoon pepper
1½ quarts beef broth
Dairy sour cream
Chopped chives
Sieved hard-cooked egg yolk

1. Carefully cook garlic in melted butter in a heavy saucepan until golden, stirring constantly. Stir in flour, basil, salt, and pepper; heat until bubbly. Gradually add broth, stirring constantly. Bring to boiling; cook 1 minute.
2. Serve hot or cold, topping each serving with a generous dollop of sour cream and a sprinkling of chives and egg yolk.

4 to 6 servings

150 *New Orleans Gumbo*

Gumbo, a Creole masterpiece, is traditionally made with filé, which is dried sassafras leaves. Because filé is not always available outside of Louisiana, okra is often substituted for it.

2 onions, chopped
½ cup butter or margarine
¼ cup flour
2 quarts chicken stock
1 can (28 ounces) tomatoes
½ pound okra, sliced
1 stalk celery, sliced
½ teaspoon thyme
1 bay leaf
½ teaspoon salt
Pinch pepper
Pinch cayenne pepper
6 hard-shell crabs
24 large peeled and deveined shrimp
24 oysters
2 cups cooked rice

1. Sauté onion in butter in a large saucepan. Mix in flour; cook until bubbly.
2. Gradually add chicken stock, tomatoes, okra, celery, and seasonings; add crabs. Simmer 1 hour.
3. Add shrimp and oysters; simmer 5 minutes.
4. Put ¼ cup rice into each soup bowl; ladle in hot gumbo.

8 servings

151 *Toasted Almond Soup*

This creamy soup is not only delicious but quick, because it is made in an electric blender.

1 cup water
1 cup salted roasted almonds
4 egg yolks
3 chicken bouillon cubes
1 small slice onion
½ teaspoon sugar
2 cups water
1 cup half-and-half

1. Put 1 cup water, almonds, egg yolks, bouillon cubes, onion, and sugar in an electric blender container. Blend until amonds are finely ground.
2. Pour into a saucepan; stir in 2 cups water. Cook over low heat about 5 minutes, or until mixture coats a spoon, stirring constantly (do not boil).
3. Stir in half-and-half and heat thoroughly without boiling. Garnish with **finely shredded orange peel**.

5 or 6 servings

152 *Crab Meat Bisque*

Bisques are cream soups usually containing shellfish, as here. Accompany any one of these bisques with crescent-shaped Dinner Rolls

½ cup chopped onion
⅓ cup chopped carrot
1 leek (white part only), minced
3 tablespoons butter or margarine
● 1 quart White Stock
1 teaspoon salt
⅛ teaspoon pepper
1 bay leaf
3 egg yolks, beaten
1 cup whipping cream
½ cup dry white wine
2 cups (8 ounces) flaked fresh crab meat
Minced parsley

1. Sauté onion, carrot, and leek in melted butter in a large saucepan. Stir in white stock, salt, pepper, and bay leaf. Cover; simmer 10 minutes.
2. Push mixture through sieve or food mill or purée in an electric blender. Return to saucepan.
3. Stir about 3 tablespoons hot soup into egg yolks. Return mixture to soup, stirring constantly.
4. Stir in whipping cream, wine, and crab meat. Heat; do not boil.
5. Sprinkle parsley over each serving.

8 servings

Lobster Bisque: Follow recipe for Crab Meat Bisque, substituting **2 cans (about 6 ounces each) lobster meat,** drained, for the crab meat.

Shrimp Bisque: Follow recipe for Crab Meat Bisque, substituting **2½ cups chopped cooked shrimp** for crab meat.

153 *Crimson Soup*

4 cups puréed drained tomatoes
   (about 2 pounds ripe tomatoes)
1 tablespoon brown sugar
1 teaspoon salt
   Few grains freshly ground black pepper
½ teaspoon grated lemon peel
2 tablespoons lemon juice
½ teaspoon grated onion
1 cup finely chopped cantaloupe
½ cup finely chopped honeydew melon
¼ cup finely chopped cucumber

1. Combine tomato purée, brown sugar, salt, pepper, lemon peel and juice, and onion. Stir in remaining ingredients.
2. Chill several hours.
3. Serve in chilled bowls. If desired, garnish each serving with a lemon slice and a sprig of parsley or watercress. Accompany with a shaker of seasoned salt and a bowl of brown sugar.

6 servings

154 Swedish Fruit Soup

1 cup dried apricots
¾ cup dried apples
½ cup dried peaches
½ cup prunes
½ cup dark seedless raisins
2 quarts water
¼ cup sugar
3 tablespoons quick-cooking
   tapioca
1 piece stick cinnamon (3 inches)
1 teaspoon grated orange peel
1 cup red raspberry fruit syrup

1. Rinse dried fruits with cold water; remove pits from prunes. Place fruits in a large kettle with the water; cover and allow to soak 2 to 3 hours.
2. Add the sugar, tapioca, cinnamon, and orange peel to fruits; let stand 5 minutes. Bring to boiling and simmer covered 1 hour, or until fruit is tender.
3. Stir in syrup; cool, then chill thoroughly.
4. Serve with **whipped cream** and **slivered blanched almonds.**

12 to 16 servings

155 Breakfast Nog

¼ cup sugar
2 egg yolks
1 quart milk
¼ teaspoon salt
⅛ teaspoon nutmeg
1 teaspoon vanilla extract

1. Beat sugar into egg yolks in a large saucepan. Stir in milk, salt, and nutmeg. Cook over low heat, stirring constantly, until mixture coats a spoon.
2. Serve hot or cold in mugs.

4 servings

Banana Nog: Prepare Breakfast Nog. Chill. Stir in **1 or 2 sliced bananas.** If desired, sprinkle each serving with **grated chocolate** and **cinnamon.**   156

Fluffy Breakfast Nog: Prepare Breakfast Nog; chill. Beat **2 egg whites** until foamy. Gradually add **3 tablespoons sugar,** beating until soft peaks form. Fold into chilled custard. Top each serving with dollop of **whipped cream.**   157

158 Cherry Breakfast Soup

1 can (about 10 ounces) dark sweet
   cherries, drained; reserve liquid
4 whole cloves
1 stick cinnamon, broken in half
  Juice of ½ lemon (about 2
   tablespoons)
2 teaspoons cornstarch
1 can (16 ounces) sliced pears,
   drained; reserve juice
1 orange, peeled and sectioned

1. Combine cherry liquid, cloves, cinnamon, and lemon juice in a saucepan; bring to boiling. Simmer 5 minutes. Remove spices with slotted spoon.
2. Combine cornstarch and pear juice; gradually add to cherry mixture. Cook until thickened, stirring constantly.
3. Stir in remaining fruit. Serve hot or cold.

6 servings

159 *Apricot-Melon Soup*

2 cups chopped melon, cantaloupe, or honeydew
2 cups apricot nectar
2 tablespoons lemon juice
Dash salt
1 pint lemon sherbet

1. Combine melon, apricot nectar, lemon juice, and salt. Chill.
2. Serve in chilled bowls. Float a scoop of sherbet on each serving.

4 servings

160 *Green Pea Potage*

Water chestnuts are a unique soup ingredient, for no matter how long they sit in the soup, they never get soggy and lose their crunch.

¼ cup dairy sour cream
1 can (about 11 ounces) condensed green pea soup
1 soup can water
¼ cup sliced water chestnuts
1 tablespoon sliced green onion
1 tablespoon lemon juice
Toasted slivered almonds

1. Blend sour cream into soup in a bowl. Gradually add water, stirring until smooth. Mix in water chestnuts, green onion, and lemon juice. Chill 4 hours.
2. Garnish chilled soup with the almonds.

3 servings

161 *Tomato-Noodle Soup*

Tomatoes and noodles join to make this reminiscent of spaghetti!

2 cans (about 10 ounces each) condensed tomato soup
2 cans (about 10 ounces each) condensed cream of celery soup
1 can (6 ounces) tomato paste
¼ cup instant minced onion
1 can (1 ounce) dried instant mixed vegetables
1 teaspoon salt
¼ teaspoon pepper
1 teaspoon crushed basil
2 quarts water
8 ounces (about 4 cups) fine egg noodles
Milk

1. Combine soups and tomato paste in a large saucepan; mix in instant minced onion, instant vegetables, salt, pepper, and basil.
2. Gradually add water, stirring constantly. Bring to boiling, stirring occasionally.
3. Add noodles gradually so the mixture continues to boil. Cook, uncovered, until noodles are tender, about 10 minutes, stirring occasionally. Blend in milk to taste.

About 3½ quarts

162 *Creamy Shrimp Gumbo*

Shrimp makes it elegant, canned soups make it quick.

1 can (about 10 ounces) condensed
    cream of chicken soup
1 soup can milk
1 can (about 10 ounces) condensed
    chicken gumbo soup
½ cup chopped cooked shrimp
¼ teaspoon soy sauce
    Garlic powder to taste

1. Blend chicken soup and milk in a saucepan.
2. Stir in remaining ingredients. Heat (do not boil).

4 to 6 servings

163 *Chilled Dilled Chicken Soup*

2 cans (about 10 ounces each)
    condensed cream of chicken
    soup
2 soup cans milk
2 teaspoons chopped green onion
    with tops
½ cup chopped cucumber
2 teaspoons chopped fresh dill or
    ½ teaspoon dill weed

1. Mix soup and milk in a bowl; blend in the remaining
ingredients.
2. Cover and refrigerate 3 to 4 hours to allow flavors to
blend.
3. Serve soup thoroughly chilled, or heat and serve.

About 6 servings

164 *Cream of Everything Soup*

Mushroom, peas, tomato, rice are all blended to perfection.

1 can (about 10 ounces) condensed
    cream of mushroom soup
1 can (about 11 ounces) condensed
    green pea soup
1 can (about 10 ounces) condensed
    tomato-rice soup
3 soup cans water
½ teaspoon crushed dill weed
¼ teaspoon crushed tarragon
    Dairy sour cream

1. Combine all ingredients in a saucepan. Cover and simmer
about 10 minutes.
2. Top individual bowls of soup with a dollop of dairy sour
cream.

About 8 servings

165 *Herbed Soup*

Two herbs here you should get to know. Basil complements most tomato dishes, while fennel, a mild licorice flavor, enhances the taste of fish.

1 can (about 10 ounces) condensed chicken gumbo soup
1 can (about 10 ounces) condensed cream of celery soup
2 soup cans water
¼ teaspoon ground fennel
¼ teaspoon crushed basil
Few grains ground ginger
Avocado Sauce

1. Blend soups, water, herbs, and ginger in a saucepan. Simmer covered about 10 minutes.
2. Serve with Avocado Sauce.

6 servings

Avocado Sauce: Combine **½ cup dairy sour cream** and **½ cup mashed ripe avocado**; blend until smooth.

16

167 *Canyon City Soup*

Seasonings in this soup give it a southwestern flavor.

1 onion, sliced
2 tablespoons margarine
½ pound frankfurters, sliced
3½ cups (28 ounces) tomatoes
2 cups (about 15 ounces) kidney beans or chili beans, drained
½ to 1 teaspoon chili powder
½ teaspoon cumin powder
½ teaspoon garlic salt
Salt and pepper

1. Sauté onion in margarine.
2. Add remaining ingredients; stir.
3. Simmer 10 minutes.

4 servings

168 *Curried Potato-Apple Soup*

1 can (about 10 ounces) condensed cream of potato soup
1 soup can milk
1 apple, quartered, pared, and cored
½ teaspoon curry powder

1. Combine all ingredients in electric blender container and blend until smooth.
2. Pour into a saucepan and heat thoroughly.
3. Garnish hot soup with **apple wedges.**

About 1 quart

169 *Zucchini Soup*

Zucchini grows so abundantly and quickly that it is a fun vegetable to watch in the garden.

2 cups diced zucchini
½ cup tomato juice
2 tablespoons chopped onion
⅛ teaspoon basil
1 package (8 ounces) cream cheese, cubed

1. Combine zucchini, tomato juice, onion, and basil; simmer 20 minutes.
2. Pour into an electric blender; add cream cheese and blend until smooth.
3. Serve hot, or chill to serve as cold soup or dip.

About 3 servings

170 *Vegetable-Sausage Soup*

1 can (about 10 ounces) condensed vegetable soup
1 soup can water
½ teaspoon prepared mustard
⅛ teaspoon pepper
1 cup cubed thuringer or cervelat sausage

1. Combine soup, water, mustard, and pepper in a saucepan. Set over moderate heat until mixture begins to simmer.
2. Add the sausage and simmer 10 minutes.

3 servings

171 *Caraway Bouillon*

1½ quarts boiling water
6 beef bouillon cubes
1 tablespoon crushed caraway seed

1. Add water to bouillon and caraway seed in a saucepan. Stir until cubes are dissolved. Cover; simmer 10 minutes.
2. Serve hot in mugs.

6 to 8 servings

172 *Vegetable Bouillon*

1 can (about 10 ounces) condensed beef broth
1 soup can water
1 can (6 ounces) cocktail vegetable juice
2 tablespoons finely chopped green pepper
3 radishes, finely chopped
½ teaspoon instant minced onion

1. Bring broth, water, and vegetable juice to boiling in a saucepan.
2. Add green pepper, radishes, and onion. Simmer, uncovered, 5 to 8 minutes.
3. Serve hot, garnished with sprigs of **parsley**.

4 servings

173 *California Cup*

Although the ingredients sound unusual, the combination is surprisingly good.

1 can (about 10 ounces) condensed
    tomato soup
½ soup can cranberry juice cocktail
½ soup can water
1 teaspoon lemon juice
    Dairy sour cream

1. Combine ingredients; chill until serving time.
2. Top each serving with dollop of sour cream.

3 servings

174 *Cabbage-Cheese Chowder*

The brisk autumn air and activities are sure to stimulate appetites.

1 can (about 10 ounces) condensed
    Cheddar cheese soup
1 soup can milk
½ teaspoon prepared mustard
4 slices (2 ounces) bologna, diced
3 cups thinly sliced cabbage

1. Combine soup, milk, and mustard in a medium saucepan. Stir in bologna and cabbage.
2. Cook over low heat until cabbage is crisp-tender, about 5 minutes.

4 servings

175 *Quick Mulligatawny*

Creamy curried chicken soup is a quick adaptation of a well-known Indian soup.

1 can (about 10 ounces) condensed
    cream of chicken soup
1 soup can milk
1 cup finely chopped cooked
    chicken
¼ cup packaged precooked rice
½ teaspoon curry powder
¼ teaspoon instant minced onion

1. Combine all ingredients in a medium saucepan.
2. Simmer 10 minutes.

4 servings

176 *Egg Drop Soup*

Oriental in origin, Egg Drop Soup is an appetizing first course.

¼ cup thinly sliced celery
2 tablespoons thinly sliced
    mushrooms
1 green onion, thinly sliced
3 cups chicken stock
½ teaspoon salt
    Few grains pepper
1 egg, well beaten

1. Combine vegetables and chicken stock in a saucepan. Stir in salt and pepper. Bring to boiling; simmer 5 minutes.
2. Reduce heat and drizzle egg slowly into stock while stirring. Stir until egg separates into shreds. Simmer 1 minute. Serve at once.

3 or 4 servings

177 *Herbed Zucchini Soup*

½ cup chopped onion
2 tablespoons bacon fat or
    margarine
4 medium zucchini, sliced (about 4
    cups)
1 can (about 10 ounces) condensed
    beef consommé or broth
2 cups water
1 teaspoon basil
½ teaspoon salt
¼ teaspoon garlic powder
⅛ teaspoon pepper
¼ cup minced parsley or 2
    tablespoons dried parsley
    Grated Parmesan cheese

1. Sauté onion in bacon fat in a large saucepan. Stir in remaining ingredients except Parmesan cheese. Heat to boiling; simmer until zucchini is tender, 3 to 5 minutes.
2. Sprinkle each serving with Parmesan cheese.

4 to 6 servings

Creamy Zucchini Soup without Cream: 178
Prepare Herbed Zucchini Soup. Purée in an electric blender. Reheat.

Breads

179 *Basic White Bread*

5½ to 6 cups flour
2 packages active dry yeast
2 tablespoons sugar
2 teaspoons salt
1 cup milk
1 cup water
2 tablespoons oil
Oil or butter

QUICK MIX METHOD

1. Combine 2 cups flour, yeast, sugar, and salt in a large mixing bowl.
2. Heat milk, water, and 2 tablespoons oil in a saucepan over low heat until very warm (120° to 130°F).
3. Add liquid to flour mixture; beat on high speed of electric mixer until smooth, about 3 minutes. Gradually stir in more flour to make a soft dough.
4. Turn onto lightly floured surface and knead until smooth and elastic (5 to 10 minutes).
5. Cover dough with bowl or pan; let rest 20 minutes.
6. For two loaves, divide dough in half and roll out two 14×7-inch rectangles; for one loaf roll out to 16×8-inch rectangle.
7. Roll up from narrow side, pressing dough into roll at each turn. Press ends to seal and fold under loaf.
8. Place in 2 greased 8×4×2-inch loaf pans or 1 greased 9×5×3-inch loaf pan; brush with oil.
9. Let rise in warm place until double in bulk (30 to 45 minutes).
10. Bake at 400°F 35 to 40 minutes.
11. Remove from pans immediately and brush with oil; cool on wire rack.

One 2-pound loaf
or two 1-pound loaves

CONVENTIONAL METHOD

1. Heat milk, sugar, oil, and salt; cool to lukewarm.
2. In a large bowl, sprinkle yeast in warm water (105° to 115°F); stir until dissolved.
3. Add lukewarm milk mixture and 2 cups flour; beat until smooth.
4. Beat in enough additional flour to make a stiff dough.
5. Turn out onto lightly floured surface; let rest 10 to 15 minutes. Knead until smooth and elastic (8 to 10 minutes).
6. Place in a greased bowl, turning to grease top. Cover; let rise in warm place until double in bulk (about 1 hour).
7. Punch down. Let rest 15 minutes.
8. Follow same shaping and baking instructions as Quick Mix Method.

You'll want to try these flavor variations to the Basic White Bread for something different. Shaping variations are also included.

Cheese Bread: Add **1 cup (4 ounces) shredded Cheddar cheese** before the last portion of the flour. — 181

Onion Bread: Omit the salt and add **1 package (1⅜ ounces) dry onion soup mix** to the warm milk. — 182

Mini Loaves: Divide dough into 10 equal pieces. Shape into loaves. Place in 10 greased 4½ × 2½ × 1½-inch loaf pans. Cover; let rise until double in bulk (about 20 minutes). Bake at 350°F 20 to 25 minutes. — 183

Braided Egg Bread: Reduce milk to ½ cup. Add **2 eggs** with warm liquid to the flour mixture. Divide dough into 3 equal pieces. Form each into a rope, 15×12 inches. Braid. Tuck ends under. Place on a greased baking sheet or 9×5×3-inch loaf pan. Cover and let rise and bake the same as basic recipe. — 184

French Bread: Omit the milk and oil and use **2 cups water.** Divide dough in half. Roll each half into 15×12-inch rectangle. Beginning at long side, roll up tightly. Seal seams. Taper the ends. With a sharp knife, make ¼-inch deep diagonal cuts along loaf tops. Cover. Let rise until less than double in bulk (about 20 minutes). Brush with water. Bake at 400°F 15 minutes, then reduce to 350°F and bake 15 to 20 minutes longer. For crisper crust, put pan of hot water in bottom of oven and 5 minutes before loaf is done, brush with glaze of **1 beaten egg white** and **1 tablespoon cold water.** — 185

186 *Flavorful Herb Bread*

The delicious aroma of the herbs baking in this bread will draw everyone into the kitchen. Be prepared.

 ¾ cup warm milk
 2 tablespoons melted bacon fat or butter
 2 tablespoons sugar
1½ teaspoons salt
 1 package active dry yeast
 ¼ cup warm water (105° to 115°F)
 1 egg
 ¼ cup chopped chives
 2 tablespoons minced parsley
 1 teaspoon crushed oregano
 3 to 3½ cups all-purpose flour

1. Heat milk, bacon fat, sugar, and salt; cool to lukewarm.
2. Sprinkle yeast over warm water in a large mixing bowl; stir until dissolved.
3. Add the liquid, egg, chives, parsley, and oregano to yeast. Stir in 2 cups flour, beating until smooth. Add enough more flour to make a stiff dough.
4. Turn dough onto floured surface; knead until smooth and elastic (10 minutes).
5. Place in a greased bowl, turning to grease top of dough. Cover; let rise in a warm place until double in bulk (1 to 1½ hours).
6. Punch dough down. Shape into a round loaf. Place in a greased 9-inch pie pan. Cover; let rise until double in bulk (about 30 minutes).
7. Bake at 400°F 10 minutes; reduce to 375°F and bake 20 to 25 minutes longer, or until bread is well browned.

1 loaf

187 *100% Whole Wheat Bread*

Whole wheat flour gives a sweet, nutty flavor to this bread and is great for toasting. Remember the loaf will be low and compact because of the bran particles cutting through the gluten structure.

4¼ to 4¾ cups whole wheat flour
2 packages active dry yeast
1 tablespoon salt
¾ cup milk
¾ cup water
2 tablespoons oil
2 tablespoons honey
1 egg (at room temperature)
Oil

1. Combine 1¾ cups flour, yeast, and salt in a large mixing bowl.
2. Heat milk, water, oil, and honey over low heat until very warm (120° to 130°F).
3. Add the liquid and egg to flour mixture; beat until smooth, about 3 minutes on high speed of electric mixer.
4. Gradually stir in more flour to make a soft dough.
5. Turn onto a lightly floured surface and knead until smooth and elastic (5 to 8 minutes).
6. Cover dough with bowl or pan; let rest 20 minutes.
7. Roll out to 16×8-inch rectangle.
8. Roll up from narrow side, pressing dough into roll at each turn. Press ends to seal and fold under loaf.
9. Place in greased 9×5×3-inch loaf pan; brush with oil.
10. Let rise in a warm place (80° to 85°F) until double in bulk (30 to 45 minutes).
11. Bake at 375°F 35 to 40 minutes.
12. Remove from pans immediately and brush with oil or butter; cool on wire rack.

1 loaf

188 *Whole Wheat-Oatmeal Bread*

2¼ cups milk
¼ cup butter or margarine
1 tablespoon salt
¼ cup firmly packed brown sugar
2½ to 2¾ cups all-purpose flour
2 cups whole wheat flour
2 packages active dry yeast
2 cups uncooked oats
⅔ cup wheat germ

1. Heat milk, butter, salt, and sugar in a saucepan until lukewarm. Pour liquid into a large mixer bowl. Add 1 cup all-purpose flour and 1 cup whole wheat flour; beat 2 minutes at medium speed of electric mixer. Add remaining whole wheat flour and yeast; beat 2 minutes at medium speed. Stir in oats, wheat germ, and enough additional all-purpose flour to make a soft dough.
2. Turn dough onto a floured surface; knead until smooth and elastic (about 10 minutes). Round dough into a ball. Place in a greased bowl; lightly grease surface of dough. Cover; let rise in a warm place until nearly double in bulk (about 1 hour).
3. Punch dough down; shape into 2 large or 8 miniature loaves. Place in greased 8×4×2-inch or 4×3×2-inch loaf pans. Let rise in a warm place until nearly double in bulk.
4. Bake at 375°F 45 minutes for large loaves or 30 minutes for miniature loaves. Remove from pans immediately; cool on wire rack.

2 large loaves or 8 miniature loaves

189 Delicatessen Rye Bread

You'll notice when making rye breads that the dough is stickier and has a different consistency than whole wheat flour doughs.

2 to 2¾ cups all-purpose or
    unbleached flour
2 cups rye flour
2 teaspoons salt
2 packages active dry yeast
1 tablespoon caraway seed
1 cup milk
¾ cup water
2 tablespoons molasses
2 tablespoons oil

1. Combine 1¾ cups all-purpose flour, salt, yeast, and caraway seed in a large mixing bowl.
2. Heat milk, water, molasses, and oil in a saucepan over low heat until very warm (120° to 130°F).
3. Add liquid gradually to flour mixture, beating on high speed of electric mixer; scrape bowl occasionally. Add 1 cup rye flour, or enough to make a thick batter. Beat at high speed 2 minutes. Stir in remaining rye flour and enough all-purpose flour to make a soft dough.
4. Turn dough onto a floured surface; knead until smooth and elastic (about 5 minutes).
5. Cover with bowl or pan and let rest 20 minutes.
6. Divide in half. Shape into 2 round loaves; place on greased baking sheets. Cover; let rise until double in bulk (30 to 45 minutes).
7. Bake at 375°F 35 to 40 minutes, or until done.

2 loaves

190 Freezer Oatmeal Bread

This recipe lets you make your own convenience foods. Allow 4 hours after you pull the loaf out of the freezer before you enjoy hot homemade bread.

12 to 13 cups all-purpose flour
 4 packages active dry yeast
 2 tablespoons salt
 2 cups milk
 2 cups water
 ½ cup honey
 ¼ cup vegetable oil
 2 cups uncooked oats
 ½ cup wheat germ
    Oil

1. Combine 2 cups flour, yeast, and salt in a large mixing bowl.
2. Heat milk, water, honey, and oil in a saucepan until very warm (120° to 130°F).
3. Add the liquid gradually to flour mixture, beating 3 minutes on high speed of electric mixer until smooth. Stir in oats, wheat germ, and enough remaining flour to make a soft dough.
4. Turn dough onto a floured surface; knead until smooth and elastic (8 to 10 minutes).
5. Divide dough in quarters. Shape each quarter into a loaf, and either place in an 8×4×2-inch loaf pan or on a baking sheet. Freeze just until firm. Remove from pan. Wrap tightly in aluminum foil or freezer wrap. Dough will keep up to 2 weeks.
6. To bake, remove wrapping and place dough in a greased 8×4×2-inch loaf pan. Thaw in refrigerator overnight or at room temperature 2 hours. Brush with oil and let rise in a warm place until double in bulk (about 2 hours).
7. Bake at 400°F 30 to 35 minutes, or until done.

4 loaves

Freezer Whole Wheat Bread: Follow recipe for Freezer Oatmeal Bread, substituting **5 cups whole wheat flour** for 5 cups all-purpose flour.

191

Freezer White Bread: Follow recipe for Freezer Oatmeal Bread, omitting oats and wheat germ and increasing flour by about 1 cup.

192

193 Family Wheat Bread

This recipe is ideal for your family's everyday bread. It not only makes wonderful sandwiches and toast, but is high in protein due to the milk, eggs, and whole grains.

5 to 6 cups all-purpose or
    unbleached flour
2 packages active dry yeast
1 tablespoon salt
2 cups milk
½ cup water
¼ cup oil
3 tablespoons honey
3 eggs
2 cups whole wheat flour

1. Combine 2½ cups all-purpose flour, yeast, and salt in a large mixing bowl.
2. Heat milk, water, oil, and honey in a saucepan until very warm (120° to 130°F).
3. Add liquid to flour mixture and beat until smooth. Add eggs and continue beating about 3 minutes on high speed of electric mixer.
4. Stir in whole wheat flour and enough all-purpose flour to make a soft dough.
5. Turn dough onto a floured surface; allow to rest 10 minutes for easier handling. Knead until smooth and elastic (about 8 minutes). Let rest 20 minutes.
6. Divide dough in half. Roll each half into a 14×9-inch rectangle. Shape into loaves. Place in greased 9×5×3-inch loaf pans.
7. Cover with plastic wrap. Refrigerate 2 to 24 hours.
8. When ready to bake, remove from refrigerator. Let stand at room temperature 10 minutes.
9. Bake at 400°F 40 minutes, or until done.

2 loaves

Variations: Substitute 1 cup of any one of the following ingredients for 1 cup of the whole wheat flour: **uncooked oats, cornmeal, cracked wheat, soybean grits, millet, wheat germ, ground sunflower seeds, bran, crushed shredded wheat cereal,** or any flour of your choice.

194

195 Refrigerator Rye Bread

This lets you do all the mixing and clean up when you have the time and just shape and bake the loaf when you want to serve hot bread.

3 to 3½ cups unbleached or
    all-purpose flour
¼ cup firmly packed brown sugar
2 packages active dry yeast
1 tablespoon salt
1 tablespoon caraway seed or
    grated orange peel
2 cups hot water
¼ cup molasses
2 tablespoons softened butter or
    margarine
3 cups rye flour
    Cornmeal

1. Combine 2 cups unbleached flour, brown sugar, yeast, salt, and caraway seed in a large mixing bowl.
2. Heat water, molasses, and butter until very warm (120° to 130°F).
3. Add liquid gradually to flour mixture and beat about 3 minutes on high speed of electric mixer. Stir in rye flour and enough unbleached flour to make a soft dough.
4. Turn dough onto a floured surface; knead until smooth and elastic (about 5 minutes). Let rest 20 minutes.
5. Divide dough in half. Shape into 2 long narrow loaves by rolling and stretching dough as for French Bread.
Place on a greased baking sheet sprinkled with cornmeal. Cover with plastic wrap or waxed paper; refrigerate 2 to 24 hours.
6. When ready to bake, remove plastic wrap carefully. Let rise in a warm place while oven is preheating, about 15 minutes. Brush loaves with water.
7. Bake at 400°F 40 minutes, or until done.

2 loaves

196 Carrot Brown Bread

The husky character of this bread makes it a good companion to soups and a tasty way to get vitamin A.

3 cups whole wheat flour
4 cups unbleached or all-purpose
   flour
2 packages active dry yeast
2 teaspoons salt
2 cups milk
½ cup water
¼ cup vegetable oil
2 tablespoons honey
2 tablespoons molasses
1 cup grated carrot

1. Mix flours.
2. Combine 2 cups flour mixture, yeast, and salt in a large mixing bowl.
3. Heat milk, water, oil, honey, and molasses in a saucepan until very warm (120° to 130°F).
4. Add liquid gradually to flour mixture, beating 3 minutes on high speed of electric mixer.
5. Stir in carrot and enough more flour to make a soft dough.
6. Turn dough onto a floured surface; allow to rest 10 minutes for easier handling. Knead until smooth and elastic (5 to 8 minutes).
7. Place dough in an oiled bowl; turn to oil top of dough. Cover; let rise in a warm place until double in bulk (about 1 hour).
8. Punch dough down; divide in half. Either shape into 2 round loaves and place on a greased baking sheet, or shape into 2 loaves and place in 2 greased 9×5×3-inch loaf pans. Cover; let rise until double in bulk (about 30 minutes).
9. Bake at 375°F 40 to 45 minutes, or until done.

2 loaves

197 Mozzarella Egg Bread

7 to 8 cups all-purpose flour
2 packages active dry yeast
1 tablespoon sugar
1 tablespoon salt
6 eggs (at room temperature)
1 cup plain yogurt
2 cups shredded mozzarella cheese
   (8 ounces)
½ cup hot tap water (120° to 130°F)

1. Combine 2 cups flour, yeast, sugar, and salt in a mixing bowl.
2. Stir eggs, yogurt, 1½ cups cheese, and water into flour mixture; beat until smooth, about 3 minutes on high speed of electric mixer.
3. Stir in enough more flour to make a soft dough.
4. Turn dough onto a floured surface; knead until smooth and elastic (5 to 8 minutes).
5. Place in an oiled bowl; turn to oil top of dough. Cover; let rise in a warm place until double in bulk (about 1 hour).
6. Punch dough down. Divide in half; shape into loaves, and place in 2 greased 9×5×3-inch loaf pans. Cover; let rise until double, about 30 minutes. Top loaves with remaining cheese.
7. Bake at 375°F 30 minutes, or until done.

2 loaves

198 Hearty Potato Bread

Potato adds wonderful flavor and moistness to bread. Now you have a chance to see why it has been an international favorite for years.

6½ to 7½ cups flour
2 packages active dry yeast
2 tablespoons sugar
1 tablespoon salt
2¼ cups hot potato water
1 cup warm unseasoned mashed
    potatoes
2 tablespoons oil

1. Combine flour, yeast, sugar, and salt in a large mixing bowl.
2. Add potato water (see Note), potatoes, and oil to flour mixture; beat about 3 minutes on high speed of electric mixer.
3. Stir in enough more flour to make a soft dough.
4. Turn dough onto a floured surface; knead until smooth and elastic (5 to 8 minutes).
5. Place in an oiled bowl; turn to oil top of dough. Cover; let rise in a warm place until double in bulk (about 1 hour).
6. Punch dough down. Divide in half; shape into loaves and place in 2 greased 9×5×3-inch loaf pans. Cover; let rise until double in bulk (about 45 minutes).
7. Bake at 375°F 40 to 45 minutes, or until done.

2 loaves

Note: To make potato water, cook 2 pared, cut-up potatoes until tender in about 3 cups water. Drain, reserving water. Mash potatoes and cool for bread.

199 Colonial Bread

2 cups whole wheat flour
2½ cups unbleached or all-purpose
    flour
¾ cup rye flour
½ cup yellow cornmeal
⅓ cup firmly packed brown sugar
2 packages active dry yeast
1 tablespoon salt
2½ cups hot tap water (120° to
    130°F)
¼ cup vegetable oil
1 egg

1. Blend flours and cornmeal. Combine 2½ cups flour mixture, sugar, yeast, and salt in a large mixing bowl.
2. Stir water, oil, and egg into flour mixture; beat until smooth, about 3 minutes on high speed of electric mixer.
3. Gradually stir in enough more flour mixture to make a soft dough.
4. Turn dough onto a floured surface; knead until smooth and elastic (5 to 8 minutes).
5. Place in an oiled bowl; turn to oil top of dough. Cover; let rise in a warm place until double in bulk (about 1 hour).
6. Punch dough down. Divide in half; shape into loaves. Place in 2 greased 9×5×3-inch loaf pans. Cover; let rise until double in bulk (about 30 minutes).
7. Bake at 375°F 35 to 40 minutes, or until done.

2 loaves

200 Cornmeal French Bread

1 cup cooked cornmeal mush (see recipe)
2 packages active dry yeast
½ cup warm water
1 cup milk, scalded
1 tablespoon sugar
2½ teaspoons salt
4¾ to 5¼ cups all-purpose flour

1. Prepare cornmeal mush; cool slightly.
2. Dissolve yeast in warm water.
3. Pour scalded milk over sugar and salt in a large bowl. Add mush and mix well; cool to lukewarm. Beat in 1 cup flour. Mix in yeast and enough additional flour to make a soft dough.
4. Turn dough onto a lightly floured surface. Knead until smooth and satiny (about 10 minutes).
5. Put dough into a greased bowl; turn to grease top. Cover; let rise in a warm place until double in bulk (about 1 hour).
6. Punch dough down; cover and let rest 10 minutes. Form into a long thin roll on greased baking sheet. With a sharp knife, cut diagonal ¼-inch-deep slits about 2½ inches apart across the top. Brush top of loaf with salt water (**1 tablespoon salt** dissolved in **¼ cup water**). Cover; let rise until double in bulk (about 45 minutes).
7. Pour boiling water into a pie pan to a ½-inch depth; set on bottom rack of oven.
8. Bake at 400°F 15 minutes; turn temperature control to 350°F and bake 30 to 35 minutes longer. About 5 minutes before bread is finished baking, baste with salt water.

1 large loaf

Cornmeal Mush: Heat **3 cups water** to boiling in a saucepan. Mix **1 cup cornmeal, 1 teaspoon salt,** and **1 cup cold water.** Pour cornmeal mixture into boiling water, stirring constantly. Cook until thickened, stirring frequently. Cover; continue cooking over low heat 10 minutes.

4 cups

201

202 Here's-To-Your-Health Bread

Just about every ingredient in this bread is good for you. Whole grains and cottage cheese provide protein. Raisins and molasses contribute important minerals, especially iron. And besides all this, it tastes delicious.

4½ cups all-purpose or unbleached flour
3 cups whole wheat flour
1 cup uncooked oats
½ cup wheat germ
2 packages active dry yeast
2 teaspoons salt
2½ cups hot tap water (120° to 130°F)
1½ cups (12 ounces) creamed cottage cheese (at room temperature)
½ cup molasses or honey
2 tablespoons vegetable oil
1 cup raisins

1. Mix flours and oats.
2. Combine 3 cups flour mixture, wheat germ, yeast, and salt in a large mixing bowl.
3. Add water, cottage cheese, molasses, and oil to flour mixture; beat until smooth, about 3 minutes on high speed of electric mixer.
4. Stir in raisins and enough more flour to make a soft dough.
5. Turn dough onto a floured surface; let rest 10 minutes for easier handling. Knead until smooth and elastic (5 to 8 minutes).
6. Place in an oiled bowl; turn dough to oil top. Cover; let rise in a warm place until double in bulk (about 1 hour).
7. Punch dough down. Divide dough in thirds; shape into loaves and place in 3 greased 9×5×3-inch loaf pans. Cover; let rise until double in bulk (about 30 minutes).
8. Bake at 375°F 30 to 35 minutes, or until done.

3 loaves

203 Cinnamon Swirl Loaves

2 packages active dry yeast
½ cup warm water
2 cups milk, heated
⅓ cup honey
1 tablespoon salt
⅓ cup shortening
5 to 5½ cups all-purpose flour
2 cups uncooked oats
½ cup firmly packed brown sugar
2 tablespoons cinnamon

1. Dissolve yeast in warm water.
2. Pour hot milk over honey, salt, and shortening in a large bowl. Cool to lukewarm. Stir in 1 cup flour. Add softened yeast and oats. Stir in enough more flour to make a soft dough.
3. Turn dough onto a lightly floured surface; knead until smooth and satiny (about 10 minutes). Round dough into a ball and place in a greased bowl. Brush lightly with melted shortening. Cover; let rise in a warm place until double in bulk (about 1 hour).
4. Punch dough down; divide in half. Roll each half into a 14×7-inch rectangle. Brush with melted butter; sprinkle with brown sugar and cinnamon. Starting with short side, roll up as for jelly roll.
5. Place in 2 greased 8×4×2-inch loaf pans. Brush lightly with **melted shortening.** Cover; let rise until nearly double in bulk (about 45 minutes).
6. Bake at 375°F 45 to 50 minutes. Remove loaves from pans and brush with **melted butter.** Cool. Drizzle with a thin confectioners' sugar glaze, if desired.

2 loaves

204 Triple Treat Bread

If you don't have dry milk, you can replace 1 cup of the water with milk for the same tasty results.

4½ cups all-purpose or unbleached flour
2 cups whole wheat flour
1 cup rye flour
½ cup firmly packed brown sugar
½ cup instant nonfat dry milk
2 packages active dry yeast
1 tablespoon salt
2 cups hot tap water (120° to 130°F)
¼ cup vegetable oil

1. Mix flour.
2. Combine 2 cups flour mixture, sugar, dry milk, yeast, and salt in a large mixing bowl.
3. Stir water and oil into flour mixture; beat until smooth, about 3 minutes on high speed of electric mixer. Stir in enough remaining flour to make a soft dough.
4. Turn dough onto a floured surface; knead until smooth and elastic (5 to 8 minutes).
5. Place in an oiled bowl; turn to oil top of dough. Cover; let rise in a warm place until double (about 45 minutes).
6. Punch dough down. Divide in half; shape into loaves and place in 2 greased 9×5×3-inch loaf pans. Cover; let rise until double in bulk (about 30 minutes).
7. Bake at 375°F 35 to 40 minutes, or until done.

2 loaves

205 Ground Nut Bread

The electric blender or food processor is perfect for grinding the nuts and sunflower seeds for this bread.

3 cups all-purpose flour
1½ cups whole wheat flour
2 packages active dry yeast
2 teaspoons salt
1¾ cups hot tap water (120° to 130°F)
¼ cup honey

1. Mix flours.
2. Combine 1¾ cups flour mixture, yeast, and salt in a large mixing bowl.
3. Add water, honey, and oil to flour mixture; beat until smooth, about 3 minutes on high speed of electric mixer.
4. Stir in oats, nuts, sunflower seeds, cornmeal, and enough more flour to make a soft dough.

2 tablespoons vegetable oil
1 cup rolled oats
1 cup ground unsalted nuts
½ cup ground unsalted hulled
   sunflower seeds
½ cup cornmeal

5. Turn dough onto a floured board; knead until smooth and elastic (5 to 8 minutes).
6. Place in an oiled bowl; turn to oil top of dough. Cover; let rise in a warm place until double in bulk (about 1 hour).
7. Punch dough down. Divide in half, then each half in thirds. Form each piece into a rope 12 to 15 inches long. For each loaf, braid 3 pieces together. Tuck ends under; place in 2 greased 9×5×3-inch loaf pans or on greased baking sheets. Cover; let rise until double in bulk (about 1 hour).
8. Bake at 375°F 35 to 40 minutes, or until done.

2 loaves

206 *Harvest Bread*

1½ cups milk
⅓ cup margarine
2 tablespoons honey
2 tablespoons light molasses
2 teaspoons salt
2 large shredded wheat biscuits,
   crumbled
½ cup warm water (105° to 115°F)
2 packages active dry yeast
2 cups whole wheat flour
¼ cup wheat germ
2 to 3 cups all-purpose flour

1. Heat milk; stir in margarine, honey, molasses, salt, and shredded wheat biscuits. Cool to lukewarm.
2. Measure warm water into a large warm bowl. Sprinkle in yeast; stir until dissolved. Add lukewarm milk mixture and whole wheat flour; beat until smooth. Stir in wheat germ and enough all-purpose flour to make a stiff dough.
3. Turn dough onto a lightly floured surface; knead until smooth and elastic (8 to 10 minutes). Place in a greased bowl; turn to grease top. Cover; let rise in a warm place until double in bulk (about 1 hour).
4. Punch dough down; divide in half. Proceed, following directions below for desired shape.
5. Cover; let rise in a warm place until double in bulk (about 1 hour). If making sheaf, make diagonal snips with scissors along the bent portion of stalks above the twist. If desired, gently brush sheaf with beaten egg.
6. Bake on lowest rack position at 400°F about 20 minutes for sheaves and 25 to 30 minutes for loaves, or until done. Remove from baking sheets and cool on wire racks.

2 loaves

To Make Round Loaves: Shape each half of dough into a smooth round ball. Press each ball slightly to flatten into rounds 6 inches in diameter. Place on greased baking sheets.

To Make Wheat Sheaf: Divide one half of dough into 18 equal pieces. Roll 2 pieces into 12-inch ropes. Twist ropes together; set aside. Roll 8 pieces into 18-inch ropes and roll remaining 8 pieces into 15-inch ropes. Place one 18-inch rope lengthwise on center of a greased baking sheet, bending top third of rope off to the left at a 45-degree angle. Place a second 18-inch rope on sheet touching the first rope but bending top third off to the right. Repeat procedure using two more 18-inch ropes, placing them along outer edges of straight section and inside bent sections so that ropes are touching. Repeat, using two of the 15-inch ropes. Repeat, starting with the long ropes, placing them on top of the arranged long ropes and slightly spreading out ropes forming bottom of sheaf. Fill in by topping with the remaining 15-inch ropes, making shorter bends in two uppermost ropes. Cut twist in half. Arrange twists side by side around center of sheaf, tuck ends underneath. Repeat with remaining half of dough.

207 Mushroom Bread

¼ cup margarine
½ pound mushrooms, finely
   chopped
1 cup finely chopped onion
2 cups milk
3 tablespoons molasses
4 teaspoons salt
¼ teaspoon pepper
½ cup warm water (105° to 115°F)
2 packages active dry yeast
1 egg
1 cup wheat germ
8 to 9 cups all-purpose flour

1. Melt 2 tablespoons margarine in a large skillet over medium heat. Add mushrooms and onion; sauté until onion is tender and liquid has evaporated. Cool.
2. Heat milk; stir in molasses, salt, and pepper. Cool to lukewarm.
3. Measure warm water into a large warm bowl. Sprinkle in yeast; stir until dissolved. Add lukewarm milk mixture, egg, wheat germ, and 2 cups flour; beat until smooth. Stir in enough additional flour to make a stiff dough.
4. Turn dough onto a lightly floured surface; knead until smooth and elastic (8 to 10 minutes). Place in a greased bowl; turn to grease top. Cover; let rise in a warm place until double in bulk (about 1 hour).
5. Meanwhile, use four 30-ounce fruit cans to prepare Mushroom Pans (see below).
6. Punch dough down; turn onto lightly floured surface.

To Make Mushrooms: Divide dough onto 4 equal pieces. Shape each piece into a smooth round ball. Place in prepared Mushroom Pans. Let rise in a warm place until double in bulk (about 1 hour). With fingertips, gently press lower edge of mushroom cap down to meet foil-covered collar. Reshape cap if necessary. If desired, brush mushrooms with a mixture of 1 egg beaten with 1 tablespoon water. Bake on lowest rack position at 400°F about 40 minutes, or until done. Carefully remove from pans and cool on wire racks.

To Make Loaves: Divide dough in half. Roll each half to a 14×9-inch rectangle. Shape into loaves. Place in 2 greased 9×5×3-inch loaf pans. Cover; let rise in a warm place until double in bulk (about 1 hour). Bake at 400°F about 45 minutes, or until done. Remove from pans and cool on wire racks.

4 mushrooms
or 2 round loaves

Mushroom Pans: Cut 4 heavy cardboard squares 2 inches wider than can opening. Trace can opening in center of squares and cut out. Cover rings with foil. Place rings over cans so they fit tightly around opening. Grease cans and foil collars well.

208 Anadama Batter Bread

1 package active dry yeast
¼ cup warm water
1 cup cornmeal
2 teaspoons salt
½ teaspoon baking soda
⅓ cup dark molasses
3 tablespoons shortening
¾ cup boiling water

1. Dissolve yeast in warm water.
2. Combine cornmeal, salt, baking soda, molasses, and shortening in a large mixer bowl. Stir in boiling water; cool to lukewarm.
3. Add softened yeast, egg, and 1 cup flour to cornmeal mixture; beat 2 minutes on medium speed of electric mixer or 300 vigorous strokes with a wooden spoon. Stir in remaining flour.

1 egg
2¼ cups all-purpose flour
Melted butter

4. Spread batter in a well-greased 2-quart casserole. Cover; let rise in a warm place until nearly double in bulk (1 to 1½ hours).
5. Bake at 350°F about 40 minutes. Remove from casserole immediately. Brush top lightly with melted butter; cool.

1 loaf

209 *Aspen Batter Bread*

4 cups all-purpose flour
2 tablespoons sugar
1 package active dry yeast
1 teaspoon salt
¼ teaspoon ginger
1 can (13 ounces) evaporated milk
½ cup hot water
2 tablespoons vegetable oil

1. Combine 2 cups flour, sugar, yeast, salt, and ginger in a large mixing bowl.
2. Heat milk, water, and oil until very warm (120° to 130°F).
3. Stir in liquid with flour mixture; beat 2 minutes by hand or with electric mixer. Cover; let rise 15 minutes.
4. Beat in remaining flour by hand. Pour into 2 greased 1-pound coffee cans. Cover with greased plastic lids; let rise in a warm place until dough rises to top of cans (or until lids pop off), about 35 minutes. Remove lids.
5. Bake at 375°F 40 to 45 minutes, or until done. Place on wire racks to cool slightly before removing loaves from cans.

2 loaves

210 *Bran-New Batter Bread*

1 cup all-purpose flour
1 package active dry yeast
2 teaspoons salt
½ cup hot water
½ cup milk
½ cup vegetable oil
⅓ cup honey
2 eggs
1 cup whole bran cereal
½ cup wheat germ
1½ cups all-purpose flour

1. Combine 1 cup flour, yeast, and salt in large mixing bowl.
2. Heat water, milk, oil, and honey until very warm (120° to 130°F).
3. Add liquid and eggs to flour mixture and beat about 3 minutes at high speed of electric mixer.
4. Beat in bran cereal, wheat germ, and remaining flour by hand. Divide mixture into 2 well-greased 1-pound coffee cans. Cover with greased plastic lids and let rise in a warm place until dough rises almost to top of cans (about 35 minutes). Remove lids.
5. Bake at 375°F 35 minutes, or until done. Place on wire racks. Cool loaves slightly, then remove from cans and place on racks to cool.

2 loaves

211 *Dilly Cottage Batter Bread*

2½ cups all-purpose flour
1 package active dry yeast
1 tablespoon instant minced onion
1 teaspoon salt
½ teaspoon dill weed, thyme, or rosemary
1 cup creamed cottage cheese (at room temperature)
½ cup hot tap water (120° to 130°F)
1 egg (at room temperature)
1 tablespoon honey
1½ cups all-purpose flour

1. Combine 1 cup flour, yeast, onion, salt, and dill weed.
2. Add cottage cheese, water, egg, and honey to flour mixture; beat 3 minutes by hand or with electric mixer.
3. Beat in remaining flour. Cover; let rise in a warm place until double in bulk (about 1 hour).
4. Stir batter down; pour into a well-greased 1½-quart round casserole. Let rise in a warm place until light (30 to 40 minutes).
5. Bake at 375°F 50 to 55 minutes, or until done.

1 loaf

212 *Basic Dinner Rolls*

4 to 4¾ cups all-purpose flour
2 tablespoons sugar
2 packages active dry yeast
1 teaspoon salt
1 cup milk
½ cup water
¼ cup butter or margarine
1 egg (at room temperature)
Melted butter (optional)

1. Combine 1½ cups flour, sugar, yeast, and salt in a mixing bowl.
2. Heat milk, water, and butter until very warm (120° to 130°F).
3. Add liquid and egg to flour mixture; beat until smooth, about 3 minutes.
4. Stir in enough remaining flour to make a soft, sticky dough.
5. Turn dough onto a floured surface; continue to work in flour until dough can be kneaded. Knead until smooth and elastic, but still soft (about 5 minutes).
6. Cover dough with bowl or pan. Let rest 20 minutes.
7. Shape dough as desired. Cover and let rise until double in bulk (about 15 minutes).
8. Bake at 425°F about 12 minutes. Cool on wire racks. Brush with butter if desired.

2 to 2½ dozen rolls

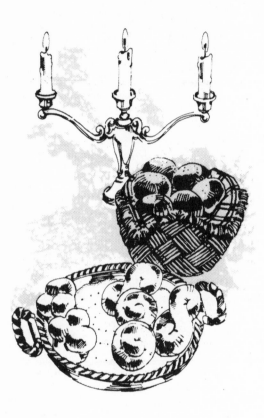

Pan Rolls: Divide dough into 24 equal pieces by first dividing dough in half and then each half into 12 equal pieces. Roll into balls. Place in a greased 13×9×2-inch baking pan. Brush with melted butter, if desired. 213

Cloverleaf Rolls: Pinch off bits of dough; roll into 1-inch balls. For each roll, place 3 balls in a greased muffin-pan well. 214

Crescents: Divide dough in half. Roll each half into a 12-inch round about ¼ inch thick. Brush with **2 tablespoons melted butter.** Cut into 12 wedges. For each crescent, roll up wedge beginning at side opposite the point. Place point-side down on a greased baking sheet; curve ends. 215

Snails: Roll dough into a rectangle ¼ inch thick. Cut off strips ½ inch wide and 5 inches long. Roll each piece of dough into a rope about 10 inches long. Wind into a flat coil, tucking ends under. Place on greased baking sheet. 216

Figure Eights: Shape strips of dough ½ inch wide and 5 inches long into 10-inch ropes as in Snails (above). For each roll, pinch ends of rope together and twist once to form a figure 8. Place on greased baking sheets. 217

Twists: Follow procedure for Figure Eights, giving each 8 an additional twist. 218

Bowknots: Roll dough into a rectangle ¼ inch thick. Cut off strips ½ inch wide and 5 inches long. Roll each strip into a smooth rope 9 or 10 inches long. Gently tie into a single or double knot. Place on a greased baking sheet. 219

Parker House Rolls: Roll dough ¼ inch thick. Brush with **3 or 4 tablespoons melted butter.** Cut with a 2½-inch round cutter. With a knife handle, make a crease across each circle slightly off center. Fold larger half over the smaller, pressing edges to seal. Place on a greased baking sheet or close together in a greased 13×9×2-inch baking pan. 220

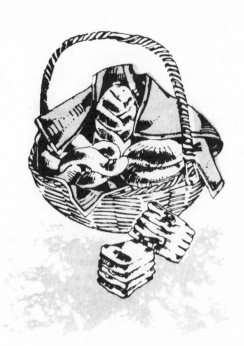

Braids: Form several ropes, ½ inch in diameter. Braid 3 ropes into a long strip; cut into 3-inch lengths. Pinch together at each end. Place on a greased baking sheet. **221**

Butterflies: Divide dough in half. Roll each half into a 24×6-inch rectangle about ¼ inch thick. Brush with **2 tablespoons melted butter.** Starting with long side, roll up dough as for jelly roll. Cut off 2-inch pieces. With handle of knife, press crosswise at center of each roll, forming a deep groove so spiral sides become visible. Place on a greased baking sheet. **222**

Fantans or Butterflake Rolls: Roll dough into a rectangle ¼ inch thick. Brush with **3 or 4 tablespoons melted butter.** Cut into 1-inch strips. Stack 6 or 7 strips; cut each into 1½-inch sections. Place on end in greased muffin-pan wells. **223**

224 *Crusty Hard Rolls*

If you like a crunchy roll, try this one. A shiny golden crust surrounds the snowy white and moist interior.

3½ to 4½ cups all-purpose flour
2 packages active dry yeast
1 tablespoon sugar
1½ teaspoons salt
1 cup hot tap water (120° to 130°F)
2 tablespoons vegetable oil
1 egg white
1 egg yolk
1 tablespoon water

1. Combine 1 cup flour, yeast, sugar, and salt in a large mixer bowl. Stir in water, oil, and egg white; beat until smooth, about 3 minutes on high speed of electric mixer. Gradually stir in more flour to make a soft dough.
2. Turn dough onto a floured surface; knead until smooth and elastic (3 to 5 minutes).
3. Cover with bowl or pan and let rest about 20 minutes.
4. Divide into 18 equal pieces. Form each into a smooth oval; place on a greased baking sheet. Slash tops lengthwise about ¼ inch deep. Let rise until double in bulk (about 15 minutes).
5. Brush with a mixture of egg yolk and 1 tablespoon water.
6. Bake at 400°F 15 to 20 minutes. For a crisper crust, place a shallow pan of hot water on lowest oven rack during baking.
1½ dozen rolls

Kaiser Rolls: Follow recipe for Crusty Hard Rolls, only flatten each of the 18 pieces of dough into 4- to 4-½-inch rounds. For each roll, lift one edge of the round and press it into center of circle. Then lift the corner of the fold and press it into the center. Continue clockwise around the circle until 5 or 6 folds have been made. Let rise and bake as directed above. **225**

226 French Crescents (Croissants)

Crescents are a lot of work but since they melt in your mouth they're worth every minute.

1 cup milk
1 tablespoon oil
1 tablespoon sugar
½ teaspoon salt
1 package compressed or active dry yeast
¼ cup warm water (105° to 115°F)
2¾ to 3 cups all-purpose flour
1 cup (½ pound) butter, softened
1 egg yolk
1 tablespoon milk

1. Heat 1 cup milk, oil, sugar, and salt in a saucepan; cool to lukewarm.
2. Dissolve yeast in warm water in a large bowl. Add milk mixture and 1 cup flour; beat until smooth. Stir in enough remaining flour to make a soft dough.
3. Turn dough onto a floured surface; continue to work in flour until dough can be kneaded. Knead until smooth and elastic (about 5 minutes).
4. Shape dough into a ball and place in an oiled bowl; turn to oil top of dough. Cover; let rise in a warm place until double in bulk (about 45 minutes).
5. Punch dough down. Roll out on floured surface to form a rectangle about ¼ inch thick.
6. Cut butter in slices (just soft enough to spread but not melted). Spread over center one-third section of rectangle. Fold each extending side over butter, pressing together the open edges to seal. Roll out again until rectangle is ⅜ inch thick. Turn dough occasionally, flouring surface lightly to prevent sticking. Fold in thirds again to make a squarish rectangle. Roll dough and fold again in the same manner. Wrap dough in waxed paper or foil; chill 30 minutes. If at any time dough oozes butter and becomes sticky while rolling, chill until butter is more firm.
7. Roll and fold again 2 more times exactly as directed before. Chill dough again another 30 minutes.
8. Roll dough into a rectangle about ⅛ inch thick. Cut into strips 6 inches wide. Cut triangles out of each strip to measure about 6×8×6 inches. Roll up each triangle of dough from a 6-inch edge, pinching tip to seal. Shape each roll into a crescent. Place, point down, 1½ inches apart on ungreased baking sheet.
9. Cover; let rise until double in bulk (30 to 45 minutes).
10. Brush each roll with mixture of egg yolk and 1 tablespoon milk.
11. Bake at 425°F 15 minutes, or until brown. Remove from baking sheet and cool on wire rack. Serve warm.

About 1½ dozen rolls

227 Pumpkin Spice Rolls

3½ to 4½ cups all-purpose flour
¼ cup firmly packed brown sugar
1 package active dry yeast
1 teaspoon salt
½ teaspoon cinnamon
¼ teaspoon nutmeg
⅛ teaspoon cloves
⅛ teaspoon ginger
1 cup milk
¼ cup water

1. Combine 1½ cups flour, brown sugar, yeast, salt, and spices in a large mixer bowl.
2. Heat milk, water, pumpkin, and oil in a saucepan until very warm (120° to 130°F).
3. Add liquid and egg to flour mixture and beat until smooth, about 3 minutes on high speed of electric mixer.
4. Stir in enough remaining flour to make a soft dough.
5. Turn dough onto floured board; continue to work in flour until dough is stiff enough to knead. Knead until smooth and elastic (about 5 minutes).

¾ cup canned pumpkin
¼ cup vegetable oil
1 egg
2 tablespoons melted butter

6. Cover with bowl or pan; let rest 20 minutes.
7. Shape into 2-inch balls; place each ball in a greased muffin-pan well. Brush with melted butter. Cover; let rise until double in bulk (about 20 minutes).
8. Bake at 375°F 20 minutes, or until done.

2 dozen rolls

228 *Potato Pan Rolls*

½ cup milk
1 tablespoon sugar
¾ teaspoon salt
2 tablespoons margarine
½ cup warm water (105° to 115°F)
1 package active dry yeast
1 egg
½ cup mashed potatoes (at room temperature)
3½ to 4½ cups all-purpose flour
Flour for dusting

1. Heat milk; stir in sugar, salt, and margarine. Cool to lukewarm.
2. Measure warm water into a large warm bowl. Sprinkle in yeast; stir until dissolved. Stir in lukewarm milk mixture, egg, mashed potatoes, and 2 cups flour. Beat until smooth. Stir in enough additional flour to make a soft dough.
3. Turn dough onto a lightly floured surface; knead until smooth and elastic (8 to 10 minutes). Place in a greased bowl; turn to grease top. Cover; let rise in a warm place until double in bulk (about 1 hour).
4. Punch dough down; turn out onto a lightly floured surface. Divide in half. Divide each half into 16 equal pieces; form into smooth balls. Place in 2 greased 9-inch round layer cake pans. Cover; let rise in a warm place until double in bulk (about 1 hour).
5. Dust rolls with flour.
6. Bake at 375°F about 25 minutes, or until done. Remove from pans and cool on wire racks.

32 rolls

229 *Brown-and-Serve Rolls*

9 to 10 cups all-purpose flour
½ cup sugar
2 packages active dry yeast
1 tablespoon salt
2 cups warm water
1 cup milk
½ cup butter or margarine

1. Stir together 3 cups flour, sugar, yeast, and salt in a large mixer bowl.
2. Heat water, milk, and butter until very warm (120° to 130°F).
3. Add liquid ingredients to flour mixture; beat until smooth, about 3 minutes on high speed of electric mixer.
4. Gradually stir in enough more flour to make a soft dough.
5. Turn out onto a floured surface; knead until smooth and elastic (5 to 8 minutes).
6. Shape dough into a ball, place in an oiled bowl, and turn to oil top of dough. Cover; let rise in a warm place until double in bulk (30 to 45 minutes).
7. Punch dough down. Divide in half. Shape each half into rolls (see page 26 for different shapes). Let rise in a warm place until double in bulk (30 to 45 minutes).
8. Bake at 375°F 20 to 25 minutes, or just until rolls begin to change color. Cool in pans 20 minutes. Finish cooling on wire racks. Wrap tightly in plastic bags and refrigerate up to 1 week, or freeze up to 2 months. Before serving, place rolls on ungreased baking sheet.
9. Bake at 400°F 10 to 12 minutes.

About 4 dozen rolls

230 Better Batter Rolls

These rolls resemble muffins in texture and shape, but the aroma as they bake is unmistakably and deliciously that of yeast. These go together quickly as they require no kneading.

3 cups all-purpose flour
1 package active dry yeast
1 teaspoon salt
1 cup hot water
¼ cup vegetable oil
¼ cup honey
1 egg

1. Combine 2 cups flour, yeast, and salt in a mixer bowl. Add water, oil, honey, and egg; beat until smooth, about 2 minutes on medium speed of electric mixer or 300 vigorous strokes by hand.
2. Beat in remaining flour by hand. Cover; let rise until double in bulk (about 30 minutes).
3. Fill greased muffin-pan wells half full. Let rise until double in bulk (about 30 minutes).
4. Bake at 400°F 10 to 12 minutes.

2 dozen rolls

231 English Muffins

3 to 3½ cups all-purpose flour
2 tablespoons sugar
1 package active dry yeast
1 teaspoon salt
¾ cup hot milk (120° to 130°F)
1 egg (at room temperature)
2 tablespoons vegetable oil
Cornmeal

1. Combine 1 cup flour, sugar, yeast, and salt in a mixer bowl.
2. Stir in milk, egg, and oil; beat until smooth, about 3 minutes on high speed of electric mixer.
3. Stir in enough remaining flour to make a soft dough.
4. Turn out onto floured board; knead until smooth and elastic (5 to 8 minutes).
5. Cover with bowl; let rest 20 minutes.
6. Roll out to ½-inch thickness. Cut into 3- or 4-inch rounds. Sprinkle with cornmeal. Cover; let rise until double in bulk (about 45 minutes).
7. Bake in a greased heavy skillet or on a griddle on top of the range over low heat 20 to 30 minutes, or until golden brown, turning once. Cool and store in an airtight container or plastic bag.
8. To serve, split with knife or fork. Toast. Serve hot.

About 1 dozen muffins

232 *Hurry-Up Dinner Rolls*

2½ to 3 cups all-purpose flour
2 tablespoons sugar
1 package active dry yeast
½ teaspoon salt
¾ cup hot tap water (120° to 130°F)
1 egg (at room temperature)
2 tablespoons vegetable oil
2 tablespoons melted butter or margarine

1. Combine 1 cup flour, sugar, yeast, and salt in a bowl. Stir in water, egg, and oil; beat until smooth. Cover; let rise in a warm place 15 minutes.
2. Stir in enough remaining flour to make a soft, sticky dough.
3. Turn dough onto a floured board; continue to work in flour until dough can be kneaded. Knead until smooth and elastic (about 3 minutes).
4. Divide dough into 16 pieces; shape into balls. Place in a greased 9-inch square pan. Brush tops with melted butter. Cover; let rise 20 minutes.
5. Bake at 425°F 8 to 10 minutes.

16 rolls

233 *Parmesan Bread Fingers*

2½ cups all-purpose biscuit mix
1 package active dry yeast
½ teaspoon salt
⅔ cup hot water
¼ cup butter or margarine, melted
¼ cup grated Parmesan cheese

1. Combine biscuit mix, yeast, and salt in a bowl.
2. Stir in water until mixture clings to itself.
3. Turn dough onto a floured surface. Knead 8 to 10 times.
4. Roll out into a 13×9-inch rectangle.
5. Brush half of butter in a 13×9×2-inch baking pan. Place dough in pan, pressing to fit. Cut crosswise into 16 strips, then lengthwise in half.
6. Brush with remaining butter and sprinkle with cheese. Cover; let rise 15 minutes.
7. Bake at 425°F 15 minutes. Turn off oven; allow sticks to remain in oven 15 minutes.

32 bread fingers

234 *Brooklyn Bagels*

4 to 5 cups all-purpose flour
1 package active dry yeast
2 teaspoons salt
1½ cups hot water (120° to 130°F)
2 tablespoons honey or sugar
1 egg white
1 teaspoon water

1. Combine 1 cup flour, yeast, and salt in a bowl.
2. Stir in hot water and honey; beat until smooth, about 3 minutes. Stir in enough remaining flour to make a soft dough.
3. Turn out onto a floured surface; continue to work in flour until dough is stiff enough to knead. Knead until smooth and elastic (about 5 minutes).
4. Cover with bowl. Let rest 15 minutes.
5. Divide into 12 equal parts. Shape each into a flattened ball. With thumb and forefinger poke a hole into center. Stretch and rotate until hole enlarges to about 1 or 2 inches. Cover; let rise about 20 minutes.
6. Boil water in a large shallow pan, about 2 inches deep. Reduce heat. Simmer a few bagels at a time about 7 minutes. Remove from pan; drain on a towel about 5 minutes. Place on a baking sheet; brush with mixture of egg white and water.
7. Bake at 375°F 30 minutes, or until done.
8. To serve, split and toast. Spread with **butter** and **jam** or **cream cheese**.

1 dozen bagels

235 *Basic Sweet Dough*

4 to 5 cups all-purpose flour
2 packages active dry yeast
1 teaspoon salt
¾ cup milk
½ cup water
½ cup melted butter
½ cup sugar
1 egg

1. Stir together 1¾ cups flour, yeast, and salt in a large mixer bowl.
2. Heat milk, water, butter, and sugar until very warm (120° to 130°F).
3. Add liquid ingredients to flour mixture; beat until smooth, about 2 minutes on electric mixer.
4. Add egg and ½ cup more flour and beat another 2 minutes.
5. Gradually add enough more flour to make a soft dough.
6. Turn out onto floured board; continue to work in flour until dough can be kneaded. Knead until smooth and elastic, but still soft (about 5 minutes).
7. Cover; let rest about 20 minutes.
8. Shape, let rise, and bake as directed in recipes that follow.

Cinnamon Rolls: Roll dough into a 13×9-inch rectangle. Spread with **2 tablespoons softened butter** or **margarine.** Sprinkle with mixture of **½ cup firmly packed brown** or **white sugar** and **2 teaspoons cinnamon.** Beginning with long side, roll dough up tightly jelly-roll fashion. Cut roll into 12 (1-inch) slices. Place slices in a greased 13×9×2-inch baking pan or greased muffin cups. Bake at 375°F 15 to 20 minutes.

1½ dozen

236

Glazed Raised Doughnuts: Follow recipe for Basic Sweet Dough. Roll out to about ½-inch thickness. Cut with doughnut cutter or make into shape of your choice, such as squares, twists, long johns, doughnut holes, or bismarcks. Let rise, uncovered, until light, 40 to 50 minutes. Fry in deep hot oil (375°F) 3 to 4 minutes, turning once. Drain on paper towels. Dip in a glaze of **1½ cups confectioners' sugar, 2 tablespoons warm water,** and **1 teaspoon vanilla extract.**

237

Apricot Crisscross Coffeecake: For one large coffeecake, roll dough into a 15×12-inch rectangle. For two small coffeecakes, divide dough in half. Roll each half into an 12×8-inch rectangle. Combine **½ cup apricot preserves, ½ cup raisins,** and **½ cup sliced almonds.** Spread half the filling lengthwise down the center of each rectangle. Make about 12 slashes, each 2 inches long, down the long sides of each coffeecake. Fold strips alternately over filling, herringbone fashion. Cover; let rise until double in bulk (50 to 60 minutes). Bake at 375°F 20 to 25 minutes for small coffeecakes and 35 to 40 minutes for large coffeecake.

238

239 *Refrigerator Sweet Dough*

5 to 6 cups all-purpose flour
2 packages active dry yeast
½ cup sugar
1½ teaspoons salt
1 cup milk
½ cup water
½ cup butter or margarine, softened
2 eggs

1. Stir 1¾ cups flour, yeast, sugar, and salt together in a large mixer bowl.
2. Heat milk, water, and butter to very warm (120° to 130°F).
3. Add liquid to dry ingredients and beat until smooth, about 2 minutes on electric mixer.
4. Add eggs and ½ cup flour and continue beating another 2 minutes.
5. Gradually stir in enough additional flour to make a soft dough.
6. Turn out onto floured board; continue to work in flour until dough can be kneaded. Knead until smooth and elastic, but still soft (5 to 8 minutes).
7. Cover with plastic wrap, then with a towel.
8. Let rest 20 minutes.
9. Divide in half and shape as desired.
10. Brush with **oil.** Cover with plastic wrap.
11. Refrigerate 2 to 24 hours. When ready to bake, remove from refrigerator and let stand 10 minutes.
12. Bake at 375°F 20 to 30 minutes.
13. Remove from pans and cool on rack.

2 coffeecakes

Cinnamon Slice Coffeecake: Follow shaping instructions as in Cinnamon Rolls ●, only omit 13×9×2-inch pan. Instead, place 6 slices, cut-side down, on bottom of a greased 10-inch tube pan. Place 6 more slices cut-side against outer side of pan. Cover first layer with remaining 6 rolls. Bake at 375°F 20 to 25 minutes.

240

Cinnamon Discs: Combine **¾ cup firmly packed brown sugar, ¾ cup white sugar, ½ cup finely chopped pecans,** and **1 teaspoon cinnamon.** Divide dough in half. Roll each half into a 12-inch square. Melt **½ cup butter.** Brush dough with 2 tablespoons of the butter. Sprinkle with ½ cup sugar mixture. Roll up jelly-roll fashion; pinch to seal edges. Cut into 1-inch slices. Place on greased baking sheets at least 3 inches apart. Cover with waxed paper. Flatten each to about 3 inches in diameter. Let rise 15 minutes. Flatten again. Brush with remaining butter; sprinkle with remaining sugar mixture. Cover with waxed paper; flatten again. Bake at 400°F 10 to 12 minutes.

241

2 dozen

Bubble Bread: Divide dough into 20 equal pieces; shape into balls. Combine **½ cup sugar or firmly packed brown sugar, ½ cup finely chopped nuts,** and **1 teaspoon cinnamon.** Melt **½ cup butter or margarine.** Roll balls in butter, then in sugar mixture. Arrange balls in a well-greased 10-inch tube pan. Cover; let rise until double in bulk (45 to 60 minutes). Bake at 350°F 30 to 35 minutes.

242

Orange Bubble Ring: Shape dough into 20 balls as for Bubble Bread. Roll each ball in **½ cup melted butter** and then a mixture of **½ cup sugar** and **1 tablespoon grated orange peel.** Arrange and bake as above.

243

Apricot Bubble Bread: Shape dough into 20 balls as for Bubble Bread; roll balls in butter, then in sugar. Arrange 10 balls in bottom of a well-greased 10-inch tube pan. Top with **¼ cup apricot preserves.** Repeat layers. Cover; let rise until double in bulk (about 45 minutes). Bake as directed.

244

245 *Sweet Maple Coffeecake*

3 to 3½ cups all-purpose flour
1 package active dry yeast
½ teaspoon salt
½ cup milk
¼ cup water
¼ cup butter or margarine
2 eggs
¼ cup honey or sugar
Maple Filling

1. Combine 1 cup flour, yeast, and salt in a mixer bowl.
2. Warm milk, water, and butter in a small saucepan.
3. Add liquid, eggs, and honey to flour mixture; beat until smooth, about 3 minutes on electric mixer.
4. Stir in enough remaining flour to make a soft, sticky dough.
5. Turn out onto floured board; continue to work in flour until dough can be kneaded. Knead until smooth and elastic, but still soft (about 5 minutes).
6. Cover with a bowl; let rest 30 minutes.
7. Divide dough in half; roll each half into a 15×12-inch rectangle. Spread with Maple Filling. Fold each rectangle in thirds, making a 15×4-inch strip. Cut in 10 equal pieces. Place strips of dough in greased 8×4×2-inch loaf pans, cut side down. Cover; let rise 30 minutes.
8. Bake at 350°F 35 to 40 minutes.

2 loaves

Maple Filling: Cream **½ cup firmly packed brown sugar** and **⅓ cup white sugar** with **¼ cup softened butter or margarine.** Stir in **¼ cup maple syrup, 2 tablespoons all-purpose flour, ½ teaspoon cinnamon,** and **½ cup chopped nuts.**

246 *Nutty Sweet Twists*

Now that you've mastered the basic yeast dough, you're ready for a new twist!

1 can (13 ounces) evaporated milk
   or 1⅔ cups milk
1 tablespoon lemon juice or
   vinegar
½ cup raisins
3 tablespoons sugar
2 tablespoons butter or margarine
3 to 3¼ cups all-purpose flour
1 package active dry yeast

1. Warm milk and lemon juice in a small saucepan. Add raisins, sugar, and 2 tablespoons butter.
2. Combine 2 cups flour, yeast, salt, and baking soda in a large mixer bowl. Stir in milk mixture and egg; beat until smooth.
3. Stir in enough remaining flour to make a soft, sticky dough.
4. Turn out onto a floured surface; continue to work in flour until dough can be kneaded. Knead until smooth and elastic,

1 teaspoon salt
½ teaspoon baking soda
1 egg
2 tablespoons butter or margarine,
    softened or melted
⅓ cup firmly packed brown sugar
⅓ cup finely chopped nuts
2 teaspoons cinnamon

but still soft (about 5 minutes). Let dough rest 5 minutes.

5. Roll dough into a 24×12-inch rectangle, about ⅛ inch thick. Spread or brush with 2 tablespoons butter. Sprinkle with a mixture of brown sugar, nuts, and cinnamon. Fold in half lengthwise, forming a 24×6-inch rectangle. Cut into 1-inch strips. For each roll, hold both ends of strip and twist. Place on greased baking sheet. (If shorter rolls are desired, cut twists in half.)

6. Bake at 375°F 10 to 15 minutes (see Note).

*2 dozen long (6-inch) twists
or 4 dozen short (3-inch) twists*

Note: For shinier twists, brush dough with mixture of **1 egg white** and **1 teaspoon water** just before baking.

Frosted Sweet Twists: Follow recipe for Nutty Sweet Twists and glaze baked rolls with a mixture of **½ cup confectioners' sugar** and **1 tablespoon milk.**

247

248 *Austrian Almond Braid*

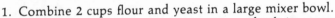

5 to 5½ cups all-purpose flour
2 packages active dry yeast
1 cup milk
½ cup sugar
½ cup shortening or butter
¼ cup water
2 teaspoons salt
2 eggs (at room temperature)
½ cup golden raisins
½ cup candied mixed fruit, chopped
½ cup chopped blanched almonds
    Almond Icing (see recipe)
    Candied fruit and nuts for
        decoration (optional)

1. Combine 2 cups flour and yeast in a large mixer bowl.

2. Heat milk, sugar, shortening, water, and salt in a saucepan over low heat until very warm (120° to 130°F), stirring to blend. Add liquid to flour-yeast mixture and beat until smooth, about 3 minutes on medium speed of electric mixer. Blend in eggs. Add 1 cup flour and beat 1 minute. Stir in fruit and almonds; add more flour to make a soft dough.

3. Turn dough onto a lightly floured surface; knead until smooth and satiny (5 to 10 minutes). Cover dough and let rest 20 minutes. Divide dough in half.

4. For each braid, take two-thirds of one portion of dough and divide into thirds. Roll each piece with hands into a 15-inch strand. Braid strands on lightly greased baking sheet. Divide remaining third into thirds; form three 18-inch strands. Braid strands loosely; place on first braid, pressing in lightly. Tuck ends of top braid under ends of bottom braid. Brush with oil. Let rise in a warm place until double in bulk (about 45 minutes).

5. Bake at 350°F 25 to 30 minutes, or until golden brown. Remove from baking sheets to wire rack. While braids are still slightly warm, ice with almond icing. Decorate with candied fruit and nuts, if desired.

2 large loaves

Almond Icing: Put **1½ cups confectioners' sugar, 2 tablespoons milk,** and **1 teaspoon almond extract** into a small bowl; stir until smooth.

249 *Sally Lunn*

5 cups all-purpose flour
½ cup sugar
1 package active dry yeast
1 teaspoon salt
1½ cups milk
½ cup butter or margarine
3 eggs
¼ cup sugar
¼ teaspoon nutmeg

1. Combine 2 cups flour, ½ cup sugar, yeast, and salt in a mixer bowl.
2. Heat milk and butter in a small saucepan.
3. Add liquid with eggs to flour mixture; beat 2 minutes by hand or with electric mixer.
4. Stir in remaining flour by hand. Cover; let rise until double in bulk (about 1 hour).
5. Stir dough down. Pour into a greased and sugared 10-inch tube pan. Cover; let rise until double in bulk (about 30 minutes).
6. Combine ¼ cup sugar and nutmeg; sprinkle over dough.
7. Bake at 400°F 40 minutes. Cool in pan 5 minutes.
8. If desired, serve hot with strawberries and whipped cream.

One large loaf

250 *Russian Kulich*

5 cups all-purpose flour
2 packages active dry yeast
1 cup milk
½ cup sugar
¼ cup oil
2 teaspoons salt
2 eggs (at room temperature)
2 teaspoons grated lemon peel
½ cup chopped blanched almonds
¼ cup raisins
¼ cup chopped candied citron
¼ cup chopped candied orange peel
¼ cup chopped candied cherries
½ cup confectioners' sugar
1 tablespoon milk
Candied fruit (optional)

1. Combine 1 cup flour and yeast in a large mixer bowl.
2. Heat 1 cup milk, sugar, oil, and salt in a saucepan over low heat until very warm (120° to 130°F), stirring to blend. Add liquid to flour-yeast mixture and beat until smooth, about 2 minutes on medium speed of electric mixer. Beat in eggs, lemon peel, almonds, raisins, and candied fruit. Add 1 cup flour and beat 1 minute on medium speed. Stir in more flour to make a soft dough.
3. Turn dough onto a lightly floured surface and knead until smooth and satiny (8 to 10 minutes). Shape into a ball and place in a lightly greased bowl; turn to grease surface. Cover; let rise in a warm place until double in bulk (about 1½ hours).
4. Punch dough down; divide into 2 or 3 equal portions and shape into balls. Let rest 10 minutes.
5. Grease generously two 46-ounce juice cans or three 1-pound coffee cans. Place dough in cans, filling about half full; brush with oil. Let rise until double in bulk (about 1 hour).
6. Bake at 350°F 30 to 35 minutes, or until golden brown. Immediately remove from cans and cool.
7. Blend confectioners' sugar and 1 tablespoon milk until smooth; ice top of loaves. Decorate with candied fruit, if desired.

2 large or 3 medium loaves

251 Cottage Raisin Puffs

Sweet enough for breakfast, but not too sweet for lunch or dinner. The cheeses add enough protein to make it a good match for one of our lighter soups.

    3 to 3½ cups all-purpose flour
    2 packages active dry yeast
 1½ teaspoons salt
    1 cup creamed cottage cheese
  ½ cup melted butter or margarine
  ½ cup hot water
  ¼ cup sugar or honey
    1 egg
      Raisin Cream Filling

1. Combine 1 cup flour, yeast, and salt in a mixer bowl.
2. Heat cottage cheese, butter, water, and sugar in a saucepan until very warm (120° to 130°F).
3. Add liquid and egg to flour mixture and beat until smooth, about 3 minutes.
4. Stir in enough remaining flour to make a soft dough.
5. Turn out onto floured board; continue to work in flour until dough can be kneaded. Knead until smooth and elastic, but still soft (about 5 minutes).
6. Place in an oiled bowl; turn to oil top of dough. Cover; let rise in warm place until double in bulk (about 1 hour).
7. Punch dough down. Roll into a rectangle 20×12 inches. Cut into 2-inch squares. Place about 1 teaspoon of Raisin Cream Filling in center of each square. Bring corners to center and press together. Place on greased baking sheets. Let rise 10 minutes.
8. Bake at 375°F 12 to 15 minutes, or until done.

2 dozen

Raisin Cream Filling: Stir **2 tablespoons milk** into **1 package (8 ounces) cream cheese, softened.** Blend in **½ cup raisins.**

Cottage Date Puffs: Prepare Cottage Raisin Puffs, substituting **chopped dates** for raisins and adding **¼ cup chopped nuts.**

252

253 Kugelhupf

    3 to 4 cups all-purpose flour
    2 packages active dry yeast
    1 cup milk
    1 cup raisins
  ½ cup water
  ½ cup sugar
  ½ cup butter
    1 teaspoon salt
    3 eggs (at room temperature)
    2 teaspoons rum extract
      Butter, softened
  ⅓ cup ground almonds
      Sifted confectioners' sugar
      Candied fruits and nuts
      Corn syrup

1. Combine 2 cups flour and yeast in a large mixer bowl.
2. Heat milk, raisins, water, sugar, ½ cup butter, and salt in a saucepan over low heat until very warm (120° to 130°F), stirring to blend; add to flour-yeast mixture and beat until smooth, about 3 minutes on medium speed of electric mixer. Blend in eggs and rum extract; add ½ cup flour and continue to beat 2 minutes. Add enough flour to make a thick batter. Cover; let rise in a warm place until double in bulk and batter is bubbly (about 1 hour).
3. Stir batter down. Spoon into two 1½-quart or three 1-quart turk's-head or other fancy molds that have been buttered and dusted with ground almonds. Cover; let rise in a warm place until double in bulk (about 30 minutes).
4. Bake at 325°F 1 hour for 1½-quart loaves or 45 minutes for 1-quart loaves. If necessary to prevent excessive browning, cover during the last 10 minutes of baking. Unmold on wire racks. Dust with confectioners' sugar. Decorate with candied fruits and nuts that have been dipped in corn syrup.

2 large or 3 small loaves

Sourdough puts a little bit of history in your loaf pan. About 6,000 years ago the Egyptians accidentally discovered that when flour was exposed to water and the wild yeast in the air, it fermented and expanded. When the fermented dough was added to bread dough, the result was a lighter bread. The "starter" was passed down from generation to generation to produce the staff of life for thousands of years.

In this country, gold prospectors carried the starter with them everywhere they went, and soon they themselves became known as Sourdoughs.

Sourdough requires a little know-how in order to nurture it and see that it performs as expected. Read these helpful hints to guide you in making sourdough breads.

Hints: Use your starter often. Don't let it become tucked away in the back of the refrigerator where you'll forget about it. Sourdough that is allowed to sit unused for 2 or 3 months will spoil and have to be discarded.

If you have replenished the starter, make sure that you wait at least 8 hours before using it.

The old sourdoughs, the name given to prospectors who always carried the sourdough starter with them, referred to the process of replenishing the starter as "sweetening" it. When replenishing, use warm water (105° to 115°F) to provide the best environment for yeast growth. Just as packaged yeast is vulnerable to too high temperatures, so is the yeast in sourdough starters.

Store your starter in the refrigerator. You may want to keep as much as 2 cups on hand so you'll be ready either for quantity baking or for sharing with a friend.

254 *Sourdough Starter*

2 cups flour
1 package active dry yeast
1 tablespoon sugar
2 cups warm potato water (105° to 115°F)

1. Combine flour, yeast, and sugar in a nonmetal mixing bowl. Stir in potato water.
2. Cover; let stand in a warm place (80° to 85°F) for 48 hours.
3. Store in covered jar in refrigerator.

To use in recipe: Stir well before use. Pour out required amount called for in recipe and use as directed.

To replenish remaining starter: Mix in 1 cup each flour and warm water until smooth. Let stand in warm place a few hours until it bubbles again before covering and replacing in refrigerator.

Note: Use in recipe or remove 1 cup starter and replenish every week.

255 Sourdough Sam's Skillet Loaves

Sourdough and an iron skillet will carry you back to the early prospecting days. For authenticity and mighty good eating, serve it with honey and butter.

1 cup sourdough starter
2½ cups warm water
2 tablespoons honey or sugar
7 to 7½ cups all-purpose flour
¼ cup vegetable oil
1 tablespoon salt
1 teaspoon baking soda
6 tablespoons butter
4 tablespoons cornmeal

1. Combine starter, water, honey, and 5 cups flour in a large nonmetal mixing bowl. Cover with plastic wrap or a wet towel; let stand at room temperature 12 hours or overnight.
2. Stir in oil. Combine salt, soda, and 1 cup flour. Stir into dough; beat until smooth.
3. Stir in enough remaining flour to make a soft dough.
4. Turn dough onto a floured surface; continue to work in flour until dough is stiff enough to knead. Knead until smooth and elastic (about 5 minutes).
5. Divide dough in half. Roll each into a 10-inch round (see Note).
6. For each loaf, melt 3 tablespoons butter in a heavy 10-inch cast-iron skillet with heat-resistant handle. Sprinkle with 2 tablespoons cornmeal. Place dough in skillet. Turn over to coat top with butter and cornmeal. Let rise 15 minutes.
7. Bake at 400°F 25 to 30 minutes, or until done.
8. Serve hot with **butter** and **honey**.

2 loaves

Note: If you don't have 2 skillets, simply allow the second dough circle to rise while the first bakes—it will just have a lighter texture.

Sweet and Sourdough Granola Bread: 256

Prepare dough as in Sourdough Sam's Skillet Loaves. After dividing dough in half, roll out each half into a 16×6-inch rectangle. Brush each with **2 tablespoons melted butter** and sprinkle with half the Granola Cinnamon Filling. Beginning with narrow end of rectangle, roll up tightly as for jelly roll; seal edges. Place loaves in 2 greased 9×5×3-inch loaf pans. Cover; let rise until double in bulk (45 to 60 minutes). Bake at 350°F 40 to 45 minutes.

Granola Cinnamon Filling: Combine **1 cup granola, ½ cup firmly packed brown sugar, ½ cup chopped dates or raisins** (optional), and **1 teaspoon cinnamon.** 257

Sourdough Apple Kuchen: 258

Prepare dough as in Sourdough Sam's Skillet Loaves. After dividing dough, roll out each half into a 10-inch round. Place dough in 2 greased 9- or 10-inch springform pans. Press dough about 1½ inches up sides of pan. Fill each kuchen with a mixture of **2 cups finely sliced pared apples, ½ cup firmly packed brown sugar, ¼ cup all-purpose flour,** and **1 teaspoon cinnamon.** Sprinkle with **¼ cup sliced almonds.** Dot with **2 tablespoons butter.** Let rise 30 minutes. Bake at 375°F 40 to 45 minutes, or until done.

259 Golden Sourdough Bread

1 package active dry yeast
1¼ cups warm water
¼ cup firmly packed brown sugar
2 teaspoons salt
⅓ cup butter or margarine
3½ to 4 cups all-purpose flour
• 1½ cups sourdough starter
3½ cups uncooked oats

1. Soften yeast in ¼ cup warm water. Pour remaining 1 cup water over sugar, salt, and butter in a large bowl. Stir in 2 cups of flour, sourdough starter, oats, and softened yeast. Stir in enough additional flour to make a stiff dough.
2. Knead dough on a floured surface until smooth and elastic (about 10 minutes). Round dough into a ball; place in a greased bowl. Lightly grease surface of dough. Cover; let rise in a warm place until nearly double in bulk (about 1 hour).
3. Punch dough down; shape into 2 round loaves. Place on greased cookie sheets. Let rise in a warm place until nearly double in bulk (about 40 minutes). Slash tops with sharp knife or kitchen shears.
4. Bake at 400°F 35 to 40 minutes. Cool on wire racks.

2 loaves

260 San Francisco Sourdough French Bread

• 1 cup sourdough starter
1½ cups warm water
2 tablespoons sugar
5 to 6 cups all-purpose flour
1 tablespoon salt
½ teaspoon baking soda

1. Combine starter, water, sugar, and 3 cups flour in a large nonmetal mixing bowl. Cover with plastic wrap or a towel; let stand at room temperature 12 hours or overnight.
2. Combine salt, soda, and 1 cup flour. Stir into dough; beat until smooth.
3. Stir in enough remaining flour to make a soft dough.
4. Turn dough onto a floured surface; continue to work in flour until dough is stiff enough to knead. Knead until smooth and elastic (5 to 8 minutes).
5. Shape dough into a long, narrow loaf by rolling and stretching dough as for French Bread (page 15). Place on a greased baking sheet. Cover; let rise in a warm place until double in bulk (1½ to 2 hours).
6. With a sharp knife, slash top ½ inch deep at 2-inch intervals. Brush loaf with **water.**
7. Bake at 375°F 30 to 35 minutes.

1 loaf

Note: For a browner and shinier crust, brush before baking with a mixture of **1 egg white** and **⅓ cup water** instead of only water.

261 Quick Buttermilk Bread

1¾ cups all-purpose flour
2 teaspoons baking powder
¾ teaspoon baking soda
1 teaspoon salt
⅓ cup firmly packed brown sugar
1½ cups uncooked oats
1 cup buttermilk
½ cup vegetable oil
2 eggs, beaten
½ cup chopped pecans

1. Mix flour, baking powder, baking soda, and salt in a bowl. Stir in brown sugar and oats. Add remaining ingredients; stir only until dry ingredients are moistened.
2. Pour batter into a greased 9×5×3-inch loaf pan.
3. Bake at 350°F 50 to 55 minutes. Cool on wire rack about 10 minutes. Remove from pan; cool thoroughly.
4. Wrap and store. (Bread will slice better if stored a day before slicing.)

1 loaf

262 Cheddar Cornbread

1 cup yellow cornmeal
1 cup all-purpose flour
1 tablespoon baking powder
1 teaspoon salt
2 cups shredded Cheddar cheese (8 ounces)
1 cup milk
¼ cup melted butter or margarine or vegetable oil
1 egg
4 slices crisply cooked bacon, crumbled
1 green pepper, sliced (optional)

1. Combine cornmeal, flour, baking powder, salt, and 1 cup cheese in a mixing bowl.
2. Combine milk, butter, and egg in a separate bowl; beat well.
3. Add liquid ingredients to dry ingredients; stir just until flour is moistened. Pour into a greased 9-inch round layer cake pan. Sprinkle with remaining cheese and bacon. Top with green pepper rings, if desired.
4. Bake at 425°F 25 minutes, or until done.

About 8 servings

263 Pleasin' Pumpkin Bread

3½ cups all-purpose flour
3 cups sugar
2 cups cooked mashed pumpkin
1 cup vegetable oil
⅓ cup water
4 eggs
2 teaspoons baking soda
1½ teaspoons salt
2 teaspoons cinnamon
½ teaspoon nutmeg
¼ teaspoon cloves
¼ teaspoon ginger

1. Put flour, sugar, baking soda, salt, and spices into a large mixing bowl; mix well. Add pumpkin, oil, water, and eggs; beat until well blended.
2. Divide batter equally into 2 greased 9×5×3-inch loaf pans.
3. Bake at 350°F 70 minutes, or until done.
4. Cool before wrapping.

2 loaves

264 *Oklahoma Oatmeal Bread*

1 cup evaporated milk
2 tablespoons vegetable oil
1 tablespoon vinegar
1 cup uncooked oats
1 cup all-purpose flour
1 cup firmly packed brown sugar
1 teaspoon baking soda
½ teaspoon salt
1 cup raisins or chopped nuts

1. Beat milk, oil, and vinegar in a mixing bowl until smooth.
2. Add oats, flour, brown sugar, baking soda, and salt; mix until well blended.
3. Stir in raisins or nuts.
4. Turn into a greased 9×5×3-inch loaf pan or two 7×4×2-inch loaf pans.
5. Bake at 350°F 50 to 60 minutes, or until done.
6. Cool before wrapping.

1 large loaf or 2 small loaves

Light, flaky biscuits are a snap to make. They can be mixed minutes before the meal and served piping hot right from the oven.

The same biscuit dough can be either rolled or dropped onto a baking sheet, depending on your preference and time. Drop biscuits are dropped by spoonfuls onto a greased baking sheet just like a cookie. Then you pop them into the oven. To produce that wonderful flakiness and shape typical of the rolled biscuit, an additional step must be taken. The dough is gently kneaded about ½ minute, rolled or patted out, and cut with a biscuit cutter. Both kinds are baked in a hot (425°-450°F) oven 10 to 12 minutes.

A technique to remember to get straight, even sides is to push the biscuit cutter evenly, straight down, without twisting. If you like soft sides, place the biscuits close together in a shallow pan. For crusty sides, allow about an inch around each biscuit on the baking sheet.

To pull piping-hot, mouth-watering biscuits out of the oven just as everyone is sitting down to dinner or breakfast, you can cheat a little on the time schedule. Prepare the biscuits, put on a baking sheet, and cover with plastic wrap. Refrigerate up to one hour before you are ready to bake. Just allow a few extra minutes for them to bake.

265 *Biscuits*

2 cups all-purpose flour
1 tablespoon baking powder
1 teaspoon salt
⅓ cup butter or shortening
¾ cup milk

1. Combine flour, baking powder, and salt in a mixing bowl. Cut in butter with pastry blender or 2 knives until mixture resembles rice kernels.
2. Stir in milk with a fork just until mixture clings to itself.
3. Form dough into a ball and knead gently 8 to 10 times on lightly floured board. Gently roll dough ½ inch thick.
4. Cut with floured biscuit cutter or knife, using an even pressure to keep sides of biscuits straight.
5. Place on ungreased baking sheet, close together for soft-sided biscuits or 1 inch apart for crusty ones.
6. Bake at 450°F 10 to 15 minutes, or until golden brown.

About 1 dozen

Southern Buttermilk Biscuits: Follow recipe for Biscuits, substituting **buttermilk** for the milk and adding ¼

266

teaspoon baking soda to the dry ingredients and reducing baking powder to 2 teaspoons.

Drop Biscuits: Follow recipe for Biscuits, increasing milk to 1 cup. Omit rolling-out instructions. Simply drop from a spoon onto a lightly greased baking sheet.

267

268 *Scones*

1⅔ cups all-purpose flour
1 tablespoon sugar
1½ teaspoons baking powder
½ teaspoon baking soda
½ teaspoon salt
½ cup shortening
½ cup buttermilk

1. Combine flour, sugar, baking powder, baking soda, and salt in a mixing bowl. Cut in shortening with pastry blender or two knives until mixture resembles rice kernels.
2. Stir in buttermilk with a fork until mixture clings to itself.
3. Form dough into a ball and knead gently about 8 times on a floured surface. Divide dough in half; roll each into a round about ½ inch thick. Cut each round into 6 wedge-shaped pieces. Place on ungreased baking sheets.
4. Bake at 450°F 8 to 10 minutes. Serve warm.

1 dozen

269 *Savory Biscuit Bread*

1½ cups all-purpose flour
1 tablespoon baking powder
½ teaspoon salt
½ teaspoon paprika
½ teaspoon celery salt
¼ teaspoon pepper
¼ teaspoon poultry seasoning
¼ cup shortening
½ cup milk (about)

1. Combine flour, baking powder, and seasonings in a mixing bowl. Cut in shortening until mixture resembles rice kernels.
2. Stir in milk with a fork just until flour is moistened.
3. Pat into a greased 8-inch round layer cake pan.
4. Bake at 450°F 10 to 15 minutes, or until done.

6 servings

270 *Dakota Bran Muffins*

1 cup all-purpose flour
1 tablespoon baking powder
½ teaspoon salt
1½ cups ready-to-eat bran flakes
1 cup milk
1 egg
¼ cup vegetable oil
¼ cup honey or sugar

1. Combine dry ingredients in a mixing bowl.
2. Combine remaining ingredients in a separate bowl; beat well.
3. Add liquid ingredients to dry ingredients; stir just until flour is moistened. Spoon batter into 12 greased muffin-pan wells.
4. Bake at 400°F 20 to 25 minutes, or until golden brown.

1 dozen

271 *Buttermilk Coffeecake*

1 cup sugar
½ cup butter or margarine, softened
2 eggs
1 teaspoon vanilla extract
2 cups all-purpose flour
1 teaspoon baking powder
1 teaspoon baking soda
½ teaspoon salt
1 cup buttermilk

Topping:
1 cup chopped nuts
1 cup sugar
⅓ cup firmly packed brown sugar
1 teaspoon cinnamon
½ cup butter or margarine

1. Cream sugar and butter; beat in eggs and vanilla extract until well blended.
2. Combine flour, baking powder, baking soda, and salt.
3. Add buttermilk and flour mixture alternately to sugar mixture, beating well after each addition.
4. For topping, combine nuts, sugar, brown sugar, and cinnamon. Cut in butter.
5. Sprinkle half of topping mixture in bottom of a greased and floured 13×9×2-inch baking pan. Pour in batter. Cover with remaining topping.
6. Bake at 350°F 25 to 30 minutes.
7. Serve warm.

1 coffeecake

272 *Rhubarb Bread*

1½ cups firmly packed brown sugar
⅔ cup vegetable oil
1 cup buttermilk
1 egg
1 teaspoon vanilla extract
2½ cups all-purpose flour
1 teaspoon salt
1 teaspoon baking soda
1½ cups finely chopped rhubarb
½ cup chopped nuts
2 tablespoons sugar

1. Beat brown sugar, oil, buttermilk, egg, and vanilla extract in a mixing bowl.
2. Mix flour, salt, and baking soda. Add to brown sugar mixture and stir until blended.
3. Stir in rhubarb and nuts.
4. Turn into 2 greased 8×4×2-inch loaf pans. Sprinkle 1 tablespoon sugar over each.
5. Bake at 325°F 1 hour, or until done.

2 loaves

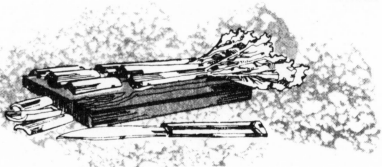

273 *Zucchini Bread*

2 cups sugar
1 cup vegetable oil
3 eggs
1 teaspoon vanilla extract
3 cups all-purpose flour
1 teaspoon salt
1 teaspoon baking soda
1 teaspoon cinnamon
2 cups shredded unpeeled zucchini
1 cup chopped nuts

1. Beat sugar, oil, eggs, and vanilla extract in a mixing bowl until fluffy.
2. Mix flour, salt, baking soda, and cinnamon. Add to egg mixture and stir until blended.
3. Stir in zucchini and nuts.
4. Turn into a greased 9×5×3-inch loaf pan.
5. Bake at 350°F 1 hour and 20 minutes, or until done.
6. Cool before wrapping.

1 loaf

274 Waffles

2 cups sifted all-purpose flour
1 tablespoon sugar
1 tablespoon baking powder
½ teaspoon salt
3 eggs, well beaten
2 cups milk
½ cup butter or margarine, melted

1. Mix flour, sugar, baking powder, and salt in a bowl.
2. Combine eggs, milk, and melted butter. Add liquid mixture to flour mixture; beat just until batter is blended.
3. Heat waffle baker. Pour enough batter into waffle baker to allow spreading to within 1 inch of edges. Lower cover and bake waffle; do not raise cover during baking. Lift cover and loosen waffle with a fork. Serve hot.

About 4 large waffles

Buttermilk Waffles: Follow recipe for Waffles; substitute **buttermilk** for milk. Decrease baking powder to 2 teaspoons and add **1 teaspoon baking soda.**   275

Wheat Germ Pecan Waffles: Follow recipe for Waffles; decrease flour to 1½ cups. Stir **½ cup toasted wheat germ** into the flour mixture. Sprinkle **3 tablespoons coarsely chopped pecans** onto the batter before baking each waffle.   276

Cheese Waffles: Follow recipe for Waffles. When batter is smooth, blend in **½ cup shredded cheese.**   277

Chocolate Waffles: Follow recipe for Waffles. Generously sprinkle **semisweet chocolate pieces** over batter before closing waffle baker.   278

Popovers, unlike the other quick breads, rely on steam as the leavening agent. (The others use baking powder or baking soda.) The steam is produced from the high amount of liquid present in popover batter. It is this steam that gives the popover its characteristic hollow interior. The crispy outside structure comes from eggs and gluten. If they turn out any other way, they just aren't popovers.

Failure of popovers to "pop" is probably due to one of two reasons. One is underbeating. The batter should be beaten vigorously to develop the gluten. The second reason may be the oven temperature. It must be hot enough to achieve a sudden rise to open up the inside of the popover.

279 Popovers

3 eggs
1 cup milk
2 tablespoons vegetable oil
½ teaspoon salt
1 cup sifted all-purpose flour

1. Beat eggs in a mixing bowl. Beat in milk, oil, and salt.
2. Beat in flour until mixture is smooth and well blended.
3. For best results, preheat iron popover pan after thoroughly coating pan wells with shortening or oil. Pour batter into 8 popover-pan wells or 8 greased heat-resistant custard cups.
4. Bake at 400°F 35 to 40 minutes, or until popovers are puffed and golden brown. Serve hot with butter.

8 popovers

Note: For a crispier popover, make slit in side of each baked popover to allow the steam to escape. Return popovers to oven for 10 minutes with the heat turned off.

280 *Sunshine Corn Muffins*

1½ cups all-purpose flour
1½ cups yellow cornmeal
1 tablespoon baking powder
⅛ teaspoon salt
1 cup milk
½ cup honey
½ cup vegetable oil
2 eggs

1. Combine dry ingredients in a mixing bowl.
2. Combine remaining ingredients in a separate bowl; beat well.
3. Add liquid ingredients to dry ingredients; stir just until flour is moistened. Spoon into 24 greased muffin-pan wells.
4. Bake at 400°F 15 to 20 minutes, or until wooden pick inserted in muffin comes out clean.

2 dozen

Sunshine Cornbread: Follow recipe for Sunshine Corn Muffins, except pour mixture into a greased 9-inch square pan. Bake at 400°F 30 minutes, or until done.

6 servings

28

282 *Lemon Chiffon Muffins*

½ cup softened butter or margarine
½ cup sugar
Grated peel of 1 lemon (about 1 tablespoon)
2 tablespoons milk
2 eggs, separated
3 tablespoons lemon juice (about 1 lemon)
1 cup all-purpose flour
1 teaspoon baking powder
¼ teaspoon salt
¼ cup chopped nuts
1 tablespoon sugar
1 teaspoon nutmeg

1. Cream butter, sugar, lemon peel, milk, and egg yolks in a mixing bowl until light and fluffy. Beat in lemon juice.
2. Combine flour, baking powder, and salt in a separate bowl. Add to batter and mix just until blended.
3. Beat egg whites until soft peaks form; fold into batter.
4. Spoon into 12 greased muffin-pan wells. Sprinkle with a mixture of nuts, sugar, and nutmeg.
5. Bake at 375°F 15 to 20 minutes, or until done.

1 dozen

283 *Maple Tree Muffins*

2 cups all-purpose flour
1 tablespoon baking powder
½ teaspoon salt
½ cup chopped nuts
⅔ cup milk
½ cup pure maple syrup or maple-blended syrup
1 egg
¼ cup vegetable oil

1. Combine flour, baking powder, salt, and nuts in a mixing bowl.
2. Combine remaining ingredients in a separate bowl; beat well.
3. Add liquid ingredients to dry ingredients; stir just until flour is moistened. Spoon into 12 greased muffin-pan wells.
4. Bake at 400°F 15 to 20 minutes, or until a wooden pick inserted in muffin comes out clean.

1 dozen

284 *Bran-Oatmeal Muffins*

¾ cup bran cereal
¾ cup milk
¼ cup butter or margarine
¼ cup molasses
1 egg
1 cup all-purpose flour

1. Combine bran cereal and milk to soften.
2. Beat butter and molasses together in a bowl. Add egg and mix well. Add bran-milk mixture.
3. Mix flour, sugar, baking powder, baking soda, and salt. Add dry ingredients to bran mixture; stir just until moistened. Stir in oats.

2 tablespoons sugar
1 teaspoon baking powder
½ teaspoon baking soda
½ teaspoon salt
1 cup uncooked oats

4. Spoon mixture into 12 greased medium-sized muffin-pan wells.
5. Bake at 400°F 15 to 18 minutes, or until golden brown.

1 dozen

Pancakes and waffles from a simple batter make possible a delicious array of combinations. Pancakes can be rolled, stuffed, or stacked with creamed meats or vegetables or sweet syrups for breakfast through dinner. You can add chopped nuts, raisins, coconut, fruits, and herbs to change the basic batter.

Two things to remember to make perfect pancakes or waffles. The batter should not be overmixed and the temperature of the griddle must be right. The dry ingredients are stirred with the liquid until just blended, and the batter should still be lumpy. You can make pancakes just how you like them, either thick or thin, by adding more or less liquid to the recipe.

The griddle is hot enough for baking when drops of cold water sprinkled on the surface dance in small beads.

285 *Pancakes*

1½ cups sifted all-purpose flour
1 tablespoon sugar
1½ teaspoons baking powder
¼ teaspoon salt
2 egg yolks, beaten
1⅓ cups milk
2 tablespoons butter or margarine, melted
2 egg whites

1. Start heating griddle or heavy skillet over low heat.
2. Mix flour, sugar, baking powder, and salt in a bowl.
3. Combine egg yolks, milk, and butter. Add liquid to flour mixture and beat until blended.
4. Beat egg whites until rounded peaks are formed. Spread beaten egg whites over batter and fold gently together.
5. Test griddle; it is hot enough for baking when drops of water sprinkled on surface dance in small beads. Lightly grease griddle, if so directed by manufacturer.
6. Pour batter onto griddle into pools about 4 inches in diameter, leaving at least 1 inch between cakes. Turn pancakes as they become puffy and full of bubbles. Turn only once.
7. Serve hot.

About 12 pancakes

Buttermilk Pancakes: Follow recipe for Pancakes; substitute **½ teaspoon baking soda** for the baking powder and **buttermilk** for the milk. Do not separate eggs. Beat eggs with buttermilk and proceed as in step 3 above.
286

Cornmeal Pancakes: Follow recipe for Pancakes. Decrease flour to ¾ cup. Mix **¾ cup yellow cornmeal** into dry ingredients.
287

Rye Pancakes: Follow recipe for Buttermilk Pancakes. Decrease flour to ¾ cup and mix in **¾ cup rye flour.** Blend **3 tablespoons molasses** into buttermilk-egg mixture.
288

Blueberry Pancakes: Follow recipe for Pancakes; gently fold **2 cups rinsed and drained blueberries** into batter after folding in beaten egg whites.
289

Jiffy quick breads from convenience foods give you a head start on the road to home baking. Some of the following recipes use a biscuit mix which has the fat and leavening agents already preblended for you. Because most of them are mixed all in one bowl and then baked, you can enjoy hot, homemade breads in a twinkling.

290 *Homemade Croutons*

Day-old bread slices
Softened butter or margarine

1. Spread both sides of bread slices with butter.
2. Stack slices and cut into cubes.
3. Spread over baking sheet.
4. Bake at 275°F 25 to 35 minutes, stirring occasionally, until dry and lightly browned.

Parmesan Croutons: Follow recipe for Homemade Croutons, except sprinkle both sides of bread with **grated Parmesan cheese** before cubing and baking.

Crusty Croutons: Follow recipe for Homemade Croutons except use **French bread** slices instead of day-old bread slices and do not cube bread. Turn slices over once during baking.

29

29

293 *Poppy Seed Cheese Bread*

1 cup shredded Cheddar cheese (4 ounces)
1 cup all-purpose biscuit mix
⅓ cup milk
1 egg
¼ cup chopped onion
1 tablespoon poppy seed

1. Combine ½ cup cheese and biscuit mix in a mixing bowl.
2. Add milk; stir just until flour is moistened. Pat dough over bottom of a greased 8- or 9-inch pie plate.
3. Combine remaining cheese, egg, and onion. Spread over biscuit dough. Sprinkle with poppy seed.
4. Bake at 425°F 15 to 20 minutes.

About 6 servings

294 *Sesame Seed Twists*

2 cups biscuit mix
¼ cup chilled butter
3 tablespoons melted butter
2 tablespoons sesame seed
1 egg yolk
1 teaspoon milk

1. Prepare biscuit mix as directed on package for rolled biscuits. Roll out on a lightly floured surface into a 12-inch square.
2. Thinly slice 3 tablespoons of butter and place on half of dough; fold other half over it. With rolling pin, gently seal open edges. Repeat procedure, using remaining chilled butter. Fold other half over, forming a 6-inch square.
3. Roll dough into a 12-inch square. Divide in half. Set one half in refrigerator.
4. Brush surface with melted butter. Sprinkle with some of the sesame seed. Cut into twelve 6×1-inch strips. Twist each strip and place on an ungreased baking sheet. Brush with mixture of egg yolk and milk. Sprinkle with more sesame seed. Repeat with other half.
5. Bake at 425°F 10 minutes.

2 dozen twists

Roast Leg of Lamb with Spicy Wine Sauce, page 184
Peach Wine Mold, page 27

295 Quick Strips

1 loaf unsliced white bread
½ cup butter or margarine, melted
¼ teaspoon garlic salt
Grated Parmesan cheese, sesame
seed, or poppy seed

1. Cut four 1¼-inch slices from loaf of bread. Cut each slice into 1-inch strips.
2. Combine butter and garlic salt in a 13×9×2-inch baking pan.
3. Toss bread strips in butter; sprinkle with cheese.
4. Bake at 350°F 20 minutes.

About 20 strips

296 Garlic Bread

1 loaf French bread
½ cup butter or margarine, softened
¼ teaspoon garlic powder or garlic salt

1. Slice bread almost through to bottom crust at 1-inch intervals.
2. Thoroughly combine butter and garlic powder. Spread on both sides of each bread slice.
3. Place on baking sheet.
4. Bake at 350°F 15 to 20 minutes, or until hot and crispy.

About 1 dozen slices

297 La Verde Slices

1 loaf Italian bread, cut diagonally in 1-inch slices
½ cup softened butter or margarine
2 tablespoons finely chopped green pepper
2 tablespoons finely chopped onion

1. Broil bread slices until golden brown on each side.
2. Combine butter, green pepper, and onion. Spread on one side of each slice.
3. Broil until lightly browned.

About 1 dozen slices

298 Sugar Buns

1 cup firmly packed brown sugar
⅓ cup butter or margarine
1 tablespoon corn syrup
½ cup chopped pecans
2 cans refrigerated dough for butterflake dinner rolls

1. Combine brown sugar, butter, and corn syrup in a saucepan; bring to boiling, stirring occasionally.
2. Stir in pecans.
3. Divide mixture evenly among 12 muffin-pan wells.
4. Place 2 rolls in each cup.
5. Bake at 375°F 15 minutes. Remove from pans immediately.

1 dozen buns

299 Cranberry Swirl Rolls

1 package (about 14 ounces) hot roll mix
1 can (16 ounces) jellied cranberry sauce
¼ cup firmly packed brown sugar
1 teaspoon cinnamon

1. Prepare hot roll mix following package directions.
2. Roll half of dough at a time into a 12×8-inch rectangle. Spread each rectangle with cranberry sauce to within 1 inch of edge. Sprinkle with brown sugar and cinnamon. Starting with a 12-inch side, roll up jelly-roll fashion. Seal edges. Cut each into 1-inch slices and place cut-side down on greased baking sheets.
3. Bake at 375°F 10 minutes, or until done.

About 2 dozen rolls

Lamb Curry, page 177

300 *Cinnamon Swirl Date Ring*

3 cups all-purpose biscuit mix
¼ cup sugar
¼ cup butter or margarine
¾ cup milk
Cinnamon-Date Filling

1. Combine biscuit mix and sugar in a mixing bowl; cut in butter until mixture resembles rice kernels.
2. Gently stir in milk just until ingredients are moistened.
3. Drop half of dough by tablespoonfuls into a greased 6-cup ring mold. Sprinkle with Cinnamon-Date Filling. Top with remaining dough.
4. Bake at 350°F 25 to 30 minutes, or until a wooden pick inserted in cake comes out clean. Invert mold onto plate; leave over cake 5 minutes. Serve warm.

One coffeecake ring

Cinnamon-Date Filling: Combine **½ cup melted butter or margarine, ½ cup chopped dates, ¼ cup chopped nuts,** and **1 teaspoon cinnamon.**

Doughnuts are more than a sweet treat during coffee breaks; they help bring people together for enjoyable conversations and can even be the whole reason for the party.

Fry cakes, as they are sometimes called, can be rolled and cut into shapes, or dropped by spoonfuls into the hot fat. In both cases the temperature of the fat is very important. The fat should be heated slowly and be maintained at 375°F throughout the cooking. If the temperature is too low, the dough will soak up too much fat; if it is too hot, the outside will brown before the inside has completely cooked.

Pour in enough oil or fat to half fill a 3- to 4-quart saucepan. This leaves enough room for the bubbling action of the doughnuts cooking.

It is helpful to have a wire basket or slotted spoon to remove the doughnuts from the oil to absorbent paper to drain.

301 *Lemon Doughnut Balls*

2 cups all-purpose flour
¼ cup sugar
1 tablespoon baking powder
1 teaspoon salt
½ teaspoon baking soda
½ cup milk
¼ cup melted butter or margarine
2 tablespoons grated lemon peel
¼ cup lemon juice
1 egg
½ cup flaked coconut
Vegetable oil or shortening
heated to 375°F
Confectioners' sugar

1. Combine flour, sugar, baking powder, salt, and baking soda in a mixing bowl.
2. Combine milk, butter, lemon peel and juice, egg, and coconut in a separate bowl; beat well.
3. Add liquid ingredients to dry ingredients. Stir just until flour is moistened.
4. Drop by teaspoonfuls into hot oil. Fry 3 minutes, or until golden brown. Drain on paper towels. Sprinkle with confectioners' sugar.

About 3 dozen

302 *Filled Berlin Doughnuts (Bismarcks)*

A hint of orange and rum extract flavors these puffy Bismarcks. Fill them with your favorite jelly.

1 package active dry yeast
¼ cup warm water
½ cup sugar
1 teaspoon salt
⅓ cup butter
1 tablespoon orange juice
2 teaspoons rum extract
1 cup milk, scalded
3½ to 4 cups all-purpose flour
2 eggs, well beaten
    Fat for deep frying heated to
      375°F
    Jam or jelly

1. Soften yeast in the warm water.

2. Put ½ cup sugar, the salt, butter, orange juice and rum extract into a large bowl. Pour scalded milk over ingredients in bowl. Stir until butter is melted. Cool to lukewarm.

3. Blend in 1 cup of the flour and beat until smooth. Stir in yeast. Add about half of the remaining flour and beat until smooth. Beat in the eggs. Then beat in enough of the remaining flour to make a soft dough.

4. Turn dough onto a lightly floured surface and let rest 5 to 10 minutes.

5. Knead until smooth and elastic. Form into a ball and put into a greased deep bowl; turn dough to bring greased surface to top. Cover; let rise in a warm place until double in bulk.

6. Punch down dough. Turn dough onto a lightly floured surface and roll ½ inch thick. Cut dough into rounds with a 3-inch cutter. Cover with waxed paper and let rise on rolling surface away from drafts and direct heat, until double in bulk (30 to 45 minutes).

7. About 20 minutes before deep frying, heat fat.

8. Fry doughnuts in heated fat. Put in only as many doughnuts at one time as will float uncrowded one layer deep in the fat. Fry 2 to 3 minutes, or until lightly browned; turn doughnuts with a fork or tongs when they rise to the surface and several times during cooking (do not pierce). Lift from fat; drain over fat for a few seconds before removing to absorbent paper. Cool.

9. Cut a slit through to the center in the side of each doughnut. Force about ½ teaspoon jam or jelly into center and press lightly to close slit. (A pastry bag and tube may be used to force jelly or jam into slit.) Shake 2 or 3 Bismarcks at one time in bag containing **sugar**.

About 2 dozen

303 *Crispy Breadsticks*

1 cup whole wheat flour
1 package active dry yeast
1 tablespoon sugar
1 teaspoon salt
⅔ cup hot water
2 tablespoons vegetable oil
1 to 1¼ cups all-purpose flour

1. Stir together whole wheat flour, yeast, sugar, and salt in a mixing bowl.
2. Blend in water and oil; beat until smooth.
3. Stir in enough flour to form a soft dough.
4. Turn onto a floured surface; continue to work in flour until dough is stiff enough to knead. Knead until smooth and elastic (about 5 minutes), working in as much flour as possible. (The more flour, the crispier the bread sticks.)
5. Cover with bowl; let rest about 30 minutes.
6. Divide dough in quarters. Divide each quarter into 8 equal pieces. For ease in shaping, allow dough to rest about 10 minutes. Roll each piece with palms of hands into 10-inch lengths.
7. Place on greased baking sheets about ½ inch apart. If desired, brush with a mixture of 1 egg white and 1 teaspoon water.
8. Bake at 325°F 20 minutes, or until golden brown and crispy.

32 bread sticks

304 *Peasant Black Bread*

3½ cups rye flour
½ cup unsweetened cocoa
¼ cup sugar
3 tablespoons caraway seed
2 packages active dry yeast
1 tablespoon instant coffee
   (powder or crystals)
2 teaspoons salt
2½ cups hot water (120°-130°F)
¼ cup vinegar
¼ cup dark molasses
¼ cup vegetable oil or melted
   butter
3½ to 4½ cups unbleached or
   all-purpose flour

1. Thoroughly mix rye flour, cocoa, sugar, caraway, yeast, coffee, and salt in a large mixing bowl.
2. Stir in water, vinegar, molasses, and oil; beat until smooth.
3. Stir in enough unbleached flour to make a soft dough.
4. Turn onto a floured surface. Knead until smooth and elastic (about 5 minutes).
5. Place in an oiled bowl; turn to oil top of dough. Cover; let rise in warm place until doubled (about 1 hour).
6. Punch dough down. Divide in half; shape each half into a ball and place in center of 2 greased 8-inch round cake pans. Cover; let rise until double in bulk (about 1 hour).
7. Bake at 350°F 40 to 45 minutes, or until done.

2 loaves

305 *Grandma Louise's Banana Loaf*

1 cup sugar
½ cup shortening
1 cup mashed fully ripe bananas
   (2 to 3 bananas)
1 egg
¼ cup buttermilk
1¾ cups all-purpose flour
1½ teaspoons baking powder
1 teaspoon baking soda
½ teaspoon salt

1. Combine sugar, shortening, bananas, egg, and buttermilk in a mixing bowl; beat well.
2. Blend remaining ingredients, add to banana mixture, and mix until blended (about 1 minute).
3. Turn into a greased 9×5×3-inch loaf pan.
4. Bake at 350°F 45 to 50 minutes, or until done.

1 loaf

306 *New England Blueberry Muffins*

In New England, they fill the muffin cups right up to the top with batter to produce these giant round-top muffins. If you like yours more petite, fill the muffin cups ⅔ full and reduce baking time by 5 minutes.

1 cup sugar
½ cup softened butter or margarine
2 eggs
½ cup milk
2 cups all-purpose flour
2 teaspoons baking powder
½ teaspoon salt
1 to 1½ cups fresh or frozen blueberries

1. Combine sugar, butter, eggs, and milk in a mixing bowl; beat well.
2. Blend flour, baking powder, and salt; add and mix until blended (about 1 minute). Fold in blueberries.
3. Spoon into 12 well-greased muffin cups, filling almost to the top of the cup.
4. Bake at 375°F 20 to 25 minutes.

12 large muffins

307 *Indian Flat Bread (Nan)*

From the northwest region of India comes Indian Flat Bread, baked at a high temperature in clay ovens. This is a richer, more sophisticated bread than the unleavened chapati eaten by most Indians. Both breads are literally the staff of life.

1 cup all-purpose flour
1 package active dry yeast
2 teaspoons salt
1 cup hot water (120°-130°F)
¼ cup buttermilk or yogurt
1 egg (at room temperature)
2 tablespoons vegetable oil
1 tablespoon honey or sugar
2 to 3 cups all-purpose flour
Melted butter (optional)
Cornmeal or sesame or poppy seeds (optional)

1. Combine 1 cup flour, yeast, and salt in a mixing bowl.
2. Stir in water, buttermilk, egg, oil, and honey; beat until smooth.
3. Stir in enough remaining flour to form a soft, sticky dough.
4. Turn onto a floured surface; continue to work in flour until dough is stiff enough to knead. Knead until smooth and elastic, but still soft (3 to 5 minutes).
5. Place in an oiled bowl; turning once to oil top of dough. Cover; let rise until double in bulk (about 45 minutes).
6. Punch dough down. Shape into 16 equal balls. Let rest 5 minutes. Roll out each ball to a ¼-inch-thick round. If desired, brush with melted butter and sprinkle with cornmeal, sesame, or poppy seeds. Set on baking sheets.
7. Bake at 450°F 5 to 8 minutes.

16 round loaves

308 *Pocket Bread*

2 cups all-purpose flour
2 packages active dry yeast
2 tablespoons sugar or honey
2 teaspoons salt
2½ cups hot water (120°-130°F)
¼ cup vegetable oil
5½ to 6 cups all-purpose flour

1. Combine 2 cups flour, yeast, sugar, and salt in a large mixing bowl.
2. Stir in water and oil; beat until smooth.
3. Stir in enough remaining flour to make a soft dough.
4. Turn onto a floured surface; continue to work in flour until stiff enough to knead. Knead until smooth and elastic (about 5 minutes).
5. Place in an oiled bowl; turn to oil top of dough. Cover; let rise in a warm place until double in bulk (about 45 minutes).
6. Punch dough down. Divide in half. Divide each half into 10 equal pieces. Roll each piece into a ball. Let dough rest 5 minutes. Roll balls into 3- or 4-inch rounds, ⅛ inch thick. Place on greased baking sheets. Cover; let rise 30 minutes (see Note).
7. Bake at 450°F 5 to 8 minutes, or until puffed and brown.

20 pocket breads

Note: Avoid pinching or creasing dough after rolling, or bread will not puff properly.

Pasta & Grains

309 Lemony Meat Sauce with Spaghetti

2 pounds ground beef
1½ cups finely chopped onion
1¼ cups chopped green pepper
2 cloves garlic, minced
¼ cup firmly packed brown sugar
1 teaspoon salt
¼ teaspoon ground black pepper
1 teaspoon thyme, crushed
½ teaspoon basil, crushed
2 cups water
2 cans (8 ounces each) tomato sauce
2 cans (6 ounces each) tomato paste
1 can (6 ounces) sliced broiled
    mushrooms (undrained)
1 tablespoon grated lemon peel
¼ cup lemon juice
1 pound enriched spaghetti
    Shredded Parmesan cheese

1. Put meat, onion, green pepper, and garlic into a heated large heavy saucepot or Dutch oven. Cook 10 to 15 minutes, cutting meat apart with fork or spoon.
2. Stir in brown sugar, salt, pepper, thyme, basil, water, tomato sauce, and tomato paste. Cover and simmer 2 to 3 hours, stirring occasionally. About 30 minutes before serving, mix in mushrooms with liquid and lemon peel and juice.
3. Meanwhile, cook spaghetti following package directions; drain.
4. Spoon sauce over hot spaghetti and sprinkle generously with cheese.

10 to 12 servings

310 *Polenta*

2 tablespoons olive oil
1 clove garlic, crushed
1 can (8 ounces) sliced mushrooms, drained, or 1 pound fresh mushrooms, sliced
1 can (16 ounces) tomatoes (undrained)
⅓ cup tomato paste
1 teaspoon salt
¼ teaspoon ground pepper
3 cups water
1½ teaspoons salt
1 cup enriched cornmeal
1 cup cold water
Grated Parmesan or Romano cheese

1. Heat olive oil and garlic in a skillet. Add mushrooms and cook about 5 minutes, stirring occasionally. When lightly browned, stir in tomatoes with liquid, tomato paste, salt, and pepper. Simmer 15 to 20 minutes.
2. Meanwhile, bring 3 cups water and 1½ teaspoons salt to boiling in a saucepan. Mix cornmeal and 1 cup cold water; stir into boiling water. Continue boiling, stirring constantly to prevent sticking, until mixture is thick. Cover, reduce heat, and cook over low heat 10 minutes or longer.
3. Turn cooked cornmeal onto warm serving platter and top with the tomato-mushroom mixture. Sprinkle with grated cheese. Serve at once.

6 to 8 servings

311 *Fried Cornmeal Mush*

1 cup enriched yellow cornmeal
1 teaspoon salt
2¼ cups milk
1½ cups water
Butter or margarine
Syrup or honey

1. Combine cornmeal, salt, and 1 cup milk. Pour remaining milk and water into a saucepan and bring to boiling. Add cornmeal mixture gradually; cook and stir until thickened. Cover and cook over low heat 10 minutes. Pour into a buttered loaf pan, mold, or other container, and chill.
2. Turn out of pan and slice ½ inch thick. Cook on lightly buttered griddle or skillet until crisp and golden, turning once. Serve with butter and syrup or honey.

6 to 8 servings

312 *Bulgur, Pilaf Style*

½ cup butter or margarine
½ cup chopped onion
½ cup chopped green pepper
2 cups bulgur (cracked wheat)
4 cups boiling water
4 chicken bouillon cubes
1 teaspoon salt
¼ teaspoon ground black pepper
1 cup shredded carrot

1. Heat butter in a skillet with heat-resistant handle. Mix in onion and green pepper. Cook until onion is tender.
2. Stir in bulgur, cover, reduce heat, and cook 10 minutes over low heat; stir once or twice to prevent sticking.
3. Add boiling water and bouillon cubes; stir until cubes are dissolved; cover tightly.
4. Cook in a 350°F oven 30 minutes. Stir in salt, pepper, and carrot. Continue cooking 15 minutes, or until liquid is absorbed and bulgur is tender.

About 8 servings

313 *Baked Hominy Grits*

1 quart milk
½ cup butter or margarine, cut in pieces
1 cup enriched white hominy grits, quick or long-cooking
1 teaspoon salt

1. Heat milk to boiling. Add butter; then add hominy grits gradually, stirring constantly. Bring to boiling and boil 3 minutes, or until mixture becomes thick, stirring constantly. Remove from heat; add salt.
2. Beat mixture at high speed of an electric mixer 5 minutes, or until grits have a creamy appearance. Turn mixture into a greased 1½-quart casserole.
3. Bake at 350°F about 1 hour. Serve hot.

6 to 8 servings

314 Spaghetti à la King Crab

Parmesan Croutons
2 cans (7½ ounces each) Alaska king
    crab or 1 pound frozen Alaska
    king crab
2 tablespoons olive oil
½ cup butter or margarine
4 cloves garlic, minced
1 bunch green onions, sliced
2 medium tomatoes, peeled and diced
½ cup chopped parsley
2 tablespoons lemon juice
¼ teaspoon basil
¼ teaspoon thyme
½ teaspoon salt
1 pound enriched spaghetti

1. Prepare Parmesan Croutons; set aside.
2. Drain canned crab and slice. Or, defrost, drain, and slice frozen crab.
3. Heat olive oil, butter, and garlic in a saucepan. Add crab, green onions, tomatoes, parsley, lemon juice, basil, thyme, and salt. Heat gently 8 to 10 minutes.
4. Meanwhile, cook spaghetti following package directions; drain.
5. Toss spaghetti with king crab sauce. Top with Parmesan Croutons. Pass additional grated Parmesan cheese.

About 6 servings

Parmesan Croutons: Put **3 tablespoons butter** into a shallow baking pan. Set in a 350°F oven until butter is melted. Slice **French bread** into small cubes to make about 1 cup. Toss with melted butter. Return to oven until golden (about 6 minutes). Sprinkle with **2 tablespoons grated Parmesan cheese** and toss.

315 White Clam Sauce for Linguine

12 ounces enriched linguine
¼ cup olive oil
½ cup chopped onion
¼ cup snipped parsley
3 cloves garlic, minced
2 tablespoons flour
¼ to ½ teaspoon salt
    Few grains pepper
3 cans (8 ounces each) minced
    clams, drained; reserve 1½ cups
    liquid

1. Cook linguine following package directions; drain and keep hot.
2. Meanwhile, heat oil in a large skillet. Add onion, parsley, and garlic; cook about 3 minutes, stirring occasionally.
3. Mix in flour, salt, and pepper; cook until bubbly. Add reserved clam liquid gradually, while blending thoroughly. Bring rapidly to boiling, stirring constantly, and boil 1 to 2 minutes. Mix in the minced clams and heat; do not boil.
4. Serve clam sauce on the hot linguine.

6 servings

316 Fiesta Zucchini-Tomato Casserole

1½ quarts water
2 packets dry onion soup mix
4 ounces enriched spaghetti, broken
⅓ cup butter or margarine
⅔ cup coarsely chopped onion
1 cup green pepper strips
2 or 3 zucchini (about ¾ pound),
    washed, ends trimmed, and
    zucchini cut in about ½-inch
    slices

1. Bring water to boiling in a saucepot. Add onion soup mix and spaghetti to the boiling water. Partially cover and boil gently about 10 minutes, or until spaghetti is tender. Drain and set spaghetti mixture aside; reserve liquid.*
2. Heat butter in a large heavy skillet. Add onion and green pepper and cook about 3 minutes, or until tender. Add zucchini; cover and cook 5 minutes. Stir in tomatoes, parsley, seasoned salt, and pepper. Cover and cook about 2 minutes, or just until heated.
3. Turn contents of skillet into a 2-quart casserole. Add

4 medium tomatoes, peeled and cut
   in wedges
¼ cup snipped parsley
1 teaspoon seasoned salt
⅛ teaspoon ground black pepper
⅔ cup shredded Swiss cheese

drained spaghetti and toss gently to mix. Sprinkle cheese over top. If necessary to reheat mixture, set in a 350°F oven until thoroughly heated before placing under broiler.

4. Set under broiler with top about 5 inches from heat until cheese is melted and lightly browned.

6 to 8 servings

*The strained soup may be stored for future use as broth or for cooking vegetables, preparing gravy or sauce, or as desired.

317 *Rice Pilaf Deluxe*

⅓ cup butter
1½ cups uncooked enriched white rice
⅓ cup chopped onion
1½ teaspoons salt
3 cans (13¾ ounces each) chicken
   broth
¾ cup golden raisins
3 tablespoons butter
¾ cup coarsely chopped pecans
½ teaspoon salt

1. Heat ⅓ cup butter in a heavy skillet. Add rice and onion and cook until lightly browned, stirring frequently.
2. Add 1½ teaspoons salt, chicken broth, and raisins; cover, bring to boiling, reduce heat, and simmer until rice is tender and liquid is absorbed (20 to 25 minutes).
3. Just before serving, heat 3 tablespoons butter in a small skillet. Add pecans and ½ teaspoon salt; heat 2 to 3 minutes, stirring occasionally.
4. Serve rice topped with salted pecans.

About 8 servings

318 *Spanish Rice au Gratin*

½ cup uncooked enriched white rice
1 cup water
½ teaspoon salt
1½ tablespoons butter or margarine
½ cup chopped onion
½ cup chopped celery
⅓ cup chopped green pepper
1 cup canned tomatoes, cut in
   pieces
½ teaspoon salt
½ teaspoon monosodium glutamate
1 teaspoon sugar
¾ teaspoon chili powder
¼ teaspoon Worcestershire sauce
1 cup (about 4 ounces) shredded
   Cheddar cheese

1. Combine rice, water, and ½ teaspoon salt in a saucepan. Bring to boiling, reduce heat, and simmer, covered, about 14 minutes.
2. Meanwhile, heat butter in a skillet. Mix in onion, celery, and green pepper. Cook until vegetables are tender. Mix in cooked rice, tomatoes, ½ teaspoon salt, monosodium glutamate, sugar, chili powder, and Worcestershire sauce. Simmer until thick.
3. Turn mixture into a greased baking dish. Top evenly with cheese.
4. Place under broiler 3 to 4 inches from heat until cheese is melted.

3 or 4 servings

319 *Cheese Risotta*

1 **cup chopped onion**
¼ **cup butter or margarine**
1 **cup uncooked white rice**
1 **can (16 ounces) tomatoes**
    (undrained)
1½ **cups water**
2 **chicken bouillon cubes**
1 **can (3 ounces) mushroom slices,**
    drained
    Dash pepper
    Few grains saffron (optional)
2 **cups (8 ounces) shredded sharp**
    Cheddar cheese

1. Sauté onion in butter in a skillet. Stir in rice; cook until lightly browned.
2. Add remaining ingredients, except cheese. Bring to a boil, stirring until bouillon cubes dissolve.
3. Place half the rice mixture in a 1½-quart casserole. Top with 1½ cups cheese. Evenly spoon remaining rice mixture over cheese.
4. Bake, covered, at 350°F 45 minutes, or until rice is tender. Remove cover; sprinkle with remaining ½ cup cheese. Bake an additional 5 minutes, or until cheese is melted.

6 servings

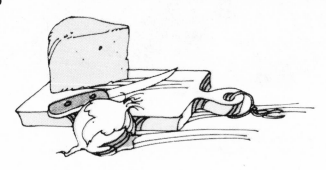

320 *Baked Rice*

1 **cup uncooked white rice**
1 **can (5 ounces) water chestnuts,**
    drained and sliced
2 **cups boiling water**
1 **package (1⅜ ounces) dry onion**
    soup mix
2 **tablespoons chopped pimento**

1. Place rice in bottom of a 1½-quart baking dish. Toast at 350°F 10 minutes, stirring occasionally until lightly browned.
2. Stir in remaining ingredients.
3. Bake, covered, at 350°F 45 minutes, or until rice is tender.

6 servings

321 *Mushroom-Rice Casserole*

1 cup uncooked white rice
½ cup slivered almonds
1 small onion, chopped
1 can (4 ounces) sliced mushrooms, drained*
¼ cup butter or margarine
2 cups water
2 chicken bouillon cubes
2 tablespoons lemon juice
1 teaspoon soy sauce
   Dash pepper
4 bacon slices, cooked and crumbled
2 tablespoons snipped parsley

1. Sauté rice, almonds, onion, and mushrooms in butter in a skillet. Stir in water, bouillon cubes, lemon juice, soy sauce, and pepper.
2. Heat to boiling. Cover and reduce heat to low. Cook until liquid is absorbed (about 20 minutes).
3. Stir in crumbled bacon and parsley. Put into a 1½-quart casserole.
4. Bake, covered, at 325°F 20 minutes, or until heated through.

6 servings

* The drained mushroom liquid can be used as part of the 2 cups water called for in the recipe.

322 *Italian Rice Casserole*

½ cup chopped onion
2 tablespoons oil
1 cup (4 ounces) shredded Cheddar cheese
1 cup sliced fresh mushrooms
¾ cup sliced pitted ripe olives
1 can (16 ounces) stewed tomatoes
1½ cups boiling water
1 package (6 ounces) long-grain and wild rice mix

1. Sauté onion in oil in a skillet. Combine with remaining ingredients. Put into a 2-quart baking dish.
2. Bake, covered, at 350°F 1 hour, or until rice is tender.

6 servings

323 *Rice Loaf*

2 cups cooked brown rice
½ cup finely chopped onion
½ cup finely chopped pecans
2 tablespoons snipped parsley
½ teaspoon salt
¼ teaspoon thyme
½ cup milk
1 egg, well beaten

1. Combine all ingredients. Put into a 1-quart casserole.
2. Bake, uncovered, at 350°F 35 to 40 minutes, or until set.

6 servings

324 *Brunch Pilaf*

1 package (6 ounces) long-grain and
    wild rice mix
½ pound pork sausage links, cut in
    1-inch pieces
½ pound fresh mushrooms, sliced
3 tablespoons butter or margarine
½ teaspoon salt
¼ teaspoon pepper
2 teaspoons instant minced onion
½ pound chicken livers, cut up

1. Prepare rice according to package directions.
2. Brown sausage in a skillet about 15 minutes. Drain and set aside.
3. Sauté mushrooms in 2 tablespoons butter. Toss with ¼ teaspoon salt, pepper, and minced onion; set aside.
4. Sauté chicken livers in remaining 1 tablespoon butter until lightly browned. Sprinkle with remaining ¼ teaspoon salt.
5. Combine all ingredients and put into a 1½-quart casserole.
6. Bake, covered, at 325°F 30 minutes, or until heated through.

6 to 8 servings

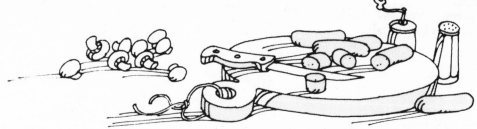

325 *Mushroom Wild Rice*

1 package (4 ounces) wild rice
1 medium green pepper, chopped
1 large onion, chopped
½ cup chopped celery
¼ cup butter or margarine
1 egg, beaten
1 can (10¾ ounces) condensed cream
    of mushroom soup
¼ cup sliced almonds
2 tablespoons snipped parsley

1. Prepare rice according to package directions.
2. Sauté green pepper, onion, and celery in butter in a skillet. Add to rice along with beaten egg. Put into a greased 1½-quart casserole.
3. Top with mushroom soup; mix slightly. Sprinkle with almonds.
4. Bake, covered, at 350°F 30 minutes, or until heated through. Sprinkle with parsley.

6 servings

326 *Wild Rice Casserole*

1 cup wild rice
2 tablespoons chopped onion
½ pound fresh mushrooms, sliced
½ cup butter or margarine
3 cups broth*
1 teaspoon salt
½ cup toasted slivered almonds

1. Sauté rice, onion, and mushrooms in butter in a skillet. Add broth and salt. Pour into a 1½-quart casserole.
2. Bake, covered, at 325°F 1 hour. Remove cover; top with almonds. Bake an additional 15 minutes, or until rice is tender. If desired, top with fresh tomato wedges.

6 servings

* Use beef broth when serving with meat and chicken broth when serving with poultry.

327 *Egg Noodle Supreme*

2 cups cooked noodles
¼ cup finely chopped green onion
1 garlic clove, minced
½ teaspoon tarragon
½ cup (2 ounces) shredded Colby cheese
½ cup milk
1 tablespoon butter or margarine, melted
½ cup dairy sour cream

1. Combine all ingredients, except sour cream. Put into a 1-quart casserole.
2. Bake, covered, at 350°F 25 minutes. Remove cover; stir in sour cream. Bake an additional 5 minutes, or until heated through.

4 servings

328 *Noodles au Gratin*

1 small onion, chopped
¼ cup butter or margarine
4 cups noodles, cooked and drained
½ cup dairy sour cream
6 slices (1 ounce each) American cheese, cut in pieces
½ teaspoon salt
½ cup milk
Paprika

1. Sauté onion in butter in a skillet. Combine with noodles, sour cream, cheese, and salt. Put into a 1½-quart casserole.
2. Pour milk over all. Sprinkle with paprika.
3. Bake, covered, at 350°F 40 minutes, or until golden brown.

6 to 8 servings

329 *Noodles Romanoff*

4 cups noodles, cooked and drained
1½ cups (12 ounces) cream-style cottage cheese
1 cup dairy sour cream
¼ cup finely chopped onion
1 teaspoon Worcestershire sauce
½ teaspoon salt
¼ teaspoon white pepper
½ cup (2 ounces) shredded Cheddar cheese
2 tablespoons snipped parsley

1. Combine all ingredients, except Cheddar cheese and parsley. Put into a 2-quart casserole. Sprinkle with cheese.
2. Bake, covered, at 325°F 40 minutes, or until heated through. Sprinkle with parsley.

6 servings

330 *Spaghetti Fromaggi*

¼ cup chopped onion
¼ cup chopped green pepper
¼ cup butter or margarine
¼ cup flour
1 teaspoon salt
¼ teaspoon pepper
3½ cups milk
1 cup (4 ounces) shredded Swiss cheese
1 cup (4 ounces) shredded Cheddar cheese
1 tablespoon Worcestershire sauce
1 tablespoon chopped pimento
1 package (16 ounces) spaghetti, cooked and drained
1 tablespoon snipped parsley

1. Sauté onion and green pepper in butter in a skillet. Stir in flour, salt, and pepper. Gradually add milk, stirring until thickened and smooth.
2. Stir in cheeses, Worcestershire sauce, pimento, and spaghetti. Put into a 3-quart casserole.
3. Bake, covered, at 350°F 45 minutes, or until heated through. Sprinkle with parsley.

8 servings

331 *Barley Italienne*

6 bacon slices, cut in 1-inch pieces
1½ cups quick-cooking barley
2¼ cups water
1 can (16 ounces) tomatoes (undrained)
1 can (8 ounces) tomato sauce
1 medium onion, sliced
1 garlic clove, minced
2 teaspoons salt
½ teaspoon oregano
¼ teaspoon pepper
8 ounces American cheese, sliced

1. Fry bacon in a skillet; drain off excess fat, reserving 2 tablespoons drippings.
2. Brown barley in bacon drippings in skillet. Add water and tomatoes. Bring to a boil; reduce heat. Cover and simmer 10 to 12 minutes, stirring occasionally.
3. Add bacon and remaining ingredients, except cheese. Cover and cook an additional 5 minutes.
4. Layer barley mixture and cheese alternately in a greased 2-quart casserole, ending with cheese on top.
5. Bake, covered, at 350°F 10 to 12 minutes, or until cheese is melted and mixture is heated through.

6 servings

332 *Barley-Mushroom Casserole*

½ cup finely chopped onion
½ pound fresh mushrooms, sliced
¼ cup butter or margarine
2 beef bouillon cubes
1 quart boiling water
1 teaspoon salt
1 cup barley

1. Sauté onion and mushrooms in butter in a skillet.
2. Dissolve bouillon cubes in boiling water. Mix with salt, barley, onion, and mushrooms. Pour into a 2-quart casserole.
3. Bake, uncovered, at 350°F 1 hour, stirring occasionally. Cover and bake an additional 30 minutes, or until barley is tender.

6 servings

Vegetables

333 *Flavor-Rich Baked Beans*

1½ quarts water
1 pound dried navy beans, rinsed
½ pound salt pork
½ cup chopped celery
½ cup chopped onion
1 teaspoon salt
¼ cup ketchup
¼ cup molasses
2 tablespoons brown sugar
1 teaspoon dry mustard
½ teaspoon ground black pepper
¼ teaspoon ground ginger

1. Grease 8 individual casseroles having tight-fitting covers. (A 2-quart casserole with lid may be used.)
2. Heat water to boiling in a large heavy saucepan. Add beans gradually to water so that boiling continues. Boil 2 minutes. Remove from heat and set aside 1 hour.
3. Remove rind from salt pork and cut into 1-inch chunks; set aside.
4. Add pork chunks to beans with celery, onion, and salt; mix well. Cover tightly and bring mixture to boiling over high heat. Reduce and simmer 45 minutes, stirring once or twice. Drain beans, reserving liquid.
5. Put an equal amount of beans and salt pork chunks into each casserole.
6. Mix one cup of bean liquid, ketchup, molasses, brown sugar, dry mustard, pepper, and ginger in a saucepan. Bring to boiling. Pour an equal amount of sauce over beans in each casserole. Cover casseroles.
7. Bake at 300°F about 2½ hours. If necessary, add more reserved bean liquid to beans during baking. Remove covers and bake ½ hour longer.

8 servings

334 *Lagered Sauerkraut with Apples*

Serve this German dish with sausage, roast pork, pork chops, or braised beef.

1 can (16 ounces) sauerkraut
1 medium apple
¾ cup beer
1 tablespoon sugar
1 tablespoon butter
½ teaspoon caraway seed
Dash pepper

1. Rinse sauerkraut in a large strainer; drain. Slice apple but do not peel.
2. Place all ingredients in a saucepan. Simmer, uncovered, for about 30 minutes, stirring occasionally, until most of liquid has evaporated and apples are tender.

4 servings

335 *Artichokes with Creamy Dill Sauce*

Cooked Artichokes
1 cup creamed cottage cheese
½ cup plain yogurt
1 tablespoon lemon juice
1 teaspoon instant minced onion
1 teaspoon sugar
½ teaspoon dill weed
½ teaspoon salt
Few grains pepper
2 parsley sprigs

1. Prepare desired number of artichokes.
2. Meanwhile, combine cottage cheese, yogurt, lemon juice, onion, sugar, dill weed, salt, pepper, and parsley in an electric blender container. Blend until smooth. Chill.
3. Serve artichokes with sauce for dipping.

About 1½ cups sauce

Cooked Artichokes: Wash **artichokes.** Cut off about 1 inch from tops and bases. Remove and discard lower outside leaves. If desired, snip off tips of remaining leaves. Stand artichokes upright in a deep saucepan large enough to hold them snugly. Add **boiling water** to a depth of 1 inch. Add **salt** (¼ teaspoon for each artichoke). Cover and boil gently 30 to 45 minutes, or until stems can easily be pierced with a fork. Drain artichokes; cut off stems.

337 *Stir-Fry Vegetables and Rice*

1 cup brown rice
¼ cup vegetable oil
1 medium onion, thinly sliced
1 cup thinly sliced carrot
1 clove garlic, crushed
1 green pepper, coarsely chopped
1 cup thinly sliced zucchini
1 cup thinly sliced mushrooms
2 cans (16 ounces each) bean sprouts, drained
¼ to ⅓ cup soy sauce

1. Cook rice following package directions; set aside.
2. Heat oil in a large skillet. Add onion, carrot, and garlic; cook and stir over medium high heat about 2 minutes.
3. Add green pepper, zucchini, and mushrooms; cook and stir 2 to 3 minutes.
4. Stir in cooked rice, bean sprouts, and soy sauce. Cook and stir 1 to 2 minutes, or until thoroughly heated.

6 to 8 servings

338 *Tangy Green Beans*

¾ pound fresh green beans, cut crosswise in pieces, or 1 package (9 ounces) frozen cut green beans
½ teaspoon salt
¼ cup butter or margarine
1 medium onion, quartered and thinly sliced
1 tablespoon wine vinegar
¼ teaspoon salt
⅛ teaspoon ground black pepper
¼ teaspoon dill weed
⅛ teaspoon crushed savory

1. Put beans and ½ teaspoon salt into a small amount of boiling water in a saucepan. Bring to boiling and cook, covered, until crisp-tender. Drain and set aside.
2. Heat 3 tablespoons butter in a skillet; add onion and cook 3 to 5 minutes. Mix in beans and cook about 4 minutes, or until thoroughly heated, stirring occasionally. Add remaining butter, wine vinegar, ¼ teaspoon salt, pepper, dill, and savory; toss over low heat until butter is melted.

About 4 servings

339 *Butter-Sauced Asparagus*

2 pounds fresh asparagus, washed,
  or 2 packages (10 ounces each)
  frozen asparagus spears, cooked
¼ cup butter
¼ cup chopped pecans
¼ cup finely chopped celery
1 tablespoon lemon juice

1. Put fresh asparagus into a small amount of boiling salted water in a skillet, bring to boiling, reduce heat, and cook 5 minutes, uncovered; cover and cook 10 minutes, or until just tender.
2. Meanwhile, heat butter in a small saucepan. Add pecans and celery and cook 5 minutes. Stir in lemon juice. Pour over asparagus and serve immediately.

About 6 servings

340 *Lima Beans New Orleans*

1 package (10 ounces) frozen lima
  beans
1 tablespoon vinegar
2 tablespoons olive oil
½ teaspoon salt
  Dash pepper
2 tablespoons chopped parsley
½ clove garlic, minced
1 teaspoon lemon juice

1. Cook lima beans following package directions; drain if necessary.
2. Add vinegar, olive oil, salt, pepper, parsley, and garlic to limas in saucepan. Heat thoroughly, then mix in lemon juice. Serve immediately.

4 servings

341 *Broccoli with Buttery Lemon Crunch*

1½ pounds broccoli, washed
¼ cup butter or margarine
½ cup coarse dry enriched bread
  crumbs
1 tablespoon grated lemon peel
3 tablespoons butter or margarine
1 small clove garlic, crushed in a
  garlic press or minced
½ teaspoon salt
  Few grains black pepper

1. Cook broccoli in a small amount of boiling salted water until just tender. (Cook uncovered 5 minutes, then cover and cook 10 to 15 minutes, or cook, covered, the full time and lift the lid 3 or 4 times during cooking.)
2. Meanwhile, heat ¼ cup butter in a large skillet; add bread crumbs and heat, stirring frequently, until well browned. Remove crumbs from butter with a slotted spoon and mix with the lemon peel.
3. Put 3 tablespoons butter, garlic, salt, and pepper into skillet; heat until butter is lightly browned. Add broccoli and turn gently until well coated with butter.
4. Arrange broccoli in a heated vegetable dish and pour remaining garlic butter over it. Top with the "lemoned" crumbs.

About 6 servings

342 *Brussels Sprouts in Herb Butter*

2 pounds fresh Brussels sprouts
⅓ cup butter
1 tablespoon grated onion
1 tablespoon lemon juice
¾ teaspoon salt
¼ teaspoon thyme
¼ teaspoon marjoram
¼ teaspoon savory

1. Cook Brussels sprouts in boiling salted water until just tender.
2. Put butter, onion, lemon juice, salt, thyme, marjoram, and savory into a saucepan. Set over low heat until butter is melted, stirring to blend.
3. When Brussels sprouts are tender, drain thoroughly and turn into a warm serving dish. Pour the seasoned butter mixture over the Brussels sprouts and toss gently to coat sprouts evenly and thoroughly.

About 8 servings

343 *Zesty Beets*

1 can or jar (16 ounces) small whole
    beets
2 tablespoons butter or margarine
2 tablespoons prepared horseradish
½ teaspoon prepared mustard
½ teaspoon seasoned salt

Heat beets in liquid; drain. Add butter, horseradish, prepared mustard, and seasoned salt; stir gently.

About 4 servings

344 *Cabbage Rolls Paprikash*

8 large cabbage leaves
2½ cups diced cooked chicken
2 tablespoons chopped onion
½ cup finely chopped celery
¼ pound chopped fresh mushrooms
1 small clove garlic, minced
½ teaspoon salt
½ teaspoon thyme leaves
1 egg, beaten
2 tablespoons butter or margarine
6 tablespoons flour
2 cups chicken broth
2 cups dairy sour cream
3 tablespoons paprika

1. Cook cabbage leaves 4 minutes in boiling salted water to cover. Drain and pat dry.
2. Mix chicken, onion, celery, mushrooms, garlic, salt, and thyme; stir in egg.
3. Place ½ cup of the chicken mixture in the center of each cabbage leaf. Fold sides of the cabbage leaf toward center, over filling, and then fold and overlap ends to make a small bundle. Fasten with wooden picks. Place in a 3-quart baking dish.
4. Heat butter in a large skillet. Blend in flour and heat until bubbly. Add chicken broth gradually, stirring until smooth. Blend in sour cream and paprika. Cook over low heat, stirring constantly, until thickened. Pour sauce over cabbage rolls. Cover baking dish.
5. Cook in a 350°F oven 35 minutes.

4 servings

345 *Cauliflower Italiana*

2 packages (10 ounces each) frozen
    cauliflower
2 tablespoons butter or margarine
½ clove garlic, minced
2 teaspoons flour
1 teaspoon salt
1 can (16 ounces) tomatoes
    (undrained)
1 small green pepper, coarsely
    chopped
¼ teaspoon oregano

1. Cook cauliflower following package directions; drain.
2. Meanwhile, heat butter with garlic in a saucepan. Stir in flour and salt and cook until bubbly.
3. Add tomatoes with liquid and bring to boiling, stirring constantly; cook 1 to 2 minutes. Stir in green pepper and oregano.
4. Pour hot sauce over cooked cauliflower.

About 6 servings

346 *Corn Spoon Bread*

1 quart milk
1 cup enriched yellow cornmeal
2 tablespoons finely chopped onion
2 tablespoons chopped parsley
4 eggs
2 tablespoons butter or margarine
2 tablespoons prepared baconlike
    pieces (a soy protein product)

1. Scald milk in top of a double boiler over simmering water.
2. Add cornmeal to scalded milk gradually, stirring constantly. Mix in onion and parsley. Cook over boiling water until thickened, about 10 minutes, stirring frequently and vigorously.
3. Meanwhile, beat eggs in a large bowl until thick and piled softly.
4. Remove double boiler top from water. Stir in butter and

2 teaspoons salt
1 teaspoon sugar
1 teaspoon baking powder
¼ teaspoon seasoned pepper
2 cups corn kernels (fresh, frozen, or canned)

baconlike pieces. Blend salt, sugar, baking powder, and seasoned pepper; stir into cornmeal mixture. Add hot mixture gradually to eggs, beating constantly. Mix in corn. Turn into a buttered 2-quart casserole.

5. Bake at 425°F 40 to 45 minutes, or until top is browned. Serve immediately.

6 to 8 servings

347 *Ratatouille with Spanish Olives*

1 medium eggplant (about 1½ pounds), pared and cut in 3 × ½-inch strips
2 zucchini, cut in ¼-inch slices
2 teaspoons salt
½ cup olive oil
2 onions, thinly sliced
2 green peppers, thinly sliced
2 cloves garlic, minced
3 tomatoes, peeled and cut in strips
1 cup sliced pimento-stuffed olives
¼ cup snipped parsley
¼ teaspoon ground pepper
   Parsley, snipped

1. Toss eggplant and zucchini with 1 teaspoon salt and let stand 30 minutes. Drain and then dry on paper toweling.
2. Heat ¼ cup oil in a large skillet and lightly brown eggplant strips and then zucchini slices. Remove with slotted spoon; set aside.
3. Heat remaining oil in the skillet; cook onions and green peppers until tender. Stir in garlic. Put tomato strips on top; cover and cook 5 minutes. Gently stir in eggplant, zucchini, olives, ¼ cup parsley, remaining salt, and the pepper.
4. Simmer, covered, 20 minutes. Uncover and cook 5 minutes; baste with juices from bottom of skillet. Serve hot or cold, garnished with parsley.

6 to 8 servings

348 *Fresh Corn Vinaigrette*

4 ears fresh corn
¼ cup vegetable oil
2 tablespoons cider vinegar
¾ teaspoon lemon juice
1½ tablespoons chopped parsley
1 teaspoon salt
½ teaspoon sugar
¼ teaspoon basil
⅛ teaspoon cayenne pepper
1 large tomato, peeled and chopped
¼ cup chopped green pepper
¼ cup chopped green onion
   Greens (optional)

1. Husk corn and remove silks. Fill a large kettle half full of water and bring to boiling. Add corn, cover, and return to boiling. Remove from heat and let stand 5 minutes. Drain and set aside to cool.
2. Mix oil, vinegar, lemon juice, parsley, salt, sugar, basil, and cayenne in a large bowl.
3. Cut corn off cob and add to bowl along with tomato, green pepper, and green onion; mix well. Cover and chill several hours.
4. Drain and serve on greens, if desired.

4 to 6 servings

Note: If desired, substitute 1½ cups (12-ounce can, drained, or 10-ounce package frozen, defrosted) whole kernel corn.

349 *Gingered Turnips*

Oriental seasonings give this often neglected vegetable new flavor appeal.

2 pounds yellow turnips, pared and cubed
1 tablespoon minced onion
1¼ cups Beef Stock
½ teaspoon ground ginger
½ teaspoon sugar
2 teaspoons soy sauce

Combine all ingredients in a saucepan; simmer covered until turnips are tender (about 15 minutes). Drain; mash turnips with potato masher or electric mixer until fluffy, adding cooking liquid as needed for desired consistency.

6 servings

350 *Fresh Peas with Basil*

2 tablespoons butter or margarine
½ cup sliced green onions with tops
1½ cups shelled fresh peas (1½ pounds)
½ teaspoon sugar
½ teaspoon salt
⅛ teaspoon ground black pepper
¼ teaspoon basil
1 tablespoon snipped parsley
½ cup water

1. Heat butter in a skillet. Add green onions and cook 5 minutes, stirring occasionally. Add peas, sugar, salt, pepper, basil, parsley, and water.
2. Cook, covered, over medium heat 10 minutes, or until peas are tender.

About 4 servings

Note: If desired, use 1 package (10 ounces) frozen green peas and decrease water to ¼ cup.

351 *Parsley-Buttered New Potatoes*

18 small new potatoes
Boiling water
1½ teaspoons salt
2 tablespoons butter
1 tablespoon snipped parsley

Scrub potatoes and put into a saucepan. Pour in boiling water to a 1-inch depth. Add salt; cover and cook about 15 minutes, or until tender. Drain and peel. Return potatoes to saucepan and toss with butter and parsley.

About 6 servings

Note: Snipped chives, grated lemon peel, and lemon juice may be used instead of parsley.

352 *Hash Brown Potatoes au Gratin*

1 package (2 pounds) frozen chopped hash brown potatoes, partially defrosted
1½ teaspoons salt
Few grains pepper
¼ cup coarsely chopped green pepper
1 jar (2 ounces) sliced pimentos, drained and chopped
2 cups milk
¾ cup fine dry enriched bread crumbs
⅓ cup soft butter
⅔ cup shredded pasteurized process sharp American cheese

1. Turn potatoes into a buttered shallow 2-quart baking dish, separating into pieces. Sprinkle with salt and pepper. Add green pepper and pimentos; mix lightly. Pour milk over potatoes. Cover with aluminum foil.
2. Cook in a 350°F oven 1¼ hours, or until potatoes are fork-tender. Remove foil; stir potatoes gently. Mix bread crumbs, butter, and cheese. Spoon over top of potatoes. Return to oven and heat 15 minutes, or until cheese is melted.

About 6 servings

353 *Potato Pancakes*

Butter or margarine (enough, melted, for a ¼-inch layer)
2 tablespoons flour
1½ teaspoons salt
¼ teaspoon baking powder
⅛ teaspoon ground black pepper
6 medium potatoes, washed
2 eggs, well beaten

1. Heat butter in a heavy skillet over low heat.
2. Combine flour, salt, baking powder, and pepper and set aside.
3. Pare and finely grate potatoes; set aside.
4. Combine flour mixture with eggs and onion.
5. Drain liquid from grated potatoes; add potatoes to egg mixture and beat thoroughly.
6. When butter is hot, spoon batter into skillet, allowing

1 teaspoon grated onion
Applesauce or maple syrup,
warmed

about 2 tablespoonfuls for each pancake and leaving about 1 inch between cakes. Cook over medium heat until golden brown and crisp on one side. Turn carefully and brown on other side. Drain on absorbent paper. Serve with applesauce or maple syrup.

About 20 pancakes

354 Lacy French-Fried Onion Rings

1 cup enriched all-purpose flour
1 teaspoon baking powder
¼ teaspoon salt
1 egg, well beaten
1 cup milk
1 tablespoon vegetable oil
4 sweet Spanish onions
Fat for deep frying heated to 375°F
Salt or garlic salt

1. Blend flour, baking powder, and salt.
2. Combine egg, milk, and oil in a bowl and beat until thoroughly blended. Beat in the dry ingredients until batter is smooth. Cover.
3. Cut off root ends of onions; slip off the loose skins. Slice onions ¼ inch thick and separate into rings.
4. Using a long-handled two-tined fork, immerse a few onion rings at a time into the batter, lift out and drain over bowl a few seconds before dropping into heated fat. Turn only once as they brown; do not crowd.
5. When rings are golden brown on both sides, lift out and drain on absorbent paper-lined cookie sheet. Sprinkle with salt and serve hot.

About 6 servings

Lacy Cornmeal Onion Rings: Follow recipe for Lacy French-Fried Onion Rings. Substitute ½ **cup enriched cornmeal** for ⅔ cup flour.

355

To Freeze French-Fried Onions: Leaving the crisp, tender rings on the absorbent paper-lined cookie sheet on which they were drained, place in freezer and freeze quickly. Then carefully remove rings to moisture-vaporproof containers with layers of absorbent paper between each layer of onions; the rings may overlap some. Cover tightly, label, and freeze.

To Reheat Frozen French-Fried Onions: Removing the desired number of onion rings, arrange them (frozen) in a single layer on a cookie sheet. Heat in a 375°F oven several minutes, or until rings are crisp and hot.

356 Turnip Custard

2 pounds turnips
1 egg, well beaten
¼ cup finely crushed soda crackers
⅔ cup (6-ounce can) undiluted
    evaporated milk
1 teaspoon salt
Few grains black pepper
1 cup (about 4 ounces) shredded
    sharp Cheddar cheese

1. Wash, pare, and cut turnips into pieces. Cook, uncovered, in boiling water to cover until turnips are tender, 15 to 20 minutes; drain. Mash and, if necessary, again drain turnips (about 2 cups mashed turnips).
2. Blend mashed turnips, egg, cracker crumbs, evaporated milk, salt, and pepper. Turn mixture into a buttered 1¼-quart baking dish. Set dish in a pan and pour in boiling water to a 1-inch depth.
3. Bake at 350°F 15 minutes. Sprinkle cheese over top. Bake 5 minutes, or until a knife inserted halfway between center and edge comes out clean. Remove from water immediately.

About 6 servings

357 *Cracked-Wheat-Stuffed Tomatoes*

½ cup cracked wheat or bulgur
1½ cups hot water
6 firm medium tomatoes, rinsed
⅛ teaspoon *each* sugar, salt, and
   pepper
3 tablespoons crushed dried mint
3 tablespoons warm water
1 small ripe avocado
1½ teaspoons salt
½ teaspoon sugar
2 tablespoons lemon juice
⅓ cup olive oil
¼ cup finely chopped green onion
¼ cup snipped parsley

1. Combine cracked wheat and hot water; set aside 30 minutes. Drain cracked wheat thoroughly and set aside.
2. Peel tomatoes. Cut off and discard a ½-inch slice from the top of each. Seed tomatoes. Scoop out pulp, chop it, and turn into a sieve to drain. Invert tomatoes on absorbent paper to drain 30 minutes. Mix ⅛ teaspoon sugar, ⅛ teaspoon salt, and pepper; sprinkle over pulp and insides of tomatoes.
3. Combine dried mint and warm water; set aside 15 minutes. Squeeze dry.
4. Peel avocado; put pulp into a bowl and mash with a fork. Beat in 1½ teaspoons salt, ½ teaspoon sugar, and lemon juice. Add oil in a thin stream, beating constantly. Mix in drained cracked wheat, tomato pulp, mint, green onion, and parsley. Fill tomatoes. Chill.

6 servings

358 *Spinach Gnocchi*

1½ cups milk
1 tablespoon butter or margarine
¼ teaspoon salt
   Few grains nutmeg
¼ cup farina
½ cup well-drained cooked chopped
   spinach
1 egg, well beaten
1 tablespoon chopped onion, lightly
   browned in 1 teaspoon butter
   or margarine
1½ cups (about 6 ounces) shredded
   Swiss cheese
2 eggs, well beaten
¾ cup milk
1 tablespoon flour
1 teaspoon salt
   Few grains nutmeg

1. Combine milk, butter, salt, and few grains nutmeg in a saucepan. Bring to boiling and add farina gradually, stirring constantly. Cook over low heat until mixture thickens.
2. Stir in spinach, egg, cooked onion, and 1 cup cheese; blend well. Set aside to cool slightly.
3. Drop mixture by tablespoonfuls close together in a well-greased shallow 9-inch baking dish or casserole. Sprinkle remaining cheese over mounds.
4. For topping, combine eggs, milk, flour, salt, and few grains nutmeg, blending well. Pour over spinach mixture in baking dish.
5. Bake at 350°F 35 to 40 minutes, or until golden brown on top. Serve at once.

4 to 6 servings

359 Apple-Stuffed Acorn Squash

2 acorn squash
2 tart apples
1½ teaspoons grated fresh lemon peel
1 tablespoon fresh lemon juice
¼ cup butter or margarine, melted
⅓ cup firmly packed brown sugar
Salt
Cinnamon
Apple and lemon slices for garnish (optional)

1. Cut squash into halves lengthwise and scoop out seedy centers. Place cut side down in baking dish and pour in boiling water to a ½-inch depth. Bake at 400°F 20 minutes.
2. Pare, core, and dice apples; mix with lemon peel and juice, 2 tablespoons butter, and brown sugar.
3. Invert squash halves and brush with remaining 2 tablespoons butter; sprinkle with salt and cinnamon.
4. Fill squash halves with apple mixture. Pour boiling water into dish to a ½-inch depth; cover and bake 30 minutes.
5. Before serving, spoon pan juices over squash. If desired, garnish with apple and lemon slices.

4 servings

360 Spinach-Bacon Soufflé

2 cups firmly packed, finely chopped fresh spinach (dry the leaves before chopping)
¼ cup finely chopped green onions with tops
½ pound sliced bacon, cooked, drained, and crumbled
3 tablespoons butter or margarine
¼ cup enriched all-purpose flour
½ teaspoon salt
¼ to ½ teaspoon thyme
1 cup milk
3 egg yolks, well beaten
4 egg whites
2 teaspoons shredded Parmesan cheese

1. Toss the spinach, green onions, and bacon together in a bowl; set aside.
2. Heat butter in a saucepan over low heat. Blend in flour, salt, and thyme. Stirring constantly, heat until bubbly. Add milk gradually, continuing to stir. Bring rapidly to boiling and boil 1 to 2 minutes, stirring constantly.
3. Remove from heat and blend spinach-bacon mixture into the sauce. Stir in the beaten egg yolks; set aside to cool.
4. Meanwhile, beat egg whites until rounded peaks are formed (peaks turn over slightly when beater is slowly lifted upright); do not overbeat.
5. Gently spread spinach-bacon mixture over the beaten egg whites. Carefully fold together until ingredients are just blended.
6. Turn mixture into an ungreased 2-quart soufflé dish (straight-sided casserole); sprinkle top with Parmesan cheese.
7. Bake at 350°F 40 minutes, or until a knife comes out clean when inserted halfway between center and edge of soufflé and top is lightly browned. Serve immediately.

6 servings

361 Spinach-Cheese Bake

2 packages (10 ounces each) frozen chopped spinach
3 eggs, beaten
¼ cup enriched all-purpose flour
1 teaspoon seasoned salt
¼ teaspoon ground nutmeg
¼ teaspoon ground black pepper
2 cups (16 ounces) creamed cottage cheese
2 cups (8 ounces) shredded Swiss or Cheddar cheese

1. Cook spinach following package directions; drain.
2. Combine eggs, flour, seasoned salt, nutmeg, and pepper in a bowl. Mix in cottage cheese, Swiss cheese, and spinach.
3. Turn into a buttered 1½-quart casserole.
4. Bake at 325°F 50 to 60 minutes.

6 to 8 servings

362 *Vegetable-Rice Medley*

3 tablespoons butter or margarine
¾ cup chopped onion
1½ pounds zucchini, thinly sliced
1 can (16 ounces) whole kernel
　golden corn, drained
1 can (16 ounces) tomatoes
　(undrained)
3 cups cooked enriched white rice
1½ teaspoons salt
¼ teaspoon ground black pepper
¼ teaspoon ground coriander
¼ teaspoon oregano leaves

Heat butter in a large saucepan. Add onion and zucchini; cook until tender, stirring occasionally. Add corn, tomatoes with liquid, cooked rice, salt, pepper, coriander, and oregano; mix well. Cover and bring to boiling; reduce heat and simmer 15 minutes.

About 8 servings

363 *Stuffed Baked Sweet Potatoes*

4 medium sweet potatoes, washed
1 small ripe banana, peeled
2 tablespoons butter or margarine
⅓ cup fresh orange juice
1 tablespoon brown sugar
1½ teaspoons salt
¼ cup chopped pecans

1. Bake sweet potatoes at 375°F 45 minutes to 1 hour, or until tender when tested with a fork.
2. Cut a lengthwise slice from each potato. Scoop out sweet potatoes into a bowl; reserve shells. Mash banana with potatoes; add butter, orange juice, brown sugar, and salt and beat thoroughly. Spoon mixture into shells. Sprinkle with pecans. Set on a cookie sheet.
3. Return to oven 12 to 15 minutes, or until heated.

4 servings

364 *Zucchini Boats*

8 medium zucchini, washed and ends
　removed
1 medium tomato, cut in small pieces
¼ cup chopped salted almonds
1 tablespoon chopped parsley
1 teaspoon finely chopped onion
½ teaspoon seasoned salt
2 teaspoons butter, melted
¼ cup cracker crumbs

1. Cook zucchini in boiling salted water until crisp-tender, 7 to 10 minutes. Drain; cool.
2. Cut zucchini lengthwise into halves; scoop out and discard centers. Chop 2 shells coarsely; set remaining shells aside. Put chopped zucchini and tomato into a bowl. Add almonds, parsley, onion, and seasoned salt; mix well.
3. Spoon filling into zucchini shells. Mix butter and cracker crumbs. Sprinkle over filling. Set on a cookie sheet.
4. Place under broiler 4 inches from heat. Broil 3 minutes, or until crumbs are golden.

6 servings

365 *German-Style Green Beans*

A savory hot bacon sauce flavored with beer is poured over green beans with palate-pleasing results. Serve with an unsauced main dish.

2 packages (9 ounces each) frozen green beans
4 slices bacon, cut in ½-inch pieces
⅓ cup finely chopped onion
¼ to ½ cup beer
2 tablespoons sugar
¼ teaspoon salt
Dash pepper

1. Cook beans according to package directions.
2. Meanwhile, fry bacon in a skillet until lightly browned. Add onion, beer, sugar, salt, and pepper. Heat to boiling.
3. Drain beans, pour beer mixture over, and toss lightly.

6 to 8 servings

366 *Beets Piquant*

¼ cup sugar
1 tablespoon cornstarch
1 teaspoon salt
½ teaspoon caraway seed
6 to 8 whole cloves
¼ cup water
1 cup beer
1 can (16 ounces) sliced beets, drained

1. In a medium saucepan, combine sugar, cornstarch, salt, caraway seed, and cloves.
2. Gradually add water and beer while stirring. Cook, stirring constantly, until thickened.
3. Add beets; heat through.

4 servings

367 *French-Style Peas*

2 cups shelled peas (see Note)
8 small boiling onions, cut in half
1 cup shredded lettuce
1 teaspoon sugar
2 teaspoons snipped parsley
2 teaspoons clarified butter
½ teaspoon salt
¼ teaspoon freshly ground pepper
¾ cup water

Combine all ingredients except water; let stand 1 hour, stirring occasionally. Transfer mixture to a saucepan; add water. Simmer covered until peas and onions are tender (about 15 minutes). Serve hot.

4 servings

Note: Two packages (10 ounces each) frozen peas can be substituted in this recipe; do not mix with other ingredients. Add to saucepan during last 5 minutes of cooking.

368 *Brussels Sprouts and Grapes*

1½ pounds fresh Brussels sprouts, cut in half
1 can or bottle (12 ounces) beer
2 teaspoons butter, melted
¼ teaspoon salt
⅛ teaspoon freshly ground white pepper
1 cup seedless white grapes
Snipped parsley

1. Simmer Brussels sprouts in beer in a covered saucepan until tender (about 8 minutes); drain.
2. Drizzle butter over sprouts; sprinkle with salt and pepper. Add grapes; heat thoroughly. Sprinkle with parsley.

6 servings

369 *Red Cabbage, Danish Style*

⅓ cup butter or margarine
1 head red cabbage (2 pounds), coarsely shredded
1 can or bottle (12 ounces) beer
⅔ cup red currant jelly
½ teaspoon salt

1. Melt butter in a large, heavy saucepan. Add cabbage; cook about 5 minutes to soften, turning frequently.
2. Stir in beer, jelly, and salt. Cover and simmer about 1½ hours, removing cover during last 30 minutes to evaporate most of liquid; stir occasionally.

10 servings, ½ cup each

370 *French-Fried Onion Rings in Beer Batter*

These light, crisp onion rings have a batter featuring a hint of beer flavor. The batter may also be used for fresh mushrooms.

1¼ cups flour
1 teaspoon baking powder
1 teaspoon salt
2 tablespoons shortening
1 egg, beaten
1 cup beer
1 large sweet Spanish onion
Oil for deep frying

1. Mix flour, baking powder, and salt in a bowl. Cut in shortening until mixture resembles fine crumbs.
2. Add egg and beer; beat until smooth.
3. Cut onion into ¼-inch-thick slices; separate into rings.
4. Using a fork, immerse a few onion rings at a time in the batter. Lift out; allow excess batter to drip off. Drop into hot oil (375°F). Fry until golden brown, turning once. Drain on paper towels. Serve hot.

50 to 60 rings; 6 to 8 servings

371 *Hash Brown Potatoes*

The potatoes absorb beer while boiling, giving the dish an unusual flavor.

6 medium boiling potatoes (2 pounds), pared and cubed
1 can or bottle (12 ounces) beer
⅓ cup chopped onion
⅓ cup chopped green pepper
¼ cup butter or margarine
½ teaspoon salt
Dash pepper

1. In a covered saucepan, boil potatoes in beer until just tender, but not mushy. Remove potatoes with a slotted spoon; chop finely.
2. Add onion and green pepper to saucepan. Add water, if needed, to just cover. Simmer, uncovered, about 5 minutes, or until tender. Drain. Mix with potatoes, salt, and pepper.
3. In a skillet, heat butter until very hot and beginning to brown. Add potato mixture. Cook over medium high heat, turning occasionally, until browned.

6 servings

372 *Beer Pilaff*

Substitute beer for water when cooking rice, and the rice takes on an intriguing flavor.

1 medium onion, chopped
2 tablespoons butter or margarine
1 chicken bouillon cube, or 1 teaspoon chicken stock base
¼ teaspoon salt
Dash pepper
¾ cup uncooked rice (not instant)
1 can or bottle (12 ounces) beer

1. Sauté onion in butter until soft.
2. Add bouillon, salt, and pepper; stir. Add rice. Cook and stir 1 minute.
3. Add beer. (If package directions specify more than 1½ cups liquid for ¾ cup uncooked rice, use water to make up the difference.)
4. Heat to boiling. Cover, reduce heat, and simmer for 15 minutes, or until tender.

2¾ cups; 4 or 5 servings

373 *Vegetable Salad with Yogurt Dressing*

Vivid colors dominate this unusual salad combination.

¾ cup Low-Fat Yogurt
2 tablespoons snipped parsley
½ cup finely chopped dill pickle
½ cup chopped tomato
1 teaspoon salt
1 cup sliced radishes
1 medium zucchini, shredded
2 medium carrots, shredded
1 large beet, shredded

1. Mix yogurt, parsley, pickle, chopped tomato, and salt; refrigerate covered 1 hour.
2. Arrange radish slices around edge of a serving plate. Arrange zucchini, carrots, and beet decoratively in center of plate. Serve yogurt mixture with salad.

4 servings

374 *Layered Casserole*

1 can (14½ ounces) asparagus spears, drained
1 can (17 ounces) green peas
1 can (8½ ounces) water chestnuts, drained and sliced
2 tablespoons chopped pimento
½ cup fine dry bread crumbs
1 can (10¾ ounces) condensed cream of mushroom soup
½ cup (2 ounces) shredded American cheese

1. Arrange asparagus spears in bottom of a 1½-quart shallow baking dish.
2. Drain peas, reserving ¼ cup liquid. Top asparagus spears with peas, water chestnuts, and pimento. Sprinkle with ¼ cup bread crumbs.
3. Combine soup with reserved ¼ cup pea liquid. Evenly spread over bread crumbs. Sprinkle with remaining ¼ cup bread crumbs and cheese.
4. Bake, uncovered, at 350°F 20 minutes, or until heated through.

6 servings

375 *Marinated Artichoke Hearts Supreme*

2 jars (6 ounces each) marinated artichoke hearts
1 garlic clove, minced
½ cup chopped onion
4 eggs, beaten
¼ cup fine dry bread crumbs
2 tablespoons snipped parsley
½ teaspoon salt
½ teaspoon oregano
¼ teaspoon pepper
¼ teaspoon Tabasco
2 cups (8 ounces) shredded Cheddar cheese

1. Cut up artichoke hearts, reserving liquid from 1 jar.
2. Pour liquid into a skillet and sauté garlic and onion.
3. Combine with eggs, bread crumbs, parsley, salt, oregano, pepper, and Tabasco. Stir in cheese and artichoke hearts. Pour into a greased 1½-quart shallow baking dish.
4. Bake, uncovered, at 325°F 30 minutes, or until set.

6 servings

376 *Sweet-and-Sour Green Beans*

8 bacon slices, cut in 1-inch pieces
½ cup sugar
1 tablespoon cornstarch
1 cup vinegar
1 large onion, thinly sliced
2 cans (16 ounces each) cut green
beans, drained

1. Fry bacon in a skillet.
2. Combine sugar and cornstarch. Blend in vinegar. Add to bacon and drippings in a skillet, stirring until thickened.
3. Put onion and beans into a 1½-quart casserole. Stir in vinegar mixture.
4. Bake, covered, at 300°F 1 hour, stirring once.

6 servings

377 *Spicy Lima Beans*

6 bacon slices, cut up
½ cup chopped onion
2 tablespoons flour
¼ teaspoon salt
Dash pepper
1 bay leaf
1 can (16 ounces) tomatoes
(undrained)
2 packages (10 ounces each) frozen
lima beans, cooked and drained
½ cup fine dry bread crumbs
2 tablespoons butter or margarine,
melted

1. Fry bacon and onion in a skillet. Stir in flour, salt, pepper, and bay leaf. Gradually add tomatoes and juice, stirring until thickened.
2. Add lima beans. Put into a 1½-quart casserole.
3. Combine bread crumbs and butter. Sprinkle over beans.
4. Bake, covered, at 350°F 20 minutes. Remove cover and bay leaf. Bake an additional 10 minutes, or until heated through.

6 servings

378 *Broccoli Casserole*

¼ cup chopped onion
¼ cup butter or margarine
2 teaspoons flour
½ cup water
1 jar (8 ounces) pasteurized process
cheese spread
2 packages (10 ounces each) frozen
chopped broccoli, thawed and
squeezed
3 eggs, well beaten
½ cup buttered bread crumbs

1. Sauté onion in butter in a skillet. Stir in flour. Gradually add water, stirring until thickened and smooth.
2. Blend in cheese until melted. Combine with broccoli and eggs. Pour into a greased 1½-quart casserole. Sprinkle with bread crumbs.
3. Bake, uncovered, at 350°F 45 minutes, or until set.

6 servings

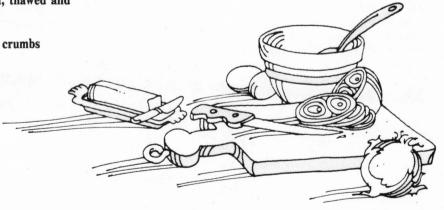

379 *Broccoli Bake*

2 packages (10 ounces each) frozen
    chopped broccoli, cooked and
    drained
1 can (10¾ ounces) condensed cream
    of mushroom soup
½ cup mayonnaise
1 cup (4 ounces) shredded Cheddar
    cheese
1 tablespoon lemon juice
½ cup crumbled cheese crackers

1. Spread broccoli in bottom of 10x6-inch baking dish.
2. Combine soup, mayonnaise, cheese, and lemon juice. Spread over broccoli. Sprinkle with cracker crumbs.
3. Bake, uncovered, at 350°F 30 minutes, or until heated through.

6 servings

380 *Broccoli-Mushroom Casserole*

1 package (10 ounces) frozen chopped
    broccoli, cooked and drained
1 can (4 ounces) mushroom slices,
    drained
2 tablespoons chopped pimento
⅓ cup dairy sour cream
½ cup chopped celery
½ teaspoon salt
    Dash pepper

1. Combine all ingredients. Put into a 1-quart casserole.
2. Bake, covered, at 350°F 25 minutes, or until heated through.

3 servings

381 *Brussels Sprouts in Broth*

2 packages (10 ounces each) frozen
    Brussels sprouts, cooked and
    drained
1 cup water
1 beef bouillon cube
2 tablespoons butter or margarine
½ cup (2 ounces) freshly grated
    Parmesan cheese

1. Put Brussels sprouts into a 1-quart casserole.
2. Heat together water, bouillon cube, and butter. Pour over Brussels sprouts. Sprinkle with cheese.
3. Bake, covered, at 325°F 20 minutes, or until heated through.

6 servings

Note: To improve flavor, cover and refrigerate Brussels sprouts, broth, and butter overnight. Add cheese before baking.

382 *Carrot-Apricot Casserole*

1 package (11 ounces) dried apricots
1 can (12 ounces) apricot nectar
2 jars (16 ounces each) tiny whole
    Belgian carrots, drained
½ cup firmly packed brown sugar
4 tablespoons butter or margarine
¼ cup slivered almonds

1. Soak apricots in nectar overnight.
2. Put 1 jar carrots into a 2-quart casserole. Top with half the apricots, half the apricot nectar, and ¼ cup brown sugar.
3. Dot with 2 tablespoons butter; repeat layers. Sprinkle with almonds.
4. Bake, covered, at 350°F 30 minutes, or until bubbly.

8 servings

383 *Marmalade Carrots*

4 cups thinly sliced carrots
⅓ cup orange juice
½ teaspoon salt
¼ teaspoon ginger
⅓ cup orange marmalade
1 tablespoon butter or margarine

1. Combine carrots, orange juice, salt, ginger, and marmalade.
2. Put into a 1½-quart casserole. Dot with butter.
3. Bake, covered, at 350°F 30 minutes, or until carrots are tender. If desired, sprinkle with snipped parsley.

8 servings

384 *Brandied Carrots*

4 cups thinly sliced carrots
¼ cup butter or margarine
¼ cup water
1 teaspoon lemon juice
½ teaspoon salt
¼ teaspoon pepper
¼ cup brandy
2 tablespoons snipped parsley

1. Put carrots into a large saucepan. Add butter and water. Cover and cook over moderate heat, stirring occasionally, until carrots are just crisp-tender (about 15 minutes).
2. Add lemon juice, salt, pepper, and brandy.
3. Put into a 1½-quart casserole. Cover and refrigerate overnight.
4. Bake, covered, at 350°F 30 minutes, or until heated through. Sprinkle with parsley.

8 servings

385 *Cabbage Casserole*

1 head cabbage, cut in 6 wedges
1½ cups (6 ounces) shredded Cheddar
    cheese
¼ cup butter or margarine
¼ cup flour
½ teaspoon seasoned salt
½ teaspoon sugar
⅛ teaspoon garlic powder
1¾ cups milk

1. Cook cabbage in **boiling salted water** about 10 minutes, or until tender.
2. Layer cabbage and 1 cup cheese in a 2-quart casserole.
3. Melt butter in a saucepan. Stir in flour, seasoned salt, sugar, and garlic powder. Gradually add milk, stirring until thickened and smooth.
4. Pour over cabbage. Sprinkle with remaining ½ cup cheese.
5. Bake, covered, at 350°F 20 minutes, or until heated through. If desired, sprinkle with paprika.

6 servings

386 *Sour Red Cabbage*

1 head red cabbage, shredded
1 onion, finely chopped
2 cooking apples, cored and cut up
¼ cup red wine vinegar
¼ cup water
1 tablespoon firmly packed brown
    sugar
1 teaspoon salt
¼ teaspoon pepper
1 tablespoon butter

1. Combine all ingredients, except butter.
2. Put into a 2-quart casserole. Dot with butter.
3. Bake, covered, at 350°F 1 hour, or until cabbage is tender.

6 servings

387 *Scalloped Corn and Broccoli*

¼ cup chopped onion
2 tablespoons butter or margarine
1 tablespoon flour
1¼ cups milk*
1 cup (4 ounces) shredded Cheddar
    cheese
1 can (12 ounces) whole kernel corn,
    drained
2 packages (10 ounces each) frozen
    broccoli spears, cooked and
    drained

1. Sauté onion in butter in a skillet. Stir in flour. Gradually add milk, stirring until thickened and smooth.
2. Add cheese, stirring until melted. Stir in corn.
3. Arrange broccoli in a 2-quart shallow baking dish.
4. Pour corn sauce over broccoli.
5. Bake, uncovered, at 350°F 30 minutes, or until heated through.

8 servings

* One-fourth cup of the drained corn liquid can be substituted for ¼ cup of the milk.

388 Creole Eggplant

1 eggplant
1¼ teaspoons salt
2 tablespoons butter or margarine
2 tablespoons flour
1 can (28 ounces) tomatoes (undrained)
½ cup chopped onion
½ cup chopped green pepper
2 tablespoons firmly packed brown sugar
¼ teaspoon pepper
¼ cup buttered bread crumbs

1. Pare and cut eggplant into cubes. Sprinkle with 1 teaspoon salt. Let stand 15 minutes.
2. Rinse and drain eggplant. Cook in **boiling water** 10 minutes; drain. Put into a 1½-quart casserole.
3. Melt butter in a saucepan. Stir in flour. Gradually add tomatoes and liquid, stirring until thickened.
4. Add onion, green pepper, brown sugar, pepper, and the remaining ¼ teaspoon salt. Pour over eggplant.
5. Bake, covered, at 350°F 15 minutes. Remove cover; sprinkle with bread crumbs. Bake an additional 5 minutes, or until heated through.

4 to 6 servings

389 Italian Eggplant Casserole

1 large eggplant
¼ cup milk
1 egg, beaten
½ cup fine dry bread crumbs
1 teaspoon salt
¼ cup shortening
1 can (8 ounces) tomato paste
1 can (8 ounces) spaghetti sauce
8 ounces mozzarella cheese, thinly sliced
½ cup (2 ounces) grated Parmesan cheese

1. Pare eggplant and cut into ¼-inch slices.
2. Combine milk and egg. Also combine bread crumbs and salt.
3. Dip eggplant into milk mixture, then bread crumbs. Fry eggplant in shortening in a skillet. Drain on absorbent paper.
4. Combine tomato paste and spaghetti sauce.
5. Alternate layers of half the eggplant, half the sauce, and half the mozzarella cheese in a 2-quart casserole. Repeat layers. Sprinkle with Parmesan cheese.
6. Bake, covered, at 350°F 30 minutes, or until heated through.

8 servings

Paprika Buttered Fish Fillets, page 362

390 *Carrot Soufflé*

3 tablespoons butter or margarine
3 tablespoons flour
1 cup milk
1 teaspoon sugar
½ teaspoon salt
¼ teaspoon pepper
2 cups mashed cooked carrots (about 1 pound fresh)
3 eggs, separated

1. Melt butter in a saucepan. Stir in flour. Gradually add milk, stirring until thickened and smooth.
2. Blend in sugar, salt, pepper, and mashed carrots. Beat in egg yolks.
3. Beat egg whites until stiff but not dry. Fold in carrot mixture. Divide in 2 buttered 1½-quart casseroles.
4. Bake, uncovered, in hot water bath at 325°F 50 minutes, or until set.

8 servings

391 *Vegetable Spoon Bread*

1 cup cornmeal
1½ teaspoons salt
1 cup cold milk
1½ cups milk, scalded
1 tablespoon butter or margarine
1 can (16 ounces) mixed vegetables, drained
5 bacon slices, cooked and crumbled
4 egg yolks
4 egg whites, beaten stiff but not dry

1. Combine cornmeal, salt, and cold milk. Add to scalded milk. Cook until thickened (about 5 minutes), stirring constantly.
2. Remove from heat; add butter, vegetables, and bacon.
3. Beat egg yolks until thick and lemon colored. Stir a small amount of cornmeal mixture into egg yolks; add egg mixture to cornmeal, stirring constantly. Fold in beaten egg white.
4. Pour into a greased 2-quart casserole or soufflé dish.
5. Bake, uncovered, at 350°F 50 to 60 minutes, or until set. Serve immediately.

6 servings

Sweet & Sour Chicken, page 341

392 *Broccoli-Stuffed Onions*

3 medium sweet Spanish onions
2 tablespoons butter or margarine
2 tablespoons flour
¼ teaspoon salt
1 cup milk
1 package (3 ounces) cream cheese,
    cut in cubes
1 package (10 ounces) frozen chopped
    broccoli, cooked and drained
½ cup (2 ounces) grated Parmesan
    cheese
1 teaspoon lemon juice

1. Peel and halve onions. Cook in **boiling salted water** 10 minutes; drain. Remove centers, leaving a ½-inch edge. Chop center portion to equal ½ cup.*
2. Melt butter in a saucepan. Stir in flour and salt. Gradually add milk, stirring until thickened and smooth. Add cream cheese, stirring until smooth.
3. Stir in broccoli, Parmesan cheese, lemon juice, and chopped onion. Spoon into onion halves. Place in a 2-quart shallow baking dish.
4. Bake, uncovered, at 375°F 20 minutes, or until heated through.

6 servings

* Use remaining onion in other casserole mixtures.

393 *Barbecue Potatoes*

8 potatoes
3 tablespoons flour
2¼ cups water
¾ cup barbecue sauce
1 tablespoon vinegar
2 teaspoons salt
2 small onions, thinly sliced
    Paprika
1 tablespoon snipped parsley

1. Pare and thinly slice potatoes. Sprinkle with flour.
2. Combine water, barbecue sauce, vinegar, and salt in a large saucepan. Stir in potato and onion. Simmer 5 minutes, stirring frequently.
3. Pour into a 3-quart casserole.
4. Bake, covered, at 350°F 1 hour, or until potatoes are tender. Sprinkle with paprika and parsley.

8 servings

394 *Mushroom Business*

1 pound fresh mushrooms, thickly
    sliced
¼ cup butter or margarine
7 slices white bread, buttered
½ cup chopped onion
½ cup chopped celery
½ cup chopped green pepper
½ cup mayonnaise
¾ teaspoon salt
¼ teaspoon pepper
2 eggs, slightly beaten
1½ cups milk
1 can (10¾ ounces) condensed cream
    of mushroom soup
1 tablespoon grated Parmesan cheese

1. Sauté mushrooms in butter in a skillet; set aside.
2. Cut 3 slices bread into 1-inch cubes. Put into a 2½-quart casserole.
3. Combine mushrooms, onion, celery, green pepper, mayonnaise, salt, and pepper. Spoon on top of bread cubes.
4. Cut 3 slices bread into 1-inch cubes and put onto mushroom mixture.
5. Combine eggs and milk. Pour over mushroom mixture. Cover and refrigerate at least 1 hour.
6. Remove from refrigerator; uncover and spoon soup overall.
7. Cut remaining slice bread into 1-inch cubes; arrange over soup. Sprinkle with Parmesan cheese.
8. Bake, uncovered, at 300°F 60 to 70 minutes, or until mixture is set.

8 servings

395 *Mashed Potato Casserole*

2 pounds potatoes
⅓ to ½ cup milk
¼ cup butter or margarine
¼ cup chopped green pepper
1 package (3 ounces) cream cheese, cut in cubes
½ cup dairy sour cream
1 teaspoon salt
1 teaspoon onion salt
Dash pepper

1. Cook potatoes in **boiling water;** drain. Mash with milk and butter.
2. Beat in remaining ingredients. Put into a 1½-quart casserole.
3. Bake, covered, at 350°F 40 minutes, or until heated through. Garnish with **parsley** and **paprika.**

6 servings

396 *Potato-Mushroom Casserole*

3 cups sliced potatoes (about 4 medium)
1 cup sliced fresh mushrooms
1 onion, thinly sliced
3 beef bouillon cubes
1½ cups boiling water
¼ teaspoon salt
¼ teaspoon thyme
Dash pepper

1. Put potatoes, mushrooms, and onion into a 1½-quart casserole.
2. Dissolve bouillon cubes in boiling water. Add salt, thyme, and pepper. Pour over vegetables.
3. Bake, covered, at 350°F 30 minutes. Remove cover and bake an additional 15 minutes, or until vegetables are tender.

6 servings

397 *Potato Stuffing*

2 cups chopped pared potatoes
¼ cup butter or margarine
1 medium apple, chopped
¾ cup chopped onion
1 garlic clove, minced
2 tablespoons snipped parsley
1 cup unflavored croutons
1½ teaspoons salt
1 egg, beaten
½ cup milk

1. Sauté potatoes in butter in a skillet 10 minutes, or until lightly browned.
2. Add remaining ingredients. Put into a 1½-quart casserole.
3. Bake, covered, at 325°F 30 minutes, or until heated through.

6 servings

398 *Deluxe Scalloped Potatoes*

1 package (5.5 ounces) scalloped
  potatoes
2 tablespoons butter or margarine
2½ cups boiling water
⅔ cup milk
⅓ cup crumbled blue cheese

1. Empty potato slices into a 1½-quart casserole. Sprinkle with sauce mix.
2. Stir in butter, water, milk, and blue cheese.
3. Bake, uncovered, at 400°F 30 to 35 minutes, or until potatoes are tender. Let stand a few minutes before serving.

4 servings

399 *Apple-Honey Sweet Potatoes*

4 sweet potatoes
4 cooking apples
½ cup honey
¼ teaspoon nutmeg

1. Bake sweet potatoes at 350°F 45 minutes, or until tender.
2. Core apples and cut into thin slices. (To avoid darkening, brush with lemon juice.)
3. Peel baked potatoes and cut into ½-inch-thick slices.
4. Alternate layers of potatoes and apples in a greased 2½-quart casserole. Drizzle with honey and sprinkle with nutmeg.
5. Bake, covered, at 350°F 20 minutes, or until heated through.

6 servings

400 *Pecan Sweet Potatoes*

¼ cup butter or margarine
2 tablespoons cornstarch
¾ cup firmly packed brown sugar
½ teaspoon salt
2 cups orange juice
2 cans (23 ounces each) sweet
  potatoes, drained
¼ cup chopped pecans

1. Melt butter in a saucepan. Blend cornstarch, brown sugar, and salt; mix with butter. Gradually add orange juice, stirring until thickened and clear.
2. Put sweet potatoes into a 1½-quart casserole. Pour sauce over sweet potatoes. Sprinkle with pecans.
3. Bake, covered, at 350°F 45 minutes, or until heated through.

8 servings

401 *Spinach Bake*

2 packages (10 ounces each) frozen chopped spinach, thawed and drained
2 cups milk
6 eggs
½ teaspoon salt
1 tablespoon instant minced onion
¾ cup (3 ounces) shredded Swiss cheese

1. Blend spinach, milk, eggs, and salt in a blender.
2. Pour into an 8-inch square baking dish. Sprinkle with onion and cheese.
3. Bake, uncovered, at 325°F 45 minutes, or until set. Let stand a few minutes. Cut into squares to serve.

6 servings

402 *Spinach-Artichoke Casserole*

1 jar (6 ounces) marinated artichoke hearts, drained
2 packages (10 ounces each) frozen chopped spinach, cooked and squeezed
1 package (8 ounces) cream cheese, softened
2 tablespoons butter or margarine, softened
¼ cup milk
½ teaspoon freshly ground pepper
¼ cup (1 ounce) grated Parmesan cheese

1. Put artichoke hearts into a 1½-quart casserole.
2. Spread spinach over artichoke hearts.
3. Beat together cream cheese and butter. Gradually add milk, beating until smooth. Spread over spinach.
4. Sprinkle pepper and Parmesan cheese over top.
5. Bake, covered, at 350°F 30 minutes. Remove cover. Garnish with **pimento strips** and **hard-cooked egg slices.** Bake an additional 10 minutes, or until heated through.

6 servings

403 *Spinach and Rice*

1 package (10 ounces) frozen chopped spinach, cooked and drained
1 can (10¾ ounces) condensed cream of mushroom soup
1½ cups boiling water
1⅓ cups packaged precooked rice
⅛ teaspoon garlic powder
1 teaspoon lemon juice
2 hard-cooked eggs, sliced
¾ cup (3 ounces) shredded Cheddar cheese
1 can (3 ounces) French-fried onions

1. Combine spinach, soup, boiling water, rice, garlic powder, and lemon juice. Put into a 1½-quart shallow baking dish.
2. Bake, covered, at 400°F 25 minutes, or until rice is tender. Remove cover and stir. Arrange eggs over top. Sprinkle with cheese. Place onions around edge. Bake an additional 5 minutes, or until cheese is melted.

4 servings

404 *Spinach Pudding*

¼ cup chopped onion
¼ cup chopped green pepper
2 tablespoons butter or margarine
1 tablespoon flour
1 teaspoon salt
1 cup milk
2 packages (10 ounces each) frozen chopped spinach, cooked and drained
2 eggs, well beaten

1. Sauté onion and green pepper in butter in a skillet. Stir in flour and salt. Gradually add milk, stirring until thickened and smooth. Remove from heat.
2. Stir in spinach and eggs. Pour into a greased 1-quart casserole. Set casserole in pan of hot water 1 inch deep.
3. Bake, uncovered, at 350°F 30 minutes, or until set. If desired, garnish with pimento strips.

6 servings

405 *Layered Tomato Casserole*

1 cup sliced celery
4 tablespoons butter or margarine
¾ teaspoon basil
½ teaspoon salt
¼ teaspoon pepper
3 tomatoes, sliced
1 large onion, sliced
1 garlic clove, minced
⅓ cup fine dry bread crumbs

1. Put celery into a 1½-quart casserole.
2. Dot with 1 tablespoon butter. Sprinkle with a little basil, a little salt, and a dash of pepper. Repeat with a layer of tomatoes and a layer of onion.
3. Sauté garlic in remaining 1 tablespoon butter. Stir in bread crumbs. Sprinkle over onion.
4. Bake, covered, at 350°F 30 minutes, or until vegetables are tender.

6 servings

406 *Baked Tomato Pudding*

1 can (20 ounces) tomatoes (undrained)
⅔ cup firmly packed brown sugar
1 teaspoon salt
½ cup water
4 slices white bread, cut in ½-inch cubes (about 3 cups)
½ cup butter or margarine, melted

1. Force tomatoes through a sieve into a saucepan; add brown sugar, salt, and water. Bring to a boil; boil 5 minutes.
2. Put bread crumbs into a 1½-quart casserole. Pour melted butter over bread cubes. Add tomato mixture and stir.
3. Bake, uncovered, at 350°F 45 minutes.

6 servings

407 *Sue's Best Zucchini*

4 small zucchini, thinly sliced
¾ cup shredded carrot
½ cup chopped onion
6 tablespoons butter or margarine, melted
2½ cups herb stuffing cubes
1 can (10¾ ounces) condensed cream of mushroom soup
½ cup dairy sour cream

1. Combine all ingredients. Put into a 1½-quart casserole.
2. Bake, covered, at 350°F 30 to 40 minutes, or until zucchini is tender, stirring once.

6 servings

408 *Sauerkraut Casserole*

1 tablespoon butter or margarine
2 large onions, chopped
6½ cups drained sauerkraut, snipped
2 medium apples, quartered, cored, and diced
1 small carrot, pared and shredded
2 medium potatoes, shredded (about 1½ cups)
½ cup dry white wine
1 to 2 tablespoons brown sugar
2 teaspoons caraway seed
½ teaspoon seasoned pepper
Brown sugar
Apple, thinly sliced

1. Heat butter in a skillet. Add onion and cook, stirring occasionally, until crisp-tender, 3 to 5 minutes.
2. Meanwhile, combine kraut, diced apple, carrot, and potato in a large bowl. Toss until mixed.
3. Add onion, wine, 1 to 2 tablespoons brown sugar, caraway seed, and seasoned pepper. Toss again. Turn into a 2-quart casserole; sprinkle generously with brown sugar.
4. Overlap thinly sliced apple on top; sprinkle again with brown sugar.
5. Heat in a 350°F oven until thoroughly heated and apples are tender.

10 to 12 servings

409 *Beets in Red Wine Sauce*

2 tablespoons butter
1 shallot, minced
2 tablespoons flour
1 jar or can (16 ounces) beets, drained and ⅓ cup liquid reserved
⅓ cup beef bouillon
⅓ cup red wine
Ground cloves (optional)

1. Melt butter in a saucepan; stir in minced shallot. Add flour, stirring constantly for 1 minute.
2. Blend reserved beef liquid, bouillon, and red wine into flour mixture; bring to boiling, stirring until sauce is smooth and thick. Sprinkle lightly with cloves, if desired.
3. Add beets and heat thoroughly.

4 to 6 servings

410 *Red Cabbage and Wine*

1 head (about 2 pounds) red
   cabbage
1 cup red wine
⅓ cup firmly packed brown sugar
1 teaspoon salt
   Few grains cayenne pepper
4 medium apples
¼ cup cider vinegar
¼ cup butter

1. Remove and discard wilted outer leaves of cabbage. Rinse, cut into quarters (discarding core), and coarsely shred (about 2 quarts, shredded). Put cabbage into a saucepan with wine, brown sugar, salt, and pepper.
2. Rinse, quarter, core, and pare apples. Add the apples to the saucepan.
3. Cover and simmer over low heat 20 to 30 minutes, or until cabbage is tender. Add vinegar and butter. Toss together lightly until butter is melted.

6 servings

411 *Celery Coronado*

3 celery hearts
1 tablespoon green pepper,
   chopped
¼ cup butter or margarine
1 cup chicken bouillon or broth
½ cup dry white wine, such as
   sauterne
1 small jar pimentos
   Sliced almonds, sautéed

1. Wash celery and split lengthwise. Sauté celery and green pepper in butter, turning celery gently.
2. Add bouillon and wine. Cover and cook over low heat until celery is tender-crisp.
3. Remove celery to heat-resistant platter and keep warm in oven.
4. Reduce the sauce until it has a glazed appearance. Pour it over the celery. Garnish with strips of pimento and sautéed almonds.

4 to 6 servings

412 *Mushrooms in Wine Sauce on Toast*

1 cup water
½ cup white wine
3 tablespoons butter
1 pound fresh mushrooms,
   cleaned
1 tablespoon flour
   Juice of ½ lemon
1 egg yolk
¼ cup light cream
4 slices toast, sliced diagonally

1. Combine water, wine, and 1 tablespoon of the butter; add to the mushrooms in a saucepan. Bring to boiling; cover and let simmer 10 minutes. Drain, reserving broth.
2. Heat 2 tablespoons butter and blend in flour. Gradually add reserved broth, stirring constantly. Bring to boiling; stir and cook 1 to 2 minutes.
3. Thinly slice the mushrooms; mix into sauce with lemon juice. Cook 5 minutes.
4. Beat the egg yolk with cream. Gradually add mushroom mixture and mix well. Serve mushrooms on toast points.

4 servings

413 *Celery and Green Pepper au Gratin*

4 cups diagonally sliced celery
2 green peppers, thinly sliced
¼ cup dry sherry
3 tablespoons butter or
   margarine, melted
1 cup soft bread crumbs
½ cup crumbled blue cheese

1. Cook celery and green pepper, covered, in a small amount of boiling salted water until crisp-tender (about 5 minutes); drain. Turn vegetables into a shallow 1½-quart baking dish and drizzle with 3 tablespoons sherry.
2. Mix remaining sherry with butter and toss with bread crumbs and blue cheese. Spoon over vegetables.
3. Set under broiler with top 3 to 4 inches from heat. Broil until top is lightly browned.

6 to 8 servings

414 *Sweet and Sour Red Cabbage*

1 head (2 pounds) red cabbage
4 tablespoons brown sugar
1 teaspoon salt
½ cup beef bouillon
¼ cup cider vinegar
4 slices bacon, diced
4 tablespoons butter
2 medium cooking (sour) apples, pared and sliced
1 cup red wine

1. Discard tough, outer leaves of cabbage and shred, as for cole slaw.
2. Combine brown sugar, salt, bouillon, and vinegar as a marinade. Let cabbage stand in marinade 1 hour or longer. (This cabbage is limp when served so can be marinated as long as you wish.)
3. Cook bacon until crisp; drain bacon pieces, and pour off all but 2 tablespoons of bacon fat.
4. Melt butter in bacon fat. Add cabbage, marinade and all. Arrange apples on top of cabbage. Cover and cook slowly 1 hour.
5. Add wine, cover, and simmer 30 minutes.

6 servings

415 *Macaroni Vegetable Medley au Vin*

2 cups (8 ounces) elbow macaroni
1 package (10 ounces) frozen mixed vegetables
2 tablespoons butter or margarine
3 ounces fresh mushrooms, chopped
½ cup chopped onion
1 can (about 10 ounces) condensed cream of celery soup
1 soup can milk
2 teaspoons Worcestershire sauce
1 teaspoon salt
¼ teaspoon white pepper
1 teaspoon dry mustard
½ cup dry sherry or dry white wine
¼ cup chopped pimento
1 cup cooked peas
½ pound Swiss cheese, shredded
Chopped parsley
Pimento strips

1. Cook macaroni and frozen vegetables following directions on package. Drain and set aside.
2. Heat butter in a skillet; add mushrooms and onion. Cook, stirring occasionally, until onion is soft; set aside.
3. In a large bowl mix soup, milk, Worcestershire sauce, salt, white pepper, dry mustard, and wine. Add chopped pimento, peas, cheese, mushroom mixture, mixed vegetables, and macaroni; mix well. Turn into a greased 2½-quart casserole.
4. Bake at 300°F until thoroughly heated, about 30 minutes. Garnish with chopped parsley and pimento strips.

About 8 servings

Meat

416 *Italian-Style Meat Stew*

¼ cup olive oil
1 pound lean beef for stew (1½-inch cubes)
1 pound lean lamb for stew (1½-inch cubes)
1 can (28 ounces) tomatoes (undrained)
1½ cups boiling water
1½ cups chopped onion
1 cup diced celery
2 teaspoons salt
½ teaspoon ground black pepper
4 large potatoes, pared and quartered (about 3 cups)
5 large carrots, pared and cut in strips (about 2 cups)
1 teaspoon basil, crushed
¼ teaspoon garlic powder
½ cup cold water
¼ cup enriched all-purpose flour

1. Heat oil in a large saucepot or Dutch oven; add meat and brown on all sides.
2. Add undrained tomatoes, boiling water, onion, celery, salt, and pepper to saucepot. Cover and simmer 1 to 1½ hours, or until meat is almost tender.
3. Add potatoes, carrots, basil, and garlic powder to saucepot; mix well. Simmer 45 minutes, or until meat and vegetables are tender when pierced with a fork.
4. Blend cold water and flour; add gradually to meat-and-vegetable mixture, stirring constantly. Bring to boiling and continue to stir and boil 1 to 2 minutes, or until sauce is thickened. (Leftover sauce may be served the following day on mashed potatoes.)

8 to 10 servings

417 Oxtail Stew

½ cup enriched all-purpose flour
1 teaspoon salt
¼ teaspoon ground black pepper
3 oxtails (about 1 pound each), disjointed
3 tablespoons butter or margarine
1½ cups chopped onion
1 can (28 ounces) tomatoes, drained (reserve liquid)
1½ cups hot water
4 medium potatoes, pared
6 medium carrots, pared
2 pounds fresh peas, shelled
1 tablespoon paprika
1 teaspoon salt
¼ teaspoon ground black pepper
¼ cup cold water
2 tablespoons flour

1. Mix ½ cup flour, 1 teaspoon salt, and ¼ teaspoon pepper in a plastic bag; coat oxtail pieces evenly by shaking two or three at a time.
2. Heat butter in a 3-quart top-of-range casserole. Add onion and cook until soft. Remove onion with a slotted spoon and set aside.
3. Put meat into casserole and brown on all sides. Return onion to casserole. Pour in the reserved tomato liquid (set tomatoes aside) and hot water. Cover tightly and simmer 2½ to 3 hours, or until meat is almost tender when pierced with a fork.
4. When meat has cooked about 2 hours, cut potatoes and carrots into small balls, using a melon-ball cutter. Cut the tomatoes into pieces.
5. When meat is almost tender, mix in potatoes, carrots, peas, paprika, 1 teaspoon salt, and ¼ teaspoon pepper. Cover and simmer 20 minutes. Stir in tomatoes and cook 10 minutes, or until meat and vegetables are tender. Put meat and vegetables into a warm dish.
6. Blend cold water and 2 tablespoons flour; add half gradually to cooking liquid, stirring constantly. Bring to boiling; gradually add only what is needed of remaining flour mixture for desired gravy consistency. Bring to boiling after each addition. Cook 3 to 5 minutes after final addition. Return meat and vegetables to casserole and heat thoroughly.

6 to 8 servings

418 Sauerbraten Moderne

1 cup wine vinegar
1 cup water
1 medium onion, thinly sliced
2 tablespoons sugar
1 teaspoon salt
5 peppercorns
3 whole cloves
1 bay leaf
2 pounds beef round steak (¾ inch thick), boneless, cut in cubes
1 lemon, thinly sliced
2 tablespoons butter or margarine
1 can (10¾ ounces) beef gravy
1 can (3 ounces) broiled sliced mushrooms (undrained)
6 gingersnaps, crumbled (about ⅔ cup)
Cooked noodles

1. Combine vinegar, water, onion, sugar, salt, peppercorns, cloves, and bay leaf in a saucepan. Heat just to boiling.
2. Meanwhile, put meat into a large shallow dish and arrange lemon slices over it. Pour hot vinegar mixture into dish. Cover and allow to marinate about 2 hours.
3. Remove and discard peppercorns, cloves, bay leaf, and lemon slices; reserve onion. Drain meat thoroughly, reserving marinade.
4. Heat butter in a skillet over medium heat. Add meat and brown pieces on all sides. Stir 1 cup of the reserved liquid with the onion into skillet. Cover, bring to boiling, reduce heat, and simmer about 45 minutes.
5. Blend beef gravy and mushrooms with liquid into mixture in skillet. Bring to boiling and simmer, loosely covered, about 20 minutes longer, or until meat is tender.
6. Add the crumbled gingersnaps to mixture in skillet and cook, stirring constantly, until gravy is thickened. Serve over noodles.

6 to 8 servings

419 *Short Ribs, Western Style*

4 medium onions, peeled and
    quartered
2 teaspoons salt
¼ teaspoon ground black pepper
½ teaspoon rubbed sage
1 quart water
1 cup dried lima beans
3 tablespoons flour
1 teaspoon dry mustard
2 to 3 tablespoons fat
2 pounds beef rib short ribs, cut in
    serving-size pieces

1. Combine onions, salt, pepper, sage, and water in a large heavy saucepot or Dutch oven. Cover, bring to boiling, reduce heat, and simmer 5 minutes. Bring to boiling again; add lima beans gradually and cook, uncovered, 2 minutes. Remove from heat, cover, and set aside to soak 1 hour.
2. Meanwhile, mix flour and dry mustard and coat short ribs evenly.
3. Heat fat in a large heavy skillet and brown short ribs on all sides over medium heat. Add meat to soaked lima beans. Bring to boiling and simmer, covered, 1½ hours, or until beans and meat are tender.

About 6 servings

420 *Kidney Bean Rice Olympian*

2 tablespoons olive oil
1½ pounds beef round steak,
    boneless, cut in 1-inch cubes
2 teaspoons salt
¼ teaspoon ground black pepper
2 large cloves garlic, crushed in a
    garlic press
2 cups beef broth
1 cup sliced celery
1 can (16 ounces) tomatoes, cut in
    pieces (undrained)
2 cans (16 ounces each) kidney
    beans (undrained)
1 large green pepper, diced
3 cups hot cooked rice
1 large head lettuce, finely shredded
3 medium onions, peeled and
    coarsely chopped

1. Heat olive oil in a large heavy skillet. Add meat and brown on all sides. Add salt, pepper, and garlic; pour in beef broth. Bring to boiling, reduce heat, and simmer, covered, about 1 hour.
2. Stir celery and tomatoes and beans with liquid into beef in skillet; bring to boiling and simmer, covered, 30 minutes. Add green pepper and continue cooking 30 minutes.
3. To serve, spoon rice onto each serving plate, cover generously with shredded lettuce, and spoon a generous portion of the bean mixture over lettuce. Top each serving with about 3 tablespoons chopped onion.

About 8 servings

421 *Lamb Crown Roast with Mint Stuffing*

8 slices enriched white bread,
    toasted and cubed
1 unpared red apple, cored and
    diced
1½ tablespoons coarsely chopped
    mint or 1½ teaspoons dried
    mint flakes
¾ teaspoon poultry seasoning

1. Combine toasted bread cubes, apple, mint, poultry seasoning, and salt in a large bowl.
2. Heat butter in a saucepan. Mix in celery and onion and cook about 5 minutes. Pour over bread mixture along with water; toss lightly.
3. Place lamb on a rack, rib ends up, in a shallow roasting pan. Fill center with stuffing.
4. Roast in a 325°F oven about 2½ hours, or until a meat

½ teaspoon salt
6 tablespoons butter
½ cup chopped celery
¼ cup chopped onion
½ cup water
1 lamb rib crown roast (5 to 6 pounds)

thermometer registers 175° to 180°F (depending on desired degree of doneness).

5. Place roast on a heated serving platter. Prepare gravy, if desired. Accompany with Parsley-Buttered New Potatoes (page 68) and Butter-Sauced Asparagus (page 65).

About 8 servings

422 *Lamb Kabobs*

1½ pounds lamb (leg, loin, or shoulder), boneless, cut in 1½-inch cubes
½ cup vegetable oil
1 tablespoon lemon juice
2 teaspoons sugar
½ teaspoon salt
½ teaspoon paprika
¼ teaspoon dry mustard
⅛ teaspoon ground black pepper
¼ teaspoon Worcestershire sauce
1 clove garlic, cut in halves
6 small whole cooked potatoes
6 small whole cooked onions
Butter or margarine, melted
6 plum tomatoes

1. Put lamb cubes into a shallow dish. Combine oil, lemon juice, sugar, salt, paprika, dry mustard, pepper, Worcestershire sauce, and garlic. Pour over meat. Cover and marinate at least 1 hour in refrigerator, turning pieces occasionally. Drain.

2. Alternately thread lamb cubes, potatoes, and onions on 6 skewers. Brush pieces with melted butter.

3. Broil 3 to 4 inches from heat about 15 minutes, or until lamb is desired degree of doneness; turn frequently and brush with melted butter. Shortly before kabobs are done, impale tomatoes on ends of skewers.

6 servings

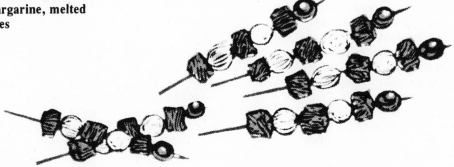

423 *Oven Lamb Stew*

2 pounds lean lamb shoulder, boneless, cut in 2-inch cubes
1¾ teaspoons salt
¼ teaspoon thyme, crushed
1 bay leaf
4 whole allspice
2 tablespoons chopped parsley
1 clove garlic, minced
¼ small head cabbage, shredded
2 leeks, thinly sliced
2 medium onions, sliced
1 cup sliced raw potatoes
4 cups water
8 small onions
4 carrots, cut in 2-inch pieces
2 white turnips, quartered

1. Put lamb into a Dutch oven. Season with salt, thyme, bay leaf, allspice, parsley, and garlic. Add cabbage, leeks, sliced onions, and potatoes. Pour in water. Cover tightly and bring rapidly to boiling.

2. Cook in a 350°F oven about 1½ hours, or until meat is tender.

3. About 30 minutes before cooking time is ended, cook whole onions, carrots, and turnips separately in boiling salted water until tender. Drain.

4. Turn contents of Dutch oven into a food mill set over a large bowl. Return meat to the Dutch oven and add the cooked onions, carrots, and turnips. Discard bay leaf and allspice; force the vegetables through food mill into the bowl containing cooking liquid (or purée vegetables in an electric blender). Heat with meat and vegetables.

6 to 8 servings

424 *Company Beef and Peaches*

1 can (8 ounces) tomato sauce with
    onions
1 can (8 ounces) sliced peaches,
    drained; reserve syrup
¾ cup beef broth
2 tablespoons brown sugar
2 tablespoons lemon juice
1 tablespoon prepared mustard
1 teaspoon Worcestershire sauce
1 clove garlic, minced
1 beef round bottom round roast or
    eye round roast, boneless (2 to 3
    pounds)
    Vegetable oil
    Salt and seasoned pepper
2 tablespoons cold water
2 teaspoons cornstarch
    Watercress or parsley

1. Turn the tomato sauce with onions into a bowl. Mix in the peach syrup (set peaches aside), beef broth, brown sugar, lemon juice, prepared mustard, Worcestershire sauce, and garlic. Set aside.
2. Cut meat across the grain into 6 to 8 slices, about ¾ inch thick.
3. Heat oil in a large skillet. Add the meat slices and brown on both sides. Sprinkle with salt and seasoned pepper. Pour the sauce mixture over the meat. Bring to boiling, reduce heat, and simmer, covered, about 1½ hours, or until meat is fork-tender; turn meat slices occasionally.
4. Overlap meat slices to one side of a heated serving platter.
5. Blend water and cornstarch; stir into sauce in skillet. Bring to boiling; cook about 1 minute. Mix in sliced peaches and heat thoroughly; spoon to the side of meat on the platter. Cover meat with sauce. Garnish with watercress.

6 to 8 servings

425 *Red-Topper Meat Loaf*

Meat loaf:
2 tablespoons butter or margarine
¾ cup finely chopped onion
¼ cup chopped green pepper
1½ pounds lean ground beef
½ pound bulk pork sausage
1 cup uncooked oats, quick or old
    fashioned
2 eggs, beaten
¾ cup tomato juice
¼ cup prepared horseradish
2 teaspoons salt
1 teaspoon dry mustard
½ teaspoon monosodium glutamate

Topping:
1 to 3 tablespoons brown sugar
1 teaspoon dry mustard
¼ cup ketchup

1. For meat loaf, heat butter in a skillet. Mix in onion and green pepper; cook about 5 minutes, or until onion is soft.
2. Meanwhile, lightly mix beef, sausage, and oats in a large bowl. Combine eggs, tomato juice, horseradish, salt, dry mustard, and monosodium glutamate; add to meat mixture and mix lightly. Turn into a 9×5×3-inch loaf pan and press lightly.
3. For topping, mix brown sugar with dry mustard and blend in ketchup. Spread over meat loaf.
4. Bake at 375°F about 1 hour. Remove from oven and allow meat to stand several minutes before slicing.

About 8 servings

426 *Liver-Apple Bake*

1 pound sliced beef liver (about ¼
    inch thick)
2 cups chopped apple
½ cup chopped onion
2 teaspoons seasoned salt
⅛ teaspoon ground black pepper
4 slices bacon, cut in thirds
    Parsley sprigs

1. Remove tubes and outer membrane from liver, if necessary. Put liver slices into a greased shallow baking dish.
2. Combine apple, onion, seasoned salt, and pepper; toss to mix. Spoon over liver. Arrange bacon pieces over top. Cover dish.
3. Cook in a 325°F oven 1 hour. Remove cover and continue cooking about 15 minutes.
4. Garnish with parsley.

4 servings

427 *Roast Leg of Lamb*

1 teaspoon salt
½ teaspoon monosodium glutamate
½ teaspoon ground black pepper
1 teaspoon seasoned salt
½ teaspoon ground marjoram
¼ teaspoon dry mustard
⅛ teaspoon ground cardamom
1 lamb leg, whole (about 6 pounds)
2 cloves garlic, cut in slivers
½ teaspoon ground thyme
Orange peel, cut in slivers
Fresh mint sprigs (optional)

1. Mix salt, monosodium glutamate, pepper, seasoned salt, marjoram, dry mustard, and cardamom; rub over lamb. Cut about 16 deep slits in roast. Toss garlic and thyme together. Insert garlic in each slit along with a sliver of orange peel.
2. Place lamb, fat side up, on a rack in a shallow roasting pan. Insert meat thermometer in center of thickest portion of meat.
3. Roast, uncovered, in a 325°F oven 2½ to 3 hours. Meat is medium done when thermometer registers 175°F and is well done at 180°F.
4. Remove meat thermometer. Place roast on a warm serving platter. Put a paper frill around end of leg bone and garnish platter with mint, if desired.

About 10 servings

428 *Pork Loin Roast*

1 pork loin roast (4 to 6 pounds)
Salt and pepper
Spiced crab apples

1. Have the meat retailer saw across the rib bones of roast at base of the backbone, separating the ribs from the backbone. Place roast, fat side up, on a rack in an open roasting pan. Season with salt and pepper. Insert meat thermometer in roast so the bulb is centered in the thickest part and not resting on bone or in fat.
2. Roast in a 350°F oven about 2½ to 3 hours, or until thermometer registers 170°F; allow 30 to 40 minutes per pound.
3. For easy carving, remove backbone, place roast on platter, and allow roast to set for 15 to 20 minutes. Garnish platter with spiced crab apples, heated if desired. Accompany with Hash Brown Potatoes au Gratin ●

8 to 10 servings

429 *Veal Glacé*

1 cup dry white wine
1½ teaspoons tarragon leaves
1½ pounds veal cutlets (about ¼ inch thick)
3 tablespoons butter
½ teaspoon salt
⅛ teaspoon ground black pepper
½ cup condensed consommé (undiluted)
½ cup dry vermouth

1. Stir tarragon into white wine. Cover; allow to stand several hours, stirring occasionally.
2. Cut meat into pieces about 3×2 inches. Heat butter in skillet until lightly browned. Add meat and brown lightly. Season with salt and pepper. Reduce heat and pour in tarragon wine mixture with the consommé and vermouth. Simmer uncovered, about 10 minutes, or until veal is tender.
3. Remove veal to a heated dish and cover. Increase heat under skillet and cook sauce until it is reduced to a thin glaze (about 10 minutes), stirring occasionally.
4. Pour glaze over meat, turning meat to coat evenly. Serve hot.

About 6 servings

Note: If desired, accompany with buttered fluffy rice tossed with chopped parsley and toasted slivered almonds.

430 *Curried Veal and Vegetables*

1 **pound veal for stew (1-inch cubes)**
2 **cups water**
1 **teaspoon salt**
3 **medium carrots, pared and cut in quarters**
½ **pound green beans**
2 **large stalks celery, cut in ½-inch slices**
3 **tablespoons butter or margarine**
2 **tablespoons flour**
½ **teaspoon curry powder**
¼ **teaspoon salt**
   Cooked rice
   Fresh parsley, snipped

1. Put veal into a large saucepan with water and 1 teaspoon salt. Cover, bring to boiling, reduce heat, and simmer 1 hour. Add carrots, green beans, and celery. Cover, bring to boiling, and simmer 1 hour, or until meat is tender.
2. Remove meat and vegetables from broth with a slotted spoon; set aside. Reserve broth.
3. Heat butter in a saucepan. Blend in flour, curry powder, and ¼ teaspoon salt. Heat until bubbly. Add reserved broth gradually, stirring until smooth. Bring to boiling, stirring constantly, and cook 1 to 2 minutes. Mix in meat and vegetables. Heat thoroughly.
4. Serve over rice. Sprinkle with parsley.

About 6 servings

431 *Saucy Ham Loaf*

Meat loaf:
1½ **pounds ground cooked ham**
½ **pound ground veal**
½ **pound ground pork**
2 **eggs, fork beaten**
½ **teaspoon salt**
⅛ **teaspoon ground black pepper**
½ **teaspoon ground nutmeg**
½ **teaspoon dry mustard**
¼ **teaspoon ground thyme**
¼ **cup finely chopped onion**
½ **cup finely chopped green pepper**
2 **tablespoons finely chopped parsley**
¾ **cup soft enriched bread crumbs**
¾ **cup apple juice**

Sauce:
⅔ **cup packed light brown sugar**
2 **teaspoons cornstarch**
1 **teaspoon dry mustard**
1 **teaspoon ground allspice**
⅔ **cup apricot nectar**
3 **tablespoons lemon juice**
2 **teaspoons vinegar**

1. Combine ham, veal, and pork with eggs, salt, pepper, nutmeg, dry mustard, and thyme in a large bowl. Add onion, green pepper, and parsley and toss to blend. Add bread crumbs and apple juice; mix thoroughly but lightly. Turn into a 9×5×3-inch loaf pan and flatten top.
2. Bake at 350°F 1 hour.
3. Meanwhile, prepare sauce for topping. Blend brown sugar, cornstarch, dry mustard, and allspice in a small saucepan. Add apricot nectar, lemon juice, and vinegar. Bring rapidly to boiling and cook about 2 minutes, stirring constantly. Reduce heat and simmer 10 minutes to allow flavors to blend.
4. Remove meat loaf from oven; pour off and reserve juices. Unmold loaf in a shallow baking pan. Spoon some of the reserved juices and then the sauce over loaf. Return to oven 30 minutes.
5. Place loaf on a warm platter and garnish as desired.

8 to 10 servings

432 *Canadian-Style Bacon and Peaches*

Roast Canadian-Style Bacon:
- 2 pounds smoked pork loin Canadian-style bacon (in one piece)
- 10 whole cloves

Orange-Spiced Peaches:
- ½ cup firmly packed brown sugar
- ⅓ cup red wine vinegar
- 1 tablespoon grated orange peel
- 2 tablespoons orange juice
- 1 teaspoon whole cloves
- ½ teaspoon whole allspice
- 1 can (29 ounces) peach halves, drained; reserve 1½ cups syrup
- Mustard Sauce

1. Remove casing from the meat and place, fat side up, on a rack in a shallow roasting pan. Stud with cloves. Insert a meat thermometer into bacon so bulb is centered. Roast, uncovered, at 325°F about 2 hours, or until thermometer registers 160°F.
2. For Orange-Spiced Peaches, stir brown sugar, wine vinegar, orange peel, orange juice, cloves, allspice, and peach syrup together in a saucepan. Bring to boiling; reduce heat and simmer 5 minutes. Mix in peaches and heat 5 minutes.
3. Remove from heat and allow peaches to cool in syrup. Refrigerate until ready to serve.
4. Shortly before meat is roasted, prepare Mustard Sauce.
5. Remove meat from oven and place on a heated serving platter. Remove thermometer. Arrange peaches on platter. Accompany with Mustard Sauce in a bowl.

About 8 servings

Mustard Sauce: Mix **1 cup firmly packed brown sugar, 2 tablespoons prepared mustard, 1 tablespoon butter or margarine, 3 tablespoons cider vinegar** in a saucepan. Stir over low heat until sugar is dissolved; heat thoroughly, stirring occasionally.

⅔ cup sauce

433 *Savory Sweetbreads*

- 1½ pounds sweetbreads
- Cold water
- ¼ cup lemon juice
- 1 teaspoon salt
- 1½ cups beef broth
- 2 stalks celery with leaves, cut in 1-inch pieces
- 2 sprigs parsley
- ¼ teaspoon savory
- ¼ teaspoon thyme
- ⅛ teaspoon ground allspice
- ⅛ teaspoon ground nutmeg
- ⅓ cup butter or margarine
- 2 tablespoons flour
- 2 teaspoons dry mustard
- 1 teaspoon monosodium glutamate
- ⅛ teaspoon ground black pepper
- 1 tablespoon vinegar
- ¼ cup coarsely snipped parsley
- Melba toast (optional)

1. Rinse sweetbreads with cold water as soon as possible after purchase. Put sweetbreads into a saucepan. Cover with cold water and add lemon juice and salt. Cover saucepan, bring to boiling, reduce heat, and simmer 20 minutes. Drain sweetbreads; cover with cold water. Drain again. (Cool and refrigerate if sweetbreads are not to be used immediately.) Remove tubes and membrane; reserve. Separate sweetbreads into smaller pieces and slice; set aside.
2. Pour broth into a saucepan. Add the tubes and membrane, celery, parsley, savory, thyme, allspice, and nutmeg. Bring to boiling and simmer, covered, 30 minutes. Strain broth, reserving 1 cup.
3. Heat butter in a skillet. Blend in flour, dry mustard, monosodium glutamate, and pepper. Heat until bubbly. Add the reserved broth and vinegar while stirring until smooth. Bring to boiling, stirring constantly, and cook until thickened. Add the sweetbreads and parsley. Heat thoroughly.
4. Serve over Melba toast, if desired.

About 6 servings

434 *Flemish Beef Stew (Carbonnade à la Flamande)*

This world-famous dish of beef, beer, and onions is from Belgium. "Carbonnade" originally meant meat grilled over hot coals or embers, but in this dish it now means slow stewing. It makes a savory, guest-pleasing party dish for a buffet dinner. Spoon it over noodles and complete the menu with a tossed salad, French bread, cake, and steins of beer to drink.

4 pounds beef chuck or round, boneless, cut in 1-inch cubes
¼ cup oil
2 tablespoons parsley flakes
2 teaspoons each thyme, sugar, and salt
½ teaspoon pepper
2 garlic cloves, minced
2 bay leaves
2 cans or bottles (12 ounces each) beer
8 medium onions, sliced
¼ cup cornstarch

1. Brown meat in oil; place in a very large casserole or two medium ones, about 2½ quarts each. Add seasonings; stir to coat meat.
2. Add beer plus a little water, if needed, to almost cover meat. Cover casseroles.
3. Bake at 300°F 1½ hours.
4. Parboil onion half covered with water, stirring frequently, until soft. Stir into meat. Cover and continue baking 1 to 1½ hours, or until meat is tender.
5. Make a paste of cornstarch and a little water. Stir into casseroles. Return to oven about 10 minutes, stirring once or twice. Serve over **noodles**.

12 to 14 servings

435 *Munich Beef*

This German-style oven beef stew has a sweet-sour gravy.

1 can or bottle (12 ounces) beer
1 medium onion, chopped
½ teaspoon salt
⅛ teaspoon pepper
1½ pounds beef chuck, boneless, cut in 1-inch cubes
4 medium carrots (¾ pound)
3 tablespoons flour
2 tablespoons currant or grape jelly
1 tablespoon grated orange or lemon peel
1 tablespoon lemon juice
4 cups cooked noodles

1. In a 2- to 2½-quart casserole, combine beer, onion, salt, and pepper. Add beef. Cover; marinate in refrigerator 10 to 24 hours, stirring occasionally.
2. Place casserole in oven (do not brown beef).
3. Bake at 300°F 1½ hours. Add carrots. Continue baking 1 hour longer, or until meat and carrots are tender.
4. Mix flour, jelly, peel, and lemon juice to a paste. Stir into stew. Bake 15 minutes more, stirring once or twice, until thickened and bubbly. Serve over noodles.

6 servings

...y Beef Stew

...subtle flavor to the gravy, although it is not a typical beer taste. The alcohol boils off early in the cooking, so the ...e served to children.

...nds beef stew meat,
...oneless, cut in 1½-inch
...ubes
... flour
...spoon salt
...spoon basil
...spoon savory or marjoram
...spoon pepper
...blespoons vegetable oil
... onions, sliced
1 can or bottle (12 ounces) beer
½ cup water
1 bay leaf
5 medium potatoes (1⅔ pounds)
1 pound carrots (8 to 10); or ½
    pound each parsnips and
    carrots

1. Dredge meat in mixture of flour, salt, basil, savory, and pepper. Reserve excess flour. Brown meat in oil. Add onion, beer, water, and bay leaf. Cover and simmer 1½ hours.
2. Pare potatoes; cut into large cubes. Slice carrots and/or parsnips. Add vegetables to stew. If necessary, add a little more water.
3. Cover and simmer 1 hour more, or until meat and vegetables are tender. Make smooth paste of reserved flour mixture and a little water. Stir into stew during last 10 minutes of cooking.

6 servings

437 *Sausage-Stuffed Rouladen with Tomato-Beer Kraut*

1 beef round steak, cut ½ inch
    thick (about 2 pounds)
    Flour
6 smoked link sausages
2 tablespoons oil
2 medium onions, sliced
1 can (16 ounces) sauerkraut,
    rinsed and drained
1 can (16 ounces) tomatoes
    (undrained)
1 can or bottle (12 ounces) beer
2 teaspoons caraway seed
1 teaspoon salt
¼ teaspoon pepper
3 tablespoons flour

1. Cut beef into 6 serving pieces approximately rectangular in shape. Dredge in flour. Pound on a floured board until as thin as possible. Roll each piece around a sausage. Fasten with wooden picks.
2. In a large skillet, brown meat in oil; set aside. Sauté onion in same skillet until golden.
3. Add sauerkraut, undrained tomatoes, beer, caraway seed, salt, and pepper. Stir. Add beef rolls. Cover and simmer 1½ to 2 hours, or until tender.
4. Transfer meat and vegetables to a serving platter, using slotted spoon. Make paste of flour and a little water; stir into cooking liquid. Cook, stirring constantly, until thickened. Pass gravy in sauceboat.

6 servings

438 *Scandinavian Sailors' Beef Casserole*

This dish is frequently served in Scandinavian homes during the winter. It is a time-honored favorite among sailors.

1½ to 2 pounds beef round steak,
    boneless, cut ½ inch thick
    Flour
3 medium onions, sliced
¼ cup margarine, oil, or butter
6 medium potatoes, pared and
    thickly sliced
1 teaspoon salt
¼ teaspoon pepper
1 can or bottle (12 ounces) beer
¼ cup minced parsley (optional)

1. Cut meat into 6 serving pieces. Dredge in flour. Pound to ¼-inch thickness.
2. Sauté onion in 2 tablespoons margarine in a large skillet; set aside.
3. In remaining margarine, brown meat on both sides in same skillet.
4. In a large casserole, layer meat, potatoes, and onion, sprinkling layers with salt and pepper.
5. Pour beer into skillet; stir up brown bits. Add to casserole.
6. Cover and bake at 350°F 1½ hours, or until meat is tender. Sprinkle with parsley. Serve with **pickled beets.**

6 servings

439 *Bachelor's Steak*

A perfect main dish for an intimate dinner for two. Complete the menu with a green vegetable or salad, plus your choice of baked potatoes, white and wild rice, or french-fried potatoes (frozen for ease of preparation). Dessert could be ice cream topped with a liqueur.

2 small single-serving steaks (rib,
    rib eye, strip, T-bone)
1 garlic clove, halved
1 can (2 to 2½ ounces) sliced
    mushrooms
¼ to ⅓ cup beer
1 tablespoon flour
¼ teaspoon salt
    Dash pepper

1. Rub meat with cut surface of garlic. Broil 2 to 3 inches from heat until as done as desired.
2. Meanwhile, drain mushroom liquid into measuring cup. Add enough beer to measure ⅔ cup total liquid.
3. Pour 2 tablespoons steak drippings into a saucepan; stir in flour, salt, and pepper until smooth. Stir in beer mixture. Cook, stirring constantly, until thickened and smooth. Add drained mushrooms; heat through.
4. Pour beer-mushroom sauce over steak and **potatoes.**

2 servings

440 *English Meat Patties*

Similar to Salisbury steaks, this dish is flavored with beer.

1 pound ground beef
½ cup fine dry bread crumbs
½ cup beer
1 small onion, finely minced
½ teaspoon salt
    Dash pepper and garlic powder
    Oil

Gravy:
2 tablespoons drippings
2 tablespoons flour
½ cup beer
½ cup water
1 teaspoon Worcestershire sauce
¼ teaspoon salt
    Dash pepper

1. Combine beef, crumbs, beer, onion, salt, and pepper. Shape into 4 patties.
2. Pan-fry in a very small amount of oil in a skillet, pouring off drippings as they accumulate. Turn once, carefully, and cook until as done as desired. Place patties on a platter; keep warm.
3. For gravy, pour off drippings from skillet; return 2 tablespoons. Stir in flour. Add beer; stir until smooth. Add water and seasonings. Cook, stirring constantly, until thickened; stir up brown bits. After gravy boils, reduce heat and simmer 2 to 3 minutes to mellow beer flavor.

4 servings

Brewerburgers: Follow recipe for English Meat Patties; omit gravy. If desired, broil or grill over coals. 441

442 *Mushroom-Beer Steaks*

1 beef round steak, cut ½ inch
    thick (2 pounds)
Flour for dredging
¼ cup shortening or cooking oil
2 large onions, sliced
2 garlic cloves, minced
1 can or bottle (12 ounces) beer
1 cup beef broth (homemade,
    canned, or from bouillon
    cubes)
¼ cup ketchup
½ teaspoon salt
¼ teaspoon pepper
1 bay leaf
1 can (4½ ounces) mushroom
    stems and pieces
¼ cup flour

1. Cut meat into 6 serving pieces. Pound with meat mallet.
2. Dredge meat in flour. Brown in shortening in a large skillet; set meat aside.
3. Add onion and garlic to skillet, adding more fat if needed. Sauté until golden. Remove.
4. To skillet add beer, broth, ketchup, salt, pepper, and bay leaf. Stir up brown bits.
5. Layer meat and onions in skillet. Cover and simmer 1 to 1½ hours, or until meat is tender. Drain mushrooms, reserving liquid. Add mushrooms during last 5 minutes.
6. Place meat, onions, and mushrooms on serving platter; cover with foil to keep warm. Measure liquid. If needed, add water to measure about 2 cups.
7. Mix ¼ cup flour, mushroom liquid, and just enough water to make a smooth paste. Stir into cooking liquid. Cook, stirring constantly, until thickened. Serve gravy over meat and a **noodle** or **potato** accompaniment.

6 servings

443 *Marinated Venison in Cream Gravy*

This marinade may be used for various kinds of game: rabbit, duck, and other birds. Cut proportions, if necessary.

1 venison roast, preferably from
    leg (4 to 5 pounds)
1 cup chopped onion
⅓ cup oil
2 cans or bottles (12 ounces each)
    beer
2 tablespoons lemon juice
2 teaspoons salt
1 teaspoon thyme
8 peppercorns
2 garlic cloves, minced
1 bay leaf
½ cup cream or half-and-half
    (about)
Flour

1. Place venison in a large glass bowl.
2. Sauté onion in oil. Stir in beer and seasonings. Pour over venison. Marinate in refrigerator 24 to 36 hours, turning occasionally.
3. Place venison and marinade in a Dutch oven. Cover.
4. Bake at 325°F 2½ hours, or until tender, basting several times. (Venison may be cooked a shorter time to rare, only if meat is from a young animal.)
5. Transfer venison to a platter. Strain cooking liquid; skim off most of fat. Measure liquid. Make a paste of cream and 2 tablespoons flour for each 1 cup cooking liquid. Combine the paste in a saucepan with liquid and cook, stirring constantly, until thickened. Season to taste. Serve in a sauceboat along with venison.

2 or 3 servings per pound

444 *Old-World Short Ribs*

Select meaty beef short ribs for this hearty and savory entrée. Serve with noodles, pouring gravy over both. Complete the meal with tossed salad, beverage, and dessert.

3 to 4 pounds beef short ribs
2 tablespoons oil
1 medium onion, chopped
1 can (8 ounces) tomato sauce
1 can or bottle (12 ounces) beer
1 teaspoon caraway seed
½ teaspoon salt
⅛ teaspoon pepper
1 bay leaf
¼ cup flour
2 to 3 cups cooked noodles

1. Brown ribs slowly in oil in a Dutch oven or deep skillet. Remove as they are browned.
2. Add onion and sauté until golden. Add tomato sauce, 1¼ cups beer, and seasonings. Return ribs.
3. Cover and simmer 1½ hours, or until tender.
4. Place ribs on platter; keep warm. Skim fat from cooking liquid (there should be about 2 cups liquid). Stir in paste made from flour and remaining ¼ cup beer. Cook, stirring constantly, until thickened. Serve gravy over ribs and noodles.

4 servings

445 *Caraway Meat Loaf*

With this meat loaf is a beer-flavored chili sauce to be poured over the slices.

1 pound ground beef
1 cup soft bread crumbs (from 2 slices white or rye bread)
1 small onion, minced
⅔ cup beer
1 egg
½ teaspoon caraway seed
½ teaspoon salt
¼ teaspoon pepper
⅓ cup chili sauce

1. Combine beef, crumbs, onion, ⅓ cup beer, egg, caraway seed, salt, and pepper.
2. Shape into a loaf. Place in a roasting pan. (Or pack into a 7 x 3½ x 2-inch loaf pan.)
3. Bake at 350°F 45 minutes.
4. Simmer chili sauce and remaining ⅓ cup beer about 5 minutes; serve over slices of meat loaf.

4 servings

446 *Breaded Pork Chops with Beer Gravy*

4 pork chops, cut ½ to ¾ inch thick
1 egg
1 tablespoon water
½ cup fine cracker crumbs (from about 12 saltines)
½ teaspoon salt
¼ teaspoon paprika
2 tablespoons oil
¾ cup beer
2 tablespoons flour
¾ cup beef bouillon
1 tablespoon ketchup

1. Dip chops in a mixture of egg and water, coating both sides. Mix crumbs, salt, and paprika. Dip egg-coated chops in this mixture, coating both sides well.
2. Brown chops slowly in oil, cooking about 15 minutes. Reduce heat; add ¼ cup beer. Cover and simmer 20 to 30 minutes, or until done.
3. Make a paste of flour and a little remaining beer. Place chops on platter. Stir flour paste, rest of beer, bouillon, and ketchup into cooking liquid. Cook, stirring constantly, until thickened. Season to taste, if desired. (Makes enough gravy to pour over meat and potatoes.)

4 servings

447 *Jiffy Beer Chili (Pronto Chili con Cerveza)*

A thick and savory chili that can be prepared in almost no time at all for cold days

½ pound ground beef
½ cup chopped onion (frozen, or 1 medium fresh)
1 can (6 ounces) tomato paste
1 can or bottle (12 ounces) beer
1 can (16 ounces) kidney beans (undrained)
1 to 1½ teaspoons chili powder
1 teaspoon sugar
1 teaspoon garlic salt
½ teaspoon oregano

1. Lightly brown ground beef and onion in a heavy medium saucepan; cook until onion is soft.
2. Add tomato paste and beer; stir up brown bits.
3. Add remaining ingredients. Cook slowly uncovered 10 to 15 minutes, or until onion is tender. Add a little water, if needed.

5 cups; 4 servings

448 *Applesauce-Topped Beef and Sausage Loaf*

Meat Loaf:
1 pound ground beef
½ pound pork sausage
½ cup dry bread or cracker crumbs
½ cup beer
1 small onion, minced
1 egg, slightly beaten
½ teaspoon salt
¼ teaspoon each sage, thyme, and garlic powder
⅛ teaspoon pepper

Topping and Sauce:
1⅓ cups applesauce
¼ cup beer

1. For meat loaf, mix ingredients. Shape into an elongated loaf. Place in a shallow roasting pan.
2. Bake at 350°F 50 minutes.
3. Spoon fat from pan. Spread ⅓ cup applesauce over meat loaf. Bake 10 minutes longer.
4. For sauce, heat 1 cup applesauce and beer to simmering; serve over meat loaf slices.

6 servings

449 *Bavarian Casserole*

A good use for leftover roast pork.

2 celery stalks, chopped
1 medium onion, chopped
3 tablespoons butter or margarine
½ teaspoon salt
¼ teaspoon sage
¼ teaspoon sugar
⅛ teaspoon pepper
1 cup beer
4 cups pumpernickel bread cubes (5 slices)
2 cups cubed cooked pork (10 ounces)

1. Sauté celery and onion in butter until soft; stir in seasonings. Add beer.
2. Place bread and pork in a 1½-quart casserole. Add beer-vegetable mixture. Stir lightly.
3. Cover and bake at 375°F 30 to 35 minutes.

4 servings

450 Savory Spareribs

4 pounds pork spareribs
1 can or bottle (12 ounces) beer
½ cup honey
2 tablespoons lemon juice
2 teaspoons salt
1 teaspoon dry mustard
¼ teaspoon pepper

1. Cut spareribs into 2-rib sections.
2. Combine remaining ingredients in a shallow glass or ceramic baking dish. Add ribs. Marinate in refrigerator at least 24 hours, turning and basting occasionally.
3. Arrange ribs in a single layer in a large baking pan; reserve marinade.
4. Bake at 350°F 1½ hours, turning once and basting frequently with marinade.

4 to 6 servings

451 Lagered Ham and Noodle Casserole

Beer delicately flavors the cheese sauce in this delicious family-style casserole.

1 medium green pepper, chopped
1 medium onion, chopped
¼ cup butter or margarine
3 tablespoons flour
½ teaspoon dry mustard
½ teaspoon salt
Dash pepper
⅓ cup instant nonfat dry milk
1 can or bottle (12 ounces) beer
1 cup shredded Cheddar cheese (4 ounces)
8 ounces uncooked medium noodles, cooked and drained
2 cups diced cooked ham (⅔ pound)

1. For sauce, slowly sauté green peeper and onion in butter until soft and almost tender. Stir in flour and seasonings.
2. Mix dry milk and ⅓ cup beer.
3. Gradually add remaining beer to flour mixture. Cook, stirring constantly, until thickened and bubbly. Add cheese; stir until melted. Remove from heat; add beer-milk mixture.
4. Combine sauce, cooked noodles, and ham. Turn into a 2½-quart casserole.
5. Bake at 350°F 20 minutes, or until heated through and bubbly.

6 servings

452 Orange-Ginger Lamb Chops

4 lamb leg sirloin or shoulder chops
1 tablespoon oil
¾ teaspoon salt
¼ teaspoon ginger
Dash pepper
1 orange, peeled
1 small to medium onion
1 can or bottle (12 ounces) beer
2 tablespoons sugar
1 tablespoon cornstarch

1. Brown chops in oil in a skillet; pour off fat. Mix salt, ginger, and pepper. Sprinkle over chops.
2. Cut off a thin slice from each end of orange. Cut remainder of orange into 4 slices. Remove seeds. Repeat with onion; do not separate into rings.
3. Top each chop with an orange slice, then an onion slice. Add 1¼ cups beer. Cover and simmer 30 minutes, or until meat is tender.
4. Transfer chops topped with orange and onion to a platter.
5. Mix sugar, cornstarch, and remaining ¼ cup beer. Add to liquid in skillet. Cook, stirring constantly, until thickened. Add dash of salt, if desired. Strain into a sauceboat. Accompany chops with rice, pouring sauce over both.

4 servings

453 *Fruited Pork Roast, Scandinavian Style*

Prunes and apple are stuffed inside a boneless pork roast to create an unusual entrée that's nice for a party or a special family meal. The slices are especially attractive. The sweetened sauce retains just a hint of beer flavor.

1 pork rolled loin roast, boneless, (3 to 3½ pounds)
8 to 10 pitted dried prunes
1 can or bottle (12 ounces) beer
½ teaspoon ginger
1 medium apple, pared and chopped
1 teaspoon lemon juice
½ teaspoon salt
Dash pepper
¼ cup flour

1. Make pocket down center of roast by piercing with a long, sharp tool such as a steel knife sharpener; leave strings on roast. (Alternate method: Remove strings. Using strong knife, cut pocket in pork by making a deep slit down length of loin, going to within ½ inch of the two ends and within 1 inch of other side.)
2. Meanwhile, combine prunes, beer, and ginger in a saucepan; heat to boiling. Remove from heat; let stand 30 minutes.
3. Mix apple with lemon juice to prevent darkening. Drain prunes, reserving liquid; pat dry with paper towels. Mix prunes and apple.
4. Pack fruit into pocket in pork, using handle of wooden spoon to pack tightly. (With alternate method of cutting pocket, tie with string at 1-inch intervals. Secure with skewers or sew with kitchen thread.)
5. Place meat on rack in a roasting pan.
6. Roast at 350°F 2 to 2½ hours, allowing 40 to 45 minutes per pound. During last 45 minutes of roasting, spoon fat from pan; baste occasionally with liquid drained from prunes.
7. Transfer meat to a platter. Skim fat from cooking liquid; measure liquid. Add a little water to roasting pan to help loosen brown bits; add to cooking liquid. Add salt, pepper, and enough additional water to measure 2 cups total. Make a paste of flour and a little more water. Combine with cooking liquid. Cook, stirring constantly, until thickened. Pass in a sauceboat for pouring over meat slices.

8 servings

454 *Piquant Lamb Kabobs*

Grill these colorful kabobs outdoors or broil inside. It's a year-round dish. If you wish, substitute tender beef cubes for the lamb.

1½ pounds boneless lamb (leg or sirloin), cut in 1-inch cubes
18 fresh medium mushrooms (about ½ pound)
¾ cup beer
1 can (6 ounces) pineapple juice (¾ cup)
2 tablespoons oil
2 teaspoons soy sauce
1 garlic clove, quartered
18 cherry tomatoes (about 1 pint)
18 green pepper squares (1 large pepper)
4 to 5 cups cooked rice

1. Place lamb cubes and whole mushrooms in a ceramic casserole.
2. Combine beer, pineapple juice, oil, soy sauce, and garlic. Pour over lamb and mushrooms. Add a little more beer, if needed.
3. Cover and refrigerate at least 6 hours, or overnight.
4. On each of 6 long skewers, alternate lamb cubes with mushrooms, cherry tomatoes, and green pepper squares. Use 3 each of the vegetables for each skewer.
5. Broil 3 inches from heat to desired doneness (about 10 to 15 minutes), turning once or twice. Watch that vegetables do not overcook.
6. Heat marinade to pass as sauce. Serve kabobs on or with rice.

6 servings

455 *Sausage in Beer*

1 can or bottle (12 ounces) beer
3 medium onions, thinly sliced
2 medium carrots, thinly sliced
1 teaspoon Worcestershire sauce
½ teaspoon salt
8 bratwurst, knockwurst, Polish sausage, or large frankfurters
8 frankfurter buns

1. Put beer, onion, carrot, Worcestershire sauce, and salt in a saucepan. Heat to boiling. Cover, reduce heat, and simmer 15 minutes.
2. Add sausage. Cover and simmer 15 minutes more, stirring occasionally.
3. Place sausages in buns. Using a slotted spoon, lift vegetables from liquid and place on sausages.

8 servings

456 *Luxemburg Stew*

2 pounds boneless veal shoulder or stew meat, cut in 1-inch cubes
⅓ cup flour
6 tablespoons butter or margarine
1 large onion, sliced
2 cans (16 ounces each) tomatoes, broken up
1 can or bottle (12 ounces) beer
6 whole cloves
1 teaspoon salt
½ teaspoon thyme
¼ teaspoon crushed rosemary
¼ teaspoon paprika
8 gingersnaps
2 tablespoons lemon juice

1. Dredge veal in flour. Brown in ¼ cup butter in a saucepot. Remove meat.
2. Add remaining 2 tablespoons butter and onion to saucepot. Sauté until golden.
3. Add veal, tomatoes with liquid, beer, and seasonings. Cover and simmer 1 hour.
4. Moisten gingersnaps with a little water; crush. Stir into meat. Simmer 5 minutes more. Add lemon juice; mix well.
5. Serve over **rice** or **noodles** or with **potatoes.**

8 servings

Note: Poultry or lean pork could be substituted for veal.

457 *German Veal Chops*

4 veal loin or rib chops
Butter or margarine
2 medium onions, sliced
1 cup dark beer
1 bay leaf
½ teaspoon salt
Dash pepper
2 tablespoons flour

1. Brown veal in butter in a skillet; set meat aside. Sauté onion in same skillet until golden.
2. Add beer, bay leaf, salt, and pepper. Cover and simmer 15 minutes.
3. Transfer veal and onion to a platter. Make a paste of flour and a little water; stir into cooking liquid in skillet. Cook, stirring constantly, until thickened and smooth. Pour over veal and onion.

4 servings

Note: If you do not have dark beer, add ½ **teaspoon molasses** to light beer.

458 *Taco Casserole*

1 pound ground beef
1 package (1.25 ounces) taco
    seasoning mix
1 cup water
1 can (15 ounces) refried beans with
    sausage
2 cups shredded lettuce
¼ cup chopped onion
1 tablespoon chopped green chilies
1 cup (4 ounces) shredded Cheddar
    cheese
Nacho-flavored tortilla chips
Chopped tomato
Sliced ripe olives
Dairy sour cream
Taco sauce

1. Brown ground beef in a skillet; drain off excess fat. Add taco mix and water. Simmer, uncovered, until mixture is thickened (about 15 minutes).
2. Lightly grease bottom of an 11x7-inch baking dish. Spread refried beans evenly on the bottom. Sprinkle with shredded lettuce, onion, and chilies; top with ground beef mixture. (If desired, cover and refrigerate until ready to finish.)
3. Bake, uncovered, at 400°F 15 minutes. Sprinkle with shredded cheese and bake an additional 5 minutes, or until cheese is melted and mixture is heated through.
4. Remove from oven and garnish with tortilla chips.
5. Serve with chopped tomato, sliced olives, sour cream, and taco sauce in separate serving dishes.

6 servings

459 *Savannah Beef and Noodles*

1 pound ground beef
1 cup chopped onion
1 can (28 ounces) tomatoes
    (undrained)
2 teaspoons salt
2 teaspoons chili powder
1 teaspoon Worcestershire sauce
3 cups cooked noodles
1 can (5¾ ounces) pitted ripe olives,
    sliced
2 cups (8 ounces) shredded Cheddar
    cheese

1. Brown ground beef and onion in a skillet; drain off excess fat. Add tomatoes, salt, chili powder, and Worcestershire sauce; simmer 30 minutes.
2. Alternate layers of half the noodles, half the meat mixture, and half the ripe olives in a 2½-quart casserole; repeat layers. Top with shredded cheese.
3. Bake, covered, at 350°F 30 minutes, or until heated through.

6 to 8 servings

460 *Easy Beefy Casserole*

1 **pound ground beef**
2 **cans (16 ounces each) tomatoes**
   (undrained)
1 **can (16 ounces) whole kernel corn,**
   drained
¼ **cup sliced stuffed olives**
½ **cup chopped green pepper**
1 **teaspoon oregano**
1½ **tablespoons instant minced onion**
1 **teaspoon salt**
½ **teaspoon pepper**
2 **cups (about 4 ounces) uncooked**
   noodles
¼ **cup (1 ounce) grated Parmesan**
   cheese

1. Brown ground beef in a skillet; drain off excess fat. Add remaining ingredients, except cheese. Put into a 2-quart casserole.
2. Bake, covered, at 350°F 25 minutes. Remove cover. Sprinkle with grated cheese and bake an additional 5 minutes, or until heated through.

6 servings

461 *Baked Steak Patties*

1 **pound ground beef**
½ **pound pork sausage meat**
2 **cups cooked white rice**
1 **egg**
6 **bacon slices**
1 **package (1⅜ ounces) dry onion**
   soup mix
3 **cups water**
2 **tablespoons flour**

1. Combine ground beef, sausage, rice, and egg. Shape to form 6 patties. Wrap each with a bacon slice; secure with wooden pick. Place in an 11x7-inch baking dish.
2. Bake, uncovered, at 350°F 30 minutes; drain off excess fat.
3. Meanwhile, combine soup mix and 2½ cups water in a saucepan. Cook, covered, 10 minutes.
4. Mix the remaining ½ cup water and flour until smooth. Gradually add to soup mixture, stirring until thickened.
5. Pour over steak patties and bake an additional 20 minutes. Remove picks before serving.

6 servings

Note: The gravy may be served with the steak patties or covered and refrigerated. Reheat and serve with mashed potatoes at the next evening's meal.

462 *Party Beef Casserole*

2 pounds ground beef
¾ cup chopped onion
1 garlic clove, minced
½ cup chopped green pepper
½ cup chopped celery
1 teaspoon salt
½ teaspoon pepper
1 can (15 ounces) tomato sauce
1 can (8 ounces) mushroom stems and
   pieces, drained
1 can (6 ounces) tomato paste
½ cup sherry
2 tablespoons Worcestershire sauce
1 package (7 ounces) shell macaroni,
   cooked and drained
1 cup (4 ounces) shredded Cheddar
   cheese

1. Brown ground beef, onion, garlic, green pepper, and celery in a skillet; drain off excess fat. Combine with remaining ingredients, except shredded cheese. Put into a 3-quart casserole.
2. Bake, covered, at 350°F 45 minutes. Sprinkle with shredded cheese and bake an additional 5 minutes, or until heated through.

8 to 10 servings

463 *Spanish Take-Along Casserole*

1½ pounds ground beef
½ cup chopped onion
¼ cup chopped green pepper
¼ cup chopped celery
1 can (8 ounces) pizza sauce
2 cups (about 4 ounces) medium
   noodles, cooked and drained
1 teaspoon salt
1 carton (16 ounces) cream-style
   cottage cheese

1. Brown ground beef, onion, green pepper, and celery in a skillet; drain off excess fat. Combine with remaining ingredients.
2. Put into a 2-quart casserole. (If desired, cover and refrigerate until ready to finish.)
3. Bake, covered, at 350°F 30 minutes, or until heated through. Garnish with **green pepper rings.**

6 to 8 servings

464 *Super Macaroni and Beef Bake*

1 package (6 ounces) elbow macaroni
1 package (8 ounces) cream cheese
1 carton (16 ounces) cream-style
cottage cheese
¼ cup dairy sour cream
1½ pounds ground beef
3 cans (8 ounces each) tomato sauce
½ cup (2 ounces) grated Parmesan
cheese

1. Cook macaroni in **boiling salted water** until just tender; rinse with cold water. Place half the macaroni in bottom of a greased 13x9-inch baking dish.
2. With mixer beat together cream cheese, cottage cheese, and sour cream; pour over macaroni. Sprinkle remaining macaroni over cheese mixture.
3. Brown ground beef in a skillet; drain off excess fat. Stir in tomato sauce. Evenly spread meat mixture over macaroni. Sprinkle with grated cheese.
4. Bake, uncovered, at 350°F 50 to 60 minutes, or until heated through.

8 servings

Note: This casserole is best when prepared a day in advance. Cover and refrigerate. Remove from refrigerator 1 hour before baking.

465 *Italian Spaghetti Bake*

1 pound ground beef
½ cup chopped onion
1 can (16 ounces) tomatoes, drained
1 can (6 ounces) tomato paste
1 garlic clove, minced
1½ teaspoons salt
½ teaspoon oregano
½ teaspoon basil
¼ teaspoon whole marjoram
1 package (7 ounces) spaghetti
2 cups milk
3 eggs
Dash of pepper
1 cup (4 ounces) grated Parmesan
cheese
1 cup (4 ounces) shredded mozzarella
cheese

1. Brown ground beef and onion in a skillet; drain off excess fat. Stir in tomatoes, tomato paste, garlic, 1 teaspoon salt, oregano, basil, and marjoram.
2. Cook spaghetti in **boiling salted water** until just tender. Spread in bottom of a 13x9-inch baking dish.
3. Combine milk, eggs, pepper, and remaining ½ teaspoon salt. Pour over spaghetti. Sprinkle with Parmesan cheese. Spoon meat mixture over Parmesan cheese. Top with mozzarella cheese.
4. Bake, uncovered, at 350°F 40 to 45 minutes, or until heated through. Let stand 10 minutes. Cut into squares to serve.

8 servings

466 *Lasagne Bolognese*

3 tablespoons butter or margarine
3 tablespoons flour
1 cup milk
1 cup whipping cream
¼ teaspoon salt
   Dash of pepper
½ pound lasagne noodles
   Meat Sauce Bolognese
1 cup (4 ounces) grated Parmesan
   cheese

1. Melt butter in a saucepan; blend in flour. Gradually add milk and cream, stirring until thickened and smooth. Add salt and pepper.
2. Cook lasagne noodles in **boiling salted water** according to package directions. Drain, rinse, and spread on a damp towel.
3. Spread a thin layer of Meat Sauce Bolognese in a 13x9-inch baking dish. Top with a layer of half the lasagne noodles, half the Meat Sauce Bolognese, half the white sauce, and half the cheese; repeat layers.
4. Bake, uncovered, at 375°F 35 to 40 minutes, or until mixture is bubbly and top is golden brown. Let stand 10 minutes. Cut into squares to serve.

8 servings

467 *Meat Sauce Bolognese*

6 bacon slices, diced
1 medium onion, chopped
½ cup chopped celery
½ cup chopped carrot
6 tablespoons butter or margarine
¼ pound chicken livers, diced
1 pound ground beef round
1 teaspoon salt
½ teaspoon oregano
¼ teaspoon nutmeg
1 bay leaf
2 tablespoons vinegar
1 can (8 ounces) tomato sauce
1 cup beef bouillon
1 cup sliced fresh mushrooms
½ cup dry white wine

1. Sauté bacon in a skillet; drain off all but 2 tablespoons fat. Add onion, celery, and carrot; cook until tender.
2. Add 2 tablespoons butter and the chicken livers. Brown lightly; add ground beef round. Cook 10 to 15 minutes, or until well browned.
3. Stir in salt, oregano, nutmeg, bay leaf, vinegar, tomato sauce, and bouillon. Cover and simmer ½ hour.
4. Sauté mushrooms in remaining 4 tablespoons butter. Add to meat sauce along with wine. Remove bay leaf. Simmer ½ hour longer.

1 quart

468 *Beef and Pea Casserole*

1 pound ground beef
1 medium onion, chopped
1 can (10¾ ounces) condensed
   tomato soup
⅓ cup water
2 cups cooked noodles
1 can (8 ounces) peas, drained*
1 can (4 ounces) sliced mushrooms,
   drained*

1. Brown ground beef and onion in a skillet; drain off excess fat. Combine with remaining ingredients. Put into a 2-quart casserole.
2. Bake, covered, at 350°F 30 minutes, or until heated through. To serve, sprinkle with **Parmesan cheese** and garnish with **pimento strips.**

6 servings

* The liquid from the peas or mushrooms may be substituted for the 1/3 cup water.

469 *Cheese, Beef, 'n' Macaroni Bake*

2 pounds ground beef
½ medium onion, chopped
1 garlic clove, minced
1 jar (15½ ounces) spaghetti sauce
1 can (16 ounces) stewed tomatoes
1 can (3 ounces) mushroom stems and pieces, drained
2 cups uncooked large macaroni shells
2 cups dairy sour cream
1 package (6 ounces) provolone cheese slices
1 cup (4 ounces) shredded mozzarella cheese

1. Brown ground beef in a skillet; drain off excess fat. Add onion, garlic, spaghetti sauce, tomatoes, and mushrooms. Mix well and simmer 20 minutes.
2. Meanwhile, prepare macaroni shells according to package directions.
3. Put the macaroni shells into a 3-quart casserole. Cover with half the meat sauce. Spread meat with half the sour cream. Top with provolone cheese.
4. Repeat macaroni, meat, and sour-cream layers. Top with mozzarella cheese.
5. Bake, covered, at 350°F 35 to 40 minutes. Remove cover. Bake an additional 10 minutes, or until cheese is lightly browned.

8 to 10 servings

470 *Mock Chop Suey Casserole*

1 pound ground beef
¾ cup chopped onion
2 cups chopped celery
1 can (10¾ ounces) condensed cream of chicken soup
1 can (10¾ ounces) condensed cream of mushroom soup
½ cup uncooked white rice
2 cups boiling water
1 tablespoon soy sauce
1 can (5 ounces) chow mein noodles

1. Brown ground beef in a skillet; drain off excess fat. Combine with remaining ingredients, except chow mein noodles. Put into a 13x9-inch baking dish.
2. Bake, covered, at 350°F 45 minutes, or until rice is tender. Uncover; sprinkle with chow mein noodles. Bake an additional 10 minutes, or until noodles are heated through.

6 servings

Gefilte Fish, page 335

471 *Beef and Rice Bake*

1 pound ground beef
1 package (1⅜ ounces) dry onion
    soup mix
¾ cup uncooked white rice
1½ cups boiling water
1 can (16 ounces) tomatoes
    (undrained)
1 cup (4 ounces) shredded Cheddar
    cheese

1. Brown ground beef in a skillet; drain off excess fat. Combine with soup mix, rice, boiling water, and tomatoes. Put into a 2-quart casserole.
2. Bake, covered, at 350°F 45 minutes, or until rice is tender. Uncover; sprinkle with cheese. Bake an additional 5 minutes, or until cheese is melted.

6 servings

472 *Easy Meatball Stroganoff*

1 tablespoon instant minced onion
½ cup milk
1½ pounds ground beef
⅔ cup quick or old-fashioned oats,
    uncooked
1 teaspoon salt
¼ teaspoon pepper
¼ teaspoon dill weed
⅛ teaspoon garlic powder
1 egg, beaten
1 can (10¾ ounces) condensed golden
    mushroom soup
½ cup dairy sour cream

1. Combine onion and milk. Mix ground beef, oats, salt, pepper, dill weed, garlic powder, egg, and onion-milk mixture.
2. Shape to form 24 meatballs. Place in a shallow 10-inch casserole. Spoon soup over meatballs.
3. Bake, covered, at 350°F 35 minutes, or until meatballs are cooked through, stirring occasionally.
4. Uncover; blend in sour cream. Serve over **hot, cooked rice.**

6 servings

473 *Sloppy Joe for a Crowd*

2¼ pounds ground beef
2½ cups chopped onion
1 cup chopped green pepper
1 bottle (14 ounces) ketchup
¼ cup firmly packed brown sugar
¼ cup lemon juice
¼ cup vinegar
¼ cup water
2 teaspoons salt
1 teaspoon pepper
1 teaspoon Worcestershire sauce
½ teaspoon prepared mustard

1. Brown ground beef, onion, and green pepper in a skillet; drain off excess fat. Combine with remaining ingredients. Put into a large oven-proof Dutch oven.
2. Bake, covered, at 325°F 1½ hours. To serve, spoon over **toasted hamburger buns.**

16 servings

Beef Stroganoff Turnovers, page 320

474 Beef-Sour Cream Casserole

4 cups cooked noodles
1 cup (8 ounces) cream-style cottage cheese
1 package (8 ounces) cream cheese
¼ cup dairy sour cream
⅓ cup instant minced onion
2 tablespoons butter or margarine, melted
1½ pounds ground beef
3 cans (8 ounces each) tomato sauce
½ teaspoon salt
1 teaspoon oregano
⅓ cup chopped green pepper
1 can (2 ounces) sliced mushrooms, drained

1. Put half the noodles into a 2-quart casserole.
2. Combine cottage cheese, cream cheese, sour cream, and onion. Spread over noodles. Cover with remaining noodles. Drizzle with butter.
3. Brown ground beef in a skillet; drain off excess fat. Add remaining ingredients. Pour over noodles. Cover and chill overnight.
4. Remove from refrigerator 1 hour before baking.
5. Bake, covered, at 375°F 45 minutes, or until heated through. To serve, sprinkle with **grated Parmesan cheese.**

8 servings

475 Biscuit-Topped Burger

1¼ pounds ground beef
3 tablespoons instant minced onion
½ cup chopped celery
1 can (8 ounces) tomato sauce
2 tablespoons sweet pickle relish
½ teaspoon chili powder
½ teaspoon horseradish
¼ teaspoon salt
1 can (10 ounces) refrigerator biscuits
1 cup (4 ounces) shredded Cheddar cheese
1 tablespoon snipped parsley
½ teaspoon celery seed

1. Brown ground beef, onion, and celery in a skillet; drain off excess fat. Add tomato sauce, pickle relish, chili powder, horseradish, and salt. Simmer 2 minutes, or until heated through.
2. Spoon into an 11x7-inch baking dish.
3. Separate biscuits; then split each biscuit into 2 layers. Place half the biscuit halves over the meat mixture.
4. Combine cheese, parsley, and celery seed. Sprinkle over biscuit layer. Top with remaining biscuit halves.
5. Bake, uncovered, at 375°F 20 to 25 minutes, or until golden brown.

5 servings

476 Texas Chili

2 pounds ground beef
2 medium onions, chopped
1 garlic clove, minced
3 tablespoons flour
2 tablespoons chili powder
2 teaspoons salt
½ teaspoon cumin
3 cups hot water
1 can (15½ ounces) kidney beans, drained

1. Brown ground beef, onion, and garlic in a skillet; drain off excess fat.
2. Combine flour, chili powder, salt, and cumin. Gradually stir in hot water. Combine with meat mixture. Pour into a 2½-quart casserole.
3. Bake, covered, at 350°F 1¼ hours. Remove cover. Add beans and bake an additional 15 minutes.

8 servings

477 Hominy-Beef Bake

2 pounds ground beef
3 medium onions, chopped
1 can (16 ounces) tomatoes (undrained)
1 can (16 ounces) whole white hominy, drained
1 can (16 ounces) whole kernel corn, drained
1 can (16 ounces) cream-style corn
1 cup sliced pitted ripe olives
2 cans (8 ounces each) tomato sauce
1 package (1.25 ounces) chili mix
1 package (6 ounces) corn tortillas, cut up

1. Brown ground beef and onion in a skillet; drain off excess fat.
2. Combine with remaining ingredients. Put into a 4-quart casserole.
3. Bake, covered, at 300°F 2 hours.

12 servings

478 Individual Burger Casseroles

1 pound ground beef
¼ cup finely chopped onion
1 teaspoon salt
¼ teaspoon oregano
2 tablespoons ketchup
1 cup plus 2 tablespoons milk
2 tablespoons butter or margarine
2 tablespoons flour
1 cup cooked mixed vegetables
2 slices American cheese, cut in 4 strips each

1. Combine ground beef, onion, ½ teaspoon salt, oregano, ketchup, and 2 tablespoons milk.
2. Divide into 4 equal portions. Evenly line bottom and sides of 4 individual casseroles with meat mixture.
3. Bake, uncovered, at 350°F 20 minutes, or until meat mixture is done. Pour off excess fat.
4. Meanwhile, melt butter in a saucepan. Stir in flour. Gradually add remaining 1 cup milk, stirring until thickened and smooth.
5. Add vegetables and remaining ½ teaspoon salt. Spoon into meat shells. Top each with crisscross of cheese strips.
6. Bake about 5 minutes or until cheese melts.

4 servings

479 *African Bobotie*

3 slices day-old bread
1½ cups milk
2 medium onions, chopped
1 garlic clove, minced
½ cup slivered almonds
½ cup raisins
1 tablespoon sugar
1 teaspoon salt
1 teaspoon curry powder
⅛ teaspoon pepper
1 tablespoon vinegar
1 teaspoon lemon juice
1½ pounds ground beef
2 eggs

1. Soak bread in milk. Squeeze milk from bread, reserving milk. Combine all ingredients, except milk and 1 egg.
2. Press mixture into an 11x7-inch baking dish.
3. Add enough milk to reserved milk to make ¾ cup. Beat together milk and remaining egg. Pour over meat mixture.
4. Bake, uncovered, at 350°F 1 hour, or until golden brown and firm to the touch.

6 servings

480 *Mediterranean Beef Casserole*

1 can (20 ounces) pineapple chunks
1 cup uncooked white rice
1 teaspoon salt
1 pound ground beef
1 egg, lightly beaten
1 cup fine soft bread crumbs
1 tablespoon instant minced onion
1 teaspoon salt
⅓ cup milk
1 tablespoon vegetable oil
1 can (16 ounces) stewed tomatoes
½ teaspoon dill weed
2 tablespoons snipped parsley

1. Drain pineapple, reserving liquid. Add enough **water** to liquid to make 2½ cups.
2. Combine liquid, rice, and 1 teaspoon of the salt in a saucepan. Bring to a boil. Cover and simmer 25 minutes, or until rice is fluffy.
3. Combine ground beef, egg, bread crumbs, onion, 1 teaspoon salt, and milk. Shape to form 1-inch balls.
4. Brown meatballs in oil in skillet; drain off excess fat.
5. Add pineapple chunks, tomatoes, dill weed, and parsley. Put into a greased 2-quart casserole.
6. Bake, covered, at 375°F 25 minutes, or until meat is done. Serve over pineapple-rice.

6 servings

481 *One 'n' One Casserole*

1 pound ground beef
1 cup uncooked white rice
1 package (1⅜ ounces) dry onion
    soup mix
1 can (10¾ ounces) condensed cream
    of mushroom soup
2½ cups boiling water
½ cup sliced green onion tops

1. Brown ground beef in a skillet; drain off excess fat. Put into a greased 2-quart casserole. Sprinkle with rice and onion soup mix.
2. Combine mushroom soup and boiling water. Pour over rice.
3. Bake, covered, at 350°F 1 hour, or until rice is tender. Remove cover. Sprinkle with onion tops.

4 servings

482 *Meatball Supper Pie*

1 pound ground beef
½ cup quick or old-fashioned oats,
    uncooked
¼ cup chopped onion
1 teaspoon salt
¼ teaspoon pepper
¼ teaspoon thyme
1¼ cups milk
1 egg, beaten
1 tablespoon butter or margarine
1 tablespoon flour
    Dash ground red pepper
½ cup (2 ounces) grated Parmesan
    cheese
1 baked 9-inch pie shell
½ cup (2 ounces) shredded American
    cheese
1 tomato, cut in wedges

1. Combine ground beef, oats, onion, salt, pepper, thyme, ¼ cup milk, and egg. Shape to form 4 dozen small meatballs.
2. Brown meatballs in a skillet; drain off excess fat.
3. Melt butter in a saucepan. Stir in flour and red pepper. Gradually add remaining 1 cup milk, stirring until thickened and smooth. Stir in Parmesan cheese.
4. Place meatballs in pie shell. Pour cheese sauce over meatballs.
5. Bake, uncovered, at 375°F 20 minutes. Sprinkle with American cheese and top with tomato wedges. Bake an additional 5 minutes. Cut into wedges to serve.

6 servings

483 *Layered Hamburger Bake*

1 **pound ground beef**
1 **medium onion, chopped**
4 **medium potatoes, pared and sliced**
¼ **teaspoon pepper**
1 **can (10½ ounces) condensed vegetable soup**
1 **can (10¾ ounces) condensed cream of mushroom soup**
½ **cup water**

1. Brown ground beef and onion in a skillet; drain off excess fat.
2. Put half of the potatoes into a greased 2-quart casserole. Top with half the meat mixture; repeat. Sprinkle with pepper.
3. Combine vegetable soup, mushroom soup, and water. Pour over meat.
4. Bake, covered, at 350°F 1 hour, or until potatoes are tender.

4 servings

484 *Tamale Pie*

1 **cup cornmeal**
1¾ **teaspoons salt**
1 **cup cold water**
2 **cups boiling water**
1 **pound ground beef**
⅓ **cup chopped onion**
2 **tablespoons flour**
½ **cup chopped pitted ripe olives**
1 **can (16 ounces) tomatoes (undrained)**
2 **teaspoons chili powder**
½ **cup cubed sharp Cheddar cheese**

1. Combine cornmeal, 1 teaspoon salt, and cold water. Slowly pour into boiling water in a saucepan, stirring constantly. Cook until thickened, stirring frequently. Cover; continue cooking over low heat about 5 minutes. Stir occasionally.
2. Brown ground beef and onion in a skillet; drain off excess fat. Add flour, olives, tomatoes, chili powder, and remaining ¾ teaspoon salt.
3. Spread mush evenly in bottom of a greased 12x8-inch baking dish. Pour meat mixture over mush. Arrange cheese cubes over meat mixture.
4. Bake, uncovered, at 350°F 20 minutes, or until casserole is bubbly.

6 servings

485 *Szededine Goulash*

2 **pounds beef stew meat, cut in 1-inch pieces**
¼ **cup vegetable oil**
2 **cups sliced onion**
1 **garlic clove, minced**
1 **teaspoon salt**
1 **can (10 ounces) tomato purée,**
1 **cup water**
1 **cup dairy sour cream**
2 **teaspoons paprika**
2 **teaspoons caraway seed**
1 **can (16 ounces) sauerkraut, rinsed and drained**
2 **tablespoons snipped parsley**

1. Brown beef in oil in a skillet. Add onion and garlic. Sauté about 5 minutes; drain off excess fat.
2. Add salt, tomato purée, and water. Put into a 2½-quart casserole.
3. Bake, covered, at 325°F 2 hours, or until meat is tender, stirring occasionally. Remove cover. Stir in sour cream, paprika, caraway seed, and sauerkraut. Bake an additional 15 minutes, or until heated through. Sprinkle with parsley.

8 servings

486 Oven Beef Bake

2 pounds beef stew meat, cut in
   1-inch cubes
1 can (10¾ ounces) condensed cream
   of mushroom soup
1 can (10½ ounces) condensed onion
   soup
¼ cup dry vermouth

1. Put meat into a 2-quart casserole.
2. Combine mushroom soup, onion soup, and vermouth. Pour over meat.
3. Bake, covered, at 325°F 3 hours, or until meat is tender. Serve with **hot, cooked noodles.**

8 servings

487 Beef Bourguignon

¼ cup flour
1 teaspoon salt
½ teaspoon freshly ground black
   pepper
2 pounds beef stew meat, cut in
   2-inch cubes
¼ cup butter or margarine
1 medium onion, chopped
2 medium carrots, chopped
1 garlic clove, minced
2 cups dry red wine
1 can (6 ounces) mushroom crowns,
   drained, reserving liquid
1 bay leaf
3 tablespoons snipped parsley
½ teaspoon thyme
1 can (16 ounces) onions, drained

1. Combine flour, salt, and pepper; coat beef cubes.
2. Brown beef in butter in a skillet. Put into a 2-quart casserole.
3. Add onion, carrots, and garlic to skillet. Cook until tender but not brown. Add wine, liquid from mushrooms, bay leaf, parsley, and thyme. Pour over meat.
4. Bake, covered, at 350°F 2½ hours. Remove cover. Add onions and mushroom crowns. Bake an additional 30 minutes, or until meat is tender.

8 servings

488 Swiss Steak Mozzarella

2 pounds beef round steak, ½ inch
   thick
3 tablespoons flour
½ cup butter or margarine
1 can (16 ounces) tomatoes, cut up
1¼ teaspoons salt
¼ teaspoon basil
½ cup chopped green pepper
1½ cups (6 ounces) mozzarella cheese

1. Cut meat into serving-size pieces; coat with flour.
2. Melt butter in a skillet. Brown meat slowly on both sides. Put into a 12x8-inch baking dish.
3. Combine tomatoes, salt, basil, and green pepper. Pour over meat.
4. Bake, covered, at 350°F 1 hour, or until meat is tender. Remove cover. Sprinkle with cheese and bake an additional 5 minutes, or until cheese is melted.

8 servings

489 *Stew with Cornbread Topping*

1½ pounds beef stew meat, cut in
    ¾-inch cubes
2 tablespoons butter or margarine
2 medium onions, sliced
1 garlic clove, minced
2¼ cups water
1 can (8 ounces) tomato sauce
¼ bay leaf
2 teaspoons salt
¼ teaspoon pepper
4 carrots, cut in 1-inch pieces
4 celery stalks, cut in 1-inch pieces
½ cup all-purpose flour
2 teaspoons baking powder
1 tablespoon sugar
1 teaspoon salt
1 cup cornmeal
1 egg, beaten
1 cup milk
2 tablespoons vegetable oil
1 tablespoon snipped parsley

1. Brown meat in butter in a skillet. Add onion and garlic, cooking until lightly brown. Stir in water, tomato sauce, bay leaf, 2 teaspoons salt, and the pepper. Put into a 2½-quart casserole.
2. Bake, covered, at 350°F 45 minutes. Remove bay leaf. Add carrots and celery. Bake, covered, an additional 25 minutes, or until meat and vegetables are tender.
3. Sift together flour, baking powder, sugar, and 1 teaspoon salt into a bowl. Mix in cornmeal. Add egg, milk, and oil. (Mix only until dry ingredients are moistened.)
4. Remove stew from oven. Pour topping over hot stew. Sprinkle with parsley.
5. Bake, uncovered, at 400°F 20 minutes, or until cornbread is golden brown.

6 servings

490 *Slow Oven Beef Stew*

2 pounds beef stew meat, cut in
    1½-inch cubes
2 medium onions, each cut in eighths
3 celery stalks, cut in 1-inch
    diagonally sliced pieces
4 medium carrots, pared and cut in
    half crosswise and lengthwise
3 cups tomato juice
⅓ cup quick-cooking tapioca
1 tablespoon sugar
2 teaspoons salt
¼ teaspoon pepper
1 bay leaf
2 medium potatoes, pared and cut in
    ¼-inch-thick slices

1. Put all ingredients, except potatoes, into a 3-quart casserole.
2. Bake, covered, at 300°F 2½ hours. Remove bay leaf and stir in potatoes. Bake, covered, an additional 1 hour, or until meat and vegetables are tender.

8 servings

491 Cornbread Tamale Pie

1 pound ground beef
½ cup chopped onion
⅓ cup chopped celery
1 can (16 ounces) tomatoes (undrained)
1 can (12 ounces) whole kernel corn, drained
1 can (8 ounces) tomato sauce
1 tablespoon chili powder
1 teaspoon salt
¼ teaspoon pepper
¼ cup all-purpose flour
1½ teaspoons baking powder
½ teaspoon salt
¾ cup cornmeal
1 egg, beaten
½ cup milk
2 tablespoons vegetable oil

1. Brown ground beef, onion, and celery in a skillet; drain off excess fat. Add tomatoes, corn, tomato sauce, chili powder, 1 teaspoon salt, and the pepper; simmer 10 minutes.
2. Sift together flour, baking powder, and ½ teaspoon salt into a bowl. Mix in cornmeal. Stir in egg, milk, and oil. (Mix only until dry ingredients are moistened.)
3. Spoon hot meat mixture into a 2-quart casserole. Top with cornbread topping.
4. Bake, uncovered, at 425°F 15 minutes, or until topping is golden brown.

6 servings

492 Beef 'n' Peppers

1 garlic clove, minced
1½ pounds lean beef, cut in 1-inch cubes
2 tablespoons shortening
1 cup sliced fresh mushrooms
2 cans (10½ ounces each) brown gravy with onions
1 green pepper, cut in strips

1. Sauté garlic and beef in hot shortening in a skillet. Put into a 1½-quart casserole.
2. Combine mushrooms and gravy in skillet with drippings. Pour over meat.
3. Bake, covered, at 350°F 2 hours, or until meat is tender. Remove cover. Add pepper strips. Bake an additional 15 minutes, or until pepper is tender but still crisp. Serve over **hot, cooked rice** or **noodles.**

6 servings

493 Yankee Steak

2 pounds beef round steak, ½ inch thick
½ cup flour
2 teaspoons salt
½ teaspoon pepper
3 tablespoons vegetable oil
2 medium onions, thinly sliced
1 can (15 ounces) tomato sauce
⅛ teaspoon garlic powder

1. Cut meat into serving-size pieces. Combine flour, salt, and pepper; pound into steak.
2. Heat oil in a skillet. Brown meat slowly on both sides. Place in a 13x9-inch baking dish. Top with onion slices.
3. Combine tomato sauce and garlic powder. Pour over meat.
4. Bake, covered, at 350°F 1 hour, or until meat is tender.

8 servings

494 *Creamy Baked Steak*

1 pound beef round tip steak
4 tablespoons flour
½ teaspoon salt
2 tablespoons vegetable oil
1 small onion, sliced
1 garlic clove, minced
1 can (10½ ounces) condensed beef
   broth
1 cup dairy sour cream
2 tablespoons sherry
1 can (3 ounces) sliced mushrooms,
   drained

1. Cut steak into serving-size pieces. Sprinkle with 1 tablespoon flour and the salt.
2. Brown meat in oil in a skillet. Add onion and garlic.
3. Combine beef broth with remaining 3 tablespoons flour. Stir into skillet. Cook, stirring constantly, until mixture thickens. Put meat and sauce into a 12x8-inch baking dish.
4. Bake, covered, at 350°F 30 minutes, or until steak is tender. Remove cover. Combine sour cream, sherry, and mushrooms. Stir into meat mixture in baking dish. Bake an additional 5 minutes, or until heated through.

3 or 4 servings

495 *Island-Style Short Ribs*

4 pounds lean beef short ribs
½ cup soy sauce
⅓ cup sugar
2 tablespoons vinegar
1 tablespoon vegetable oil
1 teaspoon ginger
½ teaspoon lemon pepper seasoning
¼ teaspoon garlic salt
1 large onion, finely chopped
¼ cup butter or margarine
2 cups water

1. Cut meat from bones; reserve the bones. Trim off as much fat as possible. Cut meat into cubes. Put meat into a bowl.
2. Combine soy sauce, sugar, vinegar, oil, ginger, lemon pepper seasoning, and garlic salt. Pour over meat. Cover and refrigerate several hours or overnight.
3. Sauté onion in butter in a skillet. Remove onion; set aside.
4. Cook meat in skillet about 10 minutes. Add onion, marinade, and water. Put into a 2-quart casserole. Top with bones.
5. Bake, covered, at 325°F 1½ hours. Remove bones and bake, uncovered, an additional 30 minutes, or until meat is tender. To serve, spoon broth over **hot, cooked rice.**

8 servings

496 *Veal Parmigiano*

1 **pound veal steak or cutlet, thinly sliced**
1 **teaspoon salt**
⅛ **teaspoon pepper**
1 **egg**
2 **cups plus 2 teaspoons water**
⅓ **cup grated Parmesan cheese**
⅓ **cup fine dry bread crumbs**
¼ **cup shortening**
1 **medium onion, finely chopped**
1 **can (6 ounces) tomato paste**
1 **teaspoon salt**
½ **teaspoon basil**
6 **slices mozzarella cheese**

1. Cut veal into 8 pieces; sprinkle with 1 teaspoon salt and the pepper.
2. Lightly beat together egg and 2 teaspoons water.
3. Combine Parmesan cheese and bread crumbs.
4. Dip veal in egg wash, then Parmesan mixture. Refrigerate at least ½ hour.
5. Brown veal on both sides in shortening in a skillet. Remove to a 1½-quart shallow baking dish.
6. Sauté onion in skillet. Stir in tomato paste, 1 teaspoon salt, and basil. Simmer 5 minutes. Pour three fourths of the sauce over veal. Top with mozzarella cheese. Pour remaining sauce over cheese.
7. Bake, uncovered, at 350°F 20 to 25 minutes, or until mixture is bubbly.

4 servings

497 *Northwoods Pork Chops*

1 **package (2¾ ounces) instant wild rice**
¼ **cup chopped celery**
¼ **cup chopped green pepper**
¼ **cup chopped onion**
6 **tablespoons butter or margarine**
4 **pork chops, ¾ inch thick**
¼ **cup flour**
2 **cups milk**
½ **teaspoon salt**
⅛ **teaspoon pepper**
½ **cup (2 ounces) shredded American cheese**

1. Prepare wild rice according to package directions.
2. Sauté celery, green pepper, and onion in 4 tablespoons butter in a skillet. Combine with wild rice. Put into a 1½-quart shallow baking dish.
3. Brown pork chops on both sides in skillet. Place on top of wild rice mixture.
4. Melt remaining 2 tablespoons butter in skillet. Blend in flour. Gradually add milk, stirring until thickened and smooth. Add salt and pepper. Pour over pork chops.
5. Bake, covered, at 350°F 1 hour, or until chops are done. Sprinkle with cheese.

4 servings

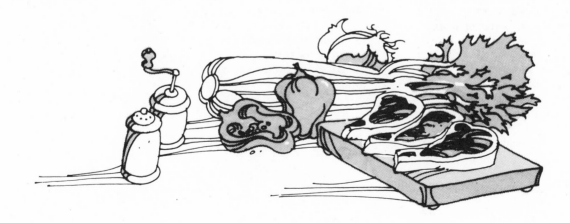

498 Golden Pork Chop Bake

6 pork chops, 1 inch thick
2 tablespoons shortening
½ cup sliced celery
1 garlic clove, minced
2 cans (10¾ ounces each) condensed
  golden mushroom soup
1⅓ cups water
1⅓ cups packaged precooked rice
½ cup chopped tomato

1. Brown pork chops on both sides in shortening in a skillet. Remove chops from skillet; drain off excess fat.
2. Sauté celery and garlic in skillet. Combine with remaining ingredients. Spoon into a 2-quart shallow baking dish.
3. Arrange chops on top of rice mixture.
4. Bake, covered, at 350°F 1 hour, or until chops are tender.

6 servings

499 Baked Stuffed Pork Chops

4 rib pork chops, 1 inch thick
1 tablespoon finely chopped onion
¼ cup diced celery
2 tablespoons butter or margarine
1 cup soft bread crumbs
½ teaspoon salt
⅛ teaspoon poultry seasoning
2 tablespoons shortening
1 can (10¾ ounces) condensed cream
  of mushroom soup
⅓ cup water

1. Trim excess fat from pork chops. Slit each chop from bone side almost to fat, making a pocket.
2. Sauté onion and celery in butter in a skillet. Combine with bread crumbs, salt, and poultry seasoning. Stuff into pockets in chops.
3. Brown chops in shortening in skillet. Place in a 10x8-inch baking dish.
4. Add soup and water to drippings in skillet. Stir to dissolve brown particles. Pour over chops.
5. Bake, covered, at 350°F 1 hour, or until chops are tender.

4 servings

500 He-Man Casserole

½ cup chopped green onion
½ cup chopped green pepper
½ cup chopped celery
6 tablespoons butter or margarine
6 tablespoons flour
  Dash pepper
1 cup chicken broth
1½ cups milk
4 cups cubed cooked ham
1 package (10 ounces) frozen peas,
  thawed
4 cups hot, cooked mashed potatoes
  (stiff)
1 egg, beaten
1 cup (4 ounces) shredded Cheddar
  cheese

1. Sauté onion, green pepper, and celery in butter in a saucepan. Stir in flour and pepper. Gradually add broth and milk, stirring until thickened and smooth.
2. Mix with ham and peas. Put into a 3-quart casserole.
3. Combine potatoes, egg, and cheese. Spoon around edge of casserole mixture.
4. Bake, uncovered, at 375°F 45 minutes, or until mixture is bubbly.

8 servings

501 *Calico Ham Bake*

1 pound cooked ham
1 package (10 ounces) sharp Cheddar
    cheese
1 medium green pepper, chopped
4 eggs, beaten
2 cups milk

1. Grind ham and cheese together. Combine with green pepper, eggs, and milk. Put into a greased 8-inch square baking dish.
2. Bake, uncovered, at 325°F 1 hour, or until browned. Cut into squares to serve.

6 servings

502 *Wild Rice-Ham Rolls*

1½ cups uncooked wild rice
½ cup sliced green onion
¼ cup snipped parsley
¼ pound fresh mushrooms, sliced
¼ cup butter or margarine
¼ cup flour
½ teaspoon salt
¼ teaspoon pepper
¼ teaspoon nutmeg
½ cup dry white wine
2 cups milk
8 slices cooked ham, about ¼ inch
    thick

1. Prepare wild rice according to package directions. Add ¼ cup green onion and the parsley.
2. Sauté remaining ¼ cup green onion and mushrooms in butter in a skillet. Stir in flour, salt, pepper, and nutmeg. Gradually add wine, then milk, stirring until thickened and smooth.
3. Combine 1 cup sauce with 2 cups wild rice. Divide evenly on top of each ham slice. Spoon remaining rice on bottom of a lightly greased 12x9-inch shallow baking dish.
4. Roll up ham rolls to enclose filling. Place seam side down on rice in casserole. Spoon remaining sauce over ham rolls.
5. Bake, uncovered, at 350°F 20 minutes, or until heated through.

8 servings

503 *Ham and Cheese Casserole Bread*

⅔ cup chopped onion
3 tablespoons vegetable oil
2 cups all-purpose biscuit mix
1 cup chopped cooked ham
2 eggs
⅔ cup milk
1 teaspoon prepared mustard
1½ cups (6 ounces) shredded Cheddar
    cheese
2 tablespoons sesame seed
2 tablespoons snipped parsley
3 tablespoons butter or margarine,
    melted

1. Sauté onion in 1 tablespoon oil in a skillet.
2. Combine biscuit mix and ham.
3. Blend the remaining 2 tablespoons oil, eggs, milk, mustard, onion, and ¾ cup cheese. Stir into ham mixture. Spoon into a greased 1½-quart round casserole. Sprinkle with remaining ¾ cup cheese, sesame seed, parsley, and butter.
4. Bake, uncovered, at 350°F minutes, or until done. Cut into wedges to serve.

6 servings

504 *Calico Supper Pie*

1 can (10 biscuits) refrigerator
    biscuits
2 cups diced cooked ham
1 large tomato, sliced
¼ cup chopped green onion
1 cup (4 ounces) shredded Cheddar
    cheese
2 eggs, separated
½ cup milk
2 tablespoons flour
¼ cup (1 ounce) grated Parmesan
    cheese
1 tablespoon snipped parsley

1. Separate dough into biscuits. Place in a 9-inch deep pie pan; press over bottom and up sides to form crust. Sprinkle with ham. Top with tomato, green onion, and Cheddar cheese.
2. Beat egg yolks. Stir in milk and flour. Pour over cheese.
3. Beat egg whites until soft peaks form. Fold in Parmesan cheese and parsley. Spread over pie. Cover edge of crust with foil.
4. Bake at 350°F 25 minutes. Remove foil. Bake an additional 10 minutes, or until crust is golden brown. Let stand a few minutes before serving.

6 servings

505 *Ham Wrap-Arounds*

8 slices cooked ham, about ¼ inch
    thick
2 packages (10 ounces each) frozen
    broccoli spears, cooked and
    drained
3 cups cubed French bread, toasted*
1½ cups dry white wine
3 cups (12 ounces) shredded Swiss
    cheese
3 tablespoons flour
2 teaspoons prepared mustard
⅛ teaspoon garlic powder

1. Wrap ham slices around broccoli spears. Place in a 12x8-inch shallow baking dish. Sprinkle with bread cubes.
2. Heat wine in a saucepan. Mix cheese and flour. Gradually add to wine while stirring until smooth. Stir in mustard and garlic powder. Pour sauce over all in dish.
3. Bake, uncovered, at 350°F 30 minutes, or until heated through.

8 servings

* To toast cubed French bread, place on a baking sheet and put into a 350°F oven about 10 minutes.

506 *Saucy Stuffed Peppers*

6 medium green peppers
1½ pounds pork sausage meat
1 cup quick or old-fashioned oats, uncooked
⅔ cup tomato juice
1 can (10¾ ounces) condensed tomato soup
¼ cup milk
1 teaspoon Worcestershire sauce
⅛ teaspoon oregano

1. Cut ¼-inch slice from the top of each green pepper; remove seeds. Cook green peppers in **boiling water** about 5 minutes; drain.
2. Brown sausage in a skillet until lightly browned; drain off excess fat. Combine meat, oats, and tomato juice.
3. Fill green peppers with meat mixture. Stand upright in a 1½-quart shallow baking dish; add a small amount of **water.**
4. Bake, uncovered, at 350°F 45 to 50 minutes, or until done.
5. Serve with sauce made by heating together the soup, milk, Worcestershire sauce, and oregano.

6 servings

507 *Ham and Asparagus Casserole*

3 tablespoons butter or margarine
3 tablespoons flour
½ teaspoon dry mustard
1½ cups milk
1½ cups (6 ounces) shredded Cheddar cheese
2 cups cubed cooked ham
1 package (10 ounces) frozen cut-up asparagus, cooked and drained
⅛ teaspoon onion powder
Dash Tabasco
½ cup toasted slivered almonds

1. Melt butter in a saucepan. Stir in flour and mustard. Gradually add milk, stirring until thickened and smooth. Add cheese, stirring until smooth.
2. Combine with ham, asparagus, onion powder, and Tabasco. Put into a 1½-quart casserole. Sprinkle with almonds.
3. Bake, uncovered, at 350°F 20 minutes, or until heated through.

4 servings

508 *Sausage-Green Bean Casserole*

3 cups hot, cooked mashed potatoes
1 pound pork sausage links, cooked and drained
1 cup (4 ounces) shredded American cheese
1 package (9 ounces) frozen cut green beans, cooked and drained
1 can (8 ounces) small whole onions, drained
1 tablespoon chopped pimento

1. Layer half of the mashed potatoes, half of the sausage, and half of the cheese in a 1½-quart casserole.
2. Combine green beans, onions, and pimento. Spoon over cheese. Top with remaining potatoes, sausage, and cheese.
3. Bake, covered, at 350°F 30 minutes, or until heated through.

6 servings

509 *Super Sausage Supper*

1 cup chopped onion
1 garlic clove, minced
3 carrots, pared and thinly sliced
2 tablespoons shortening
1 jar (32 ounces) sauerkraut, drained
2 cups apple cider
½ cup dry white wine
¼ teaspoon pepper
3 parsley sprigs
1 bay leaf
1 package (12 ounces) pork sausage links, cooked and drained
1 package (5 ounces) tiny smoked sausage links
2 links (8 ounces each) Polish sausage, cooked and drained
2 cans (16 ounces each) small white potatoes, drained
1 apple, cored and cut in chunks

1. Sauté onion, garlic, and carrot in shortening in a skillet. Add sauerkraut, apple cider, wine, pepper, parsley, and bay leaf. Bring to a boil; reduce heat and simmer 15 minutes.
2. Stir in remaining ingredients. Remove bay leaf. Put into a 3-quart casserole.
3. Bake, covered, at 350°F 1 hour.

8 servings

510 *Hearty Sausage Supper*

1 jar (16 ounces) applesauce
1 can (14 ounces) sauerkraut, drained
⅓ cup dry white wine
2 tablespoons firmly packed brown sugar
1 can (16 ounces) small white potatoes, drained
1 can (16 ounces) small whole onions, drained
1 ring (12 ounces) Polish sausage, slashed several times
1 tablespoon snipped parsley

1. Mix applesauce, sauerkraut, wine, and brown sugar. Put into a 2½-quart casserole.
2. Arrange potatoes and onions around edge of casserole. Place sausage in center.
3. Bake, covered, at 350°F 45 to 50 minutes, or until heated through. Sprinkle with parsley.

4 servings

511 *Smoked Sausage Dinner*

1 medium onion, chopped
½ cup chopped green pepper
2 tablespoons butter or margarine
1 pound smoked sausage, cut in ½-inch pieces
1 can (16 ounces) tomatoes, cut up
1 cup uncooked noodles

1. Sauté onion and green pepper in butter in a skillet. Add sausage and brown lightly; drain off excess fat.
2. Stir in remaining ingredients. Put into a 1½-quart casserole.
3. Bake, covered, at 375°F 45 minutes, or until noodles are tender, stirring once.

4 servings

512 *Lamb Curry*

1½ pounds boneless lamb shoulder, cut in ¾-inch cubes
2 tablespoons shortening
1 teaspoon salt
1 teaspoon paprika
¼ teaspoon pepper
1 large onion, sliced
1 cup sliced celery
2¼ cups water
1 teaspoon curry powder
¼ cup flour
1 cup uncooked white rice

1. Brown lamb in shortening in a large saucepan. Sprinkle with salt, paprika, and pepper. Add onion, celery, and 2 cups water. Cover and simmer 1 hour, or until tender.
2. Combine curry powder, flour, and remaining ¼ cup water. Gradually add to saucepan, stirring until thickened and smooth.
3. Meanwhile, prepare rice according to package directions. Press rice in bottom and up sides of a 2-quart casserole. Pour lamb mixture into rice shell.
4. Bake, covered, at 350°F 20 minutes, or until casserole is bubbly. Serve with **chopped peanuts, shredded coconut,** and **chutney.**

6 servings

513 *Smothered Lamb Chops*

6 lamb rib chops
2 tablespoons butter or margarine
4 medium red potatoes, pared and thinly sliced
2 large onions, sliced
1½ cups beef bouillon
2 tablespoons snipped parsley
¼ cup buttered bread crumbs

1. Brown lamb chops on both sides in butter in a skillet. Place in a 2-quart shallow baking dish.
2. Arrange potatoes over chops and onions over potatoes. Season lightly with **salt.** Pour bouillon over all.
3. Bake, covered, at 375°F 1 hour, or until chops and vegetables are tender. Combine parsley and bread crumbs. Remove cover from casserole. Sprinkle with the parsley-bread crumbs. Bake, uncovered, at 450°F 10 minutes, or until crumbs are lightly browned.

6 servings

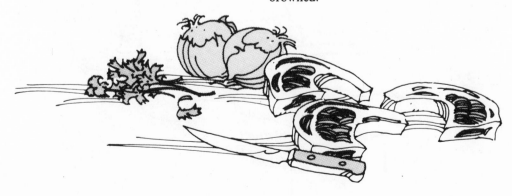

514 *Franks and Scalloped Potatoes*

6 medium potatoes, pared and thinly
  sliced
3 tablespoons finely chopped chives
3 tablespoons flour
1 teaspoon salt
¼ teaspoon pepper
3 tablespoons butter or margarine
2½ cups milk, heated
6 frankfurters, cut in pieces

1. Place one third of the potatoes in a greased 2½-quart casserole. Sprinkle with one third of the chives, one third of the flour, one third of the salt, and one third of the pepper. Dot with 1 tablespoon butter. Repeat twice. Pour milk over all.
2. Bake, covered, at 350°F 30 minutes. Remove cover. Stir in frankfurters. Bake, uncovered, an additional 50 minutes, or until potatoes are tender.

6 servings

515 *Hot Dogs in Cornbread*

1 package (8½ ounces) corn muffin
  mix
1 egg
⅓ cup milk
1 tablespoon instant minced onion
4 frankfurters, split in half lengthwise
1 teaspoon oregano
1 cup (4 ounces) shredded Cheddar
  cheese

1. Prepare corn muffin mix, using egg and milk, according to package directions. Stir onion into batter. Spread into a greased 1½-quart shallow baking dish.
2. Arrange frankfurters over batter. Sprinkle with oregano.
3. Bake, uncovered, at 400°F 15 minutes, or until golden brown. Sprinkle with cheese. Bake an additional 3 minutes, or until cheese is melted. Serve with **prepared mustard.**

4 servings

516 *Macaroni and Cheese with Franks*

1 package (8 ounces) elbow macaroni,
  cooked and drained
2 cups (8 ounces) shredded Cheddar
  cheese
1 can (13 ounces) evaporated milk
1 small onion, finely chopped
⅛ teaspoon pepper
1 package (16 ounces) frankfurters,
  cut in 1-inch pieces

1. Combine all ingredients. Put into a 2½-quart casserole.
2. Bake, covered, at 350°F 30 minutes, or until heated through, stirring occasionally.

6 servings

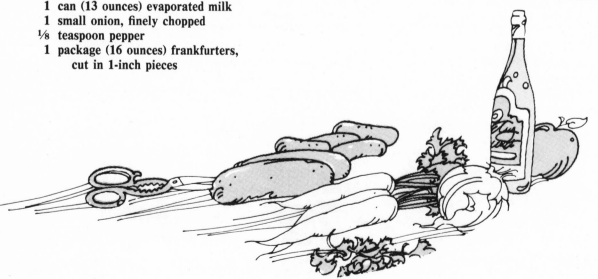

517 *Dried Beef 'n' Noodles*

1 cup diced celery
1 cup chopped onion
½ cup chopped green pepper
¼ cup shortening
2 tablespoons flour
2 cups milk
1 tablespoon Worcestershire sauce
    Dash Tabasco
½ cup (2 ounces) shredded American
    cheese
1 package (3 ounces) dried smoked
    beef, cut in pieces
2 cups cooked wide noodles
2 hard-cooked eggs, sliced

1. Sauté celery, onion, and green pepper in shortening in a skillet.
2. Stir in flour. Gradually add milk, stirring until thickened and smooth. Add Worcestershire sauce, Tabasco, and cheese, stirring until smooth. Stir in beef and noodles.
3. Put into a 1½-quart casserole. Top with hard-cooked egg slices.
4. Bake, covered, at 350°F 30 minutes, or until heated through.

4 servings

518 *Corned Beef Casserole*

½ cup chopped onion
¼ cup chopped green pepper
2 tablespoons shortening
1 can (12 ounces) corned beef, cut up
¾ cup water
1½ cups ketchup
1 package (10 ounces) frozen peas,
    thawed
1½ cups (about 6 ounces) shell
    macaroni, cooked and drained

1. Sauté onion and green pepper in shortening in a skillet. Stir in remaining ingredients. Put into a 2-quart casserole.
2. Bake, covered, at 350°F 30 minutes, or until heated through.

6 servings

519 *Hearty Sandwich Squares*

2 cups pancake mix
1 can (11 ounces) condensed Cheddar
    cheese soup
1 teaspoon prepared mustard
1¼ cups milk
8 slices (1 ounce each) luncheon meat
4 slices (1 ounce each) American
    cheese
¼ cup chopped onion
¼ cup chopped green pepper

1. Combine pancake mix, ¼ cup soup, mustard, and 1 cup milk.
2. Spread half the batter in a greased 8-inch square baking dish. Top with meat, cheese, onion, and green pepper. Spoon remaining batter over all.
3. Bake, uncovered, at 400°F 25 to 30 minutes, or until done. Cut into squares to serve. Heat together remaining soup and ¼ cup milk. Spoon over squares. Sprinkle with **snipped parsley.**

4 servings

520 *Frankfurter Supper Bake*

1 pound frankfurters
½ cup vegetable oil
1 large garlic clove, minced
8 slices bread, well toasted and cut in
    ½-inch cubes
1 cup diagonally sliced celery
2 tablespoons minced parsley
1 egg
¼ teaspoon salt
⅛ teaspoon pepper
2 cans (8 ounces each) tomato sauce
    with onions

1. Make diagonal slits at 1-inch intervals almost to bottom of each frankfurter. Set aside.
2. Mix oil and garlic and pour about half of mixture into a large skillet; heat thoroughly. Add about half of toast cubes and toss until all sides are coated and browned. Turn into a large bowl. Repeat heating oil; brown remaining toast cubes, and put into bowl along with celery and parsley.
3. Beat egg, salt, and pepper slightly. Add 1 can of tomato sauce; mix well. Pour over the crouton mixture; toss lightly.
4. Turn half of the mixture into a greased 1½-quart casserole. Put half of the franks onto the mixture. Brush franks with 1 teaspoon tomato sauce from remaining can. Repeat layers and brushing.
5. Bake, uncovered, at 350°F 45 minutes.
6. Heat remaining tomato sauce in a small saucepan and pour evenly over casserole mixture. Garnish with **parsley.**

6 servings

521 *Pear-Topped Special*

1 can (12 ounces) luncheon meat,
    shredded
2 medium onions, chopped
⅔ cup diced celery
⅓ cup slivered green pepper
4 medium potatoes, cooked, peeled,
    and cut in cubes
1 cup beef broth
½ teaspoon salt
  Few grains pepper
1 can (29 ounces) pear halves, drained
  Softened butter or margarine
¼ cup firmly packed brown sugar

1. Combine luncheon meat, onion, celery, green pepper, potato cubes, broth, salt, and pepper; toss lightly to mix. Turn into a buttered shallow 1½-quart baking dish.
2. Bake, uncovered, at 400°F 30 minutes. Arrange pear halves, cut side down, over top. Brush pears lightly with softened butter and sprinkle with brown sugar. Bake an additional 15 minutes.

About 6 servings

522 *Parmesan Macaroni Casserole*

1 package (8 ounces) cream cheese
½ teaspoon garlic salt
1 cup milk
½ cup (2 ounces) grated Parmesan
    cheese
1 can (12 ounces) luncheon meat,
    chopped
½ cup sliced celery
¼ cup chopped green pepper
1 cup (4 ounces) elbow macaroni,
    cooked and drained

1. Soften cream cheese over low heat in a saucepan. Add garlic salt. Gradually add milk, stirring until smooth.
2. Stir in remaining ingredients. Put into a greased 1½-quart casserole.
3. Bake, covered, at 350°F 25 minutes, or until heated through and lightly browned.

6 servings

523 *Pot Roast of Beef with Wine*

3- to 4-pound beef pot roast, bone-
    less (rump, chuck, or round)
2 cups red wine
2 medium onions, chopped
3 medium carrots, washed, pared,
    and sliced
1 clove garlic
1 bay leaf
¼ teaspoon pepper
4 sprigs parsley
¼ cup all-purpose flour
2 teaspoons salt
¼ teaspoon pepper
3 tablespoons butter
2 cups red wine
1 cup cold water
¼ cup all-purpose flour

1. Put the meat into a deep bowl. Add wine, onions, carrots, garlic, bay leaf, pepper, and parsley. Cover and put into re-frigerator to marinate 12 hours, or overnight; turn meat occa-sionally. Drain the meat, reserving marinade, and pat meat dry with absorbent paper.
2. Coat meat evenly with a mixture of flour, salt, and pepper.
3. Heat butter in a large saucepot; brown the meat slowly on all sides in the butter. Drain off the fat. Add the marinade and wine. Cover and bring to boiling. Reduce heat and simmer slowly 2½ to 3 hours, or until meat is tender.
4. Remove meat to a warm platter.
5. Strain the cooking liquid. Return the strained liquid to sauce-pot.
6. Pour water into a screw-top jar and add flour; cover jar tightly and shake until mixture is well blended.
7. Stirring constantly, slowly pour one half of the blended mixture into liquid in saucepot. Bring to boiling. Gradually add only what is needed of the remaining blended mixture for consistency desired. Bring gravy to boiling after each addition. Cook 3 to 5 minutes longer.
8. Serve meat with gravy.

8 to 10 servings

524 *Beef Burgundy*

This is a family-size recipe. Increase it for a party, as pictured on the cover.

2 slices bacon
2 pounds beef round tip steak, cut
    in 2-inch cubes
2 tablespoons flour
1 teaspoon seasoned salt
1 package beef stew seasoning
    mix
1 cup burgundy
1 cup water
1 tablespoon tomato paste
12 small boiling onions
4 ounces fresh mushrooms, sliced
    and lightly browned in 1
    tablespoon butter or
    margarine
16 cherry tomatoes, stems
    removed

1. Fry bacon in a Dutch oven; remove bacon. Coat meat cubes with a blend of flour and seasoned salt. Add to fat in Dutch oven and brown thoroughly. Add beef stew seasoning mix, burgundy, water, and tomato paste. Cover and simmer gently 45 minutes.
2. Peel onions and pierce each end with a fork so they will retain their shape when cooked. Add onions to beef mixture and simmer 40 minutes, or until meat and onions are tender. Add mushrooms and cherry tomatoes; simmer 3 minutes. Pour into a serving dish.

6 to 8 servings

Note: If cherry tomatoes are not available, use canned whole peeled tomatoes.

525 *Easy Corned Beef Bake*

½ package (6 ounces) noodles, cooked
    and drained
1 can (12 ounces) corned beef, cut up
1 cup (4 ounces) shredded American
    cheese
¾ cup milk
¼ cup chopped onion
½ cup fine dry bread crumbs
2 tablespoons butter or margarine

1. Combine noodles, corned beef, cheese, milk, and onion. Put into a greased 1½-quart casserole.
2. Top with bread crumbs. Dot with butter.
3. Bake, covered, at 325°F 45 minutes, or until casserole is bub-bly.

4 servings

526 Corned Beef

6-pound beef brisket corned,
   boneless
2 teaspoons whole cloves
½ cup firmly packed light brown
   sugar
¼ cup sherry

1. Put the meat into a saucepot and add enough water to cover meat. Cover saucepot tightly and bring water just to boiling over high heat. Reduce heat and simmer about 4 hours, or until meat is almost tender when pierced with a fork.
2. Remove from heat and cool in liquid; refrigerate overnight.
3. Remove meat from liquid and set on rack in roasting pan. Stud with cloves. Put brown sugar over top and press firmly.
4. Roast at 325°F 1½ hours. After roasting 30 minutes, drizzle with sherry.
5. To serve, carve meat into slices.

About 12 servings

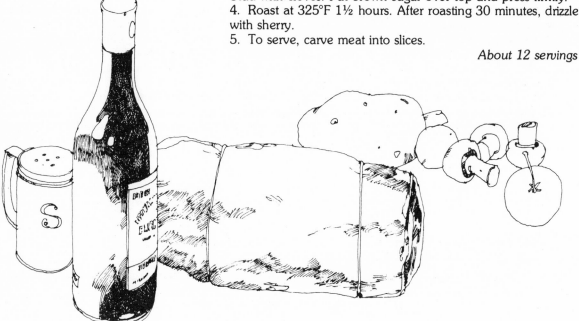

527 Roast Beef Filet with Burgundy Sauce

1 beef loin tenderloin roast, center
   cut (about 4 pounds)
  Salt and pepper
½ cup dry red wine, such as
   burgundy
  Sautéed mushroom caps
  Parsley-buttered potatoes
  Spiced crab apples
Burgundy Sauce:
½ cup warm water
¼ cup flour
1 cup beef broth
½ cup burgundy

1. Have meatman trim all but a thin layer of fat from meat and roll meat like a rib roast (but without adding fat).
2. Rub meat with salt and pepper and place in shallow roasting pan. Insert meat thermometer into center of thickest portion of roast.
3. Roast in a very hot oven, 450°F, about 45 to 60 minutes until thermometer registers 140°F (rare), basting twice with the wine after meat has cooked for 20 minutes.
4. Remove roast to heated serving platter. Garnish with sautéed mushroom caps, parsley-buttered potatoes, and spiced crab apples. Serve with Burgundy Sauce.
5. For sauce, pour off clear fat from drippings, saving ¼ cup.
6. Pour warm water into roasting pan; stir and scrape up all brown bits; strain.
7. Heat the reserved fat in a skillet; stir in flour. Slowly stir in strained liquid, beef broth, and burgundy. Cook and stir until sauce boils and thickens. Add a few drops of gravy coloring, if desired.

6 to 8 servings

528 *Boulettes of Beef Stroganoff*

1 pound ground beef round steak
1 egg, lightly beaten
⅓ cup fine fresh bread crumbs
¼ cup milk
¼ teaspoon grated nutmeg
¼ teaspoon each salt and freshly
    ground pepper
3 tablespoons paprika
¼ cup butter
¼ pound mushrooms, thinly sliced
⅓ cup finely chopped onion
¼ cup dry sherry
2 tablespoons brown sauce or
    canned beef gravy
¼ cup heavy cream
1 cup dairy sour cream
¼ cup finely chopped parsley

1. Put the meat into a mixing bowl and add the egg.
2. Soak the crumbs in milk and add this to the meat. Add the nutmeg, salt, and pepper; mix well with the hands. Shape the mixture into balls about 1½-inches in diameter. There should be about 35 to 40 meatballs.
3. Sprinkle a pan with the paprika and roll the meatballs in it.
4. Heat the butter in a heavy skillet and cook the meatballs, turning gently, until they are nicely browned, about 5 minutes. Sprinkle the mushrooms and onion between and around the meatballs and shake the skillet to distribute the ingredients evenly. Cook about 1 minute and partially cover. Simmer about 5 minutes and add the wine and brown sauce.
5. Stir in the heavy cream. Partially cover and cook over low heat about 15 minutes. Stir in the sour cream and bring just to boiling without cooking. Sprinkle with parsley and serve piping hot with **buttered fine noodles** as an accompaniment.

4 to 6 servings

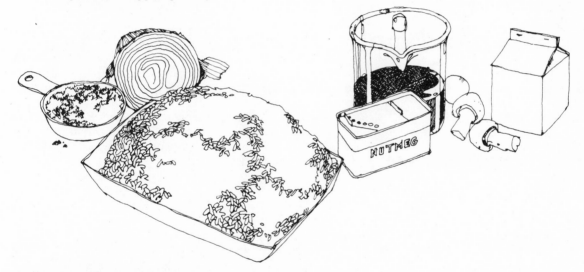

529 *Beef Stroganoff*

1½ pounds well-trimmed beef loin
    top sirloin steak, boneless
2 cups sliced mushrooms
3 tablespoons butter
1 shallot, chopped
¼ bay leaf
¾ cup dry sherry
2 tablespoons cornstarch
1 can (about 10 ounces)
    condensed beef broth
½ teaspoon salt
    Pepper to taste
1 cup dairy sour cream
1 tablespoon finely chopped
    parsley

1. Broil steak until rare. Cool thoroughly, then cut into strips.
2. Saute mushrooms in butter. Add shallot, bay leaf, and sherry; boil 5 minutes, until wine is reduced in volume to about half. Remove bay leaf.
3. Stir cornstarch into a little of the broth. Turn remaining broth over mushrooms, add cornstarch mixture, and cook-stir until sauce boils thoroughly and thickens. Add salt and pepper.
4. Just before serving, reheat sauce, then stir in sour cream and parsley and heat until simmering. Add steak strips and heat, but do not boil. Serve as soon as steak is thoroughly heated.

6 servings

530 *Tenderloin Supreme in Mushroom Sauce*

1 whole beef loin tenderloin roast
(4 to 6 pounds)
Mushroom Sauce:
⅓ cup butter
¾ cup sliced mushrooms
¾ cup finely chopped onion
1½ tablespoons flour
¾ teaspoon salt
⅛ teaspoon pepper
⅛ teaspoon thyme
1½ cups beef broth
¾ cup red wine, such as burgundy
1½ teaspoons wine vinegar
1½ tablespoons tomato paste
1½ teaspoons chopped parsley

1. Place tenderloin on rack in roasting pan. Insert roast meat thermometer in center of meat so that tip is slightly more than halfway through meat.
2. Roast, uncovered, at 425°F 45 to 60 minutes. The roast will be rare when meat thermometer registers 140°F.
3. For Mushroom Sauce, heat butter in a skillet. Add mushrooms and cook over medium heat until lightly browned and tender, stirring occasionally. Remove mushrooms with a slotted spoon, allowing butter to drain back into skillet; set aside.
4. Add onion and cook 3 minutes; blend in flour, salt, pepper, and thyme. Heat until mixture bubbles. Remove from heat.
5. Gradually add, stirring constantly, beef broth, wine, and wine vinegar. Cook rapidly until sauce thickens. Blend in the mushrooms, tomato paste, and parsley. Cook about 3 minutes.
6. Serve slices of beef tenderloin with sauce spooned over individual servings.

16 to 24 servings

531 *Roast Leg of Lamb with Spicy Wine Sauce*

1 cup dry red wine
¼ cup salad oil
1 onion, coarsely chopped
2 cloves garlic, minced
½ teaspoon Tabasco
2 teaspoons salt
1 lamb leg whole (6 to 8 pounds)
Parsley

1. Combine wine, oil, onion, garlic, Tabasco, and salt; pour over lamb. Cover and refrigerate 6 hours or overnight, turning occasionally.
2. Place lamb on rack in shallow roasting pan. Roast at 325°F about 25 minutes per pound, or until meat thermometer registers 160° to 170°F (medium); baste occasionally with marinade.
3. Garnish with parsley.

12 to 16 servings

532 *Company Affair Lamb Chops*

3 tablespoons butter
3 tablespoons flour
1 cup rich beef stock
¼ cup diced smoked pork loin,
Canadian style bacon, or lean
ham
1 tablespoon butter
¼ cup sherry
2 tablespoons minced green pepper
6 slices eggplant, cut ½ inch
thick; unpeeled
Olive oil
6 lamb loin chops
6 broiled mushroom caps

1. Melt butter in saucepan; add flour and cook until lightly browned. Gradually add beef stock and cook sauce until smooth and thick.
2. Combine bacon and butter in skillet and fry at least 2 minutes. Add sherry and green pepper and add to sauce.
3. Brush eggplant with olive oil and broil until lightly browned.
4. Broil lamb chops so that they are pink and juicy inside and crisply browned on outside.
5. Pour hot sauce over eggplant slices and place one lamb chop on each slice of eggplant. Garnish with a mushroom cap.

6 servings

533 Lamb Chops Burgundy

8 lamb loin or rib chops, cut 1½ to
    2 inches thick
½ cup burgundy
¼ cup olive oil
⅔ cup chopped red onion
½ clove garlic, minced
¼ teaspoon salt
3 peppercorns, crushed
½ teaspoon cumin seed, crushed

1. Put lamb chops into a shallow dish.
2. Combine burgundy, olive oil, red onion, garlic, salt, peppercorns, and cumin in a screw-top jar and shake to blend.
3. Pour marinade over meat. Cover and set in refrigerator to marinate about 2 hours, turning chops occasionally.
4. Remove chops from marinade and place on broiler rack. Set under broiler with tops of chops 3 to 5 inches from heat. Broil 18 to 22 minutes, or until meat is done as desired; turn once and brush occasionally with remaining marinade. To test, slit meat near bone and note color of meat.

8 servings

534 Party Lamb Chops

6 lamb loin chops, about 2 pounds
½ teaspoon salt
⅛ teaspoon pepper
2 tablespoons butter
2 tablespoons prepared mustard
1 can (16 ounces) quartered
    hearts of celery
1 cup tomato juice
½ cup dry white wine, such as
    sauterne
¼ cup finely chopped parsley

1. Sprinkle chops with salt and pepper.
2. Brown chops on both sides in butter in skillet. Spread mustard on chops.
3. Add celery and liquid from can, tomato juice, and wine. Cover and simmer 1 hour over low heat until chops are tender. Place chops on platter and keep warm.
4. Pour pan juices into blender and whirl until smooth, or beat with a rotary beater in small bowl. Pour back into skillet and reheat until bubbly and thick. Spoon over chops. Sprinkle chops with parsley.

6 servings

535 Lamb Chops with Dill Sauce

3 tablespoons butter
½ cup chopped onion
4 lamb shoulder arm chops, cut ½
    inch thick
2 tablespoons water
1 tablespoon vinegar
1 teaspoon salt
¼ teaspoon pepper
1 bay leaf
2 tablespoons butter or margarine
2 tablespoons flour
¼ teaspoon salt
    Few grains pepper
½ cup beef broth
1 tablespoon chopped fresh dill
½ cup dry white wine, such as
    chablis or sauterne
2 tablespoons vinegar

1. For chops, melt butter in a large heavy skillet with a tight-fitting cover. Add onion to fat and cook slowly, stirring occasionally, about 5 minutes. Remove onion from skillet with slotted spoon to small dish and set aside.
2. Cut through fat about every inch on outside edges of lamb chops. Be careful not to cut through to lean meat. Place chops in skillet; slowly brown both sides.
3. Meanwhile, combine water, vinegar, salt, pepper, and bay leaf; slowly add this mixture to the browned lamb. Return onion to skillet. Cover skillet and simmer 25 to 30 minutes, or until lamb is tender when pierced with a fork. If needed, add small amounts of water as lamb cooks.
4. For sauce, melt butter in small skillet over low heat. Blend flour, salt, and pepper into butter until smooth. Heat mixture until bubbly and lightly browned. Remove skillet from heat. Gradually add a mixture of the broth and fresh dill, stirring constantly.
5. Bring rapidly to boiling, stirring constantly; cook 1 to 2 minutes longer. Remove sauce from heat and gradually add wine and vinegar, stirring constantly. Serve the sauce over lamb chops.

4 servings

536 *Stuffed Veal Steak*

4 veal loin top loin chops, 1 inch thick (about 1½ pounds)
1 cup dry white wine, such as chablis
½ cup sliced mushrooms
1 green pepper, cut in ½-inch pieces
½ cup butter or margarine
½ cup all-purpose flour
1 egg, fork beaten
½ cup fine dry bread crumbs
½ cup grated Parmesan cheese
4 slices proscuitto (Italian ham)
4 slices (4 ounces) Cheddar cheese

1. Make a cut in the side of each veal chop, cutting almost all the way through. Lay each open and pound flat. Marinate meat for 1 hour in wine.
2. While meat marinates, sauté mushrooms and green pepper in butter for about 10 minutes or until tender. Remove from skillet with slotted spoon, leaving butter in skillet. Set vegetables aside.
3. Dry veal on paper towel. Bread on one side only, dipping first in flour, then in beaten egg, and last in bread crumbs mixed with Parmesan cheese.
4. Lay a slice of proscuitto on one half of unbreaded side of veal. Fold other side over. Panfry for 6 minutes on one side in butter in skillet, adding more butter if needed. Turn veal, and remove skillet from heat.
5. Insert a slice of cheese and ¼ of the mushroom-pepper mixture into the fold of each steak.
6. Return to heat and cook 6 minutes, or until meat is tender.

4 servings

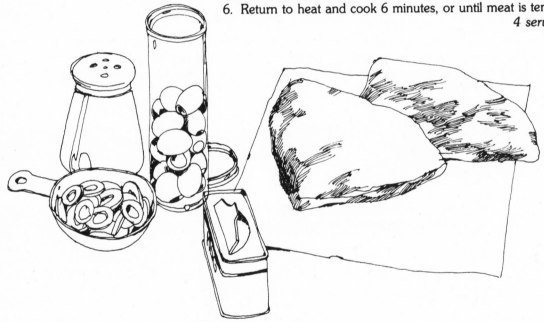

537 *Veal Cutlet in Wine with Olives*

1½ pounds veal cutlets, cut about ¼ inch thick
¼ cup all-purpose flour
1 teaspoon salt
½ teaspoon monosodium glutamate
¼ teaspoon pepper
2 to 3 tablespoons butter or margarine
⅓ cup marsala
⅓ cup sliced green olives

1. Place meat on flat working surface and pound with meat hammer to increase tenderness. Turn meat and repeat process. Cut into 6 serving-size pieces. Coat with a mixture of flour, salt, monosodium glutamate, and pepper.
2. Heat butter in skillet over low heat. Brown meat over medium heat. Add marsala and green olives. Cover skillet and cook over low heat about 1 hour, or until meat is tender when pierced with a fork.

About 6 servings

538 Veal in Wine-Mushroom Sauce

1½ pounds thin veal cutlets
1 clove garlic, peeled and cut
1 tablespoon flour
¼ cup butter or margarine
½ pound mushrooms, thinly sliced
½ teaspoon salt
 Dash white pepper
½ cup white wine, such as vermouth
1 teaspoon lemon juice (optional)
 Snipped parsley

1. Pound meat to ¼-inch thickness. Rub both sides with garlic. Cut veal into 2-inch pieces and sprinkle with flour.
2. Sauté veal, a few pieces at a time, in hot butter in a large skillet, until golden brown on both sides.
3. Return all pieces to skillet. Top with mushrooms and sprinkle with salt and pepper.
4. Add wine and cook, covered, over low heat for 20 minutes, or until fork tender, adding 1 tablespoon or so of water if necessary.
5. To serve, sprinkle with lemon juice, if desired, and parsley.

4 to 6 servings

539 Neapolitan Pork Chops

2 tablespoons olive oil
1 clove garlic, minced
6 pork loin rib chops, cut about ¾ to 1 inch thick
1 teaspoon salt
½ teaspoon monosodium glutamate
¼ teaspoon pepper
1 pound mushrooms
2 green peppers
½ cup canned tomatoes, sieved
3 tablespoons dry white wine

1. Heat oil in large heavy skillet, add minced garlic and cook until lightly browned.
2. Season pork chops with a mixture of the salt, monosodium glutamate, and pepper. Place in skillet and slowly brown chops on both sides.
3. While chops brown, clean and slice mushrooms and chop green peppers; set aside.
4. When chops are browned, add the mushrooms and peppers. Stir in tomatoes and wine, cover skillet and cook over low heat 1 to 1½ hours, depending on thickness of chops. Add small amounts of water as needed. Test the chops for tenderness by piercing with a fork.

6 servings

540 Apple-Covered Ham in Claret

2 smoked ham center slices, fully cooked, about ¾ inch thick (about ½ pound each) or 1 large center cut 1½ inches thick
½ teaspoon dry mustard
3 to 4 medium Golden Delicious apples, cored and cut in rings
4 orange slices
¾ cup dry red wine, such as claret
½ cup packed brown sugar
 Parsley sprigs

1. Place ham slices in large shallow baking dish. Sprinkle each slice with ¼ teaspoon mustard.
2. Cut unpared apple rings in half and place around outer edge of ham, slightly overlapping slices.
3. Place two orange slices in center of each ham slice.
4. Pour wine over top of ham and fruit. Then sprinkle entire dish with brown sugar.
5. Cover; cook in a 350°F oven 45 minutes. Serve on platter or from baking dish, and garnish with parsley.

6 to 8 servings

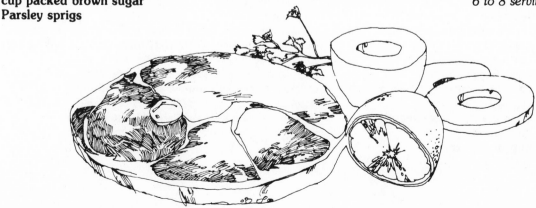

Poultry

541 *Spiced Fruited Chicken*

12 pieces frying chicken (breasts, legs, and thighs)
1½ teaspoons salt
¼ teaspoon each pepper, cinnamon, and cloves
2 garlic cloves, minced
¼ cup oil
½ cup chopped onion
1 can (13¼ ounces) crushed pineapple
1⅓ cups orange juice (about)
½ cup raisins
½ cup dry sherry

1. Rub chicken with mixture of salt, pepper, cinnamon, cloves, and garlic. Brown in oil in a heavy skillet.
2. Place browned chicken pieces in an attractive range-to-table Dutch oven.
3. Lightly brown onion in oil remaining in skillet.
4. Drain pineapple, reserving liquid. Add enough orange juice to liquid to measure 2 cups.
5. Add onion, pineapple, raisins, and orange juice mixture to chicken. Cover and simmer about 45 minutes, or until chicken is tender.
6. Remove chicken. Add sherry; cook uncovered 15 minutes longer to cook down liquid. Return chicken; heat through.

12 servings

542 *Chicken and Dumplings*

¼ cup butter or margarine
2 broiler-fryer chickens, cut in
    serving-size pieces
½ cup chopped onion
¼ cup chopped celery
2 tablespoons chopped celery leaves
1 clove garlic, minced
¼ cup enriched all-purpose flour
4 cups chicken broth
1 teaspoon sugar
2 teaspoons salt
¼ teaspoon ground black pepper
1 teaspoon basil leaves
2 bay leaves
¼ cup chopped parsley
    Basil Dumplings
2 packages (10 ounces each) frozen
    green peas

1. Heat butter in a large skillet. Add chicken pieces and brown on all sides. Remove chicken from skillet.
2. Add onion, celery, celery leaves, and garlic to fat in skillet. Cook until vegetables are tender. Sprinkle with flour and mix well. Add chicken broth, sugar, salt, pepper, basil, bay leaves, and parsley; bring to boiling, stirring constantly. Return chicken to skillet and spoon sauce over it; cover.
3. Cook in a 350°F oven 40 minutes.
4. Shortly before cooking time is completed, prepare Basil Dumplings.
5. Remove skillet from oven and turn control to 425°F. Stir peas into skillet mixture and bring to boiling. Drop dumpling dough onto stew.
6. Return to oven and cook, uncovered, 10 minutes; cover and cook 10 minutes, or until chicken is tender and dumplings are done.

About 8 servings

Basil Dumplings: Combine **2 cups all-purpose biscuit mix** and **1 teaspoon basil leaves** in a bowl. Add **⅔ cup milk** and stir with a fork until a dough is formed. Proceed as directed in recipe. 543

544 *Chicken Fricassee with Vegetables*

1 broiler-fryer chicken (about 3
    pounds), cut in serving-size
    pieces
1½ teaspoons salt
1 bay leaf
    Water
2 cups sliced carrots
2 onions, quartered
2 crookneck squashes, cut in halves
    lengthwise
2 pattypan squashes, cut in halves
    Green beans (about 6 ounces),
    tips cut off
1 can (3½ ounces) pitted ripe olives,
    drained
1 tablespoon cornstarch
2 tablespoons water

1. Place chicken pieces along with salt and bay leaf in a Dutch oven or saucepot. Add enough water to just cover chicken. Bring to boiling; simmer, covered, 25 minutes until chicken is almost tender.
2. Add carrots and onions to cooking liquid; cook, covered, 10 minutes. Add squashes and green beans to cooking liquid; cook, covered, 10 minutes, or until chicken and vegetables are tender. Remove chicken and vegetables to a warm serving dish and add olives; keep hot.
3. Blend cornstarch and 2 tablespoons water; stir into boiling cooking liquid. Boil 2 to 3 minutes. Pour gravy over chicken.

About 4 servings

545 *Chicken Polynesian Style*

2 cups chicken broth
1 package (10 ounces) frozen mixed
   vegetables
½ cup diagonally sliced celery
1½ tablespoons cornstarch
1 teaspoon monosodium glutamate
½ teaspoon sugar
½ teaspoon seasoned salt
⅛ teaspoon ground black pepper
½ teaspoon Worcestershire sauce
1 small clove garlic, minced or
   crushed in a garlic press
1 tablespoon instant minced onion
1 can (6 ounces) ripe olives, drained
   and cut in wedges
Cooked chicken, cut in 1-inch
   pieces (about 2 cups)
Chow mein noodles
Salted peanuts
Soy sauce

1. Heat ½ cup chicken broth in a saucepan. Add frozen vegetables and celery; cook, covered, until crisp-tender. Remove vegetables and set aside; reserve any cooking liquid in saucepan.
2. Mix cornstarch, monosodium glutamate, sugar, seasoned salt, and pepper; blend with ¼ cup of the chicken broth. Add remaining broth, Worcestershire sauce, garlic, and onion to the saucepan. Add cornstarch mixture; bring to boiling, stirring constantly. Cook and stir 2 to 3 minutes.
3. Mix in olives, chicken, and reserved vegetables; heat thoroughly, stirring occasionally.
4. Serve over chow mein noodles and top generously with peanuts. Accompany with a cruet of soy sauce.

About 6 servings

546 *Country Captain*

1 broiler-fryer chicken (3 to 3½
   pounds), cut in serving-size
   pieces
¼ cup enriched all-purpose flour
½ teaspoon salt
   Pinch ground white pepper
3 to 4 tablespoons lard
2 onions, finely chopped
2 medium green peppers, chopped
1 clove garlic, crushed in a garlic
   press or minced
1½ teaspoons salt
½ teaspoon ground white pepper
1½ teaspoons curry powder
½ teaspoon ground thyme
½ teaspoon snipped parsley
5 cups undrained canned tomatoes
2 cups hot cooked rice
¼ cup dried currants
¾ cup roasted blanched almonds
   Parsley sprigs

1. Remove skin from chicken. Mix flour, ½ teaspoon salt, and pinch white pepper. Coat chicken pieces.
2. Melt lard in a large heavy skillet; add chicken and brown on all sides. Remove pieces from skillet and keep hot.
3. Cook onions, peppers, and garlic in the same skillet, stirring occasionally until onion is lightly browned. Blend 1½ teaspoons salt, ½ teaspoon white pepper, curry powder, and thyme. Mix into skillet along with parsley and tomatoes.
4. Arrange chicken in a shallow roasting pan and pour tomato mixture over it. (If it does not cover chicken, add a small amount of water to the skillet in which mixture was cooked and pour liquid over chicken.) Place a cover on pan or cover tightly with aluminum foil.
5. Cook in a 350°F oven about 45 minutes, or until chicken is tender.
6. Arrange chicken in center of a large heated platter and pile the hot rice around it. Stir currants into sauce remaining in the pan and pour over the rice. Scatter almonds over top. Garnish with parsley.

About 6 servings

547 *Chicken with Fruit*

1 tablespoon flour
1 teaspoon seasoned salt
¾ teaspoon paprika
3 pounds broiler-fryer chicken
    pieces (legs, thighs, and breasts)
1½ tablespoons vegetable oil
1½ tablespoons butter or margarine
1 glove garlic, crushed in a garlic
    press or minced
⅓ cup chicken broth
2 tablespoons cider vinegar
1 tablespoon brown sugar
¼ teaspoon rosemary
1 can (11 ounces) mandarin
    oranges, drained; reserve syrup
1 jar (4 ounces) maraschino
    cherries, drained; reserve syrup
1 tablespoon water
1 tablespoon cornstarch
½ cup dark seedless raisins
Cooked rice

1. Mix flour, seasoned salt, and paprika. Coat chicken pieces.
2. Heat oil, butter, and garlic in a large heavy skillet. Add chicken pieces and brown well on all sides.
3. Mix broth, vinegar, brown sugar, rosemary, and reserved syrups. Pour into skillet; cover and cook slowly 25 minutes, or until chicken is tender.
4. Remove chicken pieces to a serving dish and keep warm; skim any excess fat from liquid in skillet. Blend water with cornstarch and stir into liquid in skillet. Add raisins, bring to boiling, stirring constantly, and cook about 5 minutes, or until mixture is thickened and smooth. Mix in orange sections and cherries; heat thoroughly.
5. Pour sauce over chicken and serve with hot fluffy rice.

About 6 servings

548 *Chicken Livers and Mushrooms*

2 pounds chicken livers, thawed if
    frozen
½ cup enriched all-purpose flour
1 teaspoon salt
¼ teaspoon ground white pepper
⅓ cup butter or margarine
1 cup orange sections, cut in halves
1 can (6 ounces) broiled mushrooms
Fresh parsley, snipped

1. Rinse chicken livers and drain on absorbent paper. Mix flour, salt, and pepper; coat chicken livers evenly.
2. Heat butter in a large skillet, add chicken livers, and cook 10 minutes, or until livers are lightly browned and tender. Mix in orange sections; heat.
3. Meanwhile, heat mushrooms in their broth in a small skillet.
4. Arrange cooked chicken livers and heated orange sections on a hot platter. Top with mushrooms and sprinkle with parsley. Serve immediately.

About 6 servings

549 *Chicken Mexicana*

3 tablespoons vegetable oil
2 broiler-fryer chickens (2½ to 3
    pounds each), cut in serving-size
    pieces
2 cans (8 ounces each) tomato sauce
1 can (13¾ ounces) chicken broth
2 tablespoons (½ envelope) dry onion
    soup mix
¾ cup chopped onion
1 clove garlic, minced
6 tablespoons crunchy peanut butter
½ cup cream
½ teaspoon chili powder
¼ cup dry sherry
Cooked rice

1. Heat oil in a large skillet. Add chicken and brown on all sides.
2. Meanwhile, combine tomato sauce, 1 cup chicken broth, soup mix, onion, and garlic in a saucepan. Heat thoroughly, stirring constantly.
3. Pour sauce over chicken in skillet. Simmer, covered, 20 minutes.
4. Put peanut butter into a bowl and blend in cream and remaining chicken broth; stir into skillet along with chili powder and sherry. Heat thoroughly. Serve with hot fluffy rice.

About 6 servings

550 Stuffed Roast Capon

½ cup butter or margarine
1½ teaspoons salt
¼ teaspoon ground black pepper
¼ teaspoon thyme
¼ teaspoon marjoram
¼ teaspoon rosemary
1½ quarts soft enriched bread cubes
½ cup milk
¼ cup chopped celery leaves
¼ cup chopped onion
1 capon (6 to 7 pounds)
Salt
Fat, melted

1. For stuffing, melt butter and mix in salt, pepper, thyme, marjoram, and rosemary.
2. Put bread cubes into a large bowl and pour in seasoned butter; lightly toss. Mix in milk, celery leaves, and onion.
3. Rub body and neck cavities of capon with salt. Fill cavities lightly with stuffing; truss bird, using skewers and cord.
4. Place, breast side up, on rack in a shallow roasting pan. Brush skin with melted fat and cover with a fat-moistened cheesecloth.
5. Roast in a 325°F oven 2½ hours, or until a meat thermometer inserted in center of inside thigh muscle registers 180° to 185°F. For easier carving, allow capon to stand about 20 minutes after removing from oven. Serve on a heated platter.

6 to 8 servings

551 Turkey 'n' Dressing Bake

3 tablespoons butter or margarine
½ cup diced celery
¼ cup minced onion
3¼ cups chicken broth (dissolve 4 chicken bouillon cubes in 3¼ cups boiling water)
5 cups coarse whole wheat bread crumbs; reserve ½ cup crumbs for topping
¼ cup snipped parsley
½ teaspoon salt
¼ teaspoon ground black pepper
1 egg, slightly beaten
2 tablespoons flour
2 eggs, beaten
⅛ teaspoon ground black pepper
¼ teaspoon crushed leaf sage
¼ teaspoon celery salt
Thin slices of cooked turkey roast (see Note)
1 tablespoon butter or margarine, melted
Parsley, snipped

1. Heat 3 tablespoons butter in a large skillet. Mix in celery and onion and cook about 5 minutes. Combine vegetables with 1¾ cups chicken broth, 4½ cups bread crumbs, ¼ cup parsley, salt, ¼ teaspoon pepper, and 1 egg. Mix lightly with a fork. Spoon the mixture over bottom of a shallow 2-quart baking dish; set aside.
2. Mix flour and ¼ cup cool broth in a saucepan until smooth; heat until bubbly. Add remaining broth gradually, stirring constantly. Cook and stir over medium heat until sauce comes to boiling; cook 2 minutes. Remove from heat and gradually add to eggs while beating. Blend in remaining pepper, sage, and celery salt.
3. Arrange the desired amount of turkey over dressing in baking dish. Pour the sauce over all.
4. Toss reserved bread crumbs with melted butter; spoon over top.
5. Bake at 350°F 30 to 40 minutes, or until egg mixture is set. Garnish generously with parsley.

6 servings

Note: Prepare frozen boneless turkey roast, following package directions.

552 *Roast Turkey with Herbed Stuffing*

Cooked Giblets and Broth
4 quarts ½-inch enriched bread
    cubes
1 cup snipped parsley
2 to 2½ teaspoons salt
2 teaspoons thyme
2 teaspoons rosemary, crushed
2 teaspoons marjoram
1 teaspoon ground sage
1 cup butter or margarine
1 cup coarsely chopped onion
1 cup coarsely chopped celery with
    leaves
1 turkey (14 to 15 pounds)
    Fat
3 tablespoons flour
¼ teaspoon salt
⅛ teaspoon ground black pepper

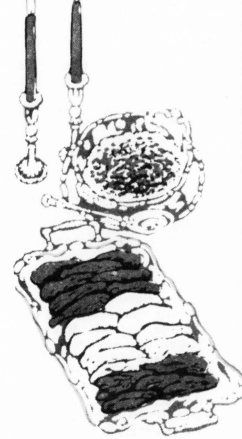

1. Prepare Cooked Giblets and Broth. Measure 1 cup chopped cooked giblets; set the broth aside.
2. Combine bread cubes, reserved giblets, and parsley in a large bowl. Blend salt, thyme, rosemary, marjoram, and sage; add to bread mixture and toss to mix.
3. Heat butter in a skillet. Mix in onion and celery; cook about 5 minutes, stirring occasionally. Toss with the bread mixture.
4. Add 1 to 2 cups broth (depending upon how moist a stuffing is desired), mixing lightly until ingredients are thoroughly blended.
5. Rinse turkey with cold water; pat dry, inside and out, with absorbent paper. Lightly fill body and neck cavities with the stuffing. Fasten neck skin to back with a skewer. Bring wing tips onto back of bird. Push drumsticks under band of skin at tail, if present, or tie to tail with cord.
6. Place turkey, breast side up, on rack in a shallow roasting pan. Brush skin with fat. Insert meat thermometer in the thickest part of the inner thigh muscle, being sure that tip does not touch bone.
7. Roast in a 325°F oven about 5 hours, or until thermometer registers 180° to 185°F. If desired, baste or brush bird occasionally with pan drippings. Place turkey on a heated platter; for easier carving, allow turkey to stand about 30 minutes.
8. Meanwhile, leaving brown residue in roasting pan, pour remaining drippings and fat into a bowl. Allow fat to rise to surface; skim off fat and measure 3 tablespoons into roasting pan. Blend flour, salt, and pepper with fat. Cook and stir until bubbly. Continue to stir while slowly adding 2 cups reserved liquid (broth and drippings). Cook, stirring constantly, until gravy thickens; scrape pan to blend in brown residue. Cook 1 to 2 minutes. If desired, mix in finely chopped cooked giblets the last few minutes of cooking.

About 25 servings

Cooked Giblets and Broth: Put **turkey neck** and **giblets** (except liver) into a saucepan with **1 large onion**, sliced, **parsley, celery with leaves, 1 medium bay leaf, 2 teaspoons salt**, and **1 quart water**. Cover, bring to boiling, reduce heat, and simmer until giblets are tender (about 2 hours); add the liver the last 15 minutes of cooking. Strain through a colander or sieve; reserve broth for stuffing. Chop giblets; set aside for stuffing and gravy.

553 Turkey-Oyster Casserole

1 tablespoon butter
2 teaspoons grated onion
4 ounces mushrooms, sliced
    lengthwise
¼ cup butter
¼ cup enriched all-purpose flour
1 teaspoon salt
¼ teaspoon ground pepper
    Few grains cayenne pepper
2 cups milk
1 egg yolk, slightly beaten
2 tablespoons chopped parsley
¼ teaspoon thyme
2 drops Tabasco
1 pint oysters (with liquor)
2 cups diced cooked turkey
    Buttered soft enriched bread
    crumbs

1. Heat 1 tablespoon butter with onion in a skillet; add mushrooms and cook over medium heat until lightly browned, stirring occasionally. Set aside.
2. Heat ¼ cup butter in a saucepan over low heat. Stir in flour, salt, pepper, and cayenne; cook until bubbly. Add milk gradually, stirring until well blended. Bring rapidly to boiling and boil 1 to 2 minutes, stirring constantly.
3. Blend a small amount of the hot sauce into egg yolk and return to remaining sauce, stirring until mixed. Stir in parsley, thyme, and Tabasco.
4. Heat oysters just to boiling; drain. Add oysters, turkey, and the mushrooms to sauce; toss lightly until thoroughly mixed.
5. Turn mixture into a buttered shallow 1½-quart baking dish. Sprinkle with crumbs.
6. Heat in a 400°F oven about 10 minutes, or until mixture is bubbly around edges and crumbs are golden brown.

About 6 servings

554 Roast Goose with Rice-and-Pickle Stuffing

3 cups cooked rice; or 1 package (6
    ounces) seasoned white and
    wild rice mix, cooked following
    package directions
1 package (7 ounces) herb-seasoned
    stuffing croutons
2 medium navel oranges, pared and
    sectioned
2 onions, chopped
1 cup cranberries, rinsed, sorted,
    and chopped
1 cup sweet mixed pickles, drained
    and chopped
¼ cup sweet pickle liquid
½ to ¾ cup butter or margarine,
    melted
2 tablespoons brown sugar
1 goose (8 to 10 pounds)
1 tablespoon salt
¼ teaspoon ground black pepper
2 tablespoons light corn syrup
1½ cups orange juice
½ cup orange marmalade

1. Combine rice, stuffing croutons, orange sections, onions, cranberries, pickles and liquid, butter, and brown sugar in a large bowl; toss lightly until blended.
2. Rinse goose and remove any large layers of fat from the body cavity. Pat dry with absorbent paper. Rub body and neck cavities with salt and pepper.
3. Lightly spoon stuffing into the neck and body cavities. Overlap neck cavity with the skin and skewer to back of goose. Close body cavity with skewers and lace with cord. Loop cord around legs; tighten slightly and tie to a skewer inserted in the back above tail. Rub skin of goose with a little salt, if desired.
4. Put remaining stuffing into a greased casserole and cover; or cook in heavy-duty aluminum foil. Set in oven with goose during final hour of roasting.
5. Place goose, breast side down, on a rack in a large shallow roasting pan.
6. Roast in a 325°F oven 2 hours, removing fat from pan several times during this period.
7. Turn goose, breast side up. Blend corn syrup and 1 cup orange juice. Brush generously over goose. Roast about 1½ hours, or until goose tests done. To test for doneness, move leg gently by grasping end of bone; when done, drumstick-thigh joint moves easily or twists out. Brush frequently during final roasting period with the orange-syrup blend.
8. Transfer goose to a heated serving platter. Spoon 2 tablespoons drippings, the remaining ½ cup orange juice, and marmalade into a small saucepan. Heat thoroughly, stirring to blend. Pour into a serving dish or gravy boat to accompany goose.

6 to 8 servings

555 *Rock Cornish Hens with Fruited Stuffing*

1½ cups herb-seasoned stuffing
    croutons
½ cup drained canned apricot
    halves, cut in pieces
½ cup quartered seedless green
    grapes
⅓ cup chopped pecans
¼ cup butter or margarine, melted
2 tablespoons apricot nectar
1 tablespoon chopped parsley
¼ teaspoon salt
4 Rock Cornish hens (1 to 1½
    pounds each), thawed if
    purchased frozen
    Salt and pepper
⅓ cup apricot nectar
2 teaspoons soy sauce

1. Combine stuffing croutons, apricots, grapes, pecans, 2 tablespoons butter, 2 tablespoons apricot nectar, parsley, and ¼ teaspoon salt in a bowl; mix lightly.
2. Sprinkle cavities of hens with salt and pepper. Fill each hen with about ½ cup stuffing; fasten with skewers and lace with cord.
3. Blend ⅓ cup apricot nectar, soy sauce, and remaining butter. Place hens, breast side up, on a rack in a shallow roasting pan; brush generously with sauce.
4. Roast in a 350°F oven about 1½ hours, or until hens are tender and well browned; baste occasionally with sauce during roasting.

4 servings

556 *Chicken with Poached Garlic*

The garlic, poached without peeling, imparts a delicate flavor to the chicken.

1 broiler-fryer chicken (2½ to 3
    pounds)
1 garlic clove, peeled and cut in
    half
    Juice of 1 lime
    Salt
    Freshly ground white pepper
16 garlic cloves (unpeeled)
½ cup Chicken Stock
¼ cup dry vermouth
    Chicken Stock
2 teaspoons arrowroot
    Cold water
¼ cup Mock Crème Fraîche
1 tablespoon snipped parsley
    Salt
    Freshly ground white pepper

1. Rinse chicken; pat dry. Place in a roasting pan. Rub entire surface of chicken with cut garlic clove. Squeeze lime juice over chicken. Sprinkle cavity and outside of chicken lightly with salt and pepper. Place remaining garlic cloves around chicken; pour in ½ cup stock and ¼ cup dry vermouth.
2. Roast in a 325°F oven about 2½ hours, or until done; meat on drumstick will be very tender. Add stock if necessary to keep garlic covered. Remove chicken to platter. Cover loosely with aluminum foil. Let stand 20 minutes before carving.
3. Spoon fat from roasting pan. Add enough stock to pan to make 1 cup of liquid. Mix arrowroot with a little cold water; stir into stock. Simmer, stirring constantly, until thickened (about 3 minutes). Stir in Mock Crème Fraîche and parsley. Season to taste with salt and pepper. Pass sauce with chicken.

4 servings

Note: To eat garlic cloves, gently press with fingers; the soft cooked interior will slip out. The flavor of the poached garlic is very delicate.

557 *Mock Crème Fraîche*

1½ cups Neufchatel cheese
6 tablespoons Low-Fat Yogurt

1. Mix cheese and yogurt in a blender or food processor until smooth and fluffy. Place in small jars; cover tightly.
2. Set jars in a warm place (100° to 125°F) for 2 hours; see Note. Cool and refrigerate. Stir before using.

About 2 cups

Note: Use an oven thermometer in making Mock Crème Fraîche, as temperature is very important. A gas oven with a pilot light will be about 125°F. Turn electric oven to as warm a setting as necessary to maintain temperature. Mock Crème Fraîche can be refrigerated up to 3 weeks.

558 Roast Chicken with Orange-Beer Sauce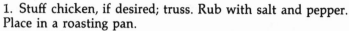

1 roasting chicken (4 to 5
    pounds)
Stuffing (optional)
Salt and pepper
1 can or bottle (12 ounces) beer
½ cup orange juice
2 tablespoons lemon juice
2 tablespoons tomato paste or
    ketchup
2 teaspoons sugar
¼ cup flour
Fresh parsley and orange slices

1. Stuff chicken, if desired; truss. Rub with salt and pepper. Place in a roasting pan.
2. Combine 1 cup beer, orange juice, lemon juice, tomato paste, and sugar. Pour a little over chicken.
3. Roast, uncovered, at 375°F 2 to 2½ hours, or until done, basting occasionally with remaining beer mixture.
4. Transfer chicken to platter; keep warm. Skim fat from drippings; measure remaining liquid. If needed, add water to make 1½ cups. Make paste with flour and remaining ½ cup beer. Combine with liquid. Cook, stirring constantly, until thickened. Season with salt and pepper to taste.
5. Garnish chicken with parsley and orange slices. Pass sauce to pour over slices after carving.

6 servings

Ham-Bread Stuffing for Chicken: Combine **3 cups fresh bread cubes, ¼ pound ground ham, 1 small onion, minced, 2 tablespoons melted butter, ½ teaspoon salt, ¼ teaspoon sage, a dash pepper,** and just enough **beer** to moisten.

559 Brewers' Chicken

You don't taste the beer in this creamy, smooth sauce, but it imparts a subtly savory flavor.

1 broiler-fryer chicken (2 to 2½
    pounds), cut up
12 small white onions; or 3
    medium onions, sliced
3 tablespoons cooking oil
¾ cup beer
1 tablespoon ketchup
½ teaspoon each thyme or
    rosemary, paprika, and salt
1 bay leaf
½ cup milk or half-and-half
3 tablespoons flour

1. In a large skillet, brown chicken and onions in oil, removing pieces as they brown. Pour off excess fat.
2. Add beer, ketchup, and seasonings to skillet. Stir up brown bits.
3. Return chicken and onions to skillet. Cover and simmer 30 to 35 minutes, or until tender.
4. With a slotted spoon, transfer chicken and onions to serving platter; keep warm. Boil down cooking liquid to about 1½ cups.
5. Stir milk into flour until smooth. Add to liquid in skillet. Cook, stirring constantly, until thickened and smooth. Strain, if desired.

4 servings

560 *Broiled Marinated Chicken*

Cook this chicken indoors in the broiler or outdoors over hot coals.

1 broiler-fryer chicken (2 to 2½ pounds), cut up
1 can or bottle (12 ounces) beer
2 tablespoons lemon juice
2 tablespoons oil
2 tablespoons honey
1 garlic clove, slivered
½ teaspoon crushed rosemary
½ teaspoon salt
⅛ teaspoon pepper

1. Place chicken in a shallow dish just large enough to hold pieces. Combine remaining ingredients; pour over chicken. Marinate in refrigerator at least 6 hours or overnight.
2. Grill or broil 6 to 8 inches from heat, basting often with marinade and turning, 30 to 40 minutes, or until tender.

4 servings

561 *African-Style Chicken*

1 broiler-fryer chicken (2 to 2½ pounds), cut up
2 tablespoons peanut or other cooking oil
1 medium onion, chopped
1 garlic clove, minced
¾ cup beer
⅓ cup ground peanuts
1 tablespoon lemon juice
1 tablespoon honey
½ teaspoon salt
¼ to ½ teaspoon dried ground chili pepper or chili powder
¼ teaspoon ginger
3 tablespoons cream or milk
2 to 3 tablespoons flour
¼ cup flaked coconut

1. Brown chicken in oil in a heavy skillet; set aside.
2. Sauté onion and garlic in same skillet until golden. Add beer, peanuts, lemon juice, honey, and seasonings; mix.
3. Return chicken to skillet. Cover and simmer 35 to 40 minutes, or until tender.
4. Place chicken on a platter; keep warm. Measure cooking liquid. Make a paste of cream and flour, using 2 tablespoons flour per 1 cup cooking liquid. Add coconut. Cook, stirring constantly, until thickened. Pour part of sauce over chicken. Pass remainder to pour over **rice** or **potatoes.**

4 servings

562 *Chicken and Rice in Beer*

Chicken, rice, and flavorings bake together in this meal-in-one casserole. Beer is used in place of water to cook the rice. Complete the dinner with a green salad and fruit or a custard dessert.

1 broiler-fryer chicken (2 to 2½ pounds), cut up
2 tablespoons oil
2 medium onions, chopped
1 garlic clove, minced
¾ cup uncooked rice (not instant)
½ green pepper, chopped
½ cup chopped fresh or canned tomatoes
1½ teaspoons salt
¼ teaspoon pepper
1 can or bottle (12 ounces) beer
2 bay leaves

1. Brown chicken in oil in a large skillet; set chicken aside.
2. In same skillet, sauté onion and garlic until golden.
3. Stir in rice, green pepper, tomatoes, 1 teaspoon salt, and pepper. Put mixture into a large, shallow baking dish.
4. Sprinkle chicken with ½ teaspoon salt; place on top of rice mixture.
5. Add beer to skillet; stir up brown bits. Pour over chicken and vegetables. Add bay leaves.
6. Cover tightly with foil or lid.
7. Bake at 375°F 40 to 60 minutes, or until chicken and rice are tender.

4 servings

563 *Crunchy Fried Chicken*

Chicken is dipped in a beer batter, then fried. The resulting coating is tender, crisp, and so delicious!

1 cup all-purpose flour
½ teaspoon salt
¼ teaspoon pepper
2 eggs
½ cup beer
1 broiler-fryer chicken (2 to 2½ pounds), cut up
Cooking oil

1. Mix flour, salt, and pepper. Beat eggs with beer; add to flour mixture. Stir until smooth.
2. Dip chicken in batter, coating pieces well. Chill 1 hour.
3. Fry chicken in hot oil ½ to 1 inch deep 15 minutes on one side. Turn; fry on other side 5 to 10 minutes, or until browned and done. Drain on absorbent paper.

4 servings

564 *Chicken Easy Oriental Style*

¼ cup flour
1 teaspoon salt
¼ teaspoon pepper
4 chicken breasts, split in halves
¼ cup shortening
1 can (10¾ ounces) condensed cream of chicken soup
¼ cup dry white wine
¼ cup milk
1 can (4 ounces) water chestnuts, drained and sliced
¼ teaspoon ground ginger

1. Combine flour, salt, and pepper; coat chicken with mixture.
2. Brown chicken in shortening in skillet. Place in a 13x9-inch baking dish.
3. Combine soup, wine, milk, chestnuts, and ginger. Pour over chicken.
4. Bake, covered, at 350°F 1 hour, or until chicken is tender. If desired, sprinkle with snipped parsley.

4 servings

565 *Chicken and Tomato Casserole*

1 broiler-fryer chicken (about 3 pounds), cut up
3 tablespoons shortening
½ cup chopped onion
¼ cup chopped green pepper
1 can (28 ounces) tomatoes (undrained)
1 can (8 ounces) tomato sauce
1 can (6 ounces) tomato paste
1 teaspoon salt
1 teaspoon oregano

1. Brown chicken in shortening in a skillet. Place in a 2-quart casserole.
2. Sauté onion and green pepper in fat in skillet. Stir in remaining ingredients and pour over chicken.
3. Bake, covered, at 350°F 1 hour, or until chicken is tender. Serve with **hot, cooked spaghetti.**

4 servings

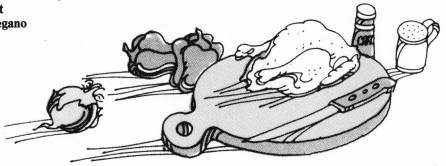

566 *Chicken Novaes*

2 jars (6 ounces each) tamales
1 can (4 ounces) sliced mushrooms, drained
2 cans (8 ounces each) tomato sauce
12 slices cooked chicken
2 cups cooked white rice
1 cup chopped green onion
2 cans (10¾ ounces each) condensed cream of chicken soup
1 cup (4 ounces) shredded Cheddar cheese
½ cup buttered bread crumbs

1. Remove paper from tamales. Cut in half crosswise and arrange in bottom of a 3-quart casserole.
2. Over the tamales, layer mushrooms, 1 can tomato sauce, chicken, rice, and onion. Top with the remaining can of tomato sauce. Spoon chicken soup over all, inserting a knife so soup will seep through.
3. Combine cheese and bread crumbs. Sprinkle over top of casserole mixture.
4. Bake, covered, at 350°F 30 minutes, or until bubbly.

12 servings

567 *Swiss Chicken Bake*

6 chicken breasts, split in halves, boned, and skin removed
1½ cups (6 ounces) shredded Swiss cheese
1 can (10¾ ounces) condensed cream of chicken soup
½ cup sherry
3 cups packaged herb stuffing mix
1 tablespoon butter or margarine

1. Place chicken breasts in a 13x9-inch baking dish. Sprinkle with cheese.
2. Combine soup and sherry; pour over Swiss cheese. Evenly spoon dressing over all. Dot with butter.
3. Bake, covered, at 350°F 1 hour, or until chicken is tender.

6 servings

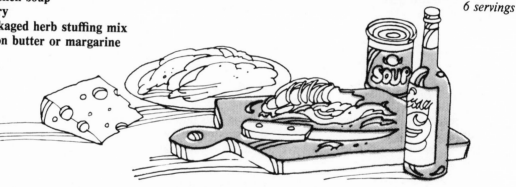

568 *Thyme-Chicken Casserole*

4 chicken breasts, split in halves
1 teaspoon salt
¼ teaspoon pepper
¼ cup butter or margarine
1 can (10¾ ounces) condensed cream of mushroom soup
¼ cup dry white wine
1 can (4 ounces) sliced mushrooms, drained
¼ cup chopped green pepper
¼ teaspoon thyme
1 tablespoon instant minced onion

1. Season chicken with salt and pepper. Brown in butter in a skillet. Arrange, skin side up, in a 13x9-inch baking dish.
2. Blend soup into drippings. Slowly stir in wine. Add remaining ingredients; heat thoroughly. Pour over chicken.
3. Bake, covered, at 350°F 50 minutes. Remove cover and bake an additional 10 minutes, or until chicken is tender.

4 servings

569 *Italian Baked Chicken*

¼ cup butter or margarine, melted
1 tablespoon lemon juice
1 broiler-fryer chicken (about 3 pounds), cut up
1 package (1½ ounces) spaghetti sauce mix
⅔ cup fine dry bread crumbs
½ to 1 cup half-and-half
1 cup (4 ounces) shredded mozzarella cheese

1. Combine butter and lemon juice. Dip chicken pieces in butter mixture.
2. Combine spaghetti sauce mix and bread crumbs; coat chicken pieces with mixture.
3. Place chicken pieces, skin side up, in a 1½-quart shallow baking dish. Pour half-and-half around and between chicken pieces.
4. Bake, covered, at 350°F 1 hour, or until chicken is tender. Top with cheese and bake 2 minutes, or until cheese is melted.

4 servings

570 *Crispy Chicken with Curried Fruit*

1 cup corn flake crumbs
½ teaspoon salt
Dash pepper
1 broiler-fryer chicken (about 3 pounds), cut up
½ cup evaporated milk
Curried Fruit

1. Combine crumbs, salt, and pepper. Dip chicken pieces in milk. Roll in crumb mixture. Place chicken pieces in a 1½-quart shallow baking dish.
2. Bake, uncovered, at 350°F with Curried Fruit 1 hour, or until chicken is tender.

4 servings

571 *Curried Fruit*

1 can (16 ounces) peach halves, drained*
1 can (8½ ounces) pineapple chunks, drained*
4 maraschino cherries
¼ cup butter or margarine, melted
½ cup firmly packed brown sugar
1 tablespoon curry powder

1. Put fruits into a 1½-quart casserole. Combine butter, brown sugar, and curry powder. Spoon over fruits.
2. Bake, covered, at 350°F 1 hour. Serve with **hot, cooked rice.**

4 servings

* The drained liquids can be refrigerated and used in gelatin salads.

572 *Chicken and Rice*

2 cups cooked white rice
½ cup milk
2 tablespoons chopped pimento
1 can (10¾ ounces) condensed cream of celery soup
1 can (10¾ ounces) condensed cream of mushroom soup
1 broiler-fryer chicken (about 3 pounds), cut up
1 package (1⅜ ounces) dry onion soup mix

1. Combine rice, milk, pimento, celery soup, and mushroom soup. Pour into a greased 13x9-inch baking dish.
2. Dip chicken pieces in **milk,** then roll in onion soup mix. Arrange chicken pieces over rice mixture.
3. Bake, covered, at 350°F 1 hour, or until chicken is tender.

4 servings

573 *Chicken and Rice Valencia*

1 broiler-fryer chicken (about 3 pounds), cut up
¼ cup olive oil
1 medium onion, finely chopped
1 medium green pepper, slivered
1 can (10 ounces) tomatoes (undrained)
1 bay leaf
¾ cup water
Dash ground saffron (optional)
1 cup drained stuffed olives
1 package (6 ounces) Spanish rice mix
½ cup chopped celery

1. Brown chicken pieces in olive oil in a skillet.
2. Add remaining ingredients, except rice and celery. Place in a 2-quart casserole.
3. Bake, covered, at 350°F 1 hour, or until chicken is tender.
4. Meanwhile, prepare rice according to package directions. Stir celery into rice. Spread on hot serving platter.
5. Remove bay leaf from chicken. Spoon chicken and sauce over rice.

4 servings

574 *Chicken Surprise*

½ cup chopped onion
1 tablespoon butter or margarine
1 tablespoon cornstarch
¾ cup orange juice
2 tablespoons prepared mustard
½ cup sherry
2 cups chopped cooked chicken
½ cup raisins
½ cup sliced celery

1. Sauté onion in butter in a skillet. Stir in cornstarch. Gradually add orange juice, then mustard and sherry, stirring until thickened and smooth.
2. Place chicken, raisins, and celery in a 1-quart casserole. Pour sauce over all; mix.
3. Bake, covered, at 325°F 30 minutes, or until heated through. Serve in **chow mein noodle** or **patty shells** and garnish with **orange twists.**

4 servings

575 *Chicken Breasts with Sour Cream*

8 chicken breasts, split in halves, boned, and skin removed
16 bacon slices
3 packages (3 ounces each) smoked sliced beef
1 can (10¾ ounces) condensed cream of mushroom soup
2 cups dairy sour cream

1. Roll each chicken breast in 1 bacon slice. (Another half bacon slice may be needed if the breast is a large one, so that all of it will be surrounded by the bacon.)
2. Shred beef and place in a 13x9-inch baking dish. Top with chicken breasts.
3. Combine soup and sour cream. Spoon over chicken breasts.
4. Bake, uncovered, at 275°F 3 hours, or until chicken is tender. Cover lightly with foil if it begins to get too brown.

8 servings

576 *Chicken Pie*

1¼ cups water
1 cup milk
1 package (⅞ ounce) chicken gravy mix
1 package (10 ounces) frozen peas, thawed
2 tablespoons chopped pimento
2 cups cubed cooked chicken
1 tablespoon finely chopped onion
1 teaspoon snipped parsley
2 cups all-purpose biscuit mix

1. Combine ¾ cup water, milk, and gravy mix in a saucepan; bring to a boil.
2. Stir in peas, pimento, and chicken; heat thoroughly.
3. Stir onion, parsley, and remaining ½ cup water into biscuit mix, stirring until thoroughly moistened.
4. Pour hot chicken mixture into an 11x7-inch shallow baking dish. Roll or pat out dough to fit top of baking dish. Set on chicken mixture.
5. Bake, uncovered, at 450°F 10 to 12 minutes, or until topping is golden brown.

6 servings

577 *Chicken Mac*

1 package (7¼ ounces) macaroni and cheese dinner
1 tablespoon instant minced onion
2 tablespoons chopped celery
2 tablespoons chopped green pepper
1 garlic clove, minced
2 tablespoons butter or margarine
1 can (8¾ ounces) whole kernel corn, drained
1 can (10¾ ounces) condensed cream of chicken soup
1½ cups chopped cooked chicken or turkey
2 tablespoons snipped parsley
⅓ cup buttered bread crumbs

1. Prepare dinner according to package directions, except use ½ cup milk.
2. Sauté onion, celery, green pepper, and garlic in butter in a skillet. Combine with corn, soup, chicken, and prepared dinner. Put into a greased 1½-quart casserole.
3. Combine parsley and bread crumbs. Sprinkle over top of casserole mixture.
4. Bake, covered, at 350°F 25 minutes, or until heated through.

4 servings

578 *Chicken Artichoke Casserole*

⅓ cup butter or margarine
¼ cup flour
1¾ cups milk
    Dash ground red pepper
1 garlic clove, minced
¼ cup (1 ounce) shredded Cheddar
    cheese
1½ ounces Gruyère cheese, cut up
2 cups chopped cooked chicken
1 can (4 ounces) button mushrooms,
    drained
1 can (14 ounces) artichoke hearts,
    drained

1. Melt butter in a saucepan. Stir in flour. Gradually add milk, stirring until thickened and smooth.
2. Add red pepper, garlic, and cheese, stirring until smooth. Blend in chicken, mushrooms, and artichoke hearts. Pour into a 2-quart casserole.
3. Bake, covered, at 350°F 30 minutes, or until heated through. Sprinkle with **paprika.**

6 servings

579 *Chicken-Green Noodle Casserole*

½ cup chopped onion
½ cup slivered almonds
1 cup sliced fresh mushrooms
¼ cup butter or margarine
3 cups cooked spinach (green) noodles
1 cup milk
2 cans (10¾ ounces each) condensed
    cream of chicken soup
3 cups chopped cooked chicken
¼ teaspoon pepper
⅓ cup buttered bread crumbs

1. Sauté onion, almonds, and mushrooms in butter in a skillet. Combine with remaining ingredients, except bread crumbs. Put into a 2½-quart casserole.
2. Bake, covered, at 350°F 30 minutes. Remove cover. Sprinkle with bread crumbs and bake an additional 15 minutes, or until heated through.

8 servings

580 *Chicken-Chip Bake*

2 cups chopped cooked chicken
2 cups sliced celery
1 can (8 ounces) pineapple chunks, drained
¾ cup mayonnaise
⅓ cup toasted slivered almonds
2 tablespoons lemon juice
2 teaspoons finely chopped onion
½ teaspoon salt
½ cup (2 ounces) shredded American cheese
1 cup crushed potato chips

1. Combine chicken, celery, pineapple, mayonnaise, almonds, lemon juice, onion, and salt. Put into a 1½-quart casserole. Sprinkle with cheese and potato chips.
2. Bake, uncovered, at 350°F 30 minutes, or until heated through.

4 to 6 servings

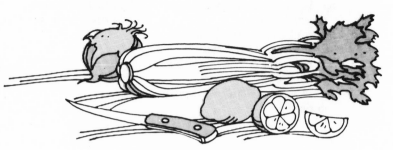

581 *Chicken Bake*

8 slices white bread, crusts removed
4 cups chopped cooked chicken or turkey
1 jar (4½ ounces) mushroom stems and pieces, drained
1 can (4 ounces) water chestnuts, drained and sliced
8 slices (1 ounce each) Cheddar cheese
¼ cup mayonnaise
4 eggs, well beaten
2 cups milk
1 teaspoon salt
2 cans (10¾ ounces each) condensed cream of mushroom soup
1 tablespoon chopped pimento
½ cup buttered bread crumbs

1. Place bread in a 13x9-inch baking dish. Top with chicken, mushrooms, water chestnuts, cheese, and mayonnaise.
2. Combine eggs, milk, and salt. Pour over all in casserole.
3. Mix soup and pimento; spread over top. Cover and refrigerate overnight.
4. Bake, covered, at 325°F 1 hour. Remove cover; sprinkle with bread crumbs and bake an additional 15 minutes, or until set. Let stand a few minutes before serving.

8 servings

582 *Hens in Wine*

1 tablespoon rosemary
1 cup dry white wine
⅓ cup flour
1 teaspoon salt
½ teaspoon pepper
1 teaspoon snipped parsley
4 Rock Cornish hens, quartered
½ cup butter or margarine
1 pound small fresh mushrooms

1. Soak rosemary in wine 1 hour.
2. Combine flour, salt, pepper, and parsley. Coat hen quarters with flour mixture.
3. Brown hen quarters in butter in a skillet. Place in a 12x8-inch baking dish. Add wine mixture.
4. Bake, uncovered, at 350°F 30 minutes.
5. Meanwhile, sauté mushrooms in butter in skillet. Add to baking dish. Bake an additional 15 minutes, or until hen quarters are tender.

4 servings

583 *Chicken à la King*

½ cup sliced fresh mushrooms
¼ cup butter or margarine
¼ cup flour
2 cups milk
1 teaspoon salt
1½ cups cooked noodles
2 cups chopped cooked chicken or
   turkey
¾ cup (3 ounces) shredded Cheddar
   cheese
1 cup cooked peas
1 tablespoon instant minced onion
2 teaspoons Worcestershire sauce
1 tablespoon ketchup
   Dash Tabasco

1. Sauté mushrooms in butter in a skillet. Stir in flour. Gradually add milk, stirring until thickened and smooth. Stir in remaining ingredients. Put into a 2-quart casserole.
2. Bake, covered, at 350°F 30 minutes, or until heated through.

4 servings

584 *Chicken and Wild Rice*

¾ cup uncooked wild rice
4 cups chopped cooked chicken
1 cup sherry
1 cup chicken broth
1 small onion, chopped
1 can (8 ounces) mushroom slices,
   drained
¼ cup butter or margarine, melted
1 can (10¾ ounces) condensed cream
   of mushroom soup
1 can (10¾ ounces) condensed cream
   of chicken soup
2 packages (10 ounces each) frozen
   broccoli or asparagus spears,
   cooked and drained
1 cup (4 ounces) shredded Cheddar
   cheese

1. Cook wild rice according to package directions.
2. Combine rice with remaining ingredients, except broccoli and cheese.
3. Spread half the rice mixture in a 13x9-inch baking dish. Top with broccoli. Evenly spread remaining rice mixture over all.
4. Bake, uncovered, at 350°F 45 minutes, or until heated through. Sprinkle with cheese and bake an additional 5 minutes, or until cheese is melted.

8 servings

585 *Turkey Pot Pie*

2 cups chopped cooked turkey
2 cans (10¾ ounces each) condensed
    cream of celery soup
½ cup milk
½ teaspoon Worcestershire sauce
    Dash pepper
6 cooked small onions
1 cup cooked cubed potato
1 cup cooked sliced carrot
⅓ cup shortening
1 cup self-rising flour
4 tablespoons cold water

1. Combine turkey, soup, milk, Worcestershire sauce, pepper, onions, potato, and carrot. Put into a 2-quart casserole.
2. Cut shortening into flour. Add water, a tablespoon at a time, mixing lightly until dough can be formed into a ball. (If necessary, add a little more water to make dough hold together.) Let rest 5 minutes.
3. Roll dough out on a lightly floured board or canvas to fit top of casserole. Cut slits to allow steam to escape. Adjust over filling; flute edges.
4. Bake, uncovered, at 425°F 20 minutes, or until pastry is golden brown.

6 servings

586 *Gefüllter Gänsebraten*
(Roast Goose with Prune-Apple Stuffing)

2 cups pitted cooked prunes
1 goose (10 to 12 pounds, ready-to-
    cook weight)
    Salt
6 medium (about 2 pounds)
    apples

1. Set out a shallow roasting pan with rack. Have prunes ready, reserving about 8 to 10 prunes for garnish.
2. If goose is frozen, thaw according to directions on package. Clean and remove any layers of fat from body cavity and opening of goose. Cut off neck at body, leaving on neck skin. Rinse and pat dry with absorbent paper. (Reserve giblets for use in gravy or other food preparation.) Rub body and neck cavities of goose with salt. Wash, core, pare and quarter apples.
3. Lightly fill body and neck cavities with the apples and prunes. To close body cavity, sew or skewer and lace with cord. Fasten neck skin to back with skewer. Loop cord around legs and tighten slightly. Place breast side down on rack in roasting pan.
4. Roast uncovered at 325°F 3 hours. Remove fat from pan as it accumulates during this period. Turn goose breast side up. Roast 1 to 2 hours longer, or until goose tests done. To test for doneness, move leg gently by grasping end of bone; drumstick-thigh joint should move easily. (Protect fingers with paper napkin.) Allow about 25 minutes per pound to estimate total roasting time.
5. To serve, remove skewers and cord. Place goose on heated platter. Remove some of the apples from goose and arrange on the platter. Garnish with the reserved prunes. For an attractive garnish, place cooked prunes on top of cooked apple rings, if desired.

8 servings

587 *Brunswick Stew*

1 chicken (about 4 pounds), disjointed
¼ cup cooking oil
1 cup coarsely chopped onion
¼ pound salt pork, chopped
4 tomatoes, peeled and quartered
2 cups boiling water
1 cup sherry
1 bay leaf
1 teaspoon Worcestershire sauce
1½ cups fresh lima or butter beans
½ cups sliced fresh okra
1½ cups fresh bread crumbs
2 tablespoons butter
Salt to taste

1. Sauté chicken in cooking oil until golden; remove chicken. Brown onion and salt pork in the same fat.
2. Put chicken, salt pork, onion, tomatoes, boiling water, sherry, bay leaf, and Worcestershire sauce into Dutch oven or saucepot. Cover and simmer 2 hours, or until chicken is tender.
3. After 1 hour, remove bay leaf; add beans and cook about 15 minutes. Add sliced okra; continue cooking about 15 minutes.
4. Sauté fresh bread crumbs in butter; stir into stew. Add salt to taste before serving.

8 servings

588 *Chicken Breasts with Noodles*

8 whole chicken breasts, flattened
Salt and pepper to taste
Dash of crushed marjoram
Butter to cover skillet
3 pounds fresh mushrooms
½ pound butter
12 ounces noodles
2 tablespoons butter
2 cups Medium White Sauce (see recipe)
1 cup cold milk
1 cup chicken broth
Hollandaise Sauce (see recipe)
½ cup dry white wine
Parmesan cheese, grated

1. Season chicken breasts with salt, pepper, and marjoram. Sauté in butter until breasts are fully cooked.
2. While chicken is cooking, wash mushrooms and cut into small pieces, then sauté in ½ pound butter.
3. Cook noodles until done; drain and work 2 tablespoons of butter gently into the noodles.
4. Make white sauce; add to it the cold milk and chicken broth. Cook mixture until thickened. Reserve while making hollandaise sauce.
5. Carefully blend hollandaise with white sauce mixture; stir in wine.
6. Butter a small roasting pan; place noodles in the bottom, add the mushrooms, and place chicken breasts on top of the mushrooms. Pour the sauce over all. Heat thoroughly in a 325°F oven about 45 minutes.
7. Remove from oven, sprinkle with grated Parmesan cheese and place under broiler to brown.

8 servings

Medium White Sauce: Melt ¼ cup butter or margarine in a saucepan. Blend in ¼ cup flour, 1 teaspoon salt, and ¼ teaspoon pepper. Cook and stir until bubbly. Gradually add 2 cups milk, stirring until smooth. Bring to boiling; cook and stir 1 to 2 minutes longer. 589

About 2 cups sauce

Hollandaise Sauce: Beat 4 egg yolks in the top of a double boiler, then beat in ½ cup cream. Cook and stir over hot water until slightly thickened. Blend in 2 tablespoons lemon juice. Cut in 4 tablespoons cold butter, a tablespoon at a time. Sauce will thicken. 590

About 1 cup sauce

591 *Chicken Curry with Rice*

⅔ cup butter or margarine
6 tablespoons chopped onion
6 tablespoons chopped celery
6 tablespoons chopped green apple
24 peppercorns
2 bay leaves
⅔ cup all-purpose flour
5 teaspoons curry powder
1 teaspoon monosodium glutamate
½ teaspoon sugar
¼ teaspoon nutmeg
5 cups milk
4 teaspoons lemon juice
1 teaspoon Worcestershire sauce
½ cup cream
¼ cup sherry
½ teaspoon Worcestershire sauce
6 cups cubed cooked chicken
Hot cooked rice

1. Heat butter in a heavy 3-quart saucepan over low heat. Add onion, celery, apple, peppercorns, and bay leaves, and cook over medium heat until lightly browned, occasionally moving and turning with a spoon.
2. Blend in flour, curry powder, monosodium glutamate, sugar, and nutmeg; heat until mixture bubbles.
3. Remove from heat and add milk gradually, stirring constantly.
4. Return to heat and bring rapidly to boiling. Stirring constantly, cook until mixture thickens; cook 1 to 2 minutes longer.
5. Remove from heat; add lemon juice and 1 teaspoon Worcestershire sauce. Strain mixture through a fine sieve, pressing vegetables against sieve to extract all sauce. Set sauce aside.
6. Reheat the curry sauce and blend in cream, sherry, and ½ teaspoon Worcestershire sauce; add chicken and cook over medium heat 2 to 3 minutes, or until mixture is thoroughly heated. Serve with rice.

8 servings

592 *Chicken à la Winegrower*

2 slices bacon, diced
2 cloves garlic, halved
1 tablespoon butter or margarine
4 chicken legs (thighs and drumsticks)
1 cup chopped onion
½ cup dry white wine
2 tablespoons chopped parsley
2 tablespoons chopped chives
1½ teaspoons salt
¼ teaspoon pepper
1 bay leaf
1 can (4 ounces) sliced mushrooms with liquid
1 cup chicken broth
2 tablespoons flour
Hot cooked rice
½ cup dairy sour cream, warmed
Chopped parsley for garnish

1. Sauté bacon and garlic in butter until bacon is partially cooked. Discard garlic.
2. Add chicken and brown on all sides.
3. Stir in onion and sauté until transparent. Add ¼ cup wine and cook a few minutes, stirring to loosen browned particles.
4. Add parsley, chives, seasonings, mushrooms, and broth. Cover and cook over low heat for 30 minutes, or until chicken is tender. Remove chicken and keep warm. Discard bay leaf.
5. Blend flour with remaining wine. Stir into sauce and cook until thickened.
6. Serve chicken on beds of fluffy rice. Top with sauce and dollops of sour cream. Garnish with parsley.

4 servings

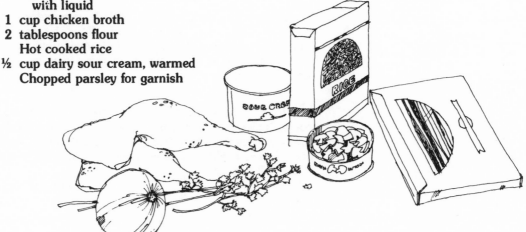

593 *Skillet Chicken and Vegetables*

1 can (about 10 ounces)
    condensed chicken broth
1 cup dry white wine, such as
    chablis
1 tablespoon instant minced onion
½ teaspoon salt
1 bay leaf
¼ teaspoon rosemary, crushed
6 half breasts of chicken
6 small carrots
6 small zucchini
2 tablespoons cornstarch
2 tablespoons cold water
3 tablespoons chopped pimento
2 tablespoons chopped parsley

1. Combine broth, wine, onion, salt, bay leaf, and rosemary in a large skillet. Heat to boiling.
2. Place chicken breasts in the boiling liquid; cover and simmer 20 minutes.
3. While chicken is cooking, pare carrots and cut in half lengthwise. Cut zucchini in half lengthwise. Add carrots and zucchini to the chicken; cover, and cook 15 minutes longer, or until chicken is tender and vegetables are crisp-tender.
4. Remove chicken and vegetables with a slotted spoon; keep warm.
5. Mix cornstarch with water and stir into liquid remaining in skillet. Cook, stirring until sauce boils thoroughly. Add pimento and parsley, and pour over chicken and vegetables.
Serve immediately.

6 servings

594 *Chicken Marengo*

1 broiler-fryer chicken (2 to 3
    pounds)
⅓ cup all-purpose flour
1 teaspoon salt
¼ teaspoon pepper
¼ cup olive oil
1 clove garlic, crushed
3 tablespoons chopped onion
4 tomatoes, quartered
1 cup white wine
    Herb Bouquet
1 cup (about 4 ounces) sliced
    mushrooms
2 tablespoons butter
½ cup sliced olives
½ cup chicken bouillon
2 tablespoons all-purpose flour

1. Disjoint chicken and cut into serving-size pieces. Rinse and pat dry with absorbent paper.
2. Coat chicken evenly with a mixture of flour, salt, and pepper.
3. Heat oil in a large skillet and brown chicken.
4. Add garlic, onion, tomatoes, wine, and Herb Bouquet to chicken; cover and simmer over low heat about ½ hour, or until thickest pieces of chicken are tender when pierced with a fork.
5. Sauté mushrooms in butter and add to chicken with olives.
6. Put bouillon and flour into screw-top jar; cover and shake well.
7. Remove chicken from skillet and discard Herb Bouquet. Gradually add bouillon-flour liquid to mixture in skillet, stirring constantly. Boil 3 to 5 minutes until mixture thickens.
8. Return chicken to sauce; cover and simmer 10 minutes. Arrange chicken on a hot platter. Cover with the sauce.

4 or 5 servings

Herb Bouquet: Tie neatly together **3 or 4 sprigs of parsley, 1 sprig thyme,** and **½ bay leaf.**

595 *Chicken a Seville*

3 tablespoons butter or margarine
½ pound fresh mushrooms, cleaned
    and halved lengthwise
3 to 4 tablespoons olive or other
    cooking oil
3 pounds chicken pieces
1 cup uncooked rice
1 large clove garlic, minced
2 cups chicken broth or bouillon

1. Heat butter in a large skillet and stir in mushrooms. Cook until lightly browned, stirring occasionally. Remove from skillet and set aside. Pour oil into skillet and heat.
2. Coat chicken pieces with a blend of **flour, salt,** and **pepper.** Fry in hot oil until browned on all sides. Remove chicken and keep warm.
3. Mix rice and garlic with oil in skillet, then stir in 1 cup of the chicken broth. Turn contents of skillet into a shallow baking dish. Put onions, browned chicken, mushrooms, and olives into dish.

12 **very small white onions**
1 **cup small pimento-stuffed olives**
1 **cup dry white wine**
¾ **teaspoon oregano**
½ **cup toasted blanched almonds, sliced**

Pour remaining broth and the wine over all. Sprinkle oregano over chicken.

4. Cook, covered, in a 375°F oven about 45 minutes, or until rice is tender. Remove from oven and top with the nuts.

About 6 servings

596 *Breast of Chicken Savannah*

4 **large chicken breasts, split**
2½ **ounces (about ¼ cup) peanut butter**
8 **thin slices cooked ham**
¼ **cup sherry**
Parmesan Sauce:
¼ **cup flour**
2 **cups milk**
½ **teaspoon salt**
6 **tablespoons freshly grated Parmesan cheese**
2 **tablespoons firm butter**

1. Lift skin on chicken breasts slightly, and spread a film of peanut butter on meat under skin; replace skin.
2. Place 1 slice of cooked ham over skin side of each breast.
3. Put sherry into a large casserole or braising pan. Add chicken pieces, ham side up; cover and cook in a 350°F oven 1 hour, or until pieces are tender.
4. Remove breasts from pan and keep warm while preparing Parmesan sauce; reserve ¼ cup pan drippings.
5. For sauce, put the pan drippings into a medium saucepan. Add flour; stir and heat until bubbly. Add milk gradually, stirring well; bring to boiling and cook 1 to 2 minutes.
6. Add salt and Parmesan cheese, stirring until cheese melts. Stir in butter, 1 tablespoon at a time.
7. Pour sauce over chicken and serve.

8 servings

597 *Canard à l'Orange*
(Roast Duckling with Orange Sauce)

2 **ducklings (4 to 5 pounds each)**
2 **teaspoons salt**
½ **teaspoon pepper**
1 **clove garlic, peeled and cut crosswise into halves**
½ **cup dry white wine**
½ **cup orange marmalade**
Sauce:
2 **tablespoons butter or margarine**
1 **can (13¾ ounces) condensed chicken broth**
½ **cup orange marmalade**
¼ **cup dry white wine**
¼ **cup orange juice**
2 **teaspoons cornstarch**
2 **teaspoons lemon juice**
2 **tablespoons slivered orange peel**

1. If frozen, let ducklings thaw according to package directions. Remove giblets, necks, and livers from ducklings. Reserve livers for sauce; if desired, reserve giblets and necks for soup stock. Remove and discard excess fat. Wash, drain, and pat dry with paper toweling. Rub cavities with salt, pepper, and garlic. Fasten neck skin of each to back with a skewer. Tuck tail ends into cavities. Tie legs together and tuck wing tips under ducklings. Prick skin generously to release fat. Place ducklings, breast side up, on a rack in a large shallow roasting pan.
2. Roast at 350°F 2 to 2½ hours or until legs can be moved easily, basting several times during roasting and removing accumulated drippings about every 30 minutes. Remove ducklings from oven and spread surface with mixture of wine and marmalade. Return to oven and continue roasting for 10 minutes.
3. For sauce, melt butter in a skillet. Add duckling livers and sauté until lightly browned. Remove and chop livers. Add chicken broth, marmalade, wine, orange juice, and cornstarch blended with lemon juice. Cook, stirring constantly over low heat for 10 minutes or until sauce bubbles and thickens. Stir in chopped livers and orange peel.
4. Transfer ducklings to a heated platter. Remove skewers and twine. Garnish, if desired, with watercress and orange slices. Reheat sauce if necessary and serve with duckling.

8 servings

598 Chicken, Cacciatore Style

¼ cup vegetable oil
1 broiler-fryer chicken (about 2½ pounds), cut in serving-size pieces
2 medium onions, sliced
2 cloves garlic, crushed in a garlic press or minced
3 tomatoes, sliced
2 medium green peppers, sliced
1 small bay leaf
1 teaspoon salt
¼ teaspoon ground black pepper
½ teaspoon celery seed
1 teaspoon crushed oregano or basil
1 can (8 ounces) tomato sauce
¼ cup dry white wine
8 ounces spaghetti, cooked

1. Heat oil in a large heavy skillet. Add chicken and brown on all sides. Remove chicken from skillet.
2. Add onion and garlic to oil remaining in skillet and cook until onion is tender but not brown; stir occasionally to cook evenly.
3. Return chicken to skillet and add the tomato, green pepper, and bay leaf.
4. Mix salt, pepper, celery seed, and oregano with tomato sauce; pour over all.
5. Cover and cook over low heat 45 minutes. Blend in wine and cook, uncovered, 20 minutes. Discard bay leaf.
6. Put cooked spaghetti onto a warm serving platter and top with the chicken pieces and sauce.

About 6 servings

599 Herb-Chicken with Mushrooms

2 tablespoons butter or margarine
1 broiler-fryer chicken (3 pounds), cut in quarters
¾ cup cider vinegar
¼ cup water
1 cup (about 3 ounces) sliced mushrooms
1 tablespoon finely chopped parsley
1 tablespoon finely chopped chives
1 teaspoon crushed tarragon
½ teaspoon thyme
½ teaspoon salt
¼ teaspoon black pepper
2 tablespoons flour
1½ cups chicken broth
½ cup sherry

1. Heat butter in a large skillet. Place chicken pieces, skin side down, in skillet and brown on all sides.
2. Meanwhile, pour a mixture of vinegar and water over the mushrooms. Let stand 10 minutes; drain.
3. When chicken is evenly browned, transfer pieces to a shallow baking dish. Sprinkle the seasonings over the chicken. Spoon drained mushrooms over the top; sprinkle evenly with flour. Pour broth and wine over all.
4. Bake at 325°F about 1 hour, or until tender.

About 4 servings

600 Roast Goose with Sauerkraut Stuffing

1 goose (ready-to-cook 10 to
    12 pounds)
1 tablespoon butter or margarine
2 large onions, chopped
6½ cups drained sauerkraut, snipped
2 medium apples, quartered,
    cored, and diced
1 small carrot, pared and shredded
2 medium potatoes, shredded
    (about 1½ cups)
½ cup dry white wine
1 to 2 tablespoons brown sugar
2 teaspoons caraway seed
½ teaspoon seasoned pepper
    Salt

1. Singe and clean goose removing any large layers of fat from the body and neck cavities. Rinse thoroughly, drain, and pat dry with absorbent paper; set aside.
2. Heat butter in a skillet; add onion and cook until crisp-tender, 3 to 5 minutes.
3. Meanwhile, combine kraut, apple, carrot, and potato in a large bowl; toss until mixed. Add the onion, wine, and a blend of brown sugar, caraway seed, and seasoned pepper; toss again.
4. Rub cavities of goose with salt; lightly spoon stuffing into the body and neck cavities. Truss goose; set, breast side up, on a rack in a shallow roasting pan.
5. Roast, uncovered, in a 325°F oven about 3½ hours, or until goose tests done. Remove stuffing to a serving dish and accompany with slices of the roast goose.

About 8 servings

601 Glazed Duckling Gourmet

2 ducklings (about 4 pounds
    each), quartered (do not use
    wings, necks, and backs) and
    skinned
1½ teaspoons salt
¼ teaspoon ground nutmeg
3 to 4 tablespoons butter
1 clove garlic, minced
1½ teaspoons rosemary, crushed
1½ teaspoons thyme
1½ cups burgundy
2 teaspoons red wine vinegar
⅓ cup currant jelly
2 teaspoons cornstarch
2 tablespoons cold water
1½ cups halved seedless green
    grapes
    Watercress

1. Remove excess fat from duckling pieces; rinse duckling and pat dry with absorbent paper. Rub pieces with salt and nutmeg.
2. Heat butter and garlic in a large skillet over medium heat; add the duckling pieces and brown well on all sides.
3. Add rosemary, thyme, burgundy, vinegar, and jelly to skillet. Bring to boiling; cover and simmer over low heat until duckling is tender (about 45 minutes). Remove duckling to a heated platter and keep it warm.
4. Combine cornstarch and water; blend into liquid in skillet; bring to boiling and cook 1 to 2 minutes, stirring constantly. Add grapes and toss them lightly until thoroughly heated.
5. Pour the hot sauce over duckling; garnish platter with watercress.

6 to 8 servings

602 *Roast Duckling with Olives*

1 duckling (about 4 pounds)
⅓ cup olive oil or other cooking oil
2 medium carrots, coarsely chopped
1 large onion, coarsely chopped
½ teaspoon salt
⅛ teaspoon seasoned pepper
¼ teaspoon rosemary
⅛ teaspoon savory
2 small stalks celery, chopped
3 sprigs parsley, chopped
1 small bay leaf
⅓ cup cognac
2 tablespoons tomato paste
2 cups hot chicken broth or bouillon
⅓ cup dry white wine
16 whole pitted green olives

1. Rinse, pat dry, and cut duckling into quarters. Remove any excess fat from pieces.
2. Heat oil in skillet; add duckling pieces and cook over medium heat until well browned on all sides. Remove pieces from skillet and keep warm.
3. Add carrots, onion, salt, seasoned pepper, rosemary, savory, celery, parsley, and bay leaf to skillet; continue cooking until carrots and onions are lightly browned. Drain off excess fat in skillet.
4. Return duck to skillet and pour cognac over it. Ignite and when flame ceases add a blend of tomato paste, chicken broth, and white wine. Cover skillet and cook in a 350°F oven about 1½ hours, or until duckling is tender.
5. Remove to heated serving platter and keep warm. Strain remaining mixture in skillet into a saucepan and add green olives. Heat until sauce is very hot and pour over duckling.

4 servings

603 *Roast Rock Cornish Hen with Wild Rice and Mushrooms*

1½ cups water
½ teaspoon salt
½ cup wild rice
2 tablespoons butter or margarine
½ pound mushrooms, sliced lengthwise through caps and stems
1 tablespoon finely chopped onion
3 tablespoons melted butter or margarine
2 tablespoons madeira
4 Rock Cornish hens, about 1 pound each
2 teaspoons salt
¼ cup unsalted butter, melted
Watercress (optional)

1. Bring the water and salt to boiling in a deep saucepan.
2. Wash rice in a sieve. Add rice gradually to water so that boiling will not stop. Boil rapidly, covered, 30 to 40 minutes, or until a kernel of rice is entirely tender when pressed between fingers. Drain rice in a colander or sieve.
3. While rice is cooking, heat 2 tablespoons butter or margarine in a skillet. Add the mushrooms and onion; cook, stirring occasionally, until mushrooms are lightly browned. Combine mushrooms, wild rice, melted butter, and madeira; toss gently until mushrooms and butter are evenly distributed throughout rice.
4. Rinse and pat hens dry with absorbent paper. Rub cavities of the hens with the salt. Lightly fill body cavities with the wild rice stuffing. To close body cavities, sew or skewer and lace with cord. Fasten neck skin to backs and wings to bodies with skewers.
5. Place hens, breast-side up, on rack in roasting pan. Brush each hen with melted unsalted butter (about 1 tablespoon).
6. Roast, uncovered, in a 350°F oven; frequently baste hens during roasting period with drippings from roasting pan. Roast 1 to 1½ hours, or until hens test done. To test, move leg gently by grasping end bone; drumstick-thigh joint moves easily when hens are done. Remove skewers, if used.
7. Transfer hens to a heated serving platter and garnish with sprigs of watercress if desired.

4 to 8 servings

Seafood

604 *Salmon Bake*

1 can (16 ounces) salmon, drained
  and flaked
1½ cups herb-seasoned stuffing
  croutons
2 tablespoons finely snipped parsley
2 tablespoons finely chopped onion
3 eggs, well beaten
1 can (10½ ounces) condensed
  cream of celery soup
½ cup milk
⅛ teaspoon ground black pepper
  Lemon, thinly sliced and cut in
    quarter-slices
  Parsley, snipped
  Sour cream sauce (prepared from
    a mix)

1. Toss salmon, stuffing croutons, parsley, and onion together in a bowl. Blend eggs, condensed soup, milk, and pepper; add to salmon mixture and mix thoroughly. Turn into a greased 1½-quart casserole.
2. Bake at 350°F about 50 minutes. Garnish center with overlapping quarter-slices of lemon and parsley.
3. Serve with hot sour cream sauce.

About 6 servings

605 *Baked Fish with Shrimp Stuffing*

1 dressed whitefish, bass, or lake
    trout (2 to 3 pounds)
Salt
1 cup chopped cooked shrimp
1 cup chopped fresh mushrooms
1 cup soft enriched bread crumbs
½ cup chopped celery
¼ cup chopped onion
2 tablespoons chopped parsley
¾ teaspoon salt
Few grains black pepper
½ teaspoon thyme
¼ cup butter or margarine, melted
2 to 3 tablespoons apple cider
2 tablespoons butter or margarine,
    melted
Parsley sprigs

1. Rinse fish under running cold water; drain well and pat dry with absorbent paper. Sprinkle fish cavity generously with salt.
2. Combine in a bowl the shrimp, mushrooms, bread crumbs, celery, onion, parsley, salt, pepper, and thyme. Pour ¼ cup melted butter gradually over bread mixture, tossing lightly until mixed.
3. Pile stuffing lightly into fish. Fasten with skewers and lace with cord. Place fish in a greased large shallow baking pan. Mix cider and 2 tablespoons melted butter; brush over fish.
4. Bake at 375°F, brushing occasionally with cider mixture, 25 to 30 minutes, or until fish flakes easily when pierced with a fork. If additional browning is desired, place fish under broiler 3 to 5 minutes. Transfer to a heated platter and remove skewers and cord. Garnish platter with parsley.

4 to 6 servings

606 *California Style Red Snapper Steaks*

6 fresh or thawed frozen red snapper
    steaks (about 2 pounds)
Salt and pepper
¼ cup butter or margarine, melted
1 tablespoon grated orange peel
¼ cup orange juice
1 teaspoon lemon juice
Dash nutmeg
Fresh orange sections

1. Arrange red snapper steaks in a single layer in a well-greased baking pan; season with salt and pepper.
2. Combine butter, orange peel and juice, lemon juice, and nutmeg; pour over fish.
3. Bake at 350°F 20 to 25 minutes, or until fish flakes easily when tested with a fork.
4. To serve, put steaks onto a warm platter; spoon sauce in pan over them. Garnish with orange sections.

6 servings

607 *Sole with Tangerine Sauce*

1 pound sole fillets
5 tablespoons butter or margarine
2 teaspoons finely shredded tangerine
    peel
½ cup tangerine juice
1 teaspoon lemon juice
1 tablespoon finely chopped parsley
1 tablespoon finely chopped green
    onion
1 bay leaf
1 tangerine, peeled, sectioned, and
    seeds removed
3 tablespoons flour
½ teaspoon salt
⅛ teaspoon ground black pepper
3 tablespoons butter or margarine
Parsley

1. Thaw fish if frozen.
2. Combine 5 tablespoons butter, tangerine peel and juice, lemon juice, 1 tablespoon parsley, green onion, and bay leaf in a saucepan. Bring to boiling and simmer over low heat until slightly thickened, stirring occasionally. Remove from heat; remove bay leaf and mix in tangerine sections. Keep sauce hot.
3. Mix flour, salt, and pepper; coat fish fillets. Heat 3 tablespoons butter in a skillet. Add fillets and fry until both sides are browned and fish flakes easily when tested with a fork.
4. Arrange fish on a hot platter and pour the hot sauce over it. Garnish with parsley.

About 4 servings

608 *Two-Layer Salmon-Rice Loaf*

Salmon layer:
- 1 can (16 ounces) salmon
- 2 cups coarse soft enriched bread crumbs
- 2 tablespoons finely chopped onion
- ½ cup undiluted evaporated milk
- 1 egg, slightly beaten
- 2 tablespoons butter or margarine, melted
- 1 tablespoon lemon juice
- 1 teaspoon salt

Rice layer:
- 3 cups cooked enriched rice
- ¼ cup finely chopped parsley
- 2 eggs, slightly beaten
- ⅔ cup undiluted evaporated milk
- 2 tablespoons butter or margarine, melted
- ¼ teaspoon salt

Sauce:
- 1 large onion, quartered and thinly sliced
- ¾ cup water
- 1 can (10¾ ounces) condensed tomato soup

1. For salmon layer, drain salmon and remove skin. Flake salmon and put into a bowl. Add bread crumbs, onion, evaporated milk, egg, butter, lemon juice, and salt; mix lightly. Turn into a buttered 9×5×3-inch loaf pan; press lightly to form a layer.
2. For rice layer, combine rice with parsley, eggs, evaporated milk, butter, and salt. Spoon over salmon layer; press lightly.
3. Set filled loaf pan in a shallow pan. Pour hot water into pan to a depth of 1 inch.
4. Bake at 375°F about 45 minutes. Remove from water immediately.
5. Meanwhile, for sauce, put onion and water into a saucepan. Bring to boiling, reduce heat, and simmer, covered, 10 minutes. Remove onion, if desired. Add condensed soup to saucepan, stir until blended, and bring to boiling.
6. Cut loaf into slices and top servings with tomato sauce.

About 8 servings

609 *Broiled Salmon*

- 6 salmon steaks, cut ½ inch thick
- 1 cup sauterne
- ½ cup vegetable oil
- 2 tablespoons wine vinegar
- 2 teaspoons soy sauce
- 2 tablespoons chopped green onion
  Seasoned salt
  Green onion, chopped (optional)
  Pimento strips (optional)

1. Put salmon steaks into a large shallow dish. Mix sauterne, oil, wine vinegar, soy sauce, and green onion; pour over salmon. Marinate in refrigerator several hours or overnight, turning occasionally.
2. To broil, remove steaks from marinade and place on broiler rack. Set under broiler with top 6 inches from heat. Broil about 5 minutes on each side, brushing generously with marinade several times. About 2 minutes before removing from broiler, sprinkle each steak lightly with seasoned salt and, if desired, top with green onion and pimento. Serve at once.

6 servings

610 *Broiled Trout*

- Trout (8- to 10-ounce fish for each serving)
- French dressing
- Instant minced onion
- Salt

1. Remove head and fins from trout, if desired. Rinse trout quickly under running cold water; dry thoroughly. Brush inside of fish with French dressing and sprinkle generously with instant minced onion and salt. Brush outside generously with French dressing.

Lemon slices
Tomato wedges
Mint sprigs or watercress

2. Arrange trout in a greased shallow baking pan or on a broiler rack. Place under broiler with top of fish about 3 inches from heat. Broil 5 to 8 minutes on each side, or until fish flakes easily; brush with dressing during broiling.

3. Remove trout to heated serving platter and garnish with lemon, tomato, and mint.

611 Trout Amandine with Pineapple

6 whole trout
Lemon juice
Enriched all-purpose flour
6 tablespoons butter or margarine
Salt and pepper
2 tablespoons butter or margarine
½ cup slivered blanched almonds
6 well-drained canned pineapple
  slices
Paprika
Lemon wedges

1. Rinse trout quickly under running cold water; dry thoroughly. Brush trout inside and out with lemon juice. Coat with flour.

2. Heat 6 tablespoons butter in a large skillet. Add trout and brown on both sides. Season with salt and pepper.

3. Meanwhile, heat 2 tablespoons butter in another skillet over low heat. Add almonds and stir occasionally until golden.

4. Sprinkle pineapple slices with paprika. Place pineapple in skillet with almonds and brown lightly on both sides. Arrange trout on a warm serving platter and top with pineapple slices and almonds. Garnish platter with lemon wedges.

6 servings

612 Planked Halibut Dinner

4 halibut steaks, fresh or thawed
  frozen (about 2 pounds)
¼ cup butter, melted
2 tablespoons olive oil
1 tablespoon wine vinegar
2 teaspoons lemon juice
1 clove garlic, minced
¼ teaspoon dry mustard
¼ teaspoon marjoram
½ teaspoon salt
⅛ teaspoon ground black pepper
2 large zucchini
1 package (10 ounces) frozen green
  peas
1 can (8¼ ounces) tiny whole carrots
  Au Gratin Potato Puffs
  Butter
  Fresh parsley
  Lemon wedges

1. Place halibut steaks in an oiled baking pan.

2. Combine butter, olive oil, vinegar, lemon juice, garlic, dry mustard, marjoram, salt, and pepper. Drizzle over halibut.

3. Bake at 450°F 10 to 12 minutes, or until halibut is almost done.

4. Meanwhile, halve zucchini lengthwise and scoop out center portion. Cook in boiling salted water until just tender.

5. Cook peas following directions on package. Heat carrots.

6. Prepare Au Gratin Potato Puffs.

7. Arrange halibut on wooden plank or heated ovenware platter and border with zucchini halves filled with peas, carrots, and potato puffs. Dot peas and carrots with butter.

8. Place platter under broiler to brown potato puffs. Sprinkle carrots with chopped parsley.

9. Garnish with sprigs of parsley and lemon wedges arranged on a skewer.

4 servings

Au Gratin Potato Puffs: Pare 1½ pounds potatoes; cook and mash potatoes in a saucepan. Add **2 tablespoons butter** and ⅓ **cup milk**; whip until fluffy. Add **2 slightly beaten egg yolks,** ½ **cup shredded sharp Cheddar cheese, 1 teaspoon salt,** and **few grains pepper;** continue whipping. Using a pastry bag with a large star tip, form mounds about 2 inches in diameter on plank. Proceed as directed in recipe.

613

614 *Tuna Fiesta*

1 can (6½ or 7 ounces) tuna, drained
    and separated in large pieces
1 can (16 ounces) stewed tomatoes,
    drained
1 can (15¼ ounces) spaghetti in
    tomato sauce with cheese
1 tablespoon ketchup
1 teaspoon seasoned salt
½ cup (about 2 ounces) shredded
    sharp Cheddar cheese
    Few grains paprika
    Fresh parsley

1. Turn tuna, stewed tomatoes, and spaghetti into a saucepan. Add ketchup, seasoned salt, cheese, and paprika; mix well. Set over medium heat, stirring occasionally, until thoroughly heated (about 8 minutes).
2. Turn into a warm serving dish; garnish with parsley. Serve at once.

About 6 servings

Note: If desired, reserve cheese and paprika for topping. Mix remaining ingredients and turn into a greased 1-quart casserole. Top with the cheese and paprika. Set in a 350°F oven 20 minutes, or until thoroughly heated. Garnish with parsley.

615 *Patio Crab Casserole*

¼ cup butter or margarine
2 cups chopped onion
1 pound frozen or 2 cans (7½
    ounces each) Alaska king crab,
    drained and sliced
½ cup snipped parsley
2 tablespoons capers
2 tablespoons snipped chives
2 pimentos, diced
1½ cups corn muffin mix
⅛ teaspoon salt
1 egg, fork beaten
½ cup milk
1 cup cream-style golden corn
6 drops Tabasco
2 cups dairy sour cream
1½ cups shredded extra sharp
    Cheddar cheese

1. Heat butter in a skillet. Add onion and cook until tender. Stir in crab, parsley, capers, chives, and pimentos; heat.
2. Meanwhile, stir corn muffin mix, salt, egg, milk, corn, and Tabasco until just moistened (batter should be lumpy). Turn into a greased shallow 3-quart dish and spread evenly to edges.
3. Spoon crab mixture and then sour cream over batter. Sprinkle cheese over all.
4. Bake at 400°F 25 to 30 minutes.
5. To serve, cut into squares.

About 12 servings

616 *Savory Oysters*

⅓ cup butter or margarine
1 can (4 ounces) sliced mushrooms,
    drained
⅓ cup chopped green pepper
½ clove garlic
2 cups coarse toasted enriched bread
    crumbs
1 quart oysters, drained (reserve
    liquor)
¼ cup cream
1 teaspoon Worcestershire sauce
1 teaspoon salt
1 teaspoon paprika
⅛ teaspoon ground mace
    Few grains cayenne pepper

1. Heat butter in a large skillet. Add mushrooms, green pepper, and garlic; cook about 5 minutes. Remove skillet from heat; discard garlic. Stir in toasted bread crumbs. Set aside.
2. Mix ¼ cup reserved oyster liquor, cream, and Worcestershire sauce.
3. Blend salt, paprika, mace, and cayenne.
4. Use about a third of crumb mixture to form a layer in bottom of a greased 2-quart casserole. Arrange about half of oysters and half of seasonings over crumbs. Repeat crumb layer, then oyster and seasoning layers. Pour the liquid mixture over all. Top with remaining crumbs.
5. Bake at 375°F 20 to 30 minutes, or until thoroughly heated and crumbs are golden brown.

6 to 8 servings

617 Scallops Gourmet

2 pounds scallops
1 cup boiling water
1 teaspoon salt
3 to 4 tablespoons lemon juice
1 medium onion, sliced
2 sprigs parsley
1 bay leaf
¼ cup butter or margarine
½ pound mushrooms, sliced lengthwise
3 tomatoes, peeled and diced
2 tablespoons butter or margarine
2 tablespoons flour
¼ teaspoon garlic powder
8 patty shells, heated
Carrot curls

1. Rinse scallops under running cold water. Put scallops into a saucepan and pour boiling water over them. Stir in salt, lemon juice, onion, parsley, and bay leaf. Cook, covered, over low heat 5 minutes; drain and reserve 1 cup of the stock. If scallops are large, cut into smaller pieces. Set aside.
2. Heat ¼ cup butter in a skillet. Add mushrooms and cook until delicately browned and tender, stirring occasionally. Remove from skillet with slotted spoon; set aside. Add diced tomatoes to skillet and cook 5 minutes. Set aside.
3. Heat 2 tablespoons butter in a saucepan. Blend in flour; heat until bubbly. Add reserved stock gradually, stirring constantly. Continue to stir and bring rapidly to boiling; cook 1 to 2 minutes.
4. Add scallops, mushrooms, tomatoes, and garlic powder to sauce; heat thoroughly.
5. To serve, spoon scallop mixture into patty shells. Garnish with carrot curls.

About 8 servings

618 Seafood Kabobs

1 lobster tail (8 ounces), cut in 6 pieces
6 scallops
6 shrimp, peeled and deveined
12 large mushroom caps
½ cup olive oil
3 tablespoons soy sauce
1 tablespoon Worcestershire sauce
2 tablespoons white wine vinegar
½ teaspoon grated lemon peel
2 tablespoons lemon juice
½ teaspoon ground pepper
2 teaspoons snipped parsley
18 (4-inch) pieces sliced bacon
12 (1-inch) squares green pepper
6 cherry tomatoes

1. Put lobster pieces, scallops, shrimp, and mushroom caps into a shallow dish.
2. Combine olive oil, soy sauce, Worcestershire sauce, vinegar, lemon peel. lemon juice, pepper, and parsley in a screwtop jar and shake vigorously. Pour the marinade over the seafood and mushroom caps and set aside for at least 2 hours.
3. Drain off marinade and reserve.
4. Wrap each piece of seafood in bacon. Thread pieces on skewers (about 10 inches each) as follows: green pepper, lobster, mushroom, scallop, mushroom, shrimp, and green pepper. Arrange on a broiler rack and brush with marinade.
5. Place under broiler 3 inches from heat. Broil 10 to 12 minutes, turning and brushing frequently with marinade. Add a cherry tomato to each skewer during the last few minutes of broiling.

6 servings

619 *Deviled Crab*

Mustard Sauce:
- 2 tablespoons dry mustard
- 2 tablespoons water
- 2 tablespoons olive oil
- 1 tablespoon ketchup
- ¼ teaspoon salt
- ¼ teaspoon Worcestershire sauce

Crab meat mixture:
- 6 tablespoons butter
- 4 teaspoons finely chopped green pepper
- 2 teaspoons finely chopped onion
- 6 tablespoons flour
- 1 teaspoon salt
- ½ teaspoon dry mustard
- 1½ cups milk
- 1 teaspoon Worcestershire sauce
- 2 egg yolks, slightly beaten
- 1 pound lump crab meat, drained
- 2 teaspoons chopped pimento
- 2 tablespoons dry sherry
- 1 cup fine dry enriched bread crumbs
- Paprika
- Butter, melted

1. For Mustard Sauce, blend dry mustard, water, olive oil, ketchup, salt, and Worcestershire sauce in a small bowl; set aside.
2. For crab meat mixture, heat butter in a large heavy saucepan. Add green pepper and onion; cook until onion is golden in color.
3. Blend flour, salt, and dry mustard; stir in. Heat until bubbly. Add milk gradually, stirring until smooth. Stir in Worcestershire sauce. Bring rapidly to boiling; cook 1 to 2 minutes.
4. Remove mixture from heat and stir a small amount of hot mixture into the egg yolks; return to saucepan and cook 3 to 5 minutes, stirring constantly.
5. Stir in crab meat and pimento; heat thoroughly. Remove from heat and blend in sherry and the Mustard Sauce.
6. Spoon into 6 shell-shaped ramekins, allowing about ½ cup mixture for each. Sprinkle top with bread crumbs and paprika; drizzle with melted butter.
7. Set in a 450°F oven about 6 minutes, or until tops are lightly browned and mixture is thoroughly heated. Serve hot.

6 servings

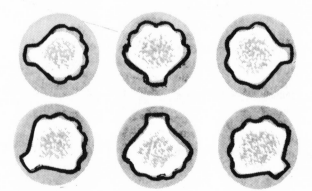

620 *Baked Flounder Superb*

- 2 pounds flounder fillets
- ½ cup fine Melba toast crumbs
- ¼ cup butter or margarine, melted
- ⅔ cup minced green onion
- 2 tablespoons snipped parsley
- ½ teaspoon poultry seasoning
- ½ pound fresh or thawed frozen sea scallops, chopped
- 1 can (4 ounces) mushroom stems and pieces, drained
- 2 tablespoons butter or margarine
- 2 tablespoons flour
- ¼ teaspoon salt
- Few grains black pepper
- 1 cup milk
- Shredded Parmesan cheese

1. Thaw fish if frozen; cut fish into 12 pieces.
2. Toss crumbs and melted butter together in a bowl. Add green onion, parsley, poultry seasoning, scallops, and mushrooms; mix well.
3. Place a piece of flounder in the bottom of each of 6 ramekins. Spoon stuffing mixture over flounder and top with remaining flounder pieces.
4. Heat butter in a saucepan. Stir in flour, salt, and pepper and cook until bubbly. Add milk gradually, stirring until smooth. Bring rapidly to boiling; boil 1 to 2 minutes, stirring constantly.
5. Spoon sauce over flounder. Sprinkle with Parmesan cheese.
6. Bake at 350°F 20 to 25 minutes. If desired, set ramekins under broiler with tops about 3 inches from heat until lightly browned; watch carefully to avoid overbrowning.

6 servings

21 Shrimp Exotica

1½ pounds deveined cooked shrimp
1 can (20 ounces) sliced pineapple, drained; reserve syrup
2 cups water
3 chicken bouillon cubes
1 cup long-grain enriched white rice
¼ cup vegetable oil
1½ cups cubed cooked ham
¼ cup chopped onion
1 clove garlic, crushed in a garlic press or minced
2 tablespoons chopped preserved or crystallized ginger
2 teaspoons soy sauce
2 teaspoons curry powder
½ teaspoon salt
1 medium green pepper, cut in strips

1. Reserve 5 or 6 whole shrimp for garnish. Cut remaining shrimp into pieces. Set aside. Cut 4 pineapple slices into pieces and set aside.
2. Bring water to boiling in a deep saucepan. Add the bouillon cubes, and when dissolved, add the rice gradually, so boiling continues. Cover pan tightly, reduce heat, and simmer 15 to 20 minutes, until a kernel is soft when pressed between fingers.
3. Heat oil in a large skillet. Add ham, onion, and garlic; heat thoroughly, turning with a spoon.
4. Blend ⅔ cup of the reserved pineapple syrup with ginger, soy sauce, curry powder, and salt; add to skillet along with green pepper and heat thoroughly. Add rice and shrimp and remaining pineapple pieces; toss until mixed. Heat thoroughly. Serve on a warm serving platter. Garnish with the pineapple slices and whole shrimp.

About 6 servings

22 Shrimp Creole

Cooked shrimp:
1 pound fresh shrimp with shells
2 cups water
2 tablespoons lemon juice
2 teaspoons salt

Sauce:
¼ cup fat
¾ cup finely chopped onion
¾ cup minced green pepper
1 can (16 ounces) tomatoes, sieved
1 teaspoon Worcestershire sauce
1 bay leaf
1½ teaspoons salt
¼ teaspoon ground black pepper
½ teaspoon sugar
½ teaspoon oregano
Cooked rice

1. For cooked shrimp, rinse shrimp under running cold water.
2. Combine water, lemon juice, and salt in a saucepan and bring to boiling. Drop shrimp into boiling water, reduce heat, and simmer, covered, until pink and tender (about 5 minutes).
3. Drain shrimp immediately and cover with cold water to chill; drain again. Remove tiny legs and peel shells from shrimp. Cut a slit to just below surface along back (curved surface) of shrimp to expose the black vein. With knife point, remove vein. Rinse shrimp quickly in cold water.
4. Reserve about ten whole shrimp for garnish and cut remainder into pieces. Refrigerate until ready to use.
5. For sauce, heat fat in a large heavy skillet. Mix in onion and green pepper and cook until vegetables are tender. Stir in sieved tomatoes, Worcestershire sauce, bay leaf, salt, pepper, sugar, and oregano. Bring mixture to boiling and simmer, uncovered, stirring occasionally. Cook about 15 minutes, or until thickened. Stir in shrimp pieces and heat thoroughly.
6. Serve shrimp mixture on hot fluffy rice and garnish with the whole shrimp.

About 4 servings

623 *Mock Lobster, Flemish Style*

The main ingredient in this dish is monk fish, which has a taste and texture somewhat similar to lobster. Served in scallop shells or ramekins, it makes a delectable fish course during a multiple-course dinner

1 pound monk fish fillets
1 can or bottle (12 ounces) beer
½ cup water
1 small onion, quartered
1 small celery stalk with top, cut in chunks
½ teaspoon salt
¼ teaspoon thyme
2 tablespoons butter or margarine
2 tablespoons flour
¼ cup cream
1 egg yolk
½ cup shredded cheese (Edam, Gruyère, Cheddar)

1. Cut fish fillets in half lengthwise; then cut each section into ¾-inch slices.
2. In a large saucepan, place beer, water, onion, celery, salt, and thyme. Heat to boiling. Add fish. Cover and simmer 4 minutes, or until fish flakes.
3. Remove fish with a slotted spoon. Drain well on paper towels. Boil stock 10 minutes to reduce; strain.
4. In another saucepan, melt butter. Stir in flour. Add ¾ cup strained stock and the cream. Cook, stirring constantly, until thickened.
5. Add a little hot mixture to egg yolk; return to pan. Cook slowly, stirring, 1 to 2 minutes. Remove from heat; adjust seasonings.
6. Gently combine fish and sauce. Spoon into scallop shells or individual ramekins. Sprinkle with cheese. Broil 2 minutes, or just until tops are lightly browned.

6 appetizer servings

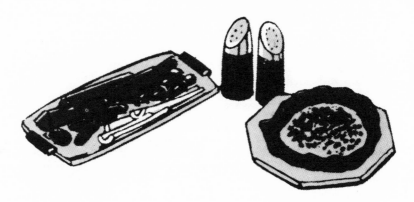

624 *Saucy Fish Fillets*

This delicately flavored entrée consists of fish poached in beer and a hollandaise-style sauce with egg yolks, cream, butter, and part of the cooking liquid.

1 pound fish fillets
1 can or bottle (12 ounces) beer
1 small onion, quartered
1 celery stalk, cut in chunks
2 tablespoons minced fresh parsley or 1 tablespoon dried parsley flakes
1 teaspoon salt
Dash white pepper
2 egg yolks
2 tablespoons cream
2 tablespoons butter or margarine

1. Thaw fish, if frozen.
2. Put beer, onion, celery, parsley, salt, and pepper in a skillet. Heat to boiling. Add fish. Cover and simmer about 8 to 10 minutes, or just until fish flakes with a fork.
3. Drain fish and put onto a deep platter. Place in a 300°F oven to keep warm. Boil cooking liquid about 5 minutes to reduce; strain.
4. In top of a double boiler, beat egg yolks with cream. Gradually stir in ½ cup hot strained cooking liquid. Cook over boiling water, stirring constantly, until thickened. Cut butter into small pieces; stir into sauce, one piece at a time. Pour sauce over fish. (Recipe makes about ¾ cup sauce.)

3 or 4 servings

625 *Tuna and Swiss Cheese Pie*

3 eggs
½ teaspoon salt
½ teaspoon dry mustard
Dash pepper
1 cup whipping cream or
half-and-half
¾ cup ale or beer
1 unbaked 9-inch pastry shell,
chilled
2 cans (6½ or 7 ounces each)
tuna, drained and flaked
6 ounces Swiss cheese, shredded
1 tablespoon flour

1. Beat eggs, salt, dry mustard, and pepper until foamy. Beat in cream and ale.
2. Cover bottom of pastry shell with a layer of tuna. Sprinkle half of cheese over tuna. Repeat layering. Sprinkle flour over cheese. Pour egg mixture over all.
3. Bake at 425°F 15 minutes. Turn oven control to 300°F and bake 25 minutes, or until a knife inserted halfway between center and edge of filling comes out clean.

6 entrée servings;
10 to 12 appetizer servings

626 *Tuna-Macaroni Bake*

1 package (7¼ ounces) macaroni
and cheese dinner
6 cups boiling water, salted
2 tablespoons butter or margarine
1 can or bottle (12 ounces) beer
¼ teaspoon salt
1 can (6½ or 7 ounces) tuna,
drained and flaked
¼ cup chopped green pepper
1 canned pimento, chopped
⅓ cup instant nonfat dry milk
2 eggs, slightly beaten

1. Cook macaroni in boiling salted water in a large saucepan, stirring occasionally, until tender (about 7 to 10 minutes). Drain; return macaroni to pan.
2. Add butter, ½ cup beer, contents of cheese sauce packet from dinner, and salt. Stir until butter is melted. Add tuna, green pepper, and pimento. (Two pimentos or ½ cup chopped green pepper may be used instead of some of each, if desired.)
3. Turn into a lightly buttered rectangular 1½-quart baking dish. Combine remaining beer, dry milk, and eggs; pour over macaroni mixture.
4. Bake at 325°F 1½ hours, or until lightly browned on edges and set.

4 servings

627 *German Beer Fish (Bier Fisch)*

This recipe is an old tradition in Germany. The sauce combines sweet, sour, and spicy flavors. In Germany, fresh carp would be used, but since good fresh carp is hard to find in this country, other fish may be substituted. It should not be too delicate in flavor.

1 whole carp, buffalo fish, or
pike (2 to 3 pounds with
head); or 1 to 1½ pounds
boneless fillets
2 tablespoons butter or margarine
1 medium onion, chopped
1 celery stalk, chopped
½ teaspoon salt
6 peppercorns
3 whole cloves
4 slices lemon
1 bay leaf
1 can or bottle (12 ounces) beer
6 gingersnaps, crushed
1 tablespoon sugar
Fresh parsley for garnish

1. Remove head from fish; discard or use to make fish stock for other recipes. Lay fish out as flat as possible, breaking bones along back.
2. Melt butter in a skillet. Add onion, celery, salt, peppercorns, and cloves; mix. Top with lemon slices and bay leaf. Place fish on top.
3. Add beer. Cover and simmer 15 to 20 minutes, or just until fish flakes with a fork. Transfer fish to a platter; cover with foil to keep warm.
4. Strain cooking liquid, pressing some of vegetables through.
5. Put gingersnaps and sugar in skillet; stir in 1½ cups strained liquid. Cook, stirring constantly, until thickened.
6. Garnish fish with fresh parsley. Pass sauce for pouring over fish and **boiled potato** accompaniment.

4 to 6 servings

628 *Tunaroni Casserole*

¼ cup chopped onion
2 tablespoons snipped parsley
2 tablespoons butter or margarine
2 tablespoons flour
½ teaspoon salt
⅛ teaspoon pepper
2 cups milk
2 cups cooked elbow macaroni
1 can (28 ounces) tomatoes, drained and cut up
2 cans (6½ or 7 ounces each) tuna, drained and flaked
¼ cup buttered bread crumbs

1. Sauté onion and parsley in butter in a skillet. Stir in flour, salt, and pepper. Gradually add milk, stirring until thickened and smooth.
2. Stir in macaroni, tomatoes, and tuna. Put into a 2-quart casserole. Sprinkle with bread crumbs.
3. Bake, covered, at 375°F 30 minutes, or until mixture is bubbly.

6 servings

629 *Seviche*

In this specialty of Mexico, the lemon juice actually "cooks" the fish.

1¼ pounds whitefish fillets, skinned and cut in 2x¼-inch strips
1 cup fresh lemon juice
2 green chilies, seeded and minced
1 teaspoon snipped fresh or ½ teaspoon dried oregano leaves
1 tablespoon snipped fresh or 1½ teaspoons dried coriander leaves
1 tablespoon olive oil
1 teaspoon salt
¼ teaspoon freshly ground pepper
2 large tomatoes, peeled, seeded, and chopped
1 medium green pepper, finely chopped
1 small yellow onion, finely chopped
¼ cup fresh lime juice
Radish slices
Ripe olives

1. Place fish in a shallow glass bowl; pour lemon juice over it. Refrigerate covered 6 hours, stirring occasionally. Drain; discard lemon juice.
2. Mix remaining ingredients except radish slices and olives with fish in a medium bowl. Refrigerate 30 minutes.
3. Serve on chilled plates; garnish with radish slices and olives. Or spoon into **fluted lemon shells.**

8 servings (½ cup each)

Walnut Torte, page 376

630 *Tuna-Idaho Casserole*

¼ cup finely chopped onion
½ cup chopped celery
3 tablespoons butter or margarine
3 tablespoons flour
1¾ cups milk
1 tablespoon lemon juice
1 teaspoon grated lemon peel
½ teaspoon salt
¼ teaspoon dill weed
Dash pepper
1 package (10 ounces) frozen peas, cooked and drained
1 can (12 ounces) tuna, drained and flaked
2 cups frozen Idaho potato puffs

1. Sauté onion and celery in butter in a saucepan. Stir in flour. Gradually add milk, stirring until thickened and smooth.
2. Add remaining ingredients, except potatoes. Spoon into a 1½-quart casserole. Top with potato puffs.
3. Bake, uncovered, at 450°F 20 minutes, or until puffs are golden brown and mixture is heated through.

4 servings

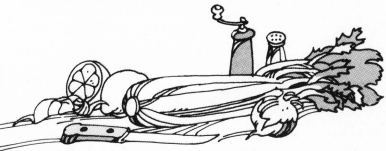

631 *Confetti Casserole*

1 can (10¾ ounces) condensed cream of mushroom soup
1 can (16 ounces) peas (undrained)
2 tablespoons chopped pimento
¼ cup chopped celery
¼ cup chopped green pepper
1 tablespoon Worcestershire sauce
2 cans (6½ or 7 ounces each) tuna, drained and flaked
1 cup (4 ounces) shredded American cheese
1 can (3 ounces) French-fried onions

1. Combine soup, peas with ½ cup liquid, pimento, celery, green pepper, and Worcestershire sauce. Mix in tuna and cheese.
2. Put half the mixture into a 2-quart casserole. Sprinkle with half the onions; repeat.
3. Bake, uncovered, at 375°F 30 minutes, or until mixture is bubbly.

6 servings

632 *Tuna-Rice Pie*

2 cups cooked white rice
2 tablespoons butter or margarine, melted
3 eggs, beaten
⅓ cup chopped pitted ripe olives
¾ cup milk
1 can (6½ or 7 ounces) tuna, drained and flaked
3 green onions, sliced
Dash ground red pepper
1 cup (4 ounces) shredded Swiss cheese

1. Combine rice, butter, 1 egg, and ripe olives. Spread evenly onto sides and bottom of a greased 9-inch pie plate.
2. Combine remaining 2 eggs, milk, tuna, onion, and red pepper. Pour into rice-lined pie plate. Sprinkle with cheese.
3. Bake, uncovered, at 350°F 15 minutes. Turn oven control to 300°F and bake an additional 10 minutes, or until set.

4 servings

Cherries Jubilee, page 331

633 *Tuna Dinner*

2 cups cooked green beans
1 can (10¾ ounces) condensed cream
   of chicken soup
1 cup mayonnaise
2 cans (7 ounces each) tuna packed in
   water (undrained)
½ cup corn flakes
1 tablespoon butter or margarine

1. Combine beans, soup, mayonnaise, and tuna. Put into a 1½-quart casserole. Top with corn flakes. Dot with butter.
2. Bake, uncovered, at 350°F 30 minutes, or until heated through.

6 servings

634 *Salmon with Rice*

1⅓ cups cooked white rice
1 can (15½ ounces) salmon, drained
   and flaked
1 large tomato, chopped
¼ cup chopped onion
1 tablespoon snipped parsley
½ cup whipping cream, whipped
½ teaspoon salt
   Dash ground red pepper
1 tablespoon lemon juice
½ cup (2 ounces) freshly grated
   Parmesan cheese

1. Combine all ingredients, except cheese. Put into a 1½-quart casserole. Sprinkle with cheese.
2. Bake, covered, at 350°F 20 minutes, or until bubbly.

4 servings

635 *Individual Salmon-Green Bean Casseroles*

1 package (9 ounces) frozen Italian
   green beans, cooked and drained
1 package (9 ounces) frozen artichoke
   hearts, cooked and drained
1 can (15½ ounces) salmon, drained
   and flaked
½ cup canned Hollandaise sauce
½ cup dairy sour cream
½ teaspoon grated lemon peel
¼ teaspoon crushed tarragon
⅛ teaspoon pepper
⅓ cup toasted slivered almonds

1. Combine beans, artichoke hearts, and salmon. Spoon into 6 individual casseroles.
2. Combine Hollandaise sauce, sour cream, lemon peel, tarragon, and pepper. Spoon evenly over salmon mixture. Sprinkle with almonds.
3. Bake, uncovered, at 350°F 20 minutes, or until heated through.

6 servings

636 *Baked Salmon Squares*

1 can (15½ ounces) salmon, drained
    and flaked
½ cup fine dry bread crumbs
1 can (10¾ ounces) condensed cream
    of celery soup
¼ cup dairy sour cream
2 eggs, beaten

1. Combine all ingredients. Put into a greased 8-inch square baking dish.
2. Bake, uncovered, at 325°F 1 hour, or until set. Cut into squares and serve with **creamed spinach.**

6 servings

637 *Shrimp and Rice Supreme*

1 medium onion, thinly sliced
⅓ cup chopped green pepper
½ cup sliced fresh mushrooms
¼ cup butter or margarine
¼ cup flour
½ teaspoon salt
    Dash ground red pepper
2 cups milk
1 tablespoon Worcestershire sauce
2 cups cooked white rice
1 pound cooked and cleaned shrimp

1. Sauté onion, green pepper, and mushrooms in butter in a skillet. Stir in flour, salt, and red pepper. Gradually add milk, stirring until thickened and smooth.
2. Combine sauce with remaining ingredients. Put into a 2-quart casserole.
3. Bake, covered, at 350°F 30 minutes, or until bubbly.

6 servings

638 *Shrimp Florentine*

1 package (10 ounces) frozen spinach,
    cooked and squeezed
1 pound cooked and cleaned shrimp
1 can (10¾ ounces) condensed cream
    of chicken soup
¼ cup sherry
1 tablespoon snipped parsley
    Dash pepper
½ cup (2 ounces) shredded Cheddar
    cheese
¼ cup buttered bread crumbs

1. Put spinach into a 1½-quart casserole.
2. Blend shrimp, soup, sherry, parsley, and pepper. Spoon over spinach.
3. Combine cheese and crumbs. Sprinkle over all.
4. Bake, covered, at 350°F 30 minutes, or until heated through.

4 servings

639 *Shrimp Lasagne*

½ cup chopped onion
1 garlic clove, minced
2 tablespoons butter or margarine
2 cans (8 ounces each) tomato sauce
1 can (6 ounces) tomato paste
½ cup water
1 tablespoon basil
2 teaspoons oregano
¼ teaspoon pepper
½ pound lasagne noodles
12 ounces cooked and cleaned shrimp
⅓ cup sliced pitted ripe olives
2 cups (8 ounces) shredded mozzarella cheese
1 carton (16 ounces) cream-style cottage cheese
½ cup (2 ounces) grated Parmesan cheese

1. Sauté onion and garlic in butter in a saucepan. Add tomato sauce, tomato paste, water, and seasonings. Simmer 25 minutes.
2. Meanwhile, cook noodles according to package directions.
3. Add shrimp and olives to sauce.
4. Layer half the noodles, half the mozzarella cheese, half the cottage cheese, and half the sauce in a 13x9-inch baking dish. Repeat layers. Sprinkle with Parmesan cheese.
5. Bake, covered, at 350°F 20 minutes. Remove cover and bake an additional 15 minutes, or until heated through. Let stand a few minutes before serving.

8 servings

640 *Seafood Creole*

1 medium onion, chopped
1 garlic clove, minced
½ cup chopped green pepper
½ cup sliced celery
3 tablespoons butter or margarine
1½ tablespoons flour
1 can (28 ounces) tomatoes (undrained)
1 bay leaf
1 teaspoon salt
1 teaspoon sugar
½ teaspoon allspice
1 tablespoon Worcestershire sauce
¼ teaspoon Tabasco
1 can (6½ or 7 ounces) tuna, drained and flaked
1 pound cooked and cleaned shrimp
1 can (7½ ounces) Alaska King crab, drained and flaked
2 tablespoons snipped parsley

1. Sauté onion, garlic, green pepper, and celery in butter in a skillet. Stir in flour. Add tomatoes, stirring until slightly thickened.
2. Combine with remaining ingredients, except parsley. Put into a 2-quart casserole.
3. Bake, covered, at 350°F 30 minutes, or until bubbly. Remove bay leaf. Sprinkle with parsley and serve over **hot, cooked rice.**

8 servings

641 *Pimento-Crab Meat Strata Supreme*

1 can (7½ ounces) Alaska King crab, drained and flaked
½ cup chopped celery
¼ cup chopped onion
¾ cup mayonnaise
Dash ground red pepper
12 slices white bread, crusts removed
Butter or margarine, softened
3 jars (4 ounces each) whole pimentos, each pimento cut in 2 or 3 large pieces
4 cups (1 pound) shredded Swiss cheese
5 eggs
3 cups milk
1 teaspoon salt
⅛ teaspoon pepper
¼ teaspoon dry mustard

1. Mix crab, celery, and onion. Blend in mayonnaise and red pepper. Set aside.
2. Spread both sides of the bread slices with butter. Place half the bread slices in a layer in a 3-quart shallow baking dish.
3. Arrange half the pimento pieces, half the crab mixture, and one third the cheese over the bread. Repeat layering, using remainder of the crab mixture, pimento, and second third of the cheese. Cover with reserved bread slices and sprinkle with the remaining cheese.
4. Beat together remaining ingredients until frothy and blended. Pour over all. Let stand 1 hour.
5. Bake, uncovered, at 325°F 1 hour, or until puffed and brown. If desired, garnish with pimento strips, green pepper strips, and sprigs of parsley.

6 to 8 servings

642 *Smoked Oyster and Corn Casserole*

1 egg, beaten
½ cup evaporated milk
1 can (16 ounces) whole kernel corn, drained
1 tablespoon instant minced onion
1 teaspoon soy sauce
1 can (3½ ounces) smoked oysters, drained
¼ cup coarsely crushed soda crackers

1. Combine egg, evaporated milk, corn, onion, and soy sauce. Put into a 1-quart casserole.
2. Scatter oysters over top. Sprinkle with cracker crumbs.
3. Bake, uncovered, at 325°F 30 minutes, or until mixture is bubbly. Stir before serving.

4 servings

643 *Savory Rice and Lobster*

1 **large lobster tail (about 10 ounces)**
 Paprika
3 **tablespoons butter or margarine**
2 **teaspoons lemon juice**
¼ **teaspoon salt**
¼ **teaspoon garlic powder**
¼ **teaspoon onion powder**
¼ **teaspoon oregano**
 Dash pepper
2 **tablespoons dry white wine**
1 **package (6 ounces) long-grain and wild rice, cooked according to package directions**

1. Cook lobster in **boiling salted water** 5 minutes.
2. Rinse lobster tail with cold water. Remove meat from shell and cut up. Sprinkle lobster pieces with paprika.
3. Brown lobster lightly in butter in a skillet. Sprinkle with lemon juice. Combine with remaining ingredients. Put into a 1-quart casserole.
4. Bake, covered, at 325°F 25 minutes, or until heated through. If desired, sprinkle with snipped parsley.

4 servings

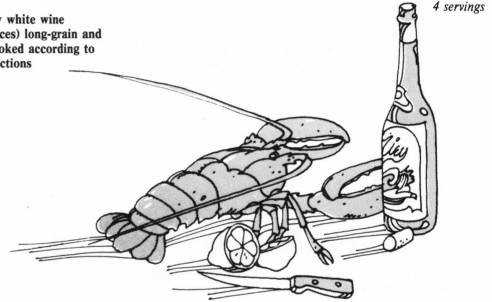

644 *Scallops au Gratin*

2 **tablespoons butter or margarine**
2 **tablespoons flour**
1 **cup milk**
1 **package (12 ounces) frozen scallops, thawed and drained**
1 **can (4 ounces) mushroom slices, drained**
¼ **cup chopped green onion**
1 **teaspoon grated lemon peel**
½ **teaspoon salt**
⅛ **teaspoon garlic powder**
½ **cup (4 ounces) shredded Cheddar cheese**
¼ **cup fine dry bread crumbs**
4 **English muffins, split and toasted**
8 **tomato slices**

1. Melt butter in a skillet. Stir in flour. Gradually add milk, stirring until thickened and smooth.
2. Stir in scallops, mushrooms, green onion, lemon peel, salt, and garlic powder. Put into a 1-quart casserole.
3. Mix cheese and bread crumbs. Sprinkle over all.
4. Bake, covered, at 325°F 25 minutes, or until mixture is bubbly. To serve, top each English muffin half with a tomato slice. Spoon scallop mixture over tomato.

4 servings

645 *Fish and Vegetable Casserole*

1½　pounds frozen fish steaks, thawed
　　　　and cut in chunks
　1　can (16 ounces) cut green beans,
　　　　drained
　1　can (16 ounces) sliced carrots,
　　　　drained
　¼　cup butter or margarine
　¼　cup flour
　1　teaspoon salt
　½　teaspoon pepper
　⅔　cup milk
1½　cups chicken broth
　1　can (10¾ ounces) condensed tomato
　　　　soup
　½　teaspoon rosemary
　3　cups hot, cooked mashed potatoes

1. Put fish, green beans, and carrots into a 2½-quart casserole.
2. Melt butter in a saucepan. Stir in flour, salt, and pepper. Gradually add milk and broth, stirring until thickened and smooth.
3. Stir in soup and rosemary. Pour over fish and vegetables.
4. Bake, covered, at 350°F 15 minutes. Remove cover and spoon potatoes around edge of casserole. Bake an additional 15 minutes, or until fish is flaky and mixture is heated through.

6 servings

646 *Seafood Continental*

　6　sole fillets
　¼　cup chopped celery
　¼　cup chopped green pepper
　⅛　teaspoon leaf tarragon
　2　tablespoons butter or margarine
1⅓　cups water
1½　cups packaged precooked rice
　½　pound cooked and cleaned shrimp,
　　　　cut up
　1　can (10¾ ounces) condensed cream
　　　　of celery soup
　⅓　cup dry white wine

1. Line the sides of 6 well-greased 6-ounce individual casseroles or custard cups with sole fillets.
2. Sauté celery, green pepper, and tarragon in butter in a saucepan. Add water; bring to a boil. Stir in rice. Cover and cook 5 minutes.
3. Stir in half the shrimp and ¼ cup soup. Spoon into fish-lined cups.
4. Bake, uncovered, at 350°F 30 minutes. Unmold onto a serving platter. Serve with sauce made by heating together remaining soup, wine, and remaining shrimp. If desired, garnish with celery leaves.

6 servings

647 Curried Prawns

1 pound large prawns, peeled
   and deveined
2 tablespoons butter
1 tablespoon chopped scallions
1 tablespoon flour
1 teaspoon curry powder
¼ cup sauterne
2 cups cream
   Hot rice

1. Sauté prawns in heated butter in skillet 2 to 3 minutes; add scallions and sauté 3 to 4 minutes longer. Sprinkle with a mixture of flour and curry powder. Cook and stir about 3 minutes.
2. Stir in the wine and cream and simmer mixture 10 minutes, stirring occasionally. Transfer prawns to a chafing dish using a slotted spoon.
3. Continue cooking the sauce over low heat to desired consistency. Add seasoning, if desired, and pour over the prawns. Serve with hot rice.

2 servings

648 Oysters in Mushroom Purée

1 pound mushrooms, coarsely
   chopped
1 quart oysters, liquor reserved
¼ cup dry sherry
½ cup soft bread crumbs
2 garlic cloves, minced
1 teaspoon salt
¼ teaspoon freshly ground
   pepper
   Beef Stock
   Watercress

1. Simmer mushrooms and 1 cup of the oysters in the sherry in a covered saucepan 8 to 10 minutes. Drain; press all moisture out of mushrooms.
2. Purée mushrooms and cooked oysters in a food processor or blender; pour into a shallow 1½-quart casserole. Stir in the bread crumbs, garlic, salt, and pepper. Stir in reserved oyster liquor. Stir in stock, if necessary, to make purée of a thick sauce consistency. Arrange remaining oysters in purée.
3. Bake covered at 350°F 20 minutes.
4. Serve in shallow bowls or ramekins. Garnish with watercress.

6 to 8 servings

649 Fresh Vegetables and Shrimp en Brochette

1¾ pounds fresh shrimp (23 to 25
   uncooked shrimp), washed,
   peeled, and deveined
1 pound fresh mushrooms (about
   12 mushrooms) with stem
   ends removed
2 medium tomatoes, quartered
2 medium green peppers, seeded
   and cut in 1½-inch cubes
2 medium onions, peeled and
   quartered
¾ cup oil
½ cup dry white wine or sherry
¼ cup chopped parsley
1 teaspoon salt
¼ teaspoon pepper

1. Combine shrimp and vegetables in a bowl.
2. Prepare marinade by combining oil, wine, parsley, salt, and pepper. Pour over shrimp and vegetables. Allow to marinate for 3 hours.
3. String shrimp on skewers alternately with vegetables. Broil about 3 inches from heat until shrimp are browned and flake easily; about 4 minutes on one side, 3 minutes on the other.

4 to 6 servings

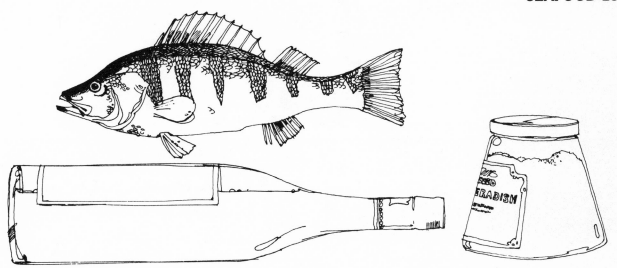

650 *Poached Fish with Horseradish Sauce*

1½ pounds fish fillets, such as perch
    or bass
Boiling water (enough to just
    cover fish)
½ cup dry white wine
1 small onion, chopped
2 tablespoons chopped parsley
1 teaspoon salt
⅛ teaspoon pepper
Horseradish Sauce:
1 cup dairy sour cream
2 to 3 tablespoons prepared
    horseradish
2 tablespoons grated lemon peel

1. For poached fish, tie fish loosely in cheesecloth to prevent breaking and place in a skillet. Add boiling water, wine, onion, parsley, salt, and pepper. Cover skillet and simmer about 10 minutes, or until fish flakes (can be separated with a fork into thin, layer-like pieces). Meanwhile, prepare sauce.
2. For sauce, blend well sour cream, horseradish, and lemon peel. Pour sauce into serving dish; set aside.
3. Drain fish; remove cheesecloth. Place fish on warm platter. Serve with sauce.

4 servings

651 *Shrimp à la King*

2 cups white wine
2 shallots, minced, or ¼ cup
    minced onion
1 cup oyster liquor, fish stock,
    or chicken broth
1½ pounds fresh shrimp, peeled
    and deveined
2 tablespoons flour
2 tablespoons butter
Juice of ¼ lemon (about 2
    teaspoons)
½ cup light cream
2 egg yolks, well beaten
Toast points
Parsley

1. Combine wine, shallots, and oyster liquor in a saucepan; bring to boiling and add shrimp. Simmer 15 minutes. Drain and reserve ¾ cup stock.
2. Meanwhile, stir flour into melted butter in a saucepan, making a roux. Blend in reserved stock; cook and stir until mixture thickens. Add shrimp and cook over low heat. Stir in lemon juice.
3. Add cream to beaten yolks. Mix well and add hot shrimp mixture, stirring constantly. Serve on toast points and garnish with parsley.

4 to 6 servings

652 *Fish Stew with Red Wine*

2 pounds fish
2 cups red wine
1 carrot, sliced
1 onion, minced
2 cloves garlic, cut in halves
1 teaspoon salt
¼ teaspoon pepper
  Herb Bouquet
3 tablespoons brandy
3 tablespoons melted butter
2 tablespoons all-purpose flour

1. Set out a deep heavy skillet with a tight-fitting cover.
2. Clean, wash, dry, and cut fish into thick slices. Put fish into skillet and add wine, carrot, onion, garlic, salt, pepper, and Herb Bouquet; bring to boiling.
3. Heat brandy in a small saucepan. Ignite brandy and immediately pour over the fish. When the flame has burned out, cover the pan. Cook fish slowly 15 to 20 minutes, or until the fish flakes when pierced with a fork. Remove fish to a warm serving dish. Keep hot. Strain and reserve cooking liquid.
4. Blend thoroughly in same skillet butter and flour. Cook over low heat until mixture bubbles. Remove from heat; gradually stir in cooking liquid. Cook rapidly; stir constantly until sauce thickens. Boil 1 to 2 minutes longer. Pour sauce over the fish.
5. Serve with **garlic croutons.** Garnish with **tiny cooked onions, sautéed mushrooms,** or **cooked shrimp.**

4 servings

Herb Bouquet: Tie together neatly **3 or 4 sprigs of parsley, 1 sprig thyme,** and **½ bay leaf.** If dry herbs are used, enclose in fine cheesecloth bag.

653 *Mussels Cooked in Wine Sauce*

2 quarts mussels
2 cups dry white wine such as chablis
1 cup finely chopped shallots
½ cup finely chopped parsley
⅓ cup unsalted butter
  Freshly ground white pepper
  Juice of ½ lemon
  Salt
Hollandaise Sauce:
2 egg yolks
2 tablespoons cream

1. Scrub mussels under running water and trim off the beards.
2. Pour wine over mussels in a saucepot; add shallots, parsley, butter, and white pepper to taste. Cover tightly and cook over high heat about 2 minutes; stir the mixture and cook, covered, 2 minutes longer, or until mussel shells open.
3. Remove the mussels from saucepot; remove and discard top shells, placing the filled bottom shells in a serving dish. Keep warm.
4. Cook the pan juice over high heat to reduce the amount by one half. Remove from heat. Add lemon juice, salt, and white pepper to taste.
5. For hollandaise sauce, in the top of a double boiler, beat egg

¼ teaspoon salt
Few grains cayenne pepper
2 tablespoons lemon juice or
tarragon vinegar
½ cup butter

yolks, cream, salt, and cayenne pepper until thick with a whisk beater. Set over hot (not boiling) water. (Bottom of double-boiler top should not touch water.)

6. Add the lemon juice gradually, while beating constantly. Cook, beating constantly with the whisk beater, until sauce is the consistency of thick cream. Remove double boiler from heat, leaving top in place.

7. Beating constantly, add the butter, ½ teaspoon at a time. Beat with whisk beater until butter is melted and thoroughly blended in. Mix with wine sauce.

8. Pour the sauce over the mussels and serve immediately.

4 servings

654 *Scallops Baked in Shells*

2 cups dry white wine
Herb Bouquet
2 pounds (1 quart) scallops
½ teaspoon salt
½ pound mushrooms
6 shallots or ¼ cup minced onions
1 tablespoon minced parsley
3 tablespoons butter
2 tablespoons water
1 teaspoon lemon juice
¼ cup melted butter
¼ cup all-purpose flour
2 egg yolks, slightly beaten
¼ cup heavy cream
⅓ cup buttered dry bread crumbs

1. Butter 6 baking shells or ramekins.
2. Heat wine in a saucepan with Herb Bouquet.
3. Wash scallops in cold water and drain.
4. Add scallops and salt to wine, cover and simmer about 10 minutes, or until tender. Remove Herb Bouquet, drain scallops, and reserve the liquid. Cut scallops into fine pieces and set aside.
5. Clean and chop mushrooms.
6. Add mushrooms, shallots, parsley, butter, water, and lemon juice to a saucepan; cover and simmer 5 to 10 minutes. Strain liquid into seasoned wine. Add vegetable mixture to scallops. Set aside.
7. Make a roux by blending butter and flour in a saucepan. Cook over low heat until mixture bubbles. Remove from heat and gradually stir in wine and vegetable liquid. Return to heat and bring rapidly to boiling, stirring constantly; cook 1 to 2 minutes longer.
8. Remove sauce from heat and add egg yolks and cream gradually, stirring vigorously. Then stir in the scallop mixture.
9. Fill shells or ramekins, piling high in center. Sprinkle with about ⅓ cup of buttered bread crumbs.
10. To brown, set shells on a baking sheet and place in oven at 450°F 8 to 10 minutes, or place under broiler 3 to 4 minutes from heat to top of the creamed mixture. Serve when browned.

6 servings

Herb Bouquet: Tie neatly together **3 or 4 sprigs of parsley, 1 sprig thyme,** and **½ bay leaf.** If dry herbs are used, enclose in fine cheesecloth bag.

655 Lobster Newburg/Crab Meat Newburg

2 cups cooked lobster meat
¼ cup butter
2 cups cream
¾ teaspoon salt
⅛ teaspoon pepper
⅛ teaspoon nutmeg
4 egg yolks, slightly beaten
2 tablespoons sherry
Toast points or cooked rice

1. Cut lobster meat into 1-inch pieces and set aside.
2. Melt butter in the top of a double boiler. Blend in cream, salt, pepper, and nutmeg; bring just to boiling. Stir in lobster and cook over low heat until lobster is thoroughly heated.
3. Vigorously stir about 3 tablespoons of hot mixture into egg yolks. Immediately blend into hot mixture. Place over simmering water and cook 3 to 5 minutes, or just until mixture thickens. Stir slowly to keep mixture cooking evenly. (Do not overcook as sauce will curdle.)
4. Remove immediately from heat and blend in sherry. Serve on toast points or cooked rice.

About 6 servings

Crab Meat Newburg: Follow recipe for Lobster Newburg substituting **2 cups cooked crab meat** for the lobster. Remove and discard bony tissue from meat.

65

657 Sole Véronique in Parchment

Baked in parchment paper, the fish retains its natural moisture and flavor.

2 pounds sole fillets
¾ teaspoon salt
3 tablespoons snipped parsley
2 teaspoons minced lemon peel
1½ cups seedless white grapes
⅔ cup dry white wine
Lemon wedges

1. Lay each fillet on a piece of parchment paper or aluminum foil, 12x12 inches. Sprinkle fillets with salt, parsley, and lemon peel. Divide grapes over fish; sprinkle with wine. Bring edges of parchment up, crimp edges and seal; place on a jelly-roll pan.
2. Bake at 350°F 20 minutes.
3. Place parchment packets on individual plates; let each person open packet. Serve with lemon wedges.

4 servings

Desserts

658 Pie-Pan Apple Dessert

1 egg
¾ cup firmly packed brown sugar
½ cup enriched all-purpose flour
1 teaspoon baking powder
¼ teaspoon salt
¼ to ½ teaspoon ground nutmeg
1½ cups chopped pared apple
½ cup chopped pecans
  Lemon Sauce, whipped cream, or
    ice cream

1. Beat egg until light and fluffy. Beat in brown sugar. Mix flour, baking powder, salt, and nutmeg; add to egg mixture and blend.
2. Stir in apple and pecans. Spread in well-greased 8- or 9-inch pie pan or plate.
3. Bake at 350°F about 30 minutes, or until top is golden brown.
4. Serve warm with Lemon Sauce or desired topping.

About 6 servings

Lemon Sauce: Mix ⅓ cup sugar, 2 teaspoons cornstarch, and a few grains salt in a saucepan. Add 1 cup boiling water gradually, stirring constantly. Continue to stir and bring to boiling; simmer 5 minutes. Remove from heat. Blend in 2 tablespoons butter, ¾ teaspoon grated lemon peel, and 1½ tablespoons lemon juice. Serve warm.

659

660 *Peaches 'n' Corn Bread, Shortcake Style*

1 cup sifted enriched all-purpose
    flour
½ teaspoon baking soda
¼ teaspoon salt
1 cup enriched yellow cornmeal
¾ cup firmly packed light brown
    sugar
1 egg, beaten
½ cup buttermilk
⅓ cup dairy sour cream
    Peach Butter Elégante
    Sweetened fresh peach slices

1. Blend flour, baking soda, salt, cornmeal, and brown sugar in a bowl; set aside.
2. Beat egg, buttermilk, and sour cream until well blended; add to dry ingredients and stir until just smooth (do not overmix).
3. Turn into a greased 11×7×1½-inch pan and spread batter evenly.
4. Bake at 425°F about 20 minutes.
5. While still warm, cut corn bread into serving-size pieces, remove from pan, and split into two layers. Spread Peach Butter Elégante generously between layers. Top with peach slices.

9 or 12 servings

Peach Butter Elégante: Thaw **1 package (10 or 12 ounces) frozen sliced peaches.** Drain peaches and cut into pieces; set aside. Put **1 cup firm unsalted butter** or **1 cup margarine** into a small mixing bowl. Beat with electric mixer on high speed just until butter is whipped. Add ½ **cup confectioners' sugar** gradually, beating thoroughly. Add the peaches, about 1 tablespoon at a time, beating thoroughly after each addition. (Do not allow butter to become too soft.) Chill until ready to use.

About 2 cups peach butter

66

662 *Spicy Peach Cobbler*

1 can (29 ounces) sliced peaches,
    drained; reserve 1 cup syrup
½ cup firmly packed brown sugar
2 tablespoons cornstarch
⅛ teaspoon salt
⅛ teaspoon ground cinnamon
⅛ teaspoon ground cloves
2 tablespoons cider vinegar
1 tablespoon butter or margarine
1 cup all-purpose biscuit mix
½ cup finely shredded sharp Cheddar
    cheese
2 tablespoons butter or margarine,
    melted
¼ cup milk

1. Put drained peaches into a shallow 1-quart baking dish. Set aside.
2. Mix brown sugar, cornstarch, salt, cinnamon, and cloves in a saucepan. Blend in reserved peach syrup and vinegar; add 1 tablespoon butter. Bring mixture to boiling, stirring frequently; cook until thickened, about 10 minutes. Pour over peaches and set in a 400°F oven.
3. Combine biscuit mix and cheese. Stir in melted butter and milk to form a soft dough. Remove dish from oven and drop dough by heaping tablespoonfuls on top of hot peaches.
4. Return to oven and bake 20 minutes, or until crust is golden brown. Serve warm.

6 servings

663 *Cantaloupe Sherbet*

2 cups ripe cantaloupe pieces
1 egg white
½ cup sugar
2 tablespoons fresh lime juice

1. Put melon pieces, egg white, sugar, and lime juice into an electric blender container. Cover and blend until smooth.
2. Turn into a shallow baking dish. Set in freezer; stir occasionally during freezing.
3. To serve, spoon into chilled dessert dishes.

About 1½ pints sherbet

Pineapple Sherbet: Follow recipe for Cantaloupe Sherbet; substitute **2 cups fresh pineapple pieces** for cantaloupe. 664

Watermelon Sherbet: Follow recipe for Cantaloupe Sherbet; substitute **2 cups watermelon pieces** for cantaloupe and, if desired, decrease sugar to ¼ cup. 665

666 *Banana-Pineapple Ice Cream*

2 cups mashed ripe bananas (about 5 medium)
1 cup sugar
1 teaspoon grated orange peel
1 teaspoon grated lemon peel
3 tablespoons lemon juice
2 tablespoons lime juice
1½ cups unsweetened pineapple juice
⅓ cup orange juice
2 cans (14½ ounces each) evaporated milk

1. Crushed ice and rock salt will be needed. Wash and scald cover, container, and dasher of a 3- or 4-quart ice cream freezer. Chill thoroughly.
2. Combine bananas, sugar, orange peel, lemon peel, lemon juice, and lime juice; blend thoroughly. Set aside about 10 minutes.
3. Stir fruit juices into banana mixture. Add evaporated milk gradually, stirring until well blended.
4. Fill chilled freezer container no more than two-thirds full with ice cream mixture. Cover tightly. Set into freezer tub. (For electric freezer, follow the directions.)
5. Fill tub with alternate layers of crushed ice and rock salt, using 8 parts ice to 1 part salt. Turn handle slowly 5 minutes. Then turn rapidly until handle becomes difficult to turn (about 15 minutes), adding ice and salt as necessary.
6. Wipe cover and remove dasher. Pack down ice cream and cover with waxed paper or plastic wrap. Replace lid. (Plug dasher opening unless freezer has a solid cover.) Repack freezer container in ice, using 4 parts ice to 1 part salt. Cover with heavy paper or cloth. Let ripen 2 hours.

About 2 quarts ice cream

667 *Quick Applesauce Whip*

1 can (16 ounces) applesauce
½ teaspoon grated lemon peel
2 teaspoons lemon juice
½ teaspoon ground cinnamon
3 egg whites
⅛ teaspoon salt
6 tablespoons sugar
Ground nutmeg

1. Combine applesauce, lemon peel, juice, and cinnamon.
2. Beat egg whites and salt until frothy. Add sugar gradually, beat well. Continue beating until rounded peaks are formed. Fold beaten egg whites into applesauce mixture.
3. Spoon immediately into dessert dishes. Sprinkle nutmeg over each serving.

About 6 servings

668 *Bananas with Royal Pineapple Sauce*

3 tablespoons dark brown sugar
2 teaspoons cornstarch
1 can (8¼ ounces) crushed pineapple (undrained)
1 tablespoon butter
⅛ teaspoon almond extract
¼ teaspoon grated lemon peel
1 tablespoon lemon juice
¼ cup butter
4 firm bananas, peeled
2 tablespoons flaked coconut

1. Mix sugar and cornstarch in a saucepan. Add pineapple with syrup, 1 tablespoon butter, and almond extract; mix well. Bring to boiling, stirring constantly until thickened.
2. Remove from heat and stir in lemon peel and juice. Set the sauce aside.
3. Heat ¼ cup butter in a heavy skillet. Add bananas; turn them by rolling to cook evenly and brown lightly. (Do not overcook or fruit will lose its shape.)
4. Allowing one-half banana per person, serve at once topped with the warm pineapple sauce. Sprinkle with coconut.

8 servings

669 *Purple Plum Crunch*

5 cups pitted, quartered fresh purple plums
¼ cup firmly packed brown sugar
3 tablespoons flour
½ teaspoon ground cinnamon
1 cup enriched all-purpose flour
1 cup sugar
1 teaspoon baking powder
¼ teaspoon salt
¼ teaspoon ground mace
1 egg, well beaten
½ cup butter or margarine, melted and cooled

1. Put plums into a shallow 2-quart baking dish or casserole.
2. Mix brown sugar, 3 tablespoons flour, and cinnamon; sprinkle over plums and mix gently with a fork.
3. Blend 1 cup flour, sugar, baking powder, salt, and mace thoroughly. Add to beaten egg and stir with a fork until mixture is crumbly. Sprinkle evenly over plums in baking dish. Pour melted butter evenly over the topping.
4. Bake at 375°F 40 to 45 minutes, or until topping is lightly browned. Serve warm.

6 to 8 servings

Note: Other fresh fruits may be substituted for the plums.

670 *Chocolate Peanut Butter Pudding*

1 small package chocolate pudding and pie filling (not instant)
1 can (14½ ounces) evaporated milk
⅔ cup water
⅓ cup peanut butter
Slightly sweetened whipped cream (optional)
Chopped salted peanuts (optional)

1. Empty pudding mix into a saucepan, then stir in evaporated milk and water.
2. Cook and stir over moderate heat until thickened, about 5 minutes. Remove from heat and stir in peanut butter. Cover and chill.
3. To serve, spoon into dessert dishes. If desired, top with whipped cream and peanuts.

4 to 6 servings

671 *Steamed Pumpkin Pudding*

Pudding:

1¼ cups fine dry bread crumbs
½ cup enriched all-purpose flour
1 cup firmly packed brown sugar
1 teaspoon baking powder
½ teaspoon baking soda
½ teaspoon salt
½ teaspoon ground cinnamon
½ teaspoon ground cloves
½ cup salad oil
½ cup undiluted evaporated milk
2 eggs
1½ cups canned pumpkin

Lemon Nut Sauce:

½ cup butter or margarine
2 cups confectioners' sugar
¼ teaspoon salt
¼ teaspoon ground ginger
¼ cup lemon juice
½ cup chopped walnuts

1. Blend bread crumbs, flour, brown sugar, baking powder, baking soda, salt, cinnamon, and cloves in a large bowl.
2. Beat oil, evaporated milk, eggs, and pumpkin. Add to dry ingredients; mix until well blended.
3. Turn into a well-greased 2-quart mold. Cover tightly with a greased cover, or tie greased aluminum foil tightly over mold. Place mold on trivet or rack in a steamer or deep kettle with a tight-fitting cover.
4. Pour in boiling water to no more than one half the height of the mold. Cover steamer, bring water to boiling, and keep boiling at all times. If necessary, add more boiling water during cooking period.
5. Steam the pudding 2½ to 3 hours, or until a wooden pick inserted in center comes out clean.
6. For Lemon Nut Sauce, beat butter in a bowl. Blend confectioners' sugar, salt, and ginger; add gradually to butter, beating well. Add lemon juice gradually, continuing to beat until blended. Mix in walnuts.
7. Remove pudding from steamer and unmold onto a serving plate. Serve pudding with Lemon Nut Sauce.

About 12 servings

Note: If pudding is to be stored and served later, unmold onto a rack and cool thoroughly. Wrap in aluminum foil or return to mold and store in a cool place. Before serving, resteam pudding about 3 hours, or until thoroughly heated.

672 *Individual Fruit Puddings*

Pudding:

2 medium oranges
1½ cups sifted enriched all-purpose flour
1 teaspoon baking soda
¼ teaspoon salt
¼ teaspoon ground cinnamon
¼ teaspoon ground cloves
¼ teaspoon ground nutmeg
¼ cup shortening
1 cup firmly packed brown sugar
1 egg, well beaten
1 cup dark seedless raisins
½ cup pitted dates, cut in pieces
½ cup walnuts, coarsely chopped

Orange Sauce:

¾ cup sugar
2 tablespoons cornstarch
⅛ teaspoon salt
¾ cup orange juice
½ cup water
1 teaspoon grated orange peel
1 tablespoon butter or margarine

1. For pudding, grease eight 5-ounce custard cups. Set aside.
2. Peel oranges; slice into cartwheels, and cut into pieces; reserve juice as it collects.
3. Blend flour, baking soda, salt, cinnamon, cloves, and nutmeg. Set aside.
4. Beat shortening; add brown sugar gradually, beating until fluffy. Add egg and beat thoroughly.
5. Mix in the orange pieces, reserved juice, raisins, dates, and walnuts. Blend in the dry ingredients.
6. Fill custard cups about two-thirds full with mixture; cover tightly with aluminum foil. Set in a pan and fill pan with water to a 1-inch depth. Cover pan with aluminum foil.
7. Cook in a 325°F oven 2 hours.
8. For Orange Sauce, mix sugar, cornstarch, and salt in a saucepan. Add orange juice and water gradually, stirring constantly. Bring to boiling, stirring constantly until thickened; cook over low heat 6 to 8 minutes, stirring occasionally.
9. Remove from heat. Blend in orange peel and butter. Keep warm.
10. Unmold puddings while hot onto dessert plates and spoon sauce over each.

8 servings

673 *Blueberry-Orange Parfaits*

2 tablespoons cornstarch
1 cup sugar
½ teaspoon salt
2 cups orange juice
2 eggs, beaten
½ teaspoon grated lemon peel
2 tablespoons sugar
2 cups fresh blueberries
Whipped cream (optional)

1. Mix cornstarch, 1 cup sugar, and salt in a heavy saucepan. Add a small amount of the orange juice and blend until smooth. Stir in remaining orange juice.
2. Bring mixture to boiling, stirring constantly, and cook 3 to 5 minutes.
3. Stir about 3 tablespoons of the hot mixture into beaten eggs; immediately blend with mixture in saucepan.
4. Cook and stir about 3 minutes. Remove from water and cool. Stir in lemon peel. Chill.
5. Meanwhile, sprinkle 2 tablespoons sugar over blueberries and allow to stand at least 30 minutes. Spoon alternating layers of custard and blueberries in parfait glasses, beginning with a layer of custard and ending with blueberries. Top with whipped cream, if desired.

6 servings

674 *Ginger-Yam Mousse*

1½ cups mashed cooked yams (about 3 medium yams)
1 cup sugar
2 teaspoons ground ginger
1 teaspoon ground nutmeg
½ teaspoon ground cinnamon
Few grains salt
3 egg yolks, fork beaten
2 cups milk
½ teaspoon grated lemon peel
½ teaspoon lemon juice
½ cup half-and-half
3 egg whites
¼ cup sugar
Whipped dessert topping
Toasted slivered almonds

1. Put mashed yams into a heavy saucepan. Blend 1 cup sugar, spices, and salt. Mix with yams, then mix in egg yolks and milk. Cook over medium heat, stirring constantly, until mixture is thick. Remove from heat when mixture just comes to boiling.
2. Cool, stirring occasionally. Blend in lemon peel, juice, and half-and-half.
3. Beat egg whites until frothy; add ¼ cup sugar gradually, continuing to beat until stiff peaks are formed. Fold into completely cooled yam mixture.
4. Turn into a 6½-cup ring mold, spreading evenly. Freeze until firm, about 3½ hours.
5. Allow mousse to soften slightly at room temperature before unmolding. Unmold onto a chilled plate. Spoon whipped dessert topping into center and sprinkle with almonds.

6 to 8 servings

675 *Citrus Bundt Cake*

¾ cup butter
2 teaspoons grated lemon peel
2 teaspoons grated orange peel
1¾ cups sugar
3 eggs
3⅓ cups sifted enriched all-purpose flour
1 tablespoon baking powder
½ teaspoon salt
1 cup milk
2 tablespoons lemon juice
2 tablespoons orange juice
⅓ cup sugar
Fruit sauce (optional)

1. Cream butter, grated peels, and 1¾ cups sugar until light and fluffy. Add eggs, one at a time, beating thoroughly after each addition.
2. Blend flour, baking powder, and salt. Mix into creamed mixture alternately with milk. Turn into a generously buttered 10-inch Bundt pan or angel food cake pan.
3. Bake at 325°F 60 to 75 minutes, or until a cake tester comes out clean. Remove from pan immediately and place on wire rack set over a shallow pan.
4. Combine fruit juices and ⅓ cup sugar in a small saucepan. Bring to boiling and boil 3 minutes. Drizzle over warm cake; cool completely before serving.
5. Slice and serve with a fruit sauce, if desired.

One 10-inch Bundt cake

676 *Chocolate Pound Cake Loaf*

3 cups sifted enriched all-purpose
    flour
2 teaspoons baking powder
¼ teaspoon salt
½ cup cocoa, sifted
1 cup butter or margarine
½ cup lard
1 tablespoon vanilla extract
½ teaspoon almond extract
3 cups sugar
1 cup eggs (5 or 6)
1¼ cups milk

1. Lightly grease (bottom only) two 9×5×3-inch loaf pans. Line bottoms with waxed paper; grease paper. Set aside.
2. Combine flour, baking powder, salt, and cocoa and blend thoroughly. Set aside.
3. Cream butter and lard with extracts in a large bowl. Add sugar gradually, creaming thoroughly after each addition. Add eggs, one at a time, beating until fluffy after each addition.
4. Beating only until blended after each addition, alternately add dry ingredients in fourths and milk in thirds to creamed mixture.
5. Turn equal amounts of batter into prepared loaf pans. Spread batter evenly. (Top of baked cakes may have a slight crack down center.) Place pans on center of oven rack so that top of batter will be at center of oven.
6. Bake at 325°F about 65 minutes, or until cake tester inserted in center comes out clean.
7. Cool cakes in pans 15 minutes on wire racks. Loosen sides with a spatula and turn onto rack. Peel off paper, turn right side up, and cool completely.

Two loaf cakes

Dutch Cocoa Loaf Cake: Follow directions for 677 Chocolate Pound Cake Loaf except substitute ⅔ **cup Dutch process cocoa** for the ½ cup cocoa and increase butter or margarine to 1½ cups; omit lard.

678 *Cranberry Upside-Down Cake*

Topping:
¼ cup butter or margarine
⅔ cup sugar
1 tablespoon grated orange peel
½ teaspoon vanilla extract
2 cups fresh cranberries, washed
    and coarsely chopped
⅓ cup sugar

Cake:
1½ cups sifted enriched cake flour
2 teaspoons baking powder
½ teaspoon salt
½ cup butter or margarine
1 teaspoon vanilla extract
½ cup sugar
1 egg
½ cup milk

1. For topping, heat butter in a saucepan. Add ⅔ cup sugar, orange peel, and vanilla extract; blend thoroughly. Spread mixture evenly in an 8×8×2-inch pan.
2. Combine cranberries and ⅓ cup sugar. Spread over mixture in pan; set aside.
3. For cake, blend flour, baking powder, and salt; set aside.
4. Cream butter with vanilla extract. Add sugar gradually, creaming until fluffy after each addition. Add egg and beat thoroughly.
5. Beating only until smooth after each addition, alternately add dry ingredients in thirds and milk in halves to creamed mixture. Turn batter over cranberry mixture and spread evenly.
6. Bake at 350°F about 50 minutes.
7. Remove from oven and let stand 1 to 2 minutes in pan on wire rack. To remove from pan, run spatula gently around sides. Cover with a serving plate and invert; allow pan to remain over cake 1 or 2 minutes. Lift pan off. Serve cake warm or cool.

One 8-inch square cake

679 *Date Spice Cake*

2¼ cups sifted enriched all-purpose flour
2 teaspoons baking powder
¼ teaspoon baking soda
½ teaspoon salt
2 teaspoons ground nutmeg
2 teaspoons ground ginger
⅔ cup shortening
1 teaspoon grated orange peel
1 teaspoon grated lemon peel
1 cup sugar
2 eggs
1 cup buttermilk
1 cup chopped dates

1. Grease a 9×9×2-inch pan. Line with waxed paper cut to fit bottom; grease paper. Set aside.
2. Blend flour, baking powder, baking soda, salt, nutmeg, and ginger.
3. Beat shortening with orange and lemon peels. Add sugar gradually, creaming until fluffy after each addition.
4. Add eggs, one at a time, beating thoroughly after each addition.
5. Beating only until smooth after each addition, alternately add dry ingredients in fourths and buttermilk in thirds to creamed mixture. Mix in dates. Turn batter into prepared pan.
6. Bake at 350°F about 45 minutes.
7. Remove from oven. Cool 5 to 10 minutes in pan on wire rack. Remove cake from pan and peel off paper; cool cake on rack.

One 9-inch square cake

680 *Carrot Cupcakes*

1½ cups sifted enriched all-purpose flour
1 teaspoon baking powder
1 teaspoon baking soda
1 teaspoon ground cinnamon
½ teaspoon salt
1 cup sugar
¾ cup vegetable oil
2 eggs
1 cup grated raw carrots
½ cup chopped nuts

1. Blend flour, baking powder, baking soda, cinnamon, and salt. Set aside.
2. Combine sugar and oil in a bowl and beat thoroughly. Add eggs, one at a time, beating thoroughly after each addition. Mix in carrots. Add dry ingredients gradually, beating until blended. Mix in nuts.
3. Spoon into paper-baking-cup-lined muffin-pan wells.
4. Bake at 350°F 15 to 20 minutes.

About 16 cupcakes

681 *Triple-Treat Walnut Bars*

½ cup butter or margarine
1 package (3 ounces) cream cheese
½ cup firmly packed dark brown sugar
1 cup whole wheat flour
⅓ cup toasted wheat germ
1 package (6 ounces) semisweet chocolate pieces
2 eggs
½ cup honey
⅓ cup whole wheat flour
⅓ cup instant nonfat dry milk
¼ teaspoon salt
¼ teaspoon ground cinnamon
¼ teaspoon ground mace
1½ cups chopped walnuts

1. Cream butter, cheese, and sugar in a bowl until light. Add 1 cup whole wheat flour and wheat germ and mix until smooth. Turn into a greased 13×9×2-inch pan; spread evenly.
2. Bake at 375°F 15 to 18 minutes, until edges are very lightly browned and top is firm.
3. Remove from oven and sprinkle with chocolate. Let stand about 5 minutes, or until chocolate softens, then spread it evenly over baked layer.
4. Combine eggs and honey; beat just until well blended. Add ⅓ cup whole wheat flour, dry milk, salt, cinnamon, mace, and walnuts; mix well. Spoon over the chocolate.
5. Return to oven and bake 18 to 20 minutes, or until top is set. Cool in pan, then cut into bars or diamonds.

About 3 dozen cookies

682 *Swiss Chocolate Squares*

Cake:
- 1 cup water
- ½ cup soft margarine
- 1½ ounces (1½ squares) unsweetened chocolate
- 2 cups enriched all-purpose flour
- 2 cups sugar
- 2 eggs
- ½ cup dairy sour cream
- 1 teaspoon baking soda
- ¼ teaspoon salt

Milk Chocolate Frosting:
- ½ cup soft margarine
- 6 tablespoons milk
- 1½ ounces (1½ squares) unsweetened chocolate
- 4½ cups confectioners' sugar
- 1 teaspoon vanilla extract
- ½ cup chopped nuts

1. For cake, combine water, margarine, and chocolate in a saucepan. Set over medium heat and bring to boiling, stirring occasionally. Remove from heat.
2. Blend flour and sugar; stir into the cooked chocolate mixture. Beat in eggs and sour cream. Blend baking soda and salt; beat in. Turn into a greased 15×10×1-inch jelly-roll pan and spread evenly.
3. Bake at 375°F 20 to 25 minutes. Cool on a wire rack.
4. For Milk Chocolate Frosting, combine margarine, milk, and chocolate in a saucepan. Set over medium heat and bring to boiling; boil 1 minute, stirring constantly. Remove from heat.
5. Stir in confectioners' sugar, adding gradually, and beat until smooth. Stir in vanilla extract.
6. Turn frosting onto warm cake and spread evenly. Sprinkle with nuts. Cool completely before cutting into squares.

1½ to 3 dozen cake squares

683 *Choco-Raisin Candy*

- ¾ cup dark seedless raisins
- ½ cup canned chocolate frosting
- Finely chopped nuts, flaked coconut, cocoa, or equal parts confectioners' sugar and cocoa

Mix raisins and chocolate frosting. Chill thoroughly. Working quickly, form mixture into 1-inch balls and coat as desired. Refrigerate before serving.

1½ dozen candy balls

684 *Peanut Butter Fudge*

- 1 cup undiluted evaporated milk
- 2 cups sugar
- ¼ cup butter or margarine
- 1 cup miniature marshmallows
- 1 jar (12 ounces) crunchy peanut butter
- 1 teaspoon vanilla extract

1. Combine evaporated milk, sugar, and butter in a heavy 10-inch skillet. Set over medium heat, bring to boiling, and boil 4 minutes, stirring constantly.
2. Remove from heat and stir in marshmallows, peanut butter, and vanilla extract until evenly blended.
3. Turn into a buttered 8-inch square pan and spread to corners. Chill before cutting into squares.

About 2 pounds fudge

Note: This fudge may be prepared in an electric skillet. Set temperature at 280°F, bring mixture to boiling, and boil about 5 minutes.

685 *Spicy Walnut Diamonds*

2½ cups sifted all-purpose flour
2 tablespoons cocoa
1½ teaspoons baking powder
1 teaspoon salt
½ teaspoon ground nutmeg
¼ teaspoon ground cloves
2 cups firmly packed brown sugar
3 eggs
½ cup honey
½ cup butter or margarine, melted
1½ cups chopped walnuts (1 cup medium and ½ cup fine)
½ cup confectioners' sugar
2 to 3 teaspoons milk

1. Blend flour, cocoa, baking powder, salt, nutmeg, and cloves.
2. Combine brown sugar and eggs in a large bowl; beat until well blended and light. Add honey, butter, and flour mixture and mix until smooth.
3. Stir in the 1 cup medium walnuts, and spread evenly in a greased 15×10×1-inch jelly-roll pan. Sprinkle the ½ cup fine walnuts over top.
4. Bake at 375°F about 20 minutes, or just until top springs back when touched lightly in center. Cool in pan.
5. Mix confectioners' sugar and enough milk to make a smooth, thin glaze. Spread over cooled layer. Cut into diamonds or bars.

About 4 dozen cookies

686 *Tropichocolate Wafers*

1½ cups sifted enriched all-purpose flour
½ teaspoon baking soda
½ teaspoon salt
½ cup cocoa
½ cup butter or margarine
½ teaspoon vanilla extract
1 cup firmly packed brown sugar
1 egg
¾ cup flaked coconut

1. Blend flour, baking soda, salt, and cocoa. Set aside.
2. Cream butter with vanilla extract. Add brown sugar gradually, creaming until fluffy. Add egg and beat thoroughly.
3. Mixing until well blended after each addition, add dry ingredients in thirds to creamed mixture. Stir in coconut.
4. Chill dough in refrigerator until easy to handle, then shape into 2 rolls about 1½ inches in diameter. Wrap each roll in waxed paper, aluminum foil, or plastic wrap. Chill several hours or overnight.
5. Remove rolls of dough from refrigerator as needed. Cut dough into ⅛-inch slices. Place slices about 1½ inches apart on lightly greased cookie sheets.
6. Bake at 400°F 5 to 8 minutes. Cool cookies on wire racks.

About 5 dozen cookies

687 *Butterscotchies*

½ cup undiluted evaporated milk
¾ cup sugar
¼ teaspoon salt
2 tablespoons butter or margarine
1 package (6 ounces) butterscotch-flavored pieces
1 teaspoon vanilla extract
1 cup flaked coconut
½ cup coarsely chopped walnuts
2 to 2½ cups crisp enriched ready-to-eat cereal

1. Put evaporated milk, sugar, salt, and butter into a heavy 2-quart saucepan. Bring to a full boil, stirring constantly, and boil 2 minutes.
2. Remove from heat. Add butterscotch pieces and vanilla extract; stir until smooth. Add coconut, walnuts, and cereal; toss lightly until well coated.
3. Drop by rounded teaspoonfuls onto a cookie sheet lined with waxed paper or aluminum foil. Allow to stand until set.

About 1½ pounds candy

688 *Peanut Blonde Brownies*

½ cup chunk-style peanut butter
¼ cup butter or margarine
1 teaspoon vanilla extract
1 cup firmly packed light brown
    sugar
2 eggs
½ cup enriched all-purpose flour
1 cup chopped salted peanuts
    Confectioners' sugar

1. Cream peanut butter, butter, and vanilla extract in a bowl. Add brown sugar gradually, beating well after each addition.
2. Add eggs, one at a time, beating thoroughly after each addition until creamy.
3. Add flour in halves, beating until blended after each addition. Stir in peanuts. Turn mixture into a greased 8×8×2-inch pan and spread evenly.
4. Bake at 350°F 30 to 35 minutes.
5. Remove from oven and cool in pan 5 minutes. Cut into 2-inch squares. Remove from pan and cool on a wire rack. Sift confectioners' sugar over tops.

16 brownies

689 *Pineapple Volcano Chiffon Pie*

2 envelopes unflavored gelatin
½ cup sugar
¼ teaspoon salt
3 egg yolks, fork beaten
½ cup water
1 can (20 ounces) crushed pineapple
    (undrained)
¼ teaspoon grated lemon peel
1 tablespoon lemon juice
3 egg whites
    Frozen dessert topping, thawed, or
    whipped dessert topping
1 baked 9-inch graham cracker crust
1 can (8¼ ounces) crushed pineapple,
    drained

1. Mix gelatin, ¼ cup sugar, and salt in the top of a double boiler.
2. Beat egg yolks and water together. Stir into gelatin mixture along with undrained pineapple.
3. Set over boiling water. Thoroughly beat mixture and continue cooking 5 minutes to cook egg yolks and dissolve gelatin, stirring constantly.
4. Remove from water; mix in lemon peel and juice. Chill, stirring occasionally until mixture mounds slightly when dropped from a spoon.
5. Beat egg whites until frothy. Gradually add remaining ¼ cup sugar, beating until stiff peaks are formed. Fold into gelatin mixture.
6. Turn filling into crust; chill.
7. Garnish pie with generous mounds of the dessert topping. Spoon on remaining crushed pineapple to resemble "volcanoes."

One 9-inch pie

690 *Cherry-Rhubarb Pie*

1 can (16 ounces) pitted tart red
    cherries (water packed),
    drained
1 pound fresh rhubarb, sliced about
    ⅛ inch thick
1¼ cups sugar
¼ cup quick-cooking tapioca
⅛ teaspoon baking soda
½ teaspoon almond extract
    Few drops red food coloring
    Pastry for a 2-crust 9-inch pie

1. Mix cherries, rhubarb, sugar, tapioca, baking soda, almond extract, and red food coloring; let stand 20 minutes.
2. Prepare pastry. Roll out enough pastry to line a 9-inch pie pan or plate; line pie pan. Roll out remaining pastry for top crust and slit pastry with knife in several places to allow steam to escape during baking.
3. Pour filling into pastry-lined pan; cover with top crust and flute edge.
4. Bake at 450°F 10 minutes. Turn oven control to 350°F and bake 40 to 45 minutes. Remove from oven and set on a wire rack. Serve warm or cooled.

One 9-inch pie

691 *Lemon-Beer Sponge Pie*

This pie bakes with a puddinglike layer on the bottom, a cakelike layer on the top. The beer flavor is subtle.

1 **unbaked 9-inch pie shell**
4 **eggs, separated**
¾ **cup sugar**
¼ **cup flour**
3 **tablespoons butter or**
  margarine, softened
2 **teaspoons grated lemon peel**
1 **can or bottle (12 ounces) beer**
2 **tablespoons lemon juice**

1. Bake pie shell at 450°F 10 minutes.
2. Beat egg whites until foamy. Gradually add half of sugar, continuing beating until stiff peaks form.
3. In a separate bowl, beat remaining sugar, flour, butter, peel and egg yolks. Mix in beer and lemon juice.
4. Fold beaten egg whites into yolk mixture. Turn into partially baked pie shell.
5. Bake at 350°F about 50 minutes, or until set. Cool to room temperature before slicing.

One 9-inch pie

692 *Peanuts-and-Beer Pie*

Peanuts and beer are frequent partners—for snacking, at the ball park, at parties. So what a natural idea it would be to combine peanuts and beer in a sweet dessert pie. It's a memorable combination. This is a chiffon-type pie made fluffy with beaten egg whites and firmed with gelatin. It goes into a prebaked shell.

  Pastry for 9-inch pie shell
1 **can or bottle (12 ounces) beer**
1 **envelope unflavored gelatin**
½ **cup packed brown sugar**
3 **eggs, separated**
1 **teaspoon vanilla extract**
6 **ounces salted peanuts (1¼**
  cups), chopped
¼ **cup granulated sugar**

1. Roll out pastry and fit into pie plate. Do not cut off excess pastry, but fold under and make high fluted sides. Prick bottom and sides thoroughly with fork.
2. Bake at 450°F 15 minutes, until light golden brown. Cool.
3. Pour beer into top of a double boiler; sprinkle with gelatin. Add brown sugar and slightly beaten egg yolks.
4. Cook over boiling water, stirring constantly, until slightly thickened and gelatin is dissolved (8 to 10 minutes). Add vanilla extract.
5. Chill until partially thickened. Stir in peanuts.
6. Beat egg whites until foamy. Gradually add granulated sugar, continuing beating until stiff peaks form. Fold in peanut-gelatin mixture. Turn into baked shell. Chill.

One 9-inch pie

693 *Cheese-Stuffed Strawberries*

A traditional French dessert, served in an elegant manner. If berries are small, slice them and serve the cheese mixture as a sauce.

½ **cup low-fat ricotta cheese**
1 **teaspoon grated lemon peel**
1 **teaspoon fresh lemon juice**
1 **teaspoon honey or sugar**
48 **large strawberries**
  Mint sprigs (optional)

1. Mix cheese, lemon peel, lemon juice, and honey in a food processor or blender until fluffy; refrigerate until chilled (about 1 hour).
2. Gently scoop centers from strawberries with melon-baller or fruit knife. Fill with cheese mixture.
3. Arrange filled strawberries on small individual plates. Garnish with mint.

4 servings

694 *Brewmaster's Poppyseed Cake*

A scrumptious, moist, and tender cake that everyone will rave about. It needs no frosting.

Cake:
- 1 package (2-layer size) regular yellow cake mix
- 1 small package instant vanilla pudding and pie filling
- 4 eggs
- 1 cup beer
- ½ cup oil
- ¼ cup poppyseed

Glaze:
- ½ cup sugar
- ½ cup beer
- ¼ cup butter

1. Place cake mix, dry pudding, eggs, beer, oil, and poppyseed in an electric mixer bowl. Blend on low speed. Then beat on medium speed for 2 minutes.
2. Turn into a well-greased and floured 10-inch Bundt or tube pan.
3. Bake at 350°F 50 to 55 minutes, or until done.
4. Cool in pan 15 minutes. Turn out on rack.
5. To prepare glaze, boil ingredients for 5 minutes. Prick warm cake with skewer in many places. Brush warm glaze generously over top and sides. Cool. (If desired, sift confectioners' sugar over top; cake needs no frosting.)

1 large cake; 16 servings

695 *Velvety Chocolate Cake*

This excellent chocolate cake has an extremely moist and tender crumb.

- 2¾ cups sifted cake flour
- 2 teaspoons baking powder
- 1 teaspoon baking soda
- ¼ teaspoon salt
- ¾ cup butter or margarine
- 1 cup packed brown sugar
- ⅔ cup granulated sugar
- 3 eggs
- 3 ounces (3 squares) unsweetened chocolate, melted and cooled
- 1 can or bottle (12 ounces) beer

1. Sift dry ingredients together.
2. Cream butter and sugars until very light and fluffy.
3. Add eggs, one at a time, beating thoroughly at medium speed of electric mixer. Beat in chocolate.
4. Add sifted dry ingredients alternately with beer, beating at low speed until blended after each addition.
5. Turn into 2 greased and waxed-paper-lined 9-inch round layer cake pans.
6. Bake at 350°F 35 minutes, or until done. Cool in pans 10 minutes; turn out on wire racks. When cool, frost with favorite icing.

One 2-layer 9-inch cake

696 *Nutmeg Cake*

A moist, flavorful cake with a very tender crumb. Fill it with Lemon-Beer Filling or Orange-Beer Filling. Frost with any white frosting.

- 3 cups sifted cake flour
- 1 tablespoon baking powder
- 2 teaspoons nutmeg
- ½ teaspoon salt
- ¾ cup butter or margarine
- 2 teaspoons vanilla extract
- 1 cup granulated sugar
- ¾ cup packed brown sugar
- 2 whole eggs
- 2 egg whites
- 1 can or bottle (12 ounces) beer
- Lemon-Beer Filling
  White frosting, any type

1. Sift dry ingredients together.
2. Cream butter with vanilla extract and sugars until light and fluffy. Add eggs and whites, one at a time, beating well after each addition (medium speed of mixer).
3. Alternately add sifted dry ingredients in thirds and beer in halves to creamed mixture, beating on low speed just until smooth after each addition.
4. Turn into 2 greased and waxed-paper-lined 9-inch round layer cake pans.
5. Bake at 350°F 30 to 35 minutes, or until cake tests done. Cool in pans about 10 minutes. Turn out onto wire racks. Cool completely before filling and frosting.

One 2-layer 9-inch cake

Note: If not making a filling requiring egg yolks, use 3 whole eggs in batter.

697 *Raisin-Nut Spice Cake*

Serve this moist, dark, and delectable cake any time of year with whipped cream, ice cream, or Beer Dessert Sauce on top. It is delicious served warm with hard sauce during the holiday season.

3 cups sifted cake flour
2 teaspoons baking powder
1 teaspoon baking soda
½ teaspoon cinnamon
½ teaspoon nutmeg
¼ teaspoon ginger
¼ teaspoon salt
1 can or bottle (12 ounces) beer
1 cup raisins (5 ounces)
¾ cup butter or margarine
1 cup sugar
½ cup molasses
2 eggs
¾ cup chopped nuts (3 ounces)
Glaze

1. Sift dry ingredients together. Set aside.
2. Heat beer and raisins to simmering; let stand about 15 minutes to plump.
3. Cream butter and sugar until light and fluffy; add molasses.
4. Add eggs, one at a time, beating well after each addition.
5. Add dry ingredients alternately in thirds with beer drained from raisins, beating just until well blended. Stir in raisins and nuts.
6. Turn into a well-greased and floured 10-inch Bundt pan or angel food cake pan (nonstick pan preferred).
7. Bake at 350°F 1 hour, or until done.
8. Let stand in pan about 10 minutes; invert onto cake rack. Cool. Cover with foil or store in airtight container. Cake slices better if made a day in advance.
9. Prepare a glaze by thinning **1 cup sifted confectioners' sugar** with **beer** or **milk.** Drizzle over cake shortly before serving.

1 large cake; 16 servings

698 *Old English Cheesecake*

Raisins, almonds, lemon peel, and beer delectably perk up the flavor of this rich dessert.

Crust:
1¼ cups all-purpose flour
¼ cup sugar
⅓ cup butter or margarine
4 tablespoons cold beer

Filling:
½ cup golden raisins (2½ ounces), chopped
⅓ cup almonds (2 ounces), finely chopped
1 tablespoon grated lemon peel
1 pound cottage cheese
½ cup flour
4 eggs
1 cup sugar
¾ cup beer
⅛ teaspoon nutmeg

1. For crust, mix flour and sugar; cut in butter until crumbly. Add beer 1 tablespoon at a time, stirring with a fork. Shape dough into a ball. Chill.
2. Roll out on floured surface to a 13- to 14-inch circle. Fold in quarters. Gently unfold in a 9-inch springform pan. Even edge of crust so it extends about 2 inches up sides of pan (1½ inches up sides if using a 10-inch pan). Prick all over with fork.
3. Bake at 425°F 10 minutes. Prick again and press to sides. Bake 10 minutes more, or until slightly golden.
4. For filling, mix chopped raisins, almonds, and peel.
5. Process cottage cheese, flour, and eggs until smooth, using food processor or electric blender. (Do in several batches in blender.)
6. Add sugar, beer, and nutmeg; blend until smooth. Stir in raisin mixture. Pour into cooled shell.
7. Bake at 300°F 1¼ to 1½ hours, or until set. Cool to room temperature for serving. Dust with **confectioners' sugar** and top with **whole unblanched almonds.**

8 to 10 servings

699 *Easy Walnut Cake*

When filled with Orange-Beer Filling or Lemon-Beer Filling, this cake doesn't even need an icing—but add one of your choice, if you wish. Otherwise, sift confectioners' sugar over the top.

1 package (2-layer size) yellow
    cake mix
Beer
Water
2 eggs
⅔ cup finely chopped walnuts
Orange-Beer Filling or
    Lemon-Beer Filling

1. Mix cake batter according to package directions. Use the exact amount of liquid called for, but substitute beer for all or part of the water. (If making Orange-Beer Filling, set aside ½ cup beer from a can for filling and use 1 cup in cake. For Lemon-Beer Filling, set aside ¾ cup beer for filling and use ¾ cup in cake. If not making beer-flavored filling, substitute beer for all of the water in cake.)
2. Blend in walnuts.
3. Turn batter into 2 greased and waxed-paper-lined 9-inch round layer cake pans.
4. Bake at 350°F 30 minutes, or until a wooden pick inserted in center comes out clean. Cool in pans 10 minutes; turn out onto wire racks. Cool completely before filling and frosting.

One 2-layer 9-inch cake

700 *Orange-Beer Filling*

⅓ cup sugar
1½ tablespoons cornstarch
⅛ teaspoon salt
½ cup beer
⅓ cup orange juice
1 egg yolk
2 teaspoons grated orange peel
2 teaspoons butter or margarine

1. In top of a double boiler, combine sugar, cornstarch, and salt. Stir in beer and orange juice. Cook over direct heat, stirring constantly, until thickened and clear.
2. Add a little hot mixture to egg yolk; return to double-boiler top. Cook over hot water, stirring constantly, 4 to 5 minutes.
3. Stir in peel and butter. Cool before spreading on cake.

About 1 cup; enough to fill two 8- or 9-inch layers

701 *Lemon-Beer Filling*

A tart filling to spread between two layers of an 8- or 9-inch cake.

½ cup sugar
2 tablespoons cornstarch
⅛ teaspoon salt
¾ cup beer
2 teaspoons grated lemon peel
2 tablespoons lemon juice
2 egg yolks

1. In top of a double boiler, combine sugar, cornstarch, and salt. Stir in beer. Cook over direct heat, stirring constantly, until thickened and clear.
2. Stir in lemon peel and juice.
3. Add a little hot mixture to egg yolks; return to double boiler top. Cook over hot water, stirring constantly, for 4 to 5 minutes. Cool before spreading on cake.

About 1 cup

702 *White Beer Icing*

3 tablespoons butter
3 cups sifted confectioners' sugar
3 to 4 tablespoons beer

1. Cream butter.
2. Add confectioners' sugar alternately with beer, until frosting is fluffy and of spreading consistency.

1⅔ cups; for tops and sides of 2 round 8- or 9-inch layers

703 *Cocoa-Beer Icing*

A light chocolate icing with a very mild beer flavor.

¼ **pound butter or margarine,**
    softened
3½ **cups sifted confectioners' sugar**
⅓ **cup cocoa**
⅛ **teaspoon salt**
⅓ **cup beer (about)**

1. Cream butter with part of confectioners' sugar.
2. Add cocoa, salt, and a little beer. Beat until smooth.
3. Add remaining sugar alternately with enough beer to make icing of spreading consistency, beating until fluffy.

2 cups; for tops and sides of two 9-inch layers

704 *Spicy Fruit Gelatin "with a Head"*

Serve this fruited gelatin dessert in pilsner glasses, if you have them, and top with whipped cream or whipped topping to simulate the foam on beer.

1 **can or bottle (12 ounces) beer**
2 **tablespoons packed brown**
    sugar
1 **stick cinnamon**
4 **whole cloves**
1 **package (3 ounces)**
    orange-flavored gelatin
1 **can (8¼ ounces) crushed**
    pineapple
    Water

1. Place beer, brown sugar, cinnamon, and cloves in a saucepan. Heat to boiling. Add gelatin; stir until dissolved.
2. Let stand at room temperature until lukewarm to mellow flavors. Remove spices.
3. Drain pineapple thoroughly, reserving liquid. Add water to liquid to measure ½ cup. Stir into gelatin mixture. Chill until partially thickened.
4. Fold in pineapple. Spoon into pilsner or parfait glasses. Chill until firm.
5. To serve, top with a "head" of whipped cream or prepared whipped topping.

4 or 5 servings

705 *Zesty Beer Ice*

You've heard of champagne sherbet, so why not a beer ice? Those who try it are in for a delicious surprise. It's especially nice on hot days or following a heavy meal. Lemon gives a zest to the taste.

1 **envelope unflavored gelatin**
2 **cans or bottles (12 ounces each)**
    beer
1 **cup sugar**
2 **teaspoons grated lemon peel**
½ **cup lemon juice**

1. Sprinkle gelatin over 1 can beer in a saucepan. Let stand 5 minutes to soften.
2. Add sugar. Cook over low heat just until dissolved.
3. Add remaining 1 can beer, lemon peel, and juice. Turn into a shallow pan.
4. Freeze until firm, stirring several times. Pack into a 1-quart covered container.

1 quart

706 *Baked Stuffed Apples*

6 **medium cooking apples (about**
    2 pounds)
½ **cup raisins**
½ **cup packed brown sugar**
1 **teaspoon cinnamon**
1 **cup beer**

1. Core apples. Remove 1-inch strip of peel around top.
2. Mix raisins, brown sugar, and cinnamon. Fill apple centers.
3. Place apples in a baking dish. Pour beer over.
4. Bake at 350°F 40 to 45 minutes, or until tender, basting occasionally.
5. Cool to room temperature, basting while cooling. Serve with its own sauce. If desired, add cream or Beer Dessert Sauce (page 76).

6 servings

707 *Beer Bread Pudding*

1½ cups milk
1 can or bottle (12 ounces) beer
3 eggs
½ cup packed brown sugar
½ teaspoon vanilla extract
¼ teaspoon cinnamon
¼ teaspoon nutmeg
¼ teaspoon salt
4 cups dry bread cubes (6 slices)

1. Scald milk and beer.
2. Beat eggs with brown sugar, vanilla extract, cinnamon, nutmeg, and salt. Add scalded milk and beer gradually while stirring. Add bread.
3. Turn into a greased 1½- or 2-quart casserole. Set in a pan of boiling water.
4. Bake at 325°F 50 minutes, or until a knife inserted in center comes out clean. Serve hot or cold.

6 servings

708 *Raisin-Beer Pudding*

Try putting beer in a simple pudding. You'll discover a surprisingly delicious and unusual flavor treat.

2 eggs
1½ cups milk
½ cup sugar
¼ cup quick-cooking tapioca
¼ teaspoon nutmeg
⅛ teaspoon salt
1 can or bottle (12 ounces) beer
½ cup raisins

1. In a heavy 2-quart saucepan, beat eggs. Add milk, sugar, tapioca, nutmeg, and salt. Let stand 5 minutes.
2. Cook, stirring constantly, to simmering. Add beer gradually while stirring; add raisins. Cook and stir just to boiling.
3. Pour into dessert dishes.

About 1 quart; 6 to 8 servings

709 *Spicy Butterscotch Pudding*

This pudding may also be put in 4 to 6 baked tart shells or an 8-inch baked pie shell.

1 package (4-serving size) butterscotch pudding and pie filling (not instant)
⅔ cup instant nonfat dry milk
1 teaspoon pumpkin pie spice
1 cup beer
1 cup water
Whipped cream or thawed frozen whipped dessert topping

1. In a heavy saucepan, combine pudding mix, dry milk, and spice. Stir in beer and water.
2. Cook over medium heat, stirring constantly, until mixture boils.
3. Pour into 4 pudding dishes. Cover surfaces with plastic wrap. Chill until set. Serve topped with whipped cream or dessert topping.

4 servings

710 Chocolate-Beer Pudding Cake

A fun dessert to make and bake. A hot chocolate-beer syrup is poured over cake batter in the pan. After baking, a puddinglike layer forms in the bottom. The cake is then inverted.

Batter:
- 1½ cups all-purpose flour
- ¾ cup sugar
- 1 tablespoon unsweetened cocoa
- 1½ teaspoons baking powder
- ½ teaspoon baking soda
- ¼ teaspoon salt
- ¾ cup beer
- ⅓ cup oil
- 1 egg, slightly beaten

Syrup:
- 1 tablespoon unsweetened cocoa
- ¾ cup beer
- ⅓ cup packed brown sugar
- ⅓ cup granulated sugar

1. For batter, mix dry ingredients; make a well in center. Add beer, oil, and egg. Beat just until smooth.
2. For syrup, make a paste of cocoa and a little beer. Add remaining beer and sugars. Heat to boiling.
3. Pour batter into a greased 8-inch square baking pan. Drizzle syrup over top.
4. Bake at 350°F 40 minutes.
5. Cool about 5 minutes. Loosen sides of cake from pan; invert onto platter. Even out pudding layer with knife. Serve warm or cool.

6 to 8 servings

711 Currant-Apple Fritters

Serve as a hot dessert sprinkled with confectioners' sugar. Or top with syrup and serve for breakfast.

- 1 cup all-purpose flour
- 1½ teaspoons baking powder
- ¼ teaspoon cinnamon
- ¼ teaspoon salt
- ½ cup beer
- ½ cup currants
- ½ cup chopped pared apple
- 2 eggs, slightly beaten
- 1 teaspoon oil
  Fat for deep frying
  Confectioners' sugar

1. Combine flour, baking powder, cinnamon, and salt. Add beer, currants, apple, eggs, and oil. Stir to blend well.
2. Drop by rounded teaspoonfuls into hot deep fat heated to 365°F. Fry until browned. Drain on paper towels.
3. Keep hot in oven until serving time. While still hot, roll in confectioners' sugar.

About 30 fritters; 6 to 8 servings

712 Peach Cobbler

- 1 can (29 ounces) sliced peaches
- 2 teaspoons lemon juice
- ¼ teaspoon cinnamon
- 1½ tablespoons cornstarch
- ¾ cup beer
- 1 cup all-purpose flour
- 1½ teaspoons baking powder
- ¼ teaspoon salt
- 3 tablespoons shortening

1. Drain peaches, reserving syrup.
2. Lightly toss together peaches, lemon juice, and cinnamon. Arrange in a buttered shallow 1½-quart baking dish, 10 x 6 inches, or 8 inches square.
3. In a small saucepan, blend cornstarch, ¼ cup reserved syrup, and ¾ cup beer. Cook, stirring constantly, until thickened and clear. Pour over peaches.
4. Bake at 400°F 10 to 15 minutes, or until bubbly.
5. Meanwhile, mix flour, baking powder, and salt. Add ½ cup more reserved syrup (or use ½ cup beer plus 1 tablespoon sugar). Stir just until dough forms a ball.
6. Drop by large spoonfuls onto peaches. Continue baking 25 minutes.

8 servings

713 *Lemon Crunch Dessert*

Lemon mixture:
- ¾ cup sugar
- 2 tablespoons flour
- ⅛ teaspoon salt
- 1 cup water
- 2 eggs, well beaten
- 1 teaspoon grated lemon peel
- ⅓ cup lemon juice

Crunch mixture:
- ½ cup butter or margarine
- 1 cup firmly packed brown sugar
- 1 cup all-purpose flour
- ½ teaspoon salt
- 1 cup whole wheat flakes, crushed
- ½ cup finely chopped walnuts
- ½ cup shredded coconut

1. For lemon mixture, mix sugar, flour, and salt in a heavy saucepan. Gradually add water, stirring until smooth. Bring mixture to boiling and cook 2 minutes.

2. Stir about 3 tablespoons of the hot mixture vigorously into beaten eggs. Immediately blend into mixture in saucepan. Cook and stir about 3 minutes.

3. Remove from heat and stir in lemon peel and lemon juice. Set aside to cool.

4. For crunch mixture, beat butter until softened; add brown sugar gradually, beating until fluffy. Add flour and salt; mix well. Add wheat flakes, walnuts, and coconut; mix thoroughly.

5. Line bottom of an 8-inch square baking dish with one third of the crunch mixture. Cover with the lemon mixture, spreading to form an even layer. Top with remaining crunch mixture.

6. Bake, uncovered, at 350°F 40 minutes, or until lightly browned. Serve warm or cold.

8 servings

714 *Hot Spicy Fruit Pot*

- 1 can (16 ounces) pear halves
- 1 can (16 ounces) peach halves
- 1 can (16 ounces) purple plums, halved and pitted
- 1 cup firmly packed brown sugar
- 1 cinnamon stick
- ¼ teaspoon nutmeg
- ¼ teaspoon allspice
- ⅛ teaspoon ginger
- ¼ cup lemon juice
- 2 teaspoons grated orange peel
- 2 tablespoons butter or margarine

1. Drain fruits, reserving 1 cup liquid. Put fruit into a buttered 2-quart casserole.

2. Combine reserved liquid with remaining ingredients, except butter. Pour over fruit. Dot with butter.

3. Bake, covered, at 350°F 30 minutes, or until bubbly. Serve hot or cold. If desired, spoon over ice cream or cake.

8 servings

715 *Buttery Baked Apples*

8 medium baking apples, cored
1 cup sugar
6 tablespoons butter or margarine
1 tablespoon cornstarch
1 tablespoon cold water
½ teaspoon vanilla extract
½ cup milk

1. Put apples into a 1½-quart baking dish. Sprinkle with sugar. Dot with butter.
2. Bake, uncovered, at 450°F 20 minutes, or until fork-tender, basting occasionally.
3. Remove baking dish from oven and apples from baking dish.
4. Combine cornstarch, water, and vanilla extract; add to milk. Stir into liquid in baking dish. Return apples to baking dish.
5. Bake an additional 8 to 10 minutes, or until sauce is thickened. To serve, spoon sauce over each apple.

8 servings

716 *Cherry-Pineapple Cobbler*

1 can (21 ounces) cherry pie filling
1 can (13¼ ounces) pineapple tidbits, drained
¼ teaspoon allspice
3 tablespoons honey
1 egg, slightly beaten
½ cup dairy sour cream
1½ cups unflavored croutons

1. Combine cherry pie filling, pineapple tidbits, allspice, and 1 tablespoon honey. Put into a 1½-quart baking dish.
2. Blend egg, sour cream, and remaining 2 tablespoons honey. Stir in croutons. Spoon over cherry-pineapple mixture.
3. Bake, uncovered, at 375°F 30 minutes, or until heated through. If desired, top with ice cream.

8 servings

717 *Indian Pudding*

3 cups milk
½ cup cornmeal
1 tablespoon butter or margarine
½ cup light molasses
½ teaspoon salt
½ teaspoon ginger
1 cup cold milk

1. Scald 2½ cups milk in top of double boiler over boiling water.
2. Combine cornmeal and the remaining ½ cup milk. Add to scalded milk, stirring constantly. Cook about 25 minutes, stirring frequently.
3. Stir in butter, molasses, salt, and ginger.
4. Pour into a greased 1½-quart baking dish. Pour the 1 cup cold milk over pudding.
5. Set in a baking pan. Pour boiling water around dish to within 1 inch of top.
6. Bake, covered, at 300°F about 2 hours. Remove cover and bake an additional 1 hour. Serve warm or cold with **cream** or **ice cream.**

6 servings

Glazed Apple Tart in Wheat Germ Crust, page 262

718 *Bread Pudding*

1 cup raisins
½ cup sherry
8 slices white bread
    Butter
4 eggs
½ cup sugar
    Dash salt
1 quart half-and-half
1½ teaspoons vanilla extract

1. Soak raisins in sherry 2 hours, stirring occasionally.
2. Trim crusts from bread and spread with butter. Place bread, buttered side down, in a 2½-quart casserole or soufflé dish.
3. Drain raisins and sprinkle over bread.
4. Beat remaining ingredients together. Pour over bread and let stand 30 minutes. Sprinkle with **cinnamon.**
5. Bake, covered, at 350°F 30 minutes. Remove cover and bake an additional 30 minutes, or until set.

8 servings

719 *Peach Meringue Pudding*

2 cans (21 ounces each) peach pie
    filling
¼ cup butter or margarine, melted
½ teaspoon cinnamon
⅛ teaspoon nutmeg
⅛ teaspoon allspice
½ cup slivered almonds
3 egg whites
½ cup sugar

1. Combine peach pie filling, butter, cinnamon, nutmeg, allspice, and almonds. Put into a 1½-quart casserole.
2. Bake, uncovered, at 350°F 30 minutes, or until bubbly. Remove from oven.
3. Beat egg whites until stiff, but not dry. Gradually beat in sugar until glossy. Evenly spread over hot peaches. Sprinkle with **cinnamon.**
4. Bake an additional 12 to 15 minutes, or until lightly browned.

6 servings

720 *Apple Cream*

6 cups sliced apples (about 2 pounds)
½ cup sugar
1 teaspoon cinnamon
1 teaspoon nutmeg
¼ cup butter or margarine
⅔ cup sugar
1 egg
½ cup flour
½ teaspoon baking powder
½ teaspoon salt
1 cup whipping cream

1. Toss the apple slices with a mixture of the ½ cup sugar, cinnamon, and nutmeg. Spread evenly in bottom of a buttered 9-inch square baking dish.
2. Cream together butter and ⅔ cup sugar. Add egg and continue beating until mixture is light and fluffy.
3. Blend flour, baking powder, and salt; beat into creamed mixture until just blended. Spread evenly over apples.
4. Bake, uncovered, at 350°F 30 minutes. Pour cream over surface and bake an additional 10 minutes, or until topping is golden brown. Serve warm with cream, if desired.

8 servings

Raspberry Mousse, page 350

721 *Favorite Apple Pudding*

6 or 7 medium firm, tart cooking
  apples, quartered, cored, pared,
  and cut in ⅛-inch slices
¾ cup firmly packed brown sugar
3 tablespoons flour
½ teaspoon salt
1 teaspoon cinnamon
¼ teaspoon nutmeg
3 tablespoons butter or margarine
1 teaspoon grated orange peel
¾ cup (3 ounces) shredded Cheddar
  cheese
5 slices white bread, toasted, buttered
  on both sides and cut in halves
¼ cup orange juice
½ cup buttered soft bread cubes

1. Arrange one third of the apple slices on bottom of a greased 2-quart casserole.
2. Thoroughly blend brown sugar, flour, salt, cinnamon, and nutmeg. Using a pastry blender or 2 knives, cut in butter and grated orange peel until mixture is in coarse crumbs. Mix in cheese.
3. Sprinkle one third of the sugar-cheese mixture over apples and cover with one half of the toast. Repeat layers. Cover the top with remaining apples and sugar-cheese mixture.
4. Pour orange juice over surface and top with the buttered bread cubes.
5. Bake, covered, at 425°F 30 minutes. Remove cover and bake an additional 10 minutes.

6 to 8 servings

722 *Baked Apricot Pudding*

1 tablespoon confectioners' sugar
1¼ cups (about 6 ounces) dried apricots
1 cup water
1½ tablespoons butter or margarine
1½ tablespoons flour
¾ cup milk
4 egg yolks
½ teaspoon vanilla extract
4 egg whites
6 tablespoons granulated sugar
  Whipped cream

1. Lightly butter bottom of a 1½-quart casserole and sift confectioners' sugar over it.
2. Put apricots and water into a saucepan. Cover; simmer 20 to 30 minutes, or until apricots are plump and tender. Force apricots through a coarse sieve or food mill (makes about ¾ cup purée).
3. Heat butter in saucepan. Stir in flour. Gradually add milk, stirring until thickened and smooth. Remove from heat.
4. Beat egg yolks and vanilla extract together until mixture is thick and lemon colored. Spoon sauce gradually into beaten egg yolks while beating vigorously. Blend in apricot purée.
5. Using clean beater, beat egg whites until frothy. Add sugar gradually, beating constantly. Continue beating until rounded peaks are formed. Spread apricot mixture gently over beaten egg whites and fold until thoroughly blended. Turn mixture into prepared casserole. Set casserole in a pan of very hot water.
6. Bake, uncovered, at 350°F 50 minutes, or until a knife inserted halfway between center and edge comes out clean. Cool slightly before serving. Top with whipped cream.

6 servings

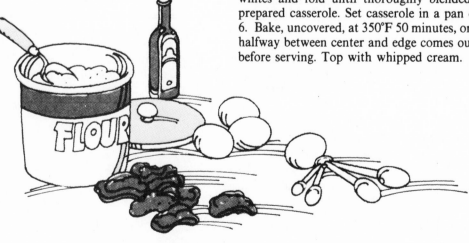

723 *Chocolate Custard*

1 package (6 ounces) semisweet
   chocolate pieces
3 tablespoons half-and-half
3 cups milk
3 eggs
1 teaspoon vanilla extract
⅓ cup sugar
¼ teaspoon salt

1. Melt 2/3 cup chocolate pieces with half-and-half in top of a double boiler over hot (not boiling) water. Stir until smooth; spoon about 1 tablespoon into each of 8 custard cups or 10 soufflé dishes. Spread evenly. Put cups into a shallow pan; set aside.
2. Scald milk. Melt remaining 1/3 cup chocolate pieces and, adding gradually, stir in scalded milk until blended.
3. Beat together eggs, vanilla extract, sugar, and salt. Gradually add milk mixture, stirring constantly. Pour into chocolate-lined cups.
4. Set pan with filled cups on oven rack and pour boiling water into pan to a depth of 1 inch.
5. Bake, uncovered, at 325°F 25 minutes, or until a knife inserted halfway between center and edge comes out clean.
6. Set cups on wire rack to cool slightly. Refrigerate and serve when thoroughly cooled. Unmold and, if desired, garnish with whipped cream rosettes.

8 to 10 servings

724 *Brazilian Pudim Moka with Chocolate Sauce*

3 cups milk
1 cup half-and-half
5 tablespoons instant coffee
2 teaspoons grated orange peel
4 eggs
1 egg yolk
½ cup sugar
½ teaspoon salt
1 teaspoon vanilla extract
  Nutmeg
  Chocolate sauce
  Chopped Brazil nuts

1. Combine milk and half-and-half in top of a double boiler and heat over simmering water until scalded.
2. Add instant coffee and orange peel, stirring until coffee is dissolved. Remove from simmering water and set aside to cool (about 10 minutes).
3. Beat together eggs and egg yolk slightly. Blend in sugar and salt.
4. Gradually add coffee mixture, stirring constantly. Mix in vanilla extract. Strain through a fine sieve into eight 6-ounce custard cups. Sprinkle with nutmeg. Set cups in pan of hot water.
5. Bake, uncovered, at 325°F 25 to 30 minutes, or until a knife inserted in center of custard comes out clean.
6. Cool and chill. To serve, invert onto serving plates. Pour chocolate sauce over top and sprinkle with Brazil nuts.

8 servings

725 *Rosy Rhubarb Swirls*

1½ cups sugar
1¼ cups water
⅓ cup red cinnamon candies
2 or 3 drops red food coloring
2¼ cups all-purpose flour
4 teaspoons baking powder
½ teaspoon salt
⅔ cup milk
⅓ cup half-and-half
3 cups finely diced fresh rhubarb (if
  tender do not peel)

1. Put sugar, water, and cinnamon candies into a saucepan. Stirring occasionally, cook over medium heat until candies are melted and mixture forms a thin syrup (about 10 minutes). Stir in food coloring.
2. Meanwhile, sift together into a bowl the flour, baking powder, and salt. Add a mixture of milk and half-and-half and stir with a fork only until dry ingredients are moistened. Turn onto a floured surface and knead lightly about 10 times with fingertips.
3. Roll dough into a 13x11x¼-inch rectangle. Spoon rhubarb evenly over dough. Beginning with longer side, roll dough and seal edges. Cut crosswise into 12 slices.
4. Pour syrup into a shallow baking dish and arrange rolls, cut side up, in syrup. Sprinkle with additional sugar (¼ to ⅓ cup) and top each roll with a small piece of **butter**.
5. Bake, uncovered, at 400°F 25 to 30 minutes. Serve warm with **half-and-half**.

12 servings

726 *Vanilla Soufflé*

1 tablespoon confectioners' sugar
¼ cup butter or margarine
3 tablespoons flour
1 cup milk
4 egg yolks
½ cup sugar
1 tablespoon vanilla extract
4 egg whites

1. Butter bottom of a 1½-quart soufflé dish (straight-sided casserole) and sift confectioners' sugar over it.
2. Heat butter in a saucepan. Stir in flour. Gradually add milk, stirring until thickened and smooth. Remove from heat.
3. Beat egg yolks, sugar, and vanilla extract together until mixture is very thick. Spoon sauce gradually into egg-yolk mixture while beating vigorously. Cool to lukewarm.
4. Using clean beater, beat egg whites until rounded peaks are formed. Spread egg-yolk mixture gently over egg whites and fold until thoroughly blended. Turn mixture into prepared soufflé dish. Set dish in a pan of very hot water.
5. Bake, uncovered, at 400°F 15 minutes. Turn oven control to 375°F and bake 30 to 40 minutes, or until a knife inserted halfway between center and edge comes out clean. Serve immediately.
6. Accompany with **puréed thawed frozen strawberries or raspberries.**

About 6 servings

727 *Wine Fruit Compote*

1 can (16 ounces) pear halves
1 can (16 ounces) cling peach halves
1 can (13½ ounces) pineapple chunks
½ lemon, thinly sliced and quartered
2 cups fruit juices and water
5 whole cloves
1 stick cinnamon
1 package (3 ounces) strawberry-flavored gelatin
2 teaspoons lemon juice
1 cup cherry kijafa wine

1. Drain fruit and reserve juice. Arrange fruit in a shallow 1½-quart dish. Scatter lemon slices over top.
2. Combine juices from fruit and water, cloves, and cinnamon in a saucepan. Heat to boiling. Simmer for 5 minutes. Strain.
3. Dissolve gelatin in the hot liquid. Add lemon juice and cherry wine. Pour over fruit. Chill 1 to 1½ hours, or until gelatin is only partly set. Baste fruit occasionally with gelatin mixture while chilling.

6 to 8 servings

728 *Elegant Creamed Peaches*

1 envelope plain gelatin
½ cup sweet red wine, such as port or muscatel
1 pint whipping cream
3 tablespoons powdered sugar
Dash salt
1 can (29 ounces) cling peach halves
½ cup glacé fruit
2 tablespoons roasted diced almonds
1 tablespoon honey
1 tablespoon sweet red wine

1. Combine gelatin and ½ cup wine in saucepan; place over low heat and stir until gelatin is dissolved.
2. Cool until mixture begins to thicken.
3. Whip cream with powdered sugar and salt.
4. Fold gelatin mixture into whipped cream. Spoon into 6 to 8 dessert dishes or 9-inch round pan.
5. Drain peaches; place cup-sides up in cream mixture.
6. Combine glacé fruit, almonds, honey, and 1 tablespoon wine. Spoon into peach cups. Chill.

6 to 8 servings

729 *Stuffed Peaches*

½ cup almond macaroon crumbs
6 large firm peaches
½ cup blanched almonds, chopped
2 tablespoons sugar
1 tablespoon chopped candied orange peel
⅓ cup sherry or Marsala
2 tablespoons sugar

1. Using an electric blender, grind enough almond macaroons to make ½ cup crumbs. Set crumbs aside.
2. Rinse, peel, and cut peaches into halves. Remove pit and a small portion of the pulp around cavity.
3. Combine and mix macaroon crumbs, chopped almonds, 2 tablespoons sugar, and orange peel.
4. Lightly fill peach halves with mixture. Put two halves together and fasten with wooden picks. Place in baking dish.
5. Pour sherry over peaches and sprinkle remaining sugar over peaches.
6. Bake at 350°F 15 minutes and serve either hot or cold.

6 servings

730 *Port Wine Molds*

1 envelope unflavored gelatin
1¼ cups sparkling water
½ cup ruby port
⅓ cup sugar

1. Soften gelatin in ½ cup of the sparkling water. Dissolve over hot water.
2. Combine remaining sparkling water, wine, and sugar; stir until sugar is dissolved. Mix in the gelatin.
3. Pour into 6 individual molds and chill until firm.
4. Unmold gelatin onto a chilled serving plate. Serve as a meat accompaniment.

6 servings

731 *Sherry Elegance*

3 envelopes unflavored gelatin
1½ cups sugar
3 cups water
1 cup plus 2 tablespoons sherry
¾ cup strained orange juice
⅓ cup strained lemon juice
9 drops red food coloring

1. Combine the gelatin and sugar in a large saucepan; mix well. Add water and stir over low heat until gelatin and sugar are dissolved.
2. Remove from heat and blend in remaining ingredients. Pour mixture into a 1½-quart fancy mold or a pretty china bowl. Chill until firm.
3. To serve, unmold gelatin onto chilled platter or serve in china bowl without unmolding. Serve with whipped cream or whipped dessert topping, if desired.

6 to 8 servings

732 Glazed Apple Tart in Wheat Germ Crust

Wheat Germ Crust (see recipe)
8 medium apples
1 cup red port
1 cup water
⅓ cup honey
2 tablespoons lemon juice
⅛ teaspoon salt
3 drops red food coloring
1 package (8 ounces) cream cheese
1 tablespoon half-and-half
1 tablespoon honey
1½ tablespoons cornstarch

1. Prepare crust and set aside to cool.
2. Pare, core, and cut apples into eighths to make 2 quarts.
3. Combine port, water, ⅓ cup honey, lemon juice, salt, and food coloring in large skillet with a cover. Add half the apples in single layer, cover, and cook slowly about 5 minutes, until apples are barely tender. Remove apples with slotted spoon and arrange in a single layer in a shallow pan. Cook remaining apples in same manner. Chill apples, saving cooking liquid for glaze.
4. Beat cream cheese with half-and-half and 1 tablespoon honey. Spread in even layer over bottom of cooled crust, saving about ¼ cup for decoration on top of tart, if desired.
5. Arrange apples over cheese.
6. Boil syrup from cooking apples down to 1 cup.
7. Mix cornstarch with 1½ tablespoons cold water. Stir into syrup, and cook, stirring, until mixture clears and thickens. Set pan in cold water, and cool quickly to room temperature. Spoon carefully over apples.
8. Chill until glaze is set before cutting.

One 10-inch tart

733 Wheat Germ Crust

1½ cups sifted all-purpose flour
3 tablespoons wheat germ
3 tablespoons packed brown sugar
¾ teaspoon salt
⅛ teaspoon cinnamon
6 tablespoons shortening
2 tablespoons butter
2 tablespoons milk (about)

1. Combine flour, wheat germ, brown sugar, salt, and cinnamon in mixing bowl.
2. Cut in shortening and butter as for pie crust.
3. Sprinkle with just enough milk to make dough stick together.
4. Press dough against bottom and up sides of 10-inch springform pan to make shell 1¾ inches deep. Prick bottom. Set on baking sheet.
5. Bake at 375°F on lowest shelf of oven for about 20 minutes, or until golden.

734 Crêpes Superbe with Wine Sauce

⅔ cup all-purpose flour
3 tablespoons sugar
¼ teaspoon salt
⅛ teaspoon baking soda
2 eggs

1. Combine the flour, sugar, salt, and baking soda in a mixing bowl; mix well.
2. Using an electric or hand rotary beater, beat the eggs; add milk, melted butter, orange peel and juice, and rum.
3. Combine egg mixture with dry ingredients and continue beat-

¾ cup milk
¼ cup butter or margarine,
    melted and cooled
1½ teaspoons grated orange peel
3 tablespoons orange juice
1 tablespoon rum

Wine Sauce:
1½ tablespoons butter or
    margarine
1½ teaspoons sugar
¾ cup apricot jam
1 cup port wine
3 tablespoons brandy
3 tablespoons Cointreau or rum

ing until smooth. (Batter should be consistency of heavy cream. Add more orange juice, if necessary.)

4. Heat and lightly butter the bottom of a 6- or 8-inch skillet. Pour in about 2 tablespoons of the batter and tilt skillet to spread batter evenly. Cook over medium heat until small bubbles form in the batter. Turn over and brown crêpe very lightly on second side. Repeat process using all the batter.

5. Keep crêpes warm by placing them in a pan over simmering water.

6. For wine sauce, heat butter in a chafing dish blazer over direct heat. Stir in sugar, jam, port wine, brandy, and Cointreau. Heat until mixture comes to boiling. Reduce heat and ignite the sauce.

7. To serve, roll crêpes jelly-roll fashion on serving plates; allow 2 or 3 per serving. Ladle hot wine sauce over them.

6 to 8 servings

735 *Chocolate Cream Cups*

1 package (3 ounces) chocolate
    or butterscotch pudding
1½ cups milk
¼ cups sherry
1 teaspoon instant coffee powder
⅛ teaspoon salt
½ cup whipping cream, whipped

Spiced Cream Topping:
½ cup whipping cream, whipped
1 tablespoon sugar
½ teaspoon instant coffee powder
⅛ teaspoon cinnamon

1. Prepare pudding mix according to package directions using milk and sherry for the liquid.

2. Add instant coffee and salt. Cover and chill.

3. Fold in whipped cream and spoon into 6 or 8 individual serving dishes. Serve with a bowl of Spiced Cream Topping.

4. For Spiced Cream Topping, whip cream; fold in sugar, instant coffee powder, and cinnamon.

6 to 8 servings

736 *Trifle*

Day-old pound cake (enough
    to line bottom of casserole)
½ cup brandy or rum
1 envelope unflavored gelatin
¼ cup cold water
5 egg yolks, slightly beaten
½ cup sugar
1½ cups milk, scalded
3 egg whites
¼ cup whipping cream, whipped

1. Cut the pound cake into 1-inch pieces. Arrange over bottom of a 2-quart shallow casserole. Pour brandy over cake pieces.

2. Soften gelatin in the cold water. Combine egg yolks with ¼ cup of the sugar in top of a double boiler. Add the scalded milk gradually, blending well. Cook over simmering water, stirring constantly until mixture coats a metal spoon. Immediately remove from heat and stir in gelatin until dissolved. Cool and chill until mixture becomes slightly thicker.

3. Beat the egg whites until frothy; gradually add the remaining ¼ cup sugar, beating constantly until stiff peaks are formed.

4. Spread egg whites and whipped cream over gelatin mixture and gently fold together. Turn into the casserole. Chill until firm.

5. When ready to serve, garnish with **candied cherries, slivered almonds,** and pieces of **angelica.** If desired, garnish with a border of sweetened whipped cream forced through a pastry bag and star decorating tube.

About 12 servings

737 *Walnut Cake*

2 cups (about 10 ounces) dark seedless raisins
⅔ cup sherry
4 cups sifted all-purpose flour
2 teaspoons baking powder
¼ teaspoon salt
1 teaspoon nutmeg
4 cups (about 1 pound) walnuts
1¼ cups butter or margarine
2 teaspoons grated orange peel
2 cups sugar
6 eggs, well beaten
⅔ cup orange juice
½ cup molasses

1. Lightly grease a 10-inch tube pan. Line bottom with waxed paper cut to fit pan. Lightly grease paper.
2. Put raisins into a bowl. Pour sherry over raisins. Set aside.
3. Sift together flour, baking powder, salt, and nutmeg and set aside.
4. Chop walnuts and set aside.
5. Cream butter and orange peel until softened. Add sugar gradually, creaming until fluffy after each addition.
6. Add eggs gradually, beating thoroughly after each addition. Set aside.
7. Drain raisins, reserving liquid. Mix liquid with orange juice and molasses.
8. Alternately add dry ingredients in fourths and liquid in thirds to creamed mixture, beating only until smooth after each addition. Finally, blend in the raisins and walnuts. Turn batter into pan, spreading evenly to edges.
9. Bake at 275°F 2½ hours, or until cake tests done. Cool completely on cooling rack and remove from pan.

One 10-inch tube cake

738 *Sherried Holiday Pudding*

1 package (14 ounces) gingerbread mix
¾ cup orange juice
¼ cup sherry
½ cup chopped walnuts
½ teaspoon grated orange peel
Golden Sherry Sauce (see recipe)
Hard Sauce Snowballs (see recipe)

1. Prepare gingerbread according to package directions using orange juice and sherry for liquid. Add walnuts and orange peel.
2. Turn batter into a well-greased 6-cup mold (batter should fill mold ½ to ⅔ full).
3. Bake at 350°F for 50 to 55 minutes, until pudding tests done. Serve warm with Golden Sherry Sauce and Hard Sauce Snowballs.

8 servings

Golden Sherry Sauce: Combine **½ cup each granulated and brown sugar (packed), ¼ cup whipping cream,** and **⅛ teaspoon salt** in saucepan. Heat slowly to boiling, stirring occasionally. Add **¼ cup sherry** and **1 teaspoon grated lemon peel.** Heat slightly to blend flavors. 739

About 1⅓ cups sauce

Hard Sauce Snowballs: Beat together **⅔ cup soft butter or margarine, 2 cups confectioners' sugar,** and **1 tablespoon sherry,** adding a little more sherry if more liquid is needed. Shape into small balls and roll in **flaked coconut.** 740

About 1½ cups or 16 balls

741 *New Orleans Holiday Pudding*

3 cups boiling water
1¼ cups prunes
1 cup dried apricots
1 cup sugar
1 teaspoon ground cinnamon
1 teaspoon ground nutmeg

1. Pour boiling water over prunes and apricots in a saucepan. Return to boiling, cover, and simmer about 45 minutes, or until fruit is tender. Drain and reserve 1 cup liquid. Set liquid aside until cold. Remove and discard prune pits.
2. Force prunes and apricots through a food mill or sieve into a large bowl. Stir in a mixture of the sugar, cinnamon, nutmeg,

1 teaspoon ground allspice
1 cup orange juice
3 tablespoons ruby port
3 envelopes unflavored gelatin
1½ cups golden raisins, plumped
2¼ cups candied cherries
⅓ cup diced candied citron
⅓ cup diced candied lemon peel
1½ cups walnuts, coarsely
    chopped
3 envelopes (2 ounces each)
    dessert topping mix, or 3
    cups whipping cream,
    whipped

and allspice, mixing until sugar is dissolved. Blend in orange juice and wine; mix thoroughly.

3. Soften gelatin in the 1 cup reserved liquid in a small saucepan. Stir over low heat until gelatin is dissolved. Stir into fruit-spice mixture. Chill until mixture is slightly thickened, stirring occasionally.

4. Blend raisins, cherries, citron, lemon peel, and walnuts into gelatin mixture.

5. Prepare the dessert topping according to package directions or whip the cream. Gently fold into fruit mixture, blending thoroughly. Turn into 10-inch tube pan. Chill until firm.

6. Unmold onto chilled serving plate.

20 to 24 servings

742 Sherry Baba Ring

1 package active dry yeast
¼ cup warm water
¼ cup hot milk
½ cup soft butter
3 tablespoons sugar
1 teaspoon salt
4 eggs
2 cups all-purpose flour
  Sherry Syrup
  Whipped cream
  Glacé fruits

1. Soften yeast in water.
2. Combine hot milk, soft butter, sugar, and salt.
3. Beat eggs. Beat in yeast mixture, then butter mixture. Beat in flour thoroughly to make a smooth, thick batter.
4. Turn into a well-buttered 2-quart mold with tube center. Let rise in a warm place until almost doubled in bulk, 1 to 1½ hours.
5. Bake at 375°F for 30 minutes, or until cake tests done. Make sherry syrup while baba is baking.
6. Remove baked baba from oven and allow to cool in pan 10 minutes. Turn baba onto a serving plate. Prick sides and top with tines of a fork. Slowly baste with sherry syrup. Let stand until syrup is almost absorbed.
7. Fill center of ring with slightly sweetened whipped cream and garnish with glacé fruits.

About 8 servings

Sherry Syrup: Simmer **1½ cups sugar** with **⅔ cup water** and **1 tablespoon grated orange peel** 10 minutes. Mix in **½ cup California Cream Sherry** and **¼ cup apricot-pineapple jam**. Simmer 5 minutes; cool.

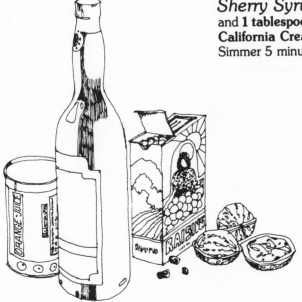

743 Biscuit Tortoni

⅓ cup confectioners' sugar
1 tablespoon sherry
½ cup plus 2 tablespoons fine dry macaroon crumbs
1 cup whipping cream, whipped
1 egg white

1. Fold sugar, sherry, and ½ cup macaroon crumbs into whipped cream until well blended.
2. Beat egg white until stiff, not dry, peaks are formed. Fold into whipped cream mixture.
3. Divide mixture equally into ten 2-inch heavy paper baking cups and sprinkle with the remaining crumbs. Freeze until firm.

10 servings

744 Sherry Almond Chiffon Pie

1 unbaked 9-inch pastry shell
¼ cup blanched almonds, toasted (see Note)
⅓ cup sugar
1 envelope unflavored gelatin
½ teaspoon salt
3 egg yolks, slightly beaten
1¾ cups milk
½ cup chilled heavy cream
3 egg whites
¼ cup sugar
3 tablespoons sherry
½ teaspoon almond extract
1 ounce (1 square) unsweetened chocolate

1. Chill a bowl and a rotary beater in refrigerator.
2. Bake pastry shell and set aside to cool.
3. Coarsely chop toasted almonds and set aside.
4. Mix ⅓ cup sugar, gelatin, and salt thoroughly in the top of a double boiler.
5. Beat egg yolks with milk until blended; add the milk mixture gradually to gelatin mixture in double boiler top, stirring constantly until blended.
6. Set over boiling water and cook, stirring constantly, until gelatin is completely dissolved, about 5 minutes.
7. Remove the gelatin mixture from heat. Cool; chill in refrigerator or over ice and water until the mixture mounds when dropped from a spoon. (If mixture is placed over ice and water, stir frequently; if placed in refrigerator, stir occasionally.)
8. Beat cream until medium consistency (piles softly) using chilled bowl and beater. Set whipped cream in refrigerator while preparing the meringue.
9. Using a clean beater, beat egg whites until frothy; add ¼ cup sugar gradually, beating well after each addition. Beat until stiff peaks are formed.
10. Fold the meringue and whipped cream into custard mixture with sherry and almond extract. Fold in the chopped toasted almonds. Turn into cooled pie shell.
11. Chill in refrigerator 2 to 3 hours, or until firm. When ready to serve, top with chocolate curls made by pulling chocolate across a shredder.

One 9-inch pie

Note: To toast almonds, place nuts in a shallow baking dish or pie pan and, if desired, brush lightly with butter, margarine, or cooking oil. Heat in a 350°F oven until delicately browned; move and turn occasionally. Or put nuts into a heavy skillet in which butter (about 1 tablespoon per cup of nuts) has been heated. Heat until nuts are lightly browned, moving and turning constantly.

Fondue

745 *Cheese Fondue with Apples*

1 can (11 ounces) condensed
    Cheddar cheese soup
2 packages (8 ounces each) cream
    cheese, softened and cut into
    pieces
1 cup dairy sour cream
½ teaspoon salt
½ teaspoon dry mustard
⅛ teaspoon garlic powder
½ teaspoon Worcestershire sauce
2 drops Tabasco
¼ cup sherry
4 or 5 apples
    Lemon juice for dipping apple
    slices

1. In a fondue pot or chafing dish, combine soup with cream cheese, blending well.
2. Add remaining ingredients, except apples; mix well. Cook over low heat, stirring occasionally, until cheese melts and mixture is smooth.
3. Meanwhile, slice apples and dip in lemon juice.
4. Keep fondue warm while dipping apple slices.

About 4½ cups fondue

746 *Cheesy Tuna-Onion Fondue*

2 cans (6½ or 7 ounces each) tuna
1 pound pasteurized process Amer-
    ican cheese, shredded (about 4
    cups)
1 cup milk
3 tablespoons chopped parsley
1 tablespoon instant minced onion
    Unsalted crackers
    Corn chips
    Potato chips

1. Drain tuna and flake, if desired.
2. Put shredded cheese into a saucepan and set over medium heat. Pour milk over the cheese. Stir until cheese is completely melted.
3. Mix in tuna, parsley, and onion. Heat thoroughly, stirring constantly.
4. Turn into a fondue saucepan and keep warm while serving with bowls of crackers, corn chips, and potato chips for dippers.

6 servings

747 Tomato Bagna Cauda

1 can (8 ounces) tomato sauce
¼ cup cooking oil
1 tablespoon anchovy paste
1 clove garlic, crushed in a garlic
   press
⅛ teaspoon pepper
¼ teaspoon tarragon leaves
   Fresh mushrooms, broccoli and
      cauliflower flowerets, celery
      sticks, carrot sticks,
      zucchini strips

1. In a fondue pot or chafing dish, stir together all ingredients except fresh vegetables. Stir over low heat until smooth and thoroughly heated.
2. Keep hot and serve fresh vegetables as dunkers.

About 1¼ cups sauce

748 Swiss Cheese Fondue

1 tablespoon cornstarch
2 tablespoons kirsch
1 clove garlic, halved
2 cups Neuchâtel or other dry
   white wine
1 pound natural Swiss cheese,
   shredded (about 4 cups)
   Freshly ground black pepper to
      taste
   Ground nutmeg to taste
1 loaf French bread, cut into
   1-inch cubes

1. Mix cornstarch and kirsch in a small bowl; set aside.
2. Rub the inside of a nonmetal fondue pot with cut surface of garlic. Pour in wine; place over medium heat until wine is about to simmer (do not boil).
3. Add cheese in small amounts to the hot wine, stirring constantly until cheese is melted. Heat cheese-wine mixture until bubbly.
4. Blend in cornstarch mixture and continue stirring while cooking 5 minutes, or until fondue begins to bubble; add seasoning.
5. Dip bread cubes in fondue. Keep the fondue gently bubbling throughout serving time.

About 6 servings

749 Brussels Sprouts with Dunking Sauce

2¼ cups chicken broth (dissolve
      2 chicken bouillon cubes in
      2¼ cups boiling water)
1 pound fresh Brussels sprouts
      (or two 10-ounce packages
      frozen Brussels sprouts)
2 tablespoons butter or margarine
1 tablespoon flour
1 teaspoon salt
½ teaspoon caraway seed
¼ teaspoon cayenne pepper
1 cup milk
1½ cups dairy sour cream

1. Heat broth in a saucepan until boiling. Add Brussels sprouts and boil, uncovered, 5 minutes. Cover and boil 5 to 10 minutes, or until just tender. (Cook frozen Brussels sprouts in the chicken broth following package directions.)
2. Meanwhile, heat butter in a fondue saucepan; stir in a mixture of flour, salt, caraway seed, and cayenne pepper. Heat until mixture bubbles. Add milk, cooking and stirring until mixture comes to boiling. Boil 1 to 2 minutes, stirring constantly.
3. Reduce heat and stir in sour cream. Heat thoroughly (do not boil). Keep sauce hot during serving.
4. Drain cooked Brussels sprouts and turn into a serving dish. Spear each sprout and dunk into the sauce.

About 8 servings

750 *Cheese Rabbit Fondue*

1 small clove garlic
2 cups beer
1 pound sharp Cheddar cheese,
    shredded (about 4 cups)
3 tablespoons flour
1 teaspoon Worcestershire sauce
½ teaspoon dry mustard
2 tablespoons chopped chives or
    green onion top (optional)
1 loaf sourdough French bread,
    cut into 1-inch cubes

1. Rub inside of a nonmetal fondue pot with garlic; discard garlic. Heat beer in the pot until almost boiling.
2. Dredge cheese in flour and add about ½ cup at a time, stirring until cheese is melted and blended before adding more.
3. When mixture is smooth and thickened, stir in Worcestershire sauce and dry mustard.
4. Sprinkle chives on top and serve with bread cubes. Keep fondue warm while serving.

4 to 6 servings

751 *Cheesy Potato Fondue*

3 cups sliced pared potatoes
3 cups water
1 tablespoon butter
1 tablespoon flour
1½ cups milk
¾ cup coarsely grated Parmesan
    or Romano cheese
2 egg yolks, fork beaten
¾ teaspoon salt
⅛ teaspoon cayenne pepper
    Cooked ham, cut into cubes
    Cherry tomatoes, halved
    Zucchini slices

1. Cook potatoes in a small amount of water until soft (about 15 minutes). Drain, reserving the water; sieve or rice potatoes.
2. Melt butter in a large fondue saucepan. Add flour and cook 1 or 2 minutes without browning.
3. Stir in potatoes with reserved water and milk. Blend until smooth and simmer 10 minutes, stirring occasionally.
4. Stir in cheese and beat in egg yolks. Continue beating until mixture is smooth, hot, and thick. Stir in salt and cayenne.
5. Serve warm with ham, tomatoes, and zucchini for dippers.

4 to 6 servings

752 *Buttermilk Fondue*

1 pound Swiss cheese, shredded
    (about 4 cups)
3 tablespoons cornstarch
½ teaspoon salt
⅛ teaspoon white pepper
¼ teaspoon dry mustard
2 cups buttermilk
1 clove garlic, split in half
1 loaf dark rye bread, cut into
    1-inch cubes

1. Toss cheese with a mixture of cornstarch, salt, pepper, and dry mustard. Set aside.
2. In a fondue saucepan, heat buttermilk with garlic over low heat. When hot, remove garlic and add cheese; stir constantly until cheese is melted.
3. Keep fondue warm over low heat while dipping bread cubes.

4 to 6 servings

753 *Beef à la Fondue*

2 teaspoons butter
1 tablespoon flour
½ cup dry white wine
8 ounces Swiss cheese, shredded
(about 2 cups)
1½ pounds beef top sirloin steak,
cut into bite-size pieces
Oil for deep frying
Sauces for dipping

1. Melt butter in top of a double boiler over boiling water. Remove from heat; add flour and part of wine, mixing to a smooth paste.
2. Add remaining wine; heat over water until thickened. Add cheese; heat until melted. Keep warm.
3. At serving time, fill a metal fondue pot half full with oil. Heat oil to 375 °F. Cook a cube of beef in the hot oil and dip it into the cheese sauce, and then into other sauces and side dishes. **Horseradish sauce** (sour cream and horseradish), **tartar sauce, mustard sauce, chopped chives** and **chutney** are suitable sauces and accompaniments. These should be in small individual dishes clustered around each place setting.

4 servings

754 *Fondue Bourguignonne*

Sauces for dipping (three or
or more)
Cooking oil
1½ to 2 pounds beef tenderloin
or sirloin, cut into 1-inch pieces

1. Prepare sauces and set aside until serving time.
2. Fill a metal fondue pot half full with oil. Heat oil to 375°F. Spear pieces of meat with dipping forks and plunge into hot oil, cooking until done as desired.
3. Dip cooked meat in desired sauce and transfer to plate. Place another piece of meat in hot oil to cook while eating cooked meat.

4 servings

755 *Velvet Lemon Sauce*

2 eggs
½ teaspoon salt
2 tablespoons lemon juice
½ cup butter, softened
Few grains white pepper
½ slice onion
½ cup hot water

1. Put eggs, salt, lemon juice, butter, pepper, and onion into an electric blender container. Blend until smooth. Add hot water, a little at a time, while blending.
2. Turn into top of double boiler. Cook over simmering water, stirring constantly until thickened (about 10 minutes).

About 1½ cups sauce

756 *Rémoulade Sauce*

1 cup mayonnaise
1½ teaspoons prepared mustard
¼ teaspoon anchovy paste
2 tablespoons finely chopped dill
pickles
1 tablespoon chopped capers
1½ teaspoons minced parsley
½ teaspoon finely crushed chervil
½ teaspoon crushed tarragon

Blend all ingredients in a small bowl. Cover; chill thoroughly.

About 1 cup sauce

757 *Paprika Sauce*

2 tablespoons butter or margarine
2 tablespoons flour
½ teaspoon salt
⅛ teaspoon pepper
1 cup milk
1 teaspoon minced onion
Few grains nutmeg
2 to 3 teaspoons paprika

1. Heat butter in a saucepan. Blend in flour, salt, and pepper; heat and stir until bubbly.
2. Gradually add milk, stirring until smooth. Bring to boiling; cook and stir 1 to 2 minutes longer.
3. Blend in onion, nutmeg, and paprika.

About 1 cup sauce

Jiffy Sauces for Fondue Bourguignonne

Onion-Chili: **Combine ½ envelope (about 1½ ounces) dry onion soup mix** and **¾ cup boiling water** in a saucepan. Cover partially and cook 10 minutes. Adding gradually, mix in **1½ tablespoons flour** mixed with **¼ cup water**. Bring to boiling, stirring constantly; cook until thickened. Remove from heat; mix in **2 tablespoons chili sauce**. 758

Onion-Horseradish: Blend **½ envelope (about 1½ ounces) dry onion soup mix, 1 tablespoon milk, 2 teaspoons prepared horseradish**, and desired amount of **snipped parsley** into **1 cup dairy sour cream**. 759

Horseradish: Blend **3 tablespoons prepared horseradish, 1 teaspoon grated onion**, and **½ teaspoon lemon juice** with **1 cup mayonnaise**. 760

Curry: Blend **1 tablespoon curry powder, 1 teaspoon grated onion**, and **½ teaspoon lemon juice** with **1 cup mayonnaise**. 761

Mustard: Blend **1 tablespoon half-and-half** with **1 cup mayonnaise** and stir in **prepared mustard** to taste. 762

Caper: Mix **1 tablespoon chopped capers** and **1 cup bottled tartar sauce**; blend in **1 tablespoon half-and-half**. 763

Béarnaise: Blend **1 tablespoon parsley flakes, ½ teaspoon grated onion, ¼ teaspoon crushed tarragon**, and **1 teaspoon tarragon vinegar** into **hollandaise sauce** prepared from a mix according to package directions. 764

Barbecue: Blend **prepared horseradish** to taste with a **bottled barbecue sauce**. 765

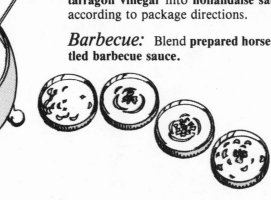

766 *Chicken Fondue*

Cooking oil
1 teaspoon salt
2 pounds chicken breasts, skinned,
    boned, and cut into ¾-inch
    cubes
Sauces for dipping

1. Pour cooking oil into a metal fondue pot, not more than half full. Heat on range to 425°F. Add salt.
2. Transfer to fondue heating element. Spear chicken cube with a fondue fork and cook in hot oil 2 to 3 minutes.
3. Dip in desired sauce.

4 servings

Note: To maintain a high enough cooking temperature, it may be necessary to return pot to kitchen range and heat oil.

767 *Easy Tomato Sauce*

1 medium clove garlic, crushed in
    a garlic press
1 teaspoon oregano
½ teaspoon thyme
1 can (8 ounces) tomato sauce
3 tablespoons grated Parmesan
    cheese
Salt and pepper to taste

Combine all ingredients in a saucepan and simmer, uncovered, 5 minutes.

768 *Béarnaise Sauce*

4 egg yolks
1 cup butter
1 tablespoon lemon juice
1 tablespoon tarragon vinegar
¼ teaspoon salt
1 teaspoon chopped parsley
1 teaspoon onion juice
Dash cayenne pepper

1. Blend egg yolks with a third of the butter in a fondue saucepan. Place over low heat. Add remaining butter as sauce thickens, stirring constantly.
2. Remove from heat and add remaining ingredients.

1 cup sauce

769 *Jiffy Curry Sauce*

⅔ cup condensed cream of celery
    soup
1½ teaspoons instant minced onion
½ teaspoon curry powder
6 tablespoons milk
1 egg, slightly beaten
1½ teaspoons butter or margarine

1. Combine soup, onion, and curry powder in a fondue saucepan; stir until well blended. Stir in milk. Heat thoroughly over low heat, stirring occasionally.
2. Stir about ¼ cup of the hot sauce into the beaten egg; immediately return mixture to fondue saucepan.
3. Cook over low heat 3 to 5 minutes, stirring occasionally to keep mixture cooking evenly. Blend in the butter.

About 1 cup sauce

770 *Sloppy Joe Fondue*

1 tablespoon butter or margarine
1 pound ground beef
1 envelope (about 1½ ounces) Sloppy Joe seasoning mix
1 can (6 ounces) tomato paste
  Water
⅓ cup chopped celery
¼ cup chopped green pepper

1. Heat butter in a large skillet. Add meat and brown, breaking into small pieces with a spoon. Stir in seasoning mix, tomato paste, and water called for in package directions. Mix in celery and green pepper. Bring to boiling, stirring occasionally.
2. Reduce heat, cover, and simmer 10 minutes, stirring occasionally.
3. Turn into a fondue saucepan and keep warm.
4. To serve, spoon over halves of **toasted buttered buns** or **English muffins.**

4 servings

771 *Oriental Chicken Fondue*

3 cups chicken broth or bouillon
2 pounds chicken breasts, skinned, boned, and cut into paper-thin strips
  Sauces for dipping

1. Heat chicken broth to boiling. Adjust heat so broth will continue to boil gently throughout dipping.
2. Spear chicken strip with a fondue fork and cook in boiling broth 2 to 3 minutes, or until chicken turns white and is tender.
3. Transfer cooked piece of chicken to plate and start cooking another before dipping in desired sauce.

4 servings

772 *Teriyaki Sauce*

½ cup pineapple juice
¼ cup brown sugar
2 tablespoons soy sauce
1 tablespoon cooking oil
¾ teaspoon ground ginger
¼ teaspoon salt
1 clove garlic, minced

Combine all ingredients in a saucepan. Heat to blend flavors.

About ⅔ cup sauce

773 *Tangy Plum Sauce*

1 can or jar (17 ounces) purple plums, drained (reserve syrup)
½ cup frozen orange juice concentrate, thawed
½ teaspoon Worcestershire sauce

Pit plums, and force through a sieve or food mill into a bowl. Blend in reserved syrup, orange juice, and Worcestershire sauce. Heat just to blend flavors.

About 1½ cups sauce

774 *Mustard Sauce*

1 cup undiluted evaporated milk
2 tablespoons dry mustard
¼ cup sugar
3 egg yolks, well beaten
⅓ cup cider vinegar

1. Scald evaporated milk in top of a double boiler over boiling water. Blend a small amount of hot evaporated milk with dry mustard until smooth; return to remaining evaporated milk along with sugar and stir until sugar is dissolved. Add a small amount of the hot mixture to the beaten egg yolks, blending well, and return to double-boiler top.
2. Cook over boiling water about 3 minutes, stirring constantly.
3. Remove from heat. Mix in vinegar. Serve hot.

About 1¼ cups sauce

775 Colby-Crab Fondue

⅓ cup butter
¾ cup dry white wine
1 pound colby cheese, shredded (about 4 cups)
2 tablespoons flour
1 can (6½ ounces) crab meat
⅛ teaspoon garlic powder
1 teaspoon salt
⅛ teaspoon Tabasco
1 teaspoon prepared mustard
1 teaspoon bottled steak sauce
1½ teaspoons Worcestershire sauce

1. Melt butter in a nonmetal fondue pot. Stir in wine and heat until bubbles appear around the edges.
2. Toss cheese with flour and stir into the hot mixture, a handful at a time. Heat and stir until completely melted.
3. Rinse, drain, and flake crab meat. Stir into cheese mixture with remaining ingredients. Heat thoroughly, stirring occasionally.
4. To serve, dip cubes of **French bread** in the warm fondue.

4 servings

776 Deep-Fried Zucchini

1¼ cups all-purpose flour
1 teaspoon salt
¼ teaspoon pepper
2 eggs, well beaten
¾ cup milk
1 teaspoon Worcestershire sauce
1 tablespoon butter or margarine, melted
  Oil for deep frying
6 medium (about 2 pounds) zucchini, cut in halves crosswise and into ¾-inch sticks lengthwise

1. Blend flour, salt, and pepper in a bowl. Add a mixture of eggs, milk, Worcestershire sauce, and butter; beat just until smooth.
2. Heat oil in a fondue pot to 365°F.
3. Dip zucchini sticks into batter, using a fork to coat evenly. Allow any excess coating to drip off.
4. Fry 2 to 3 minutes, or until golden brown. Lift from oil and drain a few seconds before removing to absorbent paper.
5. Sprinkle with **salt.**

6 servings

777 Orange Chocolate Fondue

2 packages (3¼ ounces each) chocolate pudding and pie filling
3 cups orange juice
1 cup milk
2 tablespoons butter or margarine
  Marshmallows
  Pound cake cubes
  Ladyfingers, cut in thirds
  Maraschino cherries with stems
  Walnut halves

1. In a large saucepan, mix together pudding, orange juice, and milk. Cook over low heat, stirring constantly, until mixture thickens and comes to boiling. Remove from heat.
2. Stir in butter until melted. Pour mixture into a fondue pot. Serve with marshmallows, cake cubes, ladyfingers, cherries, and walnuts.

8 servings

778 *Banana Split Fondue*

2 king-size chocolate crunch
  candy bars (about 6½
  ounces each)
1 cup milk
  Ripe bananas, cut into bite-
  size pieces
  Large marshmallows
  Maraschino cherries with
  stems

1. Break candy bars into pieces over fondue saucepan. Pour milk over candy-bar pieces.
2. Place saucepan over low heat just long enough to warm mixture. Stir occasionally until chocolate melts. If mixture becomes too thick for dipping, stir in 1 to 2 tablespoons milk.
3. Spear banana pieces and marshmallows; dip in melted chocolate. Cherries may be held by the stems for dipping.

4 to 6 servings

779 *Chocolate Fondue*

4 ounces (4 squares) unsweetened
  chocolate
1 eup sugar
½ cup whipping cream
5 tablespoons butter or margarine
2 tablespoons orange liqueur
½ teaspoon vanilla extract
  Assorted dippers (marshmallows,
  strawberries with hulls, apple
  slices, banana chunks,
  mandarin orange segments,
  cake cubes)

1. Cut up chocolate and melt in fondue pot over low heat. Stir in sugar, whipping cream, and butter.
2. Cook over low heat until thickened (about 5 minutes), stirring constantly. Stir in orange liqueur and vanilla extract.
3. Place over very low heat to keep warm while dipping.

4 servings

780 *Eggnog Fondue*

2 eggs, beaten
2 tablespoons sugar or honey
⅛ teaspoon salt
1½ cups milk
½ teaspoon vanilla extract
3 tablespoons arrowroot
3 tablespoons dark rum
  Nutmeg
  Fruitcake, cut into ¾-inch
  pieces

1. Beat together eggs, sugar, and salt. Stir in milk and vanilla extract.
2. Pour eggnog into a nonmetal fondue pot. Mix arrowroot with 1 tablespoon rum and stir into the eggnog.
3. Cook over medium heat until mixture thickens, stirring occasionally. Stir in remaining rum.
4. Keep fondue warm while dipping fruitcake pieces.

6 to 8 servings

781 *Teriyaki*

1 teaspoon ground ginger
⅓ cup soy sauce
¼ cup honey
1 clove garlic, minced
1 teaspoon grated onion
1 pound beef sirloin tip, cut into
    2x½x¼-inch strips
2 to 3 tablespoons cooking oil
1 tablespoon cornstarch
½ cup water
⅛ teaspoon red food coloring

1. Blend ginger, soy sauce, honey, garlic, and onion in a bowl. Add meat; marinate about 1 hour.
2. Remove meat, reserving marinade, and brown quickly on all sides in the hot oil in a large wok. Remove meat from wok.
3. Stir a blend of cornstarch, water, and food coloring into the reserved marinade and pour into wok. Bring rapidly to boiling and cook 2 to 3 minutes, stirring constantly.
4. Add meat to thickened marinade to glaze; remove and drain on wire rack.
5. Insert a frilled wooden pick into each meat strip and serve with the thickened marinade.

About 24 appetizers

WOK

782 *Fried Shrimp with Dunking Sauce*

2 pounds uncooked shrimp
Salt
2 eggs, slightly beaten
1 can (3 ounces) chow mein
    noodles, finely crushed
Oil for deep frying
Dunking Sauce or Zesty Sauce

1. Wash shrimp; remove shells (not tails) and black veins. Drain shrimp and sprinkle with salt.
2. Dip each shrimp into beaten egg and then into finely crushed chow mein noodles, coating well.
3. Pour oil into a wok, filling not more than a third full yet at least 1 inch deep. Heat to 375 °F.
4. Drop shrimp, about 6 at a time, into hot oil. Fry, turning as necessary, until golden, and drain on absorbent paper.
5. Serve hot with desired sauce.

About 60 appetizers

Dunking Sauce: Add enough water to **2 tablespoons dry mustard** to make a smooth paste. Blend in **½ cup soy sauce.**

Zesty Sauce: Blend **1 tablespoon ground ginger, ¼ clove garlic** (crushed in a garlic press), **¼ cup water, 2 tablespoons sugar,** and **½ cup soy sauce.**

783 *Fried Oriental Shrimp Balls*

2 pounds fresh uncooked shrimp
1 can (5 ounces) water chestnuts,
    drained and coarsely chopped
1 egg, slightly beaten
1 tablespoon cornstarch
¼ teaspoon sherry extract
½ teaspoon salt
Oil for deep frying

Sauce:

1 tablespoon cornstarch
¼ teaspoon sugar
1 tablespoon soy sauce
¾ cup chicken bouillon

1. Wash, shell, devein, and finely chop shrimp. Combine with water chestnuts, egg, cornstarch, sherry extract, and salt. Form into balls about 1 inch in diameter.
2. Pour oil into a wok, filling it not more than a third full, but at least 1 inch deep. Heat oil to 375ºF. Fry shrimp balls about 6 at a time until golden brown. Drain on paper towels and keep shrimp balls warm in a low oven, if necessary.
3. Combine ingredients for sauce in a small fondue pot. Cook over low heat until thickened, stirring constantly.
4. Keep the sauce warm and serve with hot shrimp balls.

About 4 dozen appetizers

784 *Peanut Cocktail Fritters*

½ cup boiling water
¼ cup peanut oil
¼ teaspoon salt
½ cup flour
2 eggs
1 cup finely chopped dry roasted peanuts
  Peanut oil for deep frying
  Salt

1. In a saucepan, combine water, ¼ cup peanut oil, and ¼ teaspoon salt. Bring to a full boil. Add flour all at once, and stir vigorously over low heat until mixture forms a ball and leaves sides of pan. Remove from heat.
2. Add eggs, one at a time, beating thoroughly after each is added. Stir in chopped peanuts, blending well. Form into 1-inch balls.
3. Heat oil to 365°F in a wok. Fry fritters, about 10 at a time, until golden brown (3 to 4 minutes).
4. Drain on paper towels, sprinkle with salt, and serve while hot.

5 dozen fritters

785 *Beef Sub Gum Soup*

½ pound beef round, cut into small cubes
1 tablespoon cooking oil
1 can (20 ounces) Chinese vegetables, drained
2 cans (10½ ounces each) condensed beef broth or bouillon
2 cups water
¼ cup uncooked rice
2 tablespoons soy sauce
¼ teaspoon monosodium glutamate
⅛ teaspoon pepper
1 egg, beaten

1. In a large wok, brown beef in hot oil. Chop vegetables and add to the browned meat with remaining ingredients, except egg.
2. Bring soup to boiling, stirring to blend. Cover and simmer 40 minutes.
3. Remove soup from heat and slowly stir in the egg. Let stand until egg is set.

About 6 servings

786 *Chinese Chicken-Mushroom Soup*

1 pound chicken breasts
½ teaspoon salt
1 tablespoon cooking oil
10 medium-size mushrooms, sliced
4 chicken bouillon cubes
4 cups hot water
1 tablespoon cornstarch
3 tablespoons cold water
1 tablespoon soy sauce
2 tablespoons lemon juice

1. Bone chicken breasts, remove skin, and cut into ¼-inch-wide strips, 1½ to 2 inches long. Sprinkle with salt and let stand 30 minutes.
2. Heat oil in a wok and sauté mushrooms a few minutes until golden. Remove from wok. Dissolve bouillon cubes in hot water and set aside.
3. Mix cornstarch with cold water. Stir in soy sauce. Combine with chicken bouillon in the wok. Bring to boiling, add chicken pieces, and simmer, covered, 5 minutes.
4. Add mushrooms and lemon juice to soup, adding more salt, if necessary. Heat gently without boiling.
5. Serve with a thin **lemon slice** in each bowl.

5 servings

787 Carrot Nibblers

1 pound carrots
2 to 3 tablespoons cooking oil
2 large cloves garlic, minced
1 tablespoon chopped onion
¼ cup vinegar
1½ teaspoons salt
⅛ teaspoon pepper
½ teaspoon dry mustard
1 tablespoon whole pickling spices
1 onion, thinly sliced

1. Wash and pare carrots. Cut into 3x¼-inch strips, and set aside.
2. Heat oil in a large wok. Stir in garlic and onion and cook over low heat about 5 minutes. Stir in vinegar, salt, pepper, dry mustard, spices (tied in cheesecloth), and carrots.
3. Cook, covered, over low heat about 10 minutes, or until carrots are crisp-tender. Remove spice bag and turn carrots into a shallow dish. Top with sliced onion, cover, and refrigerate overnight.

8 servings

788 Cheese Balls

4 ounces Cheddar cheese, shredded (about 1 cup)
1 teaspoon flour
¼ teaspoon salt
Dash pepper
1 egg white
Oil for deep frying

1. Mix cheese, flour, salt, and pepper.
2. Beat egg white to stiff, not dry, peaks. Fold beaten egg white into cheese mixture. Form into small balls, using a rounded tablespoon of the mixture for each.
3. Heat the oil to 365° F in a wok. Fry the cheese balls, a few at a time, until brown. Serve while warm.

12 cheese balls

789 Ham Nibbles

2 cups ground cooked ham
1 can (12 ounces) vacuum-packed whole kernel corn, drained
2 cups cheese-cracker crumbs
¼ cup mayonnaise
2 eggs, well beaten
Oil for deep frying

1. Combine the ham, corn, 1 cup of the crumbs, mayonnaise, and eggs.
2. Shape mixture into ¾- to 1-inch balls. Roll in remaining crumbs. Set aside about 30 minutes.
3. Fill a large wok with oil not more than a third full, and heat to 375°F. Fry balls uncrowded in hot fat 2 minutes, or until browned. Remove to drain on absorbent paper.
4. Serve on a heated platter accompanied with picks.

About 7 dozen appetizers

790 *Chinese Cabbage Soup*

1 chicken breast (¾ pound),
    cooked
7 cups chicken broth
6 cups sliced Chinese cabbage
    (celery cabbage)
1 teaspoon soy sauce
1¼ teaspoons salt
¼ teaspoon pepper

1. Cut chicken into strips about ⅛ inch wide and 1½ to 2 inches long. Combine with chicken broth in a large wok and heat only until hot. Add Chinese cabbage and cook 3 to 4 minutes (only until cabbage is crisp-tender; do not overcook).
2. Stir in soy sauce, salt, and pepper. Serve hot.

6 servings

Note: If desired, romaine may be substituted for the cabbage. Reduce cooking time to 1 minute

791 *Oriental Soup*

2 tablespoons cooking oil
2 cups diagonally sliced celery
½ cup chopped onion
1 can (16 ounces) bean sprouts,
    drained
1 can (5 ounces) water chestnuts,
    drained and chopped
2 quarts rich beef broth (made
    with bouillon cubes, if desired)
Salt and pepper to taste

1. In a large wok, heat oil and stir in celery and onion. Cook until crisp-tender, stirring frequently.
2. Stir in remaining ingredients and heat thoroughly.
3. Serve with crisp chow mein noodles sprinkled over individual bowls, if desired.

6 servings

792 *Spanish Chicken Soup with Sausage*

1 pound bulk pork sausage
1 teaspoon sage
1 teaspoon ground thyme
¼ teaspoon salt
½ cup finely chopped almonds
1 onion, cut into 8 wedges
1 large clove garlic, minced
1 can (10½ ounces) condensed
    chicken broth
1 can (10½ ounces) condensed
    cream of chicken soup
1 cup dry white wine
¼ cup dry sherry
¾ cup diced green pepper
1 bay leaf
⅛ teaspoon Tabasco
½ cup slivered almonds, toasted
    (see Note)
1 ounce (1 square) semisweet
    chocolate, shaved

1. Mix sausage with sage, ½ teaspoon thyme, salt, and the chopped almonds. Shape into balls about 1½ inches in diameter.
2. In a large wok, cook the meatballs over medium heat until evenly browned and thoroughly cooked. Remove meatballs from wok.
3. Stir in onion and garlic; sauté 5 minutes. Add chicken broth, condensed soup, wines, green pepper, bay leaf, Tabasco, and remaining thyme. Salt to taste.
4. Cover and simmer about 5 minutes, stirring occasionally. Uncover and simmer 10 minutes. Ladle into soup bowls and garnish with slivered almonds and shaved chocolate.

4 servings

Note: To toast almonds, spread in a shallow pan. Heat in a 350°F oven or on top of range, stirring occasionally, until almonds are lightly browned.

793 *Bacon 'n' Egg Croquettes*

3 tablespoons butter or margarine
2 tablespoons chopped onion
3 tablespoons flour
½ teaspoon salt
⅛ teaspoon pepper
¾ teaspoon dry mustard
¾ cup milk
6 hard-cooked eggs, coarsely chopped
8 slices bacon, cooked and finely crumbled
1 egg, fork beaten
2 tablespoons water
⅓ cup fine dry bread or cracker crumbs
  Oil for deep frying

1. Melt butter in a saucepan; stir in onion and cook about 2 minutes, or until tender. Stir in a mixture of flour, salt, pepper, and dry mustard. Heat until bubbly. Add milk gradually, stirring constantly. Cook and stir until mixture forms a ball.
2. Remove from heat and stir in chopped eggs and crumbled bacon. Refrigerate about 1 hour, or until chilled.
3. Shape into 8 croquettes (balls or cones). Mix egg with water. Roll croquettes in crumbs, dip into egg, and roll again in crumbs.
4. Fill a large wok no more than half full with oil. Slowly heat to 385°F. Fry croquettes without crowding in the hot oil 2 minutes, or until golden. Remove croquettes with a slotted spoon; drain over fat and place on paper towel to drain.

4 servings

Herbed Egg Croquettes: Follow recipe for Bacon 'n' Egg Croquettes. Decrease mustard to ¼ teaspoon and bacon to 4 slices. Add ½ **teaspoon summer savory,** crushed, with mustard and **4 teaspoons snipped parsley** with chopped egg.

794 *Eggs Pisto Style*

1 large clove garlic
1 cup thinly sliced onion
1 cup slivered green pepper
½ cup olive oil
1 cup thin raw potato strips
1 tablespoon chopped parsley
⅓ cup (2 ounces) diced cooked ham
2 cups small cubes yellow summer squash
2 cups finely cut peeled ripe tomatoes
2 teaspoons salt
1 teaspoon sugar
⅛ teaspoon pepper
6 eggs, beaten

1. Add garlic, onion, and green pepper to heated olive oil in a large wok; cook until softened, then remove garlic.
2. Add remaining ingredients except eggs to wok; cook over medium heat, stirring frequently, about 10 minutes, or until squash is just tender.
3. Pour beaten eggs into vegetables, and cook over low heat. With a spatula, lift mixture from bottom and sides as it thickens, allowing uncooked portion to flow to bottom. Cook until eggs are thick and creamy.

6 servings

795 *Cottage Cheese Croquettes*

3 tablespoons butter or margarine
¼ cup flour
1 teaspoon salt
  Dash pepper
½ teaspoon dill weed
1 cup milk
1 teaspoon instant minced onion
1 cup elbow macaroni, cooked and drained
1 pound (2 cups) creamed cottage cheese
1½ cups corn-flake crumbs (more if needed)
3 eggs, slightly beaten
  Oil for deep frying

1. In a 3-quart saucepan, melt butter. Blend in flour, salt, pepper, and dill weed.
2. Combine milk with onion. Add gradually to flour mixture, stirring constantly. Stir while cooking until thickened. Reduce heat and cook 2 minutes longer.
3. Stir in macaroni and cheese; mix well. Chill 1 to 2 hours, or until firm enough to handle.
4. Shape into 12 croquettes, coating with crumbs as soon as shaped. Dip in egg and again in crumbs.
5. Fill wok not more than half full with oil. Slowly heat oil to 375°F. Fry 3 croquettes at a time in hot oil until golden brown. Remove to a baking sheet lined with paper towels to drain. When all croquettes are drained, remove paper towels.
6. Bake croquettes at 350°F 10 to 15 minutes. Serve hot.

6 servings

Note: If desired, fine dry bread crumbs can be substituted for the corn-flake crumbs.

796 *Chinese Beef and Pea Pods*

1½ pounds flank steak, thinly
    sliced diagonally across grain
to 2 tablespoons cooking oil
1 bunch green onions, chopped
    (tops included)
1 or 2 packages (7 ounces each)
    frozen Chinese pea pods,
    partially thawed to separate
1 can (10½ ounces) condensed
    beef consommé
3 tablespoons soy sauce
¼ teaspoon ground ginger
2 tablespoons cornstarch
2 tablespoons cold water
1 can (16 ounces) bean sprouts,
    drained and rinsed

1. Stir-fry meat, a third at a time, in hot oil in a large wok until browned. Remove from wok and keep warm.
2. Put green onions and pea pods into wok. Stir in a mixture of condensed consommé, soy sauce, and ginger. Bring to boiling and cook, covered, about 2 minutes.
3. Blend cornstarch with water and stir into boiling liquid in wok. Stirring constantly, boil 2 to 3 minutes. Mix in the meat and bean sprouts; heat thoroughly.
4. Serve over **hot fluffy rice**.

6 servings

797 *Chinatown Chop Suey*

1¼ pounds pork, boneless
1 pound beef, boneless
¾ pound veal, boneless
3 tablespoons cooking oil
1 cup water
3 cups diagonally sliced celery
2 cups coarsely chopped onion
3 tablespoons cornstarch
¼ cup water
¼ cup soy sauce
¼ cup bead molasses
1 can (16 ounces) bean sprouts,
    drained and rinsed
2 cans (5 ounces each) water
    chestnuts, drained and sliced

1. Cut meat into 2x½x¼-inch strips. Heat oil in a large wok. Stir-fry ½ pound of meat at a time, browning pieces on all sides. Remove the meat from the wok as it is browned. When all the meat is browned, return it to the wok. Cover and cook over low heat 30 minutes.
2. Mix in 1 cup water, celery, and onions. Bring to boiling and simmer, covered, 20 minutes.
3. Blend cornstarch, the ¼ cup water, soy sauce, and molasses. Stir into meat mixture. Bring to boiling and cook 2 minutes, stirring constantly. Mix in bean sprouts and water chestnuts; heat.
4. Serve on **hot fluffy rice**.

8 servings

798 *Spicy Beef Strips*

1½ pounds beef round steak (¼
    inch thick)
2 tablespoons cooking oil
1 clove garlic
2 beef bouillon cubes
1 cup boiling water
1 tablespoon instant minced onion
½ teaspoon salt
    Few grains cayenne pepper
¼ teaspoon chili powder
¼ teaspoon ground cinnamon
¼ teaspoon ground celery seed
2 tablespoons prepared mustard

1. Cut round steak into 2x½-inch strips; set aside.
2. Heat cooking oil in a large wok. Add garlic and stir-fry until browned. Remove the garlic.
3. Add the round steak strips, half at a time, and stir-fry until browned.
4. Dissolve bouillon cubes in boiling water. Add to wok with all the ingredients; stir to mix. Cover and simmer 25 to 30 minutes, or until meat is fork-tender.
5. Serve over **hot fluffy rice**.

6 servings

799 *Nectarine Sukiyaki*

1 **tablespoon cooking oil**
2 **pounds beef sirloin steak,
    boneless, cut 1½ inches thick,
    sliced ¹⁄₁₆ inch thick, and cut
    into about 2½-inch pieces**
2 **large onions, cut in thin wedges**
8 **green onions (including tops),
    cut into 2-inch pieces**
5 **ounces fresh mushrooms, sliced
    lengthwise**
1 **can (5 ounces) bamboo shoots,
    drained and sliced**
2 **cups unpared sliced fresh
    nectarines**
½ **cup soy sauce**
½ **cup canned condensed beef broth**
2 **tablespoons sugar**

1. Heat oil in a large wok. Add meat, 1 pound at a time, and stir-fry over high heat until browned. Remove meat and set aside.
2. Arrange vegetables and nectarines in mounds in wok; top with the beef. Pour a mixture of soy sauce, condensed beef broth, and sugar over all. Simmer 3 to 5 minutes, or until onions are just tender.
3. Serve immediately over **hot fluffy rice.**

6 to 8 servings

800 *Sukiyaki*

½ **cup Japanese soy sauce (shoyu)**
½ **cup sake or sherry**
⅓ **cup sugar**
3 **tablespoons cooking oil**
1½ **pounds beef tenderloin, sliced ¹⁄₁₆
    inch thick and cut into pieces
    about 2½x1½ inches**
12 **scallions (including tops), cut
    into 2-inch lengths**
½ **head Chinese cabbage (cut
    lengthwise), cut into 1-inch
    pieces**
½ **pound spinach leaves, cut into
    1-inch strips**
2 **cups drained shirataki (or cold
    cooked very thin long egg
    noodles)**
12 **large mushrooms, sliced
    lengthwise**
12 **cubes tofu (soybean curd)**
1 **can (8½ ounces) whole bamboo
    shoots, drained and cut in large
    pieces**

1. Mix soy sauce, sake, and sugar to make the sauce; set aside.
2. Heat oil in a wok and add enough sauce to form a ¼-inch layer in bottom of wok.
3. Add half the beef and stir-fry just until pink color disappears; remove and stir-fry remaining meat, adding more of the sauce if necessary. Remove meat and set aside.
4. Arrange all other ingredients in individual mounds in skillet. Top with beef.
5. Cook until vegetables are just tender. Do not stir. Serve immediately with bowls of **hot cooked rice.**

4 servings

801 *Beef Chow Mein*

2 to 4 tablespoons cooking oil
1 pound beef tenderloin or sirloin steak, cut into 3x½x⅛-inch strips
½ pound fresh mushrooms, sliced lengthwise
2 cups sliced celery
2 green onions, sliced ½ inch thick
1 small green pepper, cut into narrow strips
1½ cups boiling water
1 teaspoon salt
½ teaspoon monosodium glutamate
⅛ teaspoon pepper
2 tablespoons cold water
2 tablespoons cornstarch
2 teaspoons soy sauce
1 teaspoon sugar
1 can (16 ounces) Chinese vegetables, drained
2 tablespoons coarsely chopped pimento

1. Heat 2 tablespoons oil in a large wok. Add beef and stir-fry until browned evenly. Remove meat; set aside.
2. Heat more oil, if necessary, in wok. Stir in mushrooms, celery, green onions, and green pepper; stir-fry 1 minute. Reduce heat and blend in boiling water, salt, monosodium glutamate, and pepper. Bring to boiling; cover and simmer 2 minutes. Remove vegetables; keep warm.
3. Bring liquid in wok to boiling and stir in a blend of cold water, cornstarch, soy sauce, and sugar. Cook and stir 2 to 3 minutes. Reduce heat; mix in the browned beef, vegetables, Chinese vegetables, and pimento. Heat thoroughly.
4. Serve piping hot with **chow mein noodles.**

4 to 6 servings

802 *Veal Scaloppine with Mushrooms*

1 tablespoon flour
¾ teaspoon salt
Pinch pepper
1 pound veal cutlets
2 tablespoons cooking oil
4 ounces fresh mushrooms, quartered lengthwise
½ cup sherry
2 tablespoons finely chopped parsley

1. Combine flour, salt, and pepper; sprinkle over veal slices. Pound slices until thin, flat, and round, working flour mixture into both sides. Cut into ¼-inch-wide strips.
2. Heat oil in a large wok. Add veal strips and stir-fry over high heat until golden.
3. Sprinkle mushrooms on top and pour sherry over all. Simmer, uncovered, about 15 minutes, or until tender.
4. Toss with parsley and serve.

4 servings

803 *Beef Polynesian*

2 tablespoons cooking oil
1 pound lean ground beef
1 can (4 ounces) mushrooms, drained
½ cup golden raisins
1 package (10 ounces) frozen green peas
½ cup beef broth
1 teaspoon curry powder
1 tablespoon soy sauce
1 orange, sliced
½ cup salted cashews
Fried Rice

1. Heat oil in a large wok. Add ground beef and separate into small pieces; cook until lightly browned.
2. Add mushrooms, raisins, peas, broth, curry powder, and soy sauce. Break block of peas apart, if necessary, and gently toss mixture to blend.
3. Arrange orange slices over top. Cover loosely and cook over low heat 15 minutes.
4. Mix in cashews and serve with Fried Rice.

About 4 servings

Fried Rice: Cook **½ cup chopped onion** in **2 tablespoons butter** until golden. Mix in **2 cups cooked rice** and **2 tablespoons soy sauce.** Cook over low heat, stirring occasionally, 5 minutes. Stir in **1 slightly beaten egg** and cook until set.

804

805 *Deep-Fried Beef Pies*

Pastry:
1 cup all-purpose flour
½ teaspoon salt
⅓ cup shortening
2 or 3 tablespoons cold water

Filling:
¾ pound lean ground beef
2 tablespoons shortening
1½ teaspoons olive oil
1 teaspoon salt
¼ teaspoon black pepper
⅛ teaspoon cayenne pepper
1 ripe tomato, peeled and cut in pieces
⅓ cup finely chopped green pepper
¼ cup finely chopped carrot
¼ cup finely chopped celery
¼ cup finely chopped onion
¼ cup finely chopped green onion
1 tablespoon chopped hot red pepper
1 tablespoon snipped parsley
1 tablespoon snipped seedless raisins
1 tablespoon chopped pitted green olives
1 tablespoon capers
¼ cup water
Oil for deep frying

1. To make pastry, sift flour and salt together into a bowl. Cut in shortening with pastry blender or two knives until pieces are the size of small peas.
2. Sprinkle water over mixture, a teaspoonful at a time, mixing lightly with a fork after each addition. Add only enough water to hold pastry together. Shape into a ball and wrap in waxed paper; chill.
3. To make filling, cook ground beef in hot shortening and olive oil in a large skillet, separating meat with a spoon. Remove from heat and drain off fat. Mix in remaining ingredients except the oil for deep frying. Cover and simmer 30 minutes.
4. Working with half the chilled pastry at a time, roll out ⅛ inch thick on a lightly floured surface. Using a lightly floured 4-inch cutter, cut into rounds. Place 1 tablespoon filling on each round. Moisten edges with cold water, fold pastry over, press edges together, and tightly seal.
5. Slowly heat the oil for deep frying in a wok to 375°F.
6. Fry one layer at a time in the heated oil until lightly browned on both sides (about 3 minutes.) Drain on absorbent paper.

About 16 pies

806 *Stir-Fry Beef and Broccoli*

2 pounds broccoli
2 pounds beef round or chuck, boneless
¼ cup olive oil
2 cloves garlic, minced
3 cups hot chicken broth
4 teaspoons cornstarch
¼ cup cold water
3 tablespoons soy sauce
1 teaspoon salt
2 cans (16 ounces each) bean sprouts, drained and rinsed

1. Cut broccoli into pieces about 2½ inches long and ¼ inch thick; set aside. Slice beef very thin and cut diagonally into 4x½-inch strips; set aside.
2. Heat 1 tablespoon olive oil with garlic in a large wok. Add half the beef and stir-fry until evenly browned. Remove cooked meat from the wok and stir-fry remaining beef, adding more olive oil, if necessary.
3. Pour 1 tablespoon olive oil in the wok. Add half the broccoli and stir-fry over high heat ½ minute. Remove cooked broccoli from the wok and stir-fry remaining broccoli ½ minute, adding more oil, if necessary.
4. Place all the broccoli in the wok; cover and cook 3 minutes. Remove broccoli and keep warm.
5. Blend into broth a mixture of cornstarch, cold water, soy sauce, and salt. Bring to boiling, stirring constantly, and cook until mixture thickens.
6. Add bean sprouts, broccoli, and beef; toss to mix. Heat thoroughly and serve over **hot fluffy rice.**

8 servings

807 *Chicken with Almonds*

2 tablespoons cooking oil
⅓ cup chopped onion
1 cup chopped celery
1 can (4 ounces) mushrooms, liquid included
2 cups diced cooked chicken
1 can (5 ounces) water chestnuts, drained and sliced
2 tablespoons cornstarch
¼ teaspoon ground ginger
3 tablespoons soy sauce
¾ cup chicken bouillon
½ cup toasted almonds

1. Heat oil in a large wok. Add onion and celery; cook until soft. Stir in mushrooms and chicken and heat gently, stirring occasionally. Mix in water chestnuts and push mixture up on sides of wok.
2. Combine cornstarch, ginger, soy sauce, and bouillon. Stir into liquid in middle of wok. Cook until sauce thickens, stirring constantly.
3. When sauce thickens, combine with chicken mixture and almonds. Serve immediately over **hot fluffy rice.**

6 servings

Note: If desired, cashew nuts may be used instead of almonds.

808 Batter-Fried Chicken

1 broiler-fryer, cut into serving pieces
1½ cups sifted flour
½ teaspoon salt
Dash pepper
1½ teaspoons baking powder
1 egg, beaten
1½ cups milk
Oil for deep frying

1. Steam chicken in a large wok until tender. Dry and refrigerate until time to fry.
2. Just before frying the chicken, combine the dry ingredients. Blend the egg with milk and combine the liquid with the dry ingredients.
3. Slowly heat oil in a wok to 375°F. Sprinkle chicken pieces with salt and pepper. Dip chicken in batter, allow excess to drain off, and fry a few pieces at a time until brown. Drain and serve either hot or cold.

2 to 4 servings

809 Good Fortune Chicken with Pineapple Piquant

1 egg, fork beaten
⅓ cup water
1 tablespoon milk
¼ cup flour
1 tablespoon cornstarch
1 tablespoon cornmeal
⅛ teaspoon baking powder
12 small chicken legs
Oil for deep frying heated to 365°F
1 tablespoon cooking oil
½ cup green pepper chunks
½ cup onion chunks
1 can (about 15 ounces) pineapple chunks (reserve syrup)
½ cup cider vinegar
½ cup packed brown sugar
2 tablespoons soy sauce
¼ cup water
1 tablespoon cornstarch

1. Beat egg, water, and milk with a mixture of flour, cornstarch, cornmeal, and baking powder in a bowl until smooth. Dip each chicken leg into the batter and drain over bowl a few seconds.
2. Fry pieces in hot oil 15 minutes, or until chicken is crisp-brown and tender. Remove with a slotted spoon and drain over fat; place on absorbent paper.
3. Meanwhile, heat 1 tablespoon cooking oil in a large wok, and cook green pepper and onion until crisp-tender, stirring occasionally. Push vegetables up on sides of wok.
4. Pour in reserved pineapple syrup; add vinegar, brown sugar, soy sauce, and a mixture of water and cornstarch. Stir until blended. Mix in pineapple. Bring rapidly to boiling, stirring constantly; cook 3 minutes.
5. Pour sauce over chicken legs and serve. If desired, add 1 tablespoon sesame seed to sauce, or sprinkle over chicken when served.

4 to 6 servings

810 *Chicken Tokay*

6	chicken breasts (about 4 pounds), skinned, boned, and split
1½	teaspoons salt
¼	teaspoon pepper
1	teaspoon crushed rosemary
3	tablespoons butter or margarine
¼	cup chopped onion
2	chicken bouillon cubes
1	cup boiling water
1	tablespoon lemon juice
4	teaspoons cornstarch
2	tablespoons cold water
1½	cups seeded and halved Tokay grapes (about 1 pound)

1. Rub chicken breasts with a mixture of the salt, pepper, and rosemary. Brown chicken slowly and evenly in hot butter in a large wok, pushing chicken up on sides of wok as it is browned.
2. Stir the onion into center of wok and cook until lightly browned, stirring occasionally. Stir chicken into onion.
3. Dissolve bouillon cubes in the boiling water and combine with lemon juice. Pour over chicken and onion. Cover and simmer until chicken is tender when pierced with a fork (about 20 minutes). Remove chicken from wok; keep hot.
4. Blend cornstarch with cold water. Stir into liquid in wok, blending thoroughly. Bring rapidly to boiling and boil 3 minutes, stirring constantly. Add grapes and chicken to wok and spoon sauce over all. Heat to serving temperature and serve immediately sprinkled with snipped **parsley**.

About 6 servings

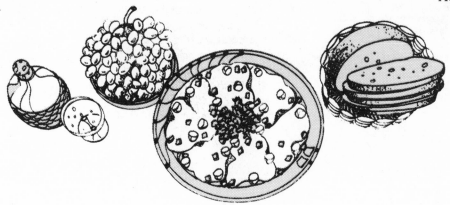

811 *Chicken Croquettes*

5 to 6	tablespoons butter or margarine
5 to 6	tablespoons flour
¼	teaspoon salt
	Few grains pepper
1½	cups milk
2	cups finely chopped or ground cooked chicken
1	tablespoon finely chopped parsley
1	tablespoon lemon juice
½	teaspoon onion juice
½	teaspoon salt
¼	teaspoon celery salt
1	cup fine dry bread crumbs
1	egg, slightly beaten
1	tablespoon milk
	Oil for deep frying

1. Heat butter in saucepan over low heat. Blend in flour, salt, and pepper. Heat until mixture is bubbly. Remove from heat and gradually stir in milk.
2. Cook rapidly, stirring constantly, until sauce thickens. Cook 1 to 2 minutes longer.
3. Mix together lightly the chicken, parsley, lemon juice, onion juice, salt, and celery salt. Combine with the sauce. Refrigerate until chilled.
4. Shape chilled mixture into balls, cones, or cylinders. Roll in bread crumbs, then dip in a mixture of the egg and milk. Roll again in bread crumbs, shaking off loose crumbs.
5. Slowly heat oil in a wok to 375°F. Deep-fry the croquettes, a few at a time, turning frequently to brown evenly. Drain on absorbent paper and serve immediately.

6 servings

Chinatown Chop Suey, page 282

812 *Oriental Pineapple Chicken*

12 chicken wings
½ teaspoon monosodium glutamate
¼ teaspoon ground ginger
2 tablespoons cooking oil
1 clove garlic, minced
Chicken broth (about 1½ cups)
1 can (8½ ounces) pineapple
    slices (reserve syrup)
½ cup soy sauce
2 tablespoons cider vinegar
2 tablespoons cornstarch
1 cup diagonally sliced celery
4 green onions, diagonally sliced
1 can (5 ounces) water chestnuts,
    drained and halved
1 can (16 ounces) bean sprouts,
    drained and rinsed
¼ cup toasted blanched almonds

1. Remove and discard tips from chicken wings; cut wings in half at joint. Toss with a mixture of monosodium glutamate and ginger.
2. Heat oil in a large wok and stir in garlic. Brown the chicken pieces.
3. Add enough chicken broth to the pineapple syrup to make 1⅔ cups liquid; gradually pour into the wok. Cover and simmer 15 minutes, or until wings are tender.
4. Push chicken up on sides of wok. Stir in a mixture of soy sauce, vinegar, and cornstarch. Add celery and green onion. Bring to boiling and cook 3 minutes, stirring constantly. Mix in water chestnuts, bean sprouts, almonds, and 2 pineapple slices, cut in large pieces. Move chicken through mixture. Heat thoroughly.
5. Turn into a heated serving dish. Garnish with remaining pineapple slices.

4 servings

813 *Pineapple Trout*

4 trout (about 6 ounces each)
1 lemon, cut in half
2 tablespoons flour
¼ teaspoon salt
Pinch pepper
2 to 3 tablespoons cooking oil
3 tablespoons finely sliced green
    onions (including tops)
5 tablespoons sugar
1½ tablespoons cornstarch
½ teaspoon ground ginger
1 can (13½ ounces) pineapple
    chunks, drained (reserve
    syrup)
¼ cup wine vinegar
1 tablespoon soy sauce
½ teaspoon bead molasses

1. Remove fins and heads from trout; rinse fish under running cold water and pat dry with absorbent paper. Rub inside of fish with lemon. Coat fish with a mixture of the flour, salt, and pepper.
2. Fry the trout in hot oil in a wok over medium heat until golden brown on one side. Turn and cook until browned on other side and fish flakes easily; sprinkle green onion over fish the last 2 or 3 minutes of cooking.
3. Transfer to a serving platter and keep warm. If desired, remove bones from fish.
4. Pour out any oil remaining in wok. Combine sugar, cornstarch, and ginger in wok. Stir in the reserved pineapple syrup plus enough water to make 1⅓ cups, the vinegar, soy sauce, and molasses. Bring rapidly to boiling; boil 2 to 3 minutes, stirring constantly. Stir in the pineapple chunks. Spoon over the fish and serve immediately.

4 servings

Eggnog Fondue, page 275

814 *Steamed Fish Slices*

1 **pound frozen sole or turbot fillets, thawed**
3 **green onions including tops, sliced**
½ **teaspoon minced ginger root**
8 **medium mushrooms, thinly sliced**
1 **tablespoon cider vinegar**
1 **tablespoon soy sauce**
1 **tablespoon cooking oil**
¼ **teaspoon sugar**
  Generous dash pepper

1. Place fish fillets on a plate, skin side down, so that they fit in a large wok. Scatter onion, ginger root, and mushrooms over fish.
2. Combine remaining ingredients and pour over fish and vegetables.
3. Steam fish 10 minutes, or until fish flakes easily (see steaming instructions, page 7), and serve immediately.

2 or 3 servings

815 *Sweet and Sour Fish*

1 **bass or other firm white fish (about 1½ pounds), cleaned and dressed with tail left on**
½ **cup flour**
2 **medium carrots, pared and cut diagonally into ⅛-inch slices**
  Oil for deep-frying
2 **green onions (including tops), sliced diagonally into ¼-inch pieces**
¼ **teaspoon ground ginger**
2 **medium green peppers, cleaned and cut in thin strips**
4 **large mushrooms, thinly sliced**
½ **teaspoon salt**
5 **tablespoons sugar**
5 **tablespoons cider vinegar**
2 **tablespoons Japanese soy sauce**
1 **tablespoon dry sherry**
2 **tablespoons cornstarch**
1 **cup cold water**

1. Rinse fish in cold water and pat dry on inside and outside. With a sharp knife or cleaver, cut off head and discard. Lay the fish on its side and split in half along the backbone, removing backbone but not the tail.
2. Make three or four diagonal cuts on each side of the fish on the inside, not the skin side. Coat the fish with flour on inside and outside. Shake off excess.
3. Place carrot slices in boiling salted water. Bring to rapid boil and cook 2 to 3 minutes. Remove and set aside to drain.
4. Heat oil in a large wok to 375°F. Lower the fish into hot oil by holding it by its tail, keeping fish open and almost flat. Deep-fry 5 to 8 minutes, or until it is golden. Lift the fish out of the oil and drain on absorbent paper toweling. Keep fish warm while making sauce.
5. Remove all but 2 tablespoons oil from wok. Stir in green onion tossed with ginger, stir-frying a minute or two. Add carrots, green pepper, and mushrooms; stir-fry 2 to 3 minutes.
6. Add salt, sugar, vinegar, soy sauce, and sherry. Combine cornstarch with water and stir into mixture in wok. Cook, stirring, until sauce is thickened and vegetables are glazed.
7. Place fish on a warm platter, pour sauce over fish, and serve.

3 or 4 servings

816 *Fried Clams*

1 **quart fresh clams, shucked**
2 **eggs, beaten**
2 **tablespoons milk**
2 **teaspoons salt**
  Few grains pepper
3 **cups dry bread crumbs**
  Oil for deep frying

1. Drain clams and set aside.
2. Combine egg, milk, salt, and pepper. Dip clams in egg mixture and roll in bread crumbs.
3. Heat oil to 350°F in a wok. Fry a few clams at a time in the hot oil 1 to 2 minutes, or until brown. Drain on absorbent paper.
4. Serve hot with **tartar sauce.**

About 6 servings

817 *Rock Lobster, Cantonese Style*

6 **South African rock lobster tails
(3 to 5 ounces each), thawed
Lime butter***
2 **cups shredded cabbage**
1½ **cups diagonally sliced celery**
1 **cup thawed frozen or fresh
peas**
6 **green onions, cut into ½-inch
pieces**
4 **carrots, cut into thin diagonal
slices**
3 to 4 **tablespoons cooking oil**
1 **cup vegetable broth**
¼ **cup soy sauce**
1 **teaspoon monosodium glutamate**
1 **teaspoon sugar**

1. Using scissors, cut away the thin underside membrane of lobster tails. Remove meat and cut into ½- to ¾-inch pieces.
2. Cook lobster pieces slowly in hot lime butter in a large wok 5 minutes, or until lobster is opaque and tender. Set aside and keep warm.
3. Cook vegetables 5 minutes in hot oil in a wok over medium heat, stirring frequently. Stir in vegetable broth, soy sauce, monosodium glutamate, and sugar. Simmer, uncovered, 10 minutes.
4. Toss lobster with vegetables; serve with **hot fluffy rice.**

6 to 8 servings

*Blend desired amount of lime juice with melted butter.

818 *Shrimp Jambalaya*

2 to 3 **tablespoons cooking oil**
½ **cup chopped onion**
½ **cup chopped green onion**
½ **cup chopped green pepper**
½ **cup chopped celery**
¼ **pound diced cooked ham**
2 **cloves garlic, minced**
2 **cups chicken broth**
3 **large tomatoes, coarsely
chopped**
¼ **cup chopped parsley**
½ **teaspoon salt**
⅛ **teaspoon pepper**
¼ **teaspoon thyme**
⅛ **teaspoon cayenne pepper**
1 **bay leaf**
1 **cup uncooked rice**
3 **cans (4½ ounces each) shrimp,
rinsed under running cold
water**
¼ **cup coarsely chopped green
pepper**

1. Heat oil in a large wok over low heat. Stir in onion, green onion, green pepper, celery, ham, and garlic. Cook over medium heat about 5 minutes, or until onion is tender, stirring occasionally.
2. Stir in chicken broth, tomatoes, parsley, salt, pepper, thyme, cayenne pepper, and bay leaf; cover and bring to boiling.
3. Add rice gradually, stirring with a fork. Simmer, covered, 20 minutes, or until rice is tender.
4. Mix in shrimp and remaining green pepper. Simmer, uncovered, about 5 minutes longer.

6 to 8 servings

819 *Noodle Supper*

½ **pound lean ground beef**
1 **teaspoon salt**
¼ **cup chopped parsley**
1 **package (1½ ounces) dry
onion soup mix**
1 **quart hot water**
1 **cup sliced carrots**
4 **ounces medium noodles**

1. Place ground beef in a large wok. Sprinkle with salt and brown lightly, stirring frequently.
2. Stir in parsley, soup mix, water, and carrots. Bring to boiling. Reduce heat and simmer 10 to 15 minutes, stirring occasionally.
3. Stir in noodles and cover. Cook about 10 minutes, or until noodles are tender.

4 servings

820 *Stir-Fried Shrimp and Vegetables*

¾ **pound fresh bean sprouts**
2 **tablespoons cornstarch**
2 **teaspoons sugar**
1½ **cups water**
2 **tablespoons Japanese soy sauce**
3 **tablespoons white wine vinegar**
½ **teaspoon pepper**
2 **tablespoons sesame oil**
1 **teaspoon salt**
1 **cup diagonally sliced celery**
6 **green onions, sliced diagonally into 1-inch pieces**
1 **cup thinly sliced fresh mushrooms**
1 **tablespoon sesame oil**
2 **cloves garlic, minced**
1 **teaspoon minced fresh ginger root**
¾ **pound cleaned and cooked shrimp**
1 **package (6 ounces) frozen snow peas, thawed and well drained**

1. Blanch bean sprouts by turning half of them into a sieve or basket and setting in a saucepan of boiling water. Boil 1 minute. Remove from water and spread out on absorbent paper to drain. Repeat with remaining bean sprouts.
2. Blend cornstarch, sugar, water, soy sauce, vinegar, and pepper; set aside.
3. Heat 2 tablespoons sesame oil in a large wok. Stir in salt, celery, green onion, and mushrooms. Stir-fry vegetables about 1 minute. Add bean sprouts and stir-fry 1 minute more. Remove vegetables from wok.
4. Heat 1 tablespoon sesame oil. Add garlic and ginger root; stir-fry briefly. Add shrimp and snow peas; stir-fry 1 minute longer. Return other vegetables to wok and mix together. Stir-fry briefly to heat.
5. Push vegetables and shrimp up sides of wok. Stir cornstarch mixture into liquid in center of wok. Cook until thickened and combine with shrimp and vegetables. Serve immediately.

4 servings

821 *Noodle Omelet*

1½ **cups (4 ounces) noodles**
3 **tablespoons butter**
2 **tablespoons chopped onion**
3 **eggs**
2 **tablespoons milk or water**
½ **teaspoon salt**
⅛ **teaspoon pepper**

1. Cook noodles according to package directions. Drain well.
2. Melt butter in a large wok over low heat. Add onion and cook until soft but not browned. Stir in noodles.
3. Meanwhile, beat eggs, milk, salt, and pepper with a fork; beat just enough to mix well. Pour over noodle mixture.
4. Cook rapidly, lifting mixture with fork, at the same time tilting wok to let uncooked egg mixture flow to bottom.
5. When mixture is set, reduce heat and cook 1 or 2 minutes longer to brown the bottom. Loosen edges and slide a spatula underneath to be sure omelet is free. Fold in half and slide out of wok onto a warm platter.

4 servings

822 *Deep-Fried Noodles*

6 **ounces fine noodles**
Oil for deep frying

1. Cook noodles in boiling salted water according to package directions. Rinse with cold water, drain, separate, and place on absorbent paper to dry.
2. Heat oil in a wok to 375°F. Place about ½ cup noodles in the hot oil. Fry until golden brown, turning once.
3. Drain on absorbent paper and sprinkle with salt, if desired. If not to be used immediately, noodles may be reheated in a 400°F oven.

4 to 6 servings

823 *Curried Rice*

1 tablespoon cooking oil
1 cup minced onion
1 cup chopped green pepper
½ cup currants
2 cups uncooked rice
1 teaspoon salt
½ teaspoon pepper
½ teaspoon curry powder
1 quart chicken broth

1. Heat oil in a large wok. Stir in onion, green pepper, and currants. Stir-fry until tender (about 10 minutes).
2. Stir in rice and seasonings; brown slightly.
3. Pour broth over rice and mix well. Bring to boiling, cover, and simmer 20 to 25 minutes, or until rice is tender.

8 servings

824 *Bacon-and-Egg Fried Rice*

10 slices bacon
½ cup chopped onion
1 cup diagonally sliced celery
1 cup sliced mushrooms
3 cups cooked rice
2 tablespoons Japanese soy sauce
1 egg, slightly beaten

1. Cook bacon, 5 slices at a time, in a large wok until crisp. Remove bacon and pour out all but 3 tablespoons bacon drippings.
2. Stir-fry onion and celery in the hot fat until almost tender. Stir in mushrooms, rice, and soy sauce. Cook 5 minutes over low heat, stirring occasionally.
3. Stir in egg and cook only until egg is set. Turn into a serving dish. Crumble bacon over top and serve immediately.

6 servings

825 *Fried Rice*

2 tablespoons butter
¾ cup uncooked rice
2 tablespoons very finely
   chopped fresh mushrooms
½ teaspoon grated onion
3 chicken bouillon cubes
2½ cups boiling water
1 tablespoon finely chopped
   carrot
1 tablespoon finely chopped
   green pepper

1. Melt butter in a wok over low heat. Add rice, mushrooms, and onion. Cook until golden brown.
2. Dissolve bouillon cubes in boiling water and stir into rice mixture. Cover and cook over low heat 30 minutes, or until rice is tender.
3. Add carrot and green pepper; toss lightly.

About 8 servings

826 *French-Style Green Beans with Water Chestnuts*

1 can (5 ounces) water chestnuts, drained, sliced, and slivered
3 tablespoons chopped onion
¼ cup butter or margarine
½ teaspoon salt
Few grains pepper
2 tablespoons lemon juice
1 teaspoon soy sauce
1 pound fresh green beans, frenched, cooked, and drained

1. Brown slivered water chestnuts and onion in hot butter in a large wok. Stir in a mixture of salt, pepper, lemon juice, and soy sauce. Heat thoroughly.
2. Add green beans and toss with sauce. Turn into a heated serving dish.

About 6 servings

827 *Old-fashioned Green Beans*

¾ pound fresh green beans
8 slices bacon, diced
2 medium potatoes, pared and cut into ½-inch pieces
1 small onion, sliced
¼ cup water
½ teaspoon salt

1. Cut green beans into 1-inch pieces. Cook in boiling salted water until tender; drain.
2. Fry bacon in a wok until crisp. Stir in green beans, potatoes, onion, water, and salt.
3. Cook, covered, over medium heat about 15 minutes, or until potatoes are tender.

About 4 servings

828 *Fried Green Pepper Strips*

2 large green peppers
½ cup fine dry bread crumbs
⅓ cup grated Parmesan cheese
1½ teaspoons salt
⅛ teaspoon pepper
1 egg, fork beaten
2 tablespoons water
Oil for frying

1. Clean green peppers and cut into ⅛-inch rings. Cut each ring into halves or thirds.
2. Coat with a mixture of bread crumbs, cheese, salt, and pepper. Dip into a mixture of egg and water. Coat again with crumb mixture. Chill 1 hour.
3. Heat a 1-inch layer of oil to 375°F in a large wok. Cover surface with chilled green pepper strips. Fry about 30 seconds, or until golden brown. Remove strips with fork or slotted spoon. Drain on absorbent paper.

4 servings

829 *Mushrooms in Sour Cream*

1½ pounds fresh mushrooms
½ cup butter
½ large clove garlic, chopped
1 small onion, sliced
¼ teaspoon paprika
2 tablespoons white wine
½ cup dairy sour cream

1. Wash mushrooms and pat dry. Slice lengthwise through caps and stems.
2. Heat butter in a large wok. Add garlic and onion; cook until onion is soft.
3. Add mushrooms and paprika; stir-fry mushrooms about 5 minutes, or until mushrooms are lightly browned.
4. Add wine to wok, reduce heat, and cook mushrooms several minutes, stirring occasionally.
5. Just before serving, blend in sour cream and heat about 1 minute. Serve immediately on **hot fluffy rice.**

4 to 6 servings

830 *Stir-Fried Peas*

1 **package (10 ounces) frozen peas, thawed**
1 **tablespoon vegetable oil**
½ **teaspoon salt**
⅛ **teaspoon pepper**
1 **medium onion, peeled, cut in half lengthwise, and sliced ¼ inch thick**

1. Drain peas on paper toweling to remove as much moisture as possible.
2. Heat oil in a large wok. Stir in salt and pepper. Add drained peas; stir-fry to coat with oil and heat through. Simmer, covered, over medium heat 2 minutes.
3. Stir in onion and continue cooking 2 minutes.
4. Serve immediately.

4 servings

831 *Summer Squash with Bacon*

2 **pounds (about 4 small) summer squash (yellow straight-neck), washed**
3 **slices bacon, diced**
¼ **cup finely chopped onion**
1 **teaspoon salt**
Few grains pepper

1. Trim ends from squash and cut squash into thin diagonal slices; set aside.
2. Cook bacon in a wok until crisp and brown. Remove bacon from wok and all but 3 tablespoons of the bacon drippings.
3. Stir in squash, onion, salt, and pepper. Cover and cook over medium heat 12 minutes, or until squash is tender. Stir in bacon and serve.

About 6 servings

832 *Creole Fried Tomatoes*

1 **small clove garlic, minced**
1 **tablespoon finely chopped parsley**
½ **teaspoon salt**
Dash pepper
¼ **cup finely chopped onion**
1 **tablespoon olive oil**
2 **large tomatoes, cut into ½- inch-thick slices**
2 **tablespoons cornmeal**
2 **teaspoons olive oil**

1. Combine garlic, parsley, salt, pepper, and onion. Mix in 1 tablespoon olive oil.
2. Spread both sides of each tomato slice with mixture. Sprinkle slices with cornmeal.
3. Heat 2 teaspoons olive oil in a large wok. Fry tomato slices until lightly browned, pushing slices up sides as they are cooked. (Additional oil may be added, if necessary.)

4 servings

833 *Mallow Sweet Potato Balls*

3 cups warm mashed sweet
    potatoes
    Salt and pepper to taste
3 tablespoons melted butter
8 large marshmallows
1 egg
1 tablespoon cold water
1 cup almonds, blanched and
    chopped
    Oil for deep frying

1. Season potatoes and add butter. Mold potato mixture around marshmallows, forming 8 balls with a marshmallow in center of each.
2. Beat egg and mix with cold water. Dip sweet potato balls in egg and then in almonds.
3. Slowly heat oil in a wok to 365°F. When oil is hot, fry sweet potato balls until brown, turning occasionally.

8 servings

834 *Zucchini Parmesan*

2 tablespoons cooking oil
1 small clove garlic, minced
4 medium zucchini, thinly sliced
⅓ cup coarsely chopped onion
1 tablespoon chopped parsley
1 teaspoon salt
⅛ teaspoon pepper
¼ teaspoon oregano
¼ teaspoon rosemary
2 cups chopped peeled tomatoes
¼ cup grated Parmesan cheese

1. Heat oil in a large wok. Add garlic and stir-fry about 1 minute. Stir in zucchini, onion, and parsley. Sprinkle with a mixture of salt, pepper, oregano, and rosemary. Stir together and cover.
2. Heat about 5 minutes over medium heat. Stir in tomatoes and cook, uncovered, 1 to 2 minutes, or until tomatoes are thoroughly heated.
3. Turn mixture into a serving dish and sprinkle with cheese.

4 or 5 servings

835 *Fried Cream*

⅓ cup sugar
¼ cup cornstarch
¼ teaspoon salt
4 egg yolks
¼ cup milk
2 cups whipping cream, scalded
½ teaspoon vanilla extract
    Fine dry bread crumbs
2 eggs, slightly beaten
    Oil for deep frying

1. Mix sugar, cornstarch, and salt in a heavy saucepan.
2. Mix egg yolks with milk; blend with dry ingredients. Add scalded cream, stirring until smooth.
3. Cook and stir mixture until thickened and smooth.
4. Remove from heat and stir in vanilla extract. Turn into a lightly greased 8-inch square dish or pan. Chill thoroughly.
5. Cut cream into squares. Coat with bread crumbs, then with slightly beaten eggs, and again with bread crumbs.
6. Pour oil into wok, filling wok not more than a third full. Heat to 365°F. Fry cream squares in hot oil until browned (about 2 minutes).

25 pieces

Chafing Dish

836 *Hot Cheese Dunk*

3 tablespoons butter or
    margarine
1 tablespoon flour
¼ teaspoon white pepper
¼ teaspoon Tabasco
½ cup instant nonfat dry milk
    solids
1 can (10½ ounces) chicken
    bouillon
½ medium onion
1 cup freshly grated Parmesan
    cheese
4 ounces Swiss cheese, shredded
    (about 1 cup)

1. In cooking pan of a chafing dish, melt butter. Blend in flour, pepper, and Tabasco.
2. Dissolve nonfat dry milk in bouillon. Gradually stir into flour mixture and add onion. Cook over medium heat, stirring constantly, until sauce thickens.
3. Remove onion and stir in cheeses until melted. Place over hot water to keep mixture warm.
4. Serve hot as a dunking sauce for cooked shrimp, ham cubes, rye toast, apple slices, or fresh uncooked vegetables.

About 2 cups dunk

Note: Dunk thickens upon standing and may be thinned with small amounts of chicken bouillon.

837 *Shrimp Mexican Style*

1 can (4 ounces) peeled green
    chilies
½ cup minced onion
3 medium cloves garlic, minced
¼ cup olive oil
2 tablespoons flour
1 cup half-and-half
8 ounces Monterey Jack cheese,
    shredded (about 2 cups)
4 ounces sharp Cheddar cheese,
    shredded (about 1 cup)
¼ cup dry white wine
½ teaspoon paprika
1 pound cooked shrimp, shelled,
    deveined, and cut in bite-size
    pieces

1. Rinse seeds from chilies; dice and set aside.
2. In cooking pan of chafing dish, sauté onion and garlic in oil over medium heat until soft but not browned. Add flour, stirring constantly. Stir over medium heat 3 minutes.
3. Gradually add half-and-half, stirring until very smooth. Add both cheeses gradually, stirring after each addition until the mixture is smooth.
4. Stir in wine, paprika, diced chilies, and shrimp. Heat thoroughly and place over simmering water to keep warm.
5. Serve warm with **corn chips**, pieces of **crisp fried tortillas**, or **crackers**.

4 to 6 servings

838 *Chili con Queso Dip*

1 **cup chopped onion**
2 **cans (4 ounces each) green
chilies, chopped and drained**
2 **large cloves garlic, mashed**
2 **tablespoons cooking oil**
1 **pound process sharp Cheddar
cheese, cut into chunks**
1 **teaspoon Worcestershire sauce**
¼ **teaspoon paprika**
¼ **teaspoon salt**
½ **cup tomato juice**

1. Sauté onion, green chilies, and garlic in oil in cooking pan of chafing dish over medium heat until onion is tender.
2. Reduce heat to low, and add remaining ingredients, except tomato juice. Cook, stirring constantly, until cheese is melted.
3. Add tomato juice gradually until dip is the desired consistency. Place over hot water to keep warm.
4. Serve with **corn chips.**

3¼ cups dip

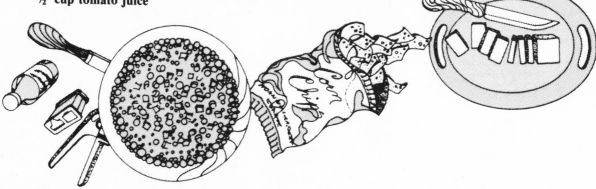

839 *Hot Cheese Dunking Sauce*

½ **cup shredded Cheddar cheese**
¾ **cup milk**
3 **tablespoons condensed cream of
mushroom soup**
⅛ **teaspoon pepper**
1½ **teaspoons Worcestershire sauce**
2 **tablespoons prepared horseradish
French bread, cut into 1-inch
cubes**

1. In cooking pan of chafing dish or in fondue pot, combine cheese and milk. Place over low heat, add soup, and stir constantly until cheese is melted,
2. Stir in pepper, Worcestershire sauce, and horseradish.
3. Keep hot in chafing dish and serve with French bread cubes.

1½ cups sauce

840 *Hot Crab Meat Dip*

2 **tablespoons butter or
margarine**
3 **tablespoons flour**
½ **teaspoon salt**
1 **cup milk**
¼ **cup shredded Cheddar
cheese**
½ **cup mayonnaise**
2 **tablespoons tomato paste**
¼ **teaspoon Worcestershire
sauce**
1 **cup flaked crab meat**

1. Melt butter in cooking pan of chafing dish. Stir in flour and salt. Add milk, stirring until mixture thickens. Blend in cheese.
2. Combine mayonnaise, tomato paste, and Worcestershire sauce. Stir in some of the hot mixture. Pour back into cooking pan. Stir in crab meat.
3. Keep warm while serving with **crackers, toast rounds, potato chips,** or **corn chips.**

About 1½ cups dip

841 *Beef Stroganoff*

1 **pound beef tenderloin, sirloin,**
  or rib, boneless, cut into
  2x½x¼-inch strips
¼ **cup flour**
½ **teaspoon salt**
  Pinch black pepper
3 **tablespoons butter or margarine**
¼ **cup finely chopped onion**
1 **cup beef broth**
1½ **tablespoons butter or margarine**
¼ **pound fresh mushrooms, sliced**
  lengthwise
½ **cup dairy sour cream**
1½ **tablespoons tomato paste**
½ **teaspoon Worcestershire sauce**

1. Coat meat strips evenly with a mixture of flour, salt, and pepper.
2. Heat 3 tablespoons butter in a large heavy skillet. Add meat strips and onion. Brown on all sides over medium heat, turning occasionally. Add broth; cover and simmer about 20 minutes.
3. Heat 1½ tablespoons butter in cooking pan of a chafing dish over medium heat. Add mushrooms and cook until lightly browned and tender. Add meat and liquid to mushrooms.
4. Blending well after each addition, add a mixture of sour cream, tomato paste, and Worcestershire sauce in small amounts. Place over simmering water and continue cooking, stirring constantly, until thoroughly heated (do not boil).

About 4 servings

842 *Hamburger Stroganoff*

1½ **pounds lean ground beef**
2 **large onions, sliced**
2 **cans (10½ ounces each) con-**
  densed cream of chicken soup
1 **pint dairy sour cream**
1 **teaspoon salt**
  Dash black pepper

1. Sauté ground beef and onions in a small amount of fat in cooking pan of a chafing dish until meat is well browned.
2. Stir in condensed soup, sour cream, salt, and pepper.
3. Cook, covered, over direct heat of chafing dish until thoroughly heated.

About 6 servings

843 *Embassy Veal Glacé*

1½ **teaspoons dry tarragon leaves**
1 **cup dry white wine**
1½ **pounds veal round steak (about**
  ¼ inch thick)
3 **tablespoons butter or margarine**
½ **teaspoon salt**
⅛ **teaspoon pepper**
½ **cup condensed beef consommé**
½ **cup dry vermouth**

1. Stir tarragon into white wine; cover and set aside ˖ral hours, stirring occasionally.
2. Cut meat into pieces about 3x2 inches. Heat butter in cooking pan of chafing dish until lightly browned. Add meat and lightly brown on both sides; season with salt and pepper.
3. Reduce heat and pour in tarragon-wine mixture with the consommé and vermouth. Simmer, uncovered, about 10 minutes, or until veal is tender.
4. Remove veal to a platter and cover.
5. Increase heat under pan and cook sauce until it is reduced to a thin glaze, stirring occasionally. Return veal to pan and spoon sauce over meat, turning meat once.
6. Cover and place over direct heat of chafing dish until warm.

About 6 servings

844 *Orange Pork Chops*

1 cup orange juice
3 tablespoons instant minced onion
2 teaspoons grated orange peel
1 tablespoon brown sugar
½ teaspoon marjoram, crushed
¼ teaspoon thyme, crushed
4 pork chops, cut about 1 inch thick
½ teaspoon salt
⅛ teaspoon pepper
  Cooking oil
  Oranges, pared and sectioned

1. Combine orange juice onion, orange peel, brown sugar, marjoram, and thyme; set aside.
2. Season pork chops with salt and pepper. Brown chops well on both sides in a small amount of oil in a heavy skillet.
3. Place chops in cooking pan of a chafing dish. Add orange juice mixture. Cook, covered, over low heat about 45 minutes, or until chops are very tender. If desired, thicken the sauce slightly with a cornstarch-water mixture.
4. Add orange sections and heat 5 to 10 minutes over direct heat of chafing dish.

4 servings

845 *Peach 'n' Pork Chop Barbecue*

6 pork chops, cut 1 inch thick
1 tablespoon fat
¼ cup lightly packed brown sugar
1 teaspoon ground cinnamon
½ teaspoon ground cloves
1 can (8 ounces) tomato sauce
6 canned cling peach halves, drained (reserve ¼ cup syrup)
¼ cup cider vinegar
1 teaspoon salt
¼ teaspoon pepper

1. Brown chops on both sides in hot fat in a large heavy skillet.
2. Meanwhile, blend a mixture of brown sugar, cinnamon, and cloves with tomato sauce, reserved peach syrup, and vinegar.
3. Place pork chops in cooking pan of chafing dish. Sprinkle with salt and pepper. Place a peach half on each chop. Pour sauce over all.
4. Cover skillet and simmer about 30 minutes, or until pork is tender; baste occasionally with the sauce.

6 servings

846 *Dutch Sausage with Gravy*

1 pound bulk pork sausage
1 to 2 tablespoons water
1 small onion, minced
1 tablespoon flour
1 cup beef broth

1. Shape sausage into 4 to 6 flat cakes. Put sausage cakes into a skillet. Add water; cover tightly and cook slowly about 5 minutes. Remove cover and cook slowly until well browned on both sides.
2. Remove cakes to cooking pan of a chafing dish and keep warm.
3. Drain off all but 3 tablespoons fat from skillet. Brown onion in the fat. Stir in flour and cook 1 minute. Stir in broth; simmer 5 minutes.
4. Pour gravy over sausage cakes and heat thoroughly.

4 to 6 servings

847 *Sausage, Hominy, and Tomato Scramble*

1 pound bulk pork sausage
½ cup fine dry bread crumbs
⅔ cup undiluted evaporated milk
½ teaspoon rubbed sage
¼ cup flour
2 cans (16 ounces each) tomatoes
1 can (20 ounces) hominy, drained
1 teaspoon salt
¼ teaspoon rubbed sage

1. Combine sausage, bread crumbs, evaporated milk, and ½ teaspoon sage. Mix well and shape into 16 balls. Roll balls in flour to coat, reserving remaining flour.
2. In cooking pan of a chafing dish, brown meatballs over low heat, turning frequently.
3. Remove all but 3 tablespoons of the fat from the pan. Stir in reserved flour, tomatoes, hominy, salt, and sage; blend well.
4. Cook, covered, over low heat about 15 minutes, or until sauce is thickened. Keep warm over chafing dish burner until ready to serve.

6 to 8 servings

848 *Ham à la Cranberry*

2 cups sugar
¼ teaspoon salt
2 cups water
1 pound (about 4 cups)
    cranberries, washed and sorted
2 teaspoons grated lemon peel
6 cups cubed cooked smoked ham
    or luncheon meat
½ cup seedless raisins (optional)

1. Combine sugar, salt, and water in a saucepan and heat to boiling. Boil, uncovered, 5 minutes. Add cranberries and continue to boil, uncovered, without stirring, about 5 minutes, or until skins pop.
2. Turn cranberry sauce into cooking pan of a chafing dish. Blend in lemon peel, ham, and raisins, if desired. Cook over direct heat until mixture starts to bubble; stir occasionally.
3. Place over simmering water to keep mixture hot. Serve over **toast triangles, patty shells,** or **hot biscuits.**

8 to 10 servings

849 *Lamb and Rice*

3 tablespoons butter or margarine
½ cup chopped onion
½ cup diced green pepper
1 can (10½ ounces) tomato purée
1 teaspoon bottled brown bouquet
    sauce
¼ cup ketchup
1 can (8¼ ounces) diced carrots
2 cups ground cooked lamb
1 teaspoon salt
1 cup packaged precooked rice
1 cup chicken bouillon

1. In cooking pan of a chafing dish, melt butter. Stir in onion and green pepper; cook over medium heat until vegetables are lightly browned.
2. Stir in remaining ingredients and cover. Cook over low heat 10 minutes, or until thoroughly heated and rice is tender.
3. Place over simmering water to keep warm.

4 to 6 servings

850 *Cherried Chicken*

> 2 large chicken breasts, skinned
> and boned
> 3 to 4 tablespoons flour
> ½ teaspoon salt
> ¼ teaspoon paprika
> ⅛ teaspoon curry powder
> 2 to 3 tablespoons butter
> ½ cup dry white wine
> 1 can (8¼ ounces) pitted dark
> sweet cherries, drained
> ¼ cup pineapple chunks

1. Dredge chicken in a mixture of flour, salt, paprika, and curry powder. Heat butter in cooking pan of a chafing dish. Cook chicken slowly in the butter until golden brown on all sides.
2. Add wine and cover pan tightly. Simmer 30 minutes, or until chicken is tender.
3. Add cherries and pineapple. Heat over simmering water until heated through.

2 servings

851 *Mexican Chicken*

> 2 tablespoons cooking oil
> 1 cup slivered almonds
> 1 cup chopped onion
> 1 medium clove garlic, minced
> ⅛ teaspoon cinnamon
> ⅛ teaspoon cloves
> ¼ teaspoon pepper
> 1 ounce (1 square) unsweetened
> chocolate, coarsely chopped
> 2 cans (7 ounces each) green
> chili sauce
> 1 can (15 ounces) tomato sauce
> 2 cups bite-size pieces cooked
> chicken or turkey

1. In cooking pan of a chafing dish, heat the oil, Sauté almonds, onion, and garlic 10 minutes over medium heat, stirring often.
2. Stir in remaining ingredients except chicken. Heat, stirring, until chocolate melts. Purée mixture in a blender or force through a food mill.
3. Return mixture to cooking pan and stir in chicken. Simmer 5 minutes.
4. Serve over **hot fluffy rice.** Garnish with **avocado** or **orange slices, dairy sour cream,** or **slivered almonds.**

4 servings

852 *Chicken Livers Superb*

> 2 pounds chicken livers
> ¼ cup flour
> 1 cup finely chopped onion
> ½ cup butter
> 5 ounces fresh mushrooms,
> cleaned, sliced lengthwise
> through stems and caps, and
> lightly browned in butter
> 2 tablespoons Worcestershire sauce
> 2 tablespoons chili sauce
> 1 teaspoon salt
> ¼ teaspoon pepper
> ½ teaspoon rosemary
> ½ teaspoon thyme
> 2 cups dairy sour cream

1. Rinse and drain chicken livers. Pat free of excess moisture with absorbent paper. Coat lightly with flour. Set aside.
2. Lightly brown onion in heated butter in a large skillet, stirring occasionally. Remove half the onion-butter mixture and set aside for second frying of livers. Add half the chicken livers and cook, occasionally moving and turning with a spoon, about 5 minutes, or until lightly browned. Turn into the cooking pan of a chafing dish. Fry remaining livers, using all the onion-butter mixture; turn into the cooking pan. Set aside.
3. After browning mushrooms, blend a mixture of Worcestershire sauce, chili sauce, salt, pepper, rosemary, and thyme with the mushrooms. Heat thoroughly.
4. Adding sour cream in small amounts at a time and stirring constantly, quickly blend with mushroom mixture. Heat thoroughly (do not boil). Mix gently with livers to coat.
5. Set cooking pan over simmering water. Before serving, garnish with wreaths of **sieved hard-cooked egg white, watercress, and sieved hard-cooked egg yolk.** Serve with buttered toasted **English muffins.**

About 8 servings

Note: If desired, blend in ¼ cup dry sauterne or sherry with the sour cream.

853 *Chicken Curry with Rice*

⅓ cup butter or margarine
3 tablespoons chopped onion
3 tablespoons chopped celery
3 tablespoons chopped green apple
12 peppercorns
1 bay leaf
⅓ cup sifted flour
2½ teaspoons curry powder
½ teaspoon monosodium glutamate
¼ teaspoon sugar
Pinch nutmeg
2½ cups milk
2 teaspoons lemon juice
½ teaspoon Worcestershire sauce
3 cups cubed cooked chicken
¼ cup cream
2 tablespoons sherry
¼ teaspoon Worcestershire sauce

1. Heat butter in a heavy saucepan over low heat. Add onion, celery, apple, peppercorns, and bay leaf. Cook over medium heat until lightly browned, stirring occasionally.
2. Blend in a mixture of flour, curry powder, monosodium glutamate, sugar, and nutmeg. Heat until mixture bubbles. Remove from heat and gradually add milk, stirring constantly.
3. Return pan to heat and bring sauce rapidly to boiling. Stirring constantly, cook until sauce thickens; cook 1 to 2 minutes longer. Remove from heat and stir in lemon juice and Worcestershire sauce. Strain sauce through a fine sieve, pressing vegetables against sieve to extract all the sauce.
4. Transfer the sauce to cooking pan of a chafing dish and place over simmering water. Blend cream, sherry, and Worcestershire sauce into the warm sauce. Add cubed chicken and cook, covered, until mixture is thoroughly heated.
5. Serve with **hot fluffy rice,** and curry condiments such as **preserved kumquats, chutney, shredded coconut,** and **finely chopped roasted peanuts.**

4 servings

854 *Chinese Chicken Crepes*

16 crepes
2 tablespoons butter or margarine
½ cup thinly sliced green onion
1 cup cooked rice
¼ cup chopped parsley
1 can (8 ounces) water chestnuts, drained and sliced
2 cups bite-size pieces cooked chicken
1 teaspoon lemon juice
Chinese Sauce

1. Prepare crepes and set aside.
2. Melt butter in a large skillet. Add green onion and rice. Cook 5 minutes over low heat, stirring occasionally.
3. Stir in parsley, water chestnuts, chicken, and lemon juice. Remove from heat and stir in 1 cup Chinese Sauce.
4. Spoon a heaping ¼ cup of chicken filling onto one end of each crepe on the unbrowned side. Roll up crepes and set aside.
5. Heat about half the remaining Chinese Sauce in the cooking pan of a chafing dish. Add half the filled crepes and heat over simmering water. As crepes are heated, serve them, and place other crepes in the sauce to heat.

8 servings

855 *Basic Crepes*

1 cup all-purpose flour
⅛ teaspoon salt
3 eggs
1½ cups milk
2 tablespoons melted butter or oil

1. Sift flour and salt. Add eggs, one at a time, beating thoroughly. Gradually add milk, mixing until blended. Add melted butter or oil and beat until smooth. (Or mix in an electric blender until smooth.)
2. Let batter stand for 1 hour before cooking crepes.
3. Heat a 7-inch skillet or crepe pan over moderately high heat. Grease lightly. Pour 3 tablespoons batter into pan and tilt pan with a swirling motion to cover bottom evenly. When brown on first side, turn over and cook other side.
4. Continue making crepes with remaining batter, greasing pan as necessary. Stack crepes on a plate or sheet of waxed paper until ready to fill.

16 crepes

856 *Chinese Sauce*

¼ cup cornstarch
4 cups chicken broth
¼ cup soy sauce
¾ cup sherry
1 teaspoon sugar

1. In a saucepan, mix cornstarch with chicken broth. Stir in remaining ingredients.
2. Cook over medium heat, stirring occasionally, until mixture thickens and comes to boiling. Remove from heat.

857 *Chicken and Ham en Crème*

¼ cup butter or margarine
¼ cup flour
½ teaspoon salt
⅛ teaspoon white pepper
½ teaspoon dry mustard
1 cup chicken broth
1½ cups cream
2 egg yolks, slightly beaten
1 cup cooked ham pieces
1½ cups cooked chicken or turkey
    pieces
¾ teaspoon grated lemon peel

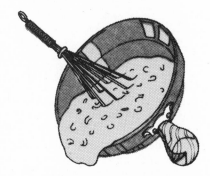

1. Heat butter in a large saucepan over low heat. Blend in a mixture of the flour, salt, pepper, and dry mustard. Heat until bubbly.
2. Gradually add chicken broth and cream, stirring constantly. Bring to boiling, stir and cook 1 to 2 minutes.
3. Vigorously stir about 3 tablespoons of the hot mixture into the egg yolks. Immediately blend into mixture in saucepan, stirring constantly. Cook and stir 2 to 3 minutes. Mix in ham, chicken, and lemon peel.
4. Turn mixture into cooking pan of a chafing dish. Place over simmering water and heat thoroughly (do not boil).

About 6 servings

Chicken and Ham Almond: Follow recipe for 858
Chicken and Ham en Crème. Omit lemon peel. Add ¾ **cup salted almonds.**

Creamed Chicken and Ham with Olives: 859
Follow recipe for Chicken and Ham en Creme. Add ¾ **cup coarsely chopped ripe olives** with chicken and ham.

860 *Chicken à la King with Ham Rolls*

⅓ cup butter or margarine
⅓ cup flour
1 cup chicken broth
1 cup milk
½ teaspoon salt
⅛ teaspoon pepper
1 teaspoon grated onion
1½ cups large-diced cooked chicken
¼ cup diced green pepper
1 pimento, diced
1 can (4 ounces) sliced mushrooms
    (liquid included)
2 tablespoons dry sherry (optional)
6 slices boiled ham
12 cooked asparagus tips

1. Melt butter in a saucepan; add flour and stir over medium heat until bubbly. Stir in broth and milk. Cook, stirring constantly, until thickened and smooth.
2. Stir in next seven ingredients and heat thoroughly. Stir in wine, if desired.
3. Roll two asparagus tips in each ham slice. Place in cooking pan of a chafing dish. Spoon chicken à la king over ham rolls and cover pan.
4. Place over simmering water until thoroughly heated.

About 6 servings

861 *Turkey Royal*

¼ cup butter or margarine
1 tablespoon minced onion
6 tablespoons flour
1 teaspoon salt
  Few grains cayenne pepper
  Few grains nutmeg
2 cans (4 ounces each) button
    mushrooms
  Milk
3 egg yolks, slightly beaten
2 cups dairy sour cream
1 tablespoon minced parsley
1 tablespoon minced chives
¼ cup pimento strips
½ cup cooked peas
2 cups cooked turkey pieces

1. Heat butter in cooking pan of a chafing dish. Add onion and cook over low heat, stirring occasionally, until onion is transparent.
2. Blend in flour, salt, cayenne, and nutmeg. Heat until bubbly. Drain mushrooms and add enough milk to mushroom liquid to make 1 cup liquid.
3. Remove cooking pan from heat and gradually add liquid, stirring constantly. Return to heat and cook over low heat until mixture thickens, stirring constantly. Cook 1 to 2 minutes longer; remove from heat.
4. Vigorously stir about 3 tablespoons of the hot mixture into the egg yolks. Immediately blend into mixture in cooking pan. Cook over simmering water 5 to 10 minutes, or until thoroughly heated. Stir slowly to keep mixture cooking evenly. Remove from heat.
5. Using a French whip, wire whisk, or fork, vigorously stir sour cream, a little at a time, into hot mixture. Mix in parsley, chives, pimento strips, peas, mushrooms, and turkey.
6. Cook over simmering water, stirring constantly, 3 to 5 minutes, or until thoroughly heated.

6 servings

Chicken Royal: Follow recipe for Turkey Royal, **862** substituting **cooked chicken** for the turkey.

863 *Salmon Rabbit*

4 ounces sharp Cheddar cheese,
    shredded (about 1 cup)
1 cup tomato purée
½ teaspoon salt
1 teaspoon prepared mustard
1 tablespoon Worcestershire sauce
2 eggs, slightly beaten
1 cup evaporated milk
1 can (16 ounces) salmon, drained

1. In cooking pan of a chafing dish, melt cheese over simmering water. Gradually blend in tomato purée, salt, mustard, and Worcestershire sauce, stirring constantly.
2. Combine eggs with milk and slowly stir into cheese mixture. Add salmon, separated into large chunks, and heat thoroughly. Serve on **hot buttered toast.**

6 servings

864 *Tuna Supreme*

⅔ cup chopped onion
1 green pepper, cut into slivers
2 tablespoons cooking oil
1 can (10¾ ounces) condensed
    tomato soup
2 teaspoons soy sauce
2 to 3 tablespoons brown sugar
1 teaspoon grated lemon peel
3 tablespoons lemon juice
2 cans (6½ or 7 ounces each)
    tuna, drained

1. Cook onion and green pepper until almost tender in hot oil in cooking pan of a large chafing dish; stir occasionally.
2. Mix in condensed tomato soup, soy sauce, brown sugar, and lemon peel and juice. Bring to boiling; simmer 5 minutes.
3. Mix in tuna, separating it into small pieces. Cover and heat thoroughly over simmering water.
4. Serve with **hot fluffy rice.** Garnish with **toasted sesame seed** and **chow mein noodles.**

About 6 servings

865 *Crab Ravigote*

¼ cup butter
¼ cup flour
1 teaspoon salt
  Few grains cayenne pepper
2 cups milk
⅔ cup chopped cooked green pepper
⅔ cup coarsely chopped pimento
2 tablespoons capers
2 teaspoons tarragon vinegar
2 cups lump crab meat
⅔ cup Hollandaise Sauce

1. Heat butter in cooking pan of a chafing dish; blend in flour, salt, and cayenne pepper; heat until bubbly. Gradually add milk, stirring constantly. Cook and stir until boiling; cook 1 minute.
2. Stir in remaining ingredients and heat thoroughly over simmering water.
3. Serve on **rusks**.

4 servings

Hollandaise Sauce: In the top of a double boiler, beat **2 egg yolks, 2 tablespoons cream, ¼ teaspoon salt,** and a **few grains cayenne pepper** until thick with a whisk beater. Set over hot (not boiling) water. Add **2 tablespoons lemon juice or tarragon vinegar** gradually, while beating constantly. Cook, beating constantly with the whisk beater, until sauce is consistency of thick cream. Remove double boiler from heat, leaving top in place. Beating constantly, add ½ **cup butter,** ½ teaspoon at a time, until the butter is melted and thoroughly blended in.

About 1 cup

866 *Lobster Newburg*

¼ cup butter or margarine
2 cups cream
¾ teaspoon salt
⅛ teaspoon pepper
⅛ teaspoon nutmeg
2 cups cooked lobster meat (1-inch pieces)
4 egg yolks, slightly beaten
2 tablespoons sherry

1. Melt butter in cooking pan of a chafing dish. Blend in cream, salt, pepper, and nutmeg. Bring just to boiling. Stir in lobster and cook over low heat until lobster is thoroughly heated.
2. Vigorously stir about 3 tablespoons of the hot mixture into the egg yolks. Immediately blend into hot mixture. Place over simmering water and cook 3 to 5 minutes, or just until mixture thickens. Stir slowly to keep mixture cooking evenly. (Do not overcook as sauce will curdle.) Remove immediately from heat.
3. Blend in sherry and serve on **toast points** or over **hot fluffy rice.**

About 6 servings

Crab Meat Newburg: Follow recipe for Lobster Newburg. Substitute **2 cups cooked crab meat** for the lobster. Remove and discard bony tissue from meat.

867 *Creamed Crab Meat and Mushrooms*

1 can (6½ ounces) crab meat
　　(about 1⅓ cups, drained)
½ pound mushrooms
　Milk
5 tablespoons butter or margarine
1 tablespoon minced onion
1 tablespoon chopped chives
1 tablespoon chopped parsley
6 tablespoons flour
1 teaspoon salt
　Few grains cayenne pepper
　Few grains nutmeg
3 egg yolks, slightly beaten
2 cups dairy sour cream
¼ cup sherry
6 Croustades

1. Remove and discard bony tissue from crab and set aside to drain.
2. Remove stems from mushroom caps. Slice both stems and caps. Set caps aside. Place stems in a small saucepan and pour in just enough cold water to barely cover the sliced stems.
3. Slowly bring to boiling, reduce heat and simmer 15 minutes. Remove from heat and drain stems, reserving liquid. Add enough milk to liquid to make 1 cup; set aside.
4. Melt butter in cooking pan of a chafing dish. Add sliced mushroom caps, drained mushroom stems, onion, chives, and parsley. Cook over medium heat until mushrooms are lightly browned and tender; stir occasionally. Remove vegetables with a slotted spoon and set aside.
5. Blend flour, salt, cayenne pepper, and nutmeg into butter in cooking pan. Heat until mixture bubbles; remove from heat.
6. Add mushroom liquid mixture gradually while stirring constantly. Return to heat and cook, stirring constantly, until mixture thickens. Cook 1 to 2 minutes longer and remove from heat.
7. Vigorously stir about 3 tablespoons of the hot mixture into the egg yolks. Immediately return to cooking pan and place over simmering water. Cook 3 to 5 minutes, stirring slowly to keep mixture cooking evenly.
8. Add the crab meat and vegetable mixture. Stirring occasionally, cook 10 to 12 minutes, or until thoroughly heated. Remove from heat.
9. Stirring vigorously with a French whip, wire whisk, or fork, add sour cream to sauce in small amounts. Stir in sherry.
10. Serve over Croustades immediately.

6 servings

868 *Croustades*

1 loaf dry bread, unsliced
　Melted butter or margarine

1. Cut bread loaf into 1¼ to 2-inch thick slices. Remove crusts and cut bread into desired shapes (see Note).
2. Brush outside and inside surfaces of shells with melted butter and place on a baking sheet.
3. Bake at 325°F 12 to 20 minutes, or until lightly browned and crisp. If shells are not to be used immediately, reheat in oven for a few minutes before filling.

6 croustades

Note: Bread slices may be cut into triangles, squares, or diamonds; or cut into rounds or fancy shapes with a large biscuit or cookie cutter. (If cutter is not deep enough, mark with it and finish cutting with the point of a sharp knife.) Following outline of shaped piece, carefully cut out center ¼ to ½ inch from edge, and down to within ¼ to ½ inch of bottom, leaving a neatly cut shell.

869 Creamed Oysters and Turkey

6 tablespoons butter or margarine
6 tablespoons flour
¾ teaspoon salt
¼ teaspoon pepper
3 cups milk or cream
1 can (2¼ ounces) deviled
    ham
3 cups cooked turkey pieces
½ pint oysters (shell particles
    removed)
8 toast cups

1. Heat butter in cooking pan of a chafing dish over direct heat. Blend in flour, salt, and pepper. Heat until mixture bubbles, stirring constantly.
2. Gradually add milk, stirring constantly; cook 1 to 2 minutes longer. Mix in the deviled ham, turkey, and oysters. Heat thoroughly, stirring occasionally. Keep hot over simmering water, if necessary.
3. Fill toast cups with creamed mixture. Serve immediately.

8 servings

Toast cups: To make 8 toast cups, cut crusts from **8 thin bread slices.** Lightly brush both sides with **melted butter or margarine** and press each slice into a muffin pan well, corners pointing up. Toast in a 325°F oven 12 to 20 minutes, or until crisp and lightly browned.

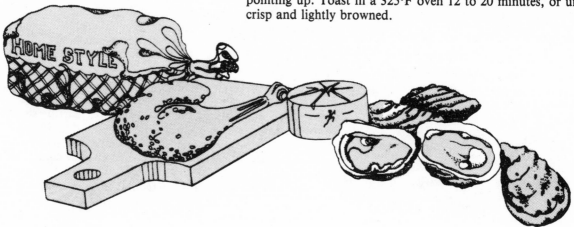

870 Oysters à la Newburg

1 pint oysters
1 teaspoon water
½ teaspoon dry mustard
¼ cup butter or margarine
2 tablespoons flour
1 teaspoon salt
⅛ teaspoon nutmeg
⅛ teaspoon pepper
2 cups half-and-half
¼ teaspoon Worcestershire sauce
4 egg yolks, slightly beaten
2 tablespoons sherry

1. Heat oysters in their own liquor just until edges curl. Drain; set aside and keep warm. Blend water with dry mustard and set aside.
2. Heat butter in top of a double boiler over direct heat. Blend in flour, salt, nutmeg, and pepper. Heat until mixture is bubbly. Remove from heat.
3. Gradually add half-and-half and Worcestershire sauce, stirring constantly. Blend mustard mixture into sauce. Bring rapidly to boiling over direct heat, stirring constantly. Cook 1 to 2 minutes longer.
4. Vigorously stir about 3 tablespoons of the hot mixture into the egg yolks. Immediately blend into mixture in top of double boiler and place over simmering water. Cook 3 to 5 minutes, stirring slowly to keep mixture cooking evenly. Remove from heat.
5. Blend in sherry; add oysters and turn into cooking pan of a chafing dish. Keep warm over simmering water and serve on crisp toast.

6 servings

371 *Oysters Royale*

6 tablespoons butter
½ clove garlic, minced
½ cup diced celery
½ cup diced green pepper
6 or 7 tablespoons flour
½ teaspoon salt
¼ teaspoon white pepper
Few grains cayenne pepper
2 cups half-and-half
1½ pints oysters, drained
(reserve ⅓ cup liquor)*
1 teaspoon prepared mustard
2 ounces Gruyère cheese, cut into pieces
¼ cup dry sherry

1. Heat butter in a saucepan. Add garlic, celery, and green pepper; cook about 5 minutes, or until vegetables are crisp-tender. Remove vegetables with a slotted spoon and set aside.
2. Blend a mixture of flour, salt, and peppers, into butter in saucepan; heat until mixture bubbles. Remove from heat; add half-and-half and reserved oyster liquor gradually, stirring constantly. Continue stirring, bring to boiling, and boil 1 to 2 minutes. Remove from heat.
3. Blend in mustard and cheese, stirring until cheese is melted. Mix in wine, vegetables, and oysters. Bring just to boiling and remove from heat. (Edges of oysters should just begin to curl.) Turn into cooking pan of a chafing dish and set over simmering water.
4. Accompany with a basket of **toasted buttered 3½-inch bread rounds** sprinkled lightly with **ground nutmeg.**

10 to 12 servings

*The amount of liquor in a pint of oysters varies; using slightly less than ⅓ cup will not affect the recipe.

372 *Neapolitan Shrimp*

3 tablespoons olive or other cooking oil
2 cloves garlic, minced
2 pounds cleaned and shelled shrimp (thawed if frozen)
8 anchovies, cut into pieces
2 cans (16 ounces each) tomatoes, forced through a food mill
8 pimento-stuffed olives, sliced
8 pitted ripe olives, sliced
2 teaspoons capers
1 teaspoon dried basil
⅛ teaspoon Tabasco
¼ teaspoon sugar

1. In cooking pan of a chafing dish, heat oil. Add garlic and cook over low heat until tender but not browned.
2. Stir in shrimp. Cook until shrimp turns pink and flesh is firm (about 5 minutes). Remove shrimp from pan and set aside.
3. Add anchovies to liquid in cooking pan; cook 1 minute. Add tomatoes and simmer over low heat 10 minutes. Add olives, capers, basil, Tabasco, and sugar. Cook, uncovered, 15 minutes.
4. Add shrimp to sauce and heat 10 minutes. Keep warm over simmering water. Serve over **hot fluffy rice.**

6 servings

373 *Shrimp Meunière*

1½ pounds uncooked shrimp, shelled
½ cup butter
1 tablespoon lime juice
¼ teaspoon salt
⅛ teaspoon freshly ground black pepper
1 teaspoon minced fresh parsley

1. Wash shelled shrimp and pat dry. Melt butter in cooking pan of a chafing dish. Stir in the shrimp and cook, turning often, until lightly browned (about 10 minutes).
2. Using a slotted spoon, remove shrimp to a warm platter. Add lime juice, salt, and pepper to butter in pan. Heat thoroughly, return the shrimp to the cooking pan, and coat with the butter sauce.
3. Sprinkle parsley over top and serve shrimp with **hot fluffy rice.**

4 to 6 servings

874 *Shrimp Aphrodite*

1 can (12 ounces) apricot
   nectar
1¼ cups water
2 tablespoons cider vinegar
2 tablespoons sugar
½ teaspoon ground ginger
½ teaspoon dry mustard
½ teaspoon dried tarragon
¼ teaspoon salt
5 cups julienned cooked ham
1½ cups thinly sliced celery
2 cups cooked shrimp, halved
   lengthwise
1 jar (4 ounces) pimentos,
   cut into strips
3 tablespoons butter
¾ cup thinly sliced white
   onion
1½ tablespoons cornstarch
3 tablespoons lime juice

1. Combine apricot nectar, water, vinegar, sugar, ginger, dry mustard, tarragon, and salt. Cover and chill at least 4 hours.
2. Combine ham, celery, shrimp, and pimento. Cover and chill.
3. When ready to serve, melt butter in cooking pan of a chafing dish. Sauté the onion until soft but not brown. Stir in the chilled apricot mixture; cover and simmer 10 minutes.
4. Stir in the chilled ham, celery, shrimp, and pimento. Cover and simmer 10 minutes. Blend cornstarch with lime juice. Stir carefully into mixture until sauce bubbles. Cook 1 to 2 minutes, stirring constantly. Serve over **hot fluffy rice.**

6 to 8 servings

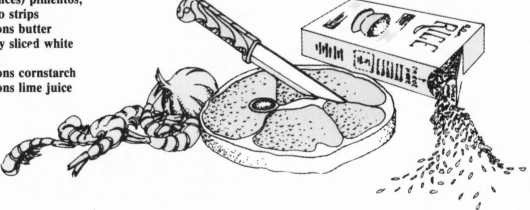

875 *Noodles with Cream and Eggs*

8 ounces medium noodles
½ cup butter
¾ cup freshly grated Parmesan
   cheese
   Freshly ground black pepper
2 egg yolks, slightly beaten
½ cup whipping cream, warmed

1. Cook noodles in boiling salted water as directed on package; drain.
2. Melt butter in cooking pan of a chafing dish. Place cooking pan over simmering water, add noodles to pan, and toss gently with butter. Sprinkle on cheese and a generous amount of pepper while tossing.
3. When cheese is well mixed and noodles are coated, stir egg yolks into the noodles.
4. Toss the noodles again and add whipping cream. Toss again and serve immediately in hot soup bowls.

4 to 6 servings

876 *Shupp Noodles*

6 ounces uncooked noodles
½ cup butter
3 eggs
½ teaspoon salt
   Pinch pepper

1. Cook noodles in boiling salted water about 10 minutes. Rinse and drain well.
2. Melt butter in cooking pan of a chafing dish. Add the cooked noodles and cook over low heat until lightly browned, stirring occasionally.
3. Beat eggs with salt and pepper, and stir into the noodles. Cook over simmering water until eggs are set.

4 to 6 servings

877 *Shrimp Creole*

¼ cup butter or margarine
½ cup chopped onion
½ cup chopped celery
⅓ cup chopped green pepper
3 tablespoons flour
1 can (16 ounces) tomatoes, sieved
1 bay leaf
1 large sprig parsley
1½ teaspoons salt
1 teaspoon sugar
¾ teaspoon Worcestershire sauce
¼ teaspoon freshly ground
  black pepper
2 or 3 drops Tabasco
¾ pound cooked shrimp

1. Heat butter in cooking pan of a chafing dish. Add onion, celery, and green pepper. Cook over medium heat, stirring occasionally, until onion is transparent and other vegetables are tender.
2. Blend in flour and heat until mixture is bubbly. Gradually stir in remaining ingredients except shrimp.
3. Simmer sauce, covered, 30 minutes. Remove bay leaf and parsley. Stir in shrimp and cook over simmering water until thoroughly heated. Serve over **hot fluffy rice**.

4 or 5 servings

878 *Shrimp in Sour Cream Sauce*

¼ cup butter or margarine
2 tablespoons olive oil
1 cup chopped scallions or
  green onions
1 pound fresh mushrooms,
  sliced
¼ cup finely chopped parsley
¼ cup Madeira
1½ pounds fresh shrimp, peeled,
  deveined, rinsed, and drained
½ to 1 teaspoon salt
⅛ teaspoon black pepper
1 cup dairy sour cream

1. Heat butter and olive oil in cooking pan of a chafing dish over direct heat. Add scallions and cook 2 minutes. Add mushrooms and cook 5 minutes. Mix in parsley and wine. Add shrimp and cook until they turn pink. Season with salt and pepper.
2. Remove from heat. Blend in sour cream and heat (*do not boil*). Sprinkle with an additional 2 teaspoons wine, if desired. Place cooking pan over hot water. Serve on **toast rounds**.

About 6 servings

879 *Spaghetti-Cheese Pie*

8 ounces spaghetti, cooked
  and drained
½ cup chopped celery
¼ cup chopped onion
1 tablespoon poppy seed
½ teaspoon salt
¼ teaspoon pepper
½ cup evaporated milk
3 tablespoons butter or margarine
8 ounces sharp Cheddar cheese,
  shredded (about 2 cups)

1. Combine spaghetti, celery, onion, poppy seed, salt, pepper, and evaporated milk in a large bowl.
2. Heat butter in cooking pan of a chafing dish. Spoon half the spaghetti mixture into the pan, spreading evenly. Sprinkle with 1½ cups cheese. Top with remaining spaghetti mixture and cheese.
3. Cover and cook over simmering water 15 to 25 minutes, running a spatula under mixture occasionally to prevent sticking.
4. Cut into six wedges and serve.

6 servings

880 *Chili Don Pedro*

8 ounces medium noodles,
  cooked and drained
1 tablespoon butter or margarine
3 cans (about 16 ounces each)
  chili with beans
8 ounces creamed cottage cheese
1 package (8 ounces) cream
  cheese, cut into ¾-inch cubes
½ cup dairy sour cream

1. Toss cooked noodles with butter; keep warm.
2. Mix chili, cheeses, and sour cream in cooking pan of a large chafing dish. Cover and simmer until the mixture is thoroughly heated, stirring occasionally. If necessary, blend in additional sour cream until of desired consistency.
3. To serve, combine noodles with the chili mixture and sprinkle **snipped parsley** over top.

8 servings

881 *Garlic-Buttered Noodles*

½ cup butter
1 clove garlic, minced
1 teaspoon salt
¼ teaspoon pepper
8 ounces medium noodles,
  cooked and drained
1 cup bread crumbs, browned
  in butter

1. Place butter, garlic, salt, and pepper in cooking pan of a chafing dish. Heat just until butter is lightly browned.
2. Place cooking pan over simmering water. Add noodles and crumbs. Toss lightly until noodles are well coated and crumbs are evenly distributed.

About 8 servings

882 *Glossy Carrots*

24 small whole carrots, pared
  and cooked
¼ cup butter or margarine
¼ cup thawed frozen orange
  juice concentrate
2 teaspoons honey
½ teaspoon ground ginger
½ teaspoon salt

1. While carrots are cooking, melt butter in cooking pan of a chafing dish. Blend in orange juice concentrate, honey, and a mixture of ginger and salt.
2. Add carrots and heat over chafing dish burner, turning carrots until well glazed.

About 4 servings

883 Corn with Mushrooms

2 tablespoons butter or margarine
¼ cup thinly sliced green onion
⅔ cup coarsely chopped mushrooms
1 can (12 ounces) whole kernel corn, drained
½ cup cream
½ teaspoon salt
⅛ teaspoon pepper
2 tablespoons snipped parsley

1. Melt butter in cooking pan of a chafing dish. Add onion and mushrooms and sauté 5 minutes.
2. Add corn and stir mixture gently over medium heat until thoroughly heated.
3. Add cream, salt, pepper, and parsley. Place over simmering water to keep warm until ready to serve.

4 to 6 servings

884 Green Beans with Tomato

1 pound fresh green beans, cut diagonally into 1-inch pieces
¼ cup butter or margarine
¼ cup finely chopped onion
1 small clove garlic, crushed in a garlic press
1 tablespoon lemon juice
2 medium-size ripe tomatoes, cut into pieces
1 tablespoon brown sugar
1 teaspoon salt
⅛ teaspoon black pepper
½ teaspoon oregano

1. Cook green beans in boiling salted water until tender; drain.
2. While beans are cooking, heat butter in cooking pan of a chafing dish. Add onion and garlic and cook over medium heat 3 minutes. Add remaining ingredients and heat thoroughly, stirring occasionally.
3. Add green beans to tomato mixture; mix gently. Place over simmering water to keep warm.

6 to 8 servings

885 Mushrooms Supreme

2 pounds mushrooms
3 tablespoons lemon juice
¼ teaspoon salt
⅛ teaspoon white pepper
½ cup butter or margarine
2 tablespoons grated onion
¼ teaspoon Worcestershire sauce
¼ teaspoon salt
¼ teaspoon white pepper
Few grains cayenne pepper
¼ cup shredded sharp Cheddar cheese

1. Remove stems from mushrooms. (Use stems for other food preparation.) Put mushroom caps into a shallow dish and drizzle with a mixture of lemon juice, ¼ teaspoon salt, and ⅛ teaspoon white pepper. Cover and marinate in refrigerator about 1 hour, turning gently several times.
2. Remove mushrooms from marinade and drain thoroughly on absorbent paper. Heat half the butter in cooking pan of a chafing dish over direct heat. Add about half the mushroom caps and half the grated onion.
3. Cook 10 to 15 minutes, or until caps are lightly browned and tender, turning with a spoon occasionally. Remove mushroom caps to a bowl and cook remaining mushrooms.
4. Place all mushroom caps in cooking pan and add Worcestershire sauce, salt, white pepper, and cayenne pepper. Toss gently to mix.
5. Sprinkle cheese over mushrooms and set pan over simmering water to keep hot while serving. Serve mushrooms on **toast triangles** and garnish with **parsley sprigs**.

6 to 8 servings

886 *Caramel Sweet Potatoes*

⅓ cup butter
½ cup walnut pieces
1 cup firmly packed brown sugar
½ teaspoon salt
½ cup orange juice
6 medium (about 2 pounds) sweet potatoes, cooked
⅓ cup brandy

1. Melt butter in cooking pan of a chafing dish. Stir in walnut pieces. Cook over moderate heat until lightly toasted.
2. Remove walnuts from pan. Add brown sugar, salt, and orange juice to butter remaining in cooking pan; stir to blend. Bring to boiling and boil 3 to 4 minutes, stirring occasionally.
3. Peel the sweet potatoes and cut in halves lengthwise. Add to the syrup with walnut pieces.
4. Place cooking pan over chafing dish burner. Heat the potatoes gently, basting with the syrup. Warm the brandy, pour over potatoes, and ignite. Serve when flames die out.

6 servings

887 *Glazed Fruit in Chafing Dish*

2 tart red apples, cored
2 tablespoons lemon juice
2 tablespoons butter
3 tablespoons brown sugar
1 large banana
½ cup pineapple chunks, fresh or unsweetened canned
1 cup pineapple juice
1 tablespoon cornstarch
Vanilla ice cream

1. Cut apples into wedges. Dip in lemon juice and place in medium-size bowl.
2. Melt butter in cooking pan of a chafing dish over medium heat. Toss apple slices with half the brown sugar and stir into melted butter. Cover and cook over medium heat 7 to 8 minutes, stirring occasionally.
3. When apple slices are almost tender, slice banana into chunks and add with pineapple to apple mixture. Sprinkle remaining brown sugar over fruit, cover, and cook several minutes until bananas are glazed.
4. Remove fruit from cooking pan. Stir in pineapple juice mixed with cornstarch. Simmer a few minutes, stirring occasionally, until sauce thickens.
5. Return fruit to sauce, warm, and serve over ice cream.

4 servings

888 *Fruit Topaz*

3 apples, pared, cored, and sliced
3 pears, pared, cored, and sliced
1 cup firmly packed light brown sugar
1 tablespoon nutmeg
1 cup golden raisins
½ cup slivered almonds
¼ cup butter or margarine
¼ cup lemon-lime carbonated beverage

1. Place apple and pear slices in cooking pan of a chafing dish. Combine sugar and nutmeg and sprinkle over fruit.
2. Sprinkle raisins and almonds over fruit. Dot top of mixture with butter. Pour carbonated beverage over all.
3. Cook over medium heat until fruit is tender (15 to 20 minutes).
4. Keep warm over simmering water while serving.

6 servings

889 *Brandied Bananas*

4 large green-tipped bananas,
　　sliced diagonally into 1-inch
　　pieces
3 tablespoons lime juice
¼ cup butter or margarine
½ cup sugar
½ cup apricot brandy
1 cup dairy sour cream or yogurt
　　Brown sugar

1. Sprinkle bananas with lime juice. Heat butter in cooking pan of a chafing dish over medium flame of chafing dish burner.
2. Add bananas and heat quickly. Stir in sugar and all but 2 tablespoons apricot brandy. Heat remaining brandy in a ladle or a large serving spoon. Ignite the warm brandy and pour over the bananas. Shake the pan gently or stir until flame dies down.
3. Serve the bananas topped with dairy sour cream and a sprinkling of brown sugar.

4 servings

890 *Peach Flambée Ambrosia*

1 tablespoon butter
¼ cup slivered almonds
2 tablespoons light brown sugar
2 tablespoons orange juice
1 package (16 ounces) frozen
　　sliced peaches, thawed
　　Vanilla ice cream
¼ cup shredded coconut
¼ cup Grand Marnier

1. Heat butter in cooking pan of a chafing dish over low heat. Add almonds and brown lightly. Stir in brown sugar and orange juice. Add peaches and heat.
2. Place scoops of vanilla ice cream in dessert dishes and sprinkle with coconut.
3. Warm liqueur in a ladle. Ignite and pour over the peaches. Shake the pan gently or stir until flames die out. Spoon over ice cream.

4 to 6 servings

891 *Strawberry-Pear Flambée*

2 packages (10 ounces each) frozen
　　strawberries
1 cup sugar
6 tablespoons butter
½ cup orange juice
1½ teaspoons grated lemon peel
1 can (29 ounces) large pear halves,
　　drained
⅓ cup cognac

1. Drain strawberries; reserve juice. Put berries through a sieve to purée. Add desired amount of reserved juice to sweeten and thin purée; set aside.
2. In cooking pan of a chafing dish, caramelize sugar with butter over medium heat. Stir in orange juice, lemon peel, and purée. Simmer sauce 1 to 2 minutes, stirring gently.
3. Place pears in sauce and roll in sauce until they are thoroughly heated and have a blush.
4. In a separate pan, heat cognac just until warm. Ignite the cognac and pour over the pears. Spoon the sauce over pears until the flames die out.
5. Serve the pears in dessert dishes with the sauce.

4 servings

892 *Crepes Suzette*

Crepes:

    1 cup all-purpose flour
    1 teaspoon sugar
    1 pinch salt
    1 egg, well beaten
    1 cup milk
    2 tablespoons butter

Sauce:

    ½ cup sugar
        Peelings (white portion removed) and juices of 1 orange and ½ lemon
    ¼ cup butter
    1 ounce Grand Marnier
    1 ounce cognac
    1 ounce Cointreau

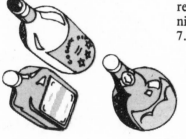

1. To prepare crepes, mix all ingredients except butter in a bowl; beat until smooth (batter should be the consistency of thin cream).
2. Put a small amount of butter in an 8-inch skillet; heat until the butter bubbles. Pour in enough batter to form a 6-inch circle, quickly rotating the pan to spread the batter thinly and evenly. Cook over medium heat about ½ minute; turn crepe and cook other side.
3. With the aid of a fork and a spoon, carefully fold the crepe in fourths. Transfer to a heated plate and keep warm. Repeat process until all the batter is used.
4. To prepare sauce, heat ¼ cup of the sugar in cooking pan of a chafing dish over low heat, stirring until sugar is caramelized. Add the citrus peelings and the butter; stir until butter is melted.
5. Add the citrus juices; cook and stir several minutes. Remove the peelings from the sauce.
6. To serve, transfer folded crepes to the sauce. Sprinkle the remaining sugar over crepes. Add the liqueurs to sauce and ignite.
7. Serve 3 crepes per person on hot dessert plates.

4 servings

893 *Emperor's Dessert (Kaiserschmarren)*

    2 tablespoons butter
    1 cup all-purpose flour
    ¼ cup sugar
    ¼ teaspoon salt
    3 eggs, beaten
    1 cup milk
    ¾ cup butter
    ¾ cup sugar
    ½ teaspoon ground cinnamon
    ½ cup golden raisins, plumped
    ½ cup flaked or sliced almonds, toasted

1. Melt 2 tablespoons butter in a heavy 6-inch skillet and set aside.
2. Combine flour, ¼ cup sugar, and salt in a bowl. Add a mixture of eggs, milk, and melted butter. Beat until smooth.
3. Heat skillet to moderately hot. Pour in just enough batter to cover bottom. Immediately tilt skillet to spread batter thinly and evenly.
4. Cook each crepe over medium heat until light brown on bottom and firm to touch on top. Turn and brown other side. As each crepe is cooked, transfer to a hot platter.
5. Using two forks, gently tear the crepes into 1-inch irregular-shaped pieces; set aside and keep warm.
6. Melt ¾ cup butter in cooking pan of a chafing dish; stir in ¾ cup sugar. Mix in cinnamon, raisins, and almonds, stirring occasionally until heated.
7. Add crepe pieces and toss lightly to coat.

8 to 10 servings

Crepes

894 *Dinner Crepes*

1 cup all-purpose flour
⅛ teaspoon salt
3 eggs
1½ cups milk
2 tablespoons melted butter or oil

1. Sift flour and salt. Add eggs, one at a time, beating thoroughly. Gradually add milk, mixing until blended. Add melted butter or oil and beat until smooth. (Or mix in an electric blender until smooth.)
2. Let batter stand for 1 hour before cooking crepes.

About 18 crepes

895 *Dessert Crepes*

1 cup all-purpose flour
¼ cup sugar
Pinch salt
3 eggs
1½ cups milk
2 tablespoons melted butter or oil
2 tablespoons brandy

1. Sift flour, sugar, and salt. Add eggs, one at a time, beating thoroughly. Gradually add milk, melted butter or oil, and brandy, beating until smooth. (Or mix in an electric blender until smooth.)
2. Let batter stand 1 hour before cooking crepes.

About 18 crepes

Cocoa Crepes: Follow recipe for Dessert Crepes; then mix **2 tablespoons cocoa** with flour, sugar, and salt, and substitute **2 tablespoons rum** for brandy.   896

897 *Wheat Crepes*

1 cup whole wheat flour
1 tablespoon sprouted wheat or
    wheat germ
3 eggs
Pinch salt
½ cup whipping cream
¾ cup water
2 tablespoons butter or margarine, melted

Make batter the same way as basic crepes

About 16 crepes

898 *Corn Crepes*

⅔ cup all-purpose flour
6 tablespoons cornmeal
3 eggs
Pinch salt
1 cup milk or cream
2 tablespoons oil

Make batter the same way as basic crepes

About 10 crepes

899 *Wafer Crepes*

2½ cups crepe batter (see Note)
Cooking oil

1. Heat a skillet or griddle over medium heat, and brush with oil.
2. Pour ½ tablespoon batter in skillet, but do not swirl the pan. Pour 3 or 4 more crepes, turn when brown, and brown on other side. Place crepes on ungreased baking sheet.
3. Bake at 350°F about 15 minutes, turning over halfway through baking. Remove from baking sheet and serve with dips, spreads, or cheese.

About 8 dozen wafers

Note: Any of the crepe batters may be used to make Wafer Crepes. If desired, batter may be thinned with a little liquid for thinner, crisper wafers.

900 *Pinwheel Party Platter*
(with Turkey, Ham, and Asparagus)

½ pound mushrooms, cleaned and chopped
5 tablespoons butter or margarine
5 tablespoons flour
½ cup water
½ cup whipping cream
¼ teaspoon salt
2 dashes pepper
¼ teaspoon dry mustard
Dash cayenne pepper
¼ pound Swiss cheese, shredded
15 dinner crepes
10 asparagus spears, cooked and salted
5 (1-ounce) slices boiled ham
5 (1-ounce) slices cooked turkey breast, lightly salted

1. Lightly sauté mushrooms in 1 tablespoon butter about 3 minutes. Set aside.
2. Melt remaining butter over low heat. Add flour and stir until smooth. Slowly stir in water and cream. Add mushrooms. Over medium heat, stir and bring to boiling. Blend in dry seasonings and Swiss cheese. Cook and stir until cheese melts.
3. Spread mixture over crepes. Pinwheels are made by placing a ham or turkey slice, tightly rolled around one asparagus spear, at the bottom edge of each crepe. Roll up, forming a tight roll. Put into a baking dish.
4. Bake at 375°F 10 minutes. Cool 30 minutes.
5. Slice each roll into 6 pinwheels. Serve with picks. Arrange in a colorful pattern on a platter.

90 hors d'oeuvres

901 *Dilled Beef Rolls*

⅓ cup dairy sour cream
2 tablespoons grated cucumber
⅛ teaspoon dill weed
Dash Worcestershire sauce
1 can (4½ ounces) roast beef spread
4 dinner crepes

1. Combine sour cream, cucumber, dill weed, and Worcestershire sauce. Let stand 30 minutes.
2. Spread roast beef mixture on the crepes. Top with a thin layer of sour cream mixture. Roll up jelly-roll fashion. Place on a cookie sheet.
3. Bake at 375°F 15 minutes.
4. Cut each roll into thirds and serve warm as a snack or hors d'oeuvres.

1 dozen hors d'oeuvres

902 Anchovy Bits

4 dinner crepes
½ cup shredded mozzarella cheese
8 to 16 anchovy fillets packed in oil, drained
¼ teaspoon garlic powder
½ teaspoon oregano

1. On each crepe sprinkle mozzarella cheese, top with 2 to 4 (depending on taste) anchovy fillets, and sprinkle with garlic powder and oregano.
2. Roll up jelly-roll fashion. Place on a cookie sheet.
3. Bake at 375°F 10 minutes.
4. Rolls can be served individually as appetizers, or each roll can be cut into bite-size pieces and served as hors d'oeuvres.

4 large appetizers or 2 dozen hors d'oeuvres

903 Cheddar-Nut Log

8 ounces sharp Cheddar cheese spread
¼ cup chopped nuts
1 tablespoon chopped parsley
3 dinner crepes
Paprika

1. Blend cheese, nuts, and parsley well. Refrigerate 30 minutes.
2. Form mixture into 3 logs. Place a log on one end of each crepe and roll. Sprinkle log with paprika. Freeze 1 hour.
3. Slice while frozen. Spear with picks and serve at room temperature.

3 nut logs

904 Sardine Pinwheels

1 can (1½ ounces) sardines in oil
1 scallion, minced
½ teaspoon dry mustard
1 to 2 tablespoons dairy sour cream
Salt and pepper
6 dinner crepes

1. Drain and mash sardines; stir in scallion, mustard, and just enough sour cream to make it spreadable. Season to taste with salt and pepper.
2. Spread on crepes and roll up jelly-roll fashion. Slice into bite-size pieces (about 6 per crepe).

About 3 dozen hors d'oeuvres

905 Red Reuben

1 can (4½ ounces) corned beef spread
4 dinner crepes
½ cup drained canned sweet 'n' sour red cabbage
½ cup shredded Swiss cheese

1. Smooth ¼ can of corned beef spread on each crepe: spread 2 tablespoons of red cabbage over corned beef. Sprinkle with 2 tablespoons cheese.
2. Roll up jelly-roll fashion.
3. Bake at 375°F 10 minutes.
4. Serve one or two as a snack or slice into bite-size pieces for hors d'oeuvres. If desired, spear with picks and dip into Dijon Sauce ●

4 rolls or 2 dozen hors d'oeuvres

906 *Beef Stroganoff Turnovers*

2 tablespoons butter or
    margarine
½ medium onion, minced
½ pound mushrooms, cleaned and
    sliced
1 pound skirt steak, cut in
    thin strips (sirloin,
    round, or flank can be
    substituted)
1 medium clove garlic, crushed in a
    garlic press
⅛ teaspoon cumin
⅛ teaspoon dill weed
⅛ teaspoon marjoram
1 teaspoon Worcestershire sauce
2 tablespoons ketchup
⅓ cup red wine
1 beef bouillon cube
    Salt and pepper
8 ounces dairy sour cream
6 dinner crepes

1. Melt butter. Sauté onion and mushrooms. Add meat strips, garlic, cumin, dill weed, marjoram, Worcestershire sauce, and ketchup. Sauté until meat is browned. Stir in wine and bouillon cube. Simmer until meat is tender. Season with salt and pepper to taste. Stir in sour cream. Cook over low heat 5 minutes.
2. Using a slotted spoon, assemble by turnover method. Place on baking sheet.
3. Bake at 350°F 10 minutes. Serve topped with any remaining sauce.

6 turnovers

907 *Steak and Kidney Pie*

½ pound lamb kidneys
⅓ cup butter or margarine
1 cup chopped onion
½ pound diced beef (top sirloin,
    round, or flank)
1 cup dry red wine
¼ teaspoon marjoram
1 small clove garlic, crushed in
    a garlic press
1 tablespoon flour
¾ cup beef broth (1 beef
    bouillon cube dissolved in ¾ cup
    boiling water)
    Salt and pepper
6 dinner crepes

1. Peel, core, and dice kidneys.
2. Melt butter. Sauté kidneys over low heat until browned. Add onion and beef. Continue cooking until onion is browned and meat is tender. Stir in wine, marjoram, and garlic. Simmer, covered, 15 minutes.
3. Stir in flour. Gradually add broth, stirring constantly. Cook until sauce thickens. Add salt and pepper to taste.
4. Assemble, using tube method. Arrange, seam side down, on a baking sheet.
5. Bake at 375°F 10 minutes. Crepe will be crisp but filling will be moist and tasty. Serve immediately.

6 filled crepes

Note: One crepe, accompanied by soup, salad, vegetable, and dessert, is a filling dinner.

908 Cannelloni

½ pound Italian sausage,
    cooked and finely chopped
1 cup cooked chopped beef
1 package (10 ounces) frozen
    chopped spinach, thawed and
    well drained
¼ cup plus 2 tablespoons
    grated Parmesan cheese
⅛ teaspoon ground thyme
⅛ teaspoon pepper
    Salt
8 dinner crepes
• ½ cup Basic White Sauce

    Nutmeg

1. Combine sausage, beef, spinach, ¼ cup cheese, thyme, pepper, and salt to taste.
2. Divide filling among crepes. Assemble, using tube method. Top with white sauce, remaining Parmesan, and nutmeg.
3. Bake at 350°F 20 minutes.

8 filled crepes

909 Creamed Chipped Beef Turnovers

• 1½ cups Basic White Sauce
2 hard-cooked eggs, chopped
5 ounces dried beef, rinsed
½ teaspoon Worcestershire sauce
8 ounces canned peas
8 dinner crepes

1. Make white sauce; stir in eggs, beef, and Worcestershire sauce. Cook 5 minutes. Stir in peas.
2. Assemble, using turnover method. Place on a baking sheet.
3. Bake at 350°F 15 minutes.

8 turnovers

910 Veal Cordon Bleu

¼ cup butter or margarine
1 pound thin veal cutlets, pounded
    and cut in short strips
2 tablespoons white wine
½ cup shredded Swiss cheese
    Salt and pepper
8 dinner crepes
¼ pound thinly sliced boiled ham
    Paprika

1. Melt butter, add veal strips, and sauté until tender. Add wine; simmer 3 minutes. Remove from heat; stir in ⅓ cup Swiss cheese. Season with salt and pepper.
2. Spread crepes out on a work surface. Divide ham slices among crepes. Spoon veal mixture onto ham. Continue assembling, using square turnover method. Place, seam side down, on a baking sheet and top with remaining cheese. Sprinkle with paprika.
3. Bake at 375°F 15 minutes. Serve piping hot.

8 filled crepes

Note: Substitute chicken for veal, if desired.

911 *Chicken Italiano*

2 whole chicken breasts (about 1 pound)
2 tablespoons oil
½ pound mushrooms, cleaned and chopped
1 can (16 ounces) stewed tomatoes
1 medium clove garlic, crushed in a garlic press
1 teaspoon oregano
½ teaspoon thyme
1 can (8 ounces) tomato sauce
⅓ cup grated Parmesan cheese
Salt and pepper
6 dinner crepes

1. Bone chicken and cut into 1-inch strips.
2. Heat oil, sauté chicken and mushrooms until chicken turns white. Stir in stewed tomatoes, garlic, oregano, thyme, tomato sauce, and 3 tablespoons grated cheese. Add salt and pepper to taste. Simmer, uncovered, 5 minutes.
3. Using a slotted spoon, spoon onto crepes. Assemble, using tube method, place on a baking sheet, and sprinkle tops of crepes with remaining cheese.
4. Bake at 375°F until cheese browns (about 15 minutes) Serve immediately with any remaining sauce.

6 filled crepes

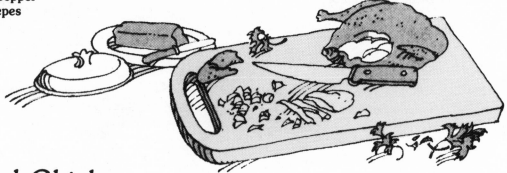

912 *Creamed Chicken*

3 tablespoons butter or margarine
¼ cup flour
1 tablespoon chopped parsley
¼ teaspoon dried tarragon
1½ cups whipping cream
2 cups diced cooked chicken
Salt and pepper
6 dinner crepes
Paprika

1. Melt butter (do not brown); stir in flour. Add parsley, tarragon, and cream. Cook until thick. Add chicken and salt and pepper to taste.
2. Divide among crepes. Fold in half; place on a baking sheet. Sprinkle with paprika.
3. Bake at 375°F 15 minutes.

6 filled crepes

913 *Curried Chicken Salad in Butterfly Crepes*

1 chicken (2½ pounds), cut in pieces
1 bay leaf
1 teaspoon thyme
½ teaspoon salt
Boiling water
¼ cup mayonnaise
¼ teaspoon curry powder
¼ teaspoon poultry seasoning
2 teaspoons curry powder
2 tablespoons chutney
⅔ cup dairy sour cream

1. Place chicken, bay leaf, thyme, and salt in a deep saucepan and cover with boiling water. Cover. Simmer, do not boil, 1 hour, or until tender.
2. While chicken is simmering, combine mayonnaise and ¼ teaspoon curry powder. Cover. Chill.
3. Remove skin and bones from chicken. Finely dice chicken; cool.
4. Mix cool chicken, poultry seasoning, remaining curry powder, and chutney. Add sour cream and mix until all ingredients are moist and mixture holds its shape. Add salt and pepper to taste.
5. Assemble crepes using butterfly method, with chicken salad

Salt and pepper
6 dinner crepes
  Chopped peanuts or cashews
  Flaked coconut
2 spiced peaches, cut in 8 wedges

for filling and topping. Garnish wings by dotting with curried mayonnaise and sprinkling with chopped nuts and coconut. Form antennae with peach wedges. Serve at room temperature.

4 servings

Note: Salad may be made in advance and stored in refrigerator until ready to assemble.

914 *Mandarin Chicken Turnovers*

1 chicken (2½ pounds)
2 scallions, minced
⅓ cup diced celery
¼ cup butter or margarine
1 can (11 ounces) mandarin oranges, drained; reserve syrup
2 teaspoons soy sauce
  Dash cayenne pepper
⅛ teaspoon minced crystallized ginger
2 teaspoons cornstarch
8 dinner crepes

1. Skin, bone, and dice chicken.
2. Sauté chicken, scallions, and celery in butter until chicken is cooked.
3. Make mandarin sauce by adding water to reserved syrup, if necessary, to equal ⅔ cup liquid. Combine this liquid with soy sauce, cayenne, ginger, and cornstarch. Stir until well blended. Cook, stirring constantly, over medium heat until mixture turns clear and thickens. Stir in mandarin oranges.
4. Stir half the sauce into hot sautéed chicken.
5. Assemble, using turnover method.
6. Serve immediately, topped with remaining sauce; or for a crispy crepe, place on a baking sheet and bake at 375°F 10 minutes. Serve immediately with remaining warm sauce.

8 turnovers

915 *Sicilian Chicken*

1 pound boned chicken
1 package (10 ounces) frozen chopped broccoli, thawed
2 tablespoons oil
¼ pound mushrooms, cleaned and sliced
● ⅔ cup Pesto Sauce
8 dinner crepes
● ½ cup Basic White Sauce
  Parsley

1. Cut chicken into 1×¼-inch strips. Drain broccoli.
2. Heat oil and sauté chicken, mushrooms, and broccoli until tender. Drain off any liquid; stir in Pesto Sauce.
3. Assemble, using square turnover method. Place on a baking sheet, separating slightly; top with white sauce.
4. Bake at 375°F 10 minutes. Serve garnished with parsley.

8 filled crepes

916 *Chicken and Shrimp Egg Roll*

3 tablespoons oil
½ pound raw chicken, cut in julienne strips*
½ pound shrimp, cleaned and diced
1 can (16 ounces) bean sprouts, well drained
⅓ cup coarsely chopped celery
8 scallions, thinly sliced
½ cup shredded cabbage
1 tablespoon soy sauce
1 teaspoon salt
12 dinner crepes
Oil for frying

1. Heat 3 tablespoons oil in skillet. Sauté chicken, stirring frequently. Add shrimp, bean sprouts, celery, scallions, and cabbage. Cook 4 minutes. Season with soy sauce and salt. Cool 10 minutes.
2. Assemble, using egg-roll method.
3. Fry in ⅛ inch heated oil in a skillet until golden. Serve hot.

12 egg rolls

Note: Egg rolls can be stored in the refrigerator or freezer. To reheat, bake at 375°F 15 minutes.

*If desired, use all chicken or all shrimp, or substitute pork for chicken.

917 *Chicken Curry Turnovers*

1 chicken (2½ pounds)
2½ tablespoons Curry Powder
3 tablespoons butter or margarine
½ cup chopped onion
¾ cup unsweetened applesauce
• 2 tablespoons Peach Chutney

Salt and pepper
6 dinner crepes

1. Skin, bone, and dice chicken. Toss chicken with Curry Powder.
2. Sauté coated chicken in butter with onion until tender. Stir in applesauce and chutney. Simmer 10 minutes.
3. Assemble, using turnover method.
4. Bake at 375°F 10 minutes.
5. Serve with Condiments for Curry.

6 turnovers

Curry Powder: Put **1 teaspoon cumin seed, 2 teaspoons coriander seed, 2½ tablespoons sesame seed, 2 teaspoons turmeric, ½ teaspoon chili powder, ¼ teaspoon ground ginger, ¼ teaspoon garlic powder,** and **1 teaspoon salt** into an electric blender container. Blend at medium-high speed until well blended and a powder. Store in a tightly covered container. **918**

⅓ cup powder

Condiments for Curry: **Chutney, chopped peanuts or cashews, chopped green pepper, flaked coconut, diced bananas, chopped raisins, quartered kumquats, sliced scallions, shredded cucumber, crushed or chunk pineapple, yogurt, diced apple, diced banana,** or **crumbled bacon.**

919 Chicken Liver and Green Grape Turnovers

1 pound chicken livers
¼ cup butter or margarine
2 tablespoons minced onion
¼ teaspoon salt
⅛ teaspoon ginger
⅛ teaspoon pepper
1 teaspoon Worcestershire sauce
1 cup seedless green grapes, cut in half
1 tablespoon sherry
1 chicken bouillon cube
¼ cup water
⅓ cup dairy sour cream
2 tablespoons chopped parsley
8 dinner crepes

1. Sauté chicken livers in butter 3 minutes. Stir in onion and sauté 4 minutes more.
2. Add salt, ginger, pepper, Worcestershire sauce, grapes, sherry, bouillon cube, and water. Simmer 3 minutes. Remove from heat. Stir in sour cream and parsley.
3. Assemble, using turnover method.
4. Bake at 350°F 10 minutes. Serve immediately.

8 turnovers

920 Chicken Polynesian Turnovers

2 chicken breasts, boned (about 1 pound)
¼ cup bottled teriyaki sauce
¼ cup oil
1 large banana, diced
1 can (8 ounces) crushed pineapple, drained; reserve juice
¼ cup chopped green pepper
1 tablespoon honey
1 tablespoon soy sauce
1 tablespoon cornstarch
4 dinner crepes

1. Cut boned chicken breasts into short strips. Marinate in teriyaki sauce for 20 minutes.
2. Heat oil; sauté chicken until tender. Stir in diced banana, crushed pineapple, and green pepper. Simmer 3 to 5 minutes to heat fruit.
3. Assemble, using turnover method. Place on a baking sheet.
4. Bake at 375°F 15 minutes.
5. While crepes are baking, make a sauce with ½ cup reserved pineapple juice, honey, soy sauce, and cornstarch; cook until mixture thickens.
6. Serve hot crepes with sauce on top. Accompany with stir-fried vegetables, if desired.

4 turnovers

921 Ham Foldovers

• 1½ cups Basic White Sauce
1 tablespoon Dijon mustard
1 pound cooked ham, cut in ¼-inch cubes
½ pound American cheese, cut in ¼-inch cubes
1 can (16 ounces) green peas, drained
8 dinner crepes
¼ pound Swiss cheese, coarsely shredded

1. Prepare sauce. Reserve ½ cup of sauce for topping.
2. To the remaining sauce, add mustard, ham, American cheese, and peas. Mix gently.
3. Divide filling among crepes. Fold crepes in half. Put on a baking sheet. Spread reserved sauce over tops of crepes and sprinkle with Swiss cheese.
4. Bake at 350°F 15 minutes. Serve at once.

8 filled crepes

Sausage Foldovers: 922 Follow recipe for Ham Foldovers; substitute **1 pound cooked Italian sausage** for ham.

923 *Turkey à la King*

2 tablespoons butter or margarine
¼ cup chopped onion
¼ pound mushrooms, cleaned and sliced
• 1½ cups Basic White Sauce

½ teaspoon Worcestershire sauce
1½ tablespoons chopped pimento
6 dinner crepes
1 cup diced cooked turkey

1. Melt butter. Sauté onion and mushrooms until tender. Stir in white sauce, Worcestershire sauce, and pimento. Simmer 5 minutes.
2. To assemble, spread crepe with some sauce, divide turkey among crepes, and proceed, using turnover method.
3. Bake at 375°F 10 minutes.
4. Keep remaining sauce warm. Serve crepes topped with remaining sauce.

6 filled crepes

Note: Substitute 1 cup diced cooked chicken, pork, or veal for turkey, if desired.

924 *Lobster Newburg*

¼ cup butter or margarine
6 tablespoons flour
1½ cups light cream
1 tablespoon cooking liquid from lobster (if possible)
3 tablespoons sherry
¼ teaspoon nutmeg
3 dashes cayenne pepper
Pinch of paprika
1 egg yolk, slightly beaten
1 egg white
2 cups cubed, cooked lobster
12 dinner crepes

1. Melt butter, stir in flour, and cook 1 minute. Slowly stir in light cream and liquid from lobster. Cook, stirring continuously, until smooth and thick.
2. Blend in sherry, nutmeg, cayenne, and paprika. Slowly add egg yolk, blend well, and cook until smooth and thick (about 3 minutes).
3. Combine half of the sauce with the lobster meat. Reserve the rest.
4. To assemble, place a heaping tablespoon of the lobster mixture on one quarter of the crepe. Brush remaining three quarters of crepe with egg white. Fold into cone-shaped packages. Place in baking dish, one cone overlapping the other, with the open part of the cone upward.
5. Bake at 375°F 10 minutes. Serve 2 for an appetizer or 3 for dinner, topped with warmed remaining sauce.

12 filled crepes

Lobster Duxelles: Sauté **½ pound sliced mushrooms** in **1 tablespoon butter or margarine** and add to the sauce. This will increase yield to fill 15 crepes. **925**

Crab Newburg: Substitute **2 cups cooked, flaked crab** for lobster. **926**

Shrimp Newburg: Sauté **⅓ cup minced celery** and **¼ pound sliced mushrooms** in **2 tablespoons butter or margarine.** Substitute **celery, mushrooms,** and **1½ cups cooked shrimp** for lobster. **927**

Scallop Newburg: Sauté **¼ pound sliced mushrooms** and **2 tablespoons snipped parsley** in **1 tablespoon butter.** Substitute **mushrooms, parsley,** and **2 cups scallops** for lobster. This will increase the filling yield slightly, so fill each crepe with 2 level tablespoons scallop mixture. **928**

929 Pesto Crab Squares

1 pound ricotta cheese
2 eggs, slightly beaten
1 teaspoon oregano
1 medium clove garlic, crushed
2 tablespoons grated Parmesan
   cheese
● ⅓ cup Pesto Sauce
6 ounces frozen king crab, drained
   well
12 dinner crepes
● 1 cup Basic White Sauce

Nutmeg

1. Beat ricotta cheese and eggs until smooth. Stir in oregano, garlic, Parmesan cheese, Pesto Sauce, and crab.
2. Assemble, using square turnover method. Arrange in baking dish so crepes are just touching. Top with Basic White Sauce; sprinkle with nutmeg.
3. Bake at 375°F 20 minutes. Cool 5 minutes before serving. Serve 1 for an appetizer; 2 for a dinner.

12 squares

930 Curried Crab Florentine

3 tablespoons butter or margarine
2 cans (7½ ounces each)
   Alaska king crab meat, drained
Salt to taste
1 scallion, chopped
1 can (4 ounces) sliced
   mushrooms, drained
1 teaspoon curry powder
Dash cayenne pepper
Dash Worcestershire sauce
1 tablespoon chutney
● 1 cup Creamy Lemon Sauce

8 dinner crepes
¼ cup flaked coconut

1. Melt butter, add crab, salt (if necessary), scallion, mushrooms, curry powder, cayenne, and Worcestershire sauce.
2. Sauté until scallions are tender and mixture is thoroughly heated. Remove from heat.
3. Stir in chutney and ¼ cup Creamy Lemon Sauce. Divide mixture among crepes and assemble, using tube method.
4. Arrange snugly in a baking dish. Top with remaining sauce and sprinkle on coconut.
5. Broil about 5 inches from source of heat 3 minutes or until lightly browned.

8 filled crepes

931 Crab Cannelloni

1 pound ricotta or cottage cheese
1 egg, slightly beaten
¼ cup grated Parmesan cheese
1 teaspoon oregano
¼ teaspoon ground thyme
1 medium clove garlic, crushed
1 teaspoon butter or margarine
2 tablespoons minced onion
½ cup diced broccoli
6 ounces frozen king crab meat,
   drained and crumbled
10 dinner crepes
● 1 cup Basic White Sauce

Nutmeg

1. Beat ricotta or cottage cheese until smooth.
2. Blend in egg, Parmesan cheese, oregano, thyme, and garlic.
3. Melt butter or margarine; sauté onion and broccoli until tender; drain well.
4. Stir onion, broccoli, and crab into cheese mixture. Assemble, using tube method; fit snugly into a baking dish.
5. Bake at 350°F 20 minutes. Cool for 5 minutes. Serve topped with warm white sauce and sprinkled with nutmeg.

10 filled crepes

932 Crab à la King

¼ cup minced onion
¼ pound mushrooms, cleaned
   and sliced
2 tablespoons butter or
   margarine
• 1½ cups Basic White Sauce

1½ teaspoons Worcestershire sauce
1 tablespoon chopped pimento
1 teaspoon lemon juice
6 ounces frozen crab meat,
   flaked
4 dinner crepes

1. Sauté onion and mushrooms in butter until tender; stir into Basic White Sauce.
2. Add Worcestershire sauce, pimento, and lemon juice to white sauce mixture; blend well.
3. Simmer 3 minutes to blend flavors. Stir ½ cup sauce into crab meat.
4. Assemble, using tube method. Place in baking pan; top with remaining sauce.
5. Bake at 375°F 15 minutes. Serve piping hot.

4 filled crepes

933 Coral Shrimp

½ cup finely chopped onion
1 tablespoon butter or margarine
• 2 cups Basic White Sauce

1 to 2 teaspoons tomato paste
¼ cup dry white wine
½ teaspoon salt
¼ teaspoon white pepper
1 pound cooked medium shrimp
   (fresh or frozen)

1. Sauté onion in butter until tender. Mix onion into white sauce. Stir in tomato paste, wine, salt, and pepper. Fold in shrimp.
2. Assemble, using tube method. Spoon extra sauce over crepes. Garnish with **fresh tomato** and **Bibb lettuce**.

12 filled crepes

934 Scallops and Broccoli au Gratin

2 tablespoons butter or margarine
5 ounces frozen chopped broccoli
1 scallion, chopped
1 pound frozen scallops
2 tablespoons white wine
1½ teaspoons lemon juice
2 dashes cayenne pepper
1 sprig parsley, chopped
⅓ cup shredded Swiss cheese
2 tablespoons grated Parmesan
   cheese
   Salt and pepper
8 dinner crepes
• ½ cup Basic White Sauce

Nutmeg

1. Melt butter. Sauté broccoli and scallion in butter until broccoli is cooked.
2. Stir in scallops, wine, lemon juice, cayenne, and parsley. Simmer until scallops are tender.
3. Drain off liquid. Stir in cheeses. Salt and pepper to taste.
4. Assemble, using square turnover method. Place on baking sheet.
5. Bake at 375°F 10 minutes. Spoon 1 tablespoon white sauce over each square, sprinkle with nutmeg, and serve.

8 squares

Note: Crab or shrimp may be substituted for scallops.

935 *Asparagus Supreme*

3 tablespoons softened butter or margarine
3 teaspoons prepared mustard
6 dinner crepes
6 slices (1 ounce each) cooked ham
18 cooked asparagus spears
6 slices Swiss cheese, cut diagonally in half
6 slices American cheese, cut diagonally in half

1. Cream butter with mustard. Spread butter mixture on crepes. Cover with a slice of ham. Place 3 asparagus spears in center of each crepe. Fold in thirds. Put on a baking sheet. Arrange 2 triangles of each cheese alternately over each crepe.
2. Broil until cheese begins to melt. Serve immediately.

6 filled crepes

936 *Mushroom Stack*

1 pound mushrooms, cleaned and finely chopped
2 tablespoons butter
● 1 cup Creamy Brown Sauce

8 dinner crepes
Parsley for garnish

1. Sauté mushrooms in butter until mushrooms are cooked and pan is almost dry. Stir in sauce.
2. Assemble by stacking 1 crepe, mushroom filling, crepe, mushroom filling, crepe, filling, crepe; form 2 stacks. Put on a baking sheet.
3. Bake at 375°F 10 minutes.
4. Cut into wedges and serve for brunch or as an appetizer. Garnish with parsley.

8 servings

Mushroom-Chicken Stack: Follow recipe for 937 Mushroom Stack. Spread contents of a **4½-ounce can chicken spread** on 2 crepes. Stack crepe, mushroom filling, crepe with chicken, crepe, mushroom, crepe. If desired, mix **1 cup Basic White Sauce** ●   and **1 cup cooked chopped spinach**; spread on each stack before serving.

938 *Spinach-Bacon Turnovers*

4 slices bacon, diced
⅓ cup chopped onion
1 package (10 ounces) frozen chopped spinach. thawed
¼ cup mayonnaise
Salt and pepper
4 dinner crepes
● 1 cup Basic White Sauce

1. Sauté bacon and onion until bacon is cooked.
2. Drain spinach well. Stir-fry spinach with bacon and onion for 3 minutes. Drain mixture well. Stir in mayonnaise and season with salt and pepper to taste.
3. Assemble, using turnover method. Place on a baking sheet.
4. Bake at 375°F 10 minutes. If desired, serve topped with white sauce and sprinkled with bacon bits.

4 turnovers

939 Tomato Rabbit

4 slices bacon, diced
2 tablespoons flour
½ cup shredded Cheddar cheese
2 tablespoons sherry
  Dash cayenne pepper
2 medium tomatoes
4 dinner crepes

1. Cook bacon until crisp. Remove bacon and drain; reserve bacon drippings.
2. To 2 tablespoons of bacon drippings add flour, ¼ cup cheese, sherry, and cayenne. Stir until well blended. Cook over medium heat until thick; cool.
3. Core tomatoes and dice. Mix tomato and cooked bacon pieces with sauce.
4. Divide sauce among crepes, fold in half, top with remaining cheese, and serve.

4 filled crepes

940 Zucchini Italiano

1 pound zucchini, diced
1 large clove garlic, crushed in a garlic press
1 can (16 ounces) tomatoes, drained and diced
½ cup chopped onion
  Salt and pepper
¼ cup grated Parmesan cheese
8 dinner crepes

1. Combine diced zucchini, garlic, tomatoes, onion, salt, and pepper in a saucepan. Simmer 25 to 30 minutes over medium heat, or until squash is tender.
2. Place crepes on a baking sheet. Drain zucchini mixture as you spoon it equally onto each crepe. Sprinkle with 2 tablespoons cheese. Fold crepes in half, brush with juice from cooked squash, and sprinkle with remaining 2 tablespoons cheese.
3. Bake at 375°F 15 minutes. Serve immediately while crisp and hot.

8 filled crepes

Note: Serve without baking, if desired.

941 Zucchini with Pesto Sauce

1 pound zucchini
  Water
3 tablespoons grated onion
½ teaspoon salt
¼ teaspoon pepper
• ⅔ cup Pesto Sauce
8 dinner crepes

1. Wash, remove stems, and dice zucchini. Place in a saucepan and cover with water. Stir in onion, salt, and pepper. Simmer 7 to 10 minutes, or until squash is tender. Drain well. Toss with Pesto Sauce. Spoon onto crepes and fold in half. Put into a baking dish.
2. Bake at 375°F 10 minutes. Serve immediately.

8 filled crepes

942 Crepes Benedict

12 eggs
  Salt and pepper
2 tablespoons butter or margarine
8 thin slices boiled ham, heated
8 dinner crepes
• 1 cup hollandaise

1. Beat eggs with salt and pepper to taste.
2. Melt butter. Soft-scramble eggs in butter.
3. To assemble, put 1 slice of ham on each crepe and spoon eggs on top. Fold crepe and ham over eggs and serve topped with warm hollandaise.

8 filled crepes

943 *Creamy Vegetable Squares*

2 tablespoons butter or margarine
2 tablespoons minced scallion
2 tablespoons grated carrot
¼ pound mushrooms, cleaned and sliced
1 package (10 ounces) frozen chopped spinach, thawed and well drained
1 pound cottage cheese
1 egg, slightly beaten
½ teaspoon Italian seasoning
¼ teaspoon ground thyme
¼ cup grated Parmesan cheese
12 dinner crepes

1. Melt butter. Sauté scallion, carrot, mushrooms, and spinach until all are tender. Drain well. Cool.
2. Beat cottage cheese and egg until well blended. Add Italian seasoning, thyme, and 2 tablespoons of grated cheese.
3. Assemble, using square turnover method. Place on a baking sheet, seam side down. Sprinkle with remaining cheese.
4. Bake at 350°F 20 minutes. Cool 5 minutes before serving.

12 filled crepes

944 *Cherries Jubilee*

1 package (16 ounces) frozen pitted tart cherries
⅓ cup sugar
¾ cup Cherry Heering
Dash salt
1 tablespoon cornstarch
1 tablespoon butter or margarine
1 tablespoon grated lemon peel
18 dessert crepes
¼ cup brandy
1 pint vanilla ice cream

1. Thaw cherries, drain, and reserve juice.
2. Combine juice (adding water to make 1 cup), sugar, ¼ cup Cherry Heering, salt, and cornstarch in chafing dish. Cook over medium heat, stirring constantly, until sauce begins to thicken. Stir in cherries, butter, and lemon peel. Simmer 3 minutes.
3. Using hot sauce method, fill chafing dish with crepes.
4. Warm ½ cup Cherry Heering and brandy in saucepan. Pour in chafing dish and ignite. When flames die down, place 3 crepes on a plate, top with vanilla ice cream, and spoon warm sauce and cherries over all.

6 servings

945 *Peach Chutney*

1 cup peach preserves
½ cup golden raisins
¼ cup chopped pecans or walnuts
¼ cup cider vinegar
½ teaspoon orange peel
1 tablespoon chopped crystallized ginger
1 teaspoon instant minced onion

1. In a saucepan, combine all ingredients. Cook 3 to 5 minutes.
2. Cool 1 hour before serving. Store in refrigerator.

1½ cups chutney

946 *Pesto Sauce*

This spicy nut-and-cheese sauce is excellent with vegetables, eggs, fish, or poultry.

1½ to 2 teaspoons dried basil
3 tablespoons chopped walnuts
3 tablespoons grated Parmesan cheese
1 medium clove garlic, crushed in a garlic press
3 sprigs fresh parsley
1 tablespoon olive oil
2 tablespoons vegetable oil
2 tablespoons butter or margarine, melted

1. In an electric blender, combine basil, nuts, cheese, garlic, and parsley. Blend at medium speed until nuts are the size of a split pea.
2. Combine oils and butter. Slowly pour this liquid into blender while it is still on medium speed. Turn off as soon as liquid is added. It's ready to serve.

About ⅓ cup sauce

947 Basic White Sauce

¼ cup butter or margarine
5 tablespoons flour
2 cups milk
¼ teaspoon salt

1. Melt butter over low heat. Stir in flour. Gradually add milk, stirring constantly. Cook and stir until mixture comes to boiling; boil 1 minute.
2. Remove from heat. Mix in salt.

2 cups sauce

Dijon Sauce: Follow recipe for Basic White Sauce; blend in **2 tablespoons Dijon mustard** after adding milk. 948

Curry Sauce: Follow recipe for Basic White Sauce; blend **2 teaspoons curry powder** and **⅛ teaspoon dry mustard** into sauce after adding milk. 949

Parmesan Sauce: Follow recipe for Basic White Sauce; after sauce has thickened, stir in **⅓ cup grated Parmesan cheese.** Remove from heat. 950

951 Standard Hollandaise

¼ pound butter or margarine
3 egg yolks
2 tablespoons lemon juice
Pinch salt
Dash nutmeg
Dash cayenne pepper
2 tablespoons hot water

1. Melt butter (do not brown) and keep hot.
2. Put egg yolks in top of double boiler over hot (not boiling) water. Beat until smooth but not fluffy. Add lemon juice and dry seasonings; drizzle in butter and hot water. Beat with a whisk until sauce begins to thicken. Do not reheat.

1 cup sauce

Béarnaise Sauce: Combine **¼ cup dry white wine, 2 scallions, chopped, ½ teaspoon dried tarragon, pinch fresh ground pepper,** and **¼ cup vinegar.** Simmer over medium heat until reduced to 2 tablespoons. Follow recipe for Standard Hollandaise. Blend in liquid along with butter. 952

Dilled Cucumber Hollandaise: Follow recipe for Standard Hollandaise; add **½ cup chopped cucumber** and **½ teaspoon dried dill weed** to mixture immediately after butter has been added. 953

Hollandaise Verde: Follow recipe for Standard Hollandaise; chop **3 sprigs parsley, 1 whole scallion,** and **1 tablespoon capers.** Combine with **2 teaspoons Worcestershire sauce** and add to mixture immediately after butter has been added. 954

955 Creamy Lemon Sauce

¼ cup whipping cream
3 ounces cream cheese, softened
2 tablespoons lemon juice
2 tablespoons butter or margarine, melted
Dash salt
Dash cayenne pepper

1. Whip cream. Gradually add small pieces of softened cream cheese. Blend in lemon juice, butter, salt, and cayenne.
2. Serve with vegetables and fish.

1 cup sauce

Creamy Brown Sauce: Follow recipe for Creamy Lemon Sauce; substitute a **beef bouillon cube** dissolved in **2 tablespoons hot water** for lemon juice. Taste before adding salt. 956

Food Processor

957 *Caraway Cheese Twists*

2 ounces sharp Cheddar cheese
    (1 cup shredded)
1 cup flour
¼ teaspoon salt
1 tablespoon shortening
8 tablespoons butter (1 stick), frozen
    and cut in 6 pieces
1 tablespoon caraway seed
3 tablespoons ice water

1. Using **shredding disc,** shred cheese and set aside.
2. Using **steel blade,** add flour, salt, shortening, and butter to bowl and process until butter is cut into flour.
3. Add caraway seed and shredded cheese to bowl. With machine on, add water through feed tube and process until dough forms into a ball.
4. Roll dough ¼ inch thick and cut into strips 4×¾ inches. Twist strips and place on baking sheet.
5. Bake at 425°F about 15 minutes.

About 3 dozen twists

958 *Spicy Steak Tartare*

1 small green onion, cleaned,
    trimmed, and cut in 1-inch
    pieces
2 tablespoons fresh parsley, cleaned
    and trimmed (1 tablespoon
    chopped)
1 radish, cleaned and trimmed
½ pound beef (sirloin, tenderloin, or
    fillet), cut in 1-inch cubes
1 egg yolk
1 tablespoon lemon juice
1 tablespoon capers
    Drop of Dijon mustard
    Salt
    Freshly ground black pepper to
    taste
3 drops Tabasco

Using **steel blade,** process green onion, parsley, and radish together until finely chopped. Add meat and remaining ingredients and process, using quick on/off motions, to desired consistency. Serve with triangles of **black bread.**

959 *Eggs in Parsley Sauce*

8 hard-cooked eggs
1 small clove garlic
2 cups fresh parsley, cleaned and
    trimmed (1 cup chopped)
1 small boiled potato, chilled
6 tablespoons lemon juice
¼ cup olive oil
½ cup vegetable oil
2 tablespoons capers or 1 small dill
    pickle
2 anchovy fillets
⅛ teaspoon pepper

1. Cut hard-cooked eggs in half lengthwise and place cut side down in a shallow serving dish.
2. Using **steel blade,** mince garlic. Add parsley and process until chopped. Add remaining ingredients and process until creamy and thoroughly blended.
3. Pour over eggs and serve.

8 servings

Note: This herb sauce is excellent served with hot or cold meats, or it makes a very tasty salad dressing.

960 *Chopped Chicken Livers*

1 pound chicken livers
3 medium onions, peeled and
    quartered
3 tablespoons chicken fat
3 hard-cooked eggs
½ teaspoon salt
⅛ teaspoon pepper

1. Wash and trim livers.
2. Using **steel blade,** process onions, with quick on/off motions, until chopped.
3. Sauté onion in chicken fat until golden. Add livers and continue to cook until no longer pink inside (10 to 15 minutes).
4. Using **plastic blade,** add livers and onion, 2 of the hard-cooked eggs, salt, and pepper to bowl and process to desired consistency. (For a smooth patélike consistency, use **steel blade.**) You may need to add additional chicken fat.
5. Chill in refrigerator for at least 2 hours. Serve garnished with **finely chopped hard-cooked egg yolk** and **fresh parsley.**

961 *Guacamole*

1 small clove garlic
2 large ripe avocados, peeled
2 tablespoons lemon juice
1 teaspoon chili powder (optional)
   Salt to taste

1. Using **steel blade,** mince garlic. Add avocado and remaining ingredients and process to desired consistency. (Remember to use quick on/off motions if a coarse, chunky consistency is desired.)
2. Serve as a dip with tortilla chips, on lettuce as a salad, or as a filling for tacos.

About 2 cups dip

Note: If not served immediately, refrigerate in a covered bowl with avocado pits immersed in guacamole. This will help prevent the avocado from darkening on standing.

962 *Gefilte Fish*

3 pounds fresh fish (whitefish, carp, and/or pike)
2 quarts water
2 teaspoons salt
½ teaspoon pepper
8 carrots, pared
4 medium onions, peeled and cut to fit feed tube
2 eggs
6 tablespoons ice water
4 tablespoons matzoh meal
2 teaspoons salt
½ teaspoon pepper

Horseradish

1. Have fish filleted, reserving head, bones, and skin.
2. In a large pot, place water, 2 teaspoons salt, ½ teaspoon pepper, 7 carrots, head, bones, and skin of fish.
3. Using **slicing disc,** slice 3½ onions (cut remaining ½ onion in half and reserve). Add sliced onion to the pot, bring to a boil, lower heat, and simmer while fish is being prepared.
4. Cut fish into 2-inch pieces. Using **steel blade,** process fish in 1-pound batches to pastelike consistency. Remove to a large bowl and repeat 2 more times with remaining fish. After all fish has been processed, thoroughly mix together by hand to blend fish together.
5. Using **steel blade,** process remaining carrot and ½ onion together until finely chopped. Remove half of this mixture from the bowl.
6. Add half of fish mixture to the bowl. To this add 1 egg, 3 tablespoons ice water, 2 tablespoons matzoh meal, 1 teaspoon salt, and ¼ teaspoon pepper. Process, using quick on/off motions, until thoroughly blended. Remove mixture from bowl and repeat procedure, using remaining ingredients.
7. Remove head, bones, and skin of fish from stock.
8. With wet hands, shape fish into shapes the size of a small baking potato and place in fish stock. Simmer slowly 2 hours.
9. Remove fish balls with a slotted spoon and place on a lettuce-lined platter. Cool and chill. Cool fish stock and save for later use for storing leftover fish.
10. Garnish with pieces of cooked carrots left over from stock and serve with freshly made horseradish.

About 20 balls

963 *Horseradish*

½ cup horseradish root, cut in 1-inch cubes
Beet juice

Using **steel blade,** process until finely chopped. Add a few drops of beet juice to get desired color. Step back from bowl before removing lid!

964 *Eggplant Caviar*

1 large eggplant (2 pounds)
1 clove garlic
1 large onion, peeled and quartered
1 small green pepper, trimmed and cut in 1-inch pieces
6 tablespoons olive oil
2 tablespoons tomato paste
2 teaspoons lemon juice
1 teaspoon salt
¼ teaspoon pepper

1. Bake eggplant in a 400°F oven for about 1 hour, or until skin is wrinkled and eggplant is soft. Cool.
2. Using **steel blade,** mince garlic. Add onion and green pepper and process until finely chopped.
3. In a skillet, sauté garlic, onion, and green pepper in 4 tablespoons olive oil until tender, but not browned.
4. When eggplant has cooled sufficiently to handle, remove the skin. Using **steel blade,** process until finely chopped.
5. Add chopped eggplant to skillet with onion mixture. Add 2 tablespoons oil and tomato paste and cook slowly, stirring occasionally, about 20 minutes.
6. Mix in lemon juice, salt, and pepper. Serve well chilled with **black bread.**

Note: The flavor of this dish improves on standing overnight. It keeps up to a week in the refrigerator.

965 *Shrimp Dumplings in Chicken Broth*

1 slice ginger
1 green onion, cut in
    1-inch pieces
½ pound fresh shrimp, shelled and
    deveined
1 egg white
½ teaspoon cornstarch
1 tablespoon sherry
2 teaspoons soy sauce
¼ teaspoon salt
8 cups chicken stock

1. Using **steel blade,** with machine on, drop ginger slice down through the feed tube and process until minced.
2. Add green onion pieces and process until finely chopped.
3. Add shrimp and process until of a pastelike consistency. Add egg white, cornstarch, sherry, soy sauce, and salt and process until thoroughly blended.
4. In a large shallow saucepan, heat chicken stock to boiling and simmer over low heat. Using two teaspoons, drop 1-inch balls of batter into simmering chicken stock. Cover and cook over medium heat until done (about 8 to 10 minutes).
5. Just before serving, garnish soup with **sliced green onion.**

About 30 (1-inch) balls or
8 servings

966 *Block Island Quahog Chowder*

1 cube (2 inches) salt pork, partially
    frozen
1 large onion, peeled and quartered
2 to 3 medium potatoes, pared and
    diced
¼ teaspoon pepper
2 dozen large quahogs (hard-shelled
    clams)

1. Using **slicing disc,** slice salt pork. In a large saucepan, cook salt pork until browned.
2. Using **steel blade,** process onion until finely chopped. Add onion to crisp salt pork and cook until onion is transparent. Remove salt pork and discard.
3. Cook diced potatoes in 1 quart water, with pepper added, until almost tender. Do not drain.
4. Meanwhile, rinse quahogs well and open with a clam knife. (If you are not adept at opening clams in this manner, see Note for an alternate method.) Be sure that all the juice is retained. Strain quahogs, and add reserved juice to saucepan with cooked onions. Using **steel blade,** process clams in two batches until finely chopped. Add to saucepan.
5. Add cooked potatoes and water they were cooked in. Add 2 cups water, more or less, if the flavor is too strong. Simmer 15 to 20 minutes but do not boil. Serve with **chowder crackers.**

8 to 10 servings

Note: An alternate method for opening clams: Rinse clams thoroughly under cold water. Place clams in a saucepan and add 2 cups water. Cook, covered, over medium heat only until shells start to open. Remove clams, reserving clam broth for chowder. Remove clams from shells and proceed as above.

967 *Escarole Soup with Tiny Meatballs*

Soup:
4 pounds beef soup bones
1 can (6 ounces) tomato paste
2½ teaspoons salt
2 quarts water
1 pound escarole, cleaned and
    drained

1. For soup, put all ingredients, except escarole, into a saucepot. Cover and simmer for 1 hour. Remove bones.

2. For meatballs, using **steel blade,** separately process bread to fine crumbs, Parmesan cheese to fine powder, and parsley until chopped; set aside. Next, mince garlic. Add meat in two batches and process until finely chopped and remove to bowl.
3. Using **plastic blade,** add chopped meat, egg, salt, pepper,

Meatballs:

1 slice dry bread, cut in quarters
   (¼ cup crumbs)
2 cubes (1 inch each) Parmesan
   cheese (¼ cup grated)
¼ cup fresh parsley, cleaned and
   trimmed (2 tablespoons
   chopped)
1 clove garlic
¾ pound beef, cut in 1-inch cubes
1 egg
½ teaspoon salt
¼ teaspoon pepper

bread crumbs, Parmesan cheese, and chopped parsley to bowl. Process, using quick on/off motions, until thoroughly blended.

4. Shape into ¾-inch balls and add to hot soup. Simmer 10 minutes.

5. Using **steel blade,** process escarole, using quick on/off motions, until coarsely chopped. Add escarole to soup and simmer 30 minutes longer.

8 servings

968 *Greens Soup*

2 cubes (1 inch each) Parmesan
   cheese (¼ cup grated)
1 pound mixed greens (lettuce,
   spinach, watercress, as well as
   any others), cleaned and trimmed
6 tablespoons butter
3 tablespoons flour
1 quart chicken stock, heated
2 egg yolks
1 cup milk

1. Using **steel blade,** separately process Parmesan cheese to a fine powder, and greens (in small batches) until coarsely chopped.

2. Sauté greens in 2 tablespoons butter for a few minutes until wilted.

3. Meanwhile, in another saucepan, melt remaining 4 tablespoons butter, add flour, and cook for 5 minutes. Add heated stock, stirring with a whisk until smooth. Add greens, cover, and simmer for 20 minutes.

4. Strain soup. Purée vegetable mixture with **steel blade** until smooth and return to soup. Heat thoroughly and remove from heat.

5. With **plastic blade** in bowl, process egg yolks and milk together. With machine on, add 1 cup hot soup through feed tube and then add all of egg mixture to soup, stirring thoroughly. Add Parmesan cheese and simmer 5 minutes, being careful not to let soup boil after egg yolks have been added.

6 servings

969 *Cranberry-Beet Borscht*

1½ cups whole cranberries
5 cups chicken stock
2 medium onions, peeled and
   quartered
½ small head cabbage
1 tablespoon sugar
1 can (8 ounces) whole beets and
   juice

1. Wash cranberries. In a large saucepan, combine cranberries and chicken stock and cook about 20 minutes, or until cranberries are soft. Sieve cranberries and return liquid to saucepan. Using **steel blade,** process sieved cranberries until puréed and return to saucepan.

2. Using **steel blade,** process onions until chopped. Add to saucepan.

3. Using **slicing disc,** slice cabbage and add to saucepan. Add sugar and simmer uncovered for about 20 minutes.

4. Just before serving, drain beets, adding juice to pan. Shred beets with **shredding disc** and add also. Simmer until thoroughly heated. Serve with a dollop of **dairy sour cream.**

6 servings

Note: This borscht can also be served chilled.

970 *Cream of Carrot Soup*

6 large carrots, pared and cut in
    1-inch pieces
1 onion, peeled and quartered
1 stalk celery, trimmed and cut in
    1-inch pieces
4 tablespoons butter
2 tablespoons flour
6 cups chicken stock
¼ cup uncooked rice
1 tablespoon sugar
    Pinch nutmeg
1 cup whipping cream

1. Using **steel blade,** process carrots, onion, and celery together until finely chopped.
2. In a large saucepan, sauté chopped vegetables in butter for about 15 minutes. Stir in flour and cook for 2 minutes.
3. Gradually add chicken stock and rice, stirring constantly with a whisk until smooth. Cook slowly for 45 minutes, or until carrots and rice are tender.
4. Strain soup, returning liquid to saucepan. Using **steel blade,** process carrot mixture until puréed and return to saucepan. Add sugar and nutmeg. Bring to a boil, add ½ cup cream, and heat thoroughly.
5. Using a mixer, whip remaining cream. Serve each portion of soup with a dollop of whipped cream.

8 servings

971 *Leek and Potato Soup*

1 pound potatoes, pared and cut to
    fit feed tube
1 pound leeks, cleaned and cut in
    3½-inch pieces
2 quarts chicken stock
½ cup whipping cream
    Chopped parsley for garnish

1. Using **slicing disc,** slice potatoes and leeks.
2. Put vegetables and chicken stock into a saucepan, partially cover, and cook for 30 minutes, or until vegetables are tender. Strain vegetables, reserving liquid.
3. Using **steel blade,** process vegetables to a smooth purée.
4. Add vegetable purée to reserved liquid and reheat to a simmer. Off heat and just before serving, stir in cream.
5. Garnish with parsley.

About 12 servings

972 *Chilean Chicken*

3 pounds chicken, cut in serving
    pieces
¾ cup flour
2 teaspoons salt
½ teaspoon pepper
2 tablespoons butter
2 tablespoons oil
1 clove garlic
1 large carrot, pared and cut in
    1-inch pieces
3 stalks celery, cleaned and cut in
    1-inch pieces
1 medium green pepper, seeded and
    cut in 1-inch pieces
1 large onion, peeled and quartered
1 teaspoon cumin
1 can (28 ounces) whole tomatoes,
    drained
1 cup pimento-stuffed olives
1 can (8 ounces) corn, drained

1. In a paper bag, dredge chicken in flour, salt, and pepper.
2. In a large skillet, brown chicken on both sides in butter and oil and remove from pan.
3. Using **steel blade,** separately process garlic until minced; carrot, celery, green pepper, and onion until finely chopped. Add to the skillet in which chicken was browned, sauté for about 5 minutes, and remove from pan.
4. Still using **steel blade,** process drained tomatoes until finely chopped.
5. Place chicken in a large Dutch oven or covered casserole. Add cooked chopped vegetables, sprinkle with cumin, and top with chopped tomatoes. Cover Dutch oven.
6. Bake at 350°F 45 minutes.
7. Using **slicing disc,** slice olives. Add sliced olives and corn and cook 15 minutes longer, or until chicken is tender. Serve with rice.

6 servings

973 *Barbecued Spareribs*

3 pounds spareribs, cracked through the center
Salt and pepper
1 small green pepper, trimmed and cut in 1-inch pieces
1 small onion, peeled and quartered
1 stalk celery, peeled and cut in 1-inch pieces
3 tablespoons butter
½ cup cider vinegar
½ cup ketchup
¼ cup brown sugar
1 tablespoon Worcestershire sauce
½ teaspoon dry mustard
½ teaspoon chili powder
2 lemon slices

1. Cut ribs into serving-size pieces, sprinkle with salt and pepper, and place, meaty side up, in a shallow roasting pan. Bake at 350°F 30 minutes, turning once.
2. Using **steel blade,** place green pepper, onion, and celery in bowl and process until coarsely chopped. In a saucepan, heat butter and sauté chopped vegetables until tender, stirring occasionally.
3. Return mixture to bowl with **steel blade.** Add remaining ingredients except lemon slices and process until puréed. Return to saucepan, add lemon slices, and simmer 10 minutes, stirring frequently. Remove from heat and set aside.
4. After ribs have baked for 30 minutes, remove them from oven and pour off excess fat. Spoon one half of the sauce over the ribs. Cover and continue baking, basting frequently, 1 to 1½ hours, or until meat is tender. Uncover the pan for the last 15 minutes.

6 servings

974 *Roast Duckling à l'Orange with Apricot-Rice Stuffing*

Duck:
1 duckling (about 4 pounds)
1 teaspoon salt
1½ cups orange juice
3 tablespoons butter

Apricot-Rice Stuffing:
2 cups cooked rice (1 cup wild and 1 cup white rice)
¼ cup fresh parsley, cleaned and trimmed (2 tablespoons chopped)
6 ounces dried apricots
1 small onion, peeled and quartered
1 stalk celery, trimmed and cut in 1-inch pieces
¼ cup orange juice
3 tablespoons butter, melted
¼ teaspoon salt
⅛ teaspoon pepper
⅛ teaspoon nutmeg
⅛ teaspoon cloves

Orange Sauce:
1 tablespoon flour
2 oranges, sectioned
2 tablespoons orange liqueur (optional)
Salt and pepper to taste

1. Rinse duckling and pat dry with paper towel. Rub cavity with salt.
2. In a saucepan, heat orange juice and butter over low heat until butter is melted. Remove from heat and using a pastry brush, brush cavity with mixture.
3. For stuffing, using **steel blade,** separately process parsley, dried apricots, onion, and celery until finely chopped. Combine all ingredients for stuffing in a large bowl and toss until thoroughly mixed.
4. Lightly fill body and neck cavity with the stuffing. Do not pack. To close body cavity, sew or skewer and lace with a cord. Fasten neck skin to back and wings to body with skewers. Place duckling, breast up, on a rack in a roasting pan. Brush with juice mixture.
5. Roast, uncovered, at 325°F 2½ to 3 hours. Brush frequently with orange juice mixture. Pour off drippings as they accumulate. When duckling is done, drumstick should move easily.
6. Place duckling on a heated platter. Pour off fat from roasting pan, reserving 2 tablespoons, leaving brown residue in the bottom. Put reserved fat into roasting pan and blend in 1 tablespoon flour, stirring constantly over medium heat until mixture bubbles. Remove from heat and continue to stir while slowly adding remaining orange juice mixture and sectioned oranges. Return to heat and cook rapidly, stirring constantly, until gravy thickens. Cook 1 to 2 minutes longer, while stirring; scrape bottom and sides of pan to blend in brown residue. Add orange liqueur and/or more orange juice to reach desired consistency. Adjust seasonings. Remove from heat, pour into gravy boat, and serve hot with duckling.

3 or 4 servings

975 *Stuffed Flank Steak*

6 slices dry bread, cut in quarters (1½ cups crumbs)
4 cubes (1 inch each) Parmesan cheese (½ cup grated)
½ cup fresh parsley, cleaned and trimmed (¼ cup chopped)
1 clove garlic
2½ medium onions, peeled and quartered
2 tablespoons butter
¼ pound mushrooms, cleaned and trimmed
¼ teaspoon tarragon
½ teaspoon salt
¼ teaspoon pepper
1 egg
1 beef flank steak (about 2 pounds)
1 carrot, pared and cut in 1-inch pieces
1 stalk celery, cut in 1-inch pieces
½ cup red wine
1 cup beef stock

1. Using **steel blade,** separately process bread to coarse crumbs, Parmesan cheese to a fine powder, and parsley until chopped; remove from bowl.
2. Still using **steel blade,** mince garlic. Add 2 onions and process until chopped.
3. In a skillet, heat butter and sauté onion and garlic until lightly browned.
4. Using **steel blade,** process mushrooms until chopped and add to skillet along with tarragon, sa!t, pepper, and parsley; cook a few minutes more.
5. Using **plastic blade,** lightly beat egg. Add bread crumbs and mushroom mixture to bowl and process, with quick on/off motions, until blended.
6. Spread the mixture on the steak. Roll lengthwise in a jelly-roll fashion and tie with string at 1-inch intervals.
7. In a heavy skillet or Dutch oven, brown the meat on all sides and remove from pan.
8. Using **steel blade,** process carrot, celery, and remaining ½ onion together until finely chopped. Add to skillet, along with wine and beef stock. Place stuffed flank steak on top and cover tightly.
9. Bake at 350°F about 2 hours, or until tender.
10. When meat is done, remove from pan, and keep warm. Using **steel blade,** process pan drippings until puréed. Add more water or milk to reach desired consistency.
11. Put steak on a platter and surround with cooked vegetables such as **sliced zucchini, julienne carrots,** and **frenched green beans.**
12. Cut steak into 1-inch slices and serve with gravy on the side.

4 to 6 servings

976 *Baked Sole in Champagne*

2 ounces Swiss cheese (1 cup shredded)
¼ cup fresh parsley, cleaned and trimmed (2 tablespoons chopped)
1 small onion, peeled and quartered
¼ pound fresh mushrooms, washed and trimmed
1 cup champagne
2 tablespoons butter
1 bay leaf
¼ cup whipping cream
4 sole fillets
Salt and pepper

1. Using **shredding disc,** shred Swiss cheese and set aside.
2. Using **steel blade,** separately process parsley until chopped, and onion until finely chopped. Set aside.
3. Using **slicing disc,** slice mushrooms.
4. In a saucepan, combine champagne, butter, bay leaf, parsley, onion, and mushrooms. Bring to boiling, reduce heat, and cook slowly until reduced by half. Remove bay leaf and mix in cream. Remove from heat.
5. Sprinkle sole fillets with salt and pepper. Place in a baking dish and pour sauce over them. Sprinkle with shredded cheese.
6. Bake at 350°F 25 minutes, or until fish is tender and top is lightly browned.

4 servings

977 *Shrimp Pancakes with Cheese Sauce*

Pancakes:
- 8 cubes (1 inch each) Parmesan cheese (1 cup grated)
- ½ pound fresh shrimp, shelled and cooked
- 2 eggs
- ¾ cup flour
- 1 cup cream
- 5 tablespoons milk
- 1 tablespoon butter, melted
- ¼ teaspoon salt

Cheese Sauce:
- 3 ounces sharp Cheddar cheese (1½ cups shredded)
- 3 tablespoons butter
- 3 tablespoons flour
- 2½ cups milk, scalded
- ¼ teaspoon salt
- ⅛ teaspoon nutmeg

1. For pancakes, using **steel blade,** process Parmesan cheese to a fine powder. Set aside.
2. Using **steel blade,** process cooked shrimp until finely chopped. Set aside.
3. Using **steel blade,** add eggs to bowl and beat lightly. Add remaining ingredients for pancakes and ½ cup grated Parmesan cheese and process until thoroughly blended.
4. In a hot well-buttered 8-inch skillet (crêpe or omelet), drop 3 tablespoons batter. Tilt pan to spread batter evenly into a 6-inch pancake. Fry until lightly browned. Turn and brown other side. Remove to a platter, cool about 1 minute, then roll up and place on a serving dish.
5. Before cooking next pancake, add 1 teaspoon melted butter to the skillet to coat bottom, and pour off excess. Cook next pancake and repeat process until all batter is used up.
6. Sprinkle rolled pancakes generously with remaining Parmesan cheese and keep them hot in a 250°F oven.

7. For sauce, using **shredding disc,** shred cheese and set aside.
8. In a saucepan, melt butter, gradually stir in flour, and cook 2 to 3 minutes. Slowly stir in milk, and continue to cook, stirring with a whisk until sauce is thickened and smooth. Add shredded cheese, salt, and nutmeg and stir until cheese is melted.
9. Serve Cheese Sauce on the side.

15 (6-inch) pancakes;
3 cups Cheese Sauce

978 *Sweet and Sour Chicken*

Sauce:
- ¾ cup chicken stock
- ¼ cup brown sugar
- ¼ cup sugar
- ½ cup vinegar
- ¼ cup ketchup
- 1 tablespoon sherry
- 1 tablespoon cornstarch
- 2 tablespoons soy sauce
- ¼ cup pineapple juice

Chicken:
- 1 chicken breast, boned, skinned, and partially frozen
- 1 clove garlic
- 2 slices fresh ginger, each slice cut in quarters (1 teaspoon minced)
- 3 tablespoons peanut oil
- 1 green pepper, cut in 1-inch pieces
- 1 tomato, cut in 1-inch pieces
- ½ cup pineapple chunks, drained (reserving liquid)

1. For sauce, combine stock, sugars, vinegar, ketchup, and sherry in a saucepan. Bring to a boil, stirring to dissolve sugar.
2. Blend cornstarch, soy sauce, and pineapple juice. Stir into mixture in saucepan and cook over low heat until thickened.

3. For chicken, using **slicing disc,** slice meat (page 13). Set aside.
4. Using **steel blade,** mince garlic and ginger root by starting machine and adding ingredients through feed tube. Set aside.
5. Heat 2 tablespoons peanut oil in a wok. Add minced garlic and ginger root and stir-fry a few seconds. Add sliced chicken and stir-fry until just tender. Remove from pan and set aside.
6. Heat 1 tablespoon peanut oil in wok and stir-fry green peppers 2 to 3 minutes. Add tomato, pineapple, and chicken and stir-fry only to heat through.
7. Remove to a serving dish and spoon sauce over the top. Serve at once with **rice.**

4 servings

979 *Veal Chops with Onion-Cheese Sauce*

6 large veal chops
Milk
4 cubes (1 inch each) Parmesan
  cheese (½ cup grated)
2 ounces Swiss cheese (1 cup
  shredded)
4 large onions, peeled and quartered
Butter (about ⅔ cup)
Flour
2 tablespoons oil
½ teaspoon salt
¼ teaspoon pepper

1. Cover veal with milk and soak for 1 hour.
2. Using **steel blade,** process Parmesan cheese to a fine powder and set aside.
3. Using **shredding disc,** shred Swiss cheese and set aside.
4. Using **steel blade,** process onions, one at a time with quick on/off motions, until finely chopped. In a large skillet, sauté onion in 4 tablespoons butter for about 5 minutes. Cover and steam onion over low heat until transparent and tender, but not browned.
5. Remove chops from milk, reserving milk in a 2-cup measure. Dry on a paper towel, then dust lightly with flour. In a separate skillet, heat 4 tablespoons butter and the oil and brown chops on both sides.
6. Lower the heat, and cook until chops are tender, turning once. Place cooked veal chops in a flat baking dish and keep warm.
7. Meanwhile, drain cooked onion and add liquid to the reserved milk. Add milk, if necessary, to fill to the 1½-cup line.
8. To the skillet in which veal chops were cooked, add enough butter to make 3 tablespoons fat. Add ¼ cup flour, stirring constantly, and cook for about 3 minutes. Slowly add milk-onion mixture, stirring with a wire whisk until smooth and thickened. Add salt, pepper, and Parmesan cheese and cook until thoroughly blended and cheese has melted.
9. Top each veal chop with some of the drained steamed onion. Pour sauce over all and sprinkle with shredded Swiss cheese.
10. Heat in a 475°F oven until cheese melts and browns lightly.

6 servings

980 *Lamb Leg on a Bed of Spinach*

Lamb:
1 lamb leg (6 pounds)
4 cloves garlic
2 carrots, pared and cut in 1-inch
  pieces
2 stalks celery, trimmed and cut in
  1-inch pieces
1 large onion, peeled and quartered
2 tablespoons fresh parsley, cleaned
  and trimmed (1 tablespoon
  chopped)
⅛ teaspoon each thyme, oregano,
  savory, and basil
1 cup beef stock

Spinach:
3 pounds spinach, cleaned and
  trimmed

1. For lamb, put lamb in a roasting pan and stud with 2 cloves garlic, cut in slivers. Bake at 400°F 15 minutes to brown.
2. Meanwhile, using **steel blade,** process remaining garlic, carrots, celery, onion, and parsley all together until finely chopped.
3. After meat has browned, remove from pan. Turn oven down to 350°F. Add chopped vegetables, spices, and beef stock to roasting pan. Place lamb on top. Cover tightly and return to oven. Roast 20 to 25 minutes per pound.
4. For spinach, put spinach into a saucepan with just the water that clings to the leaves, sprinkle with salt, and cook until almost tender (8 to 10 minutes). Remove to a colander and immediately rinse with cold water. Take the spinach in handfuls and squeeze out as much water as possible.
5. Using **steel blade** and working with small batches, process the spinach, using quick on/off motions, until chopped.
6. In an enameled pan, heat 2 tablespoons butter and add

1 teaspoon salt
6 tablespoons butter
⅛ teaspoon pepper
Pinch nutmeg

chopped spinach. Cook over high heat 2 to 3 minutes, stirring constantly, until moisture has cooked away.

7. Add remaining butter, pepper, and nutmeg. Cover and cook slowly 10 minutes until butter is absorbed and spinach is tender. Season with more salt and pepper if necessary.

8. To assemble, remove lamb from roasting pan. Let it stand at room temperature for about 15 minutes. Remove fat and strain sauce, reserving liquid. Using **steel blade,** process vegetable mixture until puréed. With machine running, add strained liquid through the feed tube. Return sauce to pan and simmer.

9. Spread spinach on a serving dish and keep warm.

10. Carve lamb into thin slices and overlap them on the bed of spinach. Serve the sauce separately.

8 servings

981 *Puffy Omelets with Crab Meat Sauce*

Crab Meat Sauce:
  1 small onion, peeled and quartered
  1 apple, pared, cored, and quartered
  1 carrot, pared and cut in 1-inch pieces
  1 stalk celery, trimmed and cut in 1-inch pieces
  6 tablespoons butter
  2 cans (7 ounces each) crab meat
  3 tablespoons flour
  2 cups milk, heated
  1 teaspoon grated lemon peel
  1 tablespoon lemon juice
  ⅛ teaspoon dry mustard
  ½ teaspoon curry powder
  ½ teaspoon salt
    Pinch nutmeg

Omelets:
  8 eggs, separated
  ½ cup milk
  1 teaspoon baking powder
  ½ teaspoon salt
  3 tablespoons butter

1. For sauce, using **steel blade,** process onion, apple, carrot, and celery together until finely chopped.

2. In a saucepan, sauté mixture in 3 tablespoons butter for 5 minutes.

3. Drain crab meat, reserving liquid. Go over crab meat carefully, removing any tendons. Measure crab meat liquid and add enough water to make ½ cup liquid. Add to vegetables; cover and simmer 20 minutes, or until tender.

4. Meanwhile, in another saucepan, melt remaining butter, add flour, and cook 2 to 3 minutes. Off heat, add heated milk and stir with a whisk until thickened and smooth. Add vegetable mixture and remaining ingredients, except crab meat. Simmer 10 minutes.

5. Strain sauce and return to saucepan. Add crab meat and heat thoroughly.

6. For omelets, using **plastic blade,** add egg yolks, milk, and baking powder to the bowl. Process until foamy and lemon colored.

7. Using a mixer, beat egg whites with salt until stiff, but not dry, peaks are formed. Gently fold in egg-yolk mixture.

8. Melt butter in a 12-inch skillet. Add egg mixture, cover, and cook over a medium-low heat 12 to 15 minutes, or until firm. Turn upside down on a platter. Top with some of Crab Meat Sauce and cut into wedges. Serve with remaining Crab Meat Sauce on the side.

6 to 8 servings

982 *Mushroom Kugel*

  5 matzoh
  ¼ cup fresh parsley, cleaned and trimmed (2 tablespoons chopped)
  2 medium onions, peeled and quartered
  ¼ pound fresh mushrooms, cleaned and trimmed
  2 tablespoons butter
  1 egg
  1 cup cottage cheese
  ½ teaspoon salt
  ¼ teaspoon pepper

1. Soak matzoh in cold water for 2 minutes. Squeeze out as much water as possible and set aside.

2. Using **steel blade,** separately process parsley and onions until chopped. Set aside.

3. Using **slicing disc,** slice mushrooms.

4. In a skillet, sauté chopped onion and sliced mushrooms in butter until onion is soft.

5. Using **plastic blade,** beat egg lightly. Add squeezed-out matzoh, mushroom-onion mixture, and remaining ingredients. Process, using quick on/off motions, until blended.

6. Pour into a buttered 2-quart casserole.

7. Bake at 375°F 40 to 45 minutes.

6 servings

983 *German Apple Pancakes*

3 small apples, pared, cored, and quartered
10 tablespoons butter
3 tablespoons sugar
1 teaspoon cinnamon
4 eggs
⅓ cup milk
¼ cup flour
¼ teaspoon salt
Confectioners' sugar

1. Using **slicing disc,** slice apples. Heat 4 tablespoons butter in a 10-inch skillet. Add apple slices, cover, and cook over medium heat until apples are almost tender, gently turning slices several times during cooking. When almost tender, sprinkle a mixture of 2 tablespoons sugar and the cinnamon evenly over the apples. Continue cooking, uncovered, until apples are just tender. Turn into a bowl and keep warm.
2. Using **plastic blade,** beat eggs thoroughly and blend in milk. Add flour, 1 tablespoon sugar, and salt and process a few seconds until blended and smooth.
3. Heat 3 tablespoons of the butter in the skillet until moderately hot. Pour in enough batter to cover bottom of skillet. Spoon about one half of the apple mixture evenly over batter. Pour in just enough batter to cover apples.
4. Bake pancake over medium heat until golden brown on the bottom. Loosen edges with a spatula and carefully turn and brown the other side.
5. When pancake is baked, remove skillet from heat and brush pancake generously with melted butter. Roll up and transfer to a warm serving platter. Sift confectioners' sugar over the top. Keep pancake hot. Repeat procedure with remaining batter and apples.

2 apple pancakes

984 *Cynthia's Cottage Cheese Pancakes*

6 eggs, separated
2 cups cottage cheese
2 tablespoons sugar
½ teaspoon salt
⅔ cup flour
Pinch cinnamon and nutmeg
⅛ teaspoon cream of tartar

1. Using **plastic blade,** process egg yolks, cottage cheese, sugar, salt, flour, cinnamon, and nutmeg until thoroughly blended.
2. Using a mixer, beat egg whites in a large bowl with cream of tartar until stiff, but not dry, peaks are formed. Gently add egg-yolk mixture to bowl and fold together.
3. Drop batter by large spoonfuls to make 4-inch pancakes on an oiled skillet or griddle. Fry until golden on both sides and puffy.
4. Sprinkle with confectioners' sugar and serve with sour cream, preserves, honey, or applesauce on the side.

About 30 (4-inch) pancakes

985 *Asparagus Supreme*

1 slice dry bread, cut in quarters
    (¼ cup crumbs)
2 ounces sharp Cheddar cheese
    (1 cup shredded)
1 small onion, peeled and quartered
2 tablespoons butter
1 tablespoon flour
¼ teaspoon salt
½ teaspoon paprika
¼ teaspoon dry mustard
½ teaspoon Worcestershire sauce
1 cup evaporated milk
2 pounds fresh asparagus, trimmed,
    cooked, and drained
1 tablespoon butter, melted

1. Using **steel blade,** process bread to fine crumbs. Set aside.
2. Using **shredding disc,** shred cheese and set aside.
3. Using **steel blade,** process onion until finely chopped. In a saucepan, cook onion in butter until tender, but not browned. Blend in flour, salt, paprika, dry mustard, and Worcestershire sauce. Heat until bubbly.
4. Remove from heat. Add evaporated milk gradually, stirring constantly. Return to heat; bring to boiling and cook 1 to 2 minutes.
5. Turn asparagus into a 1-quart shallow baking dish. Pour sauce over asparagus. Sprinkle with shredded cheese. Mix bread crumbs and melted butter together and sprinkle over the top.
6. Set under broiler with top of mixture 3 inches from heat and broil 3 to 5 minutes, or until crumbs are lightly browned and cheese is melted.

6 to 8 servings

986 *Broccoli, Sicilian Style*

1 clove garlic
1 medium onion, peeled and cut to
    fit feed tube
2 tablespoons olive oil
1½ tablespoons flour
¼ teaspoon pepper
1 cup chicken stock
3 ounces sharp Cheddar cheese (1½
    cups shredded)
½ cup ripe olives
4 anchovy fillets
2 pounds fresh broccoli, cooked and
    drained

1. Using **steel blade,** mince garlic.
2. Using **slicing disc,** slice onion.
3. In a saucepan, cook onion and garlic in olive oil until onion is soft. Blend in a mixture of flour and pepper and heat until bubbly.
4. Add chicken stock, stirring constantly. Bring to boiling and cook 1 to 2 minutes, or until sauce thickens.
5. Using **shredding disc,** shred cheese.
6. Using **slicing disc,** slice olives.
7. Using **steel blade,** process anchovy fillets until finely chopped.
8. Add shredded cheese, sliced olives, and chopped anchovy fillets to sauce. Stir over low heat until cheese melts. Pour sauce over hot broccoli and serve immediately.

6 servings

987 *Sour Cream Blintzes*

Blintzes:
1 egg
¾ cup dairy sour cream
¾ cup milk
⅛ teaspoon salt
1 teaspoon sugar
1 cup flour
1 tablespoon butter, melted

Filling:
1 carton (8 ounces) cottage cheese
1 package (8 ounces) cream cheese,
    cut in quarters
1 egg
2 tablespoons butter, melted
2 tablespoons sugar
1 teaspoon vanilla extract
¼ cup golden raisins (optional)

Apricot Sauce:
1 pound dried apricots
¾ cup sugar
    Orange liqueur (optional)

1. For blintzes, using **steel blade,** add egg, sour cream, milk, salt, and sugar to bowl. Process until light and fluffy. Add flour and butter and process until smooth.
2. Drop 2 tablespoons batter into a hot buttered 8-inch omelet or crêpe pan. Tilt pan to spread batter evenly into a 5-inch circle. Cook until light golden brown. Turn and cook other side briefly but do not brown. Repeat process until all batter is used. Remember to butter pan before each blintz is cooked and pour off excess butter.
3. Stack blintzes, browned side up, on a plate and cover with a dome-type cover to prevent them from drying out.
4. For filling, using **steel blade,** place all ingredients, except raisins, in the bowl and process until smooth and creamy. Add raisins, if desired, and process, with quick on/off motions, until blended.
5. Place a heaping tablespoon of cheese filling on each pancake. Tuck in opposite sides and roll up.
6. Arrange rolled pancakes in a buttered baking dish.
7. Set in a 350°F oven 10 to 15 minutes, or until heated through.
8. For Apricot Sauce, cover apricots with water and cook until soft. Drain, reserving juice.
9. Using **steel blade,** process until puréed, adding additional strained juice to reach desired consistency. Add sugar and process until sugar is blended into sauce. Return to saucepan and heat thoroughly. Sauce can be flavored with orange liqueur, if desired.
10. Serve with blintzes and **sour cream.**

988 *Blue Cheese Potato Salad*

5 medium potatoes, pared, cooked,
    and diced
½ teaspoon salt
¼ teaspoon pepper
4 hard-cooked eggs
3 stalks celery, trimmed and cut in
    1-inch pieces
4 green onions, trimmed and cut in
    1-inch pieces
½ medium green pepper, trimmed
    and cut in 1-inch pieces
1 cup cottage cheese
½ teaspoon dry mustard
¼ teaspoon salt
⅛ teaspoon pepper
⅔ cup (6-ounce can) evaporated milk
½ cup crumbled blue cheese
2 tablespoons cider vinegar
    Lettuce
    Green pepper slices and tomato
    wedges for garnish

1. Put potatoes into a large bowl and sprinkle with salt and pepper.
2. Using **steel blade,** process hard-cooked eggs, using quick on/off motions, until finely chopped. Add to potatoes.
3. Using **steel blade,** separately process celery, green onion, and green pepper until finely chopped. Add to potatoes and toss lightly.
4. Using **steel blade,** put cottage cheese, dry mustard, salt, pepper, evaporated milk, blue cheese, and vinegar in the bowl. Process until thoroughly blended.
5. Pour dressing over potato mixture in bowl and toss lightly and thoroughly. Chill well before serving to blend the flavors.
2. Spoon chilled potato salad into a bowl lined with lettuce. Garnish with green pepper slices and tomato wedges.

8 servings

989 *Crêpes Farcie*

Crêpes:
- ½ pound fresh spinach, cleaned and trimmed
- 2 egg yolks
- ¼ teaspoon salt
- Dash pepper
- 1 cup flour

Filling:
- 3 cubes (1 inch each) Parmesan cheese (6 tablespoons grated cheese)
- 1 medium onion, peeled and quartered
- 4 tablespoons butter
- 2 ounces mushrooms, cleaned and trimmed
- 1 pound cooked chicken, cut in 1-inch pieces
- 2 tablespoons flour
- 1 cup milk
- 1 tablespoon sherry

Sauce:
- 4 tablespoons butter
- 4 tablespoons flour
- 2 cups milk
- ¾ teaspoon salt
- ¼ teaspoon pepper
- Pinch nutmeg
- 1 tablespoon sherry
- Parmesan cheese

1. For crêpes, cook spinach and drain well. Using **steel blade,** process until finely chopped. Add egg yolks, salt, and pepper and process a few seconds until blended. Add flour and process until dough forms into a ball.
2. On a lightly floured surface, roll out dough ¹/₁₆ inch thick. Cut into 4-inch squares.
3. Add squares one at a time to boiling salted water and cook 4 to 5 minutes, or until tender. Remove with a slotted spoon and cool separately.

4. For filling, using **steel blade,** separately process Parmesan cheese to a fine powder and onion until chopped. In a saucepan, sauté chopped onion in butter until transparent.
5. Using **steel blade,** separately process mushrooms and chicken, using quick on/off motions, until finely chopped. You should have about 1½ cups chopped chicken. Add mushrooms and chicken to saucepan and cook about 5 minutes, stirring occasionally. Add flour and cook 1 or 2 minutes. Gradually add milk, stirring constantly until thickened. Mix in sherry and 2 tablespoons grated Parmesan cheese.
6. Spoon filling along center of each pasta square and roll to form a tube.

7. For sauce, in same saucepan in which chicken was cooked, melt butter and blend in flour. Stir until bubbly. Gradually add milk, stirring with a whisk until smooth. Bring to boiling. Cook and stir 1 to 2 minutes. Mix in salt, pepper, nutmeg, and sherry.
8. Spread a thin layer of sauce in a shallow baking dish. Arrange filled rolls on top and pour cream sauce over all. Sprinkle with remainder of grated Parmesan cheese.
9. Set in a 350°F oven until thoroughly heated.

4 servings

990 *Harvest Soufflé*

- 3 ounces sharp Cheddar cheese (1½ cups shredded)
- 4 tablespoons butter
- ¼ cup flour
- ¼ teaspoon salt
- ⅛ teaspoon garlic powder
- ⅓ cup milk
- 1 can (17 ounces) cream-style corn
- ½ teaspoon Worcestershire sauce
- 6 eggs, separated

1. Using **shredding disc,** shred cheese and set aside.
2. In a saucepan, melt butter, add flour, salt, and garlic powder and heat until bubbly. Remove from heat and blend in milk, corn, and Worcestershire sauce. Return to heat and bring mixture to a boil, stirring constantly. Cook 2 minutes and remove from heat.
3. Add shredded cheese and stir until cheese is melted.
4. Using **plastic blade,** add egg yolks to bowl and process until well beaten. Add corn mixture and process until thoroughly blended, stopping to scrape down sides, if necessary.
5. Using a mixer, beat egg whites until stiff, not dry, peaks are formed. Gently spread egg-yolk mixture over egg whites. Carefully fold together until just blended. Gently turn the mixture into an ungreased 2-quart soufflé dish (deep casserole with straight sides).
6. Bake at 350°F 40 to 45 minutes, or until a knife inserted in the center of the soufflé comes out clean. Serve immediately.

6 servings

991 *Bavarian Carrots*

1 pound carrots, pared and cut in
    2½-inch pieces
1 tablespoon sugar
3 slices bacon
1 large onion, peeled and quartered
2 apples, pared, cored, and
    quartered
½ cup chicken stock
½ teaspoon salt
⅛ teaspoon pepper
    Pinch nutmeg

1. Place carrots horizontally in the feed tube and slice with **slicing disc.**
2. In a saucepan, cover carrots with water and add sugar; cook until barely tender. Drain thoroughly.
3. Meanwhile, in a large saucepan, cook bacon until crisp, reserving drippings. Drain well on paper towel. Using **steel blade,** process until coarsely chopped.
4. Still using **steel blade,** process onion until chopped. Sauté in bacon drippings until golden.
5. Slice apples with **slicing disc.** Add sliced apples and chopped bacon to onions and cook together for 5 minutes. Add cooked carrots and toss gently. Add chicken stock, salt, pepper, and nutmeg and simmer for 5 minutes.

6 servings

992 *Greek-Style Carrots and Green Beans*

1 pound carrots, pared and cut in
    2½-inch pieces
1 clove garlic
1 medium onion, peeled and
    quartered
1 pound fresh green beans, cleaned,
    trimmed, and cut in 2½-inch
    pieces
2 tablespoons butter
2 tablespoons oil
1 can (15 ounces) tomato sauce
¼ teaspoon cinnamon
½ teaspoon salt
¼ teaspoon pepper

1. Place carrots horizontally in the feed tube and slice with **slicing disc.** Set aside.
2. Using **steel blade,** mince garlic. Add onion and process until chopped.
3. In a saucepan, sauté green beans, sliced carrots, onion, and garlic in butter and oil about 15 minutes.
4. Add tomato sauce, cinnamon, salt, and pepper; simmer, partially covered, until vegetables are tender (about 30 minutes).

8 servings

993 *Braised Cucumbers*

¼ cup parsley, cleaned and trimmed
    (2 tablespoons chopped)
2 medium onions, peeled and
    quartered
4 tablespoons butter
6 large cucumbers
2 tablespoons flour
½ cup chicken stock
    Salt and pepper to taste
    Pinch sugar
2 tablespoons lemon juice
1 teaspoon dried dill
½ cup dairy sour cream
    Dash nutmeg

1. Using **steel blade,** separately process parsley and onions until chopped. Set aside.
2. In a saucepan, sauté chopped onion in butter until transparent.
3. Pare cucumbers, cut in half lengthwise, and remove seeds. Cut into 3-inch lengths.
4. Add cucumbers to sautéed onions and cook until lightly browned. Add flour and cook for 2 minutes. Add chicken stock, salt, pepper, sugar, and lemon juice. Sprinkle with chopped parsley and dill and simmer for 10 minutes. Just before serving, add sour cream and nutmeg. Bring to a boil and reduce heat. Simmer for 5 minutes.

8 servings

994 *Green Salad Vinaigrette*

1 hard-cooked egg
1 clove garlic
2 tablespoons fresh parsley, cleaned
    and trimmed (1 tablespoon
    chopped)
⅛ teaspoon chervil
⅛ teaspoon tarragon
1 teaspoon Dijon mustard
1 tablespoon wine vinegar
1 tablespoon lemon juice
4 tablespoons vegetable oil
.2 tablespoons olive oil
¼ teaspoon salt
⅛ teaspoon pepper
1 head romaine lettuce

1. Using **plastic blade,** process hard-cooked egg until finely chopped. Set aside.
2. Using **steel blade,** mince garlic. Add parsley and process until chopped. Add remaining ingredients, except chopped hard-cooked egg and romaine, and process until thoroughly blended.
3. Wash and thoroughly dry romaine; tear into pieces into a salad bowl, pour dressing over lettuce, and gently toss together. Sprinkle chopped hard-cooked egg over the top.

8 servings

995 *Spinach Salad with Hot Sweet and Sour Dressing*

½ pound bacon
1 medium onion, peeled and
    quartered
1 pound fresh spinach

Dressing:
¼ cup water
¼ cup vinegar
½ cup sugar
1½ cups mayonnaise

1. Cook bacon until crisp and set aside. Reserve 1 tablespoon bacon drippings.
2. Using **steel blade,** process onion until chopped and cook in bacon drippings until golden.
3. Wash and trim spinach and drain thoroughly.
4. For dressing, combine water, vinegar, and sugar in a saucepan and boil until sugar dissolves. Add mayonnaise and onion and heat thoroughly, stirring until smooth.
5. Using **steel blade,** process bacon, using quick on/off motions, until coarsely chopped.
6. Pour hot salad dressing over spinach, sprinkle bacon over top, and toss gently.

6 to 8 servings

Note: Any leftover salad dressing can be stored in refrigerator and reheated before serving.

996 *Greek Salad*

Salad Dressing:
- ⅓ cup olive oil
- ¼ cup wine vinegar
- ½ teaspoon salt
- 1 teaspoon oregano

Salad:
- 1 large head romaine, trimmed and torn in pieces
- 1 cucumber, pared and cut in 3½-inch pieces
- 1 small bunch radishes, cleaned and trimmed
- 2 small green peppers, trimmed and cored
- 1 can (8 ounces) whole beets, drained
- 4 tomatoes
- ⅓ pound feta cheese
- Greek olives
- Anchovy fillets (optional)

1. For salad dressing, mix all ingredients and refrigerate.

2. For salad, put romaine pieces in a large salad bowl.

3. Using **slicing disc,** slice cucumber, radishes, green pepper, and beets.

4. Cut tomatoes into quarters.

5. Using **plastic blade,** process feta cheese, using quick on/off motions, until crumbled.

6. Combine prepared salad ingredients with romaine in a bowl, sprinkle with crumbled feta cheese, and top with olives and, if desired, anchovy fillets. Pour salad dressing over salad and serve.

8 servings

997 *Raspberry Mousse*

- 5 packages (10 ounces each) frozen raspberries
- 2 packages unflavored gelatin
- 2 tablespoons lemon juice
- 5 whole eggs
- 4 egg yolks
- ½ cup sugar
- 3 tablespoons raspberry liqueur (optional)
- 2½ cups whipping cream
- 2 tablespoons confectioners' sugar

1. Drain raspberries, reserving juice. Using **steel blade,** process raspberries until pureed. Strain to remove seeds. Discard seeds and set puree adiseset puree aside.

2. In a saucepan, combine lemon juice and 6 tablespoons of reserved raspberry juice. Add gelatin and stir to soften. Stir over low heat until gelatin is dissolved. Let cool.

3. Using **steel blade,** add 5 whole eggs, 4 egg yolks, and sugar to bowl. Process for about 4 to 5 minutes, until very thick. Add raspberry puree and process until combined.

4. With machine on, add cooled gelatin mixture through the feed tube. Process until thoroughly blended. Add raspberry liqueur, if desired.

5. Using a mixer, beat whipping cream until it begins to thicken. Add confectioners' sugar and continue to beat until it holds its shape. Remove one quarter of the whipped cream and save it to decorate the finished mousse.

6. Gently fold whipped cream and raspberry mixture together. Turn into a decorative crystal bowl.

7. Chill mousse until set, at least 2 hours, and decorate with remaining whipped cream put through a pastry bag.

10 to 12 servings

Microwave

998 Seafood Crackers

1 can (8 ounces) crab or shrimp,
    drained, or 1½ pounds cooked
    fresh fish
1 tablespoon sliced green onion
1 cup shredded Swiss cheese
½ cup mayonnaise
1 teaspoon lemon juice
25 crisp crackers

1. In a 1-quart mixing bowl, combine seafood, onion, cheese, mayonnaise, and lemon juice.
2. Spread 1 teaspoon filling on each cracker. Arrange 10 to 12 crackers in a circle on glass plate or waxed paper.
3. Cook 45 seconds to 1 minute, rotating dish one-quarter turn halfway through cooking time. Serve hot.

25 appetizers

999 Sweet-and-Sour Wiener Fondue

1 jar (5 ounces) currant jelly
½ cup prepared mustard
1 pound wieners, cut in bite-size
    pieces

1. In a small glass mixing bowl, combine jelly and mustard. Cook 2 minutes, stirring halfway through cooking time.
2. Add wieners and cook 3 to 4 minutes, stirring halfway through cooking time.
3. Serve warm.

60 to 70 appetizers

1,000 Stuffed Mushrooms

1 bunch green onions, chopped
¼ cup dairy sour cream
½ teaspoon Worcestershire sauce
½ teaspoon oregano
½ cup bulk pork sausage
1 pound fresh mushrooms, washed,
    drained, and stemmed

1. In a 1-quart glass casserole, blend green onions, sour cream, Worcestershire sauce, oregano, and sausage. Cook 2 to 3 minutes, stirring halfway through cooking time.
2. Stuff mushroom caps with filling. Place stem in top of filling and secure in place with wooden pick.
3. Arrange 10 to 12 mushrooms evenly around the edge of a glass pie plate and cook, covered, 6 to 8 minutes.
4. Serve warm.

25 to 30 appetizers

1,001 *Appetizer Kabobs*

8 large precooked smoked sausage links
1 can (16 ounces) pineapple chunks, drained
1 tablespoon brown sugar
2 tablespoons soy sauce
1 tablespoon vinegar

1. Arrange sausage evenly around edge of roasting rack set in a glass dish or directly on glass plate and cook 2 to 3 minutes, rotating dish one-quarter turn halfway through cooking time. Drain sausage and cut each sausage link into 5 pieces.
2. Make kabobs, using 1 sausage piece and 1 pineapple chunk threaded on a round wooden pick. Arrange evenly in a large shallow dish.
3. In a 1-cup glass measure, blend brown sugar, soy sauce, and vinegar and pour over kabobs. Refrigerate 1 or 2 hours until serving time.
4. Arrange 20 kabobs on a large glass plate and cook 2 to 3 minutes, rotating dish one-quarter turn and spooning sauce over top halfway through cooking time.
5. Cook additional kabobs as needed. Serve warm.

40 appetizers

Snackin' Nuts

¼ cup sugar
½ teaspoon cinnamon
1 tablespoon brown sugar
2 tablespoons butter
2 cups pecan halves

1. Combine sugar, cinnamon, and brown sugar; set aside.
2. In a 2-quart glass casserole, heat butter 30 seconds. Add nuts and cook 4 to 5 minutes, stirring every minute.
3. Add sugar mixture to nuts and stir to coat nuts evenly. Spread out on wooden board to cool.
4. Serve warm or cold.

2 cups nuts

Note: May be stored in freezer.

Mock Bouillabaisse

1 small onion, sliced
1 clove garlic, minced
1 bay leaf
¼ teaspoon thyme
2 tablespoons olive oil
1 can (10¾ ounces) condensed tomato soup
¾ soup can water
2 cups cooked seafood
1 teaspoon lemon juice
Dash Tabasco
3 or 4 slices French bread, toasted

1. In a 3-quart glass casserole, combine onion, garlic, bay leaf, thyme, and olive oil. Cook 3 to 4 minutes, stirring halfway through cooking time, until onion is tender.
2. Stir in soup, water, seafood, lemon juice, and Tabasco.
3. Heat 6 to 8 minutes, stirring every 2 minutes, until boiling.
4. Cover and cook an additional 2 minutes.
5. Rest 5 minutes. Ladle soup over toast in bowls.

3 or 4 servings

Leek Soup, page 36
Peasant Black Bread, page 275

Creamed Onion Soup

4 medium onions, sliced
½ cup butter
¼ cup flour
1 quart milk
2 cups chicken broth or 2 chicken
　　bouillon cubes dissolved in 2
　　cups boiling water
1 to 1½ teaspoons salt
1 egg yolk
1 tablespoon minced parsley
½ cup croutons

1. In a 3-quart glass casserole, sauté onions in butter 4 to 5 minutes, stirring every minute. Stir in flour and cook until sauce bubbles, about 1 minute.
2. Add milk slowly, stirring gently. Cook until slightly thickened, about 6 to 8 minutes, stirring every 2 minutes.
3. Add broth and cook 5 minutes, stirring twice.
4. Stir in salt to taste. Blend some of the hot soup with egg yolk and return to remaining soup. Cook 1 minute, stirring every 15 seconds.
5. Serve topped with minced parsley and croutons.

8 servings

Spaghetti Meat Sauce

1 pound ground beef
1 clove garlic, minced
1 small onion, chopped
1 can (15 ounces) tomato sauce
1 teaspoon oregano
½ teaspoon basil
½ teaspoon salt
¼ teaspoon pepper
½ cup tomato juice or ketchup

1. In a 2-quart glass casserole, brown ground beef 2 to 3 minutes, stirring to crumble.
2. Stir in garlic and onion. Cook, covered, 5 minutes, stirring halfway through cooking time.
3. Add tomato sauce, oregano, basil, salt, pepper, and tomato juice.
4. Cook, covered, 15 to 20 minutes, stirring several times. Rest, covered, 5 minutes.
5. Serve over **cooked spaghetti,** and sprinkle with **grated Parmesan cheese.**

4 servings

Gravy

¼ cup flour
¼ cup drippings
2 cups broth, water, or milk
1 teaspoon salt
¼ teaspoon pepper

1. In a 4-cup glass measure, blend flour into drippings to make a smooth paste. Gradually stir in liquid until smooth.
2. Cook 1 to 3 minutes, stirring every minute, until smooth and thickened. Add salt and pepper; stir to blend.
3. Cook 30 seconds to 1 minute.

2 cups

Pumpkin Bread

1½ cups sugar
⅓ cup salad oil
2 eggs
1 cup canned pumpkin
1½ cups all-purpose flour
¾ teaspoon salt
½ teaspoon cinnamon
½ teaspoon nutmeg
½ teaspoon cloves
½ teaspoon allspice
1 teaspoon baking soda
¼ teaspoon baking powder
½ cup coarsely chopped walnuts

1. In a large mixing bowl, blend sugar, oil, eggs, and pumpkin. When ingredients are well mixed, stir in flour, salt, cinnamon, nutmeg, cloves, allspice, baking soda, and baking powder, blending well. Stir in walnuts. Pour batter into an 8×4-inch glass dish.
2. Cook 12 to 14 minutes, rotating dish one-quarter turn every 4 minutes. Knife inserted in the center should come out clean when bread is done.
3. Rest 5 minutes and remove from pan. Serve either warm or cold with **butter** or **cream cheese.**

1 loaf bread

Strawberry Pear Flambee, page 315

Blueberry Streusel

1½ cups all-purpose flour
¾ cup uncooked oats
1 cup firmly packed brown sugar
½ teaspoon baking soda
½ teaspoon salt
½ cup butter
1 can (21 ounces) blueberry pie filling

1. In a large mixing bowl, blend flour, oats, brown sugar, baking soda, and salt. Cut butter into dry mixture until crumbly. Spread one half of mixture into an 8-inch glass baking dish, and press firmly in bottom.
2. Spread pie filling evenly over crumb mixture. Top pie filling with remaining crumb mixture.
3. Cook 12 to 15 minutes, rotating dish one-quarter turn halfway through cooking time.
4. Serve warm or cold.

8 or 9 servings

Note: Any fruit pie filling may be used.

Raisin Bran Muffins

½ cup sugar
⅓ cup shortening
1 egg
1 cup all-purpose flour
2 teaspoons baking powder
½ teaspoon baking soda
½ teaspoon salt
2 cups raisin bran flakes
1 cup buttermilk

1. In a medium mixing bowl, cream sugar and shortening. Add egg and beat until light and fluffy.
2. Add flour, baking powder, baking soda, and salt; stir to blend. Fold in raisin bran flakes and buttermilk. Stir just to moisten.
3. Line custard cups, paper drinking cups, or cupcaker with paper cups. Fill each cup no more than half full. Arrange 6 cups in a circle and cook 3 to 3½ minutes, rearranging cups halfway through cooking time.
4. Serve warm with **butter** and **jelly**.

12 to 14 muffins

Quick Cheese Bread

2½ cups all-purpose biscuit mix
1 cup shredded sharp Cheddar
 cheese
1 tablespoon poppy seed
1 egg
1 cup milk

1. In a medium mixing bowl, blend biscuit mix, cheese, poppy seed, egg, and milk. Stir just to moisten. Pour into a buttered 8-inch square glass baking dish.
2. Cook 5 to 7 minutes, rotating dish one-quarter turn halfway through cooking time. Allow to stand 5 minutes. Center will be soft but will set with standing.

9 to 12 servings

Note: A glass may be placed in the center of dish before pouring in batter to help the bread cook. A 9-inch round glass baking dish may also be used.

The bread may be browned under a conventional broiler for 1 to 2 minutes, but only if a glass ceramic baking dish is used, or the bread is transferred to a metal pan.

Quick Cheese Muffins: Follow recipe for Quick Cheese Bread. Line custard cups, paper drinking cups, or cupcaker with paper baking cups. Fill each cup half full with batter. Arrange 6 cups in a circle in microwave oven. Bake for 2 to 2½ minutes, rearranging cups halfway through cooking time.

About 1½ dozen muffins

Assorted Hot Rolls

The microwave oven is a real aid in serving piping hot rolls at every meal. Heating times may vary, depending on whether the roll has a filling, icing, or nut coating. Always undercook rolls rather than overcook them. Any complaints about dry, tough rolls are always an indication of overcooking.

Rolls (plain or sweet)

1. Place rolls in a napkin, terry towel, or napkin in a wooden bread basket.
2. Heat as follows: 1 roll, 10 to 15 seconds; 2 rolls, 20 to 30 seconds; 4 rolls, 40 to 60 seconds; and 6 rolls, 1 to 1¼ minutes. Always start with the shortest time, and heat longer if necessary.
3. Serve immediately while warm.

Peanut Butter Coffee Cake

2 cups all-purpose biscuit mix
2 tablespoons sugar
¼ cup peanut butter, chunky or
 smooth
⅔ cup milk
1 egg
½ cup jelly or jam (optional)

1. Combine biscuit mix and sugar; cut in peanut butter with a fork. Stir in milk and egg; blend evenly. Pour into a buttered 9-inch glass dish. Swirl jelly through batter, if desired.
2. Cook 8 to 10 minutes, rotating dish one-quarter turn halfway through cooking time.
3. Rest 5 minutes before serving.

4 to 6 servings

Coffee Cake Ring

½ cup butter
¾ cup brown sugar
1 egg
1 cup whole wheat pancake mix
1 teaspoon vanilla extract
¼ cup water
1 cup quick-cooking oats
½ cup butterscotch-flavored pieces
½ cup chopped walnuts

1. In a mixing bowl, blend butter, brown sugar, egg, and pancake mix.
2. Add vanilla extract, water, oats, butterscotch-flavored pieces, and walnuts. Stir until evenly blended.
3. Place small glass, open end up, in center of 8-inch glass dish. Pour batter into dish around glass.
4. Cook 4 to 6 minutes, rotating dish one-quarter turn halfway through cooking time. Rest 5 minutes.
5. Serve warm.

6 to 8 servings

Muffin Bread

5 cups all-purpose flour
2 packages active dry yeast
1 tablespoon sugar
2 teaspoons salt
2½ cups milk
½ teaspoon baking soda
1 tablespoon warm water
¼ cup cornmeal

1. In a large bowl, blend 3 cups flour, yeast, sugar, and salt.
2. In a 4-cup glass measure, heat milk 2 to 3 minutes until warm.
3. Stir milk into flour mixture and blend well. Stir in remaining flour. Cover; let rise in a warm place until doubled, about 1 hour.
4. Blend baking soda and water, then stir into batter, blending well. Divide batter in half; place in two 8×4-inch loaf dishes. Cover; let rise until doubled, about 1 hour.
5. Sprinkle 2 tablespoons cornmeal on top of each loaf.
6. Cook loaves individually 5 to 6 minutes, rotating dish one-quarter turn every 2 minutes.
7. Rest 5 minutes and remove from dish.
8. Slice and toast before serving.

2 loaves bread

Sour Cream Coffee Cake

½ cup butter
1 cup sugar
3 eggs
1 teaspoon vanilla extract
1 cup dairy sour cream
2 cups all-purpose flour
1 teaspoon baking powder
1 teaspoon baking soda
¾ cup firmly packed brown sugar
¼ cup butter
¼ cup all-purpose flour
¼ teaspoon salt
¼ teaspoon cinnamon
1 cup chopped walnuts

1. In a mixing bowl, cream butter and sugar. Add eggs and stir to blend. Stir in vanilla extract and sour cream. Add flour, baking powder, and baking soda. Stir until well mixed.
2. Line bottom of two 8-inch round glass baking dishes with waxed paper. Pour one quarter of the batter into each cake pan.
3. In a small mixing bowl, combine brown sugar, butter, flour, salt, and cinnamon; stir until crumbly. Mix in nuts.
4. Sprinkle one quarter of the nut mixture on each cake layer. Divide remaining batter between each dish, and pour over nut mixture. Cover with remaining nut mixture.
5. Cook 1 dish at a time, covered with waxed paper, 4 to 5 minutes, rotating dish one-quarter turn halfway through cooking time.
6. Rest 5 minutes before serving.

12 to 16 servings

Note: Cooked coffee cake may be frozen.

Chinese Tomato Beef

2 pounds beef steak (sirloin, round, flank, or chuck)
2 tablespoons sugar
½ cup soy sauce
1 clove garlic, minced
¼ teaspoon ginger
3 tablespoons salad oil
2 large green peppers, cut in strips
3 green onions, cut in 1-inch pieces
2 large tomatoes, peeled and cut in wedges
2 tablespoons cornstarch
¼ cup water

1. Slice steak diagonally across the grain in ⅛-inch-thick slices. Meat will slice easier if placed in the freezer 30 minutes.
2. In a 2-cup glass measure, combine sugar, soy sauce, garlic, and ginger. Pour over meat in a 9-inch baking dish. Marinate at least 30 minutes, turning meat occasionally.
3. Preheat browning dish 6 minutes. Remove meat from marinade; reserve marinade. Add oil and meat to dish. Fry meat 5 to 6 minutes in microwave oven, stirring halfway through cooking time. Drain cooking juices into marinade.
4. Stir green pepper and onion into meat. Cook 3 to 4 minutes, stirring halfway through cooking time. Top with tomato wedges.
5. In a 1-cup glass measure, combine cornstarch and water, and blend with marinade. Cook 1 to 2 minutes, stirring halfway through cooking time, until thickened. Pour over meat and vegetables and heat 1 to 2 minutes.
6. Rest 5 minutes and serve over **hot fluffy rice.**

8 servings

Marinated Flank Steak

⅓ cup soy sauce
2 tablespoons vinegar
¼ cup minced onion
¼ teaspoon garlic powder
1½ teaspoons ground ginger
2 tablespoons sugar
2 pounds beef flank steak

1. In a 2-quart glass baking dish, blend soy sauce, vinegar, onion, garlic powder, ginger, and sugar. Dip meat in mixture and marinate 4 hours, turning occasionally.
2. Cut steak into serving pieces. Pound to tenderize.
3. Return to 2-quart dish with sauce and cook, covered, 12 to 14 minutes, rotating dish one-quarter turn halfway through cooking time.
4. Serve with **hot rice.**

6 or 7 servings

Many-Way Meatballs

1 pound ground beef
¼ cup dry bread crumbs
¼ cup minced onion
1 egg
¼ teaspoon salt
1 can (10½ ounces) condensed Cheddar cheese, cream of celery, or cream of mushroom soup
½ cup water
2 tablespoons parsley flakes

1. In a mixing bowl, combine beef, bread crumbs, onion, egg, and salt. Shape into 16 meatballs, and place in a 2-quart baking dish.
2. Cook, covered, 5 to 6 minutes, stirring halfway through cooking time. Pour off drippings.
3. Stir in soup, water, and parsley. Cover and cook 6 to 8 minutes, stirring halfway through cooking time.
4. Rest 5 minutes before serving.

3 or 4 servings

Marvelous Eggs

3 tablespoons butter
1 tablespoon minced green onion
6 eggs, slightly beaten
⅓ cup milk
½ teaspoon salt
¼ teaspoon lemon juice
1 package (3 ounces) cream cheese,
    cut in ½-inch cubes

1. In a 2-quart glass casserole, heat butter 30 seconds. Add onion and cook 2 minutes, stirring once. Stir in eggs, milk, salt, and lemon juice.
2. Cook, covered, 4 to 5 minutes, stirring every 2 minutes. When almost set, lightly fold in cream cheese.
3. Cook 1 minute longer, rest 5 minutes, and serve.

4 servings

Mushroom Eggs on Toast

1 pound fresh mushrooms, cleaned
    and sliced
¼ cup butter
4 slices hot buttered toast
2 tablespoons butter
2 tablespoons flour
1 cup milk
½ cup grated Parmesan cheese
¼ teaspoon dry mustard
4 poached eggs
    Paprika (optional)

1. In a 1-quart glass casserole, cook mushrooms in ¼ cup butter 3 to 4 minutes, stirring halfway through cooking time. Cover each slice toast with one-fourth of the mushrooms.
2. In a 2-cup glass measure, heat 2 tablespoons butter 30 seconds. Stir in flour to blend. Stir in milk and cook 2 to 3 minutes, stirring every minute, until sauce becomes thick. Add cheese and dry mustard; stir to blend.
3. Place an egg on top of mushrooms on each toast slice and cover with sauce. Sprinkle with paprika, if desired.

3 or 4 servings

Confetti Eggs

2 tablespoons butter
½ cup diced ham
2 green onions, including tops,
    chopped
4 eggs
    Dash Tabasco
½ teaspoon salt
¼ teaspoon pepper

1. In a 2-quart glass casserole, cook butter, ham, and green onions 3 to 4 minutes, stirring every minute.
2. Add eggs, Tabasco, salt, and pepper; stir to blend.
3. Cook, covered, 3 to 4 minutes, stirring halfway through cooking time.
4. Rest, covered, 5 minutes.

3 or 4 servings

Tangy Pork Chops

4 to 6 pork chops
    Prepared mustard
1 can (10½ ounces) condensed cream
    of celery soup

1. Spread both sides of each pork chop with mustard and place in a 10-inch glass baking dish.
2. Cook pork chops 6 to 8 minutes, rotating dish one-quarter turn halfway through cooking time.
3. Remove drippings from pan. Pour soup over pork chops. Cook, covered, 5 to 6 minutes, rotating dish one-quarter turn halfway through cooking time.
4. Rest, covered, 5 minutes before serving.

4 to 6 servings

Breakfast Kabobs

8 ounces link pork sausage
6 ounces Canadian bacon, or 12 ounces canned luncheon meat
1 can (8 ounces) pineapple chunks, drained
16 maraschino cherries
Maple syrup
8 bamboo skewers

1. Cut each sausage link in 3 or 4 pieces. Cut bacon in small cubes.
2. Thread meat and fruit alternately on skewers. Arrange in a 2-quart glass baking dish and brush with maple syrup.
3. Cook, covered, 4 to 6 minutes, rotating one-quarter turn and basting with syrup halfway through cooking time.

4 to 6 servings

Sausage Ring

1 pound bulk pork sausage
2 eggs
2 tablespoons minced onion
½ cup bread crumbs
2 tablespoons parsley flakes

1. In a 1-quart glass casserole, blend sausage, eggs, onion, bread crumbs, and parsley flakes. Mold into a ring and place a small glass, open end up, in the center of the ring.
2. Cook 5 to 6 minutes, rotating dish one-quarter turn halfway through cooking time.
3. Rest 5 minutes, remove glass from center, and invert ring on plate to serve. Center may be filled with **cooked rice** or **noodles.** If using for breakfast, center may be filled with **scrambled eggs.**

4 or 5 servings

Note: Leftover Sausage Ring makes good sandwiches when reheated.

Fresh Ham

5- to 6-pound cook-before-eating ham

1. Place ham on roasting rack in a 2-quart glass baking dish. Shield protruding corners or shank end with foil. Do not allow foil to touch walls inside microwave oven.
2. Cook 40 to 50 minutes, allowing 8 to 9 minutes per pound. Turn ham over and rotate dish one-quarter turn halfway through cooking time.
3. Rest 10 to 15 minutes before carving or serving.

10 to 12 servings

Cooked Ham: Follow recipe for Fresh Ham, but allow 6 to 7 minutes per pound cooking time, or 30 to 40 minutes for a 5- to 6-pound ham.

Fresh Pork Roast: Follow recipe for Fresh Ham, allowing 8 to 9 minutes per pound cooking time.

Creamed Chicken Casserole

4 chicken breasts, halved
1 can (10½ ounces) condensed cream
    of chicken soup
2 tablespoons brandy
½ cup dairy sour cream
2 green onions, chopped
    Dash pepper
¼ cup cashews
    Parsley, chopped
    Paprika

1. Wash chicken and pat dry. Arrange in a 2-quart baking dish. Cook 10 to 12 minutes, rotating one-quarter turn halfway through cooking time.
2. In a mixing bowl blend soup, brandy, sour cream, onion, pepper, and cashews. Pour over chicken.
3. Cook, covered, 12 to 15 minutes, rotating one-quarter turn halfway through cooking time.
4. Garnish with parsley or paprika, if desired.

4 servings

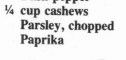

Chicken Hawaiian

1½ cups sliced celery
1 green pepper, cut in strips
3 tablespoons butter
3 cups cubed cooked chicken
1 can (21 ounces) pineapple pie
    filling
¼ cup soy sauce
2 teaspoons instant chicken bouillon
    Chow mein noodles
    Parsley (optional)

1. In a 2-quart glass casserole, blend celery, green pepper, and butter. Cook 3 to 4 minutes, stirring halfway through cooking time.
2. Add chicken, pie filling, soy sauce, and bouillon; mix well.
3. Cook, covered, 10 to 12 minutes, stirring halfway through cooking time.
4. Serve over chow mein noodles and garnish with parsley, if desired.

5 or 6 servings

Dinner Chicken Wings

2 to 3 pounds chicken wings
1 teaspoon ginger
1 teaspoon dry mustard
1 tablespoon brown sugar
⅓ cup soy sauce
3 tablespoons salad oil
3 cloves garlic, quartered
2 tablespoons sesame seed

1. Clip wing tips from each wing. Divide each wing at the joint, in two pieces. Place wing pieces in a 2-quart glass baking dish.
2. In a mixing bowl, blend ginger, mustard, brown sugar, soy sauce, oil, and garlic. Pour over chicken pieces and marinate overnight.
3. Remove the garlic pieces from the marinade. Cook the chicken in marinade 12 to 14 minutes, rotating dish one-quarter turn halfway through cooking time.
4. Rest, covered with waxed paper, 10 minutes. Pour off marinade. Sprinkle chicken with sesame seed and heat 1 minute.

5 or 6 servings

Note: Dinner Chicken Wings may be served with rice for a main dish or used as an appetizer.

Roast Turkey

8- to 15-pound turkey
2 tablespoons butter
1 tablespoon bottled brown bouquet
   sauce

1. Clean and prepare turkey for cooking as directed on turkey wrapper. Place turkey, breast down on roasting rack in a glass baking dish; cover with waxed paper.
2. Estimate the total cooking time. For an 8- to 12-pound turkey allow 7 to 8 minutes per pound, and for a 12- to 15-pound turkey allow 6 to 7 minutes per pound. Cook the turkey for a fourth of the estimated cooking time
3. Melt the butter in a custard cup and mix with the bottled brown bouquet sauce. Brush the turkey with the mixture. Cover the bottom half of wings and legs with small pieces of aluminum foil. Secure legs and wings close to body with string. Cover with waxed paper. Do not allow foil to touch inside walls of microwave oven.
4. Place turkey on its side and cook a fourth of estimated roasting time. Turn turkey on its other side and cook for another fourth of estimated roasting time. Cut strings to allow legs and wings to stand free, remove foil, place turkey breast up, and cook until turkey reaches internal temperature of 175°F. Each time turkey is turned rotate dish one-quarter turn and baste with drippings. Remove drippings as they accumulate, or additional cooking time will be needed.
5. When cooking time is up, rest the turkey 15 to 20 minutes; temperature should reach 190°F. Return to oven for additional cooking if needed.
6. Garnish with green grapes and serve.

About 2 servings per pound

Note: If desired, turkey cavity may be filled with Apple Dressing. Follow Roast Turkey recipe, but add 6 minutes per pound to the cooking time.

Apple Dressing

1½ cups finely chopped celery
 ⅔ cup finely chopped onion
  1 cup butter
  1 teaspoon salt
  1 teaspoon sage or thyme
 ½ to ¾ cup water
 12 cups dry bread cubes
  3 cups pared and chopped apple

1. In a 3-quart glass casserole, sauté celery and onion in butter 2 to 3 minutes, stirring after every minute.
2. Mix together salt, sage, and water. Pour over bread cubes, tossing lightly to mix.
3. Add bread cubes to vegetable mixture. Stir in apple, blending evenly.
4. Stuff turkey just before roasting, or cook dressing in a 3-quart casserole dish 10 to 12 minutes, rotating dish one-quarter turn halfway through cooking time.
5. Rest 5 minutes before serving.

10 to 12 servings

Note: This dressing is also good with pork chops. Extra dressing may be frozen and reheated later.

Microwave Fried Chicken

1 broiler-fryer (2½ to 3 pounds)
1 cup corn flake crumbs
¼ cup butter
  Paprika

1. Wash chicken and coat with crumbs. In a 1-cup glass measure, heat butter 45 seconds.
2. On roasting rack in a 2-quart glass baking dish, arrange chicken with meatier pieces around edges of dish, and smaller pieces, such as wings, in the center. Pour a small amount of butter over each piece. Sprinkle with paprika.
3. Cook 10 to 12 minutes. Turn chicken pieces over and coat each piece with remaining butter and paprika. Cook 10 to 12 minutes.
4. Rest 5 minutes before serving.

4 to 6 servings

Note: The chicken may be covered during cooking, which will steam the chicken, producing a soft, not crisp, skin. If the chicken is in a glass ceramic baking dish or is transferred to a metal pan, additional browning can be achieved by placing cooked chicken under a conventional broiler 1 to 2 minutes.

Paprika Buttered Fish Fillets

1 package (1 pound) frozen fish fillets
  (perch, haddock, cod, or halibut),
  thawed
  Flour
  Salt and pepper
2 tablespoons butter
  Paprika

1. Dip fillets in flour seasoned with salt and pepper; coating well. Set aside.
2. Melt butter in an 11x7-inch baking dish. Dip fillets in butter and arrange in baking dish. Sprinkle with paprika.
3. Cook, uncovered, 2 to 4 minutes. Do not turn fish over, but do rotate dish one-quarter turn halfway through cooking time.
4. Serve garnished with **cooked asparagus spears** and **carrots**.

About 4 servings

Stuffed Flounder

¼ cup chopped green onion
¼ cup butter
1 can (4 ounces) chopped mushrooms
1 can (6½ ounces) crab meat,
  drained
½ cup cracker crumbs
2 tablespoons parsley flakes
½ teaspoon salt
¼ teaspoon pepper
2 pounds flounder fillets, cut in
  serving pieces
2 tablespoons butter
2 tablespoons flour
¼ teaspoon salt
  Milk
⅓ cup sherry
1 cup shredded Cheddar cheese
½ teaspoon paprika
1 teaspoon parsley flakes

1. In a 2-quart glass casserole, combine green onion and butter and cook 2 to 3 minutes, stirring after every minute.
2. Drain mushrooms and reserve liquid. Combine mushrooms, crab meat, cracker crumbs, 2 tablespoons parsley flakes, salt, and pepper with cooked onion. Spread mixture over fish fillets. Roll up each piece of fish and secure with a wooden pick. Place seam side down in a 10-inch glass baking dish.
3. In a 4-cup glass measure, heat butter 30 seconds. Stir in flour and salt.
4. Add enough milk to reserved mushroom liquid to make 1 cup. Gradually stir milk and sherry into flour mixture. Cook sauce 2 to 3 minutes, stirring every minute, until thickened. Pour sauce over flounder.
5. Cook flounder 6 to 8 minutes, rotating dish one-quarter turn halfway through cooking time.
6. Sprinkle cheese, paprika, and 1 teaspoon parsley flakes over fish. Cook 3 to 5 minutes, or until fish flakes easily with fork.

6 to 8 servings

Fish with Caper Stuffing

1 dressed trout, pike, haddock, perch, or flounder (about 1½ pounds)
1 teaspoon salt
1 cup coarse dry bread crumbs
¼ cup capers
2 tablespoons finely chopped green onion
2 tablespoons finely chopped parsley
1 egg, slightly beaten
2 to 4 tablespoons half-and-half
Lemon wedges

1. Rinse fish under cold water; drain well and pat dry with paper towels. Sprinkle cavity with salt and set aside.
2. Combine bread crumbs, capers, green onion, and parsley. Blend egg with 2 tablespoons half-and-half and pour over bread crumb mixture. Mix until moistened, adding additional half-and-half if necessary.
3. Lightly pile stuffing into fish. Fasten with wooden picks or secure with string. Place in an 11×7-inch baking dish. Cover with waxed paper.
4. Cook fish 8 to 10 minutes, or until fish flakes when tested with a fork; rotate dish one-quarter turn halfway through the cooking time. Allow to stand 2 minutes after cooking before serving. Garnish with lemon wedges.

4 servings

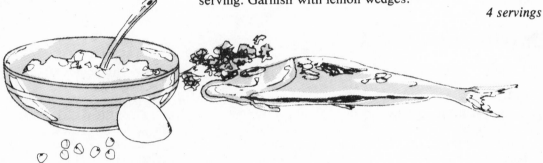

Red Snapper à l'Orange

1 pound red snapper, cut in serving pieces
2 tablespoons orange juice
1 teaspoon grated orange peel
1 tablespoon butter
½ teaspoon lemon juice
½ teaspoon salt
¼ teaspoon pepper
Parsley sprigs

1. In a 2-quart glass baking dish, arrange fish evenly around edge.
2. In a 1-cup glass measure, blend orange juice, orange peel, butter, lemon juice, salt, and pepper. Heat 30 seconds and pour over fish.
3. Cook fish, covered, 5 to 6 minutes, rotating dish one-quarter turn halfway through cooking time.
4. Rest, covered, 5 minutes before serving. Garnish with parsley.

4 servings

Sole Sauté Amandine

3 tablespoons flour
¾ teaspoon salt
¼ teaspoon pepper
1 pound sole or other white fish
   fillets
1 tablespoon oil
¼ cup butter
¼ cup sliced almonds
1 tablespoon fresh lemon juice
1 tablespoon chopped parsley

1. Combine flour, salt, and pepper in a shallow dish. Dip fillets into mixture, coating on all sides.
2. In a 10-inch glass dish, heat oil and 1 tablespoon butter 1 minute. Place fillets in dish and cover.
3. Sauté 4 to 5 minutes, turning fillets over and rotating dish one-quarter turn halfway through cooking time. Rest, covered, 5 minutes.
4. In a 1-cup glass measure, combine 3 tablespoons butter, almonds, and lemon juice. Cook and stir 1 to 2 minutes, until brown.
5. Pour sauce over fillets, sprinkle with parsley, and serve immediately.

3 or 4 servings

Salmonburgers

1 can (16 ounces) salmon
½ cup chopped onion
¼ cup salad oil
⅓ cup dry bread crumbs
2 eggs, beaten
1 teaspoon dry mustard
½ teaspoon salt
½ cup dry bread crumbs

1. Drain salmon, reserving ⅓ cup liquid; set aside.
2. In a 2-cup glass measure, cook onion in oil 2 to 2½ minutes. In a large mixing bowl, combine onion, ⅓ cup dry bread crumbs, reserved salmon liquid, eggs, mustard, salt, and salmon; mix well. Shape into 6 patties.
3. Roll patties in ½ cup bread crumbs. Place on roasting rack in a 2-quart baking dish. Cook patties 5 to 6 minutes, rotating dish one-quarter turn halfway through cooking time. Rest 5 minutes before serving.

3 or 4 servings

Salmon Ring: Follow recipe for Salmonburgers. Form mixture into a ring in a 1½-quart glass baking dish. Place a glass, open end up, in center of ring. Cook 5 to 6 minutes, rotating dish one-quarter turn halfway through cooking time. Rest 5 minutes before serving.

Shrimp Creole

3 tablespoons butter
½ cup chopped onion
½ cup thin strips green pepper
½ cup diced celery
1 clove garlic, minced
1 can (16 ounces) tomatoes, drained
1 can (8 ounces) tomato sauce
1 tablespoon Worcestershire sauce
1 teaspoon salt
1 teaspoon sugar
½ teaspoon chili powder
  Dash Tabasco
1 tablespoon cornstarch
1 pound cooked shrimp, peeled and
  deveined

1. In a 3-quart glass casserole, blend butter, onion, green pepper, celery, and garlic. Cook 3 to 4 minutes, stirring halfway through cooking time.
2. Stir in tomatoes, tomato sauce, Worcestershire sauce, salt, sugar, chili powder, and Tabasco. Cook 8 minutes, stirring every 3 minutes.
3. In a 1-cup glass measure, blend cornstarch with 2 tablespoons liquid from tomato mixture, and blend into casserole.
4. Cook 3 to 4 minutes, stirring halfway through cooking time. Fold in shrimp and heat 2 to 3 minutes.
5. Rest 10 minutes before serving.

5 or 6 servings

Lasagna

4 cups water
8 ounces lasagna noodles
1 tablespoon salad oil
1½ pounds ground beef
1 clove garlic, crushed in a garlic
  press
1 cup small curd cottage cheese
4 ounces mozzarella cheese,
  shredded
½ teaspoon salt
½ cup mayonnaise
1 jar (16 ounces) spaghetti sauce
  without meat
½ teaspoon oregano
  Grated Parmesan cheese

1. In a large pan on range, bring the water to boiling. Add noodles and salad oil. Cook 5 to 6 minutes until tender; drain.
2. In a medium glass mixing bowl, break apart ground beef. Add garlic and cook 6 to 7 minutes, stirring every 2 minutes. Drain off drippings.
3. Add cottage cheese, mozzarella cheese, salt, and mayonnaise to meat mixture; stir to blend.
4. In a 9-inch glass baking dish, place a layer of noodles on the bottom and cover with a layer of meat mixture. Continue layering with remaining noodles and meat. Pour spaghetti sauce over top and sprinkle with oregano and desired amount of Parmesan cheese.
5. Cook, covered, 6 to 8 minutes, rotating dish one-quarter turn halfway through cooking time.
6. Rest, covered, 10 minutes before serving.

4 to 6 servings

Macaroni-Franks Dinner

8 ounces macaroni
1 pound frankfurters, cut in 1-inch
  pieces
1 cup mayonnaise
2 ounces Cheddar cheese, cut in thin
  strips
½ cup sliced green onion
2 tablespoons prepared mustard
½ teaspoon salt
¼ teaspoon pepper

1. Cook macaroni as directed on package. Drain well.
2. In a 1½-quart casserole, combine frankfurters, mayonnaise, cheese, green onion, mustard, salt, and pepper; stir to blend. Stir in cooked macaroni.
3. Cook, covered, 6 to 8 minutes, rotating dish one-quarter turn halfway through cooking time.
4. Rest 5 minutes before serving.

6 to 8 servings

Tortilla Casserole

1½ pounds ground beef
 1 medium onion, chopped
 1 clove garlic, minced
 1 tablespoon chili powder
 1 can (15 ounces) tomato sauce
 ⅔ cup water
 8 corn tortillas
2½ cups shredded Cheddar cheese

1. In a 2-quart glass casserole, crumble ground beef and combine with onion and garlic. Cook 5 to 6 minutes, stirring halfway through cooking time.
2. Stir in chili powder, tomato sauce, and water. Cook 3 to 4 minutes, stirring halfway through cooking time.
3. In a 2-quart glass casserole, alternate layers of tortillas, meat sauce, and cheese, reserving ½ cup cheese for the top.
4. Cook, covered, 6 to 8 minutes, rotating dish one-quarter turn halfway through cooking time.

6 to 8 servings

Chili

 1 pound ground beef
 1 medium onion, diced
 2 teaspoons flour
 2 cans (16 ounces each) tomatoes
   (undrained)
 2 cans (16 ounces each) kidney beans
 1 tablespoon salt
 1 to 2 tablespoons chili powder
 ¼ teaspoon thyme
 1 cup water or ketchup

1. In a 3-quart glass casserole, sauté ground beef and onion 6 minutes, stirring every 2 minutes.
2. Mix flour with tomatoes and add to meat mixture. Blend in kidney beans, salt, chili powder, thyme, and water.
3. Cook, covered, 10 to 12 minutes, stirring halfway through cooking time.
4. Rest 5 minutes before serving.

4 to 6 servings

Conventional oven: Bake at 350°F 1 hour.

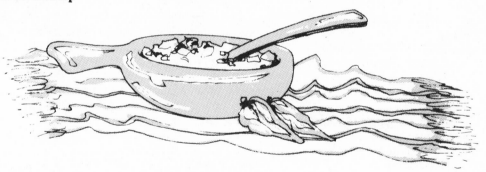

Quick Beef Pie

1½ pounds ground beef
 1 medium onion, finely chopped
 ½ teaspoon salt
 1 can (10½ ounces) condensed
   tomato soup
 1 can (16 ounces) cut green beans,
   drained
 ¼ teaspoon pepper
1½ cups seasoned mashed potatoes
 ½ cup shredded Cheddar cheese

1. In a 10-inch glass dish, crumble beef. Add onion and salt; cook 6 to 7 minutes, stirring halfway through cooking time, until browned. Drain off excess drippings.
2. Add soup, green beans, and pepper to meat mixture. Cook 3 to 4 minutes, stirring halfway through cooking time.
3. Press meat mixture into dish. Drop potatoes in mounds around edge of hot mixture, and sprinkle with cheese.
4. Cook 3 to 4 minutes, rotating dish one-quarter turn halfway through cooking time.
5. Rest 5 minutes before serving.

5 or 6 servings

Conventional oven: Bake at 350°F 25 to 30 minutes.

Note: If desired, the pie may be browned under a conventional broiler, but only if it is in a glass ceramic dish.

Macaroni in Cheese Sauce

3 cups macaroni
¼ cup butter
¼ cup flour
½ teaspoon salt
2 cups milk
½ teaspoon dry mustard
1½ cups shredded Cheddar cheese

1. Cook macaroni as directed on package.
2. In a 1½-quart glass casserole, heat butter 30 seconds. Stir in flour and salt. Add milk slowly, stirring continuously.
3. Cook 4 to 5 minutes until mixture thickens. Add mustard and cheese; stir to blend. Cook 1 minute.
4. Mix in cooked macaroni and heat 2 to 3 minutes.

5 or 6 servings

Texas Hash

1 pound ground beef
2 large onions, sliced
2 medium green peppers, chopped
½ cup chopped celery
2 cans (16 ounces each) tomatoes
¾ cup rice
½ teaspoon salt
   Pepper to taste

1. In a 3-quart glass baking dish, cook crumbled ground beef 5 minutes, stirring halfway through cooking time. Spoon off drippings.
2. Add onion, green pepper, celery, tomatoes, rice, salt, and pepper; stir to blend.
3. Cook, covered, 20 minutes, rotating dish one-quarter turn halfway through cooking time.
4. Rest, covered, 10 minutes before serving.

4 to 6 servings

Artichokes

Fresh artichokes

1. Slice off about 1 inch from top of artichoke. Cut off stem about 1 inch from base so artichoke will sit upright. Remove tough outside leaves. With scissors, clip tips of remaining leaves. Wash well.
2. Arrange artichokes upright in a glass baking dish. Cover and cook as follows: for 1 artichoke, 6 to 8 minutes; for 2, 12 to 15 minutes; for 4, 20 to 25 minutes.
3. Rest, covered, 10 minutes before serving. Serve with **lemon butter, hollandaise sauce, melted butter,** or **mayonnaise.**

Note: Artichokes may be chilled after resting and served cold.

Asparagus Amandine

2 packages (10 ounces each) frozen
   asparagus
¼ cup finely chopped almonds
¼ cup butter
1 teaspoon wine vinegar

1. Pierce asparagus packages with fork. Cook 6 to 8 minutes, rotating one-quarter turn halfway through cooking time.
2. In a 3-cup glass measure, combine almonds and butter. Cook 1 to 2 minutes, stirring halfway through cooking time. Stir in vinegar.
3. Drain asparagus well and arrange in a 10-inch glass baking

dish. Pour sauce over asparagus and cook, covered, 1 to 2 minutes.

4. Rest, covered, 5 minutes before serving.

4 to 6 servings

Note: If desired, serve cold on lettuce leaves as a salad.

Tangy Pork and Beans

2 cans (16 ounces each) pork and beans, drained
½ cup minced onion
1 cup dry white wine
½ cup firmly packed dark brown sugar
½ cup honey
1 teaspoon finely crushed bay leaf
1 teaspoon pepper
¼ teaspoon Tabasco

1. In a 2-quart glass casserole, combine pork and beans, onion, wine, brown sugar, honey, bay leaf, pepper, and Tabasco.

2. Cook, covered, 10 to 12 minutes, stirring halfway through cooking time.

3. Rest, covered, 5 minutes before serving.

6 to 8 servings

Creamed Green Beans

1 jar (8 ounces) pasteurized process cheese spread
1 can (10½ ounces) condensed cream of mushroom soup
Tabasco
1 tablespoon soy sauce
1 medium onion, chopped
3 tablespoons butter
5 fresh mushrooms, cleaned and chopped
1 can (8 ounces) water chestnuts, drained and sliced
2 cans (16 ounces each) French-style green beans, drained
Slivered almonds

1. In a 4-cup glass measure, blend cheese spread, soup, Tabasco, and soy sauce. Cook 3 to 5 minutes, stirring halfway through cooking time.

2. In a 1½-quart glass casserole, cook onion and butter 3 to 4 minutes, stirring halfway through cooking time until onions are transparent. Stir in mushrooms and water chestnuts and cook 1 minute.

3. Add green beans and soup mixture to mushroom mixture; stir to blend. Garnish with almonds.

4. Cook 5 minutes, rotating dish one-quarter turn halfway through cooking time.

5. Rest 5 minutes before serving.

6 to 8 servings

Sweet-and-Sour Beets

2 tablespoons brown sugar
1 tablespoon cornstarch
¼ teaspoon salt
1 can (8 ounces) pineapple tidbits (undrained)
1 tablespoon butter
1 tablespoon lemon juice
1 can (16 ounces) sliced beets, drained

1. In a 1-quart glass casserole, combine brown sugar, cornstarch, and salt. Stir in pineapple with its juice.

2. Cook 3 to 4 minutes, stirring after every minute, until mixture thickens.

3. Add butter, lemon juice, and beets. Cook, covered, 4 to 5 minutes, stirring halfway through cooking time.

4. Rest, covered, 5 minutes.

4 or 5 servings

Easy Broccoli Casserole

2 packages (10 ounces each) frozen
    broccoli spears
1 can (10½ ounces) condensed cream
    of mushroom soup
1 cup crushed potato chips or
    French-fried onion rings
½ cup grated Cheddar cheese

1. Pierce broccoli packages with fork. Cook broccoli 7 to 9 minutes, rotating dish one-quarter turn halfway through cooking time. Rest 5 minutes.
2. Place drained broccoli in a 2-quart glass casserole. Gently stir in soup. Sprinkle potato chips and cheese on top.
3. Cook, covered, 2 to 3 minutes. Remove cover and cook an additional 2 minutes. Serve immediately.

5 or 6 servings

Brussels Sprouts with Buttered Chestnuts

2 packages (10 ounces each) frozen
    Brussels sprouts
1 tablespoon finely chopped onion
⅔ cup sliced cooked chestnuts (see
    Note)
½ teaspoon salt

1. Pierce Brussels sprouts packages with fork. Cook 6 to 8 minutes, rotating one-quarter turn halfway through cooking.
2. In a 1-quart glass casserole, heat butter 30 seconds. Stir in onion, chestnuts, and salt, Cook 3 to 4 minutes, stirring halfway through cooking time.
3. Drain Brussels sprouts and combine with chestnut mixture. Cook, covered, 3 to 4 minutes.
4. Rest, covered, 5 minutes before serving.

6 to 8 servings

Note: To cook chestnuts, slash each chestnut crosswise through skin on flat end of shell. In a glass pie plate, arrange 20 to 24 chestnuts in an even layer. Cook 3 to 4 minutes, stirring every minute, until nuts are soft when squeezed. Rest 5 minutes. Peel off shells and use as directed.

Sweet-and-Sour Cabbage

1 small onion, chopped
3 tablespoons butter
1 cup meat stock or water
1 small head cabbage, shredded
1 small tart apple, cored and diced
3 tablespoons vinegar
1 tablespoon brown sugar
¼ teaspoon allspice
½ teaspoon salt

1. In a 2-quart glass casserole, sauté onion in butter 2 minutes, stirring after 1 minute. Stir in stock, cabbage, and apple.
2. Cover casserole and cook 6 to 8 minutes, stirring halfway through cooking time.
3. Add vinegar, brown sugar, allspice, and salt to cabbage; mix well. Cook 3 to 4 minutes.
4. Rest, covered, 5 minutes before serving.

4 to 6 servings

Orange-Glazed Carrots

6 to 8 medium carrots, pared and
    diagonally sliced
2 tablespoons butter
¼ cup brown sugar
2 tablespoons orange juice
1 teaspoon grated orange peel
1 teaspoon lemon juice
¼ teaspoon salt

1. In a 1½-quart glass casserole, combine carrots, butter, brown sugar, orange juice, orange peel, lemon juice, and salt.
2. Cover carrots and cook 10 to 12 minutes, stirring halfway through cooking time.
3. Rest, covered, 10 minutes before serving.

6 to 8 servings

Cauliflower au Gratin

½ cup butter
1 medium head cauliflower, cut in
    flowerets
¼ teaspoon garlic salt
¼ teaspoon salt
¼ teaspoon pepper
2 large tomatoes, cut in wedges
¼ cup seasoned bread crumbs
¼ cup grated Parmesan cheese
½ cup shredded Swiss cheese

1. In a 1½-quart glass casserole, heat butter 30 seconds. Add cauliflower, garlic salt, salt, and pepper, and stir to coat cauliflower with butter.
2. Cover cauliflower and cook 5 to 6 minutes, rotating dish one-quarter turn halfway through cooking time.
3. Arrange tomatoes on top of cauliflower and cook 2 minutes.
4. Add bread crumbs, Parmesan cheese, and Swiss cheese. Cook 1 to 2 minutes until cheese begins to melt.
5. Rest, covered, 5 minutes before serving.

3 or 4 servings

Sautéed Celery and Tomatoes

2 tablespoons butter
6 cups diagonally cut celery (½-inch
    slices)
½ pound cherry tomatoes, stems
    removed
½ teaspoon basil
½ teaspoon salt
¼ teaspoon pepper

1. In a 2-quart glass casserole, heat butter 30 seconds. Stir in celery. Cover and cook 10 to 12 minutes, stirring halfway through cooking time.
2. Stir tomatoes, basil, salt, and pepper into celery. Cook, covered, 3 to 4 minutes.
3. Rest, covered, 5 minutes before serving.

4 to 6 servings

Creamed Corn Casserole

2 tablespoons butter
1 egg
⅓ cup soda cracker crumbs
1 can (17 ounces) cream-style corn
½ teaspoon salt
¼ teaspoon pepper

1. In a 1-quart glass casserole, heat butter 30 seconds. Add egg, cracker crumbs, corn, salt, and pepper; blend evenly.
2. Cook 4 to 6 minutes, stirring halfway through cooking time.
3. Rest 5 minutes before serving.

4 or 5 servings

Eggplant Casserole

1 eggplant (about 1½ pounds)
Salt
Flour
½ cup salad oil for skillet
2 cans (8 ounces each) tomato sauce
1 cup thinly sliced mozzarella cheese
½ cup grated Parmesan cheese

1. Peel eggplant and cut in ½-inch-thick slices. Sprinkle both sides with salt, and set aside 20 to 30 minutes.
2. Dip eggplant slices in flour. Brown eggplant in hot microwave browning dish or in hot salad oil in hot skillet on a conventional range. Drain slices on paper towel.
3. Pour 1 can tomato sauce in a 10-inch glass baking dish. Lay eggplant slices in sauce, and cover with other can of sauce. Place mozzarella cheese over the sauce and sprinkle Parmesan cheese on top.
4. Cover with waxed paper or lid. Cook 12 to 14 minutes, rotating dish one-quarter turn halfway through cooking time.
5. Rest, covered, 5 minutes.

4 to 6 servings

Sautéed Mushrooms

2 tablespoons butter
¼ teaspoon tarragon
½ pound fresh mushrooms, cleaned and sliced
3 tablespoons chopped green onion
Salt
Pepper

1. In a 1-quart glass casserole, heat butter and tarragon 30 seconds, until butter is melted. Stir in mushrooms, cover, and cook 2 minutes.
2. Add green onion and stir to blend. Cook 3 to 4 minutes, stirring halfway through cooking time. Season with salt and pepper.
3. Rest, covered, 5 minutes before serving.

4 servings

Mustard Greens and Bacon

4 slices bacon, diced
¼ cup finely chopped onion
¾ pound mustard greens
Salt and pepper

1. In a 3-quart glass casserole, cook bacon 2 to 3 minutes, stirring halfway through cooking time.
2. Stir in onion and cover. Cook 3 to 4 minutes, stirring halfway through cooking time, until bacon is crisp. Pour off all drippings, except 1½ tablespoons.
3. Rinse and coarsely chop the mustard greens. Stir the greens into onion mixture, coating them with the drippings.
4. Cover the casserole and cook 2 to 3 minutes. Season with salt and pepper to taste.
5. Rest, covered, 5 minutes before serving.

3 or 4 servings

Note: Fresh spinach may be substituted for mustard greens.

Cooked Onions

1½ pounds small white onions
2 tablespoons butter
1 teaspoon minced sage leaves
½ teaspoon salt

1. In a 1½-quart glass casserole, combine onions, butter, sage, and salt.
2. Cook, covered, 8 to 10 minutes, stirring twice during cooking time.
3. Rest, covered, 5 minutes before serving.

4 servings

Snow Peas with Water Chestnuts

1 tablespoon salad oil or bacon
    drippings
1 can (5 ounces) water chestnuts,
    drained and sliced
½ pound fresh (or 1 10-ounce
    package frozen) snow peas
1 cup water
1 chicken bouillon cube
1 tablespoon cornstarch
2 tablespoons cold water

1. In a 1½-quart glass casserole, heat oil 15 seconds. Add water chestnuts and snow peas.
2. In a 1-cup glass measure, heat water 2 minutes. Dissolve bouillon cube and add to vegetable mixture.
3. Cook vegetables, covered, 4 to 6 minutes, stirring once halfway through cooking time.
4. Combine cornstarch and cold water; mix well. Push vegetables to one side of casserole and stir cornstarch mixture into broth.
5. Stir vegetables into sauce. Cook 2 to 4 minutes, stirring every minute, until sauce is slightly thickened. Salt to taste.

4 servings

Herbed Peas

2 packages (10 ounces each) frozen
    peas
¼ cup butter
½ cup minced onion
¼ cup minced celery
½ cup minced parsley
¼ teaspoon crushed rosemary
¼ teaspoon basil
¾ teaspoon salt

1. Pierce pea packages with fork and cook 6 to 8 minutes, rotating one-quarter turn halfway through cooking time.
2. In a 1½-quart glass casserole, heat butter 30 seconds. Stir in onion and celery. Cook 3 to 4 minutes, stirring halfway through cooking time. Add parsley, rosemary, basil, salt, and drained peas; stir to blend.
3. Cook, covered, 3 to 4 minutes, rotating dish one-quarter turn halfway through cooking time.
4. Rest, covered, 5 minutes.

6 to 8 servings

Cheesy Potato Casserole

1 package (12 ounces) frozen
    shredded hash brown potatoes
1 cup shredded Cheddar cheese
1 tablespoon flour
¼ cup chopped onion
1 teaspoon salt
¼ teaspoon pepper
1 tablespoon dried chives

1. Pierce hash brown potato package. Cook the potatoes 3 to 4 minutes, rotating one-quarter turn halfway through cooking time.
2. In a 2-quart glass casserole, blend hash brown potatoes, cheese, flour, onion, salt, pepper, and chives.
3. Cook, covered, 6 to 8 minutes, rotating dish one-quarter turn halfway through cooking time.
4. Rest, covered, 5 minutes.

4 servings

Hard Sauce

2 tablespoons butter
1 cup sifted confectioners' sugar
1 to 2 tablespoons rum or brandy
Dash salt

1. In a 2-cup glass measure, combine butter, confectioners' sugar, rum, and salt.
2. Cook 1 minute, stirring after 30 seconds. Serve hot or cold.

1½ cups

Cake-Mix Layer Cake

1 package (about 18½ ounces) cake mix

1. Prepare cake mix as directed on package, reducing the liquid by one-quarter the amount called for in mixing instructions.
2. Line bottoms of two 8-inch glass baking dishes with paper towel. Pour batter into baking dishes, filling no more than half full. Save extra batter and make cupcakes. Rest batter 10 minutes, if desired.
3. Cook, one layer at a time, 5 to 6 minutes, rotating dish one-quarter turn halfway through cooking time. When wooden pick stuck in center comes out slightly moist, cake is done.
4. Rest each layer 5 minutes before removing from dish. Cool completely before frosting.

Two 8-inch cake layers

Note: Square baking dishes hold more batter than round and will require 2 to 3 minutes more cooking time per pan.

Cake-Mix Sheet Cake: Follow recipe for Cake-Mix Layer Cake. Pour batter into an 11×7-inch glass baking dish, filling no more than half full. Cook 9 to 11 minutes, rotating one-quarter turn twice during cooking time. If cake begins to overcook in corners, shield with small pieces of foil. Cool 5 minutes before removing from dish; or cake may be left in dish. Frost when completely cool.

Apricot Almond Upside-Down Cake

⅓ cup butter
½ cup firmly packed brown sugar
1 can (16 ounces) apricot halves
½ cup blanched almonds, slivered
2 eggs
⅔ cup sugar
1 teaspoon almond extract
1 cup all-purpose flour
½ teaspoon baking powder
¼ teaspoon salt

1. In a 9-inch glass dish, heat butter 30 to 45 seconds. Blend with brown sugar and spread evenly over bottom of pan. Drain apricots and reserve juice. Arrange almonds and apricot halves over sugar mixture.
2. In a medium mixing bowl, beat eggs until thick. Using an electric mixer, beat about 5 minutes on high speed. Gradually add sugar. Add 6 tablespoons liquid from apricots and almond extract; beat well.
3. Add flour, baking powder, and salt to egg mixture; beat until well blended. Pour over fruit.
4. Cook 5 to 6 minutes, rotating dish one-quarter turn halfway through cooking time.
5. Rest 5 minutes, invert onto serving dish, and serve.

6 to 8 servings

Cupcakes

Prepared cake batter

1. Line glass custard cups, drinking cups, or cupcaker with paper baking cups. Pour 3 tablespoons batter into each cup.
2. Arrange cups in a circle on a glass plate, if not using cupcaker. Cook as follows, rotating plate or cupcaker one-quarter turn halfway through cooking time: 1 cupcake, 10 to 20 seconds; 2 cupcakes, 30 to 45 seconds; 3 cupcakes, 45 to 60 seconds; 4 cupcakes, 1 to 1¼ minutes; and 6 cupcakes, 1½ to 2 minutes.

Date Cake

Cake:
- 2 cups boiling water
- ½ cup chopped dates
- 2 teaspoons baking soda
- 1 cup butter
- 2 cups sugar
- 2 eggs
- 3 cups all-purpose flour
- 2 teaspoons vanilla extract
- 1 teaspoon salt

Topping:
- 3 tablespoons butter
- 1 cup brown sugar
- ¼ cup milk or cream
- 1 cup coarsely chopped walnuts

1. In a 4-cup glass measure, heat water about 5 to 6 minutes, to boiling. Stir in dates and sprinkle baking soda over water. Cool until just warm.
2. Cream butter with sugar and eggs. Add flour, vanilla extract, and salt to creamed mixture. Blend with date mixture and pour into a buttered 2-quart glass ceramic baking dish.
3. Cook 9 to 11 minutes, rotating dish one-quarter turn every 3 minutes.
4. Rest 5 minutes before removing from dish.
5. To make topping, heat butter 30 seconds in a 2-cup glass measure. Add brown sugar, milk, and nuts. Blend ingredients evenly and spread on top of cake.
6. Place cake under conventional broiler 1 to 2 minutes, until mixture starts to bubble. Remove and serve warm.

20 to 24 servings

Conventional oven: Bake at 350°F 45 minutes.

Apple Cake

Cake:
- 1½ cups all-purpose flour
- ¾ teaspoon baking soda
- ¾ teaspoon nutmeg
- ½ teaspoon salt
- ¼ cup salad oil
- ¾ cup sugar
- 1 egg, beaten
- 3 tablespoons buttermilk
- 1½ cups diced pared apples

Topping:
- 3 tablespoons butter, softened
- ⅓ cup firmly packed brown sugar
- 2 tablespoons milk or cream
- ¼ teaspoon vanilla extract
- ½ cup shredded coconut

1. Sift together flour, soda, nutmeg, and salt; set aside. Cream oil with sugar; beat until light and fluffy. Blend in egg.
2. Add buttermilk and flour mixture alternately to creamed mixture. Beat 2 minutes until smooth. Fold in apples.
3. Pour batter into a buttered 8-inch square glass ceramic baking dish. Cook 5 to 7 minutes, rotating dish one-quarter turn halfway through cooking time. Rest 5 minutes before removing from pan.
4. To make topping, heat butter 30 seconds in a 2-cup glass measure. Add brown sugar, milk, vanilla extract, and coconut. Stir to blend ingredients.
5. Spread evenly over top of cake and place under conventional broiler 1 to 2 minutes, until mixture starts to bubble. Remove and serve warm.

9 to 12 servings

Conventional oven: Bake at 350°F 45 minutes.

Poppy Seed Ring Cake

1 package (18½ ounces) prepared
    yellow cake mix
1 package (3¾ ounces) lemon instant
    pudding and pie filling
4 eggs
½ cup cooking oil
1 cup water
⅓ cup poppy seed
    Butter
    Sugar

1. In a large mixing bowl, combine cake mix, pudding and pie filling, eggs, oil, water, and poppy seed. Beat mixture at low speed of electric mixer until ingredients are moistened, then beat on high speed 3 to 4 minutes. If beating by hand, stir until ingredients are moistened; then beat about 150 strokes per minutes for 3 to 4 minutes.

2. Butter the bottom and sides of a 3-quart glass casserole. Sprinkle sugar over the butter. Place a drinking glass open end up in the center of the dish. Remove 1 cup of batter from the bowl and save to make cupcakes. Pour remaining batter in dish around the glass.

3. Cook 10 to 12 minutes, rotating dish one-quarter turn two times, more if needed, during cooking time. A wooden pick inserted in the cake that comes out slightly moist indicates cake is done.

4. Rest cake 5 minutes until it begins to pull away from sides of dish Remove glass from center of cake and invert cake onto serving plate. Sprinkle sifted confectioners' sugar over top, if desired.

10 to 12 servings

Note: The cake may be made in a 10-cup glass tube mold, if available.

Pineapple Upside-Down Cake

2 tablespoons butter
1 can (8 ounces) crushed pineapple
½ cup firmly packed brown sugar
6 maraschino cherries
1 package (9 ounces) yellow cake mix

1. Heat butter 30 seconds in an 8-inch round glass baking dish.

2. Drain pineapple, reserving juice.

3. Blend together butter, brown sugar, and drained pineapple; spread evenly in bottom of pan. Arrange maraschino cherries in bottom of pan.

4. Prepare cake mix as directed on package, substituting the reserved pineapple juice for water. Pour batter evenly over pineapple mixture.

5. Cook 5 to 7 minutes, rotating dish one-quarter turn halfway through cooking time. Rest 5 minutes until cake pulls away from sides of pan.

6. Invert onto serving dish.

6 to 8 servings

Note: If desired, pineapple slices may be used. Blend the melted butter and the brown sugar in baking dish and arrange slices on top. Other fruits, such as apricots or peaches, may be used, also.

Walnut Torte

4 eggs
1 cup sugar
1 cup graham cracker crumbs
½ cup chopped walnuts
1 cup apricot jam
  Whipped cream

1. Beat eggs well. Combine sugar, graham cracker crumbs, and walnuts. Add to beaten eggs, mixing well. Pour into a buttered 9-inch glass cake dish with small glass, open end up, in center of dish.
2. Cook 5 to 6 minutes, rotating dish one-quarter turn halfway through cooking time.
3. Rest 5 minutes. Invert cake on plate. Spread jam over top, and serve warm or cold with whipped cream.

One 9-inch cake

Lemon Meringue Pie

1½ cups sugar
¼ teaspoon salt
1½ cups boiling water
2 tablespoons butter
6 tablespoons cornstarch
⅓ cup lemon juice
1 tablespoon grated lemon peel
3 egg yolks, slightly beaten
1 baked 9-inch pastry pie shell
3 egg whites
6 tablespoons sugar
½ teaspoon lemon juice

1. In a 4-cup glass measure, combine 1½ cups sugar, salt, water, and butter. Cook 3 to 4 minutes, stirring halfway through cooking time until sugar is dissolved.
2. Blend cornstarch with 3 tablespoons water and stir into hot sugar mixture. Cook 2 to 3 minutes, stirring after every minute.
3. Stir in ⅓ cup lemon juice and lemon peel. Gradually add egg yolks, taking care to avoid overcooking them. Cook mixture 3 to 4 minutes, stirring after every minute. Cool and pour into pie shell.
4. Using an electric mixer, beat egg whites until stiff. Continue beating while adding 6 tablespoons sugar, 1 tablespoon at a time, until rounded peaks are formed. Beat in ½ teaspoon lemon juice.
5. Spread meringue evenly over cooked filling, sealing to edges of pie shell.
6. Bake in a conventional oven at 450°F 5 to 6 minutes, or until lightly browned.

6 or 7 servings

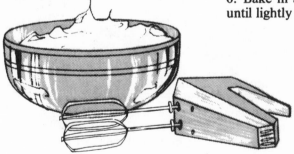

Pumpkin Pie

1 egg, beaten
1 can (14 ounces) sweetened
  condensed milk
1 can (16 ounces) cooked pumpkin
½ teaspoon salt
1 teaspoon cinnamon
¼ teaspoon nutmeg

1. Combine all ingredients except pie shell. Mix until well blended.
2. Pour filling into pie shell. Cook 4 to 5 minutes until the edges begin to set. Stir the cooked edges to the center.
3. Cook 5 to 6 minutes, until the center is almost set. Rest 10 minutes. Check to see if pie is done by inserting a knife in the center. The knife should come out clean if the pie is done.

½ teaspoon allspice
¼ cup firmly packed dark brown
   sugar
1 tablespoon flour
¼ cup hot water
1 baked 9-inch pastry pie shell

4. Cool pie before serving. Top with **whipped cream** or **vanilla ice cream** and serve.

One 9-inch pie

Conventional oven: Pour filling into unbaked pastry pie shell and bake at 375°F 50 to 55 minutes.

Brownie Pie

2 ounces (2 squares) **unsweetened chocolate**
2 tablespoons **butter**
3 **eggs,** beaten
½ cup **sugar**
¾ cup **dark corn syrup**
¾ cup **pecan halves**
1 baked 9-inch pastry pie shell

1. In a 2-cup glass measure, heat chocolate and butter 1 to 2 minutes, until melted.
2. In a large mixing bowl, combine eggs, sugar, and corn syrup; blend evenly. Slowly blend in chocolate mixture. Stir in pecan halves and pour into pie shell in glass pie plate.
3. Cook 4 to 5 minutes and rotate dish one-quarter turn.
4. Continue cooking 3 to 4 minutes until center is just beginning to set.
5. Rest pie 10 minutes. Serve slightly warm or cold with **ice cream** or **whipped cream.**

One 9-inch pie

Conventional oven: Bake at 375°F 40 to 50 minutes.

Strawberry Tarts

1 package (10 ounces) **frozen strawberries**
1 tablespoon **cornstarch**
   Dash **cinnamon**
   Dash **cloves**
½ teaspoon **lemon juice**
6 cooked pastry tart shells
   Whipped cream (optional)

1. In a 1-quart glass casserole, cook strawberries 1 to 1½ minutes. Separate berries with a fork. Add cornstarch, cinnamon, and cloves; stir to blend evenly.
2. Cook strawberries 5 to 6 minutes, stirring after every minute, until mixture is thickened and clear. Stir in lemon juice.
3. Cool slightly and spoon into tart shells. Refrigerate until ready to serve. Top with whipped cream.

6 tarts

Fresh Strawberry Pie: Follow recipe for Strawberry Tarts. Use 4 cups fresh strawberries, cook as directed above, and pour into a **9-inch baked pastry pie shell.**

Gingerbread

½ cup shortening
⅔ cup sugar
2 eggs
⅔ cup molasses
2 cups all-purpose flour
¾ teaspoon salt
¾ teaspoon ginger
¾ teaspoon cinnamon
¼ teaspoon baking soda
¾ cup boiling water

1. In a medium mixing bowl, cream shortening with sugar. Stir in eggs, one at a time. Gradually add molasses.
2. Combine flour, salt, ginger, cinnamon, and baking soda. Blend into creamed mixture. Add boiling water and mix until smooth.
3. Cut paper towel to line bottom of 9-inch glass baking dish. Pour batter into dish, filling no more than half full.
4. Cook 5 to 6 minutes, rotating dish one-quarter turn half-way through cooking time.
5. Rest 5 minutes before removing from pan. Serve with Lemon Sauce ●   or Hard Sauce ●

10 to 12 servings

Note: If desired, cupcakes may be made from mixture. Use cupcaker or custard cups lined with paper baking cups. Allow 15 seconds per cupcake.

Basic Pastry Pie Shell

4 cups all-purpose flour
1 tablespoon sugar
1 teaspoon baking powder
2 teaspoons salt
1¾ cups shortening
1 egg, beaten
⅓ cup cold water
1 tablespoon cider vinegar

1. In a large mixing bowl, combine flour, sugar, baking powder, and salt.
2. Cut in shortening with a pastry blender or two knives, until particles are the size of small peas. In a 1-cup measure, combine egg, cold water, and vinegar. Stir into flour mixture until well moistened. Chill 15 minutes.
3. Divide pastry into 5 portions and form each into a ball (see Note). Flatten one ball on a lightly floured pastry cloth, and roll to about ⅛ inch thick. Ease pastry into a 9-inch glass pie plate, and flute edges.
4. Make a waxed paper starburst pattern (follow step-by-step instructions). Center waxed paper on shell and place an 8-inch glass pie plate on top.
5. Cook pastry 3 minutes. Remove 8-inch glass pie plate and waxed paper. Rotate dish one-quarter turn and cook 2½ to 3 minutes.
6. Cool on rack.

Five 9-inch pie shells

Note: If not to be used immediately, wrap balls individually in waxed paper and freeze. When needed, remove from freezer, thaw, roll, and bake as directed.

Pastry Tart Shells: Follow recipe for Basic Pastry Pie Shell. Roll one ball on floured pastry cloth, as directed. Using an inverted 10-ounce custard cup, cut out six pastry rounds. Invert six 6-ounce glass custard cups. Cover each first with a paper towel and then a pastry round. Flute each tart edge in four evenly spaced places. Place in oven in a circle and cook 4 to 5 minutes, rearranging cups one-quarter turn halfway through cooking time. Rest 3 to 4 minutes. Place upright and carefully lift out custard cup and paper towel. Cool thoroughly before filling.

6 tart shells

Index